THE UNIVERSITY OF CHICAGO
ORIENTAL INSTITUTE PUBLICATIONS
VOLUME 117

Series Editors
Thomas A. Holland
and
Thomas G. Urban

*To the memory of
Edith Porada*

SEALS ON THE PERSEPOLIS FORTIFICATION TABLETS
VOLUME I
IMAGES OF HEROIC ENCOUNTER
PART 1: TEXT

by
MARK B. GARRISON
and
MARGARET COOL ROOT

with
Seal Inscription Readings
by
CHARLES E. JONES

ORIENTAL INSTITUTE PUBLICATIONS • VOLUME 117
THE ORIENTAL INSTITUTE OF THE UNIVERSITY OF CHICAGO
CHICAGO • ILLINOIS

Library of Congress Catalog Card Number: 97-78494

ISBN: 1-885923-12-0

ISSN: 0069-3367

The Oriental Institute, Chicago

©2001 by The University of Chicago. All rights reserved.
Published 2001. Printed in the United States of America.

The preparation of this volume of the Persepolis Seal Project was made possible in part by grants from the Program for Research Tools and Reference Works of the National Endowment for the Humanities, an independent Federal Agency, the Samuel Kress Foundation, and the Iran Heritage Foundation.

Series Editors Acknowledgments

The assistance of Dennis Campbell, Blane Conklin, Simrit Dhesi, Charles E. Jones, John A. Larson, and Leslie Schramer is acknowledged in the production of this volume.

Printed by McNaughton & Gunn, Inc., Saline, Michigan

The paper used in this publication meets the minimum requirements of American National Standard for Information Services — Permanence of Paper for Printed Library Materials, ANSI Z39.48-1984.

TABLE OF CONTENTS

ACKNOWLEDGMENTS	xi
LIST OF ABBREVIATIONS	xv
LIST OF CHARTS	xvii
LIST OF FIGURES	xix
LIST OF REFERENCES	xxi
INTRODUCTION	1
PART ONE: OVERVIEW OF THE FORTIFICATION ARCHIVE	1
Scope and Character of the Evidence	3
Seal Inscriptions and Issues of Language	7
Other Areas of Significance: Studying Seals, People, and Places	9
Seal Carving Styles in the PFS Corpus: The Case of Volume I	16
Persepolitan Modeled Style	16
Plausibly Antique Seals	17
Antique Seals	17
Fortification Style	18
Court Style	18
Mixed Styles I and Mixed Styles II	19
Broad and Flat Styles and Linear Styles	19
Diverse Styles	19
Summary	20
PART TWO: THE FORTIFICATION ARCHIVE AND ARCHAEOLOGICAL INQUIRY	23
Herzfeld's Discovery	23
Mystifications of the Record	24
Archival Deposition in Antiquity	26
Aspects of Archival Function	29
Other Sealing Archives of the Achaemenid Empire	32
Heartland Court Contexts	32
Persepolis: The Treasury	33
Persepolis: Post-Herzfeld Discoveries in the Fortification	34
Susa	35
Satrapal Court Contexts	35
Phrygia: Daskyleion	35
Egypt: Memphis	35
Egypt: Decontextualized Letters with Sealed Bullae	36
Egypt(?) to Mesopotamia(?): A Small Corpus of Decontextualized Sealed Tablets	36
Business/Legal/Temple Contexts	37
Babylonia	37
Susa	38
Palestine	38
Private (Artisanal) Context	39
Ur	39

vi   SEALS ON THE PERSEPOLIS FORTIFICATION TABLETS, VOLUME I: IMAGES OF HEROIC ENCOUNTER

PART THREE: GUIDE TO THE THREE-VOLUME CATALOG 41
    Conceptual Organization of the Material 41
        Definition of a Main Scene 42
        Volume I: Images of Heroic Encounter 42
        Volume II: Images of Human Activity 43
        Volume III: Animals, Creatures, Plants, and Geometric Devices 44
    Documentation of the Seals: Volumes I–III 44
        Numbering and Collating 44
            Hallock's Legacy 44
            The Garrison and Root Collation Effort 45
        Visual Documentation 46
            Summary of the Catalog Apparatus 46
            Study Photographs 46
            Publication Prints 46
            Composite Drawings 47
        Verbal Documentation 48
            Basic Information Header 48
            Description of Seal as Impressed Image 50
            Inscription 51
            Commentary 51
            Seal Application 52
            Bibliography 52
PART FOUR: IMAGES IN VOLUME I 53
    Meanings of Heroic Encounter 53
        Shifting Valences of the Motif in Ancient Western Asia 53
        The Heroic Encounter in Achaemenid Times 54
            Prevalence of the Motif 54
            Special Connotations within the Achaemenid Imperial Sphere 56
    Typology of Images in Volume I 60

CATALOG OF IMAGES OF HEROIC ENCOUNTER 63
COMPOSITIONAL FORMAT I: IMAGES OF HEROIC CONTROL 63
    I-A. Hero Controls Rampant Animals and/or Creatures 63
        I-A.1. Bulls 63
        I-A.2. Winged Bull Creatures 66
        I-A.3. Winged Human-faced/Human-headed Bull Creatures 82
        I-A.4. Lions 92
        I-A.5. Winged Lion Creatures 121
        I-A.6. Winged Human-faced/Human-headed Lion Creatures 149
        I-A.7. Winged Bird-headed Lion Creatures 160
        I-A.8. Bulls or Lions 169
        I-A.9. Winged Bull or Lion Creatures 171
        I-A.10. Winged Human-faced/Human-headed Bull or Lion Creatures 174
        I-A.11. Horned Animals: Deer, Gazelles, Wild Goats, Wild Sheep 182
        I-A.12. Winged Horned-Animal Creatures: Deer, Gazelles, Wild Goats, Wild Sheep 190

I-A.16. Various Composite Creatures	191
I-A.17. Mixed Animals and/or Creatures	195
I-A.18. Animals of Uncertain Type	223
I-A.19. Winged Creatures of Uncertain Type	229
I-B. Hero Holds Animals or Creatures at His Chest	252
I-B.11. Horned Animals: Deer, Gazelles, Wild Goats, Wild Sheep	252
I-B.17. Mixed Animals and/or Creatures	254
I-C. Hero Controls Inverted Animals or Creatures	256
I-C.4. Lions	256
I-C.6. Winged Human-faced/Human-headed Lion Creatures	268
I-C.7. Winged Bird-headed Lion Creatures	272
I-C.11. Horned Animals: Deer, Gazelles, Wild Goats, Wild Sheep	276
I-C.17. Mixed Animals and/or Creatures	277
I-C.18. Animals of Uncertain Type	279
I-C.19. Winged Creatures of Uncertain Type	281
I-D. Hero Controls Marchant Animals or Creatures	282
I-D.3. Winged Human-faced/Human-headed Bull Creatures	282
I-D.4. Lions	283
I-D.10. Winged Human-faced/Human-headed Bull or Lion Creatures	284
I-D.11. Horned Animals: Deer, Gazelles, Wild Goats, Wild Sheep	287
I-D.12. Winged Horned-Animal Creatures: Deer, Gazelles, Wild Goats, Wild Sheep	288
I-D.17. Mixed Animals and/or Creatures	289
I-D.18. Animals of Uncertain Type	291
I-D.19. Winged Creatures of Uncertain Type	292
I-E. Hero Controls Variously Posed Animals or Creatures	294
I-E.15. Snakes	294
COMPOSITIONAL FORMAT II: IMAGES OF HEROIC COMBAT	295
II-A. Hero Stabs Rampant Animal or Creature	295
II-A.4. Lions	295
II-A.5. Winged Lion Creatures	304
II-B. Hero Threatens Rampant Animal or Creature, Weapon Held Down behind Body	309
II-B.1. Bulls	309
II-B.2. Winged Bull Creatures	313
II-B.3. Winged Human-faced/Human-headed Bull Creatures	314
II-B.4. Lions	321
II-B.5. Winged Lion Creatures	340
II-B.6. Winged Human-faced/Human-headed Lion Creatures	349
II-B.11. Horned Animals: Deer, Gazelles, Wild Goats, Wild Sheep	354
II-B.12. Winged Horned-Animal Creatures: Deer, Gazelles, Wild Goats, Wild Sheep	358
II-B.16. Various Composite Creatures	360
II-B.18. Animals of Uncertain Type	363
II-B.19. Winged Creatures of Uncertain Type	370
II-C. Hero Threatens Rampant Animal or Creature, Weapon Held Up behind Head	378
II-C.2. Winged Bull Creatures	378
II-C.4. Lions	380

II-C.5. Winged Lion Creatures	387
II-C.6. Winged Human-faced/Human-headed Lion Creatures	395
II-C.18. Animals of Uncertain Type	396
II-C.19. Winged Creatures of Uncertain Type	397
II-E. Hero Threatens Inverted Animal or Creature, Weapon Held Down behind Body	399
II-E.4. Lions	399
II-E.18. Animals of Uncertain Type	402
II-H. Hero Threatens Marchant Animal or Creature, Weapon Held Down behind Body	403
II-H.1. Bulls	403
II-H.14. Ostriches	404
II-H.19. Winged Creatures of Uncertain Type	408
II-I. Hero Threatens Marchant Animal or Creature, Weapon Held Up behind Head	409
II-I.3. Winged Human-faced/Human-headed Bull Creatures	409
II-I.16. Various Composite Creatures	411
COMPOSITIONAL FORMAT III: COMPOSITE CONTROL AND COMBAT ENCOUNTERS	415
III-A. Two Heroic Encounters: One Control, One Combat	415
III-A.17. Mixed Animals and/or Creatures	415
III-B. One Heroic Encounter with Two Heroes: One Controlling, One Threatening	419
III-B.4. Lions	419
III-C. Two Heroic Encounters with One Hero: Hero Controls One Animal or Creature, Threatens the Other	421
III-C.5. Winged Lion Creatures	421
III-C.6. Winged Human-faced/Human-headed Lion Creatures	423
III-C.17. Mixed Animals and/or Creatures	424
III-C.18. Animals of Uncertain Type	428
III-C.19. Winged Creatures of Uncertain Type	430
III-D. Fragmentary Images Suggesting Various Control and Combat Encounters	432
III-D.20. Animals or Creatures of Unverifiable Type	432
COMPOSITIONAL FORMAT IV: OTHER HEROIC COMPOSITIONS	436
IV-A. Seated Hero Controls Rampant Animal or Creature	436
IV-A.18. Animals of Uncertain Type	436
IV-B. Hero Lifts Animal or Creature above Head	440
IV-B.18. Animals of Uncertain Type	440
APPENDIX ONE: CONCORDANCE OF SEALS TO TABLETS IN VOLUME I	443
APPENDIX TWO: PROVISIONAL LIST OF ALL SUBSUMED HALLOCK PFS NUMBERS (VOLUMES I–III)	469
APPENDIX THREE: SUMMARY DATA ON SEAL DIMENSIONS FOR VOLUME I	471
APPENDIX FOUR: STAMP SEALS IN VOLUME I GROUPED BY APPARENT CONTOUR OF SEAL FACE	485
APPENDIX FIVE: INSCRIBED SEALS IN VOLUME I BY LANGUAGE OR SCRIPT	489

TABLE OF CONTENTS

APPENDIX SIX: DISTRIBUTION OF SEALS IN VOLUME I BY STYLISTIC CATEGORIES	491
APPENDIX SEVEN: ANIMALS AND COMPOSITE CREATURES ON SEALS IN VOLUME I	497
APPENDIX EIGHT: ICONOGRAPHIC FEATURES ON SEALS IN VOLUME I	505
APPENDIX NINE: PERSONAL NAMES	529
APPENDIX TEN: OCCUPATIONAL DESIGNATIONS	533
APPENDIX ELEVEN: GEOGRAPHICAL NAMES	535
APPENDIX TWELVE: CONCORDANCE OF PFS TO CAT.NO. IN VOLUME I	539
INDEX OF ALL SEALS ON FORTIFICATION AND TREASURY TABLETS CITED IN VOLUME I	543
GENERAL INDEX	551

ACKNOWLEDGMENTS

The Persepolis Seal Project has received support in one way or another from various sources. It is a pleasure to acknowledge this assistance, starting with the University of Chicago. At the Oriental Institute, R. T. Hallock welcomed Margaret Root's efforts wholeheartedly—even to the point of sharing his office. To the late Dick Hallock, we have extended special appreciation through our dedication of *Persepolis Seal Studies* (Garrison and Root 1996). Since 1977, several Directors of the Oriental Institute attended to the periodic negotiations on the project. We thank them all for their time and efforts: John A. Brinkman, Robert McC. Adams, Janet Johnson, and William M. Sumner. We also thank Matthew Stolper for allowing Mark Garrison to work with the tablets in his office during his intensive visits to render final drawings as well as for sharing his formidable knowledge of the tablets and his insights on Achaemenid administration. We thank Charles Jones for lively discussions on the Fortification texts and for practical assistance both with the tablets themselves and in the Research Archives. Beyond that, of course, we thank Jones especially for his hard work as epigraphic consultant on the project. A task that was meant to be a revision of work already done by Hallock developed into a much more difficult labor as it became clear that many challenges in the seal inscriptions had not been addressed.

Other staff (former and current) of the Oriental Institute have also facilitated our work and we thank them warmly: Anita Ghaemi, Thomas Holland, John Larson, Ray Tindel, Thomas Urban, and Karen Wilson.

Moving to the University of Michigan, the litany of indebtedness is more complex. Margaret Root was attracted to Michigan while George Cameron was still living. He was delighted by the fact that someone was at long last working on the seal impressions on the Fortification tablets; and he was particularly pleased that the effort had been taken up by someone with substantial historical interests in Achaemenid Persian studies. Cameron's encouragement meant a great deal.

The University of Michigan has given much to this project. First of all, and perhaps in the long run most importantly, Michigan has fostered an intellectual climate that has made it possible for three generations of doctoral students so far to engage with the seals preserved on the Fortification tablets in formal seminars and in the course of research assistantships. It is this climate (in the Department of the History of Art and in the Interdepartmental Program in Classical Art and Archaeology) that produced and sustained the partnership between Margaret Root and Mark Garrison.

Garrison's dissertation on the Fortification and Treasury seals of heroic encounter (Garrison 1988) capped the first generation of Michigan doctoral students for whom exposure to the Persepolis Seal Project was *de rigueur*. In this particular case, a true collaboration emerged as a result of the dissertation process. The Persepolis Seal Project had always been too big, too complex, for one researcher able to devote sustained time to it only sporadically. Garrison's collaboration has, quite simply, made the catalog possible.

Over the years, many Michigan graduate students have served as stimulating discussants in the context of History of Art 822 when this seminar has been devoted to some aspect of the archive or closely related issues. Additionally, graduate research assistantships have formed the financial basis for crucial aspects of project work. The photographs of all the seal impressions were taken by Mark Garrison and Gail Hoffman in the early 1980s. At that time, organizational and technical support was also supplied by Victoria Jennings, Meg Morden, and Jackie Royer.

In the second generation, specialized research assistantships supervised by Root have been held by Mariana Giovino and Elspeth McIntosh Dusinberre. As this is written, a new group of graduate students is emerging. It is exciting to see the increasing and ever more varied investigative potentials of the seals unfold for a succeeding academic generation as the documentation progresses.

Michigan has supported our project financially in the form of sabbatical leaves and competitively awarded research assistantships and faculty grants. Special discretionary grants have also been awarded for specific and discrete phases in the project's history from various units: the Kelsey Museum of Archaeology, the College of Literature, Science, and the Arts, the Horace H. Rackham School of Graduate Studies, the Office of the Vice President for Research, the International Institute, and the Forsyth Fund of the Department of the History of Art.

Many individuals have facilitated the funding process at Michigan. We extend heartfelt thanks to all of them. The following have been particularly instrumental: John H. D'Arms, as former Dean of the Graduate School; Susan Lipschutz†, former Associate Dean of the Graduate School and then Associate Provost for Academic Affairs; Edie N. Goldenberg, former Dean of the College; Marvin Parnes, Assistant Vice-President for Research; John Griffiths Pedley and Elaine K. Gazda, consecutive former Directors of the Kelsey Museum of Archaeology.

Special thanks also go to Helen Baker, Jackie Monk, Jane Nye, and Lelia Raley for gracious assistance on all levels and particularly for administrative oversight of accounts at the Kelsey Museum and at the Department of the

History of Art; and to Paul Cunningham and Adeline Ryznar, past and current Project Representatives sequentially for the Division of Research Development and Administration.

With the partnership of Mark Garrison, Trinity University in San Antonio, Texas, has become a feature in the support process for our work. Here we owe thanks to all his colleagues in the Department of Classical Studies, Joan Burton, James B. Pearce, and Colin M. Wells, who not only welcomed a specialist in Iranian art into their midst, but actively encouraged his work and gave support on many levels. To Colin M. Wells we owe special thanks. As chairman of the department he showed extraordinary patience with and understanding of the complexities of this project. His support and encouragement, especially in securing release time for Garrison, have been indispensable. Thanks also to colleagues in the Department of Art History, in particular to Charles Talbot, for many thoughtful discussions on the Persepolis seals. Trinity University has provided financial support for the project in the form of work-study students. Many have worked part time on various curatorial tasks; we wish to thank in particular Nicole King. Trinity University, through the graces of William O. Walker, Jr., former Dean of the Division of Humanities and Arts, also made available special work-study funds to underwrite the inking of drawings by Laura Mosman during the academic years 1994–1998. Finally, Jim D. Stoker and Kate A. Ritson, former Chairs of the Department of Art, have for many years made available to Garrison the photographic darkroom of the Department of Art for the custom production of the publication prints. Without this support, the production of the publication prints would have been financially prohibitive.

Beyond the home institutions, numerous institutions and agencies have contributed to the Persepolis Seal Project through direct support or services. It is an honor to express gratitude to the following: the Samuel Kress Foundation (for duplication of our complete archive of negatives and for production of publication prints for Volumes I and II), the National Endowment for the Humanities (for a two-year Research Tools Grant, 1993–1995), and, most recently, a generous grant in 1999 from the Iran Heritage Foundation.

Other institutions and agencies have contributed to support individual research by Garrison and Root. It is an honor to express gratitude to the following: the John Simon Guggenheim Memorial Foundation (1985 Fellowship to Root facilitating research in Oxford), National Endowment for the Humanities (1978 Fellowship support of Root), the Department of Classics at Vassar College (all of its faculty, but especially Robert Brown, chairman of the department, for the Carl Blegen Fellowship support for Garrison during 1991–1992), and Wolfson College and the Ashmolean Museum, Oxford, for institutional privileges in support of research there.

In addition to the doctoral students acknowledged earlier for their work on the project, we cite a number of professionals who have been employed by the project for special services: Bob Moustakas (for the printing of the study photographs); Zane Udriss and Lauren Talalay (for early trials in production of collated templates for the seal drawings).

Special thanks go to Laurie E. Hall and Langley Garoutte for their extraordinarily labor-intensive custom production of publication prints from our existing negatives. This first volume, and, indeed, the photographic documentation for future volumes, would not have been possible without their dedication to the project and their photographic skills. In cases where the photographs seem inadequate, the fault lies in the elusive nature of the image itself and the resulting inadequacy of the negative.

Special thanks also go to Lorene Sterner, who worked with Margaret Root for several years producing 3:1 collated templates which formed the skeletal framework for our final drawings as rendered by Mark Garrison.

Laura Mosman, a talented graduate of Trinity University, has inked the final drawings under Mark Garrison's supervision. We owe her sincere thanks for her professionalism and her dedication to a difficult task.

Over the years Margaret Root's husband Larry Root has been our volunteer computer consultant, frequently being the catalytic agent encouraging us to move forward technologically and to think creatively about databases. We are very grateful. At a critical moment in the production of the reports from the database we received technical support from Dr. Pedar Foss, currently of DePauw University, and Alan Hogg of the University of Michigan, to whom we give warm thanks.

There are many colleagues beyond the boundaries of Chicago, Michigan, and Trinity who have offered special encouragement and support. Here we list only those whose interests have been most keenly felt: Pierre Briant, Ann Gunter, Amélie Kuhrt, Roger Moorey, Heleen Sancisi-Weerdenburg†, and David Lewis†. We also thank numerous anonymous reviewers of grant proposals who have offered useful commentary.

Friendships made in recent years between Root and members of the Iranian-American Medical Association have yielded thought-provoking dialogue on Iranian traditions as well as inspirational validation of the relevance of the seals preserved on the Fortification tablets to the interests of an audience beyond the sphere of specialist archaeologists and historians.

Finally, the late Edith Porada. Her extraordinary accomplishments in the field of glyptic documentation have been an important model for us even though our material lends itself to organizational and interpretive agendas that diverge from any particular pattern she developed. Although Miss Porada was never directly involved with our project as a collaborator or spokesperson, she gave generously of her time in informal but intense discussions at her apartment in New York. She seemed genuinely excited about the material as it began to unfold. Her probing questions about stylistic and iconographical details have remained in our minds continuously as we have pressed onward. We deeply regret that we are not able to present her with a tangible copy of the catalog. But we hope we have produced a document worthy of its dedication to her memory.

In closing, we are happy to shout Thank You to the loved ones who live this project with us: to Larry Root, Katherine, and Benjamin; and to Heather I. Sullivan and Fiona.

Mark B. Garrison and Margaret Cool Root
Ann Arbor, Michigan
December 2000

LIST OF ABBREVIATIONS

*	inscribed seal
C4 text	small cattle as tax; category of texts assigned by Hallock (1969, p. 16)
ca.	*circa*, about, approximately
Cat.No.	in parentheses after PFS number, catalog number of seal in volume
cf.	*confer*, compare
cm	centimeter(s)
comp.	complete
e.g.	*exempli gratia*, for example
esp.	especially
et al.	*etalii*, and others
F text	setting-aside of grains for seed and fodder; category of texts assigned by Hallock (1969, pp. 20–22)
f.	female personal name
fig(s).	figure(s)
Fort.	Elamite texts read by Cameron; also some anepigraphic tablets
H text	receipt by officials; category of texts assigned by Hallock (1969, pp. 23–24)
II	in parentheses after PFS number, indicates seal is forthcoming in *Seals on the Persepolis Fortification Tablets*, Volume II: *Images of Human Activity*
III	in parentheses after PFS number, indicates seal is forthcoming in *Seals on the Persepolis Fortification Tablets*, Volume III: *Animals, Creatures, Plants, and Geometric Devices*
i.e.	*id est*, that is
incl.	including
incomp.	incomplete
J text	royal provisions; category of texts assigned by Hallock (1969, pp. 24–25)
K1 text	rations for individual with religious function; category of texts assigned by Hallock (1969, pp. 25–26)
K3 text	regular monthly rations for named person without qualifications; category of texts assigned by Hallock (1969, p. 27)
L1 text	regular monthly rations with *gal makip*; category of texts assigned by Hallock (1969, pp. 27–32)
M text	special rations; category of texts assigned by Hallock (1969, pp. 35–37)
N text	mothers' rations; category of texts assigned by Hallock (1969, pp. 37–38)
n(n).	note(s)
NA	not available
ND	no date formula exists or is preserved for tablet
OD	occupational designation
no(s).	number(s)
op. cit.	*opere citato*, in the work cited
P text	daily rations; category of texts assigned by Hallock (1969, pp. 38–40)

PF	Persepolis Fortification; Persepolis Fortification tablet published by Hallock (1969)
PFa	Persepolis Fortification tablet published by Hallock (1978)
PFNN	unpublished Elamite tablets from the Persepolis Fortification, transliterated by R. T. Hallock
PFS	seal documented by impression(s) on Persepolis Fortification tablet(s)
pl(s).	plate(s)
PN	personal name
PT	Persepolis Treasury tablet published by Cameron (1948)
PTS	seal occurring in impression on Persepolis Treasury tablet(s)
Q text	travel rations; category of texts assigned by Hallock (1969, pp. 40–45)
s	stamp seal
S1 text	regular rations for animals; category of texts assigned by Hallock (1969, pp. 47–49)
S3 text	travel rations for animals; category of texts assigned by Hallock (1969, p. 50)
s.v.	*sub verbo, sub voce*, under the word
T text	letter; category of texts assigned by Hallock (1969, pp. 50–53)
U text	label; category of texts assigned by Hallock (1969, pp. 53–55)
V text	journal; category of texts assigned by Hallock (1969, pp. 55–57)
viz.	*videlicet*, namely
W text	accounts; category of texts assigned by Hallock (1969, pp. 57–69)

LIST OF CHARTS

1.	Height of Cylinder Seals in Volume I	473
2.	Distribution by Carving Styles of Cylinder Seals with Reconstructed Height in Volume I	473
3.	Height of Cylinder Seals: Modeled Style	474
4.	Height of Cylinder Seals: Mixed Styles I	474
5.	Height of Cylinder Seals: Fortification Style	475
6.	Height of Cylinder Seals: Mixed Styles II	475
7.	Height of Cylinder Seals: Court Style	476
8.	Height of Cylinder Seals: Broad and Flat Styles	476
9.	Height of Cylinder Seals: Linear Styles	477
10.	Height of Cylinder Seals: Diverse Styles	477
11.	Height of Cylinder Seals: Plausibly Antique and Antique Styles	478
12.	Diameter of Cylinder Seals in Volume I	478
13.	Distribution by Carving Styles of Cylinder Seals with Reconstructed Diameter in Volume I	479
14.	Diameter of Cylinder Seals: Modeled Style	479
15.	Diameter of Cylinder Seals: Mixed Styles I	480
16.	Diameter of Cylinder Seals: Fortification Style	480
17.	Diameter of Cylinder Seals: Mixed Styles II	481
18.	Diameter of Cylinder Seals: Court Style	481
19.	Diameter of Cylinder Seals: Broad and Flat Styles	482
20.	Diameter of Cylinder Seals: Linear Styles	482
21.	Diameter of Cylinder Seals: Diverse Styles	483
22.	Diameter of Cylinder Seals: Plausibly Antique and Antique Styles	483
23.	Distribution of All Seals in Volume I by Carving Styles	495
24.	Distribution of Cylinder Seals in Volume I by Carving Styles	495
25.	Distribution of Stamp Seals in Volume I by Carving Styles	496

LIST OF FIGURES

1. Reconstructed Drawings of Select Cylinders in Volume I: PFS 778 (Cat.No. 11), PFS 9* (Cat.No. 288), PFS 20 (Cat.No. 145), PFS 1* (Cat.No. 182), PFS 731 (Cat.No. 131), PFS 43* (Cat.No. 207), PFS 52 (Cat.No. 114), PFS 774 (Cat.No. 58), and PFS 7* (Cat.No. 4) 2

2. General Map of Persepolis and Its World 4

3. Persepolis Citadel (Takht) and Immediate Surroundings 5

4. View of the Persepolis Takht during Clearance by the Oriental Institute Persepolis Expedition 24

5. Herzfeld's Sketch of the Takht, Showing Area of Discovery of the Fortification Tablets 25

6. Excavation of the Persepolis Fortification Tablets 29

7. Sketch of PF 1092, Without the Elamite Cuneiform Text, Showing Sealing Surfaces on the Tablet: Obverse, Reverse, Left Edge, Right Edge, Upper Edge, and Bottom Edge 31

8. Study Sketch of PFS 16* by R. T. Hallock and Composite Line Drawing of PFS 16* (Cat.No. 22), Garrison and Root Publication Drawing 45

9. Stamp Seal Terminology and Schematic Drawings of Main Stamp Seal Types Relevant to the PFS Corpus .. 486

LIST OF REFERENCES

Akkermans, Peter M. M. G., and Marc Verhoeven
 1995 "An Image of Complexity: The Burnt Village at Late Neolithic Sabi Abyad, Syria." *American Journal of Archaeology* 99: 5–32.

Akurgal, Ekrem
 1956 "Les fouilles de Daskyleion." *Anatolia* 1: 20–24.

Amiet, Pierre
 1966 *Élam*. Auvers-sur-Oise: Archée.
 1972 *Glyptique susienne: Des origines à l'époque des perses achéménides. Cachets, sceaux-cylindres et empreintes antiques découverts à Suse de 1913 à 1967*. 2 Volumes. Mémoires de la Délégation archéologique en Iran 43. Paris: Librarie Orientaliste Paul Geuthner.
 1973a "Glyptique élamite, à propos de documents nouveaux." *Arts asiatiques* 26: 3–45.
 1973b "La glyptique de la fin de l'Élam." *Arts asiatiques* 28: 3–32.
 1980 *La glyptique mésopotamienne archaïque*. Second edition. Paris: Éditions du Centre national de la recherche scientifique.

d'Amore, Paola
 1992 "Glittica a cilindro achemenide: Linee di uno sviluppo tematico-cronologico." *Contributi e Materiali di Archeologia Orientale* 4: 187–267.

Aperghis, Gerassimos G.
 1998 "The Persepolis Fortification Texts – Another Look." In *Studies in Persian History: Essays in Memory of David M. Lewis*, edited by Maria Brosius and Amélie Kuhrt, pp. 35–62. Achaemenid History 11. Leiden: Nederlands Instituut voor het Nabije Oosten.
 1999 "Storehouses and Systems at Persepolis: Evidence from the Persepolis Fortification Tablets." *Journal of the Economic and Social History of the Orient* 42: 152–93.

Aruz, Joan
 1992a "Late Susa I Glyptic: Ritual Imagery, Practical Use." In *The Royal City of Susa: Ancient Near Eastern Treasures in the Louvre*, edited by Prudence O. Harper, Joan Aruz, and Françoise Tallon, pp. 43–46. New York: Metropolitan Museum of Art.
 1992b "The Neo-Elamite Period: Seals." In *The Royal City of Susa: Ancient Near Eastern Treasures in the Louvre*, edited by Prudence O. Harper, Joan Aruz, and Françoise Tallon, pp. 211–14. New York: Metropolitan Museum of Art.
 1997 "Siegel als Zeugnisse des kulturellen Austausches." In *Mit Sieben Siegeln versehen: Das Siegel in Wirtschaft und Kunst des Alten Orients*, edited by Evelyn Klengel-Brandt, pp. 138–49. Mainz: Philipp von Zabern. Berlin: Staatliche Museen zu Berlin, Vorderasiatisches Museum.

Avigad, Nahman
 1997 *Corpus of West Semitic Stamp Seals*. Revised and Completed by Benjamin Sass. Jerusalem: Israel Academy of Sciences and Humanities, Israel Exploration Society, Institute of Archaeology, Hebrew University of Jerusalem.

Badawy, Alexander
 1963 "The Architectural Symbolism of the Mammisi-Chapels in Egypt." *Chronique d'Égypte* 38: 78–90.

Balcer, Jack M.
 1979 Review of *Die Griechen in Persien*, by Josef Hofstetter. *Bibliotheca Orientalis* 36: 276–80.
 1991 "Erich Friedrich Schmidt, 13 September 1897–3 October 1964." In *Through Travellers' Eyes: European Travellers on the Iranian Monuments*, edited by Heleen Sancisi-Weerdenburg and Jan-Willem Drijvers, pp. 147–72. Achaemenid History 7. Leiden: Nederlands Instituut voor het Nabije Oosten.
 1993 *A Prosopographical Study of the Ancient Persians, Royal and Noble, c. 550–450 B.C.* Lewiston: Edwin Mellen Press.

Balkan, Kemal
 1959 "Inscribed Bullae from Daskyleion-Ergili." *Anatolia* 4: 123–28.

Bergamini, Giovanni
 1991 "Neo-Sumerian 'Vignettes'? A Methodological Approach." *Mesopotamia* 26: 101–18.

Bianchi, Francesco
 1996 "I sigilli anepigrafi della Giudea achemenide: una nuova datazione." *Studi Epigrafici e Linguistici* 13: 79–90.

Bivar, A. D. H.
 1961 "A 'Satrap' of Cyrus the Younger." *Numismatic Chronicle* 7/1: 119–27.
 1970 "A Persian Monument at Athens, and Its Connections with the Achaemenid State Seals." In *W. B. Henning Memorial Volume*, edited by Mary Boyce and Ilya Gershevitch, pp. 43–61. London: Lund Humphries.
 1975 "Religious Subjects on Achaemenid Seals." In *Mithraic Studies*, Volume 1, edited by John R. Hinnells, pp. 90–105. Manchester: Manchester University Press.

Black, Jeremy A., and Anthony Green
 1992 *Gods, Demons and Symbols of Ancient Mesopotamia: An Illustrated Dictionary*. London: British Museum Press.

Black, Jeremy A., and William J. Tait
 1995 "Archives and Libraries in the Ancient Near East." In *Civilizations of the Ancient Near East*, Volume 4, edited by Jack M. Sasson, pp. 2197–209. New York: Scribner.

Bleibtreu, Erika
 1997 "Die Siegelinhaber." In *Mit Sieben Siegeln versehen: Das Siegel in Wirtschaft und Kunst des Alten Orients*, edited by Evelyn Klengel-Brandt, pp. 92–103. Mainz: Philipp von Zabern. Berlin: Staatliche Museen zu Berlin, Vorderasiatisches Museum.

Boardman, John
   1970a "Pyramidal Stamp Seals in the Persian Empire." *Iran* 8: 19–45.
   1970b *Greek Gems and Finger Rings: Early Bronze Age to Late Classical.* New York: Harry N. Abrams.
   1988 *The Cambridge Ancient History, Plates to Volume 4: Persia, Greece and the Western Mediterranean, c. 525 to 479 B.C.* New Edition. Cambridge: Cambridge University Press.
   1998 "Seals and Signs. Anatolian Stamp Seals of the Persian Period Revisited." *Iran* 36: 1–13.

Bollweg, Jutta
   1988 "Protoachämenidische Siegelbilder." *Archaeologische Mitteilungen aus Iran* 21: 53–61.

Bonnet, Hans
   1926 *Die Waffen der Völker des Alten Orients.* Leipzig: J. C. Hinrichs.

Bordreuil, Pierre
   1986 *Catalogue des sceaux ouest-sémitiques inscrits de la Bibliothèque National, du Musée du Louvre et du Musée Biblique de Bible et Terre Sainte.* Paris: Bibliothèque Nationale.

Boucharlat, Rémy
   1987 "Les niveaux post-achéménides à Suse, secteur nord. Fouilles de l'Apadana-Est et de la Ville Royal-Ouest (1973–1978)." *Cahiers de la Délégation archéologique française en Iran* 15: 145–310.
   1990 "Suse et la Susiane à l'époque achéménide: Données archéologiques." In *Centre and Periphery*, edited by Heleen Sancisi-Weerdenburg and Amélie Kuhrt, pp. 149–75. Achaemenid History 4. Leiden: Nederlands Instituut voor het Nabije Oosten.
   1998 "À la recherche d'Ecbatane sur Tepe Hegmataneh." In *Neo-Assyrian, Median, Achaemenian and other Studies in Honor of David Stronach*, edited by R. Boucharlat, J. E. Curtis, and E. Haerinck. *Iranica Antiqua* 33: 173–86.

Boussac, Marie-Françoise, and Antonio Invernizzi, editors
   1996 *Archives et sceaux du monde hellénistique.* Bulletin de correspondance hellénique, Supplément 29. Athens: École française d'Athènes.

Breasted, Charles
   1933 "Exploring the Secrets of Persepolis." *National Geographic Magazine* 64: 381–420.

Bregstein, Linda B.
   1993 Seal Use in Fifth Century B.C. Nippur, Iraq: A Study of Seal Selection and Sealing Practices in the Murašû Archive. Ph.D. dissertation, University of Pennsylvania.
   1996 "Sealing Practices in the Fifth Century B.C. Murašû Archive from Nippur, Iraq." In *Archives et sceaux du monde hellénistique*, edited by Marie-Françoise Boussac and Antonio Invernizzi, pp. 53–63. Bulletin de correspondance hellénique, Supplément 29. Athens: École française d'Athènes.

Briant, Pierre
   1984 *L'Asie centrale et les royaumes proche-orientaux du premier millénaire (c. VIIIe–IVe siècles avant notre ère).* Mémoire 42. Paris: Éditions recherche sur les civilisations.
   1994 Multiculturalism and Unitary Empire: The Case of the Achaemenid Empire. Paper delivered in Ann Arbor, Michigan.
   1996 *Histoire de l'empire perse de Cyrus à Alexandre.* Paris: Librairie Arthème Fayard.
   1997 "Bulletin d'histoire achéménide (I)." *Topoi* Supplément 1: 5–127.

Brosius, Maria
   1991 Royal and Non-Royal Women in Achaemenid Persia (559–331 B.C.). D.Phil. thesis, Oxford University.
   1996 *Women in Ancient Persia: 559–331 B.C.* Oxford: Clarendon Press.

Buccellati, Giorgio, and Marilyn Kelly-Buccellati
   1996 "The Seals of the King of Urkesh: Evidence from the Western Wing of the Royal Storehouse AK." In *Festschrift für Hans Hirsch*, edited by Arne A. Ambros and Markus Köhbach, pp. 65–98. Wiener Zeitschrift für die Kunde des Morgenlandes 86. Vienna: Instituts für Orientalistik.

Buchanan, Briggs
   1966 *Catalogue of Ancient Near Eastern Seals in the Ashmolean Museum,* Volume 1: *Cylinder Seals.* Oxford: Clarendon Press.

Buchanan, Briggs, and P. R. S. Moorey
   1984 *Catalogue of Ancient Near Eastern Seals in the Ashmolean Museum,* Volume 2: *The Prehistoric Stamp Seals.* Oxford: Clarendon Press.
   1988 *Catalogue of Ancient Near Eastern Seals in the Ashmolean Museum,* Volume 3: *The Iron Age Stamp Seals (c. 1200–350 B.C.).* Oxford: Clarendon Press.

Burney, Ch.
   1999 "Beyond the Frontiers of Empire: Iranians and Their Ancestors." In *Neo-Assyrian, Median, Achaemenian and Other Studies in Honor of David Stronach*, edited by R. Boucharlat, J. E. Curtis, and E. Haerinck. *Iranica Antiqua* 34: 1–20.

Byron, Robert
   1982 *The Road to Oxiana.* New York: Oxford University Press. [First published 1937]

Cagni, L.; G. Giovinazzo; and S. Graziani
   1985 "Typology and Structure of Mesopotamian Documentation during the Achaemenid Period." *Annali dell'Istituto Universitario Orientale* 45: 547–83.

Calmeyer, Peter
   1980 "Textual Sources for the Interpretation of Achaemenian Palace Decorations." *Iran* 18: 55–63.
   1983 "The Persian King in the Lion's Den." *Iraq* 45: 138–39.

Cameron, George G.
   1942 "Darius' Daughter and the Persepolis Inscriptions." *Journal of Near Eastern Studies* 1: 214–18.
   1948 *Persepolis Treasury Tablets.* Oriental Institute Publications 65. Chicago: University of Chicago Press.
   1965 "New Tablets from the Persepolis Treasury." *Journal of Near Eastern Studies* 24: 167–92.
   1973 "The Persian Satrapies and Related Matters." *Journal of Near Eastern Studies* 32: 47–56.

Carter, Elizabeth
    1994 "Bridging the Gap between the Elamites and the Persians in Southeastern Khuzistan." In *Continuity and Change*, edited by Heleen Sancisi-Weerdenburg, Amélie Kuhrt, and Margaret Cool Root, pp. 65–95. Achaemenid History 8. Leiden: Nederlands Instituut voor het Nabije Oosten.

Carter, Elizabeth, and Matthew W. Stolper
    1984 *Elam: Surveys of Political History and Archaeology*. Near Eastern Studies 25. Berkeley and Los Angeles: University of California Press.

Cassin, Elena
    1987 *Le semblable et le différent. Symbolismes du pouvoir dans le proche-orient ancien*. Paris: Éditions la découverte.

Clanchy, M. T.
    1993 *From Memory to Written Record: England 1066–1307*. Second edition. Oxford: Blackwell.

Collège de France
    2000 Achemenet. http://www.achemenet.com.

Collon, Dominique
    1975 *The Seal Impressions from Tell Atchana/Alalakh*. Alter Orient und Altes Testament 27. Kevelaer: Butzon and Bercker.
    1981 "The Aleppo Workshop—A Seal Cutter's Workshop in Syria in the Second Half of the 18th Century B.C." *Ugarit-Forschungen* 13: 33–43.
    1982 *The Alalakh Cylinder Seals*. British Archaeological Reports, International Series 132. London: British Archaeological Reports.
    1986a *Catalogue of the Western Asiatic Seals in the British Museum, Cylinder Seals 3: Isin-Larsa and Old Babylonian Periods*. London: British Museum Publications.
    1986b "The Green Jasper Cylinder Seal Workshop." In *Insight through Images: Studies in Honor of Edith Porada*, edited by Marilyn Kelly-Buccellati, pp. 57–70. Bibliotheca Mesopotamica 21. Malibu: Undena.
    1987 *First Impressions: Cylinder Seals in the Ancient Near East*. Chicago: University of Chicago Press.
    1995 *Ancient Near Eastern Art*. Berkeley and Los Angeles: University of California Press.
    1996 "A Hoard of Sealings from Ur." In *Archives et sceaux du monde hellénistique*, edited by Marie-Françoise Boussac and Antonio Invernizzi, pp. 65–84. Bulletin de correspondence hellénique, Supplément 29. Athens: École française d'Athènes.
    1998 "First Catch your Ostrich." In *Neo-Assyrian, Median, Achaemenian and other Studies in Honor of David Stronach*, edited by R. Boucharlat, J. E. Curtis, and E. Haerinck. *Iranica Antiqua* 33: 25–42.

Collon, Dominique, editor
    1997 *7000 Years of Seals*. London: British Museum Press.

Cook, J. M.
    1983 *The Persian Empire*. London: J. M. Dent.

Cross, Frank M., Jr.
    1963 "The Discovery of the Samaria Papyri." *Biblical Archaeologist* 26: 110–21.
    1969 "Papyri of the Fourth Century B.C. from Daliyeh." In *New Directions in Biblical Archaeology*, edited by David N. Freedman and Jonas C. Greenfield, pp. 45–69. Garden City: Doubleday.

Curtis, C. D.
    1925 *Jewelry and Gold Work*. Sardis 13. Rome: Sindacato Italiano Arti Grafiche.

Curtis, J. E., and J. E. Reade, editors
    1995 *Art and Empire: Treasures from Assyria in the British Museum*. New York: Metropolitan Museum of Art.

Curtis, Vesta S., and St. John Simpson
    1997 "Archaeological News from Iran." *Iran* 35: 137–44.

Dalley, Stephanie
    1993 "Nineveh After 612 BC" *Altorientalische Forschungen* 20: 134–47.

Dandamayev, Muhammad A.
    1999 "Achaemenid Imperial Policies and Provincial Governments." In *Neo-Assyrian, Median, Achaemenian and Other Studies in Honor of David Stronach*, edited by R. Boucharlat, J. E. Curtis, and E. Haerinck. *Iranica Antiqua* 34: 269–82.

Delaporte, L.
    1920 *Catalogue des cylindres, cachets, et pierres gravées de style oriental*, Volume 1: *Fouilles et missions*. Paris: Librarie Hachette.

Delaunay, J. A.
    1976 "Remarques sur quelques noms de personne des archives élamites de Persepolis." *Studia Iranica* 5: 9–31.

Donbaz, Veysel, and Matthew W. Stolper
    1997 *Istanbul Murašû Texts*. Uitgaven van het Nederlands historisch-archaeologisch Instituut te Istanbul 79. Leiden: Nederlands historisch-archaeologisch Instituut te Istanbul.

Downey, Susan B.
    1988 *Mesopotamian Religious Architecture: Alexander through the Parthians*. Princeton: Princeton University Press.

Driver, Godfrey R.
    1957 *Aramaic Documents of the Fifth Century B.C.* Oxford: Clarendon Press.

Dusinberre, Elspeth R. M.
    1997a Satrapal Sardis: Aspects of Empire in an Achaemenid Capital. Ph.D. dissertation, Interdepartmental Program in Classical Art and Archaeology, University of Michigan.
    1997b "Imperial Style and Constructed Identity: A 'Graeco-Persian' Cylinder Seal from Sardis." *Ars Orientalis* 27: 99–129.
    2000 Construing Persepolis: The Ernst Herzfeld Archive at the Smithsonian Institution's Freer Archives. Unpublished paper presented at the Freer Gallery of Art and Arthur M. Sackler Gallery, Smithsonian Institution, Washington, D.C.

Dyson, Robert H., Jr., and Mary V. Harris
    1986 "The Archaeological Context of Cylinder Seals Excavated on the Iranian Plateau." In *Insight through Images: Studies in Honor of Edith Porada*, edited by Marilyn Kelly-Buccellati, pp. 79–110. Bibliotheca Mesopotamica 21. Malibu: Undena.

Ehrenberg, Erica
1999 *Uruk: Late Babylonian Seal Impressions on Eanna-Tablets.* Ausgrabungen in Uruk-Warka Endberichte 18. Mainz: Philipp von Zabern.

Ferioli, Piera, and Enrica Fiandra
1994 "Archive Techniques and Methods at Arslantepe." In *Archives before Writing. Proceedings of the International Colloquium Oriolo Romano, October 23–25, 1991,* edited by Piera Ferioli, Enrica Fiandra, Gian Giacomo Fissore, and Marcella Frangipane, pp. 149–61. Rome: Centro Internazionale di Ricerche Archeologiche Antropologiche e Storiche.

Ferioli, Piera; Enrica Fiandra; Gian Giacomo Fissore; and Marcella Frangipane, editors
1994 *Archives before Writing. Proceedings of the International Colloquium Oriolo Romano, October 23–25, 1991.* Rome: Centro Internazionale di Ricerche Archeologiche Antropologiche e Storiche.

Frankfort, Henri
1939 *Cylinder Seals.* London: Macmillan.

Freer Gallery of Art
2000 *Selected Papers of Ernst Herzfeld in the Freer Gallery of Art and Arthur M. Sackler Gallery Archives.* Washington, D.C.: Smithsonian Institution (IDC Publishers).

Friedrich, Johannes
1965 "Ein phrygisches Siegel und ein phrygisches Tontäfelchen." *Kadmos* 4: 154–56.

Frye, R. N., editor
1973 *Sasanian Remains from Qasr-i Abu Nasr: Seals, Sealings, and Coins.* Cambridge: Harvard University Press.

Garrison, Mark B.
1988 Seal Workshops and Artists in Persepolis: A Study of Seal Impressions Preserving the Theme of Heroic Encounter on the Persepolis Fortification and Treasury Tablets. Ph.D. dissertation, Interdepartmental Program in Classical Art and Archaeology, University of Michigan.
1991 "Seals and the Elite at Persepolis: Some Observations on Early Achaemenid Persian Art." *Ars Orientalis* 21: 1–29.
1995 "Tavoletta Storica: Yale Babylonian Collection 16813." In *Alessandro Magno: Storia e Mito,* edited by Tiziana Quirico, pp. 262–63. Rome: Leonardo Arte.
1996a "The Identification of Artists and Workshops in Sealed Archival Contexts: The Evidence from Persepolis." In *Archives et sceaux du monde hellénistique,* edited by Marie-Françoise Boussac and Antonio Invernizzi, pp. 29–51. Bulletin de correspondence hellénique, Supplément 29. Athens: École française d'Athènes.
1996b "A Persepolis Fortification Seal on the Tablet MDP 11 308 (Louvre Sb 13078)." *Journal of Near Eastern Studies* 55: 15–35.
1998 "The Seals of Ašbazana (Aspathines)." In *Studies in Persian History. Essays in Memory of David M. Lewis,* edited by Maria Brosius and Amélie Kuhrt, pp. 115–31. Achaemenid History 11. Leiden: Nederlands Instituut voor het Nabije Oosten.
2000 "Achaemenid Iconography as evidenced by Glyptic Art: Subject Matter, Social Function, Audience and Diffusion." In *Images as Media: Sources for the Cultural History of the Eastern Mediterranean and the Near East (1st Millennium BCE),* edited by C. Uehlinger, pp. 115–64. Fribourg: Orbis Biblicus et Orientalis.
in press "Anatolia in the Persian Period: Glyptic Insights and Perspectives from Persepolis." In *Proceedings of the First International Symposium on Anatolia in the Achaemenid Period (Bandırma, Turkey, 15–17 August 1997),* edited by T. Bakır.

Garrison, Mark B., and Paul Dion
1999 "The Seal of Ariyāramna in the Royal Ontario Museum, Toronto." *Journal of Near Eastern Studies* 58: 1–17.

Garrison, Mark B., and Margaret Cool Root
1996 *Persepolis Seal Studies: An Introduction with Provisional Concordances of Seal Numbers and Associated Documents on Fortification Tablets 1–2087.* Corrected edition 1998. Achaemenid History 9. Leiden: Nederlands Instituut voor het Nabije Oosten.

Gates, Marie-Henriette
1996 "Archaeology in Turkey." *American Journal of Archaeology* 100: 277–335.

Gershevitch, Ilya
1979 "The Alloglottography of Old Persian." *Transactions of the Philological Society* 77: 114–90.

Ghouchani, Abdullah
1991 "Identifikation eines Tellers aus dem 4. Jahrhundert H. Gh." *Archaeologische Mitteilungen aus Iran* 24: 219–21.

Gibson, McGuire, and Robert D. Biggs, editors
1977 *Seals and Sealing in the Ancient Near East.* Bibliotheca Mesopotamica 6. Malibu: Undena.

Gill, David W. J., and Christopher Chippindale
1993 "Material and Intellectual Consequences of Esteem for Cycladic Figures." *American Journal of Archaeology* 97: 601–59.

Giovinazzo, Grazia
1989 "L'expression 'ha duš ha duka' dans les textes de Persépolis." *Akkadika* 63: 12–26.
1994 "Les voyages de Darius dans les régions orientales de l'empire." *Annali dell'Istituto Universitario Orientale* 54: 32–45.

Goetze, Albrecht
1944 "Three Achaemenian Tags." *Berytus* 8: 97–101.

Goff, Beatrice L.
1956 "The Rôle of Amulets in Mesopotamian Ritual Texts." *Journal of the Warburg and Courtauld Institutes* 19: 1–39.

Gorissen, P.
1978 "Litterae Lunatae." *Ancient Society* 9: 149–63.

Graf, David F.
1994 "The Persian Royal Road System." In *Continuity and Change,* edited by Heleen Sancisi-Weerdenburg,

Amélie Kuhrt, and Margaret Cool Root, pp. 167–89. Achaemenid History 8. Leiden: Nederlands Instituut voor het Nabije Oosten.

Gragg, Gene B.
1995 "Less-Understood Languages of Ancient Western Asia." In *Civilizations of the Ancient Near East*, Volume 4, edited by Jack M. Sasson, pp. 2161–79. New York: Scribner.

Green, Anthony
1986 "The Lion-Demon in the Art of Mesopotamia and Neighbouring Regions. Materials toward the Encyclopaedia of Mesopotamian Religious Iconography, I/1." *Baghdader Mitteilungen* 17: 141–251.

Greenfield, Jonas
1962 "Studies in Aramaic Lexicography I." *Journal of the American Oriental Society* 82: 290–99.

Gropp, Douglas Marvin
1986 The Samaria Papyri from Wâdī ed-Dâliyeh: The Slave Sales. Ph.D. dissertation, Harvard University.

Gunter, Ann C., and Margaret Cool Root
1998 "Replicating, Inscribing, Giving: Ernst Herzfeld and Artaxerxes' Silver *Phiale* in the Freer Gallery of Art." *Ars Orientalis* 28: 1–38.

Guzzo, Maria G. A.
1997 "Phoenician-Punic." In *The Oxford Encyclopedia of Archaeology in the Near East* 4, edited by Eric M. Meyers, pp. 317–24. New York: Oxford University Press.

Hallock, Richard T.
1942 "Darius I, the King of the Persepolis Tablets." *Journal of Near Eastern Studies* 1: 230–32.
1969 *Persepolis Fortification Tablets*. Oriental Institute Publications 92. Chicago: University of Chicago Press.
1973 "The Persepolis Fortification Archive." *Orientalia* 42: 320–23.
1977 "The Use of Seals on the Persepolis Fortification Tablets." In *Seals and Sealing in the Ancient Near East*. Bibliotheca Mesopotamica 6, edited by McGuire Gibson and Robert D. Biggs, pp. 127–33. Malibu: Undena.
1978 "Selected Fortification Texts." *Cahiers de la Délégation archéologique française en Iran* 8: 109–36.
1985 "The Evidence of the Persepolis Tablets." In *The Cambridge History of Iran*, Volume 2: *The Median and Achaemenian Periods*, edited by Ilya Gershevitch, pp. 588–609. Cambridge: Cambridge University Press.

Handley-Schachler, Morrison
1998 "The *Lan* Ritual in the Persepolis Fortification Texts." In *Studies in Persian History: Essays in Memory of David M. Lewis*, edited by Maria Brosius and Amélie Kuhrt, pp. 195–204. Achaemenid History 11. Leiden: Nederlands Instituut voor het Nabije Oosten.

Hansen, Donald P.
1987 "The Fantastic World of Sumerian Art; Seal Impressions from Ancient Lagash." In *Monsters and Demons in the Ancient and Medieval Worlds: Papers Presented in Honor of Edith Porada*, edited by A. Farkas, P. O. Harper, and E. B. Harrison, pp. 53–63. Mainz: Philipp von Zabern.

Harper, Prudence O.
1978 *The Royal Hunter: Art of the Sasanian Empire*. New York: Asia Society in association with John Weatherhill.

Harper, Prudence O.; Joan Aruz; and Françoise Tallon, editors
1992 *The Royal City of Susa: Ancient Near Eastern Treasures in the Louvre*. New York: Metropolitan Museum of Art.

Harrington, Fred A.
1977 *A Guide to the Mammals of Iran*. Tehran: Department of the Environment.

Helms, Svend W.
1997 *Excavations at Old Kandahar in Afghanistan 1976–1978. Stratigraphy, Pottery and Other Finds*. British Archaeological Reports, International Series 686; Society for South Asian Studies Monograph 2. Oxford: Archaeopress.

Henkelman, Wouter
1995/96 "The Royal Achaemenid Crown." *Archaeologische Mitteilungen aus Iran* 28: 275–93.

Herbordt, Suzanne
1992 *Neuassyrische Glyptik des 8.–7. Jh. v. Chr*. State Archives of Assyria Studies 1. Helsinki: State Archives of Assyria.

Herrmann, Georgina
1986 *Ivories from Room SW 37 Fort Shalmaneser: Commentary and Catalogue*. Ivories from Nimrud (1949–1963) 4/1. London: British School of Archaeology in Iraq.

Herzfeld, Ernst
1934 "Recent Discoveries at Persepolis." *Journal of the Royal Asiatic Society* 1934: 226–232.
1941 *Iran in the Ancient East*. London: Oxford University Press.

Hinz, Walther
1971 "Achämenidische Hofverwaltung." *Zeitschrift für Assyriologie* 61: 260–311.
1976 *Darius und die Perser: Eine Kulturgeschichte der Achämeniden*. Baden-Baden: Holle Verlag.

Hinz, Walther, and Heidemarie Koch
1987 *Elamisches Wörterbuch*. Archaeologische Mitteilungen aus Iran, Ergänzungsband, 17. Berlin: Dietrich Reimer Verlag.

Hrouda, Barthel
1965 *Die Kulturgeschichte des assyrischen Flachbildes*. Saarbrücker Beiträge zur Altertumskunde 2. Bonn: Rudolf Habelt Verlag.

Jacobsen, Thorkild
1976 *The Treasures of Darkness: A History of Mesopotamian Religion*. New Haven and London: Yale University Press.

Jakob-Rost, Liane
　1997　*Die Stempelsiegel im Vorderasiatischen Museum Berlin.* Second edition. Mainz: Philipp von Zabern.

Jeffery, Lilian Hamilton
　1990　*The Local Scripts of Archaic Greece: A Study of the Origin of the Greek Alphabet and Its Development from the Eighth to the Fifth Centuries B.C.* Revised edition with supplement by A. W. Johnson. Oxford: Clarendon Press.

Joannès, F.
　1990　"Textes babyloniens de Suse d'époque achéménide." In *Contribution à l'histoire de l'Iran: Mélanges offerts à Jean Perrot,* edited by François Vallat, pp. 173–80. Paris: Éditions recherche sur les civilisations.

Jones, Charles E.
　1990　Document and Circumstance at the City of the Persians. Unpublished paper presented at the symposium Ancient Art for the Twenty-First Century, San Antonio Museum of Art and Trinity University, San Antonio.
　1990–94　*Pirradaziš.* Chicago: Charles E. Jones.
　1999　"Zišsabarna (*Ciçafarnah), not Uššabarna in PFS 36*." *N.A.B.U.: Nouvelles Assyriologiques Brèves et Utilitaires,* Volume 1999, Number 3. September 1999.

Jones, Charles E., and Matthew W. Stolper
　1986　"Two Late Elamite Tablets at Yale." In *Fragmenta Historiae Elamicae: Mélanges offerts à M.-J. Steve,* edited by L. de Meyer, H. Gasche, and F. Vallat, pp. 243–54. Paris: Éditions recherche sur les civilisations.

Kaim, Barbara
　1991　"Das geflügelte Symbol in der Achämenidischen Glyptik." *Archaeologische Mitteilungen aus Iran* 24: 31–34.

Kantor, Helene J.
　1962　"A Bronze Plaque with Relief Decoration from Tell Tainat." *Journal of Near Eastern Studies* 21: 93–117.

Kantor, Helene J., and Pinhas Delougaz
　1996　*Chogha Mish,* Volume 1: *The First Five Seasons of Excavations, 1961–1971.* Edited by Abbas Alizadeh. Oriental Institute Publications 101. Chicago: Oriental Institute.

Kaptan, Deniz
　1996a　"The Great King's Audience." In *Fremde Zeiten: Festschrift für Jürgen Borchhardt,* edited by F. Blakolmer, K. R. Krierer, F. Krinzinger, A. Landskron-Dinstl, H. D. Szemethy, and K. Zhuber-Okrog, pp. 259–71. Vienna: Phoibos Verlag.
　1996b　"Some Remarks About the Hunting Scenes on the Seal Impressions of Daskyleion." In *Archives et sceaux du monde hellénistique,* edited by Marie-Françoise Boussac and Antonio Invernizzi, pp. 85–100. Bulletin de correspondance hellénique, Supplément 29. Athens: École française d'Athènes.
　in press　*Catalogue of Seal Impressions on the Bullae from Ergili/Daskyleion.* Achaemenid History 12. Leiden: Nederlands Instituut voor het Nabije Oosten.

Kaptan-Bayburtluoğlu, Deniz
　1990　"A Group of Seal Impressions on the Bullae from Ergili/Daskyleion." *Epigraphica Anatolica* 16: 15–27.

Karg, Norbert
　1984　*Untersuchungen zur älteren frühdynastischen Glyptik Babyloniens: Aspekte regionaler Entwicklungen in der ersten Hälfte des 3. Jahrtausends.* Baghdader Forschungen 8. Mainz: Philipp von Zabern.

Kawami, Trudy
　1987　*Monumental Art of the Parthian Period in Iran.* Acta Iranica 26. Leiden: E. J. Brill.

Kawase, Toyoko
　1984　"Female Workers 'Pašap' in the Persepolis Royal Economy." *Acta Sumerologica* 6: 19–31.

Keel, Othmar
　1992　"Iconography and the Bible." In *The Anchor Bible Dictionary,* Volume 3, edited by David N. Freedman, pp. 358–74. New York: Doubleday.

Keel, Othmar, and Christoph Uehlinger
　1990　*Altorientalische Miniaturkunst: Die ältesten visuellen Massenkommunikationsmittel. Ein Blick in die Sammlung des Biblischen Instituts der Universität Freiburg Schweiz.* Mainz: Philipp von Zabern.

Kelly-Buccellati, Marilyn
　1977　"Towards the Use of Quantitative Analysis in Mesopotamian Sphragistics." *Mesopotamia* 12: 41–52.
　1986　"Sealing Practices at Terqa." In *Insight through Images: Studies in Honor of Edith Porada,* edited by Marilyn Kelly-Buccellati, pp. 133–42. Bibliotheca Mesopotamica 21. Malibu: Undena.
　1998　"The Workshops of Urkesh." In *Urkesh and the Hurrians. Studies in Honor of Lloyd Cotsen,* edited by Giorgio Buccellati and Marilyn Kelly-Buccellati, pp. 35–50. Urkesh/Mozan Studies 3. Bibliotheca Mesopotamica 26. Malibu: Undena.

Kent, Roland G.
　1953　*Old Persian: Grammar, Texts, Lexicon.* Second revised edition. American Oriental Series 33. New Haven: American Oriental Society.

Kleiss, W.
　1990　"Kastenmauern in der frühen iranischen Architektur." In *Contribution à l'histoire de l'Iran. Mélanges offerts à Jean Perrot,* edited by François Vallat, pp. 165–72. Paris: Éditions recherche sur les civilisations.
　1992　"Beobachtungen aus dem Burgberg von Persepolis." *Archaeologische Mitteilungen aus Iran* 25: 155–67.

Klengel-Brandt, Evelyn
　1969　"Siegelabrollungen aus dem Babylon der Spätzeit." *Oriens Antiquus* 8: 329–36.

Klengel-Brandt, Evelyn, editor
　1997　*Mit Sieben Siegeln versehen: Das Siegel in Wirtschaft und Kunst des Alten Orients.* Mainz: Philipp von Zabern. Berlin: Staatliche Museen zu Berlin, Vorderasiatisches Museum.

Koch, Heidemarie
　1977　*Die religiösen Verhältnisse der Dareioszeit: Untersuchungen an Hand der Elamischen Persepolistäfel-*

chen. Göttinger Orientforschungen III. Reihe: Iranica, Band 4. Wiesbaden: Harrassowitz
- 1981 "'Hofschatzwarte' und 'Schatzhäuser' in der Persis." *Zeitschrift für Assyriologie* 71: 232–47.
- 1983 "Zu den Lohnverhältnissen der Dareioszeit in der Persis." In *Kunst und Kultur der Achämenidenzeit und ihr Fortleben*, edited by Heidemarie Koch and D. N. MacKenzie, pp. 19–50. Archaeologische Mitteilungen aus Iran, Ergänzungsband 10. Berlin: Dietrich Reimer.
- 1986 "Die Achämenidische Poststrasse von Persepolis nach Susa." *Archaeologische Mitteilungen aus Iran* 19: 133–47.
- 1987 "Götter und ihre Verehrung im achämenidischen Persien." *Zeitschrift für Assyriologie* 77: 239–278.
- 1990 *Verwaltung und Wirtschaft im persischen Kernland zur Zeit der Achämeniden*. Beihefte zum Tübinger Atlas des Vorderen Orients Reihe B, Nr. 89. Wiesbaden: Dr. Ludwig Reichert Verlag.
- 1992 *Es Kündet Dareios der König ...: Vom Leben im persischen Grossreich*. Kulturgeschichte der Antiken Welt 55. Mainz: Philipp von Zabern.
- 1993 *Achämeniden-Studien*. Wiesbaden: Harrassowitz.
- 1994 "Zu den Frauen im Achämenidenreich." In *Iranian and Indo-European Studies. Memorial Volume of Otakar Klima*, edited by Petr Vavroušek, pp. 125–41. Prague: Enigma Corporation.

Kohl, Philip, and Stephan Kroll
- 1999 "Notes on the Fall of Horom." In *Neo-Assyrian, Median, Achaemenian and Other Studies in Honor of David Stronach*, edited by R. Boucharlat, J. E. Curtis, and E. Haerinck. *Iranica Antiqua* 34: 243–59.

Krefter, Friedrich
- 1971 *Persepolis Rekonstruktionen*. Teheraner Forschungen 3. Berlin: Deutsches Archäologisches Institut.

Kuhrt, Amélie
- 1989 "Conclusions." In *Le tribut dans l'empire perse*, edited by P. Briant and C. Herrenschmidt, pp. 217–31. Travaux de l'Institut d'études iraniennes de l'Université de la Sorbonne Nouvelle 13. Louvain and Paris: Peeters.
- 1990 "Achaemenid Babylonia: Sources and Problems." In *Centre and Periphery*, edited by Heleen Sancisi-Weerdenburg and Amélie Kuhrt, pp. 177–94. Achaemenid History 4. Leiden: Nederlands Instituut voor het Nabije Oosten.

Lambert, W. G.
- 1975 Review of *Les légendes des sceaux cassites*, by H. Limet. *Bibliotheca Orientalis* 32: 219–23.
- 1979 "Near Eastern Seals in the Gulbenkian Museum of Oriental Art, University of Durham." *Iraq* 41: 1–45.

Lecoq, Pierre
- 1983 "Un problème de religion achéménide: Ahura Mazda ou Xvarnah?" *Acta Iranica* 23: 301–26.
- 1997 *Les inscriptions de la Perse achéménide*. Paris: Gallimard.

Legrain, L.
- 1951 *Seal Cylinders*. Ur Excavations 10. London and Philadelphia: British Museum and University of Pennsylvania.

Leith, Mary J. W.
- 1997 *Wadi Daliyeh 1: The Wadi Daliyeh Seal Impressions*. Discoveries in the Judaean Desert 24. Oxford: Clarendon Press.

Lerner, Judith A.
- 1977 *Christian Seals of the Sasanian Period*. Uitgaven van het Nederlands historisch-archaeologisch Instituut te Istanbul 41. Leiden: Nederlands historisch-archaeologisch Instituut te Istanbul.

Lewis, David M.
- 1977 *Sparta and Persia*. Cincinnati Classical Studies 1. Leiden: E. J. Brill.
- 1980 "Datis the Mede." *Journal of Hellenic Studies* 100: 194–95.
- 1984 "Postscript." In *Persia and the Greeks*, by A. R. Burn, pp. 587–612. Second edition. London: Duckworth.
- 1985 "Persians in Herodotus." In *The Greek Historians: Literature and History. Papers Presented to A. E. Raubitschek*, edited by M. H. Jameson, pp. 101–17. Saratoga: Anma Libri.
- 1990 "The Persepolis Fortification Texts." In *Centre and Periphery*, edited by Heleen Sancisi-Weerdenburg and Amélie Kuhrt, pp. 1–6. Achaemenid History 4. Leiden: Nederlands Instituut voor het Nabije Oosten.
- 1994 "The Persepolis Tablets: Speech, Seal and Script." In *Literacy and Power in the Ancient World*, edited by A. K. Bowman and G. Woolf, pp. 17–32. Cambridge: Cambridge University Press.

Lockwood, William G., editor
- 1984 *Beyond Ethnic Boundaries: New Approaches in the Anthropology of Ethnicity*. Ann Arbor: University of Michigan Press.

MacGinnis, John
- 1994 "The Royal Establishment at Sippar in the 6th Century BC." *Zeitschrift für Assyriologie* 84: 198–219.
- 1995 *Letter Orders from Sippar and the Administration of the Ebabbara in the Late Babylonian Period*. Poznan: Bonami.

Mallowan, Barbara
- 1986 "Three Middle Assyrian Bronze/Copper Dogs." In *Insight through Images: Studies in Honor of Edith Porada*, edited by Marilyn Kelly-Buccellati, pp. 149–52. Bibliotheca Mesopotamica 21. Malibu: Undena.

Marcus, Michelle I.
- 1994 "In His Lips He Held a Spell." *Source: Notes in the History of Art* 13 (no. 4): 9–14.
- 1996 *Emblems of Identity and Prestige: The Seals and Sealings from Hasanlu, Iran. Commentary and Catalogue*. University Museum Monograph 84. Hasanlu Special Studies 3. Philadelphia: University Museum, University of Pennsylvania.

Mayrhofer, Manfred
- 1973 *Onomastica Persepolitana: Das Altiranische Namengut der Persepolis-Täfelchen*. Sitzungsberichte der Österreichischen Akademie der Wissenschaften, Philosophisch-historische Klasse 286. Vienna: Österreichische Akademie der Wissenschaften.
- 1978 *Supplement zur Sammlung der altpersischen Inschriften*. Sitzungsberichte der Österreichischen Akademie der Wissenschaften, Philosophisch-historische Klasse 338. Vienna: Österreichische Akademie der Wissenschaften.

Ménant, Joachim
  1886 *Recherches sur la glyptique orientale.* Paris: Maisonneuve Frères et Ch. Leclerc, Éditeurs.

Merhav, Rivka, editor
  1991 *Urartu: A Metalworking Center in the First Millennium B.C.E.* Israel Museum Catalog 324. Tel Aviv: Sabinsky Press.

Miller, Margaret C.
  1989 "Peacocks and *Tryphe* in Classical Athens." *Archaeological News* 15: 1–10.
  1997 *Athens and Persia in the Fifth Century BC: A Study in Cultural Receptivity.* Cambridge: Cambridge University Press.

Miller-Collett, Stella, and Margaret Cool Root
  1997 "An Achaemenid Seal from the Lower City." *Studia Troica* 7: 355–62.

Miroschedji, Pierre de
  1981 "Le dieu élamite au serpent et aux eaux jaillissantes." *Iranica Antiqua* 16: 1–25.
  1982 "Notes sur la glyptique de la fin de l'Élam." *Revue d'assyriologie et d'archéologie orientale* 76: 51–63.
  1985 "La fin du royaume d'Anšan et de Suse et la naissance de l'Empire perse." *Zeitschrift für Assyriologie* 75: 265–306.

Moerman, Michael
  1965 "Who are the Lue? Ethnic Identification in a Complex Civilization." *American Anthropologist* 67: 1215–30.
  1968 "Being Lue: Uses and Abuses of Ethnic Identification." In *Essays on the Problem of Tribe* (Proceedings of the 1967 Annual Spring Meeting of the American Ethnological Society), edited by June Helm, pp. 153–69. Seattle: University of Washington Press.

Moorey, P. R. S.
  1978 "The Iconography of an Achaemenid Stamp-Seal Acquired in the Lebanon." *Iran* 16: 143–54.
  1979 "Aspects of Worship and Ritual on Achaemenid Seals." In *Seventh International Congress on Iranian Art and Archaeology, Munich 1976*, pp. 218–26. Berlin: Dietrich Reimer.
  1988 "The Persian Empire." In *Cambridge Ancient History*, Volume 4, Supplement 1, edited by J. Boardman, pp. 1–94. New York: Macmillan.
  1994 *Ancient Mesopotamian Materials and Industries. The Archaeological Evidence.* Oxford: Clarendon Press.

Moortgat, Anton
  1940 *Vorderasiatische Rollsiegel.* Berlin: Verlag Gebr. Mann.

Morris, Christine
  1993 "Hands Up for the Individual! The Role of Attribution Studies in Aegean Prehistory." *Cambridge Archaeological Journal* 3: 41–66.

Mousavi, Ali
  1992 "Parsa, a Stronghold for Darius: A Preliminary Study of the Defence System of Persepolis." *East and West* 42: 203–26.
  1999 "La Ville de Parsa: quelques remarques sur la topographie at le système défensif de Persépolis." In *Neo-Assyrian, Median, Achaemenian and Other Studies in Honor of David Stronach*, edited by R. Boucharlat, J. E. Curtis, and E. Haerinck. *Iranica Antiqua* 34: 145–55.

Muscarella, Oscar W.
  1980 *The Catalogue of Ivories from Hasanlu, Iran.* University Museum Monograph 40. Hasanlu Special Studies 2. Philadelphia: University Museum, University of Pennsylvania.

Negahban, Ezat O.
  1991 *Excavations at Haft Tepe, Iran.* Philadelphia: University Museum, University of Pennsylvania.

Nijhowne, Jeanne D.
  1999 *Politics, Religion, and Cylinder Seals: A Study of Mesopotamian Symbolism in the Second Millennium B.C.* British Archaeological Reports, International Series 772. Oxford: John and Erica Hedges.

Nylander, Carl
  1983 "The Standard of the Great King: A Problem in the Alexander Mosaic." *Opuscula Romana* 14: 19–37.
  1993 "Darius III – The Coward King: Point and Counterpoint." In *Alexander the Great, Reality and Myth*, edited by J. Carlsen, B. Due, O. S. Due, and B. Poulsen, pp. 145-59. Analecta Romana Instituti Danici, Supplement 20. Rome: "L'erma" di Bretschneider.

Oelsner, Joachim
  1986 *Materialen zur babylonischen Gesellschaft und Kultur in hellenistischer Zeit.* Budapest: Eötvös Loránd Tudományegyetem.

Ouseley, William
  1821 *Travels in Various Countries of the East – More Particularly Persia.* Volume 2. London: Rodwell and Martin (1819–1823).

Owen, David I.
  1981 "Of Birds, Eggs and Turtles." *Zeitschrift für Assyriologie* 71: 29–50.

Özgen, İlknur, and Jean Öztürk
  1996 *The Lydian Treasure: Heritage Recovered.* With contributions by M. J. Mellink, C. H. Greenewalt, Jr., K. Akbiyikoğlu, and L. M. Kaye. Istanbul: Ministry of Culture, Republic of Turkey.

Özgüç, Nimet
  1980 "Seal Impressions from the Palaces at Acemhöyük." In *Ancient Art in Seals*, edited by Edith Porada, pp. 61–86. Princeton: Princeton University Press.

Paley, Samuel M.
  1986 "Inscribed Neo-Assyrian and Neo-Babylonian Cylinder Seals and Impressions." In *Insight through Images: Studies in Honor of Edith Porada*, edited by Marilyn Kelly-Buccellati, pp. 209–20. Bibliotheca Mesopotamica 21. Malibu: Undena.

Parker, Barbara
  1955 "Excavations at Nimrud, 1949–1953: Seals and Seal Impressions." *Iraq* 17: 93–125.
  1962 "Seals and Seal Impressions from the Nimrud Excavations, 1955–1958." *Iraq* 24: 26–40.

Parker, R. A., and W. H. Dubberstein
  1956 *Babylonian Chronology 626 B.C.–A.D. 75.* Brown University Studies 19. Providence: Brown University Press.

Pedersén, Olof
  1998 *Archives and Libraries in the Ancient Near East 1500–300 B.C.* Bethesda: CDL Press.

Petrie, William M. F.; E. Mackay; and G. Wainwright
  1910 *Meydum and Memphis (3).* British School of Archaeology in Egypt 18. London: British School of Archaeology.

Pittman, Holly
  1992 "The Proto-Elamite Period." In *The Royal City of Susa: Ancient Near Eastern Treasures in the Louvre,* edited by Prudence O. Harper, Joan Aruz, and Françoise Tallon, pp. 68–77. New York: Metropolitan Museum of Art.
  1994 *The Glazed Steatite Glyptic Style: The Structure and Function of an Image System in the Administration of Protoliterate Mesopotamia.* Berliner Beiträge zum vorderen Orient 16. Berlin: Dietrich Reimer Verlag.

Porada, Edith
  1947a *Seal Impressions of Nuzi.* Annual of the American Schools of Oriental Research 24. New Haven: American Schools of Oriental Research.
  1947b "Suggestions for the Classification of Neo-Babylonian Cylinder Seals." *Orientalia* 16: 145–65.
  1948 *Corpus of Ancient Near Eastern Seals in North American Collections,* Volume 1: *The Collection of the Pierpont Morgan Library.* Bollingen Series 14. New York: Pantheon Books.
  1960 "Greek Coin Impressions from Ur." *Iraq* 22: 228–34.
  1961 Review of *Persepolis 2: Contents of the Treasury and Other Discoveries,* by Erich Schmidt. *Journal of Near Eastern Studies* 20: 66–71.
  1965 *The Art of Ancient Iran.* New York: Crown Publishers.
  1979 "Achaemenid Art: Monumental and Minute." In *Highlights of Persian Art,* edited by R. Ettinghausen and E. Yarshater, pp. 57–94. Boulder: Westview Press.
  1980 "Introduction." In *Ancient Art in Seals,* edited by Edith Porada, pp. 3–30. Princeton: Princeton University Press.
  1982 "Problems of Method in the Archaeology and Art History of the Ancient Near East." *Journal of the American Oriental Society* 102: 501–06.

Porter, Paul A.
  1985 *Metaphors and Monsters. A Literary-Critical Study of Daniel 7 and 8.* Toronto: University of Toronto Press.

Posner, Ernst
  1972 *Archives in the Ancient World.* Cambridge: Harvard University Press.

Potts, Daniel T.
  1999 *The Archaeology of Elam. Formation and Transformation of an Ancient Iranian State.* Cambridge World Archaeology. Cambridge: Cambridge University Press.

Rice, E. E.
  1983 *The Grand Procession of Ptolemy Philadelphus.* London: Oxford University Press.

Richter, Gisella M. A.
  1946 "Greeks in Persia." *American Journal of Archaeology* 50: 15–30.

Roaf, Michael
  1980 "Texts about the Sculptures and Sculptors at Persepolis." *Iran* 18: 65–74.
  1983 "Sculptures and Sculptors at Persepolis." *Iran* 21: 1–164.
  1995 "Media and Mesopotamia: History and Architecture." In *Later Mesopotamia and Iran: Tribes and Empires 1600–539 BC. Proceedings of a Seminar in Memory of Vladimir G. Lukonin,* edited by J. Curtis, pp. 54–66. London: British Museum Press.

Rochberg, Francesca
  1996 "Personifications and Metaphors in Babylonian Celestial *Omina.*" *Journal of the American Oriental Society* 116: 475–85.

Root, Margaret Cool
  1976 "The Herzfeld Archive of the Metropolitan Museum of Art." *Metropolitan Museum Journal* 11: 119–24.
  1979 *The King and Kingship in Achaemenid Art: Essays on the Creation of an Iconography of Empire.* Acta Iranica 19. Leiden: E. J. Brill.
  1981 Review of *Christian Seals of the Sasanian Period,* by Judith A. Lerner. *Journal of Near Eastern Studies* 40: 61–62.
  1985 "The Parthenon Frieze and the Apadana Reliefs at Persepolis: Reassessing a Programmatic Relationship." *American Journal of Archaeology* 89: 103–20.
  1988 "Evidence from Persepolis for the Dating of Persian and Archaic Greek Coinage." *Numismatic Chronicle* 148: 1–12.
  1989 "The Persian Archer at Persepolis: Aspects of Chronology, Style and Symbolism." In *L'or perse et l'histoire greque,* edited by R. Descat, pp. 33–50. Revue des études anciennes 91. Paris: Belle Lettres.
  1990a "Circles of Artistic Programming: Strategies for Studying Creative Process at Persepolis." In *Investigating Artistic Environments in the Ancient Near East,* edited by Ann C. Gunter, pp. 115–39. Washington, D.C.: Smithsonian Institution.
  1990b *Crowning Glories: Persian Kingship and the Power of Creative Continuity.* Ann Arbor: Kelsey Museum of Archaeology.
  1991 "From the Heart: Powerful Persianisms in the Art of the Western Empire." In *Asia Minor and Egypt: Old Cultures in a New Empire,* edited by Heleen Sancisi-Weerdenburg and Amélie Kuhrt, pp. 1–29. Achaemenid History 6. Leiden: Nederlands Instituut voor het Nabije Oosten.
  1992 "Persian Art." In *The Anchor Bible Dictionary, Volume 1,* edited by David N. Freedman, pp. 440–47. New York: Doubleday.
  1993 Review of *Investigating Artistic Environments in the Ancient Near East,* edited by Ann C. Gunter. *Topoi* 3: 217–45.
  1994 "Lifting the Veil: Artistic Transmission Beyond the Boundaries of Historical Periodisation." In *Continuity and Change,* edited by Amélie Kuhrt, Heleen Sancisi-Weerdenburg, and Margaret Cool Root, pp. 9–37. Achaemenid History 8. Leiden: Nederlands Instituut voor het Nabije Oosten.
  1995 "Art and Archaeology of the Achaemenid Empire." In *Civilizations of the Ancient Near East,* Volume 4, edited by Jack M. Sasson, pp. 2615–37. New York: Scribner.

Root, Margaret Cool (*cont.*)
- 1996a Modes of Seal Application on the Persepolis Fortification Tablets: Protocol and Predilection in Re-Creative Image-Making. Communication presented at the 1996 Meeting of the American Oriental Society, Philadelphia.
- 1996b "The Persepolis Fortification Tablets: Archival Issues and the Problem of Stamps Versus Cylinder Seals." In *Archives et sceaux du monde hellénistique*, edited by Marie-Françoise Boussac and Antonio Invernizzi, pp. 3–27. Bulletin de correspondance hellénique, Supplément 29. Athens: École française d'Athènes.
- 1997 "Cultural Pluralisms on the Persepolis Fortification Tablets." *Topoi* Supplément 1: 229–52.
- 1998 "Pyramidal Stamp Seals – The Persepolis Connection." In *Studies in Persian History: Essays in Memory of David M. Lewis*, edited by Maria Brosius and Amélie Kuhrt, pp. 257–98. Achaemenid History 11. Leiden: Instituut voor het Nabije Oosten.
- 1999a "The Cylinder Seal from Pasargadae: Of Wings and Wheels, Date and Fate." In *Neo-Assyrian, Median, Achaemenian and Other Studies in Honor of David Stronach*, edited by R. Boucharlat, J. E. Curtis, and E. Haerinck. *Acta Iranica* 34: 157–90.
- 1999b Irreverent Inversions. Seal Play at the Persian Court. Paper presented at the symposium Visual Humour in World Art. Warburg Institute, London.
- 2000 "The Adams (ex-Herzfeld) Collection of Prehistoric Stamp Seals: Prospects and Quandaries." *Bulletin of the Museums of Art and Archaeology, The University of Michigan 1997–2000* 12: 9–40.
- in press "Animals in the Art of Ancient Iran." In *A History of the Animal World in the Ancient Near East*, edited by B. J. Collins, pp.169–209. Leiden: E. J. Brill.

Salje, Beate
- 1997 "Siegelverwendung im privaten Bereich. 'Schmuck' – Amulett – Grabbeigabe." In *Mit Sieben Siegeln versehen: Das Siegel in Wirtschaft und Kunst des Alten Orients*, edited by Evelyn Klengel-Brandt, pp. 124–37. Mainz: Philipp von Zabern. Berlin: Staatliche Museen zu Berlin, Vorderasiatisches Museum.

Salonen, Armas
- 1973 *Vögel und Vogelfang im alten Mesopotamien*. Helsinki: Suomalainen Tiedeakatemia.

Sami, Ali
- 1955 *Persepolis (Takht-i-Jamshid)*. Second edition. Shiraz: Musavi Printing Office.

Sancisi-Weerdenburg, Heleen
- 1991 "Nowruz in Persepolis." In *Through Travellers' Eyes: European Travellers on the Iranian Monuments*, edited by Heleen Sancisi-Weerdenburg and Jan Willem Drijvers, pp. 173–201. Achaemenid History 7. Leiden: Nederlands Instituut voor het Nabije Oosten.
- 1993 "Political Concepts in Old Persian Royal Inscriptions." In *Anfänge politischen Denkens in der Antike: Die nahöstlichen Kulturen und die Griechen*, edited by K. Raaflaub, pp. 145–63. Schriften des historischen Kollegs, Kolloquien 24. Munich: R. Oldenbourg.
- 1995 "Darius I and the Persian Empire." In *Civilizations of the Ancient Near East*, Volume 2, edited by Jack M. Sasson, pp. 1035–50. New York: Scribner.
- 1998 "Bāji." In *Studies in Persian History: Essays in Memory of David M. Lewis*, edited by Maria Brosius and Amélie Kuhrt, pp. 23–34. Achaemenid History 11. Leiden: Nederlands Instituut voor het Nabije Oosten.

Sarraf, Mohamed R.
- 1997 "Neue architektonische und städtebauliche Funde von Ekbatana-Tepe (Hamadan)." *Archaeologische Mitteilungen aus Iran and Turan* 29: 321–39.

Scheil, V.
- 1911 *Textes élamites-anzanites*. Mémoires de la Délégation en Perse 11. Paris: E. Leroux.

Schmandt-Besserat, Denise
- 1994 "Tokens: A Prehistoric Archive System." In *Archives before Writing* (Proceedings of the International Colloquium Oriolo Romano, 23–25 October 1991), edited by Piera Ferioli, Enrica Fiandra, Gian Giacomo Fissore, and Marcella Frangipane, pp. 13–28. Rome: Centro Internazionale di Richerche Archeologiche Antropologiche e Storiche.

Schmidt, Erich F.
- 1953 *Persepolis, Volume 1: Structures, Reliefs, Inscriptions*. Oriental Institute Publications 68. Chicago: University of Chicago Press.
- 1957 *Persepolis, Volume 2: Contents of the Treasury and Other Discoveries*. Oriental Institute Publications 69. Chicago: University of Chicago Press.

Schmitt, Rüdiger
- 1981 *Altpersische Siegel-Inschriften*. Sitzungsberichte der Österreichischen Akademie der Wissenschaften, Philosophisch-historische Klasse 381. Vienna: Österreichische Akademie der Wissenschaften.
- 1983 "Achaimenidisches bei Thukydides." In *Kunst, Kultur und Geschichte der Achämenidenzeit und ihr Fortleben*, edited by H. Koch and D. Mackenzie, pp. 69–86. Berlin: Dietrich Reimer Verlag.
- 1989 "Ein altiranisches Flüssigkeitsmass: *mariš." In *Indogermanica Europaea: Festschrift für Wolfgang Meid zum 60. Geburtstag am 12.11.1989*, edited by K. Heller, O. Panagl, J. Tischler, pp. 301–15. Grazer Linguistische Monographien 4. Graz: Institut für Sprachwissenschaft der Universität Graz.
- 1991 *The Bisitun Inscription of Darius the Great: Old Persian Text*. Corpus Inscriptionum Iranicarum, Part 1, Volume 1, edited by an International Committee. London: Corpus Inscriptionum Iranicarum and School of Oriental and African Studies.
- 1993 "Die Sprachverhältnisse im Achaimenidenreich." In *Lingue e culture in contatto nel mondo antico e altomedievale*, pp. 77–102. Atti dell'VIII Convegno Internazionale de Linguisti. Brescia: Paideia Editrice.
- 1995/96 "Eine Goldtafel mit angeblicher Dareios-Inschrift." *Archaeologische Mitteilungen aus Iran* 28: 269–73.

Seidl, U.
- 1990 "Altelamische Siegel." In *Contribution à l'histoire de l'Iran. Mélanges offerts à Jean Perrot*, edited by François Vallat, pp. 129–35. Paris: Éditions recherche sur les civilisations.

Shahbazi, A. S.
  1980 "An Achaemenid Symbol II: Farnah (Godgiven) Fortune 'Symbolized.'" *Archaeologische Mitteilungen aus Iran* 9: 119–47.

Sherwin-White, Susan, and Amélie Kuhrt
  1993 *From Samarkhand to Sardis. A New Approach to the Seleucid Empire*. Berkeley and Los Angeles: University of California Press.

Sievertsen, Uwe
  1992 "Das Messer vom Gebel el-Arak." *Baghdader Mitteilungen* 23: 1–75.

Starr, Chester G.
  1976 "A Sixth-Century Athenian Tetradrachm used to Seal a Clay Tablet from Persepolis." *Numismatic Chronicle* 136: 219–22.

Stein, Diana
  1993 *Das Archiv des Šilwa-Teššup*, Heft 8: *The Seal Impressions*. Wiesbaden: Harrassowitz.

Stern, Ephraim
  1971 "Seal Impressions in the Achaemenid Style in the Province of Judah." *Bulletin of the American Schools of Oriental Research* 202: 6–16.
  1990 "New Evidence on the Administrative Division of Palestine in the Persian Period." In *Centre and Periphery*, edited by Heleen Sancisi-Weerdenburg and Amélie Kuhrt, pp. 221–26. Achaemenid History 4. Leiden: Nederlands Instituut voor het Nabije Oosten.
  1994 "Assyrian and Babylonian Elements in the Material Culture of Palestine in the Persian Period." *Transeuphratène* 7: 51–62.

Stolper, Matthew W.
  1984 "The Neo-Babylonian Text from the Persepolis Fortification." *Journal of Near Eastern Studies* 43: 299–310.
  1985 *Entrepreneurs and Empire: The Murašû Archive, the Murašû Firm and Persian Rule in Babylonia*. Uitgaven van het Nederlands historisch-archaeologisch Instituut te Istanbul 54. Leiden: Nederlands historisch-archaeologisch Instituut te Istanbul.
  1990a "The Kasr Archive." In *Centre and Periphery*, edited by Heleen Sancisi-Weerdenburg and Amélie Kuhrt, pp. 195–205. Achaemenid History 4. Leiden: Nederlands Instituut voor het Nabije Oosten.
  1990b "Late Achaemenid Legal Texts from Uruk and Larsa." *Baghdader Mitteilungen* 21: 559–622.
  1992a "Elamite Administrative Tablet with Impression of a Royal Name Seal." In *The Royal City of Susa: Ancient Near Eastern Treasures in the Louvre*, edited by Prudence O. Harper, Joan Aruz, and Françoise Tallon, p. 273. New York: Metropolitan Museum of Art.
  1992b "The Murašû Texts from Susa." *Revue d'assyriologie et d'archéologie orientale* 86: 69–77.
  1994 Review of *Iranians in Achaemenid Babylonia*, by Muhammad A. Dandamayev. *Journal of the American Oriental Society* 114: 617–24.
  1996 "A Paper Chase after the Aramaic on TCL 13 193." *Journal of the American Oriental Society* 116: 517–21.

Stronach, David
  1978 *Pasargadae*. Oxford: Clarendon Press.
  1990 "On the Genesis of the Old Persian Cuneiform Script." In *Contribution à l'histoire de l'Iran: Mélanges offerts à Jean Perrot*, edited by François Vallat, pp. 195–203. Paris: Éditions recherche sur les civilisations.

Sumner, William M.
  1986 "Achaemenid Settlement in the Persepolis Plain." *American Journal of Archaeology* 90: 3–31.

Tadjvidi, Akbar
  1970 "Persepolis." *Iran* 8: 186–87.
  1976 *Danestanihaye Novin darbareye Honar va Bastanshenasie asr-e Hakkamaneshi bar bonyad-e kavoshhaye panjsaleye Takht-e Jamshid* (*New Knowledge on Achaemenid Art and Archaeology based on Five Years Researches at Persepolis*). Tehran: Ministry of Cultures and Arts [A.H. 1355].

Teissier, Beatrice
  1984 *Cylinder Seals from the Marcopoli Collection*. Berkeley: University of California Press.
  1994 *Sealing and Seals on Texts from Kültepe Karum Level 2*. Uitgaven van het Nederlands historisch-archaeologisch Instituut te Istanbul 70. Leiden: Nederlands historisch-archaeologisch Instituut te Istanbul.

Tilia, Ann B.
  1972 *Studies and Restorations at Persepolis and Other Sites of Fārs*. Istituto Italiano per il Medio ed Estremo Oriente, Reports and Memoirs 16. Rome: Istituto per il Medio ed Estremo Oriente.
  1978 *Studies and Restorations at Persepolis and Other Sites of Fārs 2*. Istituto Italiano per il Medio ed Estremo Oriente, Reports and Memoirs 18. Rome: Istituto per il Medio ed Estremo Oriente.

Tucker, Elizabeth
  1998 "The 'Nominal Conjugations' in Achaemenid Elamite." In *Studies in Persian History: Essays in Memory of David M. Lewis*, edited by Maria Brosius and Amélie Kuhrt, pp. 165–94. Achaemenid History 11. Leiden: Nederlands Instituut voor het Nabije Oosten.

Tuplin, Christopher J.
  1987 "The Administration of the Achaemenid Empire." In *Coinage and Administration in the Athenian and Persian Empires: The Ninth Oxford Symposium on Coinage and Monetary History*, edited by Ian Carradice, pp. 109–66. British Archaeological Reports, International Series 343. Oxford: British Archaeological Reports.
  1991 "Modern and Ancient Travellers in the Achaemenid Empire." In *Through Travellers' Eyes: European Travellers on the Iranian Monuments*, edited by Heleen Sancisi-Weerdenburg and Jan-Willem Drijvers, pp. 37–57. Achaemenid History 7. Leiden: Nederlands Instituut voor het Nabije Oosten.
  1997 "Achaemenid Arithmetic: Numerical Problems in Persian History." *Topoi* Supplément 1: 365–421.
  1998 "The Seasonal Migration of the Achaemenid Kings: A Report on Old and New Evidence." In *Studies in Persian History: Essays in Memory of David M. Lewis*, edited by Maria Brosius and Amélie Kuhrt, pp. 63–114. Achaemenid History 11. Leiden: Nederlands Instituut voor het Nabije Oosten.

Turkish Ministry of Culture and Tourism
  1983   *The Anatolian Civilisations* 2. Istanbul: Turkish Ministry of Culture and Tourism.

Uehlinger, Christoph
  1999   "'Powerful Persianisms' in Glyptic Iconography of Persian Period Palestine." In *The Crisis of Israelite Religion. Transformation of Religious Tradition in Exilic and Post-Exilic Times*, edited by B. Becking and M. C. A. Korpel, pp. 134–82. Leiden: E. J. Brill.

Uchitel, Alexander
  1989   "Organization of Manpower in Achaemenid Persia According to the Fortification Archive." *Acta Sumerologica* 11: 225–38.

Vallat, François
  1992   "Les prétendus fonctionnaires *unsak* des textes néo-élamites et achéménides." *DATA: Achaemenid History Newsletter* 4: 5.
  1994   "Deux tablettes élamites de l'Université de Fribourg." *Journal of Near Eastern Studies* 53: 263–74.
  1997   "L'utilisation des sceaux-cylindres dans l'archivage des lettres de Persépolis." In *Sceaux d'Orient et leur emploi*, edited by Rika Gyselen, pp. 171–73. Res Orientales 10. Bures-sur-Yvette: Groupe pour l'étude de la civilisation du Moyen-Orient.

van Buren, E. Douglas
  1939   *The Fauna of Ancient Mesopotamia as Represented in Art*. Analecta Orientalia 18. Rome: Pontificum Institutum Biblicum.

van Driel, G.
  1987   "Continuity or Decay in the Late Achaemenid Period: Evidence from Southern Mesopotamia." In *Sources, Structures and Synthesis*, edited by Heleen Sancisi-Weerdenburg, pp. 159–81. Achaemenid History 1. Leiden: Nederlands Instituut voor het Nabije Oosten.

van Loon, Maurits N.
  1986   "The Drooping Lotus Flower." In *Insight through Images: Studies in Honor of Edith Porada*, edited by Marilyn Kelly-Buccellati, pp. 245–52. Bibliotheca Mesopotamica 21. Malibu: Undena.

Veenhof, Klaas R.
  1986   "Cuneiform Archives: An Introduction." In *Cuneiform Archives and Libraries: XXXe Rencontre Assyriologique Internationale 1983*, edited by Klaas R. Veenhof, pp. 1–36. Uitgaven van het Nederlands historisch-archaeologisch Instituut te Istanbul 57. Leiden: Nederlands historische-archaeologisch Instituut te Istanbul.

Vollenweider, Marie-Louise
  1967   *Catalogue raisonné des sceaux cylindres et intailles*, Volume 1. Geneva: Musée d'Art et d'Histoire de Genève.

von der Osten, Hans H.
  1934   *Ancient Oriental Seals in the Collection of Mr. Edward T. Newell*. Oriental Institute Publications 22. Chicago: University of Chicago Press.

Vulpe, Nicola
  1994   "Irony and the Unity of the *Gilgamesh Epic*." *Journal of Near Eastern Studies* 53: 275–83.

Wallenfels, Ronald
  1990   Sealed Cuneiform Tablets from Hellenistic Uruk: An Iconographic and Prosopographic Analysis of the Private Business Documents. Ph.D. dissertation, Columbia University.
  1993   "Zodiacal Signs Among the Seal Impressions from Hellenistic Uruk." In *The Tablet and the Scroll: Near Eastern Studies in Honor of William W. Hallo*, edited by M. E. Cohen, D. C. Snell, and D. B. Weisberg, pp. 281–89. Bethesda: CDL Press.
  1994   *Uruk: Hellenistic Seal Impressions in the Yale Babylonian Collection*, Volume 1: *Cuneiform Tablets*. Deutsches Archäologisches Institut Abteilung Baghdad, Ausgrabungen in Uruk-Warka Endberichte 19. Mainz: Philipp von Zabern.

Wartke, Ralf-B.
  1997   "Materialien der Siegel und ihre Herstellungstechniken." In *Mit Sieben Siegeln versehen: Das Siegel in Wirtschaft und Kunst des Alten Orients*, edited by Evelyn Klengel-Brandt, pp. 41–61. Mainz: Philipp von Zabern. Berlin: Staatliche Museen zu Berlin, Vorderasiatisches Museum.

Waters, Matthew W.
  1997   A Survey of Neo-Elamite History. Ph.D. dissertation, University of Pennsylvania.

Weber, Ursula, and Josef Wiesehöfer
  1996   *Das Reich der Achaimeniden: Eine Bibliographie*. Archäologische Mitteilungen aus Iran, Ergänzungsband 15. Berlin: Dietrich Reimer Verlag.

Weingarten, Judith
  1983   *The Zakro Master and His Place in Prehistory*. Studies in Mediterranean Archaeology, Pocketbook 26. Göteborg: P. Åström.
  1985   "Aspects of Tradition and Innovation in the Work of the Zakro Master." In *L'iconographie minoenne*, edited by P. Darcque and J.-C. Poursat, pp. 167–80. Bulletin de correspondance hellénique, Supplément 11. Athens: École française d'Athènes.

Whiting, Robert M.
  1977   "Sealing Practices on House and Land Sale Documents at Eshnunna in the Isin-Larsa Period." In *Seals and Sealing in the Ancient Near East*, edited by McGuire Gibson and Robert D. Biggs, pp. 67–74. Bibliotheca Mesopotamica 6. Malibu: Undena.

Wiesehöfer, Josef
  1996   *Ancient Persia from 550 BC to 650 AD*. Translated by A. Azodi. London and New York: I. B. Tauris Publishers.

Wilkinson, C. K.
  1965   "The Achaemenian Remains at Qaṣr-i Abu Naṣr." *Journal of Near Eastern Studies* 24: 341–45.

Winter, Irene
  1992   Review of *Ivories from Room 37 Fort Shalmaneser: Commentary and Catalogue*, by Georgina Herrmann. *Journal of Near Eastern Studies* 51: 135–41.

Wiseman, D. J.
  1959   *Cylinder Seals of Western Asia*. London: Batchworth Press.

Wittmann, Beatrice
    1992   "Babylonische Rollsiegel des 11.–7. Jahrhunderts v. Chr." *Baghdader Mitteilungen* 23: 169–289.

Young, T. Cuyler, Jr.
    1986   "Godin Tepe Period VI/V and Central Western Iran at the End of the Fourth Millennium." In *Ǧamdat Naṣr: Period or Regional Style?*, edited by U. Finkbeiner and W. Röllig, pp. 212–28. Beihefte zum Tübinger Atlas des Vorderen Orients, Reihe B (Geisteswissenschaften) Nr. 62. Wiesbaden: Ludwig Reichert.
    1988   "The Consolidation of the Empire and Its Limits of Growth under Darius and Xerxes." In *The Cambridge Ancient History,* Volume 4: *Persia, Greece and the Western Mediterranean, c. 525 to 479 B.C.*, edited by J. Boardman, N. G. L. Hammond, D. M. Lewis, and M. Ostwald, pp. 53–111. Second edition. Cambridge: Cambridge University Press.

Younger, John
    1991   *A Bibliography for Aegean Glyptic in the Bronze Age.* Berlin: Gebr. Mann.

Zadok, Ran
    1977   "Iranians and Individuals Bearing Iranian Names in Achaemenian Babylonia." *Israel Oriental Studies* 7: 89–138.

Zettler, Richard L.
    1979   "On the Chronological Range of Neo-Babylonian and Achaemenid Seals." *Journal of Near Eastern Studies* 38: 257–70.
    1987   "Sealings as Artifacts of Institutional Administration in Ancient Mesopotamia." *Journal of Cuneiform Studies* 39: 197–240.

INTRODUCTION

PART ONE: OVERVIEW OF THE FORTIFICATION ARCHIVE

This volume is the first of a projected three-volume catalog of glyptic evidence on the art and social history of the Achaemenid Persian Empire (ca. 550–330 B.C.), particularly during the reign of Darius I.[1] The catalog documents the approximately 1,162 analytically legible seals retrieved through the collation of many thousands of impressions preserved on the 2,087 Elamite administrative tablets published by Richard T. Hallock in 1969 (hereafter referenced as the PF tablets or the PF corpus).[2] These tablets are dated (by means of date formulae in many of the texts) to the period 509–494 B.C., within the reign of Darius I. In Volume I alone, the catalog presents 312 distinct seals reconstituted from a grand total of 1,970 complete or partial impressions.[3]

Throughout, we refer to these reconstituted images as seals even though they are known to us through their impressions rather than through the seal artifacts that produced the impressions. In so doing we continue a tradition established long ago for the Persepolis excavations (Schmidt 1957, p. 4, n. 2). This terminology reinforces the fact that the reconstituted seal images were engraved on physical matrices (cylinder and stamp seals). The original seals were functioning tools in a complex bureaucratic system.[4] The implications of their presence in specific places at specific times and in specific contexts of personnel and transaction are a major topic of ongoing scholarly inquiry into the ancient Persian imperial mechanisms of governance, economic structure, and social life to which references appear throughout the catalog. The original seals represented by impressions on the tablets also held a variety of aesthetic values, amuletic and apotropaic qualities, spiritual significations, and social-political-religious valences as artifacts of personal or official identity, prestige, and adornment.[5] For all these reasons it is crucial to emphasize that the images revealed to us on the tablets are representatives of actual seals (fig. 1). When we address a particular phenomenon that relates to individual or collective impressions of a seal or specifically to the design of the image on the seal, we state this clearly.

We reference reconstituted seals with the siglum PFS (= Persepolis Fortification Seal) followed by the seal number. An asterisk (*) following a seal number indicates an inscribed seal. An "s" following a seal number indicates that the seal is a stamp seal. We refer collectively to all the seals used on the PF tablets (i.e., those tablets published in Hallock 1969) as the PFS corpus.

The texts published by Hallock in 1969 (i.e., the PF texts) are part of a much larger archive recovered during the excavations conducted by the Oriental Institute of the University of Chicago in the 1930s at the heartland imperial capital called Parša (with variants) in the Elamite language of the texts (fig. 2). This site is now universally referred to as Persepolis, the name given to it by the Greeks. Thus we maintain that convention for the sake of clarity. The whole of the archive is known today as the Persepolis Fortification tablet archive, Persepolis Fortification archive, or Fortification archive, since the tablets were discovered in rooms of a tower in the defensive complex embracing the Takht (i.e., the citadel) of the city (fig. 3).[6] We refer to the whole of this archive as the Fortification archive.

---

1. Darius, the Persian king, is referred to in Elamite as Dariyawiš in the Fortification texts. It would, however, seem affected to avoid referring to him in our narrative other than in the Hellenized form "Darius" since that is how he is consistently named by historians. Similarly for other Achaemenid kings, we use their Hellenized names throughout. Other individuals (even those for whom a Greek rendering of the name is also attested) are, however, referred to by the name as given in the Elamite texts (see *Appendix Nine: Personal Names*).

2. On these clay tablets approximately 255 seals are illegible; 273 of the tablets are unsealed or are destroyed on typical sealing surfaces. The number of actual legible seals represented reflects the status of work as of April 2000. Completion of final drawings for Volumes II and III will inevitably lead to several more collations and separations.

3. Various earlier publications by Garrison and by Root have listed slightly differing figures for the total number of seals projected for Volume I. These minor differences reflect collation efforts that persist even as this text is in press, as well as several decisions about how best to classify fragmentary or ambiguous images.

4. For traditions forming backdrops against which the Persepolis material may be discussed, see, for example, Gibson and Biggs 1977; Zettler 1987; Ferioli et al. 1994; Boussac and Invernizzi 1996.

5. For example, Goff 1956; Cassin 1987, pp. 267–79; Collon 1987, pp. 113–21; Marcus 1994; Collon 1997, pp. 16–20; Salje 1997.

6. Persepolis is often described as only comprising the buildings on the Takht. In fact, work after World War II has shown that

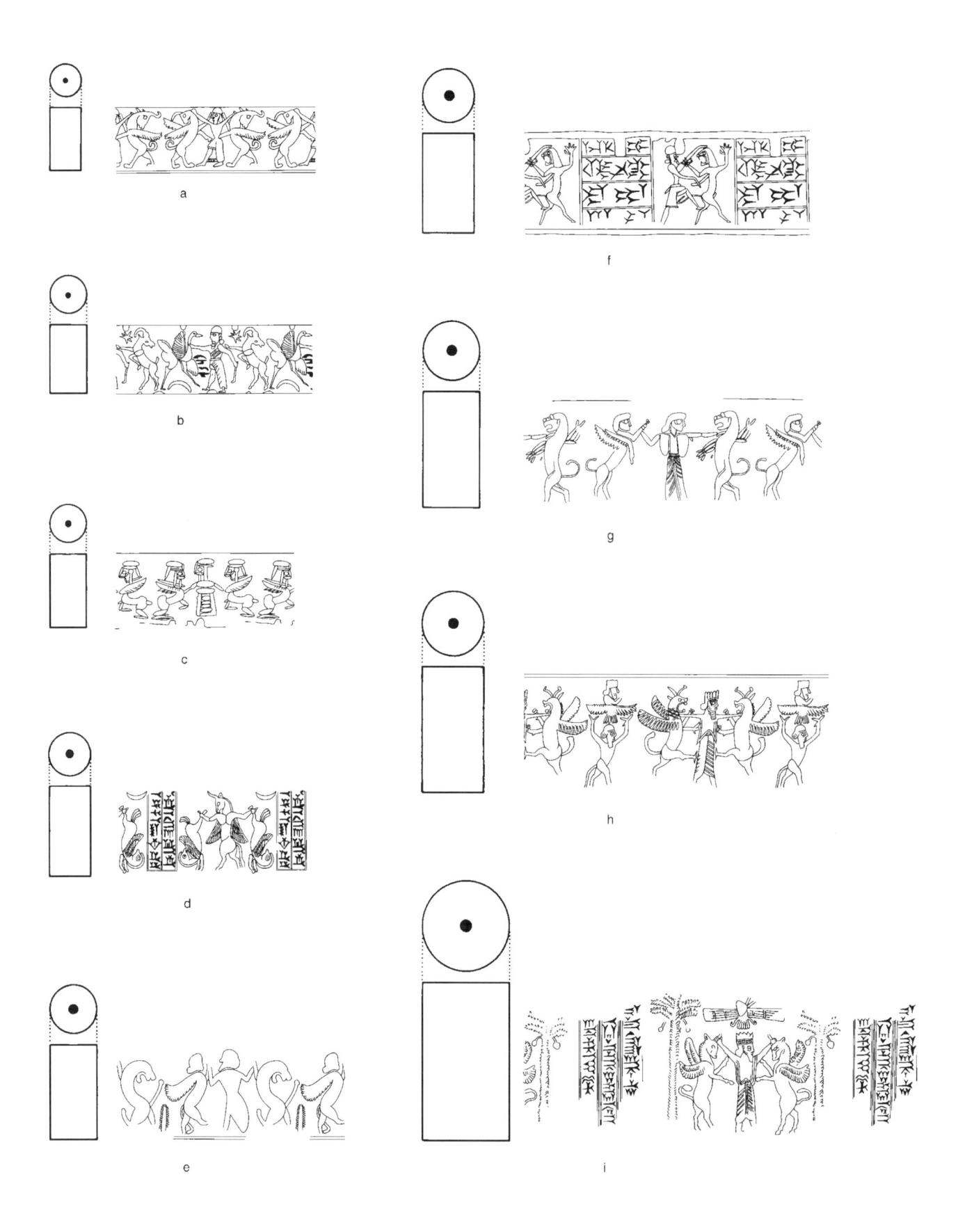

Figure 1. Reconstructed Drawings of Select Cylinders in Volume I: (*a*) PFS 778 (Cat.No. 11), (*b*) PFS 9* (Cat.No. 288), (*c*) PFS 20 (Cat.No. 145), (*d*) PFS 1* (Cat.No. 182), (*e*) PFS 731 (Cat.No. 131), (*f*) PFS 43* (Cat.No. 207), (*g*) PFS 52 (Cat.No. 114), (*h*) PFS 774 (Cat.No. 58), and (*i*) PFS 7* (Cat.No. 4). Scale 1:1

SCOPE AND CHARACTER OF THE EVIDENCE

The Fortification archive consists of inscribed tablets and also uninscribed (but sealed) tablet artifacts. Published estimates of the total number of extant clay tablets (both inscribed and anepigraphic) range between 20,000 and 30,000.[7] These figures are only approximate, in the absence to date of a systematic and comprehensive inventory of all the tablets and tablet fragments. Variation depends to some degree upon how the fragmentary tablets are counted and the number of undetected joins that may shrink the number of individual tablets. Whatever the precise tally, the Fortification archive remains one of the largest dating to the first millennium B.C. so far excavated in ancient western Asia.[8] The uninscribed but sealed tablets number in the thousands. Unofficial estimates have suggested that these may account for up to half the total number of clay artifacts in the archive. If this suggestion is roughly accurate, it still leaves approximately 15,000 complete and fragmentary inscribed tablets.

Many of the uninscribed tablets might originally have functioned in relation to additional texts (no longer preserved) that were written in Aramaic on parchment. It is also possible that some of these uninscribed tablets served different message-conveying functions within the archival system. The archival system itself was not logocentric. It incorporated seal application as a meaningful part of the communication process of record production and ultimate record product. Thus, it is important that scholarship embrace even the sealed but uninscribed tablets as "documents" — whether they were appended originally to bundles or containers of texts or to non-text commodities. In any case, the use of Aramaic on parchment is to be expected along with clay tablets inscribed in cuneiform. Aramaic was a lingua franca of the Achaemenid Empire. One Elamite text mentions a tablet on hide; numerous other PF texts refer to Babylonian scribes working on parchment ("hides") and to the procurement and preparation of hides, presumably for making parchment (Hallock 1969, p. 4).[9]

The vast majority of the preserved written documents in the Fortification archive are inscribed in cuneiform Elamite. Close to 5,000 of these Elamite texts have been read and transliterated, but many more usable ones (an "incalculable number," as Hallock [1969, p. 2] once put it) remain to be studied.[10] The Elamite language was used in the southwestern Iranian Elamite kingdom from which the Achaemenid Persians assimilated many features of culture and political texture (Carter and Stolper 1984; Potts 1999). Linguistically, it is poorly understood in comparison with many other ancient western Asiatic languages written in cuneiform (Gragg 1995, pp. 2162–64, 2178). In

---

the Takht (with its ceremonial, administrative, and military installations) looks down on an expansive urban entity in the plain that is only beginning to emerge archaeologically.

7. At the time of their discovery, Herzfeld (1934, p. 231) stated, "There are about 10,000 intact pieces [by which he meant complete tablets], 10,000 more or less complete ones, and probably more than 10,000 fragments."

8. Pedersén (1998, pp. 218–19) quantifies the Fortification archive as "thousands of clay tablets." Subsequently in his discussion of the relative size of ancient western Asiatic archives dating between 1500 and 300 B.C., Pedersén (1998, pp. 244–46) lists the Fortification archive as having "more than 2,000" texts (apparently referring only to those published by Hallock). Thus, the Fortification archive does not figure among the listing of the largest archives. Despite this confusion, Pedersén's comprehensive and impressive characterization of data on a great range of ancient western Asiatic archives within his historical parameters emphasizes the large size of the Fortification archive when we incorporate it into his synthesis.

9. See Stolper 1984 on the prominence of Babylonians in Persepolis administrative affairs.

10. Altogether, Hallock (1969; 1978) published 2,120 documents. Before his death he is known to have read and transliterated another 2,587 Elamite texts. Earlier efforts by George Cameron account for the reading of an additional ca. 150 unpublished Elamite tablets. (These tablets were returned to Tehran and are now in the Iran National Museum under the care of Dr. Abdolmajid Arfaee, who studied under Hallock in Chicago. Most of the archive remains in Chicago on research loan.) Thus, a bare minimum of ca. 4,857 Elamite tablets have been studied.

Matthew W. Stolper and Charles E. Jones are currently preparing the unpublished tablets studied by Hallock for publication in transliteration, possibly on the worldwide web. This project necessitates carefully checking Hallock's original readings against the actual documents. In advance of this finalized edition, Hallock's transliterations have been shared informally among a number of scholars, and some have thus entered published discourse on the tablets. If properly designated, the texts published by Hallock in 1969 bear the prefix PF. Those published in 1978 bear the prefix PFa. The large group of unpublished texts read by Hallock bear the prefix PFNN. The Elamite texts read by Cameron continue to be referenced with the siglum "Fort." (Hallock 1969, p. 663; Tuplin 1998, p. 64). Some anepigraphic tablets discussed in print are also referenced at the Oriental Institute by a "Fort." siglum (e.g., Fort. 60330: Starr 1976; Root 1997; Fort. 11283: Garrison 1988, pp. 401–06; Dusinberre 1997b, pp. 106–09). Cameron (1942) published one Elamite text from this group under the designation "Pers. 6754." Hallock also used this siglum a few times before his 1969 volume, but apparently he quickly dropped it in favor of the "Fort." designation. Pers. 6754 is, in any case, really Fort. 6764. (Hallock 1942, p. 230, makes the same error Cameron did and then corrects it in Hallock 1985, p. 589, n. 2.)

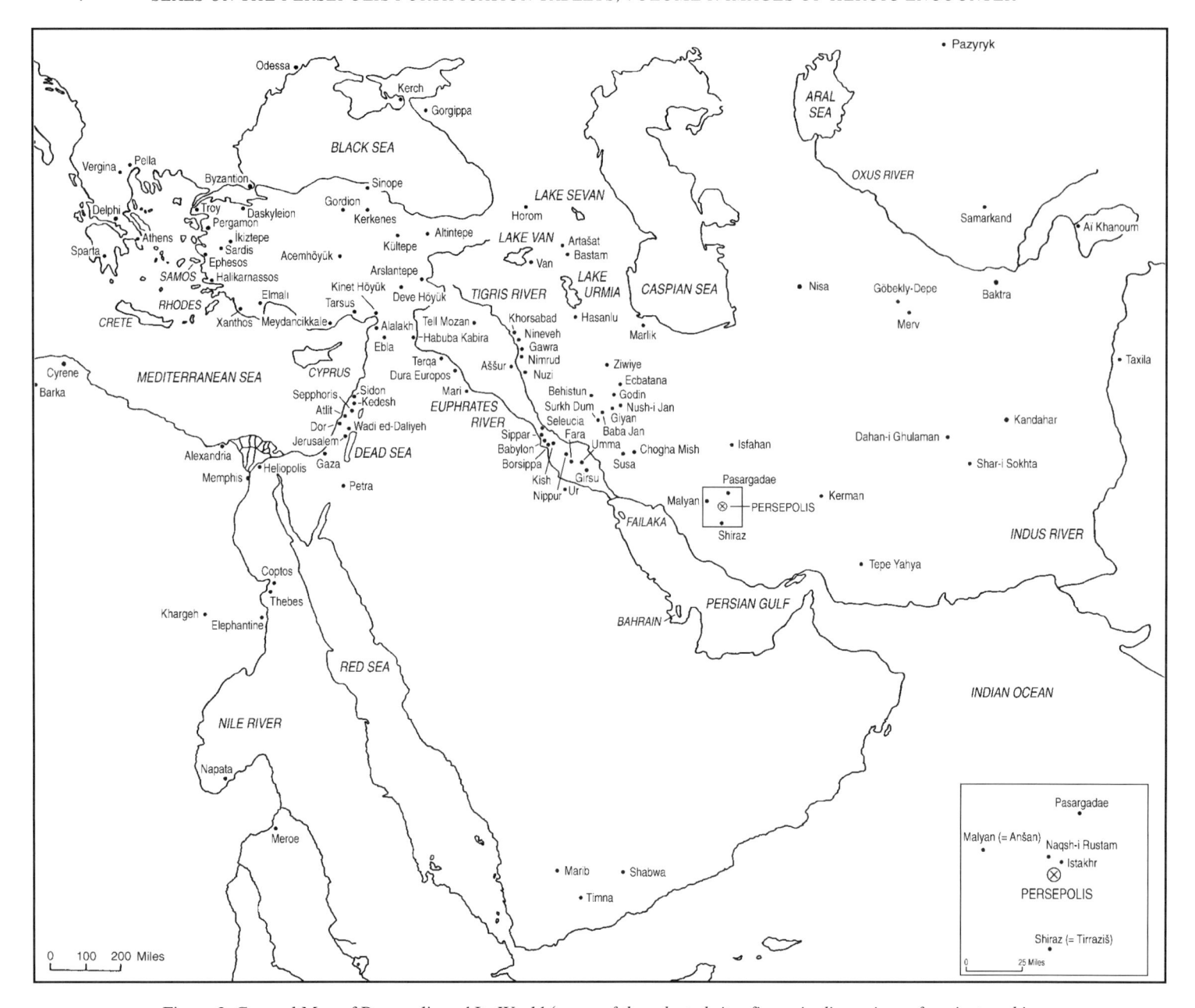

Figure 2. General Map of Persepolis and Its World (*many of the selected sites figure in discussions of ancient archives across time or of specific seals used on the PF tablets*). Scales approximate

part, this is because of the lack of a firmly established canon of texts against which the vocabulary and syntax of new texts can be analyzed.[11] The texts from the Fortification archive pose special difficulties because their subject matter involves an extremely diverse vocabulary radically different from that known through the restrictive formal rhetoric of extant monumental inscriptions in parallel trilingual versions (Elamite, Babylonian, and Old Persian) from the Achaemenid Empire. However problematic the richness of this previously unattested vocabulary, it is also a powerful positive catalyst. Hallock's sustained dedication to reading and interpreting the Elamite texts from the Fortification archive has opened up a major new chapter in the history of Achaemenid studies by making the texts available (in translation as well as transliteration) for interdisciplinary scholarly debate beyond the small community of Elamite specialists. Such debate over the possible meaning(s) of terms and notions that are crucial to interpreting historical valences of the transactions recorded in the texts is also clarifying important points of far-reaching significance to classicists as well as scholars of western Asiatic cultures (e.g., Tuplin's recent discussion of the *parasang*: 1997, pp. 404–17).

---

11. See Hallock 1969, introduction and passim; for very recent work, see, for example, Tucker 1998, which references several studies that react to Hallock's renderings.

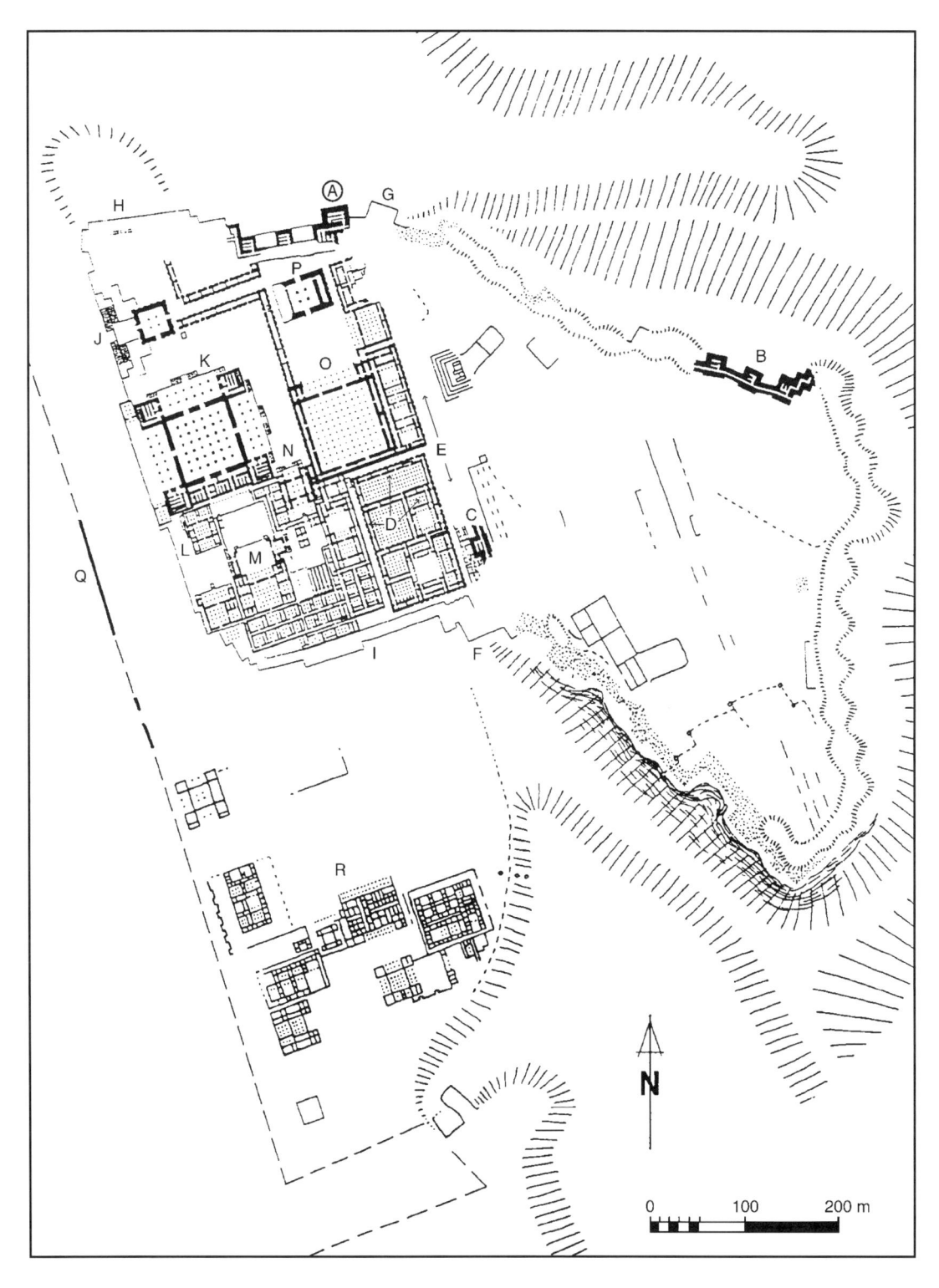

Key

Ⓐ	Northeast Sector of Fortification: Location of Fortification Archive	J	Final Ceremonial Entrance to Gate of All Lands
B	Upper Fortifications: Location of Jar with Anepigraphic Sealed Tablets (Tadjvidi 1970; 1976)	K	Apadana ("Audience Hall")
		L	Palace of Darius
C	Section of Eastern (Lower) Fortification and Garrison	M	Palace of Xerxes
D	Treasury in Final Form: Location of the Treasury Archive	N	Central Building ("Council Hall")
E	Garrison Street along East of Takht	O	Hall of One Hundred Columns ("Throne Hall")
F	Service Access at Southeast	P	Unfinished Gateway
G	Service Access at Northeast	Q	Indications of Fortifications in the Plain (Possibly a Series of Enclosures)
H	Service Access at Northwest		
I	Originally Planned Ceremonial Entrance	R	Palatial Installations in the Plain

Figure 3. Persepolis Citadel (Takht) and Immediate Surroundings (adapted from Kleiss 1992)

Approximately eighty of the Elamite tablets in the Fortification archive have been identified as bearing added ink notations in Aramaic.[12] Many of these occur on PF tablets (e.g., herein Volume I, pl. 94a) and are noted by Hallock in the relevant tablet entries in his 1969 publication. Several hundred additional tablets (perhaps almost 1,000) bear only Aramaic texts in ink.[13] Individual tablets are inscribed in Babylonian (Stolper 1984), Greek (Lewis 1977, pp. 13–14; Gorissen 1978; Balcer 1979; Schmitt 1989, pp. 303–05), and Phrygian (Friedrich 1965).

There are, then, a minimum of about 5,350 inscribed tablets on record as having been not only inventoried, but also studied and read. We stress again that our research corpus constitutes only those seals that appear on the 2,087 tablets published by Hallock in 1969 (i.e., the PF tablets).

Like Hallock's major volume of Elamite Fortification texts, our three-volume seal catalog offers a significant sampling of a much larger whole. In his 1969 opus, Hallock clearly intended to publish a representative selection of document types culled from the well-preserved Elamite tablets. The fact that our seal catalog depends upon Hallock's 1969 selection means that it is similarly representative. Furthermore, there is an obvious utility in providing a catalog of the seals specifically to accompany his massive text effort. Despite new readings of some terms rendered by Hallock in his translations, his published work remains the foundation of most text-based inquiry on the Fortification archive.[14]

Due to the specifications of our research permit it is not possible to be precise about the degree of overlap between seals occurring on the PF tablets and those occurring on other inscribed tablets in the archive. We know that the overlap is significant for the PFNN tablets, but it is also clear that new glyptic evidence awaits attention. In his post-1969 publication of an additional thirty-three Elamite tablets (the PFa tablets), Hallock (1978) tabulated the occurrence of eight seals that he recognized from his 1969 (PF) corpus and twenty-six other seals that he did not recognize as having occurred on tablets PF 1–2087. We suspect that some of those "new" seals may in fact collate with seals on the PF tablets. But even so, it is likely that overlap accounts for no more than about half of these twenty-six seals. The overlap is also significant between seals used on the PF tablets and those used on the Aramaic tablets.[15] Furthermore, we can readily see merely from examining photographs that our PFS 41 (III)[16] is the seal used on the tablet (Fort. 1771) inscribed in Greek. The seal used on the Babylonian tablet is unfortunately illegible (Stolper 1984). There is also significant overlap with the seals used on the uninscribed tablets, but these almost completely unstudied artifacts will once again yield much new material. Of only two published seals used on anepigraphic tablets, one also occurs on the PF tablets while the other does not.[17]

An additional indication of the probable degree of overlap between seals on the PF tablets and seals on other tablets in the archive derives from tablets that seem originally to have been part of the Fortification archive transaction system, but which have either found their way through the art market to museum collections or have been found at other sites within the Persepolis regional purview. For example, of the two decontextualized Fortification-type tablets now in the Biblical Institute of the University of Fribourg, one (Tablette A) is sealed with PFS 9* (Cat.No. 288; Vallat 1994, fig. 3; Keel and Uehlinger 1990, fig. 118). The other (Tablette B) is sealed with a fine cylinder that is not represented on the PF tablets (Vallat 1994, fig. 5), although it relates in composition and iconography to

---

12. Stolper 1984, p. 300. In his unpublished study of Aramaic texts from the Fortification archive ("Persepolis Aramaic Tablets") the late R. A. Bowman included eighty-three bilingual Elamite-Aramaic texts.

13. Bowman's manuscript presents readings of 492 of these monolingual Aramaic documents, and there may be as many as 500 more. Plans to revise Bowman's manuscript under the direction of D. M. Lewis have now been stalled by Lewis's tragic and untimely death.

14. Kuhrt (1989, pp. 219–20) reports something of the anxiety of the 1986 table ronde, "Le tribut dans l'empire perse," concerning the possibility that new readings of published PF texts or eventually published readings of PFNN texts might "simply invalidate conclusions arrived at on the basis of the texts available at present." She does not, however, proclaim that the inevitability of newly emerging evidence should inhibit us from exploiting the evidence we now have at our disposal. Rather, she implicitly suggests that we simply be honest about the inherent fluidities of the textual (and material) record — willing to use it but aware that we never have the last word.

15. Root had the opportunity to go over the Aramaic tablets as well as Bowman's notes and seal sketches with him in the late 1970s. The Oriental Institute kindly allowed her to look at the submitted catalog manuscript after Bowman's death, but agreement precludes actual quotation from his text at this time.

16. Roman numeral in parenthesis after PFS number indicates a seal to appear in Volume II or III.

17. The Athenian tetradrachm (Starr 1976; Root 1988, 1997) used as a seal on the anepigraphic tablet Fort. 60330 also occurs in our corpus, as PFS 1616s (III). A royal name seal of Darius occurs on the anepigraphic tablet designated Fort. 11283 as well as on others without numbers, but it is not attested in the PF corpus (Garrison 1988, pp. 401–06; Dusinberre 1997b, pp. 106–09). (This seal was given the number PFS 1683* years ago when that number represented the first number beyond designations needed for seals on the PF tablets. Under that number it was included in Garrison 1988 because of its extraordinary importance to his thesis. Nevertheless, it is not incorporated into our research permit for the present project.)

numerous seals in Volume I.[18] An Achaemenid Elamite tablet found in the excavations at Sasanian Qasr-i Abu Nasr (about thirty-five miles southwest of Persepolis) may well be part of the Fortification archive system.[19] Qasr-i Abu Nasr is probably ancient Shiraz, to be linked with Tirazziš / Širazziš of the PF texts (Frye 1973, p. 1). The tablet is sealed with a cylinder bearing an image of heroic control of winged creatures that is similar but not identical to PFS 32* (Cat.No. 180) and PFS 677* (Cat.No. 181).[20] An Achaemenid Elamite tablet from Susa (unfortunately without any specific archaeological context) is definitely related to the Fortification archive system; it is sealed with our PFS 7* (Cat.No. 4; Stolper 1992a; Garrison 1996b).

SEAL INSCRIPTIONS AND ISSUES OF LANGUAGE

Some ninety-five of the ca. 1,162 analytically legible seals used on the PF tablets (approximately 8.18%) are inscribed. (In one or two cases vestiges of apparent signs are too ephemeral to permit unqualified designation.) In Volume I, thirty-six inscribed seals are cataloged (*Appendix Five: Inscribed Seals in Volume I by Language or Script*), amounting to about 11.50% of the total number of seals in Volume I and 37.89% of all inscribed seals in the PF corpus.

The inscriptions, which for personal seals give the owner's name and often his paternity, are important documents for onomastic and prosopographical studies (e.g., Mayrhofer 1973; Delaunay 1976; Balcer 1993). The Elamite and Aramaic inscriptions also contribute significantly to the corpus of sign and letter forms for those languages in the period of the late sixth and early fifth centuries B.C. The evidence is particularly useful because it is so closely dated.

Volume I offers eight Aramaic seal inscriptions, two in Babylonian (one only tentatively classified as such), sixteen in Elamite (three of which are tentatively classified as such), two trilingual seal inscriptions (Old Persian, Elamite, and Babylonian), and five seal inscriptions in cuneiform script but in a language of uncertain identity. Additionally, on PFS 284* (Cat.No. 111) the inscription is written in Greek letters, which for the moment cannot be made to yield a recognizable personal name. In two other instances, on PFS 671* (Cat.No. 174) and PFS 677* (Cat.No. 181), the inscriptions are written in cuneiform, but in an unknown language. Further study and/or synthesis with related material may eventually clarify the writing on these seals. But it appears increasingly probable that both seals bear mock inscriptions, not meant to yield any linguistic meaning. Either alternative carries interesting implications.

Evidence of active multilingualism at the Persepolis court exists in the interplay between Elamite and Aramaic language usage on the same tablets and also in the numerous examples of Aramaic name inscriptions on seals owned by personages whose primary language ought to have been something different. A good example is the chief administrator Parnaka (= Gr. Pharnaces). An uncle of Darius the Great, he was surely a "Persian Man" in terms of kinship (see Briant 1996, pp. 437–38, 481–86, on this important individual). Presumably, the Old Persian language (at least in spoken form) figured in his life-style. One might be justified in considering Old Persian to have been his native tongue. He worked closely with scribes and other functionaries of varying language backgrounds. Two seals of Parnaka are cataloged here: PFS 9* (Cat.No. 288) and PFS 16* (Cat.No. 22). Both are inscribed in Aramaic — not in Elamite or, as one might in theory have imagined, in Old Persian.[21] Parnaka's seals occur repeatedly not only

---

18. An unprovenanced Elamite tablet now in the Yale Babylonian Collection displays impressions of a cylinder seal depicting a hero controlling winged creatures (Jones and Stolper 1986; Garrison 1995, specifically on the seal). In this case, the seal is not identical to any seal used on tablets PF 1–2087, and, like the text itself, this seal exhibits formal anomalies that separate it somewhat from the norms of the PFS corpus.

19. Wilkinson 1965, pp. 344–45, fig. 24. Jones and Stolper (1986, p. 248) state that "it cannot be shown to have belonged to the Persepolis archives," but they cautiously acknowledge the possibility. The text on this tablet has not yet been published.

20. Thanks to P. O. Harper and J. Aruz of the Metropolitan Museum of Art for facilitating firsthand study of this tablet (MMA 36.30.62).

21. The problems connected with Old Persian are many (Lecoq 1997). Among debated points are the date of its first use in written form (Stronach 1990, with references to earlier discussions), the extent to which (and the contexts in which) it was ever used as a written language as well as a spoken language (except for propagandistic purposes in official imperial contexts), and the extent to which (in written form) it was ever used except as a royal prerogative (Root 1997, pp. 234–35). To our knowledge, no tablet inscribed in Old Persian (or with added Old Persian notations) has been identified within the Fortification archive. Furthermore, there seem to be no seals inscribed monolingually in Old Persian in the PFS corpus. Old Persian occurs on our seals only in the context of the royal name seals with their trilingual displays mirroring the monu-

on the Elamite tablets (with and without added Aramaic notations), but also on the monolingual Aramaic tablets and apparently on the uninscribed tablets. The situation is even more complex when we factor in spoken language and the often occurring feature of simultaneous translation.[22] Furthermore, the codes of visual language in the interactive system were as potent as those embedded in written and spoken forms of communication.[23] The stylistic and iconographic languages of both of Parnaka's seals reverberate (each in a different way) with Assyrian reminiscences.

Kinship and language background were not, of course, the only features determining notions of identity in the Persepolis environment. Judging by the combined evidence of the seal images and their inscriptions (where applicable), there was aggressive crosscutting of cultural identity cues. Parnaka was not only a "Persian Man" by birth; he was also, we must presume, a "Persian Man" in the political sense, a representative of the policies of the quintessential "Persian Man," the Persian king.[24] It becomes particularly interesting that this person (about whom we know quite a bit) made the choices he made in seal inscription language as well as in stylistic and iconographical elements of his seals.

In summary, the seal inscriptions taken in conjunction with the seal images and the texts raise myriad issues of visual and verbal language interactions at the Persian court under Darius I. How, if at all, does the language of the seal inscription relate to the style or iconography of the seal carving? How does it relate to the administrative function of the office or official using the seal? How, if at all, does it relate to the status, rank, or other biographical information possibly available (e.g., land holdings, travel history) of the office or official using the seal?[25] How, if at all, does it relate to the ethnicity of the seal owner?[26]

In addition to addressing the above issues, the inscribed seals used on the PF tablets contribute significantly to debates about other open questions in western Asiatic glyptic studies, such as whether or not seal inscriptions in specific environments were carved by specialists in inscription carving or by the image carvers of the seals.[27] The evi-

---

mental inscriptions of Darius. Interestingly, there are some monolingual Old Persian inscriptions on royal name seals dating from the reigns of Xerxes and Artaxerxes preserved through impressions on the Persepolis Treasury tablets and the Daskyleion bullae (*Part Two: Heartland Court Contexts* and *Satrapal Court Contexts*, below). See Root 1979, pp. 118–22; Schmitt 1981, pp. 32–33, to which now add the trilingual royal name seal of Darius I discovered on Fort. 11283 (see n. 17, above) and an additional Old Persian royal name seal (of Artaxerxes) preserved on bullae from Daskyleion (Kaptan 1996b; Kaptan in press [with seal inscription readings by R. Schmitt]). See Schmitt 1981, pp. 33–34, fig. 3, for commentary on the less secure gleaning of "Darius" (but presumably Darius II) from remnants of an Old Persian-inscribed seal (SD2a) applied to bullae from Memphis (*Part Two: Other Sealing Archives of the Achaemenid Empire*, below). The evidence so far (reinforced by the PF tablets) suggests that monolingual Old Persian inscriptions on seals were rare to non-existent through the reign of Darius. Early discussions of Old Persian monolingual inscriptions on seals (e.g., Cameron 1973, pp. 51–54; Lewis 1977, pp. 2–3, esp. n. 3) need to be read in the context of this new evidence.

22. For example, Gershevitch 1979; Miroschedji 1985; Schmitt 1991, p. 19; Schmitt 1993; Vallat 1994, pp. 268–70; Lewis 1994; Root 1997, p. 232; Briant 1997, pp. 90–94, with copious recent bibliography on multilingualism in the empire. Analogies offered by work on the interfaces between orality and the written record in medieval England are useful here (Clanchy 1993).

23. See Pittman 1994 for thought-provoking commentaries on the nature of visual codes of communication embedded in seals. Although her material is from the protoliterate period, she raises important theoretical issues that will certainly be relevant to the PFS corpus.

24. See Kent 1953, pp. 137–38 (s.v. DNa), for Darius's tomb inscription in which collective military effort in service of the empire is folded into a notion of action by a "Persian Man." For the relevance of this concept of identity to the seal imagery of heroic encounter, see *Part Four: Meanings of Heroic Encounter*, below.

25. Early on, Bivar postulated that Achaemenid cylinder seals of high quality and specifically bearing Aramaic inscriptions should be considered those of senior officers of the court (Bivar 1961). The seals used on the PF tablets may ultimately inform this conjecture.

26. This is not the place to debate what different archaeologists, anthropologists, and historians mean by the term "ethnicity" (although it is an important topic of current discourse). For some time social anthropologists have questioned the usefulness of ethnicity as a concept in attempts to understand how individuals and groups construct their identities. Note, for example, Lockwood 1984 and Moerman 1965 and 1968 (with thanks to E. R. M. Dusinberre for these references). The case of ethnic makeup versus ethnic identification in the Achaemenid Empire must take into account universal features of complex fluidity; they must also factor in the specific imperial ideology of the Achaemenid dynasty as this is expressed repeatedly in the official texts and images of Darius I. Issues of naming as an indicator of literal ethnic background versus ethnic identification can be problematic, particularly in the examination of an imperial environment. See, for example, Zadok 1977; Stolper 1984; Sherwin-White and Kuhrt 1993, pp. 150–53; Stolper 1994, esp. pp. 617–18; Potts 1999, pp. 45, 337–45, 440–41.

27. Supporting Lambert 1975, Kelly-Buccellati (1977, p. 44) suggests that in most historical contexts it is unlikely that professional seal cutters were also the people who carved inscriptions on the seals.

dence of the seals used on the PF tablets does not uniformly support the idea that the seal inscriptions were the province of separate craftsmen, specially trained and professionally literate individuals.[28]

OTHER AREAS OF SIGNIFICANCE: STUDYING SEALS, PEOPLE, AND PLACES

The Fortification archive is homogeneous in overarching content, recording the procurement, storage, and disbursement of food commodities.[29] The information given in these seemingly mundane documents has radically expanded the primary source material for many aspects of the study of the Achaemenid Empire (e.g., religions practiced at the Persepolis court, economic structure, the roles and status of women at various levels of society).[30] They also broaden the interpretive horizons of Persepolis itself as an urban entity.

Evidence from the texts makes it clear that Persepolis was a magnet and a critical point along the southern east-west royal road of the empire (e.g., Koch 1986; Graf 1994; Garrison 1996b). The earliest ceremonial buildings on the Takht seem to have been designed and already in construction by around 515 B.C.[31] The fortification of the Takht appears to have been started even before that (Mousavi 1999), which is logical from a practical standpoint. Clearly, the period documented by the Fortification archive (509–494 B.C.) coincides with a time of full-scale construction activity (Root 1979; Roaf 1983). References to work crews from points far and wide abound in the texts (Roaf 1980), validating and enhancing our understanding of the chronology of this endeavor based on other types of information. And the evidence of the tablets themselves establishes that the ceremonial aspects of the heartland capital were complemented by critical regional administrative functions that linked up neatly with other zones of the empire. By the closing years of the sixth century the site was a thriving center, a locus of activity of all sorts.

An important integrative analysis of archaeological survey data with evidence from the Fortification archive renders it undeniable that the Persepolis region was richly endowed with agricultural estates which supplied the commodities enumerated in the texts (Sumner 1986). The precise geographical range of transaction sites documented in the Fortification archive is not known since the locations of most of the geographical names in the texts are unknown or not established beyond question. In general, we are dealing with an administrative region that included most of the Marv Dasht Plain, the area between Persepolis and Pasargadae, the environs of modern Shiraz, and the environs of the road running from Shiraz to Susa (Koch 1990, pp. 247–310). Exactly how close to Susa the administrative sphere of the Persepolitan system extended is still debated, but it might have reached all the way to this westernmost of the royal cities of the Persian heartland.[32] Obviously, it is possible that these purviews overlapped.

---

28. See, for example, Garrison 1998 on the scribal errors repeated on Ašbazana's second seal (PTS 14*). A different sort of argument rests in the fact that numerous inscriptions on seals impressed on the PF tablets are dynamically related to the seal's representational design. Certainly in these cases it seems implausible that a scribe stepped in at the end to add the inscription unless there was a kind of collaboration between the artist and scribe that would in itself merit special note.

29. Debates continue about what, more precisely, some of the political and economic implications of these transactions might have been. Functional analyses of specific categories of Elamite Fortification texts include, for example, Giovinazzo 1989 and Aperghis 1998, each concerned with the possibility that some of the texts are referring to commodity collection as a form of taxation.

30. Discussions using the Fortification archive as primary data are too numerous to list here. Many are referenced in the course of more specific discussions or in discrete catalog entries. In three specific categories of broad general interest, we single out Koch 1977, 1987, and 1990 and Handley-Schachler 1998 on aspects of religious practice at the Persepolis court; Kawase 1984, Uchitel 1989, Koch 1994, and Brosius 1996 on women and related issues of labor; and Lewis 1977, Bouchalat 1987, Graf 1994, Giovinazzo 1994, and Tuplin 1998 on the royal road, issues of movement patterns of the Achaemenid king around the empire, and closely related historical problems. Briant's recent and magisterial history of the Achaemenid Empire is an excellent example of the ways in which the Fortification archive has been incorporated into comprehensive re-assessments of the empire (Briant 1996, with extensive apparatus). See also Wiesehöfer's (1996) survey and the important bibliographic compendia in Jones 1990–94, Weber and Wiesehöfer 1996, Briant 1997 and ongoing (periodic literature review), and Collège de France 2000 (Achemenet.com). Similarly, articles published in the Achaemenid History Series, volumes 1–8 and 11, offer useful examples of relevant work by diverse scholars.

31. See Root 1988 and 1989 for re-affirmation gleaned through the tablets of this approximate date for the foundation deposits of the Apadana.

32. See Stolper 1992a and, in more detail, Garrison 1996a for speculations on the extent of the Persepolitan administration and a hypothetical Susian administrative region.

In contrast to this new picture of Persepolis as a locus of year-round administrative activity, the traditional view of Persepolis conjured up an elaborate imperial stage-set designed exclusively for closed-circuit royal rituals, a place open only to a select group of Persians, a hidden retreat visited rarely and certainly never by any Greek foreigners other than captive artisans until the arrival of Alexander in 331 B.C. Current re-assessments continue to explore the important concept of Persepolis as a ceremonial center (and all that may imply in terms of artistic program and political-cultic ethos) while rejecting the notion of a secret Persepolis (viz., Sancisi-Weerdenburg 1991, 1998). One is finally able to embrace the concept of a simultaneously ceremonial and working capital.

The sense of multi-culturalism at Persepolis that is offered by the PF texts and associated seals suggests a fully accessible and bustling living-working environment along a major imperial route. The result is that we must begin to problematize the ways in which the official program of ceremonial architecture and sculpture at the site was experienced by the various classes and categories of visitors whom we meet through the tablets and seals (Garrison 2000). The "opening up" of a cosmopolitan Persepolis implicit in this notion enhances the plausibility of a profound Persian impact on the culture of Athens in the classical period (Root 1985; Miller 1997).[33]

Persepolis can no longer be considered extraneous to discourse on urban civilization. Indeed, it is apparent that the seals used on the PF tablets invite a better understanding of Persepolis as an environment for vigorous artistic creativity within a veritable melting pot of cultures.[34] It is still a matter for serious analysis to consider what the nature of a Persepolis melting pot really might have been. The term is vivid in its connotations of a steaming, roiling brew of multi-cultural humanity, but it risks suggesting a haphazard, random quality that should not be taken for granted. Certainly in the sphere of official art, there is little haphazardness at Persepolis (Root 1979, passim). The mechanisms by which cross-cultural permeability of artistic interest operated in the private sphere might have involved codes and prerogatives (or at least implicit boundaries and access points) that shaped individual seal patrons' expectations, predilections, and capacities as consumers within this environment.

People in charge of the transactions recorded in the PF texts range from the previously mentioned Parnaka (PFS 9* [Cat.No. 288] and PFS 16* [Cat.No. 22]) to a host of other named officials (both elite and lesser-ranked). In many cases, the documents provide evidence for tracking the discrete and interlocking functions of specific offices (as well as officers) charged with business related to food commodities.

Recipients of the commodities include the king himself. Unfortunately, there is no known seal preserved either through ancient impressions or as a seal artifact that can be securely identified as one of the Achaemenid king's personal seals or seals of his royal office. The known seals with royal name inscriptions of the Persian Empire are the seals of officials and/or official seals, but they are not those of the king acting either as an individual or in the capacity of ruler. It is only through seals impressed in conjunction with texts that we can establish these parameters for the Achaemenid material. On the PF tablets, the royal name inscriptions uniformly declare "I, Darius ...," which may seem to proclaim a direct personal ownership of the seal by the king. But this is simply not the case.[35]

Other recipients on the PF tablets include members of the royal family such as Irtašduna (= Gr. Artystone), daughter of Cyrus and wife of Darius (PFS 38 [Cat.No. 16]), and exalted nobility such as Kambarma (= Gr. Gobryas), spear-bearer of the king and one of his most trusted allies (PFS 857s [III]). A diverse group of lesser individuals of all types (such as the camel driver using PFS 1532s [III]) are also recorded. Many individuals who are far from home, such as the man from Sardis using PFS 1321s (Cat.No. 176), are represented in the archive. Thus, although the tablets are appropriately called administrative, they are by no means limited, in the range of participants, to officials of the court. And although the tablets record disbursements made within the Persepolis region, the recipients are often people from elsewhere and their activities are often projected onto the imperial sphere.

---

33. Although Miller (1997, p. 114) maintains the inaccessibility of Persepolis to Greek ambassadors, she offers extensive evidence and learned interpretation of the pervasive multi-layered Achaemenid Persian influence on Athenian culture. Given what the PF texts present, it becomes less and less plausible to consider this demonstrated access to Achaemenid arts and morés not to have stemmed from the direct interaction of peoples at Persepolis itself, including the interactions of high-level ambassadors.

34. Dandamayev (1999) stresses the capacity of the empire to create an environment of cultural co-existence.

35. See n. 21, above, for known Achaemenid royal name seals. For additional commentary on the function of these seals, see Garrison 1991 and 1998. On royal name seals in the Neo-Assyrian milieu, see Herbordt 1992, pp. 123–36, with earlier bibliography; see Bregstein 1993, pp. 79–80, n. 71, for an interesting summary of important issues relevant to the Achaemenid material. For earlier contexts, see, for example, Buccellati and Kelly-Buccellati 1996, pp. 83–84, on usage issues of royal name seals preserved through impressions in the Tell Mozan (Urkesh) archive of the third millennium. In both the Assyrian and the third millennium contexts, a basically similar distinction to that prevailing in the Achaemenid period is drawn between royal name seals and seals actually used as a king's personal seal or his designated seal of royal office.

Sealing protocols vary according to the type of transaction recorded in the text and the status of the individual receiving goods. There are two types of texts for which the sealing praxis is clearly established. T texts (PF 1788–1860 and 2067–71) are in the form of letters. Here the addresser consistently seems to be the sole person to seal the tablet. Q texts (PF 1285–1579 and 2049–57) record disbursements relating to travel; this large group is particularly important for seal analysis since it provides access to a wide range of offices, officials, and traveling individuals. These tablets are sealed with the seal of the supplying agent or his office on the left edge. The receiver of commodities seals the tablet on the reverse (and often, but not always, on other available surfaces).[36] A third category, J texts, has been much discussed because it includes a special subset of documents dealing with goods dispensed "before" the king or dispensed "on behalf of" the king or other members of the royal family (such as royal wives). On these tablets, only a select group of seals is used to represent the oversight of activity: PFS 7* (Cat.No. 4), a royal name seal of Darius; PFS 66*a (II), PFS 66*b (II), and PFS 66*c (II), three almost identical seals (clearly meant to replicate each other) each representing a royal office of flour supply; and PFS 93* (II), a royal name seal of Cyrus of Anšan, son of Teispes and the grandfather of Cyrus the Great. But the protocols are not as straightforward as we would wish; they are definitely less transparent in their nuances than are the protocols surrounding the T and Q texts. Note, for instance, that PFS 859* (Cat.No. 205) occurs where we would expect PFS 93* (II). Personal seals used to represent some of the focal personages in these transactions can also be identified. These include Irtašduna's PFS 38 (Cat.No. 16), as well as those of other elite individuals (e.g., the apparently royal woman Irdabama using PFS 51 [II]).[37]

Even with these more or less clear-cut transactions there are complexities. Some seals of agents and agencies need to be ratified (in some sense) by the addition of the seal of a higher authority; others do not. As Hallock said in his early attempt to grapple with some questions of seal use in the archive:

> I have been contemplating the seal impressions on Persepolis tablets for about thirty-five years. In that time I have made some discoveries about the ways they were used, but I am still confused about many things. It is one of those cases in which if you are not confused you do not appreciate the problem (Hallock 1977, p. 127).

It remains impossible to be totally confident about how the specific seals used on some tablets relate to the actual individuals, offices, or groups either named or implied in the texts. In our catalog commentaries we discuss issues of seal protocol and usage (with references to the literature) when the current state of our understanding enables the seal in question to contribute to the general debate. But this catalog does not attempt to offer a synthetic and exhaustive analysis of these problems. Ultimately, it will be the documentation provided by our catalog that assists in further understanding of these matters, as scholars begin to work back and forth between the texts published by Hallock and the seal evidence as the catalog now establishes it.[38]

In addition to a lack of clarity on some basic features of how officers and offices related to one another in this very particular administrative structure, other questions involve the nature of ancient seal evidence much more broadly. These questions too are informed by the collective data offered by the PF tablets. For instance, it is well known that many individuals in ancient western Asia simultaneously owned more than one personal seal. In some cases we may be confused about sealing protocols because we are seeing one person using a variety of seals during the same period, perhaps even on the same tablet. We may not be able to distinguish between this possibility and the alternative that for some reason an additional person sealed the tablet. It is also common enough in this environment for an individual to use something other than a seal to make a mark on a tablet (e.g., thumbnail, hem of a garment, cowry shell). We have not identified any of those specific phenomena on the PF tablets, but there are a few enigmatic sealings that may represent impressions of non-seal objects, and there are two coins definitely identified as seals on the tablets (PFS 1393s [II] and PFS 1616s [III]). This suggests the possibility that doing something a little

---

36. On certain documents relating to very high status travelers, only the traveler seals the tablets.
37. Garrison (1991) offers a detailed and densely referenced discussion of the J and Q texts, particularly with reference to the seals/seal usage seen on them. Tuplin (1998, pp. 77–80) utilizes Hallock's unpublished transliterations from PFNN tablets to elaborate on some issues of J texts related to tracking the whereabouts of the king at specific dates. See Garrison 2000 for more commentary.
38. With reference apparently only to Hallock's original identifications and collation efforts on the seals, Aperghis (1998, pp. 55–56) discusses seal use on tablets bearing Hallock text types other than H (receipts by officials), J, Q, and S3 (travel rations for animals). His interesting suggestions will need to be tested against the actual material record of the tablet landscapes (Garrison and Root 1996).

spontaneous as an alternative to deploying one's normal seal(s) was acceptable behavior in the Persepolis context. We do see on the PF tablets the occasional deployment of a cylinder seal as a stamp seal (where the user presses a certain selected place in the design on the cylinder into the clay). A link between a fragmentary cylinder design deployed (for variety's sake?) as a stamping device and a full rolling of the same cylinder seal might have eluded us.[39]

Was it acceptable in the Persepolis milieu for one individual to borrow another person's seal? If so, this may further complicate attempts to sort out unclear links between a seal and a person involved in a transaction. Another complicating factor is the very real possibility that an individual possessing a seal with multiple decorated surfaces sealed some or all tablets with more than one of the images on his seal. An Achaemenid tabloid seal in the Ashmolean Museum (Moorey 1978) offers four completely different intaglio-carved surfaces from which the owner could deploy images. In this case, all the images display a coherent stylistic program deriving from a recognizable Achaemenid representational vocabulary. The same is true of the two carved surfaces of a stamp cylinder excavated at Susa (Amiet 1972, p. 285, pl. 189, no. 2205). A truncated pyramidal stamp seal found in the Persepolis Treasury preserves four designs on multiple surfaces. But in this case, the abstract altar forms on the two side faces of the seal differ dramatically in style (as well as in the contour of the edge) from the designs carved on the rectangular seal face and the square top face of the seal artifact (PT4 1087: Schmidt 1957, p. 49, pl. 18). Based on what we see in the PFS corpus, the entire visual assemblage on this seal is likely to have been a contemporary Achaemenid entity, albeit drawing upon more than one concurrent stylistic tradition. It would, however, be counter intuitive for anyone meeting this seal via discrete ancient seal impressions to consider the vestiges of these four images as deriving from the same seal. Another stamp seal retrieved during the Persepolis excavations offers an even more daunting reminder of possibilities. This seal has been interpreted as an antique Syrian artifact that was cut down to receive an additional image during the Achaemenid period, thus offering two distinct seal images with different cultural and temporal resonances carried on the same object (PT4 519: Schmidt 1957, pp. 46–47, pl. 17; Porada 1961, p. 69). Detecting and then demonstrating the deployment of multiple seal images from the same seal on the basis of our often fragmentary impressions would be a real challenge. Over time, some convincing discoveries of this nature may occur, once all the documentation on images and seal application patterns can be considered interactively.

Yet another issue in seal deployment relates specifically to elite individuals. We have already noted that only a small percentage of seals in our corpus are inscribed. Of the three exalted individuals to whom we have previously alluded (Irtašduna, Irdabama, and Kambarma), none uses an inscribed seal on the PF tablets. Unless a seal is inscribed with the name of the individual (and is not an heirloom giving, e.g., an ancestor's name), do we have any way of establishing that the seal used on behalf of that elite person is his/her own personal seal? Could it not just as plausibly be the seal of a trusted servant or agent? Quite possibly, social practice in the archive varied on this protocol. But the seals we document as representing the interests of exalted recipients of commodities (leaving the king himself aside) are unique and extremely special items. Note again, in this regard, seals of the elite individuals mentioned above: Irtašduna's PFS 38 (Cat.No. 16), Irdabama's PFS 51 (II), and Kambarma's PFS 857s (III), all of which are discussed in Garrison 1991. The consistency of this feature strongly suggests a standard practice within the PF tablets for exalted personages other than the king to be represented in the receipt of commodities by one or another of their own seals.

There is debate among glyptic specialists about who physically applied seals to tablets in the cultures of ancient western Asia. (This is a somewhat different question than that of whose seal was used to represent exalted individuals.) Was the person who applied the seal to the tablet actually the seal owner (or, in certain administrative contexts, the actual holder of the office signified by the seal)? Or was it a different person, one with professional sealing skill, presumably a scribe? As with many questions of sealing practice, close inquiry begins to suggest that standards were different in different settings and periods.[40] In her study of sealings on a corpus of Middle Assyrian tablets, Teissier suggests the likelihood that the impressions here were made by scribes rather than by the parties to the transactions (Teissier 1994, pp. 10–11). Variations and inconsistencies in the pressure applied in the rolling of cylin-

---

39. Paley (1986, pp. 210–11) discusses the occasional use of a cylinder as a stamp in Neo-Assyrian times. See also Root 1996b for further discussion of issues relating to cylinders used as stamps.

40. Gibson and Biggs (1977) made a significant impact on the field by bringing scholars together around this general topic, focusing primarily on pre-Achaemenid Near Eastern material of protoliterate and fully literate phases. Ferioli et al. (1994) now offer an excellent compendium of analyses dealing with the pre-literate and protoliterate horizon. Boussac and Invernizzi (1996) continue the 1977 inquiry focusing on the Achaemenid period and later contexts in the ancient world.

der seals seem to her well within the range that could be caused by one scribe (sometimes working hastily, sometimes with more deliberation). The variations on these tablets are not significant enough in her view to necessitate the assumption that they reflect idiosyncrasies of multiple "non-professional" individuals. On the PF tablets, the situation seems to be very different. There is a great deal of individuality expressed in the mode of application of seals on tablets, suggesting that individuals were often asserting idiosyncratic aesthetic/dialogic agendas through the manner of applying their own seals. Nothing suggests that scribes were routinely applying seals in a professional manner for non-scribes.

On the PF tablets we are able to observe the physical mode of application of particular seals, often via multiple impressions on many tablets. The information gathered by systematic effort offers insights into issues such as the degree to which seal inscriptions are privileged over representational imagery. Systematic compilations of such data from western Asia remain quite rare, but they promise to be extremely interesting as more archives can be compared across cultures and periods. Some systematic observations have, for instance, been made on the Ur III seal impressions from Umma-Drehem (Bergamini 1991) and on land sale documents from Ešnunna during the Isin-Larsa period (Whiting 1977, p. 69). In both of these late third-millennium contexts the seal inscriptions tend to be featured in the seal rolling at the expense of the coherence of the figural imagery of the seal. Bergamini (1991, p. 117) cites priority of the inscription in 108 out of 155 cases. Whiting's findings are far more radical; he reports that the inscriptions were the only part of the seal deliberately applied in the rollings of the palace officials in his corpus, with any elements of seal imagery appearing purely incidentally. The Ur III/Isin-Larsa glyptic repertoire was extremely reductive, so that dependence upon the seal inscription seems logical in this arena.[41] The PF tablets offer a very different picture. Here, we witness a veritable explosion of the imagery repertoire, and we can demonstrate that even on royal name seals it was not a necessary feature of the sealed landscape of a tablet for any application of a specific royal name seal to include even a portion of the inscription (Root 1996a).

Beyond the issue of the relative privileging of seal inscription over representation, other issues also emerge. A seal as artifact has aesthetic and symbolic dynamics by virtue of its fixed intaglio-carved image. Simultaneously, this seal has the non-fixed capacities of re-creative image making by virtue of choices the user may intentionally make in how it is impressed on the tablet. The applications of seals used on the PF tablets reveal a great deal about individual penchants for manipulation of seal images, some of them playful and evidently meant to be parodic or even somewhat subversive (e.g., PFS 17 [Cat.No. 235] on PF 46 reverse: Root 1999b). There are also many examples of seal play in which two people use their discrete seals together to make one combined image that displays careful calculation of the resulting visual effect (e.g., PFS 266* [Cat.No. 208] and PFS 1181 [Cat.No. 210] on PF 1112 left edge).

The Fortification archive is temporally circumscribed, with the dates of the texts ranging between 509 and 494 B.C.[42] These dates provide critical fixed points for the first attested use of a seal on the tablets. The date of first attested use gives a *terminus ante quem* for the production of the seal, the date before which it had to have been made. These incontrovertible dates provide critical *termini ante quem* for previously debated material in Greek and western Asiatic archaeology;[43] they also take on increasing significance in establishing scenarios in the development/invention of new styles within the court milieu (Garrison 1988; Garrison 1991; Root 1998). These efforts can then be applied to an integrative analysis of seal artifacts and impressions that are isolated from chronological or usage con-

---

41. So too with Old Babylonian seals. Kelly-Buccellati (1986, p. 138) observes in a non-quantitative discussion of the Terqa corpus that "there seems to have been more attention placed on rolling the inscription portion of the seal rather than that of the design in those cases where we have evidence of an inscription; this is common in Old Babylonian sealing practice in general." Her ongoing efforts to produce systematic compilations of data on this topic, particularly with her close attention to sealing practices at Tell Mozan, will undoubtedly assist greatly in the diachronic analysis of the question of how carvings on seal artifacts relate to the seals as image-making tools.

42. The dated texts include regnal years, often further articulated by month and day. The regnal years must refer to the thirteenth through twenty-eighth years of the reign of Darius the Great. See Cameron 1942; Parker and Dubberstein 1956; Hallock 1969.

43. See Root 1988 for fixed points provided by the evidence from the PF tablets toward resolution of debates on archaic Greek and Persian numismatic chronology.

text.[44] Similarly, the text dates allow us to perform informative analyses of the deployment of heirloom seals[45] as well as second, near duplicate, versions of original seals and new seals in different modes created for longtime archive participants to replace earlier seals.[46] Thus, although the dates given in the texts do not explicitly reveal the date of manufacture of a given seal except in rare cases such as PFS 16* (Cat.No. 22), they often provide a network of chronological indices that can be followed with potentially important results.

The repertoire of images revealed by the PFS corpus significantly expands our knowledge of artistic production and patronage mandate in the Achaemenid Empire. Studies linking images to personages offer new perspectives on many questions regarding issues of, for example, gender encoding, imagery in the service of social stratification and regionalism, social practice, and studies of realia. Perhaps one of the most interesting questions involves the interface between a powerful centralized government and the expressive capacities of social strata within such an environment. This important topic has been discussed in a very interesting way with reference to Old Babylonian and Kassite seals (Nijhowne 1999). The author concludes, with respect to this particular historical environment, that "a greater diversity in iconography may result if a centralized government loses its control over symbolic activity. ... With a breakdown of coercive authority ... individuals would assume the 'power to' express themselves using a wide variety of symbols" (p. 74). The PFS corpus contributes to this line of discourse. Its evidence suggests that for the Achaemenid Empire Nijhowne's model is not applicable. At Persepolis, there seems to have been much more flexibility and access to visual choice. Our challenge is to penetrate the nature of that flexibility and the reasons for its existence and evident viability in the Achaemenid imperial context.

The study of style on the seals used on the PF tablets has already been pioneered by Garrison with specific reference to hero seals. Through this work, the seals have been classified according to a system of stylistic categories (Garrison 1988). Part of this endeavor has also involved analysis of the seals displaying images of heroic encounter (the Volume I subset) in terms of workshop clusters and, where possible, hand attributions. As a result we are able to see an archive sealed largely (but not exclusively) by glyptic matrices that were created within a closely interacting set of workshop environments. The stylistic categories that emerge from this analysis prompt us to view the PFS corpus as the best starting point for any major attempt to review the glyptic production of the Persian Empire.[47] The PFS corpus, with its internal apparatus of fixed points and its mix of official court seals and seals of individuals, can become a basis not only for re-examining issues of style and iconography on contextually floating seal artifacts of the Achaemenid period, but also for re-examining floating seal artifacts that seem at first sight to be pre-Achaemenid, but which display certain anomalies. Seals in the PFS corpus may help to resolve some heretofore puzzling cases (e.g., Garrison and Dion 1999).

One such case is a cylinder from Susa without informative archaeological context (Louvre Sb 1475).[48] The scene displays a man in clearly Achaemenid-style Iranian riding habit (a so-called Mede) with his spear butt poised atop his foot in a fashion familiar from the figures of guards on reliefs from Persepolis and Susa.[49] Alongside this figure is an Assyro-Babylonian-type hero engaged in combat. The apparel of the hero and the particular smiting stance he assumes has made the seal seem genuinely Neo-Assyrian/Neo-Babylonian. But the garment and pose of the Mede look certifiably Achaemenid.[50] Although the domed hat is documented on an Assyrian relief of the seventh century, the entire representation, combining the tunic and leggings, the domed hat with streamer, and the

---

44. See, for example, Root 1991 for seals and impressions with Neo-Elamite characteristics; for the cylinder seal from Pasargadae, see Root 1999a. See Garrison 1991 for the royal name seal of Darius (I?), presumably from Egyptian Thebes and now in the British Museum; see Garrison and Dion 1999 for an inscribed Achaemenid seal in the Royal Ontario Museum of Toronto. For integration of chronologically fixed stylistic and iconographical evidence from the PFS corpus with a study of an excavated cylinder seal from Sardis now in the Istanbul Archaeological Museum, see Dusinberre 1997b. See Miller-Collett and Root 1997 for an Achaemenid stamp seal retrieved from a late and disturbed context during the 1988 season at Troy (now in the Çanakkale Museum).

45. For example, PFS 93* (II), the royal name seal of Cyrus of Anšan, was used for generations after its creation in the same administrative context that a royal name seal of Darius I (PFS 7* [Cat.No. 4]) was used on the PF tablets (Root 1979, p. 120; Garrison 1991, pp. 4–7).

46. For example, Garrison 1998, with special reference to the pairs PFS 1567* (II) / PTS 14* and PFS 83* [III] / PFS 11* [II]). In this volume, note the pair PFS 9* (Cat.No. 288) / PFS 16* (Cat.No. 22).

47. The efforts here are similar in implications to the classifications created by Nimet Özgüç in her study of seal impressions from Acemhöyük in Anatolia of the second millennium B.C. (Porada 1980, p. 16; Özgüç 1980).

48. Amiet 1972, pp. 275, 281, pl. 187, no. 2181; Amiet 1973b, pp. 16–17, 24, pl. 6, no. 30. See Collon 1987, p. 89, no. 414, for a convenient illustration.

49. Root (1979, pp. 279–82) urges that we abandon the idée fixe that this apparel necessarily denotes a Mede. It seems more likely that it denotes the military aspect of the Persian court.

50. Zagros peoples, presumably Medes, are represented in monumental art during the Neo-Assyrian period (e.g., as delegates to Sargon II on doorjamb reliefs of Room X at Khorsabad; Root

spear-bearing pose, is not known from any securely documented monument before the Achaemenid Empire.[51] Pierre Amiet examined the actual seal meticulously, expecting to find evidence of recutting of a Neo-Assyrian/Neo-Babylonian antique seal in order to add the "Mede" during the Achaemenid period. His examination forced him categorically to reject this possibility. He had no other option but to suggest that Louvre Sb 1475 was an Assyrianizing product of the Achaemenid period.

Struggling to come to terms with the dilemma posed by Louvre Sb 1475, Amiet struck a compromise. He made the assumption that the archaizing qualities of the seal (the Assyro-Babylonian echoes in the hero) had to reflect art production within a transitional phase chronologically between the Assyrian period and the Achaemenid period, as close as possible temporally to Neo-Assyrian times ("vers le début du VIième siècle").[52] The evidence of the PF tablets now invalidates the once-perceived necessity for this assumption. Not least, Parnaka's PFS 16* (Cat.No. 22) proves that an archaizing seal brilliantly echoing and working off Assyrian traditions could be produced at the end of the sixth century B.C. Its date of manufacture in this archaizing mode was several workshop generations removed from the final years of Assyrian power and cultural dominance. Furthermore — and this is very important — it is dated well after new and identifiably Achaemenid styles had been developed and deployed at the court (e.g., Fortification and Court Styles, as outlined below). In sum, whatever the actual date of manufacture of Louvre Sb 1475, the seals used on the PF tablets emphatically demonstrate that an Assyrianizing hero is no definitive index of even a particularly early, rather than later, Achaemenid-period date.[53]

Stylistic studies of the seals on the PF tablets also lead to more broadly significant paths of inquiry. Garrison's work demonstrates many links between seals in the archive, testifying to clusters coming from the same workshop and in some cases clearly the same "analytical individual" or even the same definitively recognizable hand.[54] Texts associated with the seals can link these clustered seals to specific owners or users. There are many implications related to patronage mandates in this research strategy. The approach also invites consideration of the ways artisanal working groups interacted as contemporary units and as units relating to various craft legacies. Hand attribution, linking a group of artifacts to a specific recognizable artistic persona based on idiosyncrasies of style, is a particularly difficult procedure in the realm of ancient seal impressions. It demands a willingness to dedicate significant resources to the production of drawings for comparative purposes that focus on line and detail, rendering as accurately as possible the nuances of style.[55] Relatively little work has yet been done in this field.[56] But in this realm, the intellectual rewards are potentially great because the effort opens up webs of archivally interrelated visual and textual information.[57]

Analysis that focuses more on workshop circles is equally important. Here we want to emphasize that the seal carving environments demonstrably flourishing in the Persepolis area were part of a tradition extending back in time. The Achaemenid Persians did not emerge in Fars out of a cultural vacuum (e.g., Root 1979, passim; Potts 1999). Craft traditions in ancient western Asia were often embedded in generational links to the past by virtue of family-based professional ties that maintained specific skills across generations (Root 1994). Scribal traditions and artistic traditions both depended upon legacies that informed developments transcending the perceived ruptures of political and military change.[58]

1979, pl. 60, fig. 60b; Roaf 1995, figs. 24–25), but they are not dressed or posed like the figure on this seal from Susa (Louvre Sb 1475).

51. Amiet (1973b, pp. 16–17, pl. 11A) makes the point, with reference to the reliefs of Aššurbanipal, that the domed hat already existed before Achaemenid times.

52. Louvre Sb 1475 is also included in Amiet's (1973b, no. 30) important discussion of glyptic production at the end of the period of Elamite independence from the Persian hegemony. However, Aruz (1992b, p. 214, no. 152) leaves open at least the possibility of an early Achaemenid date.

53. Amiet (1972, pp. 274–75) already predicted that the study of the seals on the PF tablets might enable us to re-assess the dating of first-millennium seals from Susa.

54. See Garrison 1996a, pp. 36–38, on the meaning and potentials of hand attribution.

55. Kelly-Buccellati (1977) emphasizes the importance of these agendas and the essential aspect of an effective standard of visual documentation in order for such efforts to yield persuasive results.

56. For ancient western Asia, see, for example, Porada 1947a; Collon 1975, pp. 177–78; idem 1982a; Stein 1993, pp. 126–29; Kelly-Buccellati 1998. For Aegean glyptic, see, for example, Weingarten 1983; Weingarten 1985; Morris 1993; note the excellent bibliography in Younger 1991, pp. 88–96. Hand attribution based on actual seals is more prevalent. See, for example, Collon 1986b.

57. On the potentials of hand attribution studies within the context of sealed administrative archives, see Root 1990a; Garrison 1991; Root 1993; Garrison 1996b. Note also the discussions in Gill and Chippindale 1993, pp. 636–41, and the dialogue between authors and respondents in Morris 1993. For hand attribution and workshop studies in related media from western Asia, see, for example, Muscarella 1980; Herrmann 1986; Winter 1992, pp. 136–38.

58. Waters (1997) emphasizes the importance of striving to understand the links to tradition that are manifest in the cultural activity in southwestern Iran in the poorly documented period between the fall of Susa to the Assyrian army and the official es-

In order to provide some immediately accessible descriptive framework for appreciating the stylistic categories used in this catalog and forming the basis of Garrison's project, we offer below a capsule summary of some of the main features of each broad stylistic group.[59] Although Garrison's thinking on certain stylistic categories has naturally evolved since his dissertation (1988), this early work remains the document of record for the time being for consultation on patterns and details involved in stylistic analysis of the PFS corpus. The reader can now use our illustrations and updates in Volume I in conjunction with the detailed stylistic analyses of individual seals in Garrison 1988.[60]

When changes have occurred in classification of seals from Garrison 1988 to this publication such changes are noted in the catalog entries. Selected summary data are provided here in *Appendix Three: Summary Data on Seal Dimensions for Volume I* and *Appendix Six: Distribution of Seals in Volume I by Stylistic Categories*. Material in Volumes II and III invites further commentary on the relative distribution of stylistic groups, as relevant.

SEAL CARVING STYLES IN THE PFS CORPUS: THE CASE OF VOLUME I

PERSEPOLITAN MODELED STYLE

The Persepolitan Modeled Style accounts for fifty-one seals in the Volume I corpus. It is a direct continuation of the earlier modeled carving styles of Assyria and Babylonia, but it is a phenomenon of the Achaemenid period — and probably of workshops in the Persepolis region. Only six of the Volume I seals carved in some form of a modeled style seem more likely to be antique modeled-style seals (actual representatives of the earlier Mesopotamian tradition) than to be seals in the Persepolitan Modeled Style. Five of these have been grouped in the category Plausibly Antique Seals: PFS 883* (Cat.No. 97), PFS 1122 (Cat.No. 228), PFS 1458 (Cat.No. 80), PFS 1480 (Cat.No. 257), and PFS 1658 (Cat.No. 101). The remaining seal, PFS 513 (Cat.No. 85), has been classified under Antique Seals. Indeed, PFS 513 is the only seal in Volume I that has thoroughly convinced us of its status as an heirloom product of the Neo-Assyrian period.

In the Persepolitan Modeled Style, there is a basic plastic approach to the rendering of human and animal forms. Muscular volumes swell especially in human arms, shoulders, chests, thighs, and calves, and in animal bodies (especially at the hindquarters and lower legs). There are three main expressions of the Modeled Style at Persepolis. One (Garrison's Group 1: 1988, pp. 198–215) shows large, bulky figures, but restrained modeling in the interior musculature of human and animal bodies, for example, PFS 32* (Cat.No. 180). A second (Garrison's Group 2: 1988, pp. 216–23) exhibits smaller figures, but a sometimes baroque modeling of musculature, for example, PFS 16* (Cat.No. 22). A third (Garrison's Groups 3 and 4: 1988, pp. 223–43) has quite small figures, but expressive and animated modeling of select areas of human and animal anatomy, for example, PFS 1566* (Cat.No. 218) and PFS 1* (Cat.No. 182). This third expression of the Modeled Style shows remarkable consistency in the rendering of the human form. The figure has a small, pinched waist and a narrow stomach that expands dramatically at the chest into large rounded shoulders. The whole of the torso often exhibits an elongated heart-shaped appearance. Many of the compositions of these seal designs are exceptionally dynamic. Heroes often pursue animals or creatures rather than standing in static hieratic mode. Iconography is often quite complex. Elamite inscriptions occur frequently (Garrison 2000, pp. 131–34).

Viewed in isolation, any one of the Persepolitan Modeled Style seals would most likely be taken as an heirloom from the Neo-Assyrian (eighth/seventh centuries B.C.) or the Neo-Babylonian (late seventh/mid-sixth centuries B.C.) periods. Only when viewed within the context of the whole archive can critical diagnostic patterns in the execution of these Modeled Style seals be seen. These patterns point to the contemporaneity of their execution. The repeated use of specific stylistic characteristics across a relatively large number of seals implies that these seals are not the result of maintenance and continued use of heirloom seals by random seal owners. Rather, the seals are

---

tablishment of the Persian Empire in the reign of Cyrus. Related aspects of this issue involve what really happens to sites (and the cultural commodities they contain) that have been destroyed by hostile forces. See Dalley 1993 on the Assyrian capital of Nineveh as a persistent cultural locus after the 612 B.C. destruction by the Median and Babylonian alliance.

59. For a fuller discussion of each style, its associated workshop groups, and discernible hands on seals in Volume I, see Garrison 1988.

60. Garrison plans a new study of Achaemenid glyptic styles on the basis of material across the entire three-volume corpus.

products of workshops active at the time of their use. Epigraphy also offers some assistance. PFS 1566* (Cat.No. 218) displays a remarkably well-executed design, one which serves as a paradigm for the third expression of the Modeled Style. As with several other seals used on the PF tablets carved in this type of Modeled Style, the inscription on PFS 1566* is in Elamite. This factor alone suggests the likelihood that we are dealing with a set of Persepolitan court products and certainly not with Neo-Assyrian or Neo-Babylonian court products. Moreover, the carefully integrated placement of the inscription within the design of the seal clearly indicates that the inscription was not added at a later date to an older Neo-Assyrian or Neo-Babylonian seal. Finally, the name in the seal inscription, Abbateya, confirms what the visual analysis suggests: that the manufacture of the seal is contemporary with its use in the late sixth century B.C. The name Abbateya occurs generally in the Elamite texts (e.g., PF 1182, PF 1581, PF 1584, etc.), but also specifically on PF 1852, a letter in which Abbateya is the addresser. This tablet is sealed by PFS 1566* (Cat.No. 218). The owner of PFS 1566* is beyond doubt the same Abbateya whose name occurs on the seal inscription. Abbateya was an important official active in Persepolis in the late sixth century B.C.

PFS 16* (Cat.No. 22) is another example in which the inscription and archival context confirm that we are dealing with a late sixth-century artifact, not a Neo-Assyrian heirloom. In this case, we may even isolate the date of its execution. Two texts, PF 2067 and PF 2068, state authoritatively that on the 22nd year, 3rd month, 16th day (6 June 500 B.C.), the seal we designate PFS 16* replaced Parnaka's earlier seal (PFS 9* [Cat.No. 288]). PFS 16*, surely a piece commissioned for this elite individual, was most probably executed not long before 6 June 500 B.C.

PFS 38 (Cat.No. 16), the seal of the royal wife Irtašduna, is quite large and elaborate among the seals in the PFS corpus. In addition to its Modeled Style carving, the design has many Assyrian-looking iconographic elements. Once again, viewed in isolation PFS 38 would normally pass as a Neo-Assyrian seal. The specific iconographic program of this seal viewed in its totality is, however, unique within the context of Assyrian and Achaemenid seals alike. The detailing of the garment is also unusual and finds no parallels in Neo-Assyrian seals. The soft puffy treatment of the creatures' wings and the outline of the human heads can, however, be seen on other designs from the PFS corpus, for example, PFS 113* (Cat.No. 19). The treatment of the musculature follows patterns seen commonly in Garrison's Modeled Style Group 1. Thus it clusters by idiosyncrasies of hand with other seals in the archive, suggesting contemporaneity of production during the Achaemenid period. The PFS corpus emerges as fertile ground for analysis of archaizing, its mechanisms and meanings.

PLAUSIBLY ANTIQUE SEALS

As just suggested, the identification of genuinely antique seals in the PFS corpus is difficult, in part simply because of the range of archaizing material that forces us to be particularly stringent in choosing criteria of assessment for a genuinely archaic item. This level of ambiguity exists also in the analysis of the seal artifacts excavated at Persepolis. Many of the forty-six retrieved seals and signet rings from the Chicago Expedition frankly defy traditional categorization even with the consultation of Edith Porada.[61] In Volume I, we identify nine seals that we consider most likely (but not definitely) to be antiques rather than archaizing products. Because we do not, however, have total confidence in their status as heirlooms for one reason or another, we choose to place them in the category Plausibly Antique.[62]

ANTIQUE SEALS

As noted under Persepolitan Modeled Style, PFS 513 (Cat.No. 85) is the only Volume I seal that we place definitely in the Antique category. This conservatism represents a change in perspective from Garrison 1988 to the present. The situation is somewhat different for Volume II, where there are numerous seals that are without question antiques. In the final analysis it will be most interesting to ponder the reasons for the lively deployment of archaic models for new hero seal products on the one hand and the very small number of actual heirlooms in this rep-

---

61. See Schmidt 1957, p. 42, and the frequent qualification of "presumably" after "Achaemenian" in the catalog entries. See also Porada 1961.

62. This category was not used in Garrison 1988.

resentational category on the other hand. Conversely, it will be interesting ultimately to ponder the implications of the types of antique seals (across the entire representational repertoire) that are maintained in active use in the Persepolis region during the reign of Darius I. It is well recognized that antique seals sometimes enjoyed an afterlife aboveground, in royal and temple treasuries or as personal heirlooms. But it is also generally thought that most seals were buried with their owners, while some were buried as items included in votive deposits. Other seals were not taken out of circulation but rather ended up being recut as new seals in later times probably because of the intrinsic value of their material. All this suggests that the number of antique seals kept in active use on tablets for hundreds of years was quite small and often subject to particular preselection factors.[63] It also suggests, however, that the potential for continuity and revival of antique styles in new products was deeply embedded in the social power of seals. The small size of most Achaemenid-period cylinder seals may suggest that many were cut down from old seals. If this is the case, it adds to a picture of rich availability in current workshops of antique models held at the ready as raw material for new work.

A study by Wallenfels (1990, p. 756) offers evidence from Hellenistic Uruk that the active use of any given seal ring was only about seven or eight years before being replaced. It is possible that for practical reasons seal rings were lost or damaged more quickly than cylinder and stamp seals. It is also possible that a variety of cultural factors in a given context will determine trends in the active life of old seals.[64]

FORTIFICATION STYLE

The Fortification Style accounts for a full 158 (51%) of the seals in Volume I. The term defines a local seal carving tradition previously unrecognized in glyptic research. Seals carved in the Fortification Style are generally small (see *Appendix Three: Summary Data on Seal Dimensions for Volume I*, chart 16). Carving is flat and shallow, with select areas of animal anatomy (generally the hindquarters) given a more modeled treatment. Contours of human bodies are simple, varying from rectangular, for example, on PFS 959s (Cat.No. 246), to hourglass shaped, for example, on PFS 1142 (Cat.No. 39). Outline edges tend to be sharp and flat. Human and animal appendages are thin and linear. Overall, the Fortification Style is remarkable for the plainness of its surface treatment; detailing of garments and facial features is rare. Only in a few exceptional cases does the style admit some detailing. A notable example is PFS 9* (Cat.No. 288), Parnaka's first seal. The hero's Assyrian garment has a fringe indicated on the chest and lower garment. The shape of the human and animal bodies and the flat musculature are, however, directly in the tradition of the Fortification Style. As with Modeled Style seals, seals in the Fortification Style may rework elements of Assyrian iconography. The ostrich-grasping hero on PFS 9* is one such archaizing adaptation.

COURT STYLE

The Court Style accounts for only twelve seals in Volume I,[65] but it marks an important trend in official art production of the Achaemenid court. The term, popularized by John Boardman (1970a), is conventionally associated with what Boardman calls eastern Achaemenid glyptic, by which he must be understood to mean heartland Achaemenid glyptic within the geographical and ideological frame of the empire itself. Typically, discussions of Court Style have defined it through a set of iconographic features rather than through strict stylistic criteria. Thus a seal qualifies as Court Style by virtue of the inclusion of, for example, the Persian court robe, date palms, and figures emerging from winged symbols. Actual stylistic distinctions have been articulated as qualitative judgments rather than systematic formal analyses (Garrison 1991).

---

63. Dyson and Harris (1986, p. 86) urge the gathering of as much precise, systematic, and standardized information on excavated seal artifacts as possible in order to begin to amass data for future collective analysis of issues such as routes of exchange, chronological features, patterns of usage, and elimination from active usage.

64. Obviously, seals of gods and certain other types of prestige seals (e.g., in royal families or in royal administrations) represent one general category of special material where antiques would be expected to remain in use.

65. See Garrison 1991, pp. 18–20, for discussion of the low number of Court Style seals in the PFS corpus.

The occurrence of the Court Style within the information-rich context of the PF tablets invites a critical re-evaluation of the phenomenon. Here, the Court Style exhibits two main and apparently contemporary stylistic expressions. One, for example, on PFS 7* (Cat.No. 4), shows restrained modeling in human and animal bodies and a very hard linear approach to the outline of human bodies and detailing of garments, feathers, and date palm trunks. The other expression of the style, for example, on PFS 11* (II), shows a soft outline and more plastic rendering of the musculature. These distinctions are subtle features within the overarching stylistic unity of the group. Not all seals classified as Court Style in Volume I conform strictly to the paradigms of either of these two seals, however. Like every other style, this one is a fluid phenomenon produced by artists working in close proximity with others and sharing ideas.

MIXED STYLES I AND MIXED STYLES II

The two classifications called Mixed Styles I and Mixed Styles II quite literally define clusters of seals with specific hybrid characteristics. Mixed Styles I accounts for sixteen seals in Volume I. It designates images sharing stylistic characteristics with both the Modeled Style and the Fortification Style. The connection to the Modeled Style consists mainly in the large figures, deep engraving, and sporadic use of modeling. Mixed Styles II, of which there are thirteen examples in Volume I, designates those seals sharing stylistic characteristics with both the Fortification Style and the Court Style. The overall stylistic concept here seems rooted in the Fortification Style, but aspects of the execution of detailed elements and the sometimes broad and smooth carving link these seals to the Court Style.

BROAD AND FLAT STYLES AND LINEAR STYLES

The category Broad and Flat Styles embraces a group of seals with diverse appearances, but with a homogeneous feature of broad, flat carving. These seal designs are usually executed rather coarsely. Nineteen seals in Volume I are classified in the Broad and Flat Styles. The category Linear Styles also embraces seals of diverse appearance. Fourteen seals in this classification appear in Volume I. All display a unifying feature in their simple, linear approach to the execution of form. In neither of these stylistic categories do the seals lend themselves to tidy sub-classification.

DIVERSE STYLES

There are nineteen seals in Volume I classified under Diverse Styles.[66] As the name implies, this is a catchall category frankly intended to designate a group of seals in a variety of carving styles that are distinct from the categories of production and use that seem to predominate in the archive. One subcategory of seals embraced here is a cluster of two seals, PFS 1321s (Cat.No. 176) and PFS 1309s (Cat.No. 229), that seem likely to emanate from coastal Anatolia. They are pyramidal stamp seals similar to those isolated by Boardman (1970b) as a western product representing an incipient so-called Graeco-Persian style. The Graeco-Persian glyptic phenomenon needs careful re-evaluation in light of the Persepolis sealings (Root 1991; Dusinberre 1997b; Root 1998). While the two seals just cited appear to conform securely to a carving style popular in the western sphere of the empire, another seal in Volume I suggests latent complexities. PFS 1463s (Cat.No. 231) is a stamp seal that exhibits the shape (octagonal seal face) and inclusion of a linear device in the field often associated with incipient Graeco-Persian pyramidal stamp seals. In this case, its actual carving style appears, however, to be mainstream Fortification Style. We have thus classified it with the Fortification Style. This seal, and others to appear in Volumes II and III, indicates that there was aggressive permeability in the Persepolis workshops. We have only a relatively small number of seals in the PFS corpus that seem to express direct relationships with the western sphere through their physical appearance. But this fact needs to be qualified by our evidence that active hybridization of western and heartland modes was demonstrably occurring right in the Persepolis arena.[67]

---

66. Garrison (1988) originally named this category Unknown Styles.

67. See Root 1998 for discussion of the issues involved.

Some seals classified in Volume I under Diverse Styles may ultimately emerge as representatives of an additional descriptive style category on the basis of a synthesis of documentation of the seals in Volumes II and III. This seems especially likely with a group of seals that includes various abstracted, geometric renderings of human and animal heads and linear detailing in garments, wings, etc. PFS 2 (Cat.No. 3) is the most evocative of the these seals in Volume I. On this seal, human and animal heads have a distinctive appearance due in part to the use of a round drill for indications of eyes and certain other anatomical features. Furthermore, the eyes are set within a triangular frame (for the animal creatures) or a rectangular frame (for the human figure). Linear detailing occurs in the hero's garment and in the rendering of the feathers of the wings of one of the animal creatures. At the same time, the chest and shoulders of the hero are well modeled and the contours of the creatures' bodies have a sinuous, calligraphic dynamism. PFS 1519 (Cat.No. 167) is so close stylistically to PFS 2 (Cat.No. 3) that they may be by the same artist. PFS 463 (Cat.No. 264), PFS 690 (Cat.No. 139), and PFS 740 (Cat.No. 146) exhibit similar, but more exaggerated, geometric stylizations and should be considered as part of this potential new stylistic grouping that may separate out of the Diverse Styles category.

SUMMARY

In closing this first part of the *Introduction*, we return to a point touched upon at the beginning: the importance of contemplating the seals impressed on the PF tablets as a dossier of evidence for actual seals-as-artifacts that can be notionally reconstructed on many levels. Analysis of a large corpus of glyptic evidence through impressions in an archive offers a range of statistically useful information on seal artifacts (and from an incontrovertibly genuine source). We can, for instance, establish trends in cylinder seal dimensions not only as summary tabulations, but also as a series of data broken down by, for example, stylistic categories of the representations carved onto the original seal matrices (*Appendix Three: Summary Data on Seal Dimensions for Volume I*). This type of information will eventually be important in any future project to write a more inclusive, broad-gauged survey of Achaemenid glyptic art such as that undertaken (but without access to this evidence) by d'Amore (1992). There are, however, many limitations to what we can learn about a seal matrix through study of ancient seal impressions (Root 1999a).

We cannot determine the materials with which seals of different stylistic groups were made,[68] nor can we comment upon issues such as tool marks or the nature of perforations. Often it is possible to comment upon damage sustained by a seal through observations of the ancient seal impressions. But this information is somewhat limited by the fact that the upper and lower edges of impressions (where we are most likely to detect chips) are frequently not preserved on the PF tablets. Here, the frequently used sealing surface on the left edge is very restrictive. For the same reason there are only a small number of cases for which we can supply any evidence about cylinder seal caps, the ancient mountings of the seals. This, of course, is a pity, since some of our seals must have been quite sumptuously mounted at the time of their active use in the Persepolis region.[69] Occasionally, we can detect physical signs of the recutting of seals, but this is not guaranteed.[70]

For stamp seals it is impossible to comment definitively on the back of the original seal. We can only state the apparent or probable shape and dimensions of the contour created by the seal edge and suggest by comparison what this is most likely to indicate (see *Appendix Four: Stamp Seals in Volume I Grouped by Apparent Contour of Seal Face* and accompanying fig. 9). Obviously, then, we are deprived of some crucial aspects of the material presence

---

68. Collon (1982) suggests the material out of which the seals producing the Alalakh impressions were probably made. This determination seems to derive from knowledge of the stone most commonly used on extant seal artifacts of the same milieu rather than from a strategy of empirical analysis of the impressions themselves.

69. The beautiful mountings preserved on several seals from Sardis and from other Anatolian tombs of the Persian period hint at what we are missing in terms of capacity to reconstruct the original aesthetic and prestige values of these seals (Curtis 1925; Özgen and Öztürk 1996, pp. 140–46, nos. 95–101), as does a translucent chalcedony Achaemenid scaraboid mounted in gold that was retrieved in a passage south of the Apadana at Persepolis (PT 7 67: Schmidt 1957, pp. 46–47, pl. 17).

70. A mid-third-millennium (Early Dynastic III) cylinder seal now in the British Museum was recut in antiquity to add a monolingual Old Persian private name inscription, in part obliterating the original robustly modeled animal contest scene. This is perhaps the most relevant of numerous examples one could cite of the surprises that a recutting can spring upon the investigator and of the difficulties in reading the situation accurately off a modern museum-made impression, let alone off a partially preserved and perhaps hastily applied ancient application! See Schmitt 1981, pp. 38–39, fig. 7; Collon 1987, pp. 120–22.

of these seals. Consider, for instance, a theriomorphic stamp seal from the Persepolis Treasury.[71] The oval-contoured edge of the face displays a hero clasping a horned animal (gazelle?) to his chest, while the back is in the shape of a couchant bull. As an impressed image, this would not be out of place on the PF tablets. Stylistically we would put it in the realm of the Plausibly Antique, comparable to our PFS 62 (Cat.No. 104) or our PFS 180 (Cat.No. 194), both possibly Neo-Assyrian/Neo-Babylonian Drilled Style products. The artifactual aspects of this stamp seal from Persepolis do not resolve the ambiguity of date, but they are suggestive. Stamp seals with theriomorphic backs are an established feature of Neo-Assyrian/Neo-Babylonian glyptic; in turn, they are evocative of some protoliterate Mesopotamian stamp seals.[72] Such aggressive archaisms of form are also entirely in keeping with the artistic environment at Persepolis. Indeed, it has been suggested that the conspicuous revival and flourishing of the cylinder seal in Achaemenid times (not least at Persepolis as viewed through the PFS corpus) should itself be considered an archaism (Teissier 1984, p. 45). The stamp seal from Persepolis is carved out of a multi-hued banded agate that is used occasionally in Neo-Assyrian/Neo-Babylonian glyptic. Noteworthy is the fact, however, that of the thirty-three theriomorphic stamps in the Berlin collections from excavated contexts at Aššur and Babylon which are classified as Neo-Assyrian/Neo-Babylonian, only two are apparently made of agate.[73] This stone was much favored in the Achaemenid period.[74]

There is, of course, more than enough to compensate for the limitations of the physical evidence about the seal matrix that can be gleaned from an archive of ancient impressions. In addition to the explicit information supplied by seals known through use on dated texts, there is another kind of information they contain. Implicit in the archival context is a resonance of the social encounters of the individuals applying their seals to the tablets on specific occasions. Whatever the veiled complexities of interactions might have been, the seals indicate the simultaneous presence of actual people deploying the artifacts. The sealed landscapes of the tablets are like seating-markers at a banquet table for which we know the date of the occasion, have some inkling of the purpose of the gathering, can reconstruct brief and strangely selective bio-sketches on a few of the people on the guest list, and even have a good idea of what sort of food and drink they favored. The seals themselves (when documented via these landscapes) often give voice to the guests, their symbolic and aesthetic predilections, and their cultural associations.

---

71. PT 5 1: Schmidt 1957, p. 47, pl. 17.
72. For example, von der Osten 1934, p. 15, nos. 12–17.
73. Klengel-Brandt 1997, pp. 86–87, nos. 345 (Aššur), 350 (Babylon).
74. See Wartke 1997, pp. 41–46, on sources of different stones; Moorey 1994, pp. 74–76, with important warnings about limitations in the evidence available so far and about standardization of information needed for making global observations on the usage of particular stones in particular periods. These warnings notwithstanding and bearing in mind the problems of unexcavated material, it is noteworthy that agate seals dominate the small sampling of Achaemenid cylinder seals from the Marcopoli Collection but are only marginally represented in the much larger number of Assyro-Babylonian cylinders (Teissier 1984, pp. 150–84, where only one seal out of 143 in the Assyro-Babylonian group is agate, but nine out of ten in the Achaemenid group are listed as agate). Collon (1987, p. 102) emphasizes the importance of agate in the Achaemenid period, surely an opinion based in part on her access to the complete corpus of Achaemenid cylinder seals in the British Museum collections.

PART TWO: THE FORTIFICATION ARCHIVE AND ARCHAEOLOGICAL INQUIRY

HERZFELD'S DISCOVERY

In October 1933, Charles Breasted (Secretary of the Oriental Institute of the University of Chicago) reported the discovery of the Fortification archive in these words:

> Not only have amazing works of ancient art been found, but Dr. Ernst E. Herzfeld, Field Director of the [Persepolis] Expedition, exploring for the Oriental Institute, has also uncovered a body of archives of the Persian kings, containing some 20,000 clay tablets inscribed with cuneiform characters. ... What fascinating facts these tablets may reveal, when translated, as to ancient life in Persia cannot even be imagined. It may be, indeed, that here will be found the Persians' version not only of the wars with Greece, when Darius was defeated at Marathon and Xerxes at Salamis, but new facts on Persia's spectacular invasion of Egypt, as well as the graphic record of other dramatic events of those bygone days (Breasted 1933, p. 381).

Breasted's expectations of the type of great-event history the tablets would reveal mirrored the large-scale mentality of the excavation effort itself. The focus of Ernst Herzfeld's commission at the site, in collaboration with his architect and right-hand man Friedrich Krefter, was clearance and graphic reconstruction of the palatial architectural remains of the Persepolis Takht (Krefter 1971). Working in the old manner, great teams of workers swarmed over the site removing accumulated debris by the basket-, cart-, and railcar-full (fig. 4). As luck would have it, the Fortification tablets were discovered in the process of clearing a light railway transport route for removal of excavation debris from the Takht. The trench penetrated two chambers of the Fortification containing the tablets (fig. 5).

The excitement and media hype generated by the revelation of thousands upon thousands of cuneiform tablets must have radically disrupted Herzfeld's routines and agendas. In the best of circumstances (even today) a find of this nature and magnitude creates the need for urgent triage in the field if the material is to be handled with any attention to meticulous record-keeping, safe retrieval, and recovery of small fragments.[75] But circumstances in this case were far from optimal in every way. For one thing, the tablets stumbled upon in the Persepolis operation were unbaked and had not been burned in the course of Alexander's sacking of the city. Thus they were especially friable and must have been extremely difficult to extract from the ground intact. Compounding these legitimate archaeological hardships, other issues also conspired to make this a tension-filled period for Herzfeld. His clandestine smuggling activities at the same time are now increasingly understood. They seem to have included the use of presumably unexcavated portions of the area at the eastern rim of the Takht as a secret holding place for antiquities addressed to himself in New York (Gunter and Root 1998, p. 8).

The young amateur architectural historian Robert Byron, visiting the site in the spring of 1934, was brought up short by Herzfeld's paranoid refusal to allow him to photograph any of the standing monuments (Tuplin 1991, pp. 37–41). Byron seems convinced that Herzfeld was desperately worried lest he poke about and observe whatever was going on with the small finds. There were rather few small finds actually registered during the Herzfeld years, beyond the Fortification archive itself. We are left to ponder the alternatives. Herzfeld might have been protective of the official and painstaking extraction of the Fortification tablets going on at the far northeast edge of the site, or he might have been protective of some private digging activity in an area of the central Takht, exactly the area Byron would presumably have been interested in photographing. Whatever the truth of the matter, Byron's words give a sense (albeit hostile and naively nostalgic) of the tone of things at Persepolis at the time of excavation of the tablets:

> In the old days you arrived [at Persepolis] by horse. You rode up the steps on to the platform [Takht]. You camped there, while the columns and winged beasts kept their solitude beneath the stars, and not a sound or movement disturbed the empty moonlit plain. You thought of Darius and Xerxes and

---

75. See Ferioli et al. 1994, p. 169 and passim, reinforcing how much archaeological strategies of the retrieval of sealing archives are finally able to benefit from discussions among tablet and seal specialists about what the excavator may expect to encounter in such a situation.

Figure 4. View of the Persepolis Takht during Clearance by the Oriental Institute Persepolis Expedition

Alexander. You were alone with the ancient world. ... Today you step out of a motor, while a couple of lorries thunder by in a cloud of dust. You find the approaches defended by walls. You enter by leave of a porter, and are greeted, on reaching the platform, by a light railway, a neo-German hostel, and a code of academic malice controlled from Chicago (Byron 1982, p. 167).

As the Fortification tablets were laboriously lifted from the earth they were impregnated with paraffin while still encrusted with dirt. They were packed in boxes and shipped to Chicago for study. During all of this Herzfeld was under mounting suspicion and political attack. By the close of 1934, the Oriental Institute had dismissed him as Expedition Director at Persepolis and he left Iran, never to return (Balcer 1991, p. 164). He held a residency at Princeton's Institute for Advanced Study until retirement in 1944, subsequently divesting himself of his scholarly library, papers, and antiquities collection (Root 1976, 2000). He died in Basel in 1948 at the age of 69, having published no major work on Iranian archaeology after *Iran in the Ancient East* (1941), on which see below.

MYSTIFICATIONS OF THE RECORD

This biography of Herzfeld plays a key role in the history of the study and interpretation of the Fortification tablets. Under the acrimonious (and still rather mysterious) circumstances attending his departure from Iran, Herzfeld was not generous with information. Little in the way of field notes pertaining to the discovery of the tablets exists in Chicago. Nor were any field notes discovered among the Ernst Herzfeld Papers now housed in the Freer Gallery of Art and Arthur M. Sackler Gallery Archives (Smithsonian Institution) and in the Herzfeld Archive of the Department of Ancient Near Eastern Art at the Metropolitan Museum of Art.[76] Furthermore, Erich Schmidt, Herzfeld's suc-

---

76. Comprehensive finding-aids on Herzfeld's records assist the researcher at both institutions (Freer Gallery 2000). See Root 1976 for an overview of the papers at the Metropolitan Museum of Art. Notebooks from Persepolis exist among the Smithsonian material, but they are not excavation diaries or log books per se. Thanks are due to Ms. Colleen Hennessey for gracious assistance at the Freer Gallery of Art and Arthur M. Sackler Gallery Archives.

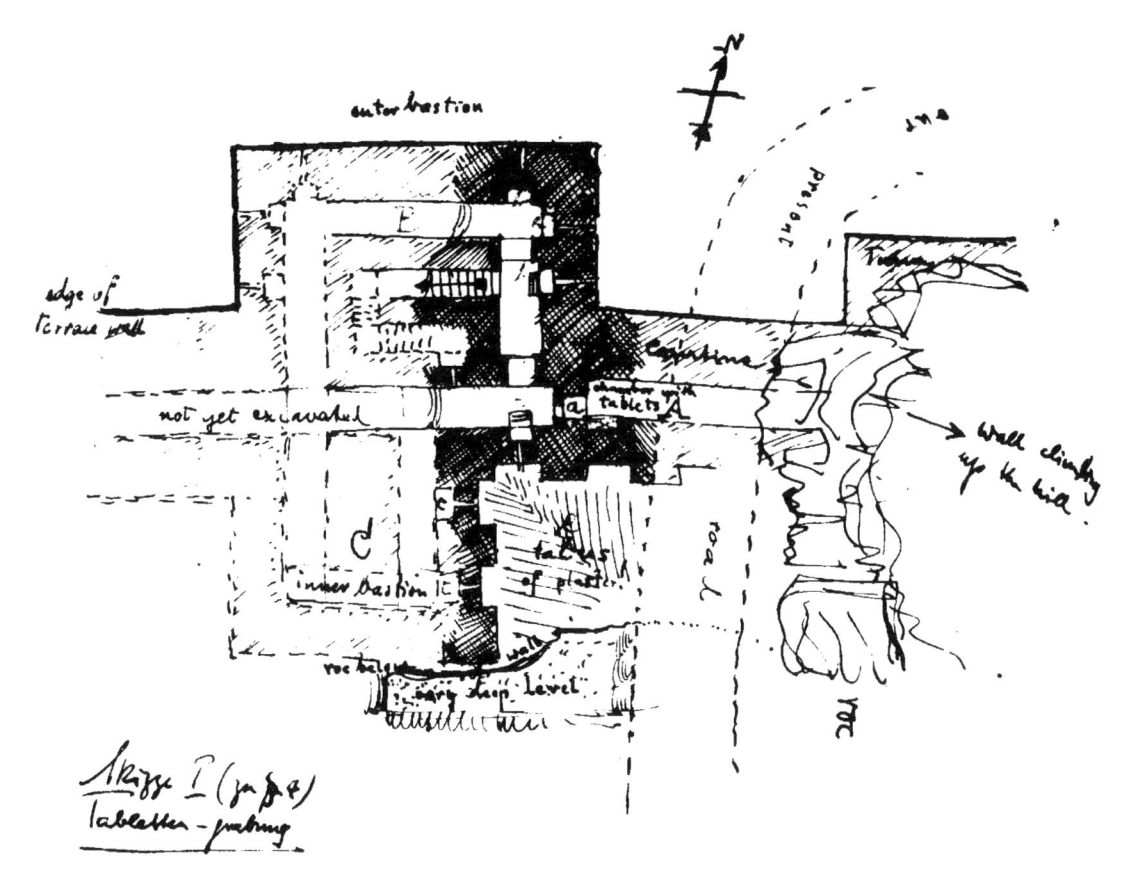

Figure 5. Herzfeld's Sketch of the Takht, Showing Area of Discovery of the Fortification Tablets

cessor as Field Director, seems to have received little anecdotal information with which to reconstruct the deposition of the tablets and their relative positioning at the point of excavation (Schmidt 1953, p. 3; 1957, p. 5, n. 11).

In his own campaigns, Schmidt steered clear of the section of the Fortification where the tablets were uncovered, continuing the original agenda to clear the monumental and ceremonial structures on the Takht. And even in Volume II of the Persepolis excavation report, dealing with artifactual finds, the Fortification tablets and their seal impressions are hardly mentioned and certainly not discussed in any way as archaeological, textual, or art historical data (Schmidt 1957). No serious effort seems to have been made in preparation for that impressive publication to grapple with the implications of the Fortification archive and its locus of excavation. The bloom of the initial excitement seen in Charles Breasted's article for *The National Geographic* had certainly faded. Although the tablets became available for study in 1937, the Great Depression and World War II altered many lives and scholarly trajectories.

A well-intentioned effort by the Oriental Institute in the late 1930s did bring in a Works Progress Administration (WPA) photographer who produced high quality professional prints of seal impressions on many of the Fortification tablets. The WPA project was obviously undertaken after the tablets had been meticulously cleaned. Tablets chosen for photography range across the entire archive, including many of the tablets eventually published by Hallock as well as many others. The criteria for selection seem to have been clarity, completeness, and beauty of the impressed images. Unfortunately, the project was not undertaken systematically or comprehensively. Neither negatives nor prints were labeled in any way, nor were they linked by any known log or work sheets to specific tablets — much less to specified surfaces on those tablets. No scale bar was used.[77] Flawed as the WPA project was, it is curious that none of these photographs were published in Schmidt 1957.

---

77. At some later time, Helene J. Kantor arranged the WPA prints (still unlabeled) into albums according to certain thematic groupings. But even so, no project was ever undertaken to identify which seal impressions on which tablets had actually been photographed. Kantor might have intended eventually to work on the seals used on the Fortification tablets. Kantor's excavations at Chogha Mish became all-absorbing, however. Due to their inherent limitations as documents of record, the WPA photographs could not facilitate a systematic investigation of the seals used specifically on the PF tablets by any subsequent researcher. If someone were now to link photographs to specific identified impressions on the PF tablets, these linked prints could potentially provide valuable evidence on images that are no longer in the pristine state they were in at the time of excavation. In some cases, rubber bands used by Hallock for decades to bind his notes to tablets have created stripes of dark stain across the seal impressions.

Meanwhile, from his vantage point at Princeton, Herzfeld remained disinclined to address any issues relating to the seals impressed on the Fortification tablets. His conflicted archaeological ethics notwithstanding, Ernst Herzfeld was a pioneer in the study of the prehistoric stamp seals of Iran, a superb draftsman, and a learned scholar of wide-ranging interests concerning Achaemenid art and inscriptions (e.g., Root 1976; Gunter and Root 1998). If political and legal intrigues had not caused major disruptions just at the critical period of discovery of the Fortification tablets, he might conceivably have taken an aggressive scholarly interest in the seal impressions on the tablets. Instead, he distanced himself from them utterly, as if in conspicuous repudiation of the beautiful and culturally informative types of things he had loved to investigate all his adult life. In his broad-gauged study of ancient Iran published after the Persepolis debacle, Herzfeld (1941) quite literally does not even allude to the seal impressions on the Fortification tablets. Enough of them are vividly preserved to make it inconceivable that Herzfeld (no matter how beleaguered) was totally oblivious to this remarkable and varied sealing assemblage as it emerged from the ground in 1933/34 under his auspices.[78] Yet he goes so far as to state, with respect to the official, monumental art tradition at Persepolis:

> It is doubtful whether another, more popular art existed. There is a group of small objects [i.e., seals deriving from other places] usually called "Graeco-Persian"; these might have been made in Asia Minor partly by Ionian and Sardian artists for Persians. ... These are not enough objects to judge, but surprising discoveries may still be made (Herzfeld 1941, p. 274).

These "surprising discoveries" had already been made. They were made by Herzfeld himself in 1933/34, and he obviously knew it! Given all the complexities and mystifications charging the atmosphere around the Fortification tablets, it is not surprising that information is hard to come by.

ARCHIVAL DEPOSITION IN ANTIQUITY

Suggestions we make now about the circumstances of discovery of the Fortification tablets and their physical maintenance in Achaemenid times must remain speculative. They are based on the following: passing (but very illuminating) published remarks by Herzfeld (1934, 1941) and bits of oral history, glimmers of light from unpublished archival material (Jones 1990; Dusinberre 2000), important observations and discoveries by the Iranian excavators at Persepolis (particularly Sami 1955) subsequent to the American expedition, analogy with better-documented situations elsewhere, and a dose of common sense.

An important question is whether or not the tablets were unearthed in an archival context or were, instead, discovered in a secondary context. Schmidt (1953, pp. 40–42) suggests that the tablets were originally maintained in Darius's earliest construction of the Treasury complex. He postulates (p. 41) that they "had been removed — sometime after 494/493 B.C. — from their original archives [in the Treasury] to be stored (or discarded) in rooms of the fortification." Schmidt bases this notion on his own discovery of the Treasury archive (see *Other Sealing Archives of the Achaemenid Empire*, below). But the two archives are of very different types — the Treasury corpus actually deals with the work of treasurers. Schmidt's suggestion is understandable from the perspective of an excavator attempting to rationalize the building history of the Treasury complex and the relation of the Treasury documents to that building history. But the line of argument does not make good sense in regard to the Fortification tablets themselves. The fact that Schmidt did not discover a Treasury archive dating to Darius and still in situ within the Treasury is not explained by the fact that the Fortification tablets were found in the Fortification. If there was at one time a Treasury archive dating to Darius, we simply do not know what happened to it. (By the same token, there was surely a Fortification type archive dating to Xerxes, but we have not yet located that either.)

---

78. Some correspondence just identified in the spring of 2000 among the Herzfeld papers in Washington document Herzfeld's concern to stabilize the tablets properly in recognition of their importance. And a series of photographs of seal impressions on the tablets still in situ lend further to the sense that Herzfeld realized full well the stunning nature of his discovery. We thank E. R. M. Dusinberre for sharing these findings made in the course of a post-doctoral fellowship with the Smithsonian Institution.

Hallock subsequently reinforced Schmidt's fairly cautious attempt to explain his (probably mistaken) view that the Fortification tablets had been removed from the Treasury to the Fortification either for storage or to be discarded. Hallock (e.g., 1973, p. 320) ultimately disseminated the idea that the tablets were "not found in their original place of deposit, but in the fortification wall, *where they had been used as fill* [emphasis ours]." He implied through these words that the tablets were used to pack a solid structure. His comments, which were not based on firsthand knowledge or particular awareness of the archaeological features of Persepolis, have been accepted uncritically and reiterated in many influential discussions (e.g., Cook 1983, p. 13; Lewis 1985, p. 106; Veenhof 1986, p. 2).

The notion that the Fortification tablets were used as construction fill certainly deserves re-assessment. Archives in the ancient Near East tended to stay accessible and active at least potentially for long periods of time — sometimes for several hundred years.[79] In this way, they served (sometimes deliberately and sometimes inadvertently) as glyptic-image repositories as well as document reference rooms. Thus it is a matter of real interest for the art historical issues embedded in our seal project to postulate an alternative scenario to Hallock's, a scenario in which the Fortification was, along with its other functions, a place of centralized administrative handling and storage of sealed documents. Exploration of this alternative scenario is also a matter of real interest for that aspect of the seal project that attempts to explore and give contextualized nuance to the seals used on the tablets as administrative tools in a final accounting activity based at Persepolis and tangibly reflected in the architectural legacy of the remains there.

Current work on the Persepolis Fortification stresses its completion as an early priority of Darius (Mousavi 1999). Thus it is entirely plausible that it was available by 509 B.C. as a locus for storage of the archive and accounts management relating to it. In fact, this does not contradict Schmidt's general impressions. He too considered the Fortification to have been built at the beginning of the Persepolis enterprise (1953, p. 41). Thus there is no disagreement about the availability of the Fortification as a facility that could have accommodated the archive from its inception (by 509 B.C. or earlier). The problem seems more related to understanding the Fortification as a wall.

Formal analysis shows that the fortification wall was an architectural system incorporating towers and rooms, with stairways to upper levels (Mousavi 1992).[80] As Herzfeld himself said (1941, p. 226), "The wall was a double one with casemates and loopholes, illustrating Sargon's description of some Median towns." The two chambers in which the Fortification tablets were unearthed were actual rooms in this system. In his limited referencing of the archaeological context of the tablets, Herzfeld did in fact describe the locus of discovery as "little archival chambers," clearly suggesting that they were found in a storage setting rather than a secondary setting where they functioned as construction fill (Herzfeld 1934, p. 231; Schmidt 1957, p. 5, n. 11). He also indicated that, in his opinion, at least some of the tablets had been maintained in an upper story (above the remains of a stairway) that had collapsed in the destruction of the site (fig. 6). At one point Herzfeld described the situation as one of active archival and also dead storage:

> At the northern angle the upper story had housed the offices of the guards, while the documents no longer used were walled up in a small room below. ... Probably the garrison was a Susian regiment of the 'immortals' (Herzfeld 1941, p. 226).

Further on, in an oblique reference embedded in a discussion of the Apadana stairway reliefs of "Susian" guards, Herzfeld (1941, p. 271) noted, "On the right side, in the upper register, the guards stand at attention. These are the Susian regiments (which have left their trace in the shape of the 30,000 Elamite tablets of their offices)." Evidently, Herzfeld, unlike Charles Breasted, imagined from the start that the Fortification texts were related to administrative functions connected directly to the place in which they were found, the northeast sector of the Fortification with its closely associated Garrison. This is interesting, as it reinforces from a different angle Herzfeld's conviction that the architectural setting of the tablets was relevant to their archival function.

The sense one derives of the archaeological context from the Iranian excavators of Persepolis, who succeeded the American team in the 1940s and 1950s, is akin to that of Herzfeld. The Iranian archaeologists' view of the situation seems to have made no impact at all on the scholarly tradition outside of Iran. Sami (1955, pp. 52–53) characterizes the locus of the Fortification tablets unambiguously as the "Royal Chancellery (Record Office)." He con-

---

79. See Black and Tait 1995 for a recent general discussion; see Pedersén 1998 for details on specific archives.

80. Kleiss (1990) offers a brief survey of casemate fortification walls in Iran that places the Persepolis system in context.

ducted further excavations at the Fortification in 1952/53, revealing two courtyards and a series of pairs of adjoining rooms. The shared wall of each set of paired chambers was pierced with an opening about ten centimeters wide.

To Sami, these small openings immediately triggered the analogy with hatchways between rooms in bank and government offices of then contemporary Iran whose purpose was to enable officials to communicate efficiently and, we may presume, even to pass documents back and forth. Thus Sami conveys an architectural design in the Fortification complex at Persepolis that was intended quite specifically to facilitate accounting activities.

Turning from Sami's mid-twentieth-century analogy back to antiquity, we note that at a number of ancient western Asiatic cities administrative documents were discovered in close proximity to a service access route and/or gateway (e.g., Root 1996b, pp. 6–9; to which add Young 1986 on Godin Tepe; Schmandt-Besserat 1994, p. 17, on ensuing symbolic associations; Pedersén 1998 more generally for examples). At Persepolis, there were service access routes to the Takht at the southeast and northwest and also, it seems, at the northeast very close to the tower in which the Fortification tablets were discovered.[81]

Very logically, tablets relating to activities concerning the movement of commodities and to activities taking place in a variety of satellite zones would have been stored close to the place where either the commodities were held at the ready or the transaction documents were brought into the central headquarters. The Persepolis Fortification tablets fit this latter scenario. Charles Jones (1990) cites evidence from the Persepolis excavation records housed in the Oriental Institute Museum archives that the Aramaic and Elamite tablets were found intermingled. In talks with Margaret Root, Professor Bowman said that Herzfeld had affirmed this to him privately. Excavation photographs show lengthy documents and small tablets together. Potentially verifying the notion that at least some clusters of the various types of clay artifacts comprising the Fortification archive were recovered in an intermingled array is the manner in which they were shipped to Chicago for long-term study purposes. As we have already noted, the tablets were not cleaned and photographed at the site. Rather, they were impregnated with paraffin for protection while still encrusted with dirt. Then they were packed in 2,353 numbered boxes (with additional large tins holding very damaged fragments). The boxes contained mixes of variously sized tablets (including, for instance, large summary documents and small single-transaction records), tablets inscribed in Aramaic and Elamite, as well as uninscribed but sealed tablets. It seems likely that the tablets were unearthed in roughly the same type of heterogeneous assemblage as was reflected in the quick on-site packing operation.[82]

The contents of the various individual boxes received in Chicago suggested no rationale to Hallock (1969, pp. 1–2). The intermingling of text types might indeed have encouraged his idea that the material had been dumped in the Fortification as construction fill. Hallock thought of the tablets in terms of the text categories he established. A rational organization of them (indicating primary deposition), from his viewpoint, might by definition have necessitated arrangement by those categories. The ancient system seems rather to have operated in a kind of functional dialogue between the various types of texts and tablet forms.[83] We return to this point below.

Our opinion is that the Fortification tablets do indeed represent an archive that was maintained intact in its original architectural setting. It is unfortunate that we cannot glean more about the deposition of the tablets and their relation to one another, but the evidence we do have points to our conclusion. By contrast, there is no evidence to support the idea that the tablets were moved to the Fortification from the Treasury — and certainly not as a convenient source of packing material. Instead, the architecture of the Fortification indicates that it incorporated business offices for working with administrative documents of a practical nature. That these offices were near the northeastern service entrance to the Takht makes good sense in the context of the nature of the archive itself.

It is widely understood that the tablets retrieved during the 1933/34 expedition must represent only the tip of the iceberg of this archive relating to food commodities; we can postulate that additional tablets, covering later years of food storage and disbursement activity in the Persepolis region, were also maintained in the Fortification and hard

---

81. See Tilia 1978, pp. 13–18; Mousavi 1992, p. 209, on evidence for an access at the northeast. All *pace* Herzfeld 1941, p. 225, who is curiously categorical to the effect that there was only the one (ceremonial) entrance to the Takht.

82. An attempt to reconstruct how the tablets lay in relation to each other at the point of their discovery may in theory proceed by tabulating the contents of each box exactly as it arrived in Chicago from Persepolis. Serial numbers were assigned (although not physically applied) to each tablet in Chicago as they were removed for extraction of the paraffin and cleaning preparatory to study (Hallock 1969, p. 1). But in reality, various discrepancies make it impossible to securely link all the tablets to these original serial numbers.

83. When Hallock undertook his extraordinary study of the Fortification tablets there was little in the way of synthetic discussion of issues relating to the archaeology of ancient archives; his focus was decipherment of a poorly understood language rather than macro-issues.

Figure 6. Excavation of the Persepolis Fortification Tablets

by the road running the length of the eastern edge of the Takht leading to the southeast service entrance.[84] We can also postulate that other archives covering different activities were maintained there in different rooms. The isolated "Tools" text recovered with the Fortification tablets (Hallock 1973) indicates leakage from one set of archive rooms to another either in antiquity or in the course of Herzfeld's clearing operation.

It would be of great interest to know what if any door sealings were recovered along with the tablet artifacts in the archival deposition. It is doubtful that careful sifting occurred in the retrieval effort, but some large fragments might have survived.[85]

ASPECTS OF ARCHIVAL FUNCTION

The Fortification archive allows us to glimpse how a recording system using textual and representational mechanisms actually might have worked in its documentation of transactions at dispersed locales relating to a wide variety of agricultural products. It is not our intention here to attempt a full explication of this difficult topic. Nevertheless, some commentary is essential to a discussion of the social functions of the seals impressed on the tablets.

The PF corpus (i.e., those tablets published by Hallock in 1969) comprises clay tablets ranging in size from ca. 2.00 cm (PF 1887) to ca. 21.70 cm (PF 1946) in greatest dimension, with the majority of the tablets fitting neatly in

---

84. See *Other Sealing Archives of the Achaemenid Empire: Heartland Court Contexts*, below, on the cache of sealed anepigraphic tablets of post-Darius I date, discovered in an upper part of the Fortification during later excavations.

85. Schmidt's (1957, p. 6) allusion to speculation by Herzfeld that labels in the Fortification archive were used in the same manner as the sealed bullae from the Treasury is confusing. Does it mean that there were also sealed bullae (as distinct from tablet-shaped artifacts) found with the Fortification archive, bullae of the type that might have sealed containers and doors?

the palm of the hand. The small tablets that fit into the palm of the hand are in the shape of a truncated lozenge, the flattened left edge of which is itself lozenge shaped and slightly concave.[86] This type of artifact may be considered the standard size and shape of the typical PF tablet.[87]

On these typically shaped tablets (fig. 7) text may be inscribed on four surfaces: upper edge, obverse, bottom edge, and reverse. Seals may be applied on as many as six surfaces: upper edge, obverse, bottom edge, reverse, left edge, and right edge. More than one seal may be applied to the same tablet surface. In *Appendix One: Concordance of Seals to Tablets in Volume I* the distribution patterns of seal impressions on tablets is keyed specifically to the seals cataloged in Volume I (those bearing images of heroic encounter).

The anepigraphic tablets and the great majority of the typically shaped Elamite and Aramaic tablets are formed of clay molded at one end around the knot of a string (Hallock 1969, pp. 77–78). On most of the tablets this string emerged at the two ends of the concave and lozenge-shaped left edge (see fig. 7c). Although the string itself disappeared long ago, the string holes at the left edge are very much in evidence on most of these tablets and are visible in many of the photographs illustrating the catalog.[88]

It is abundantly clear that the inscribed tablets were sealed before the text was written. Repeatedly, the surface preparation for the inscription invades the area of the seal impression and the subsequently applied cuneiform characters invade the seal image.

The typically shaped tablets with string seem to have been sealed and inscribed at the locales where the actual transactions occurred; this is suggested by the evidence of the texts themselves (including names of officials and places of operation) often in coordination with the evidence of the seals used on the tablets. Thus, many were sealed and inscribed in the immediate environs of Persepolis. Many others were inscribed and/or sealed in the field farther away, but still under the purview of the Persepolis regional authority.[89] Both documents created close at hand and those created far afield were brought to the Persepolis headquarters on the Takht and incorporated into the archival system. The journal (V) and account (W) texts appear to be summary compilations of the transactions and were probably composed centrally.[90]

The system seems to us complex and perhaps redundant. It is not clear at this point exactly what purposes were served by the various tablet types with string. We may be seeing a mix of tablets attached to commodities, tablets attached to other documents (as clearly with the little U text tablets), and even tablets hung around the neck of the recipient (or his/her servant) in the course of disbursement routines, all of which were eventually clipped as a receipt for the court clerks at the appropriate moment. The idea that the strings might have served to suspend the tablets from rods for storage does not seem viable.[91]

Given the apparent importance of record keeping, it is perplexing that applications of seals on the typically shaped tablets with string do not seem geared to guarantee visual verification at a later date. The case of inscribed

---

86. Designation of orientation is determined with reference to the inscribed obverse surface facing the viewer.

87. The tablets that differ most from the standard lozenge-shaped tablets are the journal and account texts (Hallock's V and W texts; see Hallock 1969, pp. 55–69), which are large rectangular tablets, and the labels (Hallock's U texts; see Hallock 1969, pp. 53–55), which are small, rounded cone-shaped tablets. These observations on the sizes and shapes of the PF tablets are also valid generally for the PFNN corpus of tablets. Many of the tablets bearing only Aramaic texts are similar in size and shape to the typically shaped PF tablets.

88. Stein (1993, p. 34, n. 113) remarks upon a similar practice in the Nuzi archive and on Middle Assyrian tablets from Aššur.

89. In various publications Hallock and others have in the past offered sometimes contradictory assessments of this issue (viz., Hallock 1977). The opinion we offer here seems now to be generally accepted.

90. All the tablets could be subjected to neutron activation analysis to test for variant clay sources since it could be argued that the tablets were shaped around the string and sealed or inscribed on site, wherever and whenever they were needed. To our knowledge, however, there are not adequate comparison data on clay beds in the region against which to interpret results yielded by the tablets themselves. Furthermore, it is certainly conceivable that containers of clay were trundled around over considerable distances, kept damp in soaked cloth, as the administrative work was carried out in the field. In this case, location of clay sources would not give us a check on the exact geographical locations of named disbursement centers. For in situ archaeological attestations of clay cores kept at the ready (in administrative establishments) for long periods of time, see Ferioli and Fiandra 1994, pp. 150–252. For relevant discussion of the issues involved in neutron activation analysis in the study of ancient archives, see Ferioli et al. 1994, for example, p. 167.

91. Root 1996b offers some comments (with comparanda from other western Asian contexts) on these issues, but they are by no means exhaustive. Included is a critique of George Cameron's theory, with reference to the similarly strung Persepolis Treasury tablets, that the string was a suspension mechanism. Vallat (1997) has now revived the theory, specifically suggesting that suspension by the left end of the tablet was intended to facilitate archival validation of the seal impression on the left edge of the hanging artifact. Our findings on seal application do not support this idea.

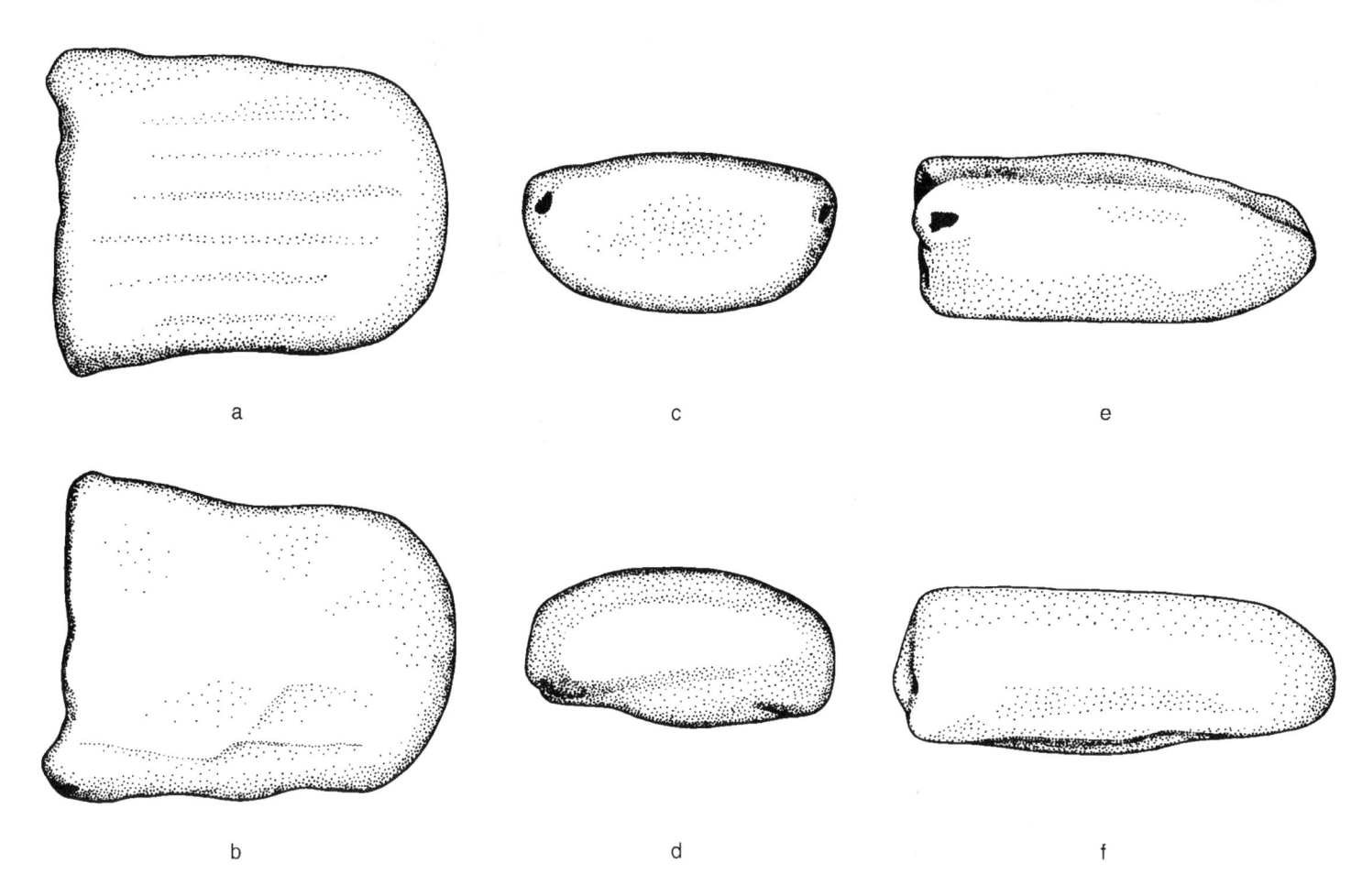

Figure 7. Sketch of PF 1092, Without the Elamite Cuneiform Text, Showing Sealing Surfaces on the Tablet: (*a*) Obverse, (*b*) Reverse, (*c*) Left Edge, (*d*) Right Edge, (*e*) Upper Edge, and (*f*) Bottom Edge. Scale 1:1

royal name seals is revealing. The inscriptions were significant to the design and meaning of these official seals. Nevertheless, incorporation of the inscription (in full or in part) was not an essential feature of the sealing protocol even for these very special seals. For multiple applications of a royal name seal on one tablet, it is not always the case that any of the impressions will present the inscription (Root 1996a). One could argue that these royal name seals were so distinctive as to be easily recognizable as authentic by any ancient bureaucrat embedded in the system. But physical evidence shows that near duplicates existed that were certainly close enough to fool even an ancient expert when seen only in a partial and perhaps idiosyncratically rolled impression (see PFS 7* [Cat.No. 4]), and there is ample testimony from western Asia of concern over forged seals. It seems inescapable that good record keeping of the food disbursement operations in the Persepolis region did not necessarily imply the capacity to verify the seals later, even though the texts on the tablets produced in the field were used later to supply information for summary texts that are also part of the archive.

For the large number of typically shaped tablets that fit in the palm of the hand, some process of verification of identity might have taken place wherever the actual sealing process occurred. Indeed, it could be that many of our seals are best understood for now as part of a performance of identity verification at the places where the commodity transactions occurred. In such a scenario, the receiver of goods might go through the process of declaring a particular seal to serve as his/her representative. This enactment might be followed up by the application of the appropriate seal(s) to the tablet (depending upon proper protocols for specific types of persons and transactions, etc.), all in the presence of the personnel involved on both sides. The seals applied by administrative agents would then testify that the agent(s) was present at this performance of identity declaration and sealing by the receiver(s) or their agent(s). After all this (and at essentially the same time), the text recording the transaction would have been added to the sealed tablet.

PF 1809, impressed only with PFS 16* of Parnaka (on left edge and right edge), has an Aramaic notation in ink written directly on top of the seal impression on the left edge (the more viable impression of the two seal applications). The Aramaic note is a terse precis of the cuneiform text on the tablet, giving date, recipient, and location of the transaction (Hallock 1969, p. 495). This is not a common practice on the PF tablets, so we do not wish to make too much of it. Nevertheless, it may reinforce the sense that it was the sealing performance that mattered more for these particular transactions than the retrieval of pristine seal image after the fact. This is especially true when taken in conjunction with what is most definitely common practice on the inscribed tablets in the archive: the seal impressions — no matter how meticulously and elegantly presented on the tablets by the seal users — are routinely invaded by the preparation of the tablet surface for receipt of the cuneiform text and then subsequently by the cuts of the signs themselves.[92]

The protocols of application and the functions of seal impressions subsequent to the moment of application are likely to have varied depending upon different social contexts even within the court environment. Thus we do not mean to suggest in our analysis of the PF tablets any universally applicable notion of sealing practice in the Achaemenid period.

OTHER SEALING ARCHIVES OF THE ACHAEMENID EMPIRE

The Fortification archive is so far a unique example of its type among those known of Achaemenid date. But there are ample indications that this uniqueness is largely a reflection of archaeological serendipity. Our PFS 7*(Cat.No. 4), a royal name seal, has been identified in an impression on an Elamite tablet of Fortification type found at Susa without recorded context (Stolper 1992a; Garrison 1996b). This link between an important office seal of the Persepolis-based sector of the imperial distribution system and a tablet found at the site of Susa seems to suggest the extended purview of the administrative authority based at Persepolis. But the picture gradually emerging also shows that there must have been archives comparable to the Fortification archive that recorded comparable transactions in which other major Achaemenid installations performed as the regional hubs of their own zones. Isolated excavated finds of Achaemenid Elamite tablets from other areas of the empire confirm the notion of multiple localized archival mechanisms in far-flung parts of the empire that echo the Persepolitan model.[93]

Below we briefly sketch the major (and primarily excavated) Achaemenid-period archival corpora so far available from court contexts in the heartland and satrapies, from legal, business, and temple contexts, and from a private archive. These corpora help contextualize features of the PF corpus and work with it to offer crucial collective evidence for glyptic studies of the Achaemenid Empire.[94] The texts of many tablets of Achaemenid date were published long ago with little or no information provided about the seals used on the tablets. As this problem is addressed retroactively through new studies, we can expect a much-expanded range of material to be incorporated into broad-based analyses of seals and seal usage in the Achaemenid Empire.[95]

HEARTLAND COURT CONTEXTS

Of the four heartland royal cities of the Achaemenid Empire (Pasargadae, Persepolis, Susa, and Ecbatana), only Persepolis has so far revealed quantitatively significant archival material, even though all but Ecbatana have been the subjects of major excavations. Controlled excavations now under way at Ecbatana (modern Hamadan) may, of course, eventually reveal sealed archives.[96]

---

92. The PF tablets are not alone in showing tablets sealed before the writing of the text; see, for example, Stein 1993, p. 34, n. 113, discussing sealing practice on certain Middle Assyrian tablets from Aššur.

93. Jones and Stolper (1986, p. 248) cite the fragments of Achaemenid Elamite tablets found in the area of the fortification at Old Kandahar in Bactria (see now Helms 1997, p. 101) and a surface find at Chogha Mish in Khuzistan. On the latter, see now Kantor and Delougaz 1996, p. 17, pl. 5k. Briant (1984, p. 59) discusses the wider implications of the Kandahar tablet. Kandahar figures as a destination in PF texts.

94. Briant (1997, pp. 15–44) surveys new finds and recent bibliography on a range of related material.

95. An important project to coordinate text and seal information on a scale useful for statistical analysis has been undertaken by Cagni, Giovinazzo, and Graziani (1985). The frustrating problems they have confronted because of a lack of information on the applied seals are evident.

96. So far most of the information concerns monumental architectural remains. But the revelation already of sections of the massive fortification system with large storage facilities nearby suggests many possibilities. See Curtis and Simpson 1997, pp. 139–40; Sarraf 1997; Boucharlat 1998.

PERSEPOLIS: THE TREASURY

The Persepolis Treasury tablets and labels are the other known published corpus of sealings on both inscribed and uninscribed clay artifacts from this heartland capital of the Achaemenid Persian Empire. They were excavated from the Treasury by Erich Schmidt. According to the terminology followed in Schmidt 1957, only the inscribed clay artifacts in this collection are termed "tablets." We follow that terminology when discussing the Treasury corpus, although we find it problematic for reasons explained below. The tablets (some 198 either complete or largely complete plus 548 smaller fragments) are built around a string emerging from the two ends of the left edge — rather similar to the typically shaped PF tablets. All the Treasury tablets are inscribed in Elamite with the exception of one Babylonian example (Cameron 1948, pp. viii, 200; Cameron 1965). The texts reflect a limited transactional sphere in administrative personnel, in locale of sealing activity, and in type of activity recorded. All deal with payments by the Persepolis Treasury from that office between 492 and 459 B.C. (Cameron 1948; Schmidt 1957, pp. 4–5; Garrison 1988, pp. 172–78). Almost all of these tablets are sealed, but with only one seal per tablet. In every case, the seal is a cylinder seal and represents an administrative agent/agency of the court Treasury.

A related corpus includes 198 sealed clay artifacts from the Treasury (plus one from the southwest tower of the Apadana) that are all called "labels" in the excavation report (Schmidt 1957, p. 5). In fact, some of these labels are similar to the anepigraphic tablets in the Fortification archive. They are tablet shaped and (like the Treasury tablets and the typically shaped Fortification tablets, both inscribed and anepigraphic) are formed around a string that emerges from the two ends of the left edge. Other clay artifacts from the group that Schmidt called "labels" are in fact what could conventionally be called "bullae," lumps of clay affixed freehand around a string, a container, or a commodity and impressed with seals. These must once have locked/labeled diplomatic gifts, other commodities, and/or document rolls.[97]

The anepigraphic tablet-shaped labels and the labels that are actually bullae are multiply sealed with a mix of seals that sometimes includes the cylinders encountered on the tablets alongside other seals: additional cylinder seals as well as stamp seals with variously contoured edges and pointed elliptical signet ring bezels. Among the seals not represented on the tablets, but only on the labels, a variety of carving styles occur, including interesting Hellenizing types as well as types in conventional Greek styles. The labels bearing impressions of administrative cylinder seals were presumably produced and sealed right at Persepolis. But some of the bulla-type labels that do not incorporate seals of the Treasury personnel as known from the tablets could well have been sealed at the points of origin of the commodities being locked/labeled. In theory, points of origin might have been anywhere within the purview of the vast Achaemenid hegemony or on its imperial horizon.

The seals impressed on the Treasury tablets and labels are the closest body of material to those of the Fortification archive. Several officials functioning in the context of the Fortification archive re-appear still active later in Treasury transactions. Four seals in the PF corpus continued to be used on the Treasury tablets:[98] PFS 113* (Cat.No. 19) = PTS 4*; PFS 71* (II) = PTS 33*; PFS 451s (II) = PTS 61s; and PFS 1084* (III) = PTS 42*. Another seal occurring on the PF tablets, PFS 1567* (II), used by Ašbazana (= Gk. Aspathines), was originally collated by Hallock (1969, p. 78) with PTS 14*. But Treasury seal PTS 14* is in fact a later version of PFS 1567* (II), displaying distinct stylistic differences (Garrison and Root 1996, p. 9; Garrison 1998). In addition to men such as Ašbazana whose presence links the two archives, it is also noteworthy that the king figures as a party in transactions in both the Fortification and Treasury archives.

Despite many links, the Fortification and Treasury archives are quite different in certain respects. The Treasury material is much more limited quantitatively. Of the seventy-seven discrete seals documented in the entire Treasury corpus, forty-three are cylinder seals and thirty-four are stamp seals and signet rings. Only seventeen of the forty-three cylinder seals represented in the entire Treasury corpus are used on the tablets. Thus, only seventeen of the seventy-seven seals can be associated with texts. Of these seventeen cylinder seals, two are used so frequently as to

---

97. The term "label" is not really appropriate for either of these types of sealed entity. Moreover, the two types should not be designated by the same term. See Ferioli and Fiandra 1994, p. 155, concerning clay items with text and seal impressions that clearly constitute what should be termed "labels." Here, the labels were found near groups of stored tablets to which their labeling texts referred.

98. We reference the seals used on the Treasury archive by the siglum PTS (= Persepolis Treasury Seal) followed by the number assigned by Schmidt 1957. An asterisk (*) following a seal number indicates an inscribed seal; an "s" following a seal number indicates a stamp seal.

account for over one-half of the total number of seal impressions on the tablets (Garrison 1988, p. 175). Obviously, the PF corpus alone is much larger with its ca. 1,417 discrete seals (including the analytically illegible ones) as opposed to only seventy-seven seals on all the published Treasury tablets and labels combined. The very small number of additional Treasury tablets that have not yet been published does not significantly alter this relationship. The very large number of still unpublished Fortification tablets does, however, significantly expand the quantitative gap in favor of that archive. When we acknowledge the added feature of the multiple applications of many of the seals on the PF tablets, the expansiveness of potential data to be derived from the PF corpus is even more evident.

Furthermore, the seals used on the PF tablets provide information on a broader cross-section of society than do those on the Treasury tablets and labels. The seals used on the Treasury tablets are restricted to those of the administrative officials involved, while the PF documents, as we have seen, frequently display the seals of individuals involved in a wide variety of administrative activities and state-related travel. Some of the Treasury bulla-type labels should perhaps be examined as a separate category of evidence in order to determine if possible the likelihood of their production at Persepolis versus far afield. A useful project would involve a return to the Treasury corpus of bulla-type labels, examining them artifactually for clues to usage (via the undersides) and locales of production/sealing (perhaps via neutron activation analysis).

Most of the seals used on the inscribed Treasury tablets are carved in the Court Style. This reflects the particular group of people and offices represented on these documents. Thus, when taken in conjunction with the seals on the PF tablets they offer important evidence on the meaning, development, and flowering of this prestigious style in the heart of the empire.

The Treasury labels sealed with cylinder seals of Treasury administrators as well as with ring bezels of unidentifiable individuals offer important evidence on the chronology of these ring seals. Since ring seals do not seem to have been used on the PF tablets but are used on Treasury labels (together with a royal name seal of Xerxes), we can establish quite close dating parameters for the emerging popularity of this seal form. Numerous Greek-style pointed elliptical ring seals appear on the Treasury labels. Once again, the associations of some of these items with closely dated seals provide rare chronological fixed points for iconographies and styles in Greek glyptic.[99]

PERSEPOLIS: POST-HERZFELD DISCOVERIES IN THE FORTIFICATION

In recent excavations in the Fortification at Persepolis, Iranian excavators have made a tantalizing discovery: a jar containing fifty-two anepigraphic sealed tablets. Tadjvidi (1970, p. 187) notes that "most of them" show the king (i.e., a crowned figure) forcing a Greek soldier to his knees. None of the seals in the PFS corpus bear an image remotely similar to this, but the same seal was used on five Treasury bulla-type labels (PTS 28: Schmidt 1957, pp. 10–11, 29, and pl. 9).[100] The scene preserved on tablets in Tadjvidi's discovery and also on the Treasury sealings (as PTS 28) includes a file of Greek captives as well as the victor spearing a kneeling Greek (see Tadjvidi 1976 for illustrations of two of the bullae from the Fortification jar). The seal represented in these impressions seems stylistically and also by association with the Treasury corpus to date to the Xerxes-Artaxerxes era. The find corroborates the notion that parts of the Fortification complex were used to house active administration archives. This assemblage, which was still contained in a jar, is hardly likely to have been discarded fill. Furthermore, it suggests that we may expect to find additional inscribed tablets in this area of the site, relating to the anepigraphic sealed tablets in the jar and expanding chronologically upon the Fortification archive of Darius I. (The nature of the business to which the Tadjvidi discovery relates remains to be determined, pending excavation and publication of linked inscribed tablets from the surrounding area.)

---

99. PTS 5*, for instance, is a royal name seal of Xerxes displaying a heroic control encounter. It appears not only on Treasury tablets but also on labels: with PTS 19 (an uninscribed Court Style cylinder that does not appear on tablets), and PTS 54s and PTS 55s (two seal rings with pointed elliptical bezels, one of which [PTS 54s] is in a Greek style). See Schmidt 1957, pp. 20–21, 36, pls. 2, 4, 13.

100. See Root 1979, pp. 182–83, for a listing and discussion of several related Achaemenid seals.

SUSA

Documented excavations at Susa have revealed no inscribed administrative tablets of Achaemenid date (though see *Business/Legal/Temple Contexts*, below). Indeed, remarkably few isolated tablets and bullae of Achaemenid date have been excavated at Susa or found in the environs (Boucharlat 1990, p. 155; Garrison 1996b). This is paradoxical in contrast to Persepolis since Susa is traditionally characterized in scholarship as the administrative capital of the Persian Empire. Several of the isolated seal impressions from Susa display close ties to earlier Elamite tradition and are generally considered pre-Achaemenid, although in certain cases they could as easily be borderline (Amiet 1973a, 1973b). Only eight sealed bullae are cataloged by Amiet as dating to the Achaemenid period, two of which display Egyptian or Egyptianizing scarab sealings. The remaining six bear impressions of seals displaying fully developed Achaemenid characteristics (Amiet 1972, pp. 284–86, pls. 37, 189–90, nos. 2202–03, 2226–29). Except for the lone Elamite tablet sealed with PFS 7* (Cat.No. 4) for which there is no documented evidence of its discovery in the Susa excavation records, none of these Susa sealings remain associated with a dated document nor do any retain association with other possible explicit chronological or socio-historical indicators (such as a name inscription).

SATRAPAL COURT CONTEXTS

Provenanced corpora of seal impressions relating to official archives at provincial government sites of the Achaemenid Empire are known from Daskyleion-Ergili (the satrapal headquarters of Phrygia) and from Memphis.[101] In both instances the seal impressions are preserved on bullae that are now divorced from their original associated texts or commodities. No archive from Sardis, satrapal capital of Lydia in the Achaemenid Empire, has yet been recovered, even in the form of detached sealed bullae.[102]

PHRYGIA: DASKYLEION

The Daskyleion material apparently represents some 193 legible individual seals multiply applied for a total of some 415 impressions. It includes two seals with the royal name inscription of Xerxes, giving one chronological anchor of 486–465 B.C., and another seal with the royal name of Artaxerxes, presumably Artaxerxes I, giving another chronological anchor of 465–425 B.C. Stylistic criteria suggest the likelihood, however, that some of the seals extend in date of manufacture down into the fourth century B.C. The Daskyleion group is the major corpus of directly court-related sealings from a western provincial palace environment. Although lacking in associated textual information, their significant number, magnificent quality, repertorial richness, and significant indications of east-west cultural exchange make these impressions a critical resource (Garrison in press). Kaptan's preliminary publications (e.g., Kaptan 1996a, 1996b) already indicate important aspects of the relationship between Greek stylistic and iconographical elements and heartland Persian elements.

EGYPT: MEMPHIS

The sealed bullae from the palace office at Memphis constitute a small corpus of sealings apparently dating to the fifth century B.C. All but one of the bullae seem to be from parcels, the exception occurring on a tablet. Twenty of the seal designs represented (nos. 21–39, 46) are clearly of Achaemenid type and date (Petrie et al. 1910, pp. 42–43, pls. 35–37). Although several seals impressed on the Memphis bullae are similar to seals in the PFS corpus,

---

101. For Daskyleion, see Akurgal 1956; Balkan 1959; Turkish Ministry of Culture and Tourism 1983, pp. 69–71; Kaptan-Bayburtluoğlu 1990; Kaptan 1996a; Kaptan 1996b; Kaptan in press. For Memphis, see Petrie et al. 1910.

102. Although remains of Achaemenid Sardis have turned out to be rich in information already, digging has not yet focused on the main areas of the Achaemenid city. See Dusinberre 1997a.

none seems to represent an identical seal. Several are extremely interesting and suggest subtle blendings of Persian and Egyptian iconography and style. One, for example, is a cylinder presenting a ritual scene involving ministrations over an animal with a seated personage looking on; another is a cylinder displaying a winged hero figure as well as a crowned scorpion-man performing as an archer, all between unusual Egyptian floral borders (Petrie et al. 1910, pls. 35–36/39, 37/46). These bullae were misplaced at the Ashmolean Museum during World War II and thus are no longer available for firsthand analysis.

EGYPT: DECONTEXTUALIZED LETTERS WITH SEALED BULLAE

The Aramaic correspondence on leather dealing with the affairs of the Achaemenid prince and satrap Aršam in Egypt deserves mention here (Driver 1957). Some thirteen written documents plus fragments comprise the archive of letters primarily dealing with the administration of royal domains in Egypt. Ten of the letters are actually from Aršam himself; they are all closely connected and form a substantively coherent group with Aršam's name running through the entirety. The letters must date to the late fifth century B.C. Although unfortunately lacking any archaeological context, the documents are extremely important for their contents. Furthermore, the leather pouch associated with the letters is a unique example demonstrating how the many couriers cited in the PF texts must have carried their "sealed documents of the king." In the leather pouch holding the Aršam correspondence were several bullae impressed with Aršam's personal cylinder seal bearing, in the field, the Aramaic inscription "seal of Aršam the prince" (Driver 1957, pp. 3–4; Moorey 1978, p. 143, fig. 8). This seal shows two dismounted equestrians in combat below a winged symbol and a crescent, with slain figures below. It is, to our knowledge, the only personal seal of an Achaemenid prince or a satrap so far securely identified as such. There is no similar seal type in the PFS corpus.

EGYPT(?) TO MESOPOTAMIA(?): A SMALL CORPUS OF DECONTEXTUALIZED SEALED TABLETS

A cluster of eight anepigraphic sealed tablets/groups of tablets with string holes (similar in shape to the typically shaped PF tablets) has been brought together by Goetze (1944) from disparate collections. Although decontextualized, specific aspects of the material raise many important issues relevant to the study of Achaemenid seals through sealed tablets. This justifies our inclusion of the group here.

All the tablets display the same four cylinder seals impressed according to the same protocol on multiple tablet surfaces. The entire collection of tablets must (because of the identical nature of tablets, seals, and sealing protocols) emanate from the same environment and the same historical moment. One of the tablets is "said to have come from" Tello (ancient Girsu) in southern Mesopotamia (Goetze 1944, p. 97). If this information is correct, then all of them presumably derive from this site. Whatever the provenance of the tablets, the four seals impressed upon them are uniformly magnificent prestige items of great intrinsic interest. They must derive from a high-level courtly administrative context. Based only on examination of the published photographs, they would classify as Court Style products. None are identical with any seal in the PFS corpus, and all of them may be about a generation later than any of the Court Style seals in the PFS corpus. One of the seals (Goetze's "d"; 1944, pp. 100–01, pl. 11) displays heraldic winged creatures flanking a name-ring crowned with volutes according to Goetze (they look more like addorsed animal protomes from the published photographs). Over this, a winged symbol hovers. The inscription, although in Aramaic letters, may render an Old Persian epithet that Goetze (1944, p. 100) tentatively reads "he who brings about good peace." Such an epithet, he argues, would have distinct royal resonance among Persians.

The Egyptian associations of the name-ring on Goetze's seal "d" suggest the possibility that the tablets were sealed at a court office in Egypt and were originally affixed to royal commodities sent from there to a palatial installation in Mesopotamian Girsu (assuming that the putative Tello provenance of the one tablet is actually correct).[103] The content of the letters of Prince Aršam (see above) is only one clear piece of evidence among many of the fluid

---

103. Goetze (1944, n. 15) offers comparandum of a seal in the Newell Collection on which the name-ring is crowned by falcon heads each wearing the Double Crown of Upper and Lower Egypt, with the Old Persian inscription inside. The inscription

exchange of imperial goods as well as services and personnel between Egypt and western Asia under the Achaemenid hegemony. A great deal of work is being done now on Achaemenid Egypt in connection with provocative new archaeological discoveries (Briant 1997, pp. 32–37). Ultimately, it may be possible to comment further on the potential links of the seals presented here with an Achaemenid-Egyptian context of production.

The tablets on which the seals are impressed are, of course, another matter. They might well have been fashioned and sealed in Egypt. But what was their ultimate trans-empire destination? Goetze (1944) expressed some skepticism about the Tello provenance for the tablets because ancient Girsu is not considered an Achaemenid site. But we are much more aware now of the archaeological and historiographic issues that have tended to mute the record of the Achaemenid presence at many sites, even sites such as Sardis where we know that presence had to have been impressive indeed (viz., Root 1991, on the problem). Although not much is currently known about Girsu for a long stretch between the early second millennium and the middle of the second century B.C., the site was apparently inhabited. Further work (or re-examination of the old records of the French mission) may yield interesting results for Achaemenid times.[104]

BUSINESS / LEGAL / TEMPLE CONTEXTS
BABYLONIA

The Murašû business archive from Nippur (454–404 B.C.) includes approximately 800 tablets inscribed in Babylonian cuneiform and bearing impressions of 657 seals. The texts and seals have now been analyzed extensively (Stolper 1985; Stolper 1992b; Bregstein 1993; Bregstein 1996; Donbaz and Stolper 1997; Pedersén 1998, p. 199). Types of seals used on the tablets include elliptical-shaped ring bezels as well as cylinders and stamps. Once visual documentation of all the Murašû evidence has been published by Bregstein and at the level necessary for fine-tuned iconographic, stylistic, and hand-attribution analysis, this corpus will offer wonderful potential similar in scope to that provided by the PFS corpus (Bregstein 1993, p. 113). Bregstein's important analyses of seal usage and of the relation of seal imagery to individual seal owners already make a major contribution to glyptic research in the Achaemenid period, particularly within the Babylonian region of the empire. Captions to seal impressions on the Murašû tablets enable more consistently secure links between seals and users named in the texts than is possible with the PF tablets. Remarkably, the latest dated texts (reign of Darius II) seem to indicate that by that time ownership of the Murašû family holdings had been transferred to Prince Aršam, the satrap of Egypt whose correspondence and personal seal we have just mentioned. The seal known through impressed bullae associated with his Egyptian correspondence is not, however, preserved on the Murašû documents.

The Kasr archive from Babylon is comprised of approximately 950 clay tablets recording lease and loan agreements (Pedersén 1998, p. 184). Those bearing dates provide a range within the reigns of Artaxerxes I and Darius II (465–404 B.C.). This collection is thus essentially contemporaneous with the Murašû archive; indeed, there is some overlap in actual seals used in these two Babylonian archives (Klengel-Brandt 1969; Stolper 1990a). The Kasr corpus exemplifies numerous problems of archive analysis for Achaemenid Mesopotamia caused by negligence in the field, inadequate recording and publication, and the negative effects of the antiquities trade, all contributing to the dismantling of the corpus (van Driel 1987; Kuhrt 1990, pp. 182–83).

A very large archive of clay tablets excavated at Sippar northwest of Babylon includes a group of some 32,000 Babylonian documents dating to the Neo-Babylonian and early Achaemenid periods (from the reign of Nabopolassar down into the second year of Xerxes [ca. 625–486 B.C.]). The archive is important not least for the information it reveals on storage procedures in a temple context at this time (Pedersén 1998, pp. 195–97). One collec-

---

was once translated (viz., Goetze 1944) as "belonging to Artaxerxes" but is rendered as "under [unter] Artaxerxes" by Schmitt (1981, pp. 34–35, fig. 4). This seal (said to have come "from Egypt") has no archaeological context, but the even more emphatic Egyptianate aspect of its iconography reinforces the possibility that the seal with name-ring impressed on these tablets studied by Goetze reflects an Egyptian milieu in the Persian court administration.

104. Downey (1988, p. 48) reviews the installation in the Seleucid era of a local ruler who created a rather remarkable environment replete with ancient statues and other evocations of Girsu's great third-millennium ruler Gudea. This suggests the possibility that earlier (Achaemenid period) antiquarian excavation and palatial installation had already occurred here and provided the link between the third-millennium antiquities and the Seleucid presentation of them.

tion of letter orders from the larger Sippar corpus includes frequent multiple seal impressions of some sixty-seven discrete seals (MacGinnis 1995, pp. 177–79, for a listing from which we derive this count of seals used). The smallness of the sample, its great chronological range, plus the heavily traditional Babylonian milieu of the archive combine to make this a rather idiosyncratic collection for purposes of analytical comparison with the PFS corpus. Interesting observations about the interplay of seals used by different categories of persons do, however, suggest ways in which heartland Persian representational strategies worked and were deployed over time in relation to local traditional forms within this particular Babylonian environment.

Additional Achaemenid material from Babylon is surveyed by Pedersén (1998, pp. 187–91; e.g., his Babylon 13, a private archive dating to Darius I and Xerxes, as yet unpublished; Babylon 14, a private or temple archive dating to Darius I; Babylon 15, the illicitly recovered archive of the Egibi family, with references). Recent work on archival material from Uruk is also now available but has come to our attention too late to be incorporated analytically here or in the catalog entries for Volume I (Ehrenberg 1999).

Archives of Hellenistic documents may in some cases preserve material actually of Achaemenid date (e.g., Oelsner 1986).

SUSA

A handful of Babylonian legal texts of Achaemenid date seem to have been drafted at Susa, even though they relate to Murašû family dealings that were centered at Nippur. They are without archaeological context, but their relation to the Murašû archive (above, *Babylonia*) particularly merits their mention here. Issues they have raised are informative on aspects of the cosmopolitanism of society during the Achaemenid Empire (Stolper 1992b).

Joannès (1990) has published two Babylonian tablets from Susa (both date to one of the Artaxerxes and are legal rather than state administrative texts). The seals used on these two documents were published by Amiet (1973a, pls. 16 [72], 17 [76: 1–6]). The carving styles and iconographies of the seals used do not have an obvious correspondence with the ethnic identifications of the names cited in the transactions (e.g., an individual using an Egyptian name does not use an Egyptian or Egyptianizing seal). This has led Joannès to suggest (p. 180) that in the multi-cultural context of the empire it would be fruitless to seek correlations between seal style/imagery and the ethnicity of the seal owner (as determined by the name the individual uses). Rather, he proposes that these variables relate to the predilections or background of the seal carver. As more scholars begin working through such questions with the published seal evidence of the PF tablets and the Murašû tablets, perhaps this important line of questioning can be addressed against a backdrop of a larger sample. It seems likely that patron choices frequently reflected within the PFS corpus are in fact related to the biography of the individual in some sense. But these choices often reflect complexly layered allusive interests in and relationships to visual culture accessible in the multi-cultural environment of the empire.

PALESTINE

The collection of sealed bullae presumably once attached to the legal papyri from the Wadi ed-Daliyeh (Cave I) in the area of Samaria north of Jerusalem is a significant corpus (Leith 1997).[105] Unfortunately, it is not derived from a controlled archaeological context. Samaria was, however, a key administrative center of the Achaemenid Empire. It is likely that the papyri belonged to Samaritan refugees who, in flight from the Macedonians in the fourth century B.C., brought their most important legal papers with them when they sought shelter in Cave I. There are some sixty-one distinct (and legible) seals used to produce the impressions on the corpus of bullae that Leith published (information culled from Leith 1997, pp. 4–5, 23, and a tally of her images); Leith's publication does not include all the bullae thought to be connected to the Wadi ed-Daliyeh corpus (Leith 1997, pp. 3–6). The papyri with which the detached sealed bullae are originally considered to have been associated have date formulae in Persian

---

105. In several instances the papyrus documents still bore sealings; there seems to be no doubt that the sealed bullae in the find are to be associated with the papyri (Leith 1997, pp. 18, 55, 87, 100, 107, 110, 213, 221, 239; Pedersén 1998, pp. 226–27).

regnal years giving parameters of 375–365 B.C. and 335 B.C. Their contents have suggested to Leith that the owners/users of the seals were affluent local people of Samaria "who administered the city and its province for their Persian overlords" (Leith 1997, p. 6; but cf. Gropp 1986, p. vi, who characterizes the owners of the documents as simply "wealthy patricians of Samaria"). This seems borne out by the representational repertoire on the seals used. Although there is some overlap in seal imagery between the Wadi ed-Daliyeh corpus and the PFS corpus, it is interesting that the winged symbol is completely absent in this corpus even from seal types which relate in other ways to heartland Achaemenid imagery. Although opinion is divided as to whether this symbol actually depicts the god Ahuramazda within the iconographical program of Achaemenid Persian art, there is little if any question that it symbolizes crucial concepts of Zoroastrian faith or Mazdaism on some level (Sancisi-Weerdenburg 1995, p. 1042; commentary on PFS 7* [Cat.No. 4], herein). Its absence from the iconography of the Wadi ed-Daliyeh seals thus suggests a capacity among this Jewish population to maintain distance from Achaemenid religious reference. For the most part, the sealings from the Wadi ed-Daliyeh archive reflect western imperial koine styles, and they are crucial evidence in ongoing investigations of cultural continuities and discontinuities between Achaemenid and Hellenistic Syro-Palestine.[106]

Numerous isolated finds of sealed bullae have been retrieved from excavations at various sites in Judah, the rival region to the south of Samaria, and its surrounding countryside (Stern 1971). They are no longer associated with documents or commodities, and it is not clear in what context the seals were used. Stern, who has published an interesting analysis of a group of these items, makes a case for administrative use based upon the representational evocations of heartland Achaemenid Persian court glyptic on these anepigraphic figural seals (Stern 1990).[107]

Active ongoing archaeology in Israel holds great potential for pursuing further (undoubtedly with ever-expanding evidence) some of the important suggestions already put forth (e.g., Uehlinger 1999).[108]

PRIVATE (ARTISANAL) CONTEXT

UR

Another type of collection is the hoard of approximately 200 ancient impressions in clay found in a coffin at Ur (Legrain 1951, pp. 47–53; Porada 1960; Bregstein 1993, pp. 65–69; Collon 1996). These impressions document seals, coins, and details on metalware. One cast of an Athenian tetradrachm has been used to establish a possible *terminus post quem* of about 460 B.C. for the burial. But there are some indications that the collection was perhaps added to much later, after 400 B.C. (Collon 1996, p. 78). This cache presumably represents an artist's collection of models. It validates the concept that glyptic artists in Achaemenid times self-consciously and systematically consulted broad-based repertoires of style and imagery. The collection is diverse in its amalgamation of Mesopotamian antique images, Achaemenid images, and Greek images, suggesting a varied set of interests on the part of this artisan's patrons in the heart of Mesopotamia during the Achaemenid Empire. It also demonstrates that imagery shared between seal, coin, and toreutic production was a critical feature of the creative environment. This is an aspect of the cultural landscape in the Persian Empire that needs more analysis.[109] The seals used on the PF tablets include at least two that are actually coins: PFS 1616s (III) (Starr 1976; Root 1997) and PFS 1393s (II) (Root 1988; Root 1989).

---

106. For example, the exciting ongoing excavation of a substantial archive of sealed bullae from a good second-century B.C. context at Kedesh of the Upper Galilee under the University of Michigan/University of Minnesota Expedition to Tel Kedesh (S. Herbert, pers. comm. [1999]).

107. Stern's dating has been disputed in Bianchi 1996.

108. See Avigad 1997 for an extensive compilation of evidence on seals and sealings in western Semitic contexts, including material of the Persian period.

109. See Moorey 1978 for some suggestions.

PART THREE: GUIDE TO THE THREE-VOLUME CATALOG

CONCEPTUAL ORGANIZATION OF THE MATERIAL

Originally this project was envisioned as a traditional *catalogue raisonné* for which the major effort would rest in searching for comparanda among published seals. In the end, it has become apparent that our main obligation is, first, to document the seals on the PF tablets visually and verbally at the highest level within our means, and, second, to integrate the seals so documented into the structure of the archive as much as possible given the current state of research in this area. Stress has thus shifted from fitting the seals used on the PF tablets into comparative relationships with previously known (and often unprovenanced) seal artifacts. The goal now is rather to provide a research tool that will enable the scholarly community to use our documentation in a variety of interpretive agendas, with the seals on the PF tablets serving as a standard of reference against which other material can be evaluated.

Each seal in the PFS corpus is documented in a discrete catalog entry. In addition, we offer a many-layered apparatus that invites intra-archival explorations across the entire PFS corpus. The sheer size of this corpus compels us, however, to divide the publication into three volumes.

We have chosen to divide the material into these three volumes according to representational categories. Catalogs of ancient western Asiatic seals, seal impressions, and ivories often arrange material by stylistic groups. Our decision to depart from that model, privileging representation, was in part based on practical considerations. It has been possible to isolate and define the different representational categories in the corpus as a first-level endeavor while work in refining our categorizations of stylistic nuance proceeds on a seal-by-seal basis. To have based the catalog structure on stylistic groupings would have meant an unacceptable deferral of publication of the volumes because it would have necessitated waiting until final interpretive work had been accomplished on every seal before publishing Volume I. In substantive rather than practical terms, one of the most remarkable aspects of the PFS corpus is the great variety of imagery it documents at the Persian court. This cultural context is often dismissed for its limited repertoire of visual expression. Thus it seems particularly important to redress the balance by allowing the reader immediate, systematic access to the representational variety and complexity highlighted through a thematic organization.[110]

Various other organizational options for our catalog might have included grouping the seals in relation to specific features of the documents with which they are associated, such as names of users. Alas, the PF tablets do not include name captions next to seal impressions, and, as we have already explained, user protocols are unambiguous for only two text types within the archive. Thus, explorations of relationships between text information about individual types of (or parties to) transactions and the seal imagery deployed in the service of these administrative activities needs to be facilitated by our catalog; such discussions will certainly continue to emerge in focused projects.

In sum, we reached our decision to organize the catalog by representational categories after weighing the options carefully. We established a hierarchy of information so as to privilege the seals as works of art, listing them first by representation and second by style. This then invites the reader to consider the seals as social tools in active use within a particular administrative environment.

The internal organization of seals in each volume seeks to show relationships between similar composition types across the entire stylistic spectrum present in the PFS corpus (see, e.g., *Part Four: Typology of Images in Volume I*, below). This organizational principle avoids imposition of an arbitrary division of the material according to presumed notions of the history of stylistic development. Instead, the organization privileges a different aspect of historicity, the historicity of active use embedded in the Fortification archive. All the seals in the PFS corpus (with their stylistic and iconographic diversity and their various social categories of users) were part of the same visible and functional world of the Persepolis region for at least a brief collective transactional moment between 509 and 494 B.C. In that sense they have their own collective internal history. They are a portfolio of visual possibilities that were all unquestionably at hand in the Persian heartland at Persepolis during the middle years of the reign of Darius I.

---

110. Bregstein (1993, pp. 71–72) similarly organizes the Murašû material in this way, giving cogent reasons for doing so.

All three volumes of the catalog follow the basic Volume I format, except for differences in organization necessitated by the more diverse subject matters offered in Volumes II and III. The final volume includes updated and comprehensive concordances and appendices synthesizing data across the entire three-volume set.

Throughout the volumes each seal (PFS) is given a catalog number (Cat.No.) alongside its PFS number. The catalog number provides an internal finding aid of sequential numbers from the first seal cataloged in Volume I to the last one cataloged in Volume III. Seals that are discussed in Volume I but cataloged in subsequent volumes are cited here by PFS number and also parenthetically by a II or a III to designate the volume in which they appear. All seals in the PFS corpus that are referred to in Volume I and also cataloged in Volume I incorporate the parenthetical catalog number. The seals are known in scholarly literature by PFS number. This should remain the case. To avoid confusion between the catalog number and the PFS number we always cite a given seal as "PFS plus number," not resorting to alternatives such as "seal plus number" just for the sake of variety.

DEFINITION OF A MAIN SCENE

Determinations of appropriate volume designation have been made on the basis of the main scene represented on each seal, whether a heroic encounter, scenes of human activity, or images of animals, creatures, plants, and geometric devices. Although so-called terminal field motifs on cylinder seals are crucial features of seal design and iconographical program (Root 1999a, pp. 160–61), they often introduce a different category of imagery (see *Appendix Eight: Iconographic Features on Seals in Volume I*, under *Terminal Field Motifs*). Thus, for instance, PFS 1071 (Cat.No. 29) is classified as a hero seal by virtue of its main scene, but this same seal bears a terminal field device of a winged symbol with figure emergent supported by two rampant, winged, human-headed bull or lion creatures with human arms in the atlas pose. This symbolic support motif exists as the main (and only) scene on numerous Achaemenid seals including examples in Volume II, but here on PFS 1071 it cedes status to the hero image for the purposes of organization of the catalog.[111] This does not mean that we discount the significance of terminal field designs. Quite the contrary, it becomes apparent when we discuss issues of seal application patterns in the PFS corpus that the catalog seeks to awaken scholarly interest in the interplay of features that we characterize (for lack of better terms) as main scenes, terminal field elements (including inscriptions), and symbols placed elsewhere in the compositional field (elements that are often called fillers rather dismissively in the literature).

VOLUME I: IMAGES OF HEROIC ENCOUNTER

It has long been recognized that images of heroic encounter enjoyed a great popularity in Achaemenid-period glyptic. They appear in all styles and in myriad iconographical and compositional variations. Images of heroic encounter account for more seal designs than any other single motif. Approximately 27% of the entire PFS corpus of analytically legible seals definitely comprise heroic scenes. A number of seals grouped in Volume III preserve only segments of rampant animals. Some of these fragmentary images must also belong to hero seals. Were we able to reconstruct them more fully, they would further swell the tally of hero seals.

The seals on the PF tablets preserving the theme of heroic encounter were first studied by Garrison (1988). A few seals that were not included in Garrison 1988 are included in Volume I. These changes are due either to better readings of seal designs resulting from further work with the tablets or to definitional adjustments to the hero category. Those seals in Garrison 1988 that have been reclassified appear in Volume II. All such changes are noted in the relevant catalog entries.

We define a scene of heroic encounter as one in which a protagonist exerts power or control over animals or creatures in a manner that explicitly transcends the plausible. Carried with this definition is a notion of an emblematic display rather than a clearly narrative scenario set in the context of, for example, a hunting scene. The line between a scene that transcends the plausible via an unrealistic display of power relationships and one that takes place

---

111. A dramatic example of the tension between main image and terminal field motif appears on an Achaemenid cylinder seal in the Louvre (Louvre AO 2405) where a controlling hero occupies the main field, but an unusually elaborate scene of a seated figure with servant and paraphernalia occupies the terminal field; see Collon 1987, pp. 150–51, no. 659.

in a more or less realistic narrative context is sometimes blurry, but overall the distinction works to create a notional system for analysis. This notional system is rarely articulated explicitly in the literature, but it is conventionally accepted. The hero is usually a male human figure, with details of dress and bearing open to much variety. There are no recognized female heroes in the PFS corpus. The hero may also be a hybrid being (such as a winged human figure) or even a composite animal creature who assumes the role of a human-type figure but has minimal human physical attributes, as on PFS 1* (Cat.No. 182). Similarly, the subject of the hero's exercise may be any type of real or fantastic creature. The range is great.

Specifically within the PFS corpus, we have attempted rigor in interpreting formal qualification as a hero scene. The heroic protagonist must demonstrably make contact with the object of his involvement or at minimum, with a fragmentary image, be most plausibly interpreted to have done so. Thus, for instance, we separate out from the corpus of potential scenes of heroic control a seal such as PFS 1312s (II). Here, the compositional format of a human flanked by fish creatures might have indicated an image of heroic control, but since no actual contact seems to be made by the central figure the seal is placed in Volume II. Similarly, there are numerous seals in Volume II displaying images of human figures in stasis confronting at a distance potentially dangerous animals or fantastic creatures. One could conceivably argue that the aura of control exists in such scenes since the psychological force of the human figure could be said to keep the creature at bay. With the feature of direct physical engagement unexpressed, however, the valences of such scenes seem to reside in another realm that is not best described by the term "heroic." Scenes depicting a protagonist leading an animal in procession are found in Volume II rather than Volume I, even though they too may in some cases share the element of the implausible with the traditional heroic encounter.

The most difficult challenges have been posed by scenes such as that on PFS 1166 (II). This seal displays a chariot hunt scene in which one passenger reaches out the back of the vehicle to grasp a large animal by the hind leg. Obviously, it shares some important features with a traditional heroic encounter, but it also crosses the line into a definite hunt scene with narrative qualities. By our decision to place this seal in Volume II rather than in Volume I, PFS 1166 (II) takes its place alongside the many other hunting scenes depicting chariots, a significant iconographical cluster that is best kept together.

We discuss aspects of the history and meanings of images of heroic encounter in *Part Four: Images in Volume I*, below.

VOLUME II: IMAGES OF HUMAN ACTIVITY

Volume II represents about 30% of the entire PFS corpus of analytically legible seals, including a wide variety of scene types best described as relating to human activity. The protagonists of this human activity can be human figures, human creatures, animals acting as humans, or fantastic creatures acting as humans. The single largest category of imagery is the archer scene, which covers at least 31% of the seals in Volume II (approximately 9.6% of the entire legible PFS corpus). As with the hero scenes, the archer scenes are extraordinarily varied in style, composition, and iconography. And as with the hero scenes, the archer scenes include an array of protagonists who depart from the traditional human form (including, e.g., centaurs). Other categories of representation include additional hunting scenes, many involving chariots; formal dispositions and processions of figures, including worship and cult scenes of Assyrian, Babylonian, and Persian types; scenes of seated figures, including presentation scenes and banquet scenes; genre scenes; and a small number of martial scenes and isolated figural studies.[112] Occasionally, seals are included in Volume II that could plausibly go in Volume III. An example is PFS 650 (II). Here a human-headed winged goat(?) participates in an animal contest scene, but this particular figure is the dominant aggressor and wields a spear in the manner of a human combatant. We have opted to include this seal with others of human activity.

---

112. Garrison 2000 illustrates an informative selection of Volume II seals.

VOLUME III: ANIMALS, CREATURES, PLANTS, AND GEOMETRIC DEVICES

Volume III is the largest, embracing approximately 43% of the analytically legible PFS corpus. It includes many examples of the age-old animal-contest motif in a variety of guises. All cases in which a hybrid creature, even if human headed (e.g., a sphinx), performs like an animal rather than a human are incorporated in Volume III. There are many isolated animal or creature studies, some of which are stunning tours de force. Isolated floral and geometric displays are less frequent, but several examples pose interesting questions concerning the use of antique seals or archaizing imagery reaching across vast temporal stretches.

DOCUMENTATION OF THE SEALS: VOLUMES I–III
NUMBERING AND COLLATING
HALLOCK'S LEGACY

In the course of his work on the Fortification texts, Richard T. Hallock became interested in the seal impressions. His interest was in their possible usefulness as verifiers of information on administrative protocols, personnel, and places as given in the texts. He painstakingly noted their occurrences in his work on the texts, and he attempted to keep track of multiple occurrences of the same seal used on different tablets. He drew sketches of many of the impressions (fig. 8). Usually these are sketches of an individual impression. They rarely represent an attempt to collate information gleaned from all recognized impressions. Nor are they intended in any way to convey stylistic information or carefully studied iconographical details.[113]

Hallock assigned numbers to the 314 seals that he thought occurred on more than one PF tablet. According to the principle of his graduated numbering scheme, PFS 1* (Cat.No. 182) occurs on the largest number of tablets; the number of tablet occurrences descends from there in the sequence of PFS 1* through PFS 314. The graduating numbers do not take into account the fact that a seal may frequently occur several times on one tablet. For Hallock, such instances did not qualify as "multiple occurrences." Hallock's scheme was devised by a scholar thinking primarily in terms of the texts, tablet by tablet, and secondarily in terms of the seals as diagnostic agents for the texts, tablet by tablet. Work that privileges exploration of the seals impressed on the tablets as social tools and works of art with inherent significance demands more focused tabulations.

Hallock's attempts to identify individual seals and to track them across the 2,087 PF tablets enabled scholars to begin discussing some aspects of seal usage with respect to the tracking of seals in the PFS 1*–314 range (by number) across Hallock's published texts. The secondary literature is by now quite vast and much of it figures in catalog entries for individual seals. For the most part, this scholarship on seal usage works with the seals conceptually (as numbers that signify discrete administrative tools and thus also signify the presence of a specific person or the location of a transaction at a specific place). Despite the fact that these interpretive studies are not dealing with the seals as visual representations, they are dependent upon the accuracy of formal analysis of the seal representations. It is only through meticulous formal analysis that distinctions between fragmentary impressions can determine accurate collations. Many of Hallock's seal identifications have now changed as a result of the Garrison and Root project (as announced in Garrison and Root 1996 with provisional concordances correcting Hallock's original collations). Potentially reinforcing Hallock's erroneous collations posthumously, photocopies of Hallock's transliterations of unpublished Elamite texts (i.e., the PFNN tablets, including notes on seals he identified as appearing on them) have enjoyed some circulation among specialist scholars (e.g., Hinz and Koch 1987). References to his seal identifications on these PFNN tablets continue to appear in more recent publications.[114] Some will need correcting on the basis of the Garrison and Root project.

---

113. See Garrison and Root 1996 for a comprehensive characterization of Hallock's efforts in this regard and explanation of the difficulties that have been caused by the informal circulation of Hallock's sketches and reliance upon them as accurate visual documentation.

114. Note for instance Brosius 1996; Tuplin 1998; Handley-Schachler 1998.

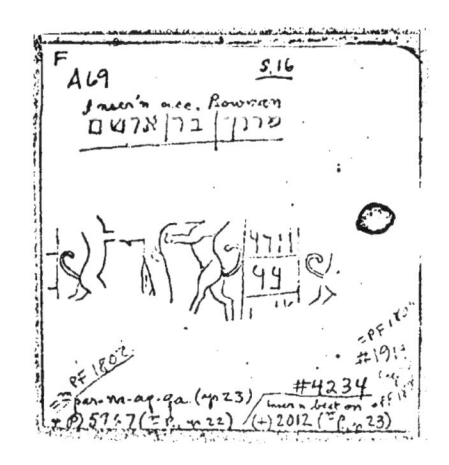

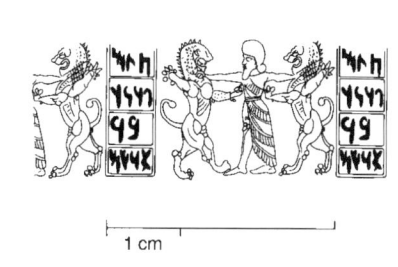

Figure 8. (Left) Study Sketch of PFS 16* by R. T. Hallock and (Right) Composite Line Drawing of PFS 16* (Cat.No. 22),
Garrison and Root Publication Drawing. Scale 1:1

THE GARRISON AND ROOT COLLATION EFFORT

The logistical difficulties of systematic and accurate collation across the entire PFS corpus using the actual tablets presented insurmountable obstacles. The impressions of individual seals (and of closely similar but not identical seals) occur on multiple surfaces of tablets across the PF corpus. Thus, in order to pursue this work, it was necessary to produce a complete photographic record of every seal impression on every tablet. Before producing this photographic record, Hallock's tablet numbers were physically applied to the tablets to guard against confusion.

It was also essential as a preliminary step to assign an arbitrary number to each seal above those tabulated through Hallock's numbers 1*–314. An inclusive numbering system had to be established in order to embed labels in the photographic shots. In order to designate these arbitrary numbers, we worked off Hallock's tablet entries in which he noted the occurrences of seals on tablet surfaces. For all those seal impressions that Hallock thought represented isolated occurrences on only one tablet (and to which he therefore did not assign a number), we started, tablet by tablet, numbering those seals beginning with the number 315. Based on Hallock's diagnosis of singly impressed seals versus multiply impressed ones, the numbering process took us to a total of 1,682 seals. This figure included analytically illegible seals as well as the legible ones that are actually cataloged in our volumes. At present, these seal numbers (of illegible as well as legible seals) range from PFS 1* to PFS 1696, owing to corrections that we have made to Hallock's initial reading of the impressions. The number of discrete seals actually signified by these initially assigned PFS numbers has currently shrunk down to approximately 1,417 (again, including illegible seals), owing to collations.

Elsewhere we discuss the details of our collation process and our standards for accepting or rejecting a collation previously made by Hallock (Garrison and Root 1996). As suggested above, our collations have altered seal identifications even among Hallock's PFS 1*–314 group. PFS 314 itself has been collated with PFS 260 (Cat.No. 225). So far Hallock's collations remain completely unchallenged only for five of the ten seals occurring on the highest numbers of tablets: PFS 1* (Cat.No. 182), PFS 2 (Cat.No. 3), PFS 3 (III), PFS 4* (Cat.No. 292), and PFS 9* (Cat.No. 288). See *Appendix Two: Provisional List of All Subsumed Hallock PFS Numbers (Volumes I–III)* for a provisional list of those Hallock seal numbers (1*–314) in Volumes I–III that have been totally subsumed by Garrison and Root collations. In certain other cases separations of some impressions from the collective cluster of impressions representing one seal have been made by Garrison and Root. *Appendix One: Concordance of Seals to Tablets in Volume I* gives the up-to-date concordance of Volume I seals as they occur in impressions on various tablet surfaces. The shrinkage in number of seals actually represented through the thousands of impressions is particularly dramatic given that the final tally also incorporates the separations of multiple seal impressions that Hallock thought represented a single seal but which actually represent two (or more) discrete original seals. Some separations have had particularly noteworthy results. Among some high-use office seals we have, for instance, identified examples of duplicate and triplicate seals (e.g., PFS 12a–b [II]; PFS 66*a–c [II]).

Our separations and collations interfere with Hallock's scheme of numbering "multiple [tablet] occurrence" seals in certain cases, but to a great extent one can still say that a low PFS number between PFS 1* (Cat.No. 182) and ex-PFS 314 (= PFS 260 [Cat.No. 225]) signifies a seal that occurs on more tablets than a seal with a high number within that same group. Examples where the system is disrupted completely include PFS 227 (III), which has now been separated into two distinct seals (PFS 227 [III] and PFS 1692 [III]) and thus is no longer what Hallock would call a multiple occurrence seal at all, even though the seal that keeps the PFS 227 designation lies within Hallock's number sequence of multiple occurrence seals.

PFS 7* (Cat.No. 4) has sustained only one separation through our efforts to correct Hallock's determinations. This one separation is, however, significant. PFS 7* is one of the most frequently discussed seals in the literature on administrative aspects of the archive (with reference to its deployment rather than its imagery). Our separation of one impression from Hallock's original cluster of collated impressions resolves what had previously been a nagging discrepancy in scholarly understanding of the sealing protocols operative for this royal name seal. Examples such as this validate the utility of devoting great attention to the visual analysis and documentation of each image, taking advantage of every impression available within the PF corpus, no matter how fragmentary.

The series of provisional lists and concordances published in *Persepolis Seal Studies* (Garrison and Root 1996) deals with all the seals across the entire three-volume PFS corpus. In the third volume, this apparatus for the entire PFS corpus appears again, in revised and freshly updated form. The information published in *Persepolis Seal Studies* includes a provisional concordance of tablets to seals; provisional concordance of seals to tablets; provisional concordance of seals on the PF tablets to seals on the Treasury tablets; list of subsumed Hallock seal numbers; and comprehensive list of merged seals. This information enables all the seals in the three volumes to be tracked across the PF archive by tablet number and also location(s) on the tablets in advance of the appearance of the last volume in this catalog.

VISUAL DOCUMENTATION

SUMMARY OF THE CATALOG APPARATUS

Each seal is represented at the head of its catalog entry by a composite drawing at two times actual size (2:1). One or more photographs of selected impressions of each seal, printed at two times actual size (2:1), appear in *Part 2: Plates* of each volume along with a repeat of the 2:1 drawing (aligned with the photographic image) for easy reference. Additionally, an assemblage of composite drawings appears in *Part 2: Plates* of each volume, highlighting selected iconographical, compositional, and/or functional features shared among seals cataloged in each volume.

STUDY PHOTOGRAPHS

Our archive of study photographs includes work sheets by tablet (subdivided by tablet surface), which were devised to record the photographic biography with roll and frame numbers of every impression, delineated by tablet surface. All study photographs incorporate a scale bar and a label giving PF tablet number and PFS number of the specific impression as designated at the time of photography. We work with prints at 3:1. As collations have ensued, these labels have been updated by hand on existing prints and in the paperwork. The specific tablet surface represented on a photograph is generally self-evident since the contours of the tablet are visible in the image. But tablet surfaces shown in each photograph are also recorded on the photograph work sheets frame by frame.

PUBLICATION PRINTS

The publication photographs in this catalog have been produced from original negatives in our study archive and have been professionally custom printed especially for this publication. They present a highly selective sampling of retrieved impressions of a given seal. Particularly for minutely detailed seals with many fragmentary impressions, it has not been possible in every case to publish photographs of enough impressions to document every detail rendered in the composite drawing. Conversely, a seal is sometimes known only through a single impression

COMPOSITE DRAWINGS

Method

Using the study photographs printed at 3:1, Root made a sketch of the seal image. Then a precise 3:1 template of the collated image was produced with reference to all the preserved impressions of the seal image. As a rule with multiple occurrence seals, a master impression was identified that provided the best possible image for establishing the critical spacing between the figures. Details were built up around that armature from all other impressions. A final 3:1 pencil drawing was made by Garrison, based on the composite template but now with intensive firsthand reference to all the actual impressions in Chicago. The pitfalls in photographing and drawing ancient seal impressions are notorious (Buchanan 1966, p. xxi; Collon 1987, pp. 5–6). One major challenge in the production of our composite 3:1 templates was to rectify distorted images as conservatively as possible, yet adequately to achieve a drawing that symbolizes an ideal seal impression. Problems of distortion abound on the seal impressions on the PF tablets. Sometimes these distortions are caused by idiosyncrasies in the way the user applied the seal. Uneven pressure can yield hills and valleys that distort spacing. Too much pressure applied with excessive backward force can yield a retracted spacing between figures; too little pressure can yield a stretched image. Fanning of the image is caused by a pivoting of the seal (usually with the lower segment arcing out). In addition to distortions caused by the seal user's idiosyncrasies of motion and force, there are also distortions of spacing caused by the smoothing and pressing of adjacent tablet surfaces in preparation for application of the cuneiform text. While the template provided a critical framework, close scrutiny against the actual tablets has been an essential follow-up. This process has usually resulted in important adjustments to the template — in fine-tuning contours, diagnosing often complex issues of seal overlays that could not be discerned adequately through photographs, and making corrections or additions in detailing. Garrison also rendered the inscription copies directly from the tablets, in consultation with Charles Jones. The drawings were inked under Garrison's supervision.

Parameters

The composite drawing of each seal design unites all linear (two-dimensional) visual information available to us through the study of all impressions of each legible seal preserved on the PF tablets. The drawing aims to be as faithful as possible a rendering of lines. It does not attempt to render volumes. (Techniques such as stippling were found to interfere, on the elaborate seals, with the legibility of critical linear details such as closely stacked garment folds or wing feathers.)

The most important goal of each drawing is to create a visual display that re-incorporates preserved information. Nothing is reconstructed. Occasionally, the occurrence of a PFS seal on a tablet not in the PF corpus has been kindly brought to our attention in an effort to clear up a difficulty in making sense out of a representational element of the seal design as preserved in impressions on the PF tablets. In these very rare cases, we have integrated that evidence into our effort to understand what the impressions in the PF corpus reveal. We have not, however, incorporated evidence from any other (non-PF) tablets into our composite drawing of representational elements of a seal if we could not see it (with the guidance of the better preserved example) on the PF tablets. A notable instance is PFS 38 (Cat.No. 16), where help from a PFNN tablet enabled us to understand what we were seeing on PF tablets. In presenting the reconstituted composite representational imagery on the seals, we consider it absolutely essential for the reader to be able to rely on the fact that the visual information we are giving is based on the particular tablets for which our extensive apparatus of appendices and indices provides links to the published documents in the PF corpus. We have encountered enough cases of nearly but not precisely identical seals to recognize the importance of not reaching conclusions about the collation of one impression with another based on assumption.

For the protocols that we followed to create the inscription copies for inscribed seals, see page 51, below.

Drawing Conventions

For cylinder seals, any line indicated at the top and bottom of the image proper represents a preserved border, cap, or seal edge. For stamp seals, the contour of the seal edge is rendered as a line, but only where this outline is actually preserved in the impression(s).[115]

In numerous cases, we do not have the complete lateral extent of the image of the original cylinder seal. In these instances, the drawing of the cylinder seal reproduces those elements that are preserved just as they are presented to us by the seal user, for example, PFS 199* (Cat.No. 305). In all cases where we have been able to compile the complete lateral extent of the image, we have included partial repeats at each end of the composite drawing. These repeats extend the drawing as if the seal had been rolled for somewhat more than one complete turn. This enables the reader to appreciate the aesthetic properties of various potentials inherent in the design depending upon how the seal user applied the seal to the tablet. Many seal designs were clearly conceived by the artists as continuous frieze patterns, with no clear breaks or edges (e.g., PFS 6 [Cat.No. 304]). Extending the drawing with repeats displays the dynamic coherence of such complex designs.

Below the drawing a horizontal line with upturned ends articulates (what we have identified as) the exact edges of the design. All elements and figures beyond these upturned edges are part of the repeats. In drawings of inscribed cylinder seals where the inscription occurs in the terminal field, the inscription is rendered on the viewer's left as the first element in the notional rolling of the cylinder (immediately after the left repeat). The inscription re-appears in toto as part or all of the repeat on the right edge. Similarly, a representational image that occupies the terminal field of a cylinder seal is placed at the left, to initiate the notional rolling (immediately after the left repeat), and re-appears as the main or only repeat element on the right edge.

A one-centimeter scale indicator is incorporated into the bar below each drawing.

VERBAL DOCUMENTATION

BASIC INFORMATION HEADER

Following the drawing of each seal is a header that briefly lists basic information about the seal according to the categories listed and explained below.

Seal Type

This category indicates whether the seal preserved through impressions is a stamp seal or a cylinder seal. In the case of stamp seals, we also characterize the contour of the seal edge if possible. Where it is impossible to be sure of the contour of the edge of a stamp seal the difficulty is sometimes the result of the application of too little pressure in the stamping process, but more often it is the result of the pressure exerted in preparing the adjacent surfaces of the still-malleable tablet for the text. This pressure against the surface bearing the stamped impression often caused distortion, to the extent that the originally crisp facets of an octagonal pyramidal stamp, for instance, have acquired the look of an oval-faced conoid or a scaraboid. Even when the contour of the stamp seal face is clear, there is a range of possibilities for the shape of the seal itself. The most prevalent possibilities in the Achaemenid heartland milieu are tabulated in figure 9, accompanying *Appendix Four: Stamp Seals in Volume I Grouped by Apparent Contour of Seal Face*.

For cylinders, it is not possible to determine from the impressions on the PF tablets whether the seal producing them was a barrel-shaped object or a straight-sided object.

Photograph(s)

This category provides references to the plate(s) on which specific impressions of the seal are illustrated.

---

115. For terminology of stamp seals, see Buchanan and Moorey 1984, p. xi; and *Appendix Four: Stamp Seals in Volume I Grouped by Apparent Contour of Seal Face*, below.

Earliest Dated Application

This category supplies the date of the earliest dated PF tablet on which the seal occurs. This date in turn supplies a precise *terminus ante quem* for the production of the seal. Where no date is given or preserved in the text(s) with which the seal is associated, the entry reads "ND."

Typology and Style

The stylistic classification, for example, Fortification Style, follows the terms and concepts explained above in *Part One: Seal Carving Styles in the PFS Corpus*. Any special notes to the reader regarding specific issues of style pertinent to the Volume II and III seals but not manifest in the Volume I corpus are included in the introductions to those volumes.

The seals in Volume I have been organized according to a coded typology of compositional formats (see *Part Four: Typology of Images in Volume I*, below). This typology is specific to the organization of the images of heroic encounter. Typologies for other motifs are described in Volumes II and III.

Language(s) (or Script) of Inscription

This category states the language(s) (or script) of the seal inscription (where present). See also *Appendix Five: Inscribed Seals in Volume I by Language or Script*.

Preserved Height of Image

This category indicates the maximum preserved height of the composite image produced from analysis of all available impressions of the seal on PF tablets.

Preserved Length/Width of Image

Maximum preserved length (cylinder seal) or width (stamp seal) of the composite image produced from analysis of all available impressions of the seal on PF tablets.

Estimated Height of Original Seal

For cylinder seals only, this figure is offered only when we can suggest the estimated height of the original seal with a high degree of probability.

Estimated Diameter of Original Seal

For cylinder seals only, this figure is offered only when we have the complete preserved length of the seal image (derived from analysis of one or many impressions), which is equivalent to the circumference of the cylinder. With a known circumference, the diameter of the original artifact can be calculated.

Every measurement has been rounded off to the nearest millimeter (e.g., 1.63 = 1.60; 1.65 = 1.70). When any dimension cannot be reconstituted with a satisfactory degree of accuracy, the entry reads "NA" (= not available).

Number of Impression(s)

This category gives the total number of individual impressions of the seal preserved on the PF tablets. Where more than one impression of the seal is preserved on the same surface of one tablet, each impression is counted separately. For a cylinder seal, a continuous extended rolling is counted as only one impression even if it extends over multiple repetitions of the seal image. But if the cylinder is picked up and placed down again (even on the same tablet surface), then each separate placement of the seal counts as a separate impression no matter how small a segment of the original seal design is included in that discrete placement. The figures in this informational category range from those for PFS 1* (Cat.No. 182) with 233 impressions (on seventy-four tablets) down to numerous seals preserved through only one impression.

Quality of Impression(s)

This category assesses the capacity to retrieve good detail from the impression(s).

Completeness of Image

This category indicates in a very general manner the completeness of a seal image. With cylinder seals we often have a full rolling of the middle of the image, with the upper and lower edges missing. With stamp seals, we often have only one or two edges of the stamp and the corresponding parts of the seal image.

DESCRIPTION OF SEAL AS IMPRESSED IMAGE

This section offers a brief description of the seal design as revealed by the composite of its impressions. The goal is to draw attention to selected aspects of composition and of detail in the seal design with as much consistency of vocabulary and focus as possible from one entry to another. This narrative is important in a documentary catalog, no matter how precise the accompanying graphic characterization of the artifact may be (Porada 1982, pp. 502–03).

The descriptions for Volume I proceed according to the following scheme:[116]

1. Overall composition of the heroic encounter: directionality of the hero, whether facing or moving to right or left; the placement of his arms; the nature of the animal(s) or creature(s) that he engages and the manner in which he engages them; any unusual feature in the pose of the hero's lower body, for example, running, kneeling, or lifting forward leg. We use the term "animal" to denote any form that occurs in nature. We use the term "creature" to denote any form that does not occur in nature (e.g., winged animals, human-headed animals). For issues involved in classifying animals/creatures, see *Appendix Seven: Animals and Composite Creatures on Seals in Volume I*.

2. Animals/creatures: directionality, pose, and how they hold their tails.

3. Iconographic details of the hero: for example, garment, headdress, beard, and hair. See *Appendix Eight: Iconographic Features on Seals in Volume I* for explanation of certain terms and criteria.

4. Iconographic details of the animals/creatures: for example, placement of wings, rendering of feathers, horns, ears, manes, whether mouths are open.

5. Figures or other elements in the terminal field, in the upper or lower spatial zones of the design field, and in areas between the hero and the animals/creatures.

6. Placement of the inscription, where applicable.

7. Preservation of the upper and/or lower edges of the seal and the occurrence of any elements that appear to be flaws in the stone rather than design elements.

Directions refer to the viewer's perspective. Thus, for instance, "the animal to the left of the hero" refers to the animal to the left of the hero from the viewer's vantage point. Only when using the possessive in referring to appendages of a specified figure do we give direction from the figure's vantage point, for example, "the hero's left arm."

As a rule, we describe symbols and beings physically rather than interpretively. Thus we avoid terms such as "sphinx" to indicate a winged human-headed lion or terms such as "demon" or "monster" to denote hybrid creatures.

---

116. Descriptions of seal designs in Volumes II and III entail additional sets of schemes because of the wide-ranging representations in these compendia. These schemes are outlined in introductory notes to the relevant volumes.

"Terminal field" is used in the catalog to describe a design feature, either representational or inscriptional, that occupies a position effectively punctuating the main figural image of the seal design. In *Appendix Eight: Iconographic Features on Seals in Volume I*, under *Terminal Field Motifs*, all these punctuating elements are itemized and keyed to specific seals.

INSCRIPTION

If the seal is inscribed, basic information on the inscription is given: language, transliteration, and translation (see *Appendix Five: Inscribed Seals in Volume I by Language or Script*). In the transliterations of Elamite inscriptions we follow conventions established by Hallock (1969, pp. 70–78). For Aramaic inscriptions we follow the conventions of Bordreuil (1986), rendering the transliterations in Latin letters. We do not attempt to vocalize Aramaic inscriptions.

We make no attempt in the copies of the seal inscriptions to reconstruct signs or letters that we are not able to see. We have, however, consulted the PFNN tablets as well as the PF tablets in making the inscription copies. This access was encouraged by the Oriental Institute specifically for the seal inscriptions. A great deal of work had already been done by Hallock on the inscriptions appearing on seals in the PF corpus. In the process, he had identified and worked with the (unpublished) PFNN tablets on which inscribed seals appear. It would have been perverse to mute that effort in order to apply a consistent regime to the study of both the representational and inscriptional elements of seals. Furthermore, the presence of Charles E. Jones, our epigraphic consultant who is on staff at the Oriental Institute, has made access to that particular material routine. The extraordinary difficulties posed by reading the seal inscriptions combined with the rather small number of inscribed seals has added to the rationalization for this different protocol. The inscription copies, and thus the transliterations and translations, sometimes then include signs or letters that are not preserved on any seal impression in the PF corpus; those signs or letters do appear on PFNN tablets.

For the trilingual royal name seals, PFS 7* (Cat.No. 4) and PFS 113*/PTS 4* (Cat.No. 19) in Volume I, where the inscription is standard and well preserved in its entirety in other exemplars, the transliteration and translation provide clearly bracketed information filling in any lacunae that can be plausibly established.

A brief commentary describes the orientation of the script on the seal and states whether or not case lines or a panel were used (see also *Appendix Eight: Iconographic Features on Seals in Volume I*). We explain difficulties in readings and suggest alternatives. Occasionally, reference to relevant texts on the PF and PFNN tablets assists in making sense of the name in the seal inscription by supplying in full a personal name that should designate the seal owner whose name may be only partially preserved on the seal inscription. When we are able to take advantage of this information we state it explicitly.

COMMENTARY

In this section we discuss issues of seal ownership and usage as well as other issues relevant to seal usage that are derived from published commentary. We also identify the owners of seals that occur with two classes of texts for which the seal protocol is straightforward: travel rations (Q texts) and letters (T texts). If a seal does not occur with one of these two types of text, or if it has not been commented upon by a scholar in a publication, we do not attempt identification of the seal owner.

The commentary section may also include a brief formal or iconographical discussion of the seal. These remarks are by no means exhaustive. Readers may turn to references cited in Garrison 1988 for a more detailed analysis of the style of a particular seal in Volume I or for a fuller analysis of the main stylistic categories more generally throughout the corpus.[117] When a seal is part of a group of seals that show exceptionally close stylistic relationships and are perhaps even the work of the same artist, this is noted in the catalog commentary. Stylistic and

---

117. Special cases of style oddities that emerge in Volumes II and III, but which are not represented in Volume I, are discussed in those contexts as they arise.

iconographical comparisons are sometimes made here with other seals in the PFS corpus. But we invite the reader to use our appendices for systematic and comprehensive access to congruencies of stylistic category and iconographical elements across the seals in the entire volume. (In Volume III, the contents of the final appendices span the three-volume set.)

Some comparisons are also made with specific artifacts from other contexts. Here, we emphasize provenanced parallels as much as possible. When we refer the reader to comparanda outside the PFS corpus, it generally serves to reinforce our interpretation of a difficult form or to highlight a particularly interesting stylistic or iconographic pedigree or debate.

Where compositional or iconographical elements on a given seal have been grouped together with related elements on other seals in drawing illustrations, references for these illustrations (pls. 174–291) are cited at the end of the commentary.

SEAL APPLICATION

This section offers a systematic characterization of how each seal was actually applied by its user(s) to the tablet surfaces. Application patterns of stamp seals are not without interest, but they do not approach the complexity of the cylinder seal information and generally require little explanation. For the cylinder seals, we used the following method. The composite drawing of each seal image was reproduced in a version extending over multiple rollings. Using a separate copy of this template for each discrete seal impression, we labeled it by PFS number, PF tablet number, and PF tablet surface location. Then we marked off the rendered segment of the seal design on the template.

Due to the very large number of impressions involved, it was impractical to include a dossier of these delineated templates in the catalog, even at a very reduced scale.[118] Instead, we have presented the data only in a summary narrative form within each catalog entry. The narrative strives for a uniform pattern of presentation. For inscribed seals, we focus preliminarily on the presence or absence of the inscription. For anepigraphic seals, we use the hero figure (in Volume I) as the initial reference point. Other protocols following the same concept are used in Volumes II and III.

BIBLIOGRAPHY

Each catalog entry ends with a bibliography citing published references to the seal. Conspicuously absent are references to the seals in Hallock 1969. Our collations and separations as well as our numbering of seals that remained unnumbered in Hallock 1969 lead us to advise that the reader use *Appendix One: Concordance of Seals to Tablets in Volume I* and *Appendix Two: Provisional List of All Subsumed Hallock PFS Numbers (Volumes I–III)* to move from a PFS number to the associated text(s) published by Hallock. We have not distinguished here between citations that represent extensive discussion and those that contain only a passing allusion. Although our initial aim was comprehensiveness, the explosion of interest in and acknowledgment of the material in a vast array of publications worldwide and covering many disciplines has made it impossible to guarantee this any longer. In a few cases where a seal cataloged in Volume I was not included in Garrison 1988, the seal entry may have no bibliography at all. For Volumes II and III, many more seals lack bibliographic citations.

---

118. This may be done as part of an online presentation of comprehensive visual evidence from the project linked to Achemenet (Collège de France 2000).

PART FOUR: IMAGES IN VOLUME I

MEANINGS OF HEROIC ENCOUNTER

SHIFTING VALENCES OF THE MOTIF IN ANCIENT WESTERN ASIA

In western Asiatic glyptic the heroic encounter is among the earliest figural representations, beginning in prehistoric times and weaving in and out of the tradition down through the Sasanian period.[119] Initially, the motif must have signified direct aspects of human interaction and power relationships with the animal world; it must have alluded explicitly to the agency of humankind in its primordial grappling with the forces of nature. But even on the earliest figural stamp seals of Mesopotamia and Iran the hero image is likely also to have symbolized emerging ideas of authority translated from the explicit level of represented meaning to a more abstract metaphorical level of human intervention, prestige, and mastery within the domain of human affairs.[120] Some scholars emphasize links to cult and divinity embedded in the heroic vision, as opposed to links with the pragmatics of power and control of resources implicit in an increasingly complex social ecology.[121] There is, however, no need to consider these factors as mutually exclusive. To some extent the motif probably never lost its primeval essences, even as it developed increasing metaphorical capacities.[122]

The hero motif clearly carried multiple valences and varying degrees and qualities of social significance in different eras and geographical and social settings throughout its long history. It also seems likely to have carried multiple valences internally within specific period-culture boundaries, depending upon variables of, for example, social status, affiliation, and sex of the owner as well as locale of usage within the larger political context.[123] In any attempt to determine nuances of meaning, the formal properties of a specific seal may hold critical cues. Differing stylistic values deployed for the same essential figural composition might have conveyed specific status or other information within the culture.[124] Furthermore, variations in compositional format may present very different moods and meanings.

---

119. Garrison (1988, pp. 24–160) provides the only in-depth scholarly survey of the history and stylistic forms of the motif in seal art from the beginnings up to the Achaemenid period. Particularly important for the seals on the PF tablets is the discussion of Neo-Assyrian and Neo-Babylonian glyptic. Bregstein 1993, pp. 73–74, includes perceptive comments on the Neo-Assyrian/Neo-Babylonian material. For a more general overview with emphasis on the early phases, see Collon 1986a, pp. 87–90. See also Moorey 1978, pp. 151–53.

120. It is increasingly clear that these figural stamp seals were among those used in the earliest so far documented evidence of seal impressions as administrative tools in long-distance trade and in other systematized aspects of socio-economic organization. See Akkermans and Verhoeven 1995, pp. 21–25; none of the seal impressions at Sabi Abyad published in this 1995 report actually represent a heroic encounter, but the figural seal types that do occur as administrative tools derive from representational dossiers familiar from assemblages of actual prehistoric figural seals excavated elsewhere (at the types of sites whence sealed goods received at Sabi Abyad were sent). These dossiers of actual seals contemporaneous with the Sabi Abyad sealings do include scenes of heroic encounter. The Sabi Abyad discovery establishes the earliest demonstrable administrative use of such seals.

121. For example, Amiet 1980, pp. 69–73; Hansen 1987, p. 61. Collon (1987, p. 197) makes the case for rejecting the idea that the hero with curls represents Gilgamesh.

122. Capacities in pre-literate and protoliterate phases for metaphorical thought and integration of complex systems of ideas via visual representation should not be underestimated. See Pittman 1994, passim, and Sieversten 1992 for commentary specifically on the functioning of seal imagery; see Rochberg 1996, esp. pp. 477–78, more generally on metaphorical processing in ancient Mesopotamia and rejection of the thesis of mythopoeic thought.

123. See Cassin 1987, pp. 131–213, on overarching ambiguities and interpretive strategies. An interesting case in point is Hasanlu on the eastern periphery of the Neo-Assyrian Empire. The Hasanlu IVB assemblage of 105 seals and sealings includes only two hero images (Marcus 1996, pp. 84 [fig. 18, no. 3; Local Style], 116 [fig. 81, no. 59; Neo-Assyrian]). This is noteworthy since the heroic encounter was an important feature of the Neo-Assyrian repertoire at the imperial center.

124. See Garrison 1988, pp. 38–50, for discussion of these issues specifically in the context of Early Dynastic glyptic.

THE HEROIC ENCOUNTER IN ACHAEMENID TIMES

PREVALENCE OF THE MOTIF

In order to comment on possible meanings of the hero motif in the Achaemenid Empire, it is important to characterize the relative prevalence of the hero image in the corpora of seals impressed on the PF tablets and on some of the other Achaemenid-period tablets and bullae that were itemized earlier (*Part Two: The Fortification Archive and Archaeological Inquiry*, above).

As noted, the hero image in its many aspects becomes the single dominant theme in the known repertoire of Achaemenid-period glyptic representation. The ca. 27% prevalence of hero seals across the large and socially diversified PFS corpus of ca. 1,162 analytically legible seals strikingly reinforces an established wisdom that roughly one-third of all Achaemenid seals bear a hero motif.[125] Heretofore this estimate has had to be based on more impressionistic data gleaned from a miscellaneous assortment of excavated and unexcavated material. Furthermore, the estimate has considered the hero image only within a pool of seals categorized by the conservative evaluations of museum and sales catalogs as Achaemenid products. Only those seals that were obviously and without ambiguity made in the Achaemenid period according to perceived notions of Achaemenid taste were considered in the pool; for example, seals on which figures wear the Persian robe or on which other quintessential indices of Achaemenid identity (stylistic or iconographic) appear to separate them conclusively from earlier products. The ca. 27% prevalence of seals of heroic encounter that we discuss on the PF tablets is instead considered within a much more inclusive assemblage.

In a discussion of the nature of the predilection for hero imagery during the Achaemenid period, the PFS corpus suggests that the phenomenon is demonstrated primarily through the commissioning of new seals (in a dramatic array of styles including archaizing ones). Some scholars may disagree with our categorization of specific hero seals as archaizing rather than pre-Achaemenid antiques, but many of the hero seals in Volume I must be archaizing products of the Achaemenid period rather than heirlooms. This display of the predilection for the image and for reworkings of its antique legacy is remarkable. With respect to the strong archaizing trend documented in the PFS hero corpus, an important point emerges: the strenuous (we might even say inexorably systematic) mining of Mesopotamian traditions is specific to the hero seals on the PF tablets. In itself this reflects a particular fascination in the Achaemenid creative context with the heroic encounter motif as a synchronic phenomenon.[126]

How does the preponderance of hero imagery in the PFS corpus compare with evidence from other archives? The corpus of sealings from the Persepolis Treasury is a mixed assemblage including bulla-type labels, some of which may in theory have been produced in distant lands of the empire or even beyond its borders (see *Part Two: The Fortification Archive and Archaeological Inquiry: Other Sealing Archives of the Achaemenid Empire*, above). We may really be looking at two bodies of material that should not be considered together for statistical purposes relating to discussion of seal usage in particular environments of the empire. But lacking the kind of access that would make full evaluation possible at this time, we focus on only a few points. On the (inscribed) Treasury tablets, only seventeen seals occur, all cylinders. Of these, thirteen display an image of heroic encounter. This yields a 76.47% prevalence of hero imagery on the inscribed Treasury tablets. Five additional hero seals occur on other clay artifacts (labels) in the assemblage. This gives a total of eighteen hero seals out of seventy-seven seals on the Treasury tablets (23.34%) when we combine definitely Persepolis-based seals with the group that may include some that were perhaps used far away, at different times, and by individuals whose identities and functions we cannot establish.[127]

From Susa, five of the eight sealings on bullae listed as Achaemenid period by Amiet (62.5%) preserve an image of heroic encounter.[128] These eight bullae include two sealed with Egyptian seals; the others are conventionally recognizable as Achaemenid. To this we add the attestation of our PFS 7* (Cat.No. 4) on the isolated Elamite Fortification-type tablet from Susa (Stolper 1992a; Garrison 1996b). The small sample renders this Susa grouping ill-suited to statistical formulation. Nevertheless, its emphatic bias toward hero imagery is worth noting.

---

125. For example, Greenfield 1962. Note that Root (1992, p. 445) accidentally inverted the figures to state that hero seals constitute *two*-thirds of the total.

126. Groups of archaizing seals in other representational categories in the PFS corpus seem generally to suggest unbroken continuities of glyptic tradition rather than the wide-ranging reworkings of multiple antique models that we see with the hero images.

127. Schmidt (1957, p. 7) cites only PTS 1*–13 as examples of the hero triumphant, but in fact PTS 37–39* and 59s–60s are also hero seals (on labels).

128. Amiet 1972, pls. 37, 189–90, nos. 2202–03, 2227–29.

The seal impressions from the satrapal court at Daskyleion contain some twenty-seven hero seals out of a total of 193, or 14% of the whole.[129] This still significant, but smaller, percentage may perhaps reflect the western location of Daskyleion and the partial attunement of its workshops and patrons to koine products less closely allied to the iconographical traditions of greater Mesopotamian art. The small corpus of administrative sealings from the palace at Memphis in Egypt also represents a regional headquarters of the empire distant from the Persian heartland and with local traditions available to offer alternative backdrops for artistic production. Here, however, seven of the twenty clearly Achaemenid seals documented by impressions (about 35%) are definitely hero seals.[130] If we place these seven hero seals in the larger context that includes twenty-four additional seals which are thoroughly Egyptian hieroglyphic items, then the prevalence of hero seals from the Memphis palace is lowered to 16.27%. This is still rather impressive.

Within the Murašû business archive from Nippur, 144 out of 614 seals cataloged by Bregstein (ca. 24%) are listed as seals displaying an image of heroic encounter (Bregstein 1993, p. 60); to Bregstein's group we would add two seals with anomalous figures (e.g., Bes) as hero that she has not classified as hero images (see Bregstein 1993, p. 82, for seals 206–07).

From the Wadi ed-Daliyeh (Samaria) corpus of detached bullae, nine seals out of some sixty-one (15%) show the heroic encounter in a fully Achaemenid mode. One other displays a heroic control scene of traditional Mesopotamian/Achaemenid compositional format, but in a Hellenizing style (Leith 1997, WD 47: 44.033). Although Leith calls this figure "Herakles," we would include this seal in the hero count for a total of 16.4% in this corpus. Another seal in the full Greek (as opposed to Hellenizing) mode of Herakles and the lion is not included in the count of hero images in this corpus. Either the about 15% or the more generous 16.4% tally of hero seals in this corpus is substantial especially given two factors: on the one hand, many seals in this corpus face the west in figural repertoire and styles, and on the other hand, even for those seals that are Achaemenid in style and iconography the avoidance of specific religious icons such as the winged symbol suggests a particularistic social environment in which certain Achaemenid images integral to the heartland repertoire were muted. If indeed anything can be made of this phenomenon, it suggests that in regions embraced by the Achaemenid Empire individuals had some systematic capacity to maintain their own identities in glyptic symbolism even as certain groups were incorporating themselves into the identity framework of the realm in various ways. Given this apparent flexibility of choice, it is interesting that so many Samaritans represented themselves on these bullae through seals with hero imagery in Achaemenid Persian mode.

Two groups of material offer a less compelling case for the dominance of the hero image. In each case, however, the situation is particular and understandable in its anomalous qualities. Of the Sippar letters published by MacGinnis, only five (ca. 7.5%) of the seals ratifying tablets securely dated to the Achaemenid period (out of some sixty-seven discrete seals used across the entire collection) display an image of heroic encounter.[131] The group is unusual for its heavy weight toward Neo-Babylonian-type worship scenes. The different story presented by the Murašû archive suggests that the location of this Sippar subset in Babylonia is probably not as much a factor in yielding a rather low number of hero seals as is the particular temple-associated context of the letters. MacGinnis suggests that the use of hero seals in this temple environment might have been the prerogative of (or at least standard issue for) the royally appointed officials. By contrast, the temple administrators in the transactions seem to have consistently used Neo-Babylonian-type worship seals.[132] Chronology may also be a factor here, since the encroachment of Achaemenid-type seals is only gradually seen on Babylonian documents under the early Persian kings (Zettler 1979).

The Ur corpus of seal impressions apparently produced to serve as an artisan's image bank reveals nine or more discrete seals of the western Asiatic type of heroic encounter out of approximately 128 seals that appear to be represented once repeat images have been collated and impressions of metalware have been removed.[133] (We have retained impressions of coins in the count since there are coin impressions used as seals in the PFS corpus.) Four additional seals documented in this collection that we do not count display heroic encounter, but in the guise of the Hel-

---

129. Personal communication from Deniz Kaptan, September 1997.

130. Petrie et al. 1910, pp. 42–43, pls. 35–37, nos. 25–27, 29–31, 46. We include here only sealings that definitely seem to come from the palace area (Petrie is not always clear on this point). Petrie classified his nos. 33–39 as Greek, but this is incorrect. They are Achaemenid products that display some koine Egyptian-Persian qualities.

131. MacGinnis 1995, C.3–C.8; Garrison and Dion 1999, p. 2, n. 4.

132. See MacGinnis 1995, p. 170, who acknowledges the extremely limited size of the sample upon which he bases these suggestions.

133. Legrain 1951, nos. 733, 751/752, 753/754, 755, 757–58, 760–62.

lenic Herakles and the lion, including one which replaces Herakles with a Bes-as-Herakles (Legrain 1951, nos. 746–49). This works out to a presence of only about 7% Mesopotamian/Achaemenid hero seals, but this collection is very idiosyncratic. It was gathered and kept presumably by one craftsman and thus indicates the range of that particular artisan's repertoire of material and interests and not the predilections of society at large. This is a rather different phenomenon from what we see in an archive of tablets that represents a sample of seals actually in use as seals within a specific period of time.

Turning briefly to excavated examples of seal artifacts clearly of Achaemenid-period manufacture, the dominance of the heroic encounter imagery (in myriad permutations) is re-affirmed. Actual seals that can be unequivocally categorized as Achaemenid in date and that emerge from controlled contexts (even loosely defined) are not plentiful.[134] Thus they can only offer a limited repertoire of hero images compared with the proliferation we find on the PF tablets. Efforts to examine the nuances of individual seal artifacts emerging from excavated contexts demonstrate important possibilities for interpreting permutations of the hero image in varying arenas of the imperial environment, particularly with reference to the Fortification archive.[135] Similarly, on Achaemenid-period seals lacking archaeological context or even a verifiable provenance, the heroic image abounds.[136] It is prevalent as well among the many unprovenanced seals of koine production such as those usually labeled "Graeco-Persian" and said to derive from the Lydian sphere (Boardman 1970a, 1970b).

SPECIAL CONNOTATIONS WITHIN THE ACHAEMENID IMPERIAL SPHERE

Who is the Achaemenid hero? What does the image of heroic encounter mean in the Achaemenid Persian context? Why does the hero image become so popular in the Achaemenid period? What are the variables of date, location, and social setting that might have determined differences in presence, iconography, and style? Here we offer a few observations meant to stimulate interest in the possibilities as scholars increasingly avail themselves of the rich visual record of the Achaemenid Empire, which is becoming accessible via seals on the PF tablets and other archives, in order to attempt systematic explorations of specific issues.

From the entire known repertoire of official Achaemenid sculpture depicting a human-form protagonist, the hero motif is the only one that is also a quantitatively significant theme on seals of the period. In monumental art, the theme is restricted to the combat encounter. The occurrence of the heroic combat in official monumental contexts may help elucidate the identity, meaning, and evident prestige of this form of the image on Achaemenid seals.

---

134. Here we see one of the implications of the problem of attempting to categorize isolated seal artifacts as opposed to impressions of those seals on a large archive of dated tablets. Relatively few excavated seals are retrieved from definitively closed, chronologically contained, and uncontaminated contexts. Even in those rare instances, there is the potential for a great chronological range to be represented. The theriomorphic stamp seal from the Persepolis Treasury that we discussed above is a case in point (Schmidt 1957, pl. 17: PT5 1). Its retrieval from the Treasury does not of course guarantee that it was made in Achaemenid times rather than earlier. Its discovery in that context does, however, open up the possibility that it is an archaizing piece made during the Achaemenid period, similar to numerous demonstrably archaizing seals used on the PF tablets. Were it known to us only as a floating artifact in a museum collection, it would be classified absolutely without question as a Neo-Babylonian seal. On problems and ambiguities posed even by the evidence of most excavated seals, see Dyson and Harris 1986.

135. The following items are representative examples rather than an exhaustive compilation of excavated hero seals that are unquestionably products of the Achaemenid period: from the Chicago Persepolis excavations, two cylinders and one stamp (Schmidt 1957, pls. 15 [PT5 413, PT5 36], 17 [PT4 519]); from Pasargadae, one cylinder (Stronach 1978, pl. 162 a–b; Root 1999a); from Horom in Urartu, a cylinder remarkably similar to the Pasargadae seal (Kohl and Kroll 1999, p. 258, fig. 7); from Susa, seven cylinders that Amiet defines as Achaemenid (Amiet 1972, pp. 285–86, pls. 189–90, nos. 2206–12); from Qasr-i Abu Nasr, one conoid stamp, with a secondary Sasanian image carved on the side face (Frye 1973, p. 39, no. 8); from Borsippa, Iraq, a very large chalcedony cylinder with a double-hero scene (Collon 1987, pp. 90–91, no. 428); from Sardis, five seals (Sardis 104 [cylinder] = Curtis 1925, pp. 39–40, pls. 10–11; Dusinberre 1997b; Sardis 111 [conoid] = Curtis 1925, p. 42, pls. 10–11; Sardis 116 [conoid] = Curtis 1925, p. 44, pls. 10–11; Sardis 119 [conoid] = Curtis 1925, p. 44, pls. 10–11; Sardis 120 [conoid] = Curtis 1925, p. 45, pls. 10–11); from Gezer, one agate stamp (Stern 1994, fig. 1c); from Samaria, one glass conoid (Stern 1994, fig. 2b); from Tell el-Heir, in northwestern Sinai, a carnelian cylinder (Collon 1987, p. 90–91, no. 423; Stern 1994, fig. 1b); from Atlit, a scaraboid with Bes as hero plus three stamps showing Herakles as hero in combat (Stern 1994, fig. 3a–d).

136. For example, among very many unexcavated and floating examples, von der Osten 1934, nos. 453–55, 465–68; Buchanan 1966, pl. 44, nos. 671, 673–75, 680, 682–83; Porada 1979, figs. 44–45, 48–49; Collon 1987, pp. 90–93, nos. 418, 420–21; Keel and Uehlinger 1990, pp. 47, 54–55 (figs. 54, 75–76); Garrison and Dion 1999. The forthcoming catalog of Achaemenid cylinder seals in the British Museum collections will provide detailed access to many examples in this category.

(By extension, it may help us to understand the meanings that would have been re-invested in an antique seal of this type used within the milieu of the Achaemenid court.)

The monumental sculptures do not depict the hero as a king in ceremonial regalia, nor do they depict a figure dressed for active battle (in the Iranian riding habit). The hero in the monumental representations never wears a crown, nor does he wear the smooth royal shoes that are a consistent feature in explicit sculptural representations of the king in ceremonial guise. And although the hero wears a Persian court robe (rather than battle garb that might hint at a direct metaphorical link between heroic combatant and brave warrior), he does bare well-muscled arms in a flash of non-hieratic charisma that departs dramatically from the static visions of explicit kingship monumentally portrayed elsewhere (Root 1990a). Root has postulated that the heroic combatant of the official sculptural program represents the specific ideological construct of a "Persian Man," as articulated in several monumental inscriptions alluding metaphorically to the far-flung military power of the Achaemenid Empire (Root 1979). In this case, the hero of Achaemenid monumental art could be read as a generic figure symbolizing the collective force of Persian power. It is possible, furthermore, that there were cultural taboos in the Iranian tradition of kingship that inhibited explicit depictions of the king in any position of potential vulnerability.[137] This may help explain the importance of rendering the monumental hero figures with ambiguous identity: kingly but not precisely the king and able to be contemplated as a flexible entity with which every person of Persian identification could associate himself. It is important to consider that the capacity of an individual to identify with the Persianness of the "Persian Man" may not have been limited to those of Persian blood lineage in this imperial context.[138]

Herein may lie a key to the extraordinary prevalence of the hero motif in the Achaemenid glyptic repertoire. The calculated ambiguity of the imagery at the highest levels of monumental art may reflect a deliberately exploited mechanism of social incorporation in an arena where many metaphors for social harmony and cooperative enterprise were systematically deployed. The very fact of the ancientness of the heroic vision in one form or another in western Asia guaranteed its receptivity, its capacity to capture the imaginations of diverse constituencies. The opportunity offered by the Achaemenid ideology of the "Persian Man" for broad ownership of the hero role further guaranteed the appeal of the imagery.

This line of argument poses a dilemma that now must be addressed head on. Numerous hero seals, made at the same time as the monumental sculptures, depict the hero in a distinctly royal crown. This is true of the royal name seals, and it is also true of a variety of other seals documented in the PFS corpus and elsewhere. The wearing of a crown not least on the high-profile royal name seals that have long been known has encouraged some scholars to see the hero in glyptic representations as a direct and explicit representation of the king (e.g., Porada 1948, p. 102; Porada 1961, p. 68; Porada 1979, pp. 82, 86, n. 68; Calmeyer 1980, p. 59; Henkelman 1995/96). The PFS corpus now proves that the hero existed in a multiplicity of guises, even on seals used actually under the nose of the king. It is not possible to employ a single equation of hero = king for Achaemenid glyptic production. In the PFS corpus the heroes range from the winged bull creature of PFS 1* (Cat.No. 182) to the classic crowned and robed royal hero of PFS 7* (Cat.No. 4). Some of the figures performing heroic feats of mastery over other creatures seem frankly humorous. The seated heroes on PFS 148 (Cat.No. 311), PFS 280 (Cat.No. 309), and PFS 435 (Cat.No. 310) suggest the possibility of a blatant parody of the vigorous but regally aloof hero of PFS 7*. These seated hero images seem to tease the beholder with the notion of an enthroned personage (a quintessential vision of hieratic kingship) playing the armchair hero. In between these poles there are many variants. We must be dealing here with multiple meanings that could lend themselves to some sorting via elements relating to the identity or status of the particular person or the particular office deploying a given seal. But the multiple variants also suggest that there was great individual freedom in this area, so that we should perhaps not overtax our interpretive strategies in the expectation that different categories of people will in all cases cluster neatly around specific manifestations of the image.

Even with seal representations that clearly show the hero wearing a royal crown, there is room for nuanced suggestions. Biblical testimony relates a tradition of gifting in the Achaemenid Empire whereby the king might offer a royal crown and robes to an honored and loyal friend.[139] It is possible that the inclusion of the crown on the royal name seals (which, as we now know, were used by administrators at the court) was a reference to this honor having

---

137. It may even be that ideologies of kingship actually inhibited the direct intervention of the Persian king in dangerous battle situations — not because the king was cowardly, but because the king was in a sense a sacred entity that could not be put at risk. See Nylander 1993.

138. Here we return to issues of fluid concepts of ethnicity and identity discussed above.

139. Esther 6:6 and 8:15. See Root 1992, p. 446. The Book of Esther is much debated in terms of date (it may well be post-Achaemenid) and nature of its authenticity (it may preserve

been bestowed upon these administrators. In this case, the crown becomes a reference to the symbolic potential or reality of a non-king acquiring an attribute of kingship as proof of his status as part of the collective identity of the "Persian Man." Such notions may not sit comfortably since they imply a courtly environment of human relationships and investments rather at odds with the sterile world of shadows and hostility that is sometimes portrayed in discussions of the Persians (on which, see Root 1991).

We wish to emphasize that this tentative suggestion about the workings of the royal name seals at least in the reigns of Darius and Xerxes does not preclude different scenarios for other types of seals. The fact that an insignium of state has a very specific meaning when deployed in an official context does not necessarily keep it from being deployed in a variety of lesser contexts, some of which will be debased to the point of triviality. Many contemporary analogies could be enlisted here to prove the point. The evidence of the PF tablets suggests that there were no image police monitoring the innuendoes of hero imagery in glyptic art and making sure things stayed serious. Interestingly, however, the heroes on the royal name seals are generally rather static and hieratic in posture (even when vestiges of modeling reveal subtle carving of musculature on a minute scale). By contrast, the animals and creatures these heroes contend with offer much more fluidity of carving and liveliness of physical affect. This difference suggests that for the royal name seals there might have been a code of appropriateness specifically regarding the hero which insulated the hero figure from some of the energetic experimentation which court artists were otherwise free to pursue, even on the same seals.

Leaving now the issue of the identity of the hero, we turn to some further comments on possible meanings of the heroic activity itself. The liminal placement and focal direction of the sculpted heroic combat scenes in the doorjambs of several buildings on the Takht at Persepolis strongly suggest that the sculptures were meant symbolically to protect interior spaces.[140] The aggressive element here represents notions of triumphant defense within the practical world of empire maintenance in terms of a more abstract realm of archaic ideals. Porada has suggested in a general way a direct link between the doorjamb heroes of Achaemenid palaces and the late Assyrian royal seal type in which a figure in the Assyrian crown (presumably a representation of the king) stabs a rampant lion (Porada 1961, p. 68; Porada 1979, p. 83). This idea does not account for the systematic avoidance of royal accoutrements on the sculptures of Achaemenid heroes (for which we have attempted to offer possible explanations above). It does, however, reinforce the clear protective message projected by the doorjamb reliefs of heroic combat since the Assyrian royal seals (known so far only through impressions on bullae) were actually office seals used to lock commodities in the palace stores.[141]

An interesting early interpretation once suggested that the image of heroic combat on palace doorjambs symbolized the triumph of the nocturnal sun, with the hero a manifestation of Mithra. The hero image was seen in a kind of cosmic point-counterpoint with the lion and bull image, where the latter was understood as a symbol of the triumph of the diurnal sun (Ouseley 1821, p. 285, n. 75). Although there is no proof of a Mithraic cult at Persepolis in the reign of Darius, it is certainly possible that notions relating to that belief system were energizing the patronage mandate there and might have informed one relevant reading of the heroic combat image at the Achaemenid court.[142] This raises the important issue of meanings embedded in the different types of beings engaged by the hero. Data from the PFS corpus will certainly inform debate on the symbolic associations of specific types of animals and creatures within the Iranian milieu (see, e.g., Burney 1999 on the bull and Indra).

narratives that are telling on some folkloristic level but not to be used as direct historical testimony).

140. See Root 1979, pp. 303–08, and catalog entries on fragments of a colossal hero statue from Susa and on doorjamb sculptures in the Palace of Darius, the Harem of Xerxes, and the Throne Hall at Persepolis; see Root 1990a for additional comments on the rhetorical strategies of the heroic combats on Persepolis doorjambs.

141. Bregstein (1993, p. 78, n. 71) objects to Porada's suggestion on the grounds that (1) the Assyrian royal seals were used for internal palace business and thus would not have been readily known outside the inner circle, and (2) about 125 years had elapsed between the last attested use of the Assyrian royal seal type and the earliest doorjambs at Persepolis. These are important points, but they do not allow for broader interpretations of the evidence. The circulation of commodities sealed with the royal seals might have been wider than we currently know. In addition, there are multiple means by which cultural knowledge about inner circle phenomena leaks to outer circles. Among the zones of leakage could be the inevitable involvement of personnel who are elusive to us but were players nonetheless in the operations and transmission of culture (artisans who make the seals, scribes and others who seal the bullae, laborers who transport and store things, etc.). Issues of the maintenance of ideas for availability across stretches of time and social differentiation are discussed in Root 1994.

142. See Koch 1977, pp. 87–88, and Koch 1987, pp. 87–89, adjusting earlier opinions that Mithra is mentioned in certain PF texts. For pre-Achaemenid Mesopotamia, Paley (1986, pp. 215–18) proposes cosmic implications on Neo-Babylonian seals of heroic combat.

Another valence of the heroic combat against animals and animal creatures was certainly as an alternative to literal representations of military combat. This blurred boundary is obvious when we look at certain Achaemenid seals showing Persian warriors fighting against human enemies. The hero-warrior sometimes grasps the enemy by the foresection of his headgear as if it were the horn of a rampant bull or the forelock of a raging lion. Occasionally, the human victim of the hero-warrior looks particularly animal-like in sinuous bodily contours.[143] It is difficult to imagine that these visual relationships were not understood and exploited by the seal carvers. It is also difficult to imagine that the allusiveness of this crossover imagery would have been lost on the seal users in a place like Persepolis where, thanks to the PF tablets, we can see a lively world of play on the motif.

The theme of heroic control poses the same questions of identity of the hero (and the beings with which he engages) that we have already addressed above.[144] In addition, it raises other issues. Although no image of control encounter is known in an Achaemenid monumental context, in glyptic art there seems to be a clear quantitative dominance of control imagery over combat imagery. In the PFS corpus, the control encounter is by far the dominant form; this is echoed in several other glyptic contexts as well, particularly where cylinder seals are a popular form.

On the PF tablets, 201 of the 312 hero seals (64.4%) display some version of the control encounter. Only 111 display combat encounters. On the Treasury corpus of sealed tablets and labels, eleven seals display control encounters (PTS 2*–7*, 9–13) and seven display combat encounters (PTS 1*, 8*, 37–39*, 59s–60s). On the Daskyleion bullae seventeen seals display a hero controlling a pair of creatures while only ten depict a hero in combat with a single creature (Kaptan, pers. comm. [1999]). Of the eight royal name seals of Darius I known to date, six display some version of hero imagery; five of these six are control encounters and only one is a combat encounter.[145]

Generally speaking, the control encounter as we witness it through seals used on the PF tablets suggests a hieratic equilibrium — a balancing of forces — that is really quite different from the combat encounter, with its suggestion of aggression either held at bay or actively thwarted through the imminent or realized smiting of the hero's antagonist. One recent attempt to understand encoded religious symbolism in the motif of heroic encounter has suggested that the hero figure in these images represents the god Bal (Bivar 1970). This theory has been subject to critique for possibly pressing the limited evidence too far (Moorey 1978, pp. 151–53). Yet such interpretive forays, as well as the learned responses they provoke, alert us to important possibilities in this multi-cultural context. The same could be said for Root's discussion of the possible relation of some Achaemenid images of heroic control of wild beasts to the notion of the "blameless one," emphasized as a personal value in Darius's eloquent tomb inscription at Naqsh-i Rustam nearby Persepolis and reiterated in the biblical story of Daniel in the Lion's Den (Root 1981; Root 1992, pp. 445–46; cf. Calmeyer 1983). As the biblical tradition transmits it, Daniel's blamelessness, rectitude, and right-minded attitude toward the Achaemenid king was demonstrated by his miraculous capacity to pacify wild beasts (Porter 1985). The numinous equilibrium Daniel achieved with the beasts, as described in the biblical passage, is suggestive of the aura of many Achaemenid seals of heroic control, where the grasp of the hero is more dance-like, more charmed than aggressive. In a similar vein, Yahweh's reference to his interactions with a variety of beasts in the Book of Job has been seen as an affirmation that the image of heroic control, or mastery, of beasts had acquired a particular spiritual overlay among Jews (Keel 1992, p. 372). A group of Achaemenid-period seals combining a heroic encounter with a scene of Neo-Babylonian-type worship before an altar presents interesting analytical possibilities that deserve further study in an attempt to fathom possible syncretistic meanings embedded in the motif.[146]

Notions of king-hero-divinity in ancient western Asiatic traditions seem to have been complex from the beginning, millennia before the added complexities of the texturing of Indo-Iranian beliefs and ideological imperatives that must be factored in when we consider the Achaemenid Empire.[147] During the Achaemenid period our evidence

---

143. See, for example, a chalcedony cylinder in the Bibliothèque Nationale and another in the British Museum (Collon 1987, pp. 162–63, nos. 744, 747). The inscribed royal name seal in the Newell Collection displays the human victim looking animal-like in bodily form (von der Osten 1934, pl. 31, no. 453).

144. The control encounter refers to balanced compositions in which a hero deals with two animals or creatures; the combat encounter refers to compositions in which a hero's attention is directed toward the stabbing or threatening of one animal or creature.

145. Royal name seals of Darius I with control encounter are: PFS 7*, PFS 113* (= PTS 4*), and PFS 1683* (not in our re-

search corpus); PTS 2* and PTS 3* (Schmidt 1957). The sole combat encounter is PTS 1*.

146. For example, Collon 1987, pp. 90–91, no. 418: a banded agate cylinder in the British Museum; Root 1990a, p. 35, no. 19: a banded agate cylinder probably of the Achaemenid period in Neo-Babylonian cut style from the University of Michigan excavations at Seleucia-on-the-Tigris (Kelsey Museum of Archaeology 94527).

147. On metaphors of kingship-heroism in Mesopotamia, see, for example, Jacobsen 1976, pp. 226–39; for the hero-king axis in the seminal Epic of Gilgamesh, see Vulpe 1994.

strongly suggests that multiple readings were both explicitly embedded in the visual record by the artist-patron collaboration and also overlaid onto the visual record by various receivers of the images.

The later images of controlling heroes on Christian seals of the Sasanian period are direct visual descendants of the heroes of Achaemenid times. In the context of the Christian minority in Sasanian times, some of the seals clearly make specific reference via captions to the Daniel story (Lerner 1977; Root 1981; Calmeyer 1983). By contrast, some images of heroes in the pagan contexts of the Parthian and Sasanian periods assert different social links, seeming to blend the age-old western Asiatic hero and the image of Hellenic Herakles as had already been done in koine products of the Achaemenid period.[148]

The question remains open as to whether visual allusions to Hellenic Herakles in Iran during the Seleucid period attest to the actual observance of a Herakles cult in the east or, rather, to the observance of an Iranian cult in Hellenized visual vocabulary (e.g., Potts 1999, p. 373). This same type of question is relevant for the deployment of varying hero imagery within the cosmopolitan multi-ethnic social environments of the Achaemenid Empire, particularly in the realm of glyptic art, with its personal connotations.

The material assembled in this catalog for the first time needs to speak for itself and to invite deeper inquiry into meanings of heroic encounter in the Achaemenid Empire from a variety of scholars according to agendas including, but certainly not limited to, those we have suggested herein.

TYPOLOGY OF IMAGES IN VOLUME I

The seals of heroic encounter are arranged according to a multi-tiered system of formal criteria. The first tier is determined by the basic action of the hero:

COMPOSITIONAL FORMAT I: IMAGES OF HEROIC CONTROL
— Balanced compositions in which a hero deals with two animals or creatures

COMPOSITIONAL FORMAT II: IMAGES OF HEROIC COMBAT
— In which a hero's attention is directed toward the stabbing or threatening of one animal or creature

COMPOSITIONAL FORMAT III: COMPOSITE CONTROL AND COMBAT ENCOUNTERS

COMPOSITIONAL FORMAT IV: OTHER HEROIC COMPOSITIONS
— Specifically, seated hero and hero holding an animal or creature above his head

Under these first-level categories of compositional format is a second tier based on two interlocking features: first, the pose of the animal(s) or creature(s) acted upon by the hero; and second, a finer description of the hero's action. These second-tier categories are:

COMPOSITIONAL FORMAT I: IMAGES OF HEROIC CONTROL
    I-A   Hero Controls Rampant Animals and/or Creatures
    I-B   Hero Holds Animals or Creatures at His Chest
    I-C   Hero Controls Inverted Animals or Creatures
    I-D   Hero Controls Marchant Animals or Creatures
    I-E   Hero Controls Variously Posed Animals or Creatures

---

148. See Root 1990a, pp. 20–21, for links between Parthian Herakles-as-Hero and earlier Assyrian and Achaemenid monumental tradition; Kawami 1987, pp. 113–35, pl. 54, for the statue of Herakles from Masjid-i Suleiman, with a different perspective on it. See Harper 1978, pp. 51–52, for heroes on Sasanian silver vessels; see, for example, Ghouchani 1991 for remarks on control imagery in late antique Iranian metalware and textiles.

COMPOSITIONAL FORMAT II: IMAGES OF HEROIC COMBAT
- II-A Hero Stabs Rampant Animal or Creature
- II-B Hero Threatens Rampant Animal or Creature, Weapon Held Down behind Body
- II-C Hero Threatens Rampant Animal or Creature, Weapon Held Up behind Head
- II-D Hero Stabs Inverted Animal or Creature [no examples]
- II-E Hero Threatens Inverted Animal or Creature, Weapon Held Down behind Body
- II-F Hero Threatens Inverted Animal or Creature, Weapon Held Up behind Head [no examples]
- II-G Hero Stabs Marchant Animal or Creature [no examples]
- II-H Hero Threatens Marchant Animal or Creature, Weapon Held Down behind Body
- II-I Hero Threatens Marchant Animal or Creature, Weapon Held Up behind Head
- II-J Hero Stabs Variously Posed Animal or Creature [no examples]
- II-K Hero Threatens Variously Posed Animal or Creature, Weapon Held Down behind Body [no examples]
- II-L Hero Threatens Variously Posed Animal or Creature, Weapon Held Up behind Head [no examples]

COMPOSITIONAL FORMAT III: COMPOSITE CONTROL AND COMBAT ENCOUNTERS
- III-A Two Heroic Encounters: One Control, One Combat
- III-B One Heroic Encounter with Two Heroes: One Controlling, One Threatening
- III-C Two Heroic Encounters with One Hero: Hero Controls One Animal or Creature, Threatens the Other
- III-D Fragmentary Images Suggesting Various Control and Combat Encounters

COMPOSITIONAL FORMAT IV: OTHER HEROIC COMPOSITIONS
- IV-A Seated Hero Controls Rampant Animal or Creature
- IV-B Hero Lifts Animal or Creature above Head

Beyond this second tier, a third tier codes the identity of the focal animal(s)/creature(s) as follows:

1. Bulls
2. Winged Bull Creatures
3. Winged Human-faced/Human-headed Bull Creatures
4. Lions
5. Winged Lion Creatures
6. Winged Human-faced/Human-headed Lion Creatures
7. Winged Bird-Headed Lion Creatures
8. Bulls or Lions
9. Winged Bull or Lion Creatures
10. Winged Human-faced/Human-headed Bull or Lion Creatures
11. Horned Animals: Deer, Gazelles, Wild Goats, Wild Sheep
12. Winged Horned-Animal Creatures: Deer, Gazelles, Wild Goats, Wild Sheep
13. Winged Human-faced/Human-headed Horned-Animal Creatures: Deer, Gazelles, Wild Goats, Wild Sheep [no examples]
14. Ostriches
15. Snakes
16. Various Composite Creatures
17. Mixed Animals and/or Creatures
18. Animals of Uncertain Type
19. Winged Creatures of Uncertain Type
20. Animals or Creatures of Unverifiable Type

Finally, a silent fourth tier codes the direction of the animal or creature's body and direction of focus of its head. This tier is not articulated by letter or number, but it is the notion dictating the final level of organization of the seals in Volume I.

CATALOG OF IMAGES OF HEROIC ENCOUNTER
COMPOSITIONAL FORMAT I: IMAGES OF HEROIC CONTROL
I-A. HERO CONTROLS RAMPANT ANIMALS AND/OR CREATURES
I-A.1. BULLS

PFS 102   Cat.No. 1

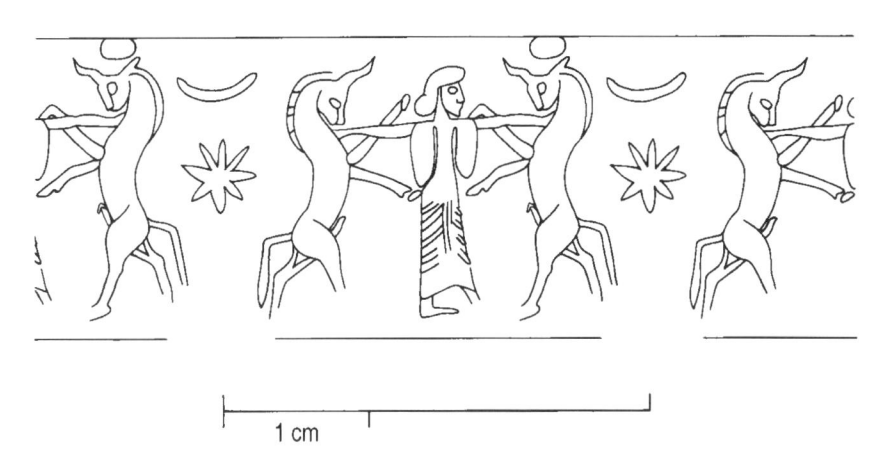

Seal Type:	Cylinder	Photographs:	Pl. 1a–b
Earliest Dated Application:	499/498 B.C.	Typology and Style:	I-A.1 — Fortification Style
Preserved Height of Image:	2.00 cm (comp.)	Preserved Length of Image:	2.90 cm (comp.)
Estimated Height of Original Seal:	2.00 cm	Estimated Diameter of Original Seal:	0.90 cm
Number of Impressions:	7	Quality of Impressions:	Fair-good

Completeness of Image: Complete except for details along lower edge

DESCRIPTION OF SEAL AS IMPRESSED IMAGE

Hero faces right, arms straight at horizontal; hero grasps two rampant bulls by throat.

Each bull holds upper foreleg straight and extends it upward toward hero's head; hoof of bull at right bends downward to touch hero's left shoulder. Each bull holds lower foreleg straight and extends it downward toward hero's hips; hoof of bull at left touches hero; tail of each bull is bent and hangs downward.

Hero wears Persian court robe; sleeves are pushed up to reveal arms and hang from either side of torso in long swags; double central pleat and diagonal folds of lower part of garment are indicated; sheath(?) projects at back. Hero has close-shaved beard or is beardless; rounded coiffure rests at back of neck.

Each bull has long curved horn that emerges from front of its head. Mane is indicated by outline along contour of neck; that of bull at left has diagonal hatching; each bull is ithyphallic.

Crescent is in upper terminal field; star is in middle terminal field.

Edge of seal is preserved at top and bottom of design; flaw or chip is along top edge above bull at right.

COMMENTARY

Koch (1990) notes only that PFS 102 is linked with PFS 60 (II) and PFS 34 (Cat.No. 73) in her Southeastern Region III. Garrison (1996a) suggests that PFS 102 may be an office seal.

The seal is a powerful creation from a series of impressive designs by a master engraver. The sense of line and modeling and the spaciousness of the carving are quite sophisticated; see Garrison (1988, 1991, and 1996a) for this important seal and the artist whose work has close ties to the Court Style.

For comparative illustrations including PFS 102, see pls. 178c (Persian court robes with sleeves pushed up in deep swags), 220c (bulls and bull creatures), 233b (ithyphallic animals/creatures), and 252c (crescents and stars).

SEAL APPLICATION (SEE *APPENDIX ONE: CONCORDANCE OF SEALS TO TABLETS IN VOLUME I*)

With one exception (PF 156, only on the reverse) PFS 102 always occurs on the reverse and upper edge of tablets with PFS 60 (II) on the left edge (the left edge of PF 157 is destroyed). On the reverse of PF 154–155 and PF 157 the seal is inverted. Impressions of the seal are carefully applied. A few applications on the reverse preserve the complete height of the seal, a phenomenon not often seen in the PFS corpus. Rollings of the seal are long, almost two complete revolutions on PF 154 and PF 157. Rollings on the very restricted surface of the upper edge show consistent vertical and lateral placement of the figural design. In five impressions the seal is rolled for at least one complete turn, preserving the entire length of the seal design. Of these five applications, one displays the bull to the left of the hero and the elements in the terminal field in the center; two display the bull to the left of the hero in the center; two display the bull to the right of the hero in the center. Of the two remaining partial rollings, one preserves only the bull to the left of the hero and the hero; one preserves only the hero and the bull to right. On the reverse of PF 154–157 the seal clearly was applied before the text since several cuneiform wedges cut deeply into the top or bottom of the impressions. PF 154 and PF 155 are the earliest dated tablets with PFS 102 and are both dated 499/498 B.C.

BIBLIOGRAPHY

Garrison 1988, pp. 363–68, 489, 495; Garrison 1991, pp. 16–17, fig. 30; Garrison 1996a, pp. 40–43, figs. 10–11; Koch 1981, p. 120; Koch 1990, pp. 75, 270.

PFS 524   Cat.No. 2

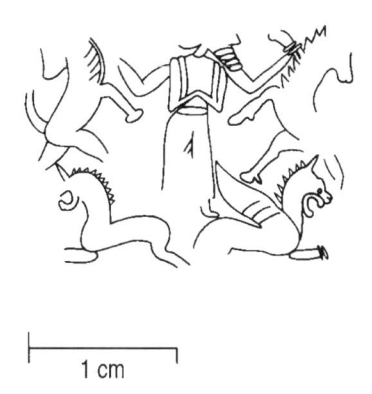

Seal Type:	Cylinder	Photograph:	Pl. 2a
Earliest Dated Application:	495 B.C.	Typology and Style:	I-A.1 — Mixed Styles II
Preserved Height of Image:	1.70 cm (incomp.)	Preserved Length of Image:	2.20 cm (incomp.)
Estimated Height of Original Seal:	NA	Estimated Diameter of Original Seal:	NA
Number of Impressions:	2	Quality of Impressions:	Fair

Completeness of Image: Large segment of middle of design survives

DESCRIPTION OF SEAL AS IMPRESSED IMAGE

Hero faces right, arms bent, and holds two rampant bulls(?) by upper foreleg (link preserved only at right). Hero stands on hindquarters of two courant addorsed horned lion creatures (creature to right is winged).

Each pedestal creature holds one foreleg straight and extended horizontally in front of its chest. Short straight horn emerges from top of head; mane is rendered by crisp serrated edge along contour of neck; mouth open in roar.

Each bull moves toward hero but turns its head away from him and strides over head of pedestal creature; each extends bent lower foreleg toward hero's waist. Bull at right places hoof of forward hind leg on wing of pedestal creature. Tail of bull at left curls upward.

Hero wears belted Persian court robe; sleeves of garment are pushed up to reveal hero's bare arms; gathered folds of sleeves are indicated, as are short segment of central pleat and two diagonal folds of lower part of garment. Long squared, segmented beard rests along hero's left arm; traces of rounded coiffure are at back of neck.

Mane of bull to left rendered by sharp edge along contour of neck and diagonal marks on neck; mane of bull to right is rendered by serrated edge along contour of neck.

COMMENTARY

PFS 524 may have been inscribed, but the terminal field is not preserved for scrutiny. Stylistically and compositionally the seal is very close to PFS 164* (Cat.No. 20) and they probably represent the same hand. Dusinberre (1997b) suggests that PFS 524 is replaced by PFS 164* (Cat.No. 20).

Pedestal creatures are not common, occurring definitively on only seven hero seals in the PFS corpus: PFS 524, PFS 31 (Cat.No. 172), PFS 36* (Cat.No. 5), PFS 164* (Cat.No. 20), PFS 396 (Cat.No. 178), PFS 523* (Cat.No. 209), and PFS 931* (Cat.No. 270). The use of pedestal creatures is documented on several Court Style seals from the Persepolis Treasury archive, for example, PTS 1*, PTS 3*, and PTS 6*. It is also documented on a royal name seal of Darius used on Fort. 11283 (Garrison 1988, pp. 401–05, designated there as PFS 1683*; Dusinberre 1997b, p. 107, fig. 7). See Dusinberre 1997b for the significance of the pedestal creatures as an elite motif in early Achaemenid glyptic, specifically with reference to a cylinder seal excavated at Sardis.

For comparative illustrations including PFS 524, see pls. 179c (Persian court robes with sleeves pushed up), 217a (hero standing atop pedestal figure[s] or other supporting element), and 223e (lions and lion creatures).

SEAL APPLICATION (SEE *APPENDIX ONE: CONCORDANCE OF SEALS TO TABLETS IN VOLUME I*)

PFS 524 occurs on the reverse (inverted) and upper edge of PF 256. PFS 523* (Cat.No. 209) is applied (also inverted) directly above PFS 524 on the reverse. Both partial rollings of PFS 524 display the hero in the center. PF 256 is dated 495 B.C.

BIBLIOGRAPHY

Dusinberre 1997b, pp. 106–07, 113, 124 (nn. 57, 59), 126 (n. 105); Garrison 1988, pp. 378–80; Garrison 1998, p. 120 (n. 12).

I-A.2. WINGED BULL CREATURES

Cat.No. 3   PFS 2

Seal Type:	Cylinder	Photographs:	Pls. 2c–d, 3a–b
Earliest Dated Application:	502 B.C.	Typology and Style:	I-A.2 — Diverse Styles
Preserved Height of Image:	1.60 cm (comp.)	Preserved Length of Image:	2.30 cm (comp.)
Estimated Height of Original Seal:	1.60 cm	Estimated Diameter of Original Seal:	0.70 cm
Number of Impressions:	111	Quality of Impressions:	Good

Completeness of Image: Complete, including what appear to be segments of cylinder caps

DESCRIPTION OF SEAL AS IMPRESSED IMAGE

Hero faces left, arms bent, and grasps two rampant winged bull creatures by muzzle.

Each creature holds forelegs slightly bent and extends them together toward hero's leg; creature to right places hooves on hero's leg. Creatures' tails curve upward with hooked terminations.

Hero wears double-belted robe with two tiers of vertical folds at lower garment. Hero is apparently beardless; small round coiffure rests at back of neck. Hero perhaps wears domed headdress.

Each creature has long curved horn that emerges from front of its head; small ear is also indicated at back of head. Two rows of feathers are indicated on each creature's wing.

Line border is at top and bottom of design; on some impressions there are hints of triangle pattern and edge, suggesting seal cap.

COMMENTARY

PFS 2 is the personal seal of Irtuppiya, the officer in charge of the grain supply from 503 to 499 B.C. He appears as the officer in charge of cattle in 507 B.C. He also acts in several other capacities in the administrative system. Hinz (1971) identifies him as the "Hofspeicherwart" and director of his "Abteilung I, 'Cerealien'" of the "Hofintendantur." Koch (1990) characterizes him as the "Leiter" of the "Intendantur" of her Elam Region VI. Irtuppiya's importance is judged by the fact that he is one of the few officials whose personal seal always occurs on its own. The seal occurs on more tablets than any other personal seal in the PF corpus.

This is a carefully worked engraving by a very fine artist. The composition is noteworthy for its generous and elegant exploitation of negative space. Human and animal heads exhibit geometric stylization with much undisguised drill work. PFS 740 (Cat.No. 146) and PFS 690 (Cat.No. 139) show similar stylization, but they are less carefully executed and probably by a different artist. PFS 740 (Cat.No. 146) is also close compositionally to PFS 2. PFS 1519 (Cat.No. 167) shows the same elegant animal and human body forms combined with a geometric approach to the heads, and it may be by the same hand as PFS 2, which sets itself apart from these seals, however, in the smooth undulating rhythm of the animal forms. The form and the decoration of the hero's garment and the treatment of the creatures' wings cannot readily be paralleled, but see PFS 740 (Cat.No. 146) for the wings. Other non-heroic scenes betray the same hand, for example, PFS 23 (III). The style of PFS 2 is close both to the Fortification Style and the Court Style in specific respects (Garrison 1988), but the particular hybridization we see here makes the seal an interesting anomaly by an individualistic artist. The treatment of faces relates to a long tradition in Elamite glyptic (Seidl 1990). The traces of possible seal caps, visible, for example, on PF 1848, are rare owing to the small surfaces of most of the tablets used in the Persepolis Fortification archive.

For comparative illustrations including PFS 2, see pls. 182a (robes with various features of detail), 204b (arm positions of heroic control), 210b (heroic attitudes of control encounter), 270f (compositions creating dynamic negative space as terminal field), 276a (evidence of original seal caps), and 282a (personal seals of supply/apportionment officers).

SEAL APPLICATION (SEE *APPENDIX ONE: CONCORDANCE OF SEALS TO TABLETS IN VOLUME I*)

As is typical of seals of important offices and officials, PFS 2 never appears with another seal. Of the many tablets on which it occurs, the normal sealing pattern is on the reverse and left edge only (twenty-nine tablets). Other sealing patterns include: the upper edge and left edge (six tablets); only the left edge (five tablets); the reverse, upper edge, and left edge (three tablets); the lower edge and left edge (one tablet); the reverse, lower edge, upper edge, and left edge (one tablet); the reverse, lower edge, and left edge (one tablet); the obverse and left edge (one tablet); only the reverse (one tablet).

On thirteen tablets the seal has been applied inverted on the reverse. Impressions of the seal tend to be meticulously applied, with little or no vertical or lateral distortion. Multiple rollings on the reverse of the tablet are arranged neatly in registers, consistently oriented. Because the cylinder is so small, the complete figural image occurs in the majority of applications, often with part of the design repeated. Of the total 111 impressions, one impression is too poorly preserved for analysis. Of the 110 remaining impressions, ninety-one show the seal rolled for at least one complete turn, preserving the entire length of the seal design. In three of these ninety-one applications, the figural design is repeated twice. Twenty-four rollings display the hero in the center; fifteen display the hero and creature to left in the center; fifteen display the hero and creature to the right; fourteen display the creature to the left of the hero; twenty-two display the creature to right of the hero; twenty display the two creatures. In the last case, when the two creatures are the central element, the focal emphasis is a wonderful negative space created by the calligraphic lines of the tails and hind legs of the two creatures.

On the reverse of many tablets the seal was clearly applied before the text since several cuneiform wedges cut into the top or bottom of the impressions. PF 1069–1070 and PF 1072–1073 are the earliest dated tablets with PFS 2 and are all dated 502 B.C.

BIBLIOGRAPHY

Aperghis 1999, pp. 181–82; Brosius 1996, pp. 157 (table 8), 159; Garrison 1988, pp. 447–50; Garrison 1991, pp. 12–13, 20, figs. 19–20; Garrison 1996b, pp. 25, 30–31; Hallock 1985, p. 600; Hinz 1971, pp. 286–87; Hinz 1976, p. 99; Koch 1986, p. 146; Koch 1990, pp. 181, 241–43, 299, 307; Koch 1992, pp. 42–43, 61; Root 1996b, p. 23, fig. 11.

Cat.No. 4 PFS 7*

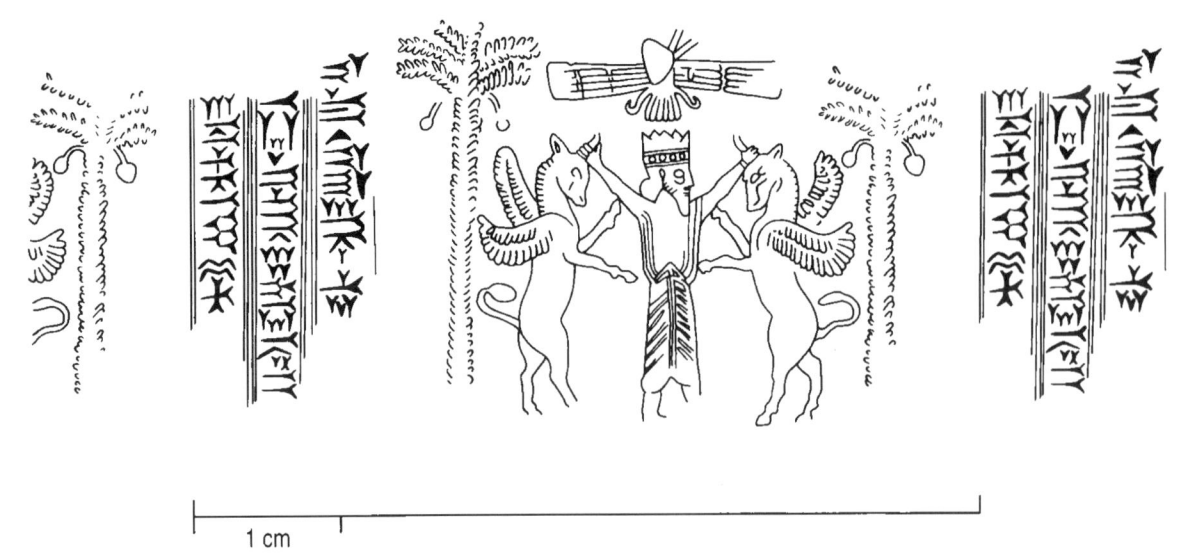

Seal Type:	Cylinder, Inscribed	Photographs:	Pl. 4a–d
Earliest Dated Application:	503/502 B.C.	Typology and Style:	I-A.2 — Court Style
Languages of Inscription:	Old Persian, Elamite, and Babylonian		
Preserved Height of Image:	2.60 cm (incomp.)	Preserved Length of Image:	5.40 cm (comp.)
Estimated Height of Original Seal:	3.00 cm	Estimated Diameter of Original Seal:	1.70 cm
Number of Impressions:	115	Quality of Impressions:	Many preserve excellent detail

Completeness of Image: Almost complete except for upper edge and lower edge

DESCRIPTION OF SEAL AS IMPRESSED IMAGE

Hero faces right, arms straight and diagonally upward above shoulder level; hero holds two rampant winged bull creatures by horn.

Each creature holds upper foreleg straight and extends it upward to place hoof at hero's arm; lower foreleg is straight and extended downward toward hero's waist; creature to right places hoof on hero's waist. Their tails curve upward with tufted terminations.

Hero wears Persian court robe; sleeves of garment are pushed up to reveal hero's bare arms; gathered folds of sleeves are indicated, as are central pleat and diagonal folds of lower part of garment. Hero wears five-pointed dentate Persian crown with studded band. Long rounded, striated beard rests over hero's left shoulder along chest; ear is clearly indicated; rounded coiffure lies at base of neck.

Each creature has two wings indicated, upper one extending diagonally upward from lower; two rows of feathers are indicated on each wing. Thick curved horn emerges from front of each creature's head; pointed ear is at back of each creature's head.

Date palms with bulbous fruit clusters frame heroic encounter. Figure emerging from winged symbol (with bird's wings and tail feathers with hooked tendrils) hovers directly above hero, facing right, and raises both arms. Figure wears Persian court robe with sleeves down. Wings are broad and rectangular with feathers indicated by long parallel horizontal lines intersected in each case by two vertical lines.

Paneled inscription is in terminal field, framed (like heroic encounter) by the two date palms.

INSCRIPTION

Old Persian, Elamite, and Babylonian

Line
1. [a-]da-ma : da-a-ra-ya-va-[…]
2. [v.ú] v.Da-ri-ya-ma-u-iš […]
3. [ana-ku ᵐ]Da-ri-iá-muš […]

Translation   I (am) Darius …

The inscription on PFS 7* has been known for some time and has been published, with previous bibliography, by Schmitt (1981). Schmitt's reading of the inscription is based on a letter that he had received from Hallock (Schmitt 1981, p. 22). The beginnings and ends of the lines are not preserved in any impression that we have studied. The beginnings of the Elamite and Babylonian lines are restored based upon the Old Persian. Restoration of the ends of the lines is more problematic since no known impression of any royal name seal of Darius preserves the ends of the lines. Published restorations of the ends of the lines follow the inscription preserved in the London Darius cylinder (Schmitt 1981, p. 19 sub SDa).

Known as SDe, the inscription is one of the standard trilingual (Old Persian, Elamite, and Babylonian) inscriptions of Darius I. The inscription is oriented along the vertical axis of the seal design, each line enclosed in its own panel, reading (from top to bottom): Old Persian, Elamite, and Babylonian. The visible signs in SDe are very similar to those found on SDa (the London Darius cylinder); the signs in SDe are slightly taller compared to the length of each line than in SDa. This may be a function of the rollings, where even a slight slippage would create a substantial difference in these proportions. It is also noteworthy that each line of the inscription in SDe appears to have its own case, which results in double lines between the Old Persian and Elamite inscriptions, and between the Elamite and Babylonian inscriptions. No other inscription on a seal of heroic encounter in the PFS corpus exhibits this characteristic. Seals with images of heroic encounter that have case lines enclosed in panels and oriented along the vertical axis of the seal are limited to PFS 7*, PFS 1* (Cat.No. 182), PFS 64* (Cat.No. 173), the royal name seal PFS 113* (Cat.No. 19), and PFS 526* (Cat.No. 216).

COMMENTARY

PFS 7* seems to have belonged to an office in charge of provisioning the king with food supplies (see Garrison 1996b; Hinz 1971, "Hofspeisenmeister"; cf. Tuplin [1998] who voices skepticism). The seal occurs only on a special type of transaction (J texts). The seal has no geographical restriction, and it seems to have important administrative authority. The seal occurs alone, or as a counter seal with PFS 66a* (II), PFS 66b* (II), or PFS 66c* (II), which are also office seals (overseeing flour deliveries) and are also found only on the J texts. The seal has, furthermore, been identified on an Achaemenid administrative tablet now in the Louvre (MDP 11 308). This tablet is a J text, and it is thought to have been found at Susa (Garrison 1996b). If MDP 11 308 is indeed from Susa, it vividly documents the wide administrative range of PFS 7*. Much of the bibliography focuses on the administrative use of the seal (e.g., Hallock 1977, Hinz 1971, Koch 1990, Garrison 1996b). Lewis (1994) considers PFS 7* one of Darius's personal seals that he gave out to a subordinate.

This masterfully carved seal is the largest preserved seal in the PFS corpus of seals of heroic encounter. The seal design is one of the early dated examples of the fully developed Court Style, formally and iconographically related to Court Style seals used on the slightly later Persepolis Treasury tablets.[1]

The identity of the figure emerging from the winged symbol, traditionally associated with the god Ahuramazda, is still a subject of dispute.[2] The disk element of the typical winged symbol with figure emergent as we know it from the monumental art of the Achaemenids (viz., Root 1979) is not included in the symbol as rendered on any examples of the motif in the PFS corpus of hero seals. Compare PFS 7* with PFS 774 (Cat.No. 58), PFS 1053 (Cat.No. 45), and PFS 1071 (Cat.No. 29). See Garrison 1988 and 1991 and Root 1989, for discussions on style and selected iconographical features of the seal design. See Porada 1979, p. 85, and Dusinberre 1997b, pp. 107–14, for commentary on the date palm and its royal associations.

For comparative illustrations including PFS 7*, see pls. 179a (Persian court robes with sleeves pushed up), 188a (Persian crowns and fluted tiaras), 190a (beards), 197b (hands), 203a (arm positions of heroic control), 218a (comparative heroic proportions), 220a (bulls and bull creatures), 232f (spectacular animal studies), 248a (deities emergent from winged symbol), 259a (date palms), 261b (paneled inscriptions with vertical case lines), 265g (trilingual [royal name] inscriptions), and 281c (office seals).

---

1. Schmidt 1957, pp. 7–10, 18–33, pls. 1–14; see Amiet 1972, no. 2203, for a sealing preserved on a bulla from Susa, similar in style and iconography.

2. Root (1979) advocates the identification with Ahuramazda, reinforced, for example, by Lecoq 1984 and Sancisi-Weerdenburg 1993 but disputed most notably by Shahbazi 1980. Brief reviews of the problem include Kaim 1991; d'Amore 1992, pp. 210–11.

SEAL APPLICATION (SEE APPENDIX ONE: CONCORDANCE OF SEALS TO TABLETS IN VOLUME I)

As mentioned above, PFS 7* is either used alone or else with PFS 66a* (II), PFS 66b* (II), or PFS 66c* (II). When it appears with any of those seals, PFS 7* always occurs only (and in isolation) on the reverse, with PFS 66a*, PFS 66b*, or PFS 66c* always on the left edge and sometimes also on additional surfaces (excluding the reverse). When it appears alone, PFS 7* tends to cover all uninscribed surfaces. On PF 722, PFS 7* occurs on all six possible sealing surfaces. Other sealing patterns include: reverse, upper edge, and left edge (six tablets); reverse and left edge (six tablets); reverse, lower edge, upper edge, and left edge (four tablets); reverse, lower edge, upper edge, right edge, and left edge (three tablets); reverse, upper edge, right edge, and left edge (two tablets); reverse, lower edge, and left edge (one tablet); reverse, lower edge, right edge, and left edge (one tablet); obverse and reverse (one tablet). On the reverse of ten tablets the seal is inverted. Impressions of the seal tend to be carefully executed, although vertical and lateral distortions occur. Multiple rollings of the seal are common on the reverse; they are neatly executed and consistently oriented. The size of the seal creates over-rolling in these cases. The large size of the seal also means that few impressions preserve the complete seal design.

Of the total 115 impressions, seventy-seven show some part of the inscription. In five impressions the seal is rolled for at least one complete turn, preserving the entire length of the seal design. Of these five applications, two display the hero in the center with partial rollings of the inscription at each end of the impression; two display the hero and the creature to left in the center with a full rolling of the inscription at the left of the impression, a partial rolling of the inscription at the right; one displays the hero and the creature to right in the center with a complete rolling of the inscription at the right of the impression and a partial rolling of the inscription at the left. Of the remaining 110 partial applications, ten display a complete rolling of the inscription in the center; one displays a complete rolling of the inscription and the date palm to right in the center; one preserves only a complete rolling of the inscription and the date palm to left; one preserves only a complete rolling of the inscription and the date palm to right; fourteen display the hero in the center; eight display the hero and the creature to left in the center (of which three preserve a partial rolling of the inscription at the left of the impression); twelve display the hero and the creature to right in the center (of which eight preserve a partial rolling of the inscription at the right of the impression); one preserves only the hero and the creature to left; five preserve only the hero and the creature to right; two display the creature to the left of the hero and a date palm in the center with a partial rolling of the inscription at the left of the impression; seven display the creature to the right of the hero and a date palm in the center with a partial rolling of the inscription at the right of the impression; one preserves only the creature to the left of the hero and a date palm; fifteen display the creature to the left of the hero in the center with a partial rolling of the inscription at the left of the impression; twenty-one display the creature to the right of the hero in the center (of which eighteen preserve a partial rolling of the inscription at the right of the impression); five display the date palm to the left of the hero in the center with a partial rolling of the inscription (in one instance a complete rolling of the inscription) at the left of the impression; six display the date palm to the right of the hero in the center with a partial rolling of the inscription (in one instance preserving a complete rolling of the inscription) at the right of the impression.

On the reverse of six tablets the seal clearly was applied before the text since several cuneiform wedges cut into the top or bottom of the impressions. PF 707 is the earliest dated tablet with PFS 7* and is dated 503/502 B.C.

BIBLIOGRAPHY

Aperghis 1999, p. 164; Dusinberre 1997b, pp. 107, 110–11, figs. 10–11; Garrison 1988, pp. 220, 255, 367, 372, 376, 377, 390, 391, 394–401, 414, 416, 474, 480, 489, 491, 530; Garrison 1991, pp. 3, 13–21, figs. 21–22; Garrison 1996a, pp. 42–45, figs. 14–15, pl. 6; Garrison 1996b, pp. 15–35, figs. 6–7; Garrison 1998, p. 128 (n. 24), p. 131 (n. 30); Garrison 2000, pp. 128–29, 130–31, 156; Garrison in press; Garrison and Dion 1999, pp. 10, 14 (n. 39); Garrison and Root 1996, pp. 11–12; Hallock 1977, pp. 127–28, pl. E (3); Harper et al. 1992, pp. 260, 273, no. 191; Hinz 1971, pp. 229–30; Koch 1990, p. 88; Lewis 1994, p. 31; Mayrhofer 1978 p. 16 sub 3.11.1; Miller-Collett and Root 1997, p. 360; Root 1979, pp. 121, 303; Root 1989, pp. 40–42, fig. 2; Root 1990b, pp. 36–37; Root 1992, pp. 445–46, fig. ART.35; Root 1996b, p. 22, figs. 6–7; Root 1997, p. 233; Root 1999a, pp. 170, 173, fig. 6; Scheil 1911, no. 308; Schmitt 1981, pp. 22 sub SDe; Stolper 1992a, p. 273, no. 191; Tuplin 1998, pp. 78–79.

PFS 36*   Cat.No. 5

Seal Type:	Cylinder, Inscribed	Photographs:	Pl. 5a–c
Earliest Dated Application:	504 B.C.	Typology and Style:	I-A.2 — Fortification Style
Language of Inscription:	Elamite		
Preserved Height of Image:	1.50 cm (incomp.)	Preserved Length of Image:	4.20 cm (comp.)
Estimated Height of Original Seal:	NA	Estimated Diameter of Original Seal:	1.30 cm
Number of Impressions:	27	Quality of Impressions:	Good

Completeness of Image: Almost complete except for upper edge, large part of lower edge and parts of inscription

DESCRIPTION OF SEAL AS IMPRESSED IMAGE

Four-winged hero faces right, arms bent, and holds two rampant winged bull creatures by upper foreleg; hero appears to stand on hindquarters of two couchant(?) addorsed winged bull creatures (wing of creature at right not preserved).

Each pedestal creature has long curved horn that emerges from front of its head; creature to left has long pointed ear at back of its head.

Each bull creature controlled by hero holds upper foreleg straight and extends it upward toward hero's wing; lower foreleg is bent and held in front of its body; tail curves upward with undulating contour and has tufted termination.

Hero wears Assyrian garment that leaves forward leg exposed; fringe is indicated along front of chest. Short pointed beard rests above hero's left shoulder; round coiffure rests at back of neck.

Each bull creature has long curved horn that emerges from front of its head; long pointed ear is at back of its head.

Large paneled inscription is in terminal field.

INSCRIPTION

Elamite

Line   1. v.Zi-iš-ša-
                 2. bar-na ša(-)
                 3. [x x (x)] ⌜x⌝

Translation   Ziššabarna

There are three lines to the inscription, oriented along the horizontal axis of the seal, separated by case lines, and enclosed in a panel. Most impressions of the seal on the PF tablets show virtually nothing of the inscription. Our reading is based mainly on the impressions of the seal on the left edge of PFNN 1046 and PFNN 1068. The name Ziššabarna is a transcription of Old Persian *Čiçafarnah.[3]

---

3. Jones's reading of the name as initially published in Garrison and Dion 1999, p. 13, caption to fig. 9, is corrected here and in Jones 1999.

Commentary

Koch (1990) suggests that the seal may belong to Rašda, an official connected with the site of Tirazziš (Shiraz). Brosius (1996, pp. 132, 139–41) seems to imply that PFS 36* is an office seal and associates both Rašda and Uštana with the seal in their function as overseeing the provisioning of rations for workers qualified as *kurtaš abbakkanaš Irdabamana*.

For the significance of the pedestal creatures as an elite motif in early Achaemenid glyptic, see Dusinberre 1997b. Other seals of heroic encounter with pedestal creatures include PFS 31 (Cat.No. 172), PFS 164* (Cat.No. 20), PFS 396 (Cat.No. 178), PFS 523* (Cat.No. 209), PFS 524 (Cat.No. 2), and PFS 931* (Cat.No. 270), with PFS 164* (Cat.No. 20), PFS 396 (Cat.No. 178), PFS 523* (Cat.No. 209), and PFS 524 (Cat.No. 2) being close parallels.[4]

This is a large and exceptionally well-executed seal. Stylistically the seal has close ties to the Court Style, especially in the treatment of the animal forms, the very formal and symmetrical composition, the inclusion of pedestal creatures, and the large paneled inscription. The design is crisply executed and well conceived, with a very delicate and light quality in the animal forms. The seal is one of the more impressive designs in Volume 1.

For comparative illustrations including PFS 36*, see pls. 204d (arm positions of heroic control), 216c (hero standing atop pedestal figure[s] or other supporting element), 262b (paneled inscriptions with horizontal case lines), and 273a (open compositions).

Seal Application (see *Appendix One: Concordance of Seals to Tablets in Volume I*)

As is typical of the seals of important officials, PFS 36* always occurs alone and usually on several surfaces of a tablet, normally the reverse and the left edge (eight tablets), also the reverse, left, and upper edge (three tablets). Impressions of the seal tend to be carefully applied and usually exhibit no distortion. Because the seal is relatively large, complete heights cannot be accommodated on the small sealing surfaces. Normally the seal user privileges the upper part of the design. On the reverse of PF 397 and PF 1076 the seal has been applied twice, one impression directly above the other. On the reverse of PF 398, PF 1028, and PF 1041 the seal is inverted.

Of the total twenty-seven impressions, eleven show some part of the inscription, but none displays the inscription alone in the center. In four impressions the seal is rolled for at least one complete turn, preserving the entire length of the seal design. Of these four applications, one displays the inscription and the creature to the left of the hero in the center; two display the inscription and the creature to the right of the hero in the center; one application is very long, preserving two complete rollings of the inscription and placing the creature to the right of the hero in the center. Of the twenty-three partial impressions, seven display the hero in the center without any traces of the inscription; seven preserve only the hero and the creature to the left; one displays the hero and the creature to the left in the center; three display the creature to the left of the hero in the center (partial rolling of the inscription at the left of the impression); one displays the creature to the right of the hero in the center; two preserve only a partial rolling of the inscription and the creature to the left of the hero; one preserves only the creature to the left of the hero; one preserves only the hero and the creature to the right. On the reverse of PF 398–399, PF 821, PF 1028, PF 1041, PF 1223, and PF 1613 the seal clearly was applied before the text since several cuneiform wedges cut into the top or bottom of the impressions. PF 1076 and PF 1612 are the earliest dated tablets with PFS 36* and are both dated 504 B.C.

Bibliography

Brosius 1996, pp. 132–25 (table 2), 136 (table 3), 137 (table 4), 139–41, 143 (table 5), 146; Dusinberre 1997b, pp. 106–07, 113, 123 (n. 57), 124 (n. 57), 126 (n. 105); Garrison 1988, pp. 287–92, 482–83; Garrison 1998, pp. 120 (n. 12), 121 (n. 15); Garrison and Dion 1999, pp. 9 (n. 19), 10 (n. 28), 12, and fig. 9; Jones 1999; Koch 1990, pp. 62–63.

---

4. Compare also a fragmentary impression of a cylinder on a bulla from Susa (Amiet 1972, pls. 37 and 189, no. 2203).

PFS 970   Cat.No. 6

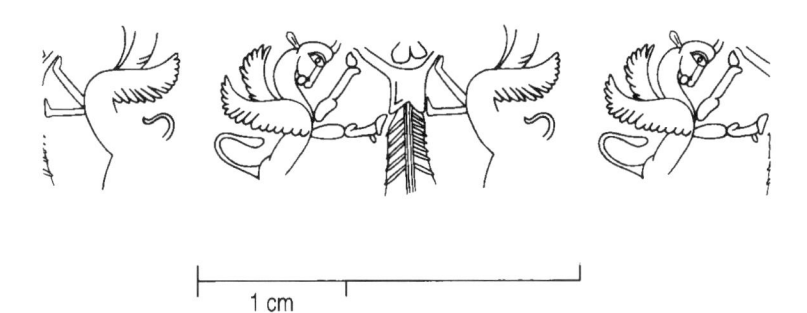

Seal Type:	Cylinder	Photograph:	Pl. 6a
Earliest Dated Application:	500 B.C.	Typology and Style:	I-A.2 — Court Style
Preserved Height of Image:	1.10 cm (incomp.)	Preserved Length of Image:	2.60 cm (comp.)
Estimated Height of Original Seal:	1.30 cm	Estimated Diameter of Original Seal:	0.80 cm
Number of Impressions:	2	Quality of Impressions:	Fair

Completeness of Image: Segment of middle of design survives along its complete length

DESCRIPTION OF SEAL AS IMPRESSED IMAGE

Hero faces right, arms straight at diagonal above shoulder level, and holds two rampant winged bull creatures probably by horn.

Each creature holds upper foreleg straight and extends it upward to place hoof on hero's arm; lower foreleg is straight and hoof is placed on hero's waist. Creature to left has long tail that curls upward with tufted termination. Creature to right has thin tail that curls upward with pointed termination.

Hero wears Persian court robe with sleeves pushed up to reveal arms; gathered folds of sleeves are indicated (on hero's right side only). Triple central pleat and diagonal folds of lower part of garment are also indicated. Squared beard rests over hero's left arm; rounded coiffure rests at back of neck.

Each creature has two wings indicated, upper extending diagonally upward from lower. Creature to left has curved horn (only partially preserved) that emerges from front of its head; long thin ear is at back of its head.

COMMENTARY

The animal forms are thinner than normally seen in the Court Style, and the rendering of the details of the hero's garment is somewhat careless; nevertheless, the sharp execution of the animal forms represents the style well. The detailing in the head and forelegs of the creature to the left is especially noteworthy and typical of the Court Style. Quite remarkable is the suggestion of a three-quarters view of this creature's face.

For comparative illustrations including PFS 970, see pls. 203f (arm positions of heroic control), 220h (bulls and bull creatures), 231f (feet of animals and creatures), and 232b (animals/creatures with distinctive perspectival elements).

SEAL APPLICATION (SEE *APPENDIX ONE: CONCORDANCE OF SEALS TO TABLETS IN VOLUME I*)

PFS 970 occurs on the left edge of both PF 848 and PF 1047. Of the two partial applications, that on PF 848 displays the hero in the center; that on PF 1047 displays the creature to the left of the hero in the center. PF 848 and PF 1047 are both dated 500 B.C.

BIBLIOGRAPHY

Garrison 1988, pp. 412, 416, 479–80.

Cat.No. 7   PFS 429

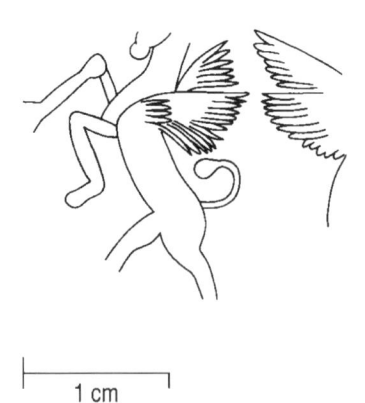

Seal Type:	Cylinder	Photograph:	Pl. 6c
Earliest Dated Application:	499/498 B.C.	Typology and Style:	I-A.2 — Modeled Style
Preserved Height of Image:	1.80 cm (incomp.)	Preserved Length of Image:	2.25 cm (incomp.)
Estimated Height of Original Seal:	NA	Estimated Diameter of Original Seal:	NA
Number of Impressions:	1	Quality of Impression:	Poor

Completeness of Image: Small segment of middle of design survives

DESCRIPTION OF SEAL AS IMPRESSED IMAGE

Only left arm of hero is preserved; arm is straight and extended diagonally upward above shoulder level to hold rampant winged bull creature by upper foreleg.

Pair of wings at far right of impression should belong to similar creature held by hero's right hand. Creature to right holds upper foreleg straight and extends it diagonally upward; lower foreleg is bent, hoof flexed, and held in front of its body. Creature appears to raise forward hind leg slightly; tail curls upward with tufted termination. Two wings are indicated, upper extending diagonally upward from lower.

COMMENTARY

The forms are large and fully modeled, suggesting a powerful and well-made design. This seal was not included in Garrison 1988.

For comparative illustrations including PFS 429, see pl. 203d (arm positions of heroic control).

SEAL APPLICATION (SEE APPENDIX ONE: CONCORDANCE OF SEALS TO TABLETS IN VOLUME I)

PFS 429 occurs once (inverted) across the lower half of the reverse of PF 121. PFS 430 (Cat.No. 56) is applied once (also inverted) across the upper half of the reverse. The partial rolling of PFS 429 preserves only the creature to the right of the hero and the wings of the creature to the left of the hero. PF 121 is dated 499/498 B.C.

BIBLIOGRAPHY

Garrison and Root 1996, p. 13.

PFS 1189   Cat.No. 8

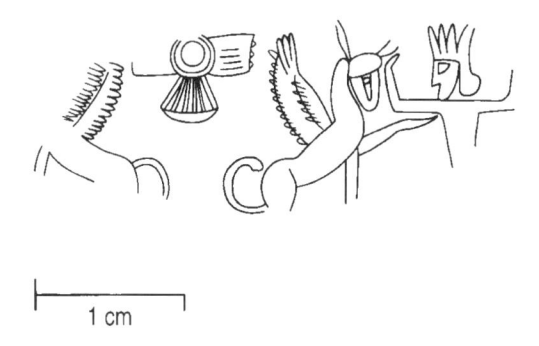

Seal Type:	Cylinder	Photograph:	Pl. 6e
Earliest Dated Application:	500 B.C.	Typology and Style:	I-A.2 — Diverse Styles
Preserved Height of Image:	1.20 cm (incomp.)	Preserved Length of Image:	3.30 cm (incomp.)
Estimated Height of Original Seal:	NA	Estimated Diameter of Original Seal:	NA
Number of Impressions:	1	Quality of Impression:	Good

Completeness of Image: Large segment of middle of design survives

Description of Seal as Impressed Image

Hero faces left, arms bent, and holds two rampant winged bull creatures by horn (contact preserved only to left of hero).

Creature to left of hero holds upper foreleg bent and extends it upward toward hero's chest; lower foreleg is straight (only partially preserved) and held down under its body; tail curls upward. Creature to right is only partially preserved; one foreleg is held down under its body; tail curls downward.

Hero wears garment of uncertain type and fluted Persian tiara. Rounded beard rests above hero's right shoulder; rounded coiffure is at back of neck.

Horn of creature to left of hero emerges from front of its head; long thin ear is at back of its head. Each creature has two rows of feathers on its wing.

Winged symbol with bird's tail is in upper terminal field.

Commentary

Details of iconography such as the winged symbol and the fluted tiara recall the Court Style, but the engraving is quite different. Animal and human heads show an abstracted geometric approach with sharp edges. Engraving seems very flat and stiff. The form of the winged symbol is unparalleled among the images of heroic encounter in the PFS corpus but seems close to one preserved on a sealing from Nineveh (Herbordt 1992, pl. 20, fig. 12). PFS 1189 is probably not from the mainstream Persepolitan workshops, and its origins may lie in more western realms of the empire.[5]

For comparative illustrations including PFS 1189, see pls. 189c (Persian crowns and fluted tiaras), 207e (arm positions of heroic control), and 249e (winged symbols).

Seal Application (see Appendix One: Concordance of Seals to Tablets in Volume I)

PFS 1189 occurs on the reverse of PF 1247. The partial rolling displays the creature to the left of the hero in the center. The seal clearly was applied before the text since several cuneiform wedges cut into the bottom of the impression. PF 1247 is dated 500 B.C.

Bibliography

Garrison 1988, p. 460.

---

5. The wing style compares well to that on an unprovenanced agate conoid classified by Boardman as "Court Style" (see Boardman 1970a, p. 42, pl. 5, fig. 120).

Cat.No. 9 PFS 1460

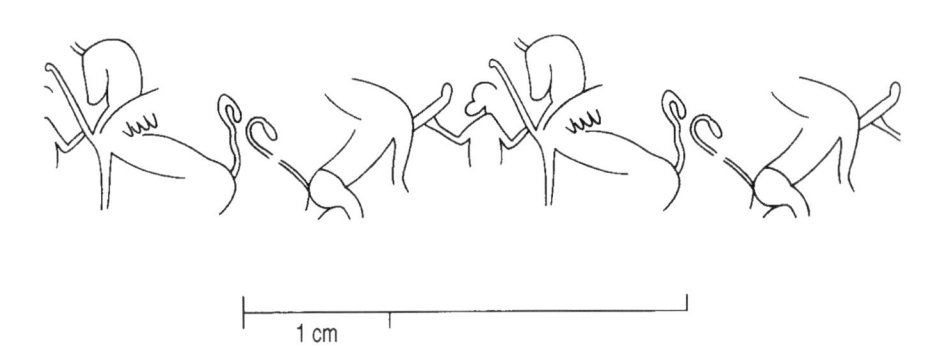

Seal Type:	Cylinder	Photograph:	Pl. 7a
Earliest Dated Application:	ND	Typology and Style:	I-A.2 — Fortification Style
Preserved Height of Image:	1.20 cm (incomp.)	Preserved Length of Image:	3.00 cm (comp.)
Estimated Height of Original Seal:	NA	Estimated Diameter of Original Seal:	0.90 cm
Number of Impressions:	1	Quality of Impression:	Very poor

Completeness of Image: Segment of middle of design survives along its complete length

DESCRIPTION OF SEAL AS IMPRESSED IMAGE

Hero faces right, arms bent, and holds two rampant winged bull creatures by upper foreleg.

Each creature holds upper foreleg straight and extends it diagonally upward. Creature to left holds lower foreleg bent and extends it vertically downward under its body; tail extends diagonally upward, hooking downward at its end with tufted termination. Creature to right holds lower foreleg straight and extends it vertically downward under its body; tail undulates vertically upward, hooking downward at its end with tufted termination.

Hero wears garment of uncertain type; rounded coiffure rests at back of his neck.

Creature to right has thin curved horn (only partially preserved) emerging from front of its head. Head of creature to left is not preserved.

COMMENTARY

Based on Q texts protocol, PFS 1460 should belong to Paršena the *barrišdama* ("elite guide"), who in PF 1577 received date rations for 108 Cappadocian workers on their way to Elam under the authority (*halmi*) of Parnaka. PF 1577 preserves the only occurrence of the name Paršena in the PF texts.

The large bull creatures and small hero make for an unusual design. The disparity in the creatures' forms is also unusual. The creature to the left is short and thick; the creature to the right is thin and elongated.

For comparative illustrations including PFS 1460, see pls. 205h (arm positions of heroic control), 219h (comparative heroic proportions), and 288g (personal seals of elite guides [*barrišdama*]).

SEAL APPLICATION (SEE *APPENDIX ONE: CONCORDANCE OF SEALS TO TABLETS IN VOLUME I*)

PFS 1460 occurs on the reverse of PF 1577. The rolling preserves the entire length of the seal design and displays the creature to the left of the hero in the center. The date of PF 1577 is unknown.

BIBLIOGRAPHY

Garrison 1988, pp. 268–70.

PFS 1499   Cat.No. 10

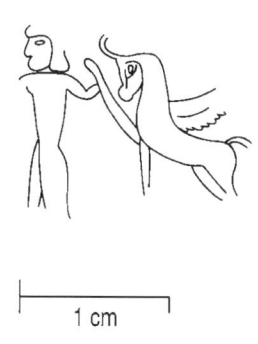

Seal Type:	Cylinder	Photograph:	Pl. 7c
Earliest Dated Application:	ND	Typology and Style:	I-A.2 — Fortification Style
Preserved Height of Image:	1.20 cm (incomp.)	Preserved Length of Image:	1.60 cm (incomp.)
Estimated Height of Original Seal:	NA	Estimated Diameter of Original Seal:	NA
Number of Impressions:	1	Quality of Impression:	Poor

Completeness of Image: Segment of middle of design survives

Description of Seal as Impressed Image

Hero faces left, arms bent, and holds two(?) rampant winged bull creatures (preserved only at right) by upper foreleg.

Creature to right holds upper foreleg straight and extends it upward toward hero's head; lower foreleg straight (only partially preserved) and held down vertically under its body.

Hero wears Assyrian garment that leaves forward leg exposed. Hero has close-shaved beard or is beardless; flattened coiffure rests at back of neck.

Thin horn curves upward from front of creature's head.

Commentary

This is a very well-made design, although the one impression of it is poor. See Garrison 1988 for this important artist, whose work is close to the Court Style.

Seal Application (see *Appendix One: Concordance of Seals to Tablets in Volume I*)

PFS 1499 occurs on the left edge of PF 1622. The reverse of the tablet is destroyed. The partial rolling preserves only the hero and the creature to the right. The date of PF 1622 is unknown.

Bibliography

Garrison 1988, pp. 352–56, 361, 382, 485–86.

Cat.No. 11 PFS 778

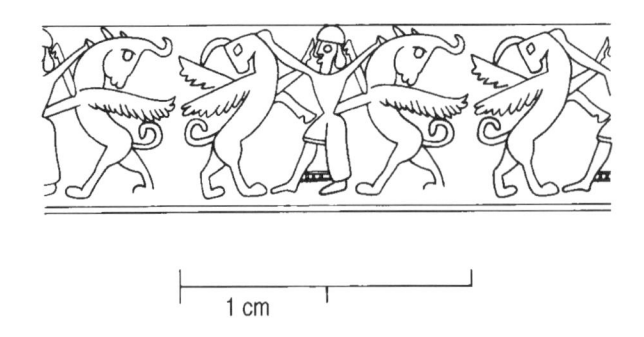

Seal Type:	Cylinder	Photograph:	Pl. 7e
Earliest Dated Application:	500/499 B.C.	Typology and Style:	I-A.2 — Fortification Style
Preserved Height of Image:	1.20 cm (comp.)	Preserved Length of Image:	2.00 cm (comp.)
Estimated Height of Original Seal:	1.20 cm	Estimated Diameter of Original Seal:	0.60 cm
Number of Impressions:	6	Quality of Impressions:	Fair-good

Completeness of Image: Complete

DESCRIPTION OF SEAL AS IMPRESSED IMAGE

Hero faces left in striding pose, arms straight at diagonal above shoulder level, and holds two rampant winged bull creatures by back of neck.

Each creature moves toward hero but turns its head away from him. Creature to left holds upper foreleg bent and extends it upward toward hero's head; lower foreleg is straight and extends downward toward hero's thigh; tail curls upward. Creature to right holds upper foreleg straight and extends it upward toward hero's head; lower foreleg is straight and extended downward to place hoof on hero's waist; tail curls upward.

Hero wears Assyrian garment that leaves forward leg exposed below knee; border is on hem along right leg; lower hem between legs is decorated with paneled design. Squared beard rests over hero's right shoulder; rounded coiffure is at back of neck. Hero perhaps wears domed headdress.

Creature to left has two wings indicated, the upper extended diagonally upward from the lower; horn of this creature curves forward from front of its head. Horn of creature to right emerges from front of its head, curling back at end; three pointed projections along contour of its neck apparently indicate mane.

Edge of seal is preserved at top of design; line border is at bottom of design.

COMMENTARY

The engraving is quite deep. The manner by which the hero holds the creatures is unique in the PFS corpus of hero seals.

For comparative illustrations including PFS 778, see pls. 177c (Assyrian garments with detailing preserved), 192d (rounded coiffures), 203e (arm positions of heroic control), and 270h (compositions creating dynamic negative space as terminal field).

SEAL APPLICATION (SEE *APPENDIX ONE: CONCORDANCE OF SEALS TO TABLETS IN VOLUME I*)

PFS 778 occurs twice (inverted) on the reverse and once on the left edge of both PF 560 and PF 1106. No other seal is used on the tablets. The rollings on the reverse are placed one directly above the other. All six impressions are complete; one displays the hero in the center; one displays the hero and the creature to the right in the center; four display the creature to the left of the hero in the center. PF 560 is the earliest dated tablet with PFS 778 and is dated 500/499 B.C.

BIBLIOGRAPHY

Garrison 1988, pp. 359–63.

PFS 1467 — Cat.No. 12

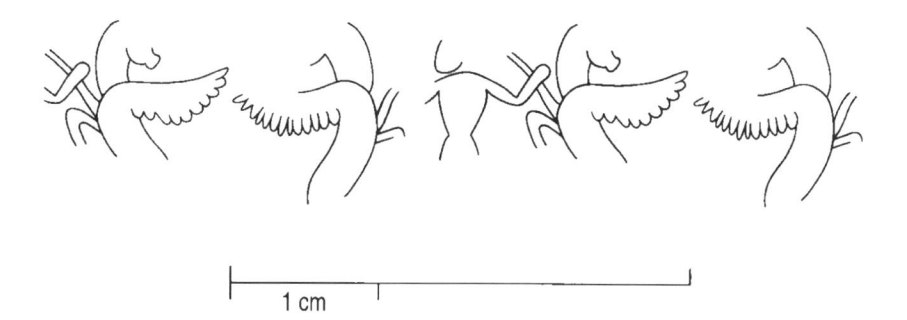

Seal Type:	Cylinder	Photograph:	Pl. 8a
Earliest Dated Application:	504/503(?) B.C.	Typology and Style:	I-A.2 — Fortification Style
Preserved Height of Image:	1.30 cm (incomp.)	Preserved Length of Image:	3.20 cm (comp.)
Estimated Height of Original Seal:	NA	Estimated Diameter of Original Seal:	1.00 cm
Number of Impressions:	2	Quality of Impressions:	Poor

Completeness of Image: Segment of middle of design survives along its complete length

DESCRIPTION OF SEAL AS IMPRESSED IMAGE

Hero faces right, arms bent (only left arm fully preserved), and holds two rampant winged bull creatures by upper foreleg (contact preserved only at right).

Each creature moves toward hero but turns its head away from him. Holds upper foreleg slightly bent, and extends it upward toward hero's head; lower foreleg is bent and held in front of its body.

Hero wears garment of uncertain type; rounded coiffure rests at back of his neck.

SEAL APPLICATION (SEE *APPENDIX ONE: CONCORDANCE OF SEALS TO TABLETS IN VOLUME I*)

PFS 1467 occurs on the reverse (inverted) and right edge of PF 1586. The partial rolling on the reverse displays the hero in the center. The partial rolling on the right edge preserves only the wings of the two creatures. The seal clearly was applied before the text on the reverse since several cuneiform wedges cut into the top of the impression. PF 1586 is dated 504/503(?) B.C.

BIBLIOGRAPHY

Garrison 1988, pp. 271–73.

Cat.No. 13   PFS 841

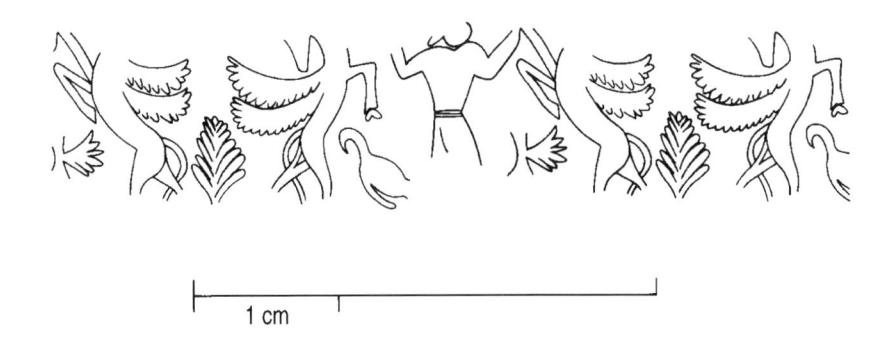

Seal Type:	Cylinder	Photograph:	Pl. 8c
Earliest Dated Application:	501/500 B.C.	Typology and Style:	I-A.2 — Mixed Styles I
Preserved Height of Image:	1.30 cm (incomp.)	Preserved Length of Image:	3.20 cm (comp.)
Estimated Height of Original Seal:	NA	Estimated Diameter of Original Seal:	1.00 cm
Number of Impressions:	1	Quality of Impression:	Good

Completeness of Image: Large segment of middle of design survives along its complete length

DESCRIPTION OF SEAL AS IMPRESSED IMAGE

Hero faces left, arms bent, and holds two rampant winged bull creatures (head of creature to right is not preserved) by upper foreleg (contact preserved only at right).

Creature to left moves toward hero but turns its head away from him. Creature holds lower foreleg bent in front of its body; long tail curves down behind its rear hind leg. Creature to right moves toward hero. Creature holds upper foreleg straight and extends it upward toward hero's head; lower foreleg is bent and held in front of its body; long tail curves down behind its rear hind leg.

Hero wears double-belted Assyrian garment that leaves forward leg exposed. Pointed beard rests over hero's right shoulder; large rounded coiffure rests at back of neck.

Each bull creature has two wings indicated, both extended horizontally outward from its back.

In lower field between hero and creature to left is long-necked bird of uncertain type, apparently in flight moving left. In lower field between hero and creature to right is another bird of uncertain type, with large tail and wings spread, in flight moving left.

Plant is in terminal field.

COMMENTARY

The tails of the bull creatures, weaving behind the legs, define a notable calligraphic feature of this image. The style is a combination of the Modeled Style (the body of the hero) and the Fortification Style (animal forms).

For comparative illustrations including PFS 841, see pls. 227e (birds), 231e (feet of animals and creatures), and 260e (various plants).

SEAL APPLICATION (SEE *APPENDIX ONE: CONCORDANCE OF SEALS TO TABLETS IN VOLUME I*)

PFS 841 occurs on the reverse of PF 644. The rolling preserves the entire length of the seal design and displays the creature to the right of the hero and the bush in the terminal field in the center. PF 644 is dated 501/500 B.C.

BIBLIOGRAPHY

Garrison 1988, pp. 249–52.

PFS 1550   Cat.No. 14

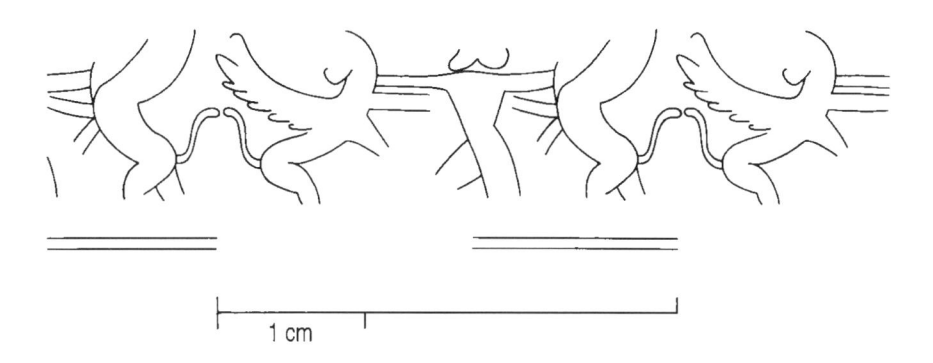

Seal Type:	Cylinder	Photograph:	Pl. 9a
Earliest Dated Application:	494/493 B.C.	Typology and Style:	I-A.2 — Modeled Style
Preserved Height of Image:	1.50 cm (incomp.)	Preserved Length of Image:	3.20 cm (comp.)
Estimated Height of Original Seal:	1.70 cm	Estimated Diameter of Original Seal:	1.00 cm
Number of Impressions:	1	Quality of Impression:	Poor

Completeness of Image: Large segment of middle and bottom of design survives along its complete length

DESCRIPTION OF SEAL AS IMPRESSED IMAGE

Hero faces left, arms straight and horizontal, and holds two rampant winged bull creatures by throat. Hero stands in vigorous striding pose, with forward leg bent.

Each creature moves toward hero but turns its head away from him. Holds upper foreleg straight, and extends it toward hero's chest; lower foreleg is straight and extended diagonally downward; creatures' tails curve upward.

Hero wears Assyrian garment that leaves forward leg exposed. Rounded beard rests over hero's right shoulder; rounded coiffure is at back of neck.

Portion of line border is preserved at bottom of design under hero and creature to right.

COMMENTARY

The overall spirit of the design of PFS 1550 is very similar to PFS 120 (Cat.No. 49), rendered in the Fortification Style.

For comparative illustrations including PFS 1550, see pl. 192h (rounded coiffures).

SEAL APPLICATION (SEE *APPENDIX ONE: CONCORDANCE OF SEALS TO TABLETS IN VOLUME I*)

PFS 1550 occurs on the reverse of PF 1769. The rolling preserves the entire length of the seal design and displays the two creatures in the center. PF 1769 is dated 494/493 B.C.

BIBLIOGRAPHY

Garrison 1988, pp. 213–14.

I-A.3. WINGED HUMAN-FACED/HUMAN-HEADED BULL CREATURES

Cat.No. 15   PFS 18

Seal Type:	Cylinder	Photographs:	Pl. 9c–d
Earliest Dated Application:	501 B.C.	Typology and Style:	I-A.3 — Fortification Style
Preserved Height of Image:	1.70 cm (incomp.)	Preserved Length of Image:	2.70 cm (comp.)
Estimated Height of Original Seal:	1.80 cm	Estimated Diameter of Original Seal:	0.90 cm
Number of Impressions:	19	Quality of Impressions:	Fair

Completeness of Image: Complete except for upper edge

DESCRIPTION OF SEAL AS IMPRESSED IMAGE

Hero faces left, in vigorous striding pose, arms bent, and holds two rampant winged human-headed creatures by upper foreleg.

Creature at left holds upper foreleg straight and extends it upward toward hero's head; lower foreleg is bent and held in front of its body. Creature raises forward hind leg as if to step on hero's forward foot; tail curves down and between its hind legs. Creature at right holds upper foreleg straight and extends it upward toward hero's head; lower foreleg is slightly curved and held downward in front of its body; tail curls sharply upward.

Hero wears double-belted baggy trousers; folds are indicated along forward leg. Hero perhaps wears domed headdress. Long pointed beard rests along hero's right shoulder; round coiffure is at back of neck.

Human head of each creature has short pointed beard. Rounded coiffure rests at back of neck of creature at left. Creature at right appears to have short-cropped coiffure and is ithyphallic.

Edge of seal is preserved at bottom of design under creatures.

COMMENTARY

Hallock identifies this seal as the personal seal of Mirayauda, a supplier of grain and flour. Koch (1990) notes that Mirayauda uses PFS 18 in years 21–23. She also notes that PFS 24 (Cat.No. 298) occurs with the personal name Mirayauda (who holds the office of *tumara*) at Umpura. It is unclear whether she considers him the same individual who uses PFS 18 (cf. Koch 1990, p. 138 and chart on p. 294). The attribution of PFS 18 to a Mirayauda is assured based upon Q texts protocol.

See Garrison 1988 for the artist and related seals. The style is elongated and flowing; the poses of the creatures and the placement of their tails adds to the pleasing calligraphic quality of the engraving.

For comparative illustrations including PFS 18, see pls. 184a (trousers), 210d (heroic attitudes of control encounter), and 233a (ithyphallic animals/creatures).

SEAL APPLICATION (SEE *APPENDIX ONE: CONCORDANCE OF SEALS TO TABLETS IN VOLUME I*)

PFS 18 occurs only on the left edge of tablets. Some applications show distortion. No application of the seal preserves the entire length of the seal design. Of the total nineteen partial rollings, one displays the hero in the center; five preserve only the hero and the creature to left; three preserve only the hero and the creature to right; three display the creature to the left of the hero in the center; seven preserve only the winged creatures. PF 1575 is the earliest dated tablet with PFS 18 and is dated 501 B.C.

BIBLIOGRAPHY

Garrison 1988, pp. 341–43, 345; Hallock 1985, p. 598; Koch 1986, pp. 141–42; Koch 1990, pp. 129 (n. 569), 138, 293–94; Root 1998, p. 275.

PFS 38   Cat.No. 16

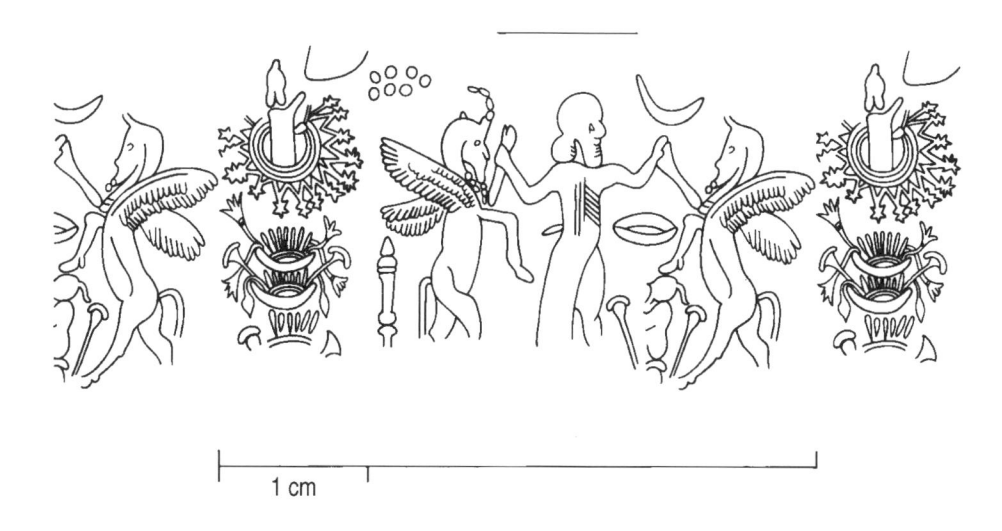

1 cm

Seal Type:	Cylinder	Photographs:	Pls. 10a–b, 11a–b
Earliest Dated Application:	501/500 B.C.	Typology and Style:	I-A.3 — Modeled Style
Preserved Height of Image:	2.40 cm (incomp.)	Preserved Length of Image:	4.00 cm (comp.)
Estimated Height of Original Seal:	NA	Estimated Diameter of Original Seal:	1.30 cm
Number of Impressions:	Minimum of 50		

Quality of Impressions: Varies from extremely poor to good, but a few preserve excellent detail

Completeness of Image: Almost complete except for upper edge and lower edge

DESCRIPTION OF SEAL AS IMPRESSED IMAGE

Hero faces right, arms bent, and holds two rampant winged human-faced bull creatures by upper foreleg.

Each creature holds upper foreleg straight and extends it upward toward hero's head; lower foreleg is bent and held in front of its body. Tail of creature at left bends down sharply; that of creature at right curves downward.

Hero wears Assyrian garment that leaves forward leg exposed; garment shows vertical and diagonal detailing on torso; sheath projects from back of hero's waist. Squared beard with horizontal striations rests over hero's left shoulder; rounded coiffure with horizontal striations is at back of neck.

On each creature two wings are depicted, lower extending diagonally downward from upper. On creature to left, three rows of feathers are indicated on upper wing, two on lower; on creature at right, two rows of feathers are indicated on upper wing, one on lower. Each creature's human face has long squared beard terminating in beaded segments over its chest. Creature to left has segmented horn that curves back from front of its head; small pointed ear is at top of its head. Creature to right has thin curved horn (only partially preserved) that emerges from front of its head.

Rhomb is in middle field between hero and creature to right; crescent is in upper field above rhomb.

Below rhomb are faint traces of another design feature, apparently a figure facing left with arms bent up to place a finger to his mouth. This figure, apparently nude, wears a pigtail and sits on a papyrus bud placed between tall papyrus stalks.

Above wings of creature to left, in terminal field, is group of seven dots arranged in two horizontal lines of three dots with seventh dot in front at right. Behind this same creature is segmented vertical object terminating in point. Also in terminal field is elaborate floral element consisting of two superimposed bowls with vegetal sprays of lotus blossoms and buds and papyrus blossoms; below this are indications of third bowl also with floral spray. Over this floral element floats figure emerging from nimbus of stars. Figure in nimbus faces right and extends upper arm diagonally upward in front of face; lower arm is held down near waist; figure appears to wear a robe and a conical headdress with knob. Figure appears likely to be beardless with large rounded chin; narrow rounded coiffure rests at back of neck. Large chip or leaf symbol appears between this figure and group of seven dots.

Portion of edge of seal is preserved at top of design above hero.

COMMENTARY

The seal is a personal seal of Irtašduna, wife of Darius I, known to Herodotus (VII.69.2) as Artystone, daughter of Cyrus and favorite wife of Darius. She uses the seal to draw royal provisions (J texts) and to ratify letters (T texts).[6]

The seal is quite large and is one of the most elaborate in the entire PFS corpus of seal designs. The design has many Assyrianizing features, including the seven dots of the Pleiades, the rhomb, the figure in the nimbus, and the elaborate floral element as terminal.[7] The detailing of the hero's garment is, however, unusual and finds no ready parallels in Neo-Assyrian seals. The soft puffy treatment of creatures' wings can be seen on designs from the PFS corpus; see, for example, PFS 113* (Cat.No. 19). The seal is probably Assyrianizing rather than Assyrian.

The small, apparently nude, figure in the lower field between the hero and the creature to the right is very poorly preserved. Previous drawings of the seal (Garrison 1991) suggested a frontal nude figure, but further examination of the tablets indicates a figure sitting on a papyrus bud, presumably an Egyptianizing Infant Horus figure.[8] (Here, the pigtail is shown at the back rather than side of the head for the sake of visibility.) The image of the Infant Horus in a papyrus thicket relates to Egyptian representations of the Horus cycle (Badawy 1963). In the Neo-Assyrian glyptic tradition Egyptianizing images of the Infant Horus more commonly show him on the lotus plant (e.g., Parker 1962, p. 39, fig. 11, pl. 22/4). The figure surrounded by a nimbus is often associated with Ištar in Assyria, with Anahita in Iran.[9] We thus suggest that it may be a female figure. The vertical object in the terminal field may be a censer, but it may conceivably be a phallic symbol (e.g., Black and Green 1992, p. 152, fig. 124). For other seals herein that have a rhomb in the design, see PFS 944 (Cat.No. 129) and PFS 1026 (Cat.No. 156). The large number of symbols in the terminal field is rare in the hero corpus; compare PFS 1236 (Cat.No. 159) and PFS 9* (Cat.No. 288). See Root 1990b and Garrison 1991 for comments on style and iconography.

For comparative illustrations including PFS 38, see pls. 176c (Assyrian garments with detailing preserved), 196a (coiffures of unusual types), 204e (arm positions of heroic control), 248e (deity emergent from nimbus of stars), 249f (rhombs), 250b (crescents), 254b (various devices and symbols), 256e (stylized floral elements), 260a (papyrus plants), 269a (terminal field motifs other than inscriptions), 272a (dense compositions), and 284e (personal seals of women).

SEAL APPLICATION (SEE *APPENDIX ONE: CONCORDANCE OF SEALS TO TABLETS IN VOLUME I*)

As is typical of seals of high-ranking individuals, PFS 38 always occurs alone on tablets that it seals. In the case of PFS 38 the seal is always applied on three or four different sealing surfaces of each tablet. The minimum fifty impressions in fact come from only eleven tablets. The reverse and upper edges often carry multiple applications of the seal. On the reverse, these applications are oriented along the horizontal axis of the seal, but there is much over-rolling of one impression by another. On the reverse of PF 730, PF 733–734, PF 1836–1839, and PF

---

6. On seven tablets bearing PFS 38, letters mandate the informing of named estate agents, for example, Dutukka and Šalamana, to execute orders made directly by Irtašduna. On the West Semitic Šalamana, see Delaunay 1976, pp. 25–26.
7. For example, Pleiades (Carter 1994, p. 66; Collon 1987, nos. 344–46, 573, 618, 739, 804, 856, 883; Herbordt 1992, pls. 2, no. 1; 4, nos. 1, 3; 5, no. 1; 6, nos. 1, 6, 7; etc.); rhomb (Bregstein 1993, no. 125, p. 519; Collon 1987, nos. 344–45, 573, 823, 881, probably Neo-Babylonian; Herbordt 1992, pls. 2, nos. 1, 8–9; 4, nos. 1, 5, 12; 5, nos. 1, 6; 6, nos. 1, 3; etc.); figure surrounded by nimbus (Herbordt 1992, pls. 1, nos. 5, 7, 9; 14, no. 24); Infant Horus in papyrus thicket (Herbordt 1992, pl. 14, nos. 14–16); vegetal device with figure in winged disk above it (Collon 1987, no. 358; Herbordt 1992, pl. 3, no. 1, after Parker 1955, p. 114, fig. 5, pl. 23 [1], occurring on a tablet dated to 650 B.C.).
8. Compare Herbordt 1992, pl. 14, nos. 14–16, impressions of stamp seals from Nimrud and Nineveh.
9. For Assyrian seals, see, for example, Herbordt 1992, pls. 1, nos. 5, 7, 9; 14, no. 24. For an Achaemenid example, see the seal from Gorgippa (Collon 1987, no. 432).

2035 the seal is inverted. The applications on the left edge tend to be much more carefully executed. The applications of PFS 38 are often very difficult to read, owing to the short, fragmentary nature of many of the impressions, distortions, and the lightness of pressure with which the seal has been applied. For these reasons we can provide only a count of the minimum number of seal applications (fifty). Distortion often occurs on the left edge and right edge of impressions.

Of the minimum fifty impressions, seven are too poorly preserved for analysis. Of the remaining forty-three applications, only three preserve at least one complete turn of the seal preserving the entire length of the seal design. All three complete rollings of the seal carefully keep the basic figural design of the heroic encounter intact, with full or partial rollings of the floral element and figure in the nimbus in the terminal field at one or both vertical edges of the impression. Of these three complete applications, one displays the hero in the center (elements in the terminal field frame the heroic encounter on both edges); one displays the hero and the creature to the left in the center (elements in the terminal field only at the left of the impression); one displays the hero and the creature to the right in the center (elements in the terminal field only at the right of the impression). Of the forty partial rollings, eight display the hero in the center; two display the hero and the creature to the left in the center; one preserves only the hero and the creature to left; eight display the creature to the left of the hero in the center; one preserves only the creature to the left of the hero; five preserve only the hero and the creature to right; three display the creature to the right of the hero in the center; two preserve only the creature to the right of the hero; one displays the creature to the left of the hero and the elements in the terminal field in the center; two display the creature to the right of the hero and the elements in the terminal field in the center; one preserves only the elements in the terminal field and the creature to the left of the hero; one preserves only the creature to the right of the hero and the elements in the terminal field; one displays the elements in the terminal field in the center; three preserve only isolated segments of the floral element in the terminal field; one preserves only the censer(?).

On the reverse of PF 733–734, PF 1836–1839, and PF 2035 the seal has clearly been applied before the text since several cuneiform wedges cut into the bottom of the impression. PF 1836 is the earliest dated tablet with PFS 38 and is dated 501/500 B.C.

BIBLIOGRAPHY

Aperghis 1999, p. 164; Brosius 1996, pp. 27–29, 50, 97, 125–27, 129, 156, 181–82; Garrison 1988, pp. 203–07, 476–77, 480, 520; Garrison 1991, pp. 7–10, 20, figs. 6–7; Garrison 1996b, pp. 25, 30; Garrison 1998, p. 121, (n. 16); Garrison in press; Garrison and Root 1996, p. 4; Hallock 1977, p. 128; Hallock 1978, pp. 110, 113, 121; Hallock 1985, p. 608; Hinz 1971, pp. 298–99; Koch 1992, pp. 235–38; Root 1990b, p. 37; Root 1999a, p. 163.

Cat.No. 17 PFS 1684

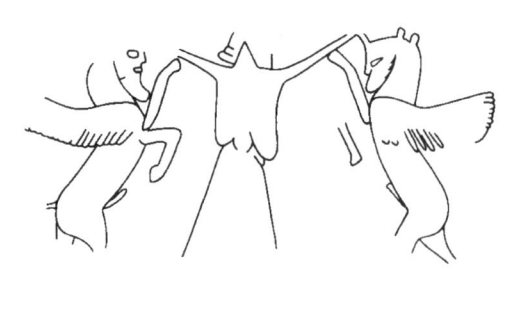

Seal Type:	Cylinder	Photograph:	Pl. 12a
Earliest Dated Application:	494 B.C.	Typology and Style:	I-A.3 — Court Style
Preserved Height of Image:	1.60 cm (incomp.)	Preserved Length of Image:	3.20 cm (incomp.)
Estimated Height of Original Seal:	NA	Estimated Diameter of Original Seal:	NA
Number of Impressions:	1	Quality of Impression:	Fair

Completeness of Image: Large segment of middle of design survives

Description of Seal as Impressed Image

Hero faces right, arms straight at diagonal above shoulder level, and holds two rampant winged human-faced bull creatures by horn (preserved only at right).

Each creature holds upper foreleg slightly bent and extends it upward to place hoof on hero's arm; lower foreleg is bent and held in front of its body. Slender tail (only partially preserved) of creature to left curves upward.

Hero wears Persian court robe with indication of belt end; sleeves are pushed up to reveal arms. Squared beard rests over hero's left shoulder; flattened coiffure with horizontal striations is at back of neck.

Creature to left has long squared beard that curls upward at its end. Creature to right has rounded beard that rests on its chest; thin curved horn (only partially preserved) emerges from front of its head; two short appendages emerging from back of its head may be ears. Each creature is ithyphallic.

Commentary

Based on Q texts protocol, PFS 1684 should belong to Šauša, who in year 28.2 (494 B.C.) received flour rations on his way to the king under the authority (*halmi*) of Bakabana. PF 1324 preserves the only occurrence of the name Šauša in the PF texts.

This large seal is a version (early?) of the Court Style where there occurs little surface detailing. See Garrison 1988, 1991, and 1996a for this important artist. Hallock mistakenly identifies the impression of PFS 1684 as collating with PFS 7* (Cat.No. 4). This is an understandable error since the seals are by the same artist.

For comparative illustrations including PFS 1684, see pls. 195h (coiffures of distinctive types/sub-types), 235h (human-headed/human-faced creatures), and 289f (personal seals of various receivers).

Seal Application (see *Appendix One: Concordance of Seals to Tablets in Volume I*)

PFS 1684 occurs on the reverse of PF 1324. The partial rolling carefully displays the hero in the center. The seal clearly was applied before the text since several cuneiform wedges cut into the bottom of the impression. PF 1324 is dated 494 B.C.

Bibliography

Garrison 1988, pp. 394–401; Garrison 1991, p. 14; Garrison 1996a, pp. 43–44, figs. 16–17; Garrison and Root 1996, p. 11.

PFS 1641   Cat.No. 18

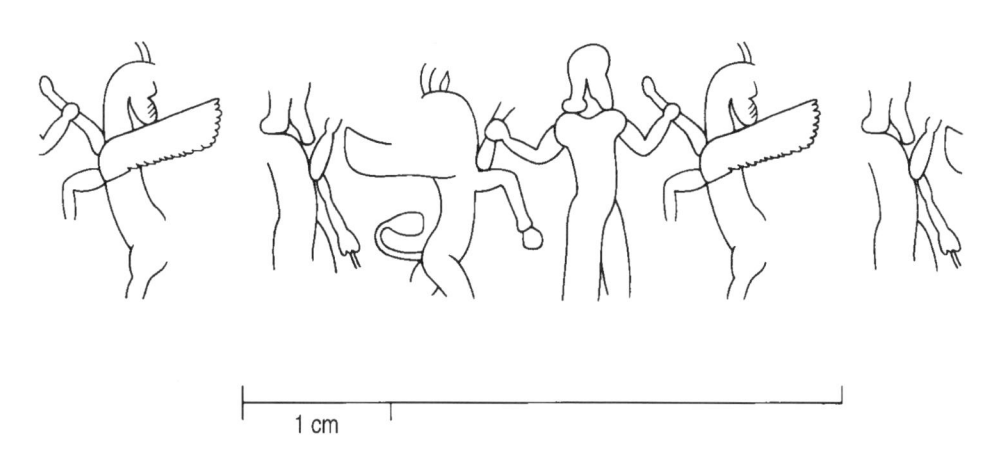

Seal Type:	Cylinder	Photograph:	Pl. 12c
Earliest Dated Application:	509/508 B.C.	Typology and Style:	I-A.3 — Modeled Style
Preserved Height of Image:	1.70 cm (incomp.)	Preserved Length of Image:	4.00 cm (comp.)
Estimated Height of Original Seal:	1.90 cm	Estimated Diameter of Original Seal:	1.30 cm
Number of Impressions:	1	Quality of Impression:	Fair

Completeness of Image: Large segment of middle of design survives along its complete length

DESCRIPTION OF SEAL AS IMPRESSED IMAGE

Hero faces right, arms bent, and holds two rampant winged human-faced bull creatures by upper foreleg.

Each creature moves toward hero but turns its head away from him. Holds upper foreleg straight, and extends it upward toward hero's head; lower foreleg is bent and held in front of its body. Tail of creature to left curves upward with large tufted termination.

Hero wears Assyrian garment that leaves forward leg exposed. Rounded beard rests over hero's left shoulder; flattened coiffure is at back of neck.

Creature to right has thick rounded beard with horizontal striations that rests over its wing. Each creature has curved horn (only partially preserved) that emerges from front of its head. Creature to left also has pointed ear at top of its head.

To left of heroic encounter, male figure seen in profile faces right and raises one arm upward toward wing of creature to left of hero with hand apparently held with flat palm parallel to picture plane; other arm is straight and held downward in front of his body with hand holding object with handle or stem. Male figure wears Assyrian garment that leaves forward leg exposed. Long squared beard rests over his chest; flattened coiffure is at back of neck.

COMMENTARY

This is a large and well-executed design. The pose of the figure in the terminal field recalls worshipers and attendants on Neo-Assyrian and Neo-Babylonian worship scenes, many of whom hold buckets.[10] Perhaps the figure in PFS 1641 also holds a bucket; compare PFS 68 (II) and PFS 166 (II). A more likely alternative for PFS 1641 would be a lotus blossom held by the stem and drooping downward (e.g., Collon 1987, no. 347). Either accoutrement supports the identification of the figure as a worshiper/cult attendant (see Paley 1986, pp. 215–16, illustrations 11, 13; van Loon 1986). Interestingly, the figure is closely integrated into the formal dynamic of the heroic encounter to the extent that the bull creatures with heads turned back appear to acknowledge his presence.

For comparative illustrations including PFS 1641, see pl. 238f (subsidiary human/human-creature figures in encounter images).

---

10. For example, Collon 1987, nos. 341, 351, 357, 379, 812, 824;
    Herbordt 1992, pls. 1, no. 5; 2, no. 2; 21, no. 2; 26, no. 1.

SEAL APPLICATION (SEE *APPENDIX ONE: CONCORDANCE OF SEALS TO TABLETS IN VOLUME I*)

PFS 1641 occurs on the reverse of PF 2087. The upper edge of the tablet is damaged. No other seal is preserved on the tablet. The seal is rolled along the longitudinal axis of the tablet. The rolling preserves the entire length of the seal design and displays the figure in the terminal field and the creature to the left of the hero in the center. The seal was clearly applied before the text since several cuneiform wedges cut into the right edge of the impression. PF 2087 is dated 509/508 B.C.

BIBLIOGRAPHY

Garrison 1988, pp. 207–10.

Cat.No. 19   PFS 113* = PTS 4*

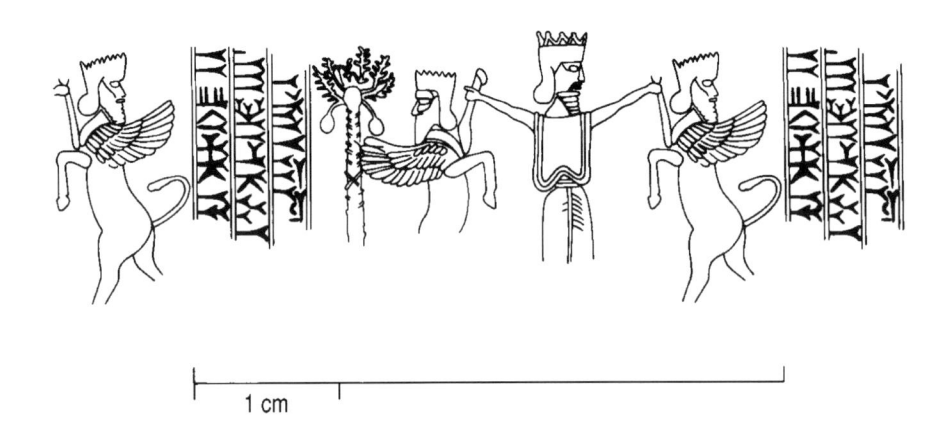

Seal Type:	Cylinder, Inscribed	Photographs:	Pl. 13a–d
Earliest Dated Application:	495/494 B.C.	Typology and Style:	I-A.3 — Court Style
Languages of Inscription:	Old Persian, Elamite, and Babylonian		
Preserved Height of Image:	1.70 cm (incomp.)	Preserved Length of Image:	3.90 cm (comp.)
Estimated Height of Original Seal:	NA	Estimated Diameter of Original Seal:	1.20 cm
Number of Impressions:	6	Quality of Impressions:	Many preserve excellent detail

Completeness of Image: Large segment of middle of design survives along its complete length

DESCRIPTION OF SEAL AS IMPRESSED IMAGE

Hero faces right, arms straight at diagonal above shoulder level, and holds two rampant winged human-headed bull creatures by upper foreleg.

Each creature moves toward hero but turns its head away from him. Each creature holds upper foreleg straight and extends it upward in front of its head; lower foreleg is bent and held in front of its body. Tail of creature at right curls upward with tufted termination.

Hero wears belted Persian court robe with sleeves pushed up to reveal hero's bare arms; gathered folds of sleeves are indicated, as are central pleat and diagonal folds of lower part of garment. Hero wears five-pointed dentate Persian crown. Squared beard in graduated horizontal segments rests over hero's left shoulder; down-turned mustache is also indicated; rounded coiffure rests at back of neck.

Creature at left has long blunt-pointed beard. Beard of creature at right is squared with vestiges of graduated segments. Each creature has rounded coiffure at back of its neck. Each creature wears Persian crown with serrated top. Wing of each creature has three rows of feathers indicated.

Behind creature at left in terminal field is date palm with bulbous fruit clusters and imbricate markings on the trunk. To left of date palm, large paneled inscription occupies remainder of terminal field.

INSCRIPTION

Old Persian, Elamite, and Babylonian

Line
1. [a-d]a-ma : da-⌈a-⌉[ra-ya-va-u-ša…]
2. [v.]⌈ú⌉ v.Da-ri-a-⌈ma-⌉[u-iš…]
3. [ana-]⌈ku⌉ ᵐDa-ri(!)-a-[iá-muš…]

Translation   I (am) Darius …

The inscription on PFS 113* has been known for some time and was published, with previous bibliography, by Schmitt (1981).

Known as SDg, the inscription is the standard trilingual (Old Persian, Elamite, and Babylonian) inscription of Darius I on seals. The inscription is oriented along the vertical axis of the seal, separated by case lines, and enclosed in a panel. It reads (from top to bottom): Old Persian, Elamite, and Babylonian. As noted by Hallock via Schmitt, the ri-sign in both the Elamite and Akkadian versions lacks a third vertical wedge. We are able to see slightly more of the beginning of the Old Persian and Elamite versions than was apparent to Hallock and Schmitt, but our reading simply confirms what they had restored. The only other inscribed seals with images of heroic encounter that show the combination of case lines enclosed in a panel and orientation along the vertical axis of the seal are PFS 64* (Cat.No. 173), PFS 1* (Cat.No. 182), PFS 526* (Cat.No. 216), and the royal name seal PFS 7* (Cat.No. 4).

COMMENTARY

This very large seal also occurs on the Treasury tablets (= PTS 4*), used, as on the PF tablets, by Baradkama, treasurer at Persepolis during 490–479 B.C. The evidence from both archives shows that he keeps this seal for some fifteen years, enjoying apparently exclusive use of it as an office seal under both Darius and Xerxes.

The seal is a masterpiece of glyptic art and an outstanding example of the fully developed Court Style; the amount of detailing in the scene is striking even for the Court Style. See Garrison 1988 and 1996a for the artist, a leading innovator in the Court Style.

For comparative illustrations including PFS 113*, see pls. 179b (Persian court robes with sleeves pushed up), 188e (Persian crowns and fluted tiaras), 191c (variously detailed beards), 220d (bulls and bull creatures), 234e (human-headed/human-faced creatures), 259b (date palms), 261d (paneled inscriptions with vertical case lines), 265h (trilingual [royal name] inscriptions), and 281g (office seals).

SEAL APPLICATION (SEE APPENDIX ONE: CONCORDANCE OF SEALS TO TABLETS IN VOLUME I)

As is typical of seals of important offices and officials, PFS 113* occurs alone on tablets, often on multiple surfaces (e.g., three surfaces of PF 879). The seal always occurs on the left edge; on PF 864 it is also on the upper edge; in PF 879 it is also on the reverse and upper edge. Impressions are carefully executed, giving preference to the upper part of the design. Of the total six impressions, five show some part of the inscription. No impression preserves the entire figural design. Of the six partial impressions, one displays the inscription in the center; one displays the date palm in the center with a full rolling of the inscription at the left of the impression; one displays the creature to the left of the hero in the center with a full rolling of the inscription at the left of the impression; two display the hero in the center; one displays the hero and the creature to the left in the center. On the reverse of PF 879 the seal clearly was applied before the text since the bottom of the impression has been smoothed and several cuneiform wedges cut into the area. PF 879 is the earliest dated tablet with PFS 113* and is dated 495/494 B.C.

BIBLIOGRAPHY

Brosius 1996, pp. 149, 150 (table 6), 151; Garrison 1988, pp. 220, 227, 255, 394–401, 480; Garrison 1991, p. 27 (n. 90); Garrison 1996a, pp. 42–44; Garrison 1996b, p. 28; Garrison 2000, pp. 128–29, 130–31, 154, fig. 3, pl. 16:3; Garrison in press; Garrison and Dion 1999, p. 10; Garrison and Root 1996, pp. 14, 18; Hinz 1971, p. 262; Koch 1981, p. 242; Koch 1990, p. 235; Koch 1992, pp. 47–49, fig. 22; Root 1979, p. 121; Root 1997, p. 233; Schmidt 1957, p. 20, pl. 4; Schmitt 1981, pp. 23–24 (SDg).

Cat.No. 20   PFS 164*

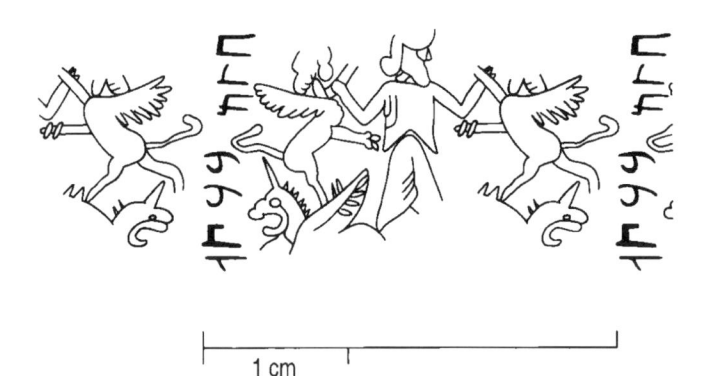

Seal Type:	Cylinder, Inscribed	Photographs:	Pl. 14a–b
Earliest Dated Application:	494 B.C.	Typology and Style:	I-A.3 — Mixed Styles II
Language of Inscription:	Aramaic		
Preserved Height of Image:	1.60 cm (incomp.)	Preserved Length of Image:	2.90 cm (comp.)
Estimated Height of Original Seal:	NA	Estimated Diameter of Original Seal:	0.90 cm
Number of Impressions:	4	Quality of Impressions:	Fair

Completeness of Image: Large segment of design preserved along its complete length

DESCRIPTION OF SEAL AS IMPRESSED IMAGE

Hero faces right in striding pose, arms bent, and holds two rampant winged human-headed bull creatures by upper foreleg. Hero stands on hindquarters of two addorsed couchant(?) winged horned lion creatures.

Each pedestal creature has two spiked projections (feathers?) extending upward from its wing; mane is rendered by crisp serrated edge along contour of its neck (pedestal creature to right has only two mane serrations preserved). Long pointed horn emerges from front of each pedestal creature's head; mouth is open in roar.

Each human-headed creature moves toward hero but turns its head away from him. Creature to left holds upper foreleg (only partially preserved) straight and extends it upward toward hero's head; lower foreleg is straight and extended toward hero's waist. Creature has only one hind leg indicated, placed on left pedestal creature's wing. Creature to right holds upper foreleg (only partially preserved) straight and extends it upward toward hero's head; lower foreleg is straight and extended outward toward hero's elbow. Creature places forward hind leg on right pedestal creature's wing; rear hind leg is bent and extended back toward right pedestal creature's snout. Each creature has long crooked tail that bends upward near its end with slightly tufted termination.

Hero wears Persian court robe with sleeves pushed up to reveal hero's bare arms; gathered folds of sleeves indicated on right side of hero's torso, as are central pleat and diagonal folds of lower part of garment. Long rounded beard crosses over hero's left shoulder; flattened coiffure curls upward at back of neck.

Creature to left has rounded striated beard resting on its wing; rounded coiffure is at back of head. Creature to right has rounded coiffure at back of its neck. Creature to right has squared striated beard resting on its wing; narrow rounded coiffure is at back of its neck.

Single line inscription is in terminal field.

INSCRIPTION

Aramaic

    Line   1.   ḤTM RRTx[...]

    Translation   Seal of PN...

There is one line to the inscription, oriented along the vertical axis of the seal. The first word is clear. The second word, presumably a PN, is very difficult to read in the impressions. The apparent variation in what we are reading as the T letter may be due to the legibility of the inscription. In the absence of supporting textual evidence, vocalization of the PN is difficult.

Commentary

Dusinberre (1997b, p. 107 [n. 59]) suggests that PFS 164* replaces PFS 524 (Cat.No. 2).

Pedestal creatures are not common, occurring definitively on only seven hero seals in the PFS corpus: PFS 31 (Cat.No. 172), PFS 36* (Cat.No. 5), PFS 396 (Cat.No. 178), PFS 523* (Cat.No. 209), PFS 524 (Cat.No. 2), and PFS 931* (Cat.No. 270) in addition to PFS 164*. The use of pedestal creatures is documented on several Court Style seals from the Treasury archive, for example, PTS 1*, PTS 3*, and PTS 6*. See Dusinberre 1997b for the significance of the pedestal creatures as an elite motif in early Achaemenid glyptic.

The style is a mix of Court Style and Fortification Style. See the commentary for PFS 524 (Cat.No. 2), which shows a similar composition and style and probably is from the same artist.

For comparative illustrations including PFS 164*, see pls. 204g (arm positions of heroic control), 216e (hero standing atop pedestal figure[s] or other supporting element), 264f (inscriptions without panels or case lines), and 272c (dense compositions).

Seal Application (see *Appendix One: Concordance of Seals to Tablets in Volume I*)

PFS 164* occurs on the upper edge and left edge of PF 969 and PF 970; no other seal appears on these tablets. Impressions generally exhibit some distortion in their lower sections. Impressions tend to be long, and all four rollings preserve the entire length of the seal design. Of these four applications, one displays the creature to the left of the hero and the inscription in the center; one displays the hero in the center; one displays the hero and the creature to left in the center; one displays the hero and the creature to right in the center. PF 969 is the earliest dated tablet with PFS 164* and is dated 494 B.C.

Bibliography

Brosius 1996, pp. 158 (table 9), 160; Dusinberre 1997b, pp. 106–07, 113, 124 (n. 59), figs. 5–6; Garrison 1988, pp. 272–73, 286, 378–80, 483; Garrison 1998, p. 120 (n. 12); Garrison and Dion 1999, p. 10.

PFS 1465   Cat.No. 21

Seal Type:	Cylinder	Photograph:	Pl. 14d
Earliest Dated Application:	507/506 B.C.	Typology and Style:	I-A.3 — Diverse Styles
Preserved Height of Image:	1.20 cm (incomp.)	Preserved Length of Image:	3.30 cm (comp.)
Estimated Height of Original Seal:	NA	Estimated Diameter of Original Seal:	1.10 cm
Number of Impressions:	3	Quality of Impressions:	Fair

Completeness of Image: Segment of middle of design survives along its complete length

Description of Seal as Impressed Image

Hero faces left, arms straight, and holds two rampant winged human-faced bull creatures by upper foreleg.

Each creature moves toward hero but turns its head away from him. Each creature holds upper foreleg straight and extends it diagonally upward. Creature to left holds lower foreleg bent and extends it downward in front of its body. Creature to right holds lower foreleg slightly bent and extends it downward toward hero's waist.

Hero wears belted garment of uncertain type. Rounded beard rests over hero's right shoulder; rounded coiffure curls slightly upward at back of neck. Diagonal striations at top of hero's head perhaps indicate decorated domed headdress.

Each creature has rounded beard that rests over its wing; curved horn (only partially preserved) emerges from front of its head; short ear is at back of head.

COMMENTARY

The design shows extensive use of the cutting wheel, especially in the hero's head and beard. The human body seems to be a thickened version of the Fortification Style, but the long cylindrical neck and the shape of the jaw are anomalous. The creature forms, although only partially preserved, are carefully executed; the details of the hooves and forelegs place the design close to the Court Style. The seal thus represents a very particular and unusual hybrid of Persepolitan styles.

For comparative illustrations including PFS 1465, see pl. 195f (coiffures of distinctive types/sub-types).

SEAL APPLICATION (SEE *APPENDIX ONE: CONCORDANCE OF SEALS TO TABLETS IN VOLUME I*)

PFS 1465 occurs on the reverse, upper edge, and left edge of PF 1580. No other seal is used on the tablet. The partial rollings on the upper edge and left edge display the hero in the center. The partial rolling on the reverse displays the creature to the left of the hero in the center. On the reverse the seal clearly was applied before the text since several cuneiform wedges cut into the top of the impression. PF 1580 is dated 507/506 B.C.

BIBLIOGRAPHY

Garrison 1988, pp. 375, 461–62.

I-A.4. LIONS

Cat.No. 22   PFS 16*

Seal Type:	Cylinder, Inscribed	Photographs:	Pl. 15a–f
Earliest Dated Application:	500 B.C.	Typology and Style:	I-A.4 — Modeled Style
Language of Inscription:	Aramaic		
Preserved Height of Image:	1.90 cm (incomp.)	Preserved Length of Image:	3.10 cm (comp.)
Estimated Height of Original Seal:	2.10 cm	Estimated Diameter of Original Seal:	1.00 cm
Number of Impressions:	43	Quality of Impressions:	Many preserve excellent detail

Completeness of Image: Almost complete except for upper edge

DESCRIPTION OF SEAL AS IMPRESSED IMAGE

Hero faces left, arms straight, and holds two rampant lions by throat.

Each lion holds one foreleg straight and places upturned paw at hero's chest; other foreleg is straight, held up and away from its body, toes splayed. Lion to left places paw of forward hind leg on hero's forward foot. Lions' tails curl upward with tufted terminations.

Hero wears double-belted Assyrian garment that leaves forward leg exposed, with fringe at hem of short undergarment visible on forward leg above knee; garment has fringe on chest and three swags of fringe on lower garment. Long rounded beard rests over hero's chest; round coiffure is at back of neck.

There is much muscular detail in each lion's body; manes are rendered by crisp serrated edge along contour of neck; mouth is open in roar.

Paneled inscription is in terminal field.

INSCRIPTION

Aramaic

Line	1. ḪTM
	2. PRNK
	3. BR
	4. ʾRŠM

Translation   Seal (of) Parnaka son of Aršam

There are four lines to the inscription, oriented along the horizontal axis of the seal, separated by case lines, and enclosed in a panel. In addition to numerous occurrences in the PF texts, the name also appears in the Aramaic inscription on PFS 9* (Cat.No. 288), the earlier seal of Parnaka. Both Hallock and Bowman copied the inscription, but neither observed the first line (ḪTM); compare, however, Cameron's reading which does include the first line.

COMMENTARY

The seal is the personal seal of Parnaka, chief functionary in the Persepolis Fortification archive and the uncle of Darius the Great.[11] PF 2067 and PF 2068 state authoritatively that on the 22nd year, third month, 16th day (6 June 500 B.C.) PFS 16* replaced Parnaka's earlier seal, PFS 9* (Cat.No. 288). As with PFS 9* (Cat.No. 288), PFS 16* never occurs with any other seal.

The seal is a masterpiece of glyptic art, a technical tour de force of Modeled Style carving. The extensive and controlled use of the drill in the design produces minute details, especially on the lion bodies (e.g., dewlaps, toes, joints of the rear hind legs). The powerful iconography and Assyrianizing style of the seal have been discussed often, as has the evidence the seal yields concerning artistic patronage. For a close parallel of the decoration on the hero's lower garment, see PFS 1582 (Cat.No. 232). The careful documentation in the texts of Parnaka's adoption of this seal, the quality of the design and the perfect arrangement of the paneled inscription suggest very strongly that PFS 16* was a commissioned piece, probably cut not long before 6 June 500 B.C. when the texts note the introduction of its use.[12]

For comparative illustrations including PFS 16*, see pls. 176b (Assyrian garments with detailing preserved), 198c (feet and shoes), 202a (arm positions of heroic control), 210c (heroic attitudes of control encounter), 222a (lions and lion creatures), 230a (feet of animals and creatures), 232g (spectacular animal studies), 262a (paneled inscriptions with horizontal case lines), and 285f (personal seals of Parnaka, son of Aršam, uncle of Darius, and Chief Functionary at Persepolis).

SEAL APPLICATION (SEE *APPENDIX ONE: CONCORDANCE OF SEALS TO TABLETS IN VOLUME I*)

As is typical of seals of important officials, PFS 16* always occurs alone on tablets that it seals. Eight tablets have three or four edges sealed with PFS 16*: upper edge, right edge, and left edge (four tablets); reverse, upper edge, right edge, and left edge (three tablets); reverse, right edge, and left edge (one tablet). Ten tablets have only one or two edges sealed with PFS 16*: right edge and left edge (five tablets); only the left edge (four tablets); upper edge and left edge (one tablet). All of these texts that are sealed once or twice are letters (T texts). The seal is never applied more than once to any single surface. On all four tablets where the seal occurs on the reverse, it is inverted. Impressions of the seal tend to be carefully applied, although a few impressions do show lateral distortion.

---

11. See Briant 1996, pp. 481–86, for Parnaka and Darius.

12. We cannot agree with Vallat's suggestion that PFS 16* should not be considered a "personal" seal of Parnaka (Vallat 1997, p. 173).

Despite the large size of the seal, almost half of the rollings preserve the complete design. Of the total forty-three impressions, two impressions are too poorly preserved for analysis. Of the forty-one remaining impressions, thirty-eight show some part of the inscription. Of these thirty-eight impressions, thirty-five preserve the complete width of the inscriptional panel, which suggests that a concerted effort was made to show the full width of the inscription when possible. The three impressions that do not preserve the inscription are all partial rollings which preserve only the heroic encounter with the hero displayed in the center.

Of the forty-one analytically viable impressions, eighteen are rolled for at least one complete turn of the seal, preserving the entire length of the seal design. Of these eighteen applications, three display the inscription in the center; one displays the inscription and the lion to the left of the hero in the center; three display the inscription and the lion to the right of the hero in the center; three display the hero and the lion to the left in the center with a complete rolling of the inscription at the left of the impression; seven display the hero and the lion to the right in the center with a complete rolling of the inscription at the right of the impression; one displays the lion to the right of the hero in the center with a complete rolling of the inscription at the right of the impression.

Of the remaining twenty-three partial rollings, one displays the inscription in the center; one preserves only the inscription; one displays the inscription and the lion to the left of the hero in the center; two preserve only the inscription and the lion to the left of the hero; three display the hero in the center; one displays the hero and the lion to the left in the center with a complete rolling of the inscription at the left of the impression; two preserve only the hero and the lion to the left; five display the hero and the lion to the right in the center with a complete (two instances) or partial rolling of the inscription at the right of the impression; five display the lion to the left of the hero in the center with a complete rolling of the inscription at the left of the impression; two display the lion to the right of the hero in the center with a complete rolling of the inscription at the right of the impression.

On the reverse of PF 667, PF 668, PF 1802, and PF 1803 the seal clearly was applied before the text since several cuneiform wedges cut into the bottom of the impressions.

On the left edge of PF 1809 an Aramaic notation is written over the impression of PFS 16* (Hallock 1969, p. 495).

PF 1802, PF 2067, and PF 2068 are the earliest dated tablets with PFS 16* and are all dated 500 B.C.

BIBLIOGRAPHY

Aperghis 1999, p. 164; Balcer 1993, p. 84; Boardman 1988, pp. 35–37, no. 35a; Cameron 1948, p. 53 (n. 52); Cook 1983, p. 89; Dusinberre 1997b, p. 112, figs. 14–15; Garrison 1988, pp. 201, 204, 217–23, 238, 249, 256, 361, 380–81, 400, 452, 478–79, 493, 521–22; Garrison 1991, pp. 9–10, figs. 11–12; Garrison 1996a, p. 45, figs. 18–19; Garrison 1998, pp. 115, 130; Garrison 2000, pp. 153–54; Garrison in press; Garrison and Dion 1999, pp. 6–7, 9–10, 13, 16, fig. 4; Garrison and Root 1996, pp. 2, 18; Hallock 1977, pp. 128–29, pl. E-7; Hinz 1971, pp. 271, 302; Koch 1990, passim, but esp. pp. 224–27; Koch 1992, pp. 26, 30–31, 33, 36–40, 61, 97; Lewis 1994, pp. 29–30; Moorey 1988, pp. 35–36, fig. 35a; Root 1990a, pp. 130–31, fig. 14; Root 1991, p. 22, fig. 9; Root 1995, p. 2634, fig. 13; Root 1996b, p. 16, figs. 1–2, 8–9; Root 1997, p. 235; Root 1999a, p. 163, fig. 4, pp. 172, 174, 179; Schmitt 1983, p. 76; Stolper 1996, p. 521 (n. 26); Vallat 1997, p. 173; Young 1988, p. 85.

PFS 49   Cat.No. 23

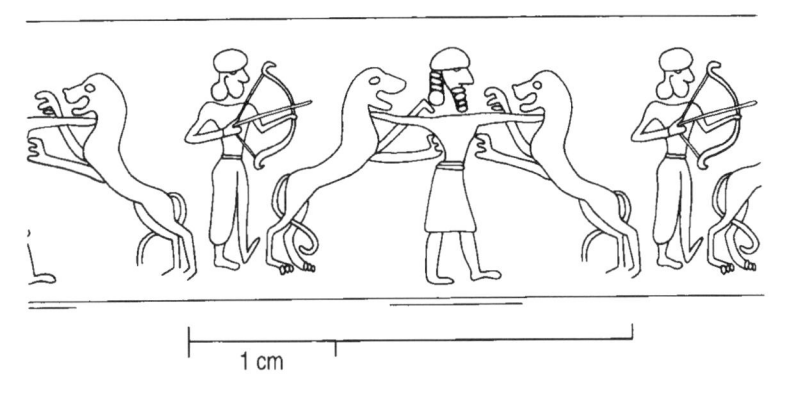

Seal Type:	Cylinder	Photographs:	Pl. 16a–c
Earliest Dated Application:	499 B.C.	Typology and Style:	I-A.4 — Fortification Style
Preserved Height of Image:	1.90 cm (comp.)	Preserved Length of Image:	3.00 cm (comp.)
Estimated Height of Original Seal:	1.90 cm	Estimated Diameter of Original Seal:	1.00 cm
Number of Impressions:	13	Quality of Impressions:	Fair

Completeness of Image: Complete

DESCRIPTION OF SEAL AS IMPRESSED IMAGE

Hero faces right, arms straight at horizontal, and holds two rampant lions by throat.

Lion to left holds upper foreleg straight and extends it upward to place paw (bent downward) at hero's head; lower foreleg is straight to place paw (toes splayed) on hero's chest; tail curves down between its hind legs with hooked termination. Lion to right holds upper foreleg straight, toes splayed, and extends it upward toward hero's head; lower foreleg is straight to place paw (toes splayed) on hero's chest; tail curves downward behind lion's hind legs.

Hero wears double-belted tunic. Rounded, segmented beard rests over hero's left shoulder; long rounded, segmented coiffure with round termination is at back of neck. Hero perhaps wears domed headdress.

Each lion has mouth open in roar.

To left of heroic encounter, archer faces right, arrow drawn in bow. Archer appears to wear belted Assyrian garment that leaves forward leg exposed and has close-shaved beard or is beardless; rounded coiffure is at back of neck. Archer perhaps wears domed headdress.

Portions of line border are preserved at bottom of design; edge of seal is preserved at top of design.

COMMENTARY

Based upon Q text protocol, PFS 49 should belong to Išbaramištima, a *barrišdama* ("elite guide"), as noted by both Koch and Lewis. The seal occurs on the reverse of Q travel rations PF 1316–1318. Rather remarkably, the text of PF 1318 actually says that "the seal of Išbaramištima was applied (to this tablet)." In year 23 he is making a trip from India to Susa with the Indian Abbatema (PF 1317–1318, PF 1556, PF 1558).

The seal is fairly large and well made. See Garrison 1988 for discussion of this important artist. The archer is an unusual addition to the scene; the seal, with others from the same workshop, has, however, several iconographic and stylistic features that tie it to the Court Style, where archers are commonly depicted (see Volume II). For a similar compositional format with an archer as secondary actor in a heroic engagement, but in a combat encounter, see PFS 1466 (Cat.No. 234). See PFS 1101 (Cat.No. 297) for somewhat related seal with a "rescuing" second hero. The archer of PFS 49 bends his left arm (rather than extending it in proper form); similarly, his left foot is flexed. These details suggest that the artist carved the archer last and had slightly less than optimal space for the figure.

For comparative illustrations including PFS 49, see pls. 191b (variously detailed beards), 193b (round coiffures), 198e (feet and shoes), 202b (arm positions of heroic control), 230d (feet of animals and creatures), 238a (subsidiary human/human-creature figures in encounter images), 246a (bows, arrows, quivers), and 288d (personal seals of elite guides [*barrišdama*]).

SEAL APPLICATION (SEE *APPENDIX ONE: CONCORDANCE OF SEALS TO TABLETS IN VOLUME I*)

With one exception (PF 1317, on the obverse), PFS 49 occurs always on the reverse of tablets; on PF 686 it occurs additionally on the upper edge and left edge; on PF 687 and PF 1556 it occurs additionally on the upper edge. On the reverse of PF 687 the seal has been applied twice, one impression directly above the other. On the reverse of PF 1316 the seal is inverted. Impressions generally exhibit little or no distortion. In ten impressions the seal is rolled for at least one complete turn, preserving the entire length of the seal design. Of these ten applications, two display the archer in the center; two display the lion to the left of the hero in the center; one displays the hero and the lion to the left in the center; one displays the hero and the lion to the right in the center; four display the lion to the right of the hero in the center. Of the remaining three partial impressions, two display the hero in the center; one displays the hero and the lion to the left in the center. On the reverse of PF 687, PF 1316, PF 1318, and PF 1556 the seal clearly was applied before the text since several cuneiform wedges cut into the top or the bottom of the impression. PF 686–687, PF 785, PF 1317–1318, PF 1556, and PF 1558 are the earliest dated tablets with PFS 49 and are all dated 499 B.C.

BIBLIOGRAPHY

Aperghis 1999, p. 164; Garrison 1988, pp. 290–91, 348–52, 484–85; Koch 1983, p. 22; Koch 1986, p. 138; Koch 1992, p. 35; Lewis 1977, p. 5; Root 1997, p. 237, fig. 2.

Cat.No. 24   PFS 63

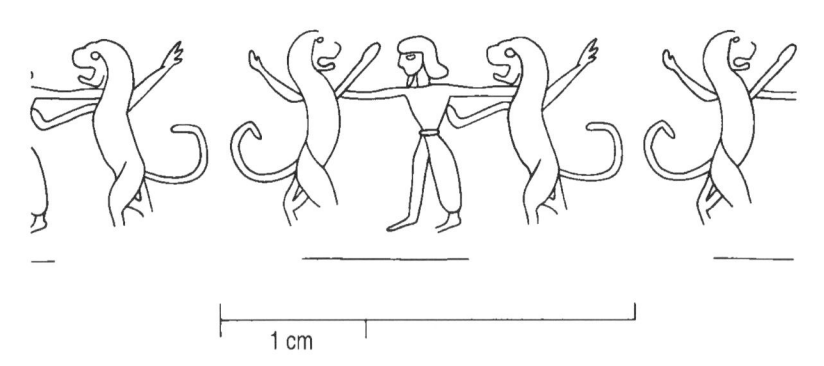

Seal Type:	Cylinder	Photographs:	Pl. 17a–b
Earliest Dated Application:	ND	Typology and Style:	I-A.4 — Fortification Style
Preserved Height of Image:	1.50 cm (incomp.)	Preserved Length of Image:	2.80 cm (comp.)
Estimated Height of Original Seal:	1.70 cm	Estimated Diameter of Original Seal:	0.90 cm
Number of Impressions:	14	Quality of Impressions:	Fair

Completeness of Image: Complete except for upper edge and lower edge

DESCRIPTION OF SEAL AS IMPRESSED IMAGE

Hero faces left, arms straight at horizontal, and holds two rampant lions by throat.

Lion to left holds one foreleg straight and extends it upward toward hero's head; other foreleg is straight, held up and away from body. Lion to right holds one foreleg straight and extends it downward to place upturned paw on hero's chest; other foreleg is straight, held up and away from body, toes splayed. Tail of each lion curls upward; that of lion at left is bent at its end.

Hero wears belted Assyrian garment that leaves forward leg exposed. Narrow pointed beard rests over hero's right shoulder; flattened coiffure curls slightly upward at back of neck.

Each lion opens mouth in roar.

Portion of edge of seal is preserved at bottom of design below hero and lion to left.

COMMENTARY

Koch (1990) assigns PFS 63 to Hiumizza, an official responsible for the apportionment of horses in the area of Parmizzan in her Southwestern Region IV.

See Garrison 1988 for the distinctive hand of this artist.

For comparative illustrations including PFS 63, see pls. 222e (lions and lion creatures) and 282d (personal seals of supply/apportionment officers).

SEAL APPLICATION (SEE *APPENDIX ONE: CONCORDANCE OF SEALS TO TABLETS IN VOLUME I*)

PFS 63 always occurs on two edges of a tablet. Normally this is the reverse and upper edge, but on PF 1687 it is the reverse and left edge, on PF 1690 the upper edge and right edge. Most impressions show significant distortion, especially at the vertical edges of the impression. In ten impressions, the seal has been rolled for at least one complete turn, preserving the entire length of the seal design. Of these ten applications, one displays the hero in the center; two display the lion to the left of the hero in the center; six display the lion to the right of the hero in the center; one displays the two lions in the center. Of the four remaining partial rollings, three display the hero in the center; one preserves only the lion to the right of the hero. On the reverse of PF 1688–1689, PF 1691, PF 1695, and PF 2064 the seal clearly was applied before the text since several cuneiform wedges cut into the top of the impression. The dates of all the tablets with PFS 63 are unknown.

BIBLIOGRAPHY

Garrison 1988, pp. 257, 359–65, 487, 489; Garrison and Dion 1999, p. 9 (n. 20); Koch 1990, p. 111 (n. 470).

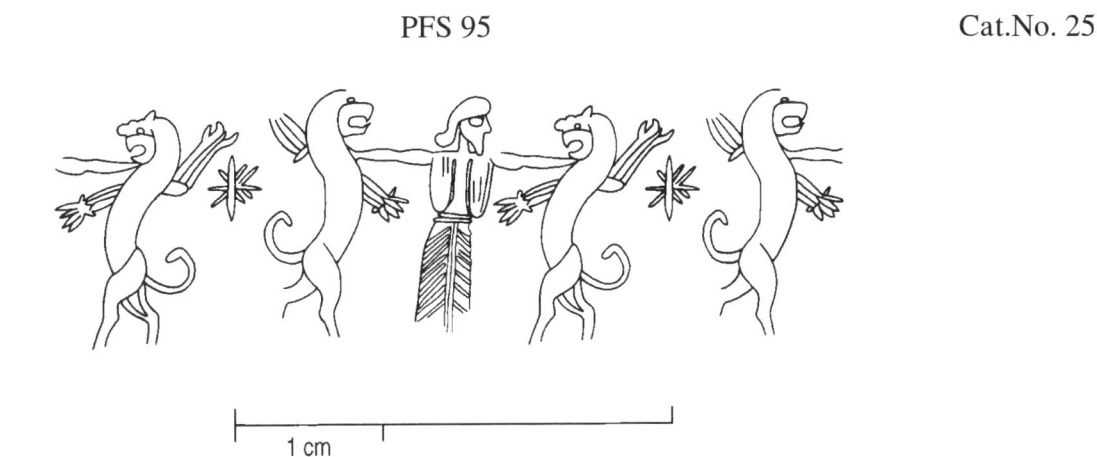

PFS 95   Cat.No. 25

Seal Type:	Cylinder	Photographs:	Pl. 18a–b
Earliest Dated Application:	500 B.C.	Typology and Style:	I-A.4 — Fortification Style
Preserved Height of Image:	1.60 cm (incomp.)	Preserved Length of Image:	3.00 cm (comp.)
Estimated Height of Original Seal:	1.90 cm	Estimated Diameter of Original Seal:	1.00 cm
Number of Impressions:	5	Quality of Impressions:	Good

Completeness of Image: Almost complete except for upper edge and lower edge

DESCRIPTION OF SEAL AS IMPRESSED IMAGE

Hero faces right, arms straight at horizontal, and holds two rampant lions by throat.

Each lion holds one foreleg straight and extends it downward toward hero's waist, toes splayed; other foreleg is straight, held up and away from its body with toes splayed; tail of each lion curls upward and is bent at termination.

Hero wears belted Persian court robe with sleeves pushed up to reveal arms. Upper part of garment hangs from either side of torso in long swag with vertical folds indicated; double central pleat and diagonal folds of lower part of garment are indicated. Short pointed beard rests on hero's left shoulder; rounded coiffure curls upward at back of neck.

Lion to right has short ear(?) emerging from top of its head. Each lion opens mouth in roar.
Star is in terminal field.

COMMENTARY

Based on Q texts protocol, PFS 95 should belong to Medumannuš, who in year 22.6 (500 B.C.; PF 1368) supplied flour. In PF 1495 flour was supplied in year 22.12 (499 B.C.), but no supplier is named. PFS 95 also occurs, however, on the following texts: the upper edge of PF 1092 (M text), where Bakaraddus and his companions received flour supplied by Mazamanna in year 23 (499/498 B.C.); the left edge of PF 1139 (M text), where Zakarna received figs supplied by Karukka in year 23.9 (December 499 and early January 498 B.C.); the left edge of PF 1234 (N text), where Irzapparra and his companions received grain and *milti* supplied by Ištimanka in year 22.10 (late December 500 B.C. and early January 499 B.C.). This pattern suggests strongly that PFS 95 is an office seal belonging to a grain/flour supply office.

The hand of PFS 95 is distinctive and unmistakable; see Garrison 1988, 1991, and 1996a for the work of this important artist, who combines stylistic features of the Fortification Style and the Court Style.

For comparative illustrations including PFS 95, see pls. 178b (Persian court robes with sleeves pushed up in deep swags), 190c (beards), 230g (feet of animals and creatures), and 253b (stars, rosettes).

SEAL APPLICATION (SEE *APPENDIX ONE: CONCORDANCE OF SEALS TO TABLETS IN VOLUME I*)

With one exception (PF 1092 on the upper edge) PFS 95 occurs only on the left edge of tablets. Impressions show little or no distortion. No impression preserves the entire length of the seal design. Of the five partial rollings, one displays the hero in the center; two preserve only the hero and the lion to the left; one preserves only the hero and the lion to the right; one displays the lion to the left of the hero in the center. PF 1368 is the earliest dated tablet with PFS 95 and is dated 500 B.C.

BIBLIOGRAPHY

Garrison 1988, pp. 363–68, 488–89; Garrison 1991, pp. 16–17, fig. 29; Garrison 1996a, pp. 40–43, figs. 8–9; Garrison and Dion 1999, p. 6 (n. 15), 9 (n. 20); Garrison and Root 1996, p. 11, fig. 4; Root 1988, p. 10.

PFS 232 — Cat.No. 26

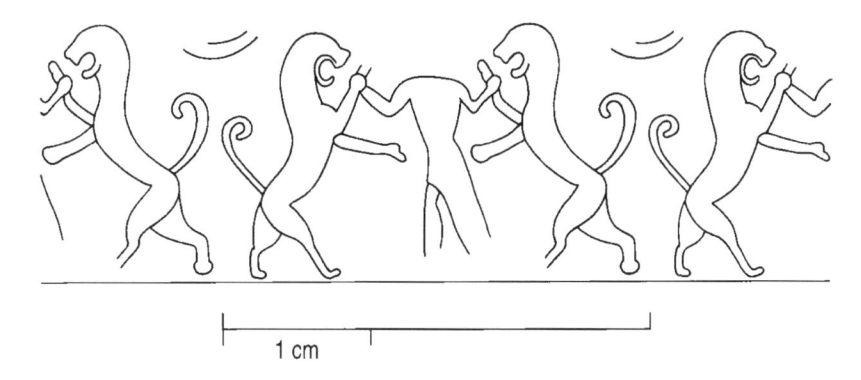

Seal Type:	Cylinder	Photographs:	Pl. 19a–b
Earliest Dated Application:	501/500(?) B.C.	Typology and Style:	I-A.4 — Fortification Style
Preserved Height of Image:	1.70 cm (incomp.)	Preserved Length of Image:	2.90 cm (comp.)
Estimated Height of Original Seal:	1.90 cm	Estimated Diameter of Original Seal:	0.90 cm
Number of Impressions:	3	Quality of Impressions:	Fair-good

Completeness of Image: Almost complete except for sections of upper edge and lower edge

Description of Seal as Impressed Image

Hero faces left, arms bent, and holds two rampant lions by upper foreleg.

Each lion holds upper foreleg straight and extends it upward toward hero's head; lower foreleg is straight and extended downward toward hero's hips. Lions' tails extend diagonally upward with curled terminations.

Hero wears Assyrian garment that leaves forward leg exposed below mid-thigh.

Each lion has mouth open in roar.

Traces of crescent are in upper terminal field.

Edge of seal is visible at bottom of design.

Commentary

The seal is fairly large and well made; see Garrison 1988 for artist and related seals.
For comparative illustrations including PFS 232, see pls. 205b (arm positions of heroic control) and 250d (crescents).

Seal Application (see Appendix One: Concordance of Seals to Tablets in Volume I)

PFS 232 occurs on the reverse of PF 37 and PF 117–118, with PFS 40 (III) always on the left edge. In its three impressions the seal is rolled for at least one complete turn, preserving the entire length of the seal design. One displays the hero in the center; two display the lion to the right of the hero in the center. On PF 117 the seal clearly was applied before the text since several cuneiform wedges cut into the top of the impression. PF 37 is the earliest dated tablet with PFS 232 and is dated 501/500(?) B.C.

Bibliography

Garrison 1988, pp. 313–16, 450.

Cat.No. 27   PFS 249

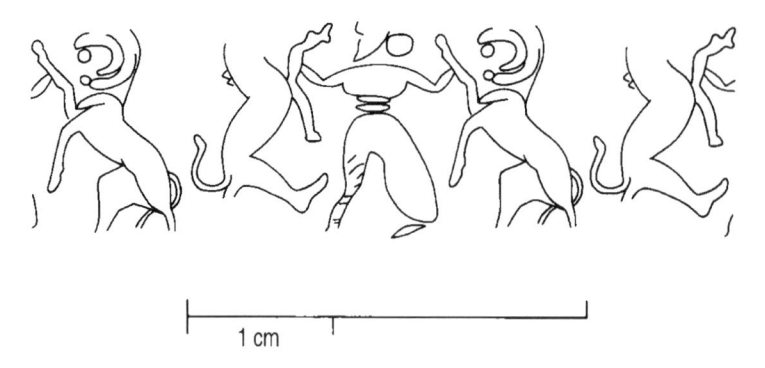

Seal Type:	Cylinder	Photographs:	Pl. 20a–b
Earliest Dated Application:	498 B.C.	Typology and Style:	I-A.4 — Fortification Style
Preserved Height of Image:	1.50 cm (incomp.)	Preserved Length of Image:	2.70 cm (comp.)
Estimated Height of Original Seal:	1.80 cm	Estimated Diameter of Original Seal:	0.90 cm
Number of Impressions:	4	Quality of Impressions:	Poor

Completeness of Image: Almost complete except for upper edge and lower edge

DESCRIPTION OF SEAL AS IMPRESSED IMAGE

Hero faces left in striding pose, arms bent, and holds two rampant lions (head of animal to left not preserved) by upper foreleg.

Each lion holds upper foreleg bent and extends it upward toward hero's head; lower foreleg is curved and held down in front of its body. Lion at left raises forward hind leg toward hero's leg; tail curls upward and is bent at its end. Tail of lion at right curves down between its hind legs.

Hero appears to wear double-belted trousers; diagonal and horizontal folds are indicated on forward leg. Pointed beard rests over hero's right shoulder; round coiffure is at back of neck.

Traces of mane are rendered by crisp serrated edge along contour of neck of lion to left. Raised leg of lion to left terminates in human-like foot. Lion to right has mouth open in roar.

COMMENTARY

See Garrison 1988 for the artist and stylistically related seals.
    For comparative illustrations including PFS 249, see pls. 184d (trousers), 193e (round coiffures), 198h (feet and shoes), and 223a (lions and lion creatures).

SEAL APPLICATION (SEE *APPENDIX ONE: CONCORDANCE OF SEALS TO TABLETS IN VOLUME I*)

PFS 249 occurs on the left edge of PF 971, PF 1641, PF 1710, and PF 2042, with PFS 248 (II) on the reverse of each tablet. Impressions tend to exhibit some distortion. The impression on the left edge of PF 2042 is too poorly preserved for analysis. Of the remaining three partial rollings, one displays the hero in the center; one preserves only the hero and the lion to the right; one preserves only the two lions. PF 971, PF 1641, and PF 2042 are the earliest dated tablets with PFS 249 and are all dated 498 B.C.

BIBLIOGRAPHY

Garrison 1988, pp. 341–43; Koch 1990, p. 38.

PFS 329

Cat.No. 28

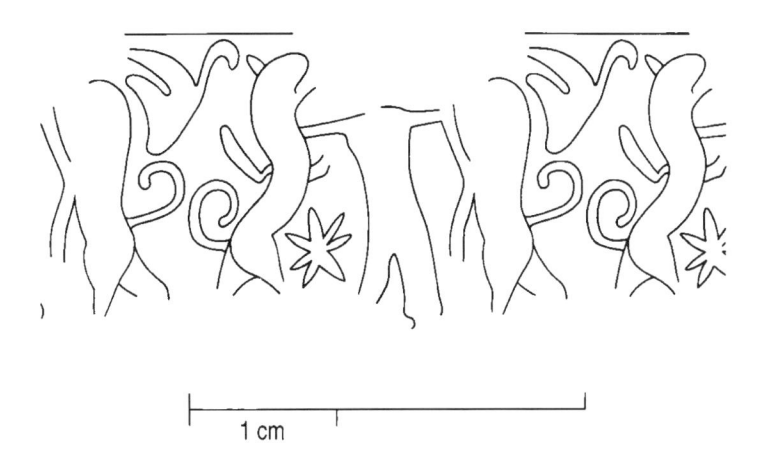

Seal Type:	Cylinder	Photograph:	Pl. 20d
Earliest Dated Application:	500/499 B.C.	Typology and Style:	I-A.4 — Mixed Styles I
Preserved Height of Image:	2.00 cm (incomp.)	Preserved Length of Image:	2.70 cm (comp.)
Estimated Height of Original Seal:	2.20 cm	Estimated Diameter of Original Seal:	0.90 cm
Number of Impressions:	2	Quality of Impressions:	Poor

Completeness of Image: Complete except for portions of upper edge and lower edge

Description of Seal as Impressed Image

Hero moves to left, has arms straight at horizontal, and holds two rampant lions, one to left by throat, one to right by upper foreleg.

Lion to left holds one foreleg bent and extends it toward hero's chest; other foreleg is bent, held up and away from its body; tail curls upward. Lion at right holds upper foreleg straight and extends it upward; lower foreleg is bent and extended downward in front of its body; tail curls upward.

Hero wears Assyrian garment that leaves forward leg exposed.

Star is in lower field between hero and lion to left.

Large bird of uncertain type in flight facing right is in upper terminal field.

Commentary

The design seems poorly executed. Although birds occur on other seals of heroic encounter in the PFS corpus, the form of this one is anomalous.

For comparative illustrations including PFS 329, see pls. 227c (birds), 253g (stars, rosettes), and 272f (dense compositions).

Seal Application (see Appendix One: Concordance of Seals to Tablets in Volume I)

PFS 329 occurs on the reverse of PF 17 (inverted) and PF 624, with PFS 328s (III) applied on the left edge of each tablet. The two rollings preserve the entire length of the seal design and show almost the same sequence, displaying the lion to the left of the hero in the center. On the reverse of PF 17 the seal clearly was applied before the text because several cuneiform wedges cut into the bottom of the impression. PF 17 and PF 624 are dated 500/499 B.C.

Bibliography

Garrison 1988, pp. 245–46; Garrison and Dion 1999, p. 9 (n. 20) (cited, before collation with PFS 329, as PFS 827).

Cat.No. 29 PFS 1071

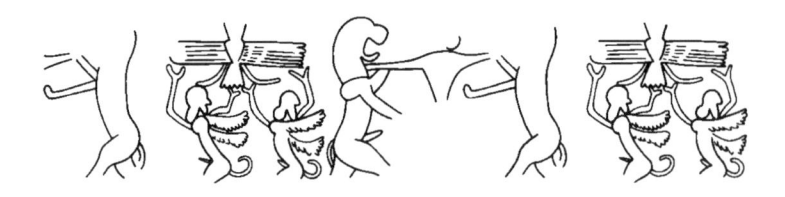

Seal Type:	Cylinder	Photograph:	Pl. 21a
Earliest Dated Application:	499/498 B.C.	Typology and Style:	I-A.4 — Mixed Styles II
Preserved Height of Image:	1.10 cm	Preserved Length of Image:	2.90 cm (comp.)
Estimated Height of Original Seal:	NA	Estimated Diameter of Original Seal:	0.90 cm
Number of Impressions:	1	Quality of Impression:	Fair

Completeness of Image: Large segment of middle of design survives along its complete length

DESCRIPTION OF SEAL AS IMPRESSED IMAGE

Hero faces left, arms straight at horizontal, and holds two rampant lions, one to left by throat, one to right by foreleg or throat.

Each lion holds upper foreleg straight and extends it upward to place paw on hero's arm. Lion to left holds lower foreleg (only partially preserved) straight and extends it downward toward hero's waist. Lion to right holds lower foreleg straight, paw turned upward, and extends it downward toward hero's chest. Lions' tails curve downward between their hind legs.

Hero wears garment of uncertain type; rounded coiffure (only partially preserved) rests at back of neck.

Lion to left is ithyphallic and has mouth open in roar.

In terminal field, two rampant winged human-headed bull or lion creatures with human arms support figure emerging from winged symbol with bird's tail and tendrils. Figure emergent wears garment of uncertain type. Supporting creatures move to left but turn their heads back to right. Each creature holds arms bent above its head in atlas pose; their tails curl upward. Each creature has two wings, upper parallel to lower. Pointed beard rests over each creature's left shoulder; rounded coiffure is at back of each creature's neck. Each creature is ithyphallic.

COMMENTARY

The figure emergent from a winged symbol and supported by one or two composite creatures appears in non-heroic scenes in the PFS corpus (e.g., PFS 122 [II]) and in Achaemenid Court Style glyptic more generally (e.g., PTS 19). In addition to PFS 1071, it also occurs on PFS 774 (Cat.No. 58) and PFS 1053 (Cat.No. 45). See the commentary on PFS 7* (Cat.No. 4) for the figure emerging from the winged symbol and for remarks on the form of the symbol. Here on PFS 1071 the disk element of the winged symbol is obscure or lacking.

For comparative illustrations including PFS 1071, see pls. 233g (ithyphallic animals/creatures), 248d (deities emergent from winged symbol), and 266f (terminal field motifs other than inscriptions).

SEAL APPLICATION (SEE APPENDIX ONE: CONCORDANCE OF SEALS TO TABLETS IN VOLUME I)

PFS 1071 occurs across the upper half of the reverse of PF 1114. Immediately below it on the lower half of the reverse PFS 1072 (Cat.No. 61) has been applied. PFS 1071 appears to have been rolled first because the lower edge has been lost, presumably owing to the application of PFS 1072 (Cat.No. 61), which is completely preserved. The rolling of PFS 1071 preserves the entire length of the seal design and displays the lion to the left of the hero and the atlas creature to his right in the center. PF 1114 is dated 499/498 B.C.

BIBLIOGRAPHY

Garrison 1988, pp. 374–78, 381–82, 430, 496; Root 1999a, p. 173, fig. 8.

PFS 1362   Cat.No. 30

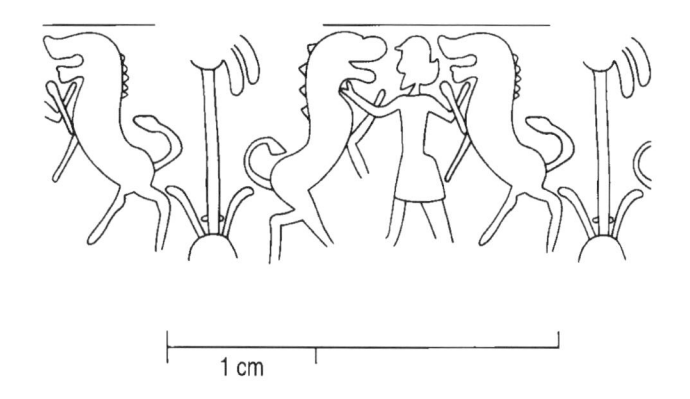

Seal Type:	Cylinder	Photograph:	Pl. 21c
Earliest Dated Application:	ND	Typology and Style:	I-A.4 — Fortification Style
Preserved Height of Image:	1.60 cm (incomp.)	Preserved Length of Image:	2.60 cm (comp.)
Estimated Height of Original Seal:	1.70 cm	Estimated Diameter of Original Seal:	0.80 cm
Number of Impressions:	1	Quality of Impression:	Fair

Completeness of Image: Almost complete except for lower edge and details

DESCRIPTION OF SEAL AS IMPRESSED IMAGE

Hero faces left, arms bent, and holds two rampant lions by throat.

Each lion holds upper foreleg straight and extends it upward toward hero's head; lower foreleg is straight (only partially preserved on lion to left) and extended downward toward hero's leg. Tail of lion to left curls upward with tufted termination. Tail of lion to right is bent upward with tufted termination.

Hero wears short tunic. Short pointed beard rests over hero's right shoulder; flattened coiffure curls upward at back of neck; short projection from front of hero's head suggests possible domed headdress with brim.

Mane of each lion is rendered by crisply serrated edge along contour of neck; each lion has mouth open in roar.

Palm tree with fronds emerging at base is in terminal field.

Portions of edge of seal are preserved at top of design above heroic encounter.

COMMENTARY

Based on Q texts protocol, PFS 1362 should belong to Harraštamka, who in PF 1464 received flour rations under the authority (*halmi*) of the king. PF 1464 preserves the only occurrence of the name Harraštamka in the PF texts.

    See Garrison 1988 for the artist.

    For comparative illustrations including PFS 1362, see pls. 185j (tunics), 258h (palm trees), and 291b (personal seals of various travelers).

SEAL APPLICATION (SEE *APPENDIX ONE: CONCORDANCE OF SEALS TO TABLETS IN VOLUME I*)

PFS 1362 occurs on the reverse of PF 1464. The rolling preserves the entire length of the seal design and displays the palm tree in the terminal field in the center. The seal clearly was applied before the text since several cuneiform wedges cut into the bottom of the impression. The date of PF 1464 is unknown.

BIBLIOGRAPHY

Garrison 1988, pp. 339–41, 488.

Cat.No. 31   PFS 1374

Seal Type:	Cylinder	Photograph:	Pl. 22a
Earliest Dated Application:	499 B.C.	Typology and Style:	I-A.4 — Mixed Styles I
Preserved Height of Image:	1.70 cm (incomp.)	Preserved Length of Image:	2.80 cm (comp.)
Estimated Height of Original Seal:	1.90 cm	Estimated Diameter of Original Seal:	0.90 cm
Number of Impressions:	1	Quality of Impression:	Fair

Completeness of Image: Almost complete except for upper edge and lower edge

DESCRIPTION OF SEAL AS IMPRESSED IMAGE

Hero faces left, arms bent, and holds two rampant lions by upper foreleg.

Each lion holds upper foreleg straight and extends it upward toward hero's head; lower foreleg is straight and extended downward toward hero's waist. Tail of each lion curves downward between its hind legs.

Hero wears Assyrian garment that leaves forward leg exposed below knee. Beard terminates in blunt point over hero's right shoulder; rounded coiffure is at back of neck.

Mane of each lion is rendered by crisp serrated edge along contour of neck; mouth is open in roar. Lion to left is ithyphallic.

Bird of uncertain type with wings spread flies to left in terminal field.

COMMENTARY

Based on Q texts protocol, PFS 1374 should belong to Kamnakka, who in year 23.1 (499 B.C.) received flour rations on his way to Persepolis under the authority (*halmi*) of Parnaka. PF 1478 preserves the only occurrence of the name Kamnakka in the PF texts.

The best parallel in Volume I for the bird in flight on PFS 1374 is found on PFS 31 (Cat.No. 172), where full preservation indicates a goose.[13]

This large seal was probably of much higher quality than the one preserved impression can convey. Figures are well modeled and well spaced. The style is a mix of Assyro-Babylonian Modeled Style and the local Fortification Style.

For comparative illustrations including PFS 1374, see pl. 291d (personal seals of various travelers).

SEAL APPLICATION (SEE *APPENDIX ONE: CONCORDANCE OF SEALS TO TABLETS IN VOLUME I*)

PFS 1374 occurs once on the reverse of PF 1478. The rolling preserves the entire length of the seal design and displays the lion to the left of the hero and the bird in the terminal field in the center. The seal clearly was applied before the text since several cuneiform wedges cut into the top of the impression. PF 1478 is dated 499 B.C.

BIBLIOGRAPHY

Garrison 1988, pp. 246–49.

---

13. See Amiet 1972, pl. 189, no. 2210, for an Achaemenid hero seal from Susa with a very similar bird in flight, this time in the terminal field between two rampant goats.

PFS 1527   Cat.No. 32

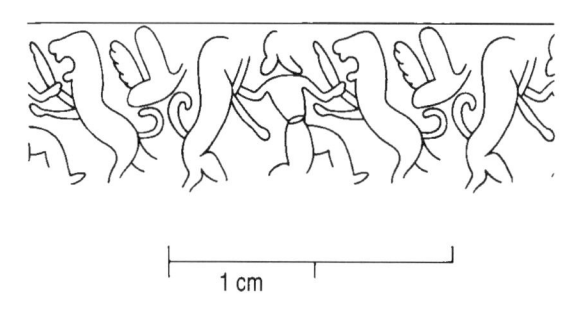

|—— 1 cm ——|

Seal Type:	Cylinder	Photograph:	Pl. 22c
Earliest Dated Application:	499/498 B.C.	Typology and Style:	I-A.4 — Fortification Style
Preserved Height of Image:	1.10 cm (incomp.)	Preserved Length of Image:	1.90 cm (comp.)
Estimated Height of Original Seal:	1.20 cm	Estimated Diameter of Original Seal:	0.60 cm
Number of Impressions:	3	Quality of Impressions:	Poor

Completeness of Image: Almost complete except for lower edge and details

DESCRIPTION OF SEAL AS IMPRESSED IMAGE

Hero faces right, arms bent, and holds two rampant lions by upper foreleg. Hero has forward leg raised and rear leg is apparently bent at knee in *knielauf*-pose.

Lion to left holds upper foreleg straight and extends it diagonally upward; lower foreleg is straight and extended downward toward hero's leg; tail curls upward. Lion to right holds upper foreleg bent and extends it upward toward hero's head; lower foreleg is straight and extended toward hero's waist; tail extends outward, curling upward at its end.

Hero appears to wear belted trousers. Long rounded beard rests over hero's left shoulder; rounded coiffure is at back of neck.

Lion to right has mouth open in roar.

Bird of uncertain type in upper terminal field alights facing right with wings upward, apparently to peck lion to left of hero.

Edge of seal is preserved at top of design.

COMMENTARY

See Garrison 1988 for the artist. The full *knielauf*-pose of the hero (with rear leg also bent) on PFS 1527 is noteworthy.[14] Although the *knielauf*-pose is assumed by a small number of heroes in the PFS corpus, it figures prominently as a pose of archers in Volume II, reinforcing the significance of the royal archer in *knielauf*-pose depicted on Achaemenid coinage.[15] In Volume I, the *knielauf*-pose is seen also on PFS 120 (Cat.No. 49), PFS 1309s (Cat.No. 229), and PFS 67 (Cat.No. 293).

For comparative illustrations including PFS 1527, see pls. 184i (trousers), 211i (heroic attitudes of control encounter), and 228d (pecking birds).

SEAL APPLICATION (SEE *APPENDIX ONE: CONCORDANCE OF SEALS TO TABLETS IN VOLUME I*)

PFS 1527 occurs twice on the reverse (inverted) and once on the upper edge of PF 1686. The applications on the reverse are placed one directly above the other and are rolled in the exact same sequence. Both applications preserve the entire length of the seal design; the lower displays the hero in the center; the upper displays the lion to the left of the hero in the center. The rolling on the upper edge preserves the entire length of the seal design and displays the hero and the lion to left in the center. PF 1686 is dated 499/498 B.C.

---

14. The *knielauf*-pose is found also on seal impressions from Assyria (e.g., Herbordt 1992, pls. 5, no. 8; 6, nos. 4–9) and Susa (Amiet 1973b, pls. 1, no. 3; 2, nos. 8–10) and seals traditionally classified as Neo-Babylonian (Wittmann 1992, pls. 20, nos. 29–34; 21, nos. 38–43, etc.). On the *knielauf*-pose in western Asiatic art, see Kantor 1962.

15. See Root 1988 and 1989 for PFS 1393s (II), the Persian archer coin used as a seal.

BIBLIOGRAPHY

Garrison 1988, pp. 335–39, 494.

Cat.No. 33 PFS 1243

	1 cm
Seal Type: Cylinder	Photograph: Pl. 23a
Earliest Dated Application: 499 B.C.	Typology and Style: I-A.4 — Fortification Style
Preserved Height of Image: 1.10 cm (incomp.)	Preserved Length of Image: 2.30 cm (incomp.)
Estimated Height of Original Seal: NA	Estimated Diameter of Original Seal: NA
Number of Impressions: 1	Quality of Impression: Poor

Completeness of Image: Segment of middle of design survives

DESCRIPTION OF SEAL AS IMPRESSED IMAGE

Hero moves to left, arms bent (only left arm preserved), and holds two rampant lions by upper foreleg (contact between hero and lion preserved only for lion at right).

Hindquarters of animal and tail curving downward between its legs at far right of impression belong to other lion held by hero (at hero's left). Lion to right of hero holds upper foreleg straight and extends it diagonally upward; lower foreleg is straight and extended downward toward hero's leg; tail curves downward between its legs.

Hero appears to wear Assyrian garment that leaves forward leg exposed.

Mane of lion to right is rendered by crisp serrated edge along contour of neck.

Rampant winged lion creature moves to left in terminal field; wings are spread to either side of its body; tail curves downward between its legs.

COMMENTARY

Based on Q texts protocol, PFS 1243 should belong to Bakadada, who is going to Persepolis in 23.8 (499 B.C.) under the authority (*halmi*) of Bakabana. The name Bakadada is common in the PF texts, and we are probably dealing with several individuals. Koch (1990, p. 245) identifies one Bakadada as a high-ranking official in her Shiraz Region II.

SEAL APPLICATION (SEE *APPENDIX ONE: CONCORDANCE OF SEALS TO TABLETS IN VOLUME I*)

PFS 1243 occurs on the reverse of PF 1297. The partial rolling displays the lion to the right of the hero in the center. The seal clearly was applied before the text since several cuneiform wedges cut into the top and bottom of the impression. PF 1297 is dated 499 B.C.

BIBLIOGRAPHY

Garrison 1988, pp. 271–73.

PFS 1276 — Cat.No. 34

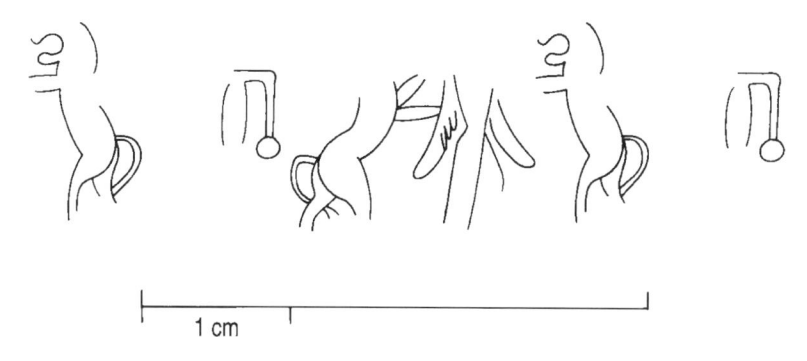

Seal Type:	Cylinder	Photograph:	Pl. 23c
Earliest Dated Application:	ND	Typology and Style:	I-A.4 — Fortification Style
Preserved Height of Image:	1.40 cm (incomp.)	Preserved Length of Image:	3.30 cm (comp.)
Estimated Height of Original Seal:	NA	Estimated Diameter of Original Seal:	1.10 cm
Number of Impressions:	2	Quality of Impressions:	Poor

Completeness of Image: Segment of middle of design survives along its complete length

DESCRIPTION OF SEAL AS IMPRESSED IMAGE

Winged hero moves to right, forward leg bent, and holds two rampant lions (actual contact not preserved).

Lion to left holds upper foreleg straight (only partially preserved) and extends it upward toward hero's head; lower foreleg is straight and paw is placed on hero's wing; tail curves downward between its hind legs with tufted termination. Lion to right holds one foreleg straight and extends it horizontally toward hero's chest; tail (only partially preserved) curves downward between its hind legs.

Hero wears Assyrian garment that leaves forward leg exposed. Two lower wings of presumably four-winged hero creature are preserved.

Lion to right has mouth open in roar.

In upper terminal field, small part of trunk and bulbous fruit cluster of date palm are preserved.

COMMENTARY

Based on Q texts protocol, PFS 1276 should belong to Mirinzamna, who in PF 1332 received flour rations at Bessitme on his way from Susa to Kerman. A Mirinzamna occurs also on the fragmentary PF 807, with PFS 931* (Cat.No. 270) and PFS 932 (illegible) used on the tablet, and in the account PFa 31, receiving wine rations for individuals going from Sagartia to Persepolis under the authority (*halmi*) of the king.

Despite poor preservation at the upper body of the hero, an originally four-winged aspect seems assured, as similarly with PFS 72 (Cat.No. 147), PFS 516 (Cat.No. 98), and PFS 1387 (Cat.No. 72). Well preserved, and thus demonstrably, two-winged human-creature heroes in the PFS corpus of heroic images almost always display the two wings emerging from the same side of the body; for example, PFS 30 (Cat.No. 291), PFS 65 (Cat.No. 241), PFS 98* (Cat.No. 217), PFS 931* (Cat.No. 270), PFS 964 (Cat.No. 260), and PFS 1566* (Cat.No. 218). The exception is PFS 1321s (Cat.No. 176), where the bird-like features of the hero make it verge toward the non-human creature category.

For comparative illustrations including PFS 1276, see pls. 259g (date palms) and 290c (personal seals of various travelers).

SEAL APPLICATION (SEE *APPENDIX ONE: CONCORDANCE OF SEALS TO TABLETS IN VOLUME I*)

PFS 1276 occurs twice on the reverse of PF 1332, one impression directly above the other. The upper impression preserves the entire length of the seal design and displays the date palm in the terminal field in the center. The partial lower impression displays the lion to the right of the hero in the center. The upper impression clearly was applied before the text since several cuneiform wedges cut into the top of the impression. The date of PF 1332 is unknown.

BIBLIOGRAPHY

Garrison 1988, pp. 287–91; Garrison and Dion 1999, p. 9 (n. 19).

Cat.No. 35　　　　　　　　　　　　　　　　PFS 1320

Seal Type:	Cylinder	Photograph:	Pl. 23e
Earliest Dated Application:	499 B.C.	Typology and Style:	I-A.4 — Fortification Style
Preserved Height of Image:	1.40 cm (incomp.)	Preserved Length of Image:	2.90 cm (incomp.)
Estimated Height of Original Seal:	NA	Estimated Diameter of Original Seal:	NA
Number of Impressions:	1	Quality of Impression:	Poor

Completeness of Image: Small segment of middle of design survives

DESCRIPTION OF SEAL AS IMPRESSED IMAGE

Hero faces left, arms bent, and holds two rampant lions by upper foreleg.

Each lion holds upper foreleg bent and extends it upward toward hero's head. Lion to left holds lower foreleg (only partially preserved) straight and extends it downward toward hero's leg.

Hero wears belted Assyrian garment that leaves forward leg exposed below knee. Large rounded coiffure is partially preserved at back of neck.

Lion to left opens mouth in roar.

In terminal field, rampant winged creature of uncertain type moves to left; tail (only partially preserved) curves downward.

COMMENTARY

Based on Q texts protocol, PFS 1320 should belong to Bakabada, who in year 23.7 (499 B.C.) received flour rations at Hidali on his way from Susa to Persepolis under the authority (*halmi*) of Bakabana. The name Bakabada occurs frequently in the PF texts, and we clearly are dealing with several individuals.

For comparative illustrations including PFS 1320, see pls. 175c (Assyrian garments) and 205f (arm positions of heroic control).

SEAL APPLICATION (SEE *APPENDIX ONE: CONCORDANCE OF SEALS TO TABLETS IN VOLUME I*)

PFS 1320 occurs on the reverse of PF 1403. The partial rolling displays the hero in the center. PF 1403 is dated 499 B.C.

BIBLIOGRAPHY

Garrison 1988, pp. 312–13.

PFS 1322

Cat.No. 36

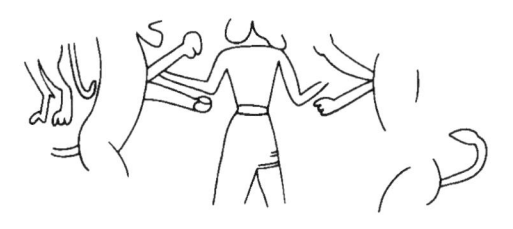

Seal Type:	Cylinder	Photograph:	Pl. 24a
Earliest Dated Application:	ND	Typology and Style:	I-A.4 — Fortification Style
Preserved Height of Image:	1.40 cm (incomp.)	Preserved Length of Image:	3.20 cm (incomp.)
Estimated Height of Original Seal:	NA	Estimated Diameter of Original Seal:	NA
Number of Impressions:	1	Quality of Impression:	Fair

Completeness of Image: Large segment of middle of design survives

Description of Seal as Impressed Image

Hero faces right, arms bent, and holds two rampant lions by upper foreleg.

Each lion holds upper foreleg straight and extends it upward toward hero's head; lower foreleg is straight and extended downward toward hero's waist. Tail (partially preserved) of lion to left curves upward. Tail of lion to right curves upward, thickening at its end with pointed termination.

Hero wears belted Assyrian garment that leaves forward leg exposed below knee; two horizontal bands are indicated on short undergarment over forward knee. Rounded beard rests over hero's left shoulder; large rounded coiffure rests at back of neck.

Lion to left has mouth open in roar.

Hind legs and tail of marchant(?) animal of uncertain type are preserved in upper terminal field. Animal moves to left.

Commentary

Based on Q texts protocol, PFS 1322 should belong to Umiša, who in PF 1405 received flour rations at Hidali on his way to Persepolis under the authority (*halmi*) of Bakabana. The name Umiša occurs also on PF 91–92 (apportioning flour), PF 1023 and PF 2105 (supplying flour), PF 1945 (assigning; *tumara* at Antarrantiš; see Koch 1990, p. 10 [n. 11], 33), and PF 1971 (receiving grain). Different seals are involved in these transactions; we seem to have several individuals. Koch (1990, p. 209 [n. 858]) concluded that the traveler in PF 1405 is not to be connected with any other individuals using the same name.

The engraving is deep but rather poorly executed.

For comparative illustrations including PFS 1322, see pl. 291a (personal seals of various travelers).

Seal Application (see *Appendix One: Concordance of Seals to Tablets in Volume I*)

PFS 1322 occurs on the upper edge of PF 1405. The partial rolling displays the hero in the center. The date of PF 1405 is unknown.

Bibliography

Garrison 1988, pp. 271–73, 482, 493.

Cat.No. 37								PFS 1020

Seal Type:	Cylinder	Photograph:	Pl. 24c
Earliest Dated Application:	500 B.C.	Typology and Style:	I-A.4 — Linear Styles
Preserved Height of Image:	0.70 cm (incomp.)	Preserved Length of Image:	1.40 cm (incomp.)
Estimated Height of Original Seal:	NA	Estimated Diameter of Original Seal:	NA
Number of Impressions:	1	Quality of Impression:	Poor

Completeness of Image: Small fragment of middle of design survives

DESCRIPTION OF SEAL AS IMPRESSED IMAGE

Hero faces right, arms straight (only right arm preserved), and (presumably) holds two rampant lions by foreleg (preserved only to left).

Lion holds one foreleg curved and extends it upward toward hero's shoulder; other foreleg is straight and held up and away from body with toes splayed.

Hero wears Persian court robe with sleeves pushed up to reveal arms; sleeve folds are indicated along outer edges. Narrow rounded beard rests over hero's left shoulder; rounded coiffure rests at back of neck.

Lion has linear detailing on neck; mouth is open in roar.

COMMENTARY

The outline linear style is very rare; see, however, PFS 294 (Cat.No. 53) for a similar style.
	For comparative illustrations including PFS 1020, see pl. 190f (beards).

SEAL APPLICATION (SEE APPENDIX ONE: CONCORDANCE OF SEALS TO TABLETS IN VOLUME I)

PFS 1020 occurs on the reverse of PF 1047. The partial rolling displays the contact between the lion to the left and the hero in the center. PF 1047 is dated 500 B.C.

BIBLIOGRAPHY

Garrison 1988, pp. 440–42, 497, 531.

PFS 385   Cat.No. 38

|—————1 cm—————|

Seal Type:	Cylinder	Photograph:	Pl. 24e
Earliest Dated Application:	495/494 B.C.	Typology and Style:	I-A.4 — Fortification Style
Preserved Height of Image:	1.80 cm (incomp.)	Preserved Length of Image:	2.90 cm (comp.)
Estimated Height of Original Seal:	2.00 cm	Estimated Diameter of Original Seal:	0.90 cm
Number of Impressions:	4	Quality of Impressions:	Fair-good

Completeness of Image: Almost complete except for upper edge and lower edge

DESCRIPTION OF SEAL AS IMPRESSED IMAGE

Hero faces left, arms bent, and holds two rampant lions by upper foreleg.

Each lion moves toward hero but turns its head away from him. Each lion holds upper foreleg straight and extends it upward toward hero's head; lower foreleg is curved, paw turned upward, and extended downward toward hero's waist. Each lion raises forward straight hind leg, paw turned upward, toward hero. Tail of lion to left curls upward. Tail of lion to right curves downward between its hind legs with tufted termination.

Hero wears double-belted Assyrian garment that leaves forward leg exposed.

Each lion has mouth open in roar. Mane and fur of lion to left is rendered by crisp serrated edge along contour of neck and belly. Lion to right is ithyphallic.

Diamond-shaped device is in upper terminal field.

Trace of edge of seal is preserved at bottom of design under lion to right.

COMMENTARY

The composition is a lively one, the lions being especially animated.

The diamond-shaped device is not cataloged by Boardman among his corpus of Anatolian symbols (nor is it among the "mason's mark" symbols [1970a, 1998]). Bregstein (1993, e.g., p. 535 no. 139) would classify this device as a "rhomb." We, however, see it as a distinct symbol that should be differentiated from the soft-contoured "rhomb" on, for example, our PFS 38 (Cat.No. 16).[16]

For comparative illustrations including PFS 385, see pls. 206g (arm positions of heroic control), 223c (lions and lion creatures), and 255d (various devices and symbols).

SEAL APPLICATION (SEE APPENDIX ONE: CONCORDANCE OF SEALS TO TABLETS IN VOLUME I)

PFS 385 occurs twice on the reverse of both PF 85 and PF 107. On each tablet the impressions are placed one directly above the other. PFS 384s (III) is applied twice along the horizontal axis of PF 85 directly below the lower impression of PFS 385. All applications preserve the entire length of the seal design; one displays the hero in the center; one displays the hero and the lion to left in the center; one displays the hero and the lion to the right in the center; one displays the two lions in the center. PF 85 and PF 107 are both dated 495/494 B.C.

---

16. A large diamond shape occurs on a seal impressed on an Assyrian tablet from Nineveh (Herbordt 1992, pl. 8, no. 5). In addition to Bregstein 1993, no. 139, a fairly good Achaemenid-period parallel for the large diamond-shaped device appears, for example, on an agate stamp seal: Keel and Uehlinger 1990, p. 55, fig. 76.

BIBLIOGRAPHY

Garrison 1988, pp. 307–08.

No. 39 PFS 1142

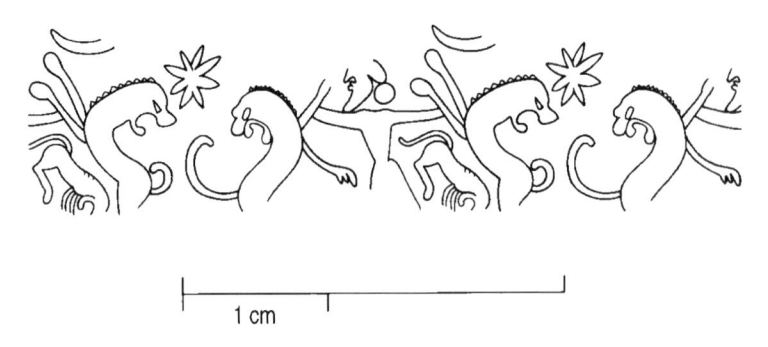

Seal Type:	Cylinder	Photograph:	Pl. 25a
Earliest Dated Application:	500/499 B.C.	Typology and Style:	I-A.4 — Fortification Style
Preserved Height of Image:	1.30 cm (incomp.)	Preserved Length of Image:	2.60 cm (comp.)
Estimated Height of Original Seal:	NA	Estimated Diameter of Original Seal:	0.80 cm
Number of Impressions:	3	Quality of Impressions:	Fair

Completeness of Image: Large segment of middle of design survives along its complete length

DESCRIPTION OF SEAL AS IMPRESSED IMAGE

Hero faces left, arms straight, and holds two rampant lions, one at left by upper foreleg, one at right by lower foreleg.

Each lion moves toward hero but turns its head away from him. Lion to left holds upper foreleg straight and extends it upward toward hero's head; lower foreleg is curved, toes splayed, and extended downward toward hero's leg; long tail curls upward. Lion to right holds forelegs straight and extends them together upward toward hero's head; short tail curls upward with tufted termination.

Hero wears garment of uncertain type; long rounded beard rests over his right shoulder; round coiffure rests at back of neck.

Mane of each lion is rendered by crisp serrated edge along contour of neck; mouth is open in roar.

Small inverted lion is in field between hero and lion to right; forelegs are curved and held together under its body; one bent hind leg is indicated; tail curves upward; mouth is open in roar.

Crescent is in field above lion to right of hero.

Star is in upper terminal field.

COMMENTARY

See Garrison 1988 for the distinctive hand of this artist in other seals. The manner in which the hero grasps the different forelegs of the lions is unusual, as is the small inverted lion between the hero and the lion to right. The inverted lion appears inert, as if suggesting the carcass of an animal.

For comparative illustrations including PFS 1142, see pls. 193i (round coiffures), 223g (lions and lion creatures), 237d (animal carcasses), 252i (crescents and stars), and 267i (terminal field motifs other than inscriptions).

SEAL APPLICATION (SEE APPENDIX ONE: CONCORDANCE OF SEALS TO TABLETS IN VOLUME I)

PFS 1142 occurs on the reverse and upper edge of PF 1198 and the reverse of PF 1234. PFS 1184 (III) is applied (inverted) directly above PFS 1142 on the reverse of PF 1234. All three impressions of PFS 1142 preserve the entire length of the seal design; that on the upper edge of PF 1198 displays the hero and lion to right in the center; that on the reverse of PF 1198 displays the lion to the left of the hero and the star in the center; that on the reverse of PF 1234 displays the lion to the right of the hero and the star in the center. On the reverse of PF 1198 the seal clearly was applied before the text since several cuneiform wedges cut into the top of the impression. PF 1198 and PF 1234 are both dated 500/499 B.C.

BIBLIOGRAPHY

Garrison 1988, pp. 335–39, 422; Garrison and Dion 1999, pp. 12, 14, fig. 10.

PFS 1146 — Cat.No. 40

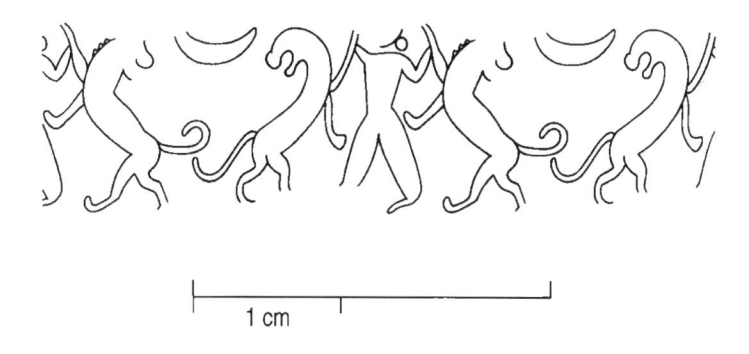

Seal Type:	Cylinder	Photograph:	Pl. 25c
Earliest Dated Application:	504/503 B.C.	Typology and Style:	I-A.4 — Fortification Style
Preserved Height of Image:	1.30 cm (incomp.)	Preserved Length of Image:	2.50 cm (comp.)
Estimated Height of Original Seal:	1.40 cm	Estimated Diameter of Original Seal:	0.80 cm
Number of Impressions:	2	Quality of Impressions:	Fair

Completeness of Image: Almost complete except for upper edge and lower edge

DESCRIPTION OF SEAL AS IMPRESSED IMAGE

Hero faces left, right arm straight above shoulder level, and left arm bent; holds two rampant lions by upper foreleg.

Each lion moves toward hero but turns head away from him. Lion to left holds upper foreleg curved and extends it upward toward hero's head; lower foreleg is curved and extended downward toward hero's leg; long tail curves downward. Lion to right holds upper foreleg straight and extends it upward toward hero's head; lower foreleg is straight, paw turned upward, and extended downward toward hero's hip; tail extends outward, curling upward at its end.

Hero appears to wear trousers. Small round coiffure rests at back of hero's neck.

Mane of lion to right is rendered by crisp serrated edge along contour of neck. Each lion has mouth open in roar.

Large crescent is in upper terminal field.

COMMENTARY

For comparative illustrations including PFS 1146, see pl. 251d (crescents).

SEAL APPLICATION (SEE *APPENDIX ONE: CONCORDANCE OF SEALS TO TABLETS IN VOLUME I*)

PFS 1146 occurs twice on the reverse of PF 1200, one application directly above the other. Both rollings preserve the entire length of the seal design; the upper rolling displays the lion to the left of the hero in the center; the lower rolling displays the hero in the center. The seal was clearly applied before the text since several cuneiform wedges cut into the bottom of the impression. PF 1200 is dated 504/503 B.C.

BIBLIOGRAPHY

Garrison 1988, pp. 305–07.

Cat.No. 41　　　　　　　　　　　　　　　　PFS 1325

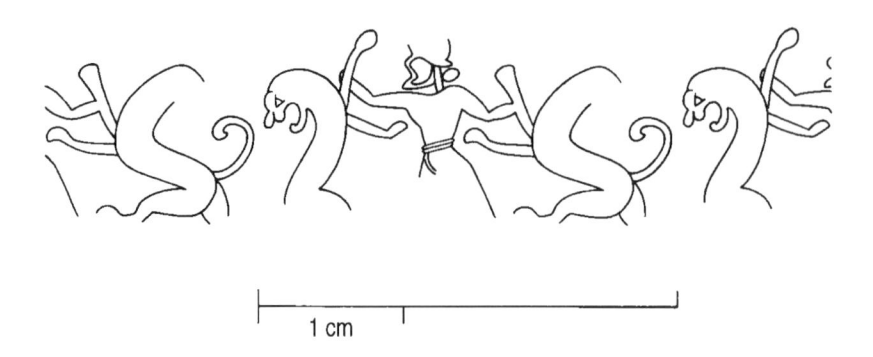

Seal Type:	Cylinder	Photograph:	Pl. 26a
Earliest Dated Application:	500/499 B.C.	Typology and Style:	I-A.4 — Mixed Styles I
Preserved Height of Image:	1.40 cm (incomp.)	Preserved Length of Image:	2.90 cm (comp.)
Estimated Height of Original Seal:	1.60 cm	Estimated Diameter of Original Seal:	0.90 cm
Number of Impressions:	1	Quality of Impression:	Fair

Completeness of Image: Segment of middle of design survives along its complete length

DESCRIPTION OF SEAL AS IMPRESSED IMAGE

Hero faces left, arms bent, and holds two rampant lions by upper foreleg.

Each lion moves toward hero but turns its head away from him; each lion holds upper foreleg straight and extends it upward toward hero's head. Lion to left holds lower foreleg straight, paw turned upward, and extends it downward toward hero's chest. Lion to right holds lower foreleg straight, paw curved, and extends it toward hero's waist. Lion to right raises forward hind leg toward hero; tail curls upward with tufted termination.

Hero appears to wear double-belted Assyrian garment with border aligned diagonally downward from waist. Hero perhaps wears domed headdress with projection at back. Hero appears to have pointed beard that rests over his right shoulder; small round coiffure rests at back of neck.

Lion to left has mouth open in roar.

COMMENTARY

Based on Q texts protocol, PFS 1325 should belong to Kammazikara, the *barrišdama* ("elite guide"), who in year 22 (500/499 B.C.) received flour rations for two Sardian men on their way from Susa to an individual named Šandupirzana (who is at Maknan) under the authority (*halmi*) of Parnaka. PF 1409 preserves the only occurrence of the name Kammazikara in the PF texts.

The animal forms are pure Fortification Style, but the geometric rendering of the hero's head is quite unusual; compare PFS 2 (Cat.No. 3). The modeled human forms are indicative of the Modeled Style.

For comparative illustrations including PFS 1325, see pls. 205g (arm positions of heroic control) and 288f (personal seals of elite guides [*barrišdama*]).

SEAL APPLICATION (SEE *APPENDIX ONE: CONCORDANCE OF SEALS TO TABLETS IN VOLUME I*)

PFS 1325 occurs on the upper edge of PF 1409. The rolling preserves the entire length of the seal design and displays the lion to the left of the hero in the center. PF 1409 is dated 500/499 B.C.

BIBLIOGRAPHY

Garrison 1988, pp. 249–52.

PFS 1440 Cat.No. 42

Seal Type:	Cylinder	Photograph:	Pl. 26c
Earliest Dated Application:	ND	Typology and Style:	I-A.4 — Fortification Style
Preserved Height of Image:	1.70 cm (incomp.)	Preserved Length of Image:	2.70 cm (comp.)
Estimated Height of Original Seal:	1.80 cm	Estimated Diameter of Original Seal:	0.90 cm
Number of Impressions:	2	Quality of Impressions:	Fair

Completeness of Image: Almost complete except for upper edge and details

DESCRIPTION OF SEAL AS IMPRESSED IMAGE

Hero faces left, arms bent, and holds two rampant lions by upper foreleg.

Each lion moves toward hero, but turns its head away from him. Each lion holds upper foreleg straight and extends it diagonally upward. Lion to left holds lower foreleg curved, extends it downward toward hero's foot; lion raises forward hind leg to place paw over foot of hero's forward leg; tail curls downward between its hind legs with tufted termination. Lion to right holds lower foreleg straight, paw turned upward, and extends it downward toward hero's leg; tail curls upward with tufted termination.

Hero appears to wear belted trousers. Pointed beard rests over hero's right shoulder; rounded coiffure rests at back of head.

Mane of lion to left is rendered by crisp serrated edge along contour of neck. Each lion has mouth open in roar.

Large crescent is in upper terminal field.

Line border is at bottom of design, serving also as ground line for figures.

COMMENTARY

Based on Q texts protocol, PFS 1440 should belong to Yaunaparza "the miller(?)," who in PF 1549 received wine rations under the authority (*halmi*) of Parnaka. PF 1549 preserves the only occurrence of the name Yaunaparza in the PF texts.

The design and style are big and bold, very similar to PFS 1083 (Cat.No. 43).

For comparative illustrations including PFS 1440, see pls. 251e (crescents), 277g (ground lines on cylinder seals), and 289e (personal seals of various receivers).

SEAL APPLICATION (SEE *APPENDIX ONE: CONCORDANCE OF SEALS TO TABLETS IN VOLUME I*)

PFS 1440 occurs on the reverse (inverted) and upper edge of PF 1549. Both rollings preserve the entire length of the seal design; that on the upper edge displays the hero and the lion to right in the center; that on the reverse displays the lion to the right of the hero in the center. On the reverse the seal clearly was applied before the text since several cuneiform wedges cut into the bottom of the impression. The date of PF 1549 is unknown.

BIBLIOGRAPHY

Garrison 1988, pp. 305–07.

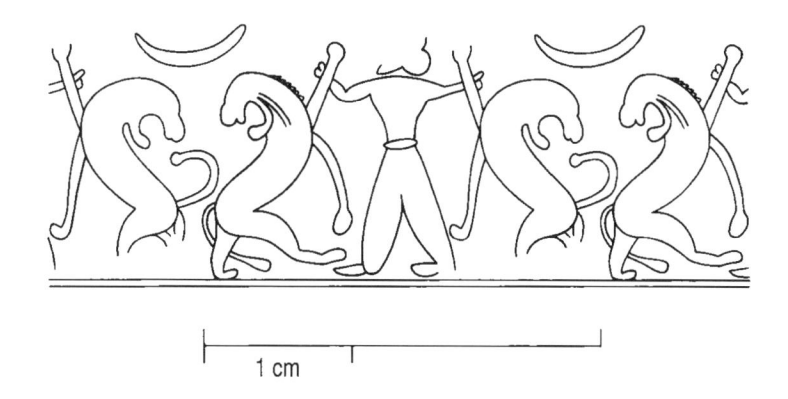

Cat.No. 43 PFS 1083

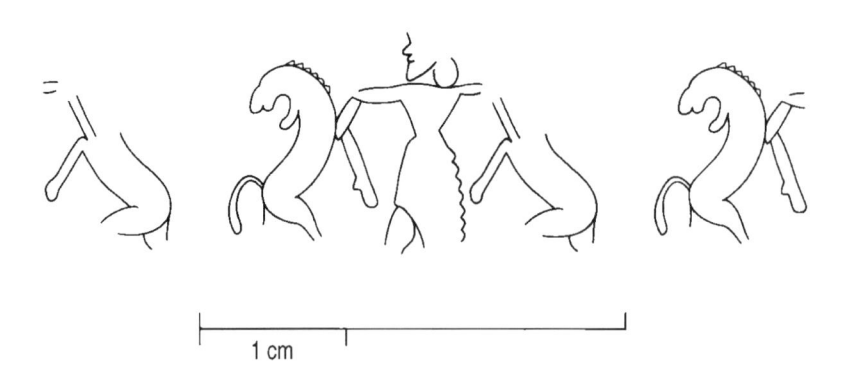

Seal Type:	Cylinder	Photograph:	Pl. 27a
Earliest Dated Application:	497/496 B.C.	Typology and Style:	I-A.4 — Fortification Style
Preserved Height of Image:	1.50 cm (incomp.)	Preserved Length of Image:	3.00 cm (comp.)
Estimated Height of Original Seal:	1.70 cm	Estimated Diameter of Original Seal:	1.00 cm
Number of Impressions:	1	Quality of Impression:	Poor

Completeness of Image: Segment of middle of design survives along its complete length

DESCRIPTION OF SEAL AS IMPRESSED IMAGE

Hero faces left, arms straight, and holds two rampant lions by upper foreleg.

Each lion moves toward hero but turns its head away from him (preserved only at left). Each lion holds upper foreleg straight and extends it upward toward hero's head; lower foreleg is straight and extended downward toward hero's leg. Tail of lion to left curves downward. Lion to right appears to raise forward hind leg toward hero.

Hero wears Assyrian garment that leaves forward leg exposed below knee; fringe(?) is indicated along back edge of lower garment. Pointed beard rests over hero's right shoulder; large rounded coiffure rests at back of neck.

Mane of lion to left is rendered by crisp serrated edge along contour of neck; mouth is open in roar.

COMMENTARY

The bold carving style is very similar to that seen on PFS 1440 (Cat.No. 42).

For comparative illustrations including PFS 1083, see pl. 271e (compositions with large empty space as terminal field).

SEAL APPLICATION (SEE *APPENDIX ONE: CONCORDANCE OF SEALS TO TABLETS IN VOLUME I*)

PFS 1083 occurs on the reverse of PF 1131. The rolling preserves the entire length of the seal design and displays the lions in the center. The seal clearly was applied before the text since several cuneiform wedges cut into the top of the impression. PF 1131 is dated 497/496 B.C.

BIBLIOGRAPHY

Garrison 1988, pp. 304–07.

PFS 1285 — Cat.No. 44

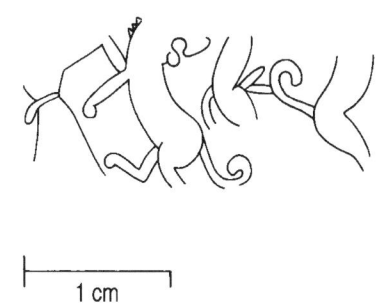

├─── 1 cm ───┤

Seal Type:	Cylinder	Photograph:	Pl. 27c
Earliest Dated Application:	500 B.C.	Typology and Style:	I-A.4 — Fortification Style
Preserved Height of Image:	1.30 cm (incomp.)	Preserved Length of Image:	2.50 cm (incomp.)
Estimated Height of Original Seal:	NA	Estimated Diameter of Original Seal:	NA
Number of Impressions:	1	Quality of Impression:	Fair

Completeness of Image: Segment of middle of design survives

DESCRIPTION OF SEAL AS IMPRESSED IMAGE

Hero holds two rampant lions by upper foreleg (connection between hero and lion preserved only for lion held by hero at right).

Hindquarters and tail of animal preserved at far right of impression belong to lion held by hero at left; tail of this lion extends upward, curling at end. Lion to right of hero moves toward hero but turns its head away from him. Lion holds upper foreleg straight and extends it diagonally upward; lower foreleg is straight, paw turned downward, and extended downward toward hero's hip. Lion raises bent forward hind leg toward hero; tail curves downward, hooking upward at its termination.

Hero wears belted garment of uncertain type. Mane of lion to right of hero is rendered by crisp serrated edge along contour of its neck; mouth is open in roar.

Suspended in middle of the terminal field are preserved hindquarters and tail of vertically disposed ithyphallic animal (quadruped) of uncertain type moving to right; tail (only partially preserved) curves downward.

COMMENTARY

Based on Q texts protocol, PFS 1285 should belong to Turpiš the *karabattiš* (caravan leader), who in year 22.9 (500 B.C.) received flour rations. A Turpiš also occurs in the Q text PF 1571, receiving grain for mules and men, using PFS 1456s (illegible). There seem to be several individuals having this name, but only the one in PF 1341 is qualified as a *karabattiš*. Koch (1990, p. 14 [n. 44]; 84 [n. 367]; 90 [n. 395]; 97 [n. 416]; 209) suggests that the Turpiš who occurs in the two Q texts is the same individual. A Turpiš supplied goats in PF 72; other occurrences of the name are found in PF 146 (*wumrudda* deposited into his account), PF 246 (grain supplier), PF 257 (wine entrusted to him), PF 380 (received grain), PF 642 (grain entrusted to him), PF 850–853 (grain supplier at Kurištiš), PF 1637 (grain supplier at Kansan), perhaps PF 1664 (grain supplier at Kurištiš), PF 1765 (received *hamura* for horses; described as a horseman for *kulla*-horses of the king), PF 1766 (suppler for horses), PF 1946 (received grain for horses), PF 1963 (account of grain received by him), PF 1971 (received grain at Tukraš), PF 1981 (reckoned account for storehouse at Tukraš), and PF 2012 (mentioned in long account text).

The composition seems somewhat crowded, but the preserved impression suggests a well-executed design.

For comparative illustrations including PFS 1285, see pl. 288b (personal seals of various men leading groups).

SEAL APPLICATION (SEE *APPENDIX ONE: CONCORDANCE OF SEALS TO TABLETS IN VOLUME I*)

PFS 1285 occurs on the reverse of PF 1341. The partial rolling displays the lion to the right of the hero and the animal in the terminal field in the center. The seal clearly was applied before the text since several cuneiform wedges cut into the bottom of the impression. PF 1341 is dated 500 B.C.

BIBLIOGRAPHY

Garrison 1988, pp. 302–04.

Cat.No. 45   PFS 1053

|— 1 cm —|

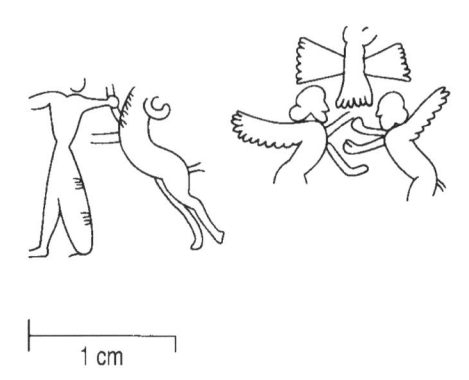

Seal Type:	Cylinder	Photograph:	Pl. 28a
Earliest Dated Application:	501/500 B.C.	Typology and Style:	I-A.4 — Fortification Style
Preserved Height of Image:	1.60 cm (incomp.)	Preserved Length of Image:	3.00 cm (incomp.)
Estimated Height of Original Seal:	NA	Estimated Diameter of Original Seal:	NA
Number of Impressions:	2	Quality of Impressions:	Poor

Completeness of Image: Segment of middle of design survives

DESCRIPTION OF SEAL AS IMPRESSED IMAGE

Hero faces left, arms straight at horizontal, and presumably holds two rampant lions (preserved only at right) by upper foreleg.

Lion to right moves toward hero but turns its head away from him. Lion holds upper foreleg curved and extends it upward toward hero's head; lower foreleg is straight (only partially preserved) and extended toward hero's waist; tail (only partially preserved) extended outward.

Hero wears Assyrian garment that leaves forward leg exposed; fringe or other decorative detailing is indicated along back edge of lower part of garment. Rounded coiffure is partially preserved at back of hero's neck.

Mane of lion to right is rendered by crisp points just inside contour of neck; mouth is open in roar.

In terminal field two rampant winged human-headed bull or lion creatures move toward each other. Creature to left holds upper foreleg straight and extends it diagonally upward; lower foreleg is bent, paw turned upward, and extended diagonally downward. Creature to right holds forelegs straight, paws turned upward, and extends them together in front of its body; tail (partially preserved) curves downward. Each creature has beard that terminates in blunt point over its chest; rounded coiffure rests at back of neck. Above creatures, figure emerges from winged symbol with bird's tail; faces right, and appears to raise arm(s) before its face (not preserved).

Figure emergent wears garment of uncertain type.

COMMENTARY

The design is well executed and ambitious. See Garrison 1988 for the important group of artists represented by PFS 1053, who frequently draw on imagery from the Court Style. See the commentary on PFS 7* (Cat.No. 4) for the figure emerging from the winged symbol and for the form of the symbol. See the commentary on PFS 1071 (Cat.No. 29) for winged symbols supported by creatures.

For comparative illustrations including PFS 1053, see pls. 248c (deities emergent from winged symbol) and 266e (terminal field motifs other than inscriptions).

SEAL APPLICATION (SEE *APPENDIX ONE: CONCORDANCE OF SEALS TO TABLETS IN VOLUME I*)

PFS 1053 occurs twice on the reverse of PF 1095, one impression directly above the other. The partial upper rolling preserves only the hero, the lion to right, and the terminal field motif. The lower rolling preserves only the terminal field motif. PF 1095 is dated 501/500 B.C.

BIBLIOGRAPHY

Dusinberre 1997b, p. 128 (n. 135); Garrison 1988, pp. 348–52, 490.

PFS 225   Cat.No. 46

Seal Type:	Cylinder	Photograph:	Pl. 28c
Earliest Dated Application:	499/498 B.C.	Typology and Style:	I-A.4 — Fortification Style
Preserved Height of Image:	1.80 cm (incomp.)	Preserved Length of Image:	3.10 cm (comp.)
Estimated Height of Original Seal:	2.00 cm	Estimated Diameter of Original Seal:	1.00 cm
Number of Impressions:	2	Quality of Impressions:	Fair

Completeness of Image: Complete except for upper edge and lower edge

DESCRIPTION OF SEAL AS IMPRESSED IMAGE

Hero faces right (with lower body turned to left), arms bent, and holds two rampant lions by top of head (left) and forelock/ear (right).

Each lion moves away from hero but turns its head back toward him. Lion to left holds upper foreleg straight and extends it vertically upward in front of its neck; lower foreleg is straight and extended vertically downward in front of its body. Lion to right holds upper foreleg straight and extends it diagonally upward; lower foreleg is straight, paw turned upward, and extended diagonally downward to rest on horned animal (deer) in terminal field. Each lion has long thin tail that curves downward between its hind legs.

Hero appears to wear belted Persian court robe with sleeves pushed up to reveal arms and lower garment hitched up over hero's right leg. Fold line of gathered sleeve is on left side of upper part of garment. Rounded beard rests over hero's left shoulder; round coiffure rests at back of neck. Hero wears conical headdress.

Lion to left has mouth open in roar and is ithyphallic. Lion to right has large curved muscle detail at shoulder; mane is rendered by flat hatching along contour of neck; short pointed ear or forelock emerges from front of head; mouth is open in roar.

Lions create heraldic group doubled by framing terminal field motif of small, heraldically posed deer rampant on either side of lower part of stylized tree of uncertain type. Deer to left holds upper foreleg bent and extends it upward toward tree; lower foreleg is bent and held down in front of its body; two-pronged antler emerges from back of its head; tail (end not preserved) curls upward. Deer to right holds upper foreleg slightly bent and extends it upward toward tree; lower foreleg is slightly bent and extended downward toward tree; antler and tail are not preserved.

120 SEALS ON THE PERSEPOLIS FORTIFICATION TABLETS, VOLUME I: IMAGES OF HEROIC ENCOUNTER

COMMENTARY

Koch (1990) assigns the seal to Da'uka, perhaps the *titikaš* (supervisor?) who received and passed on rations for workers. Da'uka worked around Tašpak in Koch's Elam Region VI.

The seal is relatively large. The design is enlivened by the terminal field image, forming a doubled-heraldic group with the lions; see a similar compositional concept in PFS 162 (Cat.No. 249), PFS 496 (Cat.No. 108), and PFS 1519 (Cat.No. 167), probably by the same artist as PFS 225 and PFS 1123 (Cat.No. 279). Overall the design is quite elaborate. For similar rendering of the shoulder muscle of the lion to right, see PFS 255 (Cat.No. 233).

For comparative illustrations including PFS 225, see pls. 186h (headdresses), 193d (round coiffures), 205a (arm positions of heroic control), 241h (heroic encounters fused with heraldic motifs), 256a (stylized trees), 269d (terminal field motifs other than inscriptions), and 284d (personal seals of various officers).

SEAL APPLICATION (SEE *APPENDIX ONE: CONCORDANCE OF SEALS TO TABLETS IN VOLUME I*)

PFS 225 occurs on the reverse of both PF 1099 and PF 1167 (inverted). The rolling on PF 1167 preserves the entire length of the seal design and displays the hero in the center. The partial rolling on PF 1099 preserves only the lion to the right of the hero. On both tablets the seal clearly was applied before the text since several cuneiform wedges cut into the top or bottom of the impressions. PF 1099 and PF 1167 are both dated 499/498 B.C.

BIBLIOGRAPHY

Garrison 1988, pp. 276–78, 281; Garrison and Dion 1999, p. 6 (n. 15); Koch 1990, pp. 158 (n. 674), 180, 187 (n. 777).

Cat.No. 47   PFS 361

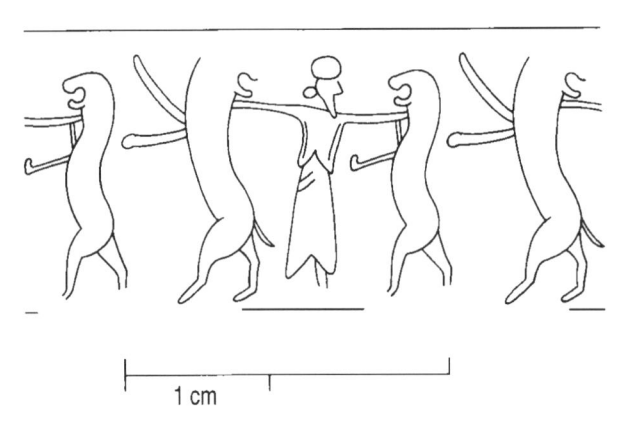

Seal Type:	Cylinder	Photograph:	Pl. 29a
Earliest Dated Application:	499/498 B.C.	Typology and Style:	I-A.4 — Mixed Styles II
Preserved Height of Image:	1.80 cm (comp.)	Preserved Length of Image:	2.20 cm (comp.)
Estimated Height of Original Seal:	1.80 cm	Estimated Diameter of Original Seal:	0.70 cm
Number of Impressions:	4	Quality of Impressions:	Very poor

Completeness of Image: Complete except for lower edge and details

DESCRIPTION OF SEAL AS IMPRESSED IMAGE

Hero faces right, arms straight at horizontal, and holds two rampant lions by throat.

Lion to left moves away from hero but turns its head back toward him. Lion holds upper foreleg straight and extends it diagonally upward; lower foreleg is straight and extended horizontally outward; short tail curves downward. Lion to right moves toward and faces hero; lion holds upper foreleg straight and extends it upward to place paw on hero's arm; lower foreleg is straight, paw turned upward, and extended toward hero's waist.

Hero wears Persian court robe with sleeves pushed up to reveal arms; gather folds of sleeves are indicated, as are two diagonal folds on lower part of garment. Long pointed beard rests across hero's left shoulder; small round coiffure rests at back of neck. Hero perhaps wears domed headdress.

Each lion has mouth open in roar.

Edge of seal is preserved at top and partially (under hero) at bottom of design.

COMMENTARY

Although the iconography and a few aspects of style indicate ties to the Court Style, the overall style is clearly related more to the Fortification Style (contra Garrison 1988, where it was classified as Court Style). This composition in a control encounter (where one animal moves away from the hero, the other animal toward him) is unusual.

SEAL APPLICATION (SEE *APPENDIX ONE: CONCORDANCE OF SEALS TO TABLETS IN VOLUME I*)

PFS 361 occurs on the reverse (inverted) and left edge of PF 55 and the reverse (inverted) and upper edge of PF 324. The impression on the left edge of PF 55 is too poorly preserved for analysis. The remaining three applications preserve the entire length of the seal design; two display the hero in the center; one displays the two lions in the center. PF 55 and PF 324 are both dated 499/498 B.C.

BIBLIOGRAPHY

Garrison 1988, pp. 412, 417, 442.

I-A.5. WINGED LION CREATURES

PFS 86   Cat.No. 48

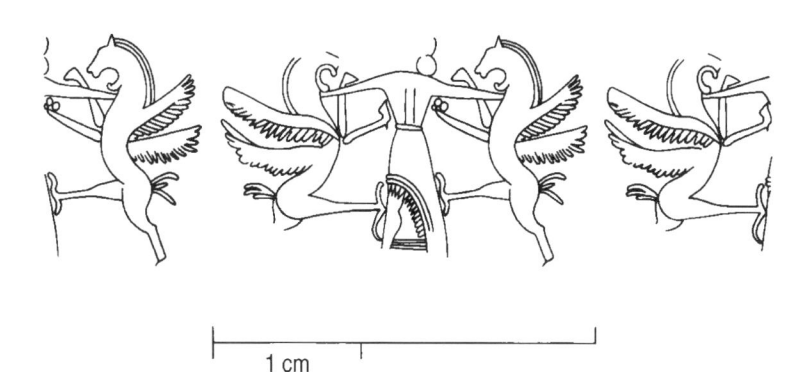

Seal Type:	Cylinder	Photographs:	Pl. 29c–d
Earliest Dated Application:	501/500 B.C.	Typology and Style:	I-A.5 — Fortification Style
Preserved Height of Image:	1.60 cm (incomp.)	Preserved Length of Image:	2.60 cm (comp.)
Estimated Height of Original Seal:	1.90 cm	Estimated Diameter of Original Seal:	0.80 cm
Number of Impressions:	8	Quality of Impressions:	Fair-good

Completeness of Image: Almost complete except for upper edge and lower edge

DESCRIPTION OF SEAL AS IMPRESSED IMAGE

Hero faces left, arms straight, and holds two rampant winged lion creatures by throat.

Each creature holds upper foreleg straight and extends it upward to wrap paw around hero's upper arm; lower foreleg is straight and extended upward to place upturned paw at hero's chest. Paw of creature to right is depicted by three small dots. Each creature lifts forward straight hind leg to place bird's foot on hero's leg; each creature has three-feathered bird's tail that curls slightly downward.

Hero wears belted Assyrian garment that leaves forward leg exposed below lower thigh; two vertical lines are on upper part of garment over chest; double border with fringe is along front of lower part of hero's garment;

lower hem of garment between hero's feet shows triple horizontal border. Round coiffure rests at back of hero's neck.

Each creature has two wings, the upper parallel to the lower; mane is rendered by smooth thin outline (double on creature to right) along contour of neck. Creature to right has short pointed ear emerging from top of its head. Each creature opens mouth in roar.

COMMENTARY

Koch (1990) suggests that PFS 86 may belong to an unnamed official connected with the treasury at Tirazziš (Shiraz).

The design is well conceived and executed. There are several decorative effects, such as the hero's elaborate garment and the crisply executed birds' feet. For the linear border on the forward edge of the hero's lower garment, see PFS 480 (Cat.No. 134) and PFS 971 (Cat.No. 171). PFS 439 (Cat.No. 150) may be the same seal, but it is too poorly preserved to make a definite collation.

For comparative illustrations including PFS 86, see pls. 176e (Assyrian garments with detailing preserved) and 230f (feet of animals and creatures).

SEAL APPLICATION (SEE *APPENDIX ONE: CONCORDANCE OF SEALS TO TABLETS IN VOLUME I*)

PFS 86 occurs on the left edge of four tablets (PF 128, PF 129, PF 131, and PF 284) and the reverse of three tablets (PF 1013–1015). On PF 1013 the seal also is applied on the upper edge. On the reverse of PF 1015 the seal is inverted. Some impressions exhibit lateral distortion. In two impressions the seal has been rolled for at least one complete turn, preserving the entire length of the seal design. Of these two applications, one displays the hero in the center; one displays the hero and the creature to the right in the center. Of the remaining six partial rollings, one displays the hero in the center; two preserve only the hero and the creature to right; two display the creature to the left of the hero in the center; one preserves only the two creatures. On the reverse of PF 1014 and PF 1015 the seal clearly was applied before the text since several cuneiform wedges cut into the top or bottom of the impressions. PF 128, PF 129, PF 131, and PF 284 are the earliest dated tablets with PFS 86 and all are dated 501/500 B.C.

BIBLIOGRAPHY

Dusinberre 1997b, p. 127 (n. 119); Garrison 1988, pp. 247–48, 297–99; Garrison and Dion 1999, p. 8 (n. 17); Koch 1990, p. 58.

PFS 120   Cat.No. 49

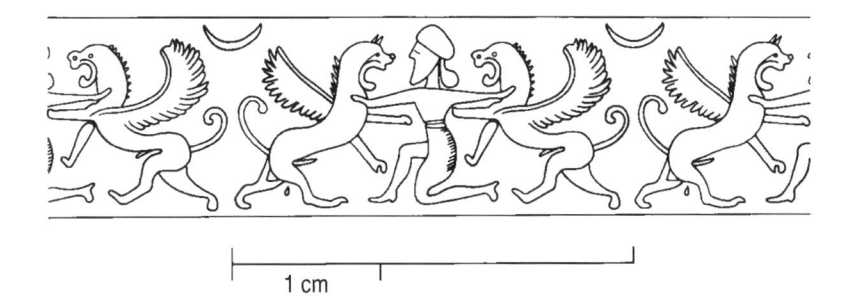

Seal Type:	Cylinder	Photographs:	Pl. 30a–c
Earliest Dated Application:	504/503(?) B.C.	Typology and Style:	I-A.5 — Fortification Style
Preserved Height of Image:	1.30 cm (comp.)	Preserved Length of Image:	2.60 cm (comp.)
Estimated Height of Original Seal:	1.30 cm	Estimated Diameter of Original Seal:	0.80 cm
Number of Impressions:	11	Quality of Impressions:	Good

Completeness of Image: Complete

DESCRIPTION OF SEAL AS IMPRESSED IMAGE

Hero faces left in *knielauf*-pose, arms straight at horizontal, and holds two rampant winged lion creatures by throat.

Each creature holds upper foreleg straight and extends it toward hero's chest; lower foreleg is straight and extended downward toward hero's legs. Their tails curve upward with tufted terminations.

Hero appears to wear belted trousers with linear detailing on rear leg. Pointed beard rests over hero's right shoulder; rounded coiffure curls upward at back of neck. Hero appears to wear flat headdress.

Mane of each creature is rendered by crisp serrated edge along contour of neck. Creature to left has two ears. Each creature has mouth open in roar and is ithyphallic.

Crescent appears in upper terminal field.

Edge of seal is visible at top and bottom of design.

COMMENTARY

PFS 120 occurs only on the long journals (V texts) and accounts (W texts). Koch (1990) assigns PFS 120 to Mawukka, a "Steuereinnehmer" (*bazikara*) at Battirakkan in her Persepolis Region I. Mawukka is under the supervision of Iršena and Bakabada. Mawukka seems to appear at many other places and to perform many other functions (if it is the same person in all texts that preserve the name).

See Garrison 1988 for the distinctive hand of this artist in other seals. The design has several peculiarities, including the *knielauf*-pose of the hero; compare PFS 67 (Cat.No. 293), PFS 1309s (Cat.No. 229), and PFS 1527 (Cat.No. 32).[17] The *knielauf*-pose is far more common in archer scenes (Volume II). Note also how the hero fills the entire height of the field and the creatures are placed diagonally in the field. This is one of the few seals of heroic encounter in which the complete figural design and all details are preserved.

For comparative illustrations including PFS 120, see pls. 184c (trousers), 186e (headdresses), 202d (arm positions of heroic control), 210g (heroic attitudes of control encounter), and 250c (crescents).

SEAL APPLICATION (SEE *APPENDIX ONE: CONCORDANCE OF SEALS TO TABLETS IN VOLUME I*)

PFS 120 occurs on various edges of eight tablets, applied either once or twice on each tablet: only on the left edge (PF 1940 and PF 2013); only on the reverse (PF 1943); only on the lower edge (PF 1945 and PF 2079); on the upper edge and left edge (PF 1965); on the reverse and left edge (PF 2001); on the reverse and upper edge (PF 2075). On the reverse of PF 1943, PF 2001, and PF 2075 the seal is inverted. Impressions are clear and carefully applied, showing little or no distortion. Often rollings are quite long; compare especially PF 2001 and

---

17. On the *knielauf*-pose in western Asiatic art, see Kantor 1962.
For comparanda from Susa, see Amiet 1973b, pl. 2, nos. 8–10.

PF 2013. All impressions preserve the entire seal design. Of the total eleven applications, one preserves four complete rollings of the seal with the figural composition intact, two in each half of the impression; one preserves two and a half rollings of the seal with the figural composition intact on the left edge and middle of the impression; one preserves two complete rollings of the seal, with the figural composition intact in the center of the impression and half scenes on each end of the impression; four preserve two full rollings of the seal with the figural composition intact in each half of the impression; one displays the hero in the center; one displays the hero and the creature to left in the center; one displays the creature to the left of the hero in the center; and one displays the two creatures in the center. On the reverse of PF 1943, PF 2001, and PF 2075 the seal clearly was applied before the text since several cuneiform wedges cut into the bottom of the impression. PF 2075 is the earliest dated tablet with PFS 120 and is dated 504/503(?) B.C.

BIBLIOGRAPHY

Garrison 1988, pp. 330–33, 345, 494; Garrison and Root 1996, p. 11; Koch 1990, pp. 32 (n. 149), 256.

Cat.No. 50   PFS 201

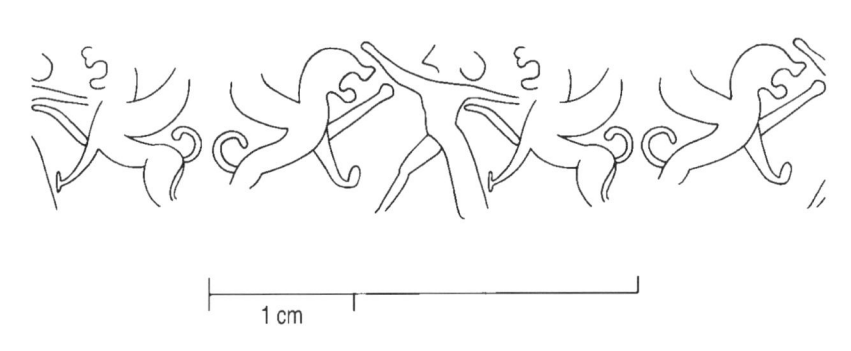

Seal Type:	Cylinder	Photographs:	Pl. 31a–b
Earliest Dated Application:	494 B.C.	Typology and Style:	I-A.5 — Fortification Style
Preserved Height of Image:	1.20 cm (incomp.)	Preserved Length of Image:	2.90 cm (comp.)
Estimated Height of Original Seal:	1.40 cm	Estimated Diameter of Original Seal:	0.90 cm
Number of Impressions:	3	Quality of Impressions:	Poor

Completeness of Image: Almost complete except for upper edge and lower edge

DESCRIPTION OF SEAL AS IMPRESSED IMAGE

Hero faces left, arms straight, and holds two rampant winged lion creatures, one to left by top of its head(?), one to right by its throat. Hero is in vigorous striding pose, with forward leg slightly bent.

Creature to left holds upper foreleg straight and extends it upward toward hero's arm; lower foreleg is straight, paw bent upward, and extended downward toward hero's lower leg. Creature to right holds upper foreleg slightly bent and extends it upward toward hero's chest; lower foreleg is slightly curved, paw turned upward, and extended downward toward hero's lower leg. Tail of each creature curls upward with tufted termination.

Hero wears Assyrian garment that leaves forward leg exposed. Large rounded coiffure rests at back of neck.

Each creature has mouth open in roar.

COMMENTARY

Lewis suggests that PFS 201 belongs to an unnamed beer supplier at Hidali. A new occurrence of this seal has been identified on the travel text PF 1543, apparently confirming this attribution. Based on Q texts protocol, PFS 201 should belong to the unnamed beer supplier, who in 27.11 (494 B.C.) supplied beer to Mella on his way from Susa to Persepolis. PFS 201 also occurs, however, on the left edge of the travel text PF 1404, where flour (not beer) was supplied by an unnamed individual. In PF 1276 (P text, daily rations), PFS 201 occurs on the reverse; beer was received by Pilpisurmu(?) at Hidali.[18] In PF 749 (K1 text, rations for individuals with religious functions), PFS 201 occurs on the left edge; beer was received by Da'upirna at Hidali.

See Garrison 1988 for the artist and workshop producing PFS 201.

For comparative illustrations including PFS 201, see pls. 174c (Assyrian garments), 210h (heroic attitudes of control encounter), and 287e (personal seals of various suppliers).

SEAL APPLICATION (SEE *APPENDIX ONE: CONCORDANCE OF SEALS TO TABLETS IN VOLUME I*)

PFS 201 occurs on the left edge of PF 749, PF 1404, and PF 1543 and on the reverse (inverted) of PF 1276. One rolling preserves the entire length of the seal design and displays the hero in the center. Of the remaining three partial rollings, one displays the hero in the center; one displays the creature to the right of the hero in the center; one displays the hero and the creature to the left in the center. On the reverse of PF 1276 the seal clearly was applied before the text since several cuneiform wedges cut into the top of the impression. PF 1543 is the earliest dated tablet with PFS 201 and is dated 494 B.C.

BIBLIOGRAPHY

Garrison 1988, pp. 333–35; Garrison and Root 1996, p. 14; Lewis 1980, p. 194; Root 1997, p. 237, fig. 4; Root 1998, p. 275.

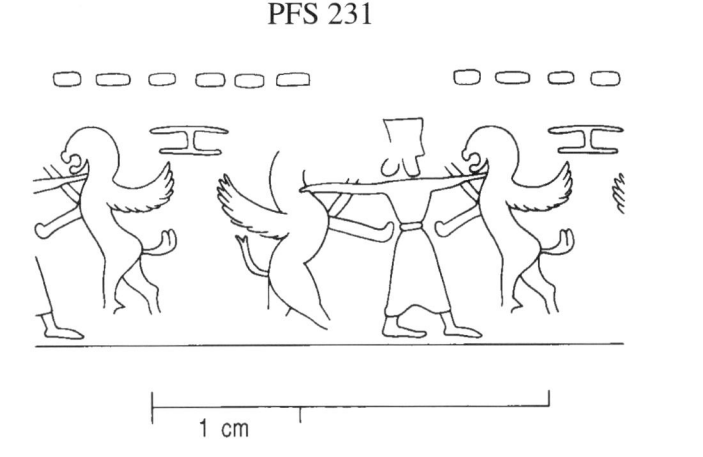

PFS 231 — Cat.No. 51

Seal type:	Cylinder	Photographs:	Pl. 32a–b
Earliest Dated Application:	500 B.C.	Typology and Style:	I-A.5 — Fortification Style
Preserved Height of Image:	1.80 cm (incl. cap)	Preserved Length of Image:	2.70 cm (comp.)
Estimated Height of Original Seal:	1.80 cm (incl. cap)	Estimated Diameter of Original Seal:	0.90 cm
Number of Impressions:	5	Quality of Impressions:	Fair

Completeness of Image: Almost complete except for portions of upper edge and lower edge

DESCRIPTION OF SEAL AS IMPRESSED IMAGE

Hero faces right, arms straight at horizontal, and holds two rampant winged lion creatures by throat.

Each creature holds upper foreleg (only partially preserved) straight and extends it upward toward hero's head; lower foreleg is straight, paw turned upward, and extended downward toward hero's waist. Tail of creature to left curves upward with forked termination. Tail of creature to right extends horizontally outward, curving upward at its end with two-pronged plume-like termination.

Hero wears belted Persian court robe with sleeves and folds not portrayed but with characteristic profile hem line. Hero wears polos headdress. Squared beard rests over hero's left shoulder; rounded coiffure rests at back of neck.

---

18. Delaunay (1976, p. 24) suggests that the name Pilpisurmu(?) is a transcription of the Greek Philippos and that therefore this person may be an Ionian.

Creature to right has mouth open in roar.

Elongated "H-shaped" device is disposed horizontally in upper terminal field.

Edge of seal is preserved at bottom of design.

Row of rectangular depressions along top of impressions probably indicates traces of studded seal cap.

COMMENTARY

Although not well preserved, the engraving appears to have been well executed, the design well composed.

The linear device is not tabulated by Boardman (1970a, fig. 3; 1998). It looks somewhat like the Phoenician-Punic (and Greek) sign for "z" (Guzzo 1997, fig. 1).

For comparative illustrations including PFS 231, see pls. 189g (polos headdresses), 255b (various devices and symbols), 267c (terminal field motifs other than inscriptions), and 276e (borders).

SEAL APPLICATION (SEE *APPENDIX ONE: CONCORDANCE OF SEALS TO TABLETS IN VOLUME I*)

PFS 231 occurs on the reverse (inverted) and upper edge of PF 1677 and PF 1703. The seal is carefully applied twice on the reverse of PF 1677, one impression directly above the other, each application rolled in the same sequence. All five rollings preserve the entire length of the seal design; one displays the hero in the center; two display the hero and the creature to left in the center; two display the hero and the creature to right in the center. On PF 1677 and PF 1703 the seal clearly was applied before the text since several cuneiform wedges cut into the relief along the bottom of the impression. PF 1677 and PF 1703 are both dated 500 B.C.

BIBLIOGRAPHY

Garrison 1988, pp. 318–19.

PFS 233 — Cat.No. 52

Seal Type:	Cylinder	Photographs:	Pl. 33a–b
Earliest Dated Application:	ND	Typology and Style:	I-A.5 — Fortification Style
Preserved Height of Image:	1.50 cm (incomp.)	Preserved Length of Image:	2.60 cm (comp.)
Estimated Height of Original Seal:	1.80 cm	Estimated Diameter of Original Seal:	0.80 cm
Number of Impressions:	6	Quality of Impressions:	Poor

Completeness of Image: Complete except for lower edge

DESCRIPTION OF SEAL AS IMPRESSED IMAGE

Hero faces right with forward leg raised, arms slightly bent at horizontal, and holds two rampant winged lion creatures by throat.

Creature to left holds upper foreleg straight and extends it upward to wrap paw around hero's upper arm; lower foreleg is straight, toes splayed, and extended upward toward hero's chest. Creature raises straight forward hind leg to place bird's foot on hero's leg. Creature to right holds upper foreleg straight and extends it upward to place paw on hero's arm; lower foreleg is straight, paw turned upward, and extended upward toward hero's elbow. Creature raises straight forward hind leg to place bird's foot on hero's knee. Each creature has short thick bird-like tail that curves slightly upward.

Hero wears double-belted Assyrian garment that leaves forward leg exposed. Squared beard rests above hero's chest; round coiffure rests at back of neck. Hero perhaps wears domed headdress.

Creature to left has double row of feathers on wing; mane is rendered by crisp serrated edge along lower contour of neck; mouth is open in roar. Creature to right has two wings, the upper extending diagonally upward from the lower; mouth is open in roar.

Line border is preserved at top edge of design.

COMMENTARY

The abstract geometric rendering of the hero's facial features recalls somewhat the human and animal heads on PFS 2 (Cat.No. 3) and stylistically related designs. See the discussion of PFS 2 (Cat.No. 3).
    For comparative illustrations including PFS 233, see pl. 211a (heroic attitudes of control encounter).

SEAL APPLICATION (SEE *APPENDIX ONE: CONCORDANCE OF SEALS TO TABLETS IN VOLUME I*)

PFS 233 occurs on the reverse and left edge of PF 328, and the reverse, upper edge, and left edge of PF 329. No other seal is used on the tablets; on both tablets the seal is inverted on the reverse. The seal has been applied twice on the reverse of PF 328, one impression directly above the other. In four impressions the seal is rolled for at least one complete turn, preserving the entire length of the seal design. Of these four applications, one displays the hero in the center; two display the creature to the right of the hero in the center; one displays the negative space in the terminal field in the center. Both of the remaining two partial impressions display the hero in the center. The dates of PF 328 and PF 329 are unknown.

BIBLIOGRAPHY

Garrison 1988, pp. 273–76.

Cat.No. 53 PFS 294

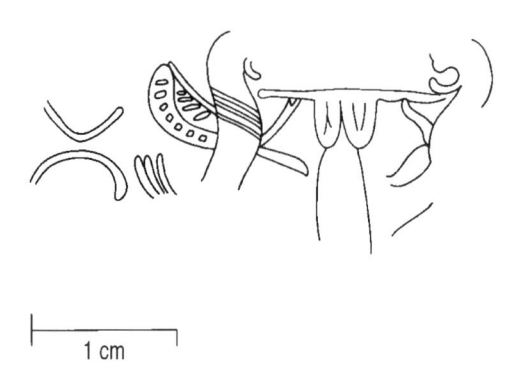

Seal Type:	Cylinder	Photograph:	Pl. 34a
Earliest Dated Application:	500 B.C.	Typology and Style:	I-A.5 — Linear Styles
Preserved Height of Image:	1.50 cm (incomp.)	Preserved Length of Image:	3.20 cm (incomp.)
Estimated Height of Original Seal:	NA	Estimated Diameter of Original Seal:	NA
Number of Impressions:	5	Quality of Impressions:	Poor

Completeness of Image: Segment of middle of design survives

DESCRIPTION OF SEAL AS IMPRESSED IMAGE

Hero has arms straight at horizontal and holds two(?) rampant winged lion creatures (wing of creature at right not preserved) by throat.

Each creature holds upper foreleg straight and extends it upward to place paw on hero's elbow; lower foreleg is straight and extended downward toward hero's hip. Creature to left has three-pronged bird's tail that curves upward.

Hero wears Persian court robe with sleeves pushed up to reveal arms; upper part of garment is rendered by two large swags of drapery with folds indicated.

Creature to left has three diagonal lines on its chest; row of studs is disposed along lower edge of wing. Each creature opens mouth in roar.

V-shaped crescent appears above inverted crescent in terminal field.

COMMENTARY

An outline linear style is used on this seal; see PFS 1020 (Cat.No. 37) for a similar style. The rendering of the upper garment is related to PFS 301 (Cat.No. 54).

It is possible but not demonstrable that the two crescent devices in the terminal field are actually the tails of two animals disposed in an unusual terminal field arrangement, with lower animal inverted.

For comparative illustrations including PFS 294, see pls. 178d (Persian court robes with sleeves pushed up in deep swags), 202e (arm positions of heroic control), and 223b (lions and lion creatures).

SEAL APPLICATION (SEE *APPENDIX ONE: CONCORDANCE OF SEALS TO TABLETS IN VOLUME I*)

PFS 294 occurs on the reverse and left edge of PF 1004 and PF 1005. No other seal is used on the tablets. On the reverse of PF 1004 the seal is applied twice; one is rolled along the longitudinal axis of the tablet at the right edge, the other rolled along the horizontal axis at the bottom. The impression on the left edge of PF 1004 is too poorly preserved for analysis. In one impression (PFS 1005 reverse) the seal is rolled to preserve the entire length of the partially retrieved seal design in the sequence shown in our drawing. This impression displays the hero and the creature to the left in the center. Of the remaining three impressions, two display the hero in the center; one displays the hero and the creature to the right in the center. On the reverse of PF 1005 the seal clearly was applied before the text since several cuneiform wedges cut into the top of the impression. PF 1004 and PF 1005 are both dated 500 B.C.

BIBLIOGRAPHY

Brosius 1996, p. 133 (table 2); Garrison 1988, pp. 440–42, 497, 531.

PFS 301   Cat.No. 54

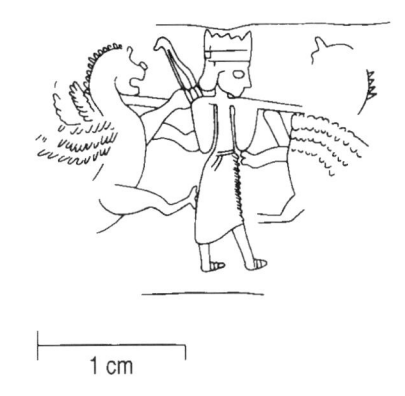

1 cm

Seal Type:	Cylinder	Photographs:	Pl. 34c–d
Earliest Dated Application:	499/498 B.C.	Typology and Style:	I-A.5 — Fortification Style
Preserved Height of Image:	1.80 cm (comp.)	Preserved Length of Image:	2.30 cm (incomp.)
Estimated Height of Original Seal:	1.80 cm	Estimated Diameter of Original Seal:	NA
Number of Impressions:	2	Quality of Impressions:	Fair

Completeness of Image: Segment of middle of design survives

DESCRIPTION OF SEAL AS IMPRESSED IMAGE

Hero faces right, arms straight at horizontal, and holds two rampant winged horned lion creatures by throat.

Creature to left holds upper foreleg straight and extends it upward to place paw on hero's shoulder; lower foreleg is curved and extended downward to place paw on hero's chest. Creature raises forward bent hind leg to place bird's foot on hero's leg. Creature to right holds upper foreleg straight and extends it upward to place paw on hero's arm; lower foreleg is straight and extended outward to place upturned paw on hero's waist. Creature raises bent forward hind leg (only partially preserved) toward hero.

Hero wears belted Persian court robe with sleeves pushed up to reveal arms; sleeves hang in long swags; folds are indicated on lower part of garment. Lower garment is hitched up over hero's forward leg. Five-pointed dentate Persian crown with studded band rests on hero's head; bow with duck-headed finial is at hero's back. Hero wears strapped Persian shoes. Hero has close-shaved beard or is beardless; flattened coiffure rests at back of neck.

Creature to left has mouth open in roar. Both creatures have short horns, crisply serrated manes, and wings with multiple rows of feathers. Creature at left has two wings.

Edge of seal is preserved at top and bottom (partially, only under hero) of design.

COMMENTARY

The detailing on the hero's shoes is unusual within the PFS corpus (even when full retrieval of the extreme lower portion of the impression allows us to examine the evidence). This seal is particularly noteworthy because the royal crown in combination with the strapped shoes is never worn by the Persian king in extant monumental sculpture (Root 1979, pp. 303–08).

See Garrison 1988, 1991, and 1996a for this important seal and the work of the artist associated with it. The artist, especially through this seal, which is one of his more accomplished designs, has close ties to the Court Style.

For comparative illustrations including PFS 301, see pls. 178e (Persian court robes with sleeves pushed up in deep swags), 188g (Persian crowns and fluted tiaras), 198j (feet and shoes), and 246d (bows, arrows, quivers).

SEAL APPLICATION (SEE *APPENDIX ONE: CONCORDANCE OF SEALS TO TABLETS IN VOLUME I*)

PFS 301 occurs on the reverse of PF 1230 and PF 1231. On both tablets, PFS 302 (II) has been applied (inverted) to the right of PFS 301 in the same horizontal plane. In both cases PFS 302 appears to have been applied after (and thus over-rolling) PFS 301. The two partial rollings of PFS 301 display the hero in the center. On the reverse of PF 1231 the seal clearly was applied before the text since several cuneiform wedges cut into the top of the impression. PF 1230 and PF 1231 are both dated 499/498 B.C.

BIBLIOGRAPHY

Garrison 1988, pp. 363–68, 489–91; Garrison 1991, pp. 16–17, fig. 301; Garrison 1996a, pp. 40–43, figs. 12–13.

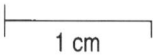

Cat.No. 55   PFS 426

Seal Type:	Cylinder	Photograph:	Pl. 35a
Earliest Dated Application:	499/498 B.C.	Typology and Style:	I-A.5 — Fortification Style
Preserved Height of Image:	1.00 cm (incomp.)	Preserved Length of Image:	1.90 cm (incomp.)
Estimated Height of Original Seal:	NA	Estimated Diameter of Original Seal:	NA
Number of Impressions:	1	Quality of Impression:	Poor

Completeness of Image: Small segment of middle of design survives

DESCRIPTION OF SEAL AS IMPRESSED IMAGE

Hero faces left, arms straight at horizontal, and holds two(?) rampant winged lion creatures by throat (preserved only at right).

Creature to right holds upper foreleg straight and extends it toward hero's chest; lower foreleg is straight (only partially preserved) and extended downward toward hero's lower body.

Hero wears garment of uncertain type; rounded coiffure rests at back of neck.

Mane of creature is rendered by crisp serrated edge along contour of neck; mouth is open in roar.

SEAL APPLICATION (SEE *APPENDIX ONE: CONCORDANCE OF SEALS TO TABLETS IN VOLUME I*)

PFS 426 occurs on the lower edge of PF 120. The partial rolling preserves only part of the hero and the creature to right. PF 120 is dated 499/498 B.C.

BIBLIOGRAPHY

Garrison 1988, pp. 320–22.

PFS 430   Cat.No. 56

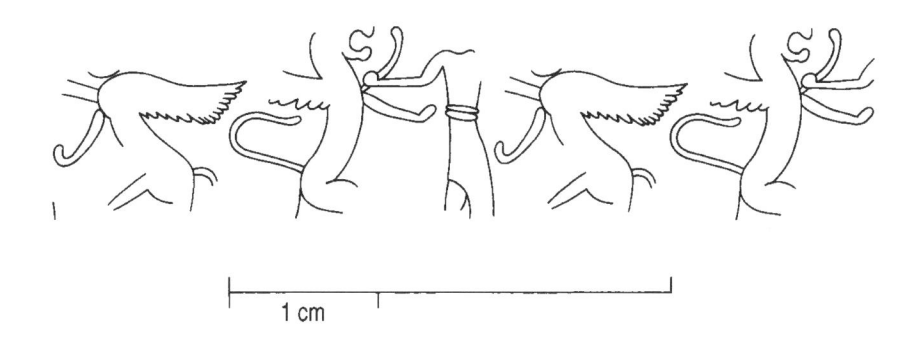

Seal Type:	Cylinder	Photograph:	Pl. 35c
Earliest Dated Application:	499/498 B.C.	Typology and Style:	I-A.5 — Fortification Style
Preserved Height of Image:	1.30 cm (incomp.)	Preserved Length of Image:	3.00 cm (comp.)
Estimated Height of Original Seal:	1.50 cm	Estimated Diameter of Original Seal:	1.00 cm
Number of Impressions:	1	Quality of Impression:	Poor

Completeness of Image: Almost complete except for upper edge and lower edge

Description of Seal as Impressed Image

Hero moves to left, arms bent (only right arm completely preserved), and holds rampant winged lion creature (at left) by upper foreleg and rampant winged lion creature possibly with human head (at right) perhaps at its head.

Creature to left holds upper foreleg curved and extends it diagonally upward; lower foreleg is slightly bent, paw turned upward, and extended downward toward hero's waist. Creature raises forward hind leg toward hero; long thin tail extends diagonally outward and then curls upward. Creature to right holds upper foreleg (only partially preserved) straight and extends it upward toward hero's chest; lower foreleg is curved, paw turned upward, and extended downward toward hero's leg. Creature raises forward hind leg toward hero; tail curves downward.

Hero wears double-belted Assyrian garment that leaves forward leg exposed below knee.

Creature to left has mouth open in roar.

Commentary

The elongated forms are typical of a large subset of seals in the Fortification Style.

Seal Application (see *Appendix One: Concordance of Seals to Tablets in Volume I*)

PFS 430 occurs along the upper half of the reverse (inverted) of PF 121. PFS 429 (Cat.No. 7) is applied once (also inverted) along the lower half of the reverse. The rolling of PFS 430 preserves the entire length of the seal design and displays the hero and the creature to right in the center. PF 121 is dated 499/498 B.C.

Bibliography

Garrison 1988, pp. 339–41.

Cat.No. 57   PFS 720

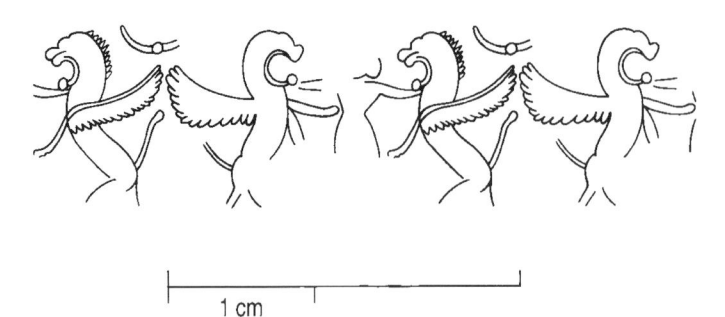

|—— 1 cm ——|

Seal Type:	Cylinder	Photograph:	Pl. 36a
Earliest Dated Application:	501/500 B.C.	Typology and Style:	I-A.5 — Fortification Style
Preserved Height of Image:	1.20 cm (incomp.)	Preserved Length of Image:	2.20 cm (comp.)
Estimated Height of Original Seal:	1.40 cm	Estimated Diameter of Original Seal:	0.70 cm
Number of Impressions:	2	Quality of Impressions:	Poor

Completeness of Image: Segment of middle of design survives along its complete length

DESCRIPTION OF SEAL AS IMPRESSED IMAGE

Hero faces left, arms straight at horizontal, and holds two rampant winged lion creatures by throat.

Creature to left holds upper foreleg straight and extends it outward toward hero's waist; lower foreleg is straight (only partially preserved) and extended diagonally downward; thin tail curves upward. Creature to right holds lower foreleg curved and extends it downward toward hero's leg; crooked tail extends diagonally upward with tufted termination.

Hero wears garment of uncertain type; rounded coiffure at back of neck.

Mane of creature to right is rendered by serrated edge along contour of its neck. Each creature opens mouth in roar.

Crescent with dot at center is in upper terminal field.

COMMENTARY

The exaggerated mouths of the lion creatures are especially nice examples of this feature in the Fortification Style.

For comparative illustrations including PFS 720, see pls. 250i (crescents) and 267f (terminal field motifs other than inscriptions).

SEAL APPLICATION (SEE *APPENDIX ONE: CONCORDANCE OF SEALS TO TABLETS IN VOLUME I*)

PFS 720 occurs on the reverse (inverted) and left edge of PF 492. The rolling on the reverse preserves the entire length of the seal design and displays the hero and the creature to right in the center. The partial rolling on the left edge preserves only the two creatures. On the reverse the seal clearly was applied before the text since several cuneiform wedges cut into the bottom of the impression. PF 492 is dated 501/500 B.C.

BIBLIOGRAPHY

Garrison 1988, pp. 298, 301.

PFS 774   Cat.No. 58

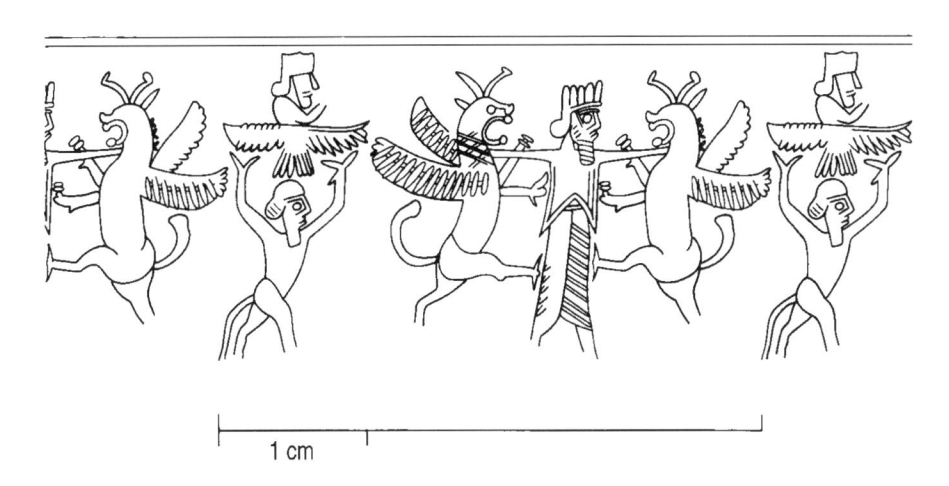

Seal Type:	Cylinder	Photograph:	Pl. 36c
Earliest Dated Application:	499/498 B.C.	Typology and Style:	I-A.5 — Court Style
Preserved Height of Image:	2.10 cm (incomp.)	Preserved Length of Image:	3.70 cm (comp.)
Estimated Height of Original Seal:	2.30 cm	Estimated Diameter of Original Seal:	1.20 cm
Number of Impressions:	2	Quality of Impressions:	Good

Completeness of Image: Almost complete except for lower edge

Description of Seal as Impressed Image

Hero faces right, arms straight at horizontal, and holds two rampant winged horned lion creatures by throat.

Each creature holds upper foreleg straight and extends it upward toward hero's head; lower foreleg is straight and extended outward to place paw on hero's chest. Each creature raises forward hind leg to place bird's foot on hero's leg; thick tail curls upward with tufted termination.

Hero wears belted Persian court robe with sleeves pushed up to reveal arms; gathered folds of sleeves are indicated, as are central pleat and diagonal folds of lower part of garment. Hero wears fluted Persian tiara with band. Long squared beard with diagonal striations rests over hero's left shoulder; rounded coiffure rests at back of neck.

Creature to left has two wings indicated, upper extending diagonally upward from its back; feathers are indicated by large oval-shaped cuts; traces of hatching are on creature's neck. Two curved horns emerge from top of its head; one to right is bent at its termination; short pointed ear emerges from back of head; mouth is open in roar. Creature to right has two wings, upper extending diagonally upward from lower; lower wing has feathers indicated by large oval-shaped cuts. Mane is rendered by three small V-shaped extensions along contour of its neck. Two curved horns emerge from top of creature's head, each bent at its termination; long pointed ear emerges from back of head; mouth is open in roar.

In terminal field is rampant human-headed bull creature with human shoulders and arms. Creature moves to and faces right; arms are bent and extended upward above its shoulders in atlas pose to support figure emerging from winged symbol with bird's tail. Creature has long tail that curves downward; long squared beard rests over its chest; rounded coiffure with diagonal striations is at back of neck. Figure emerging from winged symbol faces right and has one arm indicated, bent and held in front of its face. Figure wears garment of uncertain type; long squared beard rests over figure's arm; flattened coiffure rests at back of neck. Persian crown rises to slight point at front, back, and center.

Line border is preserved at top edge of design.

Commentary

See PFS 1071 (Cat.No. 29) and PFS 310 (II) for figure emerging from winged symbol with bird's tail held aloft by support creatures; and PFS 83* (III) for such a supporting creature as a winged bull-man. The theme is also popular in Court Style seals outside of the PFS corpus, for example, PTS 19. See the commentary on PFS 7*

(Cat.No. 4) for discussion of the figure emerging from a winged symbol and the form of the motif. See the commentary on PFS 1071 (Cat.No. 29) for winged symbols supported by creatures.

Lion creatures with the exact set of features seen in PFS 774 are difficult to trace in the PFS corpus particularly because of elusiveness of bird's feet on hind legs. For a range of representational contexts in which a similar (if not identical) creature occurs, see, for example, PFS 12a (II), PFS 12b (II), PFS 15 (III), PFS 27* (III), PFS 45* (III), PFS 66a* (II), PFS 66b* (II), PFS 66c* (II), PFS 84 (II), PFS 188* (III), PFS 224 (II), PFS 342 (III), and PFS 543* (III).[19]

Stylistically the design seems rather unrefined in comparison to other Court Style seals from Persepolis (note the schematic treatment of the creatures' paws, the hasty engraving on the wings of the rampant creatures to indicate feathers, the angularity of the Persian court robe, etc.). An excellent formal parallel for this rendering of the Persian crown occurs on the cylinder seal from Pasargadae (Root 1999a, fig. 1).

For comparative illustrations including PFS 774, see pls. 179d (Persian court robes with sleeves pushed up), 189a (Persian crowns and fluted tiaras), 202g (arm positions of heroic control), 223f (lions and lion creatures), 248b (deities emergent from winged symbol), and 266c (terminal field motifs other than inscriptions).

SEAL APPLICATION (SEE *APPENDIX ONE: CONCORDANCE OF SEALS TO TABLETS IN VOLUME I*)

PFS 774 occurs on the reverse (inverted) and left edge of PF 556. The rolling of the seal on the reverse of the tablet is long, with most of the heroic encounter at far right of the impression, partially repeated again at far left. Rolled in this manner, the terminal field motif and the creature to the left of the hero appear in the center. The partial rolling on the left edge preserves only the terminal field motif and the lion creature to the left of the hero. PF 556 is dated 499/498 B.C.

BIBLIOGRAPHY

Dusinberre 1997b, p. 127 (n. 119); Garrison 1988, pp. 377, 399–406; Garrison and Dion 1999, p. 11 (n. 36), 14 (n. 39).

---

19. See Dusinberre 1997b, figs. 1–3, p. 105, for discussion of the hero seal with similar creatures, which she calls "lion-griffins," excavated at Sardis (IAM 4581).

PFS 844   Cat.No. 59

Seal Type:	Cylinder	Photograph:	Pl. 37a
Earliest Dated Application:	500/499 B.C.	Typology and Style:	I-A.5 — Fortification Style
Preserved Height of Image:	1.40 cm (incomp.)	Preserved Length of Image:	2.30 cm (comp.)
Estimated Height of Original Seal:	1.60 cm	Estimated Diameter of Original Seal:	0.70 cm
Number of Impressions:	3	Quality of Impressions:	Poor

Completeness of Image: Almost complete except for upper edge and lower edge

Description of Seal as Impressed Image

Hero faces left, arms straight at horizontal, and holds two rampant winged horned (preserved only at right) lion creatures by throat.

Creature to left holds upper foreleg (only partially preserved) curved and extends it outward toward hero's chest; lower foreleg is straight and extended diagonally downward; tail (only partially preserved) curves upward. Creature to right holds upper foreleg curved and extends it upward to place upturned paw on hero's chest; lower foreleg is slightly bent and extended downward toward hero's leg.

Hero wears Assyrian garment that leaves forward leg exposed below knee. Short pointed beard is above hero's right shoulder; rounded coiffure rests at back of head. Hero perhaps wears domed headdress.

Creature to right has two straight horns emerging from top of its head. Each creature has mouth open in roar.

Commentary

For comparative illustrations including PFS 844, see pls. 174g (Assyrian garments) and 192e (rounded coiffures).

Seal Application (see *Appendix One: Concordance of Seals to Tablets in Volume I*)

PFS 844 occurs twice on the reverse (inverted) and once on the left edge of PF 645. No other seal is used on the tablet. On the reverse the impressions are applied one directly above the other. Impressions show marked distortion. The lower impression on the reverse preserves the entire length of the seal design and displays the hero and the creature to left in the center. The upper impression on the reverse preserves the entire length of the seal design and displays the hero and the creature to right in the center. The partial rolling on the left edge preserves only the hero and the creature to right. PF 645 is dated 500/499 B.C.

Bibliography

Garrison 1988, pp. 298, 300.

Cat.No. 60   PFS 851

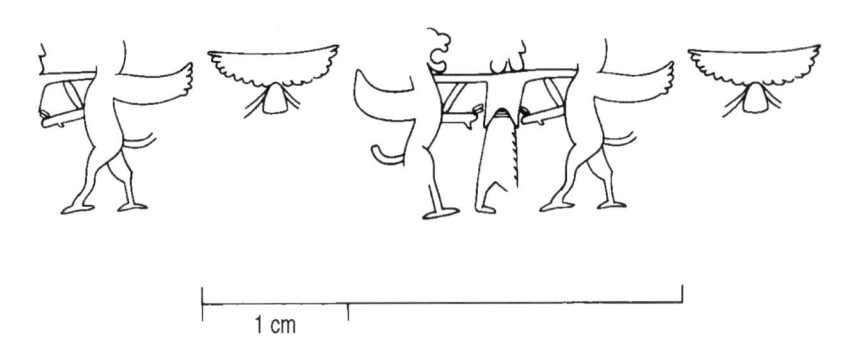

Seal Type:	Cylinder	Photograph:	Pl. 37c
Earliest Dated Application:	500/499 B.C.	Typology and Style:	I-A.5 — Mixed Styles II
Preserved Height of Image:	1.30 cm (incomp.)	Preserved Length of Image:	3.30 cm (comp.)
Estimated Height of Original Seal:	1.50 cm	Estimated Diameter of Original Seal:	1.10 cm
Number of Impressions:	1	Quality of Impression:	Poor

Completeness of Image: Large segment of middle of design survives along its complete length

DESCRIPTION OF SEAL AS IMPRESSED IMAGE

Hero faces right, arms straight at horizontal, and holds two rampant winged lion creatures by throat.

Each creature holds upper foreleg straight and extends it upward to place paw on hero's arm; lower foreleg is straight and extended outward to place paw on hero's waist; short tail curves upward.

Hero wears double-belted Persian court robe with sleeves pushed up to reveal arms; diagonal folds are indicated along front edge of lower garment. Rounded beard rests over hero's left shoulder; rounded coiffure rests at back of neck.

Each creature has bird's feet on hind legs. Creature to left has mouth open in roar.

Winged symbol with bird's tail and tendrils appears in upper terminal field; central disk is not indicated.

COMMENTARY

Human and lion creature forms closely follow norms of the Fortification Style.

For comparative illustrations including PFS 851, see pls. 179f (Persian court robes with sleeves pushed up), 249d (winged symbols), and 266d (terminal field motifs other than inscriptions).

SEAL APPLICATION (SEE *APPENDIX ONE: CONCORDANCE OF SEALS TO TABLETS IN VOLUME I*)

PFS 851 occurs on the reverse of PF 650. The rolling preserves the entire length of the seal design and displays the hero in the center. PF 650 is dated 500/499 B.C.

BIBLIOGRAPHY

Garrison 1988, pp. 373, 412, 416.

PFS 1072   Cat.No. 61

Seal Type:	Cylinder	Photograph:	Pl. 38a
Earliest Dated Application:	499/498 B.C.	Typology and Style:	I-A.5 — Mixed Styles II
Preserved Height of Image:	1.60 cm (comp.)	Preserved Length of Image:	2.50 cm (comp.)
Estimated Height of Original Seal:	1.60 cm	Estimated Diameter of Original Seal:	0.80 cm
Number of Impressions:	1	Quality of Impression:	Good

Completeness of Image: Complete except for details

DESCRIPTION OF SEAL AS IMPRESSED IMAGE

Hero faces left, arms straight at horizontal, and holds two rampant winged horned lion creatures by throat.

Each creature holds upper foreleg curved and extends it upward toward hero's head; lower foreleg is straight, paw upturned, and extended downward toward hero's waist. Creature to right raises forward hind leg and places paw above foot of hero's forward leg; tail extends outward, curling upward at its end with tufted termination. Tail of creature to right also extends outward, curling upward at its end with tufted termination.

Hero wears belted Assyrian garment that leaves forward leg exposed below mid-thigh; fringe is indicated along hem of lower garment over rear leg. Rounded beard rests over hero's right shoulder; round coiffure rests at back of neck. Hero perhaps wears domed headdress with projection at front.

Each creature has two wings, upper extending diagonally upward from lower; mane is rendered by crisp serrated edge along contour of its neck; mouth is open in roar. Creature to left has one horn (or ear?) emerging from back of its head and is ithyphallic. Creature to right has two curved horns emerging from top of its head.

Elaborate stylized tree of uncertain type is in terminal field.

Line border is preserved at top of design; edge of seal is preserved at top and bottom of design.

COMMENTARY

The style of the engraving is not easy to place, although animal forms in PFS 1072 are consistent with those found in the Fortification Style. Curiously, PFS 1071 (Cat.No. 29), which occurs on the reverse of PF 1114 along with PFS 1072, has a similarly unusual style. In Garrison 1988, it was suggested that the two seals are in fact one large double-registered seal, but this was incorrect.

    For comparative illustrations including PFS 1072, see pls. 193h (round coiffures), 199d (feet and shoes), 211f (heroic attitudes of control encounter), 231g (feet of animals and creatures), 256b (stylized trees), 269g (terminal field motifs other than inscriptions), and 276h (borders).

SEAL APPLICATION (SEE *APPENDIX ONE: CONCORDANCE OF SEALS TO TABLETS IN VOLUME I*)

PFS 1072 has been applied once along the lower half of the reverse of PF 1114. Immediately above it in the upper half of the tablet PFS 1071 (Cat.No. 29) has been applied. PFS 1072 appears to have been applied after PFS 1071 (Cat.No. 29), over-rolling the bottom of PFS 1071. The rolling of PFS 1072 preserves the entire length of the seal design and displays the creature to the right of the hero and the stylized tree in the center. PF 1114 is dated 499/498 B.C.

BIBLIOGRAPHY

Garrison 1988, pp. 374–78, 381–82, 430, 439, 496; Garrison and Dion 1999, pp. 7–8, 14, fig. 5.

Cat.No. 62   PFS 1444

Seal Type:	Cylinder	Photograph:	Pl. 38c
Earliest Dated Application:	ND	Typology and Style:	I-A.5 — Fortification Style
Preserved Height of Image:	1.60 cm (incomp.)	Preserved Length of Image:	2.80 cm (comp.)
Estimated Height of Original Seal:	1.80 cm	Estimated Diameter of Original Seal:	0.90 cm
Number of Impressions:	1	Quality of Impression:	Fair-good

Completeness of Image: Almost complete except for upper edge and lower edge

DESCRIPTION OF SEAL AS IMPRESSED IMAGE

Hero faces right, arms bent, and holds two rampant winged lion creatures by upper foreleg.

Each creature holds upper foreleg straight and extends it upward toward hero's head; lower foreleg is straight, paw upturned, and extended downward toward hero's leg. Tail of creature to left curves upward with tufted termination. Tail of creature to right curves upward, then downward with tufted termination.

Hero wears robe; rounded coiffure rests at back of hero's neck.

Mane of each creature is rendered by crisp serrated edge along contour of its neck; mouth is open in roar.

In terminal field, rampant horned animal of undetermined type moves toward hero and faces right; two rounded protrusions are at its chest and one long foreleg curves downward in front of its body. Animal has one curved horn (partially preserved) emerging from top of its head; short pointed ear emerges from back of its head. Behind horned animal, also in terminal field, is vertically disposed crescent.

To creature's left, crescent is vertically disposed in field.

COMMENTARY

Based on Q texts protocol, PFS 1444 should belong to Bakabada, who in PF 1562 received wine rations on his way to Harina under the authority (*halmi*) of the king. The name Bakabada occurs frequently in the PF texts, and we are clearly dealing with several individuals (see Koch 1990, pp. 138–39, 185–86). Other Q texts mentioning a Bakabada and carrying a seal impression belonging to him (based on Q texts protocol) are PF 1403 with PFS 1320 (Cat.No. 35) and PF 1438 with PFS 1330 (illegible).

The carving is well executed and deep, the composition lively and animated. The squared rendering of the creatures' mouths is commonly found in the Fortification Style. See Garrison 1988 for this artist and related seals.

For comparative illustrations including PFS 1444, see pls. 211h (heroic attitudes of control encounter), 251f (crescents), and 268i (terminal field motifs other than inscriptions).

SEAL APPLICATION (SEE *APPENDIX ONE: CONCORDANCE OF SEALS TO TABLETS IN VOLUME I*)

PFS 1444 occurs on the reverse of PF 1562. The rolling preserves the entire length of the seal design and displays the horned animal and the lion creature to the left of the hero in the center. The date of PF 1562 is unknown.

BIBLIOGRAPHY

Garrison 1988, pp. 313–16.

PFS 1598   Cat.No. 63

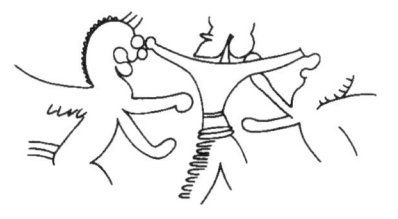

Seal Type:	Cylinder	Photograph:	Pl. 39a
Earliest Dated Application:	ND	Typology and Style:	I-A.5 — Fortification Style
Preserved Height of Image:	1.30 cm	Preserved Length of Image:	2.50 cm
Estimated Height of Original Seal:	NA	Estimated Diameter of Original Seal:	NA
Number of Impressions:	1	Quality of Impression:	Fair-good

Completeness of Image: Large segment of middle of design survives

DESCRIPTION OF SEAL AS IMPRESSED IMAGE

Hero faces left in striding pose, arms straight at diagonal, and holds two rampant winged horned lion creatures by snout (horn of creature to right is not preserved).

Creature to left holds upper foreleg straight and extends it outward toward hero's waist; lower foreleg is straight, paw upturned, and extended downward toward hero's leg; tail in two segments (only partially preserved) curves downward. Creature to right holds upper foreleg straight and extends it upward to wrap paw around hero's arm; lower foreleg is straight and extended outward toward hero's hip.

Hero appears to wear belted trousers; fringe is indicated at hips and along forward edge of front leg. Pointed beard rests over hero's right shoulder; large rounded coiffure rests at back of neck.

Creature to left has two horns (only partially preserved) emerging from front of its head; mane is indicated by serrated edge. Mane of creature at right is indicated by interior lines. Each creature has mouth open in roar.

COMMENTARY

The engraving is deep and well executed with a sharp outline. The profiles of the creatures' heads are very distinctive; see Garrison 1988 for artist and related seals.

SEAL APPLICATION (SEE *APPENDIX ONE: CONCORDANCE OF SEALS TO TABLETS IN VOLUME I*)

PFS 1598 occurs on the left edge of PF 2020. The partial rolling carefully displays the hero in the center. The date of PF 2020 is unknown.

BIBLIOGRAPHY

Garrison 1988, pp. 326–30; Garrison and Dion 1999, p. 6 (n. 15).

Cat.No. 64 PFS 673

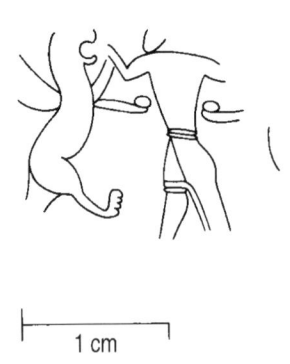

Seal Type:	Cylinder	Photograph:	Pl. 39c
Earliest Dated Application:	499/498 B.C.	Typology and Style:	I-A.5 — Modeled Style
Preserved Height of Image:	1.50 cm (incomp.)	Preserved Length of Image:	1.60 cm (incomp.)
Estimated Height of Original Seal:	NA	Estimated Diameter of Original Seal:	NA
Number of Impressions:	1	Quality of Impression:	Poor

Completeness of Image: Small segment of middle of design survives

DESCRIPTION OF SEAL AS IMPRESSED IMAGE

Hero faces left, arms bent, and holds two rampant winged lion creatures by upper foreleg (preserved only at left).

Creature to left holds upper foreleg straight and extends it upward toward hero's head; lower foreleg is straight and extended toward hero's chest. Creature raises straight forward hind leg, paw turned upward, toward hero's leg. Creature to right holds lower foreleg straight and extends it outward toward hero's chest.

Hero wears double-belted Assyrian garment that leaves forward leg exposed below knee; decorative border runs along front edge of garment over forward knee and along rear leg. Rounded beard rests over hero's right shoulder.

Creature to left has mouth open in roar.

COMMENTARY

Although poorly preserved, the engraving seems well executed.

For comparative illustrations including PFS 673, see pl. 231c (feet of animals and creatures).

SEAL APPLICATION (SEE *APPENDIX ONE: CONCORDANCE OF SEALS TO TABLETS IN VOLUME I*)

PFS 673 occurs on the left edge of PF 436. The partial rolling preserves only the hero and the creature to left with vestiges of the creature to the right. PF 436 is dated 499/498 B.C.

BIBLIOGRAPHY

Garrison 1988, pp. 207–10; Garrison and Dion 1999, p. 13 (n. 38).

PFS 882   Cat.No. 65

Seal Type:	Cylinder	Photograph:	Pl. 39e
Earliest Dated Application:	499/498 B.C.	Typology and Style:	I-A.5 — Fortification Style
Preserved Height of Image:	1.50 cm (incomp.)	Preserved Length of Image:	2.20 cm (incomp.)
Estimated Height of Original Seal:	NA	Estimated Diameter of Original Seal:	NA
Number of Impressions:	1	Quality of Impression:	Poor

Completeness of Image: Small segment of middle of design survives

DESCRIPTION OF SEAL AS IMPRESSED IMAGE

Hero faces left, arms bent, and holds two rampant winged lion creatures (one to right only partially preserved) by upper foreleg.

Each creature holds upper foreleg straight and extends it upward toward hero's head; lower foreleg is straight and extended downward toward hero's leg (at right) and waist (at left).

Hero wears belted Assyrian garment that leaves forward leg exposed below knee. Rounded beard rests over hero's right shoulder; small round coiffure rests at back of neck.

Creature to left has mouth open in roar.

COMMENTARY

See Garrison 1988 for the artist and related seals that show similar large and well-executed designs.

SEAL APPLICATION (SEE *APPENDIX ONE: CONCORDANCE OF SEALS TO TABLETS IN VOLUME I*)

PFS 882 occurs on the reverse of PF 759. The partial rolling displays the hero in the center. PF 759 is dated 499/498 B.C.

BIBLIOGRAPHY

Garrison 1988, pp. 313–16.

Cat.No. 66 PFS 1135

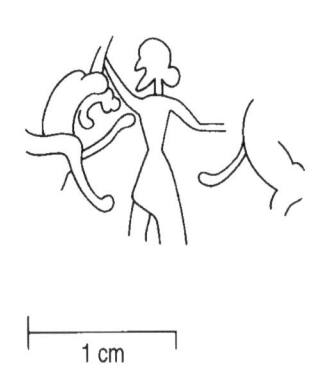

Seal Impression:	Cylinder	Photograph:	Pl. 39g
Earliest Dated Application:	499/498 B.C.	Typology and Style:	I-A.5 — Fortification Style
Preserved Height of Image:	1.30 cm (incomp.)	Preserved Length of Image:	2.00 cm (incomp.)
Estimated Height of Original Seal:	NA	Estimated Diameter of Original Seal:	NA
Number of Impressions:	1	Quality of Impression:	Poor

Completeness of Image: Small segment of middle of design survives

DESCRIPTION OF SEAL AS IMPRESSED IMAGE

Hero faces left, right arm straight at diagonal above shoulder, left arm bent, and holds rampant winged horned lion creature at left by horn; hero may hold comparable creature to right by foreleg (not preserved).

Creature to left holds upper foreleg straight and extends it upward toward hero's chest; lower foreleg is curved, paw upturned, and extended downward toward hero's leg. Creature to right has one foreleg preserved, curved and extended downward toward hero's leg.

Hero wears Assyrian garment that leaves forward leg exposed below knee. Pointed beard rests above hero's right shoulder; rounded coiffure rests at back of neck.

Large horn emerges from front of head of creature to left; mouth is open in roar.

COMMENTARY

Owing to its fragmentary preservation, the exact compositional type cannot be determined with certainty. It is possible that this is a combat encounter rather than a control encounter.

For comparative illustrations including PFS 1135, see pl. 207c (arm positions of heroic control).

SEAL APPLICATION (SEE APPENDIX ONE: CONCORDANCE OF SEALS TO TABLETS IN VOLUME I)

PFS 1135 occurs on the left edge of PF 1192. The partial rolling, now damaged on its right edge, displays the hero in the center. PF 1192 is dated 499/498 B.C.

BIBLIOGRAPHY

Garrison 1988, pp. 339–41.

PFS 1117

Cat.No. 67

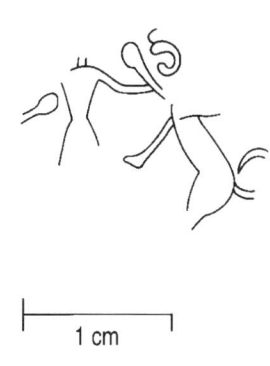

Seal Type:	Cylinder	Photograph:	Pl. 40a
Earliest Dated Application:	499/498 B.C.	Typology and Style:	I-A.5 — Fortification Style
Preserved Height of Image:	1.40 cm (incomp.)	Preserved Length of Image:	1.70 cm (incomp.)
Estimated Height of Original Seal:	NA	Estimated Diameter of Original Seal:	NA
Number of Impressions:	1	Quality of Impression:	Poor

Completeness of Image: Small segment of middle of design survives

DESCRIPTION OF SEAL AS IMPRESSED IMAGE

Hero has arm(s) bent (only his left arm preserved) and holds two(?) rampant winged lion creatures (preserved only at right) by upper foreleg.

Creature to right holds upper foreleg straight and extends it upward toward hero's head; lower foreleg is straight and extended downward toward hero's leg; tail curls upward. Mouth is open in roar. Only paw and part of foreleg of creature to left are preserved.

Hero wears garment of uncertain type.

COMMENTARY

Owing to its fragmentary preservation, the exact compositional type cannot be determined with certainty. It is possible that this is a combat encounter, rather than a control encounter.

For comparative illustrations including PFS 1117, see pl. 219d (comparative heroic proportions).

SEAL APPLICATION (SEE APPENDIX ONE: CONCORDANCE OF SEALS TO TABLETS IN VOLUME I)

PFS 1117 occurs on the left edge of PF 1176. The partial rolling preserves only the hero and the creature to right and vestige of the creature to the left. PF 1176 is dated 499/498 B.C.

BIBLIOGRAPHY

Garrison 1988, pp. 313–16.

Cat.No. 68   PFS 1091

Seal Type:	Cylinder	Photograph:	Pl. 40c
Earliest Dated Application:	499/498 B.C.	Typology and Style:	I-A.5 — Fortification Style
Preserved Height of Image:	1.30 cm (incomp.)	Preserved Length of Image:	3.10 cm (incomp.)
Estimated Height of Original Seal:	NA	Estimated Diameter of Original Seal:	NA
Number of Impressions:	1	Quality of Impression:	Poor

Completeness of Image: Segment of middle of design survives

DESCRIPTION OF SEAL AS IMPRESSED IMAGE

Hero has arms bent and holds two rampant winged lion creatures by upper foreleg.

Each creature moves toward hero but turns its head away from him. Creature to left holds upper foreleg straight and extends it diagonally upward; lower foreleg is bent and held down in front of its body; tail curls downward. Creature to right holds upper foreleg bent and extends it upward toward hero's head; lower foreleg is sharply bent and held down in front of its body.

Hero wears belted garment of uncertain type.

Each creature opens mouth in roar.

Stylized tree of uncertain type is in terminal field.

COMMENTARY

See Garrison 1988 for artist and related seals.
   For comparative illustrations including PFS 1091, see pl. 256c (stylized trees).

SEAL APPLICATION (SEE APPENDIX ONE: CONCORDANCE OF SEALS TO TABLETS IN VOLUME I)

PFS 1091 occurs on the left edge of PF 1140. The partial rolling is almost complete and displays the tree in the terminal field in the center. PF 1140 is dated 499/498 B.C.

BIBLIOGRAPHY

Garrison 1988, pp. 309–12.

PFS 132   Cat.No. 69

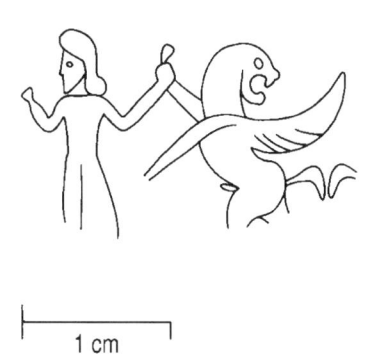

Seal Type:	Cylinder	Photographs:	Pl. 41a–b
Earliest Dated Application:	ND	Typology and Style:	I-A.5 — Fortification Style
Preserved Height of Image:	1.40 cm (incomp.)	Preserved Length of Image:	2.30 cm (incomp.)
Estimated Height of Original Seal:	NA	Estimated Diameter of Original Seal:	NA
Number of Impressions:	5	Quality of Impressions:	Poor

Completeness of Image: Small segment of middle of design survives

DESCRIPTION OF SEAL AS IMPRESSED IMAGE

Hero faces left, arms bent, and holds two(?) rampant winged lion creatures by upper foreleg (only tail of creature to left of hero is preserved).

Creature to right of hero moves toward him but turns its head away from him; creature holds upper foreleg straight and extends it diagonally upward; lower foreleg is straight and extended downward toward hero's leg; short thick tail bends downward.

Hero appears to wear Assyrian garment that leaves forward leg exposed. Pointed beard rests over hero's right shoulder; rounded coiffure rests at back of neck.

Creature to right of hero opens mouth in roar and is ithyphallic.

COMMENTARY

Koch (1990) assigns PFS 132 to Kamišdana, an official controlling grain at the warehouse (*kanti*) at Hutpirri in her Elam Region VI. The attribution to Kamišdana is assured based upon Q texts protocol; however, in Q text PF 1531, PFS 132 occurs on the left edge, the commodity supplied is beer, and the supplier is Pirišla. Has the seal changed hands?

   See Garrison 1988 for this important artist who works close to the Court Style.

   For comparative illustrations including PFS 132, see pl. 197c (hands) and 282f (personal seals of supply/apportionment officers).

SEAL APPLICATION (SEE *APPENDIX ONE: CONCORDANCE OF SEALS TO TABLETS IN VOLUME I*)

PFS 132 occurs only on the left edge of tablets. All impressions are very difficult to read. Of the five partial impressions, three preserve the hero and the creature to the right; two preserve only the hero. The dates of all the tablets with PFS 132 are unknown.

BIBLIOGRAPHY

Garrison 1988, pp. 352–56, 485; Koch 1990, pp. 299–300, 304.

146 SEALS ON THE PERSEPOLIS FORTIFICATION TABLETS, VOLUME I: IMAGES OF HEROIC ENCOUNTER

Cat.No. 70   PFS 1057

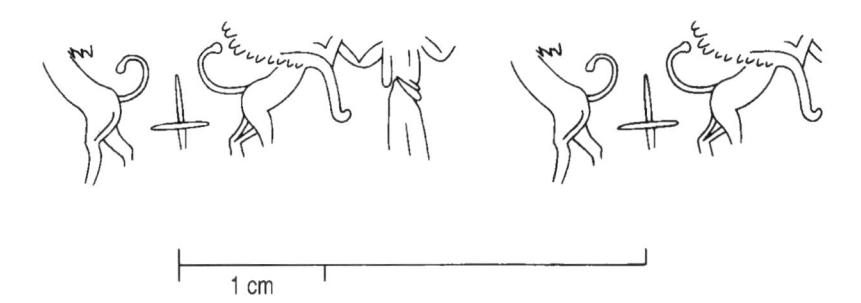

Seal Type:	Cylinder	Photograph:	Pl. 41d
Earliest Dated Application:	494/493 B.C.	Typology and Style:	I-A.5 — Mixed Styles II
Preserved Height of Image:	1.10 cm (incomp.)	Preserved Length of Image:	3.20 cm (comp.)
Estimated Height of Original Seal:	NA	Estimated Diameter of Original Seal:	1.10 cm
Number of Impressions:	1	Quality of Impression:	Fair

Completeness of Image: Segment of middle of design survives along its complete length

DESCRIPTION OF SEAL AS IMPRESSED IMAGE

Hero has arms bent and holds two rampant winged lion creatures by upper foreleg (preserved only at left).

Creature to left holds upper foreleg (only partially preserved) straight and extends it diagonally upward; lower foreleg is curved, paw upturned, and extended diagonally downward. Tail of each creature curls upward with tufted termination.

Hero wears belted Persian court robe with sleeves pushed up to reveal hero's bare arms; gathered folds of sleeves are indicated, as is central pleat of lower part of garment.

Cross appears in lower terminal field.

COMMENTARY

The cross on PFS 1057 does not appear in Boardman's (1970a, 1998) tables of linear devices represented on pyramidal stamp seals of the Persian Empire. Furthermore, simple cruciform linear devices (as distinct from the "Maltese" cross emblem and other more elaborate motifs built up from the basic cross formation) are rare in ancient Mesopotamian and Iranian art (Black and Green 1992, pp. 54–55). The device on PFS 1057 is similar in feeling to the two cruciform linear devices on a Neo-Babylonian cylinder (BM 89523) displaying a worship scene with multiple emblems in the terminal field (Collon 1987, pp. 190–91, no. 928).[20]

Although poorly preserved, the seal appears to have been well executed with a spacious design.

For comparative illustrations including PFS 1057, see pl. 255h (various devices and symbols).

SEAL APPLICATION (SEE APPENDIX ONE: CONCORDANCE OF SEALS TO TABLETS IN VOLUME I)

PFS 1057 occurs on the reverse (inverted) of PF 1101. PFS 1056 (III) is applied directly above PFS 1057. The rolling of PFS 1057 preserves the entire length of the seal design and displays the creature to the right of the hero in the center. PF 1101 is dated 494/493 B.C.

BIBLIOGRAPHY

Garrison 1988, pp. 370–74; Garrison and Dion 1999, p. 14, fig. 13; Root 1999a, p. 173, fig. 7.

---

20. See Wiseman 1959, pl. 92, for an enlarged photograph that shows crosses which unlike the cross device on PFS 1057 have a globular termination on the upper end of the vertical stroke. Wiseman interprets these crosses as "ankh-shaped signs or daggers."

PFS 1081   Cat.No. 71

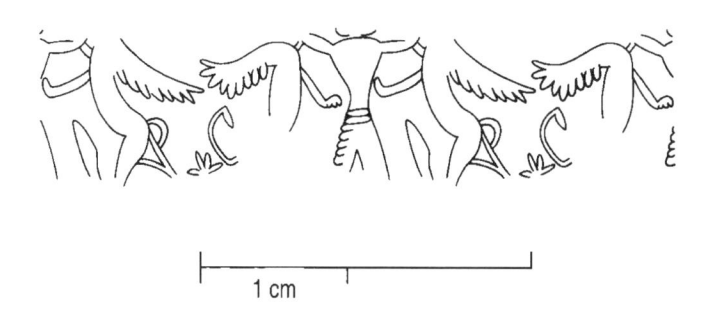

|–––––|
| 1 cm |

Seal Type:	Cylinder	Photograph:	Pl. 42a
Earliest Dated Application:	500/499 B.C.	Typology and Style:	I-A.5 — Fortification Style
Preserved Height of Image:	1.10 cm (incomp.)	Preserved Length of Image:	2.30 cm (comp.)
Estimated Height of Original Seal:	NA	Estimated Diameter of Original Seal:	0.70 cm
Number of Impressions:	1	Quality of Impression:	Good

Completeness of Image: Large segment of middle of design survives along its complete length

DESCRIPTION OF SEAL AS IMPRESSED IMAGE

Hero appears to move to left, arms bent, and holds two rampant winged lion creatures. Each creature holds upper foreleg straight and extends it upward toward hero's head.

Creature to left holds lower foreleg straight, paw upturned, and extends it downward toward hero's waist; tail curves upward, bending downward at its end. Creature to right holds lower foreleg straight, paw upturned, and extends it downward toward hero's chest; tail curves downward.

Hero appears to wear double-belted trousers; fringe or folds are indicated along front edge of garment over forward leg.

Uncertain fragmentary element appears at diagonal in lower field between hero and creature to right.

Star appears (only partially preserved) in lower terminal field.

COMMENTARY

The seal has left a clear and deep impression in the tablet. See Garrison 1988 for the artist and related seals.

SEAL APPLICATION (SEE *APPENDIX ONE: CONCORDANCE OF SEALS TO TABLETS IN VOLUME I*)

PFS 1081 occurs on the left edge of PF 1129. The rolling preserves the entire length of the seal design and carefully displays the hero in the center with the rampant creatures framing the hero at each end. PF 1129 is dated 500/499 B.C.

BIBLIOGRAPHY

Garrison 1988, pp. 309–12.

Cat.No. 72 PFS 1387

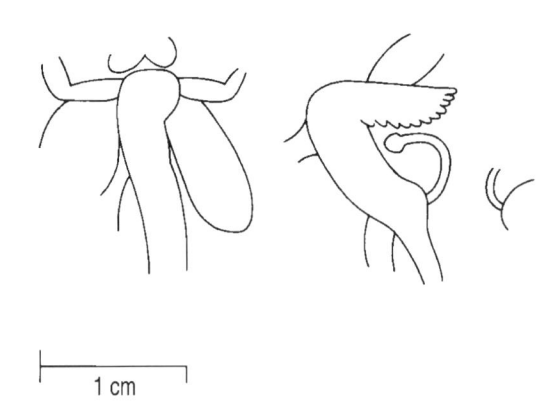

|_____|
  1 cm

Seal Type:	Cylinder	Photograph:	Pl. 42c
Earliest Dated Application:	493 B.C.	Typology and Style:	I-A.5 — Modeled Style
Preserved Height of Image:	1.70 cm (incomp.)	Preserved Length of Image:	3.40 cm (incomp.)
Estimated Height of Original Seal:	NA	Estimated Diameter of Original Seal:	NA
Number of Impressions:	1	Quality of Impression:	Fair

Completeness of Image: Segment of middle of design survives

DESCRIPTION OF SEAL AS IMPRESSED IMAGE

Winged hero faces left, arms bent, and holds two(?) rampant winged lion creatures (preserved only at right) by upper foreleg (not preserved).

Hindquarters and curled tail at far right of impression should belong to other creature held by hero. One foreleg of creature to right of hero is partially preserved. Two wings are indicated, upper emerging diagonally upward from lower; thick tail curls upward with tufted termination.

Hero wears Assyrian garment that leaves forward leg exposed; massive wing hangs downward from shoulder on either side of hero's torso. Rounded beard rests over hero's right shoulder; rounded coiffure rests at back of neck.

COMMENTARY

Based on Q texts protocol, PFS 1387 should belong to Minduka, who in year 28.10 (493 B.C.) received flour rations on his way to Persepolis under the authority (*halmi*) of the king. The name Minduka occurs also on Q texts PF 1370–1373, wherein he supplied flour rations in 22.1 and 22.2. PFS 187s (II) occurs on the left edge of PF 1370 and PFS 142 (III) occurs on the left edge of PF 1371. In the account text PF 1969, a Minduka is listed as a grain supplier at Kurarakka in years 15–17. Koch (1990, p. 114) suggests that Minduka, the supplier mentioned in these texts, was the same individual. It does not seem likely that this Minduka is the same one receiving rations in PF 1490 and using PFS 1387.

Although the design is not well preserved, the carving seems deep and the figures are well modeled and proportioned. PFS 1387 was not included in Garrison 1988; it is closely related stylistically to PFS 944 (Cat.No. 129) and PFS 1485 (Cat.No. 112). The hero almost certainly will have had two additional wings above his shoulders (see PFS 1276 [Cat.No. 34] and its commentary), but no traces remain in our single impression.

For comparative illustrations including PFS 1387, see pls. 175f (Assyrian garments), 207h (arm positions of heroic control), and 291f (personal seals of various travelers).

SEAL APPLICATION (SEE *APPENDIX ONE: CONCORDANCE OF SEALS TO TABLETS IN VOLUME I*)

PFS 1387 occurs on the reverse of PF 1490. The partial rolling preserves only the hero and the creature to right and small vestige of second creature. The seal clearly was applied before the text since several cuneiform wedges cut into the bottom of the impression. PF 1490 is dated 493 B.C.

BIBLIOGRAPHY

Garrison 1998, p. 121 (n. 15); Garrison and Dion 1999, p. 9 (n. 19).

I-A.6. WINGED HUMAN-FACED/HUMAN-HEADED LION CREATURES

PFS 34 — Cat.No. 73

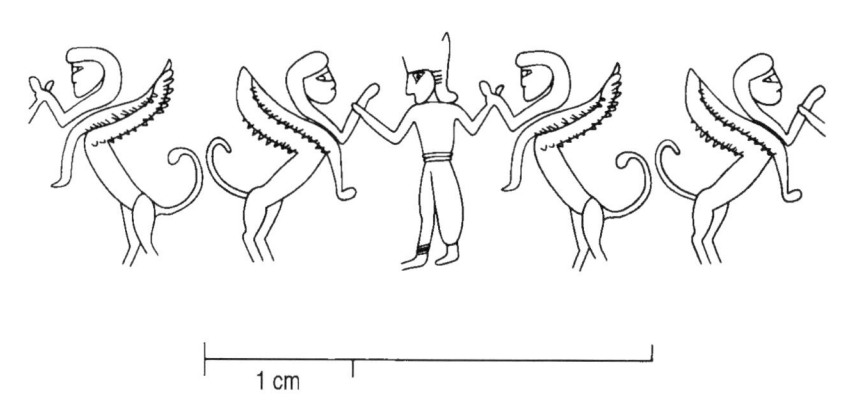

Seal Type:	Cylinder	Photographs:	Pl. 43a–b
Earliest Dated Application:	500/499 B.C.	Typology and Style:	I-A.6 — Fortification Style
Preserved Height of Image:	1.70 cm (incomp.)	Preserved Length of Image:	3.10 cm (comp.)
Estimated Height of Original Seal:	1.90 cm	Estimated Diameter of Original Seal:	1.00 cm
Number of Impressions:	12	Quality of Impressions:	Fair-good

Completeness of Image: Almost complete except for upper edge and lower edge

DESCRIPTION OF SEAL AS IMPRESSED IMAGE

Hero faces left, arms bent, and holds two rampant winged human-faced lion creatures by upper foreleg.

Each creature holds upper foreleg straight and extends it upward toward hero's head; lower foreleg is straight, paw upturned, and extended vertically downward. Creature to left holds hind legs together; tail curls upward. Creature to right holds hind legs slightly parted; tail curls upward with tufted termination.

Hero appears to wear belted trousers with horizontal striations over ankle of forward foot; one point of hero's dentate Persian crown is preserved. Rounded beard rests at hero's right shoulder; flattened striated coiffure curls upward on hero's left shoulder.

Each creature's human face appears beardless or perhaps with close-shaved beard. Two rows of feathers are indicated on wing of each creature.

COMMENTARY

Koch (1990) notes that PFS 34 often occurs in connection with tax deliveries in her Southeastern Region III. The use of PFS 34 seems connected with officials using PFS 102 (Cat.No. 1) and PFS 60 (II) in the same region. Koch suggests that PFS 34 may belong to Bakabaduš, who seems to have had control of tax collection at Šaurakkaš, Mutrizaš, Kutkuš, and especially Baktiš; he also supplied workers. PFS 34 occurs with PFS 8 (III) and PFS 13 (III) on transactions concerning tax deliveries of grain at Baktiš in her Northwestern Region V. PFS 8 and PFS 13, like PFS 34, are concerned with tax deliveries in her Northwestern Region V.

This is a handsomely engraved design and the name-piece for an important artist working close to the Court Style (see Garrison 1988). The continuous articulation from head through foreleg of each creature is especially noteworthy; see also, for example, PFS 168 (Cat.No. 74). The composition is carefully conceived and generously spaced.

For comparative illustrations including PFS 34, see pls. 184b (trousers), 188b (Persian crowns and fluted tiaras), 204c (arm positions of heroic control), 234d (human-headed/human-faced creatures), and 283c (personal seals of tax collectors).

SEAL APPLICATION (SEE *APPENDIX ONE: CONCORDANCE OF SEALS TO TABLETS IN VOLUME I*)

Several surfaces of the tablets on which PFS 34 occurs are very worn and difficult to read. With one exception (PF 151, on the reverse and upper edge) the seal occurs on only one edge: the reverse (PF 152–153 and PF 1093) or the left edge (PF 169–175). On the reverse of PF 152 and PF 1093 the seal is inverted. In four impressions the seal is rolled for at least one complete turn, preserving the entire length of the seal design. Of these four applications, two display the hero and the creature to left in the center; two display the hero and the creature to right in the center. Of the eight partial applications, one displays the hero in the center; one preserves only the hero and the creature to left; three preserve only the hero and the creature to right; two preserve only the two creatures; one displays the creature to the right of the hero in the center. On all reverses the seal clearly was applied before the text since several cuneiform wedges cut into the top or bottom of the impressions. All tablets with PFS 34 are dated 500/499 B.C.

BIBLIOGRAPHY

Dusinberre 1997b, p. 128 (n. 131); Garrison 1988, pp. 290–91, 352–56, 366, 480, 485–86; Garrison 1991, pp. 15–17, fig. 26; Garrison 2000, pp. 131, 132 (n. 45), fig. 4, pl. 17:4; Koch 1981, pp. 116–19, 121; Koch 1990, pp. 75, 149, 270, 275.

Cat.No. 74   PFS 168

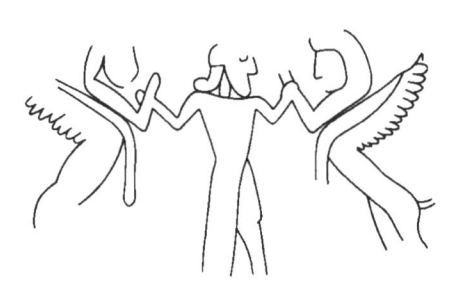

Seal Type:	Cylinder	Photograph:	Pl. 43d
Earliest Dated Application:	505/504 B.C.	Typology and Style:	I-A.6 — Fortification Style
Preserved Height of Image:	1.60 cm (incomp.)	Preserved Length of Image:	2.90 cm (incomp.)
Estimated Height of Original Seal:	NA	Estimated Diameter of Original Seal:	NA
Number of Impressions:	1	Quality of Impression:	Fair

Completeness of Image: Large segment of middle of design survives

DESCRIPTION OF SEAL AS IMPRESSED IMAGE

Hero faces right, arms bent, and holds two rampant winged human-faced lion creatures by upper foreleg.

Each creature holds upper foreleg straight and extends it upward toward hero's head; lower foreleg is straight and extended vertically downward in front of its body; tail (only partially preserved) of creature to right curves upward.

Hero wears Assyrian garment that leaves forward leg exposed below knee. Rounded beard rests over hero's left shoulder; rounded coiffure curls upward on hero's right shoulder.

Human face of each creature appears to be beardless or to have close-shaved beard, but preservation is poor in these areas.

COMMENTARY

Koch (1990) suggests that PFS 168 belongs to an unnamed official stationed, perhaps, at Pitlan(?) in her Elam Region VI.

See Garrison 1988 for this important artist who works close to the Court Style. The continuous articulation from head through foreleg of each creature is especially noteworthy; see also, for example, PFS 34 (Cat.No. 73).

For comparative illustrations including PFS 168, see pls. 174b (Assyrian garments) and 204h (arm positions of heroic control).

SEAL APPLICATION (SEE *APPENDIX ONE: CONCORDANCE OF SEALS TO TABLETS IN VOLUME I*)

PFS 168 occurs on the left edge of PF 1667. The partial rolling displays the hero in the center. PF 1667 is dated 505/504 B.C.

BIBLIOGRAPHY

Garrison 1988, pp. 352–56, 366, 475, 480, 485–86, 490; Garrison 1991, pp. 16–17, fig. 27; Koch 1990, p. 191 (n. 792).

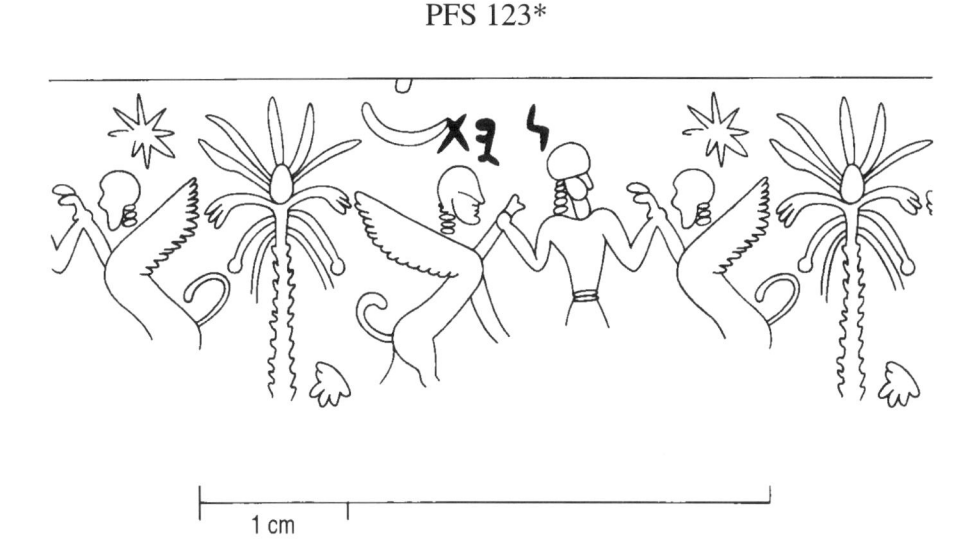

PFS 123*   Cat.No. 75

Seal Type:	Cylinder, Inscribed	Photographs:	Pl. 44a–c
Earliest Dated Application:	500/499 B.C.	Typology and Style:	I-A.6 — Mixed Styles I
Language of Inscription:	Aramaic		
Preserved Height of Image:	2.20 cm (incomp.)	Preserved Length of Image:	3.90 cm (comp.)
Estimated Height of Original Seal:	NA	Estimated Diameter of Original Seal:	1.20 cm
Number of Impressions:	7	Quality of Impressions:	Fair

Completeness of Image: Almost complete except for lower edge and details of inscription

DESCRIPTION OF SEAL AS IMPRESSED IMAGE

Hero faces right, arms bent, and holds two rampant winged human-headed lion creatures by upper foreleg.

Each creature holds upper foreleg straight and extends it upward toward hero's head. Creature to left holds lower foreleg (only partially preserved) straight and extends it diagonally downward. Tail of each creature curves upward.

Hero wears belted garment of uncertain type. Hero has squared beard; segmented, rounded coiffure rests at back of neck. Hero perhaps wears domed headdress.

Creature to left appears to be beardless or to have close-shaved beard; segmented, rounded coiffure rests at back of neck. Creature to right appears to have short rounded beard; segmented rounded coiffure rests at back of neck.

Star is in field above creature to right of hero; crescent is in field above creature to left of hero.

Date palm with fruit clusters appears in terminal field. Uncertain fragmentary element (vestige of bird in flight?) is in lower terminal field between creature to left of hero and date palm.

Three Aramaic letters are preserved between hero's head and crescent.

Edge of seal is preserved at top of design, with chip or flaw above crescent.

INSCRIPTION

Aramaic

Line   1.   [...]NS(?)T(?)[...]

Translation   ?

There is apparently one line to the inscription, oriented along the horizontal axis of the seal, located at the top edge of the design between the hero's head and the crescent. We are able to read three letters with possibly traces of a fourth, although the impressions are very poorly preserved in this area. Presumably the inscription is a PN. The forms of the S and T letters are slightly unusual, but this may be a reflection of the poor preservation. The placement of the inscription can be paralleled in the PFS corpus only by the inscription on PFS 284* (Cat.No. 111).

COMMENTARY

Although not well preserved, this large seal was well executed. Note that PFS 123* has been reclassified stylistically and has now been collated with PFS 229 (cf. Garrison 1988, pp. 281-83, 207-10).

For comparative illustrations including PFS 123*, see pls. 204f (arm positions of heroic control), 234f (human-headed/human-faced creatures), 252e (crescents and stars), 259c (date palms), and 264e (inscriptions without panels or case lines).

SEAL APPLICATION (SEE *APPENDIX ONE: CONCORDANCE OF SEALS TO TABLETS IN VOLUME I*)

PFS 123* occurs on the reverse of PF 162 and PF 219, the upper half of the reverse (inverted) on PF 220–221, the upper edge of PF 163, and the reverse and bottom edge of PF 164. PFS 171 (III) is applied directly above PFS 123* on the reverse of PF 162. PFS 230 (III) is applied directly below the impression of PFS 123* on the reverse of PF 219, 220, and 221. PFS 463 (Cat.No. 264) is applied (inverted) directly below PFS 123* on the reverse of PF 164. In four impressions the seal is rolled for at least one complete turn, preserving the entire length of the seal design. Of these four applications, one displays the hero and the creature to left in the center; one displays the hero and the creature to right in the center; one displays the date palm in the center; and one displays the date palm and creature to right of the hero in center. The remaining three partial rollings all display the date palm and the creature to the left of the hero in the center. All tablets with PFS 123* are dated 500/499 B.C.

BIBLIOGRAPHY

Brosius 1991, p. 153; Dusinberre 1997b, p. 128 (n. 131); Garrison 1988, pp. 207–10, 281–83; Garrison and Dion 1999, pp. 10, 13 (n. 38).

PFS 362

Cat.No. 76

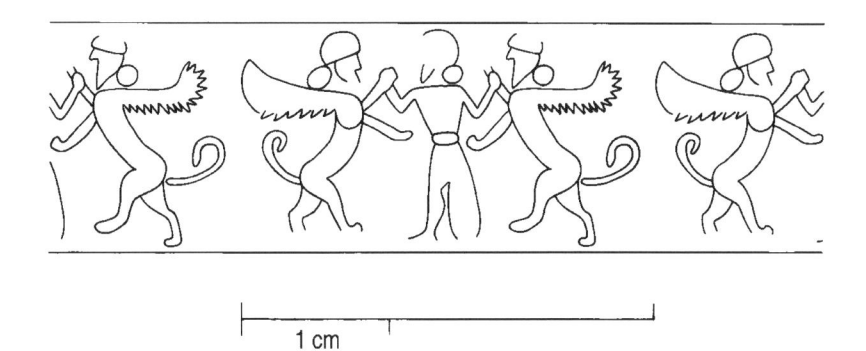

Seal Type:	Cylinder	Photograph:	Pl. 45a
Earliest Dated Application:	500/499 B.C.	Typology and Style:	I-A.6 — Fortification Style
Preserved Height of Image:	1.50 cm (comp.)	Preserved Length of Image:	2.80 cm (comp.)
Estimated Height of Original Seal:	1.50 cm	Estimated Diameter of Original Seal:	0.90 cm
Number of Impressions:	2	Quality of Impressions:	Fair

Completeness of Image: Complete except for details

DESCRIPTION OF SEAL AS IMPRESSED IMAGE

Hero faces left, arms bent, and holds two rampant winged human-headed lion creatures by upper foreleg.

Each creature holds upper foreleg straight and extends it upward toward hero's head; lower foreleg is straight, paw upturned, and extended downward toward hero's waist. Each creature raises forward bent hind leg toward hero; tail curls upward.

Hero wears belted Assyrian garment that leaves forward leg exposed. Pointed beard rests over hero's right shoulder; round coiffure rests at back of neck.

Each creature has pointed beard and round coiffure. Each creature perhaps wears domed headdress.

Edge of seal is preserved at top and bottom of design.

COMMENTARY

The style is typical Fortification Style; see Garrison 1988 for other seals by the same artist.
For comparative illustrations including PFS 362, see pl. 205c (arm positions of heroic control).

SEAL APPLICATION (SEE APPENDIX ONE: CONCORDANCE OF SEALS TO TABLETS IN VOLUME I)

PFS 362 occurs twice on the reverse of PF 56, one impression directly above the other. Both impressions preserve the entire length of the seal design. The upper rolling displays the two creatures in the center; the lower rolling displays the hero and the creature to right in the center. PF 56 is dated 500/499 B.C.

BIBLIOGRAPHY

Dusinberre 1997b, p. 128 (n. 131); Garrison 1988, pp. 271–73, 493.

Cat.No. 77   PFS 1016

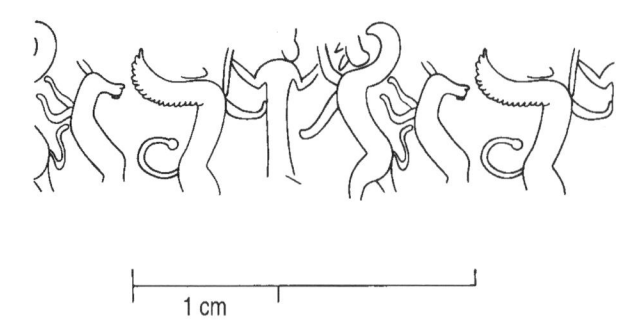

Seal Type:	Cylinder	Photograph:	Pl. 45c
Earliest Dated Application:	504 B.C.	Typology and Style:	I-A.6 — Fortification Style
Preserved Height of Image:	1.20 cm (incomp.)	Preserved Length of Image:	2.40 cm (comp.)
Estimated Height of Original Seal:	1.40 cm	Estimated Diameter of Original Seal:	0.80 cm
Number of Impressions:	1	Quality of Impression:	Poor

Completeness of Image: Almost complete except for upper edge and lower edge

DESCRIPTION OF SEAL AS IMPRESSED IMAGE

Hero faces left, arms bent, and holds two rampant winged human-headed lion creatures by upper foreleg.

Creature to left holds upper foreleg straight and extends it vertically upward; lower foreleg is curved and extended outward to place paw on hero's waist; tail curls upward with tufted termination. Creature to right holds upper foreleg bent and extends it upward toward hero's head; lower foreleg is curved and extended downward toward hero's leg; tail curves downward then upward.

Hero wears robe. Rounded coiffure rests at back of hero's neck.

Creature to right has narrow pointed beard that rests above its upper foreleg; flattened coiffure rests along wing. Creature to left has pointed beard resting along wing.

In terminal field, rampant goat moves to left but turns head back to right. Goat holds upper foreleg curved, lower foreleg bent, and extends them upward toward wing of creature to right of hero; horn emerges from top of animal's head; small beard is indicated.

COMMENTARY

The composition is more crowded than most Fortification Style designs.

SEAL APPLICATION (SEE *APPENDIX ONE: CONCORDANCE OF SEALS TO TABLETS IN VOLUME I*)

PFS 1016 occurs on the left edge of PF 1040. The rolling preserves the entire length of the seal design and displays the creature to the right of the hero in the center. PF 1040 is dated 504 B.C.

BIBLIOGRAPHY

Garrison 1988, pp. 321, 323.

PFS 399   Cat.No. 78

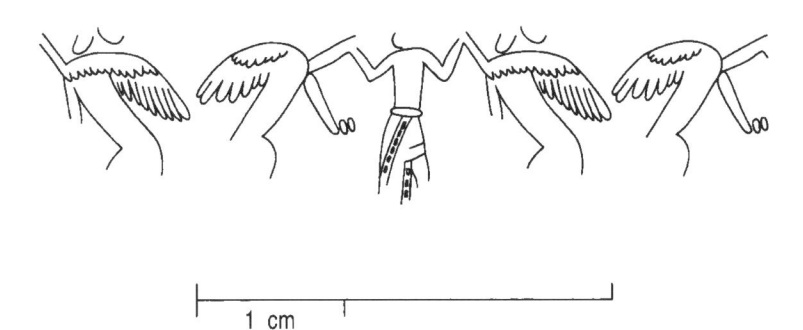

Seal Type:	Cylinder	Photograph:	Pl. 46a
Earliest Dated Application:	ND	Typology and Style:	I-A.6 — Fortification Style
Preserved Height of Image:	1.20 cm	Preserved Length of Image:	2.90 cm (comp.)
Estimated Height of Original Seal:	NA	Estimated Diameter of Original Seal:	0.90 cm
Number of Impressions:	10	Quality of Impressions:	Poor-fair

Completeness of Image: Segment of middle of design survives along its complete length

Description of Seal as Impressed Image

Hero faces right, arms bent, and holds two rampant winged human-headed lion creatures (only creature to right has head preserved) by upper foreleg.

Each creature holds upper foreleg straight and extends it upward toward hero's head. Creature to left holds lower foreleg straight and extends it downward toward hero's hip. Creature to right holds lower foreleg straight (only partially preserved) and extends it vertically downward in front of its body.

Hero wears belted Assyrian garment that leaves forward leg exposed below knee; decorative border runs along hem of short undergarment and (with stud-like detailing) along two edges of draped overgarment. Traces of rounded coiffure are at back of hero's neck.

Each creature has two rows of feathers indicated. Creature to right has squared beard that rests over its wing; traces of rounded coiffure rest at back of neck.

Commentary

For comparative illustrations including PFS 399, see pl. 230h (feet of animals and creatures).

Seal Application (see *Appendix One: Concordance of Seals to Tablets in Volume I*)

PFS 399 generally occurs on the bottom edge of tablets; on PF 326 it also occurs on the upper edge; on PF 837 it also occurs on the obverse (inverted); on PF 95 it occurs only on the reverse of the tablet, with PFS 72 (Cat.No. 147) applied (inverted) directly above it. The impressions on the upper edge of PF 326 and the bottom edge of PF 839 are too poorly preserved for analysis. Of the remaining eight impressions, six preserve one complete turn of the seal, preserving the entire length of the seal design. Of these six applications, two display the hero in the center; one displays the hero and the creature to left in the center; one displays the creature to the right of the hero in the center; two display the two creatures in the center. Of the remaining two partial rollings, one displays the hero in the center; one displays the creature to the left of the hero in the center. On the obverse of PF 837 the seal clearly was applied before the text since several cuneiform wedges cut into the bottom of the impression. The dates of all the tablets on which PFS 399 occurs are unknown.

Bibliography

Garrison 1988, pp. 276–78; Garrison and Root 1996, p. 12.

Cat.No. 79   PFS 787

Seal Type:	Cylinder	Photograph:	Pl. 46c
Earliest Dated Application:	ND	Typology and Style:	I-A.6 — Fortification Style
Preserved Height of Image:	1.50 cm (incomp.)	Preserved Length of Image:	3.00 cm (incomp.)
Estimated Height of Original Seal:	NA	Estimated Diameter of Original Seal:	NA
Number of Impressions:	2	Quality of Impressions:	Poor

Completeness of Image: Segment of middle of design survives

DESCRIPTION OF SEAL AS IMPRESSED IMAGE

Hero moves to left, arms straight (only right arm preserved) above shoulder level, and presumably holds two rampant winged human-headed lion creatures (creature at far left of preserved impressions should be the creature held to right of hero).

Each creature holds upper foreleg straight and extends it upward toward hero's head. Creature to left of hero holds lower foreleg (only partially preserved) curved and extends it downward toward hero's chest; tail curves downward then curls upward at its end. Creature presumed to be positioned to right of hero holds lower foreleg straight and extends it diagonally downward in front of its body; tail (only partially preserved) curls upward.

Hero wears Assyrian garment that leaves forward leg exposed.

Human head of creature presumed to be to right of hero has pointed beard that rests over its chest; pointed coiffure rests at back of neck.

COMMENTARY

Due to poor preservation it is impossible to be sure this is a control encounter. It could conceivably present a combat encounter, with the second rampant creature occupying the terminal field.

SEAL APPLICATION (SEE APPENDIX ONE: CONCORDANCE OF SEALS TO TABLETS IN VOLUME I)

PFS 787 occurs on the reverse (inverted) and bottom edge of PF 581. The rolling on the reverse preserves the entire length of the seal design and displays the creature to the left of the hero in the center. The partial rolling on the bottom edge displays the hero in the center. The date of PF 581 is unknown.

BIBLIOGRAPHY

Garrison 1988, pp. 304–07.

PFS 1458 — Cat.No. 80

Seal Type:	Cylinder	Photograph:	Pl. 47a
Earliest Dated Application:	501/500 B.C.	Typology and Style:	I-A.6 — Plausibly Antique: Assyro-Babylonian Modeled Style
Preserved Height of Image:	2.30 cm (incomp.)	Preserved Length of Image:	3.50 cm (incomp.)
Estimated Height of Original Seal:	2.50 cm	Estimated Diameter of Original Seal:	NA
Number of Impressions:	1	Quality of Impression:	Fair-good, but most detail is lost

Completeness of Image: Large segment of middle of design survives

DESCRIPTION OF SEAL AS IMPRESSED IMAGE

Hero faces left, arms bent, and holds two rampant winged human-headed (head preserved only at left) lion creatures by upper foreleg.

Each creature extends upper foreleg straight upward; lower foreleg is curved, paw turned downward, on creature to left. On creature to right lower foreleg is extended downward toward hero's leg, with toes splayed. Tail of creature to left curls upward with tufted termination. Two wings are indicated on creature to left, upper parallel to lower.

Hero wears Assyrian garment that leaves forward leg exposed below mid-thigh. Long squared beard rests across hero's right shoulder and chest; thick flattened coiffure rests at back of neck. Hero perhaps wears domed headdress.

Schematic head of creature to left may be beardless. Round coiffure sits atop columnar neck; another circular form denotes facial features. Creature wears domed headdress with projection at back.

COMMENTARY

PFS 1458 occurs on a Q text, but the text is somewhat unusual: "flour(?) supplied by Haturrada, Naktiš withdrew(?). Two gentlemen receive... ." Thus the seal belongs either to Naktiš (whose name occurs only here) or to one of the two gentlemen.

The large seal exhibits a heavily modeled style, with extensive use of the unmasked drill in human heads and upper bodies; the impression of the seal is very sharp and crisp. Some Neo-Assyrian Modeled Style seals are similar both as regards composition and iconography; compare also PFS 1658 (Cat.No. 101).[21] PFS 1458 may be an heirloom, but it relates closely to a group of archaizing seals in the PFS corpus of hero seals and may, rather, emerge out of a particular Persepolitan workshop environment (as per Garrison 1988).

For comparative illustrations including PFS 1458, see pl. 175g (Assyrian garments).

---

21. See, for example, Herbordt 1992, pl. 4, nos. 3, 6; 5, no. 5; 6, nos. 2, 5; 8, no. 8, for Assyrian seals displaying extensive use of drill in human heads combined with a modeled carving style.

SEAL APPLICATION (SEE *APPENDIX ONE: CONCORDANCE OF SEALS TO TABLETS IN VOLUME I*)

PFS 1458 occurs on the reverse of PF 1574. The partial rolling displays the hero in the center. The seal clearly was applied before the text since several cuneiform wedges cut into the top of the impression. PF 1574 is dated 501/500 B.C.

BIBLIOGRAPHY

Dusinberre 1997b, p. 128 (n. 131); Garrison 1988, pp. 201–03, 205, 231–32, 246, 476, 480.

Cat.No. 81   PFS 940

Seal Type: Cylinder	Photograph: Pl. 47c
Earliest Dated Application: 500 B.C.	Typology and Style: I-A.6 — Broad and Flat Styles
Preserved Height of Image: 1.30 cm (incomp.)	Preserved Length of Image: 2.70 cm (incomp.)
Estimated Height of Original Seal: NA	Estimated Diameter of Original Seal: NA
Number of Impressions: 2	Quality of Impressions: Fair

Completeness of Image: Segment of middle of design survives

DESCRIPTION OF SEAL AS IMPRESSED IMAGE

Hero moves to left, arms curved, and holds rampant winged(?) human-headed lion creature to left by middle of foreleg and holds rampant winged human-headed lion creature to right by base of foreleg.

Creature to left holds foreleg slightly bent and extends it upward toward hero's waist. Curved tail at far right of impressions should belong to this creature. Creature to right holds foreleg straight and extends it upward toward hero's head; tail curls upward.

Hero appears to wear Assyrian garment that leaves forward leg exposed below mid-thigh.

Creature at left apparently looks to left, with narrow rounded coiffure at back of head. Creature to right has beard that terminates in blunt point; rounded coiffure curls upward against back of head; three small spikes project from top of its head.

COMMENTARY

Based upon Q texts protocol, PFS 940 should belong to the wine supplier Karkašša who in year 22.2 (500 B.C.) supplied a travel group on their way from Susa to Kandahar. The seal also occurs on the left edge of PF 814 (K3 texts, rations for persons without qualification), wherein Karkašša supplied wine at Hadaran.

The awkwardly rendered figures and unusual proportions are typical of seals carved in the Broad and Flat Styles.

For comparative illustrations including PFS 940, see pls. 206j (arm positions of heroic control) and 287f (personal seals of various suppliers).

SEAL APPLICATION (SEE *APPENDIX ONE: CONCORDANCE OF SEALS TO TABLETS IN VOLUME I*)

PFS 940 occurs on the left edge of both PF 814 and PF 1550. Both rollings are partial and display the hero and the creature to right in the center. PF 1550 is the earliest dated tablet with PFS 940 and is dated 500 B.C.

BIBLIOGRAPHY

Dusinberre 1997b, p. 128 (n. 131); Garrison 1988, pp. 431, 433.

PFS 1613   Cat.No. 82

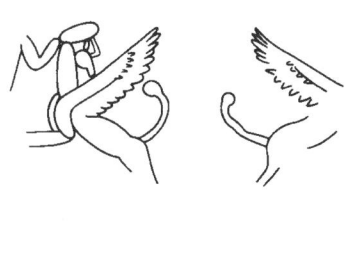

Seal Type:	Cylinder	Photograph:	Pl. 47e
Earliest Dated Application:	495 B.C.	Typology and Style:	I-A.6 — Fortification Style
Preserved Height of Image:	1.10 cm (incomp.)	Preserved Length of Image:	2.30 cm (incomp.)
Estimated Height of Original Seal:	NA	Estimated Diameter of Original Seal:	NA
Number of Impressions:	1	Quality of Impression:	Fair

Completeness of Image: Segment of middle of design survives

DESCRIPTION OF SEAL AS IMPRESSED IMAGE

Only left arm of hero is preserved; it is bent, holding rampant winged human-faced lion creature by top of head. Rampant winged creature at far right of impression should be other creature of same type held by hero with his right hand.

Both creatures move toward hero. Creature to right of hero turns its head away from him; creature holds one foreleg (only partially preserved) straight and extends it outward toward hero. Tail of each creature curls upward with tufted termination. Creature to right of hero has narrow squared beard that rests over its wing.

COMMENTARY

Based on Q texts protocol, PFS 1613 should belong to Barušiyatiš, who in year 27.8 (495 B.C.) supplied flour rations at Makkaš. Q texts PF 1290–1294, PF 1296–1297, and PF 1300–1305 record a Barušiyatiš who also supplied flour, but he used PFS 26 (Cat.No. 299; see Koch 1986, p. 140). In PF 451 (F text), PF 1704 (S1 text), and PF 1783 (S3 text) he supplied grain using PFS 26 (Cat.No. 299). There seems to be every indication that this is the same individual who used PFS 1613 on PF 2050. All of his transactions in which he used PFS 26 (Cat.No. 299) occurred in year 23 (499/498 B.C.). Apparently when he reappeared in the PF texts in year 27.8, he used a new seal, PFS 1613. PF 11 (year 28.1) and PF 330 (year 23) preserve the same Barušiyatiš who supplied grain at Parmadan; both transactions are sealed only once, with PFS 324 (illegible) and PFS 284* (Cat.No. 111) respectively.

For a similar rendering of the creatures' bodies, see PFS 1076 (Cat.No. 193); for their human faces, see PFS 2 (Cat.No. 3), PFS 233 (Cat.No. 52), PFS 690 (Cat.No. 139), PFS 740 (Cat.No. 146), and PFS 1519 (Cat.No. 167). See Garrison 1988 for this distinctive artist.

For comparative illustrations including PFS 1613, see pls. 197i (hands), 271g (compositions with large empty space as terminal field), and 285b (personal seals of Barušiyatiš, flour supplier).

SEAL APPLICATION (SEE *APPENDIX ONE: CONCORDANCE OF SEALS TO TABLETS IN VOLUME I*)

PFS 1613 occurs on the left edge of PF 2050. The partial rolling, now damaged on its right edge, displays the terminal field in the center. PF 2050 is dated 495 B.C.

BIBLIOGRAPHY

Dusinberre 1997b, p. 128 (n. 131); Garrison 1988, pp. 356–59; Garrison and Dion 1999, pp. 6 (n. 15), 11 (n. 36).

I-A.7. WINGED BIRD-HEADED LION CREATURES

Cat.No. 83   PFS 79

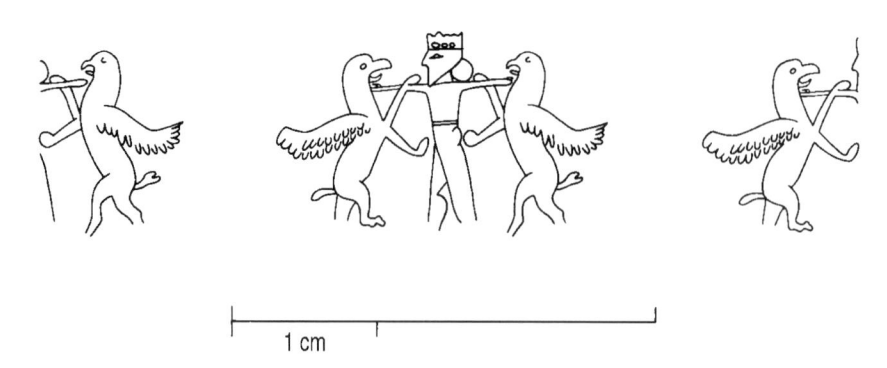

Seal Type:	Cylinder	Photographs:	Pl. 48a–b
Earliest Dated Application:	500/499 B.C.	Typology and Style:	I-A.7 — Fortification Style
Preserved Height of Image:	1.40 cm (incomp.)	Preserved Length of Image:	2.90 cm (comp.)
Estimated Height of Original Seal:	1.60 cm	Estimated Diameter of Original Seal:	0.90 cm
Number of Impressions:	17	Quality of Impressions:	Fair-good

Completeness of Image: Complete except for lower edge

DESCRIPTION OF SEAL AS IMPRESSED IMAGE

Hero faces left, arms straight at horizontal, and holds two rampant winged bird-headed lion creatures by throat.

Each creature holds upper foreleg straight and extends it upward to wrap paw around hero's arm; lower foreleg is straight, paw upturned, and extended downward toward hero's waist. Each creature raises its bent forward hind leg. Short tail of creature to left curls slightly downward. Short tail of creature to right curls upward with two pronged termination.

Hero wears belted Assyrian garment that leaves forward leg exposed; hero also wears five-pointed dentate Persian crown with studded band (three studs preserved). Pointed beard rests over hero's right shoulder; large round coiffure rests at back of neck.

Each creature has mouth open. Creature to left has two rows of feathers indicated on wing.

COMMENTARY

Koch (1990) assigns PFS 79 to an unnamed official who oversaw grain transactions at Irišdumaka, Makarkiš, and Dur, and wine transactions at Hiran, all of which lie in her Southeastern Region III. The seal occurs on the journal PF 1948, indicating that the official handled some important accounting functions.

    The seal is well composed and executed with a delicate touch. The empty terminal field is relatively large. Perhaps it was meant to receive an inscription, but the rolling patterns of the seal application suggest that the negative space created by the empty terminal field lent a distinctive aesthetic dynamic that was appreciated by the user.

    For comparative illustrations including PFS 79, see pls. 174a (Assyrian garments), 188d (Persian crowns and fluted tiaras), 202c (arm positions of heroic control), 222f (lions and lion creatures), 271a (compositions with large empty space as terminal field), and 282e (personal seals of supply/apportionment officers).

SEAL APPLICATION (SEE *APPENDIX ONE: CONCORDANCE OF SEALS TO TABLETS IN VOLUME I*)

PFS 79 always occurs alone on tablets that it seals, an indication of an office or official of some importance. The seal can occur on as many as four edges (PF 251, reverse, upper edge, right edge, and left edge) and as few as one (PF 317, upper edge; PF 1948, right edge). Other combinations are on the reverse and left edge (PF 241, PF 245, PF 250, PF 262). On the reverse of PF 241, PF 245, and PF 250 the seal has been applied twice, one impression directly above the other. The rollings of the seal are very carefully applied with little or no distortion. Rollings of the seal clearly show awareness of the figural design and the large negative space in the terminal field. In seven impressions the seal is rolled for at least one complete turn, preserving the entire length of the seal design.

Of these seven applications, two carefully display the hero in the center with the negative space of the terminal field equally balanced on the edges of the impression; three display the hero and the creature to right in the center with the negative space of the terminal field at the right; one displays the hero and the creature to left in the focal zone with the negative space of the terminal field at the left. The one application on PF 1948 is long, preserving two complete rollings of the seal; this application is carefully balanced with the negative space of the terminal field in the center flanked by a complete image of the heroic encounter framed by a repeat of the negative space of the terminal field on each end of the impression. Of the remaining ten partial impressions, nine display the hero in the center without any negative space of the terminal field at the edges of the impression; one preserves only the hero and the creature to left. On the reverse of PF 251 and PF 262 the seal clearly was applied before the text since several cuneiform wedges cut into the top of the impressions. The same is true of the right edge of PF 1948, where several cuneiform wedges cut into the terminal field at the right and left of the impression. PF 241, PF 262, and PF 317 are the earliest dated tablets with PFS 79 and are all dated 500/499 B.C.

BIBLIOGRAPHY

Brosius 1996, p. 158 (table 9); Garrison 1988, pp. 278–81; Koch 1990, pp. 108, 270, 275.

PFS 103*   Cat.No. 84

Seal Impression:	Cylinder, Inscribed	Photographs:	Pl. 49a–b
Earliest Dated Application:	500 B.C.	Typology and Style:	I-A.7 — Fortification Style
Language of Inscription:	Elamite		
Preserved Height of Image:	1.50 cm (incomp.)	Preserved Length of Image:	3.20 cm (comp.)
Estimated Height of Original Seal:	1.70 cm	Estimated Diameter of Original Seal:	1.00 cm
Number of Impressions:	14	Quality of Impressions:	Poor-fair

Completeness of Image: Complete except for upper edge and lower edge and parts of inscription

DESCRIPTION OF SEAL AS IMPRESSED IMAGE

Four-winged hero faces left, arms bent, and holds two rampant winged horned bird-headed lion creatures by upper foreleg.

Each creature holds upper foreleg straight and extends it vertically upward in front of its chest; lower foreleg is straight and extended downward toward hero's lower body. Creatures' tails are short; that of creature to left curls upward and that of creature to right extends horizontally outward, curling upward at its end with tufted termination.

Hero wears belted robe; fringe or folds are indicated along hem. Long squared beard rests over hero's chest; small round coiffure rests at back of neck. Hero appears to wear flat headdress.

Mane of creature to right is rendered by crisp serrated edge along contour of neck and head. Creature to left has short pointed horn emerging from top of its head; long pointed ear emerges from back of creature's head; two rows of feathers are indicated on its wing. Mouth of each creature is open.

Inscription fills terminal field and lower fields between hero and two creatures.

INSCRIPTION

Elamite

Line
x+1. v.d.Ša-
x+2. na-
x+3. ú(?) šak d.Ša-
x+4. ti-d.Hu-pan-na

Translation   Šanau, son of Šati-Hupan

There are four lines to the inscription oriented along the horizontal axis of the seal. Lines x+1–x+3 fill the terminal field. Line x+4 is inscribed across the length of the seal. The only reading that makes sense puts the beginning of line x+4 with the ti-sign located between the hero and the creature to right. In this way line x+4 neatly begins between the hero and the creature to right and ends with the na-sign between the hero and the creature to left. The name Šati-Hupan also occurs as the patronym in the inscription of PFS 4* (Cat.No. 292).

PN$_1$ is otherwise unattested and problematic as read. There is no attested element beginning with ša-na and preceded by the determinative for a divine name. It might alternatively be read v.An-ša-na-ú, which is also unattested and equally problematic. It is possible that we are unable to see all of the sign that we are reading here as ú, which is squeezed between the wing and the tail of one of the creatures and slightly out of the register with the remainder of line x+3. It is also possible that the ú should be read as the first sign of line x+2, yielding a reading of v.d.Ša-ú-na or v.An-ša-ú-na. None of these alternatives are attested. See also the note on the name Šati-Hupan under PFS 4* (Cat.No. 292), below.

COMMENTARY

Koch (1990) notes that PFS 103*, PFS 99 (Cat.No. 113), and PFS 228 (Cat.No. 148) are responsible for the verification of the year end accounts at Liduma in her Elam Region VI. PFS 103* never occurs with another seal. Koch assigns the seal to the "Rechnungsführer" in her Elam Region VI. Unfortunately, we are not able to verify through the PF texts that the official using PFS 103* is the individual whose name (Šanau) appears on the seal inscription. Thus we can only suggest the likelihood that PFS 103* is a personal seal of this Šanau, who uses it in his official accounting capacity.

The seal seems rather well made, better than what our impressions indicate. See Garrison 1988 for the artist and related seals. PFS 1202 (Cat.No. 137), probably by the same artist, also shows a four-winged hero.

For comparative illustrations including PFS 103*, see pls. 182c (robes with various features of detail), 264d (inscriptions without panels or case lines), 272b (dense compositions), 278c (carving anomalies), and 286c (personal seals of accountants).

SEAL APPLICATION (SEE *APPENDIX ONE: CONCORDANCE OF SEALS TO TABLETS IN VOLUME I*)

As is typical of seals of important officials and offices, PFS 103* always occurs alone on tablets that it seals, and covers multiple surfaces. PFS 103* always occurs on the reverse and left edge; in two instances (PF 240 and PF 248) PFS 103* occurs also on the bottom edge and once (PF 258) also on the upper edge. On the reverse of PF 240, PF 255, and PF 258 the seal has been applied twice, one impression directly above the other. Thus, the fourteen total impressions in fact come from only four different tablets. Rollings of the seal on the reverse tend to be long, that on PF 240 preserving almost two full revolutions of the seal. Since the first three lines of the inscription fill the terminal field and the fourth line is inscribed across the full length of the seal face, some part of the inscription is captured in every rolling of the seal. In eight impressions the seal is rolled for at least one complete turn, preserving the entire length of the seal design. Of these eight applications, one displays the hero in the center; two display the hero and the creature to right in the center; two display the creature to the left and the inscription in the center; three display the inscription in the terminal field in the center. Of the remaining six partial rollings, one preserves only the hero; two display the hero and the creature to left in the center; two display the creature to the right of the hero in the center; one preserves only the creature to the right of the hero and the inscription in the terminal field. PF 248 is the earliest dated tablet with PFS 103* and is dated 500 B.C.

BIBLIOGRAPHY

Garrison 1988, pp. 309–12; Garrison 1998, p. 121 (n. 15); Garrison and Dion 1999, p. 9 (n. 19); Koch 1990, pp. 203–05.

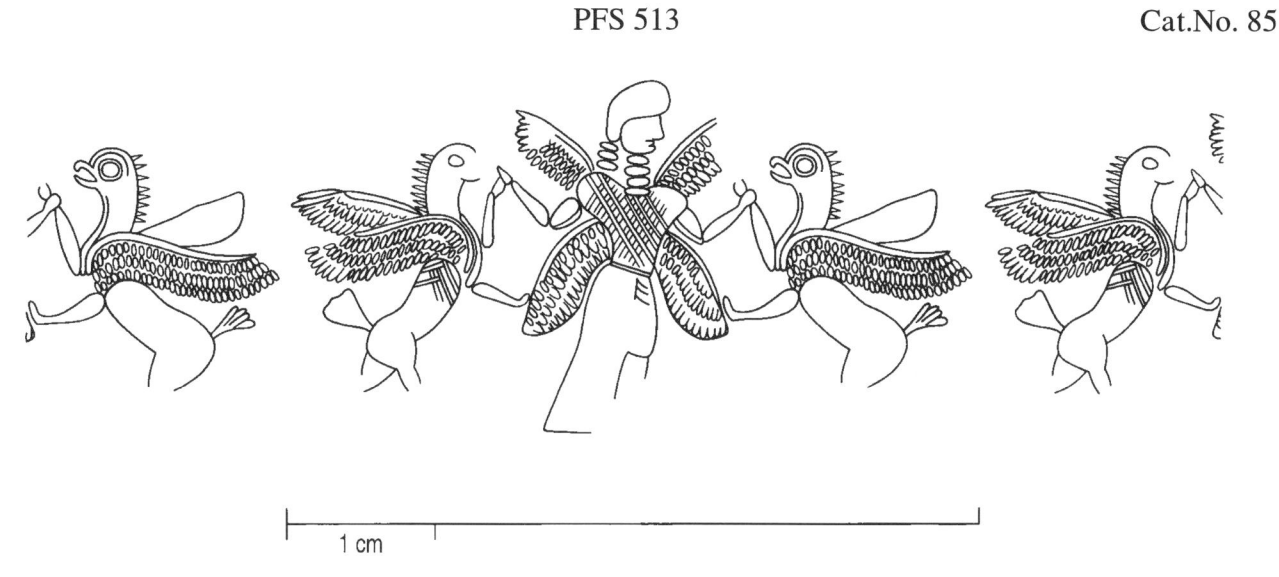

PFS 513   Cat.No. 85

Seal Type:	Cylinder	Photographs:	Pl. 50a–c
Earliest Dated Application:	503/502 B.C.	Typology and Style:	I-A.7 — Antique: Neo-Assyrian Modeled Style
Preserved Height of Image:	2.40 cm (incomp.)	Preserved Length of Image:	4.80 cm (comp.)
Estimated Height of Original Seal:	2.70 cm	Estimated Diameter of Original Seal:	1.50 cm
Number of Impressions:	10		

Quality of Impressions: Some preserve excellent detail; others are blurred and indistinct

Completeness of Image: Almost complete except for upper edge and lower edge

DESCRIPTION OF SEAL AS IMPRESSED IMAGE

Four-winged hero faces right, arms bent, and holds two rampant winged bird-headed lion creatures by upper foreleg.

Each creature holds upper foreleg straight and extends it upward toward hero's upper wing; lower foreleg is straight and extended downward to place upturned paw on hero's lower wing. Birds' tails extend diagonally upward; tail of creature to right has four feathers indicated.

Hero wears belted Assyrian garment that leaves forward leg exposed below knee; upper part of garment carries elaborate crosshatched pattern; three folds are indicated on lower part of garment over forward hip. Hero's wings are very detailed and show three rows of feathers. Long, squared, segmented beard rests over hero's chest; squared segmented coiffure rests at back of neck.

Each creature has two wings indicated, upper extending diagonally upward from lower; like hero's wings they are elaborately treated with three rows of feathers (with exception of upper wing of creature to right, which is not well preserved). Creature to left has cross-hatching on upper part of body under wings. Each creature has mane rendered by crisp spikes along contour of neck; mouth of creature to right is open.

COMMENTARY

PFS 513 is either the office seal of an accounting office or a personal seal of the unnamed accountant who uses it. The distinctive features of the seal might suggest the likelihood that it is a prized personal seal (a family heirloom?), but this cannot be demonstrated. All applications occur on accounting texts.

This is an exceptionally large and elaborately carved seal. The detailing on the design and the hard, mechanical execution draw the seal very close to select seals of the Neo-Assyrian Modeled Style and we suspect that the seal is an heirloom from the Neo-Assyrian period.[22] (Originally, Garrison [1988] placed this with other strongly archaizing seals in the Persepolitan Modeled Style.)

For comparative illustrations including PFS 513, see pls. 176f (Assyrian garments with detailing preserved), 191d (variously detailed beards), 201g (heroes as winged humans), 205d (arm positions of heroic control), 231a (feet of animals and creatures), 273f (open compositions), and 286e (personal seals of accountants).

SEAL APPLICATION (SEE *APPENDIX ONE: CONCORDANCE OF SEALS TO TABLETS IN VOLUME I*)

PFS 513 occurs on the reverse, upper edge, right edge, and left edge of PF 233, the right edge of PF 1986, the left edge of PF 1987, and the reverse, upper edge, and left edge of PF 2074. On the left edge of PF 1987 two impressions are preserved. The surface of the tablet between these two impressions is now destroyed, and there exists the possibility that we have to do here originally with one very long impression. Impressions tend to exhibit some lateral distortion. In three impressions the seal is rolled for one complete turn, preserving the entire length of the seal design. Of these three applications, two display the hero in the center; one displays the hero and the creature to left in the center. Of the remaining seven rollings, two display the hero in the center; one preserves only the hero and the creature to right; one preserves only the hero and the creature to left; two display the creature to the left of the hero in the center; one preserves only the creature to the left of the hero. On the reverse of PF 233 the seal clearly was applied before the text since several cuneiform wedges cut into the top of the impression. PF 1986 is the earliest dated tablet with PFS 513 and is dated 503/502 B.C.

BIBLIOGRAPHY

Garrison 1988, pp. 203–07, 254, 480, 520; Garrison 1998, p. 121 (n. 15); Garrison and Dion 1999, p. 9 (n. 19).

---

22. For example, Collon 1987, nos. 347–48, 350, 352; Curtis and Reade 1995, p. 185, no. 188.

PFS 819   Cat.No. 86

Seal Type:	Cylinder	Photograph:	Pl. 51a
Earliest Dated Application:	495/494 B.C.	Typology and Style:	I-A.7 — Court Style
Preserved Height of Image:	1.80 cm (incomp.)	Preserved Length of Image:	2.70 cm (comp.)
Estimated Height of Original Seal:	2.00 cm	Estimated Diameter of Original Seal:	0.90 cm
Number of Impressions:	2	Quality of Impressions:	Fair

Completeness of Image: Almost complete except for upper edge

DESCRIPTION OF SEAL AS IMPRESSED IMAGE

Hero faces right, arms straight at horizontal, and holds two rampant winged horned bird-headed lion creatures by throat.

Each creature holds upper foreleg straight and extends it upward to hero's arm; lower foreleg is straight and extended outward to place paw on hero's waist. Creatures' tails extend horizontally outward, curling upward at their ends.

Hero wears belted Persian court robe with sleeves pushed up to reveal arms; gathered folds of sleeves are indicated, as are central pleat and diagonal and horizontal folds of lower part of garment. Hero has short rounded beard; rounded coiffure rests at back of his neck.

Each creature has two wings indicated, upper extending diagonally upward from lower. Creature to right has two rows of feathers indicated on its wings. Long straight pointed horn emerges from top of creature's head. Each creature has its mouth slightly open.

Line border is preserved at bottom of design. Trace of edge of seal is preserved at bottom of design below creature to right.

COMMENTARY

The design has less surface detailing than normally seen in the Court Style, and the schematic treatment of the forepaws of the creatures and the line border are unusual in this style. The animal bodies are powerful studies, some of the heaviest in the Court Style.

For comparative illustrations including PFS 819, see pls. 179e (Persian court robes with sleeves pushed up), 202h (arm positions of heroic control), and 276g (borders).

SEAL APPLICATION (SEE *APPENDIX ONE: CONCORDANCE OF SEALS TO TABLETS IN VOLUME I*)

PFS 819 occurs on the reverse (inverted) and left edge of PF 611. No other seal is used on the tablet. The rolling on the reverse preserves the entire length of the seal design and displays the hero and the creature to right in the center. The partial rolling on the left edge displays the creature to the right of the hero in the center. PF 611 is dated 495/494 B.C.

BIBLIOGRAPHY

Garrison 1988, pp. 220, 394–401, 479–80, 529.

Cat.No. 87   PFS 981*

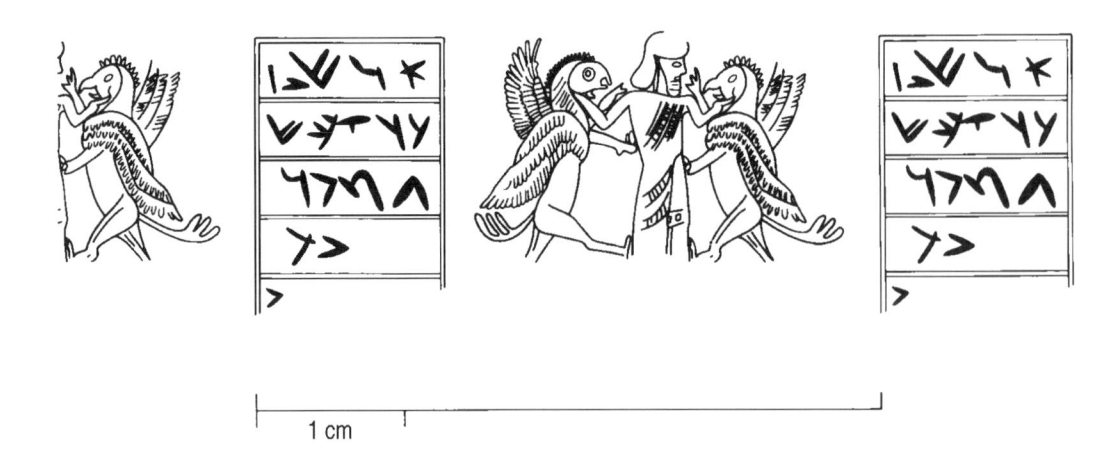

Seal Impression:	Cylinder, Inscribed	Photographs:	Pl. 52a–b
Earliest Dated Application:	500/499 B.C.	Typology and Style:	I-A.7 — Mixed Styles II
Language of Inscription:	Aramaic		
Preserved Height of Image:	1.90 cm	Preserved Length of Image:	4.20 cm (comp.)
Estimated Height of Original Seal:	NA	Estimated Diameter of Original Seal:	1.30 cm
Number of Impressions:	7	Quality of Impressions:	Good

Completeness of Image: Complete except for upper edge and lower edge and parts of inscription

DESCRIPTION OF SEAL AS IMPRESSED IMAGE

Hero faces right, arms bent, and holds two rampant winged bird-headed lion creatures by throat.

Each creature holds upper foreleg straight, toes splayed, and extends it upward toward hero's head; lower foreleg is straight and extended downward to place paw on hero's waist. Each creature raises bent forward hind leg to place bird's foot on hero's lower leg; tail curls upward terminating in three-feathered projection.

Hero wears Assyrian garment that leaves forward leg exposed below knee; two or three decorative bands are diagonally disposed across hero's chest; two bands run diagonally on lower part of garment over rear leg; decorative border is on hem of undergarment over forward knee. Squared beard with horizontal striations rests over hero's left shoulder; flattened coiffure rests at back of neck.

Each creature has two wings, lower extending diagonally downward, upper extending diagonally upward from lower; three rows of feathers are indicated. Mane/comb is rendered by crisp serrated edge along contour of neck and top of head; mouth is open.

Large paneled inscription is in terminal field.

INSCRIPTION

Aramaic

Line
1. ʾN(?)Šx
2. BR xxŠ
3. GḤ(?)WD(?)
4. [(x x)]⌈x x⌉
5. […]⌈x⌉

Translation   ʾN(?)Š … son of PN₂ …

There are five lines to the inscription, oriented along the horizontal axis of the seal, separated by case lines, and enclosed in a panel. Although the letter forms are clear, they are not particularly well executed. In the end of the first line and the middle of the second line there may be marks that are intrusive. There is nothing in the three texts with which this seal is associated to offer clues as to the vocalization of the first name.

COMMENTARY

This seal was carved by a master engraver. Stylistically the design bridges several styles, most strongly related to the Fortification Style (head of hero), Modeled Style (elaborate surface treatment, creature forms), and Court Style (human forms, creatures' wings, paneled inscription). The hero's garment bears similarities to the garment seen on PFS 16* (Cat.No. 22).

For comparative illustrations including PFS 981*, see pls. 176g (Assyrian garments with detailing preserved), 211d (heroic attitudes of control encounter), and 263b (paneled inscriptions with horizontal case lines).

SEAL APPLICATION (SEE *APPENDIX ONE: CONCORDANCE OF SEALS TO TABLETS IN VOLUME I*)

PFS 981* always occurs alone on tablets that it seals, suggesting that it is a seal of an important official or office. PFS 981* occurs on the reverse, upper edge, and left edge of PF 937 and PF 1012 and the left edge of PF 993. The seal is inverted on the reverse of PF 1012. In two impressions the seal is rolled for at least one complete turn, preserving the entire length of the seal design. These two impressions display the creature to the left of the hero in the center, with a full rolling of the inscription at the left edge of each impression. Of the remaining five partial impressions, two display the hero in the center; one displays the creature to the right of the hero and the inscription in the center; two display the creature to the right of the hero in the center, with an almost complete rolling of the inscription at the right edge of the impression. On the reverse of PF 937 and PF 1012 the seal clearly was applied before the text since several cuneiform wedges cut into the top or bottom of the impressions. PF 1012 is the earliest dated tablet with PFS 981* and is dated 500/499 B.C.

BIBLIOGRAPHY

Dusinberre 1997b, p. 127 (n. 119); Garrison 1988, pp. 368, 375, 380–83, 404, 416, 430, 496; Garrison and Dion 1999, pp. 8 (n. 17), 10.

Cat.No. 88　　　　　　　　　　　　　　PFS 1483

Seal Type:	Cylinder	Photograph:	Pl. 53a
Earliest Dated Application:	499/498 B.C.	Typology and Style:	I-A.7 — Fortification Style
Preserved Height of Image:	1.40 cm (incomp.)	Preserved Length of Image:	2.80 cm (comp.)
Estimated Height of Original Seal:	1.50 cm	Estimated Diameter of Original Seal:	0.90 cm
Number of Impressions:	1	Quality of Impression:	Poor

Completeness of Image: Almost complete except for lower edge and details

Description of Seal as Impressed Image

Hero faces left in striding pose, arms straight, and holds two rampant winged bird-headed lion creatures by throat.

Each creature holds upper foreleg curved and extends it upward toward hero's head. Creature to left holds lower foreleg straight and extends it downward toward hero's leg. Creature to right holds lower foreleg curved, paw upturned, and extends it downward toward hero's hip. Creatures' tails curl upward with tufted terminations.

Hero wears Assyrian garment that leaves forward leg exposed; indication of polos headdress is on hero's head. Beard terminates in blunt point over hero's right shoulder; flattened coiffure rests at back of neck.

Creature to right has mouth open.

Narrow vertical line appears in field above and below wing of creature to left.

V-shaped crescent is in upper terminal field.

Edge of seal is preserved at top of design.

Commentary

The vertical line in the design may suggest that PFS 1483 is a recut seal, with the line being a vestige of the earlier image. Alternatively (but less plausibly) the line may indicate a flaw in the stone that reads in an extremely regular fashion. See Garrison 1988 for the distinctive hand of this artist.

For comparative illustrations including PFS 1483, see pls. 251h (crescents) and 279d (carving anomalies).

Seal Application (see Appendix One: Concordance of Seals to Tablets in Volume I)

PFS 1483 occurs on the reverse of PF 1607. The rolling preserves the entire length of the seal design and displays the creature to the left of the hero in the center. PF 1607 is dated 499/498 B.C.

Bibliography

Garrison 1988, pp. 330–33.

I-A.8. BULLS OR LIONS

PFS 1165 — Cat.No. 89

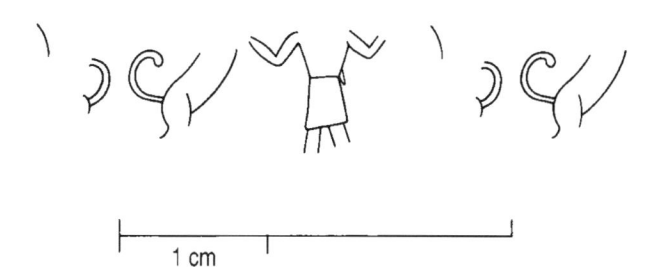

Seal Type:	Cylinder	Photograph:	Pl. 53c
Earliest Dated Application:	500/499 B.C.	Typology and Style:	I-A.8 — Fortification Style
Preserved Height of Image:	0.90 cm (incomp.)	Preserved Length of Image:	2.70 cm (comp.)
Estimated Height of Original Seal:	NA	Estimated Diameter of Original Seal:	0.90 cm
Number of Impressions:	1	Quality of Impression:	Good

Completeness of Image: Small segment of middle of design survives along its complete length

DESCRIPTION OF SEAL AS IMPRESSED IMAGE

Hero moves to left(?), arms bent, and holds two rampant bulls or lions.

Tail of each animal curls upward (with tufted termination on animal to left).

Hero wears belted tunic; short pointed projection at waist may be sheath.

COMMENTARY

Although documented by a clear impression, only a small part of the seal design emerges. The composition seems to have a spaciousness not commonly seen in the PFS corpus.

For comparative illustrations including PFS 1165, see pls. 205e (arm positions of heroic control) and 273i (open compositions).

SEAL APPLICATION (SEE *APPENDIX ONE: CONCORDANCE OF SEALS TO TABLETS IN VOLUME I*)

PFS 1165 occurs along the lower half of the reverse of PF 1217. PFS 1164 (II) is applied along the upper half of the reverse, apparently over-rolling PFS 1165. The rolling of PFS 1165 preserves the entire length of the seal design and displays the hero and the animal to right in the center. PF 1217 is dated 500/499 B.C.

BIBLIOGRAPHY

Garrison 1988, pp. 273–76.

Cat.No. 90 PFS 461

Seal Type:	Cylinder	Photograph:	Pl. 54a
Earliest Dated Application:	500/499 B.C.	Typology and Style:	I-A.8 — Fortification Style
Preserved Height of Image:	1.10 cm (incomp.)	Preserved Length of Image:	3.20 cm (comp.)
Estimated Height of Original Seal:	NA	Estimated Diameter of Original Seal:	1.00 cm
Number of Impressions:	1	Quality of Impression:	Fair

Completeness of Image: Segment of middle of design survives along its complete length

DESCRIPTION OF SEAL AS IMPRESSED IMAGE

Hero moves to right, arms bent, and holds two rampant animals (bulls or lions) by upper foreleg (preserved only to right); hero is in striding pose apparently raising his forward leg.

Animal to left holds lower foreleg curved, paw upturned, and extends it downward toward hero's leg; tail curls upward with tufted termination. Animal to right holds upper foreleg straight and extends it upward toward hero's head; lower foreleg is curved, paw upturned, and extended downward toward hero's leg. Tail (only partially preserved) curves downward.

Hero wears Assyrian garment that leaves forward leg exposed.

Eagle with folded wings and long appendages is displayed vertically in terminal field (head not preserved).

COMMENTARY

The placement and rendering of the eagle in the terminal field is unique in the PFS corpus.[23] What is preserved of the image suggests an evocation of the eagle that seems to have adorned a royal standard of the Persian king (Nylander 1983, p. 23). See Salonen 1973, pp. 80–83, on eagles and falcons in the Mesopotamian tradition. See Garrison 1988 for the artist of PFS 461 and related seals, which show similar large and well-executed designs.

For comparative illustrations including PFS 461, see pls. 227d (birds) and 268e (terminal field motifs other than inscriptions).

SEAL APPLICATION (SEE APPENDIX ONE: CONCORDANCE OF SEALS TO TABLETS IN VOLUME I)

PFS 461 occurs along the top half of the reverse (inverted) of PF 163. PFS 460 (III) is applied across the bottom half of the reverse. The rolling of PFS 461 preserves the entire length of the seal design and displays the lion to the right of the hero in the center. PF 163 is dated 500/499 B.C.

BIBLIOGRAPHY

Garrison 1988, pp. 313–16.

---

23. Compare the displayed eagle on a stone tile excavated at Persepolis in 1948 (Sami 1955, pp. 66–67) and the bird on one of the sealings from Memphis (Petrie et al. 1910, p. 42, pl. 36, no. 39).

I-A.9. WINGED BULL OR LION CREATURES

PFS 392　　　　　　　　　　　　　　　　　　　　　　　　　　　　　　　　　　　　Cat.No. 91

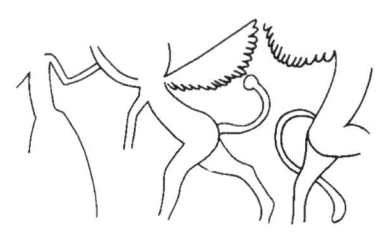

Seal Type:	Cylinder	Photograph:	Pl. 54c
Earliest Dated Application:	499/498 B.C.	Typology and Style:	I-A.9 — Fortification Style
Preserved Height of Image:	1.40 cm (incomp.)	Preserved Length of Image:	2.50 cm (incomp.)
Estimated Height of Original Seal:	NA	Estimated Diameter of Original Seal:	NA
Number of Impressions:	1	Quality of Impression:	Poor

Completeness of Image: Segment of middle of design survives

DESCRIPTION OF SEAL AS IMPRESSED IMAGE

Hero moves to left, arms bent (only left arm is completely preserved), and holds rampant winged bull or lion creature to right by upper foreleg.

Presumably the rampant winged bull or lion creature at far right of impression is other creature held by hero. This creature raises forward hind leg; tail curves downward between its hind legs with tufted termination. Creature to right of hero holds upper foreleg (only partially preserved) curved and extends it upward toward hero's head; lower foreleg (only partially preserved) is bent and extended downward in front of its body; tail curls upward with tufted termination.

Hero wears garment of uncertain type.

COMMENTARY

See Garrison 1988 for the artist and related seals.
　　For comparative illustrations including PFS 392, see pl. 218e (comparative heroic proportions).

SEAL APPLICATION (SEE *APPENDIX ONE: CONCORDANCE OF SEALS TO TABLETS IN VOLUME I*)

PFS 392 occurs on the left edge of PF 89. The partial rolling displays the creature to the right of the hero in the center. PF 89 is dated 499/498 B.C.

BIBLIOGRAPHY

Garrison 1988, pp. 313–16, 450.

Cat.No. 92   PFS 454

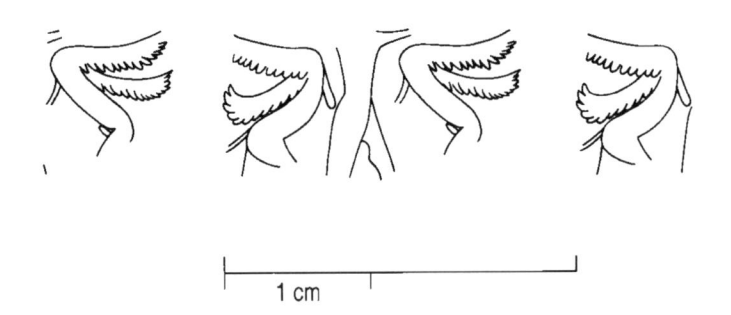

Seal Type:	Cylinder	Photograph:	Pl. 55a
Earliest Dated Application:	501/500 B.C.	Typology and Style:	I-A.9 — Fortification Style
Preserved Height of Image:	1.10 cm (incomp.)	Preserved Length of Image:	2.40 cm (comp.)
Estimated Height of Original Seal:	NA	Estimated Diameter of Original Seal:	0.80 cm
Number of Impressions:	2	Quality of Impressions:	Poor

Completeness of Image: Segment of middle of design survives along its complete length

DESCRIPTION OF SEAL AS IMPRESSED IMAGE

Hero moves to right in striding pose, arms straight at horizontal (only left arm preserved), and holds two rampant winged bull or lion creatures by throat(?).

Creature to left holds lower foreleg straight and extends it downward toward hero's hip; thin tail extends downward. Creature to right holds lower foreleg (only partially preserved) curved and extends it downward toward hero's leg. Both creatures have two wings indicated, lower extending diagonally downward from upper.

Hero wears Assyrian garment that leaves forward leg exposed.

Creature to right is ithyphallic.

COMMENTARY

Owing to the fragmentary preservation of the upper parts of all the figures, the exact composition cannot be determined; the design may show a combat encounter with the creature to left as a bystander.

For comparative illustrations including PFS 454, see pl. 271c (compositions with large empty space as terminal field).

SEAL APPLICATION (SEE *APPENDIX ONE: CONCORDANCE OF SEALS TO TABLETS IN VOLUME I*)

PFS 454 occurs on the reverse (inverted) and upper edge of PF 150. Both partial rollings display the hero in the center. On the reverse of PF 150 the seal clearly was applied before the text since several cuneiform wedges cut into the bottom of the impression. PF 150 is dated 501/500 B.C.

BIBLIOGRAPHY

Garrison 1988, pp. 298, 300.

PFS 555 Cat.No. 93

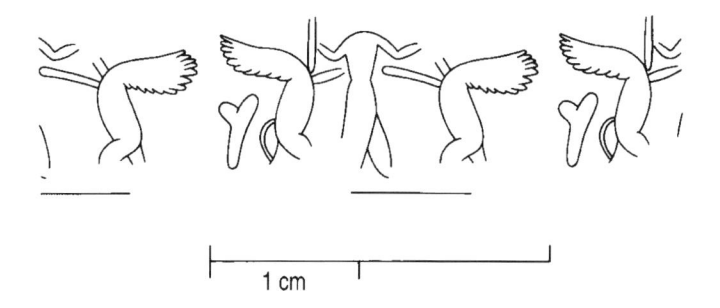

Seal Type:	Cylinder	Photograph:	Pl. 55c
Earliest Dated Application:	ND	Typology and Style:	I-A.9 — Fortification Style
Preserved Height of Image:	1.20 cm (incomp.)	Preserved Length of Image:	2.30 cm (comp.)
Estimated Height of Original Seal:	1.40 cm	Estimated Diameter of Original Seal:	0.70 cm
Number of Impressions:	1	Quality of Impression:	Poor

Completeness of Image: Complete except for upper edge and lower edge

DESCRIPTION OF SEAL AS IMPRESSED IMAGE

Hero moves to right in striding pose, arms bent, and holds two rampant winged bull or lion creatures by upper foreleg.

Creature to left holds upper foreleg straight and extends it vertically upward; lower foreleg is straight and extended upward toward hero's chest; tail curves downward. Creature to right holds upper foreleg (only partially preserved) straight and extends it diagonally upward; lower foreleg is straight and extended upward toward hero's chest.

Hero appears to wear Assyrian garment that leaves forward leg exposed.

Large Y-shaped form is behind creature to left in terminal field.

Traces of edge of seal are preserved at bottom of design below hero and creature to right.

COMMENTARY

See Garrison 1988 for the artist and related seals.
    For comparative illustrations including PFS 555, see pl. 255f (various devices and symbols).

SEAL APPLICATION (SEE *APPENDIX ONE: CONCORDANCE OF SEALS TO TABLETS IN VOLUME I*)

PFS 555 occurs along the upper half of the reverse of PF 312. Across the lower half of the reverse, but inverted, PFS 554 (II) has been applied. The rolling of PFS 555 preserves the entire length of the seal design and displays the creature to the left of the hero in the center. The date of PF 312 is unknown.

BIBLIOGRAPHY

Garrison 1988, pp. 309–12.

I-A.10. WINGED HUMAN-FACED/HUMAN-HEADED BULL OR LION CREATURES

Cat.No. 94   PFS 158

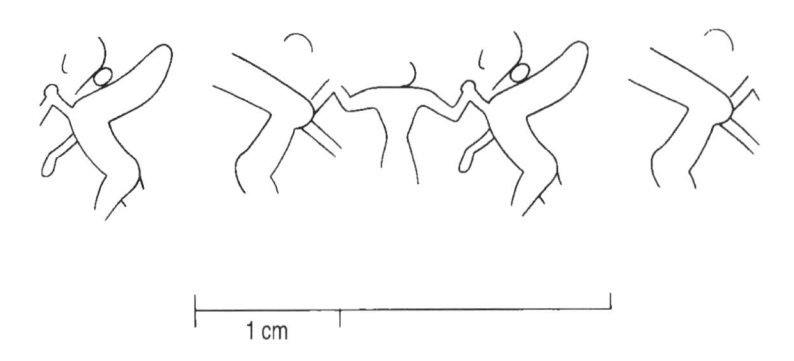

Seal Type:	Cylinder	Photograph:	Pl. 56a
Earliest Dated Application:	500/499 B.C.	Typology and Style:	I-A.10 — Fortification Style
Preserved Height of Image:	1.30 cm (incomp.)	Preserved Length of Image:	2.90 cm (comp.)
Estimated Height of Original Seal:	NA	Estimated Diameter of Original Seal:	0.90 cm
Number of Impressions:	2	Quality of Impressions:	Poor

Completeness of Image: Segment of middle of design survives along its complete length

Description of Seal as Impressed Image

Hero faces left, arms bent, and holds two rampant winged human-headed bull or lion creatures.

Each creature holds upper foreleg straight and extends it upward toward hero's head. Creature to left holds lower foreleg (only partially preserved) straight and extends it downward toward hero's leg. Creature to right holds lower foreleg bent and extends it diagonally downward.

Hero wears garment of uncertain type; rounded coiffure rests at back of neck.

Creature to right appears to have pointed beard that rests over its chest; round coiffure rests at back of neck.

Commentary

The impressions are poorly preserved and the human-headed aspect of the creature to left is tentative.

Seal Application (see *Appendix One: Concordance of Seals to Tablets in Volume I*)

PFS 158 occurs on the reverse of both PF 108 and PF 109, with PFS 154 (III) always on the left edge. On the reverse of PF 109 the seal is inverted. Both rollings preserve the entire length of the seal design, one displays the hero in the center, the other displays the hero and the creature to right in the center. On both tablets the seal clearly was applied before the text since several cuneiform wedges cut into the top or bottom of the impressions. PF 108 is the earliest dated tablet with PFS 158 and is dated 500/499 B.C.

Bibliography

Garrison 1988, pp. 297, 300.

PFS 380 Cat.No. 95

```
                    1 cm
```

Seal Type:	Cylinder	Photograph:	Pl. 56c
Earliest Dated Application:	497 B.C.	Typology and Style:	I-A.10 — Fortification Style
Preserved Height of Image:	1.30 cm (incomp.)	Preserved Length of Image:	2.20 cm (incomp.)
Estimated Height of Original Seal:	NA	Estimated Diameter of Original Seal:	NA
Number of Impressions:	1	Quality of Impression:	Poor

Completeness of Image: Large segment of middle of design survives

DESCRIPTION OF SEAL AS IMPRESSED IMAGE

Hero moves to right, arms bent, and holds two rampant winged human-headed bull or lion creatures by upper foreleg.

Each creature holds upper foreleg straight and extends it upward toward hero's head; lower foreleg is straight and extended downward toward hero's lower body. Forelegs of creature to left have two-pronged termination; tail curls upward.

Hero wears robe; vestiges of face suggest short rounded beard and large nose.

Creature to left has pointed beard. Creature to right has rounded beard; traces of rounded coiffure are at back of neck.

COMMENTARY

The image is very poorly preserved and difficult to reconstruct.

SEAL APPLICATION (SEE *APPENDIX ONE: CONCORDANCE OF SEALS TO TABLETS IN VOLUME I*)

PFS 380 occurs on the left edge of PF 72. The partial rolling displays the hero in the center. PF 72 is dated 497 B.C.

BIBLIOGRAPHY

Garrison 1988, pp. 273–76.

Cat.No. 96   PFS 945

|—1 cm—|

Seal Type:	Cylinder	Photograph:	Pl. 56e
Earliest Dated Application:	ND	Typology and Style:	I-A.10 — Linear Styles
Preserved Height of Image:	1.30 cm (incomp.)	Preserved Length of Image:	2.50 cm (incomp.)
Estimated Height of Original Seal:	NA	Estimated Diameter of Original Seal:	NA
Number of Impressions:	2	Quality of Impressions:	Poor

Completeness of Image: Large segment of middle of design survives along most of its length

DESCRIPTION OF SEAL AS IMPRESSED IMAGE

Hero faces left in striding pose, arms bent, and holds two rampant winged human-headed bull or lion creatures by upper foreleg.

Each creature holds upper foreleg straight (paw upturned on creature to right) and extends it upward toward hero's head; lower foreleg is straight, paw upturned, and extended downward toward hero's leg. Tail (only partially preserved) of creature to left extends diagonally downward.

Hero appears to wear Assyrian garment that leaves forward leg exposed below knee. Rounded coiffure rests at back of hero's neck.

Each creature has pointed beard that rests over its chest. Creature to right has flattened coiffure at back of its neck. Two rows of feathers are indicated on creatures' wings.

COMMENTARY

The poor quality of the engraving is typical of seals rendered in the Linear Styles.

For comparative illustrations including PFS 945, see pl. 175a (Assyrian garments).

SEAL APPLICATION (SEE APPENDIX ONE: CONCORDANCE OF SEALS TO TABLETS IN VOLUME I)

PFS 945 occurs on the left edge of both PF 819 and PF 1165, with PFS 236 (Cat.No. 213) on the reverse of both tablets. The two partial applications display the hero in the center. The dates of PF 819 and PF 1165 are unknown.

BIBLIOGRAPHY

Garrison 1988, pp. 435–37, 496.

PFS 883* Cat.No. 97

Seal Impression:	Cylinder, Inscribed	Photograph:	Pl. 57a
Earliest Dated Application:	498 B.C.	Typology and Style:	I-A.10 — Plausibly Antique: Assyro-Babylonian Modeled Style
Language of Inscription:	Babylonian(?)		
Preserved Height of Image:	1.30 cm (incomp.)	Preserved Length of Image:	2.40 cm (incomp.)
Estimated Height of Original Seal:	NA	Estimated Diameter of Original Seal:	NA
Number of Impressions:	1	Quality of Impression:	Fair

Completeness of Image: Segment of middle of design survives

DESCRIPTION OF SEAL AS IMPRESSED IMAGE

Four-winged hero faces right, arms bent, and holds two rampant winged human-headed bull or lion creatures by upper foreleg. Of creature to left, only foreleg, at far left of impression, and wing tip, visible at far right of single impression, are preserved.

Creature to left holds upper foreleg curved and extends it upward toward hero's wing. Creature to right holds upper foreleg slightly bent and extends it upward in front of its head; lower foreleg is straight and extended downward toward hero's lower wing; tail curves downward.

Hero appears to wear Assyrian garment that leaves forward leg exposed; fringe or folds are indicated along hero's hip; decorative border runs along front hem of garment on rear leg. Conical turban-like headdress has projection at front. Squared beard rests over hero's left shoulder; rounded wavy coiffure rests at back of neck.

Creature to right has round coiffure with striations at back of neck and top of head (domed headdress?).

Inscription is in upper terminal field.

INSCRIPTION

Babylonian(?)

Line   1. x x x
        2. x x

Translation   ?

There appear to be four or five signs disposed in the upper terminal field. The signs seem to be in two lines, oriented along the vertical axis of the seal, but, unlike all other inscriptions with images of heroic encounter so aligned in the PFS corpus, the orientation of the traces indicate that the signs should be read from the bottom to the top. Too little remains to suggest a reading.

COMMENTARY

The horned headdress, somewhat hasty engraving, heavy incision on the body of the hero, the hair of the creature at right, and the language of the inscription suggest that the seal may be an heirloom from the late Assyro-Babylonian Modeled Style.[24] The hero on PFS 594 (Cat.No. 103), a possible heirloom from the Neo-Elamite

---

24. Compare, for example, Porada 1948, pls. 115 (761–62), 116 (767); Moortgat 1940, pl. 86 (737); Buchanan 1966, pl. 43 (661); von der Osten 1934, pl. 29 (422); Lambert 1979, pls. 8 (73), 9 (75).

period, may wear similar headgear. In Garrison 1988 this seal was categorized in the Antique Style, but until more securely dated comparanda make a compelling case, we opt here for a more equivocal reading.

For comparative illustrations including PFS 883*, see pls. 187c (headdresses), 197f (hands), and 265b (inscriptions without panels or case lines).

SEAL APPLICATION (SEE *APPENDIX ONE: CONCORDANCE OF SEALS TO TABLETS IN VOLUME I*)

PFS 883* occurs on the left edge of PF 760. The partial rolling displays the hero and the creature to right in the center. PF 760 is dated 498 B.C.

BIBLIOGRAPHY

Dusinberre 1997b, p. 128 (n. 131); Garrison 1988, p. 466; Garrison 1998, p. 121 (n. 15); Garrison and Dion 1999, p. 10 (n. 28).

Cat.No. 98   PFS 516

Seal Type:	Cylinder	Photograph:	Pl. 57c
Earliest Dated Application:	500/499 B.C.	Typology and Style:	I-A.10 — Modeled Style
Preserved Height of Image:	1.30 cm (incomp.)	Preserved Length of Image:	2.70 cm (incomp.)
Estimated Height of Original Seal:	NA	Estimated Diameter of Original Seal:	NA
Number of Impressions:	1	Quality of Impression:	Poor

Completeness of Image: Small segment of upper part of design survives

DESCRIPTION OF SEAL AS IMPRESSED IMAGE

Winged hero faces right, arms bent (only right arm preserved), and holds two(?) rampant winged human-headed bull or lion creatures (creature to right not preserved) by foreleg.

Creature to left holds upper foreleg straight and extends it upward toward hero's wing.

Hero wears garment of uncertain type. Hero has long rounded(?) beard; flattened coiffure rests at back of head. Hero perhaps wears domed headdress. Two rows of feathers are indicated on hero's two preserved wings.

Creature has two wings indicated, upper extending diagonally upward from lower; two rows of feathers are on each wing. Squared segmented beard rests high above creature's chest; rounded coiffure curls upward away from neck. Creature perhaps wears domed headdress.

COMMENTARY

Although a very poorly preserved fragment, the seal seems to be large and well made. Stylistically it is related to a large number of Modeled Style seals showing exaggerated modeling and dynamic movement. The seal has been reclassified stylistically (cf. Garrison 1988). The hero almost certainly had four wings (see commentary on PFS 1276 [Cat.No. 34]).

SEAL APPLICATION (SEE *APPENDIX ONE: CONCORDANCE OF SEALS TO TABLETS IN VOLUME I*)

PFS 516 occurs along the very bottom of the reverse (inverted) of PF 239. PFS 57* (Cat.No. 239) is applied (also inverted) directly above PFS 516. The partial rolling preserves only the hero and the creature to the left. PF 239 is dated 500/499 B.C.

BIBLIOGRAPHY

Garrison 1988, pp. 281–83; Garrison 1998, p. 121 (n. 15).

PFS 370   Cat.No. 99

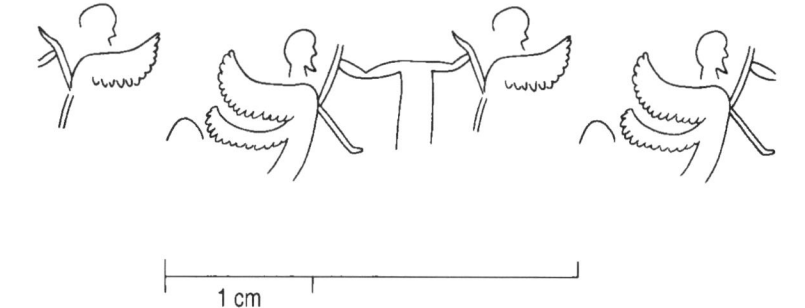

Seal Type:	Cylinder	Photograph:	Pl. 57e
Earliest Dated Application:	502 B.C.	Typology and Style:	I-A.10 — Fortification Style
Preserved Height of Image:	1.20 cm (incomp.)	Preserved Length of Image:	2.80 cm (comp.)
Estimated Height of Original Seal:	NA	Estimated Diameter of Original Seal:	0.90 cm
Number of Impressions:	1	Quality of Impression:	Very poor

Completeness of Image: Segment of middle of design survives along its complete length

DESCRIPTION OF SEAL AS IMPRESSED IMAGE

Hero has arms bent and holds two rampant winged human-headed bull or lion creatures by upper foreleg.

Creature to right moves toward hero but turns its head away from him. Each creature holds upper foreleg straight (paw bent down on creature to right) and extends it upward toward hero's head; lower foreleg is straight (paw upturned on creature to left) and extended downward toward hero's lower body.

Hero wears robe.

Creature to left has two wings, both extended horizontally outward from its back; wears short pointed beard. Creature to right has only one wing depicted.

Chip, apparently, is in lower terminal field.

COMMENTARY

The rolling of the seal is very poorly preserved, making the image difficult to read.

SEAL APPLICATION (SEE *APPENDIX ONE: CONCORDANCE OF SEALS TO TABLETS IN VOLUME I*)

PFS 370 occurs on the reverse of PF 63. The rolling preserves the entire length of the seal design and displays the hero and the creature to right in the center. The seal clearly was applied before the text since several cuneiform wedges cut into the top of the impression. PF 63 is dated 502 B.C.

BIBLIOGRAPHY

Dusinberre 1997b, p. 128 (n. 131); Garrison 1988, pp. 320, 324.

Cat.No. 100   PFS 326

Seal Type:	Cylinder	Photographs:	Pl. 58a–c
Earliest Dated Application:	495/494 B.C.	Typology and Style:	I-A.10 — Court Style
Preserved Height of Image:	1.50 cm (incomp.)	Preserved Length of Image:	2.50 cm (comp.)
Estimated Height of Original Seal:	1.70 cm	Estimated Diameter of Original Seal:	0.80 cm
Number of Impressions:	3	Quality of Impressions:	Poor-fair

Completeness of Image: Complete except for upper edge and lower edge

DESCRIPTION OF SEAL AS IMPRESSED IMAGE

Hero faces right, arms straight at diagonal above shoulder level, and holds two rampant winged horned human-headed bull or lion creatures by ear.

Each creature moves toward hero but turns its head away from him. Each creature holds upper foreleg diagonally upward to place paw at hero's arm; lower foreleg is bent and held in front of its body. Creatures' tails curl upward with tufted terminations.

Hero wears Persian court robe with sleeves pushed up to reveal arms. Lower garment blends diagonal folds of a Persian robe (on thigh of forward leg) with the contour of an Assyrian garment over rear leg. Five-pointed dentate Persian crown rests on hero's head. Long rounded beard rests over hero's left shoulder; rounded coiffure rests at back of neck.

Each creature has rounded beard over its wing; rounded coiffure rests at back of neck. Long curved horn emerges from front of each creature's head.

Crescent is in upper terminal field; in lower terminal field, bird (cock) stands facing to right. Chip is in stone under hero.

Portions of edge of seal are preserved at top of design above creature to right of hero.

COMMENTARY

The seal is small for the Court Style, and its execution does not show the care and detail seen in other examples of the style. Interestingly, the appearance of the cock is otherwise unattested in the PFS corpus of seals of heroic encounter. It seems to occur also on PFS 78 (II) and PFS 143s (II); compare van Buren 1939, p. 89. On cocks in Achaemenid glyptic, see Moorey 1978, pp. 150–51. See also Collon 1996, p. 73, pl. 19g–k, and Bregstein 1993, p. 687, no. 286, for comparanda.

    For comparative illustrations including PFS 326, see pls. 181f (hybrid garments), 188h (Persian crowns and fluted tiaras), 203c (arm positions of heroic control), 227b (birds), 250e (crescents), and 267e (terminal field motifs other than inscriptions).

SEAL APPLICATION (SEE *APPENDIX ONE: CONCORDANCE OF SEALS TO TABLETS IN VOLUME I*)

PFS 326 occurs on the reverse (inverted) and left edge of PF 13 and the reverse of PF 161. Impressions of the seal are long, on the reverse of PF 13 and PF 161 repeating the heroic encounter twice. Both of these impressions preserve the complete heroic encounter at the right of the impression and display the creature to the left of the hero in the center. The partial rolling on the left edge of PF 13 displays the creature to the left of the hero in the center. On the reverse of PF 161 the seal clearly was applied before the text since several cuneiform wedges cut into the top of the impression. PF 13 is the earliest dated tablet with PFS 326 and is dated 495/494 B.C.

BIBLIOGRAPHY

Garrison 1988, pp. 412, 416–17, 479–80; Garrison and Dion 1999, p. 6 (n. 15); Garrison and Root 1996, p. 13.

PFS 1658 — Cat.No. 101

Seal Type:	Cylinder	Photograph:	Pl. 59a
Earliest Dated Application:	500/499 B.C.	Typology and Style:	I-A.10 — Plausibly Antique: Assyro-Babylonian Modeled Style
Preserved Height of Image:	1.10 cm (incomp.)	Preserved Length of Image:	3.60 cm (incomp.)
Estimated Height of Original Seal:	NA	Estimated Diameter of Original Seal:	NA
Number of Impressions:	2	Quality of Impressions:	Poor

Completeness of Image: Segment of upper part of design survives

DESCRIPTION OF SEAL AS IMPRESSED IMAGE

Four-winged hero faces right, arms bent, and holds two rampant winged human-headed bull or lion creatures by upper foreleg.

Each creature turns its head away from hero. Each creature holds upper foreleg straight and extends it upward toward hero's wing.

Hero has long squared beard that rests over his left shoulder; large rounded coiffure rests at back of neck. Hero perhaps wears domed headdress.

Creature to left appears to have close-shaved beard or to be beardless; round coiffure rests at back of its neck. Creature to right appears to have narrow pointed beard; round coiffure rests at back of its neck.

COMMENTARY

Although poorly preserved, this must originally have been a large and well-made seal. Similar to PFS 1458 (Cat.No. 80), with which it shares many stylistic features (including the extensive use of unmasked drill work in the heads of the creatures), PFS 1658 shows connections to the Assyro-Babylonian Modeled Style and may be an heirloom, but it relates closely to a group of archaizing seals in the PFS corpus of hero seals and may, rather, emerge out of a particular Persepolitan environment (as per Garrison 1988). For comparanda, see the entry for PFS 1458 (Cat.No. 80).

SEAL APPLICATION (SEE APPENDIX ONE: CONCORDANCE OF SEALS TO TABLETS IN VOLUME I)

PFS 1658 occurs on the upper edge and right edge of PF 1256. In these restricted sealing surfaces the user has consistently given preference to the top of the seal. The partial rolling on the upper edge displays the hero in the center. The partial rolling on the right edge preserves only the creature to the left of the hero and the hero's wing. PF 1256 is dated 500/499 B.C.

BIBLIOGRAPHY

Dusinberre 1997b, p. 128 (n. 131); Garrison 1988, pp. 201–03, 231–32; Garrison 1998, p. 121 (n. 15); Garrison and Dion 1999, p. 10 (n. 28).

I-A.11. HORNED ANIMALS: DEER, GAZELLES, WILD GOATS, WILD SHEEP

Cat.No. 102　　　　　　　　　　　　　　PFS 536

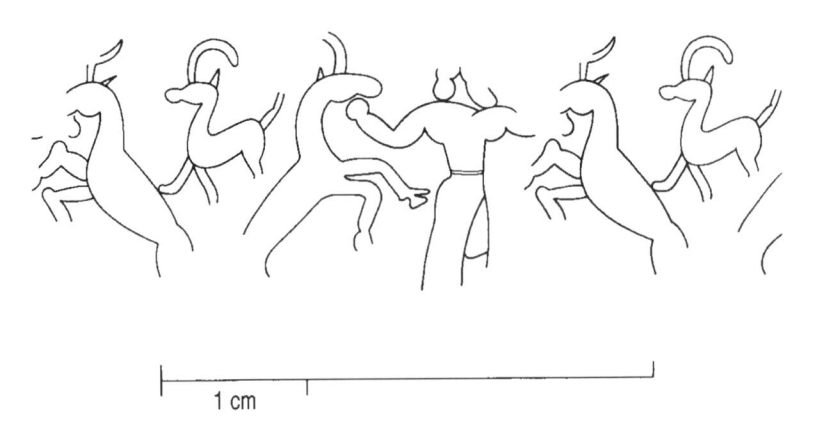

Seal Type:	Cylinder	Photographs:	Pl. 59c–d
Earliest Dated Application:	ND	Typology and Style:	I-A.11 — Modeled Style
Preserved Height of Image:	1.90 cm (incomp.)	Preserved Length of Image:	3.30 cm (comp.)
Estimated Height of Original Seal:	2.10 cm	Estimated Diameter of Original Seal:	1.10 cm
Number of Impressions:	7	Quality of Impressions:	Very poor

Completeness of Image: Almost complete except for upper edge and lower edge

Description of Seal as Impressed Image

Hero faces right, arms bent, and holds two rampant horned animals by lower jaw: wild goat at left and deer at right.

Each animal holds upper foreleg bent (cleft hoof on animal to left) and extends it upward toward hero's hip; lower foreleg is bent and held downward in front of its body.

Hero wears belted Assyrian garment that leaves forward leg exposed below knee. Long rounded beard rests over hero's left shoulder; rounded coiffure rests at back of neck.

Animal to left has long curved horn (only partially preserved) emerging from top of its head; short pointed ear is at back of head. Animal to right has branched antler (only partially preserved) emerging from top of its head; short pointed ear is at back of head.

Small marchant wild goat in upper terminal field moves to left and places one foreleg and one hind leg on backs of rampant animals; tail bends diagonally upward; large curved horn emerges from front of its head.

Commentary

The seal is relatively large and the human form is especially well modeled.

For comparative illustrations including PFS 536, see pls. 174f (Assyrian garments), 206i (arm positions of heroic control), 215d (unusual heroic attitudes), 231b (feet of animals and creatures), and 268f (terminal field motifs other than inscriptions).

Seal Application (see *Appendix One: Concordance of Seals to Tablets in Volume I*)

PFS 536 occurs on the reverse, upper edge, and left edge of PF 291, the reverse and left edge of PF 824 and the reverse (inverted) of PF 1253. On the reverse of PF 824 the seal is applied twice, one impression directly above the other. Impressions often exhibit distortion. In two impressions the seal is rolled for one complete turn, preserving the entire length of the seal design. Both applications display the rampant goat to the left of the hero in the center. Of the remaining five partial impressions, one displays the hero in the center; two preserve only the hero and the rampant goat to left; one displays the rampant goat to the left of the hero in the center; one displays the rampant goat to the left of the hero and the marchant goat in the terminal field in the center. On the reverse of PF 291 and PF 1253 the seal clearly was applied before the text since several cuneiform wedges cut into the top or bottom of the impressions. The dates of PF 291, PF 824, and PF 1253 are unknown.

BIBLIOGRAPHY

Garrison 1988, pp. 211–12.

PFS 594   Cat.No. 103

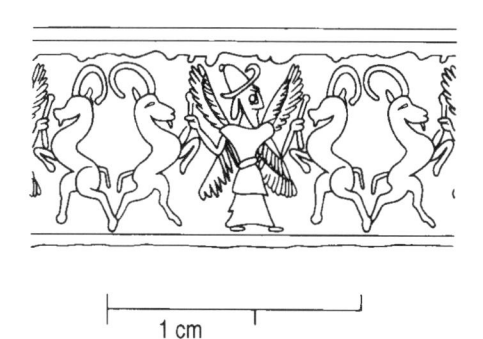

|—— 1 cm ——|

Seal Type:	Cylinder	Photograph:	Pl. 60a
Earliest Dated Application:	499/498 B.C.	Typology and Style:	I-A.11 — Plausibly Antique: Neo-Elamite
Preserved Height of Image:	1.50 cm (comp.)	Preserved Length of Image:	1.80 cm (comp.)
Estimated Height of Original Seal:	1.50 cm	Estimated Diameter of Original Seal:	0.60 cm
Number of Impressions:	1	Quality of Impression:	Excellent

Completeness of Image: Complete

DESCRIPTION OF SEAL AS IMPRESSED IMAGE

Four-winged hero faces right, arms bent, and holds two rampant wild goats by upper foreleg.

Each goat holds upper foreleg curved and extends it upward toward hero's upper wing; lower foreleg is bent and extended upward in front of its body. Goats' short tails bend downward.

Hero wears belted robe with three tiers and tall conical headdress with horn-like feature projecting at back and front and knob at top. Beard terminates in blunt point over hero's left shoulder; narrow rounded coiffure is at back of neck. Three of hero's wings have two rows of feathers indicated.

Each goat has large curved horn emerging from front of its head, pointed ear at back of head and beard.

Wide line border is at bottom of design; bottom edge is wavy. Continuous chipping invades top of design; above this is wide line border.

COMMENTARY

Many features suggest that the seal may be an heirloom from the Neo-Elamite period or else a particularly faithful rather than inventive archaizing piece. These features include the rendering of the body of the hero, as well as his elongated head, thick neck, headdress and wings, and also the compressed animal forms with their exaggerated chests.[25] The headdress has some similarity to that seen on the hero of PFS 883* (Cat.No. 97), a possible Neo-Assyrian or Neo-Babylonian heirloom. The irregular edges at the top and bottom of the design suggest the possibility that the original seal mount had been removed, damaging the stone.

For comparative illustrations including PFS 594, see pls. 182f (robes with various features of detail), 187a (headdresses), 194e (narrow rounded and/or pointed coiffures), 224e (deer, goats, sheep, and related winged creatures), 270g (compositions creating dynamic negative space as terminal field), 276b (evidence of original seal caps), and 280f (chips in seal matrices).

---

25. See Amiet 1973b, nos. 17 (impression found on a tablet from under the Palace of Darius at Susa) and 31 (cylinder from Susa), for the rendering of the hero.

SEAL APPLICATION (SEE *APPENDIX ONE: CONCORDANCE OF SEALS TO TABLETS IN VOLUME I*)

PFS 594 occurs on the reverse of PF 346. The rolling is long and carefully executed, preserving almost two full repeats of the figural design. The rolling begins at left precisely with the goat to the left of the hero and ends with the goat (partially preserved) to the right of the hero. Rolled in this manner, the two rampant goats are displayed in the center. The seal seems to have been applied before the text since one long cuneiform wedge stroke cuts into the top of the impression. PF 346 is dated 499/498 B.C.

BIBLIOGRAPHY

Garrison 1988, pp. 458–59; Garrison 1998, p. 121 (n. 15); Garrison and Dion 1999, p. 9 (n. 19).

Cat.No. 104   PFS 62

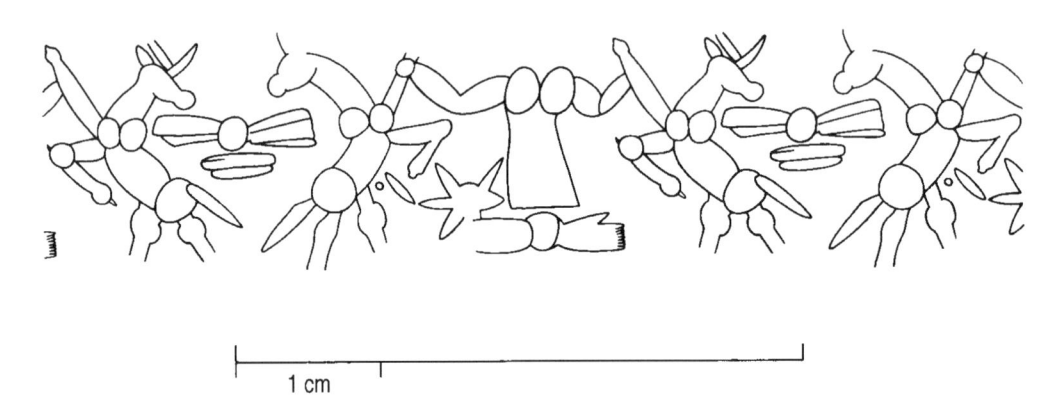

Seal Type:	Cylinder	Photographs:	Pl. 60c–d
Earliest Dated Application:	504/503 B.C.	Typology and Style:	I-A.11 — Plausibly Antique: Assyro-Babylonian Drilled Style
Preserved Height of Image:	1.70 cm (incomp.)	Preserved Length of Image:	3.90 cm (comp.)
Estimated Height of Original Seal:	NA	Estimated Diameter of Original Seal:	1.30 cm
Number of Impressions:	7	Quality of Impressions:	Poor-fair

Completeness of Image: Almost complete except for upper edge and lower edge

DESCRIPTION OF SEAL AS IMPRESSED IMAGE

Hero has arms bent and holds two rampant horned animals of undetermined type by upper foreleg; hero apparently stands atop winged symbol.

Each animal moves toward hero but turns its head away from him. Each animal holds upper foreleg straight and extends it upward toward hero's head; lower foreleg is bent and held down in front of its body; straight tail extends downward.

Hero wears robe.

Animal to left may have horn emerging from front of its head. Animal to right has two short horns emerging from front of its head and large ear at back of head.

Schematic winged symbol is in field below hero. Uncertain device (fish?, scorpion?) appears in field between hero and animal to left.

Schematic winged symbol with bird's tail is in terminal field, heraldically framed by horned animals of the heroic encounter.

COMMENTARY

Koch assigns the seal to Mikrašba, a grain supplier.

Collation of the various impressions of this seal was difficult, owing to distortion and over-rolling. The winged symbol under the hero may conceivably be an over-rolling of the winged symbol in the terminal field. The two images exhibit marked differences, however, and collation was not possible without significant alteration of the one or the other. Thus, we have kept the winged symbol under the hero in our composite drawing, although it makes for a very unusual placement of this device. Here, the winged symbol serves as an inanimate pedestal element.

The seal is relatively large. Its crude Drilled Style was popular in late Neo-Assyrian and Neo-Babylonian glyptic. An excellent stylistic parallel for the winged symbol in the terminal field is paralleled on a seal impressed on a tablet from Nineveh; and the uncertain device between the hero and the animal to the left is paralleled on another seal impressed on a tablet from Nineveh.[26] Production in this crude Drilled Style may well have continued down into Achaemenid times, however, since there exist many examples of it in the PFS corpus; compare PFS 180 (Cat.No. 194). This seal was originally categorized as a definite antique (Garrison 1988).

For comparative illustrations including PFS 62, see pls. 183a (robes of various undetailed types), 216d (hero standing atop pedestal figure[s] or other supporting element), and 249a (winged symbols).

SEAL APPLICATION (SEE *APPENDIX ONE: CONCORDANCE OF SEALS TO TABLETS IN VOLUME I*)

PFS 62 with one exception (PF 23, on the reverse) occurs only on the left edge of tablets. On the reverse of PF 23 the seal is inverted. Several applications of the seal exhibit significant distortion along the vertical axis. No rolling of the seal preserves the entire design. Of the seven partial applications, one displays the hero in the center; one displays the animal to the left of the hero in the center; two display the animal to the left of the hero and the winged symbol in the terminal field in the center; three display the animal to the right of the hero and the winged symbol in the terminal field in the center. PF 296, PF 1650, and PF 1767 are the earliest dated tablets with PFS 62 and are all dated 504/503 B.C.

BIBLIOGRAPHY

Garrison 1988, pp. 466–67; Koch 1990, p. 78 (n. 344).

---

26. Herbordt 1992, pl. 4, no. 1, p. 227 (667 B.C.); pl. 9, no. 1, p. 223 (684 B.C.), where the uncertain symbol is called a fish.

Cat.No. 105 PFS 782

|— 1 cm —|

Seal Type:	Cylinder	Photograph:	Pl. 61a
Earliest Dated Application:	499/498 B.C.	Typology and Style:	I-A.11 — Modeled Style
Preserved Height of Image:	1.70 cm (incomp.)	Preserved Length of Image:	3.00 cm (incomp.)
Estimated Height of Original Seal:	NA	Estimated Diameter of Original Seal:	NA
Number of Impressions:	1	Quality of Impression:	Poor

Completeness of Image: Segment of middle of design survives

DESCRIPTION OF SEAL AS IMPRESSED IMAGE

Four-winged hero (one upper wing not preserved) faces left in striding pose, arms bent, and holds two rampant horned animals of undetermined type by throat or upper foreleg (not preserved).

Each animal moves toward hero but turns its head away from him. Each animal holds lower foreleg bent in front of its body; tail (only partially preserved) curves upward.

Hero wears Assyrian garment that leaves forward leg exposed. Rounded beard rests over hero's right shoulder.

Animal to left has two thick pointed horns emerging from top of its head; curved ears emerge from back of head.

COMMENTARY

The human figure seems poorly executed, and overall the design is somewhat irregular.

For comparative illustrations including PFS 782, see pl. 225e (horned animals and horned-animal creatures of undetermined types).

SEAL APPLICATION (SEE APPENDIX ONE: CONCORDANCE OF SEALS TO TABLETS IN VOLUME I)

PFS 782 occurs on the reverse of PF 567. The partial rolling displays the hero in the center. PF 567 is dated 499/498 B.C.

BIBLIOGRAPHY

Garrison 1988, pp. 212, 214; Garrison 1998, p. 121 (n. 15); Garrison and Dion 1999, p. 9 (n. 19).

PFS 1489   Cat.No. 106

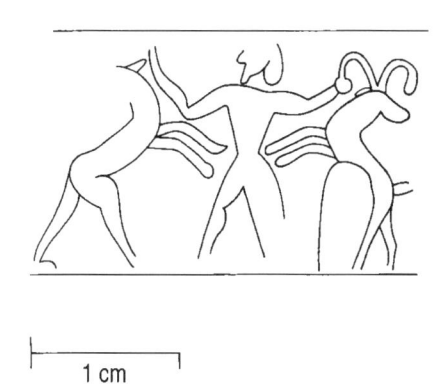

Seal Impression:	Cylinder	Photograph:	Pl. 61c
Earliest Dated Application:	ND	Typology and Style:	I-A.11 — Fortification Style
Preserved Height of Image:	1.60 cm (comp.)	Preserved Length of Image:	2.70 cm (incomp.)
Estimated Height of Original Seal:	1.60 cm	Estimated Diameter of Original Seal:	NA
Number of Impressions:	1	Quality of Impression:	Poor

Completeness of Image: Almost complete except for details and terminal field

DESCRIPTION OF SEAL AS IMPRESSED IMAGE

Hero faces left in striding pose, arms bent, and holds two rampant horned animals (wild sheep?) by horn (preserved only at right).

Each animal moves toward hero but turns its head away from him. Each animal holds forelegs slightly bent and extends them together toward hero's waist. Tail (only partially preserved) of animal to right extends outward.

Hero wears Assyrian garment that leaves forward leg exposed. Narrow squared beard rests over hero's right shoulder; rounded coiffure rests at back of neck.

Two large curved horns shown frontally emerge from top of head of animal to right; small ear is also indicated at top of head. Short pointed ear emerges from back of head of animal to left.

Edges of seal are preserved at top and bottom of design. Large chip appears to cut into lower body of animal at right.

COMMENTARY

The design appears to be very worn, or not deeply carved into the seal.

For comparative illustrations including PFS 1489, see pls. 207i (arm positions of heroic control), 224i (deer, goats, sheep, and related winged creatures), and 280i (chips in seal matrices).

SEAL APPLICATION (SEE APPENDIX ONE: CONCORDANCE OF SEALS TO TABLETS IN VOLUME I)

PFS 1489 occurs on the reverse of PF 1614. The rolling, almost complete, displays the hero in the center. The date of PF 1614 is unknown.

BIBLIOGRAPHY

Garrison 1988, pp. 305–07.

Cat.No. 107   PFS 781

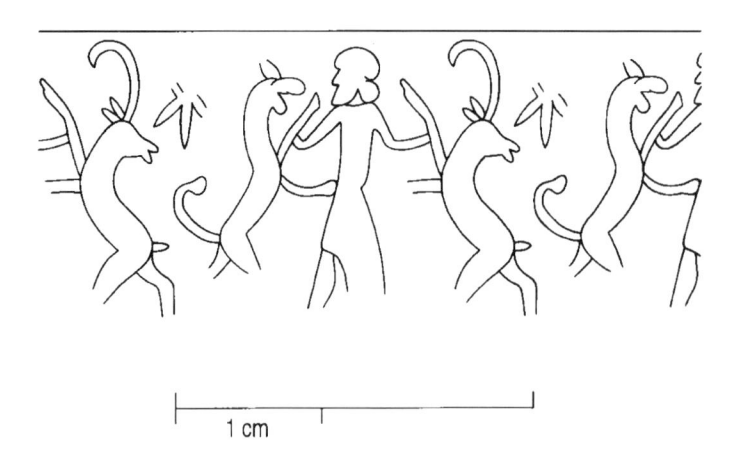

Seal Type:	Cylinder	Photograph:	Pl. 62a
Earliest Dated Application:	494/493 B.C.	Typology and Style:	I-A.11 — Fortification Style
Preserved Height of Image:	1.90 cm (incomp.)	Preserved Length of Image:	2.50 cm (comp.)
Estimated Height of Original Seal:	2.10 cm	Estimated Diameter of Original Seal:	0.80 cm
Number of Impressions:	2	Quality of Impressions:	Fair

Completeness of Image: Almost complete except for lower edge

DESCRIPTION OF SEAL AS IMPRESSED IMAGE

Hero faces left in striding pose, arms bent, and holds two rampant wild goats by upper foreleg.

Animal to left holds upper foreleg straight and extends it upward toward hero's head; lower foreleg is curved and extended downward to place paw on hero's waist; long tail (borrowed from vocabulary of lion renderings) curls upward with tufted termination. Animal to right moves toward hero but turns its head away from him. Animal holds upper foreleg slightly bent and extends it toward hero's head; lower foreleg (only partially preserved) is straight and extended outward toward hero's waist. Short pointed tail extends horizontally outward.

Hero wears Assyrian garment that leaves forward leg exposed below knee. Pointed beard rests over hero's right shoulder; rounded coiffure rests at back of neck.

Animal to left has thick horn (only partially preserved) emerging from top of its head. Animal to right has long curved horn emerging from top of its head; two pointed ears also emerge from top of head. Each animal has mouth open or is rendered with beard.

Star is in upper terminal field.

Edge of seal is preserved at top of design.

COMMENTARY

See Garrison 1988 for the artist and related seals, which show similar large and well-executed designs.

For comparative illustrations including PFS 781, see pls. 224f (deer, goats, sheep, and related winged creatures) and 270b (compositions with strong unidirectional movement).

SEAL APPLICATION (SEE *APPENDIX ONE: CONCORDANCE OF SEALS TO TABLETS IN VOLUME I*)

PFS 781 occurs on the reverse (inverted) and left edge of PF 565. No other seal is used on the tablet. Both impressions exhibit distortion. The rolling on the reverse preserves the entire length of the seal design and displays the hero in the center. The partial rolling on the left edge displays the animal to the left of the hero in the center. PF 565 is dated 494/493 B.C.

BIBLIOGRAPHY

Garrison 1988, pp. 247, 313–16.

PFS 496   Cat.No. 108

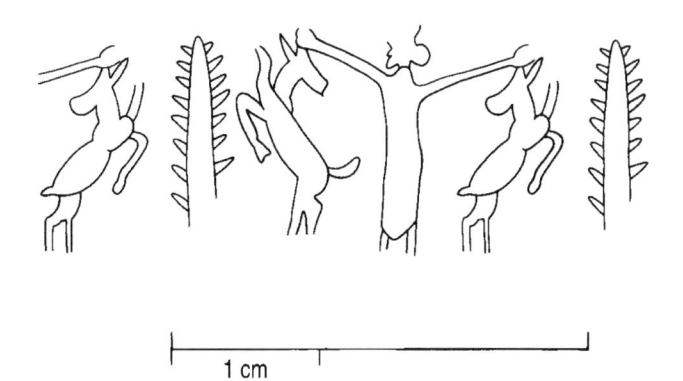

Seal Type:	Cylinder	Photograph:	Pl. 62c
Earliest Dated Application:	501/500 B.C.	Typology and Style:	I-A.11 — Broad and Flat Styles
Preserved Height of Image:	1.60 cm (incomp.)	Preserved Length of Image:	2.80 cm (comp.)
Estimated Height of Original Seal:	1.80 cm	Estimated Diameter of Original Seal:	0.90 cm
Number of Impressions:	1	Quality of Impression:	Fair

Completeness of Image: Almost complete except for upper edge and lower edge

DESCRIPTION OF SEAL AS IMPRESSED IMAGE

Hero faces left, arms straight at diagonal above shoulder level, and holds two rampant horned animals of undetermined type by horn.

Each animal moves away from hero but turns its head back toward him. Each animal holds upper foreleg curved and extends it diagonally upward; lower foreleg is bent downward in front of its body. Short tail of animal to left curls upward. Short pointed tail of animal to right extends diagonally downward.

Hero wears robe possibly suggesting Persian court robe in frontal view (with raised panel over each leg), but no sleeves or folds are indicated. Short pointed beard rests over hero's right shoulder; rounded coiffure rests at back of head.

Each animal has long pointed horn emerging from back of its head.

Schematic tree with conical trunk and short pointed branches, as on certain conifers, is in terminal field. Animals controlled by hero form heraldic group with this tree as central element.

COMMENTARY

For other scenes of heroic encounter that simultaneously create effective heraldic displays of the controlled animals flanking terminal element, see, for example, PFS 225 (Cat.No. 43), PFS 162 (Cat.No. 249), and PFS 1123 (Cat.No. 279). A rather similar tree appears on a seal used on a tablet from Nineveh (Herbordt 1992, pl. 9, no. 12, p. 248). Definitive renderings of the Persian court robe in frontal aspect, showing the dip at the hem line centered between the legs, are relatively rare in monumental relief and in glyptic (see, e.g., Root 1979, pls. 20–22, for examples on the Apadana at Persepolis). The Persianizing aspect of the garment on PFS 496 is far from certain.

For comparative illustrations including PFS 496, see pls. 181g (hybrid garments), 225d (horned animals and horned-animal creatures of undetermined types), 241i (heroic encounters fused with heraldic motifs), 257c (conifers), and 269e (terminal field motifs other than inscriptions).

SEAL APPLICATION (SEE *APPENDIX ONE: CONCORDANCE OF SEALS TO TABLETS IN VOLUME I*)

PFS 496 occurs on the reverse of PF 224. It is a long rolling preserving almost two full repeats of the figural scene. In this manner, the tree in the terminal field flanked by rampant animals becomes the center of display. PF 224 is dated 501/500 B.C.

BIBLIOGRAPHY

Garrison 1988, pp. 425–28.

I-A.12. WINGED HORNED-ANIMAL CREATURES: DEER, GAZELLES, WILD GOATS, WILD SHEEP

Cat.No. 109 PFS 341

|— 1 cm —|

Seal Type:	Cylinder	Photograph:	Pl. 63a
Earliest Dated Application:	ND	Typology and Style:	I-A.12 — Fortification Style
Preserved Height of Image:	1.60 cm (incomp.)	Preserved Length of Image:	2.70 cm (incomp.)
Estimated Height of Original Seal:	NA	Estimated Diameter of Original Seal:	NA
Number of Impressions:	1	Quality of Impression:	Poor

Completeness of Image: Segment of middle of design survives

DESCRIPTION OF SEAL AS IMPRESSED IMAGE

Hero appears to face left, arms bent, and holds two(?) rampant winged wild sheep creatures by horn (only lower body of creature to left preserved).

Each creature moves away from hero; that to right turns its head back toward him. Creature to right holds upper foreleg bent and extends it diagonally upward; lower foreleg (only partially preserved) is extended horizontally outward; tail extends diagonally upward, thickening. Short pointed tail of creature to left curves upward.

Hero wears robe. Perhaps pointed beard rests over hero's right shoulder; short-cropped(?) coiffure is above left shoulder.

COMMENTARY

See Garrison 1988 for other seals by the same distinctive hand.

For comparative illustrations including PFS 341, see pl. 224d (deer, goats, sheep, and related winged creatures).

SEAL APPLICATION (SEE *APPENDIX ONE: CONCORDANCE OF SEALS TO TABLETS IN VOLUME I*)

PFS 341 occurs on the reverse of PF 33. The partial rolling displays the hero in the center. The date of PF 33 is unknown.

BIBLIOGRAPHY

Garrison 1988, pp. 276–78.

I-A.16. VARIOUS COMPOSITE CREATURES

PFS 749 — Cat.No. 110

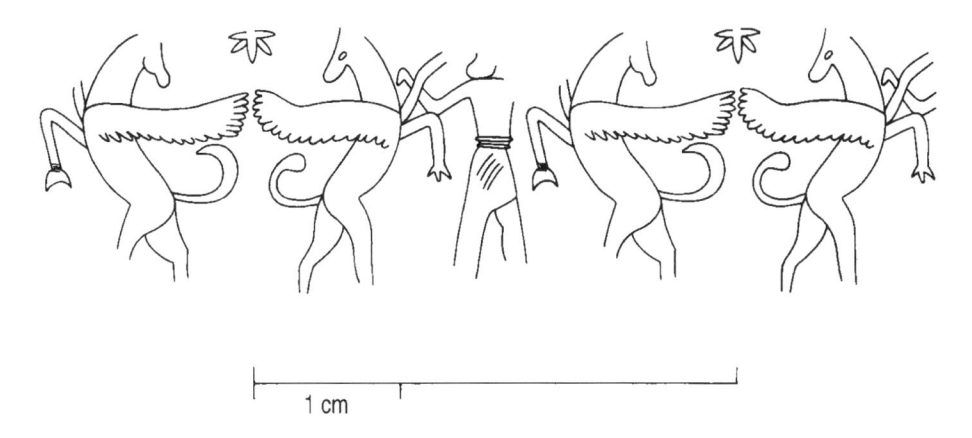

Seal Type:	Cylinder	Photograph:	Pl. 63c
Earliest Dated Application:	502/501 B.C.	Typology and Style:	I-A.16 — Fortification Style
Preserved Height of Image:	1.80 cm (incomp.)	Preserved Length of Image:	3.30 cm (comp.)
Estimated Height of Original Seal:	2.00 cm	Estimated Diameter of Original Seal:	1.10 cm
Number of Impressions:	3	Quality of Impressions:	Fair

Completeness of Image: Large segment of middle of design survives along its complete length

DESCRIPTION OF SEAL AS IMPRESSED IMAGE

Hero faces right in striding pose, arms bent, and holds two rampant winged horse creatures by throat (preserved only to left).

Each creature moves toward hero but turns its head away from him. Creature to left holds upper foreleg slightly bent and extends it upward toward hero's head; lower foreleg is bent, has three-pronged termination instead of hoof, and is extended upward in front of its body; tail curls upward with tufted termination. Creature to right holds upper foreleg (only partially preserved) straight and extends it upward toward hero's head; lower foreleg is bent, has large crescent-like termination of hoof, and is extended upward in front of its body; tail curls upward, thickening and then terminating in point.

Hero wears double-belted Assyrian garment that leaves forward leg exposed below mid-thigh; diagonal folds are indicated. Flattened coiffure rests at back of hero's neck.

Star is in upper terminal field. Horse creatures of heroic encounter form heraldic group before star.

COMMENTARY

The seal is quite large for the Fortification Style. The carving is bold and assured; see Garrison 1988 for the artist. See PFS 99 (Cat.No. 113), the only other representation of a winged horse creature on seals of heroic encounter in the PFS corpus. An important parallel for winged horse creatures in a control encounter occurs on a seal used by an Assyrian administrator in the eighth century B.C. (Bleibtreu 1997, pp. 98–99, fig. 98a–b).

For comparative illustrations including PFS 749, see pls. 197e (hands), 229f (scorpion, fish, horse, bird, and human creatures), 231d (feet of animals and creatures), and 267g (terminal field motifs other than inscriptions).

SEAL APPLICATION (SEE *APPENDIX ONE: CONCORDANCE OF SEALS TO TABLETS IN VOLUME I*)

PFS 749 occurs twice (inverted) on the reverse and once on the upper edge of PF 524. On the reverse the impressions are applied one directly above the other. The upper rolling on the reverse preserves the entire length of the seal design, placing the creature to the left of the hero in the center. The partial lower rolling on the reverse displays the creature to the left of the hero in the center. The partial rolling on the left edge preserves only the two creatures framing the terminal field. PF 524 is dated 502/501 B.C.

BIBLIOGRAPHY

Garrison 1988, pp. 304–07.

Cat.No. 111 PFS 284*

Seal Type:	Cylinder, Inscribed	Photographs:	Pl. 64a–c
Earliest Dated Application:	499/498 B.C.	Typology and Style:	I-A.16 — Diverse Styles
Language of Inscription:	Unknown		
Preserved Height of Image:	1.70 cm (comp.)	Preserved Length of Image:	3.00 cm (comp.)
Estimated Height of Original Seal:	1.70 cm	Estimated Diameter of Original Seal:	1.00 cm
Number of Impressions:	6	Quality of Impressions:	Fair

Completeness of Image: Complete except for details, and perhaps some letters of the inscription

DESCRIPTION OF SEAL AS IMPRESSED IMAGE

Hero faces left and has arms bent; in each hand he holds end of upper wing of winged double-headed lion-bird creature.

Creature moves to left on short bird-like legs; it turns one head to left, other head to right. Body and heads are lion-like. Creature has two sets of wings, upper horizontally disposed, lower diagonally disposed; on each side of its body, appendage extending from upper wing terminates in *ankh*-sign.

Hero wears belted tunic; upper part of garment stretches in folds from waist across upper arms; lower part of garment has diagonal folds. Short pointed beard rests over hero's right shoulder; large rounded coiffure rests at back of neck.

Inscription runs horizontally across upper field.

Line border is preserved at bottom of design; portions of line border are also preserved at top of design above creature.

INSCRIPTION

Greek script, language unknown

    Line   1. (?)ΚΥΜΨ(Χ?)Λ(Γ?)...ΗΠ(?)...
    Translation   ?

There is apparently one line to the inscription, oriented along the horizontal axis of the seal, across almost the full length of the top edge of the design. A horizontal bar occurs under the H. This is the only seal occurring on the tablets published by Hallock that carries an inscription in Greek letters. There is, of course, one tablet inscribed in Greek (Fort. 1771) in the Persepolis Fortification archive.

We are able to read seven letters, with space for one additional letter between the Λ and H, and for one or two additional letters between the Π and the left head of the creature.

Analysis of the lettering depends first on deciding what archaic script is represented. There seem to be two main possibilities: the Ionic script of western Asia Minor or the script of the Doric hexapolis of southwestern Asia Minor.

It is not clear where the inscription starts, or in which direction it is to be read. The orientation of the K suggests a reading from left to right, but Greek inscriptions of this date have no fixed rules. Reading from left to right, the inscription is likely to begin with the Λ, H, Π, or K. For purposes of analysis, we take the K (the letter immediately to the right of the right head of the creature) as the first letter of the inscription. We rely on Jeffery 1990, pp. 325, 345, for letter forms.

If the alphabet is Ionic, then the first letter is a K, followed by Y, M, Ψ (but in a highly elaborate form),[27] Λ, H (although probably incomplete),[28] and Π (but very unusual).[29]

If the alphabet is of the Doric hexapolis, then the first letter is K, followed by Y, M, X, Λ/Γ, H (with the same problems as above if in Ionic), and Π (with the same problems as above if in Ionic).

The H may simply indicate a rough breathing, though this is unlikely since in either Ionic or Doric it would be followed by a vowel rather than a letter. Nonetheless, it is tempting to take the H as a rough breathing mark and then read all other letters in the inscription as consonants. This solution would at least resonate with Aramaic inscriptions. The bar under the H is also a mystery. If it had occurred over the H, it conceivably could have signaled a number. One could perhaps understand the bar under the H to mark the beginning of the inscription. One further possibility is that the H is the definite article (feminine), in which case we may have an occupational designation: HΠ...KYMΨΛ...

No combination of possible letters or their ordering yields a recognizable name or occupation. Another alternative is that the inscription is purely decorative. Cuneiform-like plausibly mock inscriptions are attested on PFS 671* (Cat.No. 174) and PFS 677* (Cat.No. 181).

The location of the inscription can be paralleled in the PFS corpus of hero seals only by the Aramaic inscription on PFS 123* (Cat.No. 75).

COMMENTARY

The design is so arranged that when rolled out it appears as if the hero holds two creatures; see PFS 6 (Cat.No. 304) for a similar visual dynamic, although there the design conflates control and combat encounters. The neck of the left-facing head of the creature appears to cross in front of the neck of its right-facing mate. This suggests a pair of crossed creatures without, in fact, presenting more than a faux-crossed group. Perhaps a complete crossed pair was originally planned. The inscription in Greek script (with its oddities), the hero's garment, and the Egyptianizing iconography might suggest a koine product of Syria or coastal Anatolia. It is equally possible, however, that PFS 284* is a unique glyptic commission from a heartland Persian workshop answering a very specific set of patron directives (Root 1999a, pp. 167–68).[30]

For comparative illustrations including PFS 284*, see pls. 185c (tunics), 205i (arm positions of heroic encounter), 239e (unusual formats of heroic encounter), 243a (faux-crossed animal creatures), 254d (various devices and symbols), 264g (inscriptions without panels or case lines), 265d (mock inscriptions), and 276f (borders).

SEAL APPLICATION (SEE *APPENDIX ONE: CONCORDANCE OF SEALS TO TABLETS IN VOLUME I*)

PFS 284* occurs on the reverse (inverted) and left edge of both PF 330 and PF 2027. No other seal is applied on the tablets. The seal is applied twice on the reverse of each tablet, one impression directly above the other. Rollings exhibit marked distortion. Of the total six impressions, all but one show some part of the inscription. In two impressions the seal is rolled for one complete turn, preserving the entire length of the seal design. Of these two applications, one displays the hero in the center; one displays the hero and the inscription to the left of his head in the center. Of the remaining four partial impressions, one displays the inscription segment to the left of the hero in the center; one displays the hero in the center; one preserves only the hero and the left wings of the creature; one preserves only the body and heads of the creature. PF 330 is the earliest dated tablet with PFS 284* and is dated 499/498 B.C.

BIBLIOGRAPHY

Cameron 1942, pl. 46 G; Garrison 1988, pp. 262, 273–76; Garrison and Dion 1999, p. 10 (n. 28); Posner 1972, p. 124, fig. 28G (reprint of Cameron, op. cit., pl. 46 G); Root 1997, pp. 233–34, fig. 1; Root 1999a, pp. 167–68, fig. 5, p. 186.

---

27. The letter may also be a *sampi*, but this is unlikely.
28. There is a version of the *eta* written as a rectangle, long sides oriented vertically, with a crossbar in the middle. If the engraver failed to render the top closure of the rectangle, a figure like that on the seal would be the result.
29. The *pi* is typically written with a short right hasta, and the top bar does not project beyond the verticals on either side; the sloping shape of this letter is reminiscent of an *epsilon*, but the right hasta rules out that identification.
30. The garment is quite similar to that seen on a ca. fourteenth century "Syro-Palestinian" cylinder excavated from an early first millennium tomb in Armenia. This strange seal, with hieroglyphic inscription naming the Babylonian Kurigalzu illustrates the capacities of patron choice in glyptic invention as well as the border-crossing artistic environment of Egypt/western Asia. See Aruz 1997, 146–47, fig. 159.

Cat.No. 112   PFS 1485

Seal Type:	Cylinder	Photograph:	Pl. 65a
Earliest Dated Application:	ND	Typology and Style:	I-A.16 — Modeled Style
Preserved Height of Image:	1.60 cm (incomp.)	Preserved Length of Image:	2.70 cm (incomp.)
Estimated Height of Original Seal:	NA	Estimated Diameter of Original Seal:	NA
Number of Impressions:	2	Quality of Impressions:	Poor

Completeness of Image: Segment of middle of design survives

DESCRIPTION OF SEAL AS IMPRESSED IMAGE

Hero faces left, arms bent (only left arm preserved), and holds two winged nude female human creatures by wing or arm.

Each creature stands frontal (head not preserved), holding arms bent and extended up at each side of torso. Each creature presumably had four wings: two below arms, two above shoulders. The better preserved creature to right of hero displays two complete lower wings plus indications of one wing of the upper set. Each creature has bulbous thighs.

Hero appears to wear Assyrian garment that leaves forward leg exposed; short pointed object in front and back of waist represents sheath perhaps with hilt of dagger or sword at front. Rounded coiffure rests at back of hero's neck.

COMMENTARY

The winged, nude frontal females, unique in the PFS corpus, recall figures in Assyrian glyptic.[31] Stylistically, PFS 1485 is close to PFS 1387 (Cat.No. 72) and PFS 944 (Cat.No. 129).

For comparative illustrations including PFS 1485, see pls. 214j (frontal faces and/or bodies) and 229h (scorpion, fish, horse, bird, and human creatures).

SEAL APPLICATION (SEE APPENDIX ONE: CONCORDANCE OF SEALS TO TABLETS IN VOLUME I)

PFS 1485 occurs twice on the reverse of PF 1608, one impression directly above the other. The upper rolling is now much destroyed but originally placed the creature to the right of the hero in the center. The partial lower rolling displays the hero in the center. The date of PF 1608 is unknown.

BIBLIOGRAPHY

Brosius 1991, p. 190 (n. 49); Garrison 1988, pp. 213, 215, 495.

---

31. For example, a seal used on a tablet of late Assyrian date: Herbordt 1992, p. 206, pl. 3, no. 11, after Parker 1962, p. 38, fig. 8, pl. 21 (2).

I-A.17. MIXED ANIMALS AND/OR CREATURES

PFS 99   Cat.No. 113

Seal Type:	Cylinder	Photographs:	Pl. 65c–d
Earliest Dated Application:	504/503 B.C.	Typology and Style:	I-A.17 — Modeled Style
Preserved Height of Image:	1.40 cm (comp.)	Preserved Length of Image:	3.20 cm (comp.)
Estimated Height of Original Seal:	1.40 cm	Estimated Diameter of Original Seal:	1.00 cm
Number of Impressions:	8	Quality of Impressions:	Poor-fair

Completeness of Image: Complete except for details and small portions of upper edge and lower edge

DESCRIPTION OF SEAL AS IMPRESSED IMAGE

Hero faces right, arms bent, and holds rampant winged bull creature at left and rampant winged horse creature at right.

Bull creature at left holds upper foreleg straight and extends it upward toward hero's head; lower foreleg is slightly bent and extended downward toward hero's hip. Horse creature at right holds upper foreleg bent and extends it upward toward hero's face; lower foreleg is slightly bent and extended downward toward hero's thigh. Each creature has two wings indicated, lower wing extending slightly diagonally downward from its back, upper wing extending diagonally upward from lower wing. Tail of each creature bends downward.

Hero wears Assyrian garment that leaves forward leg exposed; diagonal folds are indicated on garment over rear leg.

Creature at left is ithyphallic.

In field between hero and creature at right is ring shape with two hooked appendages.

Flaw or chip is in lower field between hero and creature at left; three chips or flaws are in stone along lower edge. Edge of seal is preserved at top and bottom of design.

COMMENTARY

Koch (1990) notes that PFS 99, PFS 103* (Cat.No. 84), and PFS 228 (Cat.No. 148) were responsible for the verification of the year end accounts at Liduma in her Elam Region VI. PFS 99 occurs with PFS 228 (Cat.No. 148), PFS 64* (Cat.No. 173), PFS 503 (Cat.No. 307), PFS 478 (II), PFS 505 (III), PFS 477 (III), PFS 504 (III), and PFS 479 (illegible). No personal names that can be associated with these seals are preserved in the relevant texts. Brosius notes the connection of the seal with the storage of *kem* at Hidali, Liduma, and Tiliman.

Winged horses are quite rare in the PFS corpus. The winged horse creature on PFS 99 joins with the similar creatures on PFS 749 (Cat.No. 110) as the only examples on seals of heroic encounter herein.[32]

The device in the field between the hero and the horse creature has no parallel among the images of heroic encounter herein and it calls to mind linear devices on some pyramidal stamp seals from western Anatolia (Boardman 1970a, devices D.3 and D.4; cf. fig. 11, no. 83, a seal said to have come from Persepolis).

---

32. Naturalistic (non-winged, etc.) horses are represented on a small number of seals in Volume II (e.g., PFS 51 [II], PFS 93* [II], PFS 287 [II], PFS 1044 [II]; see Garrison 1991, figs. 3–4 and 1–2, for PFS 51 [II] and PFS 93* [II], respectively), on PTS 18, and on a sealing from Memphis (Petrie et al. 1910, p. 42, pl. 36, no. 38).

For comparative illustrations including PFS 99, see pls. 229e (scorpion, fish, horse, bird, and human creatures), 254c (various devices and symbols), 271b (compositions with large empty space as terminal field), 280d (chips in seal matrices), and 286b (personal seals of accountants).

SEAL APPLICATION (SEE *APPENDIX ONE: CONCORDANCE OF SEALS TO TABLETS IN VOLUME I*)

With one exception (PF 200, on the reverse), PFS 99 always occurs on the left edge of tablets. On PF 201 the seal occurs on the left edge and the reverse. On the reverse of PF 200–201 the seal is inverted. PFS 477 (III) is applied (also inverted) on the reverse of PF 200 directly above PFS 99. Some impressions show lateral distortion. In two impressions the seal is rolled for at least one complete turn, preserving the entire length of the seal design. Of these two applications, one displays the hero in the center; one displays the horse creature to the right of the hero in the center. Of the remaining six partial rollings, one displays the hero in the center; one displays the bull creature to the left of the hero in the center; three display the horse creature to the right of the hero in the center; one displays the negative space in the terminal field in the center. PF 200 is the earliest dated tablet with PFS 99 and is dated 504/503 B.C.

BIBLIOGRAPHY

Brosius 1996, pp. 137 (table 4), 138, 141; Garrison 1988, pp. 211–12; Koch 1990, pp. 204–05.

Cat.No. 114   PFS 52

Seal Type:	Cylinder	Photographs:	Pl. 66a–b
Earliest Dated Application:	504/503 B.C.	Typology and Style:	I-A.17 — Fortification Style
Preserved Height of Image:	2.00 cm (incomp.)	Preserved Length of Image:	3.30 cm (comp.)
Estimated Height of Original Seal:	2.20 cm	Estimated Diameter of Original Seal:	1.10 cm
Number of Impressions:	11	Quality of Impressions:	Fair-good

Completeness of Image: Complete except for lower edge

DESCRIPTION OF SEAL AS IMPRESSED IMAGE

Hero faces right. Right arm is bent to hold rampant winged human-headed lion creature by upper foreleg; left arm is straight at horizontal to hold rampant lion by throat.

Winged creature holds upper foreleg straight and extends it upward toward hero's head; lower foreleg is straight and extended vertically downward in front of its body. Lion holds one foreleg straight, toes splayed, and extends it downward toward hero's waist; other foreleg is straight, toes splayed, and held up and away from body. Tail of each creature curls upward with tufted termination.

Hero wears belted Persian court robe with sleeves pushed up to reveal arms; sleeves hang in long swags; V-shaped neck line indicated; double central pleat and diagonal folds of lower part of hero's garment are indicated. Hero appears to be beardless or close-shaved; flattened coiffure rests at back of neck.

Human head of winged creature is beardless or close-shaved with short-cropped coiffure. Double row of feathers are indicated on wing.

Lion has mouth open in roar.

Portions of edge of seal are preserved at top of design above rampant creature and lion.

COMMENTARY

PFS 52 often occurs with PFS 62 (Cat.No. 104), which probably belongs to Mikrašba, an important grain supplier. Names of several receivers occur on these tablets, suggesting that PFS 52 may be an office seal (see Garrison 1996a).

This is a large and impressive seal. See Garrison 1988, 1991, and 1996a for the distinctive work of this important artist who works close to the Court Style.

For comparative illustrations including PFS 52, see pls. 178a (Persian court robes with sleeves pushed up in deep swags), 206a (arm positions of heroic control), and 273b (open compositions).

SEAL APPLICATION (SEE *APPENDIX ONE: CONCORDANCE OF SEALS TO TABLETS IN VOLUME I*)

PFS 52 always occurs on the reverse of tablets, and in four instances also the upper edge (PF 296, PF 361, PF 1650, PF 1767). On all reverse surfaces the seal is inverted. Impressions tend to be clearly applied, although a few exhibit some distortion. In five impressions the seal is rolled for at least one complete turn, preserving the entire length of the seal design. Of these five applications, one displays the hero in the center; one displays the hero and the creature in the center; one displays the hero and the lion in the center; one displays the lion and the creature in the center; one displays the lion in the center. Of the remaining six partial impressions, three display the hero in the center; one preserves only the hero and the creature; one preserves only the hero and the lion; one displays the creature in the center. On PF 25, PF 361, and PF 1650 the seal clearly was applied before the text since cuneiform wedges or lines made by the scribe's stylus cut into the bottom of the impressions. PF 296, PF 1650, and PF 1767 are the earliest dated tablets with PFS 52 and are all dated 504/503 B.C.

BIBLIOGRAPHY

Garrison 1988, pp. 363–68, 480, 489–90; Garrison 1991, pp. 16–17, fig. 28; Garrison 1996a, pp. 40–43, figs. 6–7; Garrison and Dion 1999, p. 9 (n. 20).

Cat.No. 115   PFS 145

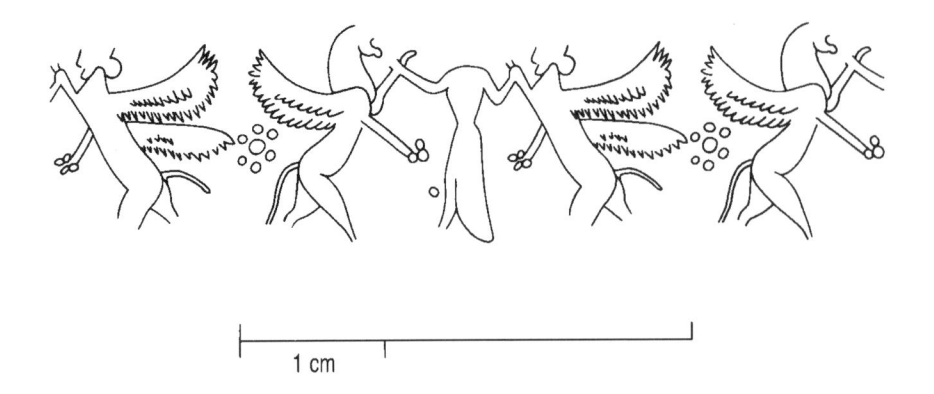

Seal Type:	Cylinder	Photographs:	Pl. 67a–b
Earliest Dated Application:	500/499 B.C.	Typology and Style:	I-A.17 — Fortification Style
Preserved Height of Image:	1.50 cm (incomp.)	Preserved Length of Image:	3.10 cm (comp.)
Estimated Height of Original Seal:	NA	Estimated Diameter of Original Seal:	1.00 cm
Number of Impressions:	6	Quality of Impressions:	Fair

Completeness of Image: Large segment of middle of design survives along its complete length

DESCRIPTION OF SEAL AS IMPRESSED IMAGE

Hero faces left, arms bent, and holds rampant winged lion creature to left and rampant winged human-headed lion creature to right by foreleg.

Each creature holds upper foreleg straight and extends it upward toward hero's head; lower foreleg is straight, toes splayed, and extended downward toward hero's leg. Tail of winged lion creature is long and curves downward. Tail of human-headed lion creature is short and curves downward.

Hero wears Assyrian garment that leaves forward leg exposed.

Winged lion creature has one wing indicated with double row of feathers; mouth is open in roar. Human-headed creature has two wings indicated, both extended horizontally back from creature's back; two rows of feathers are indicated. Beard terminates in blunt point over creature's chest; rounded coiffure rests at back of neck.

Small dot is placed in field before hero's forward leg.

Central dot surrounded by six smaller dots to form rosette appears in terminal field.

COMMENTARY

The unmasked drill work in the paws of the lions and the rosette is well executed; compare the drill work in the snouts of the lions on PFS 494 (Cat.No. 130) and the similar dot rosettes on PFS 884 (Cat.No. 123) and PFS 84 (II). See Garrison 1988 for artist and related seals.

For comparative illustrations including PFS 145, see pl. 253e (stars, rosettes).

SEAL APPLICATION (SEE APPENDIX ONE: CONCORDANCE OF SEALS TO TABLETS IN VOLUME I)

PFS 145 occurs on the reverse of PF 761–763. On PF 761 the seal also occurs on the upper edge. On the reverse of both PF 761 and PF 762 the seal is applied twice (inverted), one impression directly above the other. Rollings show marked distortion. In all six impressions the seal is rolled for at least one complete turn, preserving the entire length of the seal design. Of these six applications, one displays the hero and the creature to left in the center; three display the creature to the left of the hero in the center; one displays the creature to the right of the hero in the center; one displays the two creatures in the center. On the reverse of all three tablets the seal was clearly applied before the text since several cuneiform wedges cut into the bottom or top of the impressions. PF 763 is the earliest dated tablet with PFS 145 and is dated 500/499 B.C.

BIBLIOGRAPHY

Garrison 1988, pp. 309–12.

PFS 197   Cat.No. 116

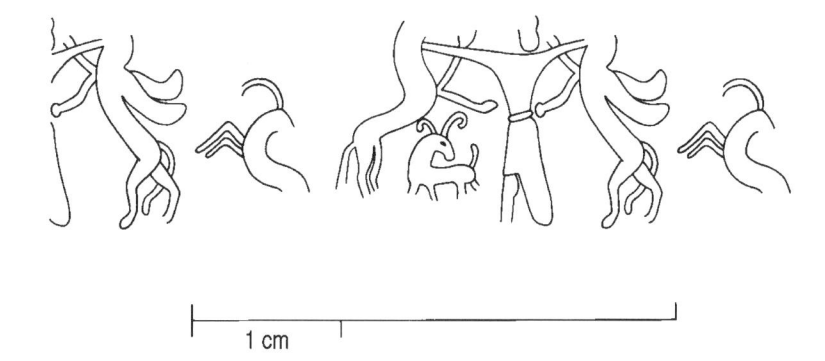

Seal Type:	Cylinder	Photograph:	Pl. 68a
Earliest Dated Application:	494/493 B.C.	Typology and Style:	I-A.17 — Fortification Style
Preserved Height of Image:	1.50 cm (incomp.)	Preserved Length of Image:	3.20 cm (comp.)
Estimated Height of Original Seal:	NA	Estimated Diameter of Original Seal:	1.00 cm
Number of Impressions:	8	Quality of Impressions:	Fair

Completeness of Image: Large segment of middle of design survives along its complete length

DESCRIPTION OF SEAL AS IMPRESSED IMAGE

Hero faces left, arms straight at slight diagonal, and holds rampant lion to left and rampant winged lion creature to right by throat.

Each animal/creature holds upper foreleg straight and extends it upward toward hero's head. Lion holds lower foreleg straight, paw upturned, and extends it downward toward hero's waist; hind legs are placed together; thick tail hangs downward. Winged lion creature holds lower foreleg slightly bent and extends it downward toward hero's waist; creature strides toward hero; tail curves downward between its hind legs.

Hero wears belted Assyrian garment that leaves forward leg exposed below knee. Rounded coiffure rests at back of neck.

Winged lion creature has two wings indicated, upper extending diagonally downward above lower.

Small marchant wild sheep is between hero and lion to left. Sheep moves to left but turns head back to right. Two long curved horns displayed frontally emerge from top of its head; short tail curves upward.

In terminal field, rampant wild goat moves to left but turns head back to right. Goat holds forelegs bent and extends them together upward in front of its body; long curved horn (only partially preserved) emerges from back of its head.

COMMENTARY

See Garrison 1988 for the artist and related seals. For the small animal nestled within the heroic scene, compare a Neo-Assyrian Modeled Style cylinder dedicated at the Samian Heraion (Aruz 1997, pp. 144–45, fig. 158).

For comparative illustrations including PFS 197, see pls. 236d (animals/creatures as secondary elements of main design field) and 268b (terminal field motifs other than inscriptions).

SEAL APPLICATION (SEE APPENDIX ONE: CONCORDANCE OF SEALS TO TABLETS IN VOLUME I)

PFS 197 occurs on the reverse and bottom edge of PF 206 and the reverse, lower edge and upper edge of PF 207, with PFS 198 (II) on the left edge of both tablets. On the reverse of both tablets the seal is inverted. On the reverse of PF 207 the seal is applied three times, the impressions stacked one above the other. On the reverse of PF 206 the seal is applied twice, one impression directly above the other. In three impressions the seal is rolled for at least one complete turn, preserving the entire length of the seal design. Of these three applications, one displays the hero in the center; two display the lion to the left of the hero in the center. Of the remaining five partial rollings, two display the hero in the center; one displays the hero and the lion creature to right in the center; one preserves only the lion to the left of the hero and the small sheep; one displays the creature to the right of the hero in the center. PF 206 and PF 207 are both dated 494/493 B.C.

BIBLIOGRAPHY

Garrison 1988, pp. 309–12.

Cat.No. 117   PFS 222

Seal Type:	Cylinder	Photographs:	Pl. 69a–b
Earliest Dated Application:	498 B.C.	Typology and Style:	I-A.17 — Broad and Flat Styles
Preserved Height of Image:	1.80 cm (comp.)	Preserved Length of Image:	2.60 cm (comp.)
Estimated Height of Original Seal:	1.80 cm	Estimated Diameter of Original Seal:	0.80 cm
Number of Impressions:	6	Quality of Impressions:	Fair

Completeness of Image: Almost complete except for parts of lower edge and details

DESCRIPTION OF SEAL AS IMPRESSED IMAGE

Hero faces left in striding pose, right arm straight to hold rampant human-faced bull creature by upper foreleg; has left arm bent to hold rampant human-faced wild sheep creature(?) by chest.

Bull creature to left actively strides toward hero. Creature holds upper foreleg bent and extends it outward toward hero's waist; lower foreleg is bent and extended downward in front of its body; long tail curves upward then downward at its end with tufted termination. Sheep creature to right holds hind legs together; creature holds upper foreleg straight and extends it upward toward hero's head; lower foreleg is bent and extended downward in front of its body. Long thick tail curves downward.

Hero wears belted Assyrian garment that leaves forward leg exposed below mid-thigh; single decorative border runs along front edge of garment; tassel hangs from belt at waist. Pointed beard rests over hero's right shoulder; small round coiffure rests at back of neck.

Each creature has long rounded beard. Beard of creature to right is narrow. Two long thin curved horns emerge from top of head of creature to right; pointed ear is at back of head.

In upper terminal field are star and crescent.

Edge of seal is visible at top of design. Portion of edge of seal is preserved at bottom of design under creature to left.

COMMENTARY

The uneven arrangement of compositional features is typical of designs found in the Broad and Flat Styles. The calligraphic quality of the animal bodies and tails is, however, unusual in this style.

For comparative illustrations including PFS 222, see pls. 177b (Assyrian garments with detailing preserved), 206e (arm positions of heroic control), 224c (deer, goats, sheep, and related winged creatures), 234g (human-headed/human-faced creatures), and 252f (crescents and stars).

SEAL APPLICATION (SEE *APPENDIX ONE: CONCORDANCE OF SEALS TO TABLETS IN VOLUME I*)

PFS 222 occurs only on the reverse of tablets, with PFS 6 (Cat.No. 304) on the left edge. On PF 1032, PF 1642, PF 1727, and PF 1761 the seal is inverted. Impressions generally exhibit marked lateral and vertical distortion.

In five impressions the seal was rolled for at least one complete turn, preserving the entire seal design. Of these five applications, one displays the hero in the center; one displays the hero and the sheep creature to right in the center; two display the bull creature to the left of the hero in the center; one displays the two creatures in the center. The remaining partial rolling displays the hero in the center. On the reverse of PF 1032, PF 1727, PF 1744, PF 1761, and PF 1762 the seal clearly was applied before the text since several cuneiform wedges cut into the top or bottom of the impressions. PF 1744 is the earliest dated tablet with PFS 222 and is dated 498 B.C.

BIBLIOGRAPHY

Garrison 1988, pp. 431–32.

PFS 552   Cat.No. 118

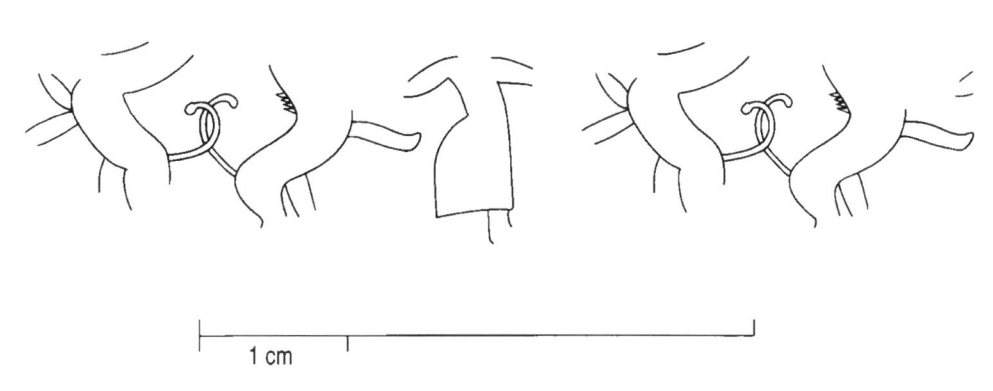

Seal Type:	Cylinder	Photograph:	Pl. 70a
Earliest Dated Application:	498/497 B.C.	Typology and Style:	I-A.17 — Modeled Style
Preserved Height of Image:	1.30 cm (incomp.)	Preserved Length of Image:	3.70 cm (comp.)
Estimated Height of Original Seal:	NA	Estimated Diameter of Original Seal:	1.20 cm
Number of Impressions:	3	Quality of Impressions:	Poor

Completeness of Image: Large segment of middle of design survives along its complete length

DESCRIPTION OF SEAL AS IMPRESSED IMAGE

Hero moves to right, arms bent(?), and holds rampant lion to left and rampant winged lion creature to right.

Lion holds lower foreleg straight and extends it downward toward hero's hip. Winged lion creature holds upper foreleg (only partially preserved) straight and extends it diagonally upward; lower foreleg (only partially preserved) is straight and extended downward toward hero's leg. Long tails of lion and lion creatures curl upward and intertwine in terminal field. Winged lion creature's tail has tufted termination.

Hero appears to wear tunic.

Traces of mane on lion are rendered by crisp serrated edge along contour of neck.

COMMENTARY

The seal is large and impressive, although poorly preserved.
    For comparative illustrations including PFS 552, see pl. 185d (tunics).

SEAL APPLICATION (SEE APPENDIX ONE: CONCORDANCE OF SEALS TO TABLETS IN VOLUME I)

PFS 552 occurs three times on the reverse of PF 310. The impressions are placed one above the other. The upper rolling preserves only the lion to the left of the hero. The middle impression is the largest and displays the hero in the center. The lower impression is very fragmentary and preserves only part of the lion to the left of the hero. PF 310 is dated 498/497 B.C.

BIBLIOGRAPHY

Garrison 1988, pp. 211–12.

Cat.No. 119									PFS 687

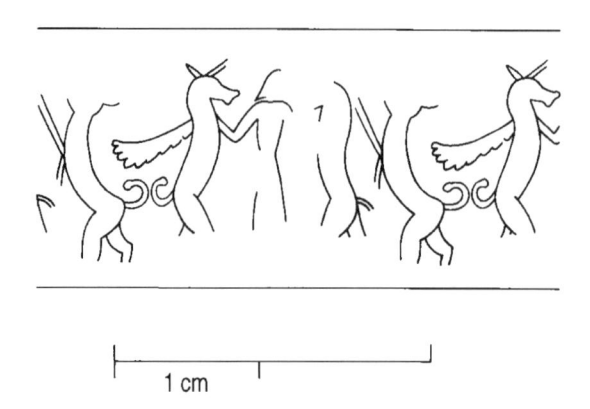

1 cm

Seal Type:	Cylinder	Photograph:	Pl. 70c
Earliest Dated Application:	497/496 B.C.	Typology and Style:	I-A.17 — Fortification Style
Preserved Height of Image:	1.70 cm (comp.)	Preserved Length of Image:	2.20 cm (comp.)
Estimated Height of Original Seal:	1.70 cm	Estimated Diameter of Original Seal:	0.70 cm
Number of Impressions:	1	Quality of Impression:	Very poor

Completeness of Image: Almost complete except for details throughout the design, especially along upper edge and lower edge

DESCRIPTION OF SEAL AS IMPRESSED IMAGE

Hero apparently faces left, arms bent, and holds rampant winged horned-animal creature to left by throat and rampant lion to right.

Tail of winged creature curls upward with tufted termination. Tail of lion (only partially preserved) curves downward.

Hero wears robe; pointed beard rests above right shoulder.

Winged creature has long thin horn (only partially preserved) emerging from top of its head; long pointed ear is at back of head.

In terminal field, rampant animal of uncertain type moves toward left but perhaps faces right. Animal holds upper foreleg straight and extends it upward toward head of rampant lion held by hero; lower foreleg (only partially preserved) is straight and extended downward toward lion's tail; tail curls upward with tufted termination.

Edge of seal is preserved at top and bottom of design.

COMMENTARY

The hero's head is not well preserved and he may face left, not right.

SEAL APPLICATION (SEE *APPENDIX ONE: CONCORDANCE OF SEALS TO TABLETS IN VOLUME I*)

PFS 687 occurs on the reverse of PF 453. The rolling preserves the entire length of the seal design and displays the lion to the right of the hero in the center. PF 453 is dated 497/496 B.C.

BIBLIOGRAPHY

Garrison 1988, pp. 309–12.

PFS 1030 Cat.No. 120

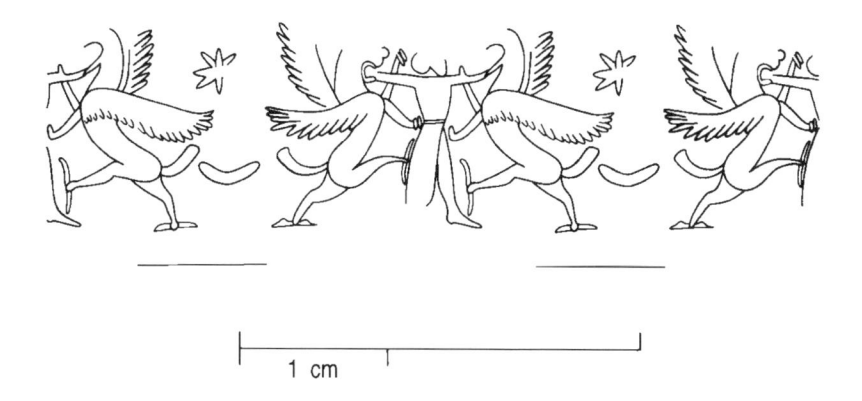

Seal Type:	Cylinder	Photograph:	Pl. 71a
Earliest Dated Application:	498 B.C.	Typology and Style:	I-A.17 — Fortification Style
Preserved Height of Image:	1.60 cm (incomp.)	Preserved Length of Image:	2.80 cm (comp.)
Estimated Height of Original Seal:	1.80 cm	Estimated Diameter of Original Seal:	0.90 cm
Number of Impressions:	3	Quality of Impressions:	Fair

Completeness of Image: Almost complete except for upper edge and lower edge

Description of Seal as Impressed Image

Hero faces right, arms straight at horizontal, and holds rampant winged lion creature to left and rampant winged bird-headed lion creature to right by their lower jaws.

Creature to left holds upper foreleg straight and extends it upward toward hero's head; lower foreleg is curved and extended downward to place paw on hero's waist. Creature raises forward curved hind leg and places bird's foot on hero's leg. Two wings are indicated, upper extending diagonally upward from lower. Creature to right holds upper foreleg straight and extends it upward toward hero's head; lower foreleg is curved, paw upturned, and extended downward toward hero's waist. Creature raises forward straight hind leg, with bird's foot, and extends it toward hero's leg. Creatures' short thick tails curve upward.

Hero wears belted Assyrian garment that leaves forward leg exposed. Beard terminates in blunt point over hero's left shoulder; large rounded coiffure rests at back of neck. Long spiky mane is indicated along contour of neck of creature to right. Each creature opens its mouth.

Star is in upper terminal field; crescent is in lower terminal field.

Traces of edge of seal are preserved at bottom of design under creature to right and terminal field.

Commentary

The design is unusually active for the Fortification Style. The carving is crisply executed.
For comparative illustrations including PFS 1030, see pl. 252h (crescents and stars).

Seal Application (see Appendix One: Concordance of Seals to Tablets in Volume I)

PFS 1030 occurs twice on the reverse of PF 1062 and once on the upper edge of PF 1118, with PFS 152 (Cat.No. 295) on the left edge of each tablet. On the reverse of PF 1062, the seal was rolled for most of its length, then picked up, inverted, and rolled again for most of its length in the same horizontal plane of the tablet. The inverted rolling displays the creature to the left of the hero in the center; the other rolling displays the hero in the center. The rolling on the upper edge preserves the entire length of the seal design and displays the bird-headed creature to the right of the hero in the center. On the reverse the seal clearly was applied before the text since several cuneiform wedges cut into the top and bottom of the impression. PF 1062 is the earliest dated tablet with PFS 1030 and is dated 498 B.C.

Bibliography

Dusinberre 1997b, p. 127 (n. 119); Garrison 1988, pp. 298–300; Garrison and Dion 1999, p. 13, fig. 11.

Cat.No. 121　　　　　　　　　　　　　　PFS 1586

Seal Type:	Cylinder	Photograph:	Pl. 71c
Earliest Dated Application:	504/503 B.C.	Typology and Style:	I-A.17 — Modeled Style
Preserved Height of Image:	1.80 cm (incomp.)	Preserved Length of Image:	3.30 cm (comp.)
Estimated Height of Original Seal:	2.00 cm	Estimated Diameter of Original Seal:	1.10 cm
Number of Impressions:	3	Quality of Impressions:	Poor

Completeness of Image: Almost complete except for lower edge

DESCRIPTION OF SEAL AS IMPRESSED IMAGE

Four-winged hero faces right, arms bent, and holds sejant winged human-headed scorpion creature with animal legs to left by beard in cupping gesture and holds rampant winged human-headed bull or lion creature to right by upper foreleg. Hero raises forward leg.

Scorpion creature's thick scorpion tail bends upward; sting at end of tail is visible above wing. Rampant bull or lion holds upper foreleg straight and extends it vertically upward in front of its face; lower foreleg is straight and extended upward to place paw on hero's lower wing. Tail bends upward with tufted termination.

Hero wears Assyrian garment that leaves forward leg exposed below knee; hero wears domed headdress with projection at front. Rounded beard rests over hero's chest; rounded segmented coiffure rests at back of neck.

Scorpion creature has long rounded beard; rounded coiffure rests at back of neck. Bull or lion creature appears to have rounded beard; large round coiffure rests at back of neck. Each creature wears domed headdress with projection at front.

COMMENTARY

PFS 1586 occurs on only one tablet, PF 1953, a journal (V text) dealing with wine transfers; it should belong to the accountant mentioned in the text, Manezza, who is located at Kurpun. The name Manezza also occurs in PF 26 (receiving grain), PF 1158 (supplying wine at Kurpun), and PF 1201 (supplying wine); the last two occurrences probably refer to the same individual mentioned in PF 1953.

For scorpion creatures in heroic encounter scenes, see a cylinder seal impression on a tablet from the Nabu Temple at Nimrud dated ca. 616 B.C. (Parker 1962, p. 36, fig. 1, pl. 19, no. 1; Herbordt 1992, p. 191, pl. 8, no. 6), where the hero also cups the creatures' beards in his hands. The intimacy of the gesture suggests that the special status of the scorpion as a symbol of fertility in ancient Mesopotamia survives on some level with some of these representations of scorpion creatures (van Buren 1939, pp. 110–12; see also Black and Green 1992, p. 161). For other scorpion creatures in this volume, see PFS 4* (Cat.No. 292) and PFS 29 (Cat.No. 302). See Garrison 1988 for the style and workshop of PFS 1586 and related seals.

For comparative illustrations including PFS 1586, see pls. 193j (round coiffures), 197h (hands), 207j (arm positions of heroic control), 215i (unusual heroic attitudes), 229c (scorpion, fish, horse, bird, and human creatures), 235g (human-headed/human-faced creatures), and 286g (personal seals of accountants).

SEAL APPLICATION (SEE APPENDIX ONE: CONCORDANCE OF SEALS TO TABLETS IN VOLUME I)

PFS 1586 occurs on the reverse, upper edge, and left edge of PF 1953. The right edge is destroyed, the left edge is damaged, affecting all impressions of PFS 1586. No other seal is preserved on the tablet. All rollings were originally very long. Each application is markedly irregular, the user apparently rolling the seal only partially, then picking it up and rolling it again. This results in a series of overlapping and incomplete impressions, which we are treating as single applications on each surface because of the difficulty in unpacking the overlaps. It is impossible to determine a central element. On the reverse of PF 1953 the seal clearly was applied before the text since several cuneiform wedges cut into the top of the impression. PF 1953 is dated 504/503 B.C.

BIBLIOGRAPHY

Dusinberre 1997b, p. 128 (n. 131); Garrison 1988, pp. 228, 240–43; Garrison 1998, p. 121 (n. 15); Garrison and Dion 1999, p. 9 (n. 19).

PFS 1654   Cat.No. 122

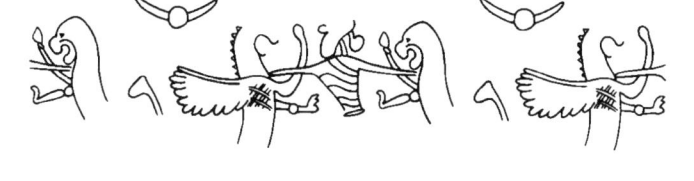

Seal Type:	Cylinder	Photograph:	Pl. 72a
Earliest Dated Application:	500 B.C.	Typology and Style:	I-A.17 — Linear Styles
Preserved Height of Image:	1.10 cm (incomp.)	Preserved Length of Image:	2.40 cm (comp.)
Estimated Height of Original Seal:	NA	Estimated Diameter of Original Seal:	0.80 cm
Number of Impressions:	2	Quality of Impressions:	Poor

Completeness of Image: Segment of middle of design survives along its complete length

DESCRIPTION OF SEAL AS IMPRESSED IMAGE

Hero faces left, arms straight, and holds rampant winged lion creature to left and rampant lion to right by throat.

Winged lion creature holds upper foreleg curved and extends it upward toward hero's head; lower foreleg is straight, toes splayed, and extended outward toward hero's waist. Lion holds upper foreleg curved and extends it upward in front of its head; lower foreleg is straight, paw upturned, and extended downward toward hero's waist; tail (only partially preserved) curls upward and is bent downward at its end with tufted termination.

Hero wears belted garment of uncertain type with diagonal striations on torso. Rounded beard rests over hero's right shoulder; round coiffure rests at back of neck.

Winged lion creature has cross-hatching on its upper body. One wing is shown; second wing may be indicated by line near upper edge of visible wing. Mane is rendered by crisp serrated edge along contour of its neck. Lion creature and lion both open mouths in roar.

Crescent with dot at center is in upper terminal field.

COMMENTARY

The crude engraving is typical of seals rendered in the Linear Styles. There is much use of a drill in the design.
   For comparative illustrations including PFS 1654, see pl. 251i (crescents).

SEAL APPLICATION (SEE *APPENDIX ONE: CONCORDANCE OF SEALS TO TABLETS IN VOLUME I*)

PFS 1654 occurs on the reverse and upper edge of PF 981. Both rollings are long, preserving the entire length of the seal design. The rolling on the upper edge preserves almost two full repeats of the figural scene; in this manner it displays the crescent in the upper terminal field in the center. The rolling on the reverse displays the lion to the right of the hero in the center. PF 981 is dated 500 B.C.

BIBLIOGRAPHY

Garrison 1988, pp. 435–37.

Cat.No. 123   PFS 884

Seal Type:	Cylinder	Photograph:	Pl. 72c
Earliest Dated Application:	498 B.C.	Typology and Style:	I-A.17 — Diverse Styles
Preserved Height of Image:	1.40 cm (incomp.)	Preserved Length of Image:	2.80 cm (comp.)
Estimated Height of Original Seal:	1.60 cm	Estimated Diameter of Original Seal:	0.90 cm
Number of Impressions:	3	Quality of Impressions:	Fair

Completeness of Image: Complete except for details, upper edge and lower edge

DESCRIPTION OF SEAL AS IMPRESSED IMAGE

Hero faces right, arms bent, and holds rampant winged human-headed creature of uncertain type at left and rampant winged lion creature at right, both by upper foreleg.

Creature to left holds upper foreleg bent, paw upturned, and extends it upward toward hero's head; lower foreleg is straight, paw turned up, and extended downward in front of its body; tail curves downward. Creature to right holds upper foreleg curved and extends it upward toward hero's head; lower foreleg is straight, toes splayed, and extended downward toward hero's leg; tail bends downward.

Hero may wear tunic. Narrow rounded beard rests above hero's left shoulder; flattened coiffure curls upward at back of neck.

Creature to left has two wings, upper one sharply curled upward from its back, lower one straight and extended diagonally upward from its back; flattened coiffure curls upward. Mouth is open, as in a lion's roar.

Rosette formed of central dot ringed by five dots is in terminal field.

COMMENTARY

The style is very unusual, although the animal forms show some link with the Fortification Style; compare PFS 1444 (Cat.No. 62). Overall, the line is very unsteady and awkward; note especially the outline of the hero's body and that of the head and neck of the creature to left. For a similar style in the rendering of the hero, see PFS 1204 (Cat.No. 136). It is fairly unusual for the creatures to have a different number of wings, and to have them rendered so differently. See PFS 145 (Cat.No. 115) and PFS 84 (II) for similar dot rosettes.

For comparative illustrations including PFS 884, see pls. 197g (hands) and 253h (stars, rosettes).

SEAL APPLICATION (SEE *APPENDIX ONE: CONCORDANCE OF SEALS TO TABLETS IN VOLUME I*)

PFS 884 occurs twice on the reverse (inverted) and once on the upper edge of PF 760. On the reverse the impressions are applied one directly above the other. The rollings on the reverse preserve the entire length of the seal design; the lower displays the two creatures in the center; the upper displays the creature to the left of the hero in the center. The partial rolling on the upper edge preserves only the two creatures. The upper rolling on the reverse clearly was applied before the text since several cuneiform wedges cut into the bottom of the impression. PF 760 is dated 498 B.C.

BIBLIOGRAPHY

Dusinberre 1997b, p. 128 (n. 131); Garrison 1988, pp. 450–52.

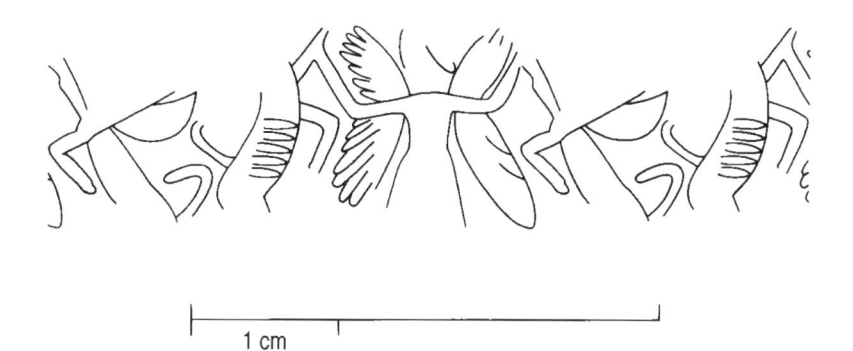

PFS 297   Cat.No. 124

Seal Type:	Cylinder	Photograph:	Pl. 73a
Earliest Dated Application:	498/487 B.C.	Typology and Style:	I-A.17 — Fortification Style
Preserved Height of Image:	1.40 cm (incomp.)	Preserved Length of Image:	3.20 cm (comp.)
Estimated Height of Original Seal:	NA	Estimated Diameter of Original Seal:	1.00 cm
Number of Impressions:	3	Quality of Impressions:	Poor

Completeness of Image: Almost complete except for upper edge and lower edge

DESCRIPTION OF SEAL AS IMPRESSED IMAGE

Four-winged hero faces right, arms bent and extended upward, and holds rampant animal of uncertain type to left and rampant winged creature of uncertain type to right, both by upper foreleg.

Animal and creature each holds upper foreleg straight and extends it upward toward hero's upper wing; lower foreleg is bent and extended downward in front of its body; tails curl upward.

Hero wears garment of uncertain type. Upper wings emerge from upper line of upper arms and curve outward; lower wings emerge from lower line of upper arms and curve outward. Blunt-pointed beard touches hero's left upper wing.

Horizontal lozenge shapes that depict fur are on body of animal to left.

COMMENTARY

The seal appears to be very worn.
    For comparative illustrations including PFS 297, see pl. 206f (arm positions of heroic control).

SEAL APPLICATION (SEE APPENDIX ONE: CONCORDANCE OF SEALS TO TABLETS IN VOLUME I)

PFS 297 occurs on the left edge of PF 98 and the reverse (inverted) and left edge of PF 99, with PFS 296* (III) also applied on the reverse of each tablet. On the reverse of PF 99 the seal is applied directly under PFS 296* (III). Impressions exhibit marked distortion and are difficult to read. Of the three partial rollings, two display the hero in the center; one displays the animal to the left of the hero in the center. PF 98 and PF 99 are both dated 498/497 B.C.

BIBLIOGRAPHY

Garrison 1988, pp. 273–76; Garrison 1998, p. 121 (n. 15); Garrison and Dion 1999, p. 9 (n. 19).

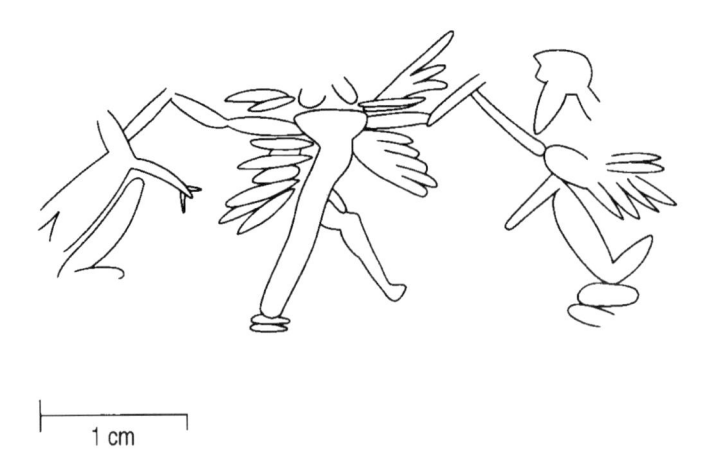

Cat.No. 125   PFS 321

Seal Type:	Cylinder	Photograph:	Pl. 73c
Earliest Dated Application:	ND	Typology and Style:	I-A.17 — Plausibly Antique: Assyro-Babylonian Cut Style
Preserved Height of Image:	2.00 cm (incomp.)	Preserved Length of Image:	4.30 cm (incomp.)
Estimated Height of Original Seal:	NA	Estimated Diameter of Original Seal:	NA
Number of Impressions:	4	Quality of Impressions:	Fair

Completeness of Image: Large segment of middle of design survives

DESCRIPTION OF SEAL AS IMPRESSED IMAGE

Four-winged hero faces right, arms bent, and holds rampant winged creature of uncertain type to left and rampant winged human-headed creature of uncertain type to right, each by upper foreleg. Hero, in active striding pose, raises bent forward leg.

Each creature holds upper foreleg straight and extends it upward toward hero's upper wing; lower foreleg is straight and held diagonally downward in front of its body. Lower foreleg of creature to left terminates in three-pronged projection.

Hero appears to wear Assyrian garment that leaves forward leg exposed. Rounded beard rests above his left shoulder; rounded coiffure rests at back of neck. Hoof-like foot terminates hero's forward leg; foot composed of two stacked lozenges emerges from garment at rear leg.

Creature to right has long pointed beard that rests over its upper foreleg; rounded(?) narrow coiffure hangs diagonally downward.

COMMENTARY

The seal is very large, with much open space. The schematic Cut Style of the engraving may indicate that it is an heirloom from a Neo-Assyrian or Neo-Babylonian context, although production in the style may well have continued into the early Achaemenid period.[33] The shape indicated along the hero's raised thigh is perhaps more likely to represent a sheath or a stray wing feather than a penis (since the hero appears to be clothed), but see PFS 152 (Cat.No. 295) for nude hero with penis indicated. Note oddities of treatment of hero's feet, the discrete shapes composing the creature to the left as well as the two lozenge-shaped elements under the creature at right.

For comparative illustrations including PFS 321, see pls. 199a (feet and shoes), 201e (heroes as winged humans), 211b (heroic attitudes of control encounter), and 273e (open compositions).

---

33. Cut Style seals have also been found in Neo-Elamite levels at Susa (see de Miroschedji 1982, pp. 51–56). The origin of the Cut Style is generally located in Babylonia (see Collon 1987, pp. 80–81; Garrison 1988, pp. 82–90; Wittmann 1992, pp. 218–24). For the style of PFS 321, see, for example, Herbordt 1992, pl. 2, no. 4, pl. 3, no. 17; Wittmann 1992, pls. 34, no. 140; 25, nos. 149–51, 153–54; 36, nos. 166–67.

SEAL APPLICATION (SEE *APPENDIX ONE: CONCORDANCE OF SEALS TO TABLETS IN VOLUME I*)

PFS 321 occurs on the reverse (inverted), bottom edge, upper edge, and right edge of PF 9. Of the four partial rollings, one displays the hero in the center; two preserve only the hero and the creature to right; one displays the creature to the left of the hero in the center. The date of PF 9 is unknown.

BIBLIOGRAPHY

Garrison 1988, pp. 439–40, 531; Garrison 1998, p. 121 (n. 15).

PFS 1017   Cat.No. 126

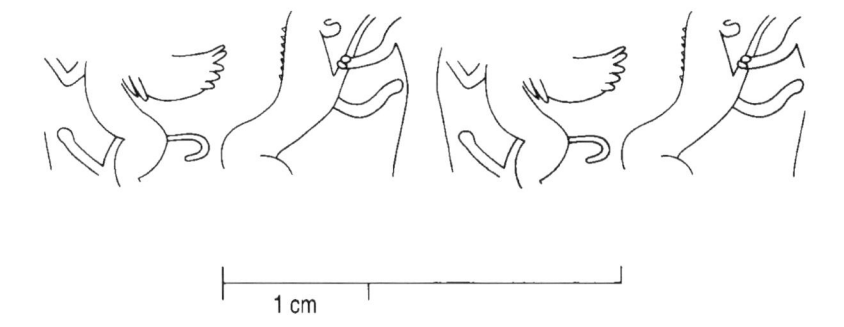

Seal Type:	Cylinder	Photograph:	Pl. 74a
Earliest Dated Application:	ND	Typology and Style:	I-A.17 — Fortification Style
Preserved Height of Image:	1.20 cm (incomp.)	Preserved Length of Image:	2.80 cm (comp.)
Estimated Height of Original Seal:	NA	Estimated Diameter of Original Seal:	0.90 cm
Number of Impressions:	1	Quality of Impression:	Fair

Completeness of Image: Large segment of middle of design survives along its complete length

DESCRIPTION OF SEAL AS IMPRESSED IMAGE

Hero, arms bent (only right arm preserved), holds rampant lion to left by upper foreleg and rampant winged bull or lion creature to right.

Lion holds upper foreleg slightly bent and extends it upward toward hero's head; lower foreleg is curved and extended downward toward hero's waist. Creature to right holds one foreleg bent and extends it upward toward hero's chest. Creature raises bent forward hind leg toward hero's leg; tail extends horizontally outward, curling downward at its end.

Hero wears robe.

Lion's mane is rendered by crisp serrated edge along contour of neck; mouth is open in roar.

SEAL APPLICATION (SEE *APPENDIX ONE: CONCORDANCE OF SEALS TO TABLETS IN VOLUME I*)

PFS 1017 occurs on the upper edge of PF 1045. The rolling preserves the entire length of the seal design and displays the hero in the center. The date of PF 1045 is unknown.

BIBLIOGRAPHY

Garrison 1988, pp. 302, 304.

Cat.No. 127   PFS 1023

Seal Type:	Cylinder	Photograph:	Pl. 74c
Earliest Dated Application:	500/499 B.C.	Typology and Style:	I-A.17 — Fortification Style
Preserved Height of Image:	1.60 cm (incomp.)	Preserved Length of Image:	3.30 cm (incomp.)
Estimated Height of Original Seal:	NA	Estimated Diameter of Original Seal:	NA
Number of Impressions:	1	Quality of Impression:	Good

Completeness of Image: Large segment of middle of design survives

DESCRIPTION OF SEAL AS IMPRESSED IMAGE

Hero faces right, arms bent, and holds rampant winged human-headed bull or lion creature by upper foreleg (left) and rampant animal of uncertain type at right (only partially preserved).

Creature to left holds upper foreleg curved and extends it diagonally upward; lower foreleg is straight and extended diagonally downward in front of its body; long thin tail curls upward. Animal to right holds one foreleg straight and extends it diagonally downward.

Hero wears Assyrian garment that leaves forward leg exposed. Long, narrow, rounded beard rests over hero's left shoulder; rounded coiffure curls upward slightly at back of neck.

Creature to left appears to have close-cropped beard; rounded coiffure rests at back of neck. Wing has two rows of feathers indicated.

In lower field between hero and creature to left is uncertain fragmentary element.

In lower field between hero and animal to right is small tree with narrow lenticular trunk and pointed branches diminishing in length toward top (as on certain conifers); two-pronged fronds(?) emerge to either side of tree (apparently growing from base).

COMMENTARY

This is a large and handsomely carved seal. The unidentifiable object in the lower field between the hero and the creature to the left may be the vestiges of a schematic animal form (possibly a pedestal creature?).[34] The two pronged elements flanking the little tree are perhaps vestiges of additional floral motifs, but compare PFS 971 (Cat.No. 171) for a completely preserved conifer with arm-like appendages projecting from lower trunk. See Garrison 1988 for the important artist of PFS 1023, who works close to the Court Style.

For comparative illustrations including PFS 1023, see pls. 207a (arm positions of heroic control), 235c (human-headed/human-faced creatures), and 257e (conifers).

SEAL APPLICATION (SEE APPENDIX ONE: CONCORDANCE OF SEALS TO TABLETS IN VOLUME I)

PFS 1023 occurs on the left edge of PF 1048. The partial rolling is very clear and carefully displays the hero in the center. PF 1048 is dated 500/499 B.C.

BIBLIOGRAPHY

Dusinberre 1997b, p. 128 (n. 131); Garrison 1988, pp. 352–56, 381, 480, 485–86, 495; Garrison and Dion 1999, p. 11 (n. 36).

---

34. Compare similar odd form on a fragmentary Neo-Assyrian seal impression from Nimrud which Herbordt interprets as an extremely abstract rendering of an animal: Herbordt 1992, p. 202, pl. 9, no. 11b.

PFS 1437s

Cat.No. 128

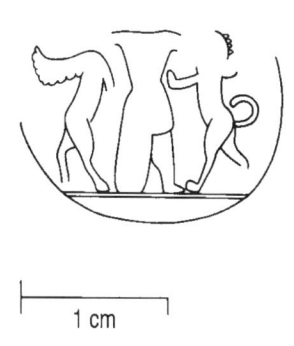

Seal Type:	Stamp, Circular Face	Photograph:	Pl. 74e
Earliest Dated Application:	494/493 B.C.	Typology and Style:	I-A.17 — Mixed Styles II
Preserved Height of Image:	1.30 cm (incomp.)	Preserved Width of Image:	1.80 cm (comp.)
Number of Impressions:	1	Quality of Impression:	Poor

Completeness of Image: Segment of middle and lower edge of design survives

DESCRIPTION OF SEAL AS IMPRESSED IMAGE

Hero moves to right in striding pose and holds rampant winged bull or lion creature to left and rampant lion to right.

Winged creature holds one foreleg (only partially preserved) straight and extends it downward in front of its body. Lion holds one foreleg straight, paw upturned, and extends it toward hero's waist; other foreleg (only partially preserved) is held up and away from body. Paw of forward hind leg steps on foot of hero's forward leg; tail curls upward.

Hero wears Assyrian garment that leaves forward leg exposed below knee.

Mane of lion is rendered by crisp serrated edge along contour of neck.

Heroic encounter is set on ground line.

COMMENTARY

Based on Q texts protocol, PFS 1437s should belong to the woman Mizapirzaka, who in year 28 (494/493 B.C.) received beer rations on her way to Persepolis under the authority (*halmi*) of Bakabana. PF 1546 preserves the only occurrence of the name Mizapirzaka in the PF texts.

The ground line is not common on stamp seals in the PFS corpus of hero scenes; compare PFS 919s (Cat.No. 259), PFS 1260s (Cat.No. 184), PFS 1321s (Cat.No. 176), and PFS 1624s (Cat.No. 261). The control encounter, owing to its spatial demands, is less common on stamp seals in the PFS corpus and in Achaemenid glyptic generally than is the combat encounter.[35]

The stamp is large and appears to have had a flat face and a quite tight circular contour. For probable seal shape, see *Appendix Four: Stamp Seals in Volume I Grouped by Apparent Contour of Seal Face* and accompanying figure 9, nos. 3a, 4c, or 5a.

For comparative illustrations including PFS 1437s, see pls. 175e (Assyrian garments), 243g (mixed animals/creatures), 275g (stamp seals), 277d (ground lines on stamp seals), and 284f (personal seals of women).

SEAL APPLICATION (SEE *APPENDIX ONE: CONCORDANCE OF SEALS TO TABLETS IN VOLUME I*)

PFS 1437s occurs on the obverse of PF 1546. The partial application is oriented along the horizontal axis of the tablet. PF 1546 is dated 494/493 B.C.

BIBLIOGRAPHY

Garrison 1988, pp. 370–74.

---

[35]. Compare, however, the Achaemenid heroic control scene with ground line on an ovoid stamp from Susa (Amiet 1972, p. 286; pl. 190, no. 2228 [= Sb 6846]); and an unprovenanced agate conoid of approximately the same face dimensions as PFS 1437s (Buchanan and Moorey 1988, no. 450).

| Cat.No. 129 | PFS 944 |

Seal Type:	Cylinder	Photograph:	Pl. 75a
Earliest Dated Application:	ND	Typology and Style:	I-A.17 — Modeled Style
Preserved Height of Image:	2.00 cm (incomp.)	Preserved Length of Image:	3.40 cm (incomp.)
Estimated Height of Original Seal:	NA	Estimated Diameter of Original Seal:	NA
Number of Impressions:	2	Quality of Impressions:	Fair

Completeness of Image: Large section of middle of design is preserved

DESCRIPTION OF SEAL AS IMPRESSED IMAGE

Hero faces right, arms bent, and holds rampant winged human-faced lion creature to right by upper foreleg.

Of animal to left of hero, only termination of foreleg near hero's waist is definitely preserved. Presumably, however, rampant bull preserved at far right of impressions represents this same animal. Bull moves toward hero but turns its head away from him; tail curls upward and thickens.

Creature to right of hero holds upper foreleg (only partially preserved) straight and extends it diagonally upward in front of its head; lower foreleg is straight and extended toward hero's waist; short straight tail extends diagonally upward, thickening. Creature has long squared beard that curves over chest, suggesting a lion's ruff as well as a human's beard.

Hero wears Assyrian garment that leaves forward leg exposed below mid-thigh.

Creature to right of hero has two wings indicated, lower extending diagonally downward from its back.

Rhomb is in lower field between hero and winged creature.

COMMENTARY

The seal is large and appears to have been well carved. The design of PFS 944 is stylistically very close to PFS 1387 (Cat.No. 72) and PFS 1485 (Cat.No. 112). For other seals in Volume I that have a rhomb in the design, see PFS 38 (Cat.No. 16) and PFS 1026 (Cat.No. 156). The human face of the lion creature, with articulated lips and nose emerging from the area that would normally display a lion's open jaws, is a distinctive feature of this seal.

For comparative illustrations including PFS 944, see pl. 249g (rhombs).

SEAL APPLICATION (SEE *APPENDIX ONE: CONCORDANCE OF SEALS TO TABLETS IN VOLUME I*)

PFS 944 occurs on the reverse (inverted) and left edge of PF 818. No other seal is used on the tablet. The partial rolling on the reverse displays the creature to the right of the hero in the center. The partial rolling on the left edge preserves only the creature and the bull. On the reverse the seal clearly was applied before the text since several cuneiform wedges cut into the bottom of the impression. The date of PF 818 is unknown.

BIBLIOGRAPHY

Garrison 1988, pp. 199–201, 203, 476.

PFS 494 — Cat.No. 130

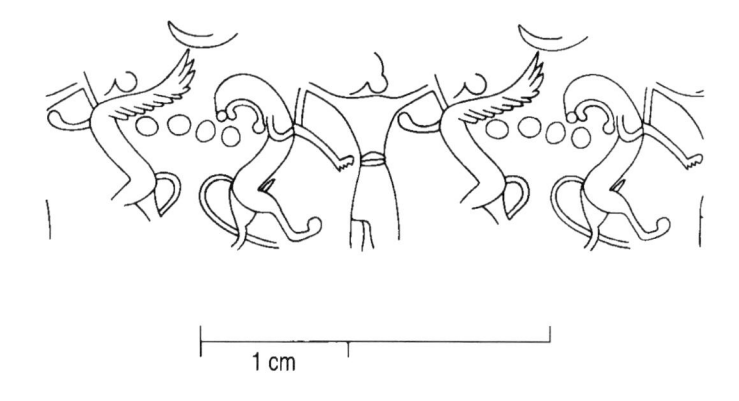

Seal Type:	Cylinder	Photograph:	Pl. 75c
Earliest Dated Application:	497/496 B.C.	Typology and Style:	I-A.17 — Fortification Style
Preserved Height of Image:	1.60 cm (incomp.)	Preserved Length of Image:	2.40 cm (comp.)
Estimated Height of Original Seal:	1.80 cm	Estimated Diameter of Original Seal:	0.80 cm
Number of Impressions:	4	Quality of Impressions:	Poor-fair

Completeness of Image: Almost complete except for upper edge and lower edge

DESCRIPTION OF SEAL AS IMPRESSED IMAGE

Hero faces left, arms straight at diagonal above shoulders, and holds rampant lion to left and rampant winged human-headed lion creature to right by upper foreleg.

Lion moves toward hero but turns its head away from him. Lion holds upper foreleg (only partially preserved) straight and extends it diagonally upward; lower foreleg is slightly curved, paw upturned and toes splayed, and extended downward toward hero's waist. Lion raises forward hind leg toward hero's leg; long tail curves downward between its hind legs. Creature to right holds upper foreleg (only partially preserved) straight and extends it diagonally upward; lower foreleg is curved and extended toward hero's chest; tail (only partially preserved) curls downward.

Hero wears double-belted Assyrian garment that leaves forward leg exposed below knee. Rounded coiffure rests at back of hero's neck.

Lion to left has mouth open in roar and is ithyphallic. Creature to right has rounded coiffure at back of its neck.

In upper terminal field is crescent; in middle terminal field are four large dots arranged in horizontal line.

COMMENTARY

In Achaemenid glyptic the snouts and mouths of lions are often highlighted in order to exaggerate the effect of a snarl or roar, and on this seal it is especially dramatic.[36] The four large dots in the terminal field of PFS 494 have no parallel in Volume I. In scale and disposition they resemble the four-dot segment of the seven-dot Pleiades formation as the cluster of dots is arranged on several Neo-Assyrian seals (e.g., Herbordt 1992, pl. 6, nos. 1 and 6). But there is absolutely no indication of three additional dots here lined up under the three at left in the visible row of four.

For comparative illustrations including PFS 494, see pls. 223d (lions and lion creatures), 243c (mixed animals/creatures), 250g (crescents), and 254f (various devices and symbols).

SEAL APPLICATION (SEE APPENDIX ONE: CONCORDANCE OF SEALS TO TABLETS IN VOLUME I)

PFS 494 occurs twice on the reverse (inverted) and once on the bottom edge and upper edge of PF 223. On the reverse the two impressions are applied one directly above the other. All four applications preserve the entire

---

36. Examples are numerous, but see in particular the cylinder seal excavated at Pasargadae (Stronach 1978, pl. 162a–b; Root 1999a, fig. 1, for a line drawing that illustrates the similarities well). On the Pasargadae seal, as on PFS 494, the lion's mouth is accented by a double line and drill work.

length of the seal design; one displays the hero in the center; one displays the hero and the creature to right in the center; one displays the lion to the left of the hero in the center; one displays the creature to the right of the hero in the center. PF 223 is dated 497/496 B.C.

BIBLIOGRAPHY

Garrison 1988, pp. 307–08.

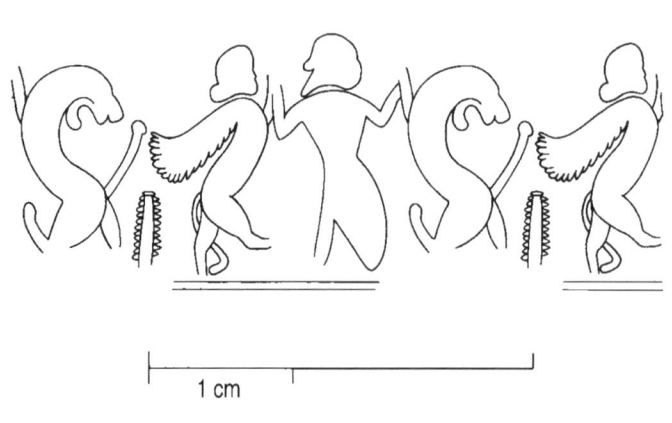

Cat.No. 131   PFS 731

Seal Type:	Cylinder	Photographs:	Pl. 76a–b
Earliest Dated Application:	499/498 B.C.	Typology and Style:	I-A.17 — Fortification Style
Preserved Height of Image:	1.70 cm (incomp.)	Preserved Length of Image:	2.70 cm (comp.)
Estimated Height of Original Seal:	1.80 cm	Estimated Diameter of Original Seal:	0.90 cm
Number of Impressions:	2	Quality of Impressions:	Fair

Completeness of Image: Almost complete except for upper edge and portions of lower edge

DESCRIPTION OF SEAL AS IMPRESSED IMAGE

Hero faces left, arms bent, and holds rampant winged human-headed lion creature to left and rampant lion to right, each by foreleg.

Winged creature holds foreleg (only partially preserved) curved and extends it diagonally upward in front of its head. Creature raises bent forward hind leg toward hero; long tail curves down between its hind legs with tufted termination. Lion moves toward hero but turns its head away from him. Lion holds foreleg (only partially preserved) straight and extends it upward in front of its neck; lion raises bent forward hind leg toward hero; thick tail extends diagonally upward with tufted termination.

Hero wears Assyrian garment that leaves forward leg exposed. Beard terminates in blunt point over hero's right shoulder; large rounded coiffure rests at back of neck.

Winged creature appears to be beardless; rounded coiffure rests at back of neck. Lion opens mouth in roar.

Stylized plant in form of vertical element with flat top and serrated edges is in lower terminal field.

Portion of line border is preserved at bottom of design below hero and creature to left.

COMMENTARY

The engraving is bold and well executed. See Garrison 1988 for artist and related seals.

For comparative illustrations including PFS 731, see pls. 243d (mixed animals/creatures) and 260d (various plants).

SEAL APPLICATION (SEE APPENDIX ONE: CONCORDANCE OF SEALS TO TABLETS IN VOLUME I)

PFS 731 occurs on the reverse of both PF 502 and PF 626. Both rollings preserve the entire length of the seal design; that on PF 502 displays the hero and the lion to the right in the center; that on PF 626 displays the lion and the winged creature in the center. PF 502 and PF 626 are both dated 499/498 B.C.

BIBLIOGRAPHY

Garrison 1988, pp. 326–30, 345.

PFS 1102 — Cat.No. 132

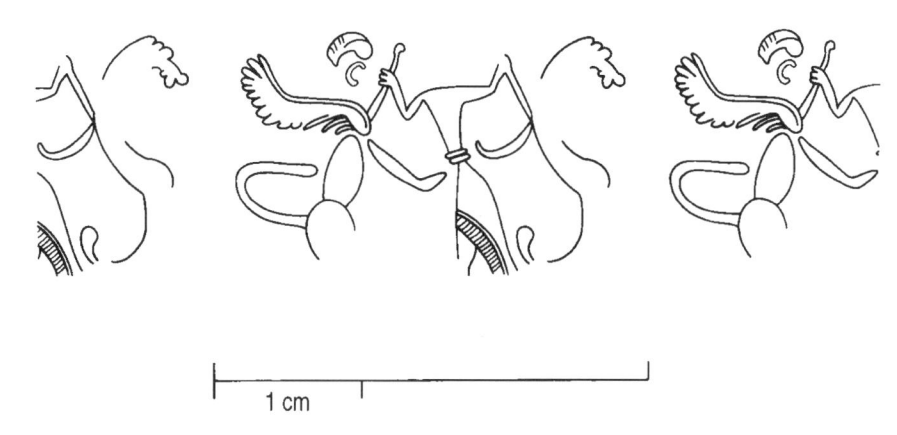

Seal Type: Cylinder	Photograph: Pl. 77a
Earliest Dated Application: 497/496 B.C.	Typology and Style: I-A.17 — Linear Styles
Preserved Height of Image: 1.60 cm (incomp.)	Preserved Length of Image: 3.00 cm (comp.)
Estimated Height of Original Seal: NA	Estimated Diameter of Original Seal: 1.00 cm
Number of Impressions: 2	Quality of Impressions: Fair

Completeness of Image: Segment of middle of design survives along its complete length

DESCRIPTION OF SEAL AS IMPRESSED IMAGE

Hero moves to left, arms bent, and holds rampant winged, apparently human-headed, lion creature to left and rampant lion to right, each by upper foreleg.

Creature to left holds upper foreleg straight and extends it upward toward hero's head; lower foreleg is straight, paw upturned, and extended downward toward hero's waist; long thick tail curves upward. Lion to right moves toward hero but turns its head away from him. Lion holds upper foreleg straight and extends it upward toward hero's head; lower foreleg is curved and extended downward toward hero's waist. Lion raises curved forward hind leg toward hero's leg.

Hero wears double-belted Assyrian garment that leaves forward leg exposed below mid-thigh; fringe is indicated along front edge of garment over knee of forward leg and rear leg.

Human-headed creature has mouth open.

COMMENTARY

The awkward figures and coarse engraving are typical of seals in the Linear Styles. The open mouth of the human-headed creature is most unusual.

For comparative illustrations including PFS 1102, see pls. 177e (Assyrian garments with detailing preserved), 211g (heroic attitudes of control encounter), and 243e (mixed animals/creatures).

SEAL APPLICATION (SEE *APPENDIX ONE: CONCORDANCE OF SEALS TO TABLETS IN VOLUME I*)

PFS 1102 occurs on the left edge of both PF 1164 and PF 1227. PFS 130 (Cat.No. 300) and PFS 1101 (Cat.No. 297) are also applied on the reverse or upper edge of each tablet. Both rollings of PFS 1102 preserve the entire length of the seal design; that on PF 1164 displays the hero in the center; that on PF 1227 displays the creature to the left of the hero in the center. PF 1164 and PF 1227 are both dated 497/496 B.C.

BIBLIOGRAPHY

Garrison 1988, pp. 437–39, 496.

Cat.No. 133 PFS 334

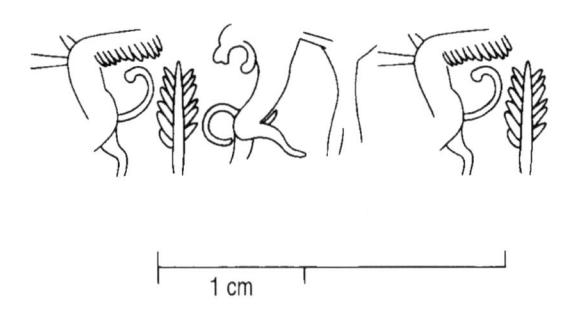

[figure: seal impression drawing with 1 cm scale bar]

Seal Type:	Cylinder	Photograph:	Pl. 77c
Earliest Dated Application:	494/493(?) B.C.	Typology and Style:	I-A.17 — Fortification Style
Preserved Height of Image:	1.10 cm (incomp.)	Preserved Length of Image:	2.30 cm (comp.)
Estimated Height of Original Seal:	NA	Estimated Diameter of Original Seal:	0.70 cm
Number of Impressions:	3	Quality of Impressions:	Poor

Completeness of Image: Almost complete except for upper edge and lower edge

DESCRIPTION OF SEAL AS IMPRESSED IMAGE

Hero apparently moves to left, arms straight, and holds rampant lion to left by foreleg and rampant winged lion creature to right, apparently also by foreleg.

Lion moves toward hero but turns its head away from him. Lion apparently holds one foreleg (only partially preserved) straight and extends it diagonally upward. Lion raises slightly bent forward hind leg toward hero; tail curls downward. Winged creature holds upper foreleg (only partially preserved) straight and extends it upward toward hero's head; lower foreleg (only partially preserved) is straight and extended outward toward hero's arm; tail curls upward with tufted termination.

Hero appears to wear Assyrian garment that leaves forward leg exposed.

Lion has mouth open in roar and is ithyphallic.

Small tree with narrow lenticular trunk and short pointed branches (as in certain conifers) is in terminal field.

COMMENTARY

See Garrison 1988 for the artist and related seals. The tree resembles the terminal motif on PFS 496 (Cat.No. 108).

For comparative illustrations including PFS 334, see pls. 243b (mixed animals/creatures) and 257b (conifers).

SEAL APPLICATION (SEE *APPENDIX ONE: CONCORDANCE OF SEALS TO TABLETS IN VOLUME I*)

PFS 334 occurs twice on the reverse and once on the upper edge of PF 26. The upper rolling on the reverse originally was long, but most of it is now destroyed, and it is unclear what elements were in the center. The lower rolling on the reverse is placed directly under the upper one, but the seal is inverted. It is long, preserving almost two full repeats of the figural design. In this manner the hero is placed in the center. The rolling on the upper edge also preserves almost two full repeats of the figural design and displays the tree in the terminal field in the center. PF 26 is dated 494/493(?) B.C.

BIBLIOGRAPHY

Garrison 1988, pp. 309–12.

PFS 480   Cat.No. 134

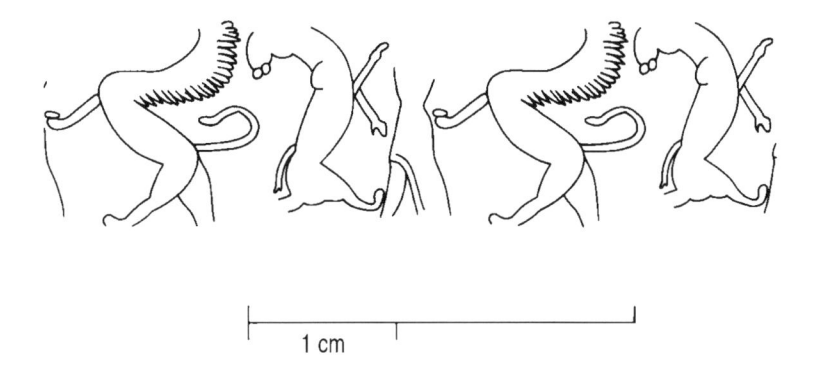

Seal Type:	Cylinder	Photograph:	Pl. 78a
Earliest Dated Application:	499/498 B.C.	Typology and Style:	I-A.17 — Modeled Style
Preserved Height of Image:	1.40 cm (incomp.)	Preserved Length of Image:	2.60 cm (comp.)
Estimated Height of Original Seal:	NA	Estimated Diameter of Original Seal:	0.80 cm
Number of Impressions:	3	Quality of Impressions:	Fair

Completeness of Image: Segment of middle of design survives along its complete length

Description of Seal as Impressed Image

Hero moves to left in striding pose.

To hero's left, rampant animal of uncertain type moves toward hero but turns its head away from him. Animal holds upper foreleg straight and extends it upward toward hero's head; lower foreleg is straight and extended downward toward hero's leg. Animal raises hind leg and places paw on hero's leg; short tail curves downward with forked termination. To right, rampant winged lion creature moves toward hero. Creature holds lower foreleg straight and extends it downward toward hero's waist. Creature raises straight forward hind leg toward hero; long tail extends horizontally outward, then curls upward, slightly bent at its termination.

Hero wears Assyrian garment that leaves forward leg exposed below knee; decorated border is along front hem of lower garment.

Commentary

Because the upper part of the body of the hero is not preserved, the composition cannot be typed with certainty. It may be a combat encounter. The engraving is of a very high quality, although forelegs of animal at left are oddly stick-like and lack integration with the shoulder.

Seal Application (see *Appendix One: Concordance of Seals to Tablets in Volume I*)

PFS 480 occurs twice on the reverse (inverted) and once on the upper edge of PF 203. On the reverse the two rollings are placed one directly above the other. The lower rolling on the reverse preserves the entire length of the seal design and displays the creature to the right of the hero in the center. The partial upper rolling on the reverse displays the hero in the center. The partial rolling on the upper edge preserves only the animal and the creature. On the reverse the seal clearly was applied before the text since several cuneiform wedges cut into the bottom of the upper impression. PF 203 is dated 499/498 B.C.

Bibliography

Garrison 1988, pp. 217, 222–23, 247–48.

Cat.No. 135 PFS 217

Seal Type:	Cylinder	Photograph:	Pl. 78c
Earliest Dated Application:	498/497 B.C.	Typology and Style:	I-A.17 — Fortification Style
Preserved Height of Image:	1.90 cm (comp.)	Preserved Length of Image:	2.80 cm (comp.)
Estimated Height of Original Seal:	1.90 cm	Estimated Diameter of Original Seal:	0.90 cm
Number of Impressions:	4	Quality of Impressions:	Fair

Completeness of Image: Complete except for upper edge and lower edge

DESCRIPTION OF SEAL AS IMPRESSED IMAGE

Hero faces left in striding pose, arms straight, and holds rampant human-headed creature of uncertain type (at left) and rampant bird-headed lion creature (at right) by upper foreleg.

Each creature moves toward hero but turns its head away from him. Each creature holds upper foreleg straight and extends it upward in front of its neck; lower foreleg is straight (paw upturned on creature to right) and extended downward toward hero's waist. Each creature raises forward hind leg slightly toward hero. Bird's tail of human-headed creature to left is short, with two feathers curving downward; lion's tail of bird-headed lion creature to right curls upward with tufted termination.

Hero wears belted Assyrian garment that leaves forward leg exposed below knee. Trace of rounded beard rests over right arm; rounded coiffure is at back of hero's neck.

Creature to left has pointed coiffure at back of its head; pointed beard defines featureless face. Creature is ithyphallic. Bird-headed creature to right has two ears emerging from back of its head; mouth is open.

Edge of seal is preserved at top and bottom of design under creature to right.

COMMENTARY

The elongated forms are typical of many seal designs in the Fortification Style.
For comparative illustrations including PFS 217, see pl. 192c (rounded coiffures).

SEAL APPLICATION (SEE *APPENDIX ONE: CONCORDANCE OF SEALS TO TABLETS IN VOLUME I*)

PFS 217 occurs on the upper edge and left edge of PF 114 and the reverse (inverted) and left edge of PF 115. No other seal is used on the tablets. In three impressions the seal is rolled for at least one complete turn, preserving the entire length of the seal design. Of these three applications, two display the hero and the creature to left in the center; one displays the creature to the right in the center. The remaining partial rolling displays the hero in the center. On the reverse of PF 115 the seal clearly was applied before the text since several cuneiform wedges cut into bottom of the impression. PF 114 and PF 115 are both dated 498/497 B.C.

BIBLIOGRAPHY

Garrison 1988, pp. 307–08.

PFS 1204 — Cat.No. 136

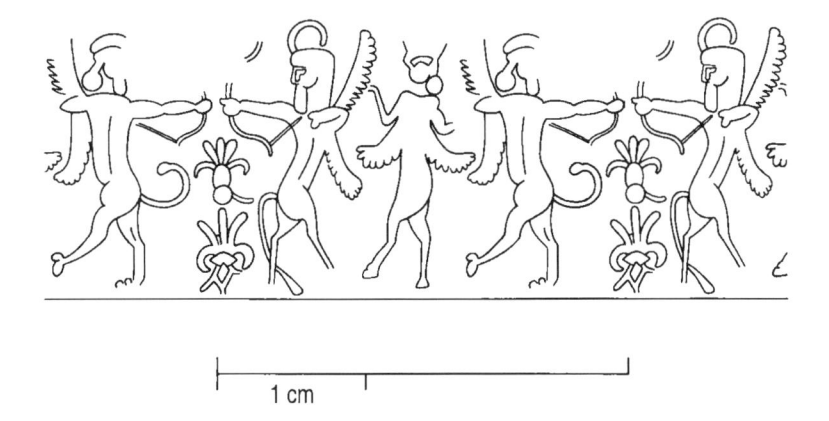

Seal Type:	Cylinder	Photograph:	Pl. 79a
Earliest Dated Application:	500 B.C.	Typology and Style:	I-A.17 — Modeled Style
Preserved Height of Image:	1.90 cm (incomp.)	Preserved Length of Image:	2.80 cm (comp.)
Estimated Height of Original Seal:	2.00 cm	Estimated Diameter of Original Seal:	0.90 cm
Number of Impressions:	1	Quality of Impression:	Good

Completeness of Image: Almost complete except for upper edge and details

DESCRIPTION OF SEAL AS IMPRESSED IMAGE

Hero is rendered as winged bull creature with human head, shoulders, and arms, with (tail-less) lower body and legs of bull. Hero faces left, arms bent, and holds rampant human-faced winged bull creature with human shoulders and arms by upper wing (at left) and (at right) rampant human-headed winged lion creature with human shoulders and arms by upper or lower wing (link not preserved). Hero raises forward leg.

Each creature moves toward hero but turns its head away from him to draw bow; each creature raises forward hind leg. On each creature two wings are indicated along vertical axis of body, upper extending diagonally upward, lower extending diagonally downward. Creature to left has long tail that curves downward between its hind legs with tufted termination. Creature to right has long tail that curls upward with tufted termination.

Hero has two horizontally disposed upward-curved wings, one on either side of torso below its arms. Human head is apparently beardless or close-shaved; round coiffure rests at back of neck.

Creature to left has long squared beard that rests across its right shoulder; long curved horn emerges from front of its head. Creature to right has rounded beard that rests over its left shoulder; rounded coiffure rests at back of neck. Creature to right wears low domed headdress.

In terminal field is elaborate stacked floral element, which serves also as focal point for archer creatures who form heraldic group shooting toward each other across the floral element.

Edge of seal is preserved at bottom of design.

COMMENTARY

The style is an unusual mix of a heavy Modeled Style (in the forms of the two archer creatures, cf. PFS 16* [Cat.No. 22]) and the Fortification Style. The rendering of the hero is, however, very unsteady, with a strange linearity in the upper body; compare PFS 884 (Cat.No. 123). The composition is striking and unusual among the images of heroic encounter in the PFS corpus. For the elaborate floral element, compare PFS 162 (Cat.No. 249) and PFS 225 (Cat.No. 46).

For comparative illustrations including PFS 1204, see pls. 200e (heroes as various composite creatures), 232d (animals/creatures with distinctive perspectival elements), 235e (human-headed/human-faced creatures), 241j (heroic encounters fused with heraldic motifs), 246g (bows, arrows, quivers), 256h (stylized floral elements), and 269h (terminal field motifs other than inscriptions).

220   *SEALS ON THE PERSEPOLIS FORTIFICATION TABLETS, VOLUME I: IMAGES OF HEROIC ENCOUNTER*

SEAL APPLICATION (SEE *APPENDIX ONE: CONCORDANCE OF SEALS TO TABLETS IN VOLUME I*)

PFS 1204 occurs on the reverse of PF 1262. The rolling is long, having been carefully applied to display the hero in the center with full repeats of the floral element on each end and a partial repeat of the winged human-headed creature at far left. The seal clearly was applied before the text since several cuneiform wedges cut into the bottom of the impression. PF 1262 is dated 500 B.C.

BIBLIOGRAPHY

Garrison 1988, pp. 450–52; Garrison 1998, p. 121 (n. 15).

Cat.No. 137   PFS 1202

Seal Type:	Cylinder	Photograph:	Pl. 79c
Earliest Dated Application:	ND	Typology and Style:	I-A.17 — Fortification Style
Preserved Height of Image:	1.40 cm (comp.)	Preserved Length of Image:	3.00 cm (incomp.)
Estimated Height of Original Seal:	1.40 cm	Estimated Diameter of Original Seal:	NA
Number of Impressions:	1	Quality of Impression:	Poor

Completeness of Image: Large segment of the complete design survives for most of its length

DESCRIPTION OF SEAL AS IMPRESSED IMAGE

Four-winged hero faces left. Hero has ovoid bird's torso and human-form lower body. From midsection of torso thin appendages emerge as arms; hero holds rampant winged bull creature to left by horn and rampant animal of uncertain type to right by foreleg.

Bull creature moves away from hero but turns its head back toward him. Bull creature holds upper foreleg (partially preserved) straight and extends it diagonally upward; lower foreleg (partially preserved) is curved and extended slightly downward; tail curves downward, hooked upward at its end. Rampant animal to right holds upper foreleg straight and extends it outward toward hero's chest; lower foreleg is curved and extended downward toward hero's lower wing.

Hero wears Assyrian garment that leaves forward leg exposed. One pair of wings emerges near top of torso curved upward on either side of hero's head; other pair emerges from short torso just below hero's arms, slanting diagonally downward and then curved upward at ends. Hero wears short rounded beard and has short-cropped coiffure. High boot(?) or unusual leg segmentation is shown on hero's forward leg.

Apparently in terminal field, rampant animal of uncertain type at far left of preserved impression moves to left, turning its head back to right (see commentary); tail (only partially preserved) curves downward.

Edge of seal is preserved at top and bottom of design.

COMMENTARY

The rampant animal in the terminal field may in fact be a repeat of the one held by the hero. Although there appear to be differences in contour between the two animals, these could reflect distortions in the sole impression available. The animals (whether two or three) all move in the same direction, creating a strong horizontal dynamic across the design; see PFS 26 (Cat.No. 299), PFS 912 (Cat.No. 138), and PFS 1188 (Cat.No. 144) for a similar arrangement of the animals.

The particular hybrid character of the hero on PFS 1202 is unique among the images of heroic encounter in the PFS corpus.[37]

See Garrison 1988 for artist and related seals.

For comparative illustrations including PFS 1202, see pls. 196f (coiffures of unusual types), 199e (feet and shoes), 200d (heroes as various composite creatures), and 270e (compositions with strong unidirectional movement).

SEAL APPLICATION (SEE *APPENDIX ONE: CONCORDANCE OF SEALS TO TABLETS IN VOLUME I*)

PFS 1202 occurs on the reverse of PF 1261. The partial rolling is almost complete, and displays the hero and the winged creature to left in the center. The date of PF 1261 is unknown.

BIBLIOGRAPHY

Garrison 1988, pp. 309–12; Garrison 1998, p. 121 (n. 15); Garrison and Dion 1999, p. 9 (n. 19).

PFS 912   Cat.No. 138

Seal Type:	Cylinder	Photograph:	Pl. 80a
Earliest Dated Application:	496 B.C.	Typology and Style:	I-A.17 — Fortification Style
Preserved Height of Image:	1.10 cm (incomp.)	Preserved Length of Image:	2.00 cm (comp.)
Estimated Height of Original Seal:	NA	Estimated Diameter of Original Seal:	0.60 cm
Number of Impressions:	1	Quality of Impression:	Very poor

Completeness of Image: Segment of middle of design survives along its complete length

DESCRIPTION OF SEAL AS IMPRESSED IMAGE

Hero faces right, arms bent, and holds rampant lion to left by top of head (not preserved) and rampant bull to right by horn.

Lion moves toward and faces hero and is part of group of two crossed lions. Lion holds foreleg curved and extends it upward toward hero's waist. Bull moves away from hero but turns its head back toward him. Bull holds foreleg bent and extends it diagonally upward in front of its neck.

Hero wears Persian court robe with sleeves pushed up to reveal his bare arms. Narrow rounded coiffure rests at back of hero's neck.

Bull has curved horn (only partially preserved) emerging from front of its head. Other lion in crossed-lion group moves and faces away from hero. Lion holds forelegs curved, paws turned up, and extends them together in front of its body; mouth is open in roar.

---

37. The short-cropped coiffure is reminiscent of the genie figure carved in relief on the preserved doorjamb of the Gatehouse at Pasargadae. The hairstyle has been linked to Neo-Elamite royal coiffure (see Stronach 1978, pp. 51–55, pls. 43–46; Root 1979, p. 48 [following Porada 1965, p. 158 n. 8]).

In field above crossed lions, small marchant animal of uncertain type moves to left but turns head back to right. Animal raises one bent foreleg in front of its body; one ear is indicated and mouth is parted.

In terminal field, rampant lion(?) moves to left, holds foreleg bent, and extends it downward in front of its body. Large feature (only partially preserved) emerges from its back, apparently vestige of crossing animal forming group with better preserved animal.

COMMENTARY

Despite the small size of the seal, the design is exceptionally busy. This fusion of heroic *control* encounter with crossed animals is unique in the PFS corpus and is an unusual composition in the history of western Asiatic glyptic. The fusion of heroic *combat* encounter with crossed animals occurs on three seals in the PFS corpus: PFS 737 (Cat.No. 281), PFS 931* (Cat.No. 270), and PFS 952 (Cat.No. 227); see the commentary for PFS 931* (Cat.No. 270). Crossed animals independent of heroic encounter action occur on three seals herein: PFS 213 (Cat.No. 140), PFS 396 (Cat.No. 178), and PFS 990 (Cat.No. 256), in addition to PFS 912. A crossed-animal group sometimes serves as an archer's quarry on seals in Volume II, for example, PFS 163 (II); and crossed animals as a central compositional element are noteworthy in Volume III, for example, PFS 3 (III).

The two animals actually held by the hero in the heroic encounter of PFS 912 move in the same direction, creating a strong horizontal dynamic across the design; PFS 1188 (Cat.No. 144) and PFS 1202 (Cat.No. 137) have a similar arrangement of the animals; note also PFS 26 (Cat.No. 299), a fused control/combat encounter. PFS 912 was not included in Garrison 1988.

For comparative illustrations including PFS 912, see pls. 178g (Persian court robes with sleeves pushed up in deep swags), 194g (narrow rounded and/or pointed coiffures), 242b (heroic encounters fused with crossed animals), and 270c (compositions with strong unidirectional movement).

SEAL APPLICATION (SEE *APPENDIX ONE: CONCORDANCE OF SEALS TO TABLETS IN VOLUME I*)

PFS 912 occurs on the reverse of PF 786. The rolling is long, preserving almost two full repeats of the figural design. In this manner, the bull to the right of the hero and the crossed lions(?) in the terminal field are displayed in the center. PF 786 is dated 496 B.C.

I-A.18. ANIMALS OF UNCERTAIN TYPE

PFS 690 — Cat.No. 139

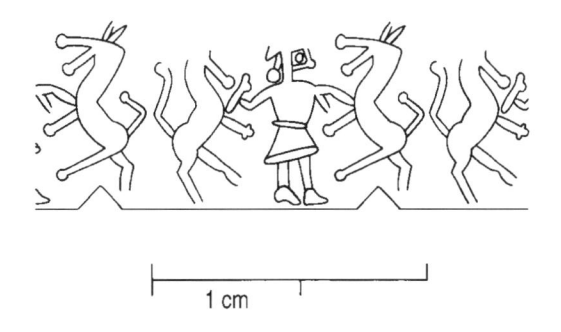

Seal Type:	Cylinder	Photograph:	Pl. 80c
Earliest Dated Application:	500/499 B.C.	Typology and Style:	I-A.18 — Diverse Styles
Preserved Height of Image:	1.30 cm (incomp.)	Preserved Length of Image:	1.90 cm (comp.)
Estimated Height of Original Seal:	1.40 cm	Estimated Diameter of Original Seal:	0.60 cm
Number of Impressions:	2	Quality of Impressions:	Fair

Completeness of Image: Complete except for details of upper edge and lower edge

DESCRIPTION OF SEAL AS IMPRESSED IMAGE

Hero faces right, arms bent, and holds two rampant animals of uncertain type by upper foreleg.

Animal to left holds upper foreleg straight and extends it upward toward hero's head; lower foreleg is straight and extended downward toward hero's waist. Animal raises straight forward hind leg toward hero; crooked tail extends diagonally upward with tufted termination. Animal to right holds upper foreleg bent and extends it upward to place paw on hero's shoulder; lower foreleg is straight and extended downward toward hero's waist. Animal raises straight forward hind leg toward hero; bent tail extends diagonally upward with tufted termination.

Hero wears belted tunic; decorative border is at hem of garment. Hero appears to wear ankle-length boots; domed(?) headdress has projection at back. Hero is apparently beardless; round coiffure rests at back of neck.

Animal to right has two long pointed ears emerging from top of its head. Each animal opens large mouth.

Edge of seal is preserved at bottom of design; chip or trace of seal cap is below animal to right.

COMMENTARY

The geometric treatment of the human head relates PFS 690 to PFS 2 (Cat.No. 3), PFS 20 (Cat.No. 145), PFS 740 (Cat.No. 146), PFS 1519 (Cat.No. 167), and PFS 1613 (Cat.No. 82). As in PFS 740 (Cat.No. 146), there is extensive use of the drill in the animal forms. PFS 690 and PFS 740 (Cat.No. 146) may be by the same artist. For the style, see the commentary on PFS 2 (Cat.No. 3).

For comparative illustrations including PFS 690, see pls. 185e (tunics), 193g (round coiffures), 199c (feet and shoes), and 276c (evidence of original seal caps).

SEAL APPLICATION (SEE APPENDIX ONE: CONCORDANCE OF SEALS TO TABLETS IN VOLUME I)

PFS 690 occurs twice on the reverse of PF 460, one application directly above the other. Both rollings preserve almost two full repeats of the figural design. The impressions show the exact same sequence, beginning and ending with a partial image of the animal to the left of the hero. In this manner the rollings display the animal to the left of the hero in the center. PF 460 is dated 500/499 B.C.

BIBLIOGRAPHY

Garrison 1988, pp. 447–50.

Cat.No. 140 PFS 213

|— 1 cm —|

Seal Type:	Cylinder	Photographs:	Pl. 81a–b
Earliest Dated Application:	500 B.C.	Typology and Style:	I-A.18 — Linear Styles
Preserved Height of Image:	1.40 cm (incomp.)	Preserved Length of Image:	3.30 cm (incomp.)
Estimated Height of Original Seal:	NA	Estimated Diameter of Original Seal:	NA
Number of Impressions:	2	Quality of Impressions:	Poor

Completeness of Image: Large segment of middle of design survives

DESCRIPTION OF SEAL AS IMPRESSED IMAGE

Hero in active striding pose moves to left, arms bent upward, and holds two rampant animals of uncertain type, one to left by upper foreleg.

Animal to left is suspended off ground. Head (with protruding tongue?) turns away from hero. Animal holds upper foreleg straight and extends it upward toward hero's head; lower foreleg is straight and extended downward toward its upper hind leg. Animal holds upper hind leg bent in front of its body; lower hind leg is bent and extended toward hero's leg; tail curves downward under its hindquarters. Animal to right holds lower foreleg straight, paw upturned, and extends it downward toward hero's leg; upper foreleg (not preserved) is presumably held upward to connect with hero's left arm. Tail (only partially preserved) curves downward.

Hero perhaps wears trousers.

In terminal field behind animal to right, small horned animal of undetermined type is vertically disposed, facing top edge of design. Animal holds one foreleg straight; one hind leg is bent. Animal displays single horn and short tail. Farther to right, two rampant long-necked winged horned-animal creatures of undetermined type cross their bodies. (Horn preserved only on creature facing left.) Body of marchant horned animal of undetermined type grows out of hindquarters of crossed creature that faces left; this horned animal faces right. Each rampant crossed creature holds forelegs together and extends them diagonally upward. Rampant creature facing right raises bent forward hind leg. Mane is rendered by crisp serrated edge along contour of neck of each composite creature.

At far right of impression are traces of what may be another animal of uncertain type vertically disposed in field. At far left of impression are tail and two legs of additional animal of uncertain type, apparently suspended on its back.

Portion of line border is preserved at upper edge of design.

COMMENTARY

Based upon Q texts protocol (PF 1440 and PF 1550), PFS 213 should belong to Zišanduš, who is described in PF 1550 as a *barrišdama* ("elite guide"). In both cases he is going from Susa to Kandahar.

The engraving style and the elaborate crowded composition have no parallels among the images of heroic encounter herein. It is tempting to suggest that the seal comes from some distant place, owing to its unusual features. It is thus interesting to note that the user of the seal is an elite guide who seems to specialize in trips to Kandahar.

The composition is not clear as preserved, especially along the right edge and left edge of the design. Crossed animals independent of the heroic encounter image also occur on PFS 396 (Cat.No. 178), PFS 912 (Cat.No. 138), and PFS 990 (Cat.No. 256). Crossed animals conflated with the heroic encounter occur on four seals: PFS 737 (Cat.No. 281), PFS 912 (Cat.No. 138), PFS 931* (Cat.No. 270), and PFS 952 (Cat.No. 227).

Crossed animals occur as a quarry of archers in Volume II and are a noteworthy focal point of compositions in Volume III. The addition of an animal growing out of one member of the crossed pair is a significant anomaly.

For comparative illustrations including PFS 213, see pls. 242e (crossed animals), 272e (dense compositions), and 288e (personal seals of elite guides [*barrišdama*]).

SEAL APPLICATION (SEE *APPENDIX ONE: CONCORDANCE OF SEALS TO TABLETS IN VOLUME I*)

PFS 213 occurs on the reverse of both PF 1440 and PF 1550. One rolling seems to preserve the entire length of the seal design and displays the vertically disposed animal in the terminal field in the center. Unfortunately, poor preservation nevertheless precludes adequate reading of the terminal field. The other (partial) rolling displays the crossed creatures in the center, but here again, poor quality of the impression inhibits our reading of the elements to its right. On the reverse of PF 1550 the seal clearly was applied before the text since several cuneiform wedges cut into the top of the impression. PF 1550 is the earliest dated tablet with PFS 213 and is dated 500 B.C.

BIBLIOGRAPHY

Garrison 1988, pp. 439–40.

PFS 501   Cat.No. 141

Seal Type:	Cylinder	Photograph:	Pl. 82a
Earliest Dated Application:	499/498 B.C.	Typology and Style:	I-A.18 — Fortification Style
Preserved Height of Image:	0.80 cm (incomp.)	Preserved Length of Image:	2.60 cm (incomp.)
Estimated Height of Original Seal:	NA	Estimated Diameter of Original Seal:	NA
Number of Impressions:	1	Quality of Impression:	Poor

Completeness of Image: Small segment of middle of design survives

DESCRIPTION OF SEAL AS IMPRESSED IMAGE

Hero moves to right, arms straight (only left arm preserved), and holds two rampant animals of uncertain type by upper foreleg (preserved only at right).

Animal to left holds lower foreleg straight and extends it downward toward hero's waist; crooked tail extends diagonally upward. Animal to right holds upper foreleg straight and extends it upward; lower foreleg is straight, paw upturned, and extended downward toward hero's waist.

Hero wears belted Assyrian garment that leaves forward leg exposed.

In terminal field, marchant animal of uncertain type moves to right but turns head back to left.

At far left of preserved impression, vestige of rampant animal may perhaps represent same animal held at hero's left.

COMMENTARY

The seal is small, even by the standards of the PFS corpus. The composition is probably as described, but since the hero's right arm is not preserved, it could conceivably be a combat encounter.

For comparative illustrations including PFS 501, see pl. 221c (animals and creatures of uncertain type).

SEAL APPLICATION (SEE *APPENDIX ONE: CONCORDANCE OF SEALS TO TABLETS IN VOLUME I*)

PFS 501 occurs on the upper edge of PF 225. The partial rolling displays the animal to the left of the hero in the center. PF 225 is dated 499/498 B.C.

BIBLIOGRAPHY

Garrison 1988, pp. 309–12.

Cat.No. 142　　　　　　　　　　　PFS 669

|─ 1 cm ─|

Seal Type:	Cylinder	Photograph:	Pl. 82c
Earliest Dated Application:	499/498 B.C.	Typology and Style:	I-A.18 — Fortification Style
Preserved Height of Image:	0.90 cm (incomp.)	Preserved Length of Image:	1.10 cm (incomp.)
Estimated Height of Original Seal:	NA	Estimated Diameter of Original Seal:	NA
Number of Impressions:	1	Quality of Impression:	Poor

Completeness of Image: Small segment of middle of design survives

DESCRIPTION OF SEAL AS IMPRESSED IMAGE

　　Hero has arms bent and appears to hold two rampant animals of uncertain type.

　　Animal to left holds lower foreleg bent and extends it downward in front of its body. Animal to right holds upper foreleg (only partially preserved) straight and extends it upward toward hero's arm; lower foreleg (only partially preserved) is straight and extended downward toward hero's leg.

　　Hero wears robe.

COMMENTARY

　　The impression is small and poorly preserved; the composition is uncertain.

SEAL APPLICATION (SEE APPENDIX ONE: CONCORDANCE OF SEALS TO TABLETS IN VOLUME I)

　　PFS 669 occurs on the reverse of PF 432. The partial rolling preserves only the hero and the animal to left, with a trace of the animal to the right. PF 432 is dated 499/498 B.C.

BIBLIOGRAPHY

Garrison 1988, pp. 276–78.

PFS 632   Cat.No. 143

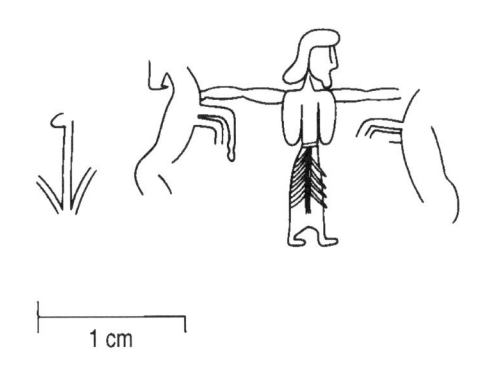

Seal Type:	Cylinder	Photographs:	Pl. 83a–b
Earliest Dated Application:	500/499 B.C.	Typology and Style:	I-A.18 — Fortification Style
Preserved Height of Image:	1.50 cm (incomp.)	Preserved Length of Image:	3.00 cm (incomp.)
Estimated Height of Original Seal:	NA	Estimated Diameter of Original Seal:	NA
Number of Impressions:	3	Quality of Impressions:	Poor

Completeness of Image: Segment of middle of design survives

Description of Seal as Impressed Image

Hero faces right, arms straight at horizontal, and holds two rampant animals of uncertain type by throat.

Each animal moves toward hero but turns its head away from him. Each animal holds forelegs bent and together in front of its body.

Hero wears belted Persian court robe with sleeves pushed up to reveal arms; sleeves hang from either side of torso in long swags; double central pleat and diagonal folds are on lower part of garment. Narrow rounded beard is suggested over hero's left shoulder; flattened coiffure rests at back of neck.

Animal to left may have short beard and is perhaps wild goat.

Plant is partially preserved in terminal field.

Commentary

See Garrison 1988, 1991, and 1996a for other, better preserved, seals from the distinctive hand of this important artist who works close to the Court Style.

For comparative illustrations including PFS 632, see pls. 178f (Persian court robes with sleeves pushed up in deep swags), 202f (arm positions of heroic control), and 260c (various plants).

Seal Application (see *Appendix One: Concordance of Seals to Tablets in Volume I*)

PFS 632 occurs on the reverse (inverted) and upper edge of PF 376 and the reverse of PF 514. Of the three partial rollings, two display the hero in the center; one preserves only the hero and the animal to left. On the reverse of PF 376 the seal clearly was applied before the text since several cuneiform wedges cut into the bottom of the impression. PF 514 is the earliest dated tablet with PFS 632 and is dated 500/499 B.C.

Bibliography

Garrison 1988, pp. 363–68; Garrison 1991, pp. 16–17; Garrison 1996a, p. 42 (n. 58).

Cat.No. 144　　　　　　　　　　PFS 1188

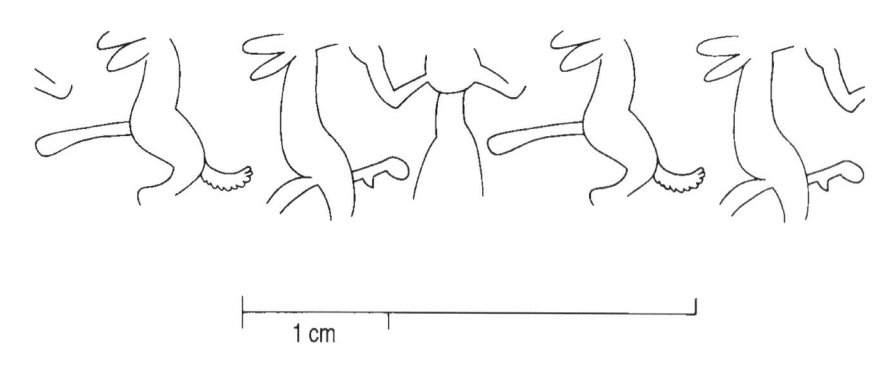

Seal Type:	Cylinder	Photograph:	Pl. 84a
Earliest Dated Application:	ND	Typology and Style:	I-A.18 — Broad and Flat Styles
Preserved Height of Image:	1.20 cm (incomp.)	Preserved Length of Image:	3.10 cm (comp.)
Estimated Height of Original Seal:	NA	Estimated Diameter of Original Seal:	1.00 cm
Number of Impressions:	2	Quality of Impressions:	Poor

Completeness of Image: Large fragment of middle of design survives along its complete length

DESCRIPTION OF SEAL AS IMPRESSED IMAGE

Hero with ovoid bird's upper torso has arms bent at shoulder level and holds two rampant animals of uncertain type.

Animal to left moves and faces away from hero; hero seems to grasp it by its horn (only partially preserved); tail of this animal extends straight out, with sharp projection at lower midpoint and large tufted termination. Animal to right moves toward and faces hero; hero may grasp it by its muzzle (link not preserved); this animal extends one foreleg diagonally downward toward hero's waist; thick tail with softly serrated edge curls upward.

Hero wears garment of uncertain type.

COMMENTARY

The anatomy of the hero is very unusual and is somewhat reminiscent of PFS 1202 (Cat.No. 137), where the hero (in that case winged) also has an ovoid bird's torso.

　For other designs showing animals/creatures in the heroic encounter moving in the same direction, see PFS 26 (Cat.No. 299) and PFS 1202 (Cat.No. 137).

　PFS 1188 was not included in Garrison 1988.

　For comparative illustrations including PFS 1188, see pls. 200f (heroes as various composite creatures) and 270d (compositions with strong unidirectional movement).

SEAL APPLICATION (SEE *APPENDIX ONE: CONCORDANCE OF SEALS TO TABLETS IN VOLUME I*)

PFS 1188 occurs on the right edge and upper edge of PF 1246, with PFS 5 (II) on the left edge. The partial rolling of PFS 1188 on the right edge displays the hero in the center. The rolling on the upper edge preserves the entire length of the seal design and displays the animal to the hero's left in the center. The date of PF 1246 is unknown.

I-A.19. WINGED CREATURES OF UNCERTAIN TYPE

PFS 20   Cat.No. 145

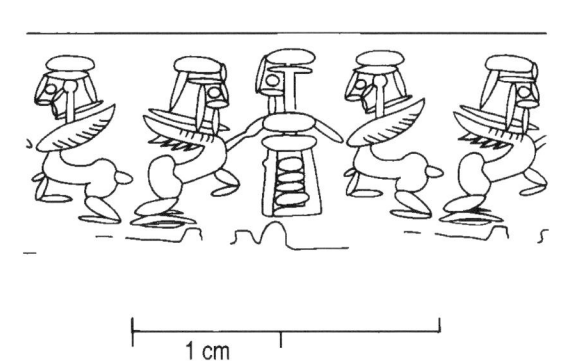

Seal Type:	Cylinder	Photographs:	Pl. 84c–d
Earliest Dated Application:	501/500(?) B.C.	Typology and Style:	I-A.19 — Diverse Styles
Preserved Height of Image:	1.40 cm (comp.)	Preserved Length of Image:	2.10 cm (comp.)
Estimated Height of Original Seal:	1.40 cm	Estimated Diameter of Original Seal:	0.70 cm
Number of Impressions:	16	Quality of Impressions:	Fair-good

Completeness of Image: Complete

DESCRIPTION OF SEAL AS IMPRESSED IMAGE

Hero faces left, arms straight at downward diagonal, and holds two rampant winged human-headed creatures of uncertain type by chest.

Each creature holds lower foreleg bent and extends it downward under its body. Upper foreleg of creature to left is not indicated; upper foreleg of creature to right is indicated by short projection. Creature to right has short tail.

Hero's robe is characterized by horizontal lozenges.

Edge of seal is preserved at top and bottom of design; lower edge of seal is irregular, suggesting three chips.

COMMENTARY

Koch (1990) suggests that PFS 20 belongs to Mamannuwiš, who oversaw a grain depot during years 21–26 (501/500–496/495 B.C.) at Kesat in her Elam Region VI.

The linear carving style of the heads recalls PFS 2 (Cat.No. 3), PFS 97 (II), and PFS 1024 (II), as well as, less similarly, PFS 1613 (Cat.No. 82), PFS 740 (Cat.No. 146), PFS 690 (Cat.No. 139) and PFS 1519 (Cat.No. 167). The hero's body recalls the Elamite "connected pieces style" (Negahban 1991, pp. 91, 101).

For comparative illustrations including PFS 20, see pls. 182b (robes with various features of detail), 217e (hero suspended high in design field), 234b (human-headed/human-faced creatures), 280b (chips in seal matrices), and 282b (personal seals of supply/apportionment officers).

SEAL APPLICATION (SEE *APPENDIX ONE: CONCORDANCE OF SEALS TO TABLETS IN VOLUME*)

PFS 20 occurs only on the left edge of tablets. All rollings appear to be carefully applied, with little or no distortion. This is especially apparent in the vertical placement of the seal on the rolling surfaces, where the user has been meticulous in retrieving as much of the seal image as possible. In twelve impressions the seal is rolled for at least one complete turn, preserving the entire length of the seal design. Of these twelve impressions, three display the hero in the center; one displays the hero and the creature to left in the center; two display the hero and the creature to right in the center; three display the two creatures in the center; two display the creature to the left of the hero in the center; one displays the creature to the right of the hero in the center. Of the remaining four partial impressions, one displays the hero in the center; one displays the hero and the creature to right in the center; one displays the creature to the left of the hero in the center; one displays the creature to the right of the hero in the center. PF 550 is the earliest dated tablet with PFS 20 and is dated 501/500(?) B.C.

BIBLIOGRAPHY

Dusinberre 1997b, p. 128 (n. 131); Garrison 1988, pp. 442–46, 531–32; Koch 1990, pp. 213, 301, 304.

Cat.No. 146								PFS 740

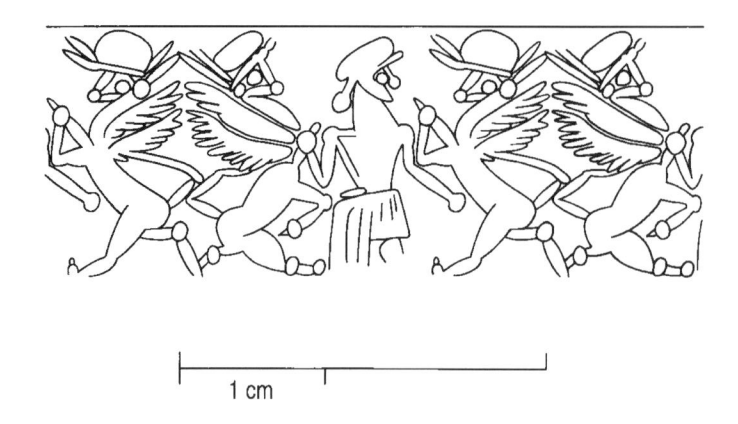

Seal Type:	Cylinder	Photograph:	Pl. 85a
Earliest Dated Application:	499/498 B.C.	Typology and Style:	I-A.19 — Diverse Styles
Preserved Height of Image:	1.70 cm (incomp.)	Preserved Length of Image:	2.50 cm (comp.)
Estimated Height of Original Seal:	1.80 cm	Estimated Diameter of Original Seal:	0.80 cm
Number of Impressions:	1	Quality of Impression:	Good

Completeness of Image: Almost complete except for lower edge

DESCRIPTION OF SEAL AS IMPRESSED IMAGE

Hero faces right, extending bent right arm to hold rampant winged human-headed creature of uncertain type by upper foreleg. Hero's left arm is bent and held down in front before rampant winged human-headed creature.

Both creatures move toward and face hero. Creature to left holds upper foreleg straight and extends it upward toward hero's shoulder; lower foreleg is bent and extended downward in front of its body; tail extends diagonally upward, bending back toward its body in two places. Creature to right of hero holds upper foreleg straight and extends it upward toward hero's head; lower foreleg is bent upward to touch upper foreleg; tail extends diagonally upward, bending back toward its body.

Hero wears variant on belted Assyrian garment that leaves forward leg exposed below knee; garment shows detailing line around outer edge on right side of hero's torso; vertical folds are indicated on lower garment. Hero wears flat headdress with projection at front; sheath projects back from hero's waist. Short pointed beard rests over hero's neck; round coiffure rests at back of neck.

Creature to left wears flat headdress with projection at front and has two long pointed ears(?) and round coiffure. Creature to right wears domed headdress with projection at front (or horn at forehead?) and has two long pointed ears(?) and round coiffure.

Edge of seal is preserved at top.

COMMENTARY

This is an unusual design since most of the visual dynamics suggest a control encounter, but the hero in fact holds only one creature. The hero turning his head away from the creature that he holds in the combat encounter would, however, be unique. More plausibly the artist may have intended a regular control encounter but simply confused the hero's left forearm and the lower foreleg of the creature to right.

The seal seems to be a debased version of the elegant PFS 2 (Cat.No. 3); the treatment of the creatures' faces is almost exactly the same. See the commentary for PFS 2 (Cat.No. 3). In PFS 740 the drill work is much more extensive, and the whole of the engraving more hasty, recalling PFS 690 (Cat.No. 139) which may be by the same hand. Compare also the treatment of heads in PFS 1519 (Cat.No. 167) and PFS 1613 (Cat.No. 82), which are, however, closer stylistically to PFS 2 (Cat.No. 3); note also the treatment of the heads n PFS 20 (Cat.No. 145) and PFS 233 (Cat.No. 52). The hero's garment faintly echoes early second-millennium Elamite renderings of narrow-waisted figures with full, vertically striated lower garments projecting from waist at a sharp right angle (cf. Amiet 1972, p. 256, pl. 175, no. 2005). But on PFS 740 the notion of the exposed forward leg of the Assyrian garment has compounded the archaizing allusions.

For comparative illustrations including PFS 740, see pls. 187b (headdresses), 235b (human-headed/human-faced creatures), and 278d (carving anomalies).

SEAL APPLICATION (SEE *APPENDIX ONE: CONCORDANCE OF SEALS TO TABLETS IN VOLUME I*)

PFS 740 occurs on the reverse of PF 513. The long rolling displays the two rampant creatures in the center. PF 513 is dated 499/498 B.C.

BIBLIOGRAPHY

Garrison 1988, pp. 447–50.

PFS 72   Cat.No. 147

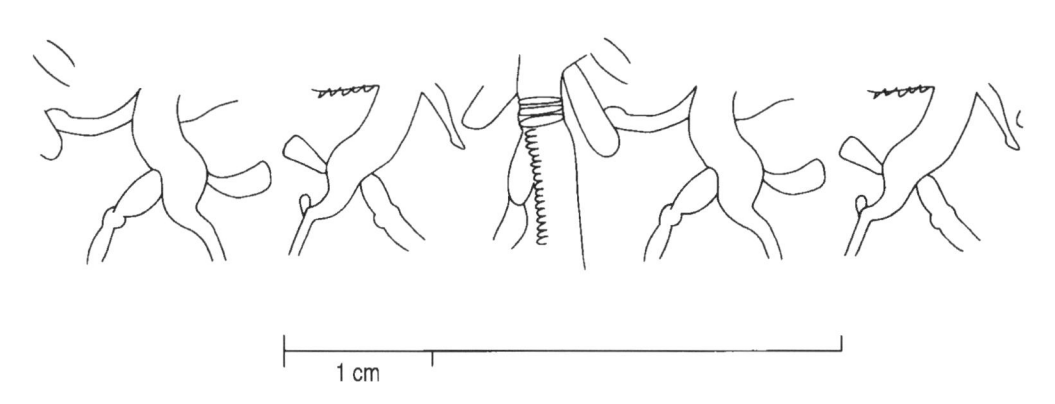

Seal Type:	Cylinder	Photograph:	Pl. 85c
Earliest Dated Application:	ND	Typology and Style:	I-A.19 — Modeled Style
Preserved Height of Image:	1.50 cm (incomp.)	Preserved Length of Image:	3.80 cm (comp.)
Estimated Height of Original Seal:	NA	Estimated Diameter of Original Seal:	1.20 cm
Number of Impressions:	8	Quality of Impressions:	Fair

Completeness of Image: Large segment of middle of design survives along its complete length

DESCRIPTION OF SEAL AS IMPRESSED IMAGE

Winged hero moves to left in striding pose and presumably holds two rampant winged creatures of uncertain type (hero's connection with creatures not preserved).

Each creature has active striding pose. Creature to left holds lower foreleg slightly bent and extends it downward toward hero's wing; thick short tail extends diagonally upward widening toward end. Creature to right holds lower foreleg slightly curved and extends it downward to place paw on hero's wing; thick short tail curves upward widening toward end.

Hero wears triple-belted Assyrian garment that leaves forward leg exposed; garment shows fringe along back leg. Two wings hang diagonally downward from each side of hero's body. Upper wings of presumed set of four are not preserved.

COMMENTARY

Koch (1990) suggests that PFS 72 belongs to Mannunda, perhaps the director of the royal bakery in her Persepolis Region I. The seal always occurs with PFS 399 (Cat.No. 78), PFS 141 (II), and, with two exceptions (PF 95 and PF 840), with PFS 90 (III). Mannunda is always listed as one of two officials receiving the flour; the other official is, with one exception (PF 840, where Mizirma receives with Mannunda), always Umardada.

Despite the looseness of line in the contours of figures and some hesitancy in the overall design, the human form seems well modeled. See PFS 1276 (Cat.No. 34) for the reconstruction of four wings on the hero.

For comparative illustrations including PFS 72, see pls. 273c (open compositions) and 284c (personal seals of various officers).

SEAL APPLICATION (SEE *APPENDIX ONE: CONCORDANCE OF SEALS TO TABLETS IN VOLUME I*)

PFS 72 occurs only on the reverse of tablets and, with one exception (PF 840), always with another seal. PFS 72 is inverted on the reverse of PF 95, with No. PFS 399 (Cat.No. 78) applied directly below it. PFS 90 (III) is applied directly below PFS 72 on the reverses of PF 326, PF 836, and PF 838. PFS 72 is inverted on the reverses of PF 835 and PF 837, and PFS 90 is applied directly below it on both tablets. PFS 72 is inverted on the reverse of PF 839, and PFS 90 is applied directly above it. PFS 72 occurs alone, inverted, on the reverse of PF 840. Rollings of the seal generally exhibit some distortion. No impression preserves the complete seal design. Of the eight partial applications, one preserves only the hero and the creature to the left; one preserves only the hero and the creature to the right; one displays the creature to the left of the hero in the center; three display the creature to the right of the hero in the center; two preserve only the creature to the right of the hero. The dates of all the tablets with PFS 72 are unknown.

BIBLIOGRAPHY

Garrison 1988, pp. 199–201; Garrison 1998, p. 121 (n. 15); Garrison and Dion 1999, p. 9 (n. 19); Garrison and Root 1996, p. 12; Koch 1990, p. 252.

Cat.No. 148　　　　　　　　　　　　　　　PFS 228

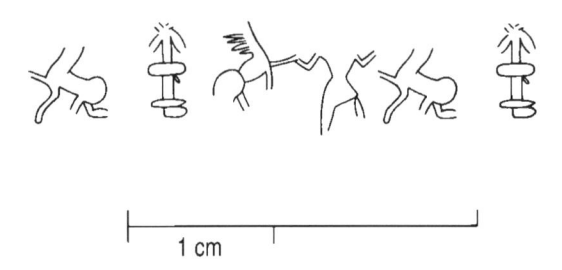

Seal Type:	Cylinder	Photograph:	Pl. 86a
Earliest Dated Application:	502/501 B.C.	Typology and Style:	I-A.19 — Fortification Style
Preserved Height of Image:	0.80 cm (incomp.)	Preserved Length of Image:	2.40 cm (comp.)
Estimated Height of Original Seal:	NA	Estimated Diameter of Original Seal:	0.80 cm
Number of Impressions:	3	Quality of Impressions:	Poor

Completeness of Image: Small segment of middle of design survives along its complete length

DESCRIPTION OF SEAL AS IMPRESSED IMAGE

Hero moves right, arms bent, and holds two rampant winged creatures of uncertain type, one to left by upper foreleg (contact with creature to right not preserved). Hero raises bent forward leg.

Creature to left holds upper foreleg straight and extends it upward toward hero's shoulder; lower foreleg (only partially preserved) is straight and extended downward in front of its body. Creature to right holds upper foreleg (only partially preserved) straight and extends it upward toward hero's elbow; lower foreleg is bent and extended downward in front of its body.

Hero appears to wear Assyrian garment that leaves forward leg exposed below knee.

In terminal field, pole with crossing horizontal bars terminates with star (only partially preserved).

COMMENTARY

Koch (1990) notes that PFS 228, PFS 99 (Cat.No. 113), and PFS 103* (Cat.No. 84) are responsible for the verification of the year end accounts at Liduma in her Elam Region VI; PFS 228 always occurs with PFS 99 (Cat.No. 113). No personal names that can be associated with these seals are preserved in the relevant texts. All three are such distinctive seals that we are nevertheless inclined to view them all as personal seals of the individual accountants.

The seal is small even by standards of the Fortification Style. The terminal field motif represents the "altar with star" seen on Neo-Babylonian seals, often in extremely reductive fashion (e.g., Jakob-Rost 1997, p. 98, no. 425). For the combination of related Babylonian cult symbols with a scene of heroic encounter, see PFS 1501 (Cat.No. 238).

For comparative illustrations including PFS 228, see pls. 248f (abstract symbols of Mesopotamian deities) and 286d (personal seals of accountants).

SEAL APPLICATION (SEE *APPENDIX ONE: CONCORDANCE OF SEALS TO TABLETS IN VOLUME I*)

PFS 228 occurs on the reverse (inverted) and bottom edge of PF 201 and the bottom edge of PF 202. PFS 99 (Cat.No. 113) has been applied directly above PFS 228 on the reverse of PF 201; PFS 479 (illegible) occurs with PFS 228 on the reverse of PF 202. Impressions of the seal are long, but very difficult to read. All three impressions preserve the entire length of the seal design; one displays the hero in the center; one displays the creature to the right of the hero in the center; one displays the terminal field motif in the center. PF 201 is the earliest dated tablet with PFS 228 and is dated 502/501 B.C.

BIBLIOGRAPHY

Garrison 1988, pp. 335–39; Koch 1990, p. 205.

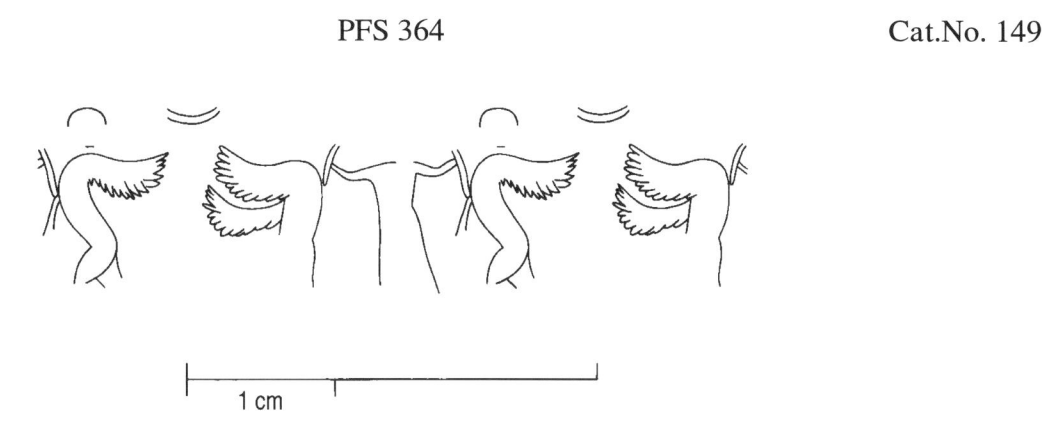

PFS 364   Cat.No. 149

Seal Type:	Cylinder	Photograph:	Pl. 86c
Earliest Dated Application:	503/502 B.C.	Typology and Style:	I-A.19 — Fortification Style
Preserved Height of Image:	1.30 cm (incomp.)	Preserved Length of Image:	2.80 cm (comp.)
Estimated Height of Original Seal:	NA	Estimated Diameter of Original Seal:	0.90 cm
Number of Impressions:	1	Quality of Impression:	Very poor

Completeness of Image: Segment of middle of design survives along its complete length

DESCRIPTION OF SEAL AS IMPRESSED IMAGE

Hero moves left(?), arms bent, and holds two rampant winged human-headed creatures of uncertain type by upper foreleg (head suggested, partially, at right only).

Each creature holds upper foreleg straight and extends it upward toward hero's head. Creature to right holds lower foreleg (only partially preserved) straight and extends it downward toward hero's lower body. Creature to left has two wings, both extended horizontally outward from its back.

Hero wears robe.

Crescent is in upper terminal field.

COMMENTARY

The impression of the seal is so poorly preserved that it is impossible definitively to read the presumably human head of the creature to the right.

For comparative illustrations including PFS 364, see pl. 250f (crescents).

SEAL APPLICATION (SEE *APPENDIX ONE: CONCORDANCE OF SEALS TO TABLETS IN VOLUME I*)

PFS 364 occurs on the reverse of PF 59. The rolling preserves the entire length of the seal design and displays the hero and the creature to left in the center. The seal clearly was applied before the text since several cuneiform wedges cut into the top of the impression. PF 59 is dated 503/502 B.C.

BIBLIOGRAPHY

Garrison 1988, pp. 320, 324.

Cat.No. 150   PFS 439

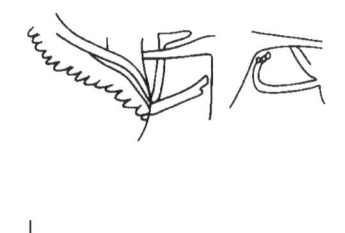

Seal Type:	Cylinder	Photograph:	Pl. 86e
Earliest Dated Application:	501/500 B.C.	Typology and Style:	I-A.19 — Fortification Style
Preserved Height of Image:	0.70 cm (incomp.)	Preserved Length of Image:	2.00 cm (incomp.)
Estimated Height of Original Seal:	NA	Estimated Diameter of Original Seal:	NA
Number of Impressions:	1	Quality of Impression:	Poor

Completeness of Image: Small segment of middle of design survives

DESCRIPTION OF SEAL AS IMPRESSED IMAGE

Hero has arms straight at horizontal and holds two(?) rampant winged creatures of uncertain type by throat (only forelegs of creature to right are preserved).

Creature to left holds upper foreleg straight, paw bent down, and extends it upward toward hero's arm; lower foreleg is straight and extended upward toward hero's chest. Creature to right holds upper foreleg straight and extends it upward to hero's arm; lower foreleg is curved, paw upturned, and extended outward to place paw on hero's chest.

Hero wears garment of uncertain type.

COMMENTARY

The preserved sealing is very difficult to read, and our drawing cannot be definitive in its details. It is possible that PFS 439 is the same seal as PFS 86 (Cat.No. 48). The style and composition are similar, and the type of transaction on which PFS 439 occurs is similar to those on which PFS 86 (Cat.No. 48) occurs, viz., receipt of commodities at a treasury, probably at Tirazziš (Shiraz); compare PF 128. Too little remains of PFS 439, however, to make a secure collation.

SEAL APPLICATION (SEE *APPENDIX ONE: CONCORDANCE OF SEALS TO TABLETS IN VOLUME I*)

PFS 439 occurs on the left edge of PF 130. The partial rolling displays the hero in the center. PF 130 is dated 501/500 B.C.

BIBLIOGRAPHY

Garrison 1988, pp. 297, 299.

PFS 547   Cat.No. 151

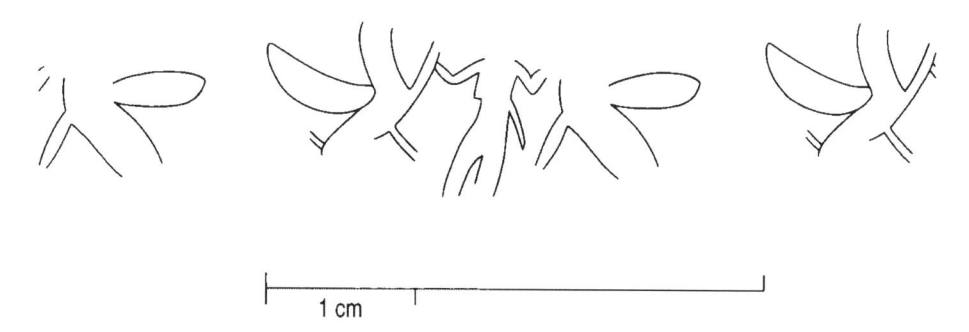

Seal Type:	Cylinder	Photograph:	Pl. 87a
Earliest Dated Application:	502/501 B.C.	Typology and Style:	I-A.19 — Broad and Flat Styles
Preserved Height of Image:	1.20 cm (incomp.)	Preserved Length of Image:	3.30 cm (comp.)
Estimated Height of Original Seal:	NA	Estimated Diameter of Original Seal:	1.10 cm
Number of Impressions:	1	Quality of Impression:	Very poor

Completeness of Image: Segment of middle of design survives along its complete length

DESCRIPTION OF SEAL AS IMPRESSED IMAGE

Hero moves to left, arms bent, and holds two rampant winged creatures of uncertain type by upper foreleg (preserved only at left).

Creature to left has long neck and holds upper foreleg (only partially preserved) straight and extends it diagonally upward; lower foreleg is straight (only partially preserved) and extended downward toward hero's leg; straight tail (only partially preserved) extends diagonally upward. Creature to right holds lower foreleg straight (only partially preserved) and extends it downward toward hero's leg.

Hero apparently wears trousers; sheath projects from back of waist.

COMMENTARY

The preservation is so poor that our drawing can only suggest a tentative rendering.

For comparative illustrations including PFS 547, see pl. 273g (open compositions).

SEAL APPLICATION (SEE *APPENDIX ONE: CONCORDANCE OF SEALS TO TABLETS IN VOLUME I*)

PFS 547 occurs on the reverse of PF 304. The one rolling preserves the entire length of the seal design and displays the creature to the left of the hero in the center. PF 304 is dated 502/501 B.C.

BIBLIOGRAPHY

Garrison 1988, pp. 431, 433–34.

Cat.No. 152   PFS 714

Seal Type:	Cylinder	Photograph:	Pl. 87c
Earliest Dated Application:	500/499 B.C.	Typology and Style:	I-A.19 — Mixed Styles I
Preserved Height of Image:	0.70 cm (incomp.)	Preserved Length of Image:	2.20 cm (incomp.)
Estimated Height of Original Seal:	NA	Estimated Diameter of Original Seal:	NA
Number of Impressions:	2	Quality of Impressions:	Poor

Completeness of Image: Small segment of middle of design survives

DESCRIPTION OF SEAL AS IMPRESSED IMAGE

Hero has arms bent and holds two rampant winged creatures of uncertain type by upper foreleg.

Each creature holds upper foreleg (only partially preserved) straight and extends it upward toward hero's head; lower foreleg is curved, paw upturned, and extended downward toward hero's waist.

Hero wears garment of uncertain type.

COMMENTARY

The human form has qualities of the Modeled Style, but the animal forms are closer to the Fortification Style.

SEAL APPLICATION (SEE *APPENDIX ONE: CONCORDANCE OF SEALS TO TABLETS IN VOLUME I*)

PFS 714 occurs twice on the reverse of PF 486, one impression directly above the other. The surface of the reverse is now very damaged. The two partial rollings display the hero in the center. PF 486 is dated 500/499 B.C.

BIBLIOGRAPHY

Garrison 1988, pp. 249–52; Root 1997, p. 239, fig. 6.

PFS 783

Cat.No. 153

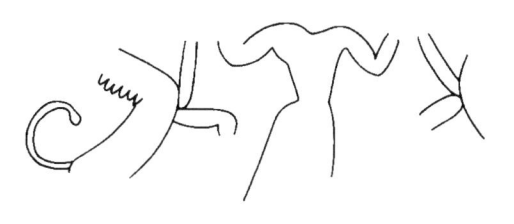

Seal Type:	Cylinder	Photograph:	Pl. 87e
Earliest Dated Application:	499/498 B.C.	Typology and Style:	I-A.19 — Mixed Styles I
Preserved Height of Image:	1.20 cm (incomp.)	Preserved Length of Image:	3.10 cm (incomp.)
Estimated Height of Original Seal:	NA	Estimated Diameter of Original Seal:	NA
Number of Impressions:	1	Quality of Impression:	Poor

Completeness of Image: Segment of middle of design survives

DESCRIPTION OF SEAL AS IMPRESSED IMAGE

Hero moves to right, arms bent, and holds two(?) rampant winged creatures of uncertain type, presumably by upper foreleg.

Each creature holds upper foreleg (only partially preserved) straight and extends it upward toward hero's head. Creature to left holds lower foreleg (only partially preserved) bent and extends it outward toward hero's waist; tail curls upward with tufted termination. Creature to right holds lower foreleg (only partially preserved) straight and extends it downward toward hero's leg.

Hero wears garment of uncertain type.

COMMENTARY

The style is typical of a large number of Mixed Styles seals that combine elements of the Modeled Style and the Fortification Style.

SEAL APPLICATION (SEE *APPENDIX ONE: CONCORDANCE OF SEALS TO TABLETS IN VOLUME I*)

PFS 783 occurs on the upper edge of PF 567. The partial rolling displays the hero in the center. PF 567 is dated 499/498 B.C.

BIBLIOGRAPHY

Garrison 1988, pp. 249–52.

Cat.No. 154   PFS 991

	1 cm	

Seal Type:	Cylinder	Photograph:	Pl. 88a
Earliest Dated Application:	500/499 B.C.	Typology and Style:	I-A.19 — Fortification Style
Preserved Height of Image:	1.00 cm (incomp.)	Preserved Length of Image:	3.10 cm (incomp.)
Estimated Height of Original Seal:	NA	Estimated Diameter of Original Seal:	NA
Number of Impressions:	2	Quality of Impressions:	Fair

Completeness of Image: Segment of middle and lower edge of design survives

DESCRIPTION OF SEAL AS IMPRESSED IMAGE

Hero moves to left in striding pose and presumably holds two rampant winged creatures of uncertain type.

Creature to left holds lower foreleg straight, paw upturned, and extends it downward toward hero's waist. Creature to right raises bent forward hind leg. Creatures' tails curl upward.

Hero appears to wear Assyrian garment that leaves forward leg exposed.

In terminal field rampant animal of uncertain type moves to right (at far right of preserved impressions); straight tail (only partially preserved) extends diagonally downward.

Edge of seal is preserved at bottom of design under hero and creature to left.

SEAL APPLICATION (SEE APPENDIX ONE: CONCORDANCE OF SEALS TO TABLETS IN VOLUME I)

PFS 991 occurs on the upper edge and left edge of PF 997. No other seal is used on the tablet. Of the two partial rollings, one displays the hero and the creature to the right in the center; the other displays the hero in the center. PF 997 is dated 500/499 B.C.

BIBLIOGRAPHY

Garrison 1988, pp. 271–73.

PFS 996   Cat.No. 155

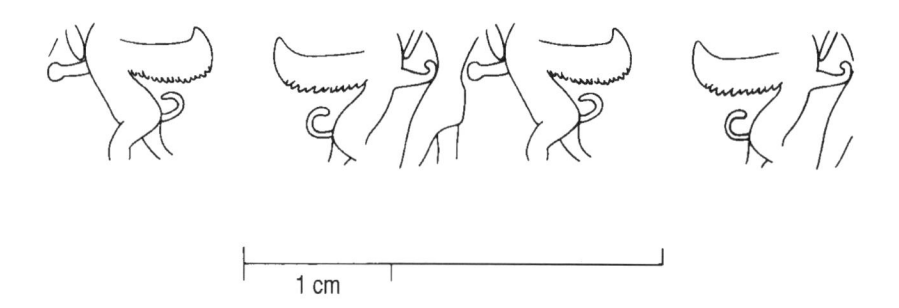

Seal Type:	Cylinder	Photograph:	Pl. 88c
Earliest Dated Application:	504 B.C.	Typology and Style:	I-A.19 — Fortification Style
Preserved Height of Image:	1.00 cm (incomp.)	Preserved Length of Image:	2.90 cm (comp.)
Estimated Height of Original Seal:	NA	Estimated Diameter of Original Seal:	0.90 cm
Number of Impressions:	1	Quality of Impression:	Fair-good

Completeness of Image: Almost complete except for upper edge and lower edge

DESCRIPTION OF SEAL AS IMPRESSED IMAGE

Hero moves to right and holds two rampant winged creatures of uncertain type.

Each creature holds upper foreleg (only partially preserved) straight and extends it upward toward hero's head. Creature to left holds lower foreleg straight and extends it outward to place upturned paw on hero's waist. Creature to right holds lower foreleg straight and extends it outward toward hero's waist. Creatures' tails curl upward.

Hero wears Assyrian garment that leaves forward leg exposed below knee.

COMMENTARY

The thick wings of the creatures draw the seal toward the Court Style. The engraving seems deep and well executed.

    For comparative illustrations including PFS 996, see pl. 271d (compositions with large empty space as terminal field).

SEAL APPLICATION (SEE *APPENDIX ONE: CONCORDANCE OF SEALS TO TABLETS IN VOLUME I*)

PFS 996 occurs on the upper edge of PF 1010. The right edge of the impression is damaged. The rolling preserves the entire length of the seal design and displays the creature to the right of the hero in the center. PF 1010 is dated 504 B.C.

BIBLIOGRAPHY

Garrison 1988, pp. 326–30, 483.

Cat.No. 156   PFS 1026

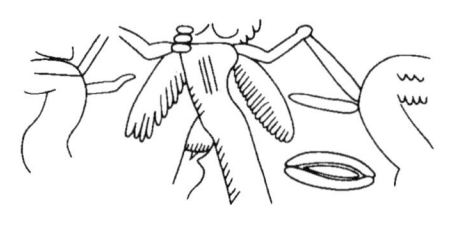

Seal Type:	Cylinder	Photograph:	Pl. 88e
Earliest Dated Application:	497 B.C.	Typology and Style:	I-A.19 — Modeled Style
Preserved Height of Image:	1.30 cm (incomp.)	Preserved Length of Image:	2.80 cm (incomp.)
Estimated Height of Original Seal:	NA	Estimated Diameter of Original Seal:	NA
Number of Impressions:	1	Quality of Impression:	Fair

Completeness of Image: Large segment of middle of design survives

DESCRIPTION OF SEAL AS IMPRESSED IMAGE

Winged hero faces left in striding pose, arms bent, and holds two rampant winged creatures of uncertain type by upper foreleg. Creature to left is human-headed; head of creature to right is not preserved.

Each creature holds upper foreleg (only partially preserved on creature to left) straight and extends it upward toward hero's head. Creature to left holds lower foreleg straight, paw upturned, and extends it upward toward hero's wing. Creature to right holds lower foreleg straight and extends it upward toward hero's wing.

Hero wears Assyrian garment that leaves forward leg exposed below knee; garment shows diagonal folds or decorative bands on chest; fringe is indicated along front edge of garment over torso and rear leg and bottom edge of garment over forward leg. Long, squared, segmented beard rests over hero's right shoulder; rounded coiffure rests at back of neck. Trace of feathered edge of third wing emerging upward behind coiffure indicates four-winged hero in fully preserved state.

Creature to right has two rows of feathers indicated on its wing. Creature to left has pointed beard.

Rhomb is in lower field between hero and creature to right.

COMMENTARY

For the rhomb, see PFS 38 (Cat.No. 16) and PFS 944 (Cat.No. 129). See PFS 1276 (Cat.No. 34) for a discussion of the format of the two-winged versus four-winged aspect of the hero as human creature.

    For comparative illustrations including PFS 1026, see pls. 211e (heroic attitudes of control encounter) and 249h (rhombs).

SEAL APPLICATION (SEE *APPENDIX ONE: CONCORDANCE OF SEALS TO TABLETS IN VOLUME I*)

PFS 1026 occurs on the left edge of PF 1059. The partial rolling displays the hero in the center. PF 1059 is dated 497 B.C.

BIBLIOGRAPHY

Garrison 1988, pp. 203–07, 520; Garrison 1998, p. 121 (n. 15); Garrison and Dion 1999, p. 9 (n. 19).

PFS 1045   Cat.No. 157

Seal Type:	Cylinder	Photograph:	Pl. 89a
Earliest Dated Application:	500/499 B.C.	Typology and Style:	I-A.19 — Linear Styles
Preserved Height of Image:	1.10 cm (incomp.)	Preserved Length of Image:	2.10 cm (comp.)
Estimated Height of Original Seal:	NA	Estimated Diameter of Original Seal:	0.70 cm
Number of Impressions:	3	Quality of Impressions:	Very poor

Completeness of Image: Segment of middle of design survives along its complete length

Description of Seal as Impressed Image

Hero moves to left, arms bent, and holds two rampant winged creatures of uncertain type by upper foreleg (preserved only at left). Hero raises bent forward leg and stands higher off bottom of seal than creatures.

Creature to left holds upper foreleg (only partially preserved) straight and extends it upward toward hero's head; lower foreleg (only partially preserved) is bent and extended downward toward hero's waist. Creature raises bent forward hind leg toward hero's foot; two wings are indicated, upper extending diagonally upward from lower. Creature to right holds lower foreleg straight, and extends it vertically downward under its body, ending in two-pronged termination. Creature raises bent forward hind leg. Creatures' tails curve downward and join in terminal field to form one tail.

Hero apparently wears trousers.

Commentary

The awkward figures and coarse engraving are typical of seals carved in the Linear Styles.

For comparative illustrations including PFS 1045, see pls. 184e (trousers), 217h (hero suspended high in design field), and 219b (comparative heroic proportions).

Seal Application (see *Appendix One: Concordance of Seals to Tablets in Volume I*)

PFS 1045 occurs on the reverse (inverted) of PF 1090 and the reverse (inverted) and upper edge of PF 1113. PFS 177 (II) is applied (inverted) directly under PFS 1045 on PF 1090. PFS 177 (II) is applied (inverted) to the left of PFS 1045 in the same horizontal plane on the reverse of PF 1113. In two impressions the seal is rolled for at least one complete turn, preserving the entire length of the seal design; that on the upper edge of PF 1113 displays the hero in the center; that on the reverse of PF 1090 displays the hero and the creature to right in the center. The remaining partial impression (PF 1113 reverse) preserves only the two creatures. PF 1113 is the earliest dated tablet with PFS 1045 and is dated 500/499 B.C.

Bibliography

Garrison 1988, pp. 437–39.

Cat.No. 158   PFS 1077

Seal Type:	Cylinder	Photograph:	Pl. 89c
Earliest Dated Application:	ND	Typology and Style:	I-A.19 — Fortification Style
Preserved Height of Image:	1.30 cm (incomp.)	Preserved Length of Image:	1.70 cm (incomp.)
Estimated Height of Original Seal:	NA	Estimated Diameter of Original Seal:	NA
Number of Impressions:	1	Quality of Impression:	Poor

Completeness of Image: Small segment of middle of design survives

DESCRIPTION OF SEAL AS IMPRESSED IMAGE

Hero faces left, arms bent, and holds two(?) rampant winged creatures of uncertain type (preserved only at left) by upper foreleg.

Creature to left holds upper foreleg straight and extends it upward toward hero's head; lower foreleg is curved, paw upturned, and extended downward in front of its body.

Hero wears belted Assyrian garment that leaves forward leg exposed below knee. Hero also wears bluntly serrated Persian crown. Rounded beard rests over hero's right shoulder; rounded coiffure rests at back of neck.

COMMENTARY

Owing to its fragmentary preservation, the composition is unclear and this seal may display a combat encounter. See Garrison 1988 for this important artist who works close to the Court Style.

For comparative illustrations including PFS 1077, see pls. 189b (Persian crowns and fluted tiaras) and 192g (rounded coiffures).

SEAL APPLICATION (SEE APPENDIX ONE: CONCORDANCE OF SEALS TO TABLETS IN VOLUME I)

PFS 1077 occurs on the left edge of PF 1123. The partial rolling preserves only the hero and the creature. The date of PF 1123 is unknown.

BIBLIOGRAPHY

Dusinberre 1997b, p. 128 (n. 131); Garrison 1988, pp. 352–56, 485.

PFS 1236   Cat.No. 159

|—— 1 cm

Seal Type:	Cylinder	Photograph:	Pl. 89e
Earliest Dated Application:	499 B.C.	Typology and Style:	I-A.19 — Fortification Style
Preserved Height of Image:	1.00 cm (incomp.)	Preserved Length of Image:	3.30 cm (incomp.)
Estimated Height of Original Seal:	NA	Estimated Diameter of Original Seal:	NA
Number of Impressions:	1	Quality of Impression:	Fair

Completeness of Image: Large segment of middle of design survives

DESCRIPTION OF SEAL AS IMPRESSED IMAGE

Hero, apparently facing right, has arms straight at horizontal and holds two rampant winged creatures of uncertain type, probably by upper foreleg (not preserved).

Creature to left holds upper foreleg (only partially preserved) straight and extends it upward toward hero's head; lower foreleg is bent and extended outward in front of its body. Bent lower foreleg is preserved of creature to right; wing at far left of impression should also belong to this creature.

Hero wears garment of uncertain type; trace of rounded beard may appear over his left arm.

Large dot is in middle field between hero and creature to left; crescent is in middle field between hero and creature to right.

Schematic date palm with bulbous fruit cluster on either side of trunk is in terminal field; stars or fronds terminating in floral elements frame tree trunk at its base.

COMMENTARY

Based upon Q texts protocol, PFS 1236 should belong to Turdumannuš(?), who in year 23.3 (499 B.C.) received flour rations, traveling on the authority (*halmi*) of Bakabana. PF 1291 is the only occurrence of the name Turdumannuš in the PF texts.

Multiple symbols in the terminal field are not common in the PFS corpus of hero seals; compare PFS 9* (Cat.No. 288) and PFS 38 (Cat.No. 16). Thus, the elements framing the lower trunk of the date palm are perhaps more likely to be floral fronds growing from its base than independent framing stars.

For comparative illustrations including PFS 1236, see pls. 254g (various devices and symbols) and 259f (date palms).

SEAL APPLICATION (SEE *APPENDIX ONE: CONCORDANCE OF SEALS TO TABLETS IN VOLUME I*)

PFS 1236 occurs on the reverse of PF 1291. The partial rolling displays the creature to the left of the hero in the center. PF 1291 is dated 499 B.C.

BIBLIOGRAPHY

Garrison 1988, pp. 326–30, 419.

Cat.No. 160   PFS 1238

Seal Type:	Cylinder	Photograph:	Pl. 90a
Earliest Dated Application:	499 B.C.	Typology and Style:	I-A.19 — Mixed Styles I
Preserved Height of Image:	0.80 cm (incomp.)	Preserved Length of Image:	2.90 cm (incomp.)
Estimated Height of Original Seal:	NA	Estimated Diameter of Original Seal:	NA
Number of Impressions:	1	Quality of Impression:	Poor

Completeness of Image: Small segment of middle of design survives

DESCRIPTION OF SEAL AS IMPRESSED IMAGE

Hero moves to left, arms bent, and holds two rampant winged creatures of uncertain type by upper foreleg (preserved only at right).

Creature to left holds lower foreleg straight, paw upturned, and extends it downward toward hero's chest. Creature to right holds upper foreleg (only partially preserved) straight and extends it diagonally upward.

Hero wears garment of uncertain type.

Uncertain fragmentary element is diagonally disposed at far left of impression in terminal field.

COMMENTARY

Based on Q texts protocol, PFS 1238 should belong to Miyara, who received flour rations in year 23.4 (499 B.C.) while on his way to Susa under the authority (*halmi*) of Parnaka. The name Miyara also occurs in PFa 24 (S1 text) and PFa 29 (journal accounting the S1 text) receiving grain rations for horses.

The seal design is very poorly preserved.

For comparative illustrations including PFS 1238, see pl. 290b (personal seals of various travelers).

SEAL APPLICATION (SEE *APPENDIX ONE: CONCORDANCE OF SEALS TO TABLETS IN VOLUME I*)

PFS 1238 occurs on the upper edge of PF 1293. The partial rolling displays the hero in the center. PF 1293 is dated 499 B.C.

BIBLIOGRAPHY

Garrison 1988, pp. 249–52.

PFS 1252   Cat.No. 161

Seal Type:	Cylinder	Photograph:	Pl. 90c
Earliest Dated Application:	493 B.C.	Typology and Style:	I-A.19 — Linear Styles
Preserved Height of Image:	1.00 cm (incomp.)	Preserved Length of Image:	1.30 cm (incomp.)
Estimated Height of Original Seal:	NA	Estimated Diameter of Original Seal:	NA
Number of Impressions:	1	Quality of Impression:	Poor-fair

Completeness of Image: Small segment of middle of design survives

DESCRIPTION OF SEAL AS IMPRESSED IMAGE

Hero (only bent right arm preserved) holds two(?) rampant winged creatures of uncertain type by upper foreleg.

Creature to left of hero holds upper foreleg straight and extends it diagonally upward; lower foreleg is straight and extended diagonally downward. Wing at far left of impression should belong to winged creature facing left and held by hero's left hand (not preserved).

COMMENTARY

Based on Q texts protocol, PFS 1252 should belong to Appumanya, who supplied flour rations to Badumašda in year 28.11 (493 B.C.). The name Appumanya occurs also in PF 40, PF 1914, and PF 1964; the variant Hapumanya occurs in PF 227, PF 806, PF 1306, and PF 1325; the variant Apmanya occurs in PF 316. Hallock transliterates both variants as Appumanya; Koch (1990, p. 315) also reads the variants as the same name. In PF 40 an Appumanya supplied *tarmu*-grain at Zakzaku; in PF 316 an Appumanya supplied a large grain shipment. In PF 1914 an Appumanya supplied wine at Razakanuš. In PF 227 and PF 806 an Appumanya received grain rations and barley loaves respectively. In the account text PF 1964 an Appumanya is described as the *raduššara*(?) for cattle at Turtukkan (see Koch 1990, p. 145, for the title). In all these transactions different seals are used. In the Q text PF 1325 an Appumanya received flour rations, using PFS 1268s (III), while traveling to Persepolis under the authority (*halmi*) of Bakabana. More study is needed to distinguish exactly how many officials are involved.

A crude outline linear style is used in this seal. Because the impression is so fragmentary, the exact composition cannot be determined with precision; the design may be a combat encounter, in which case the wing at the far left of the preserved impression would belong to a creature occupying the terminal field.

For comparative illustrations including PFS 1252, see pl. 287g (personal seals of various suppliers).

SEAL APPLICATION (SEE *APPENDIX ONE: CONCORDANCE OF SEALS TO TABLETS IN VOLUME I*)

PFS 1252 occurs on the left edge of PF 1306. The one rolling originally placed the hero and the area to the hero's right in the center, but the left edge is now damaged and preserves only part of the impression. PF 1306 is dated 493 B.C.

BIBLIOGRAPHY

Garrison 1988, pp. 440–42, 444, 497, 531.

Cat.No. 162   PFS 1388

Seal Type:	Cylinder	Photograph:	Pl. 90e
Earliest Dated Application:	500 B.C.	Typology and Style:	I-A.19 — Modeled Style
Preserved Height of Image:	1.50 cm (incomp.)	Preserved Length of Image:	3.60 cm (incomp.)
Estimated Height of Original Seal:	NA	Estimated Diameter of Original Seal:	NA
Number of Impressions:	1	Quality of Impression:	Poor

Completeness of Image: Large segment of middle of design survives

DESCRIPTION OF SEAL AS IMPRESSED IMAGE

Hero moves to right in vigorous striding pose, arms bent, and holds two rampant winged creatures of uncertain type (contact preserved only at left).

Tail of creature to left curves downward.

Hero appears to wear Assyrian garment that leaves forward leg exposed, but small swag of drapery hanging from each side of hero's torso indicates the Persian court robe with sleeves pushed up to reveal arms.

In the fields between hero and each creature inverted animal of uncertain type is suspended. Inverted animal to left is difficult to read but appears to have tail diagonally bent toward hero. Inverted animal to right turns head away from hero. Animal holds forelegs straight; one straight hind leg is extended upward toward hero's chest.

Hindquarters, tail, hind legs, and part of recurved head of third inverted animal of uncertain type occupy terminal field along with schematic bird of uncertain type in flight to left above this animal's hindquarters.

COMMENTARY

Based on Q texts protocol, PFS 1388 should belong to Mirara(?), who in year 22.4 (500 B.C.) received flour rations under the authority (*halmi*) of Parnaka. PF 1492 preserves the only occurrence of the name Mirara(?) in the PF texts.

The engraving is deep but not as broad or well executed as most Modeled Style seals; animal forms have some connections with the Fortification Style. The fusion of a Persian court robe with its lower portion echoing the Assyrian garment is also seen on PFS 17 (Cat.No. 235), PFS 326 (Cat.No. 100), PFS 1249 (Cat.No. 294), and perhaps PFS 247 (Cat.No. 245). The inverted animals in the main design field of PFS 1388 suggest animal carcasses relating to the heroic narrative. Compare PFS 17 (Cat.No. 235), PFS 243 (Cat.No. 303), PFS 1475 (Cat.No. 177), as well as PFS 256 (Cat.No. 198) and PFS 1142 (Cat.No. 39).

PFS 1388 is one of only five seals in the PFS corpus of hero seals displaying an inverted quadruped animal in the terminal field; see also PFS 17 (Cat.No. 235), PFS 243 (Cat.No. 303), PFS 256 (Cat.No. 198), and PFS 1475 (Cat.No. 177). The bird above the inverted animal on PFS 1388 is not clear. The composition with at least three inverted animals disposed in the field (in addition to the rampant creatures of the heroic encounter) is unique among seals with images of heroic encounter in the PFS corpus.

For comparative illustrations including PFS 1388, see pls. 181h (hybrid garments), 237e (animal carcasses), and 272g (dense compositions).

SEAL APPLICATION (SEE *APPENDIX ONE: CONCORDANCE OF SEALS TO TABLETS IN VOLUME I*)

PFS 1388 occurs on the reverse (inverted) of PF 1492. The partial rolling displays the hero in the center. The seal clearly was applied before the text since several cuneiform wedges cut into the bottom of the impression. PF 1492 is dated 500 B.C.

BIBLIOGRAPHY

Garrison 1988, pp. 213–14.

PFS 1447   Cat.No. 163

|—————————|
    1 cm

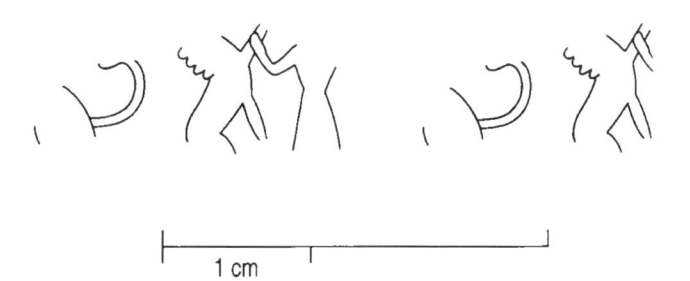

Seal Type:	Cylinder	Photograph:	Pl. 90g
Earliest Dated Application:	ND	Typology and Style:	I-A.19 — Fortification Style
Preserved Height of Image:	0.90 cm (incomp.)	Preserved Length of Image:	2.60 cm (comp.)
Estimated Height of Original Seal:	NA	Estimated Diameter of Original Seal:	0.80 cm
Number of Impressions:	1	Quality of Impression:	Fair

Completeness of Image: Segment of middle of design survives along its complete length

DESCRIPTION OF SEAL AS IMPRESSED IMAGE

Hero holds right arm bent (left arm not preserved) and holds two rampant winged creatures of uncertain type by upper foreleg (only hindquarters and tail preserved of creature to right).

Creature to left holds upper foreleg (only partially preserved) straight and extends it upward toward hero's head; lower foreleg (only partially preserved) is straight and extended downward toward hero's leg. Tail of creature to right curls upward.

Hero wears garment of uncertain type.

COMMENTARY

Based upon Q texts protocol, PFS 1447 should belong to Šappiš, who in PF 1565 received wine rations for 100 Turmiriyan workers while traveling to Elam under the authority (*halmi*) of Ziššawiš. PF 1565 preserves the only occurrence of the name Šappiš in the PF texts.

For comparative illustrations including PFS 1447, see pl. 288c (personal seals of various men leading groups).

SEAL APPLICATION (SEE *APPENDIX ONE: CONCORDANCE OF SEALS TO TABLETS IN VOLUME I*)

PFS 1447 occurs on the reverse of PF 1565. The rolling preserves the entire length of the seal design and displays the hero and the creature to right in the center. The date of PF 1565 is unknown.

BIBLIOGRAPHY

Garrison 1988, pp. 302–04.

Cat.No. 164 PFS 1535

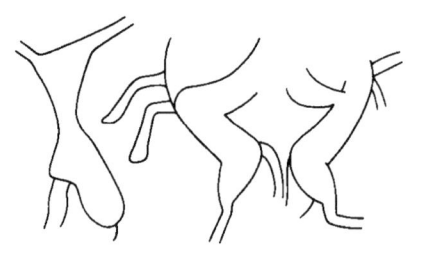

Seal Type:	Cylinder	Photograph:	Pl. 91a
Earliest Dated Application:	ND	Typology and Style:	I-A.19 — Fortification Style
Preserved Height of Image:	1.50 cm (incomp.)	Preserved Length of Image:	2.70 cm (incomp.)
Estimated Height of Original Seal:	NA	Estimated Diameter of Original Seal:	NA
Number of Impressions:	1	Quality of Impression:	Poor

Completeness of Image: Large segment of middle of design survives

DESCRIPTION OF SEAL AS IMPRESSED IMAGE

Hero moves to left in striding pose, arms straight at diagonal above shoulder level, and holds two rampant winged creatures of uncertain type by head(?).

Creature to right holds forelegs bent and extends them together in front of its body; thick tail curves downward.

Hero wears Assyrian garment that leaves forward leg exposed below mid-thigh.

At far right of impression, rampant winged creature moving to right should be creature held to left of hero. Creature holds forelegs (only partially preserved) straight, one extended diagonally upward, other diagonally downward, and raises forward hind leg.

SEAL APPLICATION (SEE APPENDIX ONE: CONCORDANCE OF SEALS TO TABLETS IN VOLUME I)

PFS 1535 occurs on the reverse of PF 1723. The partial rolling displays the creature to the right of the hero in the center. The date of PF 1723 is unknown.

BIBLIOGRAPHY

Garrison 1988, p. 321.

PFS 1630

Cat.No. 165

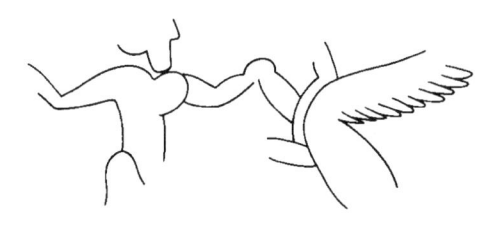

Seal Type:	Cylinder	Photograph:	Pl. 91c
Earliest Dated Application:	499/498 B.C.	Typology and Style:	I-A.19 — Modeled Style
Preserved Height of Image:	1.30 cm (incomp.)	Preserved Length of Image:	3.10 cm (incomp.)
Estimated Height of Original Seal:	NA	Estimated Diameter of Original Seal:	NA
Number of Impressions:	2	Quality of Impressions:	Poor

Completeness of Image: Small segment of middle of design survives

DESCRIPTION OF SEAL AS IMPRESSED IMAGE

Hero faces right, arms bent, and holds two(?) rampant winged creatures of uncertain type (preserved only at right).

Preserved creature holds upper foreleg straight and extends it diagonally upward toward hero's head; lower foreleg (only partially preserved) is straight and extended toward hero's chest.

Hero appears to wear Assyrian garment. Hero has squared beard that rests over his left shoulder; trace of rounded coiffure rests at back of neck.

COMMENTARY

The seal is very poorly preserved but appears to have had a large and well-executed design. Since so little of the design is preserved, it is quite possible that this is a combat encounter rather than a control encounter.

SEAL APPLICATION (SEE APPENDIX ONE: CONCORDANCE OF SEALS TO TABLETS IN VOLUME I)

PFS 1630 occurs on the reverse (inverted) and upper edge of PF 2066. The partial rolling on the reverse preserves only the hero. The partial rolling on the upper edge preserves only parts of the hero and creature. On the reverse of PF 2066 the seal clearly was applied before the text since several cuneiform wedges cut into the bottom of the impression. PF 2066 is dated 499/498 B.C.

BIBLIOGRAPHY

Garrison 1988, pp. 207–10.

Cat.No. 166   PFS 1454

Seal Type:	Cylinder	Photograph:	Pl. 92a
Earliest Dated Application:	498 B.C.	Typology and Style:	I-A.19 — Linear Styles
Preserved Height of Image:	1.30 cm (incomp.)	Preserved Length of Image:	2.30 cm (comp.)
Estimated Height of Original Seal:	NA	Estimated Diameter of Original Seal:	0.70 cm
Number of Impressions:	1	Quality of Impression:	Poor

Completeness of Image: Segment of middle of design survives along its complete length

DESCRIPTION OF SEAL AS IMPRESSED IMAGE

Hero faces left, arms straight at horizontal, and holds two rampant winged human-headed creatures of uncertain type, one to left by upper foreleg, one to right by back of head. The creature at left is certainly human-headed; that at right, apparently so (but with oddities).

Each creature moves toward hero but turns its head away from him. Creature to left holds upper foreleg straight and extends it diagonally upward; lower foreleg is straight and extended downward toward hero's body. Two wings are indicated, upper extending diagonally upward from lower. Creature to right holds upper foreleg curved and extends it upward toward hero's head; lower foreleg is straight, paw upturned, and extended downward toward hero's body. Two wings are indicated, upper extending diagonally upward from its back, lower extending diagonally downward from its back; tail (only partially preserved) curls downward.

Hero wears robe with four horizontal lozenge-shaped features stacked at bottom of preserved portion. Short rounded beard terminates above hero's right shoulder; narrow rounded coiffure rests at back of neck.

Creature to left may have short pointed beard; short pointed coiffure is at back of head. Creature to left wears flat headdress with projections at front and top. Creature to right has narrow pointed beard that rests over its wing. Projections from head of creature at right may be short horns.

Partially preserved inverted crescent-shaped element is in lower field between hero and creature to right.

COMMENTARY

The design is poorly executed. The heads of the creatures are difficult to interpret. The creature at the right may, for instance, have a bird-like head, with mouth open. Equally puzzling is the lower portion of the hero's robe in combination with the vestigial element just to the right. It is possible that the hero's lower body fuses with a couchant pedestal creature whose tail curls up between the hero and the creature to the right.

For comparative illustrations including PFS 1454, see pls. 187g (headdresses) and 217c (hero standing atop pedestal figure[s] or other supporting element).

SEAL APPLICATION (SEE *APPENDIX ONE: CONCORDANCE OF SEALS TO TABLETS IN VOLUME I*)

PFS 1454 occurs on the reverse of PF 1570. The rolling preserves the entire length of the seal design and displays the hero in the center. The seal clearly was applied before the text since several cuneiform wedges cut into the bottom of the impression. PF 1570 is dated 498 B.C.

BIBLIOGRAPHY

Garrison 1988, pp. 431–33.

PFS 1519 — Cat.No. 167

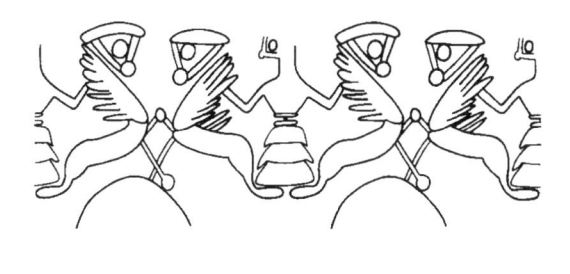

|—— 1 cm ——|

Seal Type:	Cylinder	Photograph:	Pl. 92c
Earliest Dated Application:	505/504 B.C.	Typology and Style:	I-A.19 — Diverse Styles
Preserved Height of Image:	1.40 cm (incomp.)	Preserved Length of Image:	1.70 cm (comp.)
Estimated Height of Original Seal:	1.50 cm	Estimated Diameter of Original Seal:	0.50 cm
Number of Impressions:	3	Quality of Impressions:	Poor-fair

Completeness of Image: Almost complete except for upper edge and lower edge

DESCRIPTION OF SEAL AS IMPRESSED IMAGE

Hero faces left, arms bent, and holds two rampant winged creatures of uncertain type by wing.

Each creature moves away from hero, one facing other to form heraldic group. Each creature holds upper foreleg straight and extends it diagonally upward, joining it with upper foreleg of other creature; lower foreleg is straight and extended downward, crossing lower foreleg of other creature. One hind leg is indicated for each creature, bent and extended diagonally downward.

Hero stands on lower part of hind leg of each creature. Hero wears double-belted robe with skirt of three tiers.

COMMENTARY

The heavy use of a cutting disk and drill recalls the Cut Style of Assyria and Babylonia.[38] The geometric treatment of human and animal heads that we observe on PFS 1519 is, however, a hallmark of a more distinctive group of seals in the PFS corpus. See commentary on PFS 2 (Cat.No. 3). The crowded composition is very rare in seals from the PFS corpus, although the combination of heroic encounter and heraldic group is not unknown; compare PFS 80 (Cat.No. 202), PFS 162 (Cat.No. 249), PFS 225 (Cat.No. 46), PFS 496 (Cat.No. 108), PFS 1123 (Cat.No. 279), and PFS 1204 (Cat.No. 136). The hero perched atop the feet of the animals/creatures he engages is an unusual format; compare PFS 4* (Cat.No. 292).

Despite crowding, the composition is quite carefully arranged, and the execution, although highly schematic, is in fact very accomplished. PFS 1519 shows the same elegant animal and human body forms combined with geometric approach to heads as seen on PFS 2 (Cat.No. 3), and the seals may be by the same artist. See the commentary on PFS 2 (Cat.No. 3).

For comparative illustrations including PFS 1519, see pls. 182i (robes with various features of detail), 217d (hero standing atop pedestal figure(s) or other supporting element), 270i (compositions creating dynamic negative space as terminal field), 272i (dense compositions), and 280j (chips in seal matrices).

SEAL APPLICATION (SEE *APPENDIX ONE: CONCORDANCE OF SEALS TO TABLETS IN VOLUME I*)

PFS 1519 occurs twice on the reverse and once on the upper edge of PF 1667. The rollings on the reverse are long, preserving the entire length of the seal design, one placed directly above the other. The upper rolling displays the hero and the creature to right in the center; the lower rolling displays the creature to the right of the hero in the center. The rolling on the upper edge preserves the entire length of the seal design and displays the hero and the creature to left in the center. PF 1667 is dated 505/504 B.C.

---

38. Compare, for example, Wittmann 1992, pl. 33, nos. 122–24, 129; Herbordt 1992, pl. 5, no. 7.

BIBLIOGRAPHY

Garrison 1988, p. 462.

I-B. HERO HOLDS ANIMALS OR CREATURES AT HIS CHEST
I-B.11. HORNED ANIMALS: DEER, GAZELLES, WILD GOATS, WILD SHEEP

Cat.No. 168   PFS 1217s

Seal Type:	Stamp, Circular Face	Photograph:	Pl. 92e
Earliest Dated Application:	495 B.C.	Typology and Style:	I-B.11 — Fortification Style
Preserved Height of Image:	2.10 cm (comp.)	Preserved Width of Image:	1.00 cm (incomp.)
Number of Impressions:	2	Quality of Impressions:	Poor-fair

Completeness of Image: Almost complete except for right edge and left edge

DESCRIPTION OF SEAL AS IMPRESSED IMAGE

Hero faces right and holds at his chest two vertically disposed deer (head preserved only on animal at left).

Each animal has body facing hero. Animal to left turns head away from hero.

Hero wears tunic and perhaps wears domed headdress. Rounded segmented beard rests over hero's left shoulder; rounded coiffure rests at back of neck.

Large antler emerges from back of head of deer to left.

COMMENTARY

See the commentary on PFS 201 (Cat.No. 50) for texts associated with these two seals.

The stamp has a circular contour. For probable seal shape, see *Appendix Four: Stamp Seals in Volume I Grouped by Apparent Contour of Seal Face* and accompanying figure 9, nos. 3a, 4c, or 5a. This format of heroic control fits well into the circular field and PFS 1217s admirably exploits its design potentials.

For comparative illustrations including PFS 1217s, see pls. 185i (tunics), 207f (arm positions of heroic control), 215g (unusual heroic attitudes), 224h (deer, goats, sheep, and related winged creatures), and 274f (stamp seals).

SEAL APPLICATION (SEE *APPENDIX ONE: CONCORDANCE OF SEALS TO TABLETS IN VOLUME I*)

PFS 1217s occurs on the left edge of both PF 1275 and PF 1276. Both applications are oriented along the longitudinal axis of the tablet. The seal has been carefully applied on the restricted surface of both left edges in order to display the hero in the center. PF 1275 is the earliest dated tablet with PFS 1217s and is dated 495 B.C.

BIBLIOGRAPHY

Garrison 1988, pp. 291–93.

PFS 1099   Cat.No. 169

Seal Type:	Cylinder	Photograph:	Pl. 92g
Earliest Dated Application:	ND	Typology and Style:	I-B.11 — Fortification Style
Preserved Height of Image:	1.40 cm (incomp.)	Preserved Length of Image:	2.30 cm (incomp.)
Estimated Height of Original Seal:	NA	Estimated Diameter of Original Seal:	NA
Number of Impressions:	2	Quality of Impressions:	Poor

Completeness of Image: Segment of middle of design survives

DESCRIPTION OF SEAL AS IMPRESSED IMAGE

Hero holds at his waist two wild goats vertically disposed (only goat at left is fully preserved). Hero clenches his hands together in front of his body.

Each goat is turned away from hero. Goat to left holds forelegs straight and extends them together diagonally downward in front of its body; hind legs are curved and extended diagonally downward.

Hero wears belted robe.

Goat to left has beard and single horn (only partially preserved); ear (only partially preserved) is at back of head.

To left, in terminal field, large eagle perched apparently on column looks to left. To left of eagle is pair of wings (see commentary).

COMMENTARY

This is an unusual design compositionally, iconographically, and stylistically. Stylistically the seal seems to belong with the Fortification Style, but the odd, elongated renderings of the hero's arms and torso find no ready parallels in that style.

The rendering, pose, and role in the compositional narrative of the perching eagle cannot be paralleled in the PFS corpus of hero seals. The only other eagle in Volume I also appears in the terminal field but is posed in a frontal display (PFS 461 [Cat.No. 90]). For a bird perched on a column, see an impression from Aššur of a Neo-Assyrian cylinder where the bird figures in the terminal field of a cult scene involving a worshiper and a fish-garbed priest.[39]

The pair of wings preserved at the far left of the preserved impressions of PFS 1099 suggests that the design was quite large and elaborate, apparently incorporating a genie figure of Assyrian inspiration. Compare PFS 166 (II), where a crouching monkey on a floral column occupies the terminal field flanked by two Assyrian genies facing away toward the seal design's focal element (in this case, sacred emblems rather than heroic encounter). Perhaps if PFS 1099 were fully preserved, an elaborate cult scene would usurp the heroic encounter as

---

39. Herbordt 1992, p. 80, pl. 3, no. 6.

the principal feature of the entire composition. Compare a Neo-Assyrian carnelian cylinder with a similar control encounter as terminal field element to a cult scene (Collon 1987, no. 355).

For comparative illustrations including PFS 1099, see pls. 183f (robes of various undetailed types), 207b (arm positions of heroic control), 215f (unusual heroic attitudes), 238d (subsidiary human/human-creature figures in encounter images), and 266g (terminal field motifs other than inscriptions).

SEAL APPLICATION (SEE *APPENDIX ONE: CONCORDANCE OF SEALS TO TABLETS IN VOLUME I*)

PFS 1099 occurs on the reverse and left edge of PF 1158. No other seal is used on the tablet. The two partial rollings display the eagle in the terminal field and the goat to the left of the hero in the center. The date of PF 1158 is unknown.

BIBLIOGRAPHY

Garrison 1988, pp. 293–95.

I-B.17. MIXED ANIMALS AND /OR CREATURES

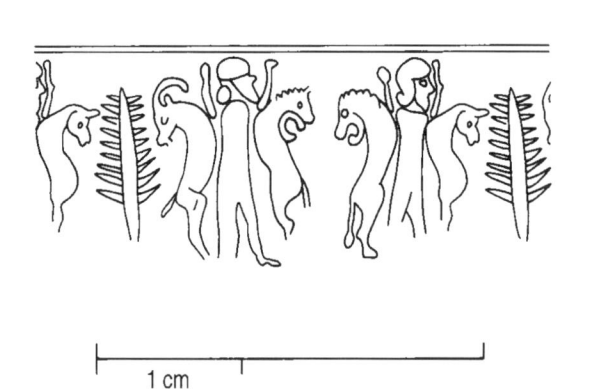

Cat.No. 170   PFS 131

Seal Type:	Cylinder	Photographs:	Pl. 93a–c
Earliest Dated Application:	501/500 B.C.	Typology and Style:	I-B.17 — Fortification Style
Preserved Height of Image:	1.50 cm (incomp.)	Preserved Length of Image:	2.70 cm (comp.)
Estimated Height of Original Seal:	1.70 cm	Estimated Diameter of Original Seal:	0.90 cm
Number of Impressions:	13	Quality of Impressions:	Poor

Completeness of Image: Almost complete except for lower edge

DESCRIPTION OF SEAL AS IMPRESSED IMAGE

Two discrete heroic encounters are depicted.

At left of design, hero, facing right, "holds" at his chest vertically disposed wild goat to left and vertically disposed lion to right. The hero does not actually have arms.

Each animal turns its head away from hero. Goat extends one foreleg vertically upward in front of hero's head; short straight tail extends diagonally downward. Lion holds one foreleg curved and extends it vertically upward in front of hero's head; tail (only partially preserved) hangs downward.

Hero wears Assyrian garment that leaves forward leg exposed; hero perhaps wears domed headdress. Beard terminates in blunt point; round coiffure rests at back of neck.

Goat has long curved horn; rounded ear is at top of head. Mane of lion is rendered by serrated edge along contour of its neck; ear (only partially preserved) emerges from front of its head; mouth is open in roar.

At right of design, second hero, facing right, "holds" to his chest vertically disposed lion to left and horned animal of undetermined type to right. The hero again does not actually have arms.

Each animal turns its head away from hero. Lion extends one foreleg vertically upward in front of hero's head; tail extends vertically downward with tufted termination. Horned animal holds one foreleg slightly bent and extends it vertically upward in front of hero's face.

Hero appears to wear Assyrian garment that leaves forward leg exposed. Pointed beard rests over hero's left shoulder; rounded coiffure curls upward at back of neck.

Mane of lion is rendered by serrated edge along contour of its neck; mouth is open in roar. Short horn emerges from front of head of horned animal; no tail is preserved.

Tree with narrow lenticular trunk and short pointed branches, diminishing in size toward top (as with certain conifers), is in terminal field.

Line border is preserved at top of design.

COMMENTARY

Koch suggests that PFS 131 belongs to an unnamed "Prüfer," who is documented at Kanduma, Šursunkiri, and Hibaš.

The doubled heroic encounter and the dense composition are unusual. Seals depicting two fully discrete heroic encounters are rare in the PFS corpus, occurring only on PFS 146 (Cat.No. 275), PFS 152 (Cat.No. 295), PFS 757 (Cat.No. 296), and PFS 1249 (Cat.No. 294) in addition to PFS 131. The clear referencing of Akkadian or Old Babylonian iconography in PFS 152 (Cat.No. 295) suggests the possibility that double-encounter seals were explored occasionally in the Achaemenid environment initially at least as an outgrowth of response to broad-based archaizing interests.[40] Beyond the PFS corpus, and generally on seals that seem later in date of production, double-encounter seals continue to have an apparently limited occurrence.[41]

Extensive drill work is visible in the head of the hero at far left. Overall the style is somewhat abstract.

For comparative illustrations including PFS 131, see pls. 206c (arm positions of heroic control), 224a (deer, goats, sheep, and related winged creatures), and 257a (conifers).

SEAL APPLICATION (SEE *APPENDIX ONE: CONCORDANCE OF SEALS TO TABLETS IN VOLUME I*)

PFS 131 occurs on the bottom edge, reverse, upper edge, right edge, and left edge of PF 235 and the reverse, upper edge, right edge, and left edge of PF 249. On PF 239 the seal occurs only on the left edge. On the reverse of PF 235 the seal is applied in three long rollings completely covering the surface. On the reverse of PF 249 the seal has been applied twice, one impression directly above the other. Impressions exhibit little distortion; those on the reverse tend to be long. In nine impressions the seal is rolled for at least one complete turn, preserving the entire length of the seal design. Of these nine applications, four display the right heroic encounter and the tree in the center; two display the left heroic encounter in the center; one displays the tree in the center; one preserves the two heroic encounters with the tree at the right edge of the impression; one preserves the two heroic encounters with the tree at the left edge of the impression. Of the remaining three partial rollings, one displays the left heroic encounter in the center; one displays the two lions in the two heroic encounters in the center; one displays the lion in the left heroic encounter in the center. On the reverse of PF 249 the seal clearly was applied before the text since several cuneiform wedges cut into the top of the impression. PF 235 and PF 249 are the earliest dated tablets with PFS 131 and are both dated 501/500 B.C.

BIBLIOGRAPHY

Garrison 1988, pp. 278–81; Koch 1990, p. 165 (n. 692).

---

40. Garrison 1991, pp. 7–10; Root 1979; eadem 1994. Double-encounter seals also occur occasionally in the Neo-Assyrian/Neo-Babylonian context where there is also significant indication of reworking of Akkadian imagery (e.g., Collon 1987, pp. 196–97, no. 965).
41. For example, the cylinder displaying a combat encounter and a control encounter used in the Murašû archive (Bregstein 1993, p. 442, no. 50 [no illustration]). Here the combat encounter is presented on pedestal creatures, further accentuating the seal's distinctive character. See also the large chalcedony cylinder from Borsippa, Iraq, BM 89337 (Collon 1987, pp. 90–91, no. 428; Wiseman 1959, pl. 105). Although not strictly speaking a hero seal, an impression from the Ur cache of the mid-fifth century B.C. is important. It displays a double hunt scene, once with a spearman and once with an archer (Collon 1987, pp. 90–91, no. 422; Legrain 1951, no. 759).

I-C. HERO CONTROLS INVERTED ANIMALS OR CREATURES
I-C.4. LIONS

Cat.No. 171   PFS 971

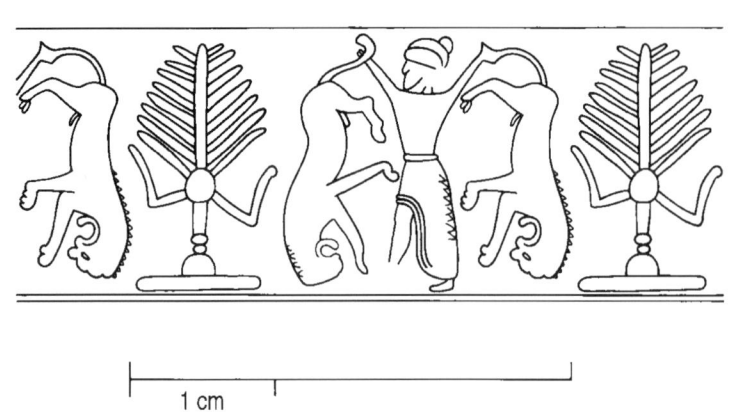

Seal Type:	Cylinder	Photographs:	Pl. 94a–b
Earliest Dated Application:	499 B.C.	Typology and Style:	I-C.4 — Mixed Styles I
Preserved Height of Image:	1.80 cm (comp.)	Preserved Length of Image:	3.00 cm (comp.)
Estimated Height of Original Seal:	1.80 cm	Estimated Diameter of Original Seal:	1.00 cm
Number of Impressions:	3	Quality of Impressions:	Excellent detail

Completeness of Image: Complete except for details

DESCRIPTION OF SEAL AS IMPRESSED IMAGE

Hero faces left in striding pose, arms straight above shoulder level, and holds two inverted lions by tail.

Each lion places forelegs and one hind leg along hero's body as if marchant. Each lion holds head straight, facing hero's body. Tail of lion to left curves vertically upward with tufted termination. Tail of lion to right curls upward and then to left with tufted termination.

Hero wears belted Assyrian garment that leaves forward leg exposed below lower thigh; double border runs along front hem of lower part of garment over forward thigh and rear leg; fringe is indicated along rear contour. Hero also wears turban-like domed headdress with knob at crown of head. Blunt-pointed beard rests over hero's right shoulder.

Mane of lion to left is rendered by blunt serrations inside contour line on neck; mouth is open in roar. Mane of lion to right is rendered by crisp serrated edge along contour of neck; mouth is open in roar. Each creature is ithyphallic.

In terminal field is tree with narrow lenticular trunk and branches diminishing in length toward top (as on certain conifers). Two bent "arms" emerge from disk at base of branches. Tree's trunk is mounted on broad-based stand.

Line border is preserved at bottom of design, serving also as ground line. Edge of seal is preserved at top.

COMMENTARY

This is an especially well-planned and well-executed design. The artist has deftly handled the difficult composition of inverted animals. The style is a mixture of Assyro-Babylonian Modeled Style traditions and the local Fortification Style.

    For comparative illustrations including PFS 971, see pls. 177d (Assyrian garments with detailing preserved), 187d (headdresses), 203g (arm positions of heroic control), and 257d (conifers).

SEAL APPLICATION (SEE *APPENDIX ONE: CONCORDANCE OF SEALS TO TABLETS IN VOLUME I*)

PFS 971 occurs on the reverse (inverted) and upper edge of PF 854 and the reverse of PF 1587, with PFS 6 (Cat.No. 304) applied on the left edge of each tablet. The impressions are crisply executed. All three impressions preserve the entire length of the seal design; that on the reverse of PF 854 displays the lion to the left of the hero and the tree in the terminal field in the center; that on the upper edge of PF 854 displays the lion to the right of the hero in the center; that on the reverse of PF 1587 displays the hero and the lion to right in the center. PF 854 is the earliest dated tablet with PFS 971 and is dated 499 B.C.

BIBLIOGRAPHY

Garrison 1988, pp. 246–49.

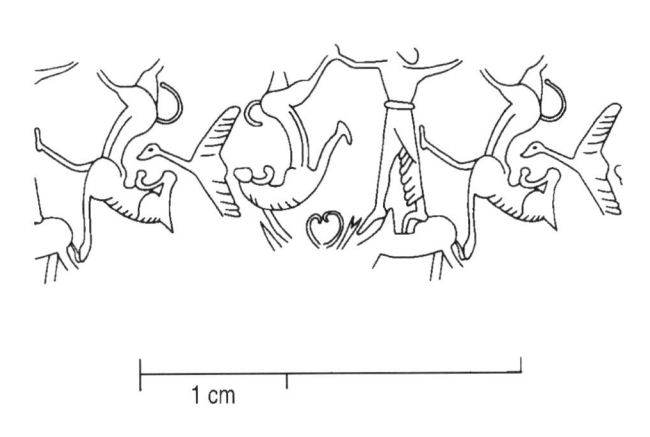

PFS 31 — Cat.No. 172

Seal Type:	Cylinder	Photographs:	Pl. 95a–e
Earliest Dated Application:	504/503 B.C.	Typology and Style:	I-C.4 — Fortification Style
Preserved Height of Image:	1.60 cm (incomp.)	Preserved Length of Image:	2.70 cm (comp.)
Estimated Height of Original Seal:	NA	Estimated Diameter of Original Seal:	0.90 cm
Number of Impressions:	13	Quality of Impressions:	Fair

Completeness of Image: Large segment of middle of design survives along its complete length

DESCRIPTION OF SEAL AS IMPRESSED IMAGE

Hero faces left, arms slightly bent at horizontal, and holds two inverted lions by hind leg. Hero stands on back of marchant humped bull moving to left, serving as pedestal animal.

Bull's hump protrudes between hero's feet; its two long horns curve toward one another. Additional linear elements to either side of horns are not comprehensible. Short tail on bull curves downward with tufted termination.

Each lion turns head away from hero. Lion to left holds one foreleg straight, paw upturned, and extends it upward toward hero's waist. Lion to left holds rear hind leg (only partially preserved) straight and extends it vertically upward; forward hind leg is extended upward toward hero's head; short tail curls downward. Lion to right holds lower foreleg slightly curved and extends it vertically downward; upper foreleg is slightly bent, paw upturned, and extended upward toward hero's leg. Lion to right holds rear hind leg (only partially preserved) bent and extends it vertically upward; forward hind leg (only partially preserved) is extended upward toward hero's head; tail curls upward.

Hero wears belted Assyrian garment that leaves forward leg exposed; fringe is indicated along forward hem of lower garment over rear leg. Rounded coiffure is partially preserved at back of hero's neck.

Mane of each lion is rendered by diagonal marks along contour of neck; mouth is open in roar. Short pointed ear emerges from back of head of lion to right.

In middle of terminal field, long-necked bird (goose) with wings spread flies to left.

COMMENTARY

This design is unusual in the PFS corpus of hero seals. Heroes on pedestal animals are rare, and this is the only example in the PFS corpus of a controlling hero standing on one rather than two creatures. See Dusinberre

(1997b, p. 123 [n. 57]) for the significance of the pedestal imagery and its socially restricted circulation. The type of animal serving as pedestal creature on PFS 31 is another anomaly. It is unfortunate that we are missing the critical area at its head. Although the humped bull is not unknown in Mesopotamian art (van Buren 1939, pp. 74–76), it is certainly rare in the extant Achaemenid repertoire (see PFS 220 [II] for another humped bull in the PFS corpus). One unprovenanced Achaemenid seal in the British Museum shows a humped bull or zebu suckling a calf (Wiseman 1959, p. 114). The best parallel in Volume I for the bird in flight on PFS 31 is found on PFS 1374 (Cat.No. 31), where, unfortunately, the neck and the head of the bird are not preserved.[42]

For comparative illustrations including PFS 31, see pls. 216b (hero standing atop pedestal figure[s] or other supporting element), 220b (bulls and bull creatures), 226d (birds), and 268a (terminal field motifs other than inscriptions).

SEAL APPLICATION (SEE *APPENDIX ONE: CONCORDANCE OF SEALS TO TABLETS IN VOLUME I*)

PFS 31, rather unusually, occurs only on the upper edge of tablets, with one exception (PF 71, on the reverse and upper edge). Applications of the seal show little or no distortion. In seven impressions the seal is rolled for at least one complete turn, preserving the entire length of the seal design. Of these seven applications, two display the hero in the center; one displays the lion to the left of the hero in the center; one displays the lion to the right of the hero in the center; three display the lion to the right of the hero and the bird in the center. Of the remaining six partial rollings, four display the hero in the center; one displays the lion to the right of the hero and the bird in the center; one displays the bird in the center. PF 58 is the earliest dated tablet with PFS 31 and is dated 504/503 B.C.

BIBLIOGRAPHY

Dusinberre 1997b, pp. 123 (n. 57), 126 (n. 105); Garrison 1988, pp. 312–13; Garrison 1998, p. 120 (n. 12); Koch 1990, p. 99 (n. 421).

---

42. Amiet 1972, pl. 189, no. 2210, for an Achaemenid heroic control seal from Susa with a rather similar bird in flight, this time in the terminal field between two rampant goats. Amiet sees the bird as an archaizing feature on this seal, and he calls it an eagle, but the neck and head area are difficult to assess in the publication.

PFS 64*   Cat.No. 173

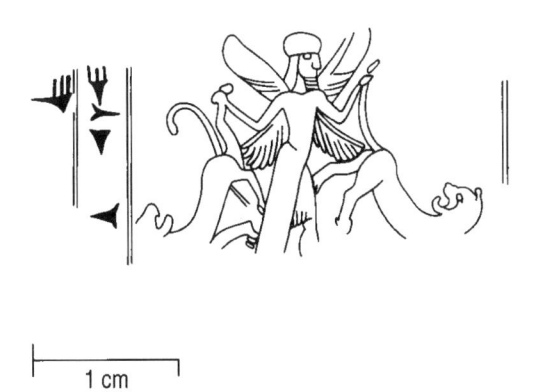

Seal Type:	Cylinder, Inscribed	Photographs:	Pl. 96a–b
Earliest Dated Application:	504/503 B.C.	Typology and Style:	I-C.4 — Fortification Style
Language of Inscription:	Uncertain		
Preserved Height of Image:	1.50 cm (incomp.)	Preserved Length of Image:	3.30 cm (incomp.)
Estimated Height of Original Seal:	NA	Estimated Diameter of Original Seal:	NA
Number of Impressions:	9	Quality of Impressions:	Fair-good

Completeness of Image: Large segment of middle of design survives

DESCRIPTION OF SEAL AS IMPRESSED IMAGE

Four-winged hero faces right in striding pose, arms bent, and holds two inverted lions, one to left by hind leg, one to right by tail.

Each lion turns head away from hero. Lion to left holds rear hind leg bent and extends it vertically upward; lion places other hind leg and one foreleg along hero's body as if marchant; tail curves upward, hooked downward at its end with tufted termination. Lion to right places rear hind leg on hero's thigh; forward hind leg is slightly bent and extended downward toward hero's leg; tail curves upward.

Hero wears Assyrian garment that leaves forward leg exposed below lower thigh; fringe is indicated along hem of garment over forward leg. Hero perhaps wears domed headdress. Squared beard with horizontal striations rests over his left shoulder; flattened coiffure rests at back of neck.

Each lion opens mouth in roar. Small projection from front of head of lion to right may be ear or forelock.

Paneled inscription is in terminal field.

INSCRIPTION

Cuneiform script, language uncertain

    Line   1. ⌈...⌉
                   2. ⌈...⌉

    Translation   ?

Two lines of the inscription are preserved, oriented along the vertical axis of the seal, separated by a case line and enclosed in a panel. Too little remains to suggest a reading. It is striking that the inscription is enclosed in a panel with a case line and oriented along the vertical axis of the seal design. The only other inscribed seals in the PFS corpus of hero seals that show this combination of features are PFS 1* (Cat.No. 182), PFS 526* (Cat.No. 216), PFS 671* (Cat.No. 174) probably with a mock inscription, and the royal name seals PFS 7* (Cat.No. 4) and PFS 113* (Cat.No. 19).

260 SEALS ON THE PERSEPOLIS FORTIFICATION TABLETS, VOLUME I: IMAGES OF HEROIC ENCOUNTER

COMMENTARY

Koch (1990) suggests that PFS 64* may belong to Tiridada, who oversaw, with a companion, the provisioning of workers at Hidali, Šursunkiri, and Kesat in her Elam Region VI. The seal also occurs on a deposit of *tarmu*-grain at Hidali under the jurisdiction of Šatra ... (PF 200).[43]

This is a beautifully conceived and executed design with a lavish use of space. The style shows some affinities with the Modeled Style, especially in the strong vertical accent through the body of the hero.

For comparative illustrations including PFS 64*, see pls. 201b (heroes as winged humans), 261c (paneled inscriptions with vertical case lines), and 284b (personal seals of various officers).

SEAL APPLICATION (SEE *APPENDIX ONE: CONCORDANCE OF SEALS TO TABLETS IN VOLUME I*)

PFS 64* always occurs on the left edge of tablets; in two instances (PF 1229 and PF 1597) it also occurs on the upper edge. Applications of the seal tend to be clear and deeply impressed, showing little or no distortion. Of the total nine impressions, three show some part of the inscription. In one impression the seal is rolled for at least one complete turn, preserving the entire length of the seal design. That rolling displays the hero in the center. Of the remaining eight impressions, two display the hero and the lion to the left in the center, with a partial rolling of the inscription at the left of the impression; five display the hero in the center; one preserves only the hero and the lion to left. PF 200 is the earliest dated tablet with PFS 64* and is dated 504/503 B.C.

BIBLIOGRAPHY

Garrison 1988, pp. 287–91, 483, 492; Garrison 1998, p. 121 (n. 15); Garrison 2000, p. 128; Garrison and Dion 1999, pp. 8 (n. 17), 10 (n. 28); Koch 1990, p. 212 (n. 872).

Cat.No. 174 PFS 671*

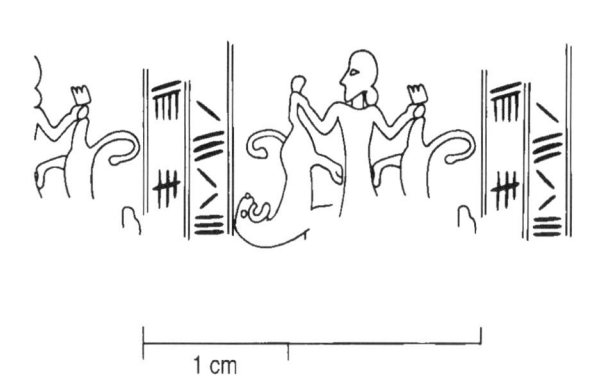

Seal Type:	Cylinder, Inscribed	Photograph:	Pl. 96d
Earliest Dated Application:	500/499 B.C.	Typology and Style:	I-C.4 — Fortification Style
Language of Inscription:	Unknown		
Preserved Height of Image:	1.40 cm (incomp.)	Preserved Length of Image:	2.30 cm (comp.)
Estimated Height of Original Seal:	NA	Estimated Diameter of Original Seal:	0.70 cm
Number of Impressions:	1	Quality of Impression:	Good

Completeness of Image: Almost complete except for upper edge and lower edge

DESCRIPTION OF SEAL AS IMPRESSED IMAGE

Hero faces left, arms bent, and holds two inverted lions by rear hind leg.

Each lion turns head away from hero. Each lion extends rear hind leg vertically upward; each lion appears to place other three legs (forelegs not well preserved) along hero's body as if marchant; each tail curls outward with tufted termination.

---

43. Koch also notes PF 2032, an inventory of grain at Kurra, Kapišda, Kemarukkaš, and Marmaš in association with PFS 64*; however, PFS 64* does not (contra Hallock) occur on this tablet.

Hero wears robe. Short pointed beard rests over hero's right shoulder; small rounded coiffure rests at back of neck.

Lion to left has mouth open in roar.

Panel for two line inscription in terminal field is filled with linear marks.

INSCRIPTION

Cuneiform-like script, language unknown

    Line   1. x x x x
                    2. x x

    Translation   ?

There are apparently two lines to the inscription, oriented along the vertical axis of the seal, separated by a case line and enclosed in a panel. The signs do not conform to any known script. Possibly they are meant deliberately to suggest cuneiform signs without actually conveying any words.

COMMENTARY

The probable mock inscription is noteworthy. Compare PFS 677* (Cat.No. 181), which may also carry an inscription but does not have the case panels as does PFS 671*. The designs and spacing around the respective cylinders of PFS 671* and PFS 677* (Cat.No. 181) could sustain an empty terminal field. In both cases, we must consider the possibility that the seal was originally carved to be anepigraphic but that the (non-literate?) purchaser subsequently asked a seal carver to add an inscription. In this scenario, the question whether or not the seal owner knew he was given a mock inscription remains open. The design of PFS 671* is well executed with a spacious feeling; note especially the negative space in the upper field.

    For comparative illustrations including PFS 671*, see pls. 261f (paneled inscriptions with vertical case lines) and 265e (mock inscriptions).

SEAL APPLICATION (SEE *APPENDIX ONE: CONCORDANCE OF SEALS TO TABLETS IN VOLUME I*)

PFS 671* occurs on the reverse of PF 434. The long rolling begins at the left with the vertical edge of the inscription panel, followed by the heroic encounter, the inscription, and ending with the inverted lion to the left of the hero. This appears to have been a very carefully applied impression, the seal user perhaps employing the vertical edge of the inscription panel as a guide to the rolling of the seal. PF 434 is dated 500/499 B.C.

BIBLIOGRAPHY

Garrison 1988, pp. 262, 278–81, 482; Garrison and Dion 1999, pp. 10 (n. 28), 13 (n. 38); Root 1997, p. 233.

Cat.No. 175   PFS 1090

| 1 cm |

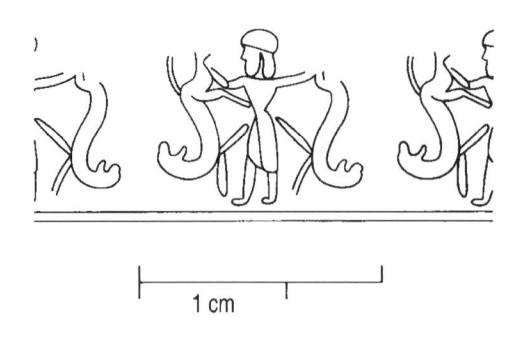

Seal Type:	Cylinder	Photograph:	Pl. 97a
Earliest Dated Application:	499/498 B.C.	Typology and Style:	I-C.4 — Fortification Style
Preserved Height of Image:	1.30 cm (incomp.)	Preserved Length of Image:	1.60 cm (comp.)
Estimated Height of Original Seal:	1.40 cm	Estimated Diameter of Original Seal:	0.50 cm
Number of Impressions:	3	Quality of Impressions:	Fair

Completeness of Image: Complete except for upper edge and details

DESCRIPTION OF SEAL AS IMPRESSED IMAGE

Hero faces left, right arm bent and left arm straight, and holds two inverted lions by hind leg.

Each lion turns head away from hero. Lion to left holds rear hind leg (only partially preserved) bent and extends it vertically upward; lion places other three legs along hero's body as if marchant. Tail (only partially preserved) curves upward. Lion to right holds one hind leg (only partially preserved) bent and extends it vertically upward; lion places straight forelegs along hero's body as if marchant.

Hero wears tunic with central split or fold. Hero perhaps wears domed headdress. Rounded beard rests over hero's right shoulder; rounded coiffure rests at back of neck.

Each lion opens mouth in roar.

Line border is preserved at bottom of design.

COMMENTARY

The design has an elegant, elongated quality; the arched scroll-like forms of the lions provide an especially calligraphic touch; see Garrison 1988 for artist and related seals. The seal is rather small, even by standards of the Fortification Style.

For comparative illustrations including PFS 1090, see pls. 185h (tunics), 271f (compositions with large empty space as terminal field), and 276i (borders).

SEAL APPLICATION (SEE APPENDIX ONE: CONCORDANCE OF SEALS TO TABLETS IN VOLUME I)

PFS 1090 occurs on the reverse (inverted), bottom edge, and upper edge of PF 1139. The three rollings all preserve the entire length of the seal design. On the reverse the seal has been rolled for two complete revolutions with the intact figural design complete in each half of the impression. The rolling on the bottom edge of PF 1139 displays the lion to the right of the hero in the center; the rolling on the upper edge of PF 1139 displays the hero and the lion to left in the center. PF 1139 is dated 499/498 B.C.

BIBLIOGRAPHY

Garrison 1988, pp. 309–12.

PFS 1321s   Cat.No. 176

Seal Type:	Stamp, Octagonal Face	Photograph:	Pl. 97c
Earliest Dated Application:	495 B.C.	Typology and Style:	I-C.4 — Diverse Styles
Preserved Height of Image:	1.90 cm (incomp.)	Preserved Width of Image:	1.20 cm (incomp.)
Number of Impressions:	1	Quality of Impression:	Good

Completeness of Image: Almost complete except for left, right, and upper edge

DESCRIPTION OF SEAL AS IMPRESSED IMAGE

Winged hero faces left in striding pose, right arm bent and left arm straight, and holds two inverted lions by tail.

Lion to right turns head away from hero (other lion's head not preserved). Each lion holds one hind leg bent and extended downward. Each lion holds foreleg straight and extended vertically downward.

Hero wears robe. Short pointed beard rests over right shoulder; rounded coiffure rests at back of neck. Short curved wing emerges from each shoulder where arm should be. "Arms" are thin appendages emerging from armpits. Hero has birds' feet.

Mane of lion to right has diagonal markings along contour of neck; mouth is open in roar.

Hero stands on double ground line. Exergue is formed by cross-hatching that meets but does not intersect upper ground line. Edge of seal is preserved at bottom and lower right of design.

COMMENTARY

Based on Q texts protocol, PFS 1321s should belong to Dauma, who in year 27.9 (495 B.C.) is receiving flour rations at Hidali while traveling from Sardis to Persepolis under the authority (*halmi*) of Artadara (Gr. Artaphernes). PF 1404 preserves the only occurrence of the name Dauma on PF tablets.

The design exhibits some connections with the class of pyramidal stamp seals with octagonal faces discussed by Boardman (1970a, 1970b) leading up to the so-called Graeco-Persian style. Specifically, the short sharply curved wings of the hero, the compressed animal forms, and the ground line with exergue below can be paralleled on numerous stamp seals that have been considered products of Graeco-Persian workshops operating in western Anatolia under a strong Greek influence. Unfortunately, the vast majority of such artifacts are without archaeological context, so that issues of chronology and social history have been difficult to assess with rigor. An extremely close iconographic parallel for PFS 1321s is, for instance, an unprovenanced seal now in Munich (Boardman 1970a, pl. 2, no. 23). A pyramidal stamp seal excavated at Sardis is less close but is also a good iconographic parallel (Curtis 1925, pls. 10–11, no. 111).[44] Despite an iconographic parallel with seals found and/or thought to be found in western Anatolia (and presumed to have been made there as well), the engraving of PFS 1321s lacks the detailing of many Graeco-Persian seals. In particular, it lacks the emphatic use of undisguised drill work (Dusinberre 1997b, pp. 109–10), deploying this technique only on the paws of the lion to the left of the hero. The plain surface treatment of PFS 1321s may in fact suggest links to the Fortification

---

44. See Dusinberre 1997b, pp. 109–10, for a succinct summary of issues plaguing the Graeco-Persian category as well as for important commentary on the role Sardis plays as the main archaeological touchstone.

Style. In this context, it is of great interest that the owner of the seal is coming from Sardis, with its strong potentials as a major production center of Graeco-Persian koine art (Dusinberre 1997a, passim). The intersection of Graeco-Persian iconography and Fortification Style stylistic links suggests the possibility of more complex hybridizations in imperial glyptic production than have previously been considered.[45] Given the fact that even the excavated pyramidal stamps from Sardis are impossible to date with precision, the usage date of PFS 1321s in 495 B.C. is a most welcome absolute fixed point.

The ground line in stamp seals is not often seen among the images of heroic encounter in the PFS corpus; compare PFS 919s (Cat.No. 259), PFS 1260s (Cat.No. 184), PFS 1437s (Cat.No. 128), and PFS 1624s (Cat.No. 261). PFS 1321s is the only seal in Volume I with an exergue.

The stamp face has an octagonal contour. For probable seal shape, see *Appendix Four: Stamp Seals in Volume I Grouped by Apparent Contour of Seal Face* and accompanying figure 9, no. 1.

For comparative illustrations including PFS 1321s, see pls. 183h (robes of various undetailed types), 199g (feet and shoes), 200g (heroes as various composite creatures), 275c (stamp seals), 277c (ground lines on stamp seals), and 290h (personal seals of various travelers).

SEAL APPLICATION (SEE *APPENDIX ONE: CONCORDANCE OF SEALS TO TABLETS IN VOLUME I*)

PFS 1321s occurs on the reverse of PF 1404, oriented along the horizontal axis of the tablet. PF 1404 is dated 495 B.C.

BIBLIOGRAPHY

Garrison 1988, pp. 461, 500; Garrison 1998, p. 121 (n. 12); Garrison and Root 1996, p. 4; Root 1997, p. 237, fig. 3; Root 1998, pp. 265–68, 271, fig. 5, pl. 7.

---

45. See Root 1998, for a preliminary attempt to reassess the issues raised by the pyramidal stamp seals of the Persian Empire, specifically with reference now to the evidence of the PFS corpus across all three volumes of our catalog.

PFS 1475   Cat.No. 177

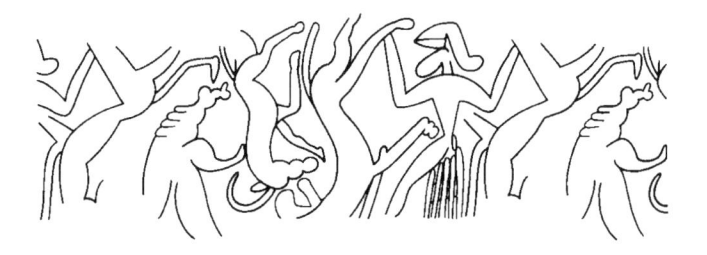

|— 1 cm —|

Seal Type:	Cylinder	Photograph:	Pl. 98a
Earliest Dated Application:	499 B.C.	Typology and Style:	I-C.4 — Diverse Styles
Preserved Height of Image:	1.50 cm (incomp.)	Preserved Length of Image:	2.90 cm (comp.)
Estimated Height of Original Seal:	1.70 cm	Estimated Diameter of Original Seal:	0.90 cm
Number of Impressions:	2	Quality of Impressions:	Fair

Completeness of Image: Complete except for upper edge and lower edge

Description of Seal as Impressed Image

Hero faces left, arms bent, and holds two inverted lions by forward hind leg. Hero has forward leg raised in striding pose.

Each lion turns head (preserved only at left) away from hero. Lion to left holds rear hind leg bent and extends it vertically upward; forward hind leg is curved and extended upward toward hero's head. Lion holds rear foreleg straight, and extends it upward toward hero's waist; forward foreleg (only partially preserved) is straight and extended diagonally downward close to its body; tail curves upward. Lion to right holds rear hind leg (only partially preserved) curved and extends it diagonally upward away from hero; forward hind leg (only partially preserved) is straight and extended upward toward hero's head. Lion holds short rear foreleg (only partially preserved) straight and extends it upward toward hero's chest; long forward foreleg (only partially preserved) is curved and extended vertically downward; crooked tail extends diagonally upward and is bent at its end with pointed termination.

Hero wears variation on Assyrian garment that leaves forward leg completely exposed; long vertical strips form lower part of garment are over rear leg. Long rounded beard rests over hero's right shoulder; rounded coiffure curls upward at back of neck.

In terminal field, inverted wild goat faces to right. Goat holds rear hind leg (only partially preserved) straight and extends it vertically upward; other hind leg and forward foreleg are posed as if marchant; rear foreleg is bent back to point vertically upward. Large curved horn emerges from front of head; short rounded ear is at top of head; tail (only partially preserved) curves upward. To left of goat, large vulture faces right, pecking at goat's hindquarters. Vulture apparently lifts one leg and places it on back of goat's neck.

Commentary

The linear style of engraving, schematic figures, and crowded composition with inverted animals seem to link the seal to Early Dynastic II glyptic (third millennium B.C.) from Susa.[46] The design, however, does recall somewhat PFS 213 (Cat.No. 140), which clearly is not Early Dynastic in date. Furthermore, the extremely small size of PFS 1475 speaks against an Early Dynastic date.

Inverted animals as elements of the terminal field occur on only five seals in Volume I: PFS 1475, PFS 17 (Cat.No. 235), PFS 243 (Cat.No. 303), PFS 256 (Cat.No. 198), and PFS 1388 (Cat.No. 162). The vulture pecking at the inverted goat on PFS 1475 in the terminal field suggests that we are meant to understand the inverted animal as a carcass (a victim of the lions now controlled by the adjacent hero?). Conceivably, this narrative is

---

46. Compare Amiet 1972, nos. 1437–39, 1440–41, 1443.

meant to be cued by the inverted animals on PFS 1388 (Cat.No. 162), PFS 256 (Cat.No. 198), and PFS 243 (Cat.No. 303) as well, even in the absence of the vulture that renders explicit the fate of the inverted animal here on PFS 1475.

For comparative illustrations including PFS 1475, see pls. 195g (coiffures of distinctive types/sub-types), 227h (birds), 237f (animal carcasses), 268j (terminal field motifs other than inscriptions), and 272h (dense compositions).

SEAL APPLICATION (SEE *APPENDIX ONE: CONCORDANCE OF SEALS TO TABLETS IN VOLUME I*)

PFS 1475 occurs twice on the reverse of PF 1596, one application directly above the other. The upper rolling preserves the entire length of the seal design and displays the inverted goat in the terminal field in the center. The partial lower impression displays the lion to the right of the hero in the center. PF 1596 is dated 499 B.C.

BIBLIOGRAPHY

Garrison 1988, pp. 465–66.

Cat.No. 178   PFS 396

Seal Type:	Cylinder	Photograph:	Pl. 98c
Earliest Dated Application:	498/497 B.C.	Typology and Style:	I-C.4 — Fortification Style
Preserved Height of Image:	1.40 cm (incomp.)	Preserved Length of Image:	2.40 cm (incomp.)
Estimated Height of Original Seal:	NA	Estimated Diameter of Original Seal:	NA
Number of Impressions:	2	Quality of Impressions:	Poor-fair

Completeness of Image: Segment of middle of design survives

DESCRIPTION OF SEAL AS IMPRESSED IMAGE

Hero moves to right in striding pose, arms straight (only left arm preserved), and holds two inverted lions (only lion to right has head preserved). Hero stands on hindquarters of addorsed winged creatures of uncertain type, almost certainly couchant (pedestal creature preserved only at right).

Lion to right turns head away from hero. Each lion holds its forelegs straight and places paws on hero's torso as if marchant.

Hero wears Assyrian garment that leaves forward leg exposed.

Lion to right has mouth open in roar.

Two rampant crossed bulls occupy terminal field. Bull facing left holds forelegs bent and extends them together in front of its body. Thick curved horn emerges from front of bull's head; small pointed ear is at top of head. Tail of bull facing right curls downward then upward. Mane of each animal is indicated by serrated edge along contour of its neck.

COMMENTARY

Although poorly preserved, this seal was extremely well executed. The rampant bulls exhibit especially fluid and crisp outlines. For the significance of the pedestal animals as an elite motif in early Achaemenid glyptic, see Dusinberre 1997b. Other hero scenes with pedestal animals in Volume I include PFS 31 (Cat.No. 172), PFS 36* (Cat.No. 5), PFS 164* (Cat.No. 20), PFS 523* (Cat.No. 209), PFS 524 (Cat.No. 2), and PFS 931* (Cat.No. 270). Other hero scenes in the PFS corpus with crossed animals independent of the heroic encounter include PFS 213 (Cat.No. 140) and PFS 990 (Cat.No. 256). PFS 396 and PFS 931* (Cat.No. 270) are the only seals in Volume I displaying both pedestal animals and crossed animals together. Crossed-animal compositions with the purposeful display qualities of PFS 396 signified an elite status in ancient western Asian glyptic and, in Achaemenid times, acquired renewed and additional symbolic valences (see Volumes II and III). For Volume I, see PFS 990 (Cat.No. 256).

For comparative illustrations including PFS 396, see pls. 216f (hero standing atop pedestal figure[s] or other supporting element), 220g (bulls and bull creatures), and 242f (crossed animals).

SEAL APPLICATION (SEE *APPENDIX ONE: CONCORDANCE OF SEALS TO TABLETS IN VOLUME I*)

PFS 396 occurs on the left edge of both PF 93 and PF 94, with PFS 241 (Cat.No. 252) applied on the reverse and upper edge of each tablet (and the right edge of PF 93). Both rollings are partial; that on PF 93 displays the negative space between the lion to the right of the hero and the crossed animals in the center; that on PF 94 displays the lion to the left of the hero in the center. PF 93 and PF 94 are both dated 498/497 B.C.

BIBLIOGRAPHY

Dusinberre 1997b, p. 124 (n. 57); Garrison 1988, pp. 291–93; Garrison 1998, p. 120 (n. 12).

PFS 381   Cat.No. 179

Seal Type:	Cylinder	Photograph:	Pl. 99a
Earliest Dated Application:	504 B.C.	Typology and Style:	I-C.4 — Fortification Style
Preserved Height of Image:	1.10 cm (incomp.)	Preserved Length of Image:	2.60 cm (comp.)
Estimated Height of Original Seal:	NA	Estimated Diameter of Original Seal:	0.80 cm
Number of Impressions:	2	Quality of Impressions:	Fair

Completeness of Image: Large segment of middle of design survives along its complete length

DESCRIPTION OF SEAL AS IMPRESSED IMAGE

Hero moves to left in striding pose, arms bent, and holds two inverted lions by tail (contact preserved only at left).

Each lion has its back to hero but turns its head toward him. Lion to left holds hind legs bent and extends them diagonally upward together. Lion holds upper foreleg straight, paw upturned, and extends it diagonally upward; lower foreleg is straight and extended diagonally downward; tail curls upward. Lion to right holds upper foreleg straight and extends it diagonally upward; lower foreleg (only partially preserved) is straight and extended downward.

Hero wears Assyrian garment that leaves forward leg exposed below knee; double border is at hem over forward and rear leg.

Each lion has mouth open in roar.

Bottom of palm tree, with framing fronds at base, is preserved in terminal field.

COMMENTARY

The pose of the lions, with their backs to the hero, is an unusual feature for this compositional type (cf. PFS 885 [Cat.No. 187]). By forcing the lions' heads to turn in toward the hero, the pose creates an awkward density in the lower portion of the design.

For comparative illustrations including PFS 381, see pl. 258e (palm trees).

SEAL APPLICATION (SEE *APPENDIX ONE: CONCORDANCE OF SEALS TO TABLETS IN VOLUME I*)

PFS 381 occurs on the reverse and upper edge of PF 76. The two rollings preserve the entire length of the seal design; that on the upper edge displays the hero in the center; that on the reverse displays the tree and lion to the left of the hero in the center. On the reverse the seal clearly was applied before the text since several cuneiform wedges cut into the top of the impression. PF 76 is dated 504 B.C.

BIBLIOGRAPHY

Garrison 1988, pp. 268–70, 493.

I-C.6. WINGED HUMAN-FACED/HUMAN-HEADED LION CREATURES

Cat.No. 180   PFS 32*

Seal Type:	Cylinder, Inscribed	Photographs:	Pl. 99c–d
Earliest Dated Application:	503 B.C.	Typology and Style:	I-C.6 — Modeled Style
Language of Inscription:	Elamite		
Preserved Height of Image:	1.70 cm (incomp.)	Preserved Length of Image:	3.40 cm (comp.)
Estimated Height of Original Seal:	NA	Estimated Diameter of Original Seal:	1.10 cm
Number of Impressions:	30	Quality of Impressions:	Poor-fair

Completeness of Image: Almost complete except for upper edge and lower edge

DESCRIPTION OF SEAL AS IMPRESSED IMAGE

Hero faces right, arms bent, and holds two inverted winged human-headed lion creatures by hind leg. Hero bends forward leg.

Each creature turns head away from hero. Creature to left holds rear hind leg straight and extends it vertically upward; forward hind leg is bent and extended downward toward hero's leg. Creature holds upper foreleg straight and extends it upward toward hero's leg; lower foreleg is straight, paw upturned, and extended vertically downward under its body; tail extends diagonally upward, hooking downward at its end. Creature to right holds rear hind leg curved and extends it vertically upward; forward hind leg is bent and extended diagonally downward. Creature holds upper foreleg (only partially preserved) slightly bent and extends it upward toward hero's leg; lower foreleg (only partially preserved) is bent and extended diagonally downward under its body; tail extends diagonally upward, hooking downward at its end with tufted termination.

Hero wears belted Assyrian garment that leaves forward leg exposed; fringe is indicated along front edge of garment. Long rounded beard with striations rests across hero's left shoulder; rounded coiffure rests at back of each creature's neck.

Human head of each creature may be beardless; small round coiffure rests at back of each creature's neck. Creature to left perhaps wears domed headdress.

Large dot in field before hero's waist is apparently unconnected to his garment.

Inscription fills terminal field.

INSCRIPTION

Elamite

Line
1. [(v.)]Šu-ud-da-⌈ya-⌉[u-]
2. ⌈da šak⌉ Ha-[tur-]
3. ⌈da⌉-da-[(na)]

Translation   Šuddayauda son (of) Haturdada

There are three lines to the inscription oriented along the vertical axis of the seal. As the reading shows, several signs are not preserved in any impression. This is especially difficult for the last name, which we, following Hallock 1977, reconstruct as Haturdada. Since neither the top nor the bottom of the seal is preserved, it is tempting to restore a *personenkeil* at the beginning of the first line and a genitive morpheme -na at the end of the third line.

COMMENTARY

PFS 32* is the personal seal of Šuddayauda, whose name occurs in the seal inscription. The name Šuddayauda occurs frequently in the PF texts; Hallock lists ninety different tablets, some with multiple occurrences of the name. Hallock identifies only one major official named Šuddayauda, whom he characterizes as an important official, an assigner and apportioner of workers. According to Hallock (1977), this Šuddayauda also used the office seal PFS 1* (Cat.No. 182), starting in year 20, while still using his personal seal. Workers whose rations and apportionments Šuddayauda specifically assigned or set are mentioned as receivers of grain, sesame, and date rations in PF 945, PF 984, PF 985, PF 986, PF 989, and PF 2043.

Koch identifies two separate major officials named Šuddayauda, one a *kurdabattiš* (Hallock: "chief of workers"), based on the occurrence of the PN and title on PF 1792 and PF 2070. This official, according to Koch, used PFS 32*. Koch places him in her Southeastern Region III. The other Šuddayauda she identifies as a *kanzabara* (Hallock: "treasurer"; Koch: "Hofschatzwart"), based upon the occurrence of the PN with PFS 1* (Cat.No. 182), a seal that she interprets as the office seal of the treasurer at Persepolis (Koch 1990, pp. 235–37).

On the thirteen tablets that actually carry PFS 32*, only six texts name a Šuddayauda specifically (PF 945, PF 984–986, PF 989, PF 2043). In these six texts he is characterized either as assigning workers or setting apportionments for workers. The other tablets that carry PFS 32* and name individuals in them include: PF 515 (Battišdana), PF 962 (workers whose apportionments were set by Bakena), PF 990 (workers whose apportionments were set by Manyakka), PF 991 (workers whose apportionments were set by Mardukka), PF 1639 and PF 1759 (both the receiving of grain by Bakuratsa the horseman), and PF 1734 (receiving of grain by Irtašbada).

The seal is large and well executed. The composition is slightly unbalanced by the large amount of negative space between the hero and the creature to the right. PFS 32* is closely paralleled in composition and spirit to the (uninscribed) seal impressed on the Fortification-type tablet from Qasr-i Abu Nasr.[47]

---

47. See *Introduction*, p. 7, above; Wilkinson 1965, fig. 24 (MMA 26.30.62).

For comparative illustrations including PFS 32*, see pl. 210e (heroic attitudes of control encounter), 264b (inscriptions without panels or case lines), and 284a (personal seals of various officers).

SEAL APPLICATION (SEE *APPENDIX ONE: CONCORDANCE OF SEALS TO TABLETS IN VOLUME I*)

PFS 32* often occurs only on the reverse and upper edge (PF 984, PF 991, PF 1734, and PF 1759), but there are many other location patterns: the reverse, upper edge, and left edge (PF 990, PF 1639, and PF 2043); the reverse, bottom edge, upper edge, and left edge (PF 515); the reverse and right edge (PF 945, the left edge is destroyed); the left edge only (PF 962); the reverse and left edge (PF 985); the reverse only (PF 986); the upper edge and left edge (PF 989). Only PF 986 may preserve a multiple rolling of the seal on one surface (reverse). On the reverse of five tablets the seal is inverted.

Impressions of the seal tend to be carefully applied, with little vertical or lateral distortion. Because the seal is relatively large, complete rollings of the scene are not common. Of the total thirty impressions, one impression is too poorly preserved for analysis. Of the twenty-nine remaining impressions, nineteen show some part of the inscription. In four impressions the seal is rolled for at least one complete turn, preserving the entire length of the seal design. Of these four applications, two display the inscription in the center; two display the hero and the creature to left in the center with a complete rolling of the inscription at the left of the impression. Of the remaining twenty-five partial rollings, one displays the inscription in the center; one preserves only the inscription; two preserve only the inscription and the creature to the left of the hero; six display the hero in the center; two preserve only the hero; four display the hero and the creature to left in the center with a partial rolling of the inscription at the left of the impression; two preserve only the hero and the creature to left; one preserves only the hero and the creature to right; four display the creature to the left of the hero in the center with a full (three instances) or partial rolling of the inscription at the left of the impression; two display the creature to the right of the hero in the center with a partial rolling of the inscription at the right of the impression.

On the reverse of eight tablets the seal clearly was applied before the text since several cuneiform wedges cut into the relief along the upper of the impression.

On PF 2043 an Aramaic notation is written over the seal impression, apparently qualifying the circumstances of the sealing agent.[48] PF 984, PF 990, PF 1734 are the earliest dated tablets with PFS 32* and are all dated 503 B.C.

BIBLIOGRAPHY

Garrison 1988, pp. 207–10, 492; Garrison and Dion 1999, p. 10 (n. 28); Garrison and Root 1996, p. 13; Hallock 1977, p. 130; Hallock 1985, pp. 595–96; Koch 1981, pp. 241–42; Koch 1990, pp. 72, 76, 244, 270, 275; Root 1996b, fig. 5; Tuplin 1987, p. 115.

---

48. Hallock (1969, p. 632) suggests a very tentative reading that is ambiguous.

PFS 677*   Cat.No. 181

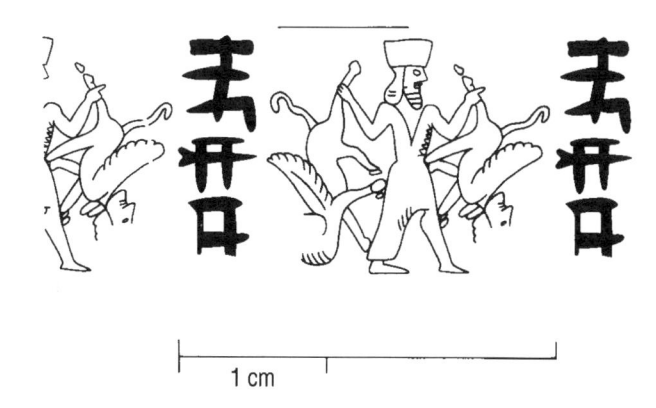

|—————1 cm—————|

Seal Type:	Cylinder, Inscribed	Photograph:	Pl. 100a
Earliest Dated Application:	502/501 B.C.	Typology and Style:	I-C.6 — Modeled Style
Language of Inscription:	Unknown		
Preserved Height of Image:	1.70 cm (incomp.)	Preserved Length of Image:	2.50 cm (comp.)
Estimated Height of Original Seal:	1.80 cm	Estimated Diameter of Original Seal:	0.80 cm
Number of Impressions:	6	Quality of Impressions:	Some preserve good detail

Completeness of Image: Almost complete except for upper edge and lower edge

DESCRIPTION OF SEAL AS IMPRESSED IMAGE

Hero faces right in striding pose, arms bent, and holds two inverted winged human-headed lion creatures by hind leg.

Each creature turns its head away from hero. Each creature holds rear hind leg upward toward hero's head; each creature places other three legs along hero's body as if marchant; creatures' crooked tails extend diagonally upward, hooked downward at end.

Hero wears Assyrian garment that leaves forward leg exposed below knee; garment apparently has deep V-neckline; fringe is indicated along chest; folds or fringe are indicated on front hem of lower part of garment over rear leg. Tall polos headdress rests on hero's head. Long rounded beard with horizontal striations rests across hero's left shoulder; rounded coiffure with horizontal striations rests at back of neck.

Diagonal markings are on head of creature to left. Creature to right may have short pointed beard; squared segmented coiffure rests at back of neck.

Three large cuneiform-like signs are arranged in vertical row in terminal field.

Portion of edge of seal is preserved at top of design above hero and creature to left.

INSCRIPTION

Cuneiform-like script, language unknown

    Line   1.   x x x
    Translation   ?

While the three signs are ordered along the vertical axis of the seal, the traces of the middle sign suggest the possibility of an orientation along the horizontal axis. The signs conform to no known script and possibly are mock signs meant to suggest the idea of an inscription.

COMMENTARY

For another probable mock inscription in cuneiform-like script, see PFS 671* (Cat.No. 174) and its commentary. See also PFS 284* (Cat.No. 111).

The engraving of PFS 677* is well executed and impressive. The compact forms of the inverted creatures create an unusually dense composition. The head of the creature to the left of the hero is poorly preserved. Possibly this creature is human-faced rather than human-headed.

For comparative illustrations including PFS 677*, see pls. 189i (polos headdresses), 211c (heroic attitudes of control encounter), 264h (inscriptions without panels or case lines), and 265f (mock inscriptions).

SEAL APPLICATION (SEE *APPENDIX ONE: CONCORDANCE OF SEALS TO TABLETS IN VOLUME I*)

PFS 677* occurs on the reverse, bottom edge, and upper edge of PF 439 and the reverse and upper edge of PF 1027. On the reverse of PF 439 the seal is applied twice, the lower impression inverted. Impressions often exhibit distortion. All six impressions preserve the entire length of the seal design; one displays the inscription and the creature to the right of the hero in the center; one displays the hero in the center, framed by the inscription on each end of the impression; two display the hero and the creature to left in the center; two display the creature to the right of the hero in the center. On the reverse of PF 1027 the seal clearly was applied before the text since several of the cuneiform-like wedges cut into the bottom of the impression. PF 439 is the earliest dated tablet with PFS 677* and is dated 502/501 B.C.

BIBLIOGRAPHY

Garrison 1988, pp. 252–55; Garrison and Dion 1999, pp. 10 (n. 28), 13 (n. 38); Root 1997, p. 233.

I-C.7. WINGED BIRD-HEADED LION CREATURES

Cat.No. 182   PFS 1*

Seal Type:	Cylinder, Inscribed	Photographs:	Pl. 100c–e
Earliest Dated Application:	506 B.C.	Typology and Style:	I-C.7 — Modeled Style
Language of Inscription:	Elamite		
Preserved Height of Image:	1.50 cm (incomp.)	Preserved Length of Image:	2.40 cm (comp.)
Estimated Height of Original Seal:	1.70 cm	Estimated Diameter of Original Seal:	0.80 cm
Number of Impressions:	233	Quality of Impressions:	Many preserve excellent detail

Completeness of Image: Complete except for upper edge and lower edge

DESCRIPTION OF SEAL AS IMPRESSED IMAGE

Hero in striding pose, rendered as rampant winged bull creature with human shoulders and arms, faces left, arms bent, and holds two inverted winged bird-headed lion creatures by hind leg.

Each creature turns head away from hero. Each creature has only one hind leg indicated, curved upward. Each creature holds forelegs straight, paws upturned, and extends them close together vertically downward; bird's tail curves upward.

Three rows of feathers are indicated on hero's wings; tail (only partially preserved) bends downward. Long curved horn emerges from front of hero's head; thick pointed ear is at top of head. Mane is rendered by outline along contour of neck.

Two rows of feathers are indicated on wing of each bird-like creature. Mane is rendered by outline along contour of neck. Creature to left has mouth open.

Crescent is in field above creature to right.

Paneled inscription is in terminal field.

INSCRIPTION

Elamite

Line
1. ⸢v.(?)⸣URU(?)-ki-su-na
2. v.Un-sa-AK(?)-TE(?)

Translation   ?

There are two lines to the inscription, oriented along the vertical axis of the seal, separated by a case line and enclosed in a panel. The shape of the signs is unusual, and a few of them are not otherwise represented in the PFS corpus. The first sign in the first line is not at all clear. The second sign in the first line is clear (if in fact it is not part of the first sign). The sign we read as URU(?) is otherwise not represented at Persepolis. An identical sign appears on an unprovenanced seal republished by Amiet (1973b, pl. 6, no. 29). The next three signs are clear. The name (if it is a name) in the first line has no obvious parallels. The first three signs in the second line are clear. The last sign or sign(s) are fairly clear, but an acceptable reading for the second line cannot be provided. Hallock's reading of GÌR (as reported by Hinz 1971) seems unlikely and appears eventually to have been dropped by Hinz since it does not appear in Hinz and Koch 1987. The signs of the inscription are placed very close together.

Hallock does not offer a published translation of the inscription. Hinz (1971) translates it as "belonging to the *Unsak*," a title that means second in command ("Vize-Intendant"), on analogy with the Treasury tablets where an individual named Saka is the "*Unsak*"; however, as mentioned, Hinz later seems to abandon this reading. Vallat (1992) suggests that *Unsak* is a personal name. The word in the second line may indeed be a title, but since we do not have a qualifier (e.g., DUMU) for the first line, it is difficult to know what to do with it. Regardless of how one reads the inscription, the meaning remains obscure. We are tempted, as Hinz, to read the second line as a title, associated with the word *unsak* (Hinz and Koch 1987, *un-sa-ak* and its associated forms, s.v.). This would be, however, the only seal inscription in the PFS corpus of hero seals (with the exceptions of the royal name seals) having a title in it. PFS 1* is, to be sure, an important seal, and so it may have warranted a special inscription.

It is striking that each line of the inscription is enclosed in a panel and oriented along the longitudinal axis of the seal design. The only other inscribed seals in Volume I that show this combination of features are PFS 64* (Cat.No. 173), PFS 526* (Cat.No. 216), and the royal name seals PFS 7* (Cat.No. 4) and PFS 113* (Cat.No. 19).

COMMENTARY

The seal belongs to a high-level office (Hinz's "Vize-Intendant"). The office represented by PFS 1* is concerned almost exclusively with rations for workers. The seal never occurs with any other seal, a usage pattern characteristic of seals employed by high-ranking offices and officers in the archive. It is first used on the PF tablets during years 15–19 by Karkiš, then during years 20–26 by Šuddayauda.

According to Hallock (1977), Šuddayauda continues to use his personal seal, PFS 32* (Cat.No. 180), during the years when he is also using the office seal PFS 1*. Koch identifies, however, two separate major officials named Šuddayauda, one of whom used PFS 32* (Cat.No. 180) (and bore the title *kurdabattiš* "chief of workers" [Hallock, op. cit.]), the other of whom used PFS 1* (and bore the title *kanzabara* "treasurer"). Hinz also links the office for which PFS 1* stands with the Treasury at Persepolis.

The design is beautifully executed and preserved. The bold modeling is typical of the strong Assyro-Babylonianizing style of many seals in the PFS corpus, but in this case the modeling is achieved on a very small seal. Nevertheless, relative to its small size, the seal is very detailed. Note especially the detailed treatment of the bull head of the hero, the indication of the thumbs of the hero's hands, and the rendering of the hero's wings. There are no exact parallels for the treatment of the hero's wings among the images of heroic encounter herein. The design of PFS 684 (Cat.No. 183) is very close compositionally and iconographically to PFS 1*, but dramatically different in feeling because poor preservation of the single impression mutes the powerful detailing that is shown in PFS 1*.

Although a bit more delicate and dance-like, the image of PFS 1* conveys the same sense of muscular demonic majesty as several proto-Elamite seals of ca. 3000 B.C., which are known through impressions on tablets from Susa.[49] It is, thus, all the more striking that this masterpiece of the Achaemenid period is carved at a height of only 1.70 cm whereas the proto-Elamite comparanda are about 2.5 times taller.[50]

For comparative illustrations including PFS 1*, see pls. 197a (hands), 200a (heroes as various composite creatures), 204a (arm positions of heroic control), 210a (heroic attitudes of control encounter), 232e (spectacular animal studies), 250a (crescents), 261a (paneled inscriptions with vertical case lines), and 281a (office seals).

SEAL APPLICATION (SEE *APPENDIX ONE: CONCORDANCE OF SEALS TO TABLETS IN VOLUME I*)

As an important office seal, PFS 1* always occurs alone on the seventy-four tablets that it seals and covers multiple surfaces: reverse, upper edge, right edge, and left edge (twenty tablets); reverse, right edge, and left edge (twenty tablets); reverse, upper edge, and left edge (eight tablets); upper edge, right edge, and left edge (ten tablets); reverse and left edge (five tablets); upper edge and left edge (five tablets); right edge and left edge (five tablets); obverse, reverse, and left edge (one tablet). On a few tablets the reverse carries multiple impressions of the seal. Of those fifty-five rollings on the reverse of tablets, sixteen are inverted. In nineteen instances the seal is applied along the vertical axis of the reverse, either at the far right or left edge of the reverse. Impressions of the seal tend to be carefully applied, although vertical and lateral distortions do occur. Because the seal is relatively small, complete rollings of the scene are fairly common. Of the total 233 impressions, fourteen impressions are too poorly preserved for analysis. Of the 219 remaining impressions, 181 show some part of the inscription. In eighty-two impressions the seal is rolled for at least one complete turn, preserving the entire length of the seal design. Of these eighty-two applications, fifteen display the inscription in the center; five display the inscription and the creature to the left of the hero in the center; nine display the inscription and the creature to the right of the hero in the center; nineteen display the hero in the center (ten of which show complete rollings of the inscription on each end of the impression); nine display the hero and the creature to the left in the center; ten display the hero and the creature to right in the center; ten display the creature to the left of the hero in the center; five display the creature to the right of the hero in the center. Of the remaining 137 partial rollings, sixteen display the inscription in the center; five display the inscription and the creature to the left of the hero in the center; eleven display the inscription and the creature to the right of the hero in the center; two preserve only the inscription; three preserve only the inscription and the creature to the left of the hero; two preserve only the inscription and the creature to the right of the hero; twenty display the hero in the center (eight of which show a partial rolling of the inscription); eight preserve only the hero; fourteen display the hero and the creature to left in the center with a partial rolling of the inscription at the left of the impression; one displays the hero and the creature to the right in the center with a partial rolling of the inscription at the right of the impression; two preserve only the hero and the creature to left; fourteen preserve only the hero and the creature to right; seventeen display the creature to the left of the hero in the center with a full or partial rolling of the inscription to left; twenty display the creature to the right of the hero in the center with a full or partial rolling of the inscription at right; two preserve only the creature to left.

On the reverse of forty-eight tablets the seal clearly was applied before the text since several cuneiform wedges cut into the top or bottom of the impressions. PF 880, PF 882, PF 883, PF 884, and PF 890 are the earliest dated tablets with PFS 1* and are all dated to 506 B.C.

BIBLIOGRAPHY

Aperghis 1999, pp. 183–85, 187–88; Brosius 1996, pp. 149, 150 (table 6), 151–52, 153–54 (table 7), 158 (table 9), 161; Garrison 1988, pp. 224–27, 256, 367, 418, 479–80, 492, 495, 522; Garrison 1998, p. 121 (n. 15); Garrison 2000, pp. 127–29, 132–33, 154, fig. 2, pl. 16:2; Garrison and Dion 1999, pp. 9 (n. 19), 10 (nn. 27–28); Garrison and Root 1996, pp. 12, 15–16; Hallock 1969, p. 78; Hallock 1977, pp. 129–31, pl. E-11; Hallock 1985, pp. 595–96; Hinz 1971, pp. 283–84; Koch 1981, pp. 233–37, 239–42; Koch 1983, p. 24 (n. 45); Koch 1990, pp. 83, 106–07, 235–36; Koch 1992, pp. 48–49; Root 1998, pp. 268–69, 273, fig. 4, pl. 6; Root in press, fig. 6.3; Stolper 1984, p. 306; Tuplin 1987, pp. 115, 130; Vallat 1992, p. 5.

---

49. For example, Pittman 1992, pp. 75–76, no. 47 (= Amiet 1966, p. 101, no. 56).

50. The seal impression on Louvre Sb 2801, cited above, measures 4.20 cm in height.

PFS 684   Cat.No. 183

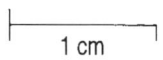

Seal Type:	Cylinder	Photograph:	Pl. 101a
Earliest Dated Application:	502/501 B.C.	Typology and Style:	I-C.7 — Modeled Style
Preserved Height of Image:	1.50 cm (incomp.)	Preserved Length of Image:	1.50 cm (incomp.)
Estimated Height of Original Seal:	NA	Estimated Diameter of Original Seal:	NA
Number of Impressions:	1	Quality of Impression:	Poor

Completeness of Image: Small segment of middle and lower parts of design survives

DESCRIPTION OF SEAL AS IMPRESSED IMAGE

Hero in striding pose, rendered as rampant winged bull creature with human torso, arms, and head, faces left, arms bent, and holds two(?) inverted winged bird-headed lion creatures by hind leg (preserved only at left).

Creature to left turns head away from hero; creature holds rear hind leg (only partially preserved) bent and extends it upward toward hero's head; forward hind leg is bent and extended outward to place paw on hero's wing. Creature holds upper foreleg straight, paw upturned, and extends it outward toward hero's lower body; lower foreleg (only partially preserved) is straight and extended vertically downward; straight tail (only partially preserved) extends diagonally upward.

Hero has rounded beard that rests over its right shoulder; rounded coiffure rests at back of neck. Tail curves downward, thickening at its end.

Preserved creature held by hero has mouth open.

COMMENTARY

The seal stylistically and iconographically is very close to PFS 1* (Cat.No. 182) and perhaps is the work of the same artist. The similarity of the iconography suggests that PFS 684 may be a less distinguished version after the PFS 1* model. Since PFS 1* is preserved through 233 impressions, whereas PFS 684 is known only through a single poorly preserved impression, point-by-point comparison is frustrated.

For comparative illustrations including PFS 684, see pl. 200c (heroes as various composite creatures).

SEAL APPLICATION (SEE APPENDIX ONE: CONCORDANCE OF SEALS TO TABLETS IN VOLUME I)

PFS 684 occurs on the reverse of PF 444. The original rolling, now much destroyed at the right, would have displayed the hero in the center. PF 444 is dated 502/501 B.C.

BIBLIOGRAPHY

Garrison 1988, pp. 224–27; Garrison 1998, p. 121 (n. 15); Garrison 2000, p. 129 (n. 42).

I-C.11. HORNED ANIMALS: DEER, GAZELLES, WILD GOATS, WILD SHEEP

Cat.No. 184   PFS 1260s

Seal Type:	Stamp, Octagonal Face	Photograph:	Pl. 101c
Earliest Dated Application:	495/494 B.C.	Typology and Style:	I-C.11 — Fortification Style
Preserved Height of Image:	1.70 cm (incomp.)	Preserved Width of Image:	1.10 cm (incomp.)
Number of Impressions:	1	Quality of Impression:	Poor

Completeness of Image: Almost complete except for left edge, lower edge, and details

DESCRIPTION OF SEAL AS IMPRESSED IMAGE

Hero faces left, arms straight, and holds two inverted horned animals of undetermined type by hind leg (animal to left only partially preserved).

Each animal holds rear hind leg bent and extends it vertically upward; forward hind leg is bent and extended downward toward hero's waist. Animal to right holds forelegs straight and extends them together downward toward hero's leg.

Hero wears Assyrian garment that leaves forward leg exposed below mid-thigh. Beard terminates in blunt point over hero's right shoulder; large rounded coiffure rests at back of head.

Horn emerges from back of head of animal to right; small rounded ear is also indicated.

Hero stands on double ground line. Edge of seal is reserved except at left and bottom.

COMMENTARY

Based on Q texts protocol, PFS 1260s should belong to Harmasula, who in year 27.10 (late December 495 B.C. and early January 494 B.C.) is going to the king under the authority (*halmi*) of Mišmina. He and his companion are described as *pirradaziš* "fast messengers."[51] A Harmasula also occurs in the account text PF 2011 (under the variant Harrumassula?), but clearly this is a different person (see Koch 1990, p. 53 note 247).

The edges of the stamp are sharp, but the design is preserved in very low, faint relief. The ground line in stamp seals is not often seen among the images of heroic encounter; see PFS 919s (Cat.No. 259), PFS 1321s (Cat.No. 176), PFS 1437s (Cat.No. 128), PFS 1624s (Cat.No. 261).

The seal face has an octagonal contour. For probable seal shape, see *Appendix Four: Stamp Seals in Volume I Grouped by Apparent Contour of Seal Face* and accompanying figure 9, no. 1. Only three other stamp seals herein, PFS 1309s (Cat.No. 229), PFS 1321s (Cat.No. 176), and PFS 1463s (Cat.No. 231), have octagonal seal faces. For discussion of the connection to the class of pyramidal stamp seals with octagonal faces leading up to the so-called Graeco-Persian style, see the entry for PFS 1321s (Cat.No. 176) and Root 1998. PFS 1260 is mainstream Fortification Style.

For comparative illustrations including PFS 1260s, see pls. 175b (Assyrian garments), 203h (arm positions of heroic control), 225g (horned animals and horned-animal creatures of undetermined types), 274g (stamp seals), 277b (ground lines on stamp seals), and 289a (personal seals of fast messengers [*piradazziš*]).

---

51. See also Lewis 1980 for *pirradaziš*, where (following Hallock) it is suggested that the term is not an occupational designation, but qualifies "the nature of the journey and the facilities to be extended to it."

SEAL APPLICATION (SEE *APPENDIX ONE: CONCORDANCE OF SEALS TO TABLETS IN VOLUME I*)

PFS 1260s occurs on the reverse of PF 1315. The one application, deeply impressed, is oriented along the horizontal axis of the tablet. PF 1315 is dated 495/494 B.C.

BIBLIOGRAPHY

Garrison 1988, pp. 291–93; Root 1998, pp. 268–69, fig. 4, pl. 6.

I-C.17. MIXED ANIMALS AND/OR CREATURES

PFS 1018   Cat.No. 185

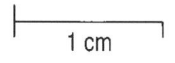

Seal Type:	Cylinder	Photograph:	Pl. 101e
Earliest Dated Application:	500/499 B.C.	Typology and Style:	I-C.17 — Fortification Style
Preserved Height of Image:	1.40 cm (incomp.)	Preserved Length of Image:	2.50 cm (incomp.)
Estimated Height of Original Seal:	NA	Estimated Diameter of Original Seal:	NA
Number of Impressions:	1	Quality of Impression:	Poor

Completeness of Image: Large section of middle and upper edge of design survives

DESCRIPTION OF SEAL AS IMPRESSED IMAGE

Hero faces left in striding pose, arms straight (only left arm preserved), and holds two inverted animals possibly of two different uncertain types by hind leg.

Each animal turns its head (partially preserved only to right) away from hero. Animal to left holds rear hind leg straight and extends it upward toward hero's head; forward hind leg (only partially preserved) is extended downward toward hero's shoulder. Animal holds one foreleg (only partially preserved) bent and extends it downward toward hero's lower leg; tail is extended diagonally upward. Animal to right holds rear hind leg bent and extends it upward toward hero's head; forward hind leg is bent and extended downward. Animal holds upper foreleg straight and extends it downward toward hero's leg; lower foreleg (only partially preserved) is straight and extended vertically downward; tail curves downward hooking upward at its end.

Hero wears Assyrian garment that leaves forward leg exposed below knee. Long beard terminates in blunt point over hero's right shoulder; large rounded coiffure rests at back of neck.

Edge of seal is preserved at top of design.

COMMENTARY

The manner in which the hero holds the animals by their forward hind legs is unusual within the PFS corpus and elsewhere.

    For comparative illustrations including PFS 1018, see pl. 219a (comparative heroic proportions).

SEAL APPLICATION (SEE *APPENDIX ONE: CONCORDANCE OF SEALS TO TABLETS IN VOLUME I*)

PFS 1018 occurs on the reverse of PF 1046. The partial rolling displays the hero in the center. The seal clearly was applied before the text since several cuneiform wedges cut into the top and bottom of the impression. PF 1046 is dated 500/499 B.C.

BIBLIOGRAPHY

Garrison 1988, pp. 318–19.

Cat.No. 186   PFS 138

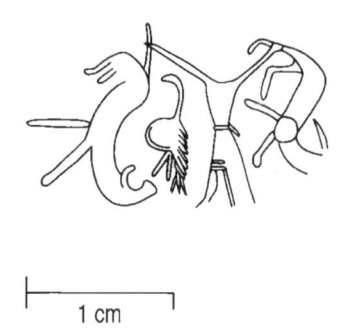

Seal Type:	Cylinder	Photograph:	Pl. 102a
Earliest Dated Application:	ND	Typology and Style:	I-C.17 — Fortification Style
Preserved Height of Image:	1.20 cm (incomp.)	Preserved Length of Image:	2.10 cm (incomp.)
Estimated Height of Original Seal:	NA	Estimated Diameter of Original Seal:	NA
Number of Impressions:	4	Quality of Impressions:	Poor

Completeness of Image: Segment of middle of design survives

DESCRIPTION OF SEAL AS IMPRESSED IMAGE

Hero moves to left in striding pose, arms straight above shoulder level, and holds inverted lion to left by tail, inverted horned animal of undetermined type to right by hind leg.

Lion has its back to hero but turns its head toward him. Lion holds hind legs bent and extends them together diagonally downward away from hero. Lion holds forelegs straight, upper one extended horizontally outward, lower one diagonally downward; tail is straight and extended vertically upward. Horned animal to right turns its head away from hero. Animal holds rear hind leg straight and extends it upward toward hero's head; forward hind leg is bent and extended downward. Animal holds upper foreleg straight and extends it upward toward hero's chest; lower foreleg is straight and extended downward toward hero's leg.

Hero wears belted Assyrian garment that leaves forward leg exposed below knee; double border is on hem of garment over forward knee; single border runs along hem of garment over rear leg. Sheath is at back of waist.

Lion has mouth open in roar. Animal to right has long straight horn emerging from back of its head.

Large long-necked bird with cascading plumage (peacock) stands facing left in field between hero and lion.

COMMENTARY

Lewis assigns PFS 138 to an unnamed supplier (of flour) at Hidali, based upon its occurrence on the Q texts PF 1405–1407. The newly identified occurrence of the seal on PF 1251 (P text, daily rations) records flour received at Hidali and so confirms the identification.

The design seems clumsy and poorly executed. Note also the different sizes of the two animals. The appearance of a peacock is unique among seals with images of heroic encounter in the PFS corpus. On the significance of the peacock as an Achaemenid prestige possession, see Miller 1989 and 1997, pp. 189–92. In the ancient Mesopotamian *representational* tradition the peacock is rare to nonexistent. It is not even listed in van Buren 1939.

For comparative illustrations including PFS 138, see pls. 203b (arm positions of heroic control), 226g (birds), 236a (animals/creatures as secondary elements of main design field), and 287d (personal seals of various suppliers).

SEAL APPLICATION (SEE *APPENDIX ONE: CONCORDANCE OF SEALS TO TABLETS IN VOLUME I*)

PFS 138 occurs only on the left edge of tablets. The four partial impressions all display the hero in the center. No tablet on which PFS 138 occurs is dated.

BIBLIOGRAPHY

Garrison 1988, pp. 312–13; Lewis 1980, p. 194.

I-C.18. ANIMALS OF UNCERTAIN TYPE

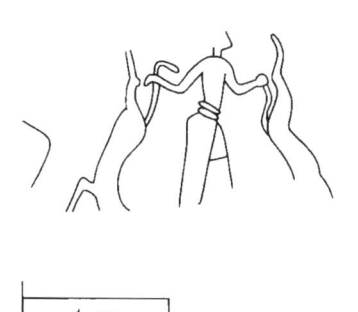

PFS 885   Cat.No. 187

Seal Type:	Cylinder	Photograph:	Pl. 102c
Earliest Dated Application:	500/499 B.C.	Typology and Style:	I-C.18 — Fortification Style
Preserved Height of Image:	1.20 cm (incomp.)	Preserved Length of Image:	2.10 cm (incomp.)
Estimated Height of Original Seal:	NA	Estimated Diameter of Original Seal:	NA
Number of Impressions:	3	Quality of Impressions:	Poor

Completeness of Image: Small segment of middle of deign survives

DESCRIPTION OF SEAL AS IMPRESSED IMAGE

Hero faces right, arms bent, and holds two inverted animals of uncertain type by tail.

Each animal has back to hero but apparently turns its head toward him (suggested by partial image at left). Animal to left holds one hind leg vertically upward. Animal holds one foreleg bent and extends it downward in front of its body; tail curves diagonally upward, bending at its end. Animal to right holds one hind leg bent and extends it diagonally upward; tail undulates vertically upward.

Hero wears double-belted Assyrian garment that leaves forward leg exposed below knee.

Traces of uncertain fragmentary object are in terminal field.

COMMENTARY

The manner in which the inverted animals seem to float away from the hero, the large amount of negative space, and the very elongated proportions of the hero's body make this an unusual seal design.

For comparative illustrations including PFS 885, see pls. 174h (Assyrian garments) and 273h (open compositions).

280 SEALS ON THE PERSEPOLIS FORTIFICATION TABLETS, VOLUME I: IMAGES OF HEROIC ENCOUNTER

SEAL APPLICATION (SEE *APPENDIX ONE: CONCORDANCE OF SEALS TO TABLETS IN VOLUME I*)

PFS 885 occurs on the left edge of PF 761, PF 763, and PF 1589. All impressions exhibit distortion. Of the three partial applications, those on PF 761 and PF 763 display the hero in the center; that on PF 1589 displays the animal to the left of the hero in the center. PF 763 is the earliest dated tablet with PFS 885 and is dated 500/499 B.C.

BIBLIOGRAPHY

Garrison 1988, pp. 293–94.

Cat.No. 188   PFS 234

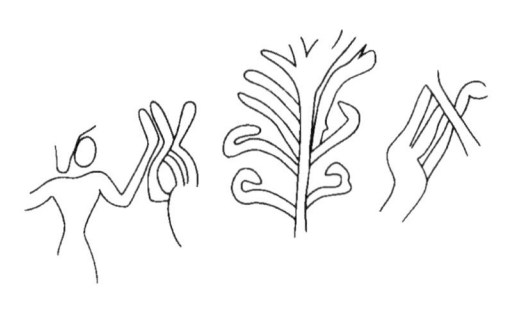

Seal Type:	Cylinder	Photograph:	Pl. 102e
Earliest Dated Application:	503/502 B.C.	Typology and Style:	I-C.18 — Broad and Flat Styles
Preserved Height of Image:	1.70 cm (incomp.)	Preserved Length of Image:	3.20 cm (incomp.)
Estimated Height of Original Seal:	NA	Estimated Diameter of Original Seal:	NA
Number of Impressions:	2	Quality of Impressions:	Fair

Completeness of Image: Segment of middle of design survives

DESCRIPTION OF SEAL AS IMPRESSED IMAGE

Hero faces left, arms bent above shoulder level, and holds two inverted animals of uncertain type by tail. Arm and inverted animal at far right of preserved impressions should be hero's arm and animal to left of hero. Only hindquarters and hind legs of animals survive.

Animal to left of hero holds hind legs straight, paw upturned on forward hind leg, and extends them upward together toward hero's head; straight tail (only partially preserved) extends diagonally upward. Animal to right holds hind legs bent and extends them vertically upward together; tail curves upward.

Hero wears garment of uncertain type. Squared beard rests over his right shoulder; large round coiffure rests at back of neck.

Asymmetric long-branched tree of uncertain type is in terminal field.

COMMENTARY

The flat carving and abstraction is typical of seals carved in the Broad and Flat Styles. For a similarly asymmetric and rangy tree, see PFS 849 (Cat.No. 189).

For comparative illustrations including PFS 234, see pl. 257f (trees of uncertain type).

SEAL APPLICATION (SEE *APPENDIX ONE: CONCORDANCE OF SEALS TO TABLETS IN VOLUME I*)

PFS 234 occurs on the reverse (inverted) of PF 336 and PF 340, with PFS 48 (III) on the left edge of each tablet. Both impressions exhibit distortion. The rolling on PF 340 preserves the entire length of the seal design and displays the tree in the center. The partial rolling on PF 336 also displays the tree in the center. PF 336 is the earliest dated tablet with PFS 234 and is dated 503/502 B.C.

BIBLIOGRAPHY

Garrison 1988, pp. 421–23.

I-C.19. WINGED CREATURES OF UNCERTAIN TYPE

PFS 849   Cat.No. 189

Seal Type:	Cylinder	Photograph:	Pl. 102g
Earliest Dated Application:	505 B.C.	Typology and Style:	I-C.19 — Mixed Styles II
Preserved Height of Image:	1.30 cm (incomp.)	Preserved Length of Image:	2.30 cm (incomp.)
Estimated Height of Original Seal:	NA	Estimated Diameter of Original Seal:	NA
Number of Impressions:	2	Quality of Impressions:	Fair

Completeness of Image: Segment of middle of design survives

DESCRIPTION OF SEAL AS IMPRESSED IMAGE

Hero faces left, arms straight, and holds two inverted winged creatures of uncertain type by hind leg (preserved only at right).

Each creature has back to hero but turns its head toward him. Tail of creature to left curves downward. Creature to right holds rear hind leg (only partially preserved) curved and extends it vertically upward; forward hind leg is slightly bent and extended diagonally upward. Creature holds upper foreleg straight, paw upturned, and extends it diagonally upward; lower foreleg (only partially preserved) is straight and extended diagonally downward; tail curves downward with tufted termination.

Hero wears belted robe. Beard terminates in blunt point over his right shoulder; rounded coiffure rests at back of neck.

Creature to right may have mouth open in roar (lower jaw not preserved) or may be based on animal with a short, narrow muzzle.

Asymmetric long-branched tree of uncertain type occupies terminal field.

COMMENTARY

The doughy texture of the hero's garment finds numerous parallels in the Court Style; compare PFS 7* (Cat.No. 4). The animal forms are typical of the Fortification Style.

    For comparative illustrations including PFS 849, see pls. 183e (robes of various undetailed types), 221e (animals and creatures of uncertain type), and 257g (trees of uncertain type).

SEAL APPLICATION (SEE *APPENDIX ONE: CONCORDANCE OF SEALS TO TABLETS IN VOLUME I*)

PFS 849 occurs on the left edge of both PF 648 and PF 1177. The two partial impressions both display the creature to the right of the hero in the center. PF 1177 is the earliest dated tablet with PFS 849 and is dated 505 B.C.

BIBLIOGRAPHY

Garrison 1988, pp. 380–81.

I-D. HERO CONTROLS MARCHANT ANIMALS OR CREATURES
I-D.3. WINGED HUMAN-FACED/HUMAN-HEADED BULL CREATURES

Cat.No. 190   PFS 1155

Seal Type:	Cylinder	Photograph:	Pl. 103a
Earliest Dated Application:	499 B.C.	Typology and Style:	I-D.3 — Fortification Style
Preserved Height of Image:	1.50 cm (incomp.)	Preserved Length of Image:	3.10 cm (comp.)
Estimated Height of Original Seal:	1.70 cm	Estimated Diameter of Original Seal:	1.00 cm
Number of Impressions:	3	Quality of Impressions:	Fair

Completeness of Image: Almost complete except for upper edge and lower edge

DESCRIPTION OF SEAL AS IMPRESSED IMAGE

Hero faces right, arms straight, and holds two marchant winged human-headed bull creatures by beard.

Each creature raises bent forward foreleg upward toward hero's waist; long tail undulates upward, bending downward at its end.

Hero wears robe. Fluted Persian tiara with multiple bands is worn low on hero's forehead. Beard terminates in blunt point over hero's left shoulder; small rounded coiffure rests at back of neck.

Each creature wears domed headdress with band low on its forehead; serrated edge and projections at back embellish headdress of creature to left. Each creature has long beard that rests along its chest (blunt pointed at left, rounded at right) and small round coiffure at back of neck.

COMMENTARY

The normal conventions of the Fortification Style have here been altered somewhat in the schematic, geometric treatment of the faces of the human-headed creatures and the weak outline of the human figure. All human heads have very low foreheads. The fluted Persian tiara is rare among the images of heroic encounter in the PFS corpus; compare PFS 139s (Cat.No. 222), PFS 326 (Cat.No. 100), PFS 774 (Cat.No. 58), and PFS 1189 (Cat.No. 8). This particular heroic composition is unique in the PFS corpus.

For comparative illustrations including PFS 1155, see pls. 183g (robes of various undetailed types), 189d (Persian crowns and fluted tiaras), 190g (beards), 207d (arm positions of heroic control), 232c (animals/creatures with distinctive perspectival elements), and 235d (human-headed/human-faced creatures).

SEAL APPLICATION (SEE *APPENDIX ONE: CONCORDANCE OF SEALS TO TABLETS IN VOLUME I*)

PFS 1155 occurs on the reverse (inverted) and upper edge of PF 1209 and the left edge of PF 1226. Two impressions preserve the entire length of the seal design; that on the upper edge of PF 1209 displays the hero and the creature to right in the center; that on the reverse of PF 1209 displays the creature to the left of the hero in the center. The partial rolling on the left edge of PF 1226 displays the hero in the center. On the reverse of PF 1209 the seal clearly was applied before the text since several cuneiform wedges cut into the top of the impression. PF 1226 is the earliest dated tablet with PFS 1155 and is dated 499 B.C.

BIBLIOGRAPHY

Garrison 1988, pp. 283–84, 482, 496; Garrison and Dion 1999, pp. 11–12, fig. 8.

I-D.4. LIONS

PFS 1300   Cat.No. 191

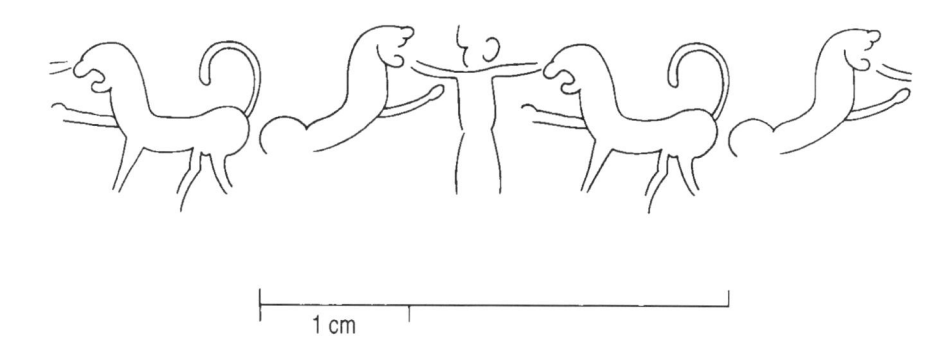

Seal Type:	Cylinder	Photograph:	Pl. 103c
Earliest Dated Application:	499 B.C.	Typology and Style:	I-D.4 — Fortification Style
Preserved Height of Image:	1.30 cm (incomp.)	Preserved Length of Image:	3.20 cm (comp.)
Estimated Height of Original Seal:	1.50 cm	Estimated Diameter of Original Seal:	1.00 cm
Number of Impressions:	2	Quality of Impressions:	Very poor

Completeness of Image: Section of middle of design survives along its complete length

DESCRIPTION OF SEAL AS IMPRESSED IMAGE

Hero faces left, arms straight, and holds one rampant lion by jaw (at left) and one marchant lion by snout (at right).

Each lion raises forward foreleg toward hero's chest. Tail of lion to right curves upward.

Hero wears robe; rounded coiffure rests at back of neck.

Each lion has mouth open in roar.

COMMENTARY

The seal occurs on both the left edge and the reverse of Q text PF 1378. Q texts sealed with single seals tend to be the seals of the receivers. If this is the case with PF 1378, PFS 1300 should belong to Bakanšakka, who in year 23.1 (499 B.C.) received flour rations on his way from Persepolis to Susa under the authority (*halmi*) of the king. A flour supplier by the name of Bakanšakka occurs in PF 837 and PF 1966. A Bakanšakka received grain rations in PF 1688. One Pandušašša is described as the wife of Bakanšakka in PF 784. Probably several different individuals are involved in these transactions (cf. Koch 1990, pp. 11 [n. 20], 73 [n. 325]).

For comparative illustrations including PFS 1300, see pl. 290e (personal seals of various travelers).

SEAL APPLICATION (SEE *APPENDIX ONE: CONCORDANCE OF SEALS TO TABLETS IN VOLUME I*)

PFS 1300 occurs on the reverse and left edge of PF 1378. No other seal is used on the tablet. The partial rolling on the reverse displays the creature to the right of the hero in the center. The partial rolling on the left edge displays the lion to the left of the hero in the center. On the reverse of PF 1378 the seal clearly was applied before the text since several cuneiform wedges cut into the top of the impression. PF 1378 is dated 499 B.C.

BIBLIOGRAPHY

Garrison 1988, pp. 284–85.

I-D.10. WINGED HUMAN-FACED/HUMAN-HEADED BULL OR LION CREATURES

Cat.No. 192   PFS 514

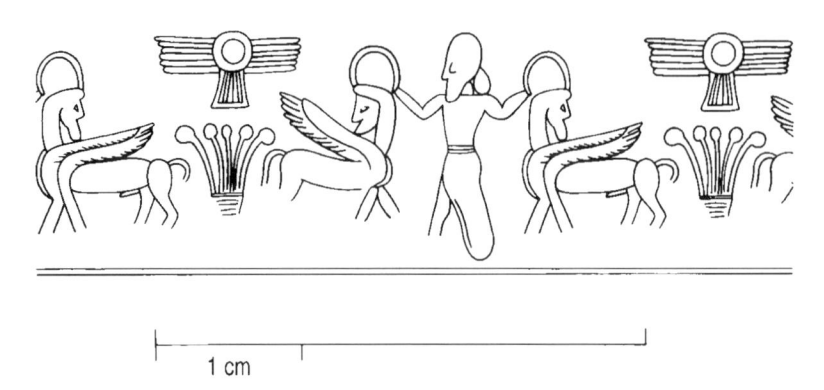

Seal Type:	Cylinder	Photograph:	Pl. 104a
Earliest Dated Application:	501/500 B.C.	Typology and Style:	I-D.10 — Fortification Style
Preserved Height of Image:	1.60 cm (incomp.)	Preserved Length of Image:	3.40 cm (comp.)
Estimated Height of Original Seal:	1.70 cm	Estimated Diameter of Original Seal:	1.10 cm
Number of Impressions:	7	Quality of Impressions:	Fair

Completeness of Image: Complete except for upper edge and details along lower edge

DESCRIPTION OF SEAL AS IMPRESSED IMAGE

Hero faces left in striding pose, arms bent, and holds two marchant winged horned human-faced bull or lion creatures by horn.

Each creature moves toward hero but turns its head away from him; their tails (partially preserved) curve downward.

Hero wears double-belted Assyrian garment that leaves forward leg exposed below mid-thigh; suggestion of border is along hem. Long squared beard rests across hero's right shoulder; round coiffure rests at back of neck.

Each creature has two rows of feathers indicated on its wing. Each creature's head has thick vertical bull-like neck; long horn emerges from front of creature's head and curves to back of head. Creature to left has short pointed beard that rests over its wing. Creature to right has long rounded beard that rests over its wing. Creature to right is ithyphallic.

Stylized papyrus plant is in lower terminal field; winged symbol with bird's tail is above papyrus in upper terminal field.

Line border is preserved at bottom of design.

COMMENTARY

This is a large seal for the Fortification Style. The creatures are very distinctive; see PFS 1076 (Cat.No. 193) for a similar hybridization. An artist (Artist of the Pendent Robe) discussed by Garrison (1991 and 1996a) shows a similar style to that of PFS 1613. The terminal field image of winged symbol over floral element is unique among seals with images of heroic encounter in the PFS corpus. The winged symbol above various versions of the "sacred tree" appears frequently on Neo-Assyrian seals depicting worshipers framing the element (e.g., on a seal impression from Nimrud: Herbordt 1992, p. 183, no. 47, pl. 3, no. 2). Occasionally a similar arrangement occurs on Neo-Assyrian hero seals (Collon 1987, pp. 79–80, no. 358).

For comparative illustrations including PFS 514, see pls. 234i (human-headed/human-faced creatures), 249c (winged symbols), 260b (papyrus plants), and 269f (terminal field motifs other than inscriptions).

SEAL APPLICATION (SEE *APPENDIX ONE: CONCORDANCE OF SEALS TO TABLETS IN VOLUME I*)

PFS 514 occurs on the reverse (inverted) of PF 234, the reverse and left edge of PF 236, and the reverse, upper edge, and left edge of PF 257. PFS 57* (Cat.No. 239) is applied (inverted) directly above PFS 514 on the reverse of PF 234. PFS 514 is rolled twice on the reverse of PF 236, one impression directly above the other. Impressions often exhibit distortion. In two impressions the seal is rolled for at least one complete turn, preserving the entire length of the seal design. Of these two applications, one displays the hero in the center; one displays the creature to the left of the hero and the terminal field in the center. Of the remaining five partial rollings, two display the hero in the center; one preserves only the hero and the creature to left; one preserves only the creature to the right of the hero; one displays the terminal field in the center. PF 257 is the earliest dated tablet with PFS 514 and is dated 501/500 B.C.

BIBLIOGRAPHY

Dusinberre 1997b, p. 128 (n. 131); Garrison 1988, pp. 252, 356–59, 480, 487, 490.

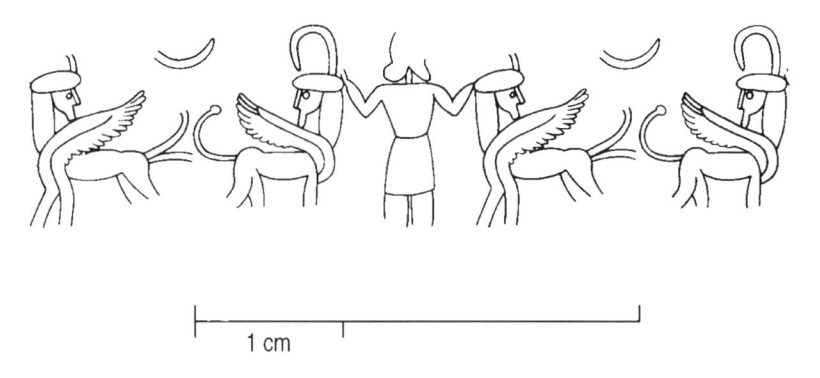

PFS 1076   Cat.No. 193

Seal Type:	Cylinder	Photograph:	Pl. 104c
Earliest Dated Application:	494 B.C.	Typology and Style:	I-D.10 — Fortification Style
Preserved Height of Image:	1.40 cm (incomp.)	Preserved Length of Image:	3.00 cm (comp.)
Estimated Height of Original Seal:	1.60 cm	Estimated Diameter of Original Seal:	1.00 cm
Number of Impressions:	3	Quality of Impressions:	Poor

Completeness of Image: Almost complete except for upper edge and lower edge

DESCRIPTION OF SEAL AS IMPRESSED IMAGE

Hero faces right, arms bent, and holds two marchant winged horned human-faced bull or lion creatures by back of head.

Each creature moves toward hero but turns its head away from him. Tail of creature to left curls upward with tufted termination. Creature to right apparently has two tails (only partially preserved), one curving upward, other curving downward.

Hero wears belted tunic and trousers. Blunt-pointed beard rests over hero's left shoulder; rounded coiffure rests at back of neck.

Narrow beard of each creature terminates in blunt point over its wing. Long curved horn emerges from back of head of creature to left, from front of head of creature at right. Horn of creature to left curves to front of head.

Crescent is in upper terminal field.

Commentary

For a similar rendering of the creatures, see PFS 1613 (Cat.No. 82) and PFS 514 (Cat.No. 192). The position of the horn on the creature at left is unusual. This may represent a miscarving (as may the two tails on the creature at right of the hero).

Hallock (1969) notes in his entry for PFS 1076 (as the unnumbered seal on PF 1120) that the seal carries an "Aramaic inscription (apparently)," but there is no trace of an inscription surviving on any impression of this seal on PF tablets.

For comparative illustrations including PFS 1076, see pls. 185g (tunics), 219c (comparative heroic proportions), and 251c (crescents).

Seal Application (see *Appendix One: Concordance of Seals to Tablets in Volume I*)

PFS 1076 occurs on the reverse (inverted) of PF 1120 and the reverse (inverted) and upper edge of PF 1212. PFS 1666 (II) is applied directly below PFS 1076 on the reverse of PF 1120. All rollings preserve the entire length of the seal design, but they are very lightly applied and thus difficult to read. The rolling on the reverse of PF 1212 displays the hero in the center. The rolling on the reverse of PF 1076 displays the creature to the right of the hero in the center. The rolling on the upper edge of PF 1212 displays the two creatures in the center. On the reverse of both tablets the seal clearly was applied before the text since several cuneiform wedges cut into the bottom of the impressions. PF 1120 is the earliest dated tablet with PFS 1076 and is dated 494 B.C.

Bibliography

Dusinberre 1997b, p. 128 (n. 131); Garrison 1988, pp. 356–59.

I-D.11. HORNED ANIMALS: DEER, GAZELLES, WILD GOATS, WILD SHEEP

PFS 180   Cat.No. 194

|⊢——⊣|
  1 cm

Seal Type:	Cylinder	Photograph:	Pl. 105a
Earliest Dated Application:	506/505 B.C.	Typology and Style:	I-D.11 — Plausibly Antique: Assyro-Babylonian Drilled Style
Preserved Height of Image:	1.40 cm (incomp.)	Preserved Length of Image:	3.80 cm (incomp.)
Estimated Height of Original Seal:	NA	Estimated Diameter of Original Seal:	NA
Number of Impressions:	6	Quality of Impressions:	Poor-fair

Completeness of Image: Segment of middle of design survives

DESCRIPTION OF SEAL AS IMPRESSED IMAGE

Four-winged hero faces right, arms bent, and holds two marchant horned animals of undetermined type by upper foreleg. Animal to left has large segmented horn or antler. Only portion of neck and forelegs is preserved of animal to right.

Animal to left moves toward hero but turns its head away from him. Animal holds upper foreleg straight and extends it upward toward hero's upper wing; curved end of tail is preserved above animal's back. Animal to right holds upper foreleg straight and extends it upward toward hero's upper wing; end of lower foreleg is preserved near hero's lower wing.

Hero wears garment of uncertain type. Hero has long, squared, segmented beard resting over his chest; long, round, segmented coiffure rests at back of neck.

Horn or antler of animal to left emerges from top of its head and bends to left (only partially preserved); large pointed ear emerges from back of head.

COMMENTARY

A crude Drilled Style such as seen in this seal was popular in late Neo-Assyrian and Neo-Babylonian glyptic.[52] This style may well have continued down into Achaemenid times since there exist several examples of it in the seals preserved on the PF tablets; compare PFS 62 (Cat.No. 104). PFS 180, as is typical of this style, is quite large. Control encounters with horned animals seem rare in the Neo-Assyrian/Neo-Babylonian repertoire, but examples of Achaemenid-period seals displaying a hero controlling horned animals (deer, wild goats) include three from Susa (Amiet 1972, p. 285, pl. 189, nos. 2207, 2209–10).

For comparative illustrations including PFS 180, see pl. 191f (variously detailed beards).

SEAL APPLICATION (SEE *APPENDIX ONE: CONCORDANCE OF SEALS TO TABLETS IN VOLUME I*)

PFS 180 occurs on the reverse, upper edge, and left edge of both PF 260 and PF 261. No other seal occurs on the tablets. On the reverse of both tablets the seal is inverted. Of the six partial impressions, two preserve only the

---

52. See Porada 1948, pp. 86–87, pl. 107, fig. 722, for discussion of the Late Drilled Style and a comparison for treatment of hero and animal forms.

hero; three display the hero in the center; one preserves only the hero and the animal to left. On the reverse of both tablets the seal clearly was applied before the text since several cuneiform wedges cut into the bottom of the impression. PF 260 is the earliest dated tablet with PFS 180 and is dated 506/505 B.C.

BIBLIOGRAPHY

Garrison 1988, pp. 466–67; Garrison 1998, p. 121 (n. 15).

I-D.12. WINGED HORNED-ANIMAL CREATURES: DEER, GAZELLES, WILD GOATS, WILD SHEEP

Cat.No. 195   PFS 719

Seal Type:	Cylinder	Photograph:	Pl. 105c
Earliest Dated Application:	503/502 B.C.	Typology and Style:	I-D.12 — Linear Styles
Preserved Height of Image:	1.30 cm (incomp.)	Preserved Length of Image:	2.30 cm (incomp.)
Estimated Height of Original Seal:	NA	Estimated Diameter of Original Seal:	NA
Number of Impressions:	2	Quality of Impressions:	Poor-fair

Completeness of Image: Segment of middle of design survives

DESCRIPTION OF SEAL AS IMPRESSED IMAGE

Hero faces right, left arm bent and right arm straight at diagonal (only partially preserved), and holds two marchant winged horned animal creatures of undetermined type by upper foreleg.

Each creature moves toward hero but turns its head away from him. Each creature raises curved forward foreleg and extends it upward toward hero's head. Creature to right has large horn or antler (only partially preserved) emerging from top of its head. Termination of long curving horn or antler (no longer preserved at juncture with creature's head) appears in field before face of creature to left. Inverted crescent(?) (partially preserved) is in field below creature to right.

Hero wears robe; hero apparently has short pointed beard.

COMMENTARY

Since the upper part of the hero's right arm is not preserved, the scene could conceivably be a combat encounter. The coarse engraving is typical of seals carved in the Linear Styles.

For comparative illustrations including PFS 719, see pl. 218g (comparative heroic proportions).

SEAL APPLICATION (SEE *APPENDIX ONE: CONCORDANCE OF SEALS TO TABLETS IN VOLUME I*)

PFS 719 occurs on the left edge of both PF 490 and PF 1127. The two partial rollings display the hero in the center. PF 490 is the earliest dated tablet with PFS 719 and is dated 503/502 B.C.

BIBLIOGRAPHY

Garrison 1988, pp. 435–38, 496.

I-D.17. MIXED ANIMALS AND/OR CREATURES

PFS 1002   Cat.No. 196

Seal Type:	Cylinder	Photograph:	Pl. 105e
Earliest Dated Application:	ND	Typology and Style:	I-D.17 — Fortification Style
Preserved Height of Image:	1.40 cm (incomp.)	Preserved Length of Image:	2.40 cm (incomp.)
Estimated Height of Original Seal:	NA	Estimated Diameter of Original Seal:	NA
Number of Impressions:	1	Quality of Impression:	Poor

Completeness of Image: Small segment of middle and upper edge of design survives

DESCRIPTION OF SEAL AS IMPRESSED IMAGE

Hero (only bent left arm preserved) holds marchant winged human-faced horned-animal creature of undetermined type by upper foreleg at right; hero holds winged creature of different undetermined type at left (contact not preserved). Hindquarters of winged creature at right of impression belong to this creature.

Creature to right of hero extends forward leg diagonally upward toward hero's shoulder; tail extends diagonally upward curving downward at its end. Long pointed beard rests over creature's chest; long curving horn emerges from front of its head. Wing of creature held to left of hero has five long thin feathers at its end; tail extends diagonally upward, hooking downward at its end.

Palm tree is in terminal field.

Line border is preserved at top of design.

COMMENTARY

See Garrison 1988 for this important artist who works close to the Court Style.

    For comparative illustrations including PFS 1002, see pls. 225f (horned animals and horned-animal creatures of undetermined types) and 258g (palm trees).

SEAL APPLICATION (SEE *APPENDIX ONE: CONCORDANCE OF SEALS TO TABLETS IN VOLUME I*)

PFS 1002 occurs on the reverse of PF 1018. The partial rolling displays the plant device in the terminal field in the center. The date of PF 1018 is unknown.

BIBLIOGRAPHY

Garrison 1988, pp. 352–56, 361.

Cat.No. 197   PFS 109

Seal Type:	Cylinder	Photographs:	Pl. 106a–b
Earliest Dated Application:	499 B.C.	Typology and Style:	I-D.17 — Fortification Style
Preserved Height of Image:	1.60 cm (incomp.)	Preserved Length of Image:	3.60 cm (incomp.)
Estimated Height of Original Seal:	NA	Estimated Diameter of Original Seal:	NA
Number of Impressions:	5	Quality of Impressions:	Poor

Completeness of Image: Large segment of middle of design survives along most of its length

DESCRIPTION OF SEAL AS IMPRESSED IMAGE

Hero faces right in striding pose, arms bent, and holds marchant lion to left and marchant winged bull creature to right, each by tail. Hero bends and lifts forward leg.

Both lion and bull creatures move away from hero. Lion to left raises one straight foreleg and extends it diagonally upward; tail curves upward with tufted termination. Tail of creature to right curves downward between its hind legs with thickened termination.

Hero appears to wear Assyrian garment that leaves forward leg exposed. Squared beard rests over hero's left shoulder; large round coiffure rests at back of neck. Hero perhaps wears domed headdress.

Four-pointed star with central dot is in field between hero's head and wing of creature to right.

COMMENTARY

Based upon Q texts protocol, sealings on the left edge of PF 1382, PF 1476, PF 1489, PF 1491, and PF 1541 indicate that PFS 109 belonged to an unnamed flour supplier or office.

The varied placement of the tails of the creatures enlivens what is otherwise a poorly executed and awkward design. The composition of marchant creatures held by the tails is unique in the PFS hero corpus. The creatures, facing one another, will have formed a heraldic group, but any terminal field element disposed between them is lost to us. The seal appears to be quite worn.

For comparative illustrations including PFS 109, see pls. 190d (beards), 193c (round coiffures), 198f (feet and shoes), 206b (arm positions of heroic control), 210f (heroic attitudes of control encounter), 218b (comparative heroic proportions), and 253c (stars, rosettes).

SEAL APPLICATION (SEE APPENDIX ONE: CONCORDANCE OF SEALS TO TABLETS IN VOLUME I)

PFS 109 occurs only on the left edge of tablets. Impressions of the seal are very difficult to read. No impression preserves the entire seal design. Of the five partial applications, four display the hero in the center; one displays the lion to the left of the hero in the center. PF 1489 is the earliest dated tablet with PFS 109 and is dated 499 B.C.

BIBLIOGRAPHY

Garrison 1988, pp. 333–35, 346.

I-D.18. ANIMALS OF UNCERTAIN TYPE

PFS 256 — Cat.No. 198

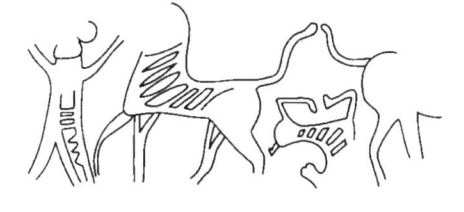

Seal Type:	Cylinder	Photograph:	Pl. 106d
Earliest Dated Application:	ND	Typology and Style:	I-D.18 — Linear Styles
Preserved Height of Image:	1.30 cm (incomp.)	Preserved Length of Image:	2.80 cm (incomp.)
Estimated Height of Original Seal:	NA	Estimated Diameter of Original Seal:	NA
Number of Impressions:	2	Quality of Impressions:	Fair

Completeness of Image: Segment of middle of design survives

DESCRIPTION OF SEAL AS IMPRESSED IMAGE

Hero faces left in striding pose, arms straight at diagonal above shoulder level, and holds two marchant animals of uncertain type (relationship preserved only at right).

Hindquarters of animal at far right of preserved impressions should belong to animal to left of hero. Animal to right of hero raises curved forward foreleg slightly to touch hero's leg. Tails of both animals curve upward.

Hero appears to wear Assyrian garment that leaves forward leg exposed; irregular designs decorate fabric along torso and rear leg. Rounded coiffure rests at back of hero's head.

Animal to right of hero has irregular rectangular and lozenge-shaped designs on its body.

Small animal of uncertain type is suspended on its back in lower terminal field. Animal's body points to right, but head turns to left; two legs are bent under its body; small tail extends downward with bent termination.

COMMENTARY

A unique outline linear style is used in the execution of this seal. The linear detailing on the human and animal bodies is also very unusual; compare, perhaps, PFS 20 (Cat.No. 145), which is, however, very different in style. The large size of the main animals and the position of the animal suspended on its back in the terminal field are also noteworthy. The small animal in the terminal field is probably a horned animal such as a goat. It relates closely to the small group of animals shown inverted in the terminal field (e.g., PFS 1475 [Cat.No. 177]); and like these, it may represent an animal carcass that narrativizes the heroic encounter. See also the comments on PFS 1388 (Cat.No. 162).

For comparative illustrations including PFS 256, see pls. 218c (comparative heroic proportions), 237c (animal carcasses), and 268c (terminal field motifs other than inscriptions).

SEAL APPLICATION (SEE APPENDIX ONE: CONCORDANCE OF SEALS TO TABLETS IN VOLUME I)

PFS 256 occurs on the left edge of both PF 1689 and PF 1690, with PFS 63 (Cat.No. 24) applied on two other surfaces of each tablet. The partial rolling on PF 1689 displays the animal to the right of the hero in the center. The left edge of PF 1690 is damaged; the preserved rolling displays the small animal in the terminal field in the center. The dates of PF 1689 and PF 1690 are unknown.

BIBLIOGRAPHY

Garrison 1988, pp. 442–46, 532.

I-D.19. WINGED CREATURES OF UNCERTAIN TYPE

Cat.No. 199   PFS 1153

Seal Type:	Cylinder	Photograph:	Pl. 106f
Earliest Dated Application:	497 B.C.	Typology and Style:	I-D.19 — Mixed Styles I
Preserved Height of Image:	0.70 cm (incomp.)	Preserved Length of Image:	1.90 cm (incomp.)
Estimated Height of Original Seal:	NA	Estimated Diameter of Original Seal:	NA
Number of Impressions:	2	Quality of Impressions:	Poor

Completeness of Image: Small segment of middle of design survives

DESCRIPTION OF SEAL AS IMPRESSED IMAGE

Hero moves to right(?), arms bent, and holds two marchant winged creatures of uncertain type by throat.

Each creature raises curved forward foreleg upward toward hero's torso (at left) and thigh (at right). Thick tail of creature to left curves upward (only partially preserved).

Hero wears garment of uncertain type.

COMMENTARY

The style cannot be placed comfortably in any one style from the PFS corpus, although the animal forms seem close to the local Fortification Style; for the style of the animals, see PFS 514 (Cat.No. 192) and PFS 1076 (Cat.No. 193). The hero's pose, rounded shoulders, and narrow waist relate the seal to many Modeled Style designs (see Garrison 1988).

SEAL APPLICATION (SEE *APPENDIX ONE: CONCORDANCE OF SEALS TO TABLETS IN VOLUME I*)

PFS 1153 occurs on the upper edge and right edge of PF 1203. The two partial rollings display the hero in the center. PF 1203 is dated 497 B.C.

BIBLIOGRAPHY

Garrison 1988, pp. 249–52, 254–55.

PFS 913   Cat.No. 200

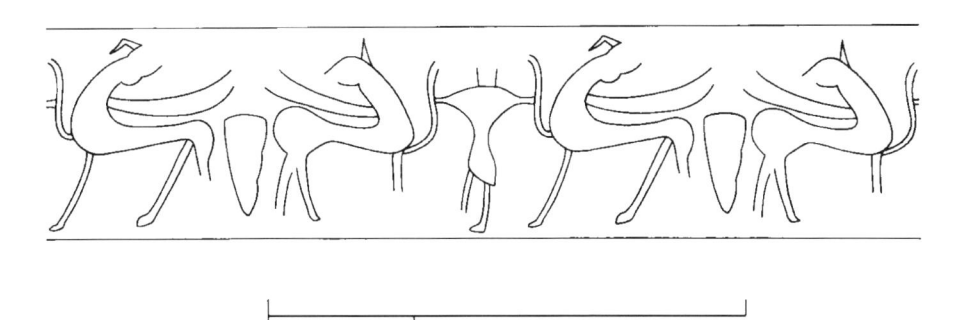

Seal Type:	Cylinder	Photograph:	Pl. 107a
Earliest Dated Application:	497/496 B.C.	Typology and Style:	I-D.19 — Linear Styles
Preserved Height of Image:	1.40 cm (comp.)	Preserved Length of Image:	3.30 cm (comp.)
Estimated Height of Original Seal:	1.40 cm	Estimated Diameter of Original Seal:	1.10 cm
Number of Impressions:	1	Quality of Impression:	Very poor

Completeness of Image: Almost complete except for details along upper edge and lower edge

DESCRIPTION OF SEAL AS IMPRESSED IMAGE

Hero moves to left, arms straight at horizontal, and holds two marchant winged creatures of uncertain type by raised foreleg.

Each creature moves toward hero but turns its head away from him. Each creature raises curved forward foreleg (only partially preserved) and extends it upward toward hero's head.

Hero wears tunic.

Creature to left has pointed ear emerging from back of its head. Bent ear (or horn?) of creature to right emerges from top of its head.

Large, elongated triangular element, point down, is in terminal field.

Edge of seal is preserved at top and bottom of design.

COMMENTARY

For a good parallel for the large triangular element, see the stamp seal of Nidintu-Anu used on a legal text from Uruk dating to 426 or 366 B.C. (Artaxerxes I or II).[53] Wallenfels (1993, p. 284) suggests that the triangular shape may refer to the Mesopotamian sky god An (Anu), as it occurs on several impressions with zodiacal imagery from Uruk of the Hellenistic period. It is possible that the triangular shape on PFS 913 (with its prominent placement in the terminal field) may relate to this hypothesis, although the representational contexts provided by PFS 913 and our comparanda here do not clarify such a link in any obvious way (e.g., through a link with a relevant theophoric name).

The poor quality of the carving is typical of seals carved in the Linear Styles.

For comparative illustrations including PFS 913, see pls. 185f (tunics), 248h (abstract symbols of Mesopotamian deities), and 267h (terminal field motifs other than inscriptions).

SEAL APPLICATION (SEE APPENDIX ONE: CONCORDANCE OF SEALS TO TABLETS IN VOLUME I)

PFS 913 occurs on the left edge of PF 786. The rolling preserves the entire length of the seal design and displays the hero in the center. PF 786 is dated 497/496 B.C.

BIBLIOGRAPHY

Garrison 1988, pp. 435–37.

---

53. Stolper 1990b, pp. 577–79, pl. 49a.

I-E. HERO CONTROLS VARIOUSLY POSED ANIMALS OR CREATURES

I-E.15. SNAKES

Cat.No. 201   PFS 418

Seal Type:	Cylinder	Photograph:	Pl. 107c
Earliest Dated Application:	500/499 B.C.	Typology and Style:	I-E.15 — Diverse Styles
Preserved Height of Image:	1.50 cm (comp.)	Preserved Length of Image:	2.60 cm (comp.)
Estimated Height of Original Seal:	1.50 cm	Estimated Diameter of Original Seal:	0.80 cm
Number of Impressions:	3	Quality of Impressions:	Poor

Completeness of Image: Complete except for parts of lower edge

DESCRIPTION OF SEAL AS IMPRESSED IMAGE

Hero (perhaps with face frontal) stands with arms outstretched but curving slightly downward. He holds two vertically disposed snakes.

Snakes undulate upward with heads rising above hero's head; each snake turns its head toward hero.

Hero wears robe.

Two triangular objects are in field above hero's head.

In terminal field stands winged creature with human body apparently facing left. Creature holds straight arms above shoulder level and has two wings (upper and lower) to either side of its body. Its head is in form of square with hooked element emerging off right upper corner and extending upward to left at diagonal. Creature wears robe. Triangular object is in field above winged creature's head.

Edge of seal is preserved at top and bottom of design.

COMMENTARY

The awkward carving style exhibits some geometric elements, such as the head of the winged creature, which may suggest a carving tradition in the Persepolis environs that had ties to archaizing Elamite modes (see, e.g., PFS 2 [Cat.No. 3]). See PFS 5 (II) for a genie rendered in a related stylistic mode. The hero with snakes is extremely rare in Achaemenid glyptic but was a significant feature in the repertoire of late prehistoric/early protohistoric stamp seals of Iran (see de Miroschedji 1981); and snake imagery played a prominent role in Elamite art before the advent of the Achaemenids.[54] A parallel for the hero with snakes on PFS 418 occurs on a cylinder from Susa assigned by Amiet to pre-Achaemenid first millennium Elamite production (Amiet 1972, p. 283, pl. 188, no. 2197).

For comparative illustrations including PFS 418, see pls. 183d (robes of various undetailed types), 206h (arm positions of heroic control), 214h (frontal faces and/or bodies), 215c (unusual heroic attitudes), 228h (fish

---

54. See Root, in press, for overview of the snake in ancient Iranian art, with discussion of issues relating to discontinuance of its popularity during the Achaemenid Empire.

and reptiles), 238b (subsidiary human/human-creature figures in encounter images), and 266b (terminal field motifs other than inscriptions).

SEAL APPLICATION (SEE *APPENDIX ONE: CONCORDANCE OF SEALS TO TABLETS IN VOLUME I*)

PFS 418 occurs twice on the reverse (one rolling placed immediately above the other) and once on the bottom edge of PF 110. All three rollings of PFS 418 preserve the entire length of the seal design. The upper rolling on the reverse displays the hero in the center. The lower rolling on the reverse displays the winged human creature in the center. The rolling on the bottom edge displays the winged human creature at the right of the impression, the hero at the left of the impression. PF 110 is dated 500/499 B.C.

BIBLIOGRAPHY

Garrison 1988, pp. 457–58; Root in press.

COMPOSITIONAL FORMAT II: IMAGES OF HEROIC COMBAT
II-A. HERO STABS RAMPANT ANIMAL OR CREATURE
II-A.4. LIONS

PFS 80   Cat.No. 202

Seal Type:	Cylinder	Photographs:	Pl. 108a–b
Earliest Dated Application:	504/503 B.C.	Typology and Style:	II-A.4 — Linear Styles
Preserved Height of Image:	1.50 cm (comp.)	Preserved Length of Image:	3.00 cm (comp.)
Estimated Height of Original Seal:	1.50 cm	Estimated Diameter of Original Seal:	1.00 cm
Number of Impressions:	11	Quality of Impressions:	Fair-good

Completeness of Image: Complete except for segment of lower edge

DESCRIPTION OF SEAL AS IMPRESSED IMAGE

Hero faces left, extending straight right arm to grasp rampant lion by upper foreleg; left arm is straight and held down behind body to hold long sword that he drives into lion's belly. Hero, in striding pose, appears to place foot on forward paw of lion's forward hind leg.

Lion moves toward and faces hero. Lion holds upper foreleg straight and extends it upward toward hero's head; lower foreleg is straight and extended downward behind hero's sword; short thick tail curls upward with tufted termination.

Hero wears short tunic with side panels and horizontal detailing. Hero wears tall conical headdress with knob (possibly Egyptianizing White Crown). Rounded beard rests over hero's right shoulder.

Lion has mouth open in roar.

In terminal field is heraldic group of two rampant lions with palm tree as central element. Each lion holds upper foreleg curved and extends it upward toward palm fronds; lower foreleg is straight and extended downward toward base of tree; tail of each lion curls upward with tufted termination. Mouth of each lion is open in roar; mane of each lion is rendered by diagonal striations on neck. In field between hind legs of lion to right of tree are two small dots.

Wide line border is along upper edge and lower edge of design.

COMMENTARY

The style is a mixture of an abstract linear approach (human figure) and the Fortification Style (animal figures and palm tree). The rendering of the human figure and headdress cannot be paralleled among hero seals in the PF corpus.[55] Although daggers are frequently represented on heroic combat seals in the corpus, long swords are rare. Actual examples of both types of weapon were excavated in the Treasury at Persepolis (Schmidt 1957, pl. 75). Herein, PFS 80 is the only seal that combines a heroic encounter of the combat type with a separate heraldic animal group. Although the heraldic lions are described above as elements of the terminal field, the heroic combat image may arguably be described thus instead. The application patterns of PFS 80 in fact suggest that its owner/user thought of the heraldic animals as the focal point (see below).

For comparative illustrations including PFS 80, see pls. 185b (tunics), 186d (headdresses), 244a (daggers and swords), 258b (palm trees), 269b (terminal field motifs other than inscriptions), 276d (borders).

SEAL APPLICATION (SEE *APPENDIX ONE: CONCORDANCE OF SEALS TO TABLETS IN VOLUME I*)

PFS 80 always occurs on the left edge of tablets. Impressions show little or no distortion. All rollings of the seal preference the heraldic group of the two lions on either side of the palm tree. In three impressions the seal is rolled for at least one complete turn, preserving the entire length of the seal design. Of these three applications, one displays the lion to the left of the palm tree in the center; one displays the lion to the right of the palm tree in the center; one displays the palm tree in the center. Of the remaining eight partial impressions, one displays the lion to the left of the palm tree in the center; three display the lion to the right of the palm tree in the center; two display the lion to the right of the palm tree and the lion held by the hero in the center; two preserve only the palm tree flanked by the lions. PF 1125, PF 1126, and PF 1215 are the earliest dated tablets with PFS 80 and are all dated 504/503 B.C.

BIBLIOGRAPHY

Garrison 1988, pp. 442–46, 497, 532; Garrison and Root 1996, p. 11.

---

55. Compare the engraving of the human figure on a scarab now in Geneva identified as Phoenician of the fourth century B.C. (Vollenweider 1967, pl. 65, no. 7).

PFS 584* — Cat.No. 203

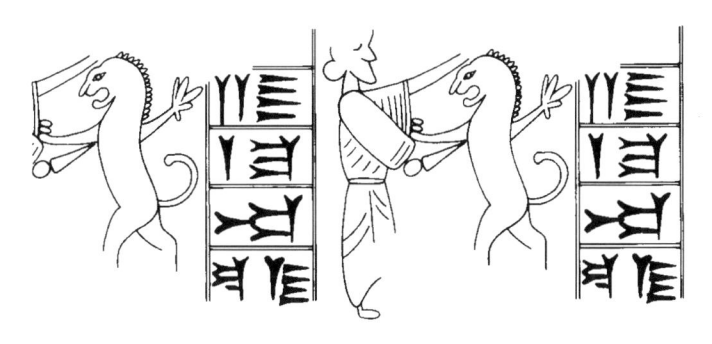

Seal Type:	Cylinder, Inscribed	Photograph:	Pl. 109a
Earliest Dated Application:	ND	Typology and Style:	II-A.4 — Court Style
Language of Inscription:	Elamite		
Preserved Height of Image:	1.90 cm (incomp.)	Preserved Length of Image:	2.50 cm (comp.)
Estimated Height of Original Seal:	NA	Estimated Diameter of Original Seal:	0.80 cm
Number of Impressions:	1	Quality of Impression:	Poor

Completeness of Image: Large segment of middle of design survives

DESCRIPTION OF SEAL AS IMPRESSED IMAGE

Hero, torso seen in profile, faces right, extending straight left arm upward to grasp rampant lion by top of head or forelock (not preserved); right arm is straight and brought forward to stab lion in chest with dagger.

Lion moves toward and faces hero. Lion holds one foreleg straight and extends it outward to place paw on hero's right arm; other foreleg is held up and away from body with toes splayed; tail curls upward with tufted termination.

Hero wears belted Persian court robe; sleeves of garment are down, wide, and billowy; folds are indicated on both sleeves and over the upper torso; central vertical fold and radiating diagonal folds occur on lower part of garment. Hero's beard terminates in blunt point over left upper arm; rounded coiffure rests at back of hero's neck.

Mane of lion is rendered by serrated edge along contour of neck; mouth is open in roar.

Large paneled inscription is in terminal field.

INSCRIPTION

Elamite

Line x+1. [...]
      x+2. KU
      x+3. MA(?)
      x+4. NA
      x+5. x x

Translation ?

Parts of five lines are preserved, oriented along the horizontal axis of the seal, separated by case lines, and enclosed in a panel. The preserved lines are unusually short, having only one or two signs. Although the preserved signs seem clear and well formed, we are unable to give a reading of the inscription.

COMMENTARY

PFS 584* was not included in Garrison 1988. The sophisticated profile rendering of the human form and the elaborately detailed garment recall somewhat the design on PFS 859* (Cat.No. 205). The compositions of the two seals are also remarkably similar. The carving style of PFS 584* appears, however, much more angular and stiff in comparison to the sureness and sophistication of the carving in PFS 859* (Cat.No. 205). The designs of both PFS 859* (Cat.No. 205) and PFS 584* have close parallels to doorjamb reliefs from Persepolis.[56]

For comparative illustrations including PFS 584*, see pls. 180b (Persian court robes with sleeves down), 199b (feet and shoes), 212i (heroic attitudes of combat encounter), 218f (comparative heroic proportions), 244e (daggers and swords), and 262g (paneled inscriptions with horizontal case lines).

SEAL APPLICATION (SEE *APPENDIX ONE: CONCORDANCE OF SEALS TO TABLETS IN VOLUME I*)

PFS 584* occurs once, inverted, on the obverse of PF 333. The one rolling of the seal displays the lion in the center. The seal clearly was applied before the text since several cuneiform wedges cut into the bottom of the impression. The date of PF 333 is unknown.

BIBLIOGRAPHY

Garrison and Dion 1999, p. 10 (n. 28).

Cat.No. 204   PFS 853

Seal Type:	Cylinder	Photograph:	Pl. 110a
Earliest Dated Application:	500/499 B.C.	Typology and Style:	II-A.4 — Mixed Styles II
Preserved Height of Image:	1.80 cm (incomp.)	Preserved Length of Image:	2.90 cm (comp.)
Estimated Height of Original Seal:	2.00 cm	Estimated Diameter of Original Seal:	0.90 cm
Number of Impressions:	2	Quality of Impressions:	Poor-fair

Completeness of Image: Complete except for upper edge, segment of lower edge, and details

DESCRIPTION OF SEAL AS IMPRESSED IMAGE

Hero faces left, extending straight right arm to grasp rampant lion by throat; left arm is straight and brought forward to stab lion in chest with dagger.

Lion moves toward and faces hero; lion lifts forward hind leg slightly. Lion holds one foreleg straight and extends it upward to place paw on hero's chest; other foreleg is straight, held up and away from body with toes splayed; long tail (only partially preserved) curves down between lion's hind legs.

Hero wears Assyrian garment that leaves forward leg exposed. Pointed coiffure curls upward at back of hero's neck.

Lion has mouth open in roar with tongue shown.

Date palm with bulbous fruit clusters to either side of its short trunk is in lower terminal field; star is in upper terminal field. To right of date palm, rampant winged bull creature moves toward it but turns head back to right. Bull creature holds upper foreleg bent and extends it diagonally upward over date palm; lower foreleg is bent and extended upward in front of its body. Long curved horn emerges from front of winged bull's head; two long

---

56. Compare, especially, the heroic encounters on the Palace of Darius (Schmidt 1953, pls. 144–46).

pointed ears emerge from top of its head; long tail (only partially preserved) curves down between winged bull's hind legs.

Edge of seal is preserved at bottom of design below rampant lion, bull creature, and date palm.

COMMENTARY

The design is more complex than the typical combat encounter. The execution of the rampant winged bull has close ties to the Court Style. For similar stylization of the tree, see PFS 971 (Cat.No. 171).

For comparative illustrations including PFS 853, see pls. 195d (coiffures of distinctive types/sub-types), 213c (heroic attitudes of combat encounter), 244f (daggers and swords), 259e (date palms), 268g (terminal field motifs other than inscriptions), 279e (carving anomalies).

SEAL APPLICATION (SEE *APPENDIX ONE: CONCORDANCE OF SEALS TO TABLETS IN VOLUME I*)

PFS 853 occurs on the reverse of both PF 685 (inverted) and PF 1487. The rolling on the reverse of PF 685 is almost complete, although very poorly preserved; it displays the two rampant animals in the center. The rolling on the reverse of PF 1487 preserves the entire length of the seal design and displays the date palm and the winged bull in the center. On the reverse of PF 1487 the seal clearly was applied before the text since several cuneiform wedges cut into the top of the impression. PF 685 is the earliest dated tablet with PFS 853 and is dated 500/499 B.C.

BIBLIOGRAPHY

Garrison 1988, pp. 370–74, 414.

PFS 859*   Cat.No. 205

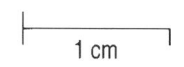

Seal Type:	Cylinder, Inscribed	Photographs:	Pl. 111a–b
Earliest Dated Application:	503/502 B.C.	Typology and Style:	II-A.4 — Court Style
Language of Inscription:	Uncertain		
Preserved Height of Image:	1.30 cm (incomp.)	Preserved Length of Image:	3.20 cm (incomp.)
Estimated Height of Original Seal:	NA	Estimated Diameter of Original Seal:	NA
Number of Impressions:	2	Quality of Impressions:	Fair

Completeness of Image: Segment of middle of design survives

DESCRIPTION OF SEAL AS IMPRESSED IMAGE

Hero, torso seen in profile, faces right, extending straight left arm upward to grasp rampant lion by forelock; right arm is straight and down, and brought forward to stab lion in chest with dagger.

Lion moves toward and faces hero. Lion holds upper foreleg straight and extends it upward to place paw on hero's left arm; lower foreleg (only partially preserved) is straight and extended downward in front of its body; lion's tail appears to curl upward with hooked termination.

Hero wears Persian court robe; sleeves of garment are pushed up to reveal hero's bare arms (sleeves on left arm pushed up only to elbow); gathered folds of sleeves are indicated. Quiver, secured to hero's back by straps, carries three arrows; tassels hang down from midsection of quiver; bow is also indicated on hero's back. Hero may be beardless; thick rounded coiffure rests at back of head.

Mane of lion is rendered by spikes along contour of neck; mouth is open in roar with pointed tongue shown. Large paneled inscription is in terminal field.

INSCRIPTION

Cuneiform script, language uncertain

Line	x+1.	[...]⌈x⌉
	x+2.	⌈x⌉ [...]⌈x⌉
	x+3.	[...]⌈x⌉

Translation　　?

Parts of three lines are preserved, oriented along the horizontal axis of the seal, separated by case lines, and enclosed in a panel. In the two impressions of the seal, the ends of the three lines are preserved to the left of the heroic scene, and the beginning of line x+2 is preserved to the right of the heroic scene. Too little remains to suggest a reading.

COMMENTARY

PFS 859* occurs on one tablet, PF 691, a J text. PFS 859* may be the personal seal of an unnamed official staffing the office in charge of cattle recorded in J texts (see Garrison 1991).

PFS 859* is a sophisticated example of the Court Style; it is also one of the early dated examples of the Court Style. The profile view of the hero, the elaborate treatment of the upper garment, and the large tasseled quiver and bow are rendered with sureness and precision. The scene has close parallels to doorjamb reliefs from Persepolis;[57] isolated non-heroic scenes from the PFS corpus seem to show the same hand, for example, PFS 35* (II). Although only partially preserved, the seal is clearly very large, perhaps originally one of the largest in the whole PFS corpus. The composition of PFS 859* is very similar to that seen on PFS 584* (Cat.No. 203).

For comparative illustrations including PFS 859*, see pls. 179g (Persian court robes with sleeves pushed up), 190e (beards), 192f (rounded coiffures), 209c (arm positions of heroic combat), 214d (profile torsos), 218i (comparative heroic proportions), 232h (spectacular animal studies), 246f (bows, arrows, quivers), 263a (paneled inscriptions with horizontal case lines), and 283b (personal seals of supply/apportionment officers).

SEAL APPLICATION (SEE *APPENDIX ONE: CONCORDANCE OF SEALS TO TABLETS IN VOLUME I*)

PFS 859* occurs on the reverse and left edge of PF 691. Because the seal is so large, both impressions show less than half of the height of the design; in both instances it is the upper half of the design that has been carefully applied. The two partial impressions display the hero and the lion in the center; that on the reverse is framed by partial rollings of the inscription on the left edge and right edge of the impression. On the reverse of PF 691 the seal clearly was applied before the text since several cuneiform wedges cut into the top of the impression. PF 691 is dated 503/502 B.C.

BIBLIOGRAPHY

Garrison 1988, pp. 412–15, 479, 491; Garrison 1991, pp. 14–15, 20, figs. 23–24; Garrison 1996b, pp. 25, 31; Garrison 2000, p. 131; Garrison in press; Garrison and Dion 1999, p. 10 (n. 28).

---

57. Compare, especially, the heroic encounters on the Palace of Darius (Schmidt 1953, pls. 144–46).

PFS 1264s
Cat.No. 206

|―――|
| 1 cm |

Seal Type:	Stamp, Oval Face	Photograph:	Pl. 111d
Earliest Dated Application:	494 B.C.	Typology and Style:	II-A.4 — Fortification Style
Preserved Height of Image:	1.60 cm (comp.)	Preserved Width of Image:	1.10 cm (incomp.)
Number of Impressions:	1	Quality of Impression:	Poor

Completeness of Image: Complete except for left and right edges and details

DESCRIPTION OF SEAL AS IMPRESSED IMAGE

Hero faces right, torso in profile, extending his straight left arm upward to grasp rampant lion by top of head; right arm is slightly curved and brought across body to stab lion in belly with dagger (only partially preserved).

Lion moves toward and faces hero. Lion holds one foreleg curved (only partially preserved) and extends it upward toward hero's chest; tail (only partially preserved) curves upward.

Hero wears robe. Hero's long squared beard rests over his chest; small rounded coiffure rests high, at back of head.

Edge of seal is preserved at upper left and bottom of design.

COMMENTARY

Based on Q texts protocol, PFS 1264s should belong to one Bakakeya, who in year 28.2 (494 B.C.) went to the king with three companions under the authority (*halmi*) of the king. He and his companions are described as *pirradaziš* "fast messengers."[58] The name Bakakeya occurs frequently in the PF and PT texts, and it is clear that we are dealing with several individuals: for example, in PF 473 a Bakakeya is the *masašiš* (OD); in PF 591–592 a Bakakeya authorizes (*halmi*) a large grain transaction; in PF 1567 a Bakakeya is the *ištimara*(?) (OD) (note that this is a Q text and the seal that belongs to this Bakakeya is PFS 1450 [illegible]); in PF 1805 a Bakakeya is the scribe; in PF 1996 a Bakakeya is the *ullira* (OD).

The seal design may have been quite well made, despite the poor impression; note especially the well-handled profile of the upper torso of the hero. The profile torso combined with the long plain robe suggests the look of "Babylonian" worshipers familiar on many Neo-Babylonian seals and on numerous seals documented through impressions in the PFS corpus (Volume II). The small size of the lion in relation to the hero is unusual. See Garrison 1988 for the hand of this distinctive artist.

The stamp face has an oval contour. For probable seal shape, see *Appendix Four: Stamp Seals in Volume I Grouped by Apparent Contour of Seal Face* and accompanying figure 9, nos. 3b or 5b.

For comparative illustrations including PFS 1264s, see pls. 214f (profile torsos), 219f (comparative heroic proportions), 274h (stamp seals), and 289b (personal seals of fast messengers [*piradazziš*]).

SEAL APPLICATION (SEE *APPENDIX ONE: CONCORDANCE OF SEALS TO TABLETS IN VOLUME I*)

PFS 1264s occurs on the upper edge of PF 1320. The partial application is oriented approximately along the longitudinal axis of the tablet. PF 1320 is dated 494 B.C.

BIBLIOGRAPHY

Garrison 1988, pp. 359–63, 487.

---

58. For the term *pirradaziš*, see the commentary for PFS 1260s (Cat.No. 184).

Cat.No. 207 PFS 43*

Seal Type:	Cylinder, Inscribed	Photographs:	Pl. 112a–b
Earliest Dated Application:	503/502 B.C.	Typology and Style:	II-A.4 — Diverse Styles
Language of Inscription:	Elamite		
Preserved Height of Image:	1.90 cm (comp.)	Preserved Length of Image:	3.10 cm (comp.)
Estimated Height of Original Seal:	1.90 cm	Estimated Diameter of Original Seal:	1.00 cm
Number of Impressions:	20	Quality of Impressions:	Good

Completeness of Image: Complete except for some signs of inscription

DESCRIPTION OF SEAL AS IMPRESSED IMAGE

Hero faces right, torso in profile, extending straight left arm upward to grasp rampant lion at top of head; right arm is curved and brought across body to stab lion in chest with dagger or sword. Hero, in vigorous striding pose, raises forward leg to place his foot on rear hind leg of lion.

Lion moves away from hero in running pose but turns its head back toward him. One foreleg is bent and extended outward to place paw with toes splayed at hero's left arm; other foreleg is bent, held up and away from body with toes splayed; long tail curves downward between hero's legs, curling upward sharply at its end.

Hero wears belted knee-length kilt that leaves forward leg exposed; detailing line is indicated at hem over rear leg; sheath projects from back of waist. Hero perhaps wears domed headdress. Narrow pointed beard rests over hero's left shoulder; squared, segmented coiffure rests at back of neck.

Lion has mouth open in roar and is ithyphallic.

Large paneled inscription is in terminal field.

Line border is at top and bottom of design. Flaws (or chips) in the seal are revealed just before and above hero's head and in first line of inscription.

INSCRIPTION

Elamite

Line
1. v.Hu-pan-
2. Ki-tin šak
3. Na-ap-
4. ⌈x-na(?)⌉

Translation   Hupan-Kitin son of Nap...

There are four lines to the inscription, oriented along the horizontal axis of the seal, separated by case lines, and enclosed in a panel. There appears to be a large chip in the seal between the hu- and the pan-signs in line 1. Compared to the other three lines, line 2 is quite crowded. The tin- and the šak-signs are written very close together. See also the commentary.

COMMENTARY

No PF text mentions the name preserved in the inscription, Hupan-Kitin. The seal seems, however, to be an office seal associated with grain supply. All texts concern the supply of grain in the Šurkutur and Tašpak regions, and PFS 43* is the only seal on the tablets. Two suppliers recur frequently, Parru and Ammamarda, with a third, Bakubeša, occurring once.

A "Hupan-Kitin, son of the king Šutur-Nahunte," was king of Susa sometime in the early sixth century B.C.[59] It is not impossible that PFS 43* is an heirloom from the Neo-Elamite period. Nothing of the ductus of the inscription indicates that the seal has to be Achaemenid Elamite. Perhaps PFS 43* even has some connections to the Susian royal family of Šutur-Nahunte. In this manner the seal would be an heirloom associated with royalty; compare PFS 93* (II) and PFS 51 (II); see Garrison 1991. Koch (1990) suggests that the seal belongs to an unnamed official, a co-worker of Uštana, director of grain cultivation in her Elam Region VI. Although citing a personal communication from Hallock to her in which he attributes PFS 43* to Uštana, she prefers to attribute PFS 45* (III) to Uštana instead, since that seal carries an inscription naming Uštana (PFS 45* is confined to the environs of Zila-Umpan). As for the identity of the owner of PFS 43*, Koch's (1990) reconstruction of the name on the seal inscription as Napša-Kitin on the basis of the occurrence of this name in PF 127 in her Elam Region IV is unsupportable since the first line of the inscription has been recovered.

The elongated figures and heavy use of the unmasked drill are unusual. The composition is, however, very popular on a select group of seals cut in the Modeled Style, where inscriptions are also common. The seal may be a generation or so older than the Persepolis Fortification archive, perhaps from Elam, although we have as yet found no good parallels in the known Neo-Elamite glyptic repertoire. Given its anomalous features either way, we are not inclined at this point to resolve the ambiguity in favor of a Plausibly Antique designation.

For comparative illustrations including PFS 43*, see pls. 180e (kilts), 186b (headdresses), 214a (profile torsos), 230c (feet of animals and creatures), 262c (paneled inscriptions with horizontal case lines), 280c (chips in seal matrices), and 281e (office seals).

SEAL APPLICATION (SEE *APPENDIX ONE: CONCORDANCE OF SEALS TO TABLETS IN VOLUME I*)

As is typical of seals of important officials and offices, PFS 43* always occurs alone on tablets that it seals. PFS 43* is always applied on the reverse and left edge of tablets. On the reverse of PF 507, PF 996, PF 1266–1267, and PF 1668 the seal is inverted. Impressions of the seal are almost always carefully applied, often they are quite long, and they show little or no distortion. Some surfaces are, however, poorly preserved and difficult to read. In general, the seal user appears to have been extremely concerned with producing careful, well-articulated rollings of the seal design. Of the total twenty impressions, nineteen show some part of the inscription. This is probably because the inscription is quite large, accounting for half of the surface of the seal design.

In fourteen impressions the seal is rolled for at least one complete turn, preserving the entire length of the seal design. Of these fourteen applications, one displays the inscription in the center; two long rollings display the heroic encounter in the center, carefully framed by full rollings of the inscription on each end of the impression; one displays the heroic encounter in the center carefully framed by partial rollings of the inscription on each end; five carefully display the complete heroic encounter at the left of the impression, the full inscription at the right; three display the lion and the full inscription in the center; two display the lion in the center. Of the remaining six partial applications, two display the hero and the lion in the center; one preserves the hero at the left of the impression, the lion at the right; three display the lion in the center. On the reverse of PF 388, PF 507, PF 580, PF 996, PF 1266–1267, PF 1668, and PF 1750 the seal clearly was applied before the text since several cuneiform wedges cut into the top or the bottom of the impressions. All tablets with PFS 43* are dated 503/502 B.C.

BIBLIOGRAPHY

Aperghis 1999, pp. 179–80, 184–85; Brosius 1996, p. 169; Garrison 1988, pp. 454–55; Garrison and Dion 1999, pp. 9 (n. 20), 10 (n. 28); Koch 1986, p. 146; Koch 1990, pp. 157, 297–98, 307.

---

59. See, for example, de Miroschedji 1982, pp. 61–62, fig. 5, for the seal which preserves this name and patronymic.

II-A.5. WINGED LION CREATURES

Cat.No. 208   PFS 266*

Seal Type:	Cylinder, Inscribed	Photographs:	Pl. 113a–c
Earliest Dated Application:	500 B.C.	Typology and Style:	II-A.5 — Mixed Styles II
Language of Inscription:	Aramaic		
Preserved Height of Image:	1.80 cm (incomp.)	Preserved Length of Image:	2.60 cm (comp.)
Estimated Height of Original Seal:	1.90 cm	Estimated Diameter of Original Seal:	0.80 cm
Number of Impressions:	4	Quality of Impressions:	Fair

Completeness of Image: Almost complete except for upper edge and lower edge and portions of inscription

DESCRIPTION OF SEAL AS IMPRESSED IMAGE

Hero faces right, extending straight left arm upward to grasp rampant winged horned lion creature by horn; right arm is straight and brought across body to stab creature in chest with dagger.

Lion creature moves toward and faces hero. Creature holds upper foreleg straight, and extends it upward toward hero's left arm; lower foreleg is straight and extended upward to place paw on hero's right arm; tail curls upward.

Hero wears double-belted Persian court robe, with sleeves not indicated; central pleat and diagonal folds are indicated on lower part of garment. Quiver on hero's back carries three arrows (tips not preserved); two tassels hang down from quiver. Squared, segmented beard rests over hero's left shoulder; flattened coiffure rests at back of head.

Muscular detail is indicated on lion creature's body; curved line runs between the creature's wing and its back. Mane is rendered by blunt serrated edge along contour of its neck; pointed horn emerges from top of creature's head; mouth is open in roar.

In lower field between hero and lion creature, bird of uncertain type is disposed vertically with wings spread in frontal display, head turned to left.

Paneled inscription is in terminal field.

INSCRIPTION

Aramaic

    Line   1. ḤTM SY
                      2. N ʾ

    Translation   Seal of SYNʾ

There appear to be two lines of the inscription, oriented along the vertical axis of the seal and enclosed in a panel. There does not appear to be a case separating the two lines of the inscription. The inscription is well executed and, apparently, complete. In the absence of textual evidence for the seal owner, it is difficult to know how to vocalize the name.

COMMENTARY

Limited understanding of M text (special rations) sealing protocols makes it impossible to assign PFS 266* to a named individual. No equivalent of the Aramaic SYN' occurs in the Elamite texts with tablets bearing the seal.

The composition is bold. Composition, iconography, and paneled inscription suggest the Court Style, but the qualities of the carving seem more at home in the Fortification Style. Given the overall commanding quality of design on PFS 266*, several details stand out: the miscarving of the bottom edge of the inscription panel; the invasion of one sign across the right border of the inscription panel; the misplaced line joining the lion creature's back to its wing; the awkward handling of the lion creature's lower foreleg; and the oddities of the Persian court robe (no sleeves and an anomalous hem line).

The bird on PFS 266* is remarkably similar in compositional deployment and general form to one on an Early Dynastic II cylinder (Collon 1987, pp. 193–94, no. 943). Less close in form, but much nearer in time is a bird on a small seal impressed on a late Neo-Elamite or early Achaemenid tablet from Susa (Amiet 1973b, pl. 2, no. 8).

For comparative illustrations including PFS 266*, see pls. 181e (hybrid garments), 208g (arm positions of heroic combat), 227a (birds), 236f (animals/creatures as secondary elements of main design field), 246c (bows, arrows, quivers), and 261h (paneled inscriptions without case lines).

SEAL APPLICATION (SEE *APPENDIX ONE: CONCORDANCE OF SEALS TO TABLETS IN VOLUME I*)

PFS 266* occurs on the left edge of PF 1097 (inverted), PF 1112, and PF 1120; on PF 1120 the seal also occurs on the upper edge. On the left edge of PF 1097 and PF 1112 the seal occurs with PFS 1181 (Cat.No. 210), one of the few examples of two seals on a left edge. PFS 266* appears to have been applied after PFS 1181 in both cases. The rolling on the left edge of PF 1097 is noteworthy since PFS 266* is inverted and PFS 1181 is upright. The application of the two seals on the left edge of PF 1112 displays both with the same orientation and is interesting because the deliberation of the application renders an impression that creates a faux double-encounter scene. See the commentary on PFS 131 (Cat.No. 170) for double-encounter images occurring on discrete seals of the Achaemenid period. The deployment of PFS 266* and PFS 1181 to yield a faux double-encounter design alerts us to the creative potentials inherent in the seal application process.

All impressions of PFS 266* exhibit marked distortion. All impressions show some part of the inscription. Only one application preserves the entire length of the seal design, placing the creature in the center with a full rolling of the inscription at the right edge of the impression, a partial rolling of the inscription at the left. Of the remaining three partial rollings, two display the creature in the center and one preserves only the creature and a full rolling of the inscription. PF 1097 and PF 1112 are the earliest dated tablets with PFS 266* and are both dated 500 B.C.

BIBLIOGRAPHY

Garrison 1988, pp. 370–74, 414; Garrison and Dion 1999, pp. 10, 13 (n. 38), 14, fig. 12.

Cat.No. 209   PFS 523*

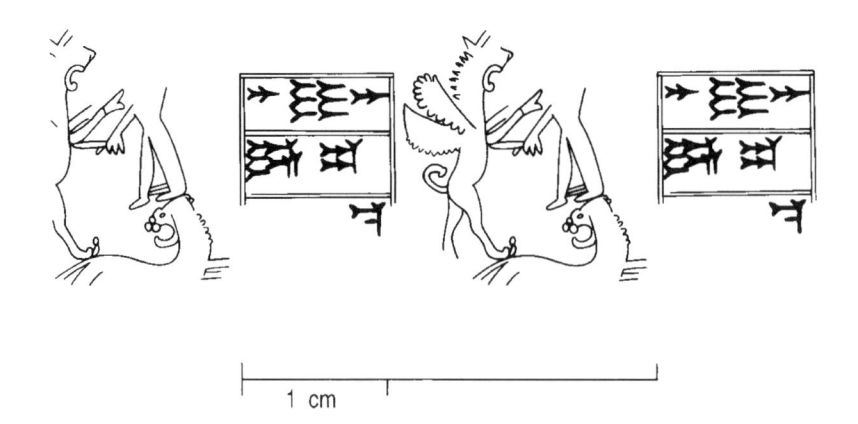

Seal Type: Cylinder, Inscribed
Earliest Dated Application: 495/494 B.C.
Language of Inscription: Uncertain
Preserved Height of Image: 1.70 cm (incomp.)
Estimated Height of Original Seal: NA
Number of Impressions: 2

Photographs: Pl. 114a–b
Typology and Style: II-A.5 — Mixed Styles II
Preserved Length of Image: 2.80 cm (comp.)
Estimated Diameter of Original Seal: 0.90 cm
Quality of Impressions: Poor-fair

Completeness of Image: Segment of middle of design survives along its complete length

DESCRIPTION OF SEAL AS IMPRESSED IMAGE

Hero faces left; left(?) arm is straight and brought across body to stab rampant winged horned lion creature in chest with dagger. Hero stands upon head of courant lion serving as pedestal animal. Pedestal lion moves to right but turns its head back to left.

Rampant creature stabbed by hero places forward hind leg on hindquarters of pedestal lion. Pedestal lion holds both forelegs (only partially preserved) straight and extends them upward together in front of its chest. Winged leonine creature moves toward and faces hero. Both forelegs are straight (upper one only partially preserved) and extended upward together toward hero's chest; short tail curls upward with tufted termination.

Hero appears to wear Assyrian garment that leaves forward leg exposed; double border is indicated along hem of garment between legs.

Rampant lion creature has two wings indicated, upper extended diagonally upward from its back, lower extended horizontally outward. Lower foreleg terminates in two-pronged projection. Horn (only partially preserved) emerges from top of creature's head; short pointed ear is at back of head; mane is rendered by spikes along contour of its neck; mouth is open in roar. Mane of pedestal lion is rendered by serrated edge along contour of its neck; mouth is open in roar.

Paneled inscription is in terminal field.

INSCRIPTION

Cuneiform script, language uncertain

Line	x+1.	HAL x HAL
	x+2.	IA AB
	x+3.	[...]⌈x⌉

Translation   ?

Three lines of inscription are preserved, oriented along the horizontal axis of the seal, separated by case lines, and enclosed in a panel. The case lines for line x+1 seem to indicate that there is not another line above this, but the evidence is not unambiguous. The signs in the first two lines of the inscription are clear, but their interpretation is uncertain. The signs, though clear (and otherwise well formed), are not well spaced within the cases. They almost seem to hang from the upper case line, leaving space in the lower portion of the case field. The second line leaves space at the right side of the case field. If the first visible line in fact begins the inscription, an alternative reading that requires the emendation of the second sign is possible. If the engraver omitted a winkelhaken following the first HAL-sign, then the second sign could be interpreted as mi, yielding the possible reading hal-mi m./Ya-ap-/[x-(x)-]{na}-… "Seal of Yap… ." The name Ya-ap occurs once on an unpublished tablet PFNN 208, which does not have PFS 523*.

COMMENTARY

Pedestal animals and composite creatures are not common, occurring definitively on only seven seal designs in Volume I: PFS 523*, PFS 31 (Cat.No. 172), PFS 36* (Cat.No. 5), PFS 164* (Cat.No. 20), PFS 396 (Cat.No. 178), PFS 524 (Cat.No. 2), and PFS 931* (Cat.No. 270). The use of pedestal animals/creatures is also documented on several Court Style seals from the Treasury archive, for example, PTS 1*, PTS 3*, and PTS 6*. Of this small group, PFS 523* is unique in displaying hero and rampant creature both atop a single pedestal animal. See PFS 31 (Cat.No. 172) for a control hero seal and PFS 931* (Cat.No. 270) for a combat hero seal with other unusual formats involving pedestal animals/creatures. See Dusinberre 1997b for the significance of the pedestal animals/creatures as an elite motif in early Achaemenid glyptic.

The seal is very tall and thin, with an exceptionally nicely executed inscription despite its odd spacing. The style has close associations with the Fortification Style, especially in the human forms.

For comparative illustrations including PFS 523*, see pls. 216g (hero standing atop pedestal figure[s] or other supporting element) and 262f (paneled inscriptions with horizontal case lines).

SEAL APPLICATION (SEE *APPENDIX ONE: CONCORDANCE OF SEALS TO TABLETS IN VOLUME I*)

PFS 523* occurs on the reverse (inverted) and left edge of PF 256. PFS 524 (Cat.No. 2) is applied (also inverted) directly below PFS 523* on the reverse. The rolling of PFS 523* on the reverse preserves the entire length of the seal design, although the left edge of the impression is damaged. The preserved rolling on the reverse displays the hero and the inscription in the center. The partial rolling on the left edge displays the hero in the center, with a partial rolling of the inscription at the right edge of the impression. PF 256 is dated 495/494 B.C.

BIBLIOGRAPHY

Dusinberre 1997b, pp. 106–07, 112, 124 (nn. 57 and 59), 126 (n. 105); Garrison 1988, pp. 374–78; Garrison and Dion 1999, p. 120 (n. 12).

Cat.No. 210   PFS 1181

Seal Type:	Cylinder	Photographs:	Pl. 115a–b
Earliest Dated Application:	500 B.C.	Typology and Style:	II-A.5 — Court Style
Preserved Height of Image:	1.60 cm (incomp.)	Preserved Length of Image:	2.80 cm (incomp.)
Estimated Height of Original Seal:	NA	Estimated Diameter of Original Seal:	NA
Number of Impressions:	3	Quality of Impressions:	Fair

Completeness of Image: Segment of middle of design survives

DESCRIPTION OF SEAL AS IMPRESSED IMAGE

Hero faces right, extending straight left arm outward to grasp rampant winged lion creature by throat; right arm is straight and brought across body to stab creature in chest with dagger.

Lion creature moves toward and faces hero. Creature holds upper foreleg straight and extends it upward to hero's left arm; lower foreleg is straight and extended downward slightly to place paw on hero's right arm; thick straight tail (only partially preserved) extends diagonally upward.

Hero wears belted Persian court robe; sleeves of garment are pushed up to reveal bare arms. Gathered folds of right sleeve are indicated in schematic fashion below hero's right arm, as are triple central pleat and diagonal folds of lower part of garment; short diagonal element emerging from back of hero's waist may be top of sheath. Narrow pointed beard rests over hero's left shoulder; rounded coiffure rests at back of neck.

Mane of lion creature is rendered by serrated edge along contour of neck; mouth is open in roar.

Behind hero, in terminal field, courant wild goat moves to right but turns its head back to left; wild goat holds forelegs straight and extends them upward together toward hero's waist. Large curved horn emerges from top of its head; short pointed ear is at back of head.

COMMENTARY

The design seems especially well conceived and executed. Note the sure handling of the hero's upper torso, the opening of the sleeved upper part of the garment and the graceful arc of the goat's horn. The composition of the heroic encounter recalls monumental doorjamb sculptures, although the less robust modeling, the schematic drapery, and the persistence of the frontal torso rather than the profile make the hero on PFS 1181 seem less close to the Persepolis reliefs than, for example, PFS 859* (Cat.No. 205).

For comparative illustrations including PFS 1181, see pls. 209d (arm positions of heroic combat), 223h (lions and lion creatures), 231h (feet of animals and creatures), 244h (daggers and swords).

SEAL APPLICATION (SEE APPENDIX ONE: CONCORDANCE OF SEALS TO TABLETS IN VOLUME I)

PFS 1181 occurs on the left edge of PF 1097, PF 1112, and PF 1228. PFS 266* (Cat.No. 208) is also applied on the left edge of PF 1097 and PF 1112, rare examples of two seals occurring together on the left edge of tablets. See the commentary on PFS 266* (Cat.No. 208) for issues raised by this very unusual and deliberate seal application pattern. PFS 266* (Cat.No. 208) appears to have been applied after PFS 1181 in both cases. PFS 1181 is inverted on PF 1097. Rollings of PFS 1181 are short. On PF 1228 the seal has been partially rolled, lifted, and partially rolled again, yielding a rolling that displays the hero in the center and a short rolling that preserves only the winged lion creature. The partial rollings on PF 1097 and PF 1112 display the hero in the center. PF 1097 and PF 1112 are the earliest dated tablets with PFS 1181 and are both dated 500 B.C.

BIBLIOGRAPHY

Garrison 1988, pp. 390, 413–15, 478–80.

II-B. HERO THREATENS RAMPANT ANIMAL OR CREATURE, WEAPON HELD DOWN BEHIND BODY

II-B.1. BULLS

PFS 1367s   Cat.No. 211

⊢—— 1 cm ——⊣

Seal Type:	Stamp, Loaf-shaped Face	Photograph:	Pl. 116a
Earliest Dated Application:	498 B.C.	Typology and Style:	II-B.1 — Fortification Style
Preserved Height of Image:	1.50 cm (comp.)	Preserved Width of Image:	1.10 cm (incomp.)
Number of Impressions:	1	Quality of Impression:	Poor

Completeness of Image: Almost complete except for right edge and lower edge

DESCRIPTION OF SEAL AS IMPRESSED IMAGE

Hero faces right, extending straight left arm outward to grasp rampant bull by throat; right arm is straight and held down behind body to hold long undulating weapon, perhaps a throw stick.

Bull moves toward and faces hero. Bull holds one foreleg bent and extends it upward in front of its body; tail curls upward with tufted termination.

Hero wears Assyrian garment that leaves forward leg exposed below knee. Narrow squared beard rests over hero's left shoulder; large rounded coiffure rests at back of neck. Hero perhaps wears domed headdress.

Curved horn emerges from front of bull's head; short pointed ear is at back of head.

Edge of seal is preserved except at upper and lower right.

COMMENTARY

Based on Q texts protocol, PFS 1367s should belong to Hiyautarra, who in year 23.11 (498 B.C.) received flour rations on his way to Susa under the authority (*halmi*) of Zišsawiš. PF 1468 preserves the only occurrence of the name Hiyautarra in the PF texts.

The hero's left arm is spindly and inarticulate compared to the robustly carved right arm with its well-articulated hand. Only one foreleg of the bull is rendered. Despite these shortcomings, this is a compelling image.

The stamp face has a loaf-shaped contour and may be a conoid or possibly a scaraboid. For probable seal shape, see *Appendix Four: Stamp Seals in Volume I Grouped by Apparent Contour of Seal Face* and accompanying figure 9, nos. 3b or 4.

For comparative illustrations including PFS 1367s, see pls. 175d (Assyrian garments), 187f (headdresses), 209f (arm positions of heroic combat), 245e (various weapons), 275d (stamp seals), 278f (carving anomalies), and 291c (personal seals of various travelers).

SEAL APPLICATION (SEE APPENDIX ONE: CONCORDANCE OF SEALS TO TABLETS IN VOLUME I)

PFS 1367s occurs on the reverse (lower left corner) of PF 1468. The one application is oriented along the horizontal axis of the tablet and preserves most of the design. PF 1468 is dated 498 B.C.

BIBLIOGRAPHY

Garrison 1988, pp. 268–70; Root 1999a, p. 185, fig. 12.

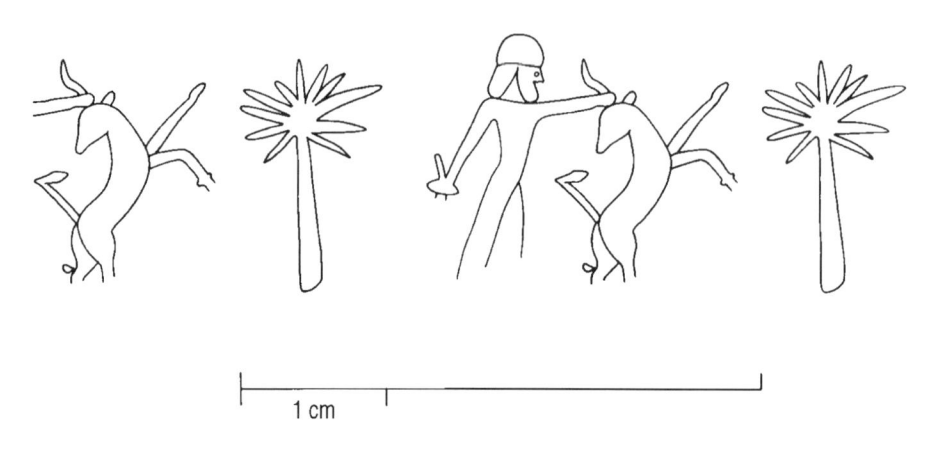

Cat.No. 212   PFS 149

Seal Type:	Cylinder	Photographs:	Pl. 116c–d
Earliest Dated Application:	498/497 B.C.	Typology and Style:	II-B.1 — Fortification Style
Preserved Height of Image:	1.80 cm (incomp.)	Preserved Length of Image:	3.60 cm (comp.)
Estimated Height of Original Seal:	2.10 cm	Estimated Diameter of Original Seal:	1.10 cm
Number of Impressions:	8	Quality of Impressions:	Fair

Completeness of Image: Almost complete except for upper edge and lower edge

DESCRIPTION OF SEAL AS IMPRESSED IMAGE

Hero faces right, extending straight left arm outward to grasp rampant bull by horn; right arm is straight and held down behind body to hold weapon of uncertain type (only curved end and hand-guard preserved).

Bull moves away from hero but turns its head back toward him. Bull holds upper foreleg straight and extends it upward in front of its neck; lower foreleg is bent and extended downward in front of body. Straight tail extends upward, bent at end with tufted termination; tiny teardrop-shaped element protrudes from rear hind leg.

Hero wears Assyrian garment that leaves forward leg exposed. Rounded beard rests over hero's left shoulder; narrow rounded coiffure rests at back of neck. Hero perhaps wears domed headdress.

Large curved horn emerges from front of bull's head; rounded ear is at top of head.

Palm tree is in terminal field.

COMMENTARY

This is a fairly large seal. The design shows affinities with the Modeled Style, especially in the vertical accent running through the hero's body. Figures are well executed, and there is a generous amount of space between them.

For comparative illustrations including PFS 149, see pls. 258c (palm trees) and 273d (open compositions).

SEAL APPLICATION (SEE APPENDIX ONE: CONCORDANCE OF SEALS TO TABLETS IN VOLUME I)

PFS 149 occurs on the reverse of PF 10 and PF 274–276. On PF 10 it also occurs on the bottom edge and upper edge; on PF 274 also on the upper edge. On the reverse of PF 10 the seal is inverted. Impressions generally exhibit some lateral distortion. In three impressions the seal is rolled for at least one complete turn, preserving the entire length of the seal design. Of these three applications, one displays the hero and the palm tree in the center; one displays the negative space behind the hero in the center; one displays the palm tree in the center. Of the remaining five partial rollings, three display the hero in the center; one preserves only the hero and the bull; one preserves only the palm tree and the hero. On the reverse of PF 275–276 the seal clearly was applied before the text since several cuneiform wedges cut into the top of the impressions. PF 274–276 are the earliest dated tablets with PFS 149 and are all dated 498/497 B.C.

BIBLIOGRAPHY

Garrison 1988, pp. 287–91.

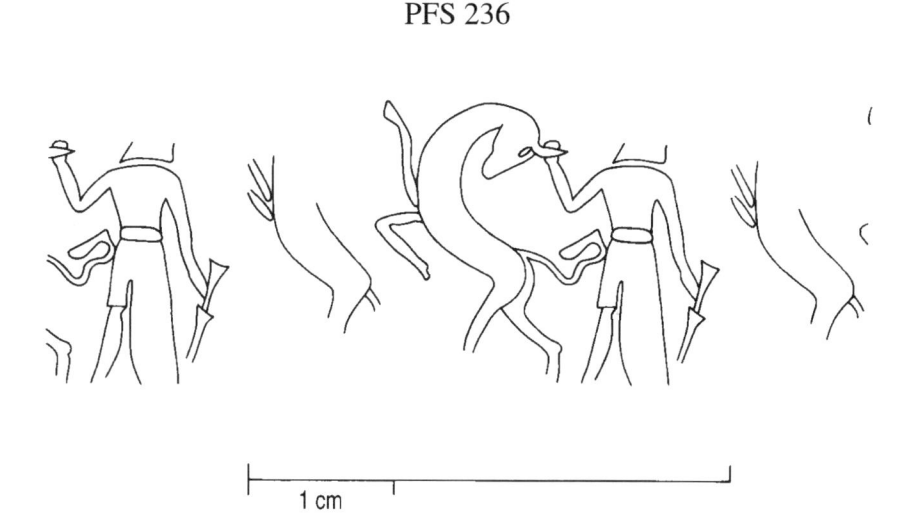

PFS 236   Cat.No. 213

Seal Type:	Cylinder	Photograph:	Pl. 117a
Earliest Dated Application:	ND	Typology and Style:	II-B.1 — Fortification Style
Preserved Height of Image:	1.90 cm (incomp.)	Preserved Length of Image:	3.30 cm (comp.)
Estimated Height of Original Seal:	2.40 cm	Estimated Diameter of Original Seal:	1.10 cm
Number of Impressions:	4	Quality of Impressions:	Fair

Completeness of Image: Almost complete except for upper and lower edge

DESCRIPTION OF SEAL AS IMPRESSED IMAGE

Hero faces left, extending bent right arm outward to grasp rampant bull by horn; left arm is straight and held down behind body to hold weapon, apparently sword (only partially preserved).

Bull moves away from hero but turns its head back toward him. Bull holds upper foreleg slightly bent and extends it upward in front of its neck; lower foreleg is bent and extended downward in front of its body; long tail curves horizontally outward, then undulates upward with tufted termination.

Hero wears belted Assyrian garment that leaves forward leg exposed below knee. Pointed beard rests over hero's right shoulder; short-cropped coiffure rests at back of neck.

Short curved horn emerges from front of bull's head.

In terminal field, rampant animal of uncertain type moves to left. Animal holds forelegs (only partially preserved) straight and extends them upward together in front of its neck; tail (only partially preserved) extends diagonally downward.

COMMENTARY

Brosius (1996, p. 170) assigns the seal to Karkiš, based on the occurrence of the name in the tablets sealed by PFS 236. Brosius does not specify whether this is the same Karkiš who uses the office seal PFS 1* (Cat.No. 182), although it seems unlikely, given the elite status of the Karkiš associated with PFS 1*.

This is a relatively large seal. The design is boldly cut and the rampant bull seems especially well executed. For comparative illustrations including PFS 236, see pls. 174d (Assyrian garments), 196d (coiffures of unusual types), and 208h (arm positions of heroic combat).

SEAL APPLICATION (SEE *APPENDIX ONE: CONCORDANCE OF SEALS TO TABLETS IN VOLUME I*)

PFS 236 occurs on the reverse (inverted) and bottom edge of PF 819 and the reverse (inverted) and upper edge of PF 1165, with PFS 945 (Cat.No. 96) on the left edge of each tablet. In three impressions the seal is rolled for at least one complete turn, preserving the entire length of the seal design. Of these three applications, one displays the heroic encounter in the center; two display the rampant bull in the center. The remaining partial rolling displays the heroic encounter in the center. On the reverse of PF 1165 the seal clearly was applied before the text since several cuneiform wedges cut into the bottom of the impression. The dates of PF 819 and PF 1165 are unknown.

BIBLIOGRAPHY

Brosius 1996, p. 170; Garrison 1988, pp. 283, 285–86, 493.

Cat.No. 214   PFS 795

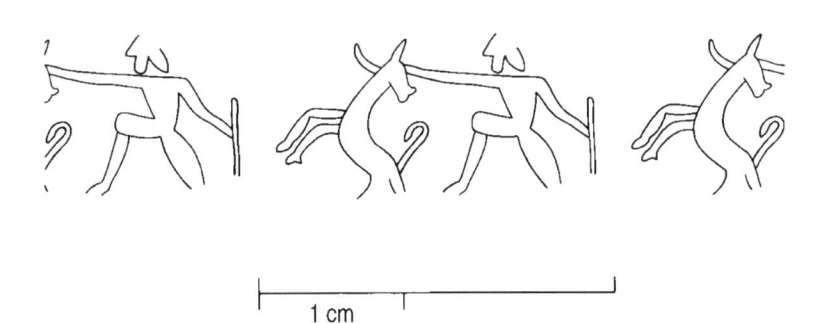

Seal Type:	Cylinder	Photograph:	Pl. 117c
Earliest Dated Application:	499/498 B.C.	Typology and Style:	II-B.1 — Fortification Style
Preserved Height of Image:	1.10 cm (incomp.)	Preserved Length of Image:	2.50 cm (comp.)
Estimated Height of Original Seal:	1.30 cm	Estimated Diameter of Original Seal:	0.80 cm
Number of Impressions:	2	Quality of Impressions:	Poor

Completeness of Image: Almost complete except for upper edge and lower edge

DESCRIPTION OF SEAL AS IMPRESSED IMAGE

Hero faces left, extending straight right arm outward to grasp rampant bull by top of head; left arm is slightly bent and held down behind body to hold long straight weapon of uncertain type (not completely preserved). Hero, in vigorous striding pose, raises bent forward leg.

Bull moves away from hero but turns its head back toward him. Bull holds forelegs slightly bent and extends them outward together in front of its body; long tail extends diagonally upward, hooking inward at its end.

Hero appears to wear Assyrian garment (poorly preserved or reductively rendered) that leaves forward leg exposed below knee. Squared beard rests over hero's right shoulder; thick pointed coiffure rests at back of neck.

Short straight horn(?) emerges from front of bull's head; long curved ear(?) is at back of head.

COMMENTARY

This composition is more often seen in seal designs cut in the Modeled Style. The seal seems poorly executed; note especially the exaggerated length of the hero's right arm and the reductive shorthand rendering the entire figure.

For comparative illustrations including PFS 795, see pl. 213b (heroic attitudes of combat encounter).

SEAL APPLICATION (SEE *APPENDIX ONE: CONCORDANCE OF SEALS TO TABLETS IN VOLUME I*)

PFS 795 occurs twice on the reverse of PF 587, one impression directly above the other. The applications are rolled in almost exactly the same sequence; they both display the rampant bull in the center. PF 587 is dated 499/498 B.C.

BIBLIOGRAPHY

Garrison 1988, pp. 320–21, 324–25.

II-B.2. WINGED BULL CREATURES

PFS 815*   Cat.No. 215

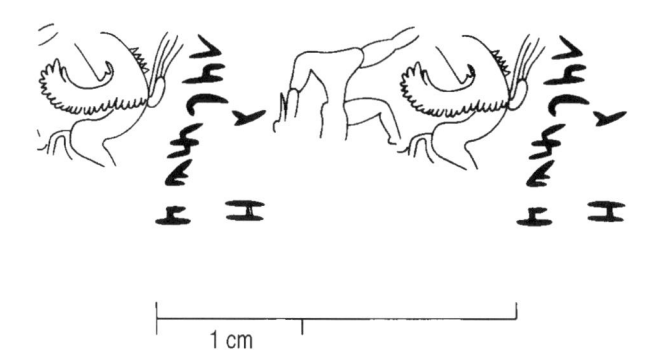

Seal Type:	Cylinder, Inscribed	Photographs:	Pl. 118a–b
Earliest Dated Application:	504/503 B.C.	Typology and Style:	II-B.2 — Modeled Style
Language of Inscription:	Aramaic		
Preserved Height of Image:	1.30 cm (incomp.)	Preserved Length of Image:	2.50 cm (comp.)
Estimated Height of Original Seal:	NA	Estimated Diameter of Original Seal:	0.80 cm
Number of Impressions:	3	Quality of Impressions:	Poor

Completeness of Image: Middle of design survives along its complete length

DESCRIPTION OF SEAL AS IMPRESSED IMAGE

Hero faces right, extending straight left arm upward to grasp rampant winged bull creature by horn (contact not preserved); left arm is held down behind body to hold weapon of uncertain type (only hilt is preserved). Hero raises bent forward leg to place foot on tail of creature.

Bull creature moves away from hero but turns its head back toward him; creature holds both forelegs slightly bent and extends them upward together in front of its neck; tail (only partially preserved) bends downward.

Hero wears Assyrian garment that leaves forward leg exposed.

Mane of bull creature is rendered by crisp serrated edge along contour of neck.

Inscription is in terminal field.

INSCRIPTION

    Aramaic

        Line   1. H[...] ⌈x⌉ [...]
                       2. RŠMLDT

        Translation   ?

There are two lines to the inscription, oriented along the vertical axis of the seal. Unlike most inscriptions, which read from the top of the seal to the bottom (regardless of language), this inscription reads from the bottom of the seal to the top (see Bordreuil 1986, no. 138, for another Aramaic seal inscription reading in the same manner). The first line is very fragmentary. According to the occurrence of this seal on PFNN 1018 (see commentary), the seal owner is Dattaparna.

COMMENTARY

In addition to its occurrence on PF 608, PFS 815* also occurs on an unpublished tablet, PFNN 1018, which is a letter (T text) sent from Dattaparna. According to T texts protocol, the sender of the letter should also seal the tablet; hence PFS 815* should belong to Dattaparna.

This is an exceptionally well-executed design. See Garrison 1988 for the style and workshop of PFS 815* and related seals.

For comparative illustrations including PFS 815*, see pls. 265a (inscriptions without panels or case lines) and 283a (personal seals of supply/apportionment officers).

SEAL APPLICATION (SEE *APPENDIX ONE: CONCORDANCE OF SEALS TO TABLETS IN VOLUME I*)

PFS 815* occurs on the reverse, upper edge, and left edge of PF 608. No other seal is used on the tablet. All impressions show some part of the inscription. The rollings on the reverse and upper edge preserve the entire length of the seal design and display the creature in the center. The partial rolling on the left edge displays the hero in the center. On the reverse of PF 608 the seal clearly was applied before the text since several cuneiform wedges cut into the top of the impression. PF 608 is dated 504/503 B.C.

BIBLIOGRAPHY

Garrison 1988, pp. 228–29, 236–40; Garrison and Dion 1999, p. 10.

II-B.3. WINGED HUMAN-FACED/HUMAN-HEADED BULL CREATURES

Cat.No. 216   PFS 526*

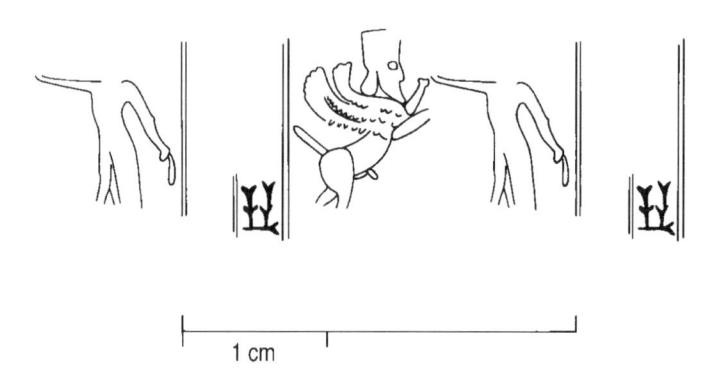

Seal Type:	Cylinder, Inscribed	Photograph:	Pl. 118d
Earliest Dated Application:	506 B.C.	Typology and Style:	II-B.3 — Fortification Style
Language of Inscription:	Uncertain		
Preserved Height of Image:	1.40 cm (incomp.)	Preserved Length of Image:	2.80 cm (comp.)
Estimated Height of Original Seal:	NA	Estimated Diameter of Original Seal:	0.90 cm
Number of Impressions:	1	Quality of Impression:	Poor

Completeness of Image: Large but uneven segment of middle of design survives along its complete length

DESCRIPTION OF SEAL AS IMPRESSED IMAGE

Hero faces left (head not preserved), extending straight right arm to grasp rampant winged human-headed bull creature by upper foreleg; left arm is straight and held down behind body to hold short slightly curved weapon of uncertain type.

Creature moves toward and faces hero. Creature holds upper foreleg straight and extends it upward in front of its head; lower foreleg is straight and extended upward toward hero's right arm; short straight tail extends diagonally upward.

Hero wears Assyrian garment that leaves forward leg exposed.

Creature wears tall polos headdress. Long beard terminates in blunt point over creature's chest; rounded coiffure rests at back of neck. One massive wing is shown, with three rows of feathers indicated; partial separation is between upper row and middle row of creature's feathers. Creature is ithyphallic.

Paneled inscription is in terminal field.

INSCRIPTION

Cuneiform script, language uncertain

    Line   1. [...] AB
                  2. [...]

    Translation   ?

It seems that there are two lines to the inscription, oriented along the vertical axis of the seal, separated by a case line, and enclosed in a panel. Only a single readable sign is preserved clearly.

The combination of vertical orientation, a case line, and a panel is noteworthy, occurring among the images of heroic encounter herein only on PFS 1* (Cat.No. 182), PFS 64* (Cat.No. 173), and the royal name seals PFS 7* (Cat.No. 4) and PFS 113* (Cat.No. 19).

COMMENTARY

The style of the seal exhibits some connections to the Court Style, such as in the three rows of feathers on the wing of the creature. Iconographically, the winged human-headed bull creature with polos and the paneled inscription of PFS 526* also draw the seal to the Court Style.

For comparative illustrations including PFS 526*, see pls. 189h (polos headdresses), 233e (ithyphallic animals/creatures), 235a (human-headed/human-faced creatures), 247h (weapons of unusual or uncertain type), and 261e (paneled inscriptions with vertical case lines).

SEAL APPLICATION (SEE *APPENDIX ONE: CONCORDANCE OF SEALS TO TABLETS IN VOLUME I*)

PFS 526* occurs on the reverse of PF 271. The rolling preserves the entire length of the seal design and carefully displays the inscription in the center. The seal clearly was applied before the text since several cuneiform wedges cut into the top of the impression. PF 271 is dated 506 B.C.

BIBLIOGRAPHY

Garrison 1988, pp. 262, 268–70, 482; Garrison 2000, p. 128; Garrison and Dion 1999, p. 10 (n. 28).

316 SEALS ON THE PERSEPOLIS FORTIFICATION TABLETS, VOLUME I: IMAGES OF HEROIC ENCOUNTER

Cat.No. 217   PFS 98*

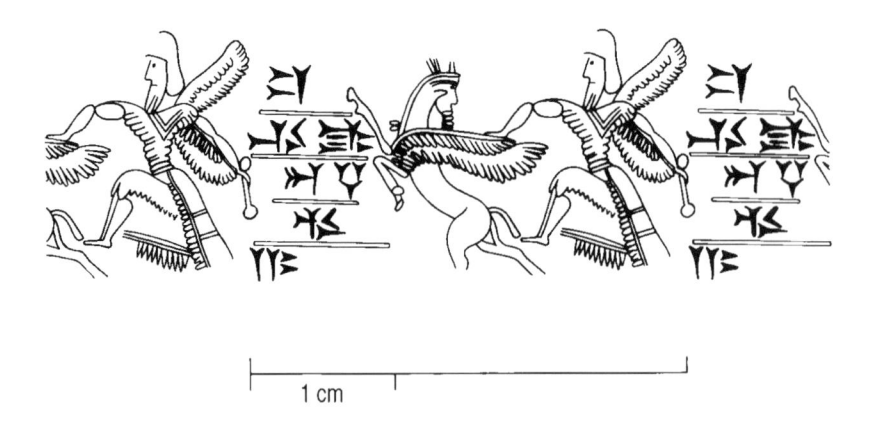

Seal Type:	Cylinder, Inscribed	Photographs:	Pl. 119a–d
Earliest Dated Application:	ND	Typology and Style:	II-B.3 — Modeled Style
Language of Inscription:	Elamite		
Preserved Height of Image:	1.60 cm (incomp.)	Preserved Length of Image:	3.00 cm (comp.)
Estimated Height of Original Seal:	1.80 cm	Estimated Diameter of Original Seal:	1.00 cm
Number of Impressions:	15	Quality of Impressions:	Many preserve good detail

Completeness of Image: Almost complete except for upper edge and lower edge

DESCRIPTION OF SEAL AS IMPRESSED IMAGE

Winged hero faces left, extending bent right arm outward (elbow up) to grasp rampant winged human-faced bull creature by wing; left arm is straight and held down behind body to hold mace. Hero, in vigorous striding pose, raises bent forward leg to place foot on rear hind leg of creature.

Creature moves away from hero in active striding pose but turns its head back toward him. Creature holds upper foreleg straight and extends it upward in front of its neck; lower foreleg is bent and extended upward in front of its body; short tail curves downward.

Hero wears elaborate double-belted Assyrian garment that leaves forward leg exposed below knee. Garment on upper torso is short-sleeved; fringe is indicated along both front edge and back edge, with V-shaped design in middle of chest. Garment is also fringed along forward leg, along whole length of rear leg, and along hem between the legs. Hem of garment between the legs also shows double decorative border; one long diagonal decorative border runs down complete length of garment on rear leg; two horizontal decorative borders are indicated on lower half of garment on rear leg. Long rounded beard with vertical striations rests over hero's right shoulder; narrow rounded coiffure rests at back of neck. One wing of hero extends diagonally upward from his shoulder; other extends diagonally downward from his back; two rows of feathers are indicated on each wing.

Human face of creature has long, squared, segmented beard that rests over its wing; mane is rendered by narrow outline along contour of creature's neck; two rounded projections at back of creature's neck may also indicate mane. Horn (only partially preserved) projects from front of creature's head; two thin projections (only partially preserved) at back of head may be ears.

Inscription with horizontal case lines is in terminal field.

INSCRIPTION

Elamite

Line   x+1. ⌈x⌉ [x-]
           x+2. ti šak
           x+3. d.Ša-
           x+4. ti-[(x-)]
           x+5. TUK-[...]

Translation   PN son of Šati-...

Five lines of the inscription are preserved, oriented along the horizontal axis of the cylinder. Four horizontal case lines mark off the lines. There is likely to have been a first line with a determinative, but it is not preserved in any impression. Both signs in line x+2 are clear. Nothing in the sign forms is distinctively late Neo-Elamite (as versus Achaemenid Elamite). Hallock (1969, p. 755) reads PN$_2$ as d.Ša-/ti-ku[?]-[…]. Collation confirms that only two horizontal wedges are evident in the final visible sign in the inscription. If the sign is complete, it is a TUK-sign. If it is incomplete, it could also be a KU- or UR-sign.

COMMENTARY

PFS 98* is very similar (even including the rare elbow-up pose of the hero) to PFS 1566* (Cat.No. 218), which is inscribed with the name of the important official Abbateya. This Abbateya is named in all texts associated with PFS 98* except PF 430 (an F text where the formula often omits reference to the appointing official). In those texts (PF 1582, PF 1583, PF 1584, and PF 1611) grain is taken to Persepolis for rations of artisans "whose apportionments are set by Abbateya." Furthermore, PFS 98* is, like PFS 1566*, the only seal used on the tablets to which it is applied. The similar style, composition, and iconography, in combination with the textual evidence, suggest that PFS 98* may be another seal of Abbateya or a seal of his agent.

The hero's garment is quite spectacular and finds no ready parallels among seals with images of heroic encounter herein. Although a bit cramped, the inscription works well compositionally with the representational image. Note especially the way the forelegs of the winged creature bracket the inscription protectively. See Garrison 1988 for the style and workshop of PFS 98* and related seals.

For comparative illustrations including PFS 98*, see pls. 176d (Assyrian garments with detailing preserved), 194b (narrow rounded and/or pointed coiffures), 208c (arm positions of heroic combat), 245b (various weapons), 263g (inscriptions without panels, with horizontal case lines), and 285c (personal seals of the official Abbateya [plausibly, PFS 98*; definitively, PFS 1566*], who sets apportionments).

SEAL APPLICATION (SEE *APPENDIX ONE: CONCORDANCE OF SEALS TO TABLETS IN VOLUME I*)

As is the case with seals of important officials and offices, PFS 98* always occurs alone on tablets that it seals and is applied on multiple surfaces: the reverse, upper edge, right edge, and left edge of PF 1582; the reverse, upper edge, and left edge of PF 430; the upper edge, right edge, and left edge of PF 1583; the reverse, bottom edge, and left edge of PF 1584; the upper edge and left edge of PF 1611. On the reverse of PF 430, PF 1582, and PF 1584 the seal is inverted. Impressions of the seal are clear and show little or no distortion. Of the fifteen impressions, fourteen show some part of the inscription. In seven impressions the seal is rolled for at least one complete turn, preserving the entire length of the seal design. Of these seven applications, one displays the inscription in the center; one displays the hero in the center, carefully framed by complete rollings of the inscription on each end of the impression; two display the hero and the inscription in the center; one displays the hero and the creature in the center; one displays the hero in the center; one displays the creature in the center. Of the remaining eight partial rollings, three preserve only the hero and the inscription; one preserves only the inscription and the creature; two display the creature in the center with the inscription at the left edge of the impression; one displays the hero in the center with a partial rolling of the inscription at the right of the impression; one preserves only the hero and the creature. On the reverse of PF 1582 the seal clearly was applied before the text since several cuneiform wedges cut into the bottom of the impression. None of the dates of tablets with PFS 98* is known.

BIBLIOGRAPHY

Garrison 1988, pp. 228–29, 233–36, 352, 479–80; Garrison 1998, p. 121 (n. 15); Garrison 2000, pp. 131–33, fig. 6, pl. 17:6; Garrison and Dion 1999, pp. 9 (n. 19), 10 (n. 28); Potts 1999, p. 348.

Cat.No. 218   PFS 1566*

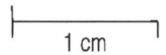

Seal Type:	Cylinder, Inscribed	Photograph:	Pl. 120a
Earliest Dated Application:	497 B.C.	Typology and Style:	II-B.3 — Modeled Style
Language of Inscription:	Elamite		
Preserved Height of Image:	1.70 cm (incomp.)	Preserved Length of Image:	3.20 cm (incomp.)
Estimated Height of Original Seal:	2.00 cm	Estimated Diameter of Original Seal:	NA
Number of Impressions:	2	Quality of Impressions:	Good

Completeness of Image: Large segment of middle of design survives including part of upper edge

DESCRIPTION OF SEAL AS IMPRESSED IMAGE

Winged hero faces right, extending bent left arm (elbow up) outward to grasp rampant winged human-faced bull creature by wing; hero's right arm is straight and held down behind body to hold curved sword; weapon terminates in point at top of hilt. Hero, in vigorous striding pose, raises bent forward leg to place his foot on rear hind leg of creature.

Creature moves away from hero but turns its head back toward him. Creature holds both forelegs (only partially preserved) bent and extends them in front of its body; tail curves down behind hero's forward leg with tufted termination.

Hero wears belted Assyrian garment that leaves forward leg exposed below knee; fringe is indicated along front edge of lower part of garment over rear leg. Hero wears domed headdress with projection at top. Long squared beard with horizontal striations on upper cheek rests along hero's chest; small flattened coiffure rests at back of neck. Upper wing extends diagonally upward from hero's shoulder; lower wing extends diagonally downward from hero's back; two rows of feathers are indicated on bottom wing, one row on top wing.

Creature has pointed beard that rests over its wing; long curved horn emerges from front of its head; thick bent ear is at top of head. Two rows of feathers are indicated on creature's wing; creature is ithyphallic.

Paneled inscription is in terminal field.

Portion of edge of seal is preserved at top of design above hero.

INSCRIPTION

Elamite

Line
1. v.Ab-ba-
2. te-ya
3. ⌈šak Ir(?)-⌉
4. [x-(x-)]⌈-x⌉

Translation   Abbateya son of Ir…

Four lines of text are preserved, oriented along the horizontal axis of the seal, separated by case lines, and enclosed in a panel. The visible signs are clear and well executed. See also the commentary (below).

COMMENTARY

From textual evidence it is clear that PFS 1566* belongs to the official Abbateya, whose name also occurs in the seal inscription. He is well known in the Fortification archive. The one tablet on which this seal appears, PF 1852, is a letter (T text) for which he is the sender. Letters are sent only by officials of very high rank (including Parnaka and Ziššawiš) and members of the royal family (including the king), placing Abbateya in a very elite circle of individuals. See PFS 98* (Cat.No. 217) for further comment on Abbateya.

This is an especially impressive and well-carved design. See Garrison 1988 for the style and workshop of PFS 1566* and related seals. This seal, clearly commissioned by Abbateya, is an excellent example of Modeled Style glyptic at the Persian court that is indisputably Assyrianizing rather than an Assyro-Babylonian heirloom.[60] It is very similar to PFS 98* (Cat.No. 217), which is also linked to Abbateya.

The horn of the winged creature suggests a wild goat, but the tail suggests a bull.

For comparative illustrations including PFS 1566*, see pls. 187h (headdresses), 191h (variously detailed beards), 199h (feet and shoes), 235f (human-headed/human-faced creatures), 244i (daggers and swords), 263d (paneled inscriptions with horizontal case lines), and 285d (personal seals of the official Abbateya [plausibly, PFS 98*; definitively, PFS 1566*], who sets apportionments).

SEAL APPLICATION (SEE *APPENDIX ONE: CONCORDANCE OF SEALS TO TABLETS IN VOLUME I*)

PFS 1566* occurs on the upper edge and left edge of PF 1852. No other seal is used on the tablet. Both impressions show some part of the inscription. The partial rolling on the left edge displays the hero in the center, with a large part of the inscription at the left of the impression. The upper edge of the tablet is much damaged; the partial rolling preserves only the inscription (at left) and the hero. PF 1852 is dated 497 B.C.

BIBLIOGRAPHY

Garrison 1988, pp. 228–29, 240–43, 479–80, 494; Garrison 1998, p. 121 (n. 15); Garrison 2000, pp. 131–34, fig. 7, pl. 18:7; Garrison and Dion 1999, pp. 9 (n. 19), 10 (n. 28).

---

60. See Collon 1987, pp. 196–97, no. 965, for one of numerous parallels for the robust modeling and musculature characteristic of Assyro-Babylonian Modeled Style and emulated so successfully in PFS 1566*.

Cat.No. 219   PFS 1227*

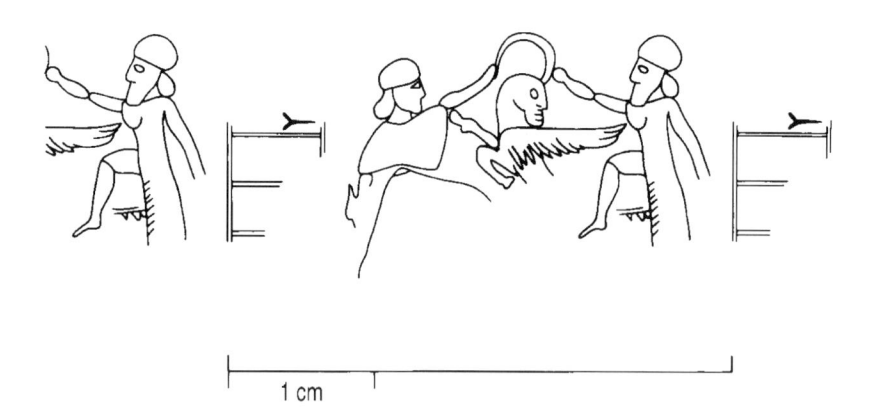

Seal Type:	Cylinder, Inscribed	Photographs:	Pl. 120c–d
Earliest Dated Application:	499/498 B.C.	Typology and Style:	II-B.3 — Modeled Style
Language of Inscription:	Uncertain		
Preserved Height of Image:	1.60 cm (incomp.)	Preserved Length of Image:	3.50 cm (comp.)
Estimated Height of Original Seal:	NA	Estimated Diameter of Original Seal:	1.10 cm
Number of Impressions:	4	Quality of Impressions:	Poor

Completeness of Image: Large but uneven segment of middle of design survives along its complete length

DESCRIPTION OF SEAL AS IMPRESSED IMAGE

Two heroes are rendered, one on either side of rampant winged human-faced bull(?) creature.

At left, one hero faces right, extending his straight left arm upward to grasp creature by tip of horn; right arm is straight and held down behind body to hold weapon (only pointed handle is preserved). Hero, in striding pose, raises bent forward leg.

Hero at left wears belted Persian court robe with sleeves down and spread wide; hero perhaps wears domed headdress. Pointed beard rests over hero's left shoulder; rounded coiffure rests at back of neck.

Creature moves toward hero at left but turns head back toward hero at right. Creature holds upper foreleg straight and extends it upward to place hoof at hero's chest; lower foreleg is bent and extended upward in front of its body.

At right, other hero faces left, extending his straight right arm upward to grasp creature by base of its horn; left arm (only partially preserved) is straight and held down behind body presumably to hold weapon (not preserved). Hero raises bent forward leg.

Hero at right wears Assyrian garment that leaves forward leg exposed below knee; fringe is indicated along front edge of garment over rear leg; decorative horizontal border and fringe are indicated on hem of garment between legs. Hero perhaps wears domed headdress. Squared beard rests over hero's right shoulder; round coiffure rests at back of neck.

Rounded beard with horizontal striations rests over creature's wing; large curved horn emerges from front of its head.

Paneled inscription is in terminal field.

INSCRIPTION

Cuneiform script, language uncertain

Line   x+1. […] ⌈x⌉
           x+2. […]
           x+3. […]
           x+4. […]

Translation   ?

There are apparently four lines to the inscription, oriented along the horizontal axis of the seal, separated by case lines, and enclosed in a panel. Only a single horizontal wedge is visible at the end of line x+1.

COMMENTARY

The Persian court robe on the hero to left finds several parallels, for example, PFS 39s (Cat.No. 221). See PFS 1566* (Cat.No. 218) on the ambiguous typology of the creature. Compare a similar (although uninscribed) double hero combat scene preserved in the Murašu archive (Bregstein 1993, p. 485, no. 93). See Garrison 1988 for the style and workshop of PFS 1227* and related seals.

For comparative illustrations including PFS 1227*, see pls. 180c (Persian court robes with sleeves down), 199f (feet and shoes), 240h (double hero encounters), and 263c (paneled inscriptions with horizontal case lines).

SEAL APPLICATION (SEE *APPENDIX ONE: CONCORDANCE OF SEALS TO TABLETS IN VOLUME I*)

PFS 1227* occurs on the reverse, bottom edge, upper edge, and left edge of PF 1282. No other seal is used on the tablet. Impressions exhibit marked distortion. Two of the total four impressions show some part of the inscription. Of the four partial rollings, two display the inscription in the center; one preserves only the hero to left and the creature; one displays the creature in the center. PF 1282 is dated 499/498 B.C.

BIBLIOGRAPHY

Garrison 1988, pp. 228–29, 233–36, 417, 479, 493; Garrison and Dion 1999, pp. 8 (n. 17), 10 (n. 28).

II-B.4. LIONS

PFS 33   Cat.No. 220

Seal Type:	Cylinder	Photographs:	Pl. 121a–b
Earliest Dated Application:	501/500 B.C.	Typology and Style:	II-B.4 — Fortification Style
Preserved Height of Image:	1.70 cm (incomp.)	Preserved Length of Image:	3.00 cm (comp.)
Estimated Height of Original Seal:	NA	Estimated Diameter of Original Seal:	1.00 cm
Number of Impressions:	21	Quality of Impressions:	Poor-fair

Completeness of Image: Large segment of middle of design survives along its complete length

DESCRIPTION OF SEAL AS IMPRESSED IMAGE

Hero faces right, extending straight left arm upward to grasp upper foreleg of rampant lion; left arm is straight and held down behind body to hold weapon of uncertain type (most of weapon not preserved).

Lion moves toward and faces hero. Lion holds upper foreleg slightly bent, paw upturned, and extends it upward toward hero's head; lower foreleg is curved, paw upturned, and extended downward toward hero's waist; tail curves upward, curling into tight spiral at its end.

Hero wears triple-belted garment of uncertain type; fringe or folds are indicated on back of garment. Long pointed beard with horizontal striations rests over hero's left shoulder; long, squared coiffure with many diagonal striations curls slightly upward at back of neck.

Lion's mane is rendered by spikes along contour of neck; mouth is open in roar.

In terminal field, rampant horned animal of undetermined type moves to right but turns its head back to left. Animal holds upper foreleg straight, hoof upturned, and extends it diagonally upward; lower foreleg is slightly bent extending downward in front of body; short tail curls down slightly. Two thin curved horns emerge from top of animal's head; pointed ear is at back of head; tiny teardrop-shaped element at lower jaw may indicate beard.

COMMENTARY

Hallock notes that PFS 33 belonged to a supplier whom he is not able to locate precisely, but he speculates that he was located near Kurdušum. Koch places the seal at her post station, Zilaba, but like Hallock, she cannot connect it with any named official. Lewis identifies the seal as an office seal of a way station, the unnamed official of which was "punctilious in use and placing of seal."

The seal seems clearly to represent an office. The commodity was always flour in the Q travel rations, but in other texts beer, grain, and exotic commodities were supplied under the jurisdiction of PFS 33.

The style is an unusual variation on the local Fortification Style; see Garrison 1988 for the distinctive hand of this artist in other seals.

For comparative illustrations including PFS 33, see pls. 195b (coiffures of distinctive types/sub-types), 222b (lions and lion creatures), and 281d (office seals).

SEAL APPLICATION (SEE *APPENDIX ONE: CONCORDANCE OF SEALS TO TABLETS IN VOLUME I*)

PFS 33 occurs only on the left edge of tablets. Rollings show little or no distortion. In eleven impressions the seal is rolled for at least one complete turn, preserving the entire length of the seal design. Of these eleven applications, four display the hero and the lion in the center; six display the lion in the center; one displays the rampant horned animal in the center. Of the remaining ten partial rollings, one displays the hero in the center; one displays the hero and the lion in the center; five preserve only the hero and the lion; one preserves only the lion and the rampant horned animal; two display the lion in the center. PF 2061 is the earliest dated tablet with PFS 33 and is dated 501/500 B.C.

BIBLIOGRAPHY

Garrison 1988, pp. 330–33; Garrison and Root 1996, p. 12; Hallock 1978, p. 113 (n. 10); Koch 1986, p. 145; Koch 1993, pp. 41, 71; Lewis 1994, p. 30.

PFS 39s
Cat.No. 221

Seal Type:	Stamp, Rounded Square Face	Photographs:	Pl. 121d–f
Earliest Dated Application:	501 B.C.	Typology and Style:	II-B.4 — Court Style
Preserved Height of Image:	1.30 cm (comp.)	Preserved Width of Image:	1.30 cm (comp.)
Number of Impressions:	10	Quality of Impressions:	Poor-fair

Completeness of Image: Complete except for details and small segment of right edge

Description of Seal as Impressed Image

Hero faces left, extending straight right arm upward to grasp forelock of rampant lion; left arm is straight and held down behind body to hold long thin weapon, probably a throw stick.

Lion moves toward and faces hero. Lion holds one foreleg straight and extends it upward toward hero's chest; other foreleg is straight, held up and away from body to left. Lion raises forward bent hind leg toward hero's leg; tail curves upward with tufted termination.

Hero wears Persian court robe with sleeves down; gathered folds of sleeves are indicated, as are double central pleat and diagonal folds of lower part of garment. Hero wears five-pointed dentate Persian crown. Narrow pointed beard rests above hero's right shoulder; rounded coiffure rests at back of neck.

Lion's mane is rendered by serrated edge; forelock emerges from front of its head; mouth is open in roar. Each paw is rendered differently, but in each case the artist has suggested splayed toes.

Edge of seal is preserved except for short passage at right.

Commentary

Koch (1990) associates the seal with grain cultivation at Kaupirriš in her Northwestern Region V. In the absence of evidence allowing us to link the seal to a specific official, for whom PFS 39s was a personal seal, we must tentatively designate it an office seal.

PFS 39s is the only example of a Court Style carving on a stamp seal in the PFS corpus of hero seals. The style is a loose version of the Court Style, far removed from the monumentality and formality of, for example, PFS 113* (Cat.No. 19). For similar stylization of the upper part of the garment, see PFS 1227* (Cat.No. 219).[61]

The stamp face has an irregular square contour with rounded corners. For probable seal shape, see *Appendix Four: Stamp Seals in Volume I Grouped by Apparent Contour of Seal Face* and accompanying figure 9, no. 2a.

For comparative illustrations including PFS 39s, see pls. 180a (Persian court robes with sleeves down), 188c (Persian crowns and fluted tiaras), 192a (rounded coiffures), 212d (heroic attitudes of combat encounter), 222c (lions and lion creatures), and 274a (stamp seals).

Seal Application (see *Appendix One: Concordance of Seals to Tablets in Volume I*)

PFS 39s occurs only on the left edge of tablets. Impressions tend to be carefully applied with little distortion, oriented along the longitudinal axis of the left edge. When the surface does not allow for a full application of the seal, i.e., PF 446, PF 782, PF 1007, and PF 1254, the user prefers the upper portion of the design. PF 1254 is the earliest dated tablet with PFS 39s and is dated 501 B.C.

---

61. Compare the image and style on a circular-faced conoid from Qasr-i Abu Nasr, now in Tehran (Wilkinson 1965, fig. 22; Frye 1973, p. 38, fig. 8).

BIBLIOGRAPHY

Brosius 1996, p. 172; Garrison 1988, pp. 235, 411, 417–18, 479; Garrison and Dion 1999, pp. 9 (n. 20), 13 (n. 38); Koch 1990, pp. 151, 291, 294; Root 1997, p. 239, figs. 6 and 8.

Cat.No. 222   PFS 139s

|—| 1 cm |—|

Seal Type:	Stamp, Circular Face	Photographs:	Pl. 122a–b
Earliest Dated Application:	499/498 B.C.	Typology and Style:	II-B.4 — Broad and Flat Styles
Preserved Height of Image:	2.10 cm (comp.)	Preserved Width of Image:	1.90 cm (comp.)
Number of Impressions:	2	Quality of Impressions:	Poor-fair

Completeness of Image: Complete except for lower right and upper left corners of design and edge

DESCRIPTION OF SEAL AS IMPRESSED IMAGE

Hero faces left, extending straight right arm outward to grasp rampant lion by throat; left arm is straight and held down behind body to hold weapon of uncertain type (only curved handle preserved).

Lion moves toward and faces hero. Lion holds one foreleg straight and extends it downward to place paw on hero's waist; other foreleg (only partially preserved) is straight, held up and away from its body; tail curls upward with tufted termination. Only one hind leg is preserved, bent and extended downward apparently to place paw on hero's forward leg (not preserved).

Hero wears robe and dentate Persian crown. Blunt-pointed beard rests over hero's right shoulder; rounded narrow coiffure rests at back of neck.

Lion has mouth open in roar; mane is indicated by narrow outline (partially preserved).

COMMENTARY

Koch assigns PFS 139s to Matukka, based upon Q texts protocol. In year 23.9 (December 499 B.C. and early January 498 B.C.) he received beer rations while on his way to Persepolis with forty men, "*halla*-makers, exerters(?)" (PF 1533; cf. the thirty "exerters(?)" named in PF 1576 in the same year) under the authorization (*halmi*) of the king. See also the entry for PFS 1428s (Cat.No. 230), another seal that Matukka seems to have used.

The composition and Persian crown faintly echo the Court Style, but the coarse engraving is typical of seals carved in the Broad and Flat Styles.

The stamp face has an irregular circular contour. For probable seal shape, see *Appendix Four: Stamp Seals in Volume I Grouped by Apparent Contour of Seal Face* and accompanying figure 9, nos. 3a, 4c, or 5a.

For comparative illustrations including PFS 139s, see pls. 183b (robes of various undetailed types), 188f (Persian crowns and fluted tiaras), 194c (narrow rounded and/or pointed coiffures), 274b (stamp seals), and 285g (personal seals of Matukka).

SEAL APPLICATION (SEE *APPENDIX ONE: CONCORDANCE OF SEALS TO TABLETS IN VOLUME I*)

PFS 139s occurs on the reverse of PF 1533 and PF 1576. On PF 1533 the seal is rotated slightly off the longitudinal axis of the tablet; on PF 1576 it is oriented along the horizontal axis of the tablet. The application on PF 1533 preserves most of the upper part of the design; that on PF 1576 preserves only the lion. On both tablets the seal clearly was applied before the text since several cuneiform wedges cut into the left edge of the impression. All tablets with PFS 139s are dated 499/498 B.C.

BIBLIOGRAPHY

Garrison 1988, pp. 375, 428–30; Garrison 1998, p. 131 (n. 32); Garrison and Root 1996, p. 14; Koch 1990, p. 194 (n. 801).

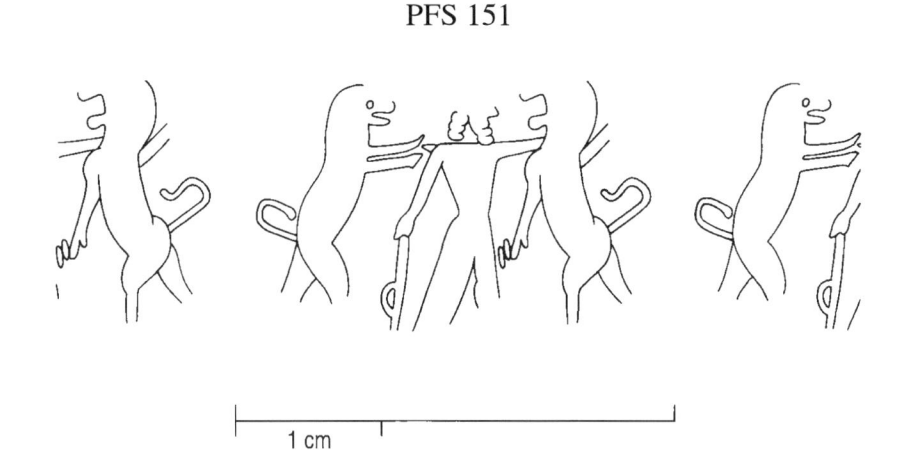

PFS 151   Cat.No. 223

Seal Type:	Cylinder	Photographs	Pl. 123a–b
Earliest Dated Application:	503/502 B.C.	Typology and Style:	II-B.4 — Fortification Style
Preserved Height of Image:	1.80 cm (incomp.)	Preserved Length of Image:	3.10 cm (comp.)
Estimated Height of Original Seal:	NA	Estimated Diameter of Original Seal:	1.00 cm
Number of Impressions:	7	Quality of Impressions:	Fair

Completeness of Image: Almost complete except for upper edge and lower edge

DESCRIPTION OF SEAL AS IMPRESSED IMAGE

Hero faces right, in striding pose, extending straight left arm outward to grasp rampant lion by throat; right arm is straight and held down behind body to hold long weapon of uncertain type with semicircular element (termination not preserved).

Lion moves toward and faces hero. Lion holds one foreleg straight, toes splayed, and extends it downward toward hero's leg; other foreleg (only partially preserved) is straight, held up and away from body; tail extends diagonally upward, hooking back and curling upward at its end.

Hero wears Assyrian garment that leaves forward leg exposed. Triangular element (tip of a strap?) projects at hero's right shoulder. Long, rounded, segmented beard rests over hero's left shoulder; rounded, segmented coiffure rests at back of neck.

Lion has mouth open in roar.

To left of hero, another rampant lion moves toward and faces hero. Lion holds forelegs straight and extends them together toward hero's shoulder; tail extends diagonally upward, hooking at its end; mouth is open.

COMMENTARY

Koch (1990) assigns PFS 151 to Šimut-ap, whose name occurs on all three transactions that carry the seal; he is active in her Elam Region VI.

The style is powerful with a sure sense of contour and modeling that draws it toward the Modeled Style.

For comparative illustrations including PFS 151, see pls. 195c (coiffures of distinctive types/sub-types), 236b (animals/creatures as secondary elements of main design field), 247e (weapons of unusual or uncertain type), and 282g (personal seals of supply/apportionment officers).

SEAL APPLICATION (SEE *APPENDIX ONE: CONCORDANCE OF SEALS TO TABLETS IN VOLUME I*)

PFS 151 occurs on the reverse (inverted) and upper edge of PF 576, the reverse of PF 577, and the upper edge and right edge of PF 590. On the reverse of PF 576 the seal is applied twice, one impression directly above the other. On the reverse of PF 577 the seal is applied twice. Both rollings run diagonally across the surface of the tablet on the same plane of the tablet surface. Impressions generally show vertical distortion on the right edge. In six impressions the seal is rolled for at least one complete turn, preserving the entire length of the seal design. These rollings of the seal tend to place the large negative space behind the lion in the terminal field at one of the ends of the impression, rather than equally balanced on both ends. Of these six complete impressions, one displays the hero and the lion to right in the center; one displays the lion in the terminal field (to the left of the hero) in the center; three display the lion to the right of the hero in the center; one displays the negative space behind the lion in the terminal field in the center. The remaining partial impression preserves only the hero and the lion to the right. PF 576 is the earliest dated tablet with PFS 151 and is dated 503/502 B.C.

BIBLIOGRAPHY

Garrison 1988, pp. 293–94; Koch 1990, p. 114 (n. 484).

Cat.No. 224   PFS 196

Seal Type:	Cylinder	Photograph:	Pl. 124a
Earliest Dated Application:	500/499 B.C.	Typology and Style:	II-B.4 — Broad and Flat Styles
Preserved Height of Image:	1.60 cm (incomp.)	Preserved Length of Image:	3.20 cm (comp.)
Estimated Height of Original Seal:	NA	Estimated Diameter of Original Seal:	1.00 cm
Number of Impressions:	2	Quality of Impressions:	Fair

Completeness of Image: Large segment of middle of design survives along its complete length

DESCRIPTION OF SEAL AS IMPRESSED IMAGE

Hero faces right, extending bent left arm upward to grasp rampant lion by forelocks; right arm is bent and held down behind body to hold weapon of uncertain type (lower portion not preserved).

Lion moves toward and faces hero. Lion holds one foreleg bent, two toes rendered, and extends it upward toward hero's arm; other foreleg is curved, held up and away from body.

Hero wears Persian court robe with sleeves pushed up to reveal hero's bare arms; gathered folds of sleeves are indicated on right side of hero's upper torso. Bow case with bow protruding is at his back; hero wears polos headdress with horizontal band. Narrow squared beard rests over hero's left shoulder; rounded coiffure rests at back of neck.

Mane of lion is rendered by spikes along contour of neck; mouth is open in roar.

Winged symbol with bird's tail and tendrils in is upper terminal field; ring placed atop each wing.

COMMENTARY

The design and iconography have associations with the Court Style, but the awkward and somewhat crude engraving is typical of the Broad and Flat Styles. The slightly curved wings on the winged symbol are noteworthy since that form (versus the broad rectangular wings) has sometimes been associated with post-Darius developments in Achaemenid art. The curved wings are best understood not as a chronological index, but rather as an index of a specific strain in rendering the image. This strain ultimately relates to Egyptian (and hence to Egyptianizing) traditions. Winged symbols rather similar to that displayed on PFS 196 may also be tracked on seals of the Neo-Assyrian period.[62]

For comparative illustrations including PFS 196, see pls. 189f (polos headdresses), 208f (arm positions of heroic combat), 222g (lions and lion creatures), 246b (bows, arrows, quivers), 249b (winged symbols), and 266a (terminal field motifs other than inscriptions).

SEAL APPLICATION (SEE *APPENDIX ONE: CONCORDANCE OF SEALS TO TABLETS IN VOLUME I*)

PFS 196 occurs on the reverse of PF 1100 and PF 1237, with PFS 64* (Cat.No. 173) on the left edge of each tablet. Both impressions preserve the entire length of the seal design, the one placing the hero and the lion in the center, the other placing the lion in the center. On the reverse of both tablets the seal clearly was applied before the text since several cuneiform wedges cut into the top of the impressions. PF 1100 is the earliest dated tablet with PFS 196 and is dated 500/499 B.C.

BIBLIOGRAPHY

Garrison 1988, pp. 428–30; Garrison and Dion 1999, pp. 9 (n. 24), 11 (n. 36), 13 (n. 38).

---

62. See Herbordt 1992, pl. 10, no. 24, for an impression from Nineveh; see Collon 1987, pp. 84–85, no. 389, for a stamp cylinder from Tarsus, Turkey.

Cat.No. 225   PFS 260

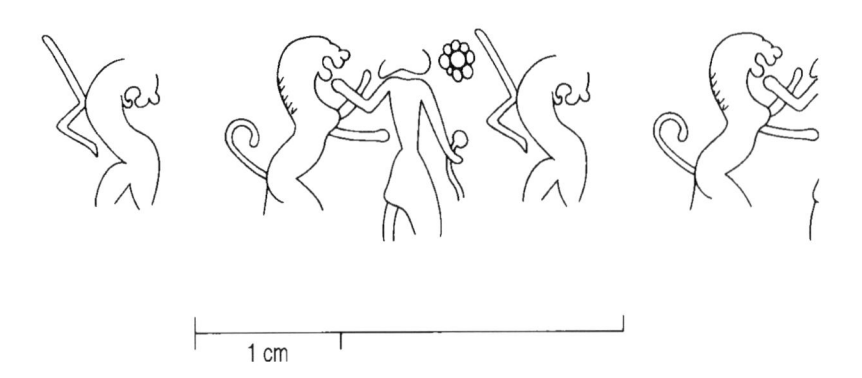

Seal Type: Cylinder	Photographs: Pl. 124c–d
Earliest Dated Application: 500/499 B.C.	Typology and Style: II-B.4 — Fortification Style
Preserved Height of Image: 1.40 cm (incomp.)	Preserved Length of Image: 2.90 cm (comp.)
Estimated Height of Original Seal: 1.60 cm	Estimated Diameter of Original Seal: 0.90 cm
Number of Impressions: 7	Quality of Impressions: Very poor

Completeness of Image: Almost complete except for upper and lower edges

DESCRIPTION OF SEAL AS IMPRESSED IMAGE

Hero faces left, extending bent right arm outward toward jaw of rampant lion; left arm is straight and held down behind body to hold curved sword (only partially preserved).

Lion moves toward and faces hero. Lion holds upper foreleg straight and extends it upward toward hero's head; lower foreleg is straight and extended horizontally toward hero's waist; tail extends diagonally upward, curling upward at its end with tufted termination.

Hero wears Assyrian garment that leaves forward leg exposed below knee. Beard terminates in blunt point over hero's right shoulder; rounded coiffure rests at back of neck.

Mane of lion is rendered by diagonal markings along back of neck; mouth is open in roar.

To right of hero, another rampant lion moves toward hero but turns its head away from him. Lion holds upper foreleg straight and extends it diagonally upward; lower foreleg is bent and extended downward in front of its body; mouth is open in roar. In upper field between hero and lion is rosette formed by large central dot and eight surrounding dots.

COMMENTARY

The poor preservation of the seal disguises what are in fact nicely engraved animal forms.

For comparative illustrations including PFS 260, see pl. 253f (stars, rosettes).

SEAL APPLICATION (SEE *APPENDIX ONE: CONCORDANCE OF SEALS TO TABLETS IN VOLUME I*)

PFS 260 occurs on the reverse, upper edge, or left edge of PF 144–148. All impressions of the seal are difficult to read; that on the reverse of PF 148 is too poorly preserved for analysis. In two impressions the seal is rolled for at least one complete turn, preserving the entire length of the seal design. Both of these applications display the hero in the center. Of the remaining four partial rollings, three display the hero in the center; one displays the lion to the left of the hero in the center. PF 144 and PF 145 are the earliest dated tablets with PFS 260 and are both dated 500/499 B.C.

BIBLIOGRAPHY

Garrison 1988, pp. 339–41.

PFS 916   Cat.No. 226

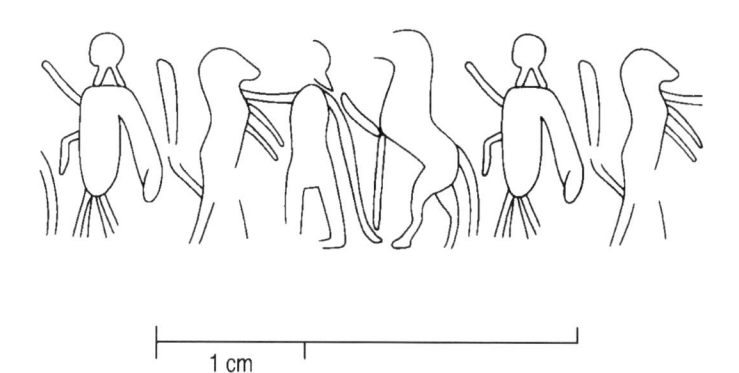

Seal Type:	Cylinder	Photograph:	Pl. 125a
Earliest Dated Application:	ND	Typology and Style:	II-B.4 — Broad and Flat Styles
Preserved Height of Image:	1.50 cm (incomp.)	Preserved Length of Image:	2.80 cm (comp.)
Estimated Height of Original Seal:	1.60 cm	Estimated Diameter of Original Seal:	0.90 cm
Number of Impressions:	1	Quality of Impression:	Poor

Completeness of Image: Almost complete except for upper and lower edges

DESCRIPTION OF SEAL AS IMPRESSED IMAGE

Hero faces left, extending straight right arm outward to grasp rampant lion by throat; left arm is curved and held down behind body, apparently merging with a long weapon of uncertain type.

Lion moves toward and faces hero. Lion holds forelegs straight and extends them downward together toward hero's waist; long tail extends diagonally upward, then bends vertically upward thickening at its termination.

Hero wears garment of uncertain type; pointed coiffure extends diagonally downward at back of hero's neck.

Behind hero, to the right, another rampant lion moves toward and faces him. Lion holds upper foreleg straight and extends it upward toward hero's shoulder; lower foreleg is straight and extended downward toward end of hero's long curved weapon; thick tail curves downward.

To right of this lion, in terminal field, rampant human-headed bird creature with quadruped's forelegs faces left. Creature holds upper foreleg straight and extends it diagonally upward in front of head; lower foreleg is bent and extended downward in front of body. Narrow beard terminates in blunt point over creature's chest; narrow rounded coiffure extends downward at back of neck. Stick-like tail feathers fan out from base of ovoid body.

COMMENTARY

See Garrison 1988 for the distinctive hand and compositions of this artist. PFS 247 (Cat.No. 245), by the same artist, displays a very similar composition, including the unusual bird creature.

For comparative illustrations including PFS 916, see pls. 194h (narrow rounded and/or pointed coiffures) and 236h (animals/creatures as secondary elements of main design field).

SEAL APPLICATION (SEE *APPENDIX ONE: CONCORDANCE OF SEALS TO TABLETS IN VOLUME I*)

PFS 916 occurs on the reverse of PF 788. The rolling preserves the entire length of the seal design and displays the bird creature in the center. The date of PF 788 is unknown.

BIBLIOGRAPHY

Garrison 1988, pp. 423–25.

Cat.No. 227 PFS 952

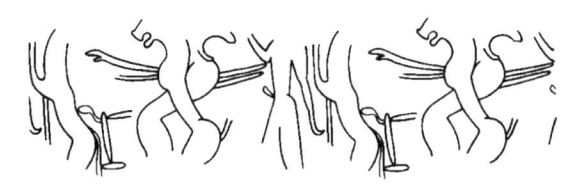

Seal Type:	Cylinder	Photograph:	Pl. 125c
Earliest Dated Application:	500 B.C.	Typology and Style:	II-B.4 — Fortification Style
Preserved Height of Image:	1.00 cm (incomp.)	Preserved Length of Image:	1.90 cm (comp.)
Estimated Height of Original Seal:	1.20 cm	Estimated Diameter of Original Seal:	0.60 cm
Number of Impressions:	1	Quality of Impression:	Poor

Completeness of Image: Almost complete except for upper edge and lower edge

DESCRIPTION OF SEAL AS IMPRESSED IMAGE

Hero faces left, extending bent right arm upward to grasp rampant lion at top of head (not preserved); left arm is straight and held down behind body to hold short curved weapon of uncertain type.

Lion is one of pair of crossed lions. Lion moves toward and faces hero. Lion holds both forelegs straight and extends them upward together toward hero's chest.

Hero appears to wear Assyrian garment that leaves forward leg exposed; projection from his waist may be short forepart of sheath.

Lion opens mouth in roar. Other lion of crossed group moves and faces to left. Lion holds both forelegs (lower foreleg only partially preserved) straight and extends them upward together in front of its body; upper foreleg has paw with one articulated toe; tail (only partially preserved) extends diagonally upward. Mouth is open.

To right of hero rampant animal of uncertain type moves toward him but turns head back toward lion of crossed pair that faces left. Animal holds upper foreleg straight and extends it vertically upward in front of its neck; lower foreleg is straight and extended vertically downward in front of its body; tail (only partially preserved) curves downward. To right of this animal is uncertain fragmentary element.

COMMENTARY

The fusion of heroic *combat* encounter and crossed animals (as on PFS 952) occurs also on PFS 931* (Cat.No. 270) and PFS 737 (Cat.No. 281); see the commentary on PFS 931* (Cat.No. 270) for discussion. The fusion of heroic *control* encounter and crossed animals occurs only on PFS 912 (Cat.No. 138). PFS 952 is remarkably close in its layout and busy exuberance to Early Dynastic prototypes of the mid-third millennium B.C.[63] The dynamics between the figures create an interlocked composition in which there is no discrete terminal field.

For comparative illustrations including PFS 952, see pls. 241f (heroic encounters merged with animal contests) and 242d (heroic encounters fused with crossed animals).

SEAL APPLICATION (SEE *APPENDIX ONE: CONCORDANCE OF SEALS TO TABLETS IN VOLUME I*)

PFS 952 occurs on the obverse of PF 826. The rolling preserves the entire length of the seal design and carefully displays the hero and the rampant animal behind him in the center with the group of crossed animals framing them at each end of the impression. The seal clearly was applied before the text since several cuneiform wedges cut into the bottom of the impression. PF 826 is dated 500 B.C.

BIBLIOGRAPHY

Garrison 1988, pp. 321, 323.

---

63. For example, Collon 1987, pp. 26–27, no. 71 (from Zinçirli, Turkey), pp. 193–94, no. 944 (from Fara, Iraq).

PFS 1122   Cat.No. 228

|—————1 cm—————|

Seal Type:	Cylinder	Photograph:	Pl. 126a
Earliest Dated Application:	499/498 B.C.	Typology and Style:	II-B.4 — Plausibly Antique: Assyro-Babylonian Modeled Style
Preserved Height of Image:	2.00 cm (incomp.)	Preserved Length of Image:	2.90 cm (comp.)
Estimated Height of Original Seal:	2.20 cm	Estimated Diameter of Original Seal:	0.90 cm
Number of Impressions:	4		

Quality of Impressions: Fair; the small impression on PF 1190 preserves much detail

Completeness of Image: Almost complete except for upper and lower edges

DESCRIPTION OF SEAL AS IMPRESSED IMAGE

Hero faces left, in striding pose, extending bent right arm outward to grasp rampant lion by upper foreleg; left arm is straight and held down behind body to hold short dagger.

Lion moves toward and faces hero. Lion holds upper foreleg (only partially preserved) curved and extends it diagonally upward; lower foreleg is curved, paw upturned, and extended downward toward hero's leg; tail curves upward, hooking downward at its end.

Hero wears triple-belted Assyrian garment that leaves forward leg exposed below knee; two layers of fringe run horizontally across hero's hips below belt; detail line is at hem of garment over forward leg. Long squared beard with horizontal striations rests over hero's chest; rounded coiffure rests high off back of head. Hooked element (dagger sheath strapped to leg?) emerges from calf of hero's forward leg.

Fur is rendered by diagonal marks along lion's belly.

Sejant dog faces left in lower field between lion and hero; two thin pointed ears emerge from front of its head.

Bird of uncertain type flies to left in upper terminal field above lion's tail and hero's left forearm; bird appears poised to peck hero's upper arm.

COMMENTARY

This is a large and well-executed design. It clearly references Neo-Assyrian and Neo-Babylonian Modeled Style glyptic in both style and iconography.[64] It may in fact be an heirloom seal, although this is far from certain. Speaking against this possibility is its very small size in comparison to most Modeled Style seals of Neo-Assyrian/Neo-Babylonian date. Speaking for an heirloom status would perhaps be the very particular (and apparently restricted) nature of the canine image.

Seated dogs such as that on PFS 1122 are associated with the goddess Gula in Mesopotamia and occur primarily on seals depicting worshipers before divine images or symbols.[65] Occasionally the seated dog appears,

---

64. See Porada 1947b, Collon 1987, p. 83, and Garrison 1988, pp. 82–105, on issues in attempting to discern distinctions between glyptic production in the Modeled Style emerging from Assyria versus Babylonia during the phase of Assyrian political dominance in the eighth and seventh centuries B.C.

65. See, for example, Wiseman 1959, p. 68 (BM 89846).

rather, in the context of an action scene, but this is rare.[66] Rarer still seems to be the appearance of the dog in a heroic encounter context.[67] PFS 1122 displays the only occurrence of the seated dog on seals with images of heroic encounter herein.[68]

For comparative illustrations including PFS 1122, see pls. 177f (Assyrian garments with detailing preserved), 213d (heroic attitudes of combat encounter), 219e (comparative heroic proportions), 227g (birds), 236i (animals/creatures as secondary elements of main design field), 244g (daggers and swords).

SEAL APPLICATION (SEE *APPENDIX ONE: CONCORDANCE OF SEALS TO TABLETS IN VOLUME I*)

PFS 1122 occurs on the reverse and left edge of PF 1178 and PF 1190. On the reverse of each tablet PFS 1121s (II) is applied directly above PFS 1122. On the left edge of each tablet PFS 1121s is applied to the right of PFS 1122. This sealing pattern is very distinctive and quite unusual for the PF tablet corpus. The impression of PFS 1122 on the left edge of PF 1178 is too poorly preserved for analysis. The rollings on the reverse of PF 1178 and PF 1190 preserve the entire length of the seal design; that on PF 1190 displays the hero in the center; that on PF 1178 displays the hero and bird in the center. The partial rolling on the left edge of PF 1190 preserves only the hero and the bird. PF 1178 is the earliest dated tablet with PFS 1122 and is dated 499/498 B.C.

BIBLIOGRAPHY

Garrison 1988, pp. 203–07, 213, 520.

---

66. See Wiseman 1959, p. 98 (BM 117716), for a cylinder inscribed in Babylonian probably dating to the pre-Achaemenid period, showing the seated dog within a scene of a horseman and a camel rider.
67. See, for example, an unprovenanced Neo-Babylonian Modeled Style seal in Fribourg showing a seated dog in the context of a heroic encounter (Collon 1987, pp. 80–81, no. 370 [height = 2.56 cm]). Far more informative is a Neo-Assyrian Modeled Style cylinder found in the excavation of the cella of the Heraion at Samos, with an inscription giving the name of a governor of Isana, south of Aššur (Aruz 1997, p. 144, fig. 158 [height = 4.00 cm]).
68. The guardian statues of seated canines excavated at Persepolis demonstrate that the icon carried potency and meaning in the Achaemenid context (Schmidt 1957, p. 70, pl. 36a–b; Sami 1955, pp. 68–69). The importance of the seated guardian dog in Elamite tradition, reinforced by the important role of the dog in Indo-Iranian (Zoroastrian?) traditions at the Persian court, may be the critical factor here (Root in press).

PFS 1309s   Cat.No. 229

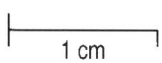

Seal Type:	Stamp, Octagonal Face	Photograph:	Pl. 126c
Earliest Dated Application:	ND	Typology and Style:	II-B.4 — Diverse Styles
Preserved Height of Image:	0.80 cm (incomp.)	Preserved Width of Image:	1.40 cm (comp.)
Number of Impressions:	1	Quality of Impression:	Fair-good

Completeness of Image: Almost complete except for right edge and lower edge

DESCRIPTION OF SEAL AS IMPRESSED IMAGE

Hero faces right, extending bent left arm outward to grasp rampant lion by upper foreleg (or jaw?); right arm is bent, elbow up, and held down behind body to hold short weapon of uncertain type. Hero appears to be in *knielauf*-pose, but rear leg is not rendered (it ought to be shown bent as if kneeling). Forward foot of hero appears to be stepping on paw of lion's forward hind leg.

Lion moves toward and faces hero. Lion holds upper foreleg straight and extends it upward to place paw on hero's arm; lower foreleg is straight and extended downward behind hero's leg; long tail curls upward with tufted termination.

Hero appears to wear belted trousers. Short pointed beard rests over hero's left shoulder; narrow pointed coiffure extends diagonally downward from back of head. Hero perhaps wears domed headdress.

Mane of lion is rendered by crisp serrated edge along contour of neck; mouth is open in roar.

In field above lion, thin undulating device with two-pronged termination may represent a snake, but this is far from certain.

Edge of seal is preserved at top and sides of design.

COMMENTARY

Based on Q texts protocol, PFS 1309s should belong to Dadaka, who in PF 1386 went to Persepolis under the authority (*halmi*) of Parnaka. The name Dadaka occurs also as a receiver on the Q text PF 1387. This seems to be the same individual mentioned in PF 1386, but a different seal was used: PFS 1310s (III). In both texts two other unnamed individuals traveled with him, and perhaps one or both of the seals PFS 1309s and PFS 1310s belonged to them. Another Dadaka (a grain handler) occurs in the J text PF 705.

The pose of the hero (with rear leg not depicted) is unusual.[69] The *knielauf*-pose is also seen on PFS 67 (Cat.No. 293), PFS 120 (Cat.No. 49), and PFS 1527 (Cat.No. 32). It is unusual in the PFS corpus that the design is oriented along the horizontal axis of the stamp face, leaving little vertical space for the figures.

The seal was not included in Garrison 1988. This design exhibits some connections with the class of pyramidal stamp seals discussed by Boardman (1970a and 1970b) as leading to the so-called Graeco-Persian style. See the discussion of PFS 1321s (Cat.No. 176).

The stamp face has an octagonal contour. For probable seal shape, see *Appendix Four: Stamp Seals in Volume I Grouped by Apparent Contour of Seal Face* and accompanying figure 9, no. 1.

For comparative illustrations including PFS 1309s, see pls. 184f (trousers), 190h (beards), 194j (narrow rounded and/or pointed coiffures), 209e (arm positions of heroic combat), 213f (heroic attitudes of combat encounter), 274i (stamp seals), 279b (carving anomalies), and 290f (personal seals of various travelers).

---

69. Compare scaraboids with kneeling archers disposed horizontally where rear leg completes the *knielauf*-type posture (Boardman 1970b, nos. 356, 376). On the *knielauf*-pose in western Asiatic art, see Kantor 1962. For comparanda from Susa, see Amiet 1973b, pl. 2, nos. 8–10.

SEAL APPLICATION (SEE *APPENDIX ONE: CONCORDANCE OF SEALS TO TABLETS IN VOLUME I*)

PFS 1309s occurs on the reverse (inverted) of PF 1386. The one application is oriented along the longitudinal axis of the tablet. The impression preserves the entire seal design except for the lower right edge. The date of PF 1386 is unknown.

BIBLIOGRAPHY

Root 1998, pp. 265, 275, fig. 6, pl. 8.

Cat.No. 230   PFS 1428s

Seal Type:	Stamp, Circular Face	Photograph:	Pl. 127a
Earliest Dated Application:	499/498 B.C.	Typology and Style:	II-B.4 — Broad and Flat Styles
Preserved Height of Image:	1.90 cm (incomp.)	Preserved Width of Image:	2.00 cm (comp.)
Number of Impressions:	1	Quality of Impression:	Good

Completeness of Image: Complete except for upper edge

DESCRIPTION OF SEAL AS IMPRESSED IMAGE

Hero faces right, extending straight left arm outward to grasp rampant lion by throat; right arm is straight and held down behind body to hold dagger.

Lion moves toward and faces hero. Lion extends right foreleg to place paw on hero's waist; other foreleg is curved up and away from body, one toe articulated. Lion slightly raises forward hind leg; tail curls upward with tufted termination.

Hero wears Persian court robe with sleeves pushed up to reveal arms; hem line suggests lower garment hitched up over forward leg. Hero wears six-pointed dentate Persian crown. Squared beard rests over hero's left shoulder; rounded coiffure rests at back of neck.

Small ear is at back of lion's head; mouth is open in roar.

Edge of seal is preserved except at top of design. Small chip, apparently, is along upper left edge of seal.

COMMENTARY

Based on Q texts protocol, PFS 1428s should belong to Matukka, who in year 23.9 (December 499 and early January 498 B.C.) received beer rations for a large traveling party (2,454 gentlemen!) on his way to Persepolis under the authority (*halmi*) of the king. A Matukka occurs in three other Q travel texts: PF 1488, receiving flour rations in year 22.12 while going to Karkiš under the authority of the king, using PFS 1385 (illegible); PF 1533, receiving beer rations in year 23.9 while going to Persepolis under the authority of the king, using PFS 139s (Cat.No. 222); and PF 1576, receiving *tarmu*-grain rations in year 23.9 while going to Persepolis under the authority of the king, using PFS 139s (Cat.No. 222). Of these texts, PF 1532–1533 and PF 1576 seem to record the same trip. Koch (1990, p. 194 note 801) assigns PFS 139s (Cat.No. 222) to Matukka since the seal only occurs on the reverse of Q texts that name Matukka as the receiver. PFS 1428s probably also belongs to him. It is very interesting to note that both seals are stamps with round contours, presumably indicating conoids, that they show almost the exact same scene, and that they belong to the same stylistic group, probably even from the same artist (see Garrison 1988).

PF 1595 records another Matukka receiving flour rations in year 22.3, sealed with PFS 1474s (illegible). PF 834 and PF 1671 mention a Matukka who was a flour and grain supplier (different seals used in all transactions). PF 1997 records a Matukka who was the *ullira* (OD).

The composition and iconography connect the seal to the Court Style, but the engraving is typical of seals carved in the Broad and Flat Styles.

The stamp face has a circular contour. For probable seal shape, see *Appendix Four: Stamp Seals in Volume I Grouped by Apparent Contour of Seal Face* and accompanying figure 9, nos. 3a, 4c, or 5a.

For comparative illustrations including PFS 1428s, see pls. 179h (Persian court robes with sleeves pushed up), 189e (Persian crowns and fluted tiaras), 275f (stamp seals), 279f (carving anomalies), 280h (chips in seal matrices), and 285h (personal seals of Matukka).

SEAL APPLICATION (SEE *APPENDIX ONE: CONCORDANCE OF SEALS TO TABLETS IN VOLUME I*)

PFS 1428s occurs on the reverse of PF 1532. The one application is carefully oriented along the vertical axis of the tablet and preserves the complete design. PF 1532 is dated 499/498 B.C.

BIBLIOGRAPHY

Garrison 1988, pp. 375, 428–30; Garrison 1998, p. 131 (n. 32).

PFS 1463s   Cat.No. 231

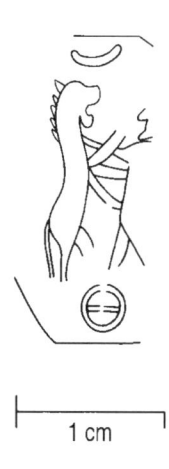

Seal Type:	Stamp, Octagonal Face	Photograph:	Pl. 127c
Earliest Dated Application:	ND	Typology and Style:	II-B.4 — Fortification Style
Preserved Height of Image:	2.00 cm (comp.)	Preserved Width of Image:	1.00 cm (incomp.)
Number of Impressions:	1	Quality of Impression:	Poor

Completeness of Image: Segment of middle and upper edge and lower edge of design survives

DESCRIPTION OF SEAL AS IMPRESSED IMAGE

Hero faces left, extending straight arm upward to grasp rampant lion by throat; other arm is apparently brought across body to stab lion in chest (no weapon discernible).

Lion moves toward and faces hero. Lion holds upper foreleg (only partially preserved) straight and extends it upward toward hero's head; lower foreleg is curved and extended downward to place paw on hero's thigh; thin tail (only partially preserved) hangs downward.

Hero wears garment of uncertain type that leaves forward leg exposed below knee and lengthens at diagonal toward back. Short pointed beard rests over hero's right shoulder.

Mane of lion is rendered by serrated edge along contour of its neck; top serration is larger than others and may represent ear; mouth is open in roar.

Crescent is in upper field; ring bisected by horizontal bar is in lower field. Edge of seal is preserved at top and bottom of design.

COMMENTARY

Based on Q texts protocol, PFS 1463s should belong to Pirdukana, who in PF 1579 received sesame rations on his way from Susa to Persepolis under the authority (*halmi*) of the king. PF 1579 preserves the only occurrence of the name Pirdukana in the PF texts.

The ring shape, bisected by horizontal bar in the lower field, has no parallels among seals with images of heroic encounter herein; nor does it appear in Boardman's (1970a, p. 23, fig. 3) chart of linear devices on pyramidal stamp seals of the western empire.[70] In seal shape, PFS 1463s may at first glance suggest the class of pyramidal seals isolated by Boardman (1970a) leading to the so-called Graeco-Persian style, but the style of PFS 1463s actually gives every indication of mainstream Fortification Style; see also the discussion of PFS 1321s (Cat.No. 176).[71] See Garrison 1988 for the hand of this distinctive artist.

PFS 1463s is close in composition to a pyramidal stamp seal picked up in the ruins of Persepolis, although here the linear device resembles that on PFS 99 (Cat.No. 113) rather than that on PFS 1463s, and it is between rather than under the hero and lion.[72] The seal from Persepolis does not, however, include a crescent in the field above. In including this feature, PFS 1463s is a unique stamp seal among seals with images of heroic encounter herein.[73]

The stamp face is flat with an octagonal contour. For probable seal shape, see *Appendix Four: Stamp Seals in Volume I Grouped by Apparent Contour of Seal Face* and accompanying figure 9, no. 1.

For comparative illustrations including PFS 1463s, see pls. 251g (crescents), 254h (various devices and symbols), 275h (stamp seals), and 291h (personal seals of various travelers).

SEAL APPLICATION (SEE *APPENDIX ONE: CONCORDANCE OF SEALS TO TABLETS IN VOLUME I*)

PFS 1463s occurs on the reverse of PF 1579. The application is oriented along the horizontal axis of the tablet. The seal clearly was applied before the text since several cuneiform wedges cut into the right edge and left edge of the impression. The date of PF 1579 is unknown.

BIBLIOGRAPHY

Garrison 1988, pp. 359–63, 487; Root 1998, pp. 270, 276, fig. 7, pl. 9.

---

70. A horizontally bisected circle occurs as a mason's mark at Sardis, however: Boardman 1998, figs. 7 and 9.
71. See Root 1998 for implications.
72. Ménant 1886, p. 165, fig. 143. It is impossible to address style based on this illustration.
73. Crescents in upper field do occur on numerous hero stamp seals of Achaemenid date from Mesopotamia, for example, Stolper 1990b, pl. 49a; Bregstein 1993, nos. 73, 110, 135, 136. Note with crescent above (Amiet 1972, pl. 190, no. 2229).

PFS 1582   Cat.No. 232

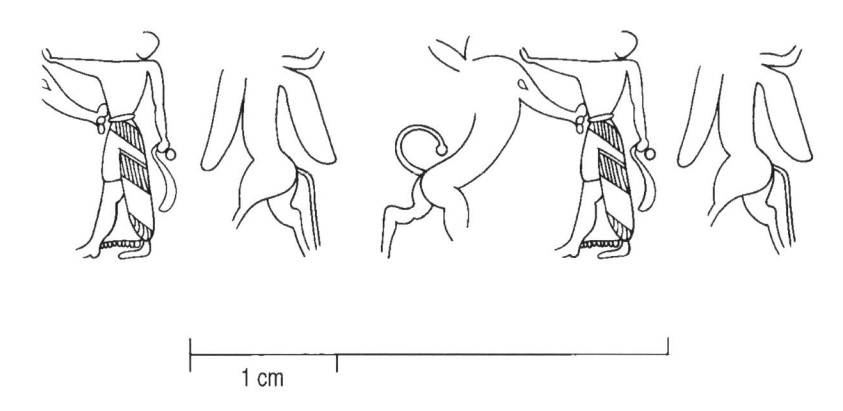

Seal Type:	Cylinder	Photograph:	Pl. 128a
Earliest Dated Application:	503/502 B.C.	Typology and Style:	II-B.4 — Mixed Styles I
Preserved Height of Image:	1.50 cm (incomp.)	Preserved Length of Image:	3.30 cm (comp.)
Estimated Height of Original Seal:	1.70 cm	Estimated Diameter of Original Seal:	1.00 cm
Number of Impressions:	2	Quality of Impressions:	Good

Completeness of Image: Almost complete except for upper edge and lower edge and details

DESCRIPTION OF SEAL AS IMPRESSED IMAGE

Hero faces left, extending straight right arm outward to grasp rampant lion by throat; left arm is straight and held down behind body to hold curved sword.

Lion moves toward and faces hero. Lion holds one foreleg straight, toes articulated, and extends it downward to place paw on hero's waist; other foreleg (only partially preserved) is straight, held up and away from body; tail curls upward with tufted termination.

Hero wears belted Assyrian garment that leaves forward leg exposed below knee; garment has two diagonal swags of fringe at hip and thigh over rear leg, one at hem over rear leg; fringe is also indicated along hem of garment between legs of hero. Large flattened coiffure rests at back of hero's neck.

In terminal field, rampant winged bull creature with human arms moves to left. Creature holds "arm" (only partially preserved) bent at elbow in atlas pose. Long thin tail (only partially preserved) bends downward; wing extends diagonally downward on either side of its body.

COMMENTARY

PFS 1582 occurs only once, on the journal (V text) PF 1942; thus it should belong to the unnamed accountant of that text.

The seal is large, the design well executed. Stylistically the seal seems closer to the Fortification Style than the Modeled Style, although the animal forms are well modeled. The decoration on the hero's lower garment finds a close parallel in PFS 16* (Cat.No. 22) of the Modeled Style. Owing to the way the seal has been applied (see below), we cannot be certain of the spacing between the heroic encounter and the bull creature in the terminal field. The preserved upraised arm of this creature strongly suggests that it supports a winged symbol that has not been preserved on either of our two impressions. If so, the spacing between hero and bull creature might have been greater than we have indicated here. A parallel for the motif of a bull creature supporting a winged symbol is PFS 774 (Cat.No. 58).

For comparative illustrations including PFS 1582, see pls. 177i (Assyrian garments with detailing preserved), 199i (feet and shoes), 232i (spectacular animal studies), 244j (daggers and swords), 266i (terminal field motifs other than inscriptions), and 286f (personal seals of accountants).

SEAL APPLICATION (SEE *APPENDIX ONE: CONCORDANCE OF SEALS TO TABLETS IN VOLUME I*)

PFS 1582 occurs along the bottom of the reverse (inverted) of PF 1942. The right edge is destroyed, and this also damages the application of the seal on the reverse. No other seal is preserved on the tablet. The rolling on the reverse is long, but in fact the seal has been picked up once in the course of its application, resulting in two rollings in the same horizontal zone. The rolling at left preserves the entire length of the seal design, that at right is partial. Both rollings display the rampant lion in the center. The seal clearly was applied first, then the scribe marked off horizontal lines for the text with his stylus. In doing so, the lower edge of the impression was removed and a line of the text written over it. PF 1942 is dated 503/502 B.C.

BIBLIOGRAPHY

Garrison 1988, pp. 253, 256–57; Garrison and Dion 1999, pp. 7–9, 13, fig. 6.

Cat.No. 233 PFS 255

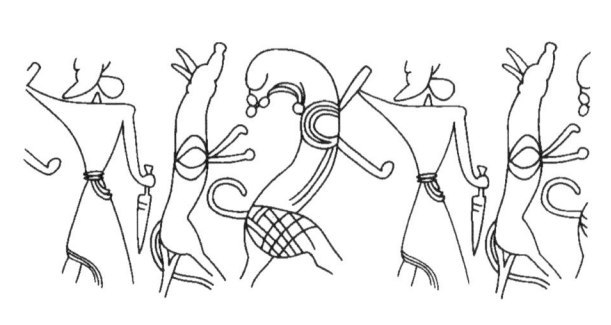

Seal Type:	Cylinder	Photograph:	Pl. 129a
Earliest Dated Application:	500/499 B.C.	Typology and Style:	II-B.4 — Fortification Style
Preserved Height of Image:	1.70 cm (incomp.)	Preserved Length of Image:	2.30 cm (comp.)
Estimated Height of Original Seal:	2.00 cm	Estimated Diameter of Original Seal:	0.70 cm
Number of Impressions:	2	Quality of Impressions:	Fair

Completeness of Image: Almost complete except for upper edge and lower edge

DESCRIPTION OF SEAL AS IMPRESSED IMAGE

Hero faces left, extending straight right arm upward to grasp rampant lion by upper foreleg; left arm is straight (wrist bent upward) and held down behind body to hold dagger.

Lion moves toward hero but turns its head away from him. Lion holds upper foreleg straight and extends it upward toward hero's head; lower foreleg is straight, paw upturned, and extended downward toward hero's waist. Lion raises forward hind leg, slightly bent, toward hero; tail extends horizontally outward and curled upward.

Hero wears double-belted Assyrian garment that leaves forward leg exposed below knee; curved folds are at back of hip; double border is indicated along hem of garment. Long pointed beard rests over hero's right shoulder; round coiffure rests at back of neck.

Musculature of lion's body is marked by curved element at shoulder, parallel lines on chest, and hatching on hindquarters; mouth is open in roar.

In terminal field, rampant long-eared animal of uncertain type moves toward and faces right; animal holds long snout upward. Animal holds upper foreleg straight, paw turned down, and extends it upward toward rampant lion's snout; lower foreleg is straight and extended outward toward rampant lion's back; thin tail curves downward between animal's hind legs. Two curved elements mark musculature at its shoulder.

COMMENTARY

The sharp outlines of the figures, the large size of the figures, and the deep engraving are unusual in the Fortification Style. The seal has other distinctive qualities, such as the rendering of the beard of the hero, the unusual shortened proportions of his arms, and the elaborate surface treatment of the lion's body; this last is especially unusual in the Fortification Style. The curved folds at the hero's hip are a Persianizing feature added to the Assyrian-type garment. For the curvilinear rendering of the muscles on the lion's shoulder, see also PFS 225 (Cat.No. 46).

For comparative illustrations including PFS 255, see pls. 181d (hybrid garments), 222h (lions and lion creatures), and 278e (carving anomalies).

SEAL APPLICATION (SEE *APPENDIX ONE: CONCORDANCE OF SEALS TO TABLETS IN VOLUME I*)

PFS 255 occurs on the reverse of PF 522 and PF 634 (inverted), with PFS 122 (II) on the left edge of each tablet. Both impressions preserve the entire length of the seal design. That on PF 522 displays the animal to the right of the hero in the center; that on PF 634 displays the hero in the center. PF 634 is dated 500/499 B.C.

BIBLIOGRAPHY

Garrison 1988, pp. 278, 320, 323–24, 422.

PFS 1466   Cat.No. 234

Seal Type:	Cylinder	Photograph:	Pl. 129c
Earliest Dated Application:	503/502 B.C.	Typology and Style:	II-B.4 — Fortification Style
Preserved Height of Image:	1.50 cm (incomp.)	Preserved Length of Image:	2.60 cm (comp.)
Estimated Height of Original Seal:	NA	Estimated Diameter of Original Seal:	0.80 cm
Number of Impressions:	3	Quality of Impressions:	Poor

Completeness of Image: Large segment of middle of design survives along its complete length

DESCRIPTION OF SEAL AS IMPRESSED IMAGE

Hero moves to left, extending straight right arm upward apparently to grasp rampant lion (point of contact not preserved); left arm is straight, hand upturned, and held down behind body to hold curved sword.

Lion moves away from hero but turns its head back toward him. Lion holds upper foreleg (only partially preserved) slightly bent and extends it diagonally upward; lower foreleg is straight and extended diagonally downward; tail (only partially preserved) curves downward.

Hero wears Assyrian garment that leaves forward leg exposed below knee; long fringe is indicated along bottom edge of lower part of garment.

Lion has mouth open in roar.

To left of lion is figure wearing double-belted Persian court robe with sleeves pushed up (arms not preserved); large swag of drapery is indicated on either side of figure's upper torso. To right of figure in Persian court robe, in lower field, is floral element (only partially preserved). Above this device is long thin irregular arc-shaped element (only partially preserved).

COMMENTARY

The figure wearing the Persian court robe with sleeves pushed up for action is certainly an archer, and the arc-shaped element to the right of him must be his drawn bow.[74] For a similar compositional format with an archer

---

74. See Collon 1987, pp. 162–63, no. 744, for an Achaemenid seal with a similarly shaped and proportioned bow.

as secondary actor in heroic engagement, but in a control encounter, see PFS 49 (Cat.No. 23). See also PFS 1101 (Cat.No. 297) for a somewhat related seal with a "rescuing" second hero.

For comparative illustrations including PFS 1466, see pls. 177g (Assyrian garments with detailing preserved), 238e (subsidiary human/human-creature figures in encounter images), 246h (bows, arrows, quivers), and 260f (various plants).

SEAL APPLICATION (SEE *APPENDIX ONE: CONCORDANCE OF SEALS TO TABLETS IN VOLUME I*)

PFS 1466 occurs twice on the reverse (inverted) and once on the left edge of PF 1585. No other seal is used on the tablet. The applications on the reverse, placed one directly above the other, are rolled in the same sequence and preserve the entire length of the seal design. The rollings display the hero in the center. The partial rolling on the left edge preserves only the rampant lion. PF 1585 is dated 503/502 B.C.

BIBLIOGRAPHY

Garrison 1988, pp. 302–04; Garrison 1998, p. 120 (n. 12).

II-B.5. WINGED LION CREATURES

Cat.No. 235   PFS 17

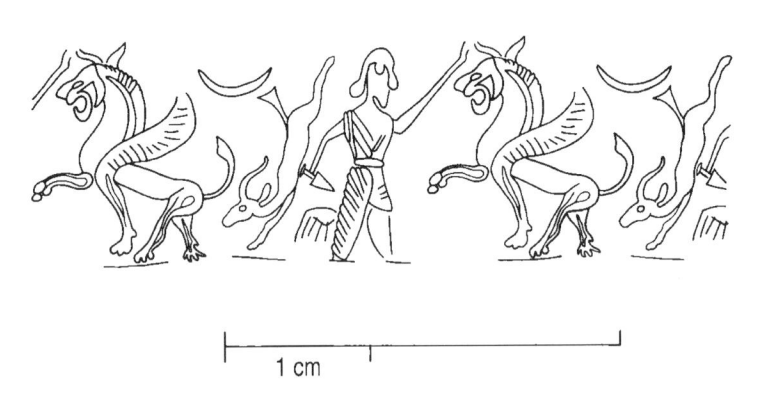

Seal Type:	Cylinder	Photographs:	Pl. 130a–c
Earliest Dated Application:	501 B.C.	Typology and Style:	II-B.5 — Fortification Style
Preserved Height of Image:	1.50 cm (incomp.)	Preserved Length of Image:	2.70 cm (comp.)
Estimated Height of Original Seal:	1.60 cm	Estimated Diameter of Original Seal:	0.90 cm
Number of Impressions:	24	Quality of Impressions:	Fair

Completeness of Image: Complete except for upper edge and segments of lower edge

DESCRIPTION OF SEAL AS IMPRESSED IMAGE

Hero faces right, extending straight left arm upward to grasp rampant winged horned lion creature by horn; right arm is bent and held down behind body to hold dagger.

Lion creature moves toward and faces hero. Creature holds upper foreleg curved and extends it outward toward hero's leg; lower foreleg is extended downward under its body; tail curves upward, thickening at its end with flat termination.

Hero wears belted Assyrian garment that leaves forward leg exposed below knee; stacked vertical folds at right shoulder indicate Persianizing sleeve pushed up to reveal hero's bare arm; diagonal folds are indicated on chest; diagonal folds (or fringe) are also indicated on whole length of rear leg; three short folds (or fringe) are indicated on garment over forward leg. Short pointed beard rests over hero's left shoulder; small rounded coiffure rests at back of neck.

Lion's body has detailing lines on legs; mane is rendered by rounded serrated edge along contour of lion's neck. Curved horn emerges from front of its head; long pointed ear is at back of head; mouth is open in roar.

In terminal field, slender horned animal of undetermined type is inverted in field at slight diagonal. Animal extends one hind leg upward, one foreleg straight downward; short straight tail extends up and away from body, thickening at its end with flat termination. Long curved horn emerges from front of animal's head; large ear is at back of head. Crescent is in upper terminal field between rampant lion and inverted animal.

Portions of lower edge of seal are preserved at bottom of design. Chip apparently is in lower field behind hero.

COMMENTARY

Koch (1990) identifies the seal as the personal seal of Ušaya, a wine supplier to travelers in her Southwestern Region IV and Northwestern Region V. Ušaya seems located at Manda, the most important wine center in Koch's Northwestern Region V. The attribution is confirmed by the occurrence of PFS 17 on the left edge the Q texts PF 1557–1559 and PF 1562–1565, which name Ušaya as the wine supplier. In Q text PF 1577, Ušaya supplied dates.

The engraving is crisply executed; the body and the legs of the winged horned lion creature are especially sharp and precise. The interior detailing lines on its legs are very unusual. An animal figure occurs quite frequently as the terminal element in seal designs of heroic encounter in the PFS corpus, but inverted animals occur on only five of these seals: PFS 17, PFS 243 (Cat.No. 303), PFS 256 (Cat.No. 198), PFS 1388 (Cat.No. 162), and PFS 1475 (Cat.No. 177); see the commentary on PFS 1475 (Cat.No. 177).

For comparative illustrations including PFS 17, see pls. 181a (hybrid garments), 225a (horned animals and horned-animal creatures of undetermined types), 237a (animal carcasses), and 287b (personal seals of various suppliers).

SEAL APPLICATION (SEE *APPENDIX ONE: CONCORDANCE OF SEALS TO TABLETS IN VOLUME I*)

On twenty-two tablets PFS 17 is applied on the left edge; on PF 46 it is also applied on the reverse in two rollings on the same horizontal plane. Applications of the seal tend to exhibit marked distortion. In four impressions the seal is rolled for at least one complete turn, preserving the entire length of the seal design. Of these four applications, three display the inverted horned animal in the center; one displays the heroic encounter in the center. Of the remaining twenty partial impressions, two preserve only the hero (at right) and the inverted animal; two display the inverted animal in the center; seven preserve only the creature and the inverted animal; five preserve the lion creature in the center flanked by partial forms of the hero and the inverted animal; three display only the lion creature and most of the hero minus his weapon-bearing lower arm; and one displays an almost complete rendering of the lion creature alone with the head of the inverted animal preserved to the right. On the reverse of PF 46 the seal was rolled for part of its length, picked up and inverted, then partially applied in the same horizontal plane. The resulting image shows an upright hero holding an inverted hero by his forward foot. PF 1156 is the earliest dated tablet with PFS 17 and is dated 501 B.C.

BIBLIOGRAPHY

Garrison 1988, pp. 343–46; Koch 1990, pp. 131, 133, 294.

Cat.No. 236   PFS 298s

Seal Type:	Stamp, Circular Face	Photographs:	Pl. 131a–b
Earliest Dated Application:	500 B.C.	Typology and Style:	II-B.5 — Fortification Style
Preserved Height of Image:	1.50 cm (comp.)	Preserved Width of Image:	1.80 cm (comp.)
Number of Impressions:	4	Quality of Impressions:	Fair

Completeness of Image: Almost complete except for lower edge and details

DESCRIPTION OF SEAL AS IMPRESSED IMAGE

Hero faces right, extending straight left arm (only partially preserved) toward upper foreleg of rampant winged horned lion creature; right arm (only partially preserved) is held down behind body.

Creature moves toward and faces hero. Creature holds upper foreleg curved, paw turned down, and extends it upward toward hero's head; lower foreleg is bent and extended in front of its body.

Hero wears Assyrian garment that leaves forward leg exposed below mid-thigh. Hero also wears domed headdress with knob. Long pointed beard rests over hero's left shoulder; rounded coiffure rests at back of neck.

Horn (only partially preserved) emerges from front of creature's head.

Edge of seal is preserved except at bottom of design.

COMMENTARY

Based upon Q texts protocol, PFS 298s should belong to Išbakatukka. In PF 1477, Išbakatukka (and, it would seem, the eight men with him) is described as an Arabian. In both PF 1477 and PF 1539, Išbakatukka went to the king in year 22.8 (500 B.C.) under the authorization (*miyatukkam* and *halmi* respectively) of Bakabana, and so the tablets probably record the same trip at different post stations.

Impressions are very poorly preserved, and there is much distortion.

The stamp face has a circular contour. For probable seal shape, see *Appendix Four: Stamp Seals in Volume I Grouped by Apparent Contour of Seal Face* and accompanying figure 9, nos. 3a, 4c, or 5a.

For comparative illustrations including PFS 298s, see pls. 186i (headdresses), 274c (stamp seals), and 290a (personal seals of various travelers).

SEAL APPLICATION (SEE *APPENDIX ONE: CONCORDANCE OF SEALS TO TABLETS IN VOLUME I*)

PFS 298s occurs twice (inverted) on the reverse of both PF 1477 and PF 1539. On PF 1477 the impressions are placed next to each other and oriented diagonally to the vertical axis of the tablet. On PF 1539 the impressions are placed next to each other and oriented along the vertical axis of the tablet. All impressions are partial. On both tablets the seal clearly was applied before the text since several cuneiform wedges cut into the bottom of the impressions. PF 1477 and PF 1539 are both dated 500 B.C.

BIBLIOGRAPHY

Garrison 1988, pp. 326–30, 338–39, 345.

PFS 312   Cat.No. 237

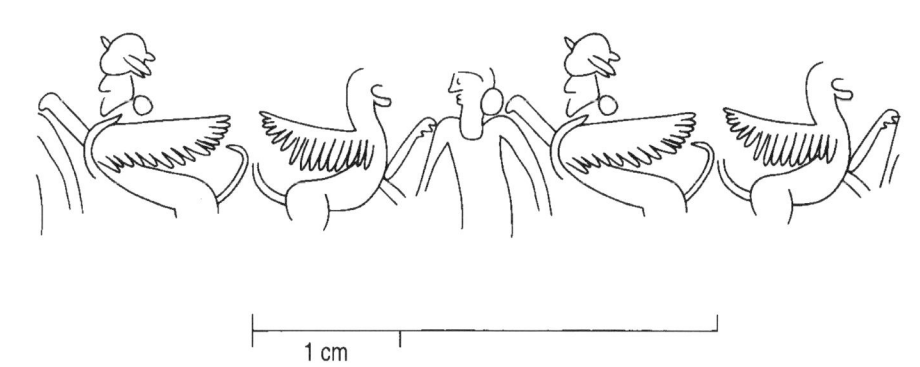

|— 1 cm —|

Seal Type:	Cylinder	Photograph:	Pl. 132a
Earliest Dated Application:	499/498 B.C.	Typology and Style:	II-B.5 — Mixed Styles I
Preserved Height of Image:	1.40 cm (incomp.)	Preserved Length of Image:	3.20 cm (comp.)
Estimated Height of Original Seal:	NA	Estimated Diameter of Original Seal:	1.00 cm
Number of Impressions:	3	Quality of Impressions:	Poor

Completeness of Image: Middle of design survives along its complete length

DESCRIPTION OF SEAL AS IMPRESSED IMAGE

Hero faces left, extending straight right arm (only partially preserved) downward apparently to grasp rampant winged lion creature by lower foreleg (point of contact not preserved); left arm (only partially preserved) is slightly bent and held down behind body.

Lion creature moves toward and faces hero. Creature holds upper foreleg straight and extends it upward to place paw (toes splayed) at hero's shoulder; lower foreleg (only partially preserved) is extended downward toward hero's waist; tail (only partially preserved) curves upward.

Hero wears garment of uncertain type; hero has long squared beard that rests on his chest; round coiffure rests at back of neck.

Lion creature has mouth open in roar.

To right of hero, rampant winged human-headed lion creature moves toward and faces hero. Creature holds upper foreleg straight and extends it upward toward hero's head; tail curves upward. Beard terminates in blunt point over its chest; round coiffure rests at back of neck. Creature wears domed headdress that has projections at sides and back.

COMMENTARY

Tuplin (1987, p. 130) seems to suggest in a parenthetical note a direct link between PFS 312 and the official Šuddayauda on PF 1105, but the reasoning is not clear. On Šuddayauda, see the commentary for PFS 1* (Cat.No. 182). PFS 312 may rather have been used on both PF 1105 and PF 1140 by Matēna. This cannot, however, be more than a plausible suggestion.

    The figures in the design seem curiously proportioned. Garrison (1988) originally classified the style of this seal differently.

    For comparative illustrations including PFS 312, see pls. 193f (round coiffures), 209b (arm positions of heroic combat), and 236g (animals/creatures as secondary elements of main design field).

SEAL APPLICATION (SEE APPENDIX ONE: CONCORDANCE OF SEALS TO TABLETS IN VOLUME I)

PFS 312 occurs on the upper edge and right edge of PF 1105 and the upper edge of PF 1140. Impressions exhibit some distortion. In two impressions the seal has been rolled for at least one complete turn, preserving the entire length of the seal design. Of these two applications, one displays the lion creature to the left of the hero in the center; one displays the human-headed creature to the right of the hero in the center. The remaining partial impression displays the hero and the human-headed creature to right in the center. PF 1105 and PF 1140 are both dated 499/498 B.C.

BIBLIOGRAPHY

Dusinberre 1997b, p. 128 (n. 131); Garrison 1988, pp. 281–83, 493–94; Tuplin 1987, p. 130 (n. 77).

Cat.No. 238 PFS 1501

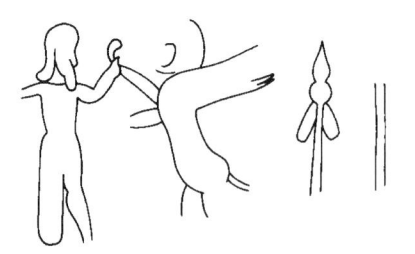

Seal Type:	Cylinder	Photograph:	Pl. 132c
Earliest Dated Application:	500/499 B.C.	Typology and Style:	II-B.5 — Fortification Style
Preserved Height of Image:	1.50 cm (incomp.)	Preserved Length of Image:	2.50 cm (incomp.)
Estimated Height of Original Seal:	NA	Estimated Diameter of Original Seal:	NA
Number of Impressions:	1	Quality of Impression:	Poor

Completeness of Image: Segment of middle of design survives

DESCRIPTION OF SEAL AS IMPRESSED IMAGE

Hero faces right, extending bent left arm upward to grasp rampant winged lion creature by upper foreleg; right arm (only partially preserved) is held behind body.

Creature moves toward and faces hero. Creature holds upper foreleg straight, paw upturned, and extends it upward toward hero's head; lower foreleg (only partially preserved) is straight and extended toward hero's waist; thin tail (only partially preserved) is curved downward.

Hero wears Assyrian garment that leaves forward leg exposed. Long rounded beard rests over hero's left shoulder; rounded coiffure curls upward slightly at back of neck.

Creature has mouth open in roar.

In terminal field at right of impression is pole terminating in triangular spade above circular element with pendent streamers. Shaft of another pole is preserved at far right of impression.

COMMENTARY

The design is very difficult to read; its partial preservation could allow for the reconstruction of a control encounter rather than a combat encounter.

The symbols in the terminal field represent the spade of Marduk and stylus of Nabu, which are unusual additions to what is otherwise a typical hero seal in the Fortification Style. Similarly in the Murašû archive from Nippur, only one design in the published corpus incorporates the spade of Marduk adjacent to a heroic encounter scene.[75] It is interesting that this combination of Babylonian symbols with scenes of heroic encounter is apparently so rare within the Babylonian context of the Achaemenid Empire as well as within the heartland Persian context, even though in both archives many seals devoted exclusively to the Babylonian worship scene deploy these symbols (see Volume II).[76]

For comparative illustrations including PFS 1501, see pls. 209g (arm positions of heroic combat), 248i (abstract symbols of Mesopotamian deities), and 266h (terminal field motifs other than inscriptions).

---

75. Bregstein 1993, p. 515, no. 121 (no drawing). Compare also an unprovenanced Assyro-Babylonian cylinder (Teissier 1984, pp. 44, 182–83, no. 286).

76. Examples of actual seals combining the heroic encounter with symbolic elements of a Babylonian worship scene include two banded agate cylinders (Collon 1987, pp. 90–91, no. 418 [BM 89324, ex-Layard]; Root 1990b, p. 35, no. 19 [Kelsey Museum 94527, Michigan excavations at Seleucia-on-the-Tigris]).

SEAL APPLICATION (SEE *APPENDIX ONE: CONCORDANCE OF SEALS TO TABLETS IN VOLUME I*)

PFS 1501 occurs on the reverse of PF 1624. The partial rolling displays the rampant creature in the center. The seal clearly was applied before the text since several cuneiform wedges cut into the bottom of the impression. PF 1624 is dated 500/499 B.C.

BIBLIOGRAPHY

Garrison 1988, pp. 291–93.

PFS 57*   Cat.No. 239

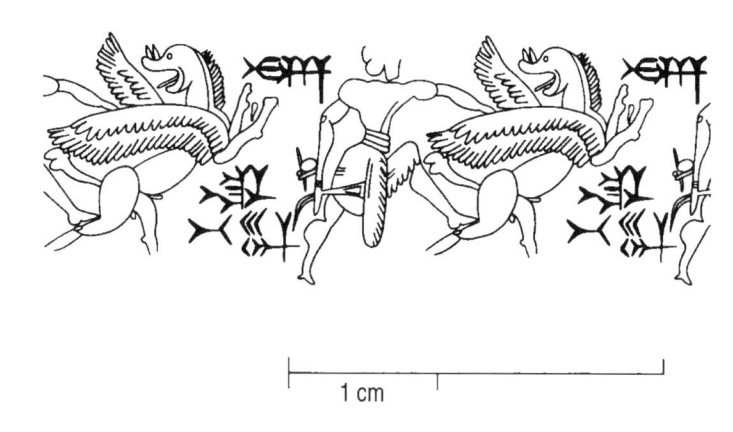

Seal Type:	Cylinder, Inscribed	Photograph:	Pl. 133a
Earliest Dated Application:	501/500 B.C.	Typology and Style:	II-B.5 — Modeled Style
Language of Inscription:	Elamite		
Preserved Height of Image:	1.70 cm (incomp.)	Preserved Length of Image:	2.60 cm (comp.)
Estimated Height of Original Seal:	2.00 cm	Estimated Diameter of Original Seal:	0.80 cm
Number of Impressions:	19	Quality of Impressions:	Many preserve excellent detail

Completeness of Image: Almost complete except for upper edge and lower edge

DESCRIPTION OF SEAL AS IMPRESSED IMAGE

Hero faces right, extending slightly bent left arm (elbow up) outward to grasp rampant winged horned lion creature by lower wing; right arm is bent and held down behind body to hold large weapon with downward-curved terminal and looped forepart (abutting garment lappet). Hero, in vigorous striding pose, raises his bent forward leg to place foot on rear hind leg of creature.

Creature moves away from hero in rampant running pose but turns its head back toward him. Creature holds upper foreleg straight and extends it diagonally upward in front of its neck; lower foreleg is slightly bent and extended upward in front of its neck; tail is curved slightly upward with thickened two-pronged termination.

Hero wears triple-belted kilt with fringed lappet and tight-fitting short-sleeved garment on torso; fringe is also indicated along hem of kilt over forward leg and along back edge of rear leg. Egg-shaped object is affixed to hero's right arm, held in place by apparatus with vertical and horizontal elements. Squared beard rests over hero's left shoulder; small rounded coiffure rests at back of neck.

Creature has two wings indicated, upper one extending diagonally upward from lower; two rows of feathers are indicated on each wing. Two short pointed horns emerge from top of creature's snout; creature's mouth is open, revealing long tongue. Mane is rendered by closely packed spikes along contour of neck; creature is ithyphallic.

Inscription fills terminal field.

INSCRIPTION

> Elamite
>
> > Line 1. Zir-
> > 2. ra-
> > 3. BAD-AH
> >
> > Translation Zirra...

Three lines of text are preserved, without case lines, oriented along the horizontal axis of the seal. The sign forms are consistent with late Neo-Elamite. The inscription is, presumably, a personal name. It is possible that the inscription is incomplete. We normally expect a personal name determinative at the beginning of the inscription. There is space for a sign below the zir-sign.

COMMENTARY

Both Hallock and Koch assign PFS 57* to Mirinzana, based, presumably, on the evidence of the letter PF 1858 addressed by Mirinzana and sealed with PFS 57*. The account text PF 2003 also carries this seal but does not refer to Mirinzana. Hallock says that he was heavily involved in accounts; Koch (1990) identifies him as a "Rechnungsprüfer" at Kurpun in her Southeastern Region III and also in her Elam Region VI. He travels frequently and in different places examines the accounts of barley, animal, and wine stocks. PF 2003, which carries his seal, is an account text for Ziršamattiš in Koch's Southwestern Region IV.

This is an extremely well-composed and executed design. See Garrison 1988 for discussion of the style and workshop of PFS 57* and related seals. It shares many features with PFS 98* (Cat.No. 217) and PFS 1566* (Cat.No. 218).

The inscription suggests a pre-owned seal if, indeed, Mirinzana was the owner at the time of the Persepolis Fortification archive. Nevertheless, all internal evidence of style and workshop clustering strongly suggests that this is a relatively contemporary seal.

Despite good detail preserved in many impressions, the hero's weapon and the object affixed to his right forearm pose a challenge. The weapon is apparently a sling, with the loop-like detailing at its wide end suggesting the place for the projectile to be inserted. The object attached to the hero's forearm seems to be an egg-shaped projectile at the ready within some type of pin-and-thong device. Bonnet (1926, pp. 114–17, fig. 53) presents a wide variety of slings, several of which are close to the example here.

For comparative illustrations including PFS 57*, see pls. 180f (kilts), 247c (projectiles, slings), 264c (inscriptions without panels or case lines), and 286a (personal seals of accountants).

SEAL APPLICATION (SEE *APPENDIX ONE: CONCORDANCE OF SEALS TO TABLETS IN VOLUME I*)

Application of PFS 57* varies. It occurs on the reverse, upper edge, and left edge of PF 231 and PF 237; on the reverse and left edge of PF 234; on the reverse only of PF 239 and PF 2003; on the reverse, upper edge, right edge, and left edge of PF 242; on the upper edge and left edge of PF 331; and on the right edge only of PF 1858. On all reverse surfaces except PF 231 the seal is inverted. On the reverse of PF 231 and PF 242 the seal is applied twice, one impression directly above the other. PFS 514 (Cat.No. 192) is applied above the impression of PFS 57* on the reverse of PF 234. PFS 516 (Cat.No. 98) is applied above the impression of PFS 57* on the reverse of PF 239. Impressions of PFS 57* are clear and deep, showing little or no distortion. Of the total nineteen impressions, all show some part of the inscription. In nine impressions the seal is rolled for at least one complete turn, preserving the entire length of the seal design. Of these nine impressions, four display the inscription in the center; two display the creature and the inscription in the center; one displays the hero and the inscription in the center; two display the hero in the center. Of the remaining ten partial impressions, three display the inscription in the center; two display the hero in the center; two preserve only the hero (at the left of the impression) and the creature; one displays the creature in the center; two preserve only the creature. On the reverse of PF 231, PF 234, PF 237, and PF 239 the seal clearly was applied before the text since several cuneiform wedges cut into the bottom of the impressions. PF 231 is the earliest dated tablet with PFS 57* and is dated 501/500 B.C.

BIBLIOGRAPHY

Aperghis 1999, p. 163; Garrison 1988, pp. 228–34, 352, 479–80; Garrison 2000, pp. 131–33, fig. 5, pl. 17:5; Garrison and Dion 1999, p. 10 (n. 28); Hallock 1978, p. 113; Koch 1990, pp. 102, 109, 222–23; Koch 1992, p. 35.

PFS 265   Cat.No. 240

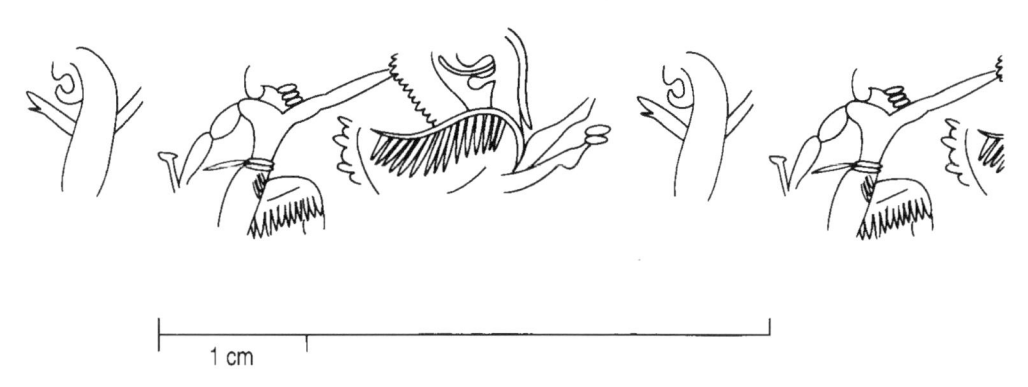

Seal Type:	Cylinder	Photographs:	Pl. 134a–b
Earliest Dated Application:	500 B.C.	Typology and Style:	II-B.5 — Modeled Style
Preserved Height of Image:	1.40 cm (incomp.)	Preserved Length of Image:	4.10 cm (comp.)
Estimated Height of Original Seal:	NA	Estimated Diameter of Original Seal:	1.30 cm
Number of Impressions:	5	Quality of Impressions:	Poor

Completeness of Image: Segment of middle of design survives along its complete length

DESCRIPTION OF SEAL AS IMPRESSED IMAGE

Hero faces right, extending straight left arm upward to grasp rampant winged lion creature by upper wing; right arm is straight and held down behind body to hold weapon of uncertain type (only handle preserved). Hero, in vigorous striding pose, raises bent forward leg.

Lion creature moves away from hero but turns its head back toward him. Creature holds forelegs slightly bent and extended upward together in front of body; paw rendered as two ovals on lower foreleg.

Hero appears to wear double-belted Assyrian garment that leaves forward leg exposed below knee; fringe is indicated at top of rear leg and along hem of garment over forward leg; sheath projects from back of waist. Squared segmented beard rests over hero's left shoulder; rounded coiffure rests at back of neck.

Creature has two wings indicated, upper extending diagonally upward from lower; lower wing has row of large feathers along upper edge. Mane is rendered by outline along contour of creature's neck; mouth is open with long curved tongue protruding.

In terminal field, rampant lion moves toward and faces winged lion creature. Lion holds forelegs straight and extends them upward to either side of body. Preserved paw shows schematic splayed toes; mouth is open in roar.

COMMENTARY

Although poorly preserved, the seal was clearly quite large and well carved. See Garrison 1988 for the style and workshop of PFS 265 and related seals. In Garrison 1988, PFS 1179 was discussed as a seal design very similar to PFS 265. Subsequent scrutiny has shown that they are in fact the same seal.

    For comparative illustrations including PFS 265, see pls. 209a (arm positions of heroic combat) and 268d (terminal field motifs other than inscriptions).

SEAL APPLICATION (SEE APPENDIX ONE: CONCORDANCE OF SEALS TO TABLETS IN VOLUME I)

PFS 265 occurs on the obverse and right edge of PF 1097, the right edge of PF 1112, and the reverse (inverted) and upper edge of PF 1228. The seal is applied along the longitudinal axis on the obverse of PF 1097. Of the five partial impressions, two display the hero in the center; three display the rampant lion in the center. On the reverse of PF 1228 the seal clearly was applied before the text since several cuneiform wedges cut into the bottom of the impression. PF 1097 and PF 1112 are the earliest dated tablets with PFS 265 and are both dated 500 B.C.

BIBLIOGRAPHY

Garrison 1988, pp. 230–33, 252, 257, 366, 479–80, 489, 495.

Cat.No. 241   PFS 65

Seal Type:	Cylinder	Photograph:	Pl. 135a
Earliest Dated Application:	501/500 B.C.	Typology and Style:	II-B.5 — Modeled Style
Preserved Height of Image:	1.60 cm (incomp.)	Preserved Length of Image:	2.70 cm (comp.)
Estimated Height of Original Seal:	NA	Estimated Diameter of Original Seal:	0.90 cm
Number of Impressions:	12	Quality of Impressions:	Fair-poor

Completeness of Image: Almost complete except for upper edge and lower edge

DESCRIPTION OF SEAL AS IMPRESSED IMAGE

Two winged heroes stand on either side of rampant four-winged lion creature.

Hero to left faces right, extending slightly bent left arm (elbow up) to grasp lion creature by lower wing; right arm is bent and held down behind body to hold weapon of uncertain type (only top of hilt preserved).

Hero to left wears triple-belted Assyrian garment that leaves forward leg exposed; fringe is indicated along forward edge of garment over rear leg. Hero perhaps wears domed headdress. Long, squared, segmented beard rests over hero's chest; narrow rounded coiffure rests at back of neck.

Hero to right faces left, extending slightly bent right arm (elbow up) to grasp creature by lower wing; left arm is straight and held down behind body to hold weapon of uncertain type (only top of hilt preserved).

Hero to right wears Assyrian garment that leaves forward leg exposed; fringe is indicated along forward edge of garment over rear leg; horizontal border is indicated on hem of garment between legs of hero. Hero perhaps wears domed headdress. Rounded, segmented beard rests over hero's chest; rounded, upward curling coiffure rests at back of neck. Each hero has two wings, upper extending diagonally upward from his shoulder, lower extending diagonally downward from his back.

Lion creature moves to left but turns its head back to right. Forelegs are bent, toes splayed, and extended outward to either side of its body; thick tail is curved upward. Fur of lion creature is rendered by crisp serrated edge along contour of lower belly; mouth is open in roar.

Head of standing(?) bird (apparently a parrot) faces right in lower field between creature and hero to left.

COMMENTARY

Koch notes that PFS 65 is associated with several officials connected with the treasury at Tirazziš (Shiraz); thus it is probably an office seal.

The design and execution are unusual. The disposition of the wings of the lion creature, combined with its forelegs reading like human arms, suggests a subtle double entendre in which the object of the heroic combat encounter serves also as the hero creature in a control encounter. The elbow-up convention for the heroes is an Assyrianizing feature not commonly found in the PFS corpus of hero seals (but cf. PFS 98* [Cat.No. 217] and PFS 1566* [Cat.No. 218]; see also, e.g., Herbordt 1992, pl. 6, no. 5).

The appearance of a parrot is also unusual. A parallel occurs in the form of a carved handle from a serpentine tray excavated in the Treasury at Persepolis (Schmidt 1957, pls. 53, no. 4, 54, no. 4).

For comparative illustrations including PFS 65, see pls. 208b (arm positions of heroic combat), 226e (birds), 240e (double hero encounters), and 281f (office seals).

SEAL APPLICATION (SEE *APPENDIX ONE: CONCORDANCE OF SEALS TO TABLETS IN VOLUME I*)

PFS 65 always occurs on the reverse of tablets that it seals. In one instance, PF 128, it also occurs on the bottom edge and upper edge; in one instance, PF 130, also on the bottom edge; and in one instance, PF 230, also on the left edge. On the reverse of PF 128 and PF 284 the seal is applied twice, one impression directly above the other. Several impressions show marked lateral distortion. In seven impressions the seal is rolled for at least one complete turn, preserving the entire length of the seal design. Of these seven applications, four display the hero to left in the center; two display the two heroes in the center; one displays the lion creature in the center. Of the remaining five partial rollings, one displays the hero to left in the center; two display the hero to right in the center; two preserve only the hero to left and the lion creature. On the reverse of PF 129 and PF 284 the seal clearly was applied before the text since several cuneiform wedges cut into the top of the impressions. All tablets with PFS 65 are dated 501/500 B.C.

BIBLIOGRAPHY

Garrison 1988, pp. 224–27, 493; Garrison 1998, p. 121 (n. 5); Garrison and Dion 1999, p. 8 (n. 17); Koch 1990, p. 58.

II-B.6. WINGED HUMAN-FACED/HUMAN-HEADED LION CREATURES

PFS 58   Cat.No. 242

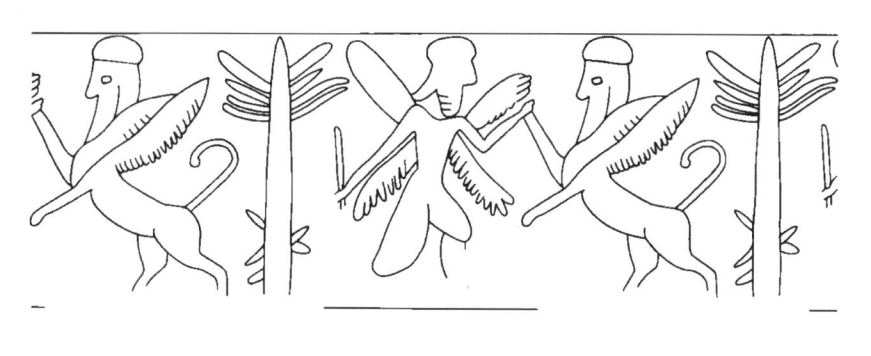

Seal Type:	Cylinder	Photographs:	Pl. 136a–b
Earliest Dated Application:	500/499 B.C.	Typology and Style:	II-B.6 — Mixed Styles I
Preserved Height of Image:	1.80 cm (comp.)	Preserved Length of Image:	3.20 cm (comp.)
Estimated Height of Original Seal:	1.80 cm	Estimated Diameter of Original Seal:	1.00 cm
Number of Impressions:	10	Quality of Impressions:	Fair

Completeness of Image: Almost complete except for segments of lower edge

DESCRIPTION OF SEAL AS IMPRESSED IMAGE

Four-winged hero faces right, extending bent left arm upward to grasp rampant winged human-faced creature by upper foreleg; right arm is straight and held diagonally down behind body to hold long weapon of uncertain type (only upper part preserved). Hero raises bent forward leg.

Lion creature moves toward and faces hero. Creature holds upper foreleg straight and extends it upward; lower foreleg is straight and extended downward toward hero's knee; straight tail is extended diagonally upward, curled inward with tufted termination.

Hero wears Assyrian garment that leaves forward leg exposed below knee. Rounded beard with horizontal striations rests over hero's left shoulder; narrow pointed coiffure curls upward at back of neck.

Lion creature has long pointed beard that rests over its chest; lion creature perhaps wears domed headdress. Two rows of feathers are indicated on its wing.

Schematic palm tree is in terminal field; multiple shoots emerge from lower trunk of tree.

Edge of seal is preserved at top of design; portion of edge of seal is preserved at bottom of design below hero.

COMMENTARY

Based upon the newly identified occurrence of PFS 58 on the Q text PF 1410, the seal should belong to Parru the flour supplier. All other occurrences of PFS 58 concern grain and flour supplied by various people at Liduma (or transported there from another place) and received (or apportioned) by Manaka. PFS 58 occurs on the reverse of these transactions in PF 14, PF 78, PF 80–81, PF 134, and PF 2015, with PFS 59 (III) on the left edge. PFS 58 occurs on both the reverse and the left edge of PF 79 without any other seal. PFS 58 occurs on the reverse of PF 82 without any other seal.

A Parru who is a supply officer at Šurkutur and Tašpak is often named in the Q texts; he, however, used PFS 5 (II). Koch (1990, p. 304) assigns PFS 59 to Manaka, whose name often occurs in texts sealed with PFS 58, based upon its occurrence on the left edge of PF 1682–1683 (naming Manaka as the supplier). If Koch is correct in assigning PFS 59 to Manaka, it suggests that PFS 58 is an office seal of a supply office in the area near Liduma. Various scenarios could reconcile the occurrence of PFS 58 on a Q text under Parru's authority, but the issue needs further study.

The thin forms of the hero's upper body are typical of the Fortification Style; however, the more massive lower body and the large animal forms of the lion creature suggest the Modeled Style. For very similar treatment of the winged hero, see PFS 6 (Cat.No. 304).

For comparative illustrations including PFS 58, see pls. 186c (headdresses) and 258a (palm trees).

SEAL APPLICATION (SEE *APPENDIX ONE: CONCORDANCE OF SEALS TO TABLETS IN VOLUME I*)

PFS 58 always occurs on the reverse of tablets with the sole exception of PF 1410 where it occurs only on the left edge. On PF 79 it occurs on the left edge as well as the reverse. On all reverse surfaces the seal is inverted. Impressions show little or no distortion. In four impressions the seal has been rolled for at least one complete turn, preserving the entire length of the seal design. Of these four applications, three display the hero in the center; one displays the creature and the palm tree in the center. Of the remaining six partial rollings, two preserve only the hero (at the left of the impression) and the creature; two display the creature in the center; two display the palm tree in the center. On the reverse of PF 14, PF 58, PF 81, PF 134, and PF 2015 the seal clearly was applied before the text since several cuneiform wedges cut into the bottom of the impressions. PF 14, PF 78–82, PF 134, and PF 2015 are the earliest dated tablets with PFS 58 and are all dated 500/499 B.C.

BIBLIOGRAPHY

Garrison 1988, p. 455; Garrison 1998, p. 121 (n. 15); Garrison and Dion 1999, p. 9 (n. 19).

PFS 902   Cat.No. 243

Seal Type:	Cylinder	Photograph:	Pl. 137a
Earliest Dated Application:	ND	Typology and Style:	II-B.6 — Fortification Style
Preserved Height of Image:	1.70 cm (incomp.)	Preserved Length of Image:	2.20 cm (incomp.)
Estimated Height of Original Seal:	NA	Estimated Diameter of Original Seal:	NA
Number of Impressions:	1	Quality of Impression:	Poor

Completeness of Image: Small segment of middle of design survives

DESCRIPTION OF SEAL AS IMPRESSED IMAGE

Hero faces left, apparently in striding pose, extending bent right arm outward to grasp rampant winged human-headed lion creature by foreleg; hero's left arm is not preserved.

Creature moves toward and faces hero. Creature holds one preserved foreleg straight and extends it upward toward hero's head.

Hero appears to wear Assyrian garment that leaves forward leg exposed. Rounded beard rests over hero's right shoulder; rounded coiffure rests at back of neck.

Creature has beard that terminates in blunt point; rounded coiffure rests at back of neck.

At far left of preserved impression, in terminal field, snout of presumably rampant lion appears, facing right. Star is in upper field between lion's snout and human-headed creature.

COMMENTARY

The fragmentary preservation of this impression allows the possibility that the scene is a control, rather than a combat, encounter.

For comparative illustrations including PFS 902, see pl. 253i (stars, rosettes).

SEAL APPLICATION (SEE APPENDIX ONE: CONCORDANCE OF SEALS TO TABLETS IN VOLUME I)

PFS 902 occurs on the left edge of PF 773. The partial rolling preserves only what our drawing shows. The date of PF 773 is unknown.

BIBLIOGRAPHY

Dusinberre 1997b, p. 128 (n. 131); Garrison 1988, pp. 283–85.

Cat.No. 244   PFS 1632*

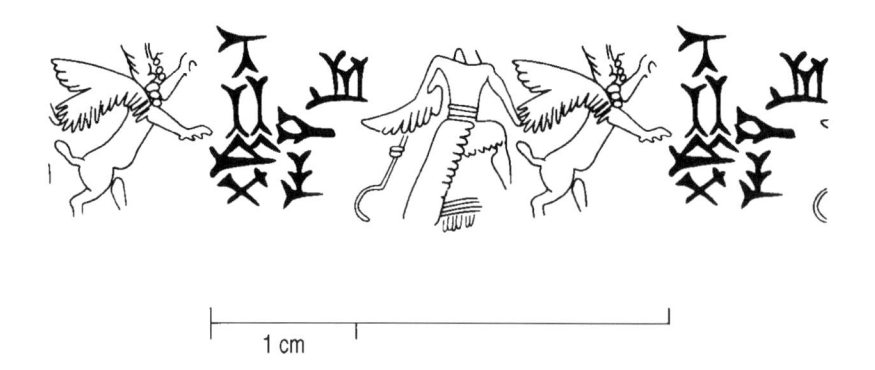

Seal Type:	Cylinder, Inscribed	Photograph:	Pl. 137c
Earliest Dated Application:	504 B.C.	Typology and Style:	II-B.6 — Modeled Style
Language of Inscription:	Babylonian		
Preserved Height of Image:	1.40 cm (incomp.)	Preserved Length of Image:	3.20 cm (comp.)
Estimated Height of Original Seal:	NA	Estimated Diameter of Original Seal:	1.00 cm
Number of Impressions:	4	Quality of Impressions:	Fair

Completeness of Image: Middle of design survives along its entire length

DESCRIPTION OF SEAL AS IMPRESSED IMAGE

Winged hero faces right, extending straight left arm downward to grasp lower wing of rampant winged human-faced (only beard preserved) lion creature; right arm is straight and held down behind body to hold curved sword. Hero, in striding pose, raises bent forward leg to place foot (not preserved) on rear hind leg of creature.

Creature moves and faces away from hero. Upper foreleg is straight, extended diagonally upward in front of face; lower foreleg is straight and extended diagonally downward in front of its body, toes splayed. Two wings are indicated, upper disposed horizontally from its body, lower disposed diagonally downward from upper wing; short thick tail bends upward.

Hero wears double-belted Assyrian garment that leaves forward leg exposed below knee; fringe is indicated at hem along rear leg and at hem over forward leg; horizontal border and fringe are indicated on hem of garment between legs. Squared beard rests over hero's left shoulder. Single wing is attached to right forearm.

Creature has long, rounded, segmented beard.

Inscription is in terminal field.

INSCRIPTION

Babylonian

Line
1. [(x)][ᵈ]AMAR.UTU-PAP [(x)]
2. [(x)] ŠÁ AN [(x)]
3. [(x)] BA [(x)]

Translation   ?

The inscription is reversed in its impression; i.e., it would be readable on the cylinder itself. Three lines of text are preserved, without case lines, oriented along the vertical axis of the seal. The beginning and the end of the inscription are missing. It is not clear how many signs (if any) might fit in the missing portions. An empty space before the BA in the last line is clearly visible. The inscription may include the PN Marduk-nāṣir; compare the PN Marduk-nāṣir responsible for workers in PT 25:9–10. Too little remains to suggest a reading.

For both the reversal of the script and the forms of some of the signs, see a seal preserved via impressions from Susa (Amiet 1973b, pl. 2, no. 6 = Delaporte 1920, pl. 48:18). PFS 1632* is the only inscribed seal of heroic encounter in the PFS corpus with a reversed inscription, but the Babylonian inscription on PFS 108* (II) is also reversed.

COMMENTARY

PFS 1632* occurs only on PF 2070. The text, fortunately, is a letter, a category of texts the sealing protocol for which is well understood (letters are always sealed only by the addresser). The addresser in PF 2070 is Raubasa (and his companion[s]), and he is communicating to Parnaka about the sending out of "tax handlers" and the accounting of sheep and goats. We learn more about Raubasa in PF 2025, a C4 text sealed by Parnaka with PFS 9* (Cat.No. 288). There, Raubasa and his companions are described as *m.KUR.lg zakkip* "payers(?) of the land" (cf. Koch 1990, pp. 96 and 99, a "Steuereinnehmer"). Again they are responsible for collecting animals as tax for the king under the supervision of Parnaka. The fact that Raubasa addresses a letter indicates that he is an official of fairly high rank.

See Garrison 1988 for the style and workshop of PFS 1632* and related seals. The positioning of the solitary wing on the hero is unique among seals with images of heroic encounter in the PF corpus.

For comparative illustrations including PFS 1632*, see pls. 201j (heroes as winged humans), 265c (inscriptions without panels or case lines), and 283d (personal seals of tax collectors).

SEAL APPLICATION (SEE *APPENDIX ONE: CONCORDANCE OF SEALS TO TABLETS IN VOLUME I*)

PFS 1632* occurs on the obverse, upper edge, right edge, and left edge of PF 2070. No other seal is used on the tablet. All impressions show some part of the inscription. In three impressions the seal has been rolled for at least one complete turn, preserving the entire length of the seal design. The rollings on the upper edge (damaged at right) and left edge (damaged at right) display the creature in the center, with two full rollings of the inscription included. The application on the right edge is damaged and displays the heroic encounter in the center framed by full rollings of the inscription on the left edge and right edge. The partial rolling on the obverse preserves only the creature and the inscription (at right). PF 2070 is dated 504 B.C.

BIBLIOGRAPHY

Garrison 1988, pp. 228–29, 240–43, 480, 493; Garrison 1998, p. 121 (n. 15); Garrison and Dion 1999, pp. 9 (n. 19), 10 (n. 28).

II-B.11. HORNED ANIMALS: DEER, GAZELLES, WILD GOATS, WILD SHEEP

Cat.No. 245   PFS 247

Seal Type: Cylinder	Photographs: Pl. 138a–b
Earliest Dated Application: 500/499 B.C.	Typology and Style: II-B.11 — Broad and Flat Styles
Preserved Height of Image: 1.60 cm (incomp.)	Preserved Length of Image: 2.80 cm (comp.)
Estimated Height of Original Seal: 1.80 cm	Estimated Diameter of Original Seal: 0.90 cm
Number of Impressions: 3	Quality of Impressions: Fair

Completeness of Image: Almost complete except for lower edge

DESCRIPTION OF SEAL AS IMPRESSED IMAGE

Hero faces left, extending bent right arm downward to grasp rampant wild goat by throat; left arm projects out to hold large saw-like weapon with jagged edge behind body.

Goat moves toward and faces hero; goat holds upper foreleg straight, lower foreleg bent, and extends them together downward toward hero's leg; short pointed tail extends diagonally upward.

Hero wears Assyrian garment that leaves forward leg exposed below knee (perhaps with Persianizing sleeves pushed up to reveal arms); diagonal folds are indicated on upper and lower areas of garment. Hero perhaps has short pointed beard; narrow pointed coiffure projects diagonally downward.

Goat has long thick curved horn emerging from front of its head.

To right of hero rampant deer moves toward and faces hero. Deer holds upper foreleg straight and extends it upward toward hero's shoulder; lower foreleg is straight, foot upturned, and extended downward toward end of hero's weapon; short pointed tail extends diagonally downward. Antler emerges at top of its head; long pointed ears are at back of head; mouth is slightly parted.

In terminal field rampant winged human-headed bird creature with ovoid bird's body and tail faces left. Creature holds forelegs (human arms) straight and extends them upward together toward head of rampant deer. Beard is squared; narrow pointed coiffure projects diagonally downward from back of head. Wing tip has trefoil termination; triangular device is below wing tip.

In upper terminal field is six-finned fish inverted.

Edge of seal is preserved at top of design.

COMMENTARY

See Garrison 1988 for the distinctive hand and compositions of the artist. The deer to the right of the hero relates closely to the heroic combat image. PFS 916 (Cat.No. 226), by the same artist, is very similar, although it lacks the distinctive and somewhat ambiguous element in the upper terminal field. Given the legacy of antique glyptic traditions drawn upon in the Achaemenid period, either a fish or a branch is a viable interpretation of the upper terminal element on PFS 247. It feels very close to an Early Dynastic seal known through an impression from Fara. There, the device is clearly a branch suspended in the upper terminal field (Collon 1987, pp. 156–57, no. 702). Fish are also symbols of great significance in earlier Mesopotamian tradition; and the form of the element on PFS 247 is convincingly fish-like.[77] The small triangle in the bottom zone of the terminal field below the wing of the bird creature may allude to the Mesopotamian god Anu (Wallenfels 1993, p. 284).

For comparative illustrations including PFS 247, see pls. 181c (hybrid garments), 194d (narrow rounded and/or pointed coiffures), 228f (fish and reptiles), 229g (scorpion, fish, horse, bird, and human creatures), 236e (animals/creatures as secondary elements of main design field), 247g (weapons of unusual or uncertain type), 248g (abstract symbols of Mesopotamian deities), and 278b (carving anomalies).

SEAL APPLICATION (SEE *APPENDIX ONE: CONCORDANCE OF SEALS TO TABLETS IN VOLUME I*)

PFS 247 occurs on the reverse of PF 1661 and PF 1743 and the upper edge of PF 1675, with PFS 6 (Cat.No. 304) on the left edge of each tablet. Impressions of the seal are extremely clear and apparently have been carefully applied to privilege the bird creature. Impressions exhibit little or no distortion. All rollings preserve the entire length of the seal design; two display the deer behind the hero and the bird creature in the center; one displays the bird creature and the goat to the left of the hero in the center. On the reverse of PF 1661 the seal clearly was applied before the text since several cuneiform wedges cut into the top of the impression. PF 1661 is the earliest dated tablet with PFS 247 and is dated 500/499 B.C.

BIBLIOGRAPHY

Garrison 1988, pp. 423–25.

PFS 959s   Cat.No. 246

1 cm

Seal Type:	Stamp, Circular Face	Photograph:	Pl. 139a
Earliest Dated Application:	ND	Typology and Style:	II-B.11 — Fortification Style
Preserved Height of Image:	1.90 cm (incomp.)	Preserved Width of Image:	2.00 cm (comp.)
Number of Impressions:	2	Quality of Impressions:	Fair

Completeness of Image: Almost complete except for left, right edge, and lower edge

DESCRIPTION OF SEAL AS IMPRESSED IMAGE

Hero faces right, extending straight left arm upward to grasp rampant wild goat by horn; right arm is slightly curved and held down behind body to hold dagger.

Goat moves away from hero but turns its head back toward him. Goat holds forelegs bent, extended upward together in front of its body; short tail curls upward.

Hero wears knee-length tunic; hero perhaps wears domed headdress. Beard with horizontal striations terminates in blunt point over hero's left shoulder; rounded coiffure rests at back of neck.

---

77. Black and Green 1992, p. 82. For a very late example, see an inscribed Neo-Babylonian seal (Collon 1987, pp. 152–53, no. 676). Bregstein (1993, pp. 102, 203, cat. no. 443) lists only one seal in the Murašû corpus with a fish "filler motif" (not illustrated).

Goat has one long curved horn emerging from front of its head and short beard under chin; small curled ear is at back of head.

Edges of seal are preserved at lower left and upper right of design.

COMMENTARY

The engraving is probably of a much higher quality than what the impressions on PF 834 preserve. The plain surface treatment and simply rendered forms are excellent examples of the Fortification Style. Compare an unprovenanced chalcedony conoid (Buchanan and Moorey 1988, no. 373).

The impressions of PFS 959s reveal a large stamp with a convex face and loosely circular contour. For probable seal shape, see *Appendix Four: Stamp Seals in Volume I Grouped by Apparent Contour of Seal Face* and accompanying figure 9, nos. 3a, 4c, or 5a.

For comparative illustrations including PFS 959s, see pl. 274e (stamp seals).

SEAL APPLICATION (SEE *APPENDIX ONE: CONCORDANCE OF SEALS TO TABLETS IN VOLUME I*)

PFS 959s occurs on the reverse (inverted) and left edge of PF 834. The partial impressions are both rotated slightly off the longitudinal axis of the tablet. The date of PF 834 is unknown.

BIBLIOGRAPHY

Garrison 1988, pp. 264–68; Garrison and Dion 1999, p. 11, fig. 7.

Cat.No. 247   PFS 1311s

Seal Type:	Stamp, Oval Face	Photographs:	Pl. 139c–d
Earliest Dated Application:	ND	Typology and Style:	II-B.11 — Modeled Style
Preserved Height of Image:	1.80 cm (incomp.)	Preserved Width of Image:	1.30 cm (incomp.)
Number of Impressions:	2	Quality of Impressions:	Poor

Completeness of Image: Large segment of design survives

DESCRIPTION OF SEAL AS IMPRESSED IMAGE

Hero faces right, extending straight left arm upward to grasp rampant horned animal of undetermined type by horn; right arm (only partially preserved) is curved and held down behind body (probably to hold weapon). Hero raises bent forward leg to place foot on hind leg of animal.

Animal moves away from hero but turns its head (not preserved) back toward him. Only small part of upper foreleg near body is preserved; lower foreleg is bent and extended in front of body.

Hero wears Assyrian garment that leaves forward leg exposed.

Thick curved horn emerges from animal's head.

Edge of seal is preserved at upper left, upper right, and lower right of design.

COMMENTARY

Based on Q texts protocol, PFS 1311s should belong to Napidan, who in PF 1388 went to Persepolis under the authority (*halmi*) of Bakabana. PF 1388 preserves the only occurrence of the name Napidan in the PF texts.

See Garrison 1988 for the style and workshop of PFS 1311s and related seals.

The stamp face has an oval contour. For probable seal shape, see *Appendix Four: Stamp Seals in Volume I Grouped by Apparent Contour of Seal Face* and accompanying figure 9, nos. 3b or 5b.

For comparative illustrations including PFS 1311s, see pls. 213g (heroic attitudes of combat encounter), 275a (stamp seals), 290g (personal seals of various travelers).

SEAL APPLICATION (SEE *APPENDIX ONE: CONCORDANCE OF SEALS TO TABLETS IN VOLUME I*)

PFS 1311s occurs on the reverse and upper edge of PF 1388. On the reverse the seal is oriented along the horizontal axis of the tablet; the partial application preserves only the hero. The partial application on the upper edge preserves the hero and the animal. On the reverse the seal clearly was applied before the text since cuneiform wedges cut into the lower edge and right edge of the impression. The date of PF 1388 is unknown.

BIBLIOGRAPHY

Garrison 1988, pp. 229, 243.

PFS 1391   Cat.No. 248

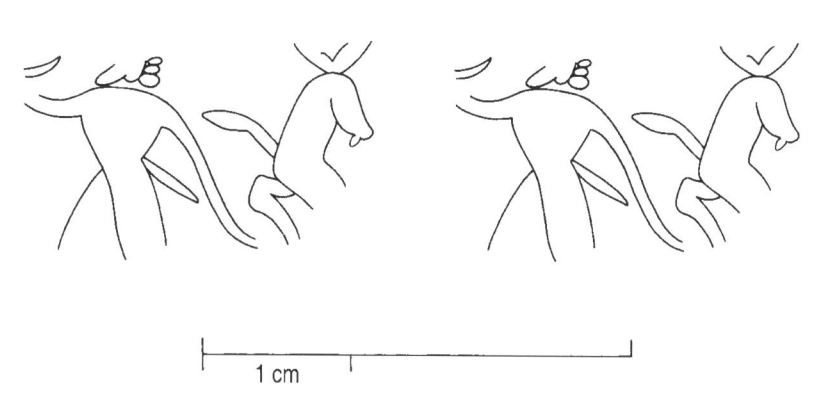

Seal Type:	Cylinder	Photograph:	Pl. 140a
Earliest Dated Application:	499 B.C.	Typology and Style:	II-B.11 — Mixed Styles I
Preserved Height of Image:	1.50 cm (incomp.)	Preserved Length of Image:	2.80 cm (comp.)
Estimated Height of Original Seal:	NA	Estimated Diameter of Original Seal:	0.90 cm
Number of Impressions:	1	Quality of Impression:	Poor

Completeness of Image: Segment of middle of design survives

DESCRIPTION OF SEAL AS IMPRESSED IMAGE

Hero faces left, apparently in striding pose, extending his curved right arm (only partially preserved) outward toward rampant horned animal of undetermined type; left arm is curved and held down behind body to hold long curved sword(?) that merges with arm.

Animal moves away from hero but turns its head back toward him. Animal holds upper foreleg bent and extends it diagonally upward; lower foreleg is bent and extended upward in front of its body.

Hero wears Assyrian garment that leaves forward leg exposed; sheath projects from back of waist. Long rounded beard rests along hero's right shoulder; rounded, segmented coiffure rests at back of neck.

Animal has short beard; two large horns (only partially preserved) emerge from top of its head.

In field above hero's right arm, partially preserved crescent-shaped element is probably termination of animal's horn.

COMMENTARY

Based on Q texts protocol, PFS 1391 should belong to Misraka, who in year 23.5 (499 B.C.) received flour rations under the authority (*halmi*) of Parnaka. PF 1494 preserves the only occurrence of the name Misraka in the PF texts; Hallock suggests that the name Misranka in PF 1493 is the same name as Misraka in PF 1494, but Misranka uses a different seal, PFS 1390s (III), making the link less compelling although certainly still possible.

A large area between the hero and the rampant animal is not preserved, and it is not clear exactly how the two figures interact over such a large space. There does not seem to be enough room for another animal. If indeed the partially preserved crescent-shaped element above the hero's right arm is the end of the animal's horn, this would imply that the hero is grasping the horn. The exaggerated and unarticulated extension of the hero's left arm suggests the legitimacy of reconstructing a similarly exaggerated horn on the animal.

The human forms suggest the Modeled Style, the animal forms the Fortification Style.

For comparative illustrations including PFS 1391, see pl. 289d (personal seals of various receivers).

SEAL APPLICATION (SEE *APPENDIX ONE: CONCORDANCE OF SEALS TO TABLETS IN VOLUME I*)

PFS 1391 occurs on the reverse of PF 1494. The rolling preserves the entire length of the seal design and displays the hero in the center. PF 1494 is dated 499 B.C.

BIBLIOGRAPHY

Garrison 1988, pp. 253–54.

II-B.12. WINGED HORNED-ANIMAL CREATURES: DEER, GAZELLES, WILD GOATS, WILD SHEEP

Cat.No. 249   PFS 162

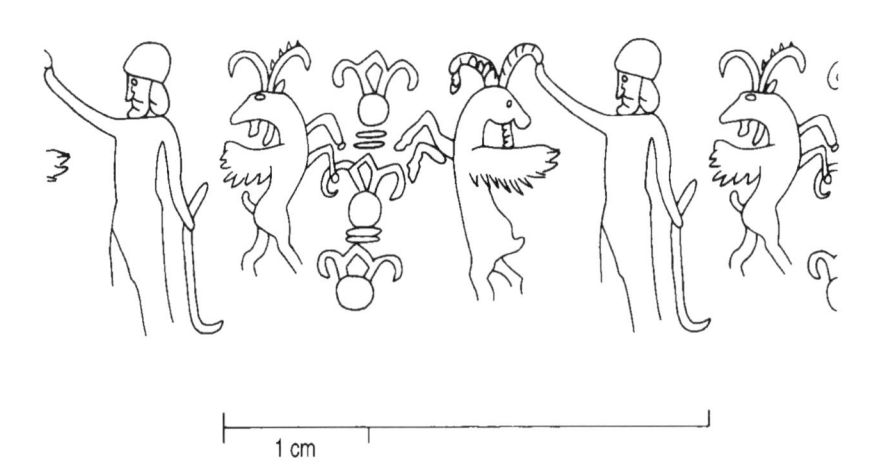

Seal Type:	Cylinder	Photographs:	Pl. 141a–b
Earliest Dated Application:	ND	Typology and Style:	II-B.12 — Fortification Style
Preserved Height of Image:	2.00 cm (incomp.)	Preserved Length of Image:	3.30 cm (comp.)
Estimated Height of Original Seal:	2.30 cm	Estimated Diameter of Original Seal:	1.10 cm
Number of Impressions:	3	Quality of Impressions:	Fair

Completeness of Image: Almost complete except for upper and lower edge

DESCRIPTION OF SEAL AS IMPRESSED IMAGE

Hero faces left, extending straight right arm upward to grasp rampant winged wild sheep creature by horn; left arm is curved and held down behind body to hold long curved sword.

Winged creature moves away from hero but turns its head back toward him. Creature holds forelegs bent and extends them upward together in front of its body; short thick tail curves slightly upward.

Hero wears Assyrian garment that leaves forward leg exposed; hero perhaps wears domed headdress. Long rounded up-curving beard with striations rests over hero's right shoulder; rounded coiffure rests at back of neck.

Winged creature grasped by hero has two curved horns and long beard with striations.

In terminal field, another rampant winged horned wild sheep creature moves to right but turns its head back to left. Together with stylized stacked floral element to its right, this creature completes a terminal field heraldic group with creature held by hero. Creature in terminal field holds forelegs bent and extends them upward together in front of its body; short tail curls upward. Two curved horns emerge from top of creature's head; horn to right has serrated edge along upper contour; small pointed ear emerges from back of its head. Creature has beard and throat mane.

COMMENTARY

Koch (1990) suggests that the seal may belong to Matiša, a "Landvogt" (*da'ubattiš*), which Hallock translates as "police officer(?)," in her Northwestern Region V and Elam Region VI.

The fusion of the heroic encounter motif and the motif of heraldic animals is also found on PFS 225 (Cat.No. 46), probably by the same artist, PFS 496 (Cat.No. 108), and PFS 1519 (Cat.No. 167). PFS 162 is, however, the only example where this fusion is contrived with a combat encounter. The stacked floral element in the terminal field, recalling Neo-Assyrian designs, finds a parallel in PFS 1204 (Cat.No. 136).

For comparative illustrations including PFS 162, see pls. 212f (heroic attitudes of combat encounter), 224b (deer, goats, sheep, and related winged creatures), 241g (heroic encounters fused with heraldic motifs), 256f (stylized floral elements), and 269c (terminal field motifs other than inscriptions).

SEAL APPLICATION (SEE *APPENDIX ONE: CONCORDANCE OF SEALS TO TABLETS IN VOLUME I*)

PFS 162 occurs on the reverse of PF 825, PF 1249, and PF 1902. On PF 825 and PF 1902 the seal is inverted and rolled somewhat off the horizontal axis of the tablet. Impressions are well executed. Of the three partial impressions, one displays the hero in the center; one displays the hero and the creature to left in the center; one displays the creature to the left of the hero and the floral element in the center. The dates of PF 825, PF 1249, and PF 1902 are unknown.

BIBLIOGRAPHY

Garrison 1988, pp. 276–78, 452; Koch 1990, p. 139; Root 1998, p. 269.

II-B.16. VARIOUS COMPOSITE CREATURES

Cat.No. 250   PFS 125

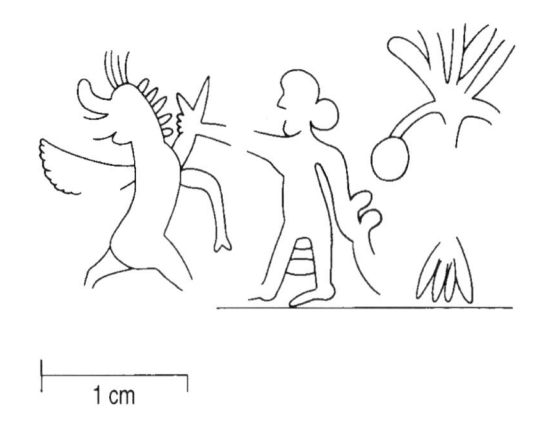

|— 1 cm —|

Seal Type:	Cylinder	Photograph:	Pl. 142a
Earliest Dated Application:	499/498 B.C.	Typology and Style:	II-B.16 — Broad and Flat Styles
Preserved Height of Image:	2.00 cm (incomp.)	Preserved Length of Image:	3.30 cm (incomp.)
Estimated Height of Original Seal:	2.20 cm	Estimated Diameter of Original Seal:	NA
Number of Impressions:	1	Quality of Impression:	Fair

Completeness of Image: Large segment of middle of design and lower edge survives

DESCRIPTION OF SEAL AS IMPRESSED IMAGE

Hero faces left, extending straight right arm to grasp rampant winged creature of uncertain type with horns by upper foreleg; left arm is straight and held down behind body to hold curved sword (only partially preserved) with two projections at hilt.

Creature moves toward hero but turns its head away from him. Creature holds upper foreleg (with elongated bifurcated hoof) straight and extends it diagonally upward in front of neck; lower foreleg (with cleft hoof) is bent and extended downward in front of body.

Hero wears garment of uncertain type with stacked horizontal lozenge-shaped features between legs. Rounded beard rests over hero's right shoulder; large rounded coiffure rests at back of neck.

Creature has elongated curling snout. Mane is rendered by five large spikes along contour of neck; two long horns (only partially preserved) emerge from top of creature's head.

To right of hero, in terminal field, is date palm (only partially preserved) with bulbous fruit clusters (one preserved). Four-pronged element forms base of tree trunk.

Portions of edge of seal are preserved at bottom of design below hero and date palm.

COMMENTARY

As is typical of this style, animal features are exaggerated and not easily categorized.

For comparative illustrations including PFS 125, see pls. 192b (rounded coiffures), 247d (weapons of unusual or uncertain type), and 259d (date palms).

SEAL APPLICATION (SEE APPENDIX ONE: CONCORDANCE OF SEALS TO TABLETS IN VOLUME I)

PFS 125 occurs on the reverse of PF 1632. The partial rolling displays the hero in the center. PF 1632 is dated 499/498 B.C.

BIBLIOGRAPHY

Garrison 1988, pp. 431–32.

PFS 10   Cat.No. 251

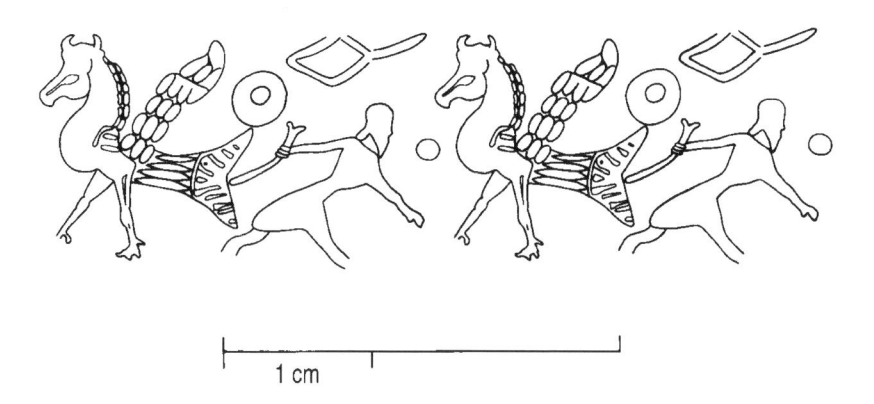

|—— 1 cm ——|

Seal Type:	Cylinder	Photographs:	Pl. 142c–e
Earliest Dated Application:	500 B.C.	Typology and Style:	II-B.16 — Fortification Style
Preserved Height of Image:	1.60 cm (incomp.)	Preserved Length of Image:	2.70 cm (comp.)
Estimated Height of Original Seal:	1.80 cm	Estimated Diameter of Original Seal:	0.90 cm
Number of Impressions:	32	Quality of Impressions:	Fair

Completeness of Image: Almost complete except for upper and lower edge

DESCRIPTION OF SEAL AS IMPRESSED IMAGE

Hero faces right, legs spread apart, and stretches one straight arm downward in posture of athletic motion toward large marchant winged fish-bull creature; other arm is straight and held down behind body to hold weapon with two-pronged terminal (apparently a sling).

Creature moves toward and faces hero. Creature consists of bull's forepart, one wing, and the lower body and caudal fin of a fish. Large ring shape rests directly on top of fin.

Hero appears to wear knee-length tunic. Pointed beard rests over hero's left shoulder; narrow rounded coiffure rests at back of neck.

Creature has two short curved horns emerging from top of its head. Mane, wing, and fin have tightly packed bead-like detailing.

Large dot is in field between hero's shoulder and creature's chest. Diamond-shaped device with horizontal projection is in field above hero.

COMMENTARY

Hallock associates the seal with an office of flour supply at Kurdušum, used by Haturdada in years 22 and 23 and also used by Ummanana. Koch (1990) identifies Haturdada as a supply authorizer of grain during years 21–28 at Kurdušum in her Elam Region VI. She also notes that Haturdada later used PFS 55 (III). Despite Hallock's suggestion of its occasional use by Ummanana, the attribution of PFS 10 to Haturdada is assured owing to numerous occurrences of PFS 10 on the left edge of Q texts that name Haturdada as the supplier.

The placement of the large dot in the relatively generous spacing between the hero and the creature creates a visual punctuation at this point in the composition, especially in an extended rolling. The composition and the athletic pose of the hero suggest that the large dot may be a spherical projectile that has just been hurled from the sling held by the hero.[78] See PFS 4* (Cat.No. 292) for a spherical object that is apparently a projectile held aloft in the hero's right hand; see PFS 57* (Cat.No. 241) for related imagery. Neither the diamond-shaped device nor the ring device occurs in Boardman's tables of linear devices (Boardman 1970a, figs. 3–4). Nor do they find parallels elsewhere so far.[79] They are unique in the PFS corpus across all three volumes, although PFS 131s (II) may preserve vestiges of a similar ring.

---

78. For a representation of balls held in slings by Assyrian soldiers, see a relief of Sennacherib from Nineveh (Hrouda 1965, pl. 60, no. 1: BM 124775).

79. Somewhat similar rings appear in the field on a recut Old Babylonian seal from the Ullu Burun shipwreck (Collon 1987, pp. 135–36, no. 570). Compare also a ring symbol on a Neo-Assyrian cylinder from Tepe Sialk (Collon 1987, pp. 86, 88, no. 417).

Overall, the style of the carving seems linked to the Fortification Style; however, the composition, the nature of the winged creature and the detailing on its body cannot be paralleled. This creature may be related to similar composite creatures found in Urartian art.[80]

Our proposed reading of the narrative content of the heroic encounter between hero and creature on PFS 10 represents a change from Garrison 1988, pp. 335–36, where the scene was described as portraying the hero reaching to grasp the creature while wielding a weapon in his other hand, ready to strike. Although the alternate reading (based on further close scrutiny of the tablets) moves PFS 10 somewhat to the margins of a true heroic encounter, it is closely associated with heroic scenes in structure.

For comparative illustrations including PFS 10, see pls. 194a (narrow rounded and/or pointed coiffures), 215a (unusual heroic attitudes), 229d (scorpion. fish, horse, bird, and human creatures), 247b (projectiles, slings), 254a (various devices and symbols), and 287a (personal seals of various suppliers).

SEAL APPLICATION (SEE *APPENDIX ONE: CONCORDANCE OF SEALS TO TABLETS IN VOLUME I*)

PFS 10 occurs only on the left edge of tablets that it seals. Impressions of the seal tend to be fragmentary and often show marked distortion. In eight impressions the seal is rolled for at least one complete turn, preserving the entire length of the seal design. Of these eight applications, six present the hero at the right of the impression, with the creature at the left ("behind" him). Only one presents the hero in proper narrative placement, at the left of the impression, with the creature to the right. The last displays the creature in the center framed by the athletic hero. Of the remaining twenty-four partial impressions, three preserve only the hero; five preserve only the creature. Sixteen preserve segments of the hero and the creature together. Of these, only four present the hero at the left (in narrative relation to the creature), while twelve present the hero at the right of the impression. PF 1309–1311, PF 1366, PF 1461, PF 1477, PF 1499, PF 1507, PF 1519, and PF 1534 are the earliest dated tablets with PFS 10 and are all dated 500 B.C.

BIBLIOGRAPHY

Brosius 1996, p. 137 (table 4); Garrison 1988, pp. 326, 335–39, 418; Hallock 1977, p. 132; Hallock 1985, pp. 598–99; Koch 1990, pp. 178, 208, 300, 304; Koch 1993, p. 78.

---

80. Compare, for example, Merhav 1991, pp. 148–49, nos. 5–7; 154, no. 13; 156, fig. 3; 157, no. 14; 168–69, nos. 5–7.

II-B.18. ANIMALS OF UNCERTAIN TYPE

PFS 241   Cat.No. 252

Seal Type:	Cylinder	Photograph:	Pl. 143a
Earliest Dated Application:	498/497 B.C.	Typology and Style:	II-B.18 — Fortification Style
Preserved Height of Image:	1.20 cm (incomp.)	Preserved Length of Image:	2.70 cm (comp.)
Estimated Height of Original Seal:	NA	Estimated Diameter of Original Seal:	0.90 cm
Number of Impressions:	5	Quality of Impressions:	Poor

Completeness of Image: Almost complete except for upper edge and lower edge

Description of Seal as Impressed Image

Hero moves to left, extending bent right arm upward toward rampant animal of uncertain type possibly with horns; left arm is slightly bent and held down behind body to hold undulating weapon of uncertain type with hooked end. Hero raises bent forward leg.

Animal holds upper foreleg straight and extends it upward to place paw or hoof on hero's elbow; lower foreleg is straight and extended downward toward hero's lower leg; thick straight tail (only partially preserved) extends diagonally upward.

Hero appears to wear Assyrian garment that leaves forward leg exposed below knee.

Animal appears to have two curved horns (only partially preserved) emerging from top of its head; mouth appears open in roar, but face and upper jaw are not preserved.

Rampant lion is poised at diagonal above animal held by hero. Lion holds one foreleg bent and extends it upward toward other animal's neck; mouth is open in roar.

Commentary

See Garrison 1988 for the distinctive hand of this artist. The composition of this image conflates the themes of heroic encounter and animal contest (viz., many seals in Volume III). The lion to left of heroic combat group relates closely to the action of this group.

For comparative illustrations including PFS 241, see pls. 241d (heroic encounters merged with animal contests) and 247f (weapons of unusual or uncertain type).

Seal Application (see *Appendix One: Concordance of Seals to Tablets in Volume I*)

PFS 241 occurs on the reverse, upper edge, and right edge of PF 93 and the reverse and upper edge of PF 94, with PFS 396 (Cat.No. 178) on the left edge of each tablet. In three impressions the seal is rolled for at least one complete turn, preserving the entire length of the seal design. Of these three applications, one displays the hero in the center; one displays the hero and the rampant lion in the upper terminal field in the center; one displays the lion in the upper terminal field in the center. Of the remaining two partial rollings, one displays the hero in the center; one displays the animal creature held by the hero in the center. On the reverse of both tablets the seal clearly was applied before the text since several cuneiform wedges cut into the top of the impressions. All tablets with PFS 241 are dated 498/497 B.C.

Bibliography

Garrison 1988, pp. 335–39, 494.

Cat.No. 253   PFS 1315s

Seal Type:	Stamp, Square Face	Photographs:	Pl. 143c–d
Earliest Dated Application:	ND	Typology and Style:	II-B.18 — Broad and Flat Styles
Preserved Height of Image:	1.00 cm (comp.)	Preserved Width of Image:	0.90 cm (comp.)
Number of Impressions:	4	Quality of Impressions:	Poor

Completeness of Image: Complete except for details

DESCRIPTION OF SEAL AS IMPRESSED IMAGE

Hero faces left, extending right arm (only partially preserved) upward toward upright seated animal of uncertain type; left arm is straight and held down behind body. Hero's legs are bent in quasi-*knielauf*-pose; his body is suspended in design field.

Animal is seated facing hero; one bent hind leg is indicated, extending under hero; one foreleg extends toward hero's thigh. Thick tail curves upward behind animal.

Hero apparently wears trousers. Domed headdress has streamer attached at top. Hero has short pointed beard; small rounded coiffure at back of head.

Thick ear emerges from back of animal's head. Animal has curving snout; mouth is open in roar.

All edges of seal are preserved.

COMMENTARY

PFS 1315s occurs on two Q texts. In PF 1393, Q texts protocol indicates that PFS 1315s should belong to Ammasuzawiš(?), who is going to the place Barrikana under the authority (*halmi*) of the king. PF 1393 preserves the only occurrence of the name in the PF texts. In PF 1573, Q texts protocol indicates that PFS 1315s should belong to Maudadda, who (with thirteen men) received three sheep while on the way from Susa to Parribana under the authority (*halmi*) of the king. Perhaps the same person received travel rations (PF 1429, the tablet is not sealed) for himself and one companion and two boys in year 24.8 (498 B.C.) under the authority (*halmi*) of Ziššawiš. PF 772 records a Maudadda who was a magus; PF 836 records a Maudadda who was a flour supplier. In PF 1107 a Maudadda and his companions received wine rations for workers at Parmizzan (apportionments set by Karkiš). The letters PF 1833–1834 seem to deal with the same Maudadda mentioned in PF 1107; according to the letters wine rations were issued to him as *hadazanam* for horses quartered at Parmizzan. A journal (PF 1957) mentions the name Maudadda in association with a storehouse. Another journal (PF 2073) qualifies a Maudadda as an *ullira* (OD, translated by Hallock as "delivery man"). Clearly, we have to do with several individuals here, and only the one in the Q text PF 1429 may be the same person who uses PFS 1315s on PF 1573 (suggested also by Koch 1990, p. 202 [n. 834]). Koch (1990, pp. 11 [n. 18], 122) suggests that the *ullira* in PF 2073 may be the same individual mentioned in PF 1957. The reason two separate individuals appear to be using this seal in Q texts is not yet understood.

PFS 1315s is quite small. The design appears to be a heroic encounter, but it is difficult to interpret. The seal was not included in Garrison 1988.

The stamp face is flat, with roughly square contour. For probable seal shape, see *Appendix Four: Stamp Seals in Volume I Grouped by Apparent Contour of Seal Face* and accompanying figure 9, nos. 2b or 7a.

For comparative illustrations including PFS 1315s, see pls. 184g (trousers), 187e (headdresses), 213h (heroic attitudes of combat encounter), 217i (hero suspended high in design field), 219g (comparative heroic proportions), 221g (animals and creatures of uncertain type), and 275b (stamp seals).

SEAL APPLICATION (SEE *APPENDIX ONE: CONCORDANCE OF SEALS TO TABLETS IN VOLUME I*)

PFS 1315s occurs twice on the obverse of PF 1393 and twice on the reverse of PF 1573. The two applications on PF 1393 are oriented along the horizontal axis of the tablet, one placed directly above the other. Both impressions originally preserved the full face of the seal, but damage to the tablet makes both impressions difficult to read. The two applications on PF 1573 are oriented along the horizontal axis of the tablet (the lower impression is rotated counterclockwise slightly), one placed directly above the other. Both impressions preserve the full face of the seal, but they are, nevertheless, very difficult to read. The dates of PF 1393 and PF 1573 are unknown.

PFS 1375s   Cat.No. 254

Seal Type:	Stamp, Square Face	Photograph:	Pl. 144a
Earliest Dated Application:	ND	Typology and Style:	II-B.18 — Broad and Flat Styles
Preserved Height of Image:	1.50 cm (comp.)	Preserved Width of Image:	1.10 cm (incomp.)
Number of Impressions:	1	Quality of Impression:	Poor

Completeness of Image: Large segment of design survives except at left and at lower edge

DESCRIPTION OF SEAL AS IMPRESSED IMAGE

Hero faces left, extending bent right arm outward to grasp rampant animal of uncertain type by upper foreleg.

Animal moves toward and faces hero. Animal holds upper foreleg (only partially preserved) straight and extends it upward toward hero's head; lower foreleg is extremely long, hanging down and terminating in large flat paw.

Hero apparently wears trousers. Rounded beard rests over hero's right shoulder; hair is gathered in ponytail at back of head.

Large pointed ear emerges from back of animal's head.

Half-oval device is disposed vertically in field at far right.

Edge of seal is preserved at top, right, and bottom right of design.

COMMENTARY

Based on Q texts protocol, PFS 1375s should belong to Kapiša, who in PF 1479 received flour rations under the authority (*halmi*) of the king. PF 1479 preserves the only occurrence of the name Kapiša in the PF texts.

The design is somewhat unclear in terms of how animal and hero are interacting. The half-oval device may represent a bow.

The stamp face has a rounded square contour. For probable seal shape, see *Appendix Four: Stamp Seals in Volume I Grouped by Apparent Contour of Seal Face* and accompanying figure 9, nos. 2b or 7a.

For comparative illustrations including PFS 1375s, see pls. 184h (trousers), 196g (coiffures of unusual types), 221h (animals and creatures of uncertain type), 275e (stamp seals), and 291e (personal seals of various travelers).

SEAL APPLICATION (SEE *APPENDIX ONE: CONCORDANCE OF SEALS TO TABLETS IN VOLUME I*)

PFS 1375s occurs on the reverse of PF 1479, oriented along the horizontal axis of the tablet. The application of the seal originally presented the entire figural design. The date of PF 1479 is unknown.

BIBLIOGRAPHY

Garrison 1988, pp. 425–28, 433, 445.

Cat.No. 255   PFS 167

Seal Type:	Cylinder	Photographs:	Pl. 144c–d
Earliest Dated Application:	500/499 B.C.	Typology and Style:	II-B.18 — Fortification Style
Preserved Height of Image:	1.60 cm (incomp.)	Preserved Length of Image:	2.50 cm (comp.)
Estimated Height of Original Seal:	1.80 cm	Estimated Diameter of Original Seal:	0.80 cm
Number of Impressions:	3	Quality of Impressions:	Fair

Completeness of Image: Almost complete except for upper edge and lower edge

DESCRIPTION OF SEAL AS IMPRESSED IMAGE

Hero faces right, extending bent left arm outward to grasp rampant animal of uncertain type by upper foreleg; right arm is straight and held down behind body to hold curved sword. Hero raises bent forward leg.

Animal moves toward hero but turns its head away from him. Animal holds its upper foreleg (only partially preserved) curved and extends it upward toward hero's head; lower foreleg, with cleft hoof, is bent and extended downward in front of its body. Animal raises bent forward hind leg (with hoof) toward hero's leg.

Hero wears belted Assyrian garment that leaves forward leg exposed. Short pointed beard rests over hero's left shoulder; small rounded coiffure rests at back of neck.

Animal has musculature indicated on its neck and hindquarters; animal is ithyphallic.

To right of animal held by hero, rampant lion moves left. Lion holds upper foreleg (only partially preserved) straight and extends it diagonally upward; lower foreleg (only partially preserved) is straight and extended downward in front of its body; tail curls downward with tufted termination. Mane is indicated by serrated edge along contour of neck; mouth is open in roar. Above lion, rampant winged bull or lion creature faces left (head not preserved). Creature holds one foreleg straight and extends it outward toward rampant lion's head; one hind leg is bent and extended upward in front of its body; other hind leg is curled downward; long tail (only partially preserved) bends vertically upward.

COMMENTARY

The crowded composition is noteworthy and finds no ready parallels among seals with images of heroic encounter herein. As with PFS 241 (Cat.No. 252) the scene displays a fusion of heroic encounter and animal contest, but here on PFS 167, the addition of the winged creature behind and above the lion creates an extremely dense visual field.

For comparative illustrations including PFS 167, see pls. 196c (coiffures of unusual types), 241c (heroic encounters merged with animal contests), 244b (daggers and swords), and 272d (dense compositions).

SEAL APPLICATION (SEE APPENDIX ONE: CONCORDANCE OF SEALS TO TABLETS IN VOLUME I)

PFS 167 occurs on the left edge of PF 22, PF 572, and PF 629. One impression preserves the entire length of the seal design, displaying the winged creature in the terminal field at the center. Of the remaining two partial impressions, one displays the hero in the center; one displays the winged creature in the terminal field in the center. PF 22 is the earliest dated tablet with PFS 167 and is dated 500/499 B.C.

BIBLIOGRAPHY

Garrison 1988, pp. 255, 270–71.

PFS 990 Cat.No. 256

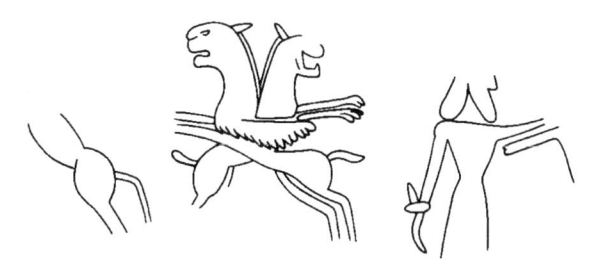

|—— 1 cm ——|

Seal Type:	Cylinder	Photograph:	Pl. 145a
Earliest Dated Application:	505 B.C.	Typology and Style:	II-B.18 — Fortification Style
Preserved Height of Image:	1.60 cm (incomp.)	Preserved Length of Image:	3.70 cm (incomp.)
Estimated Height of Original Seal:	NA	Estimated Diameter of Original Seal:	NA
Number of Impressions:	3	Quality of Impressions:	Fair

Completeness of Image: Segment of middle of design survives along most of its length

DESCRIPTION OF SEAL AS IMPRESSED IMAGE

Hero faces right, extending straight left arm to grasp rampant animal of uncertain type; right arm is straight and held down behind body to hold short curved dagger.

Only one foreleg of animal, held straight and extended diagonally downward toward hero's chest, is preserved. Perhaps rampant animal body preserved at far left of impression belongs to this same animal held by hero; long tail of animal at left bends downward.

Hero wears garment of uncertain type. Hero has long rounded beard resting over his left shoulder; rounded coiffure rests at back of neck.

Pair of crossed rampant quadrupeds is in terminal field. Quadruped facing left is winged lion creature. Creature holds forelegs (only partially preserved) straight and extends them outward together; short tail curves downward. Mane is rendered by thin outline along contour of neck; pointed ear is at back of head; mouth is slightly open. Animal facing right is lion (also with shortened tail). Lion holds forelegs straight, toes splayed, and extends them outward; short tail curves slightly upward. Mane is rendered by thin outline along contour of neck; pointed ear is at back of head; mouth is open in roar.

COMMENTARY

Crossed animals or creatures in the terminal field independent of the heroic encounter image also occur on PFS 213 (Cat.No. 140), PFS 396 (Cat.No. 178), and PFS 912 (Cat.No. 138). See the commentary for PFS 396 (Cat.No. 178), the only other seal in Volume I in which the crossed pair is displayed with the monumental force evident here on PFS 990.

For comparative illustrations including PFS 990, see pls. 242g (crossed animals) and 268h (terminal field motifs other than inscriptions).

SEAL APPLICATION (SEE *APPENDIX ONE: CONCORDANCE OF SEALS TO TABLETS IN VOLUME I*)

PFS 990 occurs on the reverse (inverted), upper edge, and left edge of PF 995. No other seal is used on the tablet. Of the three partial rollings, that on the upper edge preserves only the hero and part of the crossed animal group; those on the reverse and left edge display the negative space behind the hero in the center. On the reverse of the tablet the seal clearly was applied before the text since several cuneiform wedges cut into the bottom of the impression. PF 995 is dated 505 B.C.

BIBLIOGRAPHY

Garrison 1988, pp. 287–91.

Cat.No. 257   PFS 1480

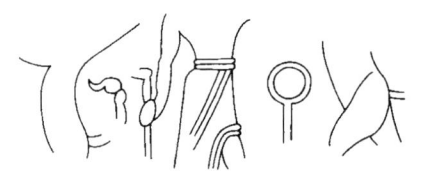

Seal Type:	Cylinder	Photograph:	Pl. 145c
Earliest Dated Application:	ND	Typology and Style:	II-B.18 — Plausibly Antique: Assyro-Babylonian Modeled Style
Preserved Height of Image:	1.00 cm (incomp.)	Preserved Length of Image:	2.60 cm (incomp.)
Estimated Height of Original Seal:	NA	Estimated Diameter of Original Seal:	NA
Number of Impressions:	3	Quality of Impressions:	Fair-good

Completeness of Image: Segment of middle of design survives

DESCRIPTION OF SEAL AS IMPRESSED IMAGE

Hero moves to right, extending raised left arm (not preserved) toward rampant animal of uncertain type; right arm is straight and held down behind body to hold weapon of uncertain type (only upper portion preserved).

Animal moves toward hero; tail (only partially preserved) appears to curve upward.

Hero wears double-belted Assyrian garment that leaves forward leg exposed below knee; double diagonal border is on overfold of lower part of garment and along hem.

Ring atop pole is in field between hero and animal with which he engages.

At far left of impression, in terminal field, rampant lion(?) moves to left. Lion(?) holds forelegs (only partially preserved) upward to either side of body; thick tail curls upward with elaborate tufted termination.

COMMENTARY

The engraving is well modeled, the execution very fine and crisp. The deep modeling and large size of the seal may suggest that it is a Neo-Assyrian or Neo-Babylonian antique.

The large ring device atop a pole relates to three linear devices assembled by Boardman as features of Achaemenid period glyptic in the western regions, although in none of these comparanda is the device apparently disposed with the ring at the top.[81]

For comparative illustrations including PFS 1480, see pls. 177h (Assyrian garments with detailing preserved) and 254i (various devices and symbols).

SEAL APPLICATION (SEE *APPENDIX ONE: CONCORDANCE OF SEALS TO TABLETS IN VOLUME I*)

PFS 1480 occurs twice on the reverse (inverted) and once on the left edge of PF 1603. The two impressions on the reverse are placed on the lower half of the reverse, one above the other. No other seal is used on the tablet. The partial upper rolling on the reverse preserves only the hero (at the right of the impression) and the lion(?) in the terminal field. The partial lower rolling preserves only the hero. The partial rolling on the left edge displays the hero in the center flanked by the other figures and is the most complete impression available. The upper impression on the reverse clearly was applied before the text since several cuneiform wedges cut into the bottom of the impression. The date of PF 1603 is unknown.

BIBLIOGRAPHY

Garrison 1988, pp. 213–14.

---

81. Boardman 1970a, fig. 3, nos. D1, D7, D46. D7 and D46 are also known as countermarks on coins of the Achaemenid period (ibid., fig. 4). See also Boardman 1998, figs. 9–12, for closely related mason's marks from Sardis, Pasargadae, Susa, and Persepolis.

PFS 1286   Cat.No. 258

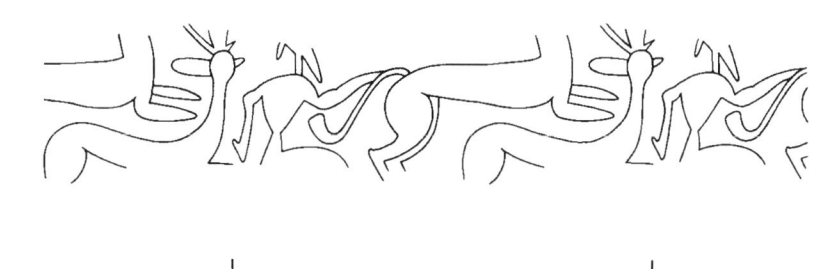

Seal Type:	Cylinder	Photograph:	Pl. 145e
Earliest Dated Application:	499 B.C.	Typology and Style:	II-B.18 — Modeled Style
Preserved Height of Image:	1.10 cm (incomp.)	Preserved Length of Image:	2.90 cm (comp.)
Estimated Height of Original Seal:	NA	Estimated Diameter of Original Seal:	0.90 cm
Number of Impressions:	1	Quality of Impression:	Fair

Completeness of Image: Large segment of middle of design survives along its complete length

DESCRIPTION OF SEAL AS IMPRESSED IMAGE

Hero faces right, extending curved left arm upward to grasp courant animal of uncertain type by tail; right arm is bent and held down behind body apparently to hold short hooked weapon of uncertain type that merges with arm. Hero raises bent forward leg (only partially preserved; rear leg not preserved).

Animal grasped by hero moves away from him to jump onto back of courant deer. Animal grasped by hero extends short forelegs together in front of its body; tail curves downward, hooking upward at its end with thickened termination.

Hero wears garment of uncertain type; hero has long pointed beard; narrow pointed coiffure extends downward from back of head.

Courant deer moves to right but turns its head back to left. Schematic large muzzle and small ear are indicated; antlers are only partially preserved. Although forepart occupies terminal field, this animal is a fully integrated secondary figure in main design field.

COMMENTARY

Based on Q texts protocol, PFS 1286 should belong to Mannuya, who in year 22.9 (499 B.C.) received flour rations for himself, two companions, and two servants while on the way from Susa to Matezziš. In the text Mannuya is qualified as *kazabara* (variant of *kanzabara*), a treasurer, who took silver from Susa to Matezziš. *Kanzabara* is an OD that occurs more commonly in the Persepolis Treasury tablets (in the PF texts it occurs in only one other instance, PF 1947, designating one Šarbaladda?). In the Treasury texts the term identifies the treasurer at Persepolis (Hinz 1971, pp. 261–62, calls the official the "Hofschatzwart"). Using the evidence of the Treasury tablets, Hinz (1971) and Koch (1990, pp. 235–37) reconstruct a list of treasurers at Persepolis from year 14 of Darius to year 7 of Artaxerxes. This list does not include the Mannuya who used PFS 1286 on the travel text PF 1342. Koch (1990, p. 27) simply says that Mannuya the *kanzabara* is a "Schatzwart" and comments no further. Treasuries occur at sites other than Persepolis (Hinz 1971, pp. 266–67; Koch 1990, p. 235). Perhaps Mannuya, the *kanzabara* who used PFS 1286, was the treasurer at one of these other places. Koch says that there was a treasury at Matezziš, but she does not explicitly connect Mannuya to it. In any case, the OD would seem to distinguish Mannuya as an official of significant rank.

The name Mannuya occurs in four other published texts besides PF 1342: PF 741, PF 794, PF 1941, and PF 1942. No other text qualifies him as *kanzabara*. PF 1941 and PF 1942, two journal texts, clearly concern a Mannuya with the OD *tumara* ("grain handler" [Hallock 1969, s.v.]; "Cerealien-Kommissar" [Hinz 1971, p. 287]). Koch (1990, p. 9) suggests that the grain supplier Mannuya mentioned in PF 741 may be the same individual as the *tumara* mentioned in PF 1941 and PF 1942. Koch (1990, pp. 8 and 250) also equates Mannuya the *tumara* with one Manuš, qualified as *tumara* in PF 54, who received grain shipments for royal stores in PF 1943. Mannuya's cohort, the *ullira* ("delivery man" [Hallock 1969, s.v.]; "Beschaffungsbeamter" [Koch 1990, p. 8]) was Manmakka. The Mannuya mentioned in PF 1941 and PF 1942 served as the *tumara* at Persepolis from years 14 to 20 (Koch 1990, p. 258).

PF 1942 preserves the mention of another Mannuya who is qualified as the *matira* in year 19 at a grain warehouse at Kansakam (Koch 1990, pp. 253 and 260).

It is an open question whether Mannuya the *tumara* at Persepolis during years 14–20 was the same individual as Mannuya the *kanzabara* who received travel rations in year 22 and used PFS 1286. Chronological considerations certainly do not exclude this possibility, and we may have to do here with an administrator of considerable ability who moved up the bureaucratic ladder.

The seal was not included in Garrison 1988.

For comparative illustrations including PFS 1286, see pls. 213e (heroic attitudes of combat encounter), 221f (animals and creatures of uncertain type), and 290d (personal seals of various travelers).

SEAL APPLICATION (SEE *APPENDIX ONE: CONCORDANCE OF SEALS TO TABLETS IN VOLUME I*)

PFS 1286 occurs once on the reverse of PF 1342, with PFS 21 (II) on the left edge. The rolling is complete and displays the hero in the center. PF 1342 is dated 499 B.C.

II-B.19. WINGED CREATURES OF UNCERTAIN TYPE

Cat.No. 259   PFS 919s

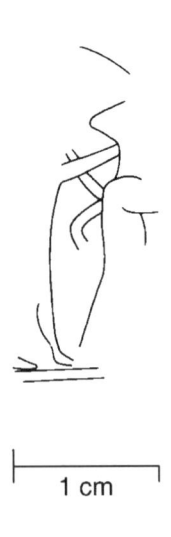

Seal Type:	Stamp, Circular Face	Photograph:	Pl. 146a
Earliest Dated Application:	500/499 B.C.	Typology and Style:	II-B.19 — Broad and Flat Styles
Preserved Height of Image:	2.30 cm (incomp.)	Preserved Width of Image:	1.00 cm (incomp.)
Number of Impressions:	2	Quality of Impressions:	Very poor

Completeness of Image: Small segment of middle of design survives

DESCRIPTION OF SEAL AS IMPRESSED IMAGE

Hero moves to right (only his left side is preserved). Hero extends straight left arm upward to grasp rampant winged creature of uncertain type by throat.

Creature moves toward and faces hero. Creature extends upper foreleg (only partially preserved) upward toward hero's head; lower foreleg (only partially preserved) is bent and extended downward in front of body.

Horizontal band at bottom of design serves as ground line.

Small section of edge of seal is preserved at upper right.

COMMENTARY

Owing to the fragmentary preservation of these impressions, it is possible that the scene is a control rather than a combat encounter; combat designs are more common, however, on stamp seals owing to the restricted surface of the stamp face.

The ground line in stamp seals is not often seen among seals with images of heroic encounter in the PFS corpus. See PFS 1260s (Cat.No. 184) and PFS 1321s (Cat.No. 176) for stamp seals with octagonal contours and ground line; see PFS 1437s (Cat.No. 128) and PFS 1624s (Cat.No. 261) for stamp seals with circular or oval contours and ground lines.[82]

The stamp face can only be reconstructed as having a circular shape. For probable seal shape, see *Appendix Four: Stamp Seals in Volume I Grouped by Apparent Contour of Seal Face* and accompanying figure 9, nos. 3a, 4c, or 5a.

For comparative illustrations including PFS 919s, see pls. 274d (stamp seals) and 277a (ground lines on stamp seals).

SEAL APPLICATION (SEE *APPENDIX ONE: CONCORDANCE OF SEALS TO TABLETS IN VOLUME I*)

PFS 919s occurs on the upper edge and left edge of PF 793. Both applications are partial. That on the left edge is too poorly preserved for analysis owing to damage. PF 793 is dated 500/499 B.C.

BIBLIOGRAPHY

Garrison 1988, pp. 428–30.

PFS 964   Cat.No. 260

Seal Type:	Cylinder	Photograph:	Pl. 146c
Earliest Dated Application:	497/496 B.C.	Typology and Style:	II-B.19 — Modeled Style
Preserved Height of Image:	1.70 cm (incomp.)	Preserved Length of Image:	3.40 cm (incomp.)
Estimated Height of Original Seal:	NA	Estimated Diameter of Original Seal:	NA
Number of Impressions:	1	Quality of Impression:	Poor

Completeness of Image: Segment of middle of design survives

DESCRIPTION OF SEAL AS IMPRESSED IMAGE

Winged hero moves to right, extending one arm straight outward, presumably to grasp rampant winged bird-headed creature of uncertain type that is preserved at far left of impression; hero's other arm is not preserved.

Creature moves toward and faces hero; thick tail extends diagonally upward.

Hero wears Assyrian garment that leaves forward leg exposed below knee. Hero has two wings, upper extending diagonally upward from lower. Torso is rendered in profile.

Crescent is in field above creature's wing.

---

82. Compare the conoid stamp seal from Qasr-i Abu Nasr with hero image and ground line (Wilkinson 1965, p. 344, figs. 22–23; Frye 1973, p. 37, no. 8).

COMMENTARY

For comparative illustrations including PFS 964, see pls. 201i (heroes as winged humans) and 251b (crescents).

SEAL APPLICATION (SEE *APPENDIX ONE: CONCORDANCE OF SEALS TO TABLETS IN VOLUME I*)

PFS 964 occurs on the reverse of PF 842. The partial rolling preserves only the hero (at the right of the impression) and the creature. PF 842 is dated 497/496 B.C.

BIBLIOGRAPHY

Garrison 1988, pp. 199–201; Garrison 1998, p. 121 (n. 15).

Cat.No. 261   PFS 1624s

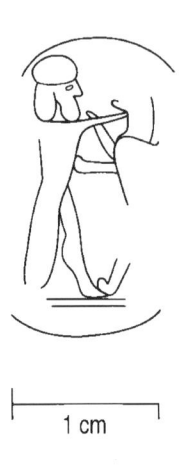

Seal Type:	Stamp, Oval Face	Photograph:	Pl. 146e
Earliest Dated Application:	495/494 B.C.	Typology and Style:	II-B.19 — Fortification Style
Preserved Height of Image:	2.20 cm (comp.)	Preserved Width of Image:	1.10 cm (incomp.)
Number of Impressions:	2	Quality of Impressions:	Fair

Completeness of Image: Large segment of middle of design survives

DESCRIPTION OF SEAL AS IMPRESSED IMAGE

Hero faces right, extending straight left arm to grasp rampant winged creature of uncertain type by throat; right arm is not preserved.

Creature moves toward and faces hero. Creature holds upper foreleg straight and extends it upward to hero's arm; lower foreleg is straight and extended outward to hero's chest. Paw of forward hind leg steps on foot of hero's forward leg.

Hero wears Assyrian garment that leaves forward leg exposed. Rounded beard rests over hero's left shoulder; rounded coiffure rests at back of neck. Hero perhaps wears domed headdress.

Band at bottom of design serves as ground line.

COMMENTARY

The ground line in stamp seals is seen occasionally among seals with images of heroic encounter in the PFS corpus; see, for example, PFS 1260s (Cat.No. 184) and PFS 1321s (Cat.No. 176) for octagonal-faced stamp seals and PFS 919s (Cat.No. 259) and PFS 1437s (Cat.No. 128) for circular-faced seals.[83]

The stamp face has a circular contour. For probable seal shape, see *Appendix Four: Stamp Seals in Volume I Grouped by Apparent Contour of Seal Face* and accompanying figure 9, nos. 3a, 4c, or 5a.

---

[83]. Compare the conoid stamp seal from Qasr-i Abu Nasr (Wilkinson 1965, p. 344, figs. 22–23; Frye 1973, p. 37, no. 8).

For comparative illustrations including PFS 1624s, see pls. 175h (Assyrian garments), 231i (feet of animals and creatures), 275i (stamp seals), and 277e (ground lines on stamp seals).

SEAL APPLICATION (SEE *APPENDIX ONE: CONCORDANCE OF SEALS TO TABLETS IN VOLUME I*)

PFS 1624s occurs twice on the obverse of PF 2059, both applications oriented along the horizontal axis of the tablet. The impressions are placed next to each other, the left one pressed slightly over the right one. Both impressions are partial. PF 2059 is dated 495/494 B.C.

BIBLIOGRAPHY

Garrison 1988, pp. 291–93.

PFS 338   Cat.No. 262

Seal Type:	Cylinder	Photograph:	Pl. 147a
Earliest Dated Application:	500/499 B.C.	Typology and Style:	II-B.19 — Fortification Style
Preserved Height of Image:	1.00 cm (incomp.)	Preserved Length of Image:	2.80 cm (comp.)
Estimated Height of Original Seal:	NA	Estimated Diameter of Original Seal:	0.90 cm
Number of Impressions:	4	Quality of Impressions:	Very poor

Completeness of Image: Large segment of middle of design survives along its entire length

DESCRIPTION OF SEAL AS IMPRESSED IMAGE

Hero moves to right, apparently to grasp rampant winged creature of uncertain type (hero's left arm is not preserved); right arm is curved and held down behind body to hold curved weapon of uncertain type (only partially preserved).

Creature extends upper foreleg (only partially preserved) upward toward hero's arm; lower foreleg, paw upturned, is extended downward toward hero's leg; short, straight tail extends diagonally upward with thickened three-pronged termination.

Hero appears to wear Assyrian garment that leaves forward leg exposed.

In terminal field, rampant animal of uncertain type moves left toward winged creature confronting hero. Animal holds upper foreleg (only partially preserved) straight and extends it diagonally upward; lower foreleg is curved, paw upturned, and extended downward toward creature's wing; tail (only partially preserved) curves downward.

COMMENTARY

The animal in the terminal field may perhaps be better described as an integral member of the heroic encounter group. Lacking preservation of the directional focus of the heads of the creature and the animal, the degree of integration remains unclear.

SEAL APPLICATION (SEE *APPENDIX ONE: CONCORDANCE OF SEALS TO TABLETS IN VOLUME I*)

PFS 338 occurs twice on the reverse (inverted) and once on the upper edge and left edge of PF 31. The rollings on the reverse are applied one above the other. In two impressions the seal is rolled for at least one complete turn, preserving the entire length of the seal design. Of these two applications, one displays the hero and the winged creature in the center; one displays the rampant animal behind the hero in the center. The remaining two partial rollings preserve only the hero and the winged creature. PF 31 is dated 500/499 B.C.

BIBLIOGRAPHY

Garrison 1988, pp. 304–07.

Cat.No. 263   PFS 344

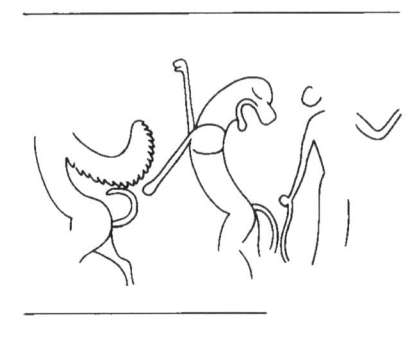

Seal Type:	Cylinder	Photograph:	Pl. 147c
Earliest Dated Application:	499/498 B.C.	Typology and Style:	II-B.19 — Fortification Style
Preserved Height of Image:	1.90 cm (comp.)	Preserved Length of Image:	2.50 cm (incomp.)
Estimated Height of Original Seal:	1.90 cm	Estimated Diameter of Original Seal:	NA
Number of Impressions:	2	Quality of Impressions:	Very poor

Completeness of Image: Large segment of middle of design survives

DESCRIPTION OF SEAL AS IMPRESSED IMAGE

Hero faces right, extending bent left arm outward, apparently to grasp rampant winged creature of uncertain type that is preserved at far left of one impression; hero's right arm is straight and held down behind body to hold curved sword (not completely preserved).

Rampant winged creature at far left of the one relevant impression moves toward hero; tail curls upward.

Hero wears garment of uncertain type; hero has rounded coiffure at back of his neck.

Behind hero, in terminal field, rampant lion moves away from him but turns its head back toward him. Lion holds upper foreleg straight, paw turned down, and extends it diagonally upward; lower foreleg is straight and extended downward toward winged creature's tail. Tail (only partially preserved) curves downward; mouth is open in roar.

Edge of seal is preserved at top and bottom of design.

COMMENTARY

The seal is very poorly preserved, despite retrieval of its upper and lower edges. The suggested interaction between the hero and the rampant winged creature at far left of the impressions is not certain.

SEAL APPLICATION (SEE APPENDIX ONE: CONCORDANCE OF SEALS TO TABLETS IN VOLUME I)

PFS 344 occurs on the reverse and left edge of PF 35. The rolling on the reverse displays the entire preserved length of the seal design (as shown in the composite drawing) and displays the winged creature and lion in the center. The partial rolling on the left edge displays the lion in the center. PF 35 is dated 499/498 B.C.

BIBLIOGRAPHY

Garrison 1988, pp. 320, 324.

PFS 463   Cat.No. 264

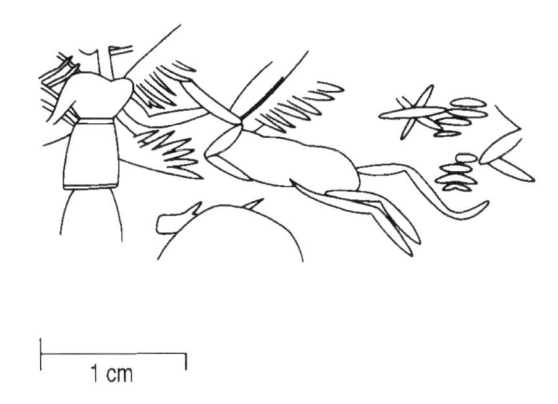

Seal Type:	Cylinder	Photograph:	Pl. 147e
Earliest Dated Application:	498/497 B.C.	Typology and Style:	II-B.19 — Diverse Styles
Preserved Height of Image:	1.60 cm (incomp.)	Preserved Length of Image:	3.50 cm (incomp.)
Estimated Height of Original Seal:	NA	Estimated Diameter of Original Seal:	NA
Number of Impressions:	1	Quality of Impression:	Very poor

Completeness of Image: Segment of middle of design survives

DESCRIPTION OF SEAL AS IMPRESSED IMAGE

Four-winged hero extends bent left arm outward to grasp courant winged creature of uncertain type by upper foreleg; hero's right arm (only partially preserved) is held behind body.

Creature moves in flying gallop toward hero. Creature holds upper foreleg straight and extends it upward toward hero's upper wing; lower foreleg is bent and held against body; long bent tail extends outward and then downward, curling up at its end.

Hero wears long belted robe, with two-tiered skirt (border at hem of first tier).

Below courant winged creature a horizontal fish faces left, almost entirely obliterated by large chip in stone.

At right of preserved impression, in terminal field, are two uneven stacks of four lozenge-shaped devices; to left of upper stack is star. To right of these elements straight upper foreleg and bent lower foreleg of another animal (courant?) are partially preserved.

COMMENTARY

The seal is very poorly preserved; the design could be a control encounter in which the hero grasps the second creature by its tail, but this seems unlikely. It is impossible to be sure how the second animal relates to the hero group. The schematic execution suggests links to the earlier Assyro-Babylonian Cut Style. For a similar style, see PFS 321 (Cat.No. 125). The seal was not included in Garrison 1988.

For comparative illustrations including PFS 463, see pls. 182e (robes with various features of detail), 201f (heroes as winged humans), 221b (animals and creatures of uncertain type), 228i (fish and reptiles), and 280e (chips in seal matrices).

SEAL APPLICATION (SEE *APPENDIX ONE: CONCORDANCE OF SEALS TO TABLETS IN VOLUME I*)

PFS 463 is rolled (inverted) across the midsection of the reverse of PF 164. Two other seals are applied on the same surface (both applied upright): PFS 123* (Cat.No. 75) at the top and PFS 464 (III) at the bottom. PFS 463 appears to have been applied after the other two seals. The one rolling of PFS 463 displays the winged creature at center. PF 164 is dated 498/497 B.C.

Cat.No. 265   PFS 818

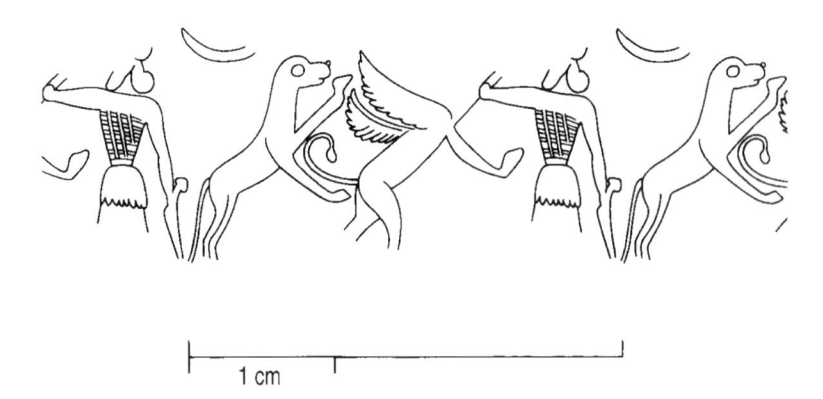

Seal Type:	Cylinder
Earliest Dated Application:	501/500 B.C.
Preserved Height of Image:	1.60 cm (incomp.)
Estimated Height of Original Seal:	NA
Number of Impressions:	5
Photographs:	Pl. 148a–b
Typology and Style:	II-B.19 — Modeled Style
Preserved Length of Image:	3.00 cm (comp.)
Estimated Diameter of Original Seal:	1.00 cm
Quality of Impressions:	Poor

Completeness of Image: Large segment of middle of design survives along its complete length

DESCRIPTION OF SEAL AS IMPRESSED IMAGE

Hero faces left, extending straight right arm upward to grasp rampant winged creature of uncertain type by upper foreleg; left arm is straight and held down behind body to hold sword.

Creature moves toward hero. Creature holds upper foreleg (only partially preserved) straight and extends it upward toward hero's head; lower foreleg, paw upturned, is extended downward toward hero's waist; tail curls upward with tufted termination.

Hero wears belted two-tiered garment of uncertain type with fringe edging top tier; hatched pattern is over chest. Rounded beard rests over hero's right shoulder; rounded coiffure rests at back of neck.

Creature has two wings indicated.

Rampant animal of uncertain type moves right toward winged creature. Animal holds upper foreleg straight, paw upturned, and extends it upward toward creature's upper wing; lower foreleg is curved and extended downward toward creature's rear hind leg. Animal holds hind legs together; straight tail extends downward.

Crescent is in upper terminal field between animal and hero.

COMMENTARY

The animal relates closely to the heroic encounter group, suggesting fusion with the animal contest theme.
    For comparative illustrations including PFS 818, see pls. 182h (robes with various features of detail), 241e (heroic encounters merged with animal contests), and 251a (crescents).

SEAL APPLICATION (SEE APPENDIX ONE: CONCORDANCE OF SEALS TO TABLETS IN VOLUME I)

PFS 818 occurs twice on the reverse and once on the left edge of PF 610 and once on the upper edge and left edge of PF 859. The rollings on the reverse of PF 610 are applied one directly above the other. No other seal is used on the tablets. The rolling on the upper edge of PF 859 preserves the entire length of the seal design and displays the winged creature and the animal in the center. Of the remaining four partial impressions, two preserve only the hero and the animal; one displays the winged creature in the center; one preserves only the winged creature and the animal. PF 610 is the earliest dated tablet with PFS 818 and is dated 501/500 B.C.

BIBLIOGRAPHY

Garrison 1988, pp. 217, 222–23, 485–86.

PFS 1025*

Cat.No. 266

Seal Type:	Cylinder, Inscribed	Photograph:	Pl. 148d
Earliest Dated Application:	497 B.C.	Typology and Style:	II-B.19 — Court Style
Language of Inscription:	Elamite(?)		
Preserved Height of Image:	0.80 cm (incomp.)	Preserved Length of Image:	3.50 cm (incomp.)
Estimated Height of Original Seal:	NA	Estimated Diameter of Original Seal:	NA
Number of Impressions:	1	Quality of Impression:	Poor

Completeness of Image: Small segment of lower middle of design survives

DESCRIPTION OF SEAL AS IMPRESSED IMAGE

Hero appears to move to right toward rampant winged creature of uncertain type.

Creature moves toward hero. Creature raises straight forward hind leg up toward hero's waist; tail (only partially preserved) curves downward.

Hero wears garment of uncertain type.

Paneled inscription is in terminal field.

INSCRIPTION

Elamite(?)

Line   x+1. [...]⌜x x⌝
                x+2. [...]⌜x⌝ DA

Translation   ?

Two lines of inscription are preserved, oriented along the horizontal axis of the seal, and divided by a case line. With the exception of the last sign in line x+2, only illegible traces remain. Too little of the inscription remains to suggest a reading.

COMMENTARY

Poor preservation does not permit secure identification of the composition. The same is true for a detailed stylistic analysis, but the inscription and careful execution suggest the Court Style.

    For comparative illustrations including PFS 1025*, see pl. 263i (inscriptions without panels, with horizontal case lines).

SEAL APPLICATION (SEE APPENDIX ONE: CONCORDANCE OF SEALS TO TABLETS IN VOLUME I)

PFS 1025* occurs on the reverse of PF 1059. The partial rolling displays the inscription at far right of the impression, and the heroic encounter at far left, thus placing the negative space between the creature and the inscription in the center. The seal clearly was applied before the text since several cuneiform wedges cut into the bottom of the impression. PF 1059 is dated 497 B.C.

BIBLIOGRAPHY

Garrison 1988, pp. 412, 416; Garrison and Dion 1999, p. 10 (n. 28).

II-C. HERO THREATENS RAMPANT ANIMAL OR CREATURE, WEAPON HELD UP BEHIND HEAD

II-C.2. WINGED BULL CREATURES

Cat.No. 267　　　　　　　　　　　　　　　　PFS 939

Seal Type:	Cylinder	Photograph:	Pl. 149a
Earliest Dated Application:	ND	Typology and Style:	II-C.2 — Fortification Style
Preserved Height of Image:	1.60 cm (incomp.)	Preserved Length of Image:	2.30 cm (comp.)
Estimated Height of Original Seal:	1.70 cm	Estimated Diameter of Original Seal:	0.70 cm
Number of Impressions:	3	Quality of Impressions:	Fair

Completeness of Image: Almost complete except for lower edge

DESCRIPTION OF SEAL AS IMPRESSED IMAGE

Hero faces left, extending straight right arm upward to grasp rampant winged bull creature by horn; hero extends bent left arm upward behind head to hold weapon of uncertain type (only small circular element is preserved).

Creature moves toward and faces hero. Creature holds upper foreleg slightly bent and extends it upward to hero's upper arm; lower foreleg is straight and extended outward toward hero's waist; tail curls upward with tufted termination.

Hero wears belted Assyrian garment that leaves forward leg exposed below knee. Squared beard rests over hero's right shoulder; narrow rounded coiffure rests at back of neck.

Creature has two wings indicated, upper extending diagonally upward from lower. Horn (only partially preserved) emerges from front of creature's head; large triangular ear is at back of head. Creature is ithyphallic.

In terminal field, bird of uncertain type with wings spread in flight moves to left.

Edge of seal is preserved at top of design.

COMMENTARY

The seal is exceptionally well executed and is an excellent example of the Fortification Style at its best.

　　For comparative illustrations including PFS 939, see pls. 194i (narrow rounded and/or pointed coiffures), 227f (birds), and 233f (ithyphallic animals/creatures).

SEAL APPLICATION (SEE *APPENDIX ONE: CONCORDANCE OF SEALS TO TABLETS IN VOLUME I*)

PFS 939 occurs twice on the reverse (inverted) and once on the upper edge of PF 814. On the reverse the impressions are applied one directly above the other. The three impressions preserve the entire length of the seal design; two on the reverse display the hero in the center; one on the upper edge displays the creature in the center. The date of PF 814 is unknown.

BIBLIOGRAPHY

Garrison 1988, pp. 264–68.

PFS 1612   Cat.No. 268

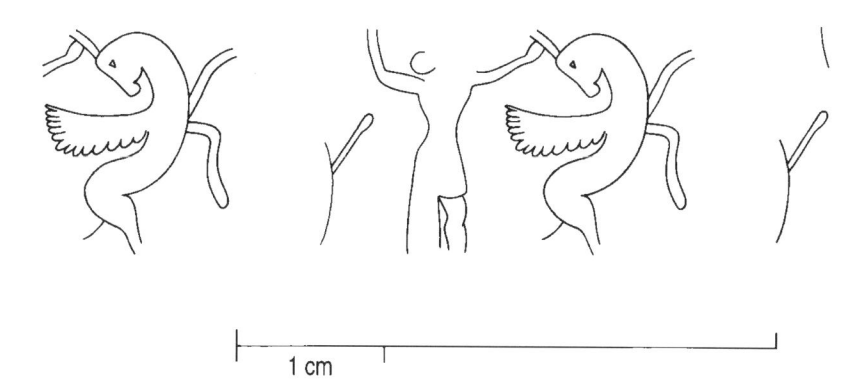

Seal Type:	Cylinder	Photograph:	Pl. 149c
Earliest Dated Application:	495 B.C.	Typology and Style:	II-C.2 — Mixed Styles I
Preserved Height of Image:	1.70 cm (incomp.)	Preserved Length of Image:	3.10 cm (comp.)
Estimated Height of Original Seal:	2.00 cm	Estimated Diameter of Original Seal:	1.00 cm
Number of Impressions:	1	Quality of Impression:	Poor

Completeness of Image: Large segment of middle of design survives along its complete length

DESCRIPTION OF SEAL AS IMPRESSED IMAGE

Hero faces right, extending left arm upward to grasp rampant winged bull creature by horn; hero extends bent right arm upward behind head (presumably to hold weapon, not preserved).

Creature moves away from hero but turns its head back toward him. Creature holds upper foreleg bent (only partially preserved) and extends it diagonally upward in front of its neck; lower foreleg is bent and extended downward in front of body.

Hero wears Assyrian garment that leaves forward leg exposed from mid-thigh. Rounded coiffure rests at back of hero's neck.

Long horn (only partially preserved) emerges from front of creature's head.

In terminal field, very poorly preserved rampant animal of uncertain type moves right toward hero; animal holds its one foreleg straight and extends it upward toward hero's arm.

COMMENTARY

Based on Q texts protocol, PFS 1612 should belong to Barnuš, who in year 27.8 (495 B.C.) received flour rations for a relatively large traveling party at Makkaš while on the way to Susa under the authority (*halmi*) of the king. In PF 2050 he is described as *karamaraš* (OD). Apparently the same Barnuš (described as the *karamaraš* of Ištibara [PN]) appears in the Q text PF 1537, where he received beer rations under the authority (*halmi*) of Šaman, but he used a different seal, PFS 1431 (II).

Despite its poor preservation, it is clear that this is a very well-executed design.

For comparative illustrations including PFS 1612, see pl. 288a (personal seals of various men leading groups).

SEAL APPLICATION (SEE *APPENDIX ONE: CONCORDANCE OF SEALS TO TABLETS IN VOLUME I*)

PFS 1612 occurs on the reverse of PF 2050. The rolling, now damaged by a crack running along the longitudinal axis of the tablet, is long and displays the rampant winged creature and rampant terminal animal in the center. PF 2050 is dated 495 B.C.

BIBLIOGRAPHY

Garrison 1988, pp. 245–46.

II-C.4. LIONS

Cat.No. 269 PFS 807

Seal Type:	Cylinder	Photograph:	Pl. 150a
Earliest Dated Application:	500/499 B.C.	Typology and Style:	II-C.4 — Modeled Style
Preserved Height of Image:	1.00 cm (incomp.)	Preserved Length of Image:	1.60 cm (incomp.)
Estimated Height of Original Seal:	NA	Estimated Diameter of Original Seal:	NA
Number of Impressions:	2	Quality of Impression:	Poor

Completeness of Image: Segment of middle of design survives

DESCRIPTION OF SEAL AS IMPRESSED IMAGE

Hero moves to right, extending bent left arm upward to grasp rampant lion presumably by forelock (contact not preserved); hero raises bent right arm upward presumably to hold weapon (not preserved). Hero raises bent forward leg.

Lion moves toward and faces hero. Lion holds one foreleg straight and extends it downward to place paw on hero's raised thigh; other foreleg is bent and extended upward away from body.

Hero apparently wears belted Assyrian garment that leaves forward leg exposed; sheath projects from back of waist. Long pointed beard rests over hero's left shoulder.

Lion opens mouth in roar.

COMMENTARY

The seal was not included in Garrison 1988; see, however, Garrison 1988, pp. 227–43, for discussion of the style and workshop of related seals.

For comparative illustrations including PFS 807, see pl. 212j (heroic attitudes of combat encounter).

SEAL APPLICATION (SEE *APPENDIX ONE: CONCORDANCE OF SEALS TO TABLETS IN VOLUME I*)

PFS 807 occurs on the left edge of PF 600. The rolling is incomplete and has been interrupted. The figure of the hero appears once at the left edge of the surface. Thereafter a second partial rolling preserves the hero and the lion. PF 600 is dated 500/499 B.C.

PFS 931*   Cat.No. 270

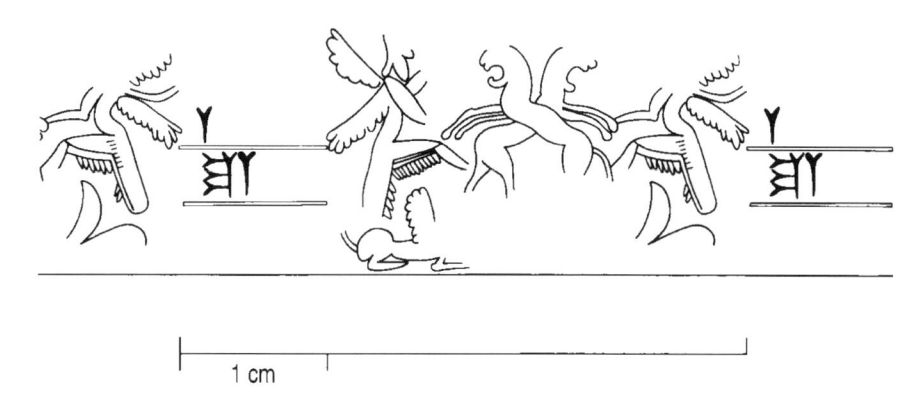

Seal Type:	Cylinder, Inscribed	Photograph:	Pl. 150c
Earliest Dated Application:	ND	Typology and Style:	II-C.4 — Modeled Style
Language of Inscription:	Elamite(?)		
Preserved Height of Image:	1.60 cm (incomp.)	Preserved Length of Image:	3.80 cm. (comp.)
Estimated Height of Original Seal:	NA	Estimated Diameter of Original Seal:	1.20 cm
Number of Impressions:	2	Quality of Impression:	Poor

Completeness of Image: Segment of middle and lower zone of design survives along its complete length

DESCRIPTION OF SEAL AS IMPRESSED IMAGE

One double encounter is depicted.

Two rampant lions cross bodies in center of design. To either side of this central group a two-winged hero stands on couchant winged creature of uncertain type.

Hero at left faces right, extending left arm (only partially preserved) upward toward head of lion facing him; hero extends right arm (only partially preserved) downward toward forelegs of same lion. Hero raises bent forward leg upward in vigorous striding pose apparently to place foot (not preserved) on hind leg of lion facing away from him. Hero is shown with profile torso.

Lion facing hero at left moves toward and faces him. Lion extends forelegs together downward, slightly bent, toward hero's forward leg; tail (only partially preserved) curves downward.

Hero at left wears Assyrian garment that leaves forward leg exposed below knee; decorative border and fringe are indicated along hem of garment over forward leg; fringe is indicated also along front edge of garment over rear leg. Rounded beard rests over his left upper arm; narrow rounded coiffure lies at back of hero's neck.

Lion facing hero at left has mouth open in roar.

Hero at right faces left, extending bent right arm downward to grasp upper foreleg of lion facing him; hero extends bent left arm (only partially preserved) upward behind head (presumably to hold weapon). Hero raises bent forward leg upward in vigorous striding pose apparently to place foot (not preserved) on hind leg of lion facing away from him. Hero is shown with profile torso.

Lion facing hero at right moves toward and faces him. Lion extends forelegs together downward, slightly bent, toward hero's forward leg.

Hero at right wears Assyrian garment that leaves forward leg exposed below knee; decorative border and fringe are indicated along hem of garment over forward leg and along front edge of garment over rear leg.

Lion facing hero at right has mouth open in roar.

Each winged pedestal creature, on which one of heroes stands, faces toward the central group of crossed lions. Tail of pedestal creature at left (only partially preserved) curves upward.

Inscription with case lines is in terminal field.

Lower edge of seal is preserved along complete length.

INSCRIPTION

Elamite(?)

Line   x+1. ⌜x⌝ [...]
        x+2. ⌜x⌝ [...]

Translation   ?

Two lines of inscription are preserved, oriented along the horizontal axis of the seal, with case lines. The two partially preserved signs are illegible.

COMMENTARY

The fusion of crossed animals with the action of heroic encounter scenes is rare in first millennium B.C. glyptic, at least according to evidence available at present. Only four examples are documented in the PFS corpus: PFS 931*, PFS 737 (Cat.No. 281), PFS 912 (Cat.No. 138), and PFS 952 (Cat.No. 227). When this fused imagery does occur, it seems to suggest the reworking specifically of heroic combat images of the Early Dynastic, Akkadian, and Old Babylonian periods (mid-third millennium B.C. through early centuries of the second millennium B.C.). PFS 931* evokes in general terms the monumentality and clarified compositional dynamics of certain Akkadian seals.[84] The elegant PFS 931* should be compared to PTS 8* (inscribed in Old Persian with the name of Xerxes) on the Persepolis Treasury tablets (Schmidt 1957, p. 22, pl. 5). On PTS 8* the two heroes combating crossed lions are dressed in Persian garb and their poses are less active. It is not clear whether they also stand on pedestal creatures, as do the heroes on PFS 931*.

Pedestal creatures supporting the actors on seals of heroic encounter are almost as rare in the PFS corpus as are crossed animals/creatures playing the role of controlled beings. Pedestal creatures occur definitively on only seven seals of heroic encounter in the PFS corpus: PFS 931*, PFS 31 (Cat.No. 172), PFS 36* (Cat.No. 5), PFS 164* (Cat.No. 20), PFS 396 (Cat.No. 178), PFS 523* (Cat.No. 209), and PFS 524 (Cat.No. 2).[85] In contrast to the extreme rarity of crossed animals figuring in the action of heroic encounter scenes, the crossed animal motif occurs quite frequently as a quarry of archers on seals of Volume II, for example, PFS 163 (II); and it figures significantly as a focal motif on seals of Volume III, for example, PFS 3 (III). In these two non-heroic scenarios the crossed animal motif finds parallels on seals beyond the Persepolis environs.[86]

For discussion of seals displaying two heroes involved in one encounter, but in a different format, see the commentary on PFS 1101 (Cat.No. 297).

The seal was not included in Garrison 1988; see, however, Garrison 1988, pp. 227–43, for discussion of the style and workshop of related seals.

For comparative illustrations including PFS 931*, see pls. 201h (heroes as winged humans), 214e (profile torsos), 217b (hero standing atop pedestal figure[s] or other supporting element), 240f (double hero encounters), 242c (heroic encounters fused with crossed animals), and 263h (inscriptions without panels, with horizontal case lines).

SEAL APPLICATION (SEE *APPENDIX ONE: CONCORDANCE OF SEALS TO TABLETS IN VOLUME I*)

PFS 931* occurs on the reverse and upper edge of PF 807. The rolling of PFS 931* on the reverse is complete and displays the inscription and the hero to the left of the crossed animals in the center. The rolling on the upper edge is complete and displays the inscription in the center. The date of PF 807 is unknown.

BIBLIOGRAPHY

Dusinberre 1997b, p. 124 (n. 61); Garrison and Dion 1999, pp. 9 (n. 9), 10 (n. 28).

---

84. For example, a cylinder from Tello now in the Louvre (Collon 1987, pp. 32–33, no. 95). Here, although the heroes are not standing on pedestal creatures, the composition exhibits the two distinct heroes combating from opposite sides the pair of crossed animals.
85. See Dusinberre 1997b for the significance of pedestal animals as an elite motif in early Achaemenid glyptic. At the time Dusinberre's article was written, the composition of the PFS 931* design was not fully understood due to the poor preservation of the two impressions. It is now clear that PFS 931* should belong in her listing in n. 57 rather than in n. 61.
86. For example, Amiet 1973b, pls. 7, no. 63 (archer seal with crossed animals from Susa); 5, no. 20 (seal impression from Susa with crossed animals as focal motif).

PFS 709　　　　　　　　　　　　　　　　　　　　　　　　　　　Cat.No. 271

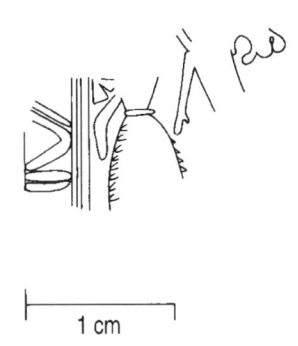

Seal Type:	Cylinder	Photograph:	Pl. 150e
Earliest Dated Application:	497/496 B.C.	Typology and Style:	II-C.4 — Fortification Style
Preserved Height of Image:	1.20 cm (incomp.)	Preserved Length of Image:	1.80 cm (incomp.)
Estimated Height of Original Seal:	NA	Estimated Diameter of Original Seal:	NA
Number of Impressions:	1	Quality of Impression:	Poor

Completeness of Image: Uneven segment of middle of design survives

DESCRIPTION OF SEAL AS IMPRESSED IMAGE

Hero apparently faces right, right arm presumably held up behind head wielding weapon (not preserved).

To right, rampant lion moves toward hero but turns its head away from him. Lion holds upper foreleg (only partially preserved) straight and extends it diagonally upward; lower foreleg is straight and extended downward in front of its body; mouth is open in roar.

Hero wears belted robe; fringe is indicated along both front edge and back edge of garment.

Linear elements attached to hero's back probably represent bottom edge of quiver and/or bow slung over hero's right shoulder.

To left, in terminal field, is partially preserved device consisting of vertical panel containing two horizontal elements, V-shaped element, and traces of diagonal element.

COMMENTARY

The design is difficult to reconstruct, but it has the main compositional scheme of a combat encounter. The element at left of the preserved design recalls the better-preserved device on PFS 435 (Cat.No. 310). In both designs the device is a symbol traditionally described as the "temple gate" or "temple shrine." Glyptic parallels occur from a range of periods.[87]

For comparative illustrations including PFS 709, see pls. 182g (robes with various features of detail), 246e (bows, arrows, quivers), and 255g (various devices and symbols).

SEAL APPLICATION (SEE APPENDIX ONE: CONCORDANCE OF SEALS TO TABLETS IN VOLUME I)

PFS 709 occurs on the left edge of PF 482. The partial rolling displays the hero in the center. PF 482 is dated 497/496 B.C.

BIBLIOGRAPHY

Garrison 1988, pp. 341–43.

---

87. See, for example, an Early Dynastic III banquet scene (Porada 1948, p. 16, no. 108, pl. 17, no. 108) and a Neo-Assyrian Linear Style worship scene (Porada 1948 p. 78, no. 652, pl. 95, no. 652). See also the "late Neo-Assyrian" cylinder excavated in the Persepolis Treasury (Schmidt 1957, pp. 43, 45, pl. 16: PT4 484).

Cat.No. 272   PFS 272*

Seal Type: Cylinder, Inscribed
Seal Type:	Cylinder, Inscribed	Photographs:	Pl. 151a–b
Earliest Dated Application:	ND	Typology and Style:	II-C.4 — Modeled Style
Language of Inscription:	Elamite		
Preserved Height of Image:	1.40 cm (incomp.)	Preserved Length of Image:	3.00 cm (incomp.)
Estimated Height of Original Seal:	NA	Estimated Diameter of Original Seal:	NA
Number of Impressions:	3	Quality of Impressions:	Fair

Completeness of Image: Segment of middle of design survives along most of its length

DESCRIPTION OF SEAL AS IMPRESSED IMAGE

Hero moves to left, extending bent right arm downward (elbow up) to grasp rampant lion by foreleg; left arm and upper body are not preserved. Hero raises bent forward leg to place foot on hindquarters of lion.

Lion moves away from hero in active striding pose but turns its head back toward him. Lion holds one foreleg slightly bent and extends it upward away from its body to left. Other foreleg is straight and extended downward behind forward leg of hero; underside of paw, with toes splayed, appears beyond hero's leg. Long tail curves between hero's legs, curling upward at its end.

Hero wears belted kilt; fringe is indicated along hem of garment over forward knee and between legs; band border is indicated along rear leg; sheath projects from back of waist.

Fur is rendered by crisp serrated edge along belly of lion; mane is indicated by spikes along contour of neck. Mouth is open in roar with pointed tongue indicated. Lion is ithyphallic.

Large paneled inscription is in terminal field.

Chip, apparently, is along lower right edge of inscription panel; another chip occurs in middle of third line of inscription.

INSCRIPTION

Elamite

Line   x+1. [...]
        x+2. ti-Hu-pan
        x+3. šak Kan-du(?)-
        x+4. ⌈x-x-na⌉

Translation   Šati(?)-Hupan son of Kandu...

Three lines of inscription are preserved, oriented along the horizontal axis of the seal, separated by case lines, and enclosed in a panel. The panel on the right side continues upward beyond the top case line and should indicate that there is another line of the inscription (our line x+1).

The du-sign in line x+3 is problematic since it lacks the small horizontal wedge at the upper left. Note how the last two horizontal wedges of the pan-sign in line x+2 actually overlap and extend beyond the vertical panel. It is reasonable to restore the first name as Šati(?)-Hupan (see PFS 4* [Cat.No. 292]). The texts with which PFS 272* is associated offer no assistance in determining the PN in the inscription.

COMMENTARY

See Garrison 1988 for style and workshop of PFS 272* and related seals. The rendering of this image is dramatic, with effective details.

For comparative illustrations including PFS 272*, see pls. 180g (kilts), 212h (heroic attitudes of combat encounter), 218d (comparative heroic proportions), and 262e (paneled inscriptions with horizontal case lines).

SEAL APPLICATION (SEE *APPENDIX ONE: CONCORDANCE OF SEALS TO TABLETS IN VOLUME I*)

PFS 272* occurs on the left edge of PF 1691, PF 1695, and PF 2064, with PFS 63 (Cat.No. 24) on the reverse and upper edge of each tablet. All impressions show some part of the inscription. Of the three partial impressions, one preserves only a full rolling of the inscription; one preserves a full rolling of the inscription and the lion; one displays the lion in the center with a partial rolling of the inscription at the left and the hero at the right. The dates of all tablets with PFS 272* are unknown.

BIBLIOGRAPHY

Garrison 1988, pp. 228–29, 236–40; Garrison and Dion 1999, pp. 9 (n. 20), 10 (n. 28).

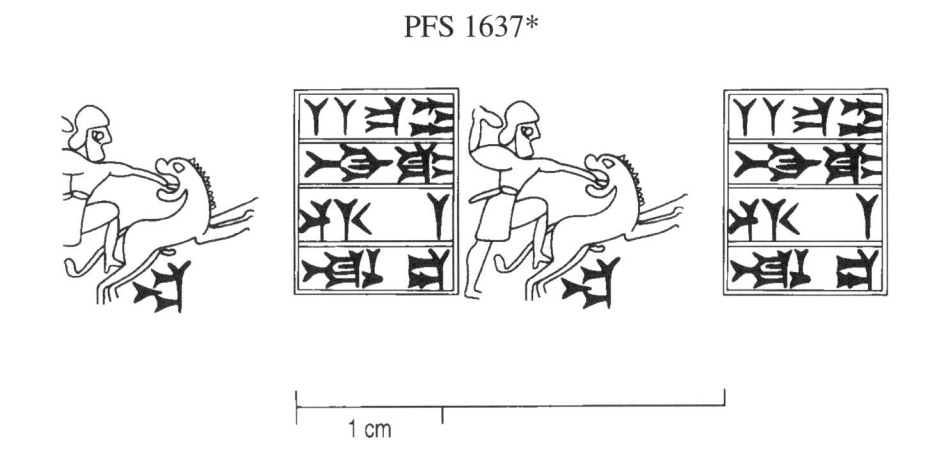

PFS 1637*   Cat.No. 273

Seal Type:	Cylinder, Inscribed	Photograph:	Pl. 151d
Earliest Dated Application:	ND	Typology and Style:	II-C.4 — Modeled Style
Language of Inscription:	Elamite		
Preserved Height of Image:	1.50 cm (incomp.)	Preserved Length of Image:	2.90 cm (comp.)
Estimated Height of Original Seal:	1.70 cm	Estimated Diameter of Original Seal:	0.90 cm
Number of Impressions:	1	Quality of Impression:	Good

Completeness of Image: Complete except for upper edge and lower edge and portions of inscription

DESCRIPTION OF SEAL AS IMPRESSED IMAGE

Hero faces right, extending straight left arm to grasp tongue inside mouth of rampant lion; hero extends bent right arm upward behind head to hold dagger. Hero, in striding pose, raises bent forward leg to place his foot on lion's hind leg.

Lion moves away from hero but turns its head back toward him. Lion holds both forelegs straight and extended upward in front of body; long tail curves downward behind hero's forward leg, bending upward at its end with thickened termination.

Hero wears belted kilt; sheath projects from back of waist. Squared beard rests over hero's left shoulder; rounded coiffure rests at back of neck.

Mane of lion is rendered by crisp serrated edge along contour of neck; mouth is open in roar with tongue indicated. Lion is ithyphallic.

In field below lion is na-sign; paneled inscription is in terminal field.

INSCRIPTION

Elamite

Line
1. v.Ma(?)-x-
2. ak šak
3. Hu-⌈x-⌉
4. ra-du(!)-
5. na

Translation   Ma...ak(?) son of Hu...radu

There are five lines to the inscription. The first four lines are oriented along the horizontal axis of the seal, separated by case lines, and enclosed in a panel. The na-sign of line 5 is oriented along the horizontal axis of the seal and occurs outside of the panel under the rampant lion. Line 1 appears to begin with the DIŠ-sign, followed by another vertical wedge that we take to be a component of the second sign, perhaps ma, though the left-hand vertical wedge is separated from the rest of the sign. In line 3, only a vertical wedge of the second sign is preserved. All the remaining signs are clearly written and well formed.

COMMENTARY

Neither of the personal names in the seal inscription occurs in PF 2085, the sole tablet bearing PFS 1637*.

The placement of the hero's hand, grasping the tongue in the open mouth of the lion, is unique in the PFS corpus. See Garrison 1988 for the style and workshop of PFS 1637* and related seals.

For comparative illustrations including PFS 1637*, see pls. 209h (arm positions of heroic combat), 213i (heroic attitudes of combat encounter), 233i (ithyphallic animals/creatures), and 263e (paneled inscriptions with horizontal case lines).

SEAL APPLICATION (SEE *APPENDIX ONE: CONCORDANCE OF SEALS TO TABLETS IN VOLUME I*)

PFS 1637* occurs on the reverse of PF 2085. The rolling originally was very long, but the left half of it was covered over by the cuneiform text. The remaining impression preserves the entire length of the seal design and displays the inscription and the hero in the center. PFS 12b (II) appears directly under PFS 1637*. The date of PF 2085 is unknown.

BIBLIOGRAPHY

Garrison 1988, pp. 228–29, 236–40; Garrison and Dion 1999, p. 10 (n. 28).

II-C.5. WINGED LION CREATURES

PFS 100 — Cat.No. 274

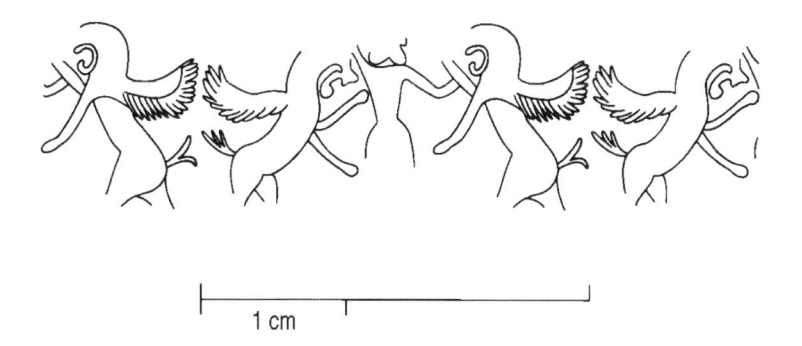

|— 1 cm —|

Seal Type:	Cylinder	Photographs:	Pl. 152a–b
Earliest Dated Application:	500/499 B.C.	Typology and Style:	II-C.5 — Fortification Style
Preserved Height of Image:	1.30 cm (incomp.)	Preserved Length of Image:	2.70 cm (comp.)
Estimated Height of Original Seal:	NA	Estimated Diameter of Original Seal:	0.90 cm
Number of Impressions:	4	Quality of Impressions:	Fair

Completeness of Image: Large segment of middle of design survives along its complete length

DESCRIPTION OF SEAL AS IMPRESSED IMAGE

Hero presumably faces right, extending bent left arm outward to grasp rampant winged lion creature by upper foreleg; hero extends straight right arm (only partially preserved) upward behind head (presumably to hold weapon).

Creature moves toward and faces hero. Creature holds upper foreleg (only partially preserved) straight and extends it upward toward hero's head; lower foreleg is straight, paw upturned, and extended downward toward hero's leg; short bifurcated tail extends diagonally upward.

Hero wears garment of uncertain type; hero has rounded beard over his left shoulder; rounded coiffure rests at back of neck.

Creature has mouth open in roar.

To left of hero rampant winged lion creature moves right toward hero. Creature holds upper foreleg slightly curved and extended upward toward hero's chest; lower foreleg is straight and extended downward toward hero's thigh; short tail with three-pronged termination extends diagonally upward; mouth is open in roar.

COMMENTARY

Koch (1990) assigns PFS 100 to Irdabada, a grain official in her Elam Region VI. She places him at Hutpirri.

The composition at first glance appears to show a control encounter, but the angle of the raised right arm of the hero seems to indicate a combat encounter. This particular compositional variation is rare among seals of heroic encounter in the PFS corpus.

SEAL APPLICATION (SEE APPENDIX ONE: CONCORDANCE OF SEALS TO TABLETS IN VOLUME I)

PFS 100 occurs only on the left edge of tablets that it seals. A few impressions show lateral distortion. No impression preserves the entire length of the seal design. Of the four partial applications, one displays the hero in the center; one displays the creature to the right of the hero in the center; one preserves only the creature to the right of the hero; one preserves only the two creatures. PF 467 and PF 469 are the earliest tablets with PFS 100 and are both dated 500/499 B.C.

BIBLIOGRAPHY

Garrison 1988, pp. 326–30, 335; Koch 1990, p. 69 (n. 307).

Cat.No. 275   PFS 146

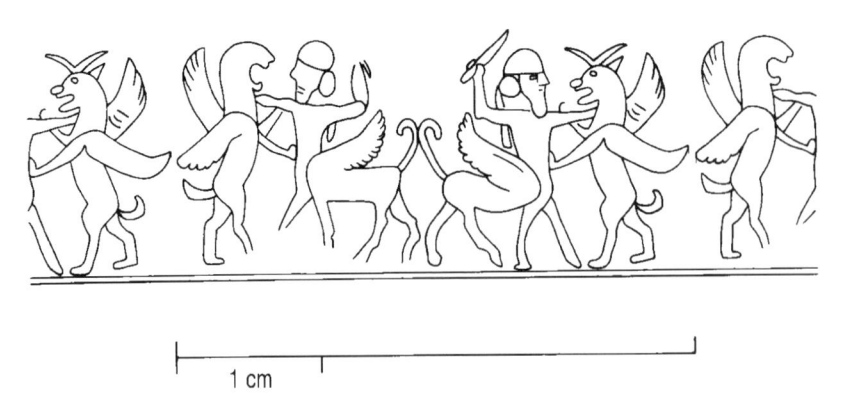

Seal Type: Cylinder
Earliest Dated Application: 501(?) B.C.
Preserved Height of Image: 1.70 cm (incomp.)
Estimated Height of Original Seal: 1.90 cm
Number of Impressions: 5

Photograph: Pl. 152d
Typology and Style: II-C.5 — Fortification Style
Preserved Length of Image: 3.60 cm (comp.)
Estimated Diameter of Original Seal: 1.10 cm
Quality of Impressions: Fair

Completeness of Image: Complete except for upper edge and details

DESCRIPTION OF SEAL AS IMPRESSED IMAGE

Two discrete heroic encounters are depicted. The two heroes are marchant winged human-headed bull or lion creatures with human torsos and arms. They stand back to back, tails curling upward and touching.

Hero at left faces left, extending straight right arm outward to grasp rampant winged lion creature by throat; hero extends bent right arm upward behind head to hold weapon of uncertain type (only pointed end of hilt is preserved).

Winged lion creature moves right, toward hero. Creature holds upper foreleg straight and extends it upward to place paw on hero's upper arm; lower foreleg is straight and extended downward to place paw at hero's waist; short thick tail curves upward.

Hero at left has rounded, striated beard that rests over its right shoulder; round coiffure rests high, at back of head. Pointed object under left arm represents end of streamer (only partially preserved) attached to his domed headdress.

Winged lion creature has two wings indicated, upper extending diagonally upward from its back, lower extending diagonally downward; mouth is open in roar.

Hero at right faces right, extending straight left arm outward to grasp rampant winged horned lion creature by throat; hero extends bent right arm upward behind head to hold dagger.

Winged horned lion creature moves left toward hero. Lion creature holds upper foreleg straight and extended upward to hero's upper arm; lower foreleg is straight and extended downward to place paw on hero's waist; short thick tail curves upward.

Hero at right has long rounded beard that rests along chest; round coiffure rests high, at back of head. Streamer hangs from domed headdress.

Winged horned lion creature has two wings indicated, upper extending diagonally upward from its neck, lower extending diagonally downward. Two long curved horns emerge from top of its head; triangular-shaped ear is at back of head; creature has mouth open in roar.

Line border is preserved at bottom of design.

COMMENTARY

Based upon Q texts protocol, PFS 146 should belong to Karkiš, described as "of the place Šurauša, formerly of Babylon" in PF 1541, in which he received beer rations in year 23.12 (498 B.C.) while on his way to Šurauša under the authorization (*halmi*) of the king. The seal also occurs on the reverse of PF 862–863, where again

Karkiš received rations. In PF 682 (H text, receipts by officials) he received beer rations in year 20+xth while on his way to Šurauša under the authorization (*halmi*) of the king. In PF 683 (H text) he received rations in year 23.12 at Naširmannu under the authorization (*halmi*) of the king. These texts seem concerned with one and the same trip. This individual is distinct from the Karkiš who was a high-ranking official and used PFS 1* (Cat.No. 182).

The design is unique, interesting, and also well executed. The two scenes of heroic encounter are mirror images. The curved tails of the hero creatures combine with their rear hind legs to create an elegant negative space. See the commentary on PFS 131 (Cat.No. 170) for discussion of designs with two discrete heroic encounters depicted.

For comparative illustrations including PFS 146, see pls. 186g (headdresses), 200b (heroes as various composite creatures), 240a (double encounter images), and 289c (personal seals of various receivers).

SEAL APPLICATION (SEE *APPENDIX ONE: CONCORDANCE OF SEALS TO TABLETS IN VOLUME I*)

PFS 146 occurs on the reverse of PF 682–683 and PF 1541; on PF 683 it also occurs on the bottom edge. On the reverse of PF 682–683 the seal is inverted. On the reverse of PF 1541 the seal is applied twice, one impression directly above the other. Applications of the seal are clear and show little or no distortion. In four impressions the seal is rolled for at least one complete turn, preserving the entire length of the seal design. Of these four applications, two display the right heroic encounter in the center; one displays the winged lion creature in the left heroic encounter in the center; one displays the winged lion creature in the right heroic encounter in the center. The remaining partial rolling displays the two heroes in the center. On the reverse of PF 682 the seal clearly was applied before the text since several cuneiform wedges cut into the bottom of the impression. PF 682 is the earliest dated tablet with PFS 146. The year, as rendered by Hallock (1969, p. 212), is "20 + xth year" — or 502 B.C. + x. Thus we have given 501 B.C.(?) as the earliest dated application in the catalog header.

BIBLIOGRAPHY

Garrison 1988, pp. 264–68; Garrison 1998, p. 121 (n. 15).

Cat.No. 276   PFS 1406

Seal Type:	Cylinder	Photograph:	Pl. 153a
Earliest Dated Application:	500 B.C.	Typology and Style:	II-C.5 — Fortification Style
Preserved Height of Image:	1.60 cm (incomp.)	Preserved Length of Image:	3.20 cm (incomp.)
Estimated Height of Original Seal:	NA	Estimated Diameter of Original Seal:	NA
Number of Impressions:	1	Quality of Impression:	Poor

Completeness of Image: Segment of middle of design survives

DESCRIPTION OF SEAL AS IMPRESSED IMAGE

Hero faces right, extending bent left arm upward to grasp rampant winged horned lion creature by horn; hero extends bent right arm upward behind head to hold weapon of uncertain type (only partially preserved).

Creature moves left toward hero. Creature holds upper foreleg bent and extends it upward toward hero's waist; lower foreleg (only partially preserved) is straight and extends vertically downward; short pointed tail extends diagonally downward.

Hero wears Assyrian garment that leaves forward leg exposed. Short pointed beard rests above hero's left shoulder; rounded coiffure rests at back of neck. Corner of polos headdress is preserved at back of head.

Thick horn (only partially preserved) emerges from top of creature's head. Mane is rendered by blunt serrations along edged contour of neck; edging is also indicated along upper contour of wing. Fur is rendered along front of chest by series of small dots; mouth is open in roar.

At far right of impression, in terminal field, very poorly preserved winged(?) creature of uncertain type moves to left but turns its head (on very long neck) back to right; creature (marchant?) holds one foreleg straight and extends it diagonally upward in front of chest.

COMMENTARY

Based on Q texts protocol, PFS 1406 should belong to Ratešda the *hupika* (OD), who in year 22.3 (500 B.C.) received flour rations while on his way to Arachosia under the authority (*halmi*) of the king. PF 1510 preserves the only occurrence of the name Ratešda in the PF texts.

See Garrison 1988 for this important artist, who appears to work in the manner of the artist of PFS 49 (Cat.No. 23).

For comparative illustrations including PFS 1406, see pl. 291g (personal seals of various travelers).

SEAL APPLICATION (SEE *APPENDIX ONE: CONCORDANCE OF SEALS TO TABLETS IN VOLUME I*)

PFS 1406 occurs on the reverse of PF 1510. The partial rolling displays the winged creature held by hero in the center. The seal clearly was applied before the text since several cuneiform wedges cut into the top of the impression. PF 1510 is dated 500 B.C.

BIBLIOGRAPHY

Garrison 1988, pp. 290–91, 348–52, 495.

PFS 54*   Cat.No. 277

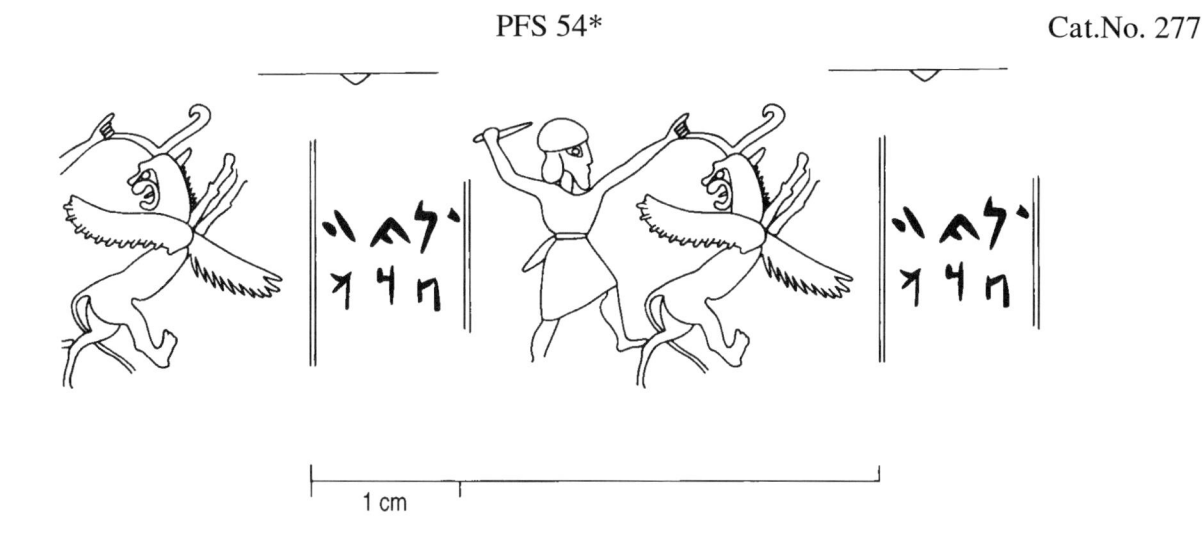

Seal Type:	Cylinder, Inscribed	Photographs:	Pl. 154a–c
Earliest Dated Application:	504/503 B.C.	Typology and Style:	II-C.5 — Modeled Style
Language of Inscription:	Aramaic		
Preserved Height of Image:	2.00 cm (incomp.)	Preserved Length of Image:	3.90 cm (comp.)
Estimated Height of Original Seal:	2.20 cm	Estimated Diameter of Original Seal:	1.20 cm
Number of Impressions:	10	Quality of Impressions:	Fair

Completeness of Image: Almost complete except for parts of upper edge, lower edge and some signs of the inscription

DESCRIPTION OF SEAL AS IMPRESSED IMAGE

Hero faces right, extending straight left arm upward to grasp horn of rampant winged horned lion creature; hero extends bent right arm upward behind head to hold dagger. Hero, in striding pose, raises forward leg to place his foot on rear hind leg of creature.

Creature moves away from hero but turns its head back toward him. Creature holds both forelegs straight and extends them diagonally upward in front of neck. Creature raises forward hind leg, paw upturned; tail curves downward between its hind legs.

Hero wears belted tunic; sheath projects from back of waist. Hero perhaps wears domed headdress. Beard terminates in blunt point over left shoulder; rounded coiffure rests at back of neck.

Two wings are indicated on creature, one extended to each side of its body. Two long horns with hooked terminations emerge from top of creature's head; pointed ear is at back of head. Mane is rendered by finely serrated edge along contour of neck; mouth is open in roar with small pointed tongue indicated. Paw of forward hind leg is flexed and looks rather like human foot.

Paneled inscription is in terminal field.

Portions of chipped edge of seal are preserved at top of design above inscription.

INSCRIPTION

Aramaic

    Line   x+1. [...]
                   x+2. NH⌈x⌉
                   x+3. ḤDK
                   x+4. [...]

    Translation   ?

There appear to be at least three lines in the inscription oriented along the horizontal axis of the seal. There seems to be enough space for a fourth line, but no traces survive. The inscription is set off by two vertical panels, but no horizontal case lines are visible in any impression. The letters that we can discern appear as copied, but we are unable to suggest a reading.

COMMENTARY

Koch (1990) assigns PFS 54* to Naptaš, a subordinate of Uštana, director of grain cultivation in her Elam Region VI. Naptaš traveled frequently and his seal occurs with control officials of various places.

This is a large seal. See Garrison 1988 for the style and workshop of PFS 54* and related seals.

For comparative illustrations including PFS 54*, see pls. 185a (tunics), 222d (lions and lion creatures), 230e (feet of animals and creatures), and 261g (paneled inscriptions without case lines).

SEAL APPLICATION (SEE *APPENDIX ONE: CONCORDANCE OF SEALS TO TABLETS IN VOLUME I*)

PFS 54* occurs on the reverse of PF 448, PF 506, PF 558, PF 575, PF 1021, and PF 1181; on PF 1037 it occurs on the reverse and left edge; on PF 972 and PF 1019 the seal occurs only on the upper edge. On the reverse of PF 448, PF 506, PF 588, PF 575, PF 1019, and PF 1037 the seal is inverted. Rollings shows little or no distortion. Of the total ten impressions, seven preserve some part of the inscription. In only one impression is the seal rolled for at least one complete turn, preserving the entire length of the seal design. This rolling displays the inscription in the center. Of the remaining nine partial rollings, two display the inscription at the left of the impression, the hero at the right; two display the creature in the center, one with a full rolling of the inscription at the right of the impression, the other with a partial rolling of the inscription at the right of the impression; two preserve only the creature and the inscription (at the right of the impression); two preserve only the hero (at the left of the impression) and the creature; one preserves only the creature. On PF 1021 and PF 1037 the seal clearly was applied before the text since several cuneiform wedges cut into the top or bottom of the impressions. PF 448, PF 506, PF 558, PF 575, PF 1019, and PF 1181 are the earliest dated tablets with PFS 54* and are all dated 504/503 B.C.

BIBLIOGRAPHY

Aperghis 1999, pp. 176–78; Garrison 1988, pp. 228–29, 236–40, 332, 494; Garrison and Dion 1999, p. 10; Koch 1986, pp. 146–47; Koch 1990, pp. 156–57, 297–98, 307.

Cat.No. 278   PFS 769*

Seal Type:	Cylinder, Inscribed	Photograph:	Pl. 155a
Earliest Dated Application:	498/497 B.C.	Typology and Style:	II-C.5 — Modeled Style
Language of Inscription:	Elamite		
Preserved Height of Image:	1.60 cm (incomp.)	Preserved Length of Image:	3.60 cm (incomp.)
Estimated Height of Original Seal:	1.80 cm	Estimated Diameter of Original Seal:	NA
Number of Impressions:	3	Quality of Impressions:	All preserve excellent detail

Completeness of Image: Large segment of middle of design survives for most of its length

DESCRIPTION OF SEAL AS IMPRESSED IMAGE

Hero faces right, extending bent left arm upward to grasp sejant winged horned lion creature by horn; hero extends bent right arm upward behind head, presumably to hold weapon (not preserved). Hero, in striding pose, raises bent forward leg to place his foot on hindquarters of creature.

Creature's body faces right, its head turned back toward hero. Creature holds upper foreleg straight and extends it diagonally upward, touching or almost touching inscription panel; lower foreleg is straight and extended downward; thick tail curls upward with forked termination.

Hero wears double-belted kilt that leaves forward leg exposed; fringe is indicated at front edge of garment along rear leg; curved sheath projects from back of waist. Short pointed beard rests over hero's left shoulder; rounded coiffure rests at back of neck. Hero perhaps wears domed headdress.

Mane of creature is rendered by rounded projections along contour of neck. Long curved horn emerges from front of creature's head; large ear is at back of head; creature has mouth open in roar with pointed tongue indicated.

Large paneled inscription is in terminal field.

INSCRIPTION

Elamite

Line
 x+1. [x] AN ⌈x⌉
 x+2. šak I-[(x)-]na
 x+3. ⌈x x (x)⌉-ik
 x+4. [...]

Translation PN_1 son of PN_2

Four lines of the inscription are preserved, oriented along the horizontal axis of the seal, separated by case lines, and enclosed in a panel. Too little of the inscription remains to suggest a reading. There is no apparent overlap or join between the components of the inscription that appear to either side of the heroic encounter. It is tempting to join the two sections in the drawing, but they make the inscription no clearer, and experiments with placing them together tended to disguise problems of spacing. Therefore, the drawing here presents the inscription as preserved on the impressions.

COMMENTARY

See Garrison 1988 for the style and workshop of PFS 769* and related seals.

For comparative illustrations including PFS 769*, see pls. 180h (kilts), 213a (heroic attitudes of combat encounter), 218h (comparative heroic proportions), and 262h (paneled inscriptions with horizontal case lines).

SEAL APPLICATION (SEE *APPENDIX ONE: CONCORDANCE OF SEALS TO TABLETS IN VOLUME I*)

PFS 769* occurs twice on the reverse and once on the left edge of PF 548. The rollings on the reverse are applied one directly above the other. All three rollings are extremely carefully applied and show some part of the inscription. The three rollings all display the hero and the creature in the center, with partial rollings of the inscription at the right edge and left edge of the impressions. PF 548 is dated 498/497 B.C.

BIBLIOGRAPHY

Garrison 1988, pp. 228–29, 236–40, 352, 479–80; Garrison and Dion 1999, p. 10 (n. 28).

Cat.No. 279 PFS 1123

|—————————————|
  1 cm

Seal Type:	Cylinder	Photograph:	Pl. 155c
Earliest Dated Application:	ND	Typology and Style:	II-C.5 — Linear Styles
Preserved Height of Image:	1.50 cm (incomp.)	Preserved Length of Image:	2.70 cm (comp.)
Estimated Height of Original Seal:	1.70 cm	Estimated Diameter of Original Seal:	0.90 cm
Number of Impressions:	3	Quality of Impressions:	Fair

Completeness of Image: Almost complete except for upper edge and lower edge

DESCRIPTION OF SEAL AS IMPRESSED IMAGE

Hero faces left, right leg bent, extending straight right arm upward to grasp rampant winged lion creature by snout; hero extends left arm (only partially preserved) upward behind head (presumably to hold weapon).

Creature moves away from hero but turns its head back toward him. Creature holds upper foreleg straight and extends it diagonally upward in front of neck; lower foreleg, paw upturned, is extended straight downward. Apparently creature has two tails. Upper tail is short and curves upward, lower tail is long and thin and curves upward with tufted termination.

Hero wears Assyrian garment that leaves forward leg exposed. Short pointed beard rests over hero's right shoulder; small rounded coiffure rests at back of neck.

Lion creature has mouth open in roar.

Six-pointed star is in lower field below belly of rampant winged lion creature grasped by hero.

In terminal field, rampant winged wild goat creatures pose heraldically to either side of elaborate stylized tree of uncertain type (only partially preserved). Each goat creature moves toward tree but turns its head away. Each creature holds upper foreleg (only partially preserved) diagonally upward toward tree; lower foreleg is bent and extended downward to place hoof on tree. Creature to left has one long curved horn emerging from top of its head; pointed ear is at back of head. Short tail curves upward with tufted termination. Creature to right has two wings, upper wing extending upward from lower wing; short tail curves downward. Tree consists of series of long thin vertical elements. Angular branch terminating in three dots emerges from either side of lower part of tree; two sets of downward-curving elements are preserved at top.

COMMENTARY

The composition could conceivably be a control encounter (with the hero grasping horn of the rampant winged goat creature immediately to the right). The hero's bent forward leg favors the combat scenario.

The style is a curious mix of Linear Styles (for the human forms) and the Fortification Style (for the animal forms). The composition is quite sophisticated, interlocking the two themes of heroic encounter and heraldic group, by careful placement of animal forelegs and wings. The combination of heroic encounter with heraldic animals or creatures forming a discrete unit in the terminal field occurs occasionally herein; compare PFS 80 (Cat.No. 202) and PFS 225 (Cat.No. 46).

For a similar stylization of trees among the images of heroic encounter in Volume I, see PFS 225 (Cat.No. 46) and PFS 1072 (Cat.No. 61).

For comparative illustrations including PFS 1123, see pls. 224g (deer, goats, sheep, and related winged creatures), 253j (stars, rosettes), and 256d (stylized trees).

Seal Application (see *Appendix One: Concordance of Seals to Tablets in Volume I*)

PFS 1123 occurs on the reverse, upper edge, and left edge of PF 1179. No other seal is used on the tablet. Two rollings preserve the entire length of the seal design; that on the reverse displays the hero and the winged goat creature to right in the center; that on the upper edge displays the tree in the center. The partial rolling on the left edge displays the heroic encounter in the center. On the reverse the seal clearly was applied before the text since several cuneiform wedges cut into the top of the impression. The date of PF 1179 is unknown.

Bibliography

Garrison 1988, pp. 437–39, 496, 531.

II-C.6. WINGED HUMAN-FACED/HUMAN-HEADED LION CREATURES

PFS 414   Cat.No. 280

Seal Type:	Cylinder	Photograph:	Pl. 156a
Earliest Dated Application:	497/496 B.C.	Typology and Style:	II-C.6 — Fortification Style
Preserved Height of Image:	1.30 cm (incomp.)	Preserved Length of Image:	1.90 cm (incomp.)
Estimated Height of Original Seal:	NA	Estimated Diameter of Original Seal:	NA
Number of Impressions:	1	Quality of Impression:	Poor

Completeness of Image: Segment of middle of design survives

Description of Seal as Impressed Image

 Hero faces left, extending straight right arm (only partially preserved) upward to grasp rampant winged human-headed lion creature; left arm is not preserved.

 Creature moves right toward hero. Creature holds upper foreleg curved and extended upward to hero's right arm; lower foreleg is bent in two places and extended downward to place upturned paw at hero's waist; straight tail (only partially preserved) extends diagonally downward.

 Hero wears belted garment of uncertain type; upper part of garment has triangular decoration in its center and series of small rectangles along outer edge; fringe is indicated along hip. Pointed beard rests over hero's right shoulder.

 Creature has two wings, upper wing extended diagonally upward from its back, lower wing extended diagonally downward from its back. Creature's beard terminates in blunt point over its chest; rounded coiffure is at back of head. Creature is ithyphallic.

Commentary

 Owing to its fragmentary preservation, the exact nature of the composition cannot be determined. The hard, linear contours of the human figure and the elaborate decoration on the garment are unusual in the Fortification Style.

396 SEALS ON THE PERSEPOLIS FORTIFICATION TABLETS, VOLUME I: IMAGES OF HEROIC ENCOUNTER

For comparative illustrations including PFS 414, see pls. 182d (robes with various features of detail), 233d (ithyphallic animals/creatures), and 234h (human-headed/human-faced creatures).

SEAL APPLICATION (SEE APPENDIX ONE: CONCORDANCE OF SEALS TO TABLETS IN VOLUME I)

PFS 414 occurs on the left edge of PF 106. The partial rolling preserves only the hero and the creature to left. PF 106 is dated 497/496 B.C.

BIBLIOGRAPHY

Dusinberre 1997b, p. 128 (n. 131); Garrison 1988, pp. 254–55, 297, 300–01, 483.

II-C.18. ANIMALS OF UNCERTAIN TYPE

Cat.No. 281   PFS 737

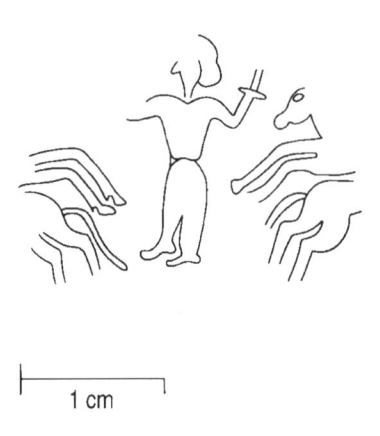

Seal Type:	Cylinder	Photograph:	Pl. 156c
Earliest Dated Application:	ND	Typology and Style:	II-C.18 — Broad and Flat Styles
Preserved Height of Image:	1.70 cm (incomp.)	Preserved Length of Image:	2.40 cm (incomp.)
Estimated Height of Original Seal:	NA	Estimated Diameter of Original Seal:	NA
Number of Impressions:	1	Quality of Impression:	Fair

Completeness of Image: Segment of middle of design survives

DESCRIPTION OF SEAL AS IMPRESSED IMAGE

Hero faces left, extending right arm (only partially preserved) toward group of two crossed rampant animals of uncertain type; hero extends bent left arm upward behind head to hold weapon of uncertain type (only part of blade and hand-guard preserved).

Each animal in group holds forelegs bent and extended outward together in front of body; each tail curves downward.

Hero apparently wears belted trousers. Pointed beard rests above hero's chest; rounded coiffure rests at back of head.

COMMENTARY

The coarse carving is typical of seals carved in the Broad and Flat Styles. The fusion of heroic *combat* encounter with crossed animals, as in PFS 737, occurs on only two other seals herein, PFS 931* (Cat.No. 270) and PFS 952 (Cat.No. 227). The fusion of heroic *control* encounter with crossed animals occurs once on PFS 912 (Cat.No. 138). See the commentary on PFS 931* (Cat.No. 270) for a discussion of crossed animals.

For comparative illustrations including PFS 737, see pls. 217g (hero suspended high in design field) and 242a (heroic encounters fused with crossed animals).

SEAL APPLICATION (SEE *APPENDIX ONE: CONCORDANCE OF SEALS TO TABLETS IN VOLUME I*)

PFS 737 occurs on the reverse of PF 510. The partial rolling carefully displays the hero in the center framed by the forelegs and hind legs of the crossed animals at each end of the impression. The date of PF 510 is unknown.

BIBLIOGRAPHY

Garrison 1988, pp. 421–23.

II-C.19. WINGED CREATURES OF UNCERTAIN TYPE

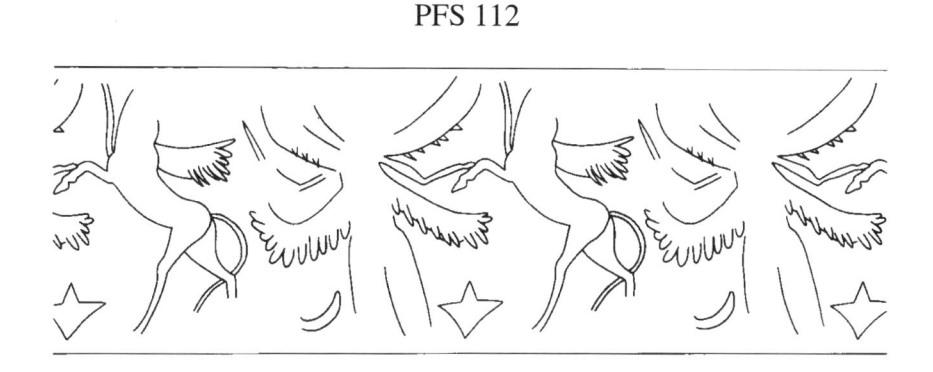

PFS 112   Cat.No. 282

Seal Type:	Cylinder	Photograph:	Pl. 156e
Earliest Dated Application:	502 B.C.	Typology and Style:	II-C.19 — Fortification Style
Preserved Height of Image:	1.90 cm (comp.)	Preserved Length of Image:	2.70 cm (comp.)
Estimated Height of Original Seal:	1.90 cm	Estimated Diameter of Original Seal:	0.90 cm
Number of Impressions:	7	Quality of Impressions:	Poor

Completeness of Image: Almost complete except for details along upper edge and lower edge

DESCRIPTION OF SEAL AS IMPRESSED IMAGE

Four-winged hero moves to right(?), extending bent left arm outward to grasp rampant winged creature of uncertain type by lower hind leg; hero extends bent right arm upward behind head to hold dagger.

Creature moves left toward hero but must turn its head away from him (based on position of neck and available space). Creature holds upper foreleg curved and extended vertically upward in front of neck; lower foreleg is slightly bent and extended upward toward hero's lower wing; tail curves downward between its legs.

Hero appears to wear Assyrian garment that leaves forward leg exposed.

Winged creature has one wing emerging from base of long, muscular neck.

Crescent (only partially preserved) is in lower field below hero's lower right wing; fragmentary star or a trefoil shape is in lower field below hero's lower left wing.

Edge of seal is preserved at top and bottom of design.

COMMENTARY

PFS 112 occurs only on the reverse of L1 texts (regular monthly rations with *gal makip*) and always with PFS 6 (Cat.No. 304), the personal seal of Manukka, a supplier of workers and animals in Koch's (1990) Shiraz Region II and Persepolis Region I, on the left edge. The texts seem to deal with the supplying of one work group.

All impressions of the seal are very poor and have low relief. The seal appears to have been very worn. The trefoil shape is unique among seals of heroic encounter in the PFS corpus. It is not a common symbol elsewhere, but it is similar to the trefoil floral device atop two poles on an Achaemenid cylinder purchased in Iraq in the nineteenth century and now in the British Museum (BM 89352: Collon 1987, pp. 182–83, no. 864). On BM 89352, the well-preserved detailing reveals floral qualities.

For comparative illustrations including PFS 112, see pls. 201c (heroes as winged humans), 208d (arm positions of heroic combat), and 252d (crescents and stars).

SEAL APPLICATION (SEE *APPENDIX ONE: CONCORDANCE OF SEALS TO TABLETS IN VOLUME I*)

With one exception (PF 980, on the upper edge only) PFS 112 always occurs on the reverse of tablets that it seals. On PF 1674 the seal occurs both on the reverse and the upper edge. On the reverse of PF 977–979 and PF 1031 the seal is inverted. Most impressions exhibit lateral distortion. Because of the small size of the seal, all seven impressions preserve the entire seal design. Of these seven applications, five display the hero in the center; two display the creature in the center. On the reverse of PF 977–979 and PF 1674 the seal clearly was applied before the text since several cuneiform wedges cut into the bottom or top of the impressions. PF 977 and PF 978 are the earliest dated tablets with PFS 112 and are both dated 502 B.C.

BIBLIOGRAPHY

Garrison 1988, pp. 313–16; Garrison 1998, p. 121 (n. 15); Koch 1990, p. 45.

Cat.No. 283   PFS 1119

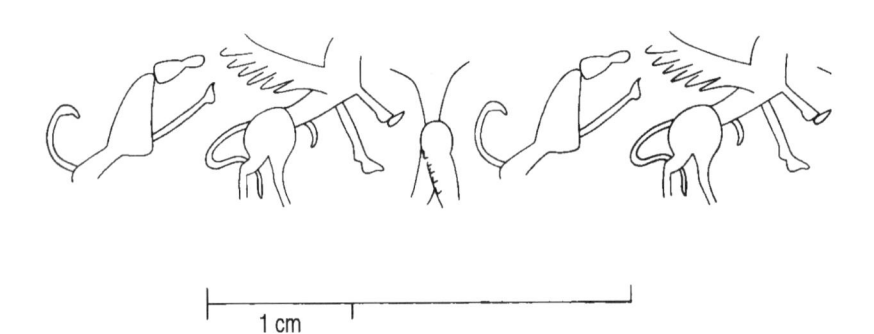

Seal Type:	Cylinder	Photograph:	Pl. 157a
Earliest Dated Application:	505/504 B.C.	Typology and Style:	II-C.19 — Diverse Styles
Preserved Height of Image:	1.20 cm (incomp.)	Preserved Length of Image:	2.90 cm (comp.)
Estimated Height of Original Seal:	NA	Estimated Diameter of Original Seal:	0.90 cm
Number of Impressions:	1	Quality of Impression:	Fair

Completeness of Image: Large segment of middle of design survives along its complete length

DESCRIPTION OF SEAL AS IMPRESSED IMAGE

Hero moves to left, apparently extending right arm (only partially preserved) toward rampant winged creature of uncertain type; hero apparently extends left arm (only partially preserved) upward behind head (presumably to hold weapon).

Creature moves right toward hero. Creature holds upper foreleg straight, hoof upturned and extended downward toward hero's waist; lower foreleg is straight, hoof upturned and extended downward toward hero's leg. Tail curves downward between its hind legs. Curved element protruding from belly apparently indicates ithyphallic aspect.

Hero apparently wears belted Assyrian garment that leaves forward leg exposed; fringe is indicated along front edge of garment over rear leg.

In terminal field, rampant animal of uncertain type moves right toward rear of creature held by hero. Animal holds one foreleg straight and extended upward toward creature's wing; tail curls upward.

COMMENTARY

The deep engraving recalls the Modeled Style, but the outline is very hard and linear and the animal forms are quite thin (closer to the Fortification Style). The carving of the forepart of the animal in the terminal field is an anomaly. Its shared traits with a seal acquired in Samarkand (Collon 1987, no. 602) raise intriguing questions.

For comparative illustrations including PFS 1119, see pl. 233h (ithyphallic animals/creatures).

SEAL APPLICATION (SEE *APPENDIX ONE: CONCORDANCE OF SEALS TO TABLETS IN VOLUME I*)

PFS 1119 occurs on the reverse of PF 1177, with PFS 1060 (III) above it. The rolling preserves the entire length of the seal design and displays the hero and the rampant animal in the terminal field in the center. PF 1177 is dated 505/504 B.C.

BIBLIOGRAPHY

Garrison 1988, pp. 459–60.

II-E. HERO THREATENS INVERTED ANIMAL OR CREATURE, WEAPON HELD DOWN BEHIND BODY

II-E.4. LIONS

PFS 114 — Cat.No. 284

Seal Type:	Cylinder	Photograph:	Pl. 157c
Earliest Dated Application:	499 B.C.	Typology and Style:	II-E.4 — Fortification Style
Preserved Height of Image:	1.60 cm (comp.)	Preserved Length of Image:	2.20 cm (comp.)
Estimated Height of Original Seal:	1.60 cm	Estimated Diameter of Original Seal:	0.70 cm
Number of Impressions:	4	Quality of Impressions:	Fair
Completeness of Image: Complete except for details			

DESCRIPTION OF SEAL AS IMPRESSED IMAGE

Hero faces left, extending bent right arm upward to grasp slightly inverted lion in upper field by hind leg; left arm is straight and held down behind body to hold curved sword.

Lion, moving away from hero but turning its head back toward him, is posed in midair above fallen horned animal. Lion holds both forelegs straight, paw of upper foreleg upturned, and extends them diagonally downward in front of body. Lion holds rear hind leg slightly bent, paw turned down, and extended upward toward hero's head; forward hind leg is bent and extended vertically downward below body; thick tail curves downward between hind legs.

Hero wears Assyrian garment that leaves forward leg exposed below knee; fringe is indicated along edge of garment over rear leg. Rounded coiffure rests at back of hero's neck. Hero appears to wear flat headdress.

Lion has mouth open in roar and is ithyphallic.

Inverted horned animal of undetermined type below lion faces to left, fallen onto its bent forelegs. Animal holds rear hind leg bent and extended upward toward hero's knee; forward hind leg is bent and extended diagonally downward under body. Short tail curls downward. Two thin curved horns emerge from top of animal's head.

Eight-petaled rosette is in upper terminal field between hero and lion.

Edge of seal is preserved at top and bottom of design.

COMMENTARY

The design is unique among seals with images of heroic encounter in the PFS corpus, recalling the protection imagery of the Early Dynastic I period (see Garrison 1988, pp. 37–39), and it shares some compositional features with PFS 190 (Cat.No. 286). PFS 114 suggests a clear narrative link between the fallen horned animal, the raging lion, and the hero. The horned animal is thus best considered a secondary feature of the main design field.

For comparative illustrations including PFS 114, see pls. 198g (feet and shoes), 208e (arm positions of heroic combat), 225b (horned animals and horned-animal creatures of undetermined types), 241a (heroic encounters merged with animal contests), 253d (stars, rosettes).

SEAL APPLICATION (SEE *APPENDIX ONE: CONCORDANCE OF SEALS TO TABLETS IN VOLUME I*)

PFS 114 occurs only on the reverse of tablets that it seals. On all PF tablets the seal is inverted. PFS 224 (II) is applied directly above PFS 114 on the reverse of PF 1162; PFS 130 (Cat.No. 300) is applied directly under PFS 114 on the reverse of PF 1163. Some impressions exhibit lateral distortion. Because the seal is so small, rollings tend to be long, and all impressions preserve the entire length of the seal design. Of these four applications, one preserves almost two complete rollings of the seal with the figural design intact in each half; one displays the hero with the animals behind him in the center; two display the two animals in the center with the hero framing the scene on each end of the impression. On the reverse of PF 1161, PF 1163, and PF 1206 the seal clearly was applied before the text since several cuneiform wedges cut into the top or bottom of the impressions. PF 1161–1163 are the earliest dated tablets with PFS 114 and are all dated 499 B.C.

BIBLIOGRAPHY

Garrison 1988, pp. 271, 283, 285, 372.

PFS 153   Cat.No. 285

|— 1 cm —|

Seal Type:	Cylinder	Photograph:	Pl. 158a
Earliest Dated Application:	498/497 B.C.	Typology and Style:	II-E.4 — Diverse Styles
Preserved Height of Image:	1.10 cm (incomp.)	Preserved Length of Image:	2.30 cm (incomp.)
Estimated Height of Original Seal:	NA	Estimated Diameter of Original Seal:	NA
Number of Impressions:	3	Quality of Impressions:	Poor

Completeness of Image: Segment of middle of design survives

DESCRIPTION OF SEAL AS IMPRESSED IMAGE

    Hero faces left, extending bent right arm outward to hold inverted lion by rear hind leg; left arm is straight and held down behind body to hold curved sword (only partially preserved).

    Lion turns head away from hero. Lion holds rear hind leg straight and extended diagonally upward; forward hind leg is bent and extended downward toward hero's waist. Lion holds upper foreleg straight and extends it outward toward hero's waist; lower foreleg (only partially preserved) is straight and extended vertically downward under its body.

    Hero wears schematic belted Persian court robe with sleeves pushed up; squared pattern and vertical folds are indicated on upper garment. Belt tie projects from front of waist. Rounded coiffure is partially preserved at back of hero's neck.

    Lion has mouth open in roar.

    At far right of preserved impressions, in terminal field, rampant horned animal of undetermined type moves right toward hero but turns its head away from him. Animal holds upper foreleg bent and extended upward toward hero's left arm; lower foreleg is bent and extended outward in front of its body. Curved horn emerges from back of its head; short rounded ear is also indicated at back of head. Crescent-like shape is in upper terminal field between horned animal and hero (see commentary).

COMMENTARY

    The segmented geometric rendering of the human body is without parallel in the PFS corpus. The animal forms seem to be compressed versions of the Fortification Style.

    The crescent-like shape is probably the termination of the animal's horn, with the join not visible in these faint impressions.

SEAL APPLICATION (SEE *APPENDIX ONE: CONCORDANCE OF SEALS TO TABLETS IN VOLUME I*)

    PFS 153 occurs on the left edge of PF 146–148, with PFS 260 (Cat.No. 225) always on the reverse. All three partial rollings display the hero in the center. All tablets with PFS 153 are dated 498/497 B.C.

BIBLIOGRAPHY

    Garrison 1988, p. 456.

II-E.18. ANIMALS OF UNCERTAIN TYPE

Cat.No. 286 PFS 190

|—— 1 cm ——|

Seal Type:	Cylinder	Photographs:	Pl. 158c–d
Earliest Dated Application:	504/503 B.C.	Typology and Style:	II-E.18 — Diverse Styles
Preserved Height of Image:	1.40 cm (incomp.)	Preserved Length of Image:	3.20 cm (comp.)
Estimated Height of Original Seal:	NA	Estimated Diameter of Original Seal:	1.00
Number of Impressions:	3	Quality of Impressions:	Poor

Completeness of Image: Segment of middle of design survives along its complete length

DESCRIPTION OF SEAL AS IMPRESSED IMAGE

Hero faces right, extending bent left arm outward to grasp inverted animal of uncertain type by hind leg; right arm is straight and held down behind body to hold wide sword. Hero raises bent forward leg.

Animal slants diagonally downward away from hero. Animal holds rear hind leg bent and extends it upward toward hero's shoulder; forward hind leg is bent and extended downward toward hero's leg. Animal holds forelegs (only partially preserved) bent and extended downward together under its body.

Hero appears to wear belted Assyrian garment that leaves forward leg exposed below knee. Beard terminates in blunt point over hero's left shoulder; narrow squared coiffure rests at back of neck.

To right of animal held by hero, marchant horned animal of undetermined type with lowered head moves and faces to left, thus forming heraldic group with animal held by hero. Thick tail (only partially preserved) curves upward; two bent horns emerge from top of its head. Suspended above heraldic pair, large marchant animal of uncertain type (poorly preserved) moves to left. Animal holds one foreleg bent and extends it outward to left; one hind leg is bent, hoof(?) upturned, and extended diagonally downward under its body. Tail (apparently) extends diagonally downward then bends upward.

COMMENTARY

Koch (1990) suggests that PFS 190 may belong to Ummurdak. In three transactions, PF 356–358, all left edges of which are sealed by PFS 29 (Cat.No. 302), he received barley to be used for the god(?) from Ammamarda at Hišema in Koch's Elam Region VI. On PF 356–357, the reverses carry PFS 190. On PF 358, however, the reverse carries PFS 606 (II); is this another seal of Ummurdak, or is it that of someone else receiving the rations in his name?

The elongated linear style, abstract figures, and ambitious, animal-dominated composition recall features of Early Dynastic II glyptic.[88] PFS 190 shares some compositional features with PFS 114 (Cat.No. 284). This particular conflation of the heroic encounter and inverted heraldic animals is, however, unique. Although no animal in the composition discretely occupies the terminal field, the heraldic image created by the confronting heads of the two lower animals produces a terminal field motif.

---

88. Compare Amiet 1980, pl. 60 (814); perhaps also Amiet 1980, pls. 116 (1561B, from Luristan), and pl. 119 (1585, possibly from Susa); many examples in Karg 1984, pls. 2–3. PFS 190 is considerably smaller than most Early Dynastic II seals.

Although daggers are frequently represented on heroic combat seals in the corpus, long straight swords are rare. Actual examples of both types of weapon were excavated in the Treasury at Persepolis (Schmidt 1957, pl. 75).

For comparative illustrations including PFS 190, see pl. 236c (animals/creatures as secondary elements of main design field).

SEAL APPLICATION (SEE *APPENDIX ONE: CONCORDANCE OF SEALS TO TABLETS IN VOLUME I*)

PFS 190 occurs on the reverse of PF 356 and the reverse and upper edge of PF 357, with PFS 29 (Cat.No. 302) on the left edge of each tablet. The complexity of the design makes the impressions difficult to read, but they generally exhibit little distortion. All three applications preserve the entire length of the seal design; one displays the hero in the center; one displays the animal to the right of the hero in the center; one displays the animal in the upper field in the center. On the reverse of both tablets the seal clearly was applied before the text since several cuneiform wedges cut into the top of the impressions. PF 356 is the earliest dated tablet with PFS 190 and is dated 504/503 B.C.

BIBLIOGRAPHY

Garrison 1988, pp. 465–66; Koch 1990, p. 193 (n. 797).

II-H. HERO THREATENS MARCHANT ANIMAL OR CREATURE, WEAPON HELD DOWN BEHIND BODY

II-H.1. BULLS

PFS 614   Cat.No. 287

Seal Type:	Cylinder	Photograph:	Pl. 159a
Earliest Dated Application:	498/497 B.C.	Typology and Style:	II-H.1 — Fortification Style
Preserved Height of Image:	1.00 cm (incomp.)	Preserved Length of Image:	3.00 cm (incomp.)
Estimated Height of Original Seal:	NA	Estimated Diameter of Original Seal:	NA
Number of Impressions:	2	Quality of Impressions:	Poor-fair

Completeness of Image: Large segment of upper half of design survives

DESCRIPTION OF SEAL AS IMPRESSED IMAGE

Hero faces right, extending straight left arm upward to grasp marchant bull by horn; right arm (only partially preserved) is straight and held down behind body (presumably to hold weapon).

Bull moves toward and faces hero. Bull raises bent forward foreleg toward hero; long tail (only partially preserved) curls upward.

Hero wears garment of uncertain type; pointed beard rests over his left shoulder; rounded coiffure curls upward at back of neck.

Bull has long curved horn emerging from front of its head; rounded ear is at back of head.

Crescent (only partially preserved) is in field above bull.

Behind hero, in terminal field, are traces of floral element (only partially preserved).

Edge of seal is preserved at top of design.

COMMENTARY

The design seems to have been well executed with generous spacing between figures. The seal was not included in Garrison 1988.

For comparative illustrations including PFS 614, see pls. 250h (crescents) and 256g (stylized floral elements).

SEAL APPLICATION (SEE *APPENDIX ONE: CONCORDANCE OF SEALS TO TABLETS IN VOLUME I*)

PFS 614 occurs on the reverse and upper edge of PF 364. The rolling on the upper edge is too poorly preserved for analysis. The partial rolling on the reverse displays the hero in the center. On the reverse the seal clearly was applied before the text since several cuneiform wedges cut into the top of the impression. PF 364 is dated 498/497 B.C.

II-H.14. OSTRICHES

Cat.No. 288   PFS 9*

Seal Type:	Cylinder, Inscribed	Photographs:	Pl. 159c–e
Earliest Dated Application:	505 B.C.	Typology and Style:	II-H.14 — Fortification Style
Language of Inscription:	Aramaic		
Preserved Height of Image:	1.30 cm (comp.)	Preserved Length of Image:	2.10 cm (comp.)
Estimated Height of Original Seal:	1.30 cm	Estimated Diameter of Original Seal:	0.70 cm
Number of Impressions:	107	Quality of Impressions:	Fair

Completeness of Image: Complete

DESCRIPTION OF SEAL AS IMPRESSED IMAGE

Hero faces left in striding pose, extending straight right arm outward to grasp marchant ostrich by throat; left arm is bent and held down behind body to hold weapon with bent end (perhaps a throw stick).

Ostrich moves toward and faces hero. Ostrich extends one wing vertically upward above its body, other diagonally downward under its body; plume-shaped tail extends diagonally upward.

Hero wears belted Assyrian garment that leaves forward leg exposed below knee; two diagonal bands are indicated on chest; fringe is indicated along forward edge of lower part of garment over rear leg. Hero perhaps wears domed headdress. Long, rounded, segmented beard rests along hero's chest; rounded, segmented coiffure rests at back of neck.

In terminal field, rampant wild goat moves toward hero but turns its head away from him. Goat holds upper foreleg straight and extends it toward hero's shoulder; lower foreleg is bent and extended downward in front of body; short tail curves upward. Large curved horn emerges from front of goat's head; small pointed ear is at back of head; short beard is indicated. Star is in upper terminal field between hero and goat.

Inscription is in middle field between hero and ostrich. Inverted crescent is below ostrich.

Edge of seal is preserved at top and bottom of design. Three chips appear along bottom edge of seal; two chips are along top edge.

INSCRIPTION

Aramaic

Line   1. PRNK

Translation   Parnaka

The inscription is in one line, oriented along the vertical axis of the seal. In addition to numerous occurrences in the PF texts, the name Parnaka also appears in the Aramaic inscription on PFS 16* (Cat.No. 22), the second seal of Parnaka.

COMMENTARY

The seal is the personal seal of Parnaka, chief functionary in the Fortification archive and uncle of Darius the Great.[89] This is his first seal, which was replaced by PFS 16* (Cat.No. 22), also a heroic encounter but of the control type, on 6 June 500 B.C.; see PF 2067 and PF 2068. The seal has no administrative or geographical restriction. Most of the bibliography concentrates on the administrative use of PFS 9* and its replacement by PFS 16*. Vallat has published a Fortification-type tablet (purchased on the art market and now in Fribourg) that carries an impression of PFS 9*.

The seal image has strong ties to Neo-Assyrian glyptic in a tradition with roots in the Middle Assyrian period; however, PFS 9* is rendered in the Fortification Style.[90] It is clearly not a Neo-Assyrian heirloom with an inscription added later.[91] The composition is extremely well conceived; note especially how the inverted crescent, inscription, star, and hero's weapon create a frame around the hero, leading the eye immediately to this figure; the inscription seems to act as a caption. The carefully arranged composition also yields clear, easily-read impressions. The large number of symbols in the terminal field is rare in the PFS hero corpus; compare PFS 38 (Cat.No. 16) and PFS 1236 (Cat.No. 159). There is an effective attempt to show the lower wing foreshortened as it emerges from the far side of the ostrich's body.[92] The only other ostriches in Volume I appear on PFS 263 (Cat.No. 289) and PFS 29 (Cat.No. 302).

For comparative illustrations including PFS 9*, see pls. 176a (Assyrian garments with detailing preserved), 191a (variously detailed beards), 193a (round coiffures), 198b (feet and shoes), 212b (heroic attitudes of combat encounter), 226a (birds), 232a (animals/creatures with distinctive perspectival elements), 245a (various weapons), 252a (crescents and stars), 264a (inscriptions without panels or case lines), 280a (chips in seal matrices), and 285e (personal seals of Parnaka, son of Aršam, uncle of Darius, Chief Functionary at Persepolis).

SEAL APPLICATION (SEE *APPENDIX ONE: CONCORDANCE OF SEALS TO TABLETS IN VOLUME I*)

As is the case with PFS 16* (Cat.No. 2), PFS 9* always occurs alone on tablets that it seals. PF 9* occurs on five surfaces of PF 268. More commonly, the seal is applied to four or three surfaces: the reverse, upper edge, right edge, and left edge of PF 247, PF 267, PF 273, PF 654–656, PF 658–659, PF 661–662, PF 666, PF 1788, PF 1792, and PF 1797; the obverse, upper edge, right edge, and left edge of PF 2025; and the upper edge, right edge, and left edge of PF 657, PF 660, PF 664, PF 1790, PF 1793, PF 1795, PF 1796, and PF 1801. The seal also occurs on only two surfaces: the reverse and left edge of PF 253; the upper edge and left edge of PF 1789 and PF 1791; and the right edge and left edge of PF 1794. The reverse and upper edge often carry two impressions

---

89. See Briant 1996, pp. 481–86, on Parnaka in relation to Darius.

90. For the hero and ostrich in combat encounter on Neo-Assyrian seal impressions from Nineveh, see, for example, Herbordt 1992, pl. 5, nos. 3, 5. See Collon 1998 for the motif in Mesopotamian glyptic imagery.

91. *Pace* Keel in Keel and Uehlinger 1990, pp. 87–92, fig. 118 with caption.

92. A similar subtlety occurs on a seal, dated by the excavator to the Middle Assyrian period, excavated at Kinet Höyük (Gates 1996, p. 294, fig. 13) and on a seal impressed on a tablet from Nineveh dated 685 B.C. (Herbordt 1992, p. 235, pl. 5, no. 5).

of the seal; on PF 267 the reverse carries three impressions of the seal, yielding six applications in total for the one tablet. Thus, although the actual number of tablets on which this seal occurs in the corpus published by Hallock (1969) is relatively modest (twenty-eight), the number of applications of the seal is nonetheless quite large. This pattern of seal rolling is also found with Parnaka's later seal; see the observations in the entry for PFS 16* (Cat.No. 22). It probably reflects his status as the official in charge of the operations of the system. On ten of the sixteen tablets on which the seal occurs on the reverse the impressions are inverted. Impressions of the seal vary. Some are carefully applied, but others are poorly applied with vertical and lateral distortion. Because the seal is relatively small, complete rollings of the seal are very common.

Of the total 107 impressions, ten are too poorly preserved for analysis. Of the remaining ninety-seven impressions, ninety-five show some part of the inscription. This is due to the high number of complete rollings of the seal. In seventy-eight impressions the seal is rolled for at least one complete turn, preserving the entire length of the design; in three applications at least two complete turns of the seal are preserved (here the central element is always the heroic encounter with the inscription repeated three times).

Of these seventy-eight complete applications, six display the hero in the center; thirteen display the hero and the ostrich (i.e., the heroic encounter) in the center; thirteen display the hero and the goat in the center; fourteen display the ostrich in the center; twenty-three display the goat in the center; nine display the goat and the ostrich in the center. Of the remaining nineteen partial rollings, seven display the hero in the center; five preserve only the hero and the ostrich; four preserve only the hero and the goat; one displays the ostrich in the center; one preserves only the goat; one preserves only the goat and the ostrich.

On the reverse of twelve tablets the seal clearly was applied before the text since several cuneiform wedges cut into the relief along the top or bottom the impressions. PF 1788 is the earliest dated tablet with PFS 9* and is dated 505 B.C.

BIBLIOGRAPHY

Aperghis 1999, p. 165; Balcer 1993, p. 84; Boardman 1988, pp. 35–37 (no. 35b); Brosius 1996, pp. 145 (n. 55), 150 (table 6), 157 (table 8), 159; Cameron 1948, p. 53 (n. 51); Dusinberre 1997b, p. 112, figs. 12–13; Garrison 1988, pp. 241, 243, 262, 264–68, 271–72, 282, 525; Garrison 1991, pp. 8–9, figs. 9–10; Garrison 1998, p. 130; Garrison 2000, pp. 153–54; Garrison in press; Garrison and Dion 1999, p. 10; Garrison and Root 1996, pp. 2, 12; Hallock 1977, pp. 128–29, pl. E-6; Hallock 1978, p. 113; Hinz 1971, pp. 271, 302; Keel and Uehlinger 1990, fig. 118; Koch 1990, passim, but esp. pp. 224–27; Koch 1992, pp. 26, 30–31, 33, 36–40, 61, 97, figs. 13, 16; Lewis 1994, pp. 29–30; Moorey 1988, pp. 36–37, fig. 35b; Root 1990a, pp. 130–31; Root 1997, p. 235; Root 1999a, pp. 163, 179–80, 184, fig. 10; Vallat 1994, pp. 264–71, fig. 3; Wiesehöfer 1996, pl. 13a.

PFS 263

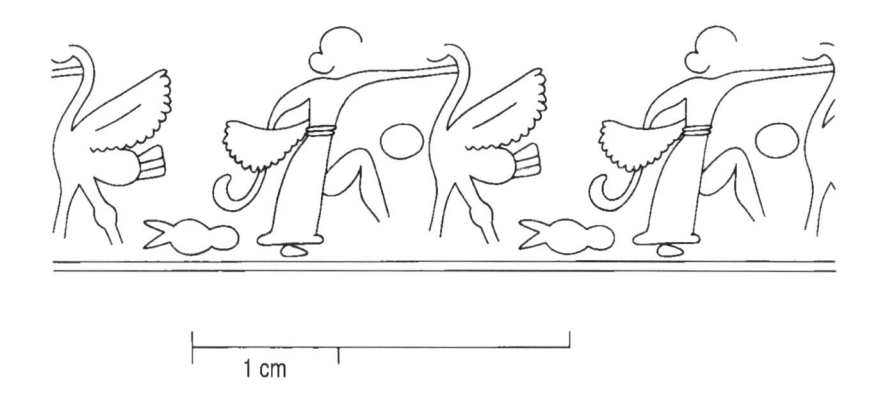

Cat.No. 289

Seal Type:	Cylinder	Photograph:	Pl. 160a
Earliest Dated Application:	503/502 B.C.	Typology and Style:	II-H.14 — Modeled Style
Preserved Height of Image:	1.60 cm (incomp.)	Preserved Length of Image:	2.60 cm (comp.)
Estimated Height of Original Seal:	1.70 cm	Estimated Diameter of Original Seal:	0.80 cm
Number of Impressions:	2	Quality of Impressions:	Poor-fair

Completeness of Image: Large segment of design survives along its complete length

DESCRIPTION OF SEAL AS IMPRESSED IMAGE

Winged hero faces right, extending straight left arm to grasp marchant ostrich by throat; right arm is bent and held down behind body to hold curved sword. Hero's wing apparently extends across his right arm (preservation is very poor in this passage). Hero raises bent forward leg toward ostrich.

Ostrich moves toward and faces hero; thick straight tail extends diagonally upward.

Hero wears double-belted Assyrian garment that leaves forward leg exposed. Single wing emerges from back at waist level. Hero has rounded coiffure at back of neck.

Ostrich has three feathers indicated on its tail.

In field between hero and ostrich is large ovoid dot. In lower terminal field is bulbous shape with two pronged termination (apparently fish, horizontal facing right).

Line border serving as ground line is preserved at bottom of design.

COMMENTARY

The large ovoid dot between the hero and the ostrich plausibly represents an ostrich egg. The ostrich was not only a fearsome bird, but it was also the producer of the marvelous large eggs that were prized and decorated as luxury objects in ancient western Asia and exported to the west, for example, to Etruria during the Orientalizing period.[93] This interpretation of the ovoid element would lend an interesting narrative dynamic to the encounter between this hero and ostrich. The fish would be interpreted as a symbol of Ea in a Mesopotamian context (Black and Green 1992, p. 82).

See Garrison 1988 for the style and workshop of PFS 263 and related seals.

For comparative illustrations including PFS 263, see pls. 198i (feet and shoes), 201d (heroes as winged humans), 212g (heroic attitudes of combat encounter), 226h (birds), 228g (fish and reptiles), 244d (daggers and swords), 254e (various devices and symbols), and 267d (terminal field motifs other than inscriptions).

SEAL APPLICATION (SEE *APPENDIX ONE: CONCORDANCE OF SEALS TO TABLETS IN VOLUME I*)

PFS 263 is rolled across the reverse of PF 1630 and PF 1631, in both cases neatly placed along the midsection of the tablet and preserving more than one complete rolling of the seal design. On PF 1630, the ostrich is displayed in the center of the rolling. On PF 1631, the hero is displayed in the center. PF 1630 is the earliest dated tablet with PFS 263 and is dated 503/502 B.C.

---

93. See Rice 1983, p. 90, on the ostrich in Greek and Roman traditions and its role in the procession of Ptolemy II, which specifically evokes numerous allusions to the Achaemenid imperial past. See also Frankfort 1939, pp. 203–04; Collon 1995, p. 64, no. 54; Owen 1981; and especially now Collon 1998 for a study of the motif of hero, ostrich, and egg in Mesopotamian glyptic art.

BIBLIOGRAPHY

Garrison 1988, p. 243.

II-H.19. WINGED CREATURES OF UNCERTAIN TYPE

Cat.No. 290   PFS 246

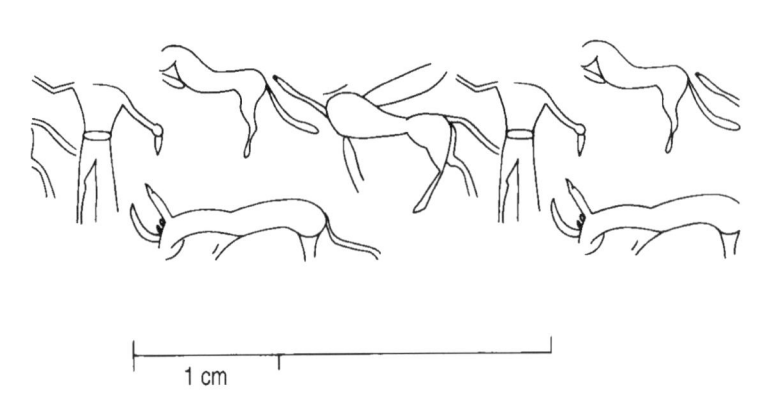

Seal Type:	Cylinder	Photographs:	Pl. 161a–b
Earliest Dated Application:	507/506 B.C.	Typology and Style:	II-H.19 — Fortification Style
Preserved Height of Image:	1.50 cm (incomp.)	Preserved Length of Image:	2.90 cm (comp.)
Estimated Height of Original Seal:	NA	Estimated Diameter of Original Seal:	0.90 cm
Number of Impressions:	6	Quality of Impressions:	Very poor

Completeness of Image: Segment of middle of design survives along its complete length

DESCRIPTION OF SEAL AS IMPRESSED IMAGE

Hero moves to left, extending bent right arm upward (only partially preserved) to grasp marchant winged creature of uncertain type by wing; left arm is straight and held down behind body to hold short dagger.

Creature moves away from hero, suspended in middle design field. Creature holds forward foreleg straight and extends it diagonally upward in front of its chest; long tail curves downward.

Hero wears belted Assyrian garment that leaves forward leg exposed.

In terminal field, two animals are placed one above the other. Upper animal is rampant animal of uncertain type, suspended in field, moving and facing left; long tail curves downward. Lower animal is marchant horned animal of undetermined type, head lowered, moving and facing left; tail (only partially preserved) bends downward. Two horns, one curved, other straight, emerge from top of head as if seen frontally; two small rounded ears are between horns on top of head.

COMMENTARY

The spatial arrangement of the design is quite unusual among seals with images of heroic encounter in the PFS corpus.

For comparative illustrations including PFS 246, see pls. 174e (Assyrian garments), 217f (hero suspended high in design field), 221a (animals and creatures of uncertain type), and 244c (daggers and swords).

SEAL APPLICATION (SEE *APPENDIX ONE: CONCORDANCE OF SEALS TO TABLETS IN VOLUME I*)

PFS 246 occurs on the reverse (inverted) and upper edge of PF 796 and PF 1698, with PFS 202 (III) on the left edge of each tablet. On the reverse of PF 796 the seal is applied three times, the impressions stacked one above the other. In two impressions the seal has been rolled for at least one complete turn, preserving the entire length of the seal design. Of these two applications, one displays the winged creature and the animals in the terminal field in the center; one displays the animals in the terminal field in the center. Of the remaining four partial impressions, one displays the hero in the center; two display the winged creature in the center; one preserves only the winged creature and the animal in the upper terminal field. On the reverse of PF 1698 the seal clearly was applied before the text since several cuneiform wedges cut into the bottom of the impression. PF 796 is the earliest dated tablet with PFS 246 and is dated 507/506 B.C.

BIBLIOGRAPHY

Garrison 1988, pp. 283, 285–86.

II-I. HERO THREATENS MARCHANT ANIMAL OR CREATURE, WEAPON HELD UP BEHIND HEAD

II-I.3. WINGED HUMAN-FACED/HUMAN-HEADED BULL CREATURES

PFS 30   Cat.No. 291

Seal Type:	Cylinder	Photographs:	Pl. 162a–d
Earliest Dated Application:	500/499 B.C.	Typology and Style:	II-I.3 — Modeled Style
Preserved Height of Image:	1.50 cm (incomp.)	Preserved Length of Image:	3.10 cm (comp.)
Estimated Height of Original Seal:	1.70 cm	Estimated Diameter of Original Seal:	1.00 cm
Number of Impressions:	34	Quality of Impressions:	Good

Completeness of Image: Almost complete except for upper edge and lower edge

DESCRIPTION OF SEAL AS IMPRESSED IMAGE

Winged hero faces right, extending slightly bent left arm upward to grasp marchant winged human-faced bull creature by horn; hero extends bent right arm upward behind head to hold weapon, probably a curved sword (only partially preserved). Hero raises bent forward leg to place his foot on forward foreleg of creature.

Creature moves toward and faces hero; tail curves upward to run parallel to back.

Hero has two wings, upper extending diagonally upward from his shoulder, lower extending diagonally downward from his back. Hero wears belted Assyrian garment that leaves forward leg exposed; bottom edge of garment stretches between hero's feet and shows squared border pattern. Beard terminates in blunt point along hero's left shoulder.

Creature's human face has long blunt-pointed beard; thick curved horn emerges from front of its head; small pointed ear or horn is at top of head and long pointed ear or horn is at back of head.

In terminal field, bird of uncertain type stands facing left as if to peck bull creature. Star is above bird.

Trace of ground line is preserved below winged creature.

COMMENTARY

PFS 30 always occurs alone on tablets that it seals, indicating an office or official of importance. Hallock and Koch note administrative links between PFS 30 and PFS 3 (III). PFS 30 was used (years 22–25) less often than PFS 3, but there are no apparent distinctions in the types of transactions (*pace* Hallock who considers that PFS 30 was not used in more southerly places). Hallock identifies both PFS 3 (III) and PFS 30 as belonging to scribal offices. Koch (1990) assigns PFS 30 to an unnamed official in charge of cereals in her Northwestern Region V.

In part because preservation is usually so poor on the upper and lower parts of the seal impressions on the PF tablets, it is rare to retrieve detailing such as we see on the hem of this hero's garment; compare, for example, PFS 86 (Cat.No. 48) and PFS 98* (Cat.No. 217). Decorated hems of the Assyrian garment are found on numerous Assyro-Babylonian seals.[94]

The style is a softened Modeled Style. The composition shows affinities with a large number of seals from the PFS corpus of hero seals (see Garrison 1988).

The thin line preserved under the middle section of the bull creature seems to be a ground line supporting the bull creature alone. The line appears to be too high to run under the reconstructed rear leg of the hero and thus does not suggest a vestige of the edge line of the seal itself. (There is, however, significant distortion in the impressions at this area.) The use of a thin line border to set off one or more discrete elements in a multi-figure composition is an occasional device in glyptic art. A cylinder of later Achaemenid date from Gorgippa (the "Nereid Coffin" find) is one parallel (Collon 1987, no. 432). Sometimes more elaborate bases set off an isolated figure, as the creature on a base grasped by a hero standing on the "ground" in an Assyrian cylinder (Collon 1987, no. 380).

For comparative illustrations including PFS 30, see pls. 177a (Assyrian garments with detailing preserved), 198d (feet and shoes), 201a (heroes as winged humans), 212c (heroic attitudes of combat encounter), 226c (birds), 228a (pecking birds), 253a (stars, rosettes), 267a (terminal field motifs other than inscriptions), and 277f (ground lines on cylinder seals).

SEAL APPLICATION (SEE *APPENDIX ONE: CONCORDANCE OF SEALS TO TABLETS IN VOLUME I*)

As is typical of seals of important offices and officials, PFS 30 always occurs alone on tablets that it seals and often is applied on three or four surfaces of a tablet: the reverse, upper edge, and left edge of PF 870, PF 1594, and PF 1660; the reverse, upper edge, right edge, and left edge of PF 965; the upper edge and left edge of PF 1640, PF 1720, and PF 1721; and multiple rollings on PF 1862, PF 1866, PF 1874–1876 (U texts). The thirty-four impressions in fact come from only twelve tablets. Applications of the seal tend to be carefully rolled, with little or no distortion. In eight impressions the seal is rolled for at least one complete turn, preserving the entire length of the seal design. Of these eight impressions, three display the hero in the center; two display the hero and the creature in the center; one displays the creature in the center; two display the bird and star in the terminal field in the center. Of the remaining twenty-six partial impressions, two preserve only the hero; ten preserve only the hero (at the left of the impression) and the front part of the creature; ten preserve only the creature; four display the bird and star in the terminal field in the center. PF 1594 and PF 1640 are the earliest dated tablets with PFS 30 and are both dated 500/499 B.C.

BIBLIOGRAPHY

Brosius 1996, p. 168; Garrison 1988, pp. 252–53, 255–56; Garrison 1998, p. 121 (n. 15); Hallock 1977, p. 131; Hallock 1985, p. 597; Koch 1990, p. 296; Tuplin 1987, p. 115.

---

94. Compare, for example, Collon 1987, nos. 369–70, 965; Porada 1948, no. 747; Herbordt 1992, pls. 5 (no. 8), 6 (no. 4); Wittmann 1992, pls. 22 (no. 51), 25 (no. 67), etc.

II-I.16. VARIOUS COMPOSITE CREATURES

PFS 4* Cat.No. 292

Seal Type:	Cylinder, Inscribed	Photographs:	Pl. 163a–b
Earliest Dated Application:	504 B.C.	Typology and Style:	II-I.16 — Modeled Style
Language of Inscription:	Elamite		
Preserved Height of Image:	1.90 cm (incomp.)	Preserved Length of Image:	3.60 cm (comp.)
Estimated Height of Original Seal:	2.10 cm	Estimated Diameter of Original Seal:	1.20 cm
Number of Impressions:	102	Quality of Impressions:	Many preserve excellent detail

Completeness of Image: Complete except for upper edge and lower edge

DESCRIPTION OF SEAL AS IMPRESSED IMAGE

Hero faces right, in striding pose, extending straight left arm downward to grasp marchant winged human-headed scorpion creature at chest; hero extends bent right arm upward behind head to hold spherical object.

Scorpion creature moves toward and faces hero.

Hero wears double-belted kilt that falls to point between legs; garment shows detailing line at hem and along front edge; thick vertical fold runs down middle of garment with diagonal striations over hero's rear leg. Sheath projects from back of hero's waist. Hero wears flat headdress with knob at top. Rounded beard with horizontal striations rests over hero's chest; rounded coiffure rests at back of neck.

Creature has scorpion body and tail, bird's legs and feet, and human head. Segmented tail curves upward with sting on its end appearing above wing. Two rows of feathers are indicated on its wing. Long, blunt-pointed, segmented beard rests over its chest; ponytail coiffure rests at back of neck. Creature wears banded domed headdress with knob at top; two short vertical projections emerge together from front of headdress.

Another marchant, winged, bird-legged human-headed scorpion creature is behind hero, moving toward and facing him. This creature is similar to the one at right but with several notable differences in details. Long squared beard with horizontal striations rests over its chest; ponytail coiffure has wavy contours. Creature wears banded conical headdress with knob at top; two vertical projections, widely spaced, emerge from front of headdress.

Hero stands upon forward foot of each creature.

Inscription fills terminal field and main design fields above and below hindquarters of the human-headed scorpion creatures.

Small mark near hero's left elbow may be flaw in stone.

INSCRIPTION

> Elamite
>
> Line
> 1. [v.]⌈d.⌉¹Hu-pan-⌈a-⌉
> 2. ah-
> 3. pi
> 4. šak d.
> 5. Ša-⌈ti⌉-Hu-pan
>
> Translation   Hupanʾahpi son of Šati-Hupan

The five line inscription is oriented along the horizontal axis of the seal and separated by irregular case lines. A diagonal mark crossing the fourth (lowest) line divider near the second sign of the fourth line does not appear to be part of the inscription and may be a chip in the stone or an error in the engraving. The arrangement of the inscription completely fills the terminal field and integrates itself with the figural design. The ša-sign in the fifth line is out of register, about half way between the fourth and fifth lines, although it clearly belongs at the beginning of the fifth line. This placement of the sign nicely fills the field under the scorpion creature at right, and this may account for its appearance out of its register.

The sign forms are generally consistent with those used in Elamite inscriptions on seals in the PFS corpus. The rendering of the heads of the wedges changes considerably starting in the second line.

Both of the names occurring in the inscription of PFS 4* are well known in Elamite. The name Hupanʾahpi also appears (as the father of a woman Šeraš) in the inscription on PFS 77* (II). The name Šati-Hupan occurs as the patronym in the inscription on PFS 103* (Cat.No. 84) and is restored on the inscription on PFS 272* (Cat.No. 272). The name may also occur on PFNN 2543:2f. written ša-ti-⌈d.(?)GAL(?)⌉.

COMMENTARY

Hallock (1977) identifies PFS 4* as an important office seal, connected mainly with texts recording payment of regular monthly rations for groups of workers and animals. He also recognizes that the seal was used in a limited number of years (years 17–23) and in a limited geographical region. The seal always occurs alone, a usage pattern characteristic of seals employed by high-ranking offices and officers in the archive. The name occurring on almost every text sealed by PFS 4* is Iršena, who, in a few other texts, carries the title *kurdabattiš*.[95] At the same time as he seemed to use PFS 4*, Iršena also seemed to fill other administrative roles in other areas. Koch (1990) places PFS 4* (and Iršena for the most part) in her Elam Region VI. The seal occurs by itself on one Q text (on the reverse and upper edge of PF 1333; left edge is destroyed), but Iršena is not named in it (the supplier is one Ištimanka, the receiver Akkiya; if the normal protocol for Q texts were at work here, Akkiya, whose name occurs only here in the PF texts, would be the official using the seal).

Aside from its occurrence on PFS 4* and PFS 77* (II), the name Hupanʾahpi is not otherwise attested at Persepolis.

PFS 4* and its inscription raise the interesting issue of a seal with a personalized inscription used in the archive as an office seal, with no evident connection between the names in the inscription and the names in the texts. Both Hinz and Koch suggest that the seal is an heirloom from the Neo-Elamite period. The stylistic analysis of Garrison 1988 suggests a date in the early Achaemenid period.

The seal is relatively large. For the scorpion creatures in an Assyrian Modeled Style heroic encounter, see a cylinder seal impression on a tablet from the Nabu Temple at Nimrud dated ca. 616 B.C.[96] Human-headed winged scorpion creatures are rare in the PFS corpus, with only two other seals among seals with images of heroic encounter herein including this iconography: PFS 29 (Cat.No. 302) and PFS 1586 (Cat.No. 121). The spherical object cupped in the upraised hand of the hero on PFS 4* is difficult to explain except as a projectile weapon the hero is about to hurl at the scorpion creature facing him. See PFS 10 (Cat.No. 251) for a very different composition that also seems to involve a projectile weapon. An Assyrian Modeled Style cylinder from the Samian Heraion shows one hero holding a small spherical or egg-shaped object in one hand, but here he seems to be displaying the object to one of the flanking creatures rather than poised to hurl the object at the creature.[97]

---

95. See Koch 1990, pp. 237–45, for a discussion of the title.
96. Parker 1962, p. 36, fig. 1, pl. 19, no. 1; Herbordt 1992, pl. 8, no. 6.
97. Aruz 1997, pp. 144–45, fig. 158; Collon 1987, pp. 136–37, no. 572.

The creature to the left of the hero could legitimately be classified as part of the terminal field, but the hero's stance, poised upon both creatures equally, suggests the appropriateness of assigning this creature to the main field. The two creatures serve in a modified way as pedestal figures.

See Garrison 1988 for discussion of the style and workshop of PFS 4* and related seals.

For comparative illustrations including PFS 4*, see pls. 180d (kilts), 186a (headdresses), 198a (feet and shoes), 208a (arm positions of heroic combat), 212a (heroic attitudes of combat encounter), 216a (hero standing atop pedestal figure[s] or other supporting element), 229a (scorpion, fish, horse, bird, and human creatures), 234a (human-headed/human-faced creatures), 247a (projectiles, slings), 263f (inscriptions without panels with horizontal case lines), and 281b (office seals).

SEAL APPLICATION (SEE *APPENDIX ONE: CONCORDANCE OF SEALS TO TABLETS IN VOLUME I*)

As is typical of important office seals, PFS 4* always occurs alone on tablets that it seals and often is applied on three or four edges of a tablet: the reverse, upper edge, right edge, and left edge of PF 405–406, PF 873, PF 925, PF 927–928; the reverse, upper edge, and left edge of PF 403, PF 847, PF 874–876, PF 915–916, PF 918–920, PF 922–923, PF 930–932, PF 934, and PF 936; the upper edge, right edge, and left edge of PF 1022; the reverse and left edge of PF 404 and PF 917; the upper edge and left edge of PF 804, PF 921, PF 924, PF 926, PF 929, PF 933, PF 935, and PF 2041; the reverse and upper edge of PF 1333; and the right edge and left edge of PF 2045. On ten of the twenty-six tablets on which the seal occurs on the reverse the impressions are inverted. On the reverse of three tablets the seal is rolled along the vertical axis of the tablet. Only one multiple rolling of PFS 4* on a single surface (PF 931, the reverse) is documented in the PF tablets. Impressions of the seal tend to be poorly applied, with some distortion. Because the seal is relatively large, there are few impressions that preserve the complete design, although many impressions preserve almost all of the image. Of the total 102 impressions, two impressions are too poorly preserved for analysis. Of the remaining 100 impressions, ninety-eight show some part of the inscription, which reflects the fact that the inscription is integrated with the figural design. In twenty-three impressions, the seal is rolled for at least one complete turn, preserving the entire length of the seal design.

Of these twenty-three applications, three display the inscription in the center; one displays the inscription and the creature to the right of the hero in the center; three display the inscription and the creature to the left of the hero in the center; three display the hero in the center; one displays the hero and the creature to right in the center; nine display the hero and the creature to left in the center (of which four preserve a complete rolling of the inscription at the left of the impression); one displays the creature to the right of the hero in the center with a complete rolling of the inscription at the right of the impression; two display the creature to the left of the hero in the center with a complete rolling of the inscription at the left of the impression. Of the remaining seventy-seven partial rollings, eleven display the inscription in the center; two display the inscription and the creature to the left of the hero in the center; two preserve only a partial rolling of the inscription and the creature to the left of the hero; eight display the hero in the center; four display the hero and the creature to right in the center with a partial rolling of the inscription at the right of the impression; fifteen display the hero and the creature to left in the center with a partial rolling of the inscription at the left of the impression; two preserve only the hero and the creature to right; two preserve only the hero and the creature to left; six display the creature to the right of the hero in the center with a partial rolling of the inscription at the right of the impression; twenty-three display the creature to the left of the hero in the center with a partial or full (seven instances) rolling of the inscription at the left of the impression; one preserves only the creature to the right of the hero; one preserves only the creature to the left of the hero.

On the reverse of twenty-four tablets the seal was clearly applied before the text since several cuneiform wedges cut into the top or bottom of the impressions. PF 403 is the earliest dated tablet with PFS 4* and is dated 504 B.C.

BIBLIOGRAPHY

Aperghis 1999, p. 186; Brosius 1996, pp. 148, 150 (table 6), 156–57 (table 8), 158 (table 9), 159–60, 179; Garrison 1988, pp. 228–29, 230–33, 479, 480, 524; Garrison and Dion 1999, p. 10 (n. 28); Hallock 1977, pp. 129–31, pl. F–1; Hallock 1985, p. 596; Hinz 1971, p. 281; Koch 1990, pp. 137 (n. 609), 186, 240–41; Wallenfels 1994, p. 10.

Cat.No. 293   PFS 67

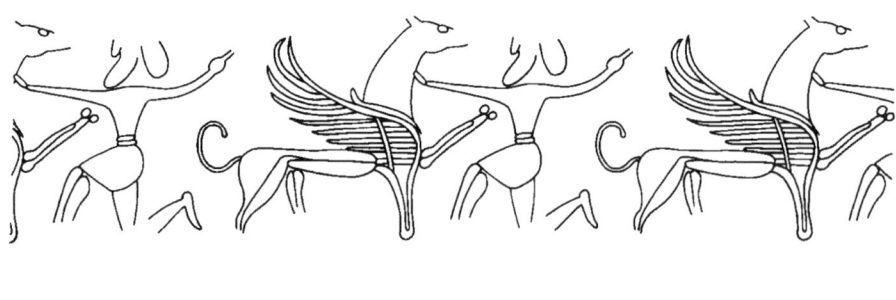

Seal Type:	Cylinder	Photographs:	Pl. 164a–b
Earliest Dated Application:	500/499 B.C.	Typology and Style:	II-I.16 — Fortification Style
Preserved Height of Image:	1.50 cm (incomp.)	Preserved Length of Image:	2.70 cm (comp.)
Estimated Height of Original Seal:	NA	Estimated Diameter of Original Seal:	0.90 cm
Number of Impressions:	7	Quality of Impressions:	Poor-fair

Completeness of Image: Almost complete except for upper edge and lower edge

DESCRIPTION OF SEAL AS IMPRESSED IMAGE

Hero faces left, both knees bent in *knielauf*-pose, extending straight right arm outward to grasp marchant winged horse(?) creature by throat; hero extends bent left arm upward behind head to hold weapon of uncertain type (only small segment preserved).

Creature moves toward and faces hero. Creature raises forward foreleg and extends it upward toward hero's arm; tail curves downward then curls upward.

Hero wears double-belted tunic. Long rounded beard is over hero's right shoulder; rounded coiffure rests at back of neck.

Creature's body has much interior linear detail; wing consists of series of long thin feathers; ear (only partially preserved) emerges from back of creature's head.

COMMENTARY

Koch assigns PFS 67 to Kuntukka, an official involved in the grain supply at Tirazziš (Shiraz).

The extensive detailing seen on the body of the creature is not often found among seals with images of heroic encounter in the PFS corpus. The composition and proportions of the figures are also unusual.[98] See Garrison 1988 for the artist, who seems to prefer this type of detailing and rather unusual designs. The full *knielauf*-pose of the hero on PFS 67 is assumed by only three other heroes in the PFS corpus: PFS 120 (Cat.No. 49), PFS 1309s (Cat.No. 229), and PFS 1527 (Cat.No. 32). See the commentary on PFS 1527 (Cat.No. 32) for more discussion. The creature resembles a winged horse in what is preserved of its head and neck, but see PFS 99 (Cat.No. 113) and PFS 749 (Cat.No. 110) for more secure examples of the rare winged horse creature.

For comparative illustrations including PFS 67, see pls. 212e (heroic attitudes of combat encounter) and 287c (personal seals of various suppliers).

SEAL APPLICATION (SEE *APPENDIX ONE: CONCORDANCE OF SEALS TO TABLETS IN VOLUME I*)

PFS 67 occurs only on the left edge of tablets that it seals. Impressions show little or no distortion. No impression preserves the complete seal design. Of the seven partial rollings, one preserves only the hero; one displays the hero in the center; four preserve only the hero (at the right of the impression) and the creature; one displays the creature in the center. PF 1149 is the earliest dated tablet with PFS 67 and is dated 500/499 B.C.

BIBLIOGRAPHY

Garrison 1988, pp. 326, 335–39, 346, 494–95; Garrison and Root 1996, p. 13; Koch 1990, p. 265.

---

98. On the *knielauf*-pose in western Asiatic art, see Kantor 1962.
For comparanda from Susa, see Amiet 1973b, pl. 2, nos. 8–10.

COMPOSITIONAL FORMAT III: COMPOSITE CONTROL AND COMBAT ENCOUNTERS

III-A. TWO HEROIC ENCOUNTERS: ONE CONTROL, ONE COMBAT

III-A.17. MIXED ANIMALS AND/OR CREATURES

PFS 1249   Cat.No. 294

Seal Type: Cylinder	Photograph: Pl. 164d
Earliest Dated Application: 498 B.C.	Typology and Style: III-A.17 — Fortification Style
Preserved Height of Image: 1.00 cm (incomp.)	Preserved Length of Image: 3.20 cm (incomp.)
Estimated Height of Original Seal: NA	Estimated Diameter of Original Seal: NA
Number of Impressions: 1	Quality of Impression: Fair

Completeness of Image: Large segment of middle of design survives

DESCRIPTION OF SEAL AS IMPRESSED IMAGE

Two discrete heroic encounters are depicted.

At far left of preserved impression, hero faces left and holds at his chest two animals vertically disposed: animal of uncertain type at left and lion at right.

Each animal turns its head away from hero. Tail of lion to right (only partially preserved) hangs downward; tail of animal at left is not preserved.

Hero of group at left wears Assyrian garment that leaves forward leg exposed below knee. Pointed beard rests over hero's right shoulder; rounded coiffure rests at back of neck.

Mane of animal to left is rendered by narrow band with striations along contour of neck. Lion to right has mouth slightly open.

To right of lion held by hero of group at left, bird of uncertain type alights facing left with wings spread and upward (as if to peck at lion).

Second heroic encounter appears at far right of impression. Hero moves to left, presumably to grasp rampant animal of uncertain type (contact not preserved); left arm (only partially preserved) is held down behind body to hold large curved weapon, probably a curved sword (only partially preserved).

Rampant animal moves away from hero; tail (only partially preserved) curves downward.

Hero of group at right wears elaborate double-belted garment. Sleeves of Persian type are preserved to either side of his upper torso, pushed up to shoulders. Lower garment appears to be Assyrian garment that leaves forward leg exposed below mid-thigh; thick fringe is indicated along edge of garment.

COMMENTARY

Based on Q texts protocol, PFS 1249 should belong to Irtena, who received flour rations in year 23.12 (498 B.C.) while traveling under the authority (*halmi*) of Ziššawiš. The name Irtena occurs in six other texts: PF 166, PF 549, PF 668, PF 1145, PF 1281, and PF 1443. PF 1281 and PF 1443 are also Q texts, and on each the receiver is named as Irtena, but the tablets are sealed with different seals, PFS 1225 (II) and PFS 160* (III) respectively. We are probably dealing with several individuals (see Koch 1990, pp. 165 [n. 695], 176–77).

The exact nature of the interaction between the hero with the weapon (at right end of impression) and the rampant animal is not clear. His garment appears to be some combination of the Persian court robe with sleeves (upper part) and the Assyrian garment (lower part). The motif of the hero clasping one or two animals to his chest is not common in Achaemenid glyptic.[99] By the same token, it is rendered in relief sculpture at Persepolis only on the jambs of two doorways.[100] See the commentary on PFS 131 (Cat.No. 170) for discussion of double encounter scenes.

The seal seems to have been quite large in diameter.

For comparative illustrations including PFS 1249, see pls. 207g (arm positions of heroic control), 215h (unusual heroic attitudes), 228c (pecking birds), 240d (double encounter images), and 243f (mixed animals/creatures).

SEAL APPLICATION (SEE *APPENDIX ONE: CONCORDANCE OF SEALS TO TABLETS IN VOLUME I*)

PFS 1249 occurs on the reverse of PF 1304. The partial rolling displays the bird in the center. PF 1304 is dated 498 B.C.

BIBLIOGRAPHY

Garrison 1988, pp. 302–04.

Cat.No. 295   PFS 152

Seal Type:	Cylinder	Photographs:	Pl. 165a–e
Earliest Dated Application:	501/500 B.C.	Typology and Style:	III-A.17 — Modeled Style
Preserved Height of Image:	1.70 cm (comp.)	Preserved Length of Image:	3.40 cm (comp.)
Estimated Height of Original Seal:	1.70 cm	Estimated Diameter of Original Seal:	1.10 cm
Number of Impressions:	8	Quality of Impressions:	Good

Completeness of Image: Complete except for details

DESCRIPTION OF SEAL AS IMPRESSED IMAGE

Two discrete heroic encounters are depicted.

At left, hero faces right, extending bent left arm outward to hold small inverted bull (calf) by hind leg; right arm is straight and held down behind body to hold curved sword.

Calf faces downward, chest toward hero. Calf holds one hind leg bent and extends it vertically upward; calf holds forelegs straight and extends them together downward toward hero's knee; long thin straight tail extends diagonally upward to right. Two large ears emerge from back of its head.

---

99. Herein, see compositional format I-B: PFS 131 (Cat.No. 170), PFS 1099 (Cat.No. 169), and PFS 1217s (Cat.No. 168). Note also a stamp seal from Persepolis (Schmidt 1957, pl. 17: PT5 1)

and a cylinder in the British Museum displaying Bes as hero in the terminal field (Collon 1987, pp. 182–83, no. 864).

100. Palace of Darius: Schmidt 1953, pl. 147; Root 1979, pp. 76–86; Root 1990b, pp. 20–21.

Hero at left wears triple-belted kilt. Rounded segmented beard rests over hero's left shoulder; rounded coiffure with striations rests at back of neck. Hero perhaps wears domed headdress.

To right of calf, rampant lion moves toward and faces hero. Lion holds one foreleg straight, toes splayed, and extends it downward toward calf held by hero; other foreleg is straight, toes splayed, and held up and away from its body. Lion slightly raises forward hind leg; long tail curves upward; mouth is slightly open.

To right of lion stands nude hero; upper body and head are frontal and lower body is in profile directed left (penis indicated). Hero holds arms bent and drawn up to chest with elbows pointing outward. From hero's right arm hangs long thick curving form (only partially preserved); from hero's left arm hangs thin curved form. Both forms presumably represent snakes suspended from hero's arms. Three long curls extend outward on each side of hero's head. Hero perhaps wears domed headdress.

To right, rampant winged lion creature moves toward nude hero but turns its head away from him. Creature holds upper foreleg straight, toes splayed, and extends it upward toward nude hero's head; lower foreleg is extended downward toward snake; long tail curves upward. Wing has double row of feathers; creature has bird's feet on hind legs. Mouth is open in roar; creature is ithyphallic.

Above wing tip of creature is small uncertain fragmentary element; indications of another element are between creature's tail and wing. Both may be chips in seal surface or small vestiges of design feature no longer preserved for analysis.

Vertical line extends up almost complete height of design field between rampant winged creature and hero with calf, serving as terminal element for entire double hero image.

Edge of seal is preserved at top and bottom of design.

COMMENTARY

This is the most unusual and most blatantly archaizing seal design in Volume I. Neither the crowded and busy scene in its entirety, nor the two heroic encounters individually, is paralleled.[101] The only features that find parallels in the PFS corpus of seal designs are the stylistic treatment of the two rampant animal forms, which are very close to several seals in the Fortification Style (see Garrison 1996b, for similar style). The frontal nude hero with curly hair is a bit of archaism that is very striking. The doubling of the heroic encounter also evokes antique practice.[102] Overall the seal shows a mixture of styles, which reflect its archaizing inspiration.

Perhaps the seal has been recut. Note that the rampant winged creature is elevated anomalously in the design field. Furthermore, the fragmentary traces next to its wing and the adjacent vertical line may be the remnants of an erased inscription.

See the commentary on PFS 131 (Cat.No. 170) for discussion of seals with two discrete heroic encounters depicted.

For comparative illustrations including PFS 152, see pls. 196b (coiffures of unusual types), 206d (arm positions of heroic control), 214g (frontal faces and/or bodies), 220f (bulls and bull creatures), 228e (fish and reptiles), 233c (ithyphallic animals/creatures), and 240b (double encounter images).

SEAL APPLICATION (SEE *APPENDIX ONE: CONCORDANCE OF SEALS TO TABLETS IN VOLUME I*)

PFS 152 occurs on the left edge of both PF 1062 and PF 1118, the upper edge of PF 1094, the upper edge and right edge of PF 1116–1117, and the reverse of PF 1951. Applications of the seal are clear; a few exhibit some

---

101. For interesting comparanda of Achaemenid date for the format (but not the style) of the hero holding the inverted animal, see the cylinder from the Pasargadae excavations (Stronach 1978, pl. 162a–b; Collon 1987, no. 425; Root 1999a) and the double hero cylinder found at Borsippa, Iraq (Collon 1987, no. 428). An early cylinder that conflates compositional aspects of the hero holding an inverted animal with the frontal hero grasping an animal in the crook of his arm is a late Early Dynastic lapis cylinder from Abu Salabikh (Collon 1987, no. 82).

102. For the frontal hero with curls and double-hero composition beginning in the Early Dynastic period but achieving a floruit in the Akkadian period, see Collon 1987, pp. 27, 32, 193; Garrison 1988, pp. 36–58. The frontal hero may ultimately relate to Lahmu (formerly associated with the hero/king Gilgamesh): Black and Green 1992, pp. 114–15. A revival of the frontal nude hero comparable to that on PFS 152 (although in combat versus an ostrich rather than grasping snakes) is seen on a cylinder impressed on a late Elamite-early Achaemenid tablet from Susa (see Amiet 1973b, pp. 7–8, pl. 1, no. 3, for preliminary publication as well as important discussion of the archaizing and dating issues). The hero with snakes goes back to late prehistory. In pre-Achaemenid Elamite traditions in southwestern Iran, the snake was associated with various deities. See, for example, Aruz 1992a, pp. 45–46, no. 18; Pittman 1992, pp. 54–55, no. 21; Miroschedji 1981.

lateral distortion. In two impressions the seal is rolled for at least one complete turn, preserving the entire length of the seal design. PF 1951 preserves a beautiful rolling that shows two and a half revolutions of the seal, placing the frontal nude hero in the center. The other complete rolling (on PF 1094) also displays the frontal nude hero in the center. Of the remaining six partial impressions, one displays the hero holding the calf in the center; one displays the hero holding the calf and the vertical line behind him in the center; two display the vertical line in the center; one displays the rampant lion and the frontal nude hero in the center; one displays the rampant lion in the center. PF 1951 is the earliest dated tablet with PFS 152 and is dated 501/500 B.C.

BIBLIOGRAPHY

Garrison 1988, pp. 253, 257–58, 366, 495; Garrison and Dion 1999, p. 9 (n. 20); Root 1996b, fig. 4; Root in press.

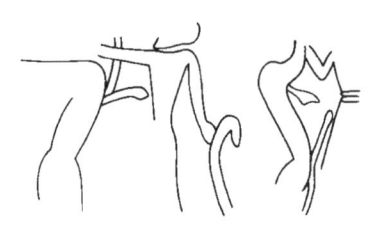

Cat.No. 296 PFS 757

Seal Type:	Cylinder	Photograph:	Pl. 166a
Earliest Dated Application:	501/500 B.C.	Typology and Style:	III-A.17 — Fortification Style
Preserved Height of Image:	1.40 cm (incomp.)	Preserved Length of Image:	2.30 cm (incomp.)
Estimated Height of Original Seal:	NA	Estimated Diameter of Original Seal:	NA
Number of Impressions:	1	Quality of Impression:	Poor

Completeness of Image: Segment of middle of design survives

DESCRIPTION OF SEAL AS IMPRESSED IMAGE

Two discrete heroic encounters are depicted.

At left of preserved impression, hero faces left, extending straight right arm upward toward rampant winged creature of uncertain type (contact not preserved); left arm is curved and held down behind body to hold large curved sword (partially preserved).

Creature moves toward hero. Creature holds upper foreleg curved and extends it diagonally upward; lower foreleg is straight and extended upward toward hero's chest.

Hero wears garment of uncertain type; hero has short pointed beard that rests over his right shoulder; rounded coiffure rests at back of neck.

At right of preserved impression, right side of the second hero is preserved. Hero has right arm bent to hold inverted animal of uncertain type by hind leg.

Animal holds hind leg held by hero curved and extended diagonally upward; other hind leg (with hoof) appears as if from far side of hindquarters and points toward hero's waist. Animal holds upper foreleg straight and extends it upward along hero's leg; lower foreleg (only partially preserved) is curved and extended downward along hero's leg.

Hero wears double-belted garment of uncertain type.

COMMENTARY

See commentary on PFS 131 (Cat.No. 170) for discussion of double encounter images.

This seal was not included in Garrison 1988.

For comparative illustrations including PFS 757, see pl. 240c (double encounter images).

SEAL APPLICATION (SEE *APPENDIX ONE: CONCORDANCE OF SEALS TO TABLETS IN VOLUME I*)

PFS 757 occurs on the reverse of PF 533. The partial rolling displays the hero of the left group (with his sword) and the inverted animal of the group to the right in the center. PF 533 is dated 501/500 B.C.

III-B. ONE HEROIC ENCOUNTER WITH TWO HEROES: ONE CONTROLLING, ONE THREATENING

III-B.4. LIONS

PFS 1101   Cat.No. 297

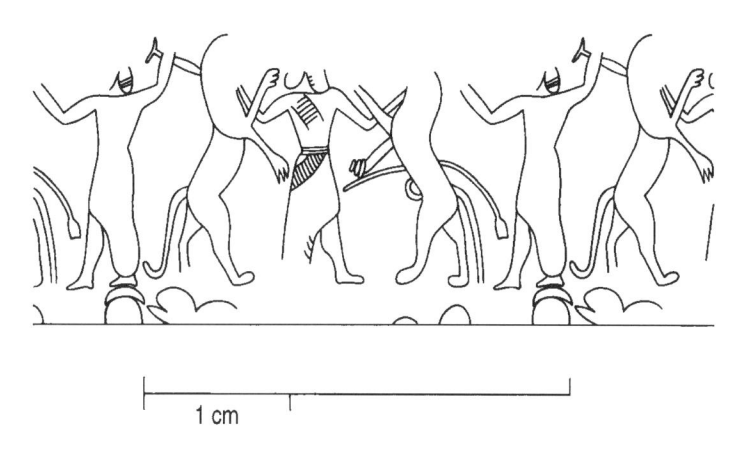

Seal Type:	Cylinder	Photographs:	Pl. 166c–d
Earliest Dated Application:	497/496 B.C.	Typology and Style:	III-B.4 — Mixed Styles I
Preserved Height of Image:	1.90 cm (incomp.)	Preserved Length of Image:	3.00 cm (comp.)
Estimated Height of Original Seal:	2.20 cm	Estimated Diameter of Original Seal:	1.00 cm
Number of Impressions:	3	Quality of Impressions:	Fair-good

Completeness of Image: Almost complete except for upper edge and details

DESCRIPTION OF SEAL AS IMPRESSED IMAGE

One double hero encounter is depicted.

Hero at left faces right, has arms bent, and holds two rampant lions by throat.

Each lion moves toward and faces hero. Lion to left holds upper foreleg straight, toes splayed, and extends it upward toward hero's head; lower foreleg is straight, toes splayed, an extended downward toward hero's hip. Tail curves downward, hooking upward at its end. Lion to right holds upper foreleg (only partially preserved) straight and extends it upward toward hero's head; lower foreleg is straight, toes splayed, and extended downward toward hero's leg; tail curves downward. Lion is apparently penetrated by arrow that droops downward behind lion's hindquarters. Half-circle at lower belly below arrow probably indicates ithyphallic lion.

Hero controlling two lions wears double-belted Assyrian garment that leaves forward leg exposed below knee; wide diagonal band is across chest and hip; fringe is indicated along front edge of lower part of garment over rear leg. Squared beard with horizontal striations rests over hero's left shoulder; rounded coiffure rests at back of neck.

To right of control encounter, second hero faces left and extends bent right arm upward to grasp rampant lion penetrated by arrow and controlled by other hero. Hero extends bent left arm upward behind head to stab neck of lion with dagger. Hero wears Assyrian garment that leaves forward leg exposed below knee. Narrow rounded coiffure with striations rests at back of hero's neck. Along bottom edge of design under rampant lions and dagger-wielding hero are various shapes; all are certainly chips in stone with exception of inverted crescent shape under rear foot of dagger-wielding hero. Crescent shape may be design element rather than flaw, but this is far from certain (see commentary).

Edge of seal is preserved at bottom of design.

COMMENTARY

Double hero scenes are rare in the PFS corpus. The double hero encounter displayed in PFS 1101 is particularly interesting because its asymmetry evokes a subtle narrative that reaches back ultimately to a group of Early Dynastic renderings which tell a story of attack by the hero of a predatory beast or beasts in defense of a domestic animal. One version of this narrative type is seen on a cylinder from Ur in which two rampant lions are attacking an inverted sheep. To the right of one lion the hero has grabbed this beast by the tail and is simultaneously stabbing it in the back of the neck. PFS 1101, with the controlling hero assuming the place of the ravaged sheep, is set up very similarly so that the combat hero appears to be coming to his rescue.[103] A good Achaemenid parallel for the double hero imagery of PFS 1101 is found in a cylinder seal impressed on a tablet from the Murašû archive that displays a combat encounter against a single lion creature in which a second hero joins the attack against the creature form the other side (Bregstein 1993, p. 485, no. 93 [no illustration]). See PFS 931* (Cat.No. 270) for a different double hero format. The narrative dynamic of PFS 1101 is somewhat related to that of PFS 49 (Cat.No. 23) and PFS 1466 (Cat.No. 234), where an archer appears as a secondary actor on the margin of a conventional scene of heroic encounter.

The various shapes along the bottom edge of impressions of PFS 1101 look to be chips in the stone, but the feet and paws of the figures are clearly preserved above them. The significant space between the feet of the figures and the bottom edge of the seal, combined with these chips, suggests that perhaps the seal once had a deep cap mount which was no longer in place when the seal was used on PF 1164 and PF 1227. Severe chipping might have occurred during or as a result of removal of the lower mount.

The design is well executed and carefully composed. The style shows a mixture of the Persepolitan Modeled Style and the Fortification Style.

For comparative illustrations including PFS 1101, see pls. 176h (Assyrian garments with detailing preserved), 240g (double hero encounters), 245h (spears), 279c (carving anomalies), and 280g (chips in seal matrices).

SEAL APPLICATION (SEE *APPENDIX ONE: CONCORDANCE OF SEALS TO TABLETS IN VOLUME I*)

PFS 1101 occurs on the upper edge of PF 1164 and twice on the reverse (inverted) of PF 1227. On both tablets PFS 130 (Cat.No. 300) is applied on the reverse and PFS 1102 (Cat.No. 132) on the left edge. PFS 130 (Cat.No. 300) is rolled directly above PFS 1101 on the reverse of PF 1227. On the reverse of PF 1227 the impressions of PFS 1101 are applied one directly above the other. The lower impression is now very damaged. In two impressions the seal is rolled for one complete turn, preserving the entire length of the seal design; the rolling on the upper edge of PF 1164 and the upper rolling on the reverse of PF 1227 both display the lion to the right of the controlling hero in the center. The partial lower rolling on the reverse of PF 1227 displays the controlling hero in the center. PF 1164 and PF 1227 are both dated 497/496 B.C.

BIBLIOGRAPHY

Garrison 1988, pp. 246–49, 326–30.

---

103. Collon 1987, pp. 28–29, no. 83. An equally interesting variant (which is less close to PFS 1101) is shown on an Early Dynastic III lapis seal from Abu Salabikh (ibid., pp. 28–29, no. 78). Here, a lion is attacking a bull (but they form a crossed animal group). Two spear-wielding heroic protectors of the flock converge on the lion from either side.

III-C. TWO HEROIC ENCOUNTERS WITH ONE HERO: HERO CONTROLS ONE ANIMAL OR CREATURE, THREATENS THE OTHER

III-C.5. WINGED LION CREATURES

PFS 24   Cat.No. 298

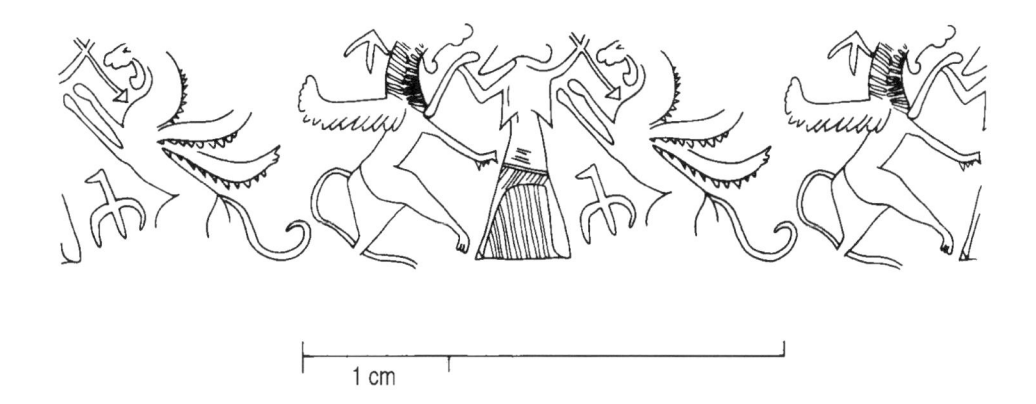

Seal Type: Cylinder	Photograph: Pl. 167a
Earliest Dated Application: 504/503 B.C.	Typology and Style: III-C.5 — Fortification Style
Preserved Height of Image: 1.60 cm (incomp.)	Preserved Length of Image: 3.30 cm (comp.
Estimated Height of Original Seal: NA	Estimated Diameter of Original Seal: 1.10 cm
Number of Impressions: 16	Quality of Impressions: Fair-good

Completeness of Image: Large segment of middle of design survives along its complete length

DESCRIPTION OF SEAL AS IMPRESSED IMAGE

Hero faces left, extending bent right arm downward to grasp rampant winged lion creature at left by upper foreleg; hero extends curved left arm upward holding spear poised to stab second rampant winged lion creature in chest.

Each creature moves toward and faces hero. Creature to left holds upper foreleg curved and extends it upward toward hero's head; lower foreleg is straight, toes splayed, and extended downward toward hero's thigh. Creature raises forward hind leg, paw turned downward, and extends it toward hero's foot (not preserved); long tail curves down between its hind legs. Creature to right holds both forelegs straight and extends them upward together toward hero's chest; long tail curves down, curling upward at its end. Creature has two wings, lower wing extending diagonally downward from upper wing.

Upper part of hero's garment conforms to conventions for the Persian court robe with sleeves pushed up to reveal arms; lower part of garment is of uncertain type, with multiple diagonal folds. Long pointed beard rests over hero's right arm; rounded coiffure rests at back of neck.

Creature to left has two rows of diagonal striations on neck, perhaps to indicate mane; mouth is open in roar. Mane of creature to right is rendered by crisp serrated edge along contour of neck; mouth is open in roar.

Abstractly rendered bird of uncertain type is displayed with wings spread, head pointing toward hero, in field between hero and creature to right; arrowhead symbol is in field behind neck of winged lion creature to left.

COMMENTARY

Koch notes that this seal often occurs with the name of the supplier Mirayauda at the post station Umpuranuš. Certainly, the fact that those Q texts (travel rations) which were sealed by PFS 24 (PF 1384–1385, PF 1388–1390, PF 1393–1394) always carried the seal on the left edge and always named Mirayauda as the supplier suggests that he used PFS 24 on those tablets. But Mirayauda also clearly used PFS 18 (Cat.No. 15), definitively during years 21–23. Was his use of PFS 18 (Cat.No. 15) simultaneous with or sequential to his use of PFS 24? Unfortunately, none of the Q texts bearing PFS 24 (and securely linked to Mirayauda) are dated. Of the two transactions carrying PFS 24 that are dated, one (PF 537, year 19) does not mention Mirayauda; and the other

(PF 348, year 23) names Parsauka, not Mirayauda, as supplier. Koch tentatively suggests that PFS 24 might be Mirayauda's earlier seal, but she has not taken PF 348 into account. If, as PF 348 indicates, Parsauka used PFS 24 here, then PFS 24 would appear to be an office seal of the station Umpuranuš.

Neither the abstract rendering of the bird nor the use of an arrowhead form as a linear device has a parallel among seals with images of heroic encounter in the PFS corpus. It is possible that the arrowhead device indicates a second abstract bird in flight, this time pointing upward into zone where preservation of details fails us.

The engraving, although somewhat coarse and hurried, is quite well executed.

For comparative illustrations including PFS 24, see pls. 181b (hybrid garments), 190b (beards), 226b (birds), 239b (unusual formats of heroic encounter), 245f (spears), and 255a (various devices and symbols).

SEAL APPLICATION (SEE *APPENDIX ONE: CONCORDANCE OF SEALS TO TABLETS IN VOLUME I*)

With one exception (PF 348, applied twice only on the reverse) PFS 24 occurs only on the left edge of tablets that it seals. On the left edge of PF 1385 the application of PFS 24 has been over-rolled by PFS 1308* (II) with careful calculation of visual effect. Rollings of the seal tend to be carefully applied, stressing the central zone of the figural design. In only one impression (on PF 1394) is the seal rolled for at least one complete turn, preserving the entire length of the seal design. This rolling displays the hero in the center. Of the remaining fifteen partial impressions, six display the hero in the center; two preserve only the hero; three preserve only the hero (at the right of the impression) and the creature to the left; two preserve only the hero (at the left of the impression) and the creature to right; one displays the creature to the left of the hero in the center; one preserves only he creature to the left of the hero. On the reverse of PF 348, the seal was partially rolled, picked up, and rolled again in the same horizontal plane. PF 595 is the earliest dated tablet with PFS 24 and is dated 504/503 B.C.

BIBLIOGRAPHY

Garrison 1988, pp. 316–18, 422; Garrison and Root 1996, p. 16, figs. 5a–b; Koch 1990, pp. 129 (n. 569), 138–40, 293–94; Root 1996a.

III-C.6. WINGED HUMAN-FACED/HUMAN-HEADED LION CREATURES

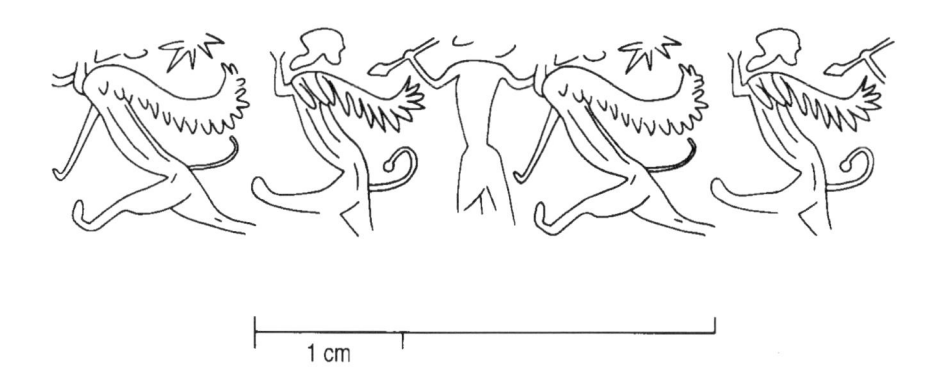

PFS 26   Cat.No. 299

Seal Type:	Cylinder	Photographs:	Pl. 167c–d
Earliest Dated Application:	499 B.C.	Typology and Style:	III-C.6 — Fortification Style
Preserved Height of Image:	1.40 cm (incomp.)	Preserved Length of Image:	3.10 cm (comp.)
Estimated Height of Original Seal:	NA	Estimated Diameter of Original Seal:	1.00 cm
Number of Impressions:	14	Quality of Impressions:	Fair

Completeness of Image: Almost complete except for upper edge and lower edge

DESCRIPTION OF SEAL AS IMPRESSED IMAGE

Hero faces left, extending bent left arm outward to grasp rampant winged human-headed lion creature by upper foreleg; hero extends bent right arm outward to hold spear aimed at back of second rampant winged human-headed lion creature.

Creature to left moves away from hero in vigorous striding pose but turns its head back toward him. Creature holds one foreleg bent and extends it upward in front of its body. Creature raises curved forward hind leg; tail curls upward with tufted termination. Creature to right, in vigorous striding pose, moves toward and faces hero. Creature holds upper foreleg (only partially preserved) straight and extends it upward in front of its head; lower foreleg is straight, paw upturned, and extended downward toward hero's leg. Creature raises bent forward hind leg, paw upturned, toward hero's leg; thin tail curves upward.

Hero wears Assyrian garment that leaves forward leg exposed below knee. Hero has pointed beard (only partially preserved); apparently large rounded coiffure (only partially preserved) rests at back of neck.

Each creature has striations along length of its body. Human head of creature to left has rounded beard over its chest; flattened coiffure rests at back of neck. Human head of creature to right has short pointed beard resting over its chest; rounded coiffure (only partially preserved) rests at back of neck.

Star (only partially preserved) is in field above wing of creature to right.

COMMENTARY

Koch identifies the seal owner as Barušiyatiš, a supplier probably from the post station Parmadan, based upon Q texts protocol. See also the commentary for PFS 1613 (Cat.No. 82), which appears to be another seal used by this individual.

The design is similar to that seen on PFS 24 (Cat.No. 298). PFS 26 has, however, a greater sense of dynamic motion. Both animals move in the same direction, creating a strong pull across the design from right to left; see PFS 912 (Cat.No. 138), PFS 1202 (Cat.No. 137), and PFS 1188 (Cat.No. 144) for designs herein that have two animals moving in the same direction. The composition of PFS 26 is infused with a sense of narrative sequence rather than emblematic stasis through the device of having one creature run away from the hero.

For comparative illustrations including PFS 26, see pls. 270a (compositions with strong unidirectional movement) and 285a (personal seals of Barušiyatiš, flour supplier).

SEAL APPLICATION (SEE *APPENDIX ONE: CONCORDANCE OF SEALS TO TABLETS IN VOLUME I*)

PFS 26 occurs only on the left edge of tablets that it seals. Rollings of the seal tend to be carefully applied with little or no distortion. In no impression is the seal rolled for one complete turn, but six impressions preserve almost the entire length of the seal design. All six of these rollings display the hero in the center. Of the remaining eight partial impressions, three preserve the hero (at the right of the impression) and the creature to the left of the hero; three preserve only the two creatures; one preserves only the creature to the left of the hero; one preserves only the creature to the right of the hero. PF 1290–1294, PF 1296–1297, and PF 1704 are the earliest dated tablets with PFS 26 and are all dated 499 B.C.

BIBLIOGRAPHY

Garrison 1988, pp. 317–18, 422; Koch 1986, p. 140.

III-C.17. MIXED ANIMALS AND/OR CREATURES

Cat.No. 300   PFS 130

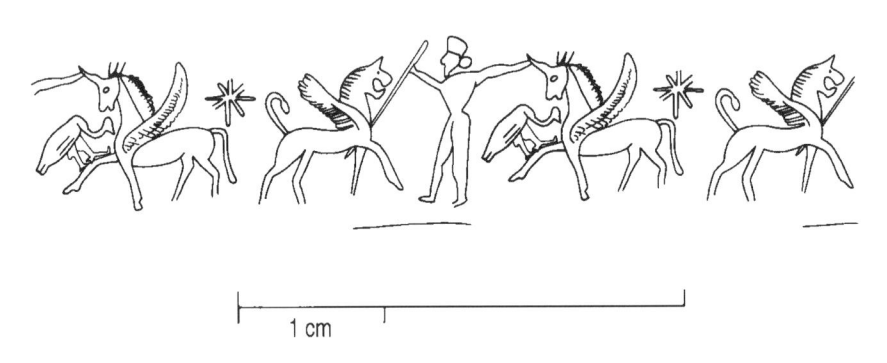

Seal Type:	Cylinder	Photographs:	Pl. 168a–b
Earliest Dated Application:	499 B.C.	Typology and Style:	III-C.17 — Fortification Style
Preserved Height of Image:	1.20 cm (incomp.)	Preserved Length of Image:	3.00 cm (comp.)
Estimated Height of Original Seal:	1.40 cm	Estimated Diameter of Original Seal:	1.00 cm
Number of Impressions:	5	Quality of Impressions:	Fair-good

Completeness of Image: Complete except for upper edge and lower edge

DESCRIPTION OF SEAL AS IMPRESSED IMAGE

Hero faces left, extending straight left arm behind him to grasp marchant winged bull at right by horn; hero holds right arm straight and diagonally upward to hold spear that penetrates chest of marchant winged lion creature at left (point of spear visible below creature).

Each creature moves toward and faces hero. Winged lion creature raises bent forward foreleg toward hero; tail extends diagonally upward, curving downward at its end with tufted termination. Winged bull raises bent forward foreleg toward hero; long tail bends downward. Vulture facing right perches on bull creature's foreleg, pecking at its chest.

Hero perhaps wears trousers and flat headdress. Pointed beard rests over hero's right shoulder; round coiffure rests at back of neck.

Mane of winged lion creature is indicated by diagonal markings on its neck. Short pointed ear emerges from front of its head; mouth is open. Mane of winged bull is rendered by serrated edge along contour of neck; two rows of feathers are indicated on its wing. Curved horn emerges from front of its head; two straight ears (only partially preserved) are at back of head; bull creature holds mouth open.

Star is in upper terminal field.

Portion of edge of seal is preserved at bottom of design below hero and lion creature.

COMMENTARY

Koch (1990) suggests that PFS 130 belongs to Bakabana (not the same person as the satrap of Elam), who received and passed on wine and grain rations to workers in Koch's Southeastern Region III.

The engraving is extremely well executed and the design is lively.

A good parallel for the vulture occurs on a stamp seal impression on an envelope from Fort Shalmanesar at Nimrud.[104]

For comparative illustrations including PFS 130, see pls. 186f (headdresses), 220e (bulls and bull creatures), 226f (birds), 228b (pecking birds), 245g (spears), and 267b (terminal field motifs other than inscriptions).

SEAL APPLICATION (SEE *APPENDIX ONE: CONCORDANCE OF SEALS TO TABLETS IN VOLUME I*)

PFS 130 occurs on the reverse of PF 1163–1164 and PF 1227 and on the upper edge and right edge of PF 1162. PFS 114 (Cat.No. 284) is applied directly above PFS 130 on the reverse of PF 1163. PFS 1101 (Cat.No. 297) is applied (inverted) directly below PFS 130 on the reverse of PF 1227. Impressions of the seal tend to be clearly applied and show little or no distortion. In three impressions the seal has been rolled for at least one complete turn, preserving the entire seal design. Of these three applications, one displays the hero in the center; two display the hero and the lion creature to left in the center. Of the remaining two partial rollings, one displays the hero in the center; one displays the bull creature to the right of the hero in the center. On PF 1164 the seal clearly was applied before the text since several cuneiform wedges cut into the top of the impression. PF 1162 and PF 1163 are the earliest dated tablets with PFS 130 and are both dated 499 B.C.

BIBLIOGRAPHY

Garrison 1988, pp. 359–63, 422, 480; Koch 1990, p. 105.

---

104. Parker (1962, p. 37, fig. 3, pl. 22: 2) identifies the bird as an ibis. See Salonen 1973, pp. 81–82, on vultures in the Mesopotamian tradition.

Cat.No. 301 PFS 447

|—1 cm—|

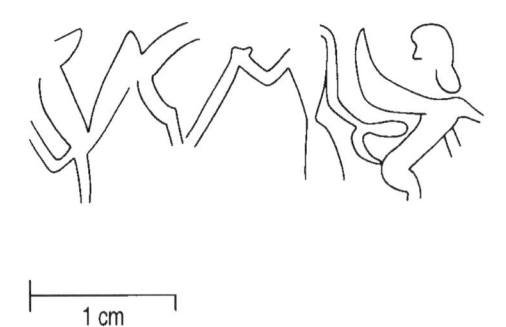

Seal Type:	Cylinder	Photograph:	Pl. 168d
Earliest Dated Application:	498/497 B.C.	Typology and Style:	III-C.17 — Fortification Style
Preserved Height of Image:	1.30 cm (incomp.)	Preserved Length of Image:	3.10 cm (incomp.)
Estimated Height of Original Seal:	NA	Estimated Diameter of Original Seal:	NA
Number of Impressions:	1	Quality of Impression:	Very poor

Completeness of Image: Segment of middle of design survives

DESCRIPTION OF SEAL AS IMPRESSED IMAGE

Hero moves to left and extends bent left arm downward to grasp rampant winged human-headed lion creature by tail; hero holds right arm bent and extends it downward holding spear(?) that he drives into lower hind leg of inverted long-necked animal of uncertain type.

Speared animal moves away from hero, hindquarters high in air as if jumping. Animal holds forward foreleg (only partially preserved) bent and extends it upward in front of its neck; lower foreleg (only partially preserved) is straight and extended vertically downward under its body. Animal holds lower hind leg (engaged by spear) bent and extends it diagonally downward under its body; upper hind leg (only partially preserved) is curved and diagonally extended upward to right.

Hero wears garment of uncertain type.

Human-headed creature to right moves away from hero but turns its head back toward him. Creature holds both forelegs (only partially preserved) diagonally downward in front of its body; tail curls upward with large tufted termination. Long rounded coiffure rests at back of its neck.

COMMENTARY

The composition is not clear in all details.
    For comparative illustrations including PFS 447, see pl. 239g (unusual formats of heroic control).

SEAL APPLICATION (SEE APPENDIX ONE: CONCORDANCE OF SEALS TO TABLETS IN VOLUME I)

PFS 447 occurs on the reverse of PF 137. The partial rolling displays the hero in the center. PF 137 is dated 498/497 B.C.

BIBLIOGRAPHY

Garrison 1988, pp. 344, 346.

PFS 29   Cat.No. 302

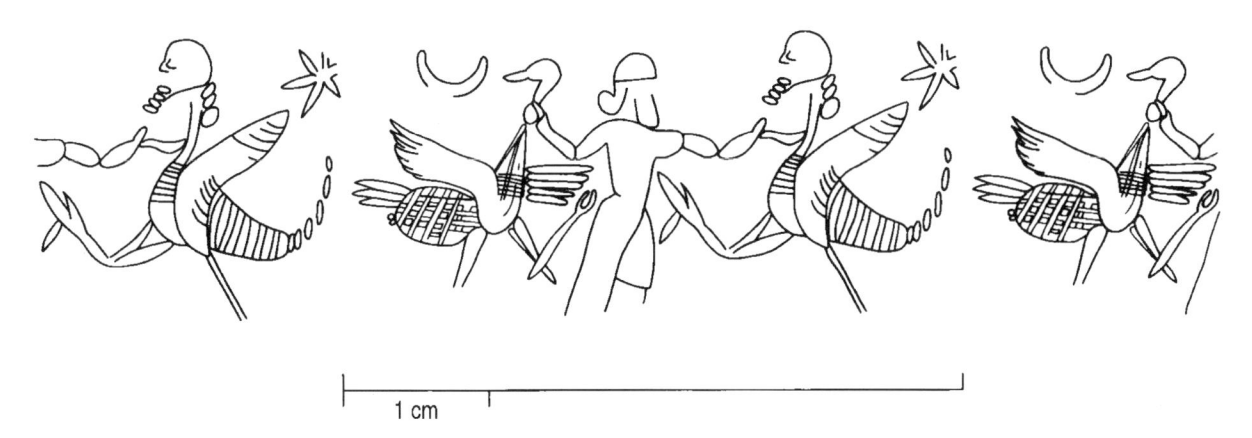

Seal Type:	Cylinder	Photographs:	Pl. 169a–d
Earliest Dated Application:	504/503 B.C.	Typology and Style:	III-C.17 — Modeled Style
Preserved Height of Image:	1.90 cm (incomp.)	Preserved Length of Image:	4.20 cm (comp.)
Estimated Height of Original Seal:	NA	Estimated Diameter of Original Seal:	1.30 cm
Number of Impressions:	17	Quality of Impressions:	Fair

Completeness of Image: Large segment of middle of design survives along its complete length

DESCRIPTION OF SEAL AS IMPRESSED IMAGE

Hero faces right, extending bent left arm outward holding dagger that he drives into throat of marchant winged human-headed scorpion creature; hero extends bent right arm outward to grasp marchant ostrich by throat.

Ostrich moves toward hero but turns its head away from him. Ostrich raises bent forward leg toward hero's waist; leg terminates in two-pronged appendage. Wings are spread to each side of ostrich's body; tail, held straight out, consists of three horizontal segments.

Scorpion creature moves toward and faces hero. Creature raises bent forward leg toward hero's chest; leg terminates in three-pronged appendage. Beaded scorpion tail curves upward.

Hero wears Assyrian garment that leaves forward leg exposed below knee. Long squared beard rests over hero's left shoulder; rounded coiffure curls upward at back of neck. Hero perhaps wears domed headdress.

Thumb is indicated on hero's right hand.

Ostrich body is decorated with waffle pattern; striations are indicated on neck. Its left wing consists of graduated series of horizontal segments detached from body; its right wing makes continuous curve from chest.

Head of scorpion creature has squared segmented beard; long, rounded, segmented coiffure is at back of long thin neck. Many detail lines are on creature's body and wing.

Crescent is in field above wing of ostrich; star is above tail of scorpion creature.

COMMENTARY

Koch (1990) links this seal with Ammamarda, an official concerned with grain during years 18–22 at Hišema in her Elam Region VI.

    The seal is very large. The design shows much detailing in the creatures' bodies; note especially the segmentation of the scorpion body, its beaded tail, the waffle pattern of the ostrich body and its segmented wing and tail. The spread wings and back-turned head of the ostrich create a lively compositional dynamic. The ostrich and scorpion creatures are holdovers from Assyro-Babylonian glyptic see PFS 9* (Cat.No. 288) and PFS 263 (Cat.No. 289) for other ostriches and for discussions of their significance; see PFS 4* (Cat.No. 292) and PFS 1586 (Cat.No. 121) for scorpion creatures. For human-headed scorpion creatures in an image of heroic encounter of Neo-Assyrian date, see a cylinder seal impression on a tablet from the Nabu Temple at Nimrud dated ca. 616 B.C. (Herbordt 1992, p. 191, pl. 8, no. 6 = Parker 1962, p. 36, fig. 1, pl. 19, no. 1), where the scorpion creatures also raise one leg toward the hero. The modeling in the human form of the hero of PFS 29 is very rich.

For comparative illustrations including PFS 29, see pls. 229b (scorpion, fish, horse, bird, and human creatures), 230b (feet of animals and creatures), 234c (human-headed/human-faced creatures), 239c (unusual formats of heroic encounter), 252b (crescents and stars), and 282c (personal seals of supply/apportionment officers).

SEAL APPLICATION (SEE *APPENDIX ONE: CONCORDANCE OF SEALS TO TABLETS IN VOLUME I*)

PFS 29 occurs only on the left edge of tablets that it seals. Although the rollings of this seal are not consistently presented along the longitudinal axis of the tablets, little distortion occurs. In no impression is the entire length of the seal design preserved. Of the seventeen partial impressions, two display the hero in the center; five preserve only the hero (at the right of the impression) and the ostrich; five preserve only the hero (at the left of the impression) and the scorpion creature; one preserves only the scorpion creature; and one preserves the area defined by the hindquarters of scorpion creature and ostrich. The three remaining impressions occur over-rolled on the left edge of PF 555: one preserves the lower body of the hero; one preserves the ostrich; one preserves segments of the scorpion creature's tail. PF 356 is the earliest dated tablet with PFS 29 and is dated 504/503 B.C.

BIBLIOGRAPHY

Aperghis 1999, pp. 165–68, 175, 190; Garrison 1988, pp. 207–10, 521; Koch 1990, p. 303.

III-C.18. ANIMALS OF UNCERTAIN TYPE

Cat.No. 303   PFS 243

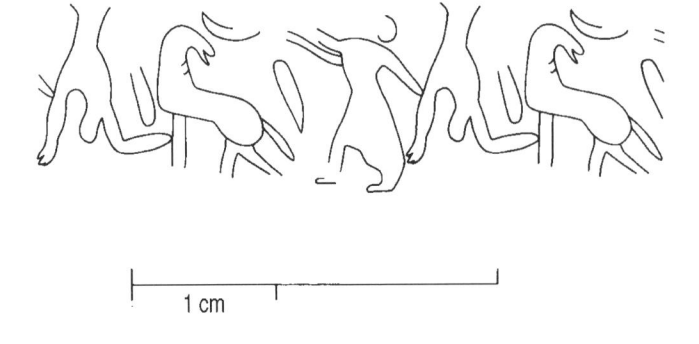

Seal Type:	Cylinder	Photograph:	Pl. 170a
Earliest Dated Application:	500/499 B.C.	Typology and Style:	III-C.18 — Broad and Flat Styles
Preserved Height of Image:	1.30 cm (incomp.)	Preserved Length of Image:	2.50 cm (comp.)
Estimated Height of Original Seal:	NA	Estimated Diameter of Original Seal:	0.80 cm
Number of Impressions:	7	Quality of Impressions:	Fair

Completeness of Image: Segment of middle of design survives along its complete length

DESCRIPTION OF SEAL AS IMPRESSED IMAGE

Hero faces left, extending straight right arm (only partially preserved) upward to combat rampant animal of uncertain type; left arm is straight and held down behind body at diagonal, touching or grasping foreleg of inverted horned animal of undetermined type. Slightly curved element meeting hero's chest under right arm may be part of elongated curved sword held at midsection by hero.

Hero may wear Persian court robe with sleeves not indicated; contour of lower part of garment suggests Persian robe slightly hitched up over hero's right leg. Rounded coiffure rests at back of neck.

To left of hero, the rampant animal combatted by hero moves to left but turns head back toward hero. Animal holds forward foreleg straight and extends it diagonally upward in front of its body; straight tail extends diagonally downward; mouth is parted.

To right of hero, inverted horned animal appears to be suspended inert; long horn bends to right.

Elongated lozenge with one pointed end is diagonally suspended in field between hero and animal to left. Crescent shape (only partially preserved) in field above animal to left appears to be end of blade of weapon (curved sword?) held by hero.

COMMENTARY

The design appears to be a heroic encounter, but there are elements that are not precisely understood. The hero clearly seems to be doing something active with his upraised right arm. The reconstruction of the hero's action suggested in the description above implies a somewhat awkwardly held and exaggerated weapon. This would be consistent with other features of the design (e.g., the horn of the inverted animal). It is also possible, however, that this seal has been recut, resulting in vestigial forms.

The lozenge with one pointed end seems to be an isolated device rather than a part of an otherwise obscure animal. Shapes of uncertain meaning, sometimes quite similar to this one, occur on certain Neo-Assyrian and Neo-Babylonian seals and the usage occasionally persists in products of the Achaemenid period.[105] It is also noteworthy, however, that the composition of PFS 243 echoes Early Dynastic II glyptic; and the Early Dynastic II contest images frequently incorporate shapes in the field, often of uncertain meaning to us.[106]

For a discussion of the inert inverted animal as possibly representing the carcass of a ravaged animal, see the commentary on PFS 1475 (Cat.No. 177).

See Garrison 1988 for the hand and distinctive compositions of this artist.

For comparative illustrations including PFS 243, see pls. 225c (horned animals and horned-animal creatures of undetermined types), 237b (animal carcasses), 239d (unusual formats of heroic encounter), and 255c (various devices and symbols).

SEAL APPLICATION (SEE *APPENDIX ONE: CONCORDANCE OF SEALS TO TABLETS IN VOLUME I*)

PFS 243 occurs on the reverse (inverted) and upper edge of PF 1682, the upper edge and right edge of PF 1683, and the reverse (inverted), upper edge, and left edge of PF 1701. In three impressions the seal is rolled for at least one complete turn, preserving the entire length of the seal design. Of these three applications, two display the hero in the center; one displays the hero and the pointed lozenge in the center. Of the four remaining partial rollings, two display the hero in the center; one preserves only the hero and the inverted animal; one preserves only the pointed lozenge and the rampant animal. On the reverse of PF 1682 and PF 1701 the seal clearly was applied before the text since several cuneiform wedges cut into the top of the impressions. PF 1682 and PF 1683 are the earliest dated tablets with PFS 243 and are both dated 500/499 B.C.

BIBLIOGRAPHY

Garrison 1988, pp. 423–25.

---

105. For example, Herbordt 1992, pl. 8, no. 11b (impression from Nineveh). Possibly the pointed lozenge on PFS 243 is a clumsy rendering of an elongated triangle shape. In this case, it would plausibly symbolize Anu; compare Stolper 1990b, pl. 49b (impression of an Achaemenid-period seal on a legal text from Uruk dating to 426 or 366 B.C.).

106. For example, Karg 1984, pl. 2, nos. 9 and 11, from Fara; pl. 3, nos. 7 and 10, from Ur and Susa respectively.

III-C.19. WINGED CREATURES OF UNCERTAIN TYPE

Cat.No. 304   PFS 6

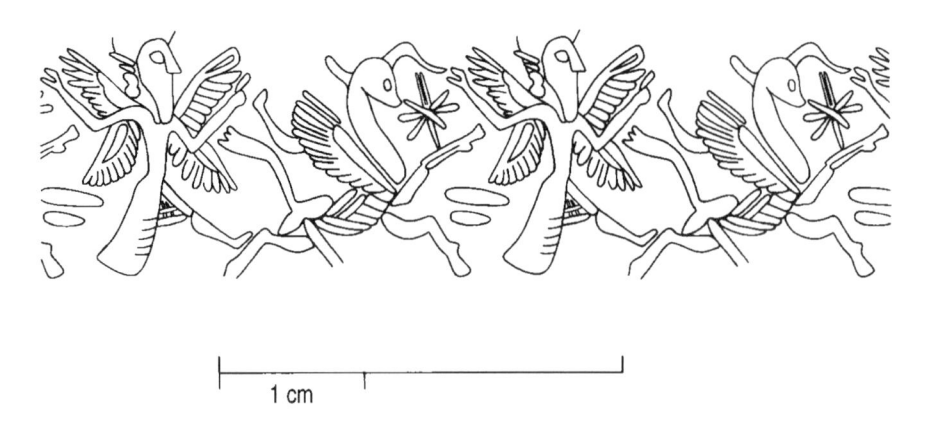

Seal Type: Cylinder	Photographs: Pl. 170c–d
Earliest Dated Application: 503/502 B.C.	Typology and Style: III-C.19 — Diverse Styles
Preserved Height of Image: 1.60 cm (incomp.)	Preserved Length of Image: 2.80 cm (comp.)
Estimated Height of Original Seal: 1.90 cm	Estimated Diameter of Original Seal: 0.90 cm
Number of Impressions: 32	Quality of Impressions: Poor-fair

Completeness of Image: Complete except for upper edge and lower edge

DESCRIPTION OF SEAL AS IMPRESSED IMAGE

Four-winged hero faces right, extending bent left arm outward apparently to grasp curved sword (with break in preservation) that extends down to touch wing of courant winged creature of uncertain type. Hero extends bent right arm behind him with hand open to grasp horn of same creature. Hero, in vigorous striding pose, raises forward leg to place his foot on hind leg of creature.

Creature holds upper foreleg bent and extends it upward toward hero's right arm; lower foreleg is bent and extended diagonally downward; rear hind leg stretches back in full stride; forward hind leg (only partially preserved) extends forward under body. Thick bent tail extends upward with serrated termination.

Hero wears Assyrian garment that leaves forward leg exposed; fringe is indicated over rear leg of lower part of garment; decorative pattern of horizontal borders interspersed with small vertical elements decorates garment stretched between hero's legs. Long squared beard rests across hero's left shoulder; rounded wavy coiffure rests at back of neck. Hero perhaps wears domed headdress with projection at back (top not preserved).

Creature's body consists of series of segmented elements. Long curved horn emerges from front of its head; large rounded ear rests at back of neck.

Star is in field between creature's head and upper foreleg; two lozenge-shaped elements are placed horizontally one above the other in field between creature's forelegs.

COMMENTARY

Koch (1990) identifies PFS 6 as the personal seal of Manukka, a supplier of workers and animals in her Shiraz Region II and Persepolis Region I. As she notes, PFS 6 also occurs, however, on PF 857–858, where grain was supplied by Hatarbanuš.

The style has some connection with the Fortification Style, especially in the shape of the hero's body and its plain surface treatment. The disjointed and elongated animal forms are, however, unusual; for the wing, see PFS 2 (Cat.No. 3). The composition whereby one animal wraps around the cylindrical surface so as to appear in its impressed state to be on both sides of the hero is an old one in the glyptic of western Asia. It is rare in the PFS corpus of hero seals, appearing again only in PFS 284* (Cat.No. 111), a control encounter, and probably in PFS 896 (Cat.No. 308).

The seal appears to be quite worn; all impressions are blurred and difficult to read.

For comparative illustrations including PFS 6, see pls. 195a (coiffures of distinctive types/sub-types), 239a (unusual formats of heroic encounter), and 278a (carving anomalies).

SEAL APPLICATION (SEE *APPENDIX ONE: CONCORDANCE OF SEALS TO TABLETS IN VOLUME I*)

With one exception (PF 1776, reverse), PFS 6 occurs only on the left edge of tablets that it seals. Impressions of the seal apparently are carefully applied, but owing to the shallowness of the carving, they are not always easy to read. In nine impressions the seal is rolled for at least one complete turn, preserving the entire length of the seal design. These complete rollings often appear, however, to be incomplete, owing to the unusual nature of the design (displaying elements of both the control and combat encounter). Of these nine applications, one displays the hero in the center; two display the creature in the center; six display the hero at the right of the impression, the creature at the left. Of the remaining twenty-three impressions, one displays the hero in the center; two preserve only the hero; four preserve the hero at the left of the impression, the creature at the right; ten preserve the hero at the right of the impression, the creature at the left; six preserve only the creature. PF 1180 is the earliest dated tablet with PFS 6 and is dated 503/502 B.C.

BIBLIOGRAPHY

Garrison 1988, p. 453; Garrison 1998, p. 121 (n. 15); Koch 1990, pp. 45, 56–57, 263, 265.

III-D. FRAGMENTARY IMAGES SUGGESTING VARIOUS CONTROL AND COMBAT ENCOUNTERS

III-D.20. ANIMALS OR CREATURES OF UNVERIFIABLE TYPE

Cat.No. 305   PFS 199*

Seal Type:	Cylinder, Inscribed	Photographs:	Pl. 171a–b
Earliest Dated Application:	503/502 B.C.	Typology and Style:	III-D.20 — Modeled Style
Language of Inscription:	Elamite(?)		
Preserved Height of Image:	1.80 cm (incomp.)	Preserved Length of Image:	3.60 cm (incomp.)
Estimated Height of Original Seal:	NA	Estimated Diameter of Original Seal:	NA
Number of Impressions:	2	Quality of Impressions:	Poor

Completeness of Image: Segment of middle of the design survives

DESCRIPTION OF SEAL AS IMPRESSED IMAGE

At far left of impressions, hero faces left, holds both arms (upper arm only partially preserved) straight, and extends them outward in front of his body. His left hand rests atop a horizontal element, possibly the foreleg of an animal or creature of unverifiable type (not preserved).

At far right of impressions, rampant winged lion creature moves right; appendage at its throat suggests extended human arm, but angle does not link with hero at left. Creature holds one foreleg (only partially preserved) straight and extends it diagonally downward; short tail extends diagonally upward, hooking upward at its end in segmented termination.

Hero wears double-belted Assyrian garment that leaves forward leg exposed below knee; double border is on hem of garment over forward leg. Long squared beard with horizontal striations rests over hero's chest; flattened coiffure rests at back of neck. Torso is in profile.

Mane of creature is rendered by spikes along contour of its neck; mouth is open in roar.

Paneled inscription is in terminal field.

INSCRIPTION

Elamite(?)

Line   x+1. ⌜x⌝[...]
        x+2. RA BA UD
        x+3. x x x

Translation   ?

Three lines of the inscription are preserved, oriented along the horizontal axis of the seal, separated by case lines, and enclosed in a panel. The inscription is illegible. The forms appear to be Elamite. All the case lines show marked distortion. Distortion is also seen in the shapes of the wedges. Vertical wedges appear to be made with a single straight vertical line from which only a single branch diverges, normally to the right. This same formation is evident in many of the horizontal wedges, with the branch diverting to the top if the wedge is in the upper part of a sign, and diverting toward the bottom if the wedge is on the bottom of a sign. Wedges in the middle of a sign appear to be more symmetrical.

Three(?) signs appear to be indicated in the third line, but the exact reading is not clear. The diagonal line between the second and third sign does not appear to be part of the inscription.

COMMENTARY

The seal is relatively large and may have incorporated two discrete heroic encounters of which only parts of each have been retrieved.

For comparative illustrations including PFS 199*, see pls. 191g (variously detailed beards), 214b (profile torsos), and 262d (paneled inscriptions with horizontal case lines).

SEAL APPLICATION (SEE *APPENDIX ONE: CONCORDANCE OF SEALS TO TABLETS IN VOLUME I*)

PFS 199* occurs on the reverse of PF 499 and the obverse of PF 557, with PFS 106 (III) on the left edge of each tablet. On PF 499 the seal is inverted. Both applications show marked vertical and lateral distortion, which may be due as much to the execution of the design as to the rolling of the seal. Both partial impressions carefully display the inscription in the center. On the reverse of PF 557 the seal clearly was applied before the text since several cuneiform wedges cut into the top of the impression. PF 499 and PF 557 are both dated 503/502 B.C.

BIBLIOGRAPHY

Garrison 1988, pp. 212, 215; Garrison and Dion 1999, p. 10 (n. 28).

PFS 373   Cat.No. 306

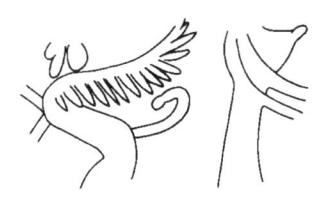

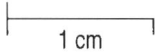

Seal Type:	Cylinder	Photograph:	Pl. 171d
Earliest Dated Application:	504/503 B.C.	Typology and Style:	III-D.20 — Fortification Style
Preserved Height of Image:	1.20 cm (incomp.)	Preserved Length of Image:	2.00 cm (incomp.)
Estimated Height of Original Seal:	NA	Estimated Diameter of Original Seal:	NA
Number of Impressions:	1	Quality of Impression:	Poor

Completeness of Image: Small segment of middle of design survives

DESCRIPTION OF SEAL AS IMPRESSED IMAGE

Hero moves to right, torso in profile, extending both arms down and forward to engage animal or creature of unverifiable type (not preserved). Above hero's left arm, passage of carving appears to represent initial rendering of a frontal torso, with left arm upraised.

Behind hero, rampant winged human-headed bull or lion creature faces left. Creature holds upper foreleg (only partially preserved) straight and extends it diagonally upward; lower foreleg (only partially preserved) is straight and extended diagonally downward; tail extends diagonally upward, curling at its end with tufted termination.

Hero wears robe that incorporated sleeve (spread wide) of Persian court robe at originally carved left arm (upraised).

Rounded beard of creature terminates over its chest; rounded coiffure rests at back of neck.

COMMENTARY

Too little of the design survives to guarantee its identification as a heroic encounter. What is preserved suggests an initial plan to depict a combat encounter with the hero's left arm holding the creature at the head while stabbing it in the belly with the right arm. This composition was then changed to depict both arms held diagonally downward, with no attempt to erase the vestigial raised left arm with sleeve. The seal is interesting as an example of a flawed carving that was nevertheless in circulation as an active seal (see Root 1999a).

For comparative illustrations including PFS 373, see pls. 214c (profile torsos) and 279a (carving anomalies).

SEAL APPLICATION (SEE *APPENDIX ONE: CONCORDANCE OF SEALS TO TABLETS IN VOLUME I*)

PFS 373 occurs on the left edge of PF 64. The partial rolling preserves only the hero (at the right of the impression) and the creature. PF 64 is dated 504/503 B.C.

BIBLIOGRAPHY

Garrison 1988, pp. 271–73; Root 1999a, pp. 184–85, fig. 11.

Cat.No. 307   PFS 503

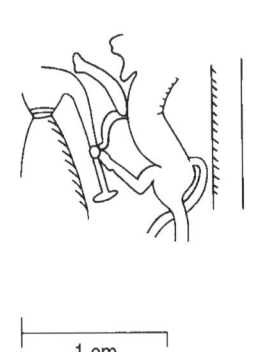

Seal Type:	Cylinder	Photograph:	Pl. 171f
Earliest Dated Application:	498/497 B.C.	Typology and Style:	III-D.20 — Modeled Style
Preserved Height of Image:	1.20 cm (incomp.)	Preserved Length of Image:	1.50 cm (incomp.)
Estimated Height of Original Seal:	NA	Estimated Diameter of Original Seal:	NA
Number of Impressions:	1	Quality of Impression:	Poor

Completeness of Image: Small fragment of middle of design survives

DESCRIPTION OF SEAL AS IMPRESSED IMAGE

Hero moves to left. Right arm is not preserved; left arm is straight and held down behind body to hold hammer-like weapon. Animal or creature grasped by hero is of unverifiable type (not preserved).

Hero wears double-belted garment of uncertain type; fringe is indicated along back edge.

Behind hero, rampant lion moves toward and faces hero. Lion holds upper foreleg bent and extends it upward toward hero's head; lower foreleg is curved and extended downward to place upturned paw on hero's hand. Lion raises bent forward hind leg to place paw on hero's weapon; long thick tail (only partially preserved) curves downward between its hind legs. Mane is indicated by diagonal lines along contour of neck; mouth is open in roar.

Trunk of palm(?) tree is to right of lion in terminal field.

COMMENTARY

Although poorly preserved, the design appears to have been well executed and quite large. The rendering of the lion is in the tradition of the Fortification Style (where it was placed by Garrison 1988), but the hero seems closely related to human figures of a group of artists in the Modeled Style. Despite the loss to us of the animal or creature engaged by the hero, the combat encounter seems secure.

For comparative illustrations including PFS 503, see pls. 245c (various weapons) and 258f (palm trees).

SEAL APPLICATION (SEE *APPENDIX ONE: CONCORDANCE OF SEALS TO TABLETS IN VOLUME I*)

PFS 503 occurs on the reverse (inverted) of PF 226. The surface of the reverse of the tablet is very poorly preserved. PFS 504 (III) is applied along the longitudinal axis of the reverse above and to the right of the rolling of PFS 503. PFS 502 (III) is applied to the right of PFS 503, apparently over-rolling it. The partial rolling of PFS 503, now much damaged, preserves only what our drawing indicates. PF 226 is dated 498/497 B.C.

BIBLIOGRAPHY

Garrison 1988, pp. 312–13.

PFS 896   Cat.No. 308

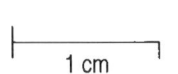

Seal Type:	Cylinder	Photograph:	Pl. 172a
Earliest Dated Application:	498/497 B.C.	Typology and Style:	III-D.20 — Broad and Flat Styles
Preserved Height of Image:	0.90 cm (incomp.)	Preserved Length of Image:	2.10 cm (incomp.)
Estimated Height of Original Seal:	NA	Estimated Diameter of Original Seal:	NA
Number of Impressions:	1	Quality of Impression:	Fair

Completeness of Image: Segment of middle of design survives

DESCRIPTION OF SEAL AS IMPRESSED IMAGE

Winged hero faces right, extending straight left arm (only partially preserved) upward; hero holds right arm bent and extends it outward to grasp tail possibly belonging to marchant(?) winged creature of uncertain type (only end of tail and edge of a wing preserved).

Hero wears garment of uncertain type. Large rounded beard rests over left upper arm; squared coiffure rests at back of neck. Single wing grows out of hero's right shoulder.

Star is in field in front of hero's chest; crescent is in upper field above hero's right hand.

COMMENTARY

The composition is not clear as preserved. The upward movement of the hero's left arm suggests that he may hold a weapon with which he attacks the front end of the same winged creature whose tail he appears to hold in his right hand. See PFS 6 (Cat.No. 304) for a similar compositional format involving only one creature who is engaged by the hero at both front and rear. Despite this good parallel for such a composition, the evidence for PFS 896 remains ambiguous. The distance between the tail and the edge of the wing yields an extremely elongated creature here, if we reconstruct both elements as belonging to the same creature. Perhaps the tail belongs to an inverted animal and the wing belongs to a rampant winged creature engaged by the hero's left hand.

The coarse engraving may be an unusual variation of types of carving found in the Broad and Flat Styles.

For comparative illustrations including PFS 896, see pls. 194f (narrow rounded and/or pointed coiffures), 195e (coiffures of distinctive types/sub-types), 239h (unusual formats of heroic encounter), and 252g (crescents and stars).

SEAL APPLICATION (SEE *APPENDIX ONE: CONCORDANCE OF SEALS TO TABLETS IN VOLUME I*)

PFS 896 occurs on the upper edge of PF 770. The partial rolling of the single impression preserves only what our drawing shows. PF 770 is dated 498/497 B.C.

BIBLIOGRAPHY

Garrison 1988, pp. 431, 433; Garrison 1998, p. 121 (n. 15).

COMPOSITIONAL FORMAT IV: OTHER HEROIC COMPOSITIONS

IV-A. SEATED HERO CONTROLS RAMPANT ANIMAL OR CREATURE

IV-A.18. ANIMALS OF UNCERTAIN TYPE

Cat.No. 309   PFS 280

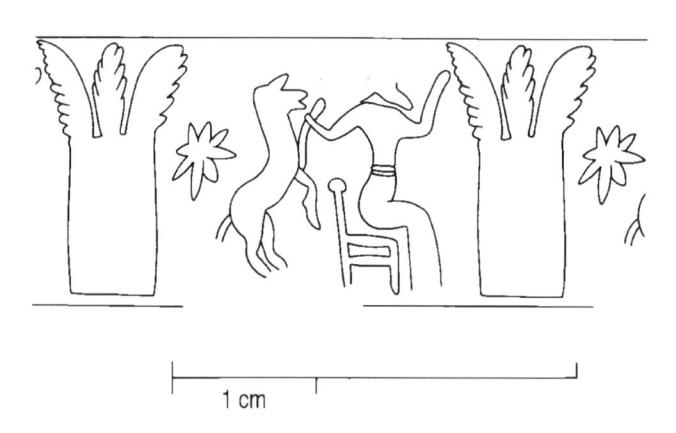

Seal Type:	Cylinder	Photographs:	Pl. 172c–d
Earliest Dated Application:	502/501 B.C.	Typology and Style:	IV-A.18 — Fortification Style
Preserved Height of Image:	1.80 cm (comp.)	Preserved Length of Image:	2.80 cm (comp.)
Estimated Height of Original Seal:	1.80 cm	Estimated Diameter of Original Seal:	0.90 cm
Number of Impressions:	2	Quality of Impressions:	Fair

Completeness of Image: Almost complete except for details

DESCRIPTION OF SEAL AS IMPRESSED IMAGE

Hero sits in chair facing right. Hero holds right arm bent behind him, grasping rampant animal of uncertain type by upper foreleg; hero holds left arm bent and extends it upward.

Rampant animal moves toward and faces hero. Animal holds upper foreleg slightly curved and extends it upward toward hero's head; lower foreleg is bent and extended downward in front of its body; tail (only partially preserved) curves downward.

Hero wears double-belted robe. Long beard terminates in blunt point over hero's left shoulder. Hero's chair consists of two legs, seat, horizontal support, and straight back with knob-like finial.

Large ear emerges from animal's head.

Large palm tree in terminal field has broad rectangular base from which emerge three leafy fronds. Large star is also in terminal field between tree and rampant animal.

Edge of seal is preserved at top of design; segment of edge of seal is preserved at bottom of design below hero and tree.

COMMENTARY

The tree on PFS 280 is almost a duplicate of the tree seen on PFS 148 (Cat.No. 311). Both seals also display a seated hero reaching behind him to grasp the animal. Major differences are found in the reversed orientation of PFS 148 (Cat.No. 311) and in the addition to that seal design of a second animal in place of the star.

For comparative illustrations including PFS 280, see pl. 258d (palm trees).

SEAL APPLICATION (SEE *APPENDIX ONE: CONCORDANCE OF SEALS TO TABLETS IN VOLUME I*)

PFS 280 occurs on the reverse of both PF 1616 (inverted) and PF 1617, with PFS 281 (II) also on the reverse and PFS 282 (III) on the left edge of each tablet. PFS 280 is applied directly above PFS 281 on both tablets. The rolling of PFS 280 on the reverse of PF 1617 preserves the entire length of the seal design and displays the hero in the center. The partial rolling on the reverse of PF 1616 displays the star and the rampant animal in the center. On both tablets the seal clearly was applied before the text since several cuneiform wedges cut into the bottom or top of the impressions. PF 1616 is the earliest dated tablet with PFS 280 and is dated 502/501 B.C.

BIBLIOGRAPHY

Garrison 1988, pp. 344–45, 423.

PFS 435   Cat.No. 310

Seal Type:	Cylinder	Photograph:	Pl. 172f
Earliest Dated Application:	498/497 B.C.	Typology and Style:	IV-A.18 — Broad and Flat Styles
Preserved Height of Image:	1.90 cm (incomp.)	Preserved Length of Image:	2.80 cm (incomp.)
Estimated Height of Original Seal:	NA	Estimated Diameter of Original Seal:	NA
Number of Impressions:	1	Quality of Impression:	Good

Completeness of Image: Large segment of middle of design survives

DESCRIPTION OF SEAL AS IMPRESSED IMAGE

Hero sits in chair facing right. Hero holds right arm bent behind him, grasping rampant animal of uncertain type by foreleg; hero holds left arm bent and extends it upward in front of his head; two vertical elements (only partially preserved) project upright from his left hand (weapon of uncertain type?).

Rampant animal moves toward and faces hero. Animal holds one foreleg straight and extends it upward toward hero's head. Animal raises bent forward hind leg toward hero's chair; short tail extends downward under its hindquarters.

Hero wears double-belted robe; fringe is indicated by diagonal markings along front edge and back edge of garment over lower legs. Squared beard rests over hero's left shoulder; flattened coiffure rests at back of neck.

Hero's chair consists of two legs, seat, and straight back; legs are slanted outward.

Creature has double horizontal detailing at its shoulder; mane is rendered by crisp serrated edge along contour of neck.

Large rectangular device (only partially preserved) fills terminal field before hero; device consists of panel with interior linear decoration crowned by two converging arced triangles. Vertical line at far left of preserved impression may be right edge of this device.

COMMENTARY

The device in the terminal field is traditionally described as a symbol for the temple gate or temple shrine. Glyptic parallels occur from a range of periods in Mesopotamia.[107] See PFS 709 (Cat.No. 271) for a similar device only partially preserved. The object held in the hero's left hand remains enigmatic.

This engraving is a fine example of one type of carving found in the Broad and Flat Styles.

For comparative illustrations including PFS 435, see pls. 239f (unusual formats of heroic encounter) and 255e (various devices and symbols).

SEAL APPLICATION (SEE *APPENDIX ONE: CONCORDANCE OF SEALS TO TABLETS IN VOLUME I*)

PFS 435 occurs on the left edge of PF 124. The partial rolling displays the hero in the center. PF 124 is dated 498/497 B.C.

BIBLIOGRAPHY

Garrison 1988, pp. 343, 345, 421–23, 496.

---

107. For example, an Early Dynastic III banquet scene (Porada 1948, p. 16, no. 108, pl. 17, no. 108) and a Neo-Assyrian Linear Style worship scene (ibid., p. 78, no. 652, pl. 95, no. 652). Note the crude "late Assyrian" cylinder seal excavated in the Persepolis Treasury displaying the temple gate symbol in the terminal field of a heroic combat scene (Schmidt 1957, p. 45, pl. 16: PT4 484), where the Gate image is described as a "panel filled with problematic symbols" (ibid., p. 43).

PFS 148 — Cat.No. 311

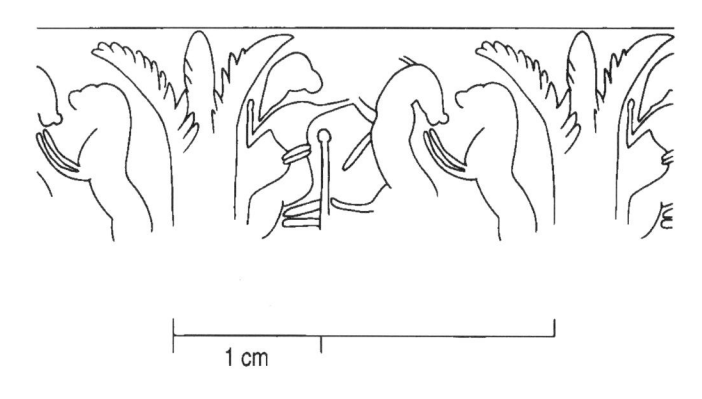

Seal Type:	Cylinder	Photographs:	Pl. 173a–b
Earliest Dated Application:	501/500 B.C.	Typology and Style:	IV-A.18 — Fortification Style
Preserved Height of Image:	1.40 cm (incomp.)	Preserved Length of Image:	2.60 cm (comp.)
Estimated Height of Original Seal:	1.70 cm	Estimated Diameter of Original Seal:	0.80 cm
Number of Impressions:	6	Quality of Impressions:	Poor

Completeness of Image: Almost complete except for lower edge and details

Description of Seal as Impressed Image

Hero sits in chair facing left. Hero holds left arm straight behind him, grasping rampant animal of uncertain type by foreleg; hero holds right arm bent and extends it upward.

Rampant animal moves toward hero but turns its head away from him. Animal holds upper foreleg straight and extends it upward to join with hero's left arm; lower foreleg is straight and extended downward in front of its body. Animal raises forward hind leg, touching back of hero's chair.

Hero wears double-belted robe. Long pointed beard rests over hero's right shoulder; rounded coiffure rests at back of neck.

Hero's chair (only partially preserved) consists of seat, cushion(?), and straight back with knob-like finial.

Rampant animal has thin curved projection (partially preserved ear? horn?) emerging from back of its head.

To right of animal held by hero, rampant lion moves toward and faces animal held by hero. Lion holds forelegs curved and extends them upward together toward muzzle of animal held by hero.

Large palm tree, in terminal field, has broad rectangular base from which emerge three leafy fronds.

Edge of seal is preserved at top of design.

Commentary

See PFS 280 (Cat.No. 309) for the tree and the composition.

The style of PFS 148 seems close to that of PFS 1459 (II), where vestiges of a similarly shaped tree appear.

For comparative illustrations including PFS 148, see pls. 183c (robes of various undetailed types), 215b (unusual heroic attitudes), and 241b (heroic encounters merged with animal contests).

Seal Application (see *Appendix One: Concordance of Seals to Tablets in Volume I*)

PFS 148 occurs on the reverse, bottom edge, and upper edge of PF 445, the reverse of PF 563, and the reverse and bottom edge of PF 601. Although the impressions are difficult to read, they exhibit little distortion. In three impressions the seal is rolled for at least one complete turn, preserving the entire length of the seal design. Of these three applications, one displays the rampant animal behind the hero in the center; one displays the tree and the rampant lion in the center; one displays the rampant lion in the center. Of the remaining three partial impressions, one displays the hero in the center; one displays the tree and the hero in the center; one preserves only the tree and the hero. PF 445 is the earliest dated tablet with PFS 148 and is dated 501/500 B.C.

Bibliography

Garrison 1988, pp. 344–45, 423.

440 SEALS ON THE PERSEPOLIS FORTIFICATION TABLETS, VOLUME I: IMAGES OF HEROIC ENCOUNTER

IV-B. HERO LIFTS ANIMAL OR CREATURE ABOVE HEAD

IV-B.18. ANIMALS OF UNCERTAIN TYPE

Cat.No. 312   PFS 538

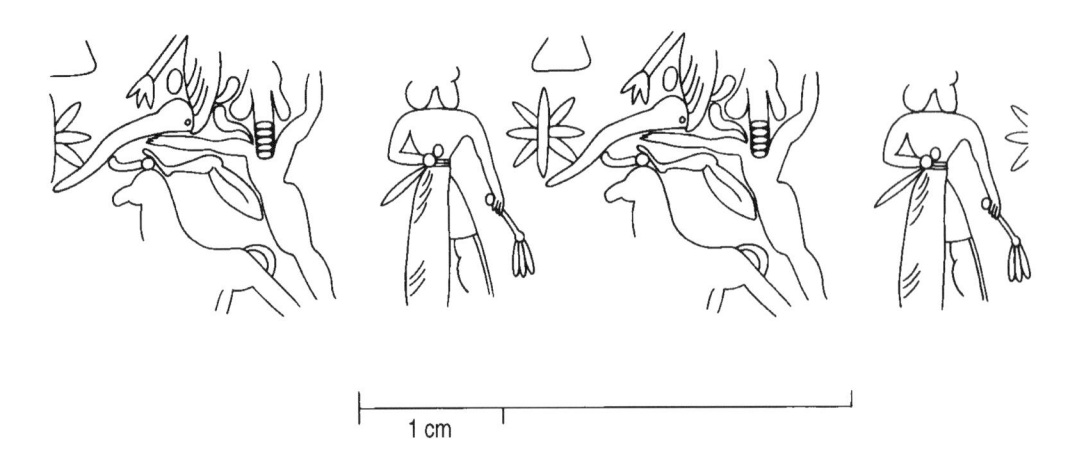

Seal Type:	Cylinder	Photograph:	Pl. 173d
Earliest Dated Application:	ND	Typology and Style:	IV-B.18 — Modeled Style
Preserved Height of Image:	2.00 cm (incomp.)	Preserved Length of Image:	3.40 cm (comp.)
Estimated Height of Original Seal:	NA	Estimated Diameter of Original Seal:	1.10 cm
Number of Impressions:	4	Quality of Impressions:	Fair; little detail preserved

Completeness of Image: Large segment of middle of design survives along its complete length

DESCRIPTION OF SEAL AS IMPRESSED IMAGE

Hero, face frontal, moves to left, extending straight right arm outward to support fantastic elongated snout of inverted creature of uncertain type (rear portion not preserved); hero holds left arm slightly bent and extended upward above his head. Hero, in dramatic striding pose, vigorously raises bent forward leg to place foot on head of marchant bull.

Long crooked snout of inverted creature extends diagonally downward. Creature holds one foreleg straight, extending diagonally downward with tripartite termination. Oval-shaped element lies between foreleg and neck; curved horn emerges from top of creature's head; curved ear(?) also is at top of head.

Marchant bull moves toward and faces left; curved horn emerges from top of bull's head; tail (only partially preserved) is curved downward.

Hero appears to be nude. Long, rounded, segmented beard rests along hero's chest; rounded mass of hair appears on either side of face.

To left of encounter group, star is in middle field. Above star is truncated triangular element, plausibly tail of winged symbol.

Flanking these symbols at left is male figure who moves toward and faces hero. Male figure holds right arm bent to place hand on hilt of sword (in sheath) at waist; sheathed sword projects diagonally downward from waist; male figure has left arm straight and extends it downward in front of his body to hold flail. Male figure wears double-belted Assyrian garment that leaves forward leg exposed below knee; folds are indicated by diagonal markings on garment over rear leg. Rounded beard rests over his left shoulder; thick rounded coiffure rests at back of neck.

COMMENTARY

The engraving and composition are exceptional for seals of heroic encounter in the PFS corpus, but see PFS 152 (Cat.No. 295) for a similarly archaizing nude hero with frontal face.[108] The bizarre inverted creature is probably to be reconstructed with its back arching over so that its rump is supported by the hero's upraised left hand. Such a reconstruction posits significant additional height to the seal — enough to accommodate a winged symbol completing the tail element preserved above the star. The marchant bull, against which the hero braces his right foot, may (with the hoof of its backward-extended rear leg) also provide a pedestal for the hero. This area of the design is not preserved. The composition of a hero holding an animal above his head is an archaism evoking Akkadian and Old Babylonian glyptic.[109] The weapon-bearing figure in the composition is separated from the heroic action on PFS 538 by the large star. Furthermore, although he stands at attention, he is not shown in action as an equal participant in the heroic encounter. Interestingly, however, an excellent parallel for the flail occurs on a cylinder with a double heroic encounter from Borsippa, Iraq, of Achaemenid date (Collon 1987, pp. 90, 93, no. 428).

For comparative illustrations including PFS 538, see pls. 191e (variously detailed beards), 196e (coiffures of unusual types), 197d (hands), 214i (frontal faces and/or bodies), 215e (unusual heroic attitudes), 221d (animals and creatures of uncertain type), 238c (subsidiary human/human-creature figures in encounter images), and 245d (various weapons).

SEAL APPLICATION (SEE *APPENDIX ONE: CONCORDANCE OF SEAS TO TABLETS IN VOLUME I*)

PFS 538 occurs twice on the reverse (inverted) and once on the upper edge and left edge of PF 293. On the reverse the impressions of the seal are applied one directly above the other. Of the four partial applications, one displays the hero in the center; one preserves only the hero and the standing figure; two display the standing figure in the center. The date of PF 293 is unknown.

BIBLIOGRAPHY

Garrison 1988, p. 212,

---

108. Compare the seal impression from Susa that also has a frontal nude hero with raised forward leg rendered in a Modeled Style (Amiet 1973b, pl. 1, no. 3). The frontal hero may ultimately relate to Lahmu, formerly associated with the hero/king Gilgamesh; see Black and Green 1992, pp. 114–15.

109. The composition is revived also in Assyro-Babylonian glyptic, for example, Collon 1987, pp. 196–97, no. 966; see the summary of the theme of the heroic encounter in the Neo-Assyrian period in Garrison 1988, pp. 82–98.

APPENDIX ONE

CONCORDANCE OF SEALS TO TABLETS IN VOLUME I

Concordance of all seals in Volume I and the tablets (and surfaces) on which they occur. The PFS number(s) of any other seal(s) applied to a cited tablet surface are also provided; these seals span the entire PFS corpus, Volumes I–III, including analytically illegible seals. Multiple impressions of an individual seal on a tablet are not indicated except for U text tablets, which are read as only having an obverse and left edge (= base) because of their rounded conical shapes; see PFS 30 (Cat.No. 291), below.

PFS No. (Cat.No.)	PF (Tablet)	Obverse	Bottom Edge	Reverse	Upper Edge	Right Edge	Left Edge	Additional PFS on Tablet and Location or Note
PFS 1* (Cat.No. 182)	409	–	–	×	×	×	×	–
	410	–	–	×	–	×	×	–
	411	–	–	×	×	–	×	–
	412	–	–	×	–	–	×	–
	808	–	–	×	×	–	×	–
	809	–	–	×	×	×	×	–
	863	–	–	×	–	×	×	–
	871	–	–	–	×	×	×	–
	872	–	–	–	×	×	×	–
	877	–	–	×	×	–	×	–
	878	–	–	×	×	×	×	–
	880	–	–	×	×	×	×	–
	881	–	–	×	×	–	×	–
	882	–	–	–	×	–	×	–
	883	–	–	×	×	×	×	–
	884	–	–	–	×	×	×	–
	885	–	–	×	×	×	×	–
	886	–	–	–	×	×	×	–
	887	–	–	×	–	×	×	–
	888	–	–	×	×	×	×	–
	889	–	–	–	–	×	×	–
	890	–	–	–	×	×	×	–
	891	–	–	×	×	×	×	–
	892	–	–	–	×	–	×	–
	893	–	–	–	–	×	×	–
	894	–	–	×	×	×	×	–
	895	–	–	×	–	×	×	–
	896	–	–	–	×	×	×	–
	897	–	–	–	×	×	×	–
	898	–	–	×	×	–	×	–
	899	–	–	–	×	–	×	–
	900	–	–	×	×	–	×	–
	901	–	–	×	×	×	×	–
	902	–	–	–	–	×	×	–
	903	–	–	×	–	–	×	–
	904	–	–	–	×	×	×	–

Appendix One: Concordance of Seals to Tablets in Volume I (*cont.*)

PFS No. (Cat.No.)	PF (Tablet)	Obverse	Bottom Edge	Reverse	Upper Edge	Right Edge	Left Edge	Additional PFS on Tablet and Location or Note
PFS 1* (Cat.No. 182) (*cont.*)								
	905	–	–	×	–	×	×	—
	906	–	–	×	×	×	×	—
	907	–	–	×	–	–	×	—
	908	–	–	×	–	×	×	—
	939	–	–	×	–	×	×	—
	940	–	–	×	–	×	×	—
	941	–	–	×	×	×	×	—
	942	–	–	×	×	×	×	—
	943	–	–	×	–	×	×	—
	944	–	–	×	–	×	×	—
	946	–	–	×	–	×	×	—
	947	–	–	–	×	–	×	—
	948	–	–	×	–	×	×	—
	949	–	–	×	–	–	×	—
	950	–	–	×	–	×	×	—
	951	–	–	×	–	×	×	—
	952	–	–	–	–	×	×	—
	953	–	–	×	×	×	×	—
	954	–	–	×	×	×	×	—
	955	–	–	×	×	×	×	—
	956	–	–	×	×	×	×	—
	957	–	–	×	–	×	×	—
	958	–	–	×	–	×	×	—
	959	–	–	×	–	×	×	—
	960	–	–	×	–	×	×	—
	961	×	–	×	–	–	×	—
	983	–	–	×	×	×	×	—
	987	–	–	×	–	–	×	—
	988	–	–	×	–	×	×	—
	1026	–	–	–	×	×	×	—
	1133	–	–	×	×	–	×	—
	1134	–	–	×	–	×	×	—
	1135	–	–	–	×	–	×	—
	1136	–	–	×	×	×	×	—
	1137	–	–	–	–	×	×	—
	1150	–	–	×	×	×	×	—
	1151	–	–	×	×	–	×	—
	2040	–	–	×	×	–	×	—
PFS 2 (Cat.No. 3)	15	–	–	×	–	–	×	—
	113	–	–	×	–	–	×	—
	442	–	–	×	–	–	×	—
	465	–	–	×	–	–	–	—
	466	–	×	×	–	–	×	—
	540	–	×	×	×	–	×	—
	542	–	–	×	–	–	×	—
	544	–	–	×	–	–	×	—
	585	–	–	×	–	–	×	—
	598	–	–	×	–	–	×	—

Appendix One: Concordance of Seals to Tablets in Volume I (*cont.*)

PFS No. (Cat.No.)	PF (Tablet)	Obverse	Bottom Edge	Reverse	Upper Edge	Right Edge	Left Edge	Additional PFS on Tablet and Location or Note
PFS 2 (Cat.No. 3) (*cont.*)								
	613	–	×	–	–	–	×	—
	710	–	–	–	–	–	×	—
	832	–	–	×	–	–	×	—
	1000	–	–	×	–	–	×	—
	1001	–	–	×	–	–	×	—
	1049	–	–	×	–	–	×	—
	1050	–	–	×	–	–	×	—
	1051	–	–	×	–	–	×	—
	1052	–	–	×	×	–	×	—
	1053	–	–	–	×	–	×	—
	1055	–	–	×	–	–	×	—
	1056	–	–	–	×	–	×	—
	1057	–	–	×	–	–	×	—
	1065	–	–	×	–	–	×	—
	1067	–	–	×	–	–	×	—
	1068	–	–	×	–	–	×	—
	1069	–	–	–	×	–	×	—
	1070	–	–	–	×	–	×	—
	1071	–	–	–	×	–	×	—
	1072	–	–	–	–	–	×	—
	1073	–	–	–	–	–	×	—
	1187	–	–	×	×	–	×	—
	1188	–	–	–	×	–	×	—
	1189	–	–	×	–	–	×	—
	1605	–	–	×	–	–	×	—
	1606	–	–	×	–	–	×	—
	1651	–	–	×	–	–	×	—
	1681	–	–	×	–	–	×	—
	1699	–	–	–	–	–	×	—
	1700	×	–	–	–	–	×	—
	1709	–	–	×	–	–	×	—
	1715	–	–	×	×	–	×	—
	1716	–	–	–	–	–	×	—
	1748	–	–	×	–	–	×	—
	1845	–	–	×	–	–	×	—
	1846	–	–	×	–	–	×	—
	1847	–	–	×	–	–	×	—
	1848	–	–	×	–	–	×	—
PFS 4* (Cat.No. 292)	403	–	–	×	×	–	×	—
	404	–	–	×	–	–	×	—
	405	–	–	×	×	×	×	—
	406	–	–	×	×	×	×	—
	804	–	–	–	×	–	×	—
	847	–	–	×	×	–	×	—
	873	–	–	×	×	×	×	—
	874	–	–	×	×	–	×	—
	875	–	–	×	×	–	×	—
	876	–	–	×	×	–	×	—

Appendix One: Concordance of Seals to Tablets in Volume I (*cont.*)

PFS No. (Cat.No.)	PF (Tablet)	Obverse	Bottom Edge	Reverse	Upper Edge	Right Edge	Left Edge	Additional PFS on Tablet and Location or Note
PFS 4* (Cat.No. 292) (*cont.*)								
	915	–	–	×	×	–	×	—
	916	–	–	×	×	–	×	—
	917	–	–	×	–	–	×	—
	918	–	–	×	×	–	×	—
	919	–	–	×	×	–	×	—
	920	–	–	×	×	–	×	—
	921	–	–	–	×	–	×	—
	922	–	–	×	×	–	×	—
	923	–	–	×	×	–	×	—
	924	–	–	–	×	–	×	—
	925	–	–	×	×	×	×	—
	926	–	–	–	×	–	×	—
	927	–	–	×	×	×	×	—
	928	–	–	×	×	×	×	—
	929	–	–	–	×	–	×	—
	930	–	–	×	×	–	×	—
	931	–	–	×	×	–	×	—
	932	–	–	×	×	–	×	—
	933	–	–	–	×	–	×	—
	934	–	–	×	×	–	×	—
	935	–	–	–	×	–	×	—
	936	–	–	×	×	–	×	—
	1022	–	–	–	×	×	×	—
	1333	–	–	×	×	–	–	—
	2041	–	–	–	×	–	×	—
	2045	–	–	–	Destroyed	×	×	—
PFS 6 (Cat.No. 304)	382	–	–	–	–	–	×	—
	383	–	–	–	–	–	×	—
	789	–	–	–	–	–	×	—
	816	–	–	–	–	–	×	PFS 943 (III): reverse
	854	–	–	–	–	–	×	PFS 971 (Cat.No. 171): reverse, upper edge
	855	–	–	–	–	–	×	—
	857	–	–	–	–	–	×	PFS 972 (III): reverse, upper edge
	858	–	–	–	–	–	×	—
	976	–	–	–	–	–	×	—
	977	–	–	–	–	–	×	PFS 112 (Cat.No. 282): reverse
	978	–	–	–	–	–	×	PFS 112 (Cat.No. 282): reverse
	979	–	–	–	–	–	×	PFS 112 (Cat.No. 282): reverse
	980	–	–	–	–	–	×	PFS 112 (Cat.No. 282): upper edge
	1031	–	–	–	–	–	×	PFS 112 (Cat.No. 282): reverse
	1032	–	–	–	–	–	×	PFS 222 (Cat.No. 117): reverse
	1180	–	–	–	–	–	×	—
	1587	–	–	–	–	–	×	PFS 971 (Cat.No. 171): reverse
	1642	–	–	–	–	–	×	PFS 222 (Cat.No. 117): reverse
	1661	–	–	–	–	–	×	PFS 247 (Cat.No. 245): reverse
	1662	–	–	–	–	–	×	—
	1674	–	–	–	–	–	×	PFS 112 (Cat.No. 282): reverse, upper edge
	1675	–	–	–	–	–	×	PFS 247 (Cat.No. 245): upper edge

Appendix One: Concordance of Seals to Tablets in Volume I (*cont.*)

PFS No. (Cat.No.)	PF (Tablet)	Obverse	Bottom Edge	Reverse	Upper Edge	Right Edge	Left Edge	Additional PFS on Tablet and Location or Note
PFS 6 (Cat.No. 304) (*cont.*)								
	1727	–	–	–	–	–	×	PFS 222 (Cat.No. 117): reverse
	1728	–	–	–	–	–	×	—
	1731	–	–	–	–	–	×	—
	1732	–	–	–	–	–	×	—
	1743	–	–	–	–	–	×	PFS 247 (Cat.No. 245): reverse
	1744	–	–	–	–	–	×	PFS 222 (Cat.No. 117): reverse
	1761	–	–	–	–	–	×	PFS 222 (Cat.No. 117): reverse
	1762	–	–	–	–	–	×	PFS 222 (Cat.No. 117): reverse
	1763	–	–	–	–	–	×	PFS 1546 (III): reverse
	1776	–	–	×	–	–	–	PFS 1556 (III): left edge
PFS 7* (Cat.No. 4)	697	–	–	×	×	×	×	—
	698	–	–	×	×	–	×	—
	699	–	–	×	–	–	–	PFS 66c* (II): upper edge, right edge, left edge
	700	–	–	×	–	–	–	PFS 66c* (II): upper edge, right edge, left edge
	701	–	–	×	–	–	–	PFS 66a* (II): right edge, left edge
	702	–	–	×	–	–	–	PFS 66a* (II): bottom edge, upper edge, right edge, left edge
	703	–	–	×	–	–	–	PFS 66b* (II): upper edge, right edge, left edge
	704	–	–	×	–	–	–	PFS 66b* (II): upper edge, right edge, left edge
	705	–	×	×	–	–	×	—
	706	–	–	×	×	×	×	—
	707	–	–	×	×	–	×	—
	708	–	–	×	×	–	×	—
	709	–	–	×	×	–	×	—
	711	–	×	×	–	×	×	—
	712	–	–	×	×	–	×	—
	713	–	–	×	–	–	×	—
	714	–	×	×	×	–	×	—
	715	–	×	×	×	×	×	—
	716	–	×	×	×	–	×	—
	717	–	–	×	–	–	×	—
	718	–	×	×	×	×	×	—
	719	–	–	×	–	–	×	—
	720	–	×	×	×	–	×	—
	721	–	×	×	×	×	×	—
	722	×	×	×	×	×	×	—
	723	×	–	×	–	–	–	PFS 861 (illegible): left edge
	724	–	–	×	×	–	×	—
	725	–	–	×	–	–	×	—
	726	–	–	×	–	–	×	—
	727	–	–	×	–	–	×	—
	2034	–	×	×	×	–	×	—
PFS 9* (Cat.No. 288)	247	–	–	×	×	×	×	—
	253	–	–	×	–	–	×	—
	267	–	–	×	×	×	×	—
	268	×	–	×	×	×	×	—
	273	–	–	×	×	×	×	—
	654	–	–	×	×	×	×	—

Appendix One: Concordance of Seals to Tablets in Volume I (*cont.*)

PFS No. (Cat.No.)	PF (Tablet)	Obverse	Bottom Edge	Reverse	Upper Edge	Right Edge	Left Edge	Additional PFS on Tablet and Location or Note
PFS 9* (Cat.No. 288) (*cont.*)								
	655	–	–	×	×	×	×	—
	656	–	–	×	×	×	×	—
	657	–	–	–	×	×	×	—
	658	–	–	×	×	×	×	—
	659	–	–	×	×	×	×	—
	660	–	–	–	×	×	×	—
	661	–	–	×	×	×	×	—
	662	–	–	×	×	×	×	—
	664	–	–	–	×	×	×	—
	666	–	–	×	×	×	×	—
	1788	–	–	×	×	×	×	—
	1789	–	–	–	×	–	×	—
	1790	–	–	–	×	×	×	—
	1791	–	–	–	×	–	×	—
	1792	–	–	×	×	×	×	—
	1793	–	–	–	×	×	×	—
	1794	–	–	–	–	×	×	—
	1795	–	–	–	×	×	×	—
	1796	–	–	–	×	×	×	—
	1797	–	–	×	×	×	×	—
	1801	–	–	–	×	×	×	—
	2025	×	–	–	×	×	×	—
PFS 10 (Cat.No. 251)	83	–	–	–	–	–	×	PFS 239 (II): reverse
	87	–	–	–	–	–	×	PFS 239 (II): reverse
	685	–	–	–	–	–	×	PFS 853 (Cat.No. 204): reverse
	785	–	–	–	–	–	×	PFS 49 (Cat.No. 23): reverse
	1081	–	–	–	–	–	×	PFS 1036s (III): reverse
	1170	–	–	–	–	–	×	PFS 1107 (III): reverse
	1199	–	–	–	–	–	×	PFS 1036s (III): reverse
	1309	–	–	–	–	–	×	PFS 1254 (III): reverse
	1310	–	–	–	–	–	×	PFS 1255s (III): reverse
	1311	–	–	–	–	–	×	PFS 1256 (II): reverse
	1361	–	–	–	–	–	×	PFS 1290s (III): reverse
	1365	–	–	–	–	–	×	PFS 1689 (II): reverse
	1366	–	–	–	–	–	×	PFS 1292s (III): upper edge
	1401	–	–	–	–	–	×	PFS 251 (III): reverse
	1451	–	–	–	–	–	×	PFS 1346 (III): reverse
	1461	–	–	–	–	–	×	—
	1462	–	–	–	–	–	×	PFS 1359 (II): upper edge
	1474	–	–	–	–	–	×	PFS 1371 (II): reverse
	1477	–	–	–	–	–	×	PFS 298s (Cat.No. 236): reverse
	1478	–	–	–	–	–	×	PFS 1374 (Cat.No. 31): reverse
	1485	–	–	–	–	–	×	PFS 1382 (III): reverse
	1488	–	–	–	–	–	×	PFS 1385 (illegible): reverse
	1493	–	–	–	–	–	×	PFS 1390s (III): reverse
	1496	–	–	–	–	–	×	PFS 1394s (III): reverse
	1499	–	–	–	–	–	×	PFS 1396 (III): reverse PFS 1690 (III): reverse

Appendix One: Concordance of Seals to Tablets in Volume I (*cont.*)

PFS No. (Cat.No.)	PF (Tablet)	Obverse	Bottom Edge	Reverse	Upper Edge	Right Edge	Left Edge	Additional PFS on Tablet and Location or Note
PFS 10 (Cat.No. 251) (*cont.*)								
	1507	–	–	–	–	–	×	PFS 270s (III): reverse
	1519	–	–	–	–	–	×	PFS 1414s (II): reverse
	1520	–	–	–	–	–	×	PFS 1415 (III): reverse
	1522	–	–	–	–	–	×	PFS 1418 (III): upper edge
	1523	–	–	–	–	–	×	PFS 1419 (III): reverse
	1534	–	–	–	–	–	×	PFS 270s (III): reverse
	1540	–	–	–	–	–	×	PFS 1433 (illegible): upper edge
PFS 16* (Cat.No. 22)	665	–	–	–	×	×	×	—
	667	–	–	×	×	×	×	—
	668	–	–	×	×	×	×	—
	669	–	–	–	×	×	×	—
	1798	–	–	–	–	–	×	—
	1799	–	–	–	–	×	×	—
	1800	–	–	–	–	–	×	—
	1802	–	–	×	–	×	×	—
	1803	–	–	×	×	×	×	—
	1804	–	–	–	×	×	×	—
	1805	–	–	–	–	–	×	—
	1806	–	–	–	–	×	×	—
	1807	–	–	–	–	×	×	—
	1808	–	–	–	–	×	×	—
	1809	–	–	–	–	×	×	—
	1810	–	–	–	×	×	×	—
	2067	–	–	–	×	–	×	—
	2068	–	–	–	–	–	×	—
PFS 17 (Cat.No. 235)	46	–	–	×	–	–	×	—
	47	–	–	–	–	–	×	PFS 357 (III): reverse
	48	–	–	–	–	–	×	PFS 358 (II): reverse
	303	–	–	–	–	–	×	PFS 546 (II): reverse
	339	–	–	–	–	–	×	PFS 590 (II): reverse
	683	–	–	–	–	–	×	PFS 146 (Cat.No. 275): bottom edge, reverse
	684	–	–	–	–	–	×	PFS 852s (III): reverse
	1114	–	–	–	–	–	×	PFS 1071 (Cat.No. 29): reverse PFS 1072 (Cat.No. 61): reverse
	1154	–	–	–	–	–	×	PFS 189 (II): reverse
	1155	–	–	–	–	–	×	PFS 189 (II): reverse
	1156	–	–	–	–	–	×	PFS 1098 (III): reverse
	1557	–	–	–	–	–	×	PFS 1442 (III): reverse, upper edge
	1558	–	–	–	–	–	×	PFS 49 (Cat.No. 23): reverse
	1559	–	–	–	–	–	×	PFS 1443s (illegible): reverse
	1562	–	–	–	–	–	×	PFS 1444 (Cat.No. 62): reverse
	1563	–	–	–	–	–	×	PFS 1445s (II): reverse
	1564	–	–	–	–	–	×	PFS 1446s (III): reverse
	1565	–	–	–	–	–	×	PFS 1447 (Cat.No. 163): reverse
	1567	–	–	–	–	–	×	PFS 1450 (illegible): obverse
	1577	–	–	–	–	–	×	PFS 1460 (Cat.No. 9): reverse
	1764	–	–	–	–	–	×	PFS 188* (III): obverse
	1780	–	–	–	–	–	×	PFS 1560 (III): reverse

Appendix One: Concordance of Seals to Tablets in Volume I (*cont.*)

PFS No. (Cat.No.)	PF (Tablet)	Obverse	Bottom Edge	Reverse	Upper Edge	Right Edge	Left Edge	Additional PFS on Tablet and Location or Note
PFS 18 (Cat.No. 15)	349	–	–	–	–	–	×	PFS 596 (III): reverse
	408	–	–	–	–	–	×	PFS 648s (II): reverse
	541	–	–	–	–	–	×	PFS 68 (II): bottom edge, reverse, upper edge
	1095	–	–	–	–	–	×	PFS 1053 (Cat.No. 45): reverse
	1096	–	–	–	–	–	×	PFS 1054 (II): reverse
	1247	–	–	–	–	–	×	PFS 1189 (Cat.No. 8): reverse
	1261	–	–	–	–	–	×	PFS 1202 (Cat.No. 137): reverse
	1374	–	–	–	–	–	×	PFS 1297 (III): reverse
	1375	–	–	–	–	–	×	PFS 1298 (III): reverse
	1376	–	–	–	–	–	×	PFS 1292s (III): reverse
	1377	–	–	–	–	–	×	PFS 223 (II): reverse
	1379	–	–	–	–	–	×	PFS 1302s (III): reverse
	1381	–	–	–	–	–	×	PFS 295 (III): obverse, reverse
	1383	–	–	–	–	–	×	PFS 1306s (illegible): reverse
	1386	–	–	–	–	–	×	PFS 1309s (Cat.No. 229): reverse
	1392	–	–	–	–	–	×	PFS 1314s (II): reverse
	1575	–	–	–	–	–	×	PFS 1459 (II): reverse
	1685	–	–	–	–	–	×	PFS 68 (II): reverse, upper edge
	1735	–	–	–	–	–	×	PFS 1541 (II): reverse
PFS 20 (Cat.No. 145)	277	–	–	–	–	–	×	PFS 53 (III): reverse
	305	–	–	–	–	–	×	PFS 53 (III): reverse
	311	–	–	–	–	–	×	PFS 53 (III): reverse
	352	–	–	–	–	–	×	PFS 53 (III): reverse
	550	–	–	–	–	–	×	PFS 53 (III): reverse
	745	–	–	–	–	–	×	PFS 111 (III): reverse
	746	–	–	–	–	–	×	PFS 111 (III): reverse
	747	–	–	–	–	–	×	PFS 111 (III): reverse
	748	–	–	–	–	–	×	PFS 111 (III): reverse
	1058	–	–	–	–	–	×	PFS 212 (III): reverse
	1609	–	–	–	–	–	×	PFS 1486 (II): reverse
	1610	–	–	–	–	–	×	PFS 212 (III): reverse
	1680	–	–	–	–	–	×	PFS 1525 (illegible): reverse
	1773	–	–	–	–	–	×	PFS 1554 (illegible): upper edge
	1850	–	–	–	–	–	×	PFS 53 (III): reverse
	1851	–	–	–	–	–	×	PFS 53 (III): reverse
PFS 24 (Cat.No. 298)	313	–	–	–	–	–	×	PFS 557 (III): obverse, bottom edge, reverse, upper edge
	348	–	–	×	–	–	–	PFS 137 (II): left edge
	350	–	–	–	–	–	×	PFS 598 (III): reverse
	537	–	–	–	–	–	×	PFS 68 (II): obverse, reverse
	595	–	–	–	–	–	×	PFS 802 (II): obverse
	788	–	–	–	–	–	×	PFS 916 (Cat.No. 226): reverse
	1248	–	–	–	–	–	×	PFS 1190 (III): reverse
	1384	–	–	–	–	–	×	PFS 1307 (III): reverse
	1385	–	–	–	–	–	×	PFS 1308* (II): reverse, upper edge, left edge
	1388	–	–	–	–	–	×	PFS 1311s (Cat.No 247): reverse, upper edge
	1389	–	–	–	–	–	×	PFS 1312s (II): reverse
	1390	–	–	–	–	–	×	PFS 1313s (III): reverse
	1393	–	–	–	–	–	×	PFS 1315s (Cat.No. 253): obverse

Appendix One: Concordance of Seals to Tablets in Volume I (*cont.*)

PFS No. (Cat.No.)	PF (Tablet)	Obverse	Bottom Edge	Reverse	Upper Edge	Right Edge	Left Edge	Additional PFS on Tablet and Location or Note
PFS 24 (Cat.No. 298) (*cont.*)								
	1394	–	–	–	–	–	×	PFS 1316 (II): reverse
	1653	–	–	–	–	–	×	PFS 1514 (II): reverse
PFS 26 (Cat.No. 299)	451	–	–	–	–	–	×	PFS 188* (III): reverse
	1290	–	–	–	–	–	×	PFS 187s (II): upper edge
	1291	–	–	–	–	–	×	PFS 1236 (Cat.No. 159): reverse
	1292	–	–	–	–	–	×	PFS 1237s (III): upper edge
	1293	–	–	–	–	–	×	PFS 1238 (Cat.No. 160): upper edge
	1294	–	–	–	–	–	×	PFS 1239 (III): reverse
	1296	–	–	–	–	–	×	PFS 1242s (III): upper edge
	1297	–	–	–	–	–	×	PFS 1243 (Cat.No. 33): reverse
	1300	–	–	–	–	–	×	PFS 1246 (III): reverse
	1301	–	–	–	–	–	×	—
	1304	–	–	–	–	–	×	PFS 1249 (Cat.No. 294): reverse
	1305	–	–	–	–	–	×	PFS 1250s (II): upper edge
	1704	–	–	–	–	–	×	PFS 289*s (II): reverse, upper edge
	1783	–	–	–	–	–	×	PFS 1562 (III): upper edge
PFS 29 (Cat.No. 302)	356	–	–	–	–	–	×	PFS 190 (Cat.No. 286): reverse
	357	–	–	–	–	–	×	PFS 190 (Cat.No. 286): reverse, upper edge
	358	–	–	–	–	–	×	PFS 606 (II): reverse, upper edge
	434	–	–	–	–	–	×	PFS 671* (Cat.No. 174): reverse
	435	–	–	–	–	–	×	PFS 15 (III): reverse
	551	–	–	–	–	–	×	PFS 195 (II): reverse, upper edge
	553	–	–	–	–	–	×	PFS 15 (III): reverse
	554	–	–	–	–	–	×	PFS 772 (III): reverse, upper edge
	555	–	–	–	–	–	×	PFS 689 (III): reverse
	798	–	–	–	–	–	×	PFS 186s (II): reverse
	1102	–	–	–	–	–	×	PFS 1693s (III): reverse
	1441	–	–	–	–	–	×	PFS 1333s (II): upper edge
	1672	–	–	–	–	–	×	PFS 1521 (illegible): upper edge
	1747	–	–	–	–	–	×	PFS 15 (III): reverse
	1770	–	–	–	–	–	×	PFS 15 (III): reverse
PFS 30 (Cat.No. 291)	870	–	–	×	×	–	×	—
	965	–	–	×	×	×	×	—
	1594	–	–	×	×	–	×	—
	1640	–	–	–	×	–	×	—
	1660	–	–	×	×	–	×	—
	1720	–	–	–	×	–	×	—
	1721	–	–	–	×	–	×	—
	1862	3×	–	–	–	–	×	Note: U text tablet: three impressions on side and one on base
	1866	3×	–	–	–	–	×	Note: U text tablet: three impressions on side and one on base
	1874	2×	–	–	–	–	×	Note: U text tablet: two impressions on side and one on base
	1875	3×	–	–	–	–	×	Note: U text tablet: three impressions on side and one on base
	1876	×	–	–	–	–	×	Note: U text tablet: one impression on side and one on base

Appendix One: Concordance of Seals to Tablets in Volume I (*cont.*)

PFS No. (Cat.No.)	PF (Tablet)	Obverse	Bottom Edge	Reverse	Upper Edge	Right Edge	Left Edge	Additional PFS on Tablet and Location or Note
PFS 31 (Cat.No. 172)	58	–	–	–	×	–	–	PFS 363 (III): left edge
	59	–	–	–	×	–	–	PFS 92 (III): left edge
								PFS 364 (Cat.No. 149): reverse
	60	–	–	–	×	–	–	PFS 366 (III): reverse, left edge
	61	–	–	–	×	–	–	PFS 366 (III): left edge
								PFS 368 (illegible): reverse
	62	–	–	–	×	–	–	PFS 92 (III): left edge
	63	–	–	–	×	–	–	PFS 92 (III): left edge
								PFS 370 (Cat.No. 99): reverse
	65	–	–	–	×	–	Destroyed	PFS 92 (III): reverse
	66	–	–	–	×	–	–	PFS 92 (III): left edge
								PFS 374 (illegible): obverse
	68	–	–	–	×	–	–	PFS 92 (III): left edge
								PFS 376 (illegible): reverse
	69	–	–	–	×	–	–	PFS 92 (III): left edge
	70	–	–	–	×	–	–	PFS 92 (III): reverse
								PFS 377 (illegible): left edge
	71	–	–	×	×	–	–	PFS 366 (III): left edge
PFS 32* (Cat.No. 180)	515	–	×	×	×	–	×	—
	945	–	–	×	–	×	Destroyed	—
	962	–	–	–	–	–	×	—
	984	–	–	×	×	–	–	PFS 42 (III): left edge
	985	–	–	×	–	–	×	—
	986	–	–	×	–	–	–	PFS 986 (III): left edge
	989	–	–	–	×	–	×	—
	990	–	–	×	×	–	×	—
	991	–	–	×	×	–	–	PFS 42 (III): left edge
	1639	–	–	×	×	–	×	—
	1734	–	–	×	×	–	–	PFS 42 (III): left edge
	1759	–	–	×	×	–	–	PFS 1545s (III): left edge
	2043	–	–	×	×	–	×	—
PFS 33 (Cat.No. 220)	100	–	–	–	–	–	×	PFS 191 (II): obverse, bottom edge, reverse, upper edge
	103	–	–	–	–	–	×	PFS 191 (II): obverse, bottom edge, reverse, upper edge
	1017	–	–	–	–	–	×	PFS 1000 (II): reverse
	1060	–	–	–	–	–	×	PFS 1027s (II): reverse
	1153	–	–	–	–	–	×	PFS 1097 (III): reverse
	1186	–	–	–	–	–	×	PFS 706* (II): reverse
	1219	–	–	–	–	–	×	PFS 1097 (III): reverse
	1317	–	–	–	–	–	×	PFS 49 (Cat.No. 23): obverse
	1359	–	–	–	–	–	×	PFS 1289s (III): upper edge
	1431	–	–	–	–	–	×	PFS 1327 (II): obverse
	1452	–	–	–	–	–	×	PFS 1347s (II): upper edge
	1481	–	–	–	–	–	×	PFS 1379 (III): reverse
	1487	–	–	–	–	–	×	PFS 853 (Cat.No. 204): reverse
	1503	–	–	–	–	–	×	PFS 1400s (illegible): reverse
	1515	–	–	–	–	–	×	PFS 1411s (III): obverse
	1524	–	–	–	–	–	×	PFS 1420 (III): reverse

Appendix One: Concordance of Seals to Tablets in Volume I (*cont.*)

PFS No. (Cat.No.)	PF (Tablet)	Obverse	Bottom Edge	Reverse	Upper Edge	Right Edge	Left Edge	Additional PFS on Tablet and Location or Note
PFS 33 (Cat.No. 220) (*cont.*)								
	1765	–	–	–	–	–	×	PFS 1547 (III): reverse
	1778	–	–	–	–	–	×	PFS 1558 (III): obverse
	1785	–	–	–	–	–	×	PFS 289*s (II): reverse, upper edge
	1786	–	–	–	–	–	×	PFS 311 (II): upper edge
	2061	–	–	–	–	–	×	PFS 1626s (III): reverse
PFS 34 (Cat.No. 73)	151	–	–	×	×	Destroyed	–	PFS 60 (II): left edge
	152	–	–	×	–	–	–	PFS 60 (II): left edge
	153	–	–	×	–	–	–	PFS 60 (II): left edge
	169	–	–	–	–	–	×	PFS 8 (III): upper edge
								PFS 13 (III): reverse
	170	–	–	–	–	–	×	PFS 8 (III): reverse
								PFS 13 (III): reverse
	171	–	–	–	–	–	×	PFS 8 (III): reverse
								PFS 13 (III): reverse
	172	–	–	–	–	–	×	PFS 8 (III): reverse
								PFS 13 (III): reverse
	173	–	–	–	–	–	×	PFS 8 (III): reverse
								PFS 13 (III): reverse
	174	–	–	–	–	–	×	PFS 8 (III): reverse
								PFS 13 (III): reverse
	175	–	–	–	–	–	×	PFS 8 (III): reverse
								PFS 13 (III): reverse
	1093	–	–	×	–	–	–	PFS 1051 (III): left edge
PFS 36* (Cat.No. 5)	397	–	–	×	–	–	×	—
	398	–	–	×	–	–	×	—
	399	–	–	×	×	–	×	—
	821	–	–	×	–	–	×	—
	849	–	–	×	–	–	×	—
	1028	–	–	×	×	–	×	—
	1041	–	–	×	×	–	×	—
	1076	–	–	×	–	–	×	—
	1223	–	–	×	–	–	×	—
	1612	–	–	×	–	–	×	—
	1613	–	–	×	–	–	×	—
PFS 38 (Cat.No. 16)	730	–	×	×	×	–	×	—
	731	–	×	×	×	–	×	—
	732	–	–	×	×	×	×	—
	733	–	–	×	×	–	×	—
	734	–	–	×	×	–	×	—
	1835	×	–	×	×	–	×	—
	1836	–	–	×	×	–	×	—
	1837	–	–	×	×	–	×	—
	1838	–	–	×	×	×	×	—
	1839	–	–	×	×	×	×	—
	2035	–	–	×	×	–	×	—
PFS 39s (Cat.No. 221)	445	–	–	–	–	–	×	PFS 148 (Cat.No. 311): bottom edge, reverse, upper edge
	446	–	–	–	–	–	×	PFS 685 (III): reverse
	486	–	–	–	–	–	×	PFS 714 (Cat.No. 152): reverse

Appendix One: Concordance of Seals to Tablets in Volume I (*cont.*)

PFS No. (Cat.No.)	PF (Tablet)	Obverse	Bottom Edge	Reverse	Upper Edge	Right Edge	Left Edge	Additional PFS on Tablet and Location or Note
PFS 39s (Cat.No. 221) (*cont.*)								
	535	–	–	–	–	–	×	PFS 760 (illegible): reverse
	563	–	–	–	–	–	×	PFS 148 (Cat.No. 311): reverse
	601	–	–	–	–	–	×	PFS 148 (Cat.No. 311): bottom edge, reverse
	606	–	–	–	–	–	×	PFS 813* (II): bottom edge, reverse
	782	–	–	–	–	–	×	PFS 73* (III): reverse
	1007	–	–	–	–	–	×	PFS 143s (II): reverse
								PFS 1677 (illegible): upper edge
	1254	–	–	–	–	–	×	—
PFS 43* (Cat.No. 207)	388	–	–	×	–	–	×	—
	507	–	–	×	–	–	×	—
	580	–	–	×	–	–	×	—
	653	–	–	×	–	–	×	—
	996	–	–	×	–	–	×	—
	1266	–	–	×	–	–	×	—
	1267	–	–	×	–	–	×	—
	1668	–	–	×	–	–	×	—
	1713	–	–	×	–	–	×	—
	1750	–	–	×	–	–	×	—
PFS 49 (Cat.No. 23)	686	–	–	×	×	–	×	—
	687	–	–	×	×	–	–	PFS 856 (III): left edge
	785	–	–	×	–	–	–	PFS 10 (Cat.No. 251): left edge
	1316	–	–	×	–	–	–	PFS 55 (III): left edge
								PFS 1261s (III): upper edge
	1317	×	–	–	–	–	–	PFS 33 (Cat.No. 220): left edge
	1318	–	–	×	–	–	–	PFS 84 (II): left edge
	1556	–	–	×	×	–	–	—
	1558	–	–	×	–	–	–	PFS 17 (Cat.No. 235): left edge
PFS 52 (Cat.No. 114)	25	–	–	×	–	–	–	PFS 62 (Cat.No. 104): left edge
	296	–	–	×	×	–	–	PFS 62 (Cat.No. 104): left edge
	361	–	–	×	×	–	–	PFS 611 (II): left edge
	1621	–	–	×	–	–	–	PFS 1498s (III): left edge
	1650	–	–	×	×	–	–	PFS 62 (Cat.No. 104): left edge
	1767	–	–	×	×	–	–	PFS 62 (Cat.No. 104): left edge
	1768	–	–	×	–	–	–	PFS 62 (Cat.No. 104): left edge
								PFS 1548 (II): upper edge
PFS 54* (Cat.No. 277)	448	–	–	×	–	–	–	PFS 313 (III): left edge
	506	–	–	×	–	–	–	PFS 5 (II): left edge
	558	–	–	×	–	–	–	PFS 776 (III): left edge
	575	–	–	×	–	–	–	PFS 5 (II): left edge
	972	–	–	–	×	–	–	PFS 5 (II): left edge
	1019	–	–	–	×	–	–	PFS 273s (II): left edge
	1021	–	–	×	–	–	–	PFS 5 (II): left edge
	1037	–	–	×	–	–	×	—
	1181	–	–	×	–	–	–	PFS 184 (II): left edge
PFS 57* (Cat.No. 239)	231	–	–	×	×	–	×	—
	234	–	–	×	–	–	×	PFS 514 (Cat.No. 192): reverse
	237	–	–	×	×	–	×	—

Appendix One: Concordance of Seals to Tablets in Volume I (*cont.*)

PFS No. (Cat.No.)	PF (Tablet)	Obverse	Bottom Edge	Reverse	Upper Edge	Right Edge	Left Edge	Additional PFS on Tablet and Location or Note
PFS 57* (Cat.No. 239) (*cont.*)								
	239	–	–	×	–	–	–	PFS 131 (Cat.No. 170): left edge
								PFS 516 (Cat.No. 98): reverse
	242	–	–	×	×	×	×	—
	331	–	–	–	×	–	×	—
	1858	–	–	–	–	×	–	—
	2003	–	–	×	–	–	–	—
PFS 58 (Cat.No. 242)	14	–	–	×	–	–	–	PFS 59 (III): left edge
	78	–	–	×	–	–	–	PFS 59 (III): left edge
	79	–	–	×	–	–	×	—
	80	–	–	×	–	–	–	PFS 59 (III): left edge
	81	–	–	×	–	–	–	PFS 59 (III): left edge
	82	–	–	×	–	–	–	—
	134	–	–	×	–	–	–	PFS 59 (III): left edge
	1410	–	–	–	–	–	×	PFS 1660s (III): reverse
	2015	–	–	×	–	–	–	PFS 59 (III): left edge
PFS 62 (Cat.No. 104)	23	–	–	×	–	–	–	PFS 333 (illegible): left edge
	25	–	–	–	–	–	×	PFS 52 (Cat.No. 114): reverse
	296	–	–	–	–	–	×	PFS 52 (Cat.No. 114): reverse, upper edge
	1650	–	–	–	–	–	×	PFS 52 (Cat.No. 114): reverse, upper edge
	1767	–	–	–	–	–	×	PFS 52 (Cat.No. 114): reverse, upper edge
	1768	–	–	–	–	–	×	PFS 52 (Cat.No. 114): reverse
								PFS 1548 (II): upper edge
	2063	–	–	–	–	–	×	PFS 1627 (II): reverse, upper edge
PFS 63 (Cat.No. 24)	1687	–	–	×	–	–	×	—
	1688	–	–	×	×	–	–	—
	1689	–	–	×	×	–	–	PFS 256 (Cat.No. 198): left edge
	1690	–	–	–	×	×	–	PFS 256 (Cat.No. 198): left edge
	1691	–	–	×	×	–	–	PFS 272* (Cat.No. 272): left edge
	1695	–	–	×	×	–	–	PFS 272* (Cat.No. 272): left edge
	2064	–	–	×	×	–	–	PFS 272* (Cat.No. 272): left edge
PFS 64* (Cat.No. 173)	200	–	–	–	–	–	×	PFS 99 (Cat.No. 113): reverse
								PFS 477 (III): reverse
								PFS 478 (II): upper edge
	1100	–	–	–	–	–	×	PFS 196 (Cat.No. 224): reverse
	1128	–	–	–	–	–	×	PFS 211 (II): upper edge
	1220	–	–	–	–	–	×	PFS 1173 (III): reverse
	1229	–	–	–	×	–	×	—
	1237	–	–	–	–	–	×	PFS 196 (Cat.No. 224): reverse
	1597	–	–	–	×	–	×	—
PFS 65 (Cat.No. 241)	128	–	×	×	×	–	–	PFS 86 (Cat.No. 48): left edge
	129	–	–	×	–	–	–	PFS 86 (Cat.No. 48): left edge
	130	–	×	×	–	–	–	PFS 439 (Cat.No. 150): left edge
	131	–	–	×	–	–	–	PFS 86 (Cat.No. 48): left edge
	230	–	–	×	–	–	×	—
	284	–	–	×	–	–	–	PFS 86 (Cat.No. 48): left edge
PFS 67 (Cat.No. 293)	137	–	–	–	–	–	×	PFS 447 (Cat.No. 301): reverse
	368	–	–	–	–	–	×	PFS 618s (illegible): reverse
	484	–	–	–	–	–	×	PFS 35* (II): reverse

Appendix One: Concordance of Seals to Tablets in Volume I (*cont.*)

PFS No. (Cat.No.)	PF (Tablet)	Obverse	Bottom Edge	Reverse	Upper Edge	Right Edge	Left Edge	Additional PFS on Tablet and Location or Note
PFS 67 (Cat.No. 293) (*cont.*)								
	1149	–	–	–	–	–	×	PFS 1094 (III): bottom edge, reverse
	1270	–	–	–	–	–	×	PFS 1211 (II): reverse
	1634	–	–	–	–	–	×	PFS 220 (II): reverse
	1733	–	–	–	–	–	×	PFS 35* (II): reverse
PFS 72 (Cat.No. 147)	95	–	–	×	–	–	–	PFS 141 (II): left edge PFS 399 (Cat.No. 78): reverse
	326	–	–	×	–	–	–	PFS 90 (III): reverse PFS 141 (II): left edge PFS 399 (Cat.No. 78): bottom edge, upper edge
	835	–	–	×	–	–	–	PFS 90 (III): reverse, upper edge PFS 141 (II): left edge PFS 399 (Cat.No. 78): bottom edge
	836	–	–	×	–	–	–	PFS 90 (III): reverse, upper edge PFS 141 (II): left edge PFS 399 (Cat.No. 78): bottom edge
	837	–	–	×	–	–	–	PFS 90 (III): reverse, upper edge PFS 141 (II): left edge PFS 399 (Cat.No. 78): obverse, bottom edge
	838	–	–	×	–	–	–	PFS 90 (III): reverse, upper edge PFS 141 (II): left edge PFS 399 (Cat.No. 78): bottom edge
	839	–	–	×	–	–	–	PFS 90 (III): reverse, upper edge PFS 141 (II): left edge PFS 399 (Cat.No. 78): bottom edge
	840	–	–	×	–	–	–	PFS 141 (II): left edge PFS 399 (Cat.No. 78): bottom edge
PFS 79 (Cat.No. 83)	241	–	–	×	–	–	×	—
	245	–	–	×	–	–	×	—
	250	–	–	×	–	–	×	—
	251	–	–	×	×	×	×	—
	262	–	–	×	–	–	×	—
	317	–	–	–	×	–	–	—
	1948	–	–	–	–	×	–	—
PFS 80 (Cat.No. 202)	425	–	–	–	–	–	×	PFS 349 (II): reverse PFS 659 (III): reverse
	536	–	–	–	–	–	×	PFS 761 (illegible): reverse PFS 762 (illegible): obverse
	1125	–	–	–	–	–	×	PFS 101 (II): reverse PFS 276 (II): reverse
	1126	–	–	–	–	–	×	PFS 101 (II): reverse PFS 276 (II): upper edge
	1132	–	–	–	–	–	×	PFS 1086 (illegible): reverse
	1215	–	–	–	–	–	×	PFS 101 (II): reverse PFS 1044 (II): upper edge
	1608	–	–	–	–	–	×	PFS 1485 (Cat.No. 112): reverse
	1628	–	–	–	–	–	×	PFS 205s (III): reverse
	1629	–	–	–	–	–	×	PFS 205s (III): reverse
	1702	–	–	–	–	–	×	PFS 1531 (III): reverse
	1771	–	–	–	–	–	×	PFS 1552s (III): reverse

Appendix One: Concordance of Seals to Tablets in Volume I (*cont.*)

PFS No. (Cat.No.)	PF (Tablet)	Obverse	Bottom Edge	Reverse	Upper Edge	Right Edge	Left Edge	Additional PFS on Tablet and Location or Note
PFS 86 (Cat.No. 48)	128	–	–	–	–	–	×	PFS 65 (Cat.No. 241): bottom edge, reverse, upper edge
	129	–	–	–	–	–	×	PFS 65 (Cat.No. 241): reverse
	131	–	–	–	–	–	×	PFS 65 (Cat.No. 241): reverse
	284	–	–	–	–	–	×	PFS 65 (Cat.No. 241): reverse
	1013	–	–	×	×	–	–	PFS 221 (II): left edge
	1014	–	–	×	–	–	–	PFS 221 (II): left edge
	1015	–	–	×	–	–	–	PFS 221 (II): left edge
PFS 95 (Cat.No. 25)	1092	–	–	–	×	–	–	PFS 206 (II): left edge PFS 1048s (II): left edge
	1139	–	–	–	–	–	×	PFS 1090 (Cat.No. 175): bottom edge, reverse, upper edge
	1234	–	–	–	–	–	×	PFS 1142 (Cat.No. 39): reverse PFS 1184 (III): reverse
	1368	–	–	–	–	–	×	PFS 1293 (III): upper edge
	1495	–	–	–	–	–	×	PFS 1393s (II): reverse
PFS 98* (Cat.No. 217)	430	–	–	×	×	–	×	—
	1582	–	–	×	×	×	×	—
	1583	–	–	–	×	×	×	—
	1584	–	×	×	–	–	×	—
	1611	–	–	–	×	–	×	—
PFS 99 (Cat.No. 113)	120	–	–	–	–	–	×	PFS 426 (Cat.No. 55): bottom edge PFS 427 (III): reverse
	121	–	–	–	–	–	×	PFS 428 (III): bottom edge PFS 429 (Cat.No. 7): reverse PFS 430 (Cat.No. 56): reverse PFS 431 (III): upper edge
	161	–	–	–	–	–	×	PFS 326 (Cat.No. 100): reverse PFS 458 (II): upper edge PFS 459 (illegible): right edge
	200	–	–	×	–	–	–	PFS 64* (Cat.No. 173): left edge PFS 477 (III): reverse PFS 478 (II): upper edge
	201	–	–	×	–	–	×	PFS 228 (Cat.No. 148): bottom edge, reverse
	202	–	–	–	–	–	×	PFS 228 (Cat.No. 148): bottom edge PFS 479 (illegible): reverse
	226	–	–	–	–	–	×	PFS 502 (III): reverse PFS 503 (Cat.No. 307): reverse PFS 504 (III): reverse
PFS 100 (Cat.No. 274)	467	–	–	–	–	–	×	PFS 695 (II): reverse
	468	–	–	–	–	–	×	PFS 696 (III): reverse
	469	–	–	–	–	–	×	PFS 697 (illegible): reverse
	627	–	–	–	–	–	×	PFS 831 (III): reverse
PFS 102 (Cat.No. 1)	154	–	–	×	×	–	–	PFS 60 (II): left edge
	155	–	–	×	×	–	–	PFS 60 (II): left edge
	156	–	–	×	–	–	–	PFS 60 (II): left edge
	157	–	–	×	×	–	Destroyed	—
PFS 103* (Cat.No. 84)	240	–	×	×	–	–	×	—
	248	–	×	×	–	–	×	—
	255	–	–	×	–	–	×	—
	258	–	–	×	×	–	×	—

Appendix One: Concordance of Seals to Tablets in Volume I (*cont.*)

PFS No. (Cat.No.)	PF (Tablet)	Obverse	Bottom Edge	Reverse	Upper Edge	Right Edge	Left Edge	Additional PFS on Tablet and Location or Note
PFS 109 (Cat.No. 197)	1382	–	–	–	–	–	×	PFS 295 (III): reverse
	1476	–	–	–	–	–	×	PFS 1373 (III): reverse
	1489	–	–	–	–	–	×	PFS 1386s (III): upper edge
	1491	–	–	–	–	–	×	PFS 219 (III): reverse
	1506	–	–	–	–	–	×	PFS 1402s (II): reverse
	1541	–	–	–	–	–	×	PFS 146 (Cat.No. 275): reverse
PFS 112 (Cat.No. 282)	977	–	–	×	–	–	–	PFS 6 (Cat.No. 304): left edge
	978	–	–	×	–	–	–	PFS 6 (Cat.No. 304): left edge
	979	–	–	×	–	–	–	PFS 6 (Cat.No. 304): left edge
	980	–	–	–	×	–	–	PFS 6 (Cat.No. 304): left edge
	1031	–	–	×	–	–	–	PFS 6 (Cat.No. 304): left edge
	1674	–	–	×	×	–	–	PFS 6 (Cat.No. 304): left edge
PFS 113* (Cat.No. 19)	864	–	–	–	×	–	×	—
	865	–	–	–	–	–	×	—
	879	–	–	×	×	–	×	—
PFS 114 (Cat.No. 284)	1161	–	–	×	–	–	–	PFS 105s (II): left edge
	1162	–	–	×	–	–	–	PFS 105s (II): left edge PFS 130 (Cat.No. 300): upper edge, right edge PFS 224 (II): reverse
	1163	–	–	×	–	–	–	PFS 70s (III): left edge PFS 130 (Cat.No. 300): reverse PFS 1100 (illegible): upper edge
	1206	–	–	×	–	–	–	PFS 105s (II): left edge PFS 224 (II): upper edge
PFS 120 (Cat.No. 49)	1940	–	–	–	–	–	×	—
	1943	–	–	×	–	–	–	—
	1945	–	×	–	–	–	Destroyed	—
	1965	–	–	–	×	–	×	—
	2001	–	–	×	–	–	×	—
	2013	–	–	–	–	–	×	—
	2075	–	–	×	×	–	–	—
	2079	–	×	–	–	Destroyed	Destroyed	—
PFS 123* (Cat.No. 75)	162	–	–	×	–	–	–	PFS 171 (III): reverse PFS 172 (III): left edge
	163	–	–	–	×	–	–	PFS 171 (III): obverse, bottom edge PFS 172 (III): left edge PFS 460 (III): reverse PFS 461 (Cat.No. 90): reverse
	164	–	×	×	–	–	–	PFS 462 (III): obverse PFS 463 (Cat.No. 264): reverse PFS 464 (III): reverse, upper edge PFS 465 (II): left edge
	219	–	–	×	–	–	–	PFS 230 (III): reverse PFS 306 (II): obverse PFS 307 (II): left edge PFS 486 (illegible): bottom edge, upper edge
	220	–	×	×	–	–	–	PFS 230 (III): reverse, upper edge PFS 306 (II): obverse PFS 307 (II): left edge
	221	–	–	×	–	–	–	PFS 230 (III): reverse, upper edge PFS 306 (II): obverse PFS 307 (II): left edge

Appendix One: Concordance of Seals to Tablets in Volume I (*cont.*)

PFS No. (Cat.No.)	PF (Tablet)	Obverse	Bottom Edge	Reverse	Upper Edge	Right Edge	Left Edge	Additional PFS on Tablet and Location or Note
PFS 125 (Cat.No. 250)	1632	–	–	×	–	–	–	PFS 1505 (III): left edge
PFS 130 (Cat.No. 300)	1162	–	–	–	×	×	–	PFS 105s (II): left edge
								PFS 114 (Cat.No. 284): reverse
								PFS 224 (II): reverse
	1163	–	–	×	–	–	–	PFS 70s (III): left edge
								PFS 114 (Cat.No. 284): reverse
								PFS 1100 (illegible): upper edge
	1164	–	–	×	–	–	–	PFS 1101 (Cat.No. 297): upper edge
								PFS 1102 (Cat.No. 132): left edge
	1227	–	–	×	–	–	–	PFS 1101 (Cat.No. 297): reverse
								PFS 1102 (Cat.No. 132): left edge
PFS 131 (Cat.No. 170)	235	–	×	×	×	×	×	—
	239	–	–	–	–	–	×	PFS 57* (Cat.No. 239): reverse
								PFS 516 (Cat.No. 98): reverse
	249	–	–	×	×	×	×	—
PFS 132 (Cat.No. 69)	105	–	–	–	–	–	×	PFS 413 (III): reverse
	475	–	–	–	–	–	×	PFS 701s (III): reverse
	1335	–	–	–	–	–	×	PFS 1278s (II): reverse
	1336	–	–	–	–	–	×	PFS 1280 (III): reverse
	1531	–	–	–	–	–	×	PFS 1426s (II): reverse
PFS 138 (Cat.No. 186)	1251	–	–	–	–	–	×	PFS 1193 (II): reverse
	1405	–	–	–	–	–	×	PFS 1322 (Cat.No. 36): upper edge
	1406	–	–	–	–	–	×	PFS 1323 (illegible): upper edge
	1407	–	–	–	–	–	×	PFS 1324 (illegible): reverse, upper edge
PFS 139s (Cat.No. 222)	1533	–	–	×	–	–	–	PFS 40 (III): left edge
	1576	–	–	×	–	–	–	PFS 40 (III): left edge
PFS 145 (Cat.No. 115)	761	–	–	×	×	–	–	PFS 885 (Cat.No. 187): left edge
	762	–	–	×	–	–	–	PFS 886 (illegible): left edge
	763	–	–	×	–	–	–	PFS 885 (Cat.No. 187): left edge
PFS 146 (Cat.No. 275)	682	–	–	×	–	–	–	PFS 40 (III): left edge
	683	–	×	×	–	–	–	PFS 17 (Cat.No. 235): left edge
	1541	–	–	×	–	–	–	PFS 109 (Cat.No. 197): left edge
PFS 148 (Cat.No. 311)	445	–	×	×	×	–	–	PFS 39s (Cat.No. 221): left edge
	563	–	–	×	–	–	–	PFS 39s (Cat.No. 221): left edge
	601	–	×	×	–	–	–	PFS 39s (Cat.No. 221): left edge
PFS 149 (Cat.No. 212)	10	–	×	×	×	–	–	PFS 323 (III): left edge
	274	–	–	×	×	–	–	PFS 150 (III): left edge
	275	–	–	×	–	–	–	PFS 150 (III): left edge
	276	–	–	×	–	–	–	PFS 150 (III): left edge
PFS 151 (Cat.No. 223)	576	–	–	×	×	–	–	PFS 5 (II): left edge
	577	–	–	×	–	–	–	PFS 5 (II): left edge
	590	–	–	–	×	×	–	PFS 799 (III): left edge
PFS 152 (Cat.No. 295)	1062	–	–	–	–	–	×	PFS 1030 (Cat.No. 120): reverse
	1094	–	–	–	×	–	–	PFS 1052 (II): left edge
	1116	–	–	–	×	×	–	PFS 308 (II): left edge
	1117	–	–	–	×	×	–	PFS 308 (II): left edge
	1118	–	–	–	–	–	×	PFS 1030 (Cat.No. 120): upper edge
	1951	–	–	×	–	–	–	PFS 1585 (II): left edge
PFS 153 (Cat.No. 285)	146	–	–	–	–	–	×	PFS 260 (Cat.No. 225): upper edge
	147	–	–	–	–	–	×	PFS 260 (Cat.No. 225): upper edge
	148	–	–	–	–	–	×	PFS 260 (Cat.No. 225): reverse, upper edge

Appendix One: Concordance of Seals to Tablets in Volume I (*cont.*)

PFS No. (Cat.No.)	PF (Tablet)	Obverse	Bottom Edge	Reverse	Upper Edge	Right Edge	Left Edge	Additional PFS on Tablet and Location or Note
PFS 158 (Cat.No. 94)	108	–	–	×	–	–	–	PFS 154 (III): left edge
	109	–	–	×	–	–	–	PFS 154 (III): left edge
PFS 162 (Cat.No. 249)	825	–	–	×	–	–	–	—
	1249	–	–	×	–	–	–	PFS 1191 (III): left edge
	1902	–	–	×	–	–	–	PFS 1575 (illegible): left edge
PFS 164* (Cat.No. 20)	969	–	–	–	×	–	×	—
	970	–	–	–	×	–	×	—
PFS 167 (Cat.No. 255)	22	–	–	–	–	–	×	PFS 331 (II): reverse, upper edge
	572	–	–	–	–	–	×	PFS 45* (III): reverse
	629	–	–	–	–	–	×	PFS 45* (III): bottom edge, reverse
PFS 168 (Cat.No. 74)	1667	–	–	–	–	–	×	PFS 1519 (Cat.No. 167): reverse, upper edge
PFS 180 (Cat.No. 194)	260	–	–	×	×	–	×	—
	261	–	–	×	×	–	×	—
PFS 190 (Cat.No. 286)	356	–	–	×	–	–	–	PFS 29 (Cat.No. 302): left edge
	357	–	–	×	×	–	–	PFS 29 (Cat.No. 302): left edge
PFS 196 (Cat.No. 224)	1100	–	–	×	–	–	–	PFS 64* (Cat.No. 173): left edge
	1237	–	–	×	–	–	–	PFS 64* (Cat.No. 173): left edge
PFS 197 (Cat.No. 116)	206	–	×	×	–	–	–	PFS 198 (II): left edge
	207	–	×	×	×	–	–	PFS 198 (II): left edge
PFS 199* (Cat.No. 305)	499	–	–	×	–	–	–	PFS 106 (III): left edge
								PFS 728 (illegible): upper edge
	557	×	–	–	–	–	–	PFS 106 (III): left edge
								PFS 775 (illegible): reverse
PFS 201 (Cat.No. 50)	749	–	–	–	–	–	×	PFS 867s (III): reverse
	1276	–	–	×	–	–	–	PFS 1217s (Cat.No. 168): left edge
	1404	–	–	–	–	–	×	PFS 1321s (Cat.No. 176): reverse
	1543	–	–	–	–	–	×	PFS 1434s (II): reverse
PFS 213 (Cat.No. 140)	1440	–	–	×	–	–	–	PFS 1332s (illegible): left edge
	1550	–	–	×	–	–	–	PFS 940 (Cat.No. 81): left edge
PFS 217 (Cat.No. 135)	114	–	–	–	×	–	×	—
	115	–	–	×	–	–	×	—
PFS 222 (Cat.No. 117)	1032	–	–	×	–	–	–	PFS 6 (Cat.No. 304): left edge
	1642	–	–	×	–	–	–	PFS 6 (Cat.No. 304): left edge
	1727	–	–	×	–	–	–	PFS 6 (Cat.No. 304): left edge
	1744	–	–	×	–	–	–	PFS 6 (Cat.No. 304): left edge
	1761	–	–	×	–	–	–	PFS 6 (Cat.No. 304): left edge
	1762	–	–	×	–	–	–	PFS 6 (Cat.No. 304): left edge
PFS 225 (Cat.No. 46)	1099	–	–	×	–	–	–	PFS 1055 (illegible): left edge
	1167	–	–	×	–	–	–	PFS 41 (III): left edge
PFS 228 (Cat.No. 148)	201	–	×	×	–	–	–	PFS 99 (Cat.No. 113): reverse, left edge
	202	–	×	–	–	–	–	PFS 99 (Cat.No. 113): left edge
								PFS 479 (illegible): reverse
PFS 231 (Cat.No. 51)	1677	–	–	×	×	–	–	PFS 21 (II): left edge
	1703	–	–	×	×	–	–	PFS 21 (II): left edge
PFS 232 (Cat.No. 26)	37	–	–	×	–	–	–	PFS 40 (III): left edge
	117	–	–	×	–	–	–	PFS 40 (III): left edge
	118	–	–	×	–	–	–	PFS 40 (III): left edge
PFS 233 (Cat.No. 52)	328	–	–	×	–	–	×	—
	329	–	–	×	×	–	×	—

Appendix One: Concordance of Seals to Tablets in Volume I (*cont.*)

PFS No. (Cat.No.)	PF (Tablet)	Obverse	Bottom Edge	Reverse	Upper Edge	Right Edge	Left Edge	Additional PFS on Tablet and Location or Note
PFS 234 (Cat.No. 188)	336	–	–	×	–	–	–	PFS 48 (III): left edge
	340	–	–	×	–	–	–	PFS 48 (III): left edge
PFS 236 (Cat.No. 213)	819	–	×	×	–	–	–	PFS 945 (Cat.No. 96): left edge
	1165	–	–	×	×	–	–	PFS 945 (Cat.No. 96): left edge
PFS 241 (Cat.No. 252)	93	–	–	×	×	×	–	PFS 396 (Cat.No. 178): left edge
	94	–	–	×	×	–	–	PFS 396 (Cat.No. 178): left edge
PFS 243 (Cat.No. 303)	1682	–	–	×	×	–	–	PFS 59 (III): left edge
	1683	–	–	–	×	×	–	PFS 59 (III): left edge
	1701	–	–	×	×	–	×	—
PFS 246 (Cat.No. 290)	796	–	–	×	×	–	–	PFS 202 (III): left edge
	1698	–	–	×	×	–	–	PFS 202 (III): left edge
PFS 247 (Cat.No. 245)	1661	–	–	×	–	–	–	PFS 6 (Cat.No. 304): left edge
	1675	–	–	–	×	–	–	PFS 6 (Cat.No. 304): left edge
	1743	–	–	×	–	–	–	PFS 6 (Cat.No. 304): left edge
PFS 249 (Cat.No. 27)	971	–	–	–	–	–	×	PFS 248 (II): reverse
	1641	–	–	–	–	–	×	PFS 248 (II): reverse
	1710	–	–	–	–	–	×	PFS 248 (II): reverse
	2042	–	–	–	–	–	×	PFS 248 (II): reverse
PFS 255 (Cat.No. 233)	522	–	–	×	–	–	–	PFS 122 (II): left edge
	634	–	–	×	–	–	–	PFS 122 (II): left edge
PFS 256 (Cat.No. 198)	1689	–	–	–	–	–	×	PFS 63 (Cat.No. 24): reverse, upper edge
	1690	–	–	–	–	–	×	PFS 63 (Cat.No. 24): upper edge, right edge
PFS 260 (Cat.No. 225)	144	–	–	–	–	–	×	PFS 452 (illegible): upper edge
	145	–	–	–	×	–	×	—
	146	–	–	–	×	–	–	PFS 153 (Cat.No. 285): left edge
	147	–	–	–	×	–	–	PFS 153 (Cat.No. 285): left edge
	148	–	–	×	×	–	–	PFS 153 (Cat.No. 285): left edge
PFS 263 (Cat.No. 289)	1630	–	–	×	–	–	–	PFS 309 (II): left edge
	1631	–	–	×	–	–	–	PFS 309 (II): left edge
PFS 265 (Cat.No. 240)	1097	×	–	–	–	×	–	PFS 264 (III): upper edge PFS 266* (Cat.No. 208): left edge PFS 1181 (Cat.No. 210): left edge
	1112	–	–	–	–	×	–	PFS 264 (III): upper edge PFS 266* (Cat.No. 208): left edge PFS 1181 (Cat.No. 210): left edge
	1228	–	–	×	×	–	–	PFS 1181 (Cat.No. 210): left edge
PFS 266* (Cat.No. 208)	1097	–	–	–	–	–	×	PFS 264 (III): upper edge PFS 265 (Cat.No. 240): obverse, right edge PFS 1181 (Cat.No. 210): left edge
	1112	–	–	–	–	–	×	PFS 264 (III): upper edge PFS 265 (Cat.No. 240): right edge PFS 1181 (Cat.No. 210): left edge
	1120	–	–	–	×	–	×	PFS 1076 (Cat.No. 193): reverse PFS 1666 (II): reverse
PFS 272* (Cat.No. 272)	1691	–	–	–	–	–	×	PFS 63 (Cat.No. 24): reverse, upper edge
	1695	–	–	–	–	–	×	PFS 63 (Cat.No. 24): reverse, upper edge
	2064	–	–	–	–	–	×	PFS 63 (Cat.No. 24): reverse, upper edge
PFS 280 (Cat.No. 309)	1616	–	–	×	–	–	–	PFS 281 (II): reverse PFS 282 (III): left edge
	1617	–	–	×	–	–	–	PFS 281 (II): reverse PFS 282 (III): left edge

Appendix One: Concordance of Seals to Tablets in Volume I (*cont.*)

PFS No. (Cat.No.)	PF (Tablet)	Obverse	Bottom Edge	Reverse	Upper Edge	Right Edge	Left Edge	Additional PFS on Tablet and Location or Note
PFS 284* (Cat.No. 111)	330	–	–	×	–	–	×	—
	2027	–	–	×	–	–	×	—
PFS 294 (Cat.No. 53)	1004	–	–	×	–	–	×	—
	1005	–	–	×	–	–	×	—
PFS 297 (Cat.No. 124)	98	–	–	–	–	–	×	PFS 296* (III): reverse
	99	–	–	×	–	–	×	PFS 296* (III): reverse
PFS 298s (Cat.No. 236)	1477	–	–	×	–	–	–	PFS 10 (Cat.No. 251): left edge
	1539	–	–	×	–	–	–	PFS 56 (III): left edge
PFS 301 (Cat.No. 54)	1230	–	–	×	–	–	–	PFS 302 (II): reverse, upper edge PFS 303 (III): left edge
	1231	–	–	×	–	–	–	PFS 302 (II): reverse, upper edge PFS 303 (III): left edge
PFS 312 (Cat.No. 237)	1105	–	–	–	×	×	–	PFS 193 (III): upper edge PFS 1063s (III): left edge
	1140	–	–	–	×	–	–	PFS 193 (III): reverse PFS 1091 (Cat.No. 68): left edge PFS 1092 (III): right edge
PFS 321 (Cat.No. 125)	9	–	×	×	×	×	–	PFS 5 (II): left edge
PFS 326 (Cat.No. 100)	13	–	–	×	–	–	×	—
	161	–	–	×	–	–	–	PFS 99 (Cat.No. 113): left edge PFS 458 (II): upper edge PFS 459 (illegible): right edge
PFS 329 (Cat.No. 28)	17	–	–	×	–	–	–	PFS 328s (III): left edge
	624	–	–	×	–	–	–	PFS 328s (III): left edge
PFS 334 (Cat.No. 133)	26	–	–	×	×	–	–	PFS 1644 (III): left edge
PFS 338 (Cat.No. 262)	31	–	–	×	×	–	×	PFS 337 (III): bottom edge
PFS 341 (Cat.No. 109)	33	–	–	×	–	–	–	PFS 342 (III): left edge
PFS 344 (Cat.No. 263)	35	–	–	×	–	–	×	—
PFS 361 (Cat.No. 47)	55	–	–	×	–	–	×	—
	324	–	–	×	×	–	–	PFS 571 (illegible): left edge
PFS 362 (Cat.No. 76)	56	–	–	×	–	–	–	PFS 163 (II): left edge
PFS 364 (Cat.No. 149)	59	–	–	×	–	–	–	PFS 31 (Cat.No. 172): upper edge PFS 92 (III): left edge
PFS 370 (Cat.No. 99)	63	–	–	×	–	–	–	PFS 31 (Cat.No. 172): upper edge PFS 92 (III): left edge
PFS 373 (Cat.No. 306)	64	–	–	–	–	–	×	PFS 366 (III): reverse PFS 372 (III): upper edge
PFS 380 (Cat.No. 95)	72	–	–	–	–	–	×	PFS 50* (II): reverse PFS 94 (III): upper edge
PFS 381 (Cat.No. 179)	76	–	–	×	×	–	–	PFS 1645 (III): left edge
PFS 385 (Cat.No. 38)	85	–	–	×	–	–	–	PFS 55 (III): left edge PFS 384s (III): reverse
	107	–	–	×	–	–	–	PFS 415s (III): upper edge PFS 417 (III): left edge
PFS 392 (Cat.No. 91)	89	–	–	–	–	–	×	PFS 391 (illegible): reverse
PFS 396 (Cat.No. 178)	93	–	–	–	–	–	×	PFS 241 (Cat.No. 252): reverse, upper edge, right edge
	94	–	–	–	–	–	×	PFS 241 (Cat.No. 252): reverse, upper edge
PFS 399 (Cat.No. 78)	95	–	–	×	–	–	–	PFS 72 (Cat.No. 147): reverse PFS 141 (II): left edge

Appendix One: Concordance of Seals to Tablets in Volume I (*cont.*)

PFS No. (Cat.No.)	PF (Tablet)	Obverse	Bottom Edge	Reverse	Upper Edge	Right Edge	Left Edge	Additional PFS on Tablet and Location or Note
PFS 399 (Cat.No. 78) (*cont.*)								
	326	–	×	–	×	–	–	PFS 72 (Cat.No. 147): reverse PFS 90 (III): reverse PFS 141 (II): left edge
	835	–	×	–	–	–	–	PFS 72 (Cat.No. 147): reverse PFS 90 (III): reverse, upper edge PFS 141 (II): left edge
	836	–	×	–	–	–	–	PFS 72 (Cat.No. 147): reverse PFS 90 (III): reverse, upper edge PFS 141 (II): left edge
	837	×	×	–	–	–	–	PFS 72 (Cat.No. 147): reverse PFS 90 (III): reverse, upper edge PFS 141 (II): left edge
	838	–	×	–	–	–	–	PFS 72 (Cat.No. 147): reverse PFS 90 (III): reverse, upper edge PFS 141 (II): left edge
	839	–	×	–	–	–	–	PFS 72 (Cat.No. 147): reverse PFS 90 (III): reverse, upper edge PFS 141 (II): left edge
	840	–	×	–	–	–	–	PFS 72 (Cat.No. 147): reverse PFS 141 (II): left edge
PFS 414 (Cat.No. 280)	106	–	–	–	–	–	×	PFS 181* (II): reverse
PFS 418 (Cat.No. 201)	110	–	×	×	–	–	–	PFS 419 (II): left edge
PFS 426 (Cat.No. 55)	120	–	×	–	–	–	–	PFS 99 (Cat.No. 113): left edge PFS 427 (III): reverse
PFS 429 (Cat.No. 7)	121	–	–	×	–	–	–	PFS 99 (Cat.No. 113): left edge PFS 428 (III): bottom edge PFS 430 (Cat.No. 56): reverse PFS 431 (III): upper edge
PFS 430 (Cat.No. 56)	121	–	–	×	–	–	–	PFS 99 (Cat.No. 113): left edge PFS 428 (III): bottom edge PFS 429 (Cat.No. 7): reverse PFS 431 (III): upper edge
PFS 435 (Cat.No. 310)	124	–	–	–	–	–	×	PFS 434 (III): reverse
PFS 439 (Cat.No. 150)	130	–	–	–	–	–	×	PFS 65 (Cat.No. 241): bottom edge, reverse
PFS 447 (Cat.No. 301)	137	–	–	×	–	–	–	PFS 67 (Cat.No. 293): left edge
PFS 454 (Cat.No. 92)	150	–	–	×	×	–	–	PFS 60 (II): left edge
PFS 461 (Cat.No. 90)	163	–	–	×	–	–	–	PFS 123* (Cat.No. 75): upper edge PFS 171 (III): obverse, bottom edge PFS 172 (III): left edge PFS 460 (III): reverse
PFS 463 (Cat.No. 264)	164	–	–	×	–	–	–	PFS 123* (Cat.No. 75): bottom edge, reverse PFS 462 (III): obverse PFS 464 (III): reverse, upper edge PFS 465 (II): left edge
PFS 480 (Cat.No. 134)	203	–	–	×	×	–	–	PFS 481 (III): left edge
PFS 494 (Cat.No. 130)	223	–	×	×	×	–	–	PFS 495 (III): left edge
PFS 496 (Cat.No. 108)	224	–	–	×	–	–	–	PFS 497 (III): right edge PFS 498 (III): left edge
PFS 501 (Cat.No. 141)	225	–	–	–	×	–	–	PFS 493 (III): reverse PFS 499s (II): left edge

Appendix One: Concordance of Seals to Tablets in Volume I (*cont.*)

PFS No. (Cat.No.)	PF (Tablet)	Obverse	Bottom Edge	Reverse	Upper Edge	Right Edge	Left Edge	Additional PFS on Tablet and Location or Note
PFS 503 (Cat.No. 307)	226	–	–	×	–	–	–	PFS 99 (Cat.No. 113): left edge PFS 502 (III): reverse PFS 504 (III): reverse
PFS 513 (Cat.No. 85)	233	–	–	×	×	×	×	—
	1986	–	–	–	–	×	–	PFS 108* (III): left edge
	1987	–	–	–	–	–	×	PFS 1591 (II): obverse, upper edge, right edge PFS 1662 (II): reverse
	2074	–	–	×	×	Destroyed	×	—
PFS 514 (Cat.No. 192)	234	–	–	×	–	–	–	PFS 57* (Cat.No. 239): reverse, left edge
	236	–	–	×	–	–	×	—
	257	–	–	×	×	–	×	—
PFS 516 (Cat.No. 98)	239	–	–	×	–	–	–	PFS 57* (Cat.No. 239): reverse PFS 131 (Cat.No. 170): left edge
PFS 523* (Cat.No. 209)	256	–	–	×	–	–	×	PFS 524 (Cat.No. 2): reverse, upper edge
PFS 524 (Cat.No. 2)	256	–	–	×	×	–	–	PFS 523* (Cat.No. 209): reverse, left edge
PFS 526* (Cat.No. 216)	271	–	–	×	–	–	–	PFS 527 (III): upper edge, left edge
PFS 536 (Cat.No. 102)	291	–	–	×	×	–	×	—
	824	–	–	×	–	–	×	—
	1253	–	–	×	–	–	–	PFS 89 (III): left edge
PFS 538 (Cat.No. 312)	293	–	–	×	×	–	×	—
PFS 547 (Cat.No. 151)	304	–	–	×	–	–	–	PFS 548 (III): left edge
PFS 552 (Cat.No. 118)	310	–	–	×	–	–	–	PFS 553 (II): left edge
PFS 555 (Cat.No. 93)	312	–	–	×	–	–	–	PFS 554 (II): reverse PFS 556 (II): left edge
PFS 584* (Cat.No. 203)	333	×	–	–	–	–	–	—
PFS 594 (Cat.No. 103)	346	–	–	×	–	–	–	PFS 1673 (III): left edge
PFS 614 (Cat.No. 287)	364	–	–	×	×	–	–	PFS 154 (III): left edge
PFS 632 (Cat.No. 143)	376	–	–	×	×	–	–	PFS 633 (II): left edge
	514	–	–	×	–	–	–	PFS 742 (illegible): bottom edge, left edge
PFS 669 (Cat.No. 142)	432	–	–	×	–	–	–	PFS 122 (II): left edge
PFS 671* (Cat.No. 174)	434	–	–	×	–	–	–	PFS 29 (Cat.No. 302): left edge
PFS 673 (Cat.No. 64)	436	–	–	–	–	–	×	PFS 15 (III): reverse
PFS 677* (Cat.No. 181)	439	–	×	×	×	–	–	PFS 678 (II): left edge
	1027	–	–	×	×	–	–	—
PFS 684 (Cat.No. 183)	444	–	–	×	–	–	–	PFS 42 (III): left edge
PFS 687 (Cat.No. 119)	453	–	–	×	–	–	–	—
PFS 690 (Cat.No. 139)	460	–	–	×	–	–	–	PFS 69 (III): left edge
PFS 709 (Cat.No. 271)	482	–	–	–	–	–	×	PFS 708 (II): reverse, upper edge
PFS 714 (Cat.No. 152)	486	–	–	×	–	–	–	PFS 39s (Cat.No. 221): left edge
PFS 719 (Cat.No. 195)	490	–	–	–	–	–	×	PFS 718 (II): reverse
	1127	–	–	–	–	–	×	PFS 1078 (illegible): reverse
PFS 720 (Cat.No. 57)	492	–	–	×	–	–	×	—
PFS 731 (Cat.No. 131)	502	–	–	×	–	–	–	PFS 732 (III): left edge
	626	–	–	×	–	–	–	PFS 732 (III): left edge
PFS 737 (Cat.No. 281)	510	–	–	×	–	–	–	PFS 185 (III): left edge
PFS 740 (Cat.No. 146)	513	–	–	×	–	–	–	PFS 5 (II): left edge
PFS 749 (Cat.No. 110)	524	–	–	×	×	–	–	PFS 702 (III): left edge
PFS 757 (Cat.No. 296)	533	–	–	×	–	–	–	PFS 758 (illegible): left edge
PFS 769* (Cat.No. 278)	548	–	–	×	–	–	×	—

Appendix One: Concordance of Seals to Tablets in Volume I (*cont.*)

PFS No. (Cat.No.)	PF (Tablet)	Obverse	Bottom Edge	Reverse	Upper Edge	Right Edge	Left Edge	Additional PFS on Tablet and Location or Note
PFS 774 (Cat.No. 58)	556	–	–	×	–	–	×	—
PFS 778 (Cat.No. 11)	560	–	–	×	–	–	×	—
	1106	–	–	×	–	–	×	—
PFS 781 (Cat.No. 107)	565	–	–	×	–	–	×	—
PFS 782 (Cat.No. 105)	567	–	–	×	–	–	–	PFS 783 (Cat.No. 153): upper edge
								PFS 784 (II): left edge
PFS 783 (Cat.No. 153)	567	–	–	–	×	–	–	PFS 782 (Cat.No. 105): reverse
								PFS 784 (II): left edge
PFS 787 (Cat.No. 79)	581	–	×	×	–	–	–	PFS 788 (III): upper edge
								PFS 789 (illegible): left edge
PFS 795 (Cat.No. 214)	587	–	–	×	–	–	–	PFS 796 (illegible): left edge
PFS 807 (Cat.No. 269)	600	–	–	–	–	–	×	PFS 806 (illegible): reverse
PFS 815* (Cat.No. 215)	608	–	–	×	×	–	×	—
PFS 818 (Cat.No. 265)	610	–	–	×	–	–	×	—
	859	–	–	–	×	–	×	—
PFS 819 (Cat.No. 86)	611	–	–	×	–	–	×	—
PFS 841 (Cat.No. 13)	644	–	–	×	–	–	–	PFS 842 (III): upper edge
								PFS 843 (II): left edge
PFS 844 (Cat.No. 59)	645	–	–	×	–	–	×	—
PFS 849 (Cat.No. 189)	648	–	–	–	–	–	×	PFS 848* (II): obverse, reverse
	1177	–	–	–	–	–	×	PFS 1060 (III): reverse
								PFS 1119 (Cat.No. 283): reverse
PFS 851 (Cat.No. 60)	650	–	–	×	–	–	–	PFS 258s (III): left edge
PFS 853 (Cat.No. 204)	685	–	–	×	–	–	–	PFS 10 (Cat.No. 251): left edge
	1487	–	–	×	–	–	–	PFS 33 (Cat.No. 220): left edge
PFS 859* (Cat.No. 205)	691	–	–	×	–	–	×	—
PFS 882 (Cat.No. 65)	759	–	–	×	–	–	–	PFS 881s (III): left edge
PFS 883* (Cat.No. 97)	760	–	–	–	–	–	×	PFS 884 (Cat.No. 123): reverse, upper edge
PFS 884 (Cat.No. 123)	760	–	–	×	×	–	–	PFS 883* (Cat.No. 97): left edge
PFS 885 (Cat.No. 187)	761	–	–	–	–	–	×	PFS 145 (Cat.No. 115): reverse, upper edge
	763	–	–	–	–	–	×	PFS 145 (Cat.No. 115): reverse
	1589	–	–	–	–	–	×	PFS 1471 (illegible): reverse
PFS 896 (Cat.No. 308)	770	–	–	–	×	–	–	PFS 895 (III): left edge
PFS 902 (Cat.No. 243)	773	–	–	–	–	–	×	PFS 900s (II): reverse
								PFS 901 (II): reverse
PFS 912 (Cat.No. 138)	786	–	–	×	–	–	–	PFS 913 (Cat.No. 200): left edge
PFS 913 (Cat.No. 200)	786	–	–	–	–	–	×	PFS 912 (Cat.No. 138): reverse
PFS 916 (Cat.No. 226)	788	–	–	×	–	–	–	PFS 24 (Cat.No. 298): left edge
PFS 919s (Cat.No. 259)	793	–	–	–	×	–	×	PFS 920 (illegible): bottom edge
PFS 931* (Cat.No. 270)	807	–	–	×	×	–	–	PFS 932 (illegible): left edge
PFS 939 (Cat.No. 267)	814	–	–	×	×	–	–	PFS 940 (Cat.No. 81): left edge
PFS 940 (Cat.No. 81)	814	–	–	–	–	–	×	PFS 939 (Cat.No. 267): reverse, upper edge
	1550	–	–	–	–	–	×	PFS 213 (Cat.No. 140): reverse
PFS 944 (Cat.No. 129)	818	–	–	×	–	–	×	—
PFS 945 (Cat.No. 96)	819	–	–	–	–	–	×	PFS 236 (Cat.No. 213): bottom edge, reverse
	1165	–	–	–	–	–	×	PFS 236 (Cat.No. 213): reverse, upper edge
PFS 952 (Cat.No. 227)	826	×	–	–	–	–	–	PFS 21 (II): left edge
PFS 959s (Cat.No. 246)	834	–	–	×	–	–	×	PFS 960 (II): reverse
								PFS 1685 (III): upper edge
PFS 964 (Cat.No. 260)	842	–	–	×	–	–	–	PFS 136 (III): left edge

Appendix One: Concordance of Seals to Tablets in Volume I (*cont.*)

PFS No. (Cat.No.)	PF (Tablet)	Obverse	Bottom Edge	Reverse	Upper Edge	Right Edge	Left Edge	Additional PFS on Tablet and Location or Note
PFS 970 (Cat.No. 6)	848	–	–	–	–	–	×	—
	1047	–	–	–	–	–	×	PFS 1020 (Cat.No. 37): reverse
PFS 971 (Cat.No. 171)	854	–	–	×	×	–	–	PFS 6 (Cat.No. 304): left edge
	1587	–	–	×	–	–	–	PFS 6 (Cat.No. 304): left edge
PFS 981* (Cat.No. 87)	937	–	–	×	×	–	×	—
	993	–	–	–	–	–	×	—
	1012	–	–	×	×	–	×	—
PFS 990 (Cat.No. 256)	995	–	–	×	×	–	×	—
PFS 991 (Cat.No. 154)	997	–	–	–	×	–	×	—
PFS 996 (Cat.No. 155)	1010	–	–	–	×	–	–	PFS 157 (II): left edge
PFS 1002 (Cat.No. 196)	1018	–	–	×	–	–	–	PFS 1003 (III): left edge
PFS 1016 (Cat.No. 77)	1040	–	–	–	–	–	×	PFS 1015 (III): reverse
PFS 1017 (Cat.No. 126)	1045	–	–	–	×	–	–	—
PFS 1018 (Cat.No. 185)	1046	–	–	×	–	–	–	PFS 21 (II): left edge
PFS 1020 (Cat.No. 37)	1047	–	–	×	–	–	–	PFS 970 (Cat.No. 6): left edge
PFS 1023 (Cat.No. 127)	1048	–	–	–	–	–	×	PFS 1022 (III): reverse, upper edge
PFS 1025* (Cat.No. 266)	1059	–	–	×	–	–	–	PFS 1026 (Cat.No. 156): left edge PFS 1680 (II): upper edge
PFS 1026 (Cat.No. 156)	1059	–	–	–	–	–	×	PFS 1025* (Cat.No. 266): reverse PFS 1680 (II): upper edge
PFS 1030 (Cat.No. 120)	1062	–	–	×	–	–	–	PFS 152 (Cat.No. 295): left edge
	1118	–	–	–	×	–	–	PFS 152 (Cat.No. 295): left edge
PFS 1045 (Cat.No. 157)	1090	–	–	×	–	–	–	PFS 89 (III): left edge PFS 177 (II): reverse
	1113	–	–	×	×	–	–	PFS 177 (II): reverse PFS 628 (III): left edge
PFS 1053 (Cat.No. 45)	1095	–	–	×	–	–	–	PFS 18 (Cat.No. 15): left edge
PFS 1057 (Cat.No. 70)	1101	–	–	×	–	–	–	PFS 1056 (III): reverse PFS 1058 (II): left edge PFS 1059 (illegible): right edge
PFS 1071 (Cat.No. 29)	1114	–	–	×	–	–	–	PFS 17 (Cat.No. 235): left edge PFS 1072 (Cat.No. 61): reverse
PFS 1072 (Cat.No. 61)	1114	–	–	×	–	–	–	PFS 17 (Cat.No. 235): left edge PFS 1071 (Cat.No. 29): reverse
PFS 1076 (Cat.No. 193)	1120	–	–	×	–	–	–	PFS 266* (Cat.No. 208): upper edge, left edge PFS 1666 (II): reverse
	1212	–	–	×	×	–	–	PFS 1159s (II): left edge
PFS 1077 (Cat.No. 158)	1123	–	–	–	–	–	×	PFS 1648 (III): reverse, upper edge
PFS 1081 (Cat.No. 71)	1129	–	–	–	–	–	×	PFS 19 (III): reverse PFS 22 (II): reverse
PFS 1083 (Cat.No. 43)	1131	–	–	×	–	–	–	PFS 1084* (III): upper edge PFS 1085 (II): left edge
PFS 1090 (Cat.No. 175)	1139	–	×	×	×	–	–	PFS 95 (Cat.No. 25): left edge
PFS 1091 (Cat.No. 68)	1140	–	–	–	–	–	×	PFS 193 (III): reverse PFS 312 (Cat.No. 237): upper edge PFS 1092 (III): right edge
PFS 1099 (Cat.No. 169)	1158	–	–	×	–	–	×	—
PFS 1101 (Cat.No. 297)	1164	–	–	–	×	–	–	PFS 130 (Cat.No. 300): reverse PFS 1102 (Cat.No. 132): left edge
	1227	–	–	×	–	–	–	PFS 130 (Cat.No. 300): reverse PFS 1102 (Cat.No. 132): left edge

Appendix One: Concordance of Seals to Tablets in Volume I (*cont.*)

PFS No. (Cat.No.)	PF (Tablet)	Obverse	Bottom Edge	Reverse	Upper Edge	Right Edge	Left Edge	Additional PFS on Tablet and Location or Note
PFS 1102 (Cat.No. 132)	1164	–	–	–	–	–	×	PFS 130 (Cat.No. 300): reverse PFS 1101 (Cat.No. 297): upper edge
	1227	–	–	–	–	–	×	PFS 130 (Cat.No. 300): reverse PFS 1101 (Cat.No. 297): reverse
PFS 1117 (Cat.No. 67)	1176	–	–	–	–	–	×	PFS 1116 (III): reverse
PFS 1119 (Cat.No. 283)	1177	–	–	×	–	–	–	PFS 849 (Cat.No. 189): left edge PFS 1060 (III): reverse
PFS 1122 (Cat.No. 228)	1178	–	–	×	–	–	×	PFS 1121s (II): reverse, left edge
	1190	–	–	×	–	–	×	PFS 1121s (II): reverse, left edge
PFS 1123 (Cat.No. 279)	1179	–	–	×	×	–	×	—
PFS 1135 (Cat.No. 66)	1192	–	–	–	–	–	×	PFS 1134s (III): reverse
PFS 1142 (Cat.No. 39)	1198	–	–	×	×	–	–	PFS 1143 (II): left edge
	1234	–	–	×	–	–	–	PFS 95 (Cat.No. 25): left edge PFS 1184 (III): reverse
PFS 1146 (Cat.No. 40)	1200	–	–	×	–	–	–	PFS 184 (II): left edge
PFS 1153 (Cat.No. 199)	1203	–	–	–	×	×	–	PFS 1152s (illegible): left edge PFS 1154 (illegible): reverse
PFS 1155 (Cat.No. 190)	1209	–	–	×	×	–	–	PFS 1156 (II): left edge
	1226	–	–	–	–	–	×	PFS 261* (II): reverse
PFS 1165 (Cat.No. 89)	1217	–	–	×	–	–	–	PFS 1164 (II): reverse PFS 1166 (II): left edge PFS 1167 (III): upper edge
PFS 1181 (Cat.No. 210)	1097	–	–	–	–	–	×	PFS 264 (III): upper edge PFS 265 (Cat.No. 240): obverse, right edge PFS 266* (Cat.No. 208): left edge
	1112	–	–	–	–	–	×	PFS 264 (III): upper edge PFS 265 (Cat.No. 240): right edge PFS 266* (Cat.No. 208): left edge
	1228	–	–	–	–	–	×	PFS 265 (Cat.No. 240): reverse, upper edge
PFS 1188 (Cat.No. 144)	1246	–	–	–	×	×	–	PFS 5 (II): left edge
PFS 1189 (Cat.No. 8)	1247	–	–	×	–	–	–	PFS 18 (Cat.No. 15): left edge
PFS 1202 (Cat.No. 137)	1261	–	–	×	–	–	–	PFS 18 (Cat.No. 15): left edge
PFS 1204 (Cat.No. 136)	1262	–	–	×	–	–	–	PFS 21 (II): left edge
PFS 1217s (Cat.No. 168)	1275	–	–	–	–	–	×	—
	1276	–	–	–	–	–	×	PFS 201 (Cat.No. 50): reverse
PFS 1227* (Cat.No. 219)	1282	–	×	×	×	–	×	—
PFS 1236 (Cat.No. 159)	1291	–	–	×	–	–	–	PFS 26 (Cat.No. 299): left edge
PFS 1238 (Cat.No. 160)	1293	–	–	–	×	–	–	PFS 26 (Cat.No. 299): left edge
PFS 1243 (Cat.No. 33)	1297	–	–	×	–	–	–	PFS 26 (Cat.No. 299): left edge
PFS 1249 (Cat.No. 294)	1304	–	–	×	–	–	–	PFS 26 (Cat.No. 299): left edge
PFS 1252 (Cat.No. 161)	1306	–	–	–	–	–	×	PFS 1251s (illegible): reverse
PFS 1260s (Cat.No. 184)	1315	–	–	×	–	–	–	PFS 55 (III): left edge
PFS 1264s (Cat.No. 206)	1320	–	–	–	×	–	–	PFS 23 (III): left edge
PFS 1276 (Cat.No. 34)	1332	–	–	×	–	–	–	PFS 1275 (illegible): left edge
PFS 1285 (Cat.No. 44)	1341	–	–	×	–	–	–	PFS 21 (II): left edge
PFS 1286 (Cat.No. 258)	1342	–	–	×	–	–	–	PFS 21 (II): left edge
PFS 1300 (Cat.No. 191)	1378	–	–	×	–	–	×	—
PFS 1309s (Cat.No. 229)	1386	–	–	×	–	–	–	PFS 18 (Cat.No. 15): left edge
PFS 1311s (Cat.No. 247)	1388	–	–	×	×	–	–	PFS 24 (Cat.No. 298): left edge
PFS 1315s (Cat.No. 253)	1393	×	–	–	–	–	–	PFS 24 (Cat.No. 298): left edge
	1573	–	–	×	–	–	Destroyed	—

Appendix One: Concordance of Seals to Tablets in Volume I (*cont.*)

PFS No. (Cat.No.)	PF (Tablet)	Obverse	Bottom Edge	Reverse	Upper Edge	Right Edge	Left Edge	Additional PFS on Tablet and Location or Note
PFS 1320 (Cat.No. 35)	1403	–	–	×	–	–	–	—
PFS 1321s (Cat.No. 176)	1404	–	–	×	–	–	–	PFS 201 (Cat.No. 50): left edge
PFS 1322 (Cat.No. 36)	1405	–	–	–	×	–	–	PFS 138 (Cat.No. 186): left edge
PFS 1325 (Cat.No. 41)	1409	–	–	–	×	–	–	PFS 5 (II): left edge
PFS 1362 (Cat.No. 30)	1464	–	–	×	–	–	–	PFS 37 (III): left edge
PFS 1367s (Cat.No. 211)	1468	–	–	×	–	–	–	—
PFS 1374 (Cat.No. 31)	1478	–	–	×	–	–	–	PFS 10 (Cat.No. 251): left edge
PFS 1375s (Cat.No. 254)	1479	–	–	×	–	–	–	PFS 1376 (illegible): left edge
PFS 1387 (Cat.No. 72)	1490	–	–	×	–	–	–	PFS 23 (III): left edge
PFS 1388 (Cat.No. 162)	1492	–	–	×	–	–	–	PFS 1389 (illegible): left edge
PFS 1391 (Cat.No. 248)	1494	–	–	×	–	–	–	PFS 1392 (illegible): left edge
PFS 1406 (Cat.No. 276)	1510	–	–	×	–	–	–	PFS 56 (III): left edge
PFS 1428s (Cat.No. 230)	1532	–	–	×	–	–	–	PFS 40 (III): left edge
PFS 1437s (Cat.No. 128)	1546	×	–	–	–	–	–	PFS 1438 (III): left edge
PFS 1440 (Cat.No. 42)	1549	–	–	×	×	–	–	PFS 250 (II): left edge
PFS 1444 (Cat.No. 62)	1562	–	–	×	–	–	–	PFS 17 (Cat.No. 235): left edge
PFS 1447 (Cat.No. 163)	1565	–	–	×	–	–	–	PFS 17 (Cat.No. 235): left edge
PFS 1454 (Cat.No. 166)	1570	–	–	×	–	–	–	PFS 1455 (illegible): left edge
PFS 1458 (Cat.No. 80)	1574	–	–	×	–	–	–	PFS 107 (III): left edge
PFS 1460 (Cat.No. 9)	1577	–	–	×	–	–	–	PFS 17 (Cat.No. 235): left edge
PFS 1463s (Cat.No. 231)	1579	–	–	×	–	–	–	PFS 1464 (III): left edge
PFS 1465 (Cat.No. 21)	1580	–	–	×	×	–	×	—
PFS 1466 (Cat.No. 234)	1585	–	–	×	–	–	×	—
PFS 1467 (Cat.No. 12)	1586	–	–	×	–	×	–	PFS 89 (III): left edge
PFS 1475 (Cat.No. 177)	1596	–	–	×	–	–	–	PFS 84 (II): left edge
PFS 1480 (Cat.No. 257)	1603	–	–	×	–	–	×	—
PFS 1483 (Cat.No. 88)	1607	–	–	×	–	–	–	PFS 117 (II): left edge
PFS 1485 (Cat.No. 112)	1608	–	–	×	–	–	–	PFS 80 (Cat.No. 202): left edge
PFS 1489 (Cat.No. 106)	1614	–	–	×	–	–	–	PFS 1490 (III): left edge
PFS 1499 (Cat.No. 10)	1622	–	–	Destroyed	–	–	×	—
PFS 1501 (Cat.No. 238)	1624	–	–	×	–	–	–	PFS 61 (II): left edge
PFS 1519 (Cat.No. 167)	1667	–	–	×	×	–	–	PFS 168 (Cat.No. 74): left edge
PFS 1527 (Cat.No. 32)	1686	–	–	×	×	–	–	PFS 1528 (III): left edge
PFS 1535 (Cat.No. 164)	1723	–	–	×	–	–	–	PFS 5 (II): left edge
PFS 1550 (Cat.No. 14)	1769	–	–	×	–	–	–	PFS 1551 (III): left edge
PFS 1566* (Cat.No. 218)	1852	–	–	–	×	–	×	—
PFS 1582 (Cat.No. 232)	1942	–	–	×	–	Destroyed	–	—
PFS 1586 (Cat.No. 121)	1953	–	–	×	×	Destroyed	×	—
PFS 1598 (Cat.No. 63)	2020	–	–	–	–	–	×	PFS 1597 (II): reverse
PFS 1612 (Cat.No. 268)	2050	–	–	×	–	–	–	PFS 1613 (Cat.No. 82): left edge
PFS 1613 (Cat.No. 82)	2050	–	–	–	–	–	×	PFS 1612 (Cat.No. 268): reverse
PFS 1624s (Cat.No. 261)	2059	×	–	–	–	–	–	PFS 1342 (II): left edge
PFS 1630 (Cat.No. 165)	2066	–	–	×	×	–	–	PFS 1631 (III): left edge
PFS 1632* (Cat.No. 244)	2070	×	–	–	×	×	×	—
PFS 1637* (Cat.No. 273)	2085	–	–	×	–	–	–	PFS 12b (II): reverse
PFS 1641 (Cat.No. 18)	2087	–	–	×	Destroyed	–	–	—
PFS 1654 (Cat.No. 122)	981	–	–	×	×	–	–	PFS 985 (III): left edge
PFS 1658 (Cat.No. 101)	1256	–	–	–	×	×	–	PFS 732 (III): left edge
PFS 1684 (Cat.No. 17)	1324	–	–	×	–	–	–	PFS 23 (III): left edge

APPENDIX TWO

PROVISIONAL LIST OF ALL SUBSUMED HALLOCK PFS NUMBERS (VOLUMES I–III)

This appendix lists those Hallock (1969) seal numbers (PFS 1*–PFS 314) that have been collated with other seal numbers.

Subsumed PFS Number		Collated PFS Number
PFS 88	=	PFS 33 (Cat.No. 220)
PFS 119	=	PFS 80 (Cat.No. 202)
PFS 147	=	PFS 61 (II)
PFS 159	=	PFS 154 (III)
PFS 200	=	PFS 142 (III)
PFS 204	=	PFS 120 (Cat.No. 49)
PFS 208	=	PFS 185 (III)
PFS 214	=	PFS 99 (Cat.No. 113)
PFS 215	=	PFS 143s (II)
PFS 218	=	PFS 117 (II)
PFS 229	=	PFS 123* (Cat.No. 75)
PFS 242	=	PFS 86 (Cat.No. 48)
PFS 259	=	PFS 92 (III)
PFS 267	=	PFS 248 (II)
PFS 274	=	PFS 28 (III)
PFS 275	=	PFS 101 (II)
PFS 277	=	PFS 221 (II)
PFS 300	=	PFS 41 (III)
PFS 304	=	PFS 101 (II)
PFS 314	=	PFS 260 (Cat.No. 225)

APPENDIX THREE

SUMMARY DATA ON SEAL DIMENSIONS FOR VOLUME I

CYLINDER SEALS

Of the 294 cylinder seals included in Volume I, we are able to reconstruct both the approximate height and the approximate diameter for 119 seals (= 40% of the total number of cylinder seals in Volume I). We are able to reconstruct the height (but not the diameter) for an additional eight cylinder seals, giving a total of 127 cylinder seals for which we are able to reconstruct the height (= 43% of the total number of cylinder seals in Volume I). We are able to reconstruct the diameter (but not the height) on an additional seventy-three cylinder seals, giving a total of 192 cylinder seals for which we are able to reconstruct the diameter (= 65% of the total number of cylinder seals in Volume I). 102 seals have neither a reconstructed height nor a reconstructed diameter (= 35% of the total number of cylinder seals in Volume I).

CYLINDER SEAL HEIGHT

The distribution of height of the 127 cylinder seals for which we can reconstruct the height appears in chart 1. As can be seen, there is a significant clustering of cylinder seals in the range from 1.40 cm to 2.00 cm; 103 cylinder seals fall in this range. This is 81% of the total sample of 127 cylinder seals for which we can reconstruct the height. Within this clustering we can see another significant clustering in the range from 1.70 cm to 1.80 cm; forty-three cylinder seals fall in this range, accounting for 42% of the 103 cylinder seals falling in the range from 1.40 cm to 2.00 cm and 34% of the total sample of 127 cylinder seals for which we can reconstruct the height. Percentages fall off dramatically beyond the 1.40 cm to 2.00 cm range. The largest known complete cylinder seal height, 3.00 cm, is represented by one example, PFS 7* (Cat.No. 4), a royal name seal.[1]

Chart 2 shows the distribution by carving styles of the 127 cylinder seals for which the height can be reconstructed. Cylinder seals carved in the Fortification Style greatly outnumber those in all other carving styles (thus it is understandable that sixty-seven cylinder seals with known complete height are in the Fortification Style, representing 53% of the total sample of 127 cylinder seals for which we can reconstruct the height). This also means that it is difficult to draw any definitive conclusions from the data. Charts 3–11 present the distribution by individual carving style of cylinder seals for which we can reconstruct the height. We again stress the difficulty of making general statements from the limited data for other carving styles, but we may suggest that Modeled Style cylinder seals (chart 3) tend to be larger than Fortification Style cylinder seals (chart 5). Ten Modeled Style cylinder seals fall in the range from 1.90 cm to 2.20 cm, representing 53% of all Modeled Style cylinder seals seals for which the height can be reconstructed; compare the seventeen Fortification Style cylinder seals which fall in the same range, representing only 25% of all Fortification Style cylinder seals for which the height can be reconstructed. The seals in the Plausibly Antique Styles (chart 11), as well as the one cylinder seal in Volume I that has been categorically designated Antique, also generally are taller than the norm in the Fortification Style. Another interesting observation is the very wide spread of height among the small sample of Court Style cylinder seals (chart 7). Only five Court Style cylinder seals have a reconstructed height, but they cover (1.30–3.00 cm) almost the full range of reconstructed height of cylinder seals in Volume I. It has been argued that the Court Style is a special phenomenon, in both function and in genesis, and the pattern of height of cylinder seals cut in the Court Style may serve to reinforce the experimental nature of the style.[2]

---

1. The dimensions of a few seals in the archive, although they cannot be reconstructed with certainty, would rival or even exceed those of PFS 7* (Cat.No. 4). The preserved height of PFS 859* (Cat.No. 205), carved in the Court Style, is 1.20 cm, and this measures only the head and chest of the hero. Even if the hero is not standing on a pedestal creature and/or there is no device such as a winged disk or crescent in the upper field, a full reconstruction of the height of this seal would be 3.00 cm at the minimum.
2. Compare Garrison 1988, pp. 383–94, 471–75, 528–30, 543–46; Garrison 1991, pp. 13–21.

CYLINDER SEAL DIAMETER

The distribution of the 192 cylinder seals for which we can reconstruct the diameter appears in chart 12. As was seen in the examination of the height of cylinder seals, there are significant cluster patterns. 151 cylinder seals have a diameter that falls in the range from 0.80 cm to 1.10 cm, representing 79% of the total sample of 192 cylinder seals for which the diameter can be reconstructed. Within this clustering, we can see another significant clustering in the range from 0.90 cm to 1.00 cm; ninety-eight cylinder seals fall in this range, accounting for 65% of the 151 cylinder seals falling in the range from 0.80 cm to 1.10 cm and 51% of the total sample of 192 cylinder seals for which the diameter can be reconstructed. Percentages fall off very dramatically above the 1.10 cm size. As we move down the size scale, the fall of percentages from 0.80 cm to 0.70 cm is about the same as the fall in percentages from 1.10 cm to 1.20 cm. The jump from 0.70 cm to 0.60 cm is, however, pronounced. The largest reconstructed cylinder seal diameter, 1.70 cm, is represented by one example, again the royal name cylinder seal PFS 7* (Cat.No. 4).

Chart 13 shows the distribution by carving styles of the 192 cylinder seals for which the diameter can be reconstructed. As with cylinder seals with reconstructed height, the Fortification Style accounts for just over half of the sample (ninety-eight cylinder seals with a reconstructed diameter occur in the Fortification Style, representing 51% of the total sample of 192 cylinder seals with a reconstructed diameter). As may be expected, a pattern in seal diameter emerges which is similar to that seen in seal height. Charts 14–22 present the distribution by individual carving style of cylinder seals for which the diameter can be reconstructed. We stress again the difficulty of making general statements from the limited data for carving styles other than the Fortification Style. We do see, however, that the diameter of Modeled Style cylinder seals tends to be larger than the diameter of Fortification Style cylinder seals. The differences are not as dramatic as with cylinder seal height, since the range of cylinder seal diameter (0.50–1.70 cm) is smaller than the range of cylinder seal height (0.50–3.00 cm). Fifteen Modeled Style cylinder seals fall in the range from 1.10 cm to 1.30 cm (chart 14), representing 47% of all Modeled Style cylinder seals for which the diameter can be reconstructed; compare the ten Fortification Style cylinder seals which fall in the same range (chart 16), representing only 10% of all Fortification Style cylinder seals for which the diameter can be reconstructed. The seven Court Style cylinder seals are spread widely across the size range (chart 18), as was the case with seal height in this style. The royal name seal PFS 7* (Cat.No. 4), from the Court Style, has the largest reconstructed diameter (1.70 cm) in the corpus of seals from Volume I.

STAMP SEALS

Only eighteen stamp seals occur in this Volume. This represents a small percentage (6%) of the total 312 seals in Volume I. Volumes II–III contain greater numbers and percentages of stamp seals. One comment on the nature of these eighteen stamp seals in Volume I deserves attention: thirteen of the eighteen stamp seals (72%) occur on Q texts, always belonging to the receiver (i.e., individuals moving through the Persepolitan administrative system, often coming from or going to distant locations).

The contours of the faces of stamp seals in Volume I fall in four distinct categories of shape (see also *Appendix Four: Stamp Seals in Volume I Grouped by Apparent Contour of Seal Face*): circular: PFS 139s (Cat.No. 222), PFS 298s (Cat.No. 236), PFS 919s (Cat.No. 259), PFS 959s (Cat.No. 246), PFS 1217s (Cat.No. 168), PFS 1428s (Cat.No. 230), PFS 1437s (Cat.No. 128), and PFS 1624s (Cat.No. 261); oval or loaf-shaped: PFS 1264s (Cat.No. 206), PFS 1311s (Cat.No. 247), and PFS 1367s (Cat.No. 211); square or rectangular: PFS 39s (Cat.No. 221), PFS 1315s (Cat.No. 253), and PFS 1375s (Cat.No. 254); and octagonal: PFS 1260s (Cat.No. 184), PFS 1309s (Cat.No. 229), PFS 1321s (Cat.No. 176), and PFS 1463s (Cat.No. 231).

Of the eight circular contours, we can reconstruct the dimensions completely on five examples: PFS 139s (Cat.No. 222), PFS 298s (Cat.No. 236), PFS 959s (Cat.No. 246), PFS 1428s (Cat.No. 230), and PFS 1437s (Cat.No. 128); and only the height on two examples: PFS 1217s (Cat.No. 168) and PFS 1624s (Cat.No. 261). The largest preserved circular contour, PFS 959s (Cat.No. 246), is 2.10 (height) × 2.00 (width) cm. The smallest, PFS 1437s (Cat.No. 128), is 1.70 × 1.80 cm. For one seal, PFS 919s (Cat.No. 259), dimensions cannot be reconstructed, but the overall character of the preserved impression suggests a circular contour. Of the two oval contours, PFS 1264s (Cat.No. 206) is 1.60 × 1.20 cm and PFS 1311s (Cat.No. 247) is 1.90 × 1.40 cm, while the closely related stamp with loaf-shaped contour, PFS 1367s (Cat.No. 211), measures 1.50 × 1.20 cm. Of the four octagonal contours, we can reconstruct the dimensions completely on two examples, PFS 1260s (Cat.No. 184) and PFS 1309s (Cat.No. 229), and only the height on two examples, PFS 1321s (Cat.No. 176) and PFS 1463s (Cat.No. 231). The largest preserved octagonal contour, PFS 1260s (Cat.No. 184), measures 1.80 × 1.20 cm; the smallest, PFS 1309s (Cat.No. 229), measures 0.90 × 1.40 cm. We can reconstruct the dimensions completely on all three of the square/rectangular contours. The largest, PFS 1375s (Cat.No. 254), measures 1.50 × 1.20 cm; the smallest, PFS 1315s (Cat.No. 253), measures 1.00 × 0.90 cm.

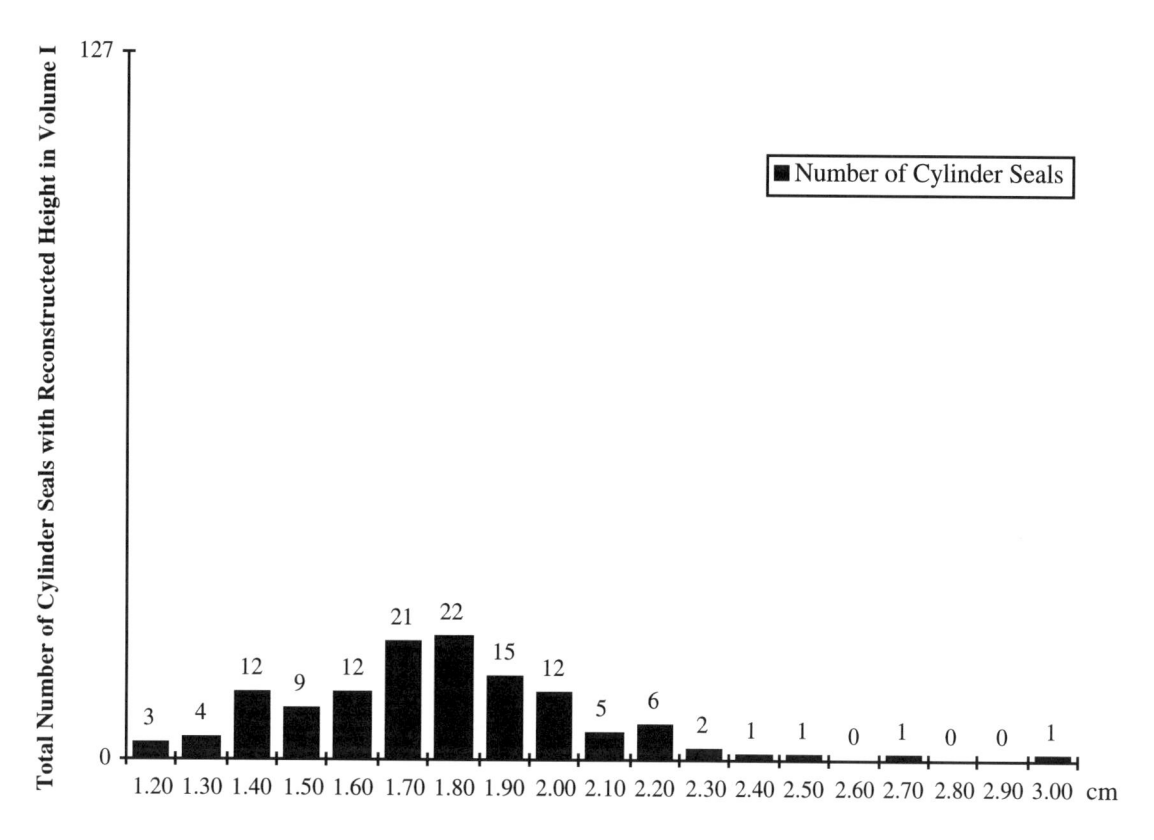

APPENDIX THREE: SUMMARY DATA ON SEAL DIMENSIONS FOR VOLUME I 473

Chart 1. Height of Cylinder Seals in Volume I

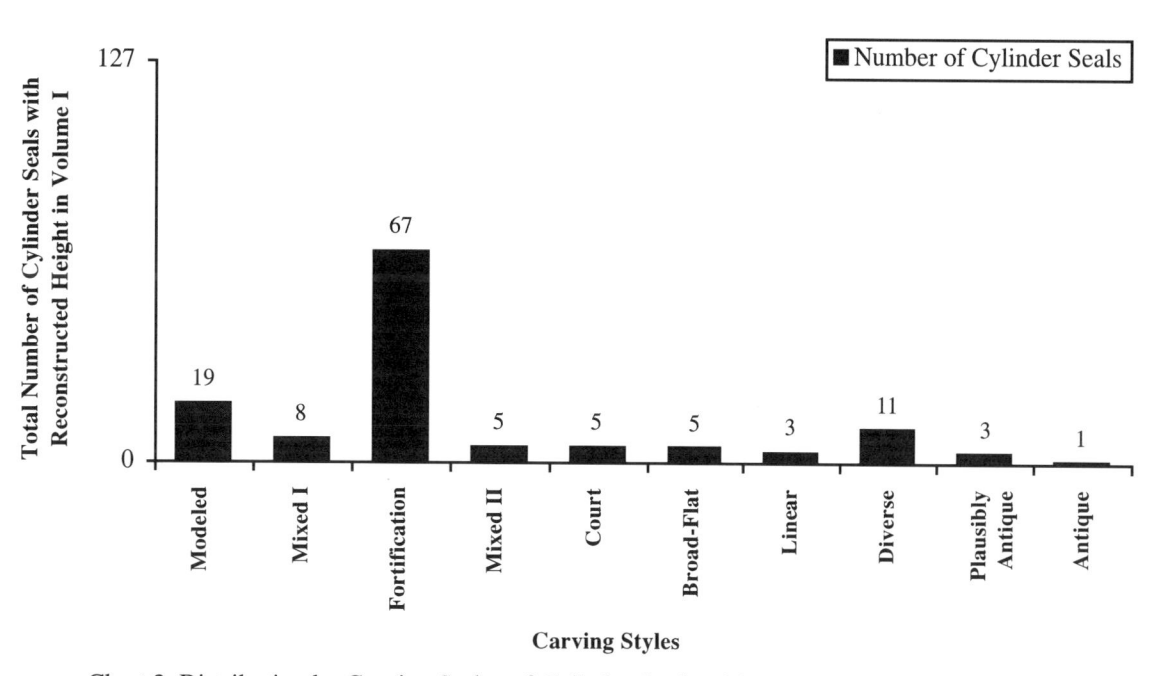

Chart 2. Distribution by Carving Styles of Cylinder Seals with Reconstructed Height in Volume I

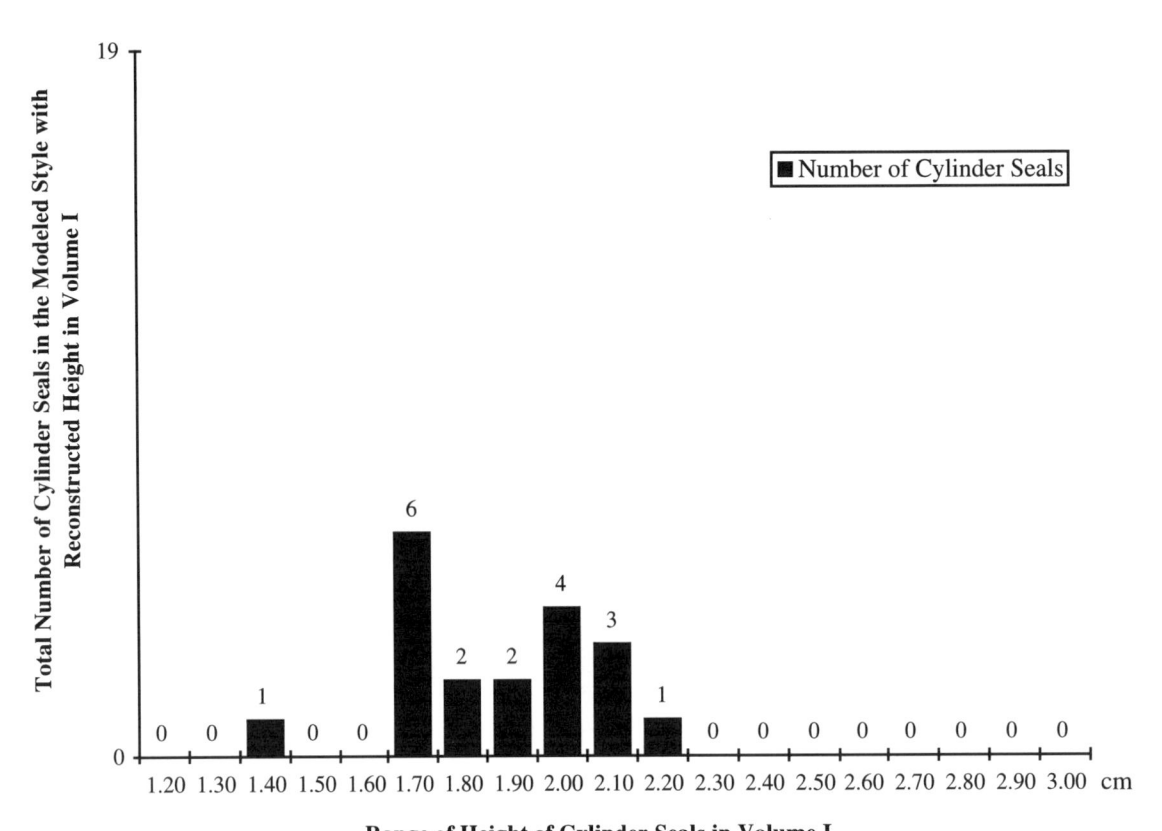

Chart 3. Height of Cylinder Seals: Modeled Style

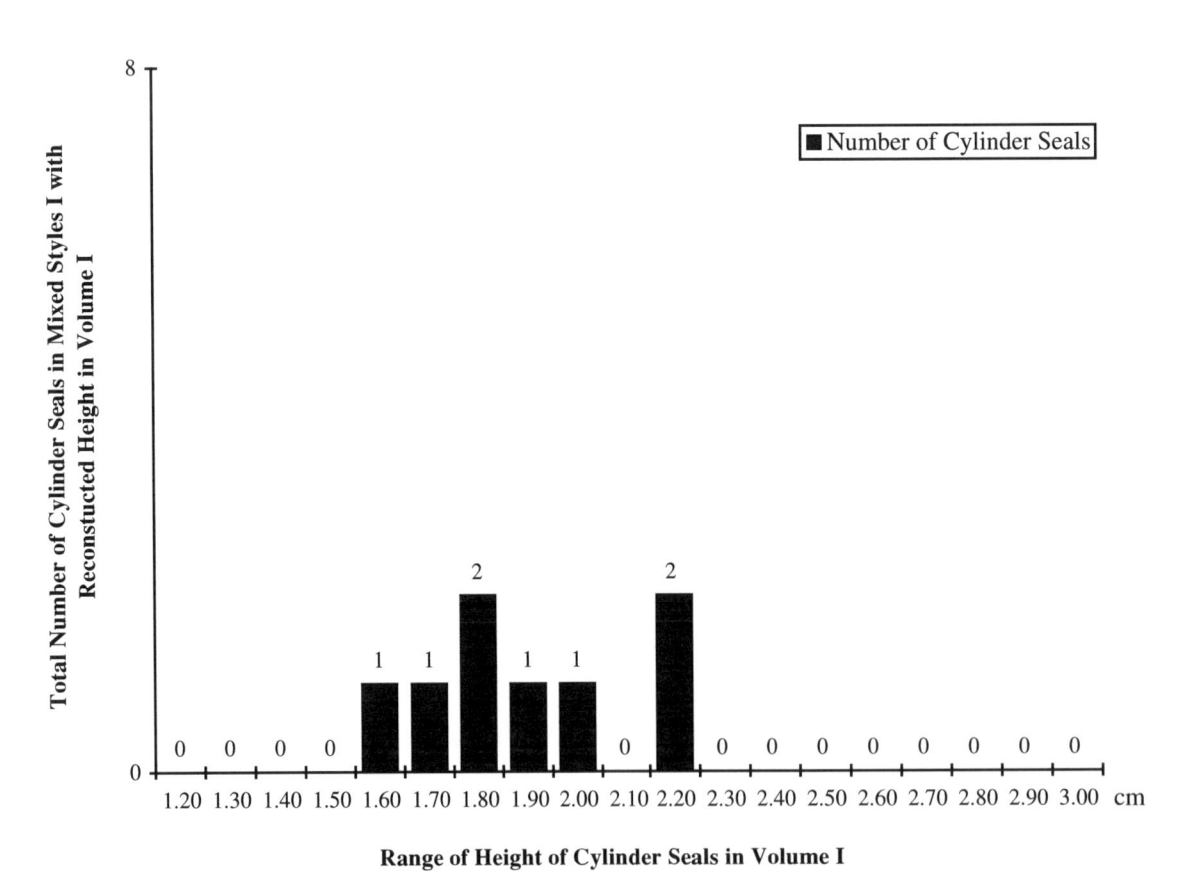

Chart 4. Height of Cylinder Seals: Mixed Styles I

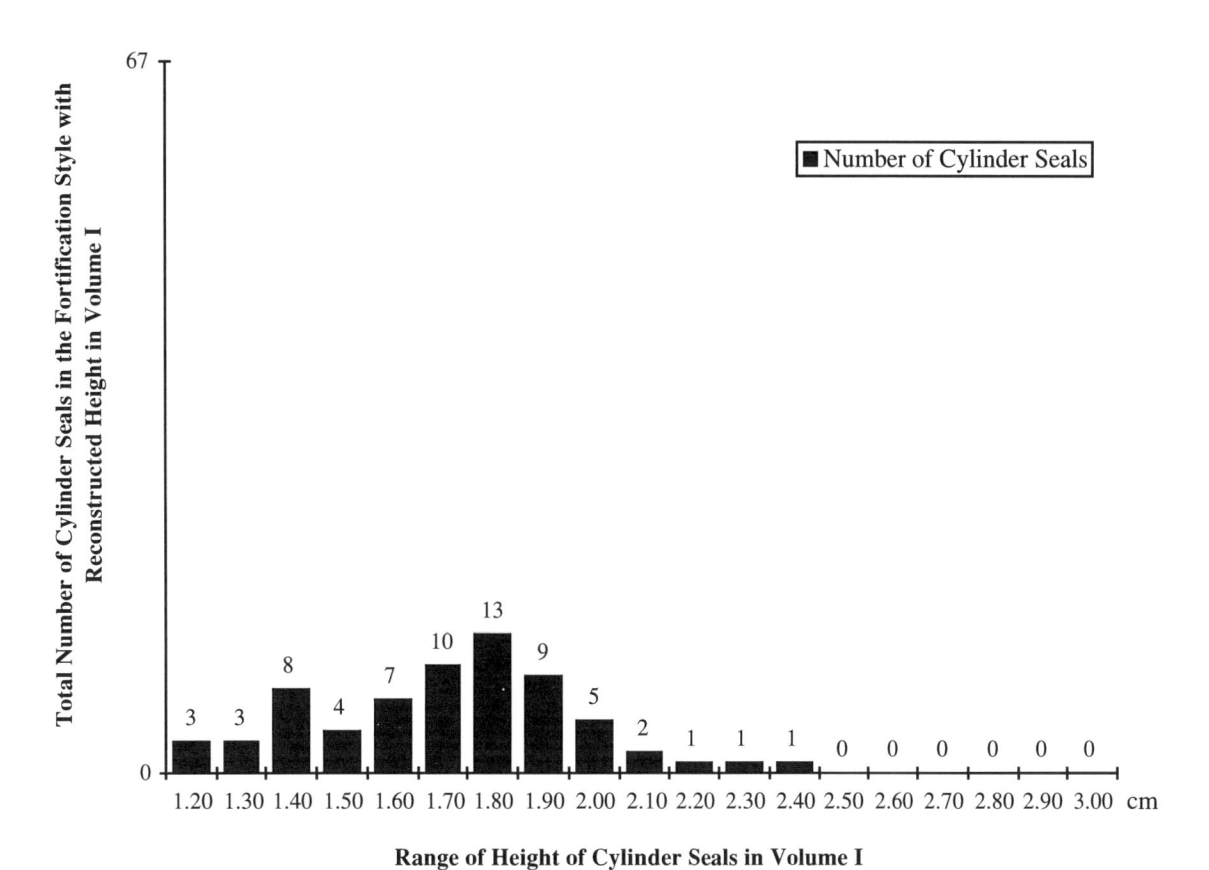

Chart 5. Height of Cylinder Seals: Fortification Style

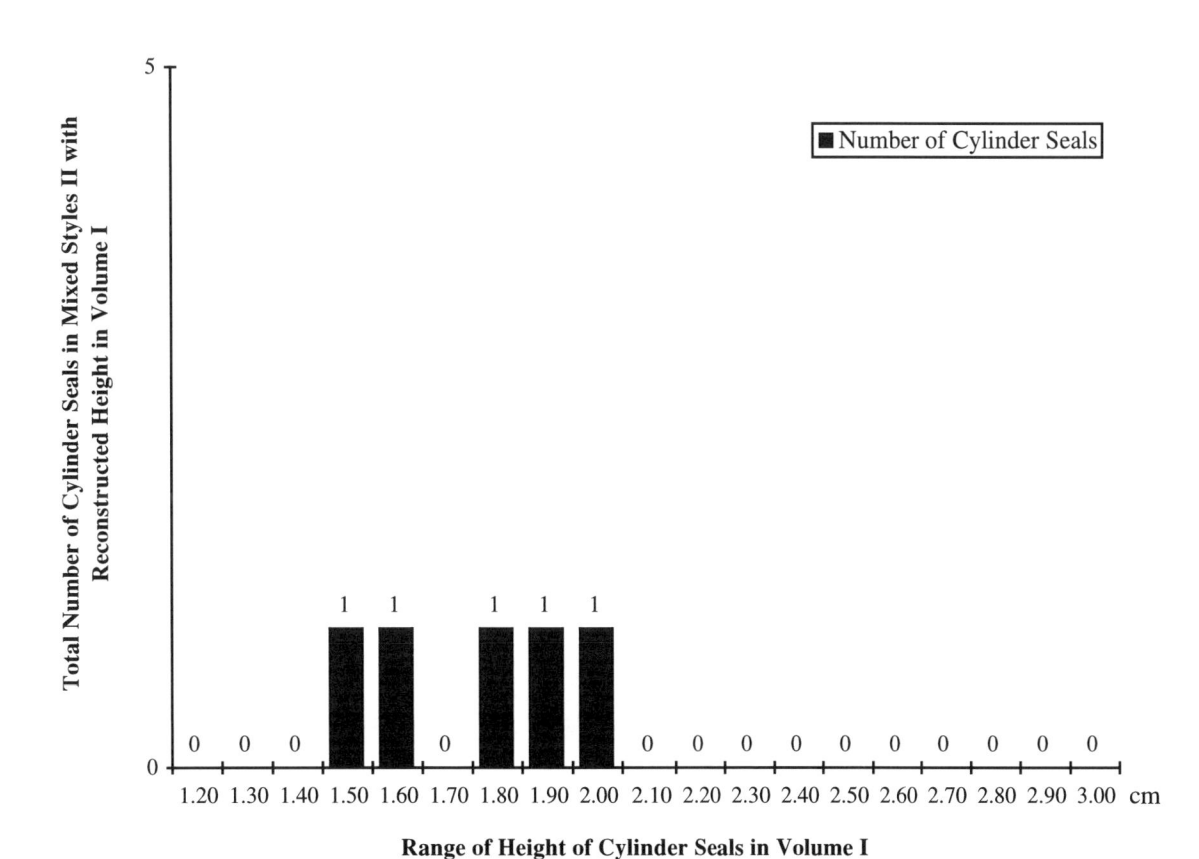

Chart 6. Height of Cylinder Seals: Mixed Styles II

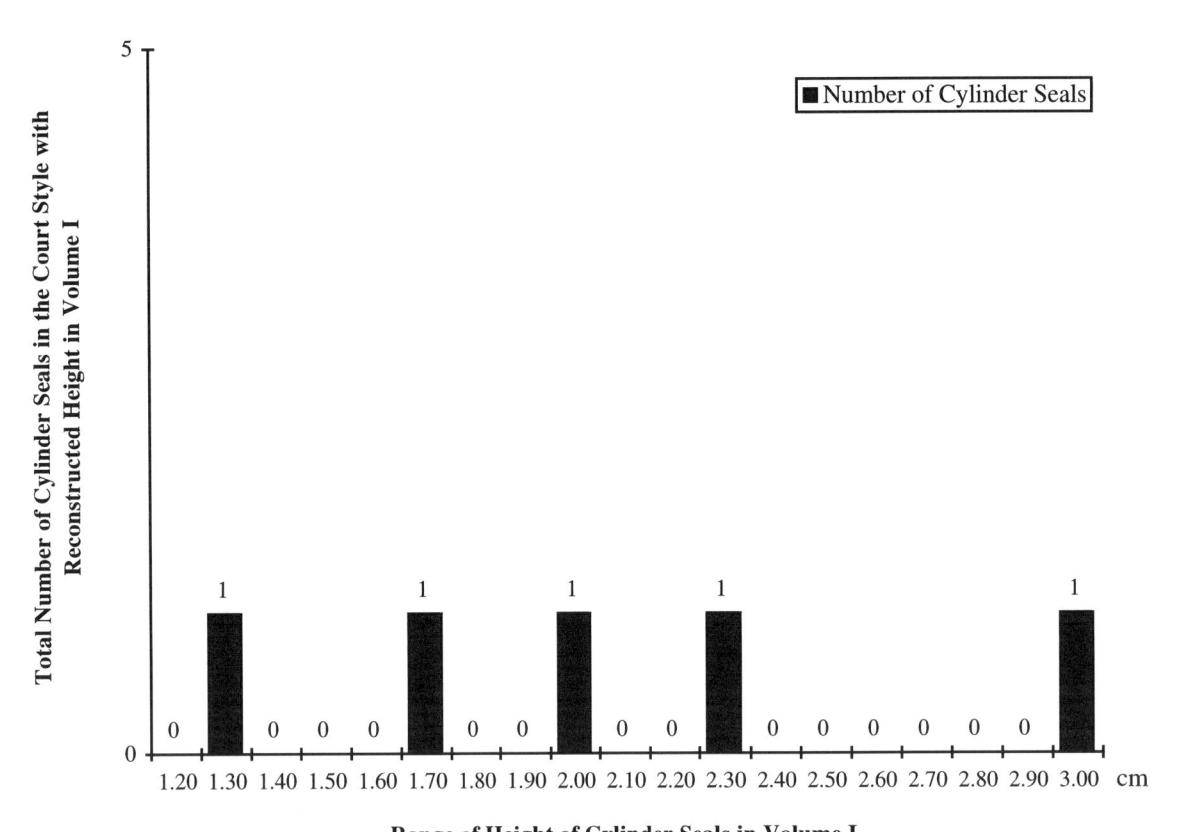

Chart 7. Height of Cylinder Seals: Court Style

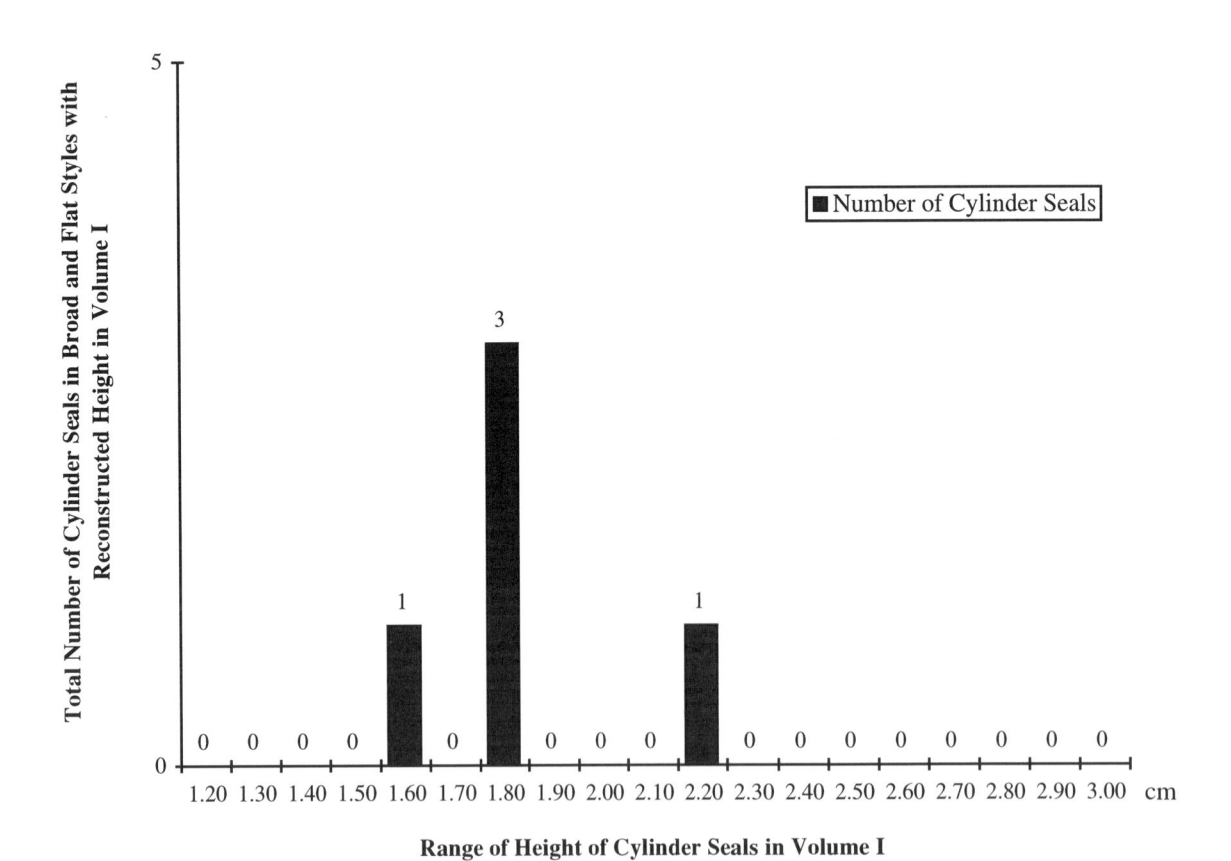

Chart 8. Height of Cylinder Seals: Broad and Flat Styles

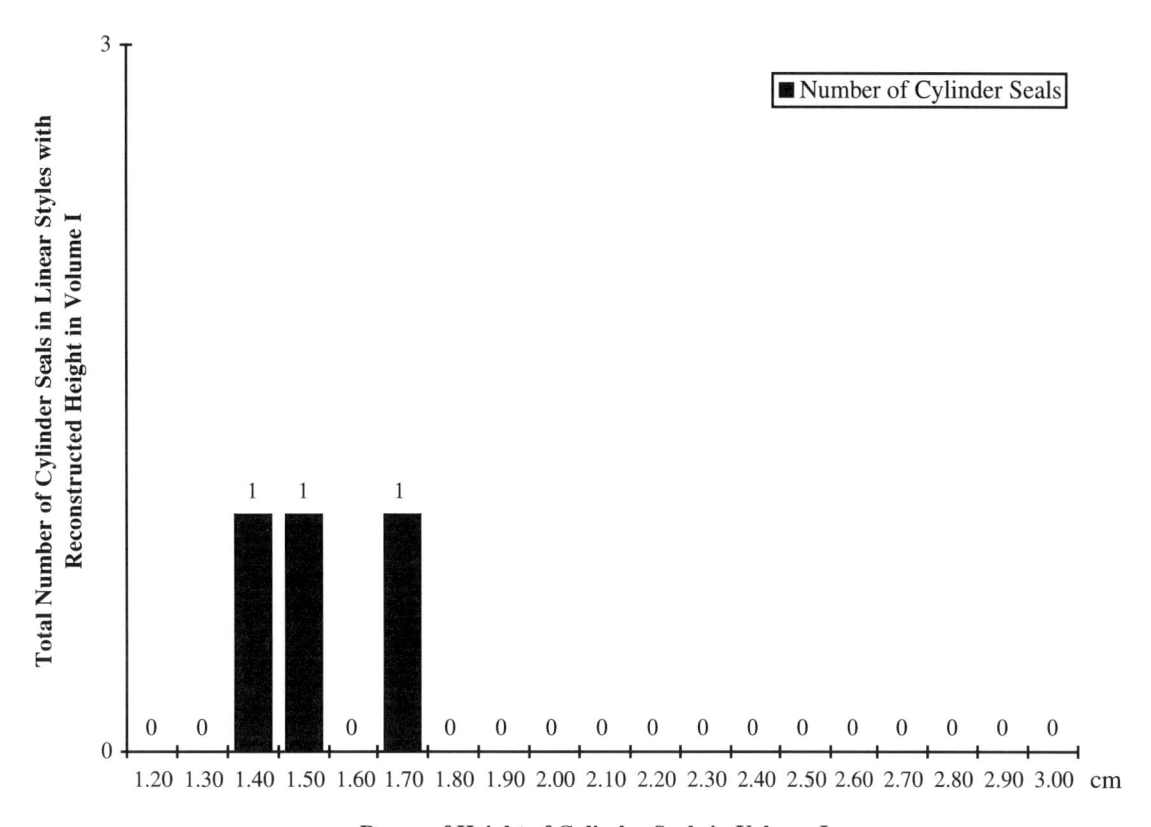

Chart 9. Height of Cylinder Seals: Linear Styles

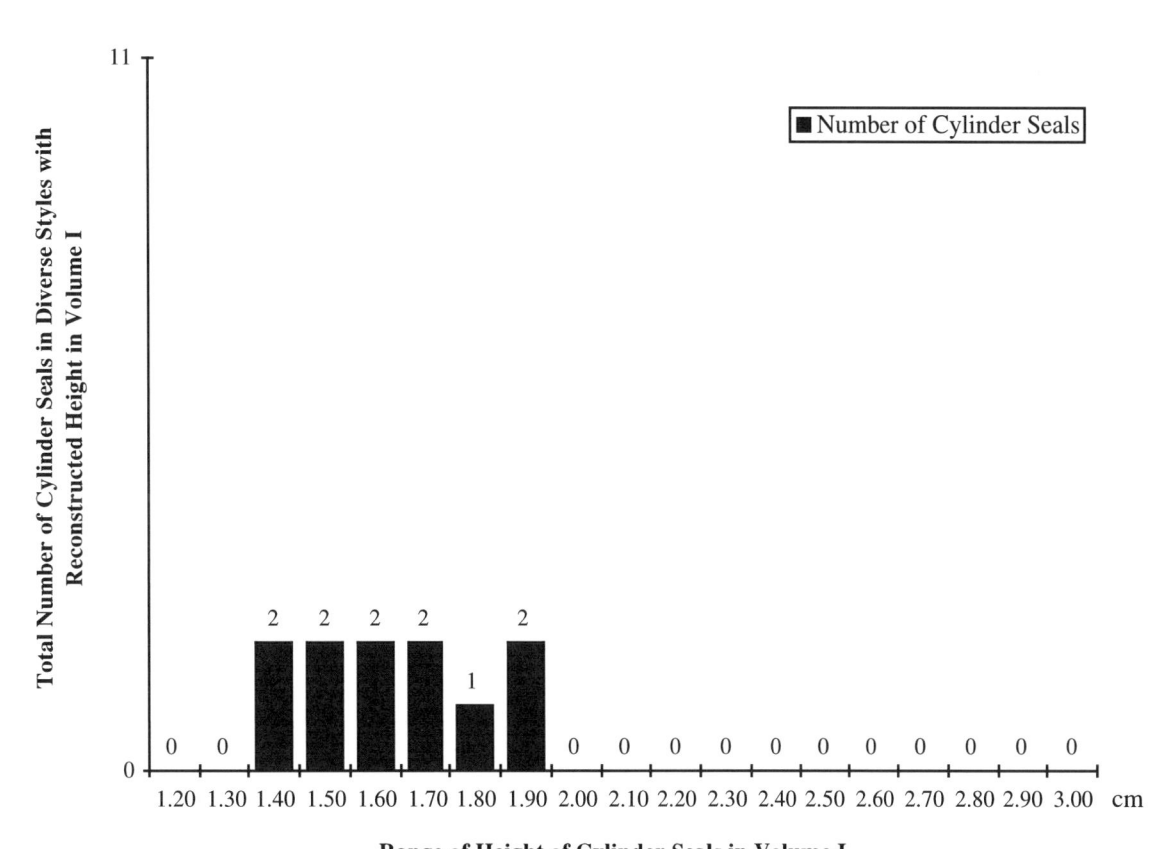

Chart 10. Height of Cylinder Seals: Diverse Styles

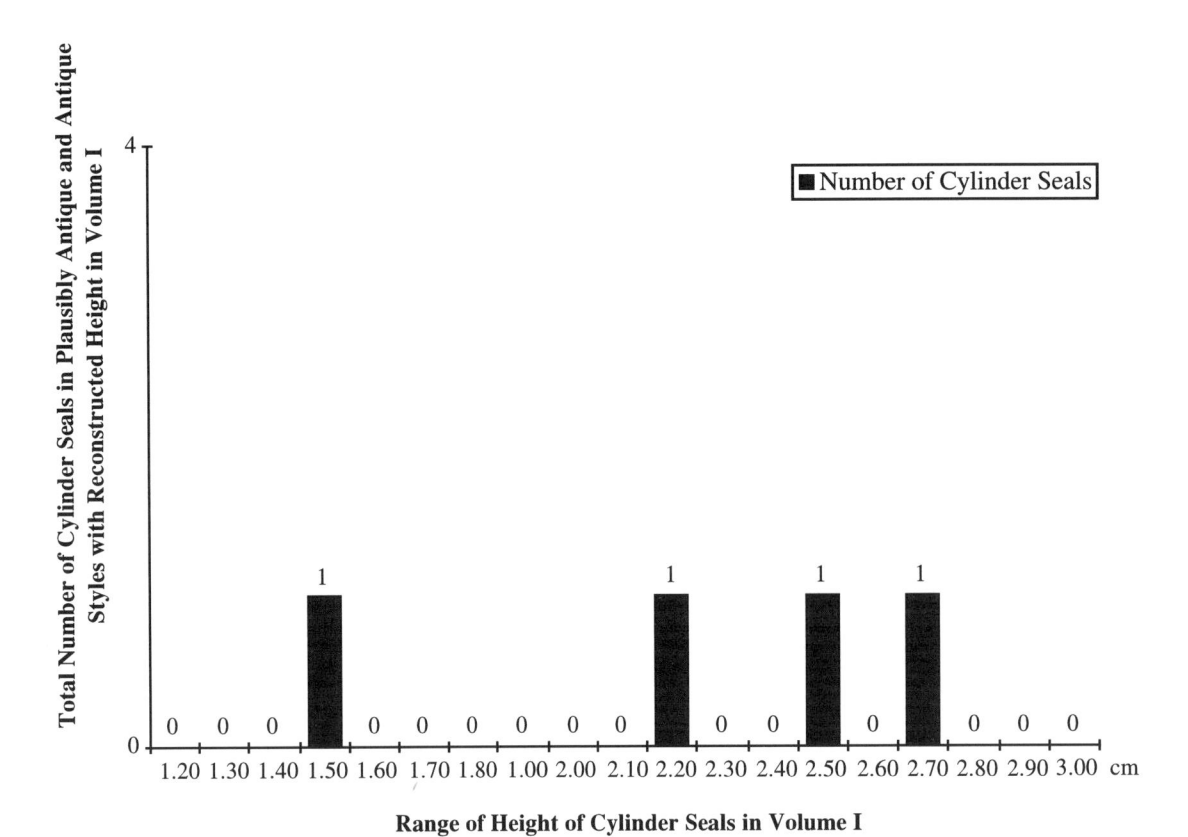

Chart 11. Height of Cylinder Seals: Plausibly Antique and Antique Styles

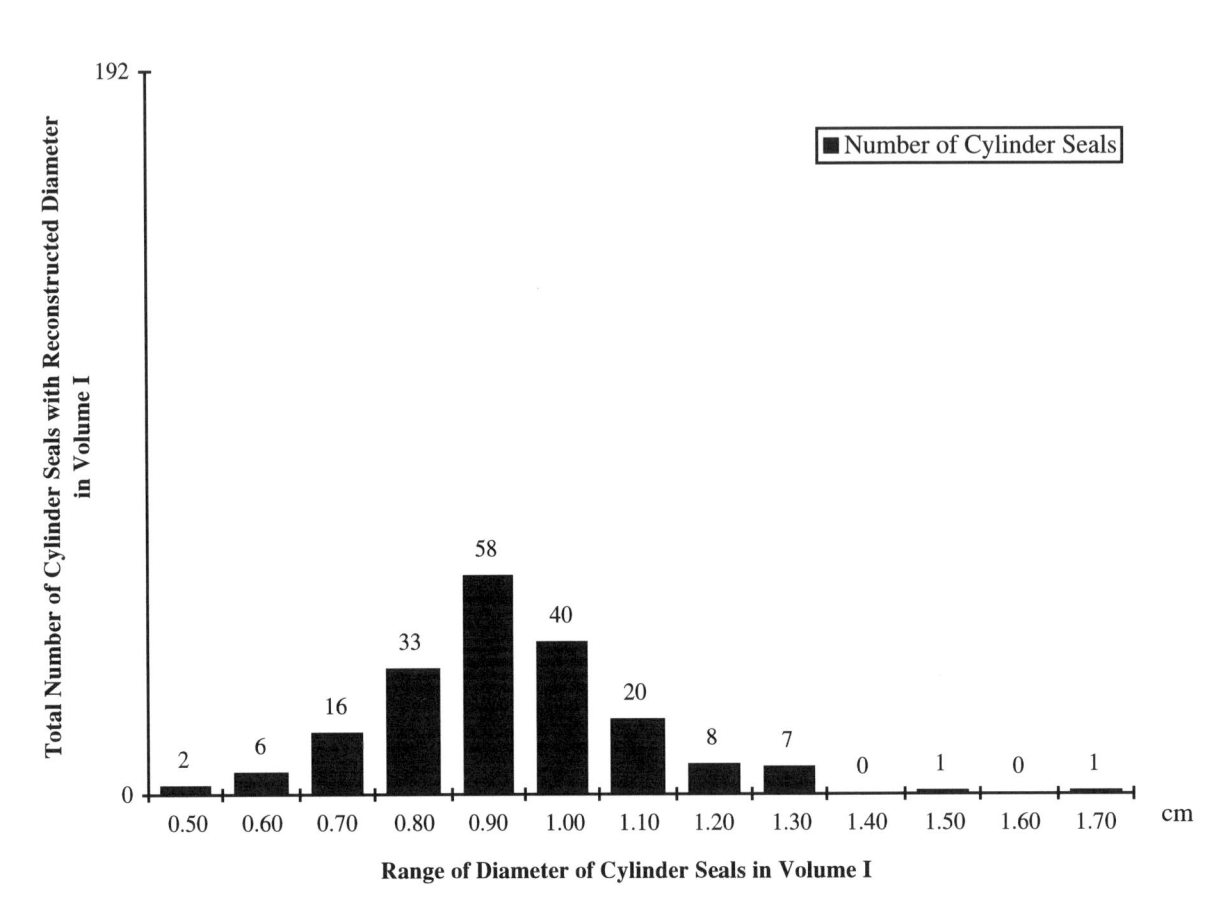

Chart 12. Diameter of Cylinder Seals in Volume I

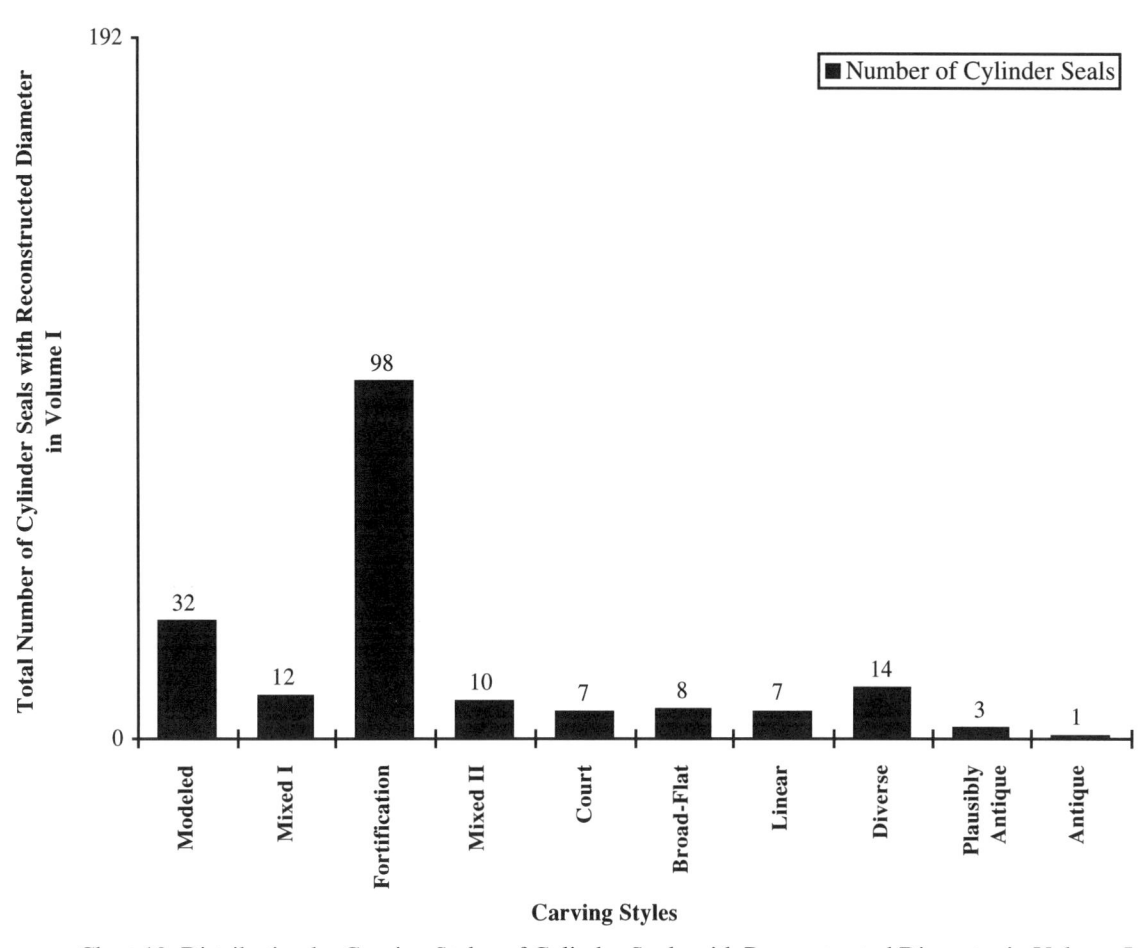

APPENDIX THREE: SUMMARY DATA ON SEAL DIMENSIONS FOR VOLUME I 479

Chart 13. Distribution by Carving Styles of Cylinder Seals with Reconstructed Diameter in Volume I

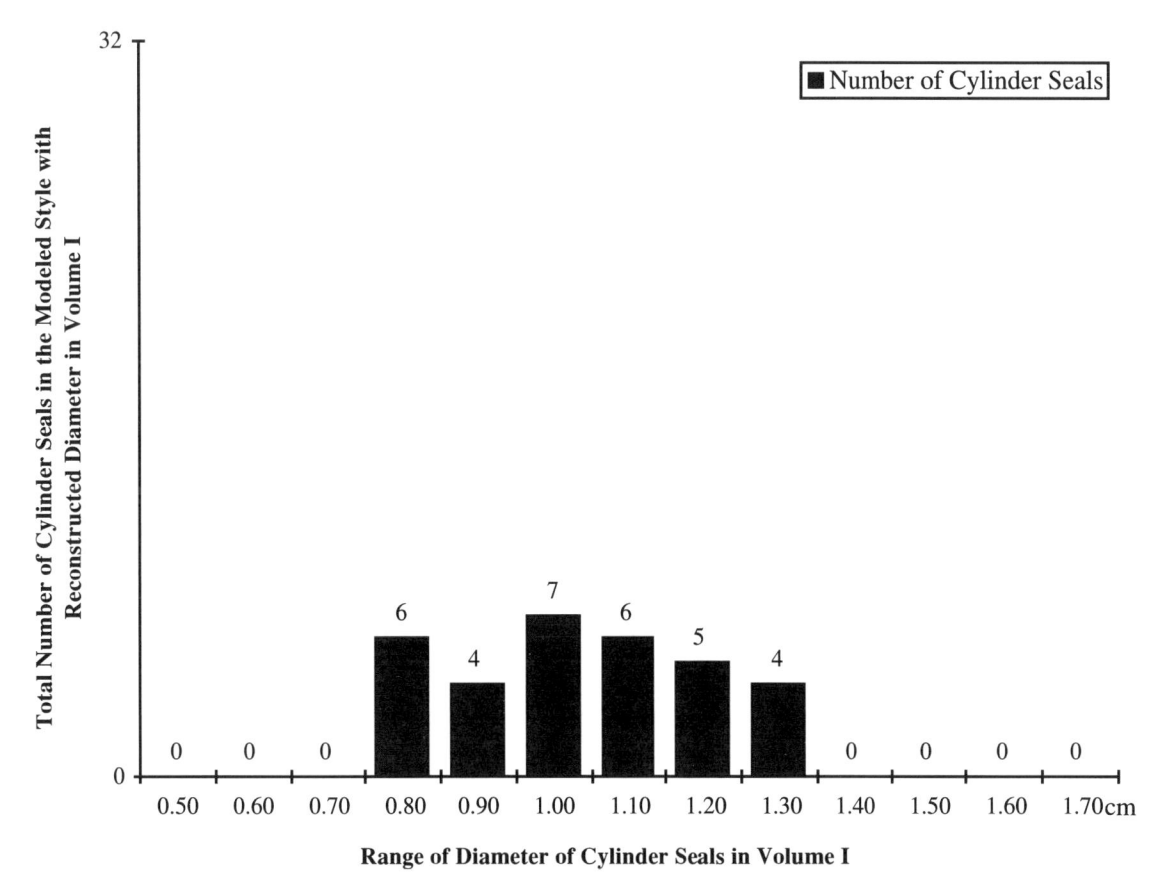

Chart 14. Diameter of Cylinder Seals: Modeled Style

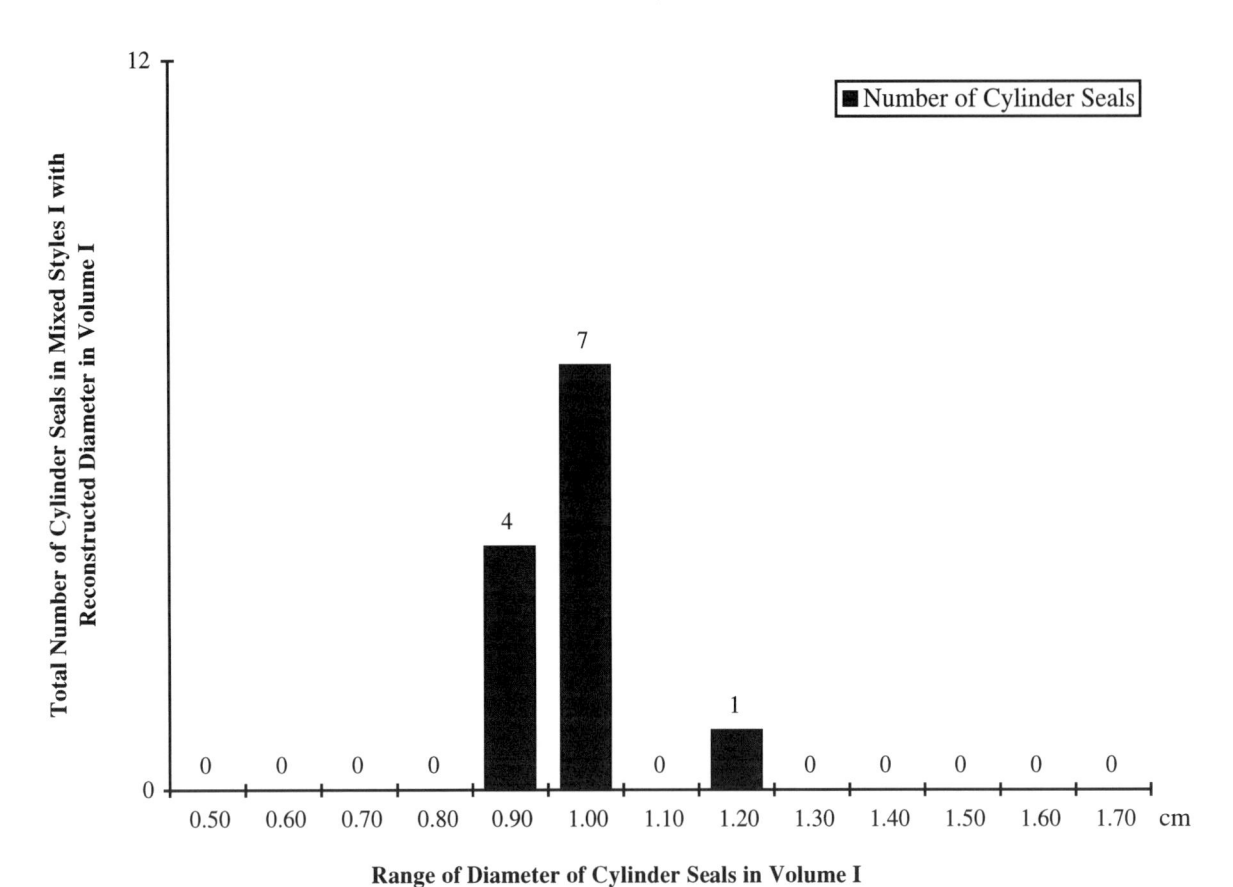

Chart 15. Diameter of Cylinder Seals: Mixed Styles I

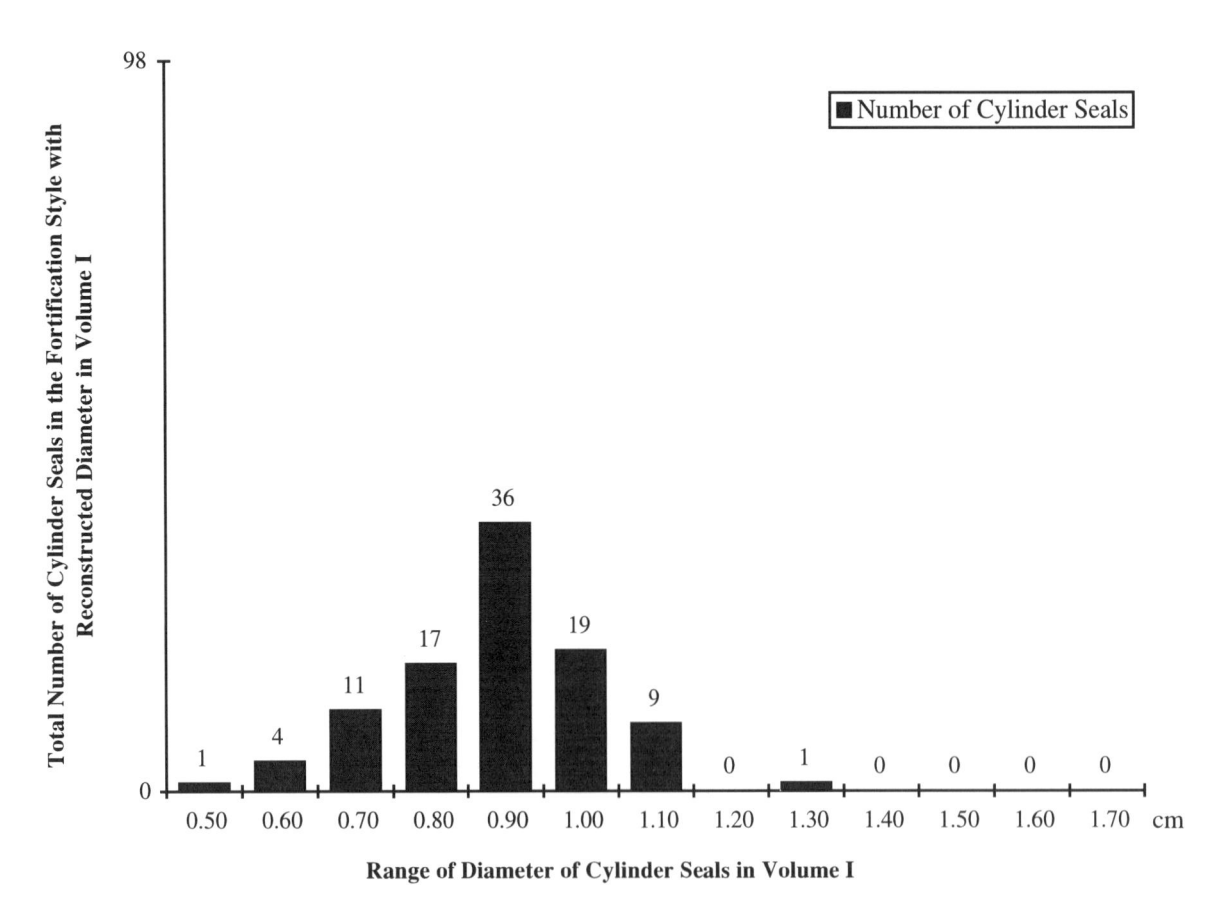

Chart 16. Diameter of Cylinder Seals: Fortification Style

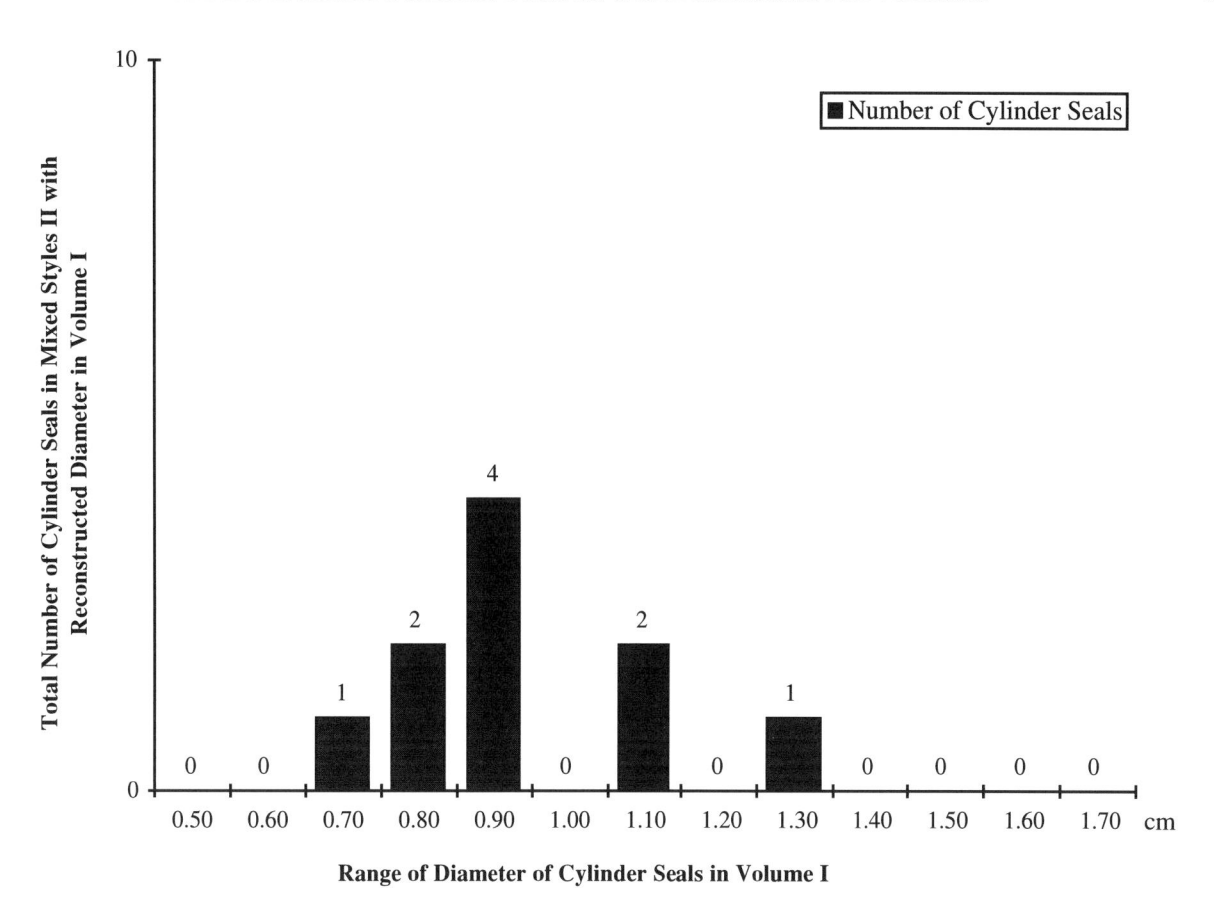

APPENDIX THREE: SUMMARY DATA ON SEAL DIMENSIONS FOR VOLUME I 481

Chart 17. Diameter of Cylinder Seals: Mixed Styles II

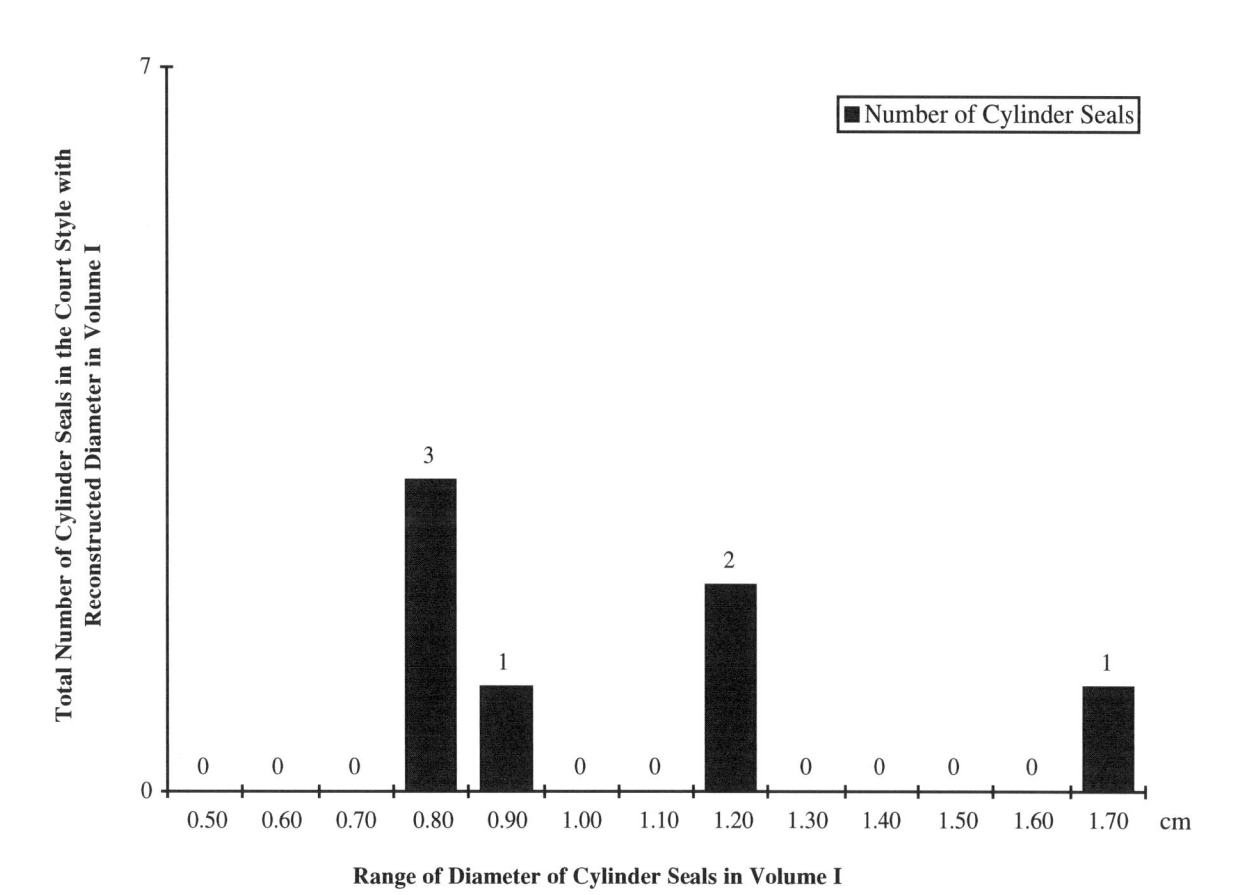

Chart 18. Diameter of Cylinder Seals: Court Style

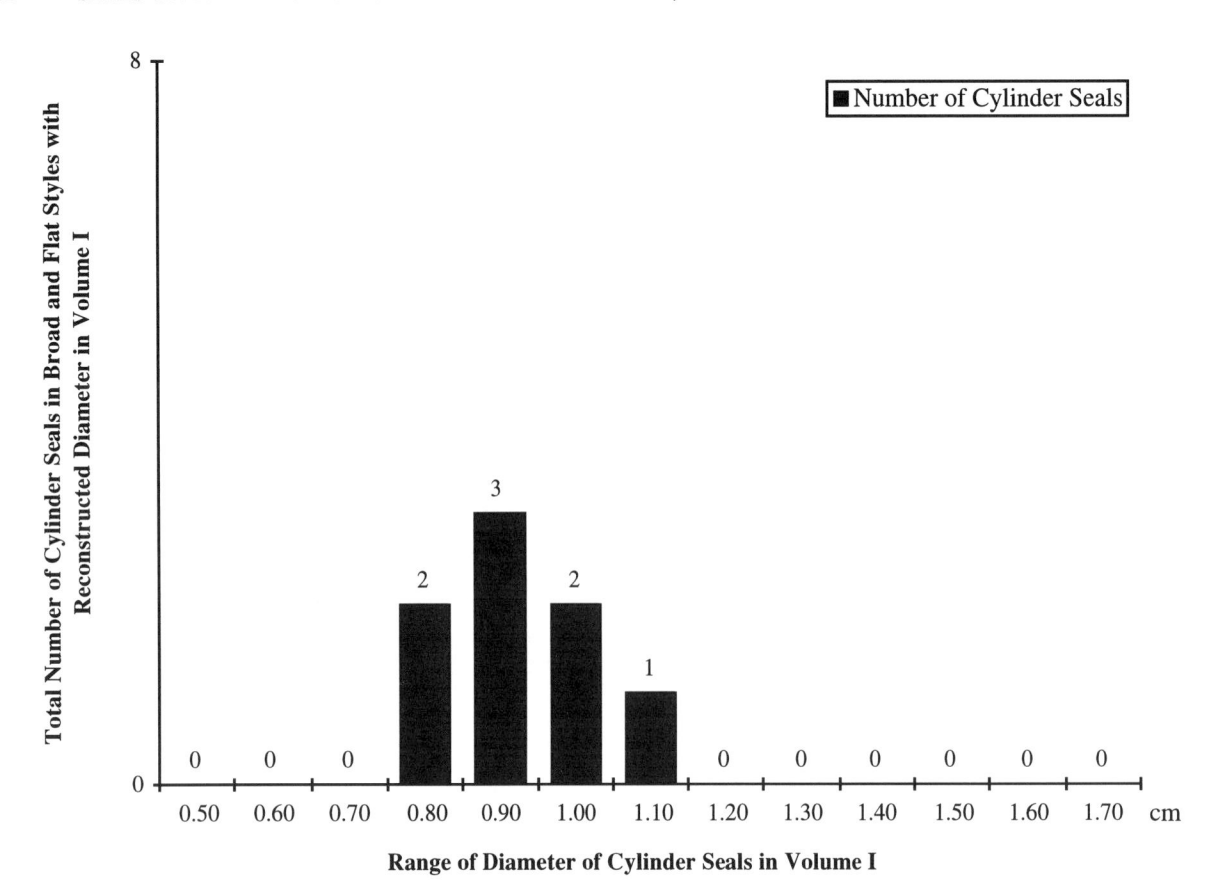

Chart 19. Diameter of Cylinder Seals: Broad and Flat Styles

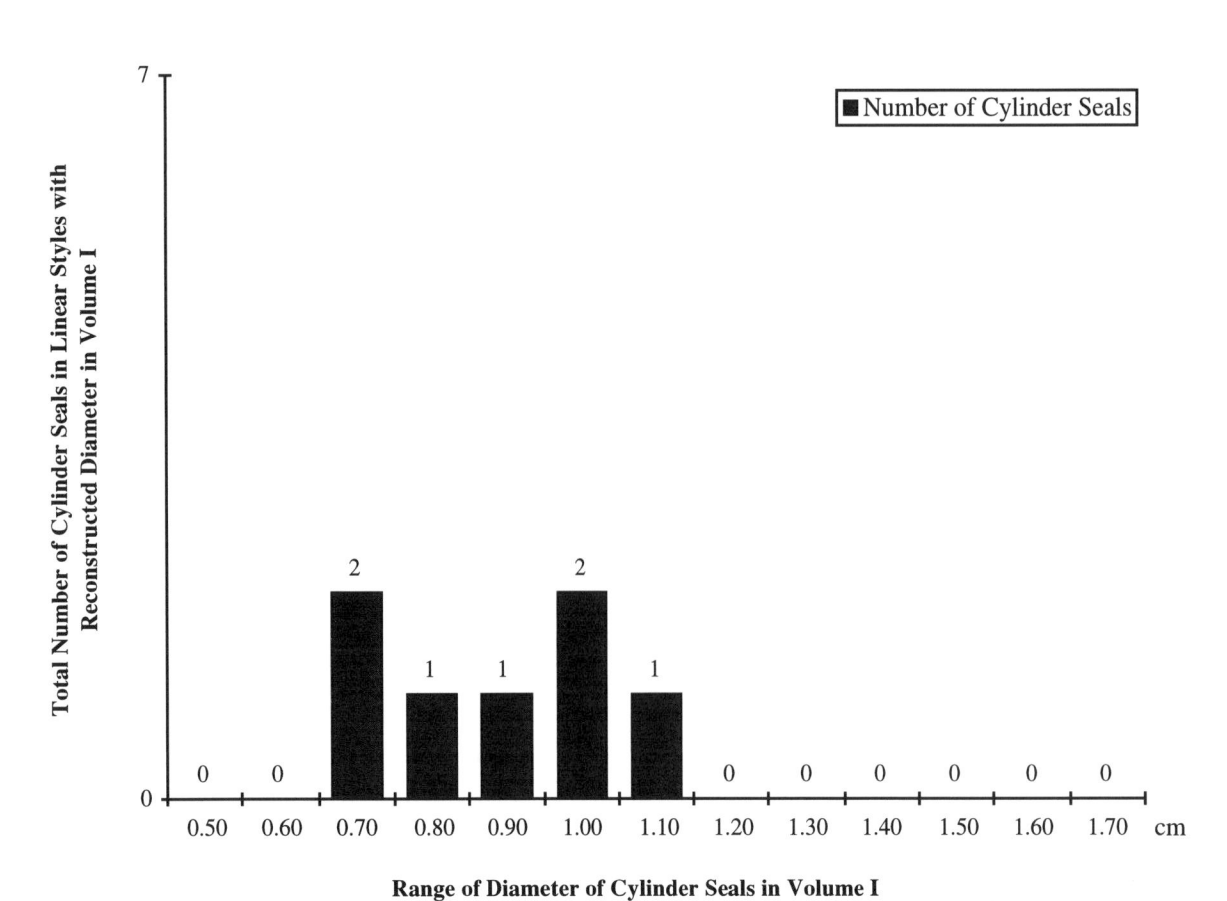

Chart 20. Diameter of Cylinder Seals: Linear Styles

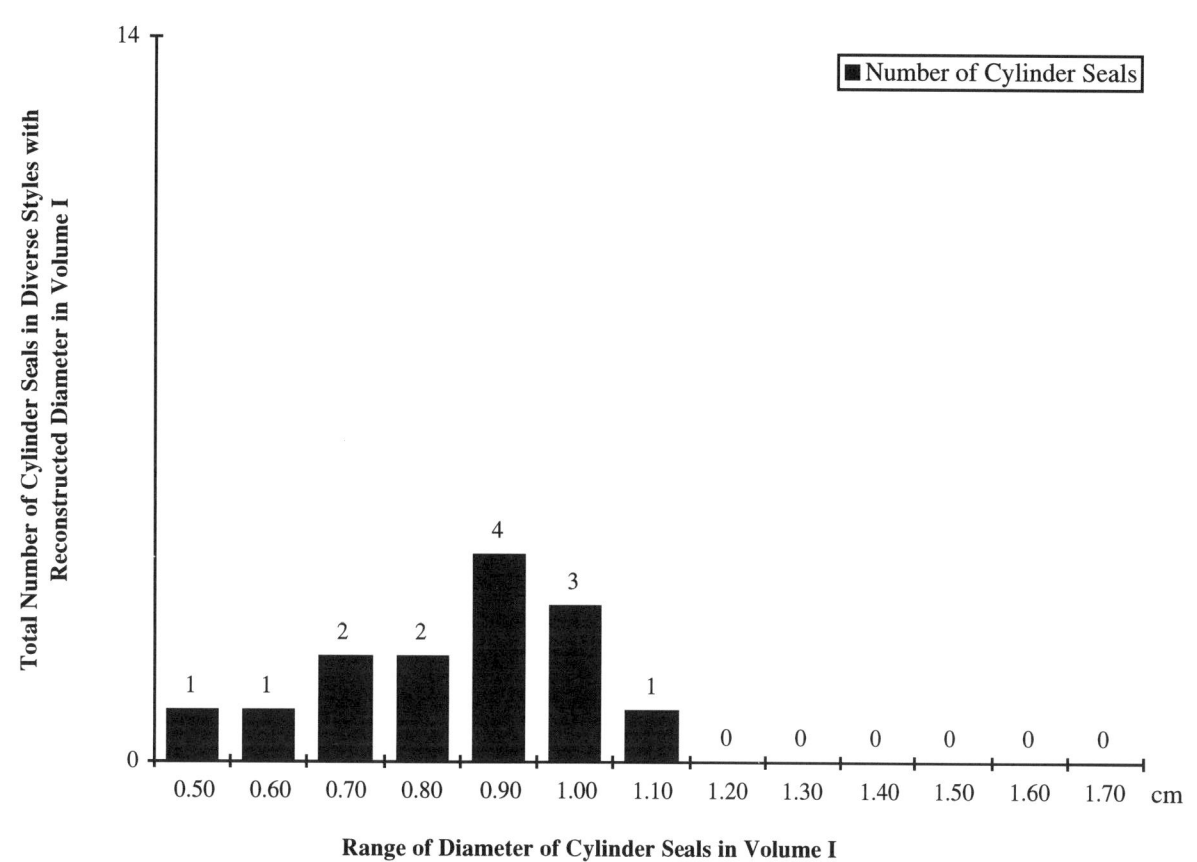

APPENDIX THREE: SUMMARY DATA ON SEAL DIMENSIONS FOR VOLUME I 483

Chart 21. Diameter of Cylinder Seals: Diverse Styles

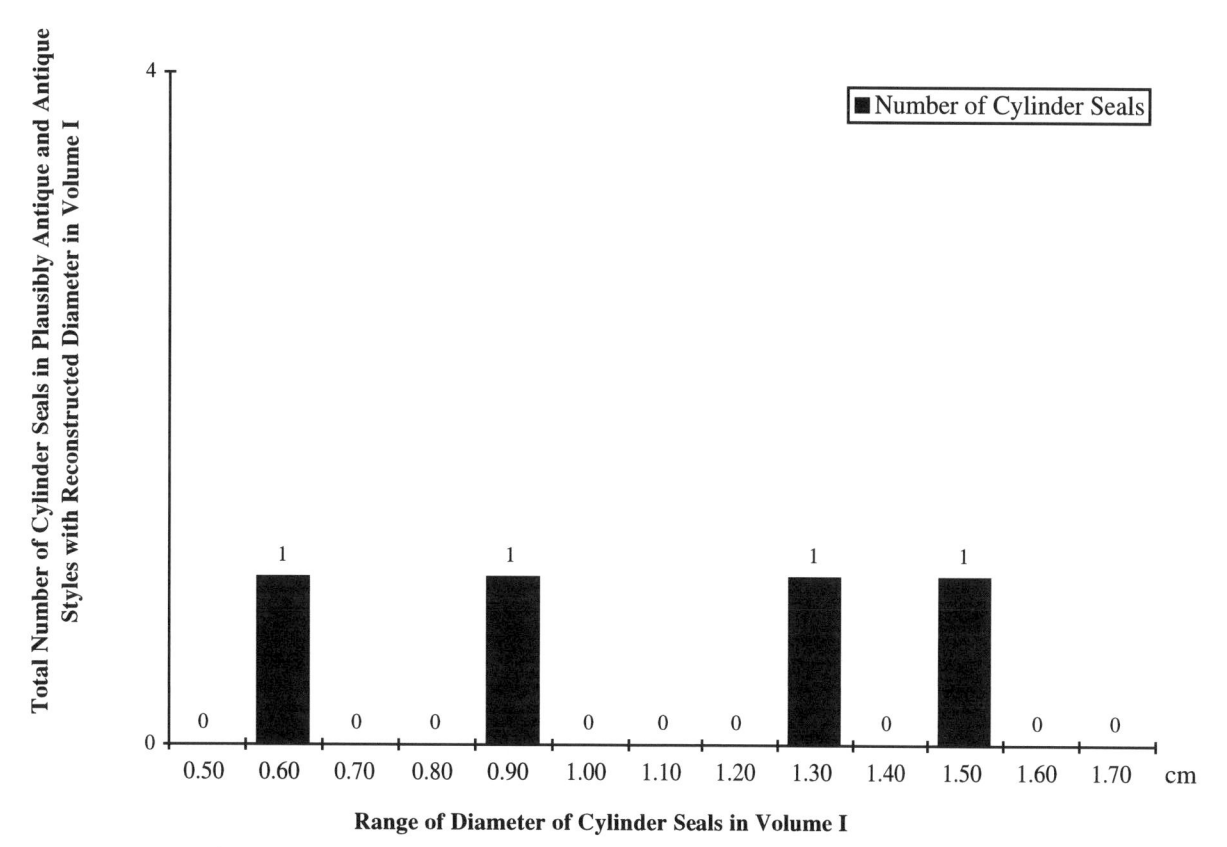

Chart 22. Diameter of Cylinder Seals: Plausibly Antique and Antique Styles

APPENDIX FOUR

STAMP SEALS IN VOLUME I GROUPED BY APPARENT CONTOUR OF SEAL FACE

It is rarely possible to be definitive in reconstructing the nature of the seal shape that produced an ancient stamp seal impression. On the PF tablets, where texts were added after the seals were applied (thus causing distortions on tablet surfaces), this is especially the case. We can only suggest probabilities in a general way, based on what is retrieved of the contour of the seal edge in a given impression or set of impressions. The difficulties are sometimes significant enough that confusions between identification of a partially rolled cylinder seal impression and a faintly impressed stamp seal impression have had to be sorted out (Garrison and Root 1996, pp. 18–19).

An examination of actual stamp seals in conjunction with the contours of their seal faces as revealed by their impressions even under optimal museum conditions shows how many variables may exist.[1]

Circular contours on seals used on the PF tablets are most likely to have been produced by conoids of varying back shape (fig. 9, no. 3a); less often they might have been made by disks (fig. 9, no. 5a), the stamp faces of stamp-cylinders (fig. 9, no. 8), or the occasional scaraboid with a roughly circular rather than a loaf-shaped or oval face (fig. 9, no. 4c). Volume I does not include impressions representing any stamp seal that particularly suggests identification as a stamp-cylinder.[2] There are, however, possibilities of the stamp-cylinder in Volume III. The stamp-cylinder was a type in great currency in administrative echelons of Urartu prior to the founding of the Achaemenid Empire, and thus the seal type might have had a greater impact in Achaemenid contexts than we are generally aware based on the largely unprovenanced collections of Achaemenid seal artifacts generally considered as representing the repertoire.[3]

Oval-shaped contours are most likely to have been produced by conoids (fig. 9, no. 3b), disks (fig. 9, no. 5b), or scaraboids (fig. 9, no. 4a). Often the scaraboid yields a loaf-shaped contour. Theriomorphic stamp seals can yield quite a range of contours in impression, some of which can come very close to a true oval, while most are truncated or egg-shaped and some yield elongated rectangular impressions or drop-shaped impressions (fig. 9, no. 9). Although Volume I does not include any seals the impressions of which suggest theriomorphic seal matrices, the type had some currency in Assyro-Babylonian contexts; and one such seal was excavated at Persepolis (see *Introduction*). There are some stamp seals in Volume III once again that might have been made by theriomorphic stamps.

Square or rectangular contours of stamp seals retrieved on the PF tablets are likely to have been produced by pyramidal stamps of variously-shaped backs (fig. 9, no. 2) or by tabloids and cuboids (sometimes called "plaques" [fig. 9, nos. 6–7]). Other rectangular shapes may be produced by particular theriomorphic stamps and by images carved on side faces of tabloids or cuboids. An image carved on the side face of a pyramidal stamp seal may also appear rectangular in contour via its impression. Generally, the square and rectangular contours produced by cuboids and tabloids are more crisply defined at the corners than are those produced by pyramidal stamps with square or rectangular faces, which tend to yield rounded corners.

The octagonal face of the pyramidal stamp seal with faceted side faces (fig. 9, no. 1) is usually distinctive in impressions in the PFS corpus, but even in the controlled setting of the museum, impressions of this type of seal sometimes mute the octagonal contour of the face of the actual matrix.

No pointed oval contour (signifying use of a pointed elliptical ring bezel as a stamping device) has been identified across the entire PFS corpus.

It is possible that an image engraved on the side face of a stamp seal has been impressed on tablets in the PFS corpus and not recognized as such. An image on the broad and somewhat rounded side face of a conoid or pyramidal stamp could easily yield an impression that looks like a fragment of a cylinder seal (i.e., with no perceptible edges), especially if pressed only gently into the clay tablet.

The following list of Volume I stamp seals annotates the seals by suggested stamp seal type, which is keyed to figure 9 (below). The schematic drawings in figure 9 illustrate actual examples of such seals at approximately 1:1.

---

1. See, for example, the ranges displayed in Buchanan and Moorey 1984; Jakob-Rost 1997, pp. 64–107.
2. A very small diameter in the ca. 0.80–1.00 cm range would be one potential diagnostic (see *Appendix Three, Chart 12, Diameter of Cylinder Seals in Volume I*). Others may include, for example, some specific usage pattern whereby a certain stamp seal was consistently used on the same tablet along with a certain cylinder seal — both having the identical diameter.
3. See, for example, Collon 1987, pp. 84–87, for stamp-cylinders from excavations of the first-millennium Urartian site of Bastam.

OCTAGONAL FACE

PFS 1260s (Cat.No. 184), fig. 9, no. 1
PFS 1309s (Cat.No. 229), fig. 9, no. 1
PFS 1321s (Cat.No. 176), fig. 9, no. 1
PFS 1463s (Cat.No. 231), fig. 9, no. 1

RECTANGULAR OR SQUARE FACE

PFS 39s (Cat.No. 221), fig. 9, no. 2a
PFS 1315s (Cat.No. 253), fig. 9, nos. 2b or 7a
PFS 1375s (Cat.No. 254), fig. 9, nos. 2b or 7a

CIRCULAR FACE

PFS 139s (Cat.No. 222), fig. 9, nos. 3a, 4c, or 5a
PFS 298s (Cat.No. 236), fig. 9, nos. 3a, 4c, or 5a
PFS 919s (Cat.No. 259), fig. 9, nos. 3a, 4c, or 5a
PFS 959s (Cat.No. 246), fig. 9, nos. 3a, 4c, or 5a
PFS 1217s (Cat.No. 168), fig. 9, nos. 3a, 4c, or 5a
PFS 1428s (Cat.No. 230), fig. 9, nos. 3a, 4c, or 5a
PFS 1437s (Cat.No. 128), fig. 9, nos. 3a, 4c, or 5a
PFS 1624s (Cat.No. 261), fig. 9, nos. 3a, 4c, or 5a

OVAL OR LOAF-SHAPED FACE

PFS 1264s (Cat.No. 206), fig. 9, nos. 3b or 5b
PFS 1311s (Cat.No. 247), fig. 9, nos. 3b or 5b
PFS 1367s (Cat.No. 211), fig. 9, nos. 3b or 4

TOTAL: 18 STAMP SEALS

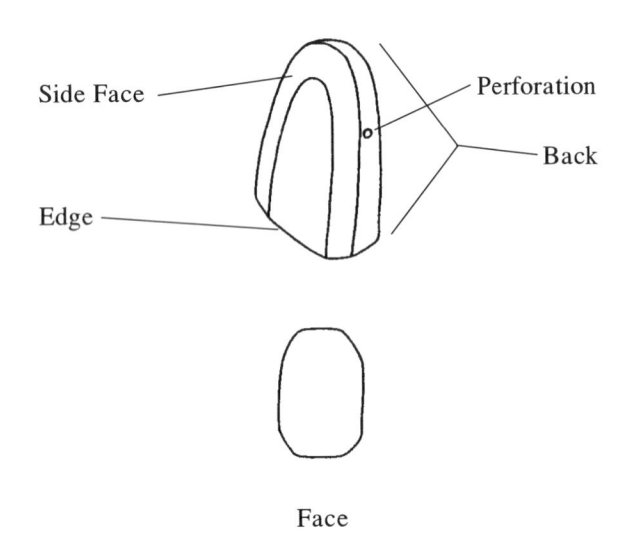

1. Pyramidal Stamp with Octagonal Face

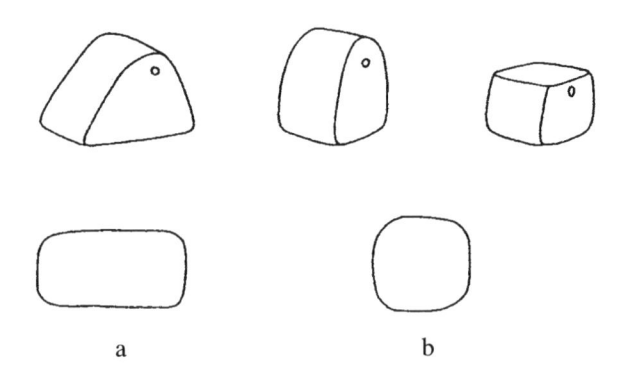

2. Pyramidal Stamps with (*a*) Rectangular or (*b*) Square Face

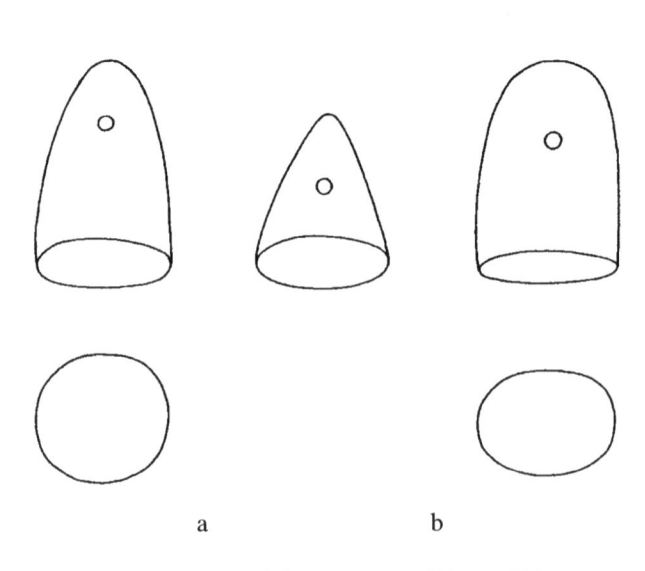

3. Conoids with (*a*) Circular or (*b*) Oval Face

Figure 9. Stamp Seal Terminology and Schematic Drawings of Main Stamp Seal Types Relevant to the PFS Corpus

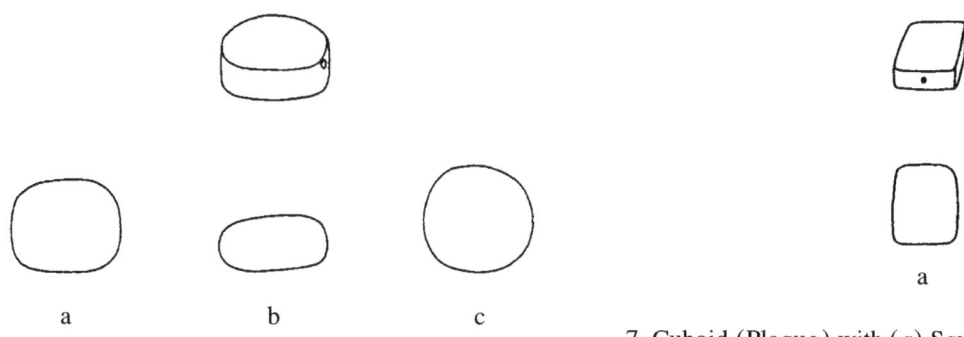

APPENDIX FOUR: STAMP SEALS IN VOLUME I GROUPED BY APPARENT CONTOUR OF SEAL FACE 487

4. Scaraboid with (*a*) Oval to Rounded-Square, (*b*) Loaf-shaped, or (*c*) Circular Face

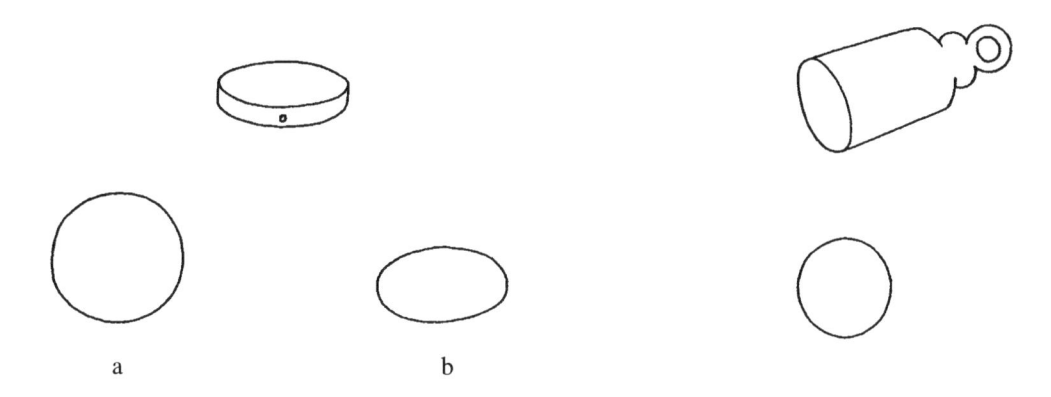

7. Cuboid (Plaque) with (*a*) Square Faces and (*b*) Rectangular Side Faces (not shown)

5. Disk with (*a*) Circular or (*b*) Oval Face

8. Stamp-cylinder with Circular Stamp Face

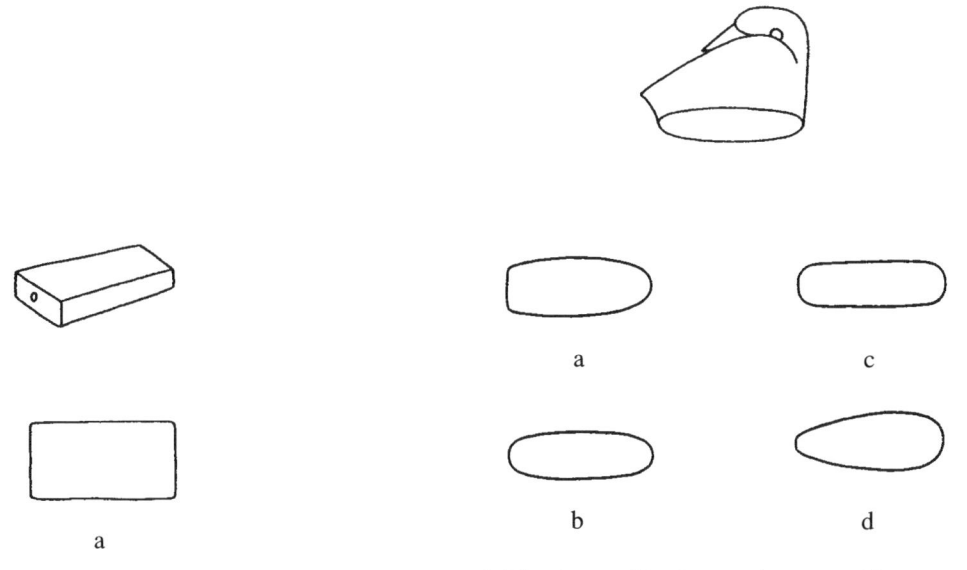

6. Tabloid with (*a*) Rectangular Faces and (*b*) Rectangular Side Faces (not shown)

9. Theriomorphic Stamps (e.g., Duck) with Variously Shaped Faces: (*a*) Truncated Oval, (*b*) Oval, (*c*) Rounded Rectangle, and (*d*) Tear-drop Shape

Figure 9 (*cont.*). Stamp Seal Terminology and Schematic Drawings of Main Stamp Seal Types Relevant to the PFS Corpus

APPENDIX FIVE

INSCRIBED SEALS IN VOLUME I BY LANGUAGE OR SCRIPT

ARAMAIC

PFS 9* (Cat.No. 288)
PFS 16* (Cat.No. 22)
PFS 54* (Cat.No. 277)
PFS 123* (Cat.No. 75)
PFS 164* (Cat.No. 20)
PFS 266* (Cat.No. 208)
PFS 815* (Cat.No. 215)
PFS 981* (Cat.No. 87)

BABYLONIAN

PFS 1632* (Cat.No. 244)

BABYLONIAN(?)

PFS 883* (Cat.No. 97)

ELAMITE

PFS 1* (Cat.No. 182)
PFS 4* (Cat.No. 292)
PFS 32* (Cat.No. 180)
PFS 36* (Cat.No. 5)
PFS 43* (Cat.No. 207)
PFS 57* (Cat.No. 239)
PFS 98* (Cat.No. 217)
PFS 103* (Cat.No. 84)
PFS 272* (Cat.No. 272)
PFS 584* (Cat.No. 203)
PFS 769* (Cat.No. 278)
PFS 1566* (Cat.No. 218)
PFS 1637* (Cat.No. 273)

ELAMITE(?)

PFS 199* (Cat.No. 305)
PFS 931* (Cat.No. 270)
PFS 1025* (Cat.No. 266)

TRILINGUAL (OLD PERSIAN, ELAMITE, AND BABYLONIAN)

PFS 7* (Cat.No. 4)
PFS 113* = PTS 4* (Cat.No. 19)

CUNEIFORM SCRIPT: LANGUAGE UNCERTAIN

PFS 64* (Cat.No. 173)
PFS 523* (Cat.No. 209)
PFS 526* (Cat.No. 216)
PFS 859* (Cat.No. 205)
PFS 1227* (Cat.No. 219)

CUNEIFORM-LIKE SCRIPT: LANGUAGE UNKNOWN

PFS 671* (Cat.No. 174)
PFS 677* (Cat.No. 181)

GREEK SCRIPT: LANGUAGE UNKNOWN

PFS 284* (Cat.No. 111)

APPENDIX SIX

DISTRIBUTION OF SEALS IN VOLUME I BY STYLISTIC CATEGORIES

Global observations on patterns of the distribution of the carving styles are presented in Volume III. A few interesting trends are noted here preliminarily and only with reference to the seals in Volume I. By far the preferred styles for cylinder seals (chart 24) are the Modeled Style (17% of all cylinder seals in Volume I) and the Fortification Style (51% of all cylinder seals in Volume I). The distribution of carving styles in stamp seals (chart 25) exhibits a few differences from the distribution of carving styles in cylinder seals. The Fortification Style is also the preferred style in stamp seals (44% of the total number of stamp seals in Volume I), but the percentage of stamp seals carved in Broad and Flat Styles is large (28% of the total number of stamp seals in Volume I; only 5% of the total number of cylinder seals in Volume I is carved in Broad and Flat Styles). This distribution may suggest that artists working in Broad and Flat Styles specialized in stamp seal production. The lack of any stamp seals, or only a very low percentage of them, in the Modeled Style, Mixed Styles I, Mixed Styles II, Court Style, and Linear Styles reinforces the impression that stamp seal carvers might have been found only in selected workshops.

Distribution of all 312 seals in Volume I by stylistic categories is presented in chart 23. Chart 24 presents distribution of the 294 cylinder seals, and chart 25 presents distribution of the eighteen stamp seals in Volume I by stylistic category.

MODELED STYLE

- PFS 1* (Cat.No. 182)
- PFS 4* (Cat.No. 292)
- PFS 16* (Cat.No. 22)
- PFS 29 (Cat.No. 302)
- PFS 30 (Cat.No. 291)
- PFS 32* (Cat.No. 180)
- PFS 38 (Cat.No. 16)
- PFS 54* (Cat.No. 277)
- PFS 57* (Cat.No. 239)
- PFS 65 (Cat.No. 241)
- PFS 72 (Cat.No. 147)
- PFS 98* (Cat.No. 217)
- PFS 99 (Cat.No. 113)
- PFS 152 (Cat.No. 295)
- PFS 199* (Cat.No. 305)
- PFS 263 (Cat.No. 289)
- PFS 265 (Cat.No. 240)
- PFS 272* (Cat.No. 272)
- PFS 429 (Cat.No. 7)
- PFS 480 (Cat.No. 134)
- PFS 503 (Cat.No. 307)
- PFS 516 (Cat.No. 98)
- PFS 536 (Cat.No. 102)
- PFS 538 (Cat.No. 312)
- PFS 552 (Cat.No. 118)
- PFS 673 (Cat.No. 64)

MODELED STYLE (*cont.*)

- PFS 677* (Cat.No. 181)
- PFS 684 (Cat.No. 183)
- PFS 769* (Cat.No. 278)
- PFS 782 (Cat.No. 105)
- PFS 807 (Cat.No. 269)
- PFS 815* (Cat.No. 215)
- PFS 818 (Cat.No. 265)
- PFS 931* (Cat.No. 270)
- PFS 944 (Cat.No. 129)
- PFS 964 (Cat.No. 260)
- PFS 1026 (Cat.No. 156)
- PFS 1204 (Cat.No. 136)
- PFS 1227* (Cat.No. 219)
- PFS 1286 (Cat.No. 258)
- PFS 1311s (Cat.No. 247)
- PFS 1387 (Cat.No. 72)
- PFS 1388 (Cat.No. 162)
- PFS 1485 (Cat.No. 112)
- PFS 1550 (Cat.No. 14)
- PFS 1566* (Cat.No. 218)
- PFS 1586 (Cat.No. 121)
- PFS 1630 (Cat.No. 165)
- PFS 1632* (Cat.No. 244)
- PFS 1637* (Cat.No. 273)
- PFS 1641 (Cat.No. 18)

51 TOTAL

MIXED STYLES I

PFS 58 (Cat.No. 242)
PFS 123* (Cat.No. 75)
PFS 312 (Cat.No. 237)
PFS 329 (Cat.No. 28)
PFS 714 (Cat.No. 152)
PFS 783 (Cat.No. 153)
PFS 841 (Cat.No. 13)
PFS 971 (Cat.No. 171)
PFS 1101 (Cat.No. 297)
PFS 1153 (Cat.No. 199)
PFS 1238 (Cat.No. 160)
PFS 1325 (Cat.No. 41)
PFS 1374 (Cat.No. 31)
PFS 1391 (Cat.No. 248)
PFS 1582 (Cat.No. 232)
PFS 1612 (Cat.No. 268)

16 TOTAL

FORTIFICATION STYLE

PFS 9* (Cat.No. 288)
PFS 10 (Cat.No. 251)
PFS 17 (Cat.No. 235)
PFS 18 (Cat.No. 15)
PFS 24 (Cat.No. 298)
PFS 26 (Cat.No. 299)
PFS 31 (Cat.No. 172)
PFS 33 (Cat.No. 220)
PFS 34 (Cat.No. 73)
PFS 36* (Cat.No. 5)
PFS 49 (Cat.No. 23)
PFS 52 (Cat.No. 114)
PFS 63 (Cat.No. 24)
PFS 64* (Cat.No. 173)
PFS 67 (Cat.No. 293)
PFS 79 (Cat.No. 83)
PFS 86 (Cat.No. 48)
PFS 95 (Cat.No. 25)
PFS 100 (Cat.No. 274)
PFS 102 (Cat.No. 1)
PFS 103* (Cat.No. 84)
PFS 109 (Cat.No. 197)
PFS 112 (Cat.No. 282)
PFS 114 (Cat.No. 284)
PFS 120 (Cat.No. 49)
PFS 130 (Cat.No. 300)
PFS 131 (Cat.No. 170)
PFS 132 (Cat.No. 69)
PFS 138 (Cat.No. 186)
PFS 145 (Cat.No. 115)

FORTIFICATION STYLE (cont.)

PFS 146 (Cat.No. 275)
PFS 148 (Cat.No. 311)
PFS 149 (Cat.No. 212)
PFS 151 (Cat.No. 223)
PFS 158 (Cat.No. 94)
PFS 162 (Cat.No. 249)
PFS 167 (Cat.No. 255)
PFS 168 (Cat.No. 74)
PFS 197 (Cat.No. 116)
PFS 201 (Cat.No. 50)
PFS 217 (Cat.No. 135)
PFS 225 (Cat.No. 46)
PFS 228 (Cat.No. 148)
PFS 231 (Cat.No. 51)
PFS 232 (Cat.No. 26)
PFS 233 (Cat.No. 52)
PFS 236 (Cat.No. 213)
PFS 241 (Cat.No. 252)
PFS 246 (Cat.No. 290)
PFS 249 (Cat.No. 27)
PFS 255 (Cat.No. 233)
PFS 260 (Cat.No. 225)
PFS 280 (Cat.No. 309)
PFS 297 (Cat.No. 124)
PFS 298s (Cat.No. 236)
PFS 301 (Cat.No. 54)
PFS 334 (Cat.No. 133)
PFS 338 (Cat.No. 262)
PFS 341 (Cat.No. 109)
PFS 344 (Cat.No. 263)
PFS 362 (Cat.No. 76)
PFS 364 (Cat.No. 149)
PFS 370 (Cat.No. 99)
PFS 373 (Cat.No. 306)
PFS 380 (Cat.No. 95)
PFS 381 (Cat.No. 179)
PFS 385 (Cat.No. 38)
PFS 392 (Cat.No. 91)
PFS 396 (Cat.No. 178)
PFS 399 (Cat.No. 78)
PFS 414 (Cat.No. 280)
PFS 426 (Cat.No. 55)
PFS 430 (Cat.No. 56)
PFS 439 (Cat.No. 150)
PFS 447 (Cat.No. 301)
PFS 454 (Cat.No. 92)
PFS 461 (Cat.No. 90)
PFS 494 (Cat.No. 130)
PFS 501 (Cat.No. 141)

FORTIFICATION STYLE (*cont.*)
    PFS 514 (Cat.No. 192)
    PFS 526* (Cat.No. 216)
    PFS 555 (Cat.No. 93)
    PFS 614 (Cat.No. 287)
    PFS 632 (Cat.No. 143)
    PFS 669 (Cat.No. 142)
    PFS 671* (Cat.No. 174)
    PFS 687 (Cat.No. 119)
    PFS 709 (Cat.No. 271)
    PFS 720 (Cat.No. 57)
    PFS 731 (Cat.No. 131)
    PFS 749 (Cat.No. 110)
    PFS 757 (Cat.No. 296)
    PFS 778 (Cat.No. 11)
    PFS 781 (Cat.No. 107)
    PFS 787 (Cat.No. 79)
    PFS 795 (Cat.No. 214)
    PFS 844 (Cat.No. 59)
    PFS 882 (Cat.No. 65)
    PFS 885 (Cat.No. 187)
    PFS 902 (Cat.No. 243)
    PFS 912 (Cat.No. 138)
    PFS 939 (Cat.No. 267)
    PFS 952 (Cat.No. 227)
    PFS 959s (Cat.No. 246)
    PFS 990 (Cat.No. 256)
    PFS 991 (Cat.No. 154)
    PFS 996 (Cat.No. 155)
    PFS 1002 (Cat.No. 196)
    PFS 1016 (Cat.No. 77)
    PFS 1017 (Cat.No. 126)
    PFS 1018 (Cat.No. 185)
    PFS 1023 (Cat.No. 127)
    PFS 1030 (Cat.No. 120)
    PFS 1053 (Cat.No. 45)
    PFS 1076 (Cat.No. 193)
    PFS 1077 (Cat.No. 158)
    PFS 1081 (Cat.No. 71)
    PFS 1083 (Cat.No. 43)
    PFS 1090 (Cat.No. 175)
    PFS 1091 (Cat.No. 68)
    PFS 1099 (Cat.No. 169)
    PFS 1117 (Cat.No. 67)
    PFS 1135 (Cat.No. 66)
    PFS 1142 (Cat.No. 39)
    PFS 1146 (Cat.No. 40)
    PFS 1155 (Cat.No. 190)
    PFS 1165 (Cat.No. 89)
    PFS 1202 (Cat.No. 137)

FORTIFICATION STYLE (*cont.*)
    PFS 1217s (Cat.No. 168)
    PFS 1236 (Cat.No. 159)
    PFS 1243 (Cat.No. 33)
    PFS 1249 (Cat.No. 294)
    PFS 1260s (Cat.No. 184)
    PFS 1264s (Cat.No. 206)
    PFS 1276 (Cat.No. 34)
    PFS 1285 (Cat.No. 44)
    PFS 1300 (Cat.No. 191)
    PFS 1320 (Cat.No. 35)
    PFS 1322 (Cat.No. 36)
    PFS 1362 (Cat.No. 30)
    PFS 1367s (Cat.No. 211)
    PFS 1406 (Cat.No. 276)
    PFS 1440 (Cat.No. 42)
    PFS 1444 (Cat.No. 62)
    PFS 1447 (Cat.No. 163)
    PFS 1460 (Cat.No. 9)
    PFS 1463s (Cat.No. 231)
    PFS 1466 (Cat.No. 234)
    PFS 1467 (Cat.No. 12)
    PFS 1483 (Cat.No. 88)
    PFS 1489 (Cat.No. 106)
    PFS 1499 (Cat.No. 10)
    PFS 1501 (Cat.No. 238)
    PFS 1527 (Cat.No. 32)
    PFS 1535 (Cat.No. 164)
    PFS 1598 (Cat.No. 63)
    PFS 1613 (Cat.No. 82)
    PFS 1624s (Cat.No. 261)
                              158 TOTAL

MIXED STYLES II
    PFS 164* (Cat.No. 20)
    PFS 266* (Cat.No. 208)
    PFS 361 (Cat.No. 47)
    PFS 523* (Cat.No. 209)
    PFS 524 (Cat.No. 2)
    PFS 849 (Cat.No. 189)
    PFS 851 (Cat.No. 60)
    PFS 853 (Cat.No. 204)
    PFS 981* (Cat.No. 87)
    PFS 1057 (Cat.No. 70)
    PFS 1071 (Cat.No. 29)
    PFS 1072 (Cat.No. 61)
    PFS 1437s (Cat.No. 128)
                              13 TOTAL

COURT STYLE
    PFS 7* (Cat.No. 4)
    PFS 39s (Cat.No. 221)
    PFS 113* (Cat.No. 19)
    PFS 326 (Cat.No. 100)
    PFS 584* (Cat.No. 203)
    PFS 774 (Cat.No. 58)
    PFS 819 (Cat.No. 86)
    PFS 859* (Cat.No. 205)
    PFS 970 (Cat.No. 6)
    PFS 1025* (Cat.No. 266)
    PFS 1181 (Cat.No. 210)
    PFS 1684 (Cat.No. 17)
                    12 TOTAL

BROAD AND FLAT STYLES
    PFS 125 (Cat.No. 250)
    PFS 139s (Cat.No. 222)
    PFS 196 (Cat.No. 224)
    PFS 222 (Cat.No. 117)
    PFS 234 (Cat.No. 188)
    PFS 243 (Cat.No. 303)
    PFS 247 (Cat.No. 245)
    PFS 435 (Cat.No. 310)
    PFS 496 (Cat.No. 108)
    PFS 547 (Cat.No. 151)
    PFS 737 (Cat.No. 281)
    PFS 896 (Cat.No. 308)
    PFS 916 (Cat.No. 226)
    PFS 919s (Cat.No. 259)
    PFS 940 (Cat.No. 81)
    PFS 1188 (Cat.No. 144)
    PFS 1315s (Cat.No. 253)
    PFS 1375s (Cat.No. 254)
    PFS 1428s (Cat.No. 230)
                    19 TOTAL

LINEAR STYLES
    PFS 80 (Cat.No. 202)
    PFS 213 (Cat.No. 140)
    PFS 256 (Cat.No. 198)
    PFS 294 (Cat.No. 53)
    PFS 719 (Cat.No. 195)
    PFS 913 (Cat.No. 200)
    PFS 945 (Cat.No. 96)
    PFS 1020 (Cat.No. 37)
    PFS 1045 (Cat.No. 157)
    PFS 1102 (Cat.No. 132)
    PFS 1123 (Cat.No. 279)
    PFS 1252 (Cat.No. 161)

LINEAR STYLES (*cont.*)
    PFS 1454 (Cat.No. 166)
    PFS 1654 (Cat.No. 122)
                    14 TOTAL

DIVERSE STYLES
    PFS 2 (Cat.No. 3)
    PFS 6 (Cat.No. 304)
    PFS 20 (Cat.No. 145)
    PFS 43* (Cat.No. 207)
    PFS 153 (Cat.No. 285)
    PFS 190 (Cat.No. 286)
    PFS 284* (Cat.No. 111)
    PFS 418 (Cat.No. 201)
    PFS 463 (Cat.No. 264)
    PFS 690 (Cat.No. 139)
    PFS 740 (Cat.No. 146)
    PFS 884 (Cat.No. 123)
    PFS 1119 (Cat.No. 283)
    PFS 1189 (Cat.No. 8)
    PFS 1309s (Cat.No. 229)
    PFS 1321s (Cat.No. 176)
    PFS 1465 (Cat.No. 21)
    PFS 1475 (Cat.No. 177)
    PFS 1519 (Cat.No. 167)
                    19 TOTAL

PLAUSIBLY ANTIQUE
    ASSYRO-BABYLONIAN CUT STYLE
        PFS 321 (Cat.No. 125)

    ASSYRO-BABYLONIAN DRILLED STYLE
        PFS 62 (Cat.No. 104)
        PFS 180 (Cat.No. 194)

    ASSYRO-BABYLONIAN MODELED STYLE
        PFS 883* (Cat.No. 97)
        PFS 1122 (Cat.No. 228)
        PFS 1458 (Cat.No. 80)
        PFS 1480 (Cat.No. 257)
        PFS 1658 (Cat.No. 101)

    NEO-ELAMITE
        PFS 594 (Cat.No. 103)
                      9 TOTAL

ANTIQUE
    NEO-ASSYRIAN MODELED STYLE
        PFS 513 (Cat.No. 85)
                      1 TOTAL

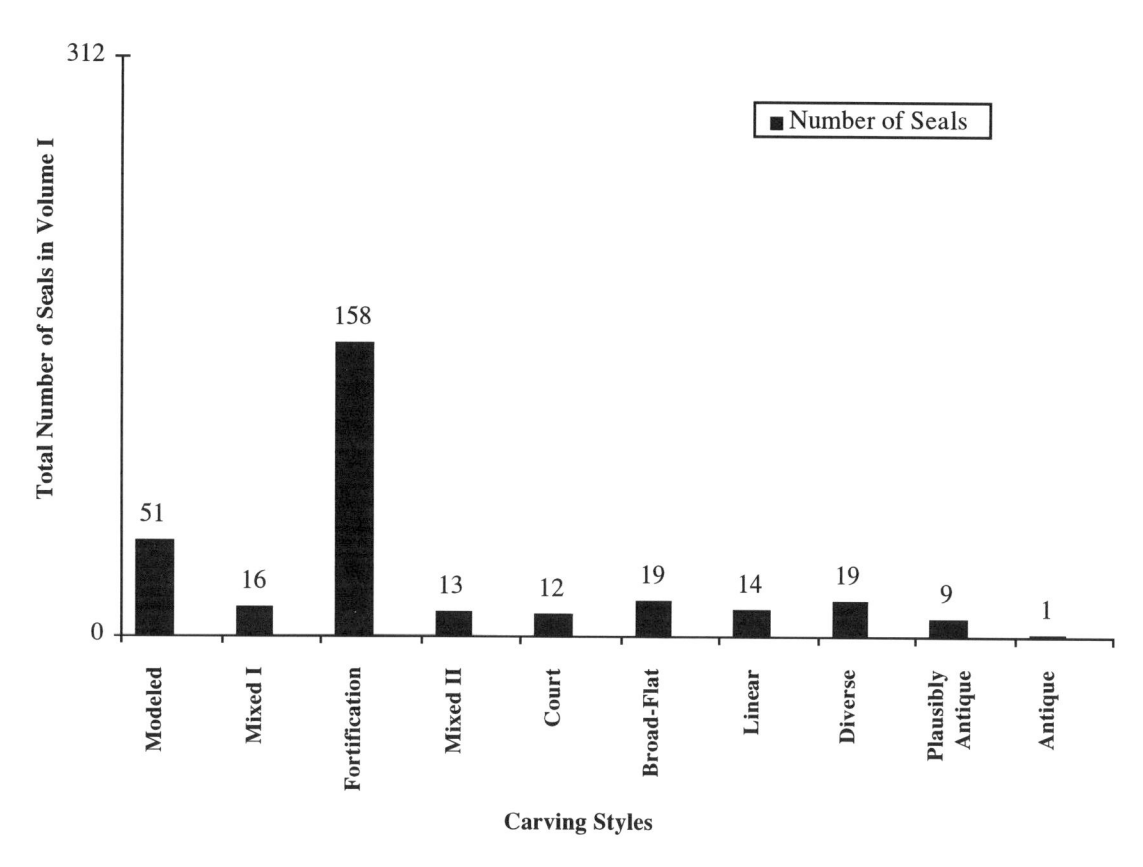

Chart 23. Distribution of All Seals in Volume I by Carving Styles

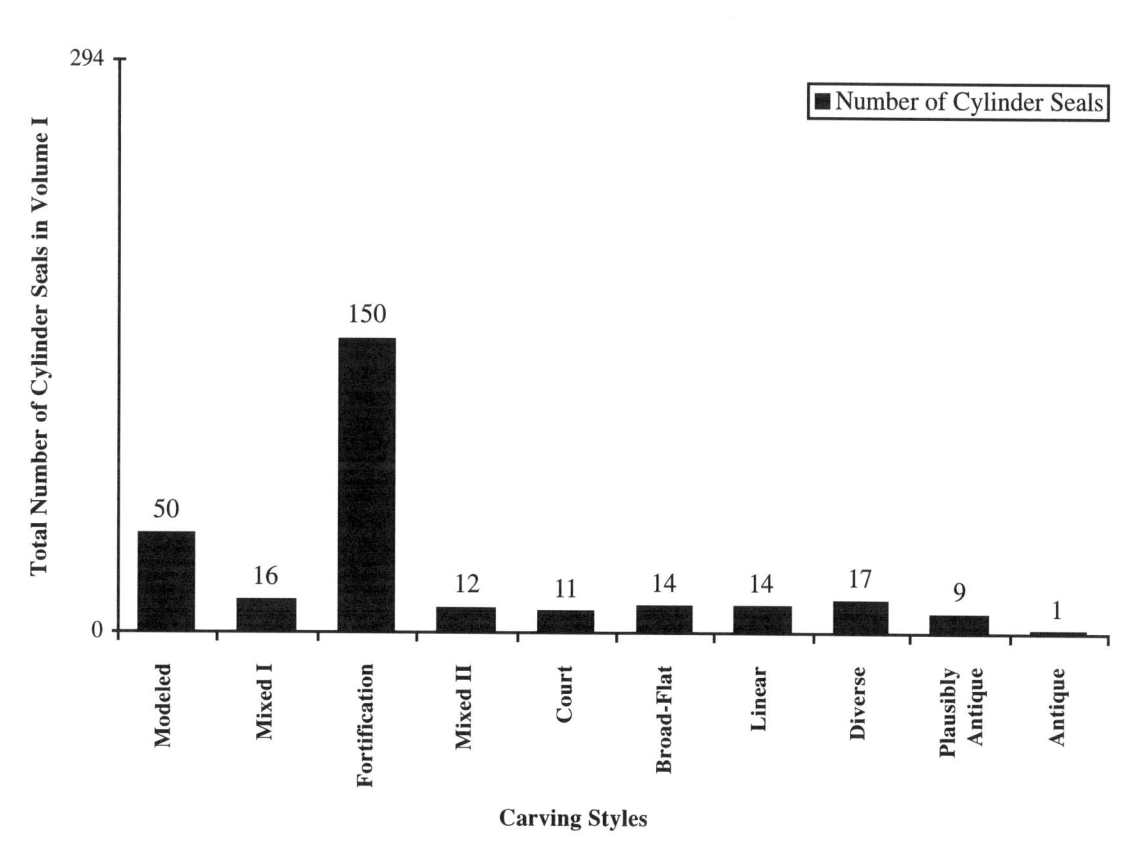

Chart 24. Distribution of Cylinder Seals in Volume I by Carving Styles

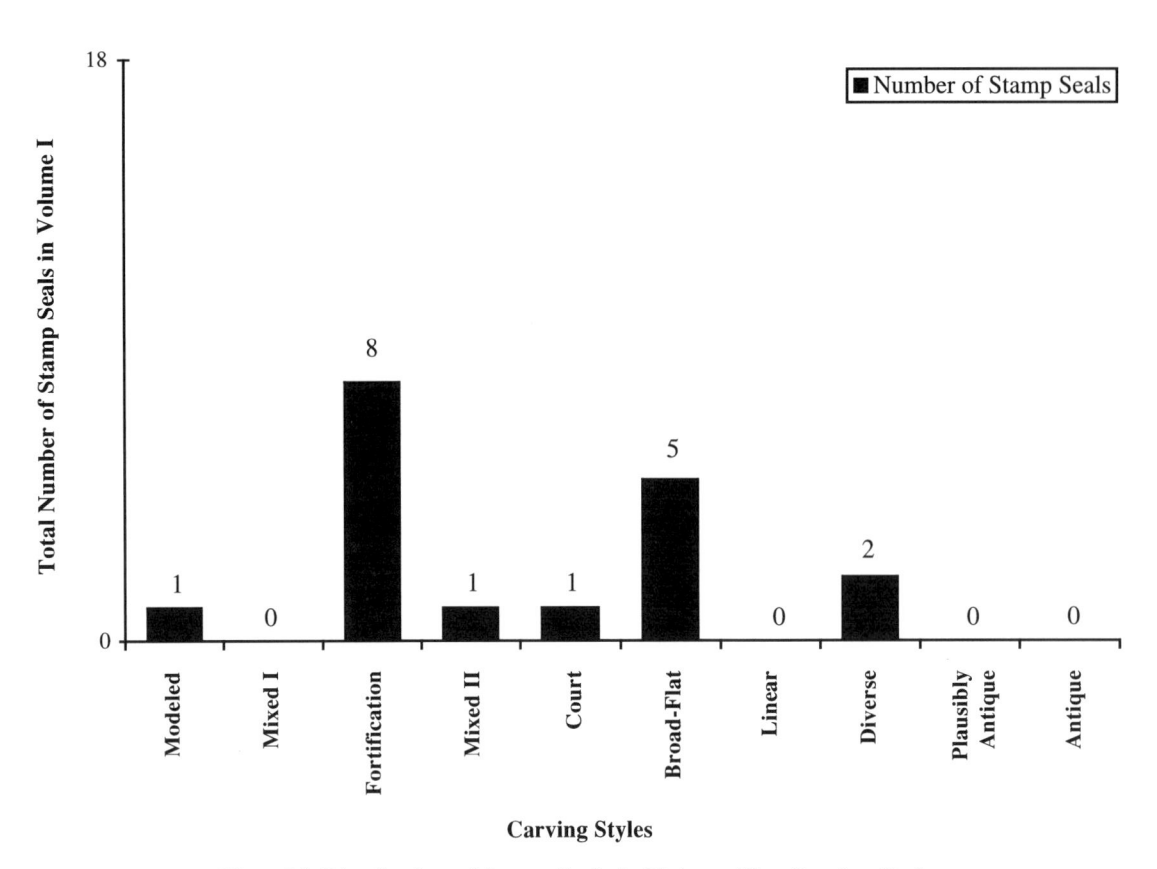

Chart 25. Distribution of Stamp Seals in Volume I by Carving Styles

APPENDIX SEVEN

ANIMALS AND COMPOSITE CREATURES ON SEALS IN VOLUME I

SCOPE

This appendix itemizes the occurrence of all animals and composite creatures in the PFS corpus of seals with the image of heroic encounter (Volume I), excluding human figures with no hybrid characteristics. It does not distinguish between primary participants in the heroic encounter scenes and other figures in the seal designs. (See *Appendix Eight: Iconographic Features on Seals in Volume I* for functional itemizations of animals and creatures within compositional formats of the seal design.) Characterizations of specific attributes of animals and creatures are limited here to the essential attitude of the body (e.g., rampant) and selected major distinguishing features of the anatomy (e.g., human-headed). Groupings of comparative illustrations cited in the catalog entries (pls. 174–291) may highlight additional physical features of animals and creatures beyond those indicated in this appendix.

TERMS

The terms used here for various types of animals/creatures flaunt no scientific pretensions. They selectively describe the selectively represented physical attributes of an array of fauna as products of the artistic imagination. This warning notwithstanding, there are numerous cases in which an animal or creature has been depicted with deliberate attention to aggregate or isolated features of extraordinary verism. Many of the animals and creatures in the PFS corpus can be clearly identified as belonging to a certain type of animal or (for composite creatures) to a certain base type: e.g., LION (for a non-fanciful lion) or LION CREATURE (for a lion with fanciful elements such as wings). In a small number of cases the base identity of a composite creature is itself a composite of recognizable types, for example, a LION-BIRD CREATURE. At the opposite end of the spectrum, many animals/creatures represented in the PFS corpus cannot be securely assigned to a specific base type (even when they are well preserved). These are labeled as animals and creatures of uncertain type. Composite creatures frequently labeled in western literature as sphinxes (lion-based creatures) or centaurs (horse-based creatures) are here itemized by their physical characteristics rather than by those terms.

Between the securely identifiable and the uncertain are cases where the base identity is tentatively offered. Here, a "(?)" is attached to the seal listing. There are, furthermore, numerous quadruped representations that are difficult to distinguish specifically as either a bull or a lion. In these cases, a separate bull or lion category appears. The most difficult challenges occur with the variety of horned animals that are primarily either the deer, gazelles, wild goats (ibexes), or wild (short-haired) sheep that were all part of the ancient Iranian environment and shared many physical attributes that seem often to be drawn upon with imaginative combinations on the seals in the PFS corpus (e.g., Harrington 1977, pp. 28, 34, 46, 52, 62). The female wild goat and wild sheep are, in nature, difficult for the casual observer to distinguish except by color markings. It is thus quite possible that nuances (including gendered ones) of the animal world embedded in the artistry of the seals in this catalog may completely elude us at present. The outward splaying horns of the wild sheep, male and female (as opposed to the almost parallel horns of the wild goat), do tend to be rendered in art as a frontal pair rather than a single horn in profile. This guideline is useful but not foolproof. When elements of artistic license are added to the mix-and-match scenarios of tail lengths, beards, and horn/antler shapes on the more flamboyant male representatives of all these animals, the problems of identification are multiplied. For some examples we simply resort to labeling them horned animals (or horned-animal creatures), type undetermined. For others, where some cue directs us and is not absolutely contradicted by another element, we suggest a more precise identity.

AVIATE ANIMALS/CREATURES
    Bird
        Cock, standing — PFS 326 (Cat.No. 100)
        Eagle
            Displayed with wings folded — PFS 461 (Cat.No. 90)
            Perched atop column with wings folded — PFS 1099 (Cat.No. 169)
        Goose, in flight with wings spread wide — PFS 31 (Cat.No. 172)
        Ostrich, marchant — PFS 9* (Cat.No. 288), PFS 29 (Cat.No. 302), PFS 263 (Cat.No. 289)
        Parrot, standing(?) — PFS 65 (Cat.No. 241)
        Peacock, standing, tail feathers cascading — PFS 138 (Cat.No. 186)
        Uncertain type
            Alighting with wings upward, pecking — PFS 1249 (Cat.No. 294), PFS 1527 (Cat.No. 32)
            Displayed with wings spread wide — PFS 24 (Cat.No. 298), PFS 266* (Cat.No. 208)
            In flight — PFS 123*(?) (Cat.No. 75), PFS 329 (Cat.No. 28), PFS 841 (Cat.No. 13), PFS 1122 (Cat.No. 228)
                Wings spread wide — PFS 939 (Cat.No. 267), PFS 841 (Cat.No. 13), PFS 1374 (Cat.No. 31), PFS 1388 (Cat.No. 162)
            Standing, pecking — PFS 30 (Cat.No. 291)
        Vulture, perched, pecking — PFS 130 (Cat.No. 300), PFS 1475 (Cat.No. 177)
    Bird creature with quadruped's forelegs, rampant, human-headed — PFS 247 (Cat.No. 245), PFS 916 (Cat.No. 226)

DEER (*see* QUADRUPEDS: Horned animal: Deer, below)

FISH, INSECTS, REPTILES
    Fish
        Horizontal — PFS 263 (Cat.No. 289), PFS 463 (Cat.No. 264)
        Inverted — PFS 247 (Cat.No. 245)
    Fish-bull creature, marchant, winged — PFS 10 (Cat.No. 251)
    Scorpion creature
        Marchant, winged, human-headed — PFS 4* (Cat.No. 292), PFS 29 (Cat.No. 302)
        Sejant, winged, human-headed — PFS 1586 (Cat.No. 121)
    Snake
        Horizontal — PFS 1309s(?) (Cat.No. 229)
        Vertically disposed
            Suspended from hero's arms — PFS 152 (Cat.No. 295)
            Undulating upward — PFS 418 (Cat.No. 201)

GOAT (*see* QUADRUPEDS: Horned animal: Wild goat, below)

HUMAN CREATURES
    Female with four wings, frontal nude — PFS 1485 (Cat.No. 112)
    Male
        With bird's ovoid torso — PFS 1188 (Cat.No. 144)
        With four wings — PFS 6 (Cat.No. 304), PFS 36* (Cat.No. 5), PFS 58 (Cat.No. 242), PFS 64* (Cat.No. 173), PFS 72(?) (Cat.No. 147), PFS 103* (Cat.No. 84), PFS 112 (Cat.No. 282), PFS 180 (Cat.No. 194), PFS 297 (Cat.No. 124), PFS 321 (Cat.No. 125), PFS 418 (Cat.No. 201), PFS 463 (Cat.No. 264), PFS 513 (Cat.No. 85), PFS 516(?) (Cat.No. 98), PFS 594 (Cat.No. 103), PFS 782 (Cat.No. 105), PFS 883* (Cat.No. 97), PFS 1026 (Cat.No. 156), PFS 1276(?) (Cat.No. 34), PFS 1387(?) (Cat.No. 72), PFS 1586 (Cat.No. 121), PFS 1658 (Cat.No. 101)
            And bird's ovoid torso — PFS 1202 (Cat.No. 137)
        With single wing — PFS 263 (Cat.No. 289), PFS 896 (Cat.No. 308), PFS 1632* (Cat.No. 244)
        With two wings — PFS 30 (Cat.No. 291), PFS 65 (Cat.No. 241), PFS 98* (Cat.No. 217), PFS 931* (Cat.No. 270), PFS 964 (Cat.No. 260), PFS 1099 (Cat.No. 169), PFS 1566* (Cat.No. 218)
            And bird's feet — PFS 1321s (Cat.No. 176)

IBEX (*see* QUADRUPEDS: Horned animal: Wild goat, below)

QUADRUPEDS
- Animal of uncertain type
    - Courant — PFS 1286 (Cat.No. 258)
    - Inverted — PFS 190 (Cat.No. 286), PFS 234 (Cat.No. 188), PFS 447 (Cat.No. 301), PFS 757 (Cat.No. 296), PFS 885 (Cat.No. 187), PFS 1018 (Cat.No. 185), PFS 1388 (Cat.No. 162)
    - Marchant — PFS 190 (Cat.No. 286), PFS 256 (Cat.No. 198), PFS 501 (Cat.No. 141), PFS 912 (Cat.No. 138), PFS 1322(?) (Cat.No. 36), PFS 1406(?) (Cat.No. 276)
    - Rampant — PFS 148 (Cat.No. 311), PFS 213 (Cat.No. 140), PFS 236 (Cat.No. 213), PFS 243 (Cat.No. 303), PFS 246 (Cat.No. 290), PFS 255 (Cat.No. 233), PFS 280 (Cat.No. 309), PFS 297 (Cat.No. 124), PFS 338 (Cat.No. 262), PFS 435 (Cat.No. 310), PFS 480 (Cat.No. 134), PFS 501 (Cat.No. 141), PFS 632 (Cat.No. 143), PFS 669 (Cat.No. 142), PFS 687 (Cat.No. 119), PFS 690 (Cat.No. 139), PFS 737 (Cat.No. 281), PFS 818 (Cat.No. 265), PFS 952 (Cat.No. 227), PFS 990 (Cat.No. 256), PFS 991 (Cat.No. 154), PFS 1023 (Cat.No. 127), PFS 1119 (Cat.No. 283), PFS 1188 (Cat.No. 144), PFS 1202 (Cat.No. 137), PFS 1249 (Cat.No. 294), PFS 1375s (Cat.No. 254), PFS 1480 (Cat.No. 257), PFS 1612 (Cat.No. 268)
        - Ithyphallic — PFS 167 (Cat.No. 255)
    - Seated upright — PFS 1315s (Cat.No. 253)
    - Suspended on its back — PFS 213(?) (Cat.No. 140), PFS 256 (Cat.No. 198)
    - Vertically disposed — PFS 213 (Cat.No. 140), PFS 1249 (Cat.No. 294)
        - Ithyphallic — PFS 1285 (Cat.No. 44)
- Animal creature of uncertain type
    - Couchant, winged — PFS 396 (Cat.No. 178), PFS 931* (Cat.No. 270)
    - Courant, winged — PFS 463 (Cat.No. 264)
        - Horned — PFS 6 (Cat.No. 304)
    - Inverted
        - Held aloft — PFS 538 (Cat.No. 312)
        - Winged — PFS 849 (Cat.No. 189)
    - Marchant, winged — PFS 246 (Cat.No. 290), PFS 896 (Cat.No. 308), PFS 913 (Cat.No. 200), PFS 1153 (Cat.No. 199), PFS 1406(?) (Cat.No. 276)
    - Rampant
        - Horned — PFS 241(?) (Cat.No. 252)
        - Human-headed, ithyphallic — PFS 217 (Cat.No. 135)
        - Winged — PFS 72 (Cat.No. 147), PFS 112 (Cat.No. 282), PFS 228 (Cat.No. 148), PFS 297 (Cat.No. 124), PFS 321 (Cat.No. 125), PFS 338 (Cat.No. 262), PFS 344 (Cat.No. 263), PFS 439 (Cat.No. 150), PFS 547 (Cat.No. 151), PFS 714 (Cat.No. 152), PFS 757 (Cat.No. 296), PFS 783 (Cat.No. 153), PFS 818 (Cat.No. 265), PFS 919s (Cat.No. 259), PFS 991 (Cat.No. 154), PFS 996 (Cat.No. 155), PFS 1025* (Cat.No. 266), PFS 1045 (Cat.No. 157), PFS 1077 (Cat.No. 158), PFS 1236 (Cat.No. 159), PFS 1238 (Cat.No. 160), PFS 1252 (Cat.No. 161), PFS 1320 (Cat.No. 35), PFS 1388 (Cat.No. 162), PFS 1447 (Cat.No. 163), PFS 1519 (Cat.No. 167), PFS 1535 (Cat.No. 164), PFS 1624s (Cat.No. 261), PFS 1630 (Cat.No. 165)
            - Bird-headed — PFS 964 (Cat.No. 260)
            - Horned — PFS 125 (Cat.No. 250)
            - Human-headed — PFS 20 (Cat.No. 145), PFS 321 (Cat.No. 125), PFS 364 (Cat.No. 149), PFS 740 (Cat.No. 146), PFS 884 (Cat.No. 123), PFS 1026 (Cat.No. 156), PFS 1454 (Cat.No. 166)
                - Horned(?) — PFS 1454 (Cat.No. 166)
            - Ithyphallic — PFS 1119 (Cat.No. 283)
- Bull (*see also* QUADRUPEDS: Bull or lion, below)
    - Inverted calf — PFS 152 (Cat.No. 295)
    - Marchant — PFS 538 (Cat.No. 312), PFS 614 (Cat.No. 287)

QUADRUPEDS (*cont.*)

   Bull (*cont.*)

      Rampant — PFS 149 (Cat.No. 212), PFS 236 (Cat.No. 213), PFS 396 (Cat.No. 178), PFS 524(?) (Cat.No. 2), PFS 795 (Cat.No. 214), PFS 912 (Cat.No. 138), PFS 944 (Cat.No. 129), PFS 1367s (Cat.No. 211)

         Ithyphallic — PFS 102 (Cat.No. 1)

   Bull, humped

      Marchant, head lowered — PFS 31 (Cat.No. 172)

   Bull creature *(see also* QUADRUPEDS: Bull or lion creature, below; *Appendix Eight: Iconographic Features on Seals in Volume I: ATLAS FIGURES; HEROES AS COMPOSITE CREATURES; SUPPORTING FIGURES BELOW FIGURE EMERGENT AND/OR WINGED SYMBOL)*

      Couchant(?), winged — PFS 36* (Cat.No. 5)

      Marchant, winged — PFS 109 (Cat.No. 197), PFS 130 (Cat.No. 300)

         Human-faced — PFS 30 (Cat.No. 291)

         Human-headed — PFS 1155 (Cat.No. 190)

      Rampant

         Human-faced — PFS 222 (Cat.No. 117)

         Human-headed with human shoulders and arms — PFS 774 (Cat.No. 58)

         Winged — PFS 2 (Cat.No. 3), PFS 7* (Cat.No. 4), PFS 36* (Cat.No. 5), PFS 429 (Cat.No. 7), PFS 778 (Cat.No. 11), PFS 815* (Cat.No. 215), PFS 841 (Cat.No. 13), PFS 853 (Cat.No. 204), PFS 970 (Cat.No. 6), PFS 1189 (Cat.No. 8), PFS 1202 (Cat.No. 137), PFS 1460 (Cat.No. 9), PFS 1467 (Cat.No. 12), PFS 1499 (Cat.No. 10), PFS 1550 (Cat.No. 14), PFS 1612 (Cat.No. 268)

            Human-faced — PFS 38 (Cat.No. 16), PFS 98* (Cat.No. 217), PFS 1227*(?) (Cat.No. 219), PFS 1465 (Cat.No. 21), PFS 1641 (Cat.No. 18)

            Ithyphallic — PFS 1566* (Cat.No. 218), PFS 1684 (Cat.No. 17)

            Human-headed — PFS 18 (Cat.No. 15), PFS 113* (Cat.No. 19), PFS 164* (Cat.No. 20)

            Ithyphallic — PFS 18 (Cat.No. 15), PFS 526* (Cat.No. 216)

         Ithyphallic — PFS 99 (Cat.No. 113), PFS 939 (Cat.No. 267)

         With human arms — PFS 1582 (Cat.No. 232)

      Standing (as a hero or archer)

         Winged with human shoulders and arms — PFS 1* (Cat.No. 182)

            Human-faced — PFS 1204 (Cat.No. 136)

            Human-headed — PFS 1204 (Cat.No. 136)

         Human-headed with human torso and arms, — PFS 684 (Cat.No. 183)

   Bull or lion, rampant — PFS 461 (Cat.No. 90), PFS 1165 (Cat.No. 89)

   Bull or lion creature

      Marchant winged

         Human-faced, horned — PFS 514 (Cat.No. 192), PFS 1076 (Cat.No. 193)

            Ithyphallic — PFS 514 (Cat.No. 192)

         Human-headed with human torso and arms — PFS 146 (Cat.No. 275)

         Rampant, winged — PFS 167 (Cat.No. 255), PFS 392 (Cat.No. 91), PFS 454 (Cat.No. 92), PFS 555 (Cat.No. 93), PFS 1017 (Cat.No. 126), PFS 1437s (Cat.No. 128)

            Human-headed — PFS 158 (Cat.No. 94), PFS 370 (Cat.No. 99), PFS 373 (Cat.No. 306), PFS 380 (Cat.No. 95), PFS 516 (Cat.No. 98), PFS 883* (Cat.No. 97), PFS 945 (Cat.No. 96), PFS 1023 (Cat.No. 127), PFS 1053 (Cat.No. 45), PFS 1586 (Cat.No. 121), PFS 1658 (Cat.No. 101)

            Horned — PFS 326 (Cat.No. 100)

            Ithyphallic with human arms — PFS 1071 (Cat.No. 29)

         Ithyphallic — PFS 454 (Cat.No. 92)

   Dog, sejant — PFS 1122 (Cat.No. 228)

QUADRUPEDS (*cont.*)

    Horned animal

        Deer

            Courant — PFS 1286 (Cat.No. 258)

            Rampant — PFS 225 (Cat.No. 46), PFS 247 (Cat.No. 245), PFS 536 (Cat.No. 102)

            Vertically disposed — PFS 1217s (Cat.No. 168)

        Type undetermined

            Inverted — PFS 17 (Cat.No. 235), PFS 114 (Cat.No. 284), PFS 138 (Cat.No. 186), PFS 243 (Cat.No. 303), PFS 1260s (Cat.No. 184)

            Marchant — PFS 180 (Cat.No. 194), PFS 190 (Cat.No. 286), PFS 213 (Cat.No. 140)

                Head lowered — PFS 246 (Cat.No. 290)

            Rampant — PFS 33 (Cat.No. 220), PFS 62 (Cat.No. 104), PFS 153 (Cat.No. 285), PFS 496 (Cat.No. 108), PFS 782 (Cat.No. 105), PFS 1311s (Cat.No. 247), PFS 1391 (Cat.No. 248), PFS 1444 (Cat.No. 62)

            Vertically disposed — PFS 131 (Cat.No. 170), PFS 213 (Cat.No. 140)

        Wild goat

            Courant — PFS 1181 (Cat.No. 210)

            Inverted — PFS 1475 (Cat.No. 177)

            Marchant — PFS 536 (Cat.No. 102)

            Rampant — PFS 9* (Cat.No. 288), PFS 197 (Cat.No. 116), PFS 247 (Cat.No. 245), PFS 536 (Cat.No. 102), PFS 594 (Cat.No. 103), PFS 781 (Cat.No. 107), PFS 959s (Cat.No. 246), PFS 1016 (Cat.No. 77)

            Vertically disposed — PFS 131 (Cat.No. 170), PFS 1099 (Cat.No. 169)

        Wild sheep

            Marchant — PFS 197 (Cat.No. 116)

            Rampant — PFS 1489(?) (Cat.No. 106)

    Horned-animal creature

        Type undetermined

            Marchant, winged — PFS 719 (Cat.No. 195), PFS 1002(?) (Cat.No. 196)

                Human-faced — PFS 1002 (Cat.No. 196)

            Rampant, winged — PFS 213 (Cat.No. 140), PFS 687 (Cat.No. 119)

        Wild goat creature

            Rampant, winged — PFS 1123 (Cat.No. 279)

        Wild sheep creature

            Rampant, human-faced — PFS 222(?) (Cat.No. 117)

            Rampant, winged — PFS 162 (Cat.No. 249), PFS 341 (Cat.No. 109)

    Horse creature

        Marchant, winged — PFS 67(?) (Cat.No. 293)

        Rampant, winged — PFS 99 (Cat.No. 113), PFS 749 (Cat.No. 110)

    Ibex (*see* QUADRUPEDS: Horned animals: Wild goat, above)

    Lion (*see also* QUADRUPEDS: Bull or lion, above)

        Courant — PFS 523* (Cat.No. 209)

        Inverted — PFS 31 (Cat.No. 172), PFS 64* (Cat.No. 173), PFS 138 (Cat.No. 186), PFS 153 (Cat.No. 285), PFS 381 (Cat.No. 179), PFS 396 (Cat.No. 178), PFS 671* (Cat.No. 174), PFS 1090 (Cat.No. 175), PFS 1142 (Cat.No. 39), PFS 1321s (Cat.No. 176), PFS 1475 (Cat.No. 177)

            Ithyphallic — PFS 114 (Cat.No. 284), PFS 971 (Cat.No. 171)

        Marchant — PFS 109 (Cat.No. 197), PFS 1300 (Cat.No. 191)

        Rampant — PFS 33 (Cat.No. 220), PFS 49 (Cat.No. 23), PFS 80 (Cat.No. 202), PFS 148 (Cat.No. 311), PFS 151 (Cat.No. 223), PFS 167 (Cat.No. 255), PFS 197 (Cat.No. 116), PFS 225 (Cat.No. 46), PFS 232 (Cat.No. 26), PFS 241 (Cat.No. 252), PFS 249 (Cat.No. 27), PFS 255 (Cat.No. 233), PFS 260 (Cat.No. 225), PFS 329 (Cat.No. 28), PFS 344 (Cat.No. 263), PFS 361 (Cat.No. 47), PFS 385 (Cat.No. 38), PFS 503 (Cat.No. 307), PFS 552 (Cat.No. 118), PFS 687 (Cat.No. 119), PFS 709 (Cat.No. 271), PFS 731 (Cat.No. 131), PFS 859* (Cat.No. 205), PFS 902 (Cat.No. 243), PFS 912 (Cat.No. 138), PFS 916

QUADRUPEDS (*cont.*)

   Lion (*cont.*)

      Rampant (*cont.*)

         (Cat.No. 226), PFS 931* (Cat.No. 270), PFS 952 (Cat.No. 227), PFS 990 (Cat.No. 256), PFS 1017 (Cat.No. 126), PFS 1053 (Cat.No. 45), PFS 1071 (Cat.No. 29), PFS 1083 (Cat.No. 43), PFS 1101 (Cat.No. 297), PFS 1102 (Cat.No. 132), PFS 1122 (Cat.No. 228), PFS 1142 (Cat.No. 39), PFS 1146 (Cat.No. 40), PFS 1243 (Cat.No. 33), PFS 1264s (Cat.No. 206), PFS 1276 (Cat.No. 34), PFS 1285 (Cat.No. 44), PFS 1300 (Cat.No. 191), PFS 1309s (Cat.No. 229), PFS 1320 (Cat.No. 35), PFS 1322 (Cat.No. 36), PFS 1325 (Cat.No. 41), PFS 1362 (Cat.No. 30), PFS 1374 (Cat.No. 31), PFS 1440 (Cat.No. 42), PFS 1463s (Cat.No. 231), PFS 1466 (Cat.No. 234), PFS 1527 (Cat.No. 32), PFS 1654 (Cat.No. 122)

         Forelegs extended on either side of body — PFS 16* (Cat.No. 22), PFS 63 (Cat.No. 24), PFS 65 (Cat.No. 241), PFS 39s (Cat.No. 221), PFS 52 (Cat.No. 114), PFS 95 (Cat.No. 25), PFS 139s (Cat.No. 222), PFS 151 (Cat.No. 223), PFS 152 (Cat.No. 295), PFS 196 (Cat.No. 224), PFS 265 (Cat.No. 240), PFS 329 (Cat.No. 28), PFS 584* (Cat.No. 203), PFS 807 (Cat.No. 269), PFS 853 (Cat.No. 204), PFS 1020 (Cat.No. 37), PFS 1428s (Cat.No. 230), PFS 1437s (Cat.No. 128), PFS 1480(?) (Cat.No. 257), PFS 1582 (Cat.No. 232)

           Ithyphallic — PFS 43* (Cat.No. 207), PFS 272* (Cat.No. 272)

         Ithyphallic — PFS 225 (Cat.No. 46), PFS 334 (Cat.No. 133), PFS 385 (Cat.No. 38), PFS 494 (Cat.No. 130), PFS 1071 (Cat.No. 29), PFS 1101 (Cat.No. 297), PFS 1374 (Cat.No. 31), PFS 1637* (Cat.No. 273)

      Vertically disposed — PFS 131 (Cat.No. 170), PFS 1249 (Cat.No. 294)

   Lion-bird creature with two heads, rampant, winged — PFS 284* (Cat.No. 111)

   Lion creature (*see also* QUADRUPEDS: Bull or lion creature, above)

      Couchant(?), winged, horned — PFS 164* (Cat.No. 20)

      Courant, horned — PFS 524 (Cat.No. 2)

         Winged — PFS 524 (Cat.No. 2)

      Inverted, winged

         Bird-headed — PFS 1* (Cat.No. 182), PFS 684 (Cat.No. 183)

         Human-headed — PFS 32* (Cat.No. 180), PFS 677* (Cat.No. 181)

      Marchant, winged — PFS 130 (Cat.No. 300)

      Rampant

         Bird-headed — PFS 217 (Cat.No. 135)

         Winged — PFS 24 (Cat.No. 298), PFS 100 (Cat.No. 274), PFS 145 (Cat.No. 115), PFS 146 (Cat.No. 275), PFS 197 (Cat.No. 116), PFS 199* (Cat.No. 305), PFS 201 (Cat.No. 50), PFS 231 (Cat.No. 51), PFS 265 (Cat.No. 240), PFS 294 (Cat.No. 53), PFS 312 (Cat.No. 237), PFS 334 (Cat.No. 133), PFS 426 (Cat.No. 55), PFS 430 (Cat.No. 56), PFS 480 (Cat.No. 134), PFS 552 (Cat.No. 118), PFS 673 (Cat.No. 64), PFS 720 (Cat.No. 57), PFS 882 (Cat.No. 65), PFS 884 (Cat.No. 123), PFS 990 (Cat.No. 256), PFS 1057 (Cat.No. 70), PFS 1081 (Cat.No. 71), PFS 1091 (Cat.No. 68), PFS 1117 (Cat.No. 67), PFS 1123 (Cat.No. 279), PFS 1181 (Cat.No. 210), PFS 1243 (Cat.No. 33), PFS 1387 (Cat.No. 72), PFS 1444 (Cat.No. 62), PFS 1501(Cat.No. 238), PFS 1654 (Cat.No. 122)

           Bird-footed — PFS 86 (Cat.No. 48), PFS 233 (Cat.No. 52), PFS 851 (Cat.No. 60), PFS 1030 (Cat.No. 120)

             Bird-headed — PFS 981* (Cat.No. 87), PFS 1030 (Cat.No. 120)

             Horned — PFS 301 (Cat.No. 54), PFS 774 (Cat.No. 58)

             Ithyphallic — PFS 152 (Cat.No. 295)

           Bird-headed — PFS 79 (Cat.No. 83), PFS 513 (Cat.No. 85), PFS 1483 (Cat.No. 88)

             Horned — PFS 103* (Cat.No. 84), PFS 819 (Cat.No. 86)

           Forelegs extended on either side of body, four-winged — PFS 65 (Cat.No. 241)

           Horned — PFS 17 (Cat.No. 235), PFS 54* (Cat.No. 277), PFS 146 (Cat.No. 275), PFS 266* (Cat.No. 208), PFS 298s (Cat.No. 236), PFS 523* (Cat.No. 209), PFS 844 (Cat.No. 59), PFS 1072 (Cat.No. 61), PFS 1135 (Cat.No. 66), PFS 1406 (Cat.No. 276), PFS 1598 (Cat.No. 63)

             Ithyphallic — PFS 57* (Cat.No. 239), PFS 1072 (Cat.No. 61)

QUADRUPEDS (*cont.*)
- Lion creature (*cont.*)
    - Rampant (*cont.*)
        - Winged (*cont.*)
            - Human-faced — PFS 34 (Cat.No. 73), PFS 58 (Cat.No. 242), PFS 168 (Cat.No. 74), PFS 944 (Cat.No. 129), PFS 1613 (Cat.No. 82), PFS 1632* (Cat.No. 244)
            - Human-headed — PFS 26 (Cat.No. 299), PFS 52 (Cat.No. 114), PFS 123* (Cat.No. 75), PFS 145 (Cat.No. 115), PFS 312 (Cat.No. 237), PFS 362 (Cat.No. 76), PFS 399 (Cat.No. 78), PFS 447 (Cat.No. 301), PFS 494 (Cat.No. 130), PFS 731 (Cat.No. 131), PFS 787 (Cat.No. 79), PFS 902 (Cat.No. 243), PFS 940 (Cat.No. 81), PFS 1016 (Cat.No. 77), PFS 1102 (Cat.No. 132), PFS 1458 (Cat.No. 80)
            - Ithyphallic — PFS 414 (Cat.No. 280)
        - Ithyphallic — PFS 120 (Cat.No. 49), PFS 132 (Cat.No. 69)
    - Sejant, winged, horned — PFS 769* (Cat.No. 278)
    - Standing (as archer)
        - Winged, with human shoulders and arms — PFS 1204 (Cat.No. 136)
- Sheep, wild (*see* QUADRUPEDS: Horned animal: Wild sheep, above)

APPENDIX EIGHT

ICONOGRAPHIC FEATURES ON SEALS IN VOLUME I

SCOPE

This appendix lists in alphabetical order design elements and features, motifs and realia, and forms of certain, probable, or possible symbolic significance within the Persian imperial milieu that occur in conjunction with the heroic encounter imagery on the seals cataloged in Volume I.

TERMS

Weapons

Precise identifications of weapons are sometimes impossible even when they are completely preserved. Generally we label a short straight-bladed weapon a dagger, whereas a long straight or curved weapon is labeled a sword. We avoid special terms for subtypes of daggers and swords, preferring the general term curved sword, for instance, to cover all the many variants of such a category (e.g., scimitar) because such terms mean different things to different audiences. For a range of types, see Bonnet 1926. Some of the slightly undulating weapons seem to be throw sticks rather than swords (Bonnet 1926, pp. 108–14); and interesting examples of slings and projectiles add another dimension to the repertoire of realia in Achaemenid glyptic. If a weapon that cannot be classified is preserved enough to provide any basis for discussion, it is itemized as a weapon of uncertain type; otherwise, nothing is itemized.

Garments

The majority of garments in Volume I echo faithfully or faintly the Assyrian robe that wraps around the body over a short undergarment (Hrouda 1965, pl. 1, nos. 6–8). These garments are designated the Assyrian garment because the Assyrianizing element is an important iconographic feature. Use of the term does not, however, imply that the seals in question date to the Neo-Assyrian period. The Persian court robe also has specific and clear cultural associations. Other garment types are simply itemized in generic descriptive terms (e.g., kilt, robe, trousers, tunic). When a garment is partially preserved but not enough to be associated with any of these categories, it is described as a garment of uncertain type. If a garment is essentially not preserved, nothing is itemized.

Many human heads seem to be adorned with a domed headdress, where a line at the bottom cuts clear across the head at brow level and the cap rises to a smooth dome. The contour of this headdress evokes the felt cap worn frequently by men represented in Achaemenid art dressed in the Iranian riding habit of tunic, trousers, and sometimes also the sleeved coat (see Koch 1993, pp. 117–35, on this and the related headgear). But here on the hero seals in the PFS corpus, the headdress is often worn by figures in combination with various other costumes (most notably, the Assyrian garment). In some cases the domed headdress is without doubt an article of apparel. In other cases it is not, however, absolutely certain that the intention was to depict a headdress or whether, instead, the appearance is simply a by-product of the drill technique for rendering the rounded head.

Symbols and Symbolic Associations

The catalog entries in Volumes I–III are not intended to offer in-depth commentary on iconographical features. The entries do, however, document the range of forms that in some occurrences (if not in all) embody specific symbolical meanings relating to divine, cosmic, magical, and royal/dynastic realms. This documentation creates a databank of such material that exists across the entire corpus of seals used on the PF tablets.

Traditionally, catalog compendia of glyptic images have identified abstract symbols and symbolically-allusive figural representations with specific divine, cosmic, magical, and royal/dynastic realms (e.g., the figure emerging from a winged symbol as Ahuramazda). Many readers will be accustomed to seek this information via these specific equivalences. In an attempt to assist those readers, the list below gives in the left-hand column specific divine, cosmic, magical, and royal/dynastic terms. In the right-hand column are the finding-aids in this appendix (and/or in *Appendix Seven*) by which the reader can search for the abstract symbols and symbolically-allusive figural representations that may be associated with these terms. As mentioned, the catalog entries themselves are not meant to offer in-depth commentary on these iconographical features; thus, in numerous instances, these associated meanings have not been noted in the catalog. It may be increasingly possible, on the basis of the data compiled across all three volumes, to establish valences of meaning for images that are not included in this list (e.g., crossed animals, pedestal animals, etc.). In addition to the Iranian/Zoroastrian gods (Ahuramazda, Anahita, and Mithra) the associations noted here embrace traditions of Greater Mesopotamia (including pre-Achaemenid Elam) and Egypt.

List of Divine, Cosmic, Magical, and Royal/Dynastic Terms and the Appendix Finding-Aids

Divine, Cosmic, Magical, and Royal/Dynastic Terms	*Appendix Finding-Aids*
AHURAMAZDA	DEVICES AND SYMBOLS: Figure emergent: From winged symbol; Winged symbol
ANAHITA	DEVICES AND SYMBOLS: Figure emergent: From nimbus of stars
ANU	DEVICES AND SYMBOLS: Triangle shape
DEATH-REBIRTH	DEVICES AND SYMBOLS: Drooping lotus
DEMONS	ATLAS FIGURES; HEROES AS COMPOSITE CREATURES; *Appendix Seven: Animals and Composite Creatures on Seals in Volume I*: QUADRUPEDS: Bull creature; Bull or lion creature; Lion creature
EA	DEVICES AND SYMBOLS: Fish
GENIES	HUMAN/HUMAN-CREATURE FIGURES OTHER THAN HEROES
GULA	DEVICES AND SYMBOLS: Dog, sejant
HORUS BIRTH CYCLE	DEVICES AND SYMBOLS: Infant Horus in papyrus plant
INŠUŠINAK, NAPIRIŠA, NINGIŠZIDA	DEVICES AND SYMBOLS: Snake
IŠTAR	DEVICES AND SYMBOLS: Figure emergent: From nimbus of stars; Rhomb; Rosette; Star; TREES: Date palm; *Appendix Seven: Animals and Composite Creatures on Seals in Volume I*: QUADRUPEDS: Lion; Lion creature
KINGSHIP/ROYALTY	DEVICES AND SYMBOLS: Rosette; TREES: Date palm
LAHMU	HEROES AS NUDE, FRONTALLY-FACED FIGURES
LIFE	DEVICES AND SYMBOLS: *Ankh*
MARDUK	DEVICES AND SYMBOLS: Spade of Marduk
MITHRA	*Appendix Seven: Animals and Composite Creatures on Seals in Volume I*: QUADRUPEDS: Bull; Bull creature
NABU	DEVICES AND SYMBOLS: Stylus of Nabu
PLEIADES/SEVEN GODS	DEVICES AND SYMBOLS: Dots, seven
SÎN/MOON	DEVICES AND SYMBOLS: Crescent

ANIMAL CARCASSES(?)
    Inverted (*see also* TERMINAL FIELD MOTIFS: Animal or creature [quadruped], below)
        Animals of uncertain type — PFS 1388 (Cat.No. 162)
        Horned animal of undetermined type — PFS 17 (Cat.No. 235), PFS 243 (Cat.No. 303)
        Small lion — PFS 1142 (Cat.No. 39)
        Wild goat pecked by vulture — PFS 1475 (Cat.No. 177)

ANIMAL CARCASSES(?) (*cont.*)

    Suspended on its back (*see also* TERMINAL FIELD MOTIFS: Animal or creature [quadruped], below)

        Small animal of uncertain type — PFS 256 (Cat.No. 198)

ANIMAL CREATURES OTHER THAN HEROES IN HUMAN ATTITUDES (*see also* HEROES AS COMPOSITE CREATURES, below) — PFS 774 (Cat.No. 58), PFS 1071 (Cat.No. 29), PFS 1204 (Cat.No. 136), PFS 1582 (Cat.No. 232)

ANIMALS AND CREATURES AS SECONDARY ELEMENTS OF MAIN DESIGN FIELD

    Bird — PFS 24 (Cat.No. 298), PFS 65 (Cat.No. 241), PFS 123*(?) (Cat.No. 75), PFS 130 (Cat.No. 300), PFS 138 (Cat.No. 186), PFS 266* (Cat.No. 208), PFS 841 (Cat.No. 13), PFS 1249 (Cat.No. 294)

    Fish, insects, reptiles

        Fish — PFS 62(?) (Cat.No. 104), PFS 463 (Cat.No. 264)

        Scorpion creature, winged, human-headed — PFS 4* (Cat.No. 292)

        Snake(?) — PFS 1309s (Cat.No. 229)

    Quadrupeds (*see also* PEDESTAL ANIMAL(S)/CREATURE(S), below)

        Animal of uncertain type

            Inverted — PFS 114 (Cat.No. 284), PFS 1388 (Cat.No. 162)

            Marchant — PFS 190 (Cat.No. 286), PFS 912 (Cat.No. 138)

            Rampant — PFS 818 (Cat.No. 265), PFS 952 (Cat.No. 227)

        Bull

            Marchant — PFS 538 (Cat.No. 312)

        Bull or lion creature, winged — PFS 167 (Cat.No. 255)

        Deer

            Courant — PFS 1286 (Cat.No. 258)

            Rampant — PFS 247 (Cat.No. 245)

        Dog

            Sejant — PFS 1122 (Cat.No. 228)

        Horned animal of undetermined type

            Inverted — PFS 243 (Cat.No. 303)

            Marchant — PFS 190 (Cat.No. 286)

        Lion

            Inverted (small) — PFS 1142 (Cat.No. 39)

            Rampant — PFS 148 (Cat.No. 311), PFS 151 (Cat.No. 223), PFS 152 (Cat.No. 295), PFS 167 (Cat.No. 255), PFS 241 (Cat.No. 252), PFS 260 (Cat.No. 225), PFS 503 (Cat.No. 307), PFS 916 (Cat.No. 226)

                Second in crossed pair — PFS 912 (Cat.No. 138), PFS 952 (Cat.No. 227)

        Lion creature, winged

            Rampant — PFS 100 (Cat.No. 274), PFS 152 (Cat.No. 295), PFS 312 (Cat.No. 237)

        Wild sheep

            Marchant — PFS 197 (Cat.No. 116)

ANKH (*see* DEVICES AND SYMBOLS: *Ankh*, below)

ARCHERS DRAWING THE BOW (*see also* ANIMAL CREATURES OTHER THAN HEROES IN HUMAN ATTITUDES, above; HUMAN/HUMAN-CREATURE FIGURES OTHER THAN HEROES, below; TERMINAL FIELD MOTIFS: Human/Human-creature figure, below; WEAPONS: Arrow[s]; Bow; Bow case; Quiver, below) — PFS 49 (Cat.No. 23), PFS 1204 (Cat.No. 136), PFS 1466 (Cat.No. 234)

ARROWHEAD (*see* DEVICES AND SYMBOLS: Arrowhead, below; WEAPONS: Arrow[s], below)

ATLAS FIGURES (*see also* SUPPORTING FIGURES BELOW FIGURE EMERGENT AND/OR WINGED SYMBOL, below; TERMINAL FIELD MOTIFS: Supporting figures, below) — PFS 774 (Cat.No. 58), PFS 1071 (Cat.No. 29), PFS 1582 (Cat.No. 232)

BEARDS OF HEROES

    Beardless or close-shaved — PFS 2 (Cat.No. 3), PFS 52 (Cat.No. 114), PFS 102 (Cat.No. 1), PFS 301 (Cat.No. 54), PFS 690 (Cat.No. 139), PFS 859* (Cat.No. 205), PFS 1204 (Cat.No. 136), PFS 1499 (Cat.No. 10)

    Long

        Pointed or blunt-pointed — PFS 18 (Cat.No. 15), PFS 24 (Cat.No. 298), PFS 148 (Cat.No. 311), PFS 255 (Cat.No. 233), PFS 280 (Cat.No. 309), PFS 298s (Cat.No. 236), PFS 361 (Cat.No. 47), PFS 807 (Cat.No. 269), PFS 1018 (Cat.No. 185), PFS 1286 (Cat.No. 258)

        Striated — PFS 33 (Cat.No. 220)

        Rounded — PFS 16* (Cat.No. 22), PFS 67 (Cat.No. 293), PFS 146 (Cat.No. 275), PFS 164* (Cat.No. 20), PFS 326 (Cat.No. 100), PFS 516(?) (Cat.No. 98), PFS 536 (Cat.No. 102), PFS 990 (Cat.No. 256), PFS 1142 (Cat.No. 39), PFS 1391 (Cat.No. 248), PFS 1475 (Cat.No. 177), PFS 1501 (Cat.No. 238), PFS 1527 (Cat.No. 32)

        Narrow — PFS 1023 (Cat.No. 127)

        Segmented — PFS 9* (Cat.No. 288), PFS 151 (Cat.No. 223), PFS 538 (Cat.No. 312)

        Striated — PFS 7* (Cat.No. 4), PFS 32* (Cat.No. 180), PFS 98* (Cat.No. 217), PFS 677* (Cat.No. 181)

        Up-curving — PFS 162 (Cat.No. 249)

        Squared — PFS 6 (Cat.No. 304), PFS 29 (Cat.No. 302), PFS 103* (Cat.No. 84), PFS 312 (Cat.No. 237), PFS 514 (Cat.No. 192), PFS 1264s (Cat.No. 206), PFS 1458 (Cat.No. 80), PFS 1658 (Cat.No. 101)

        Segmented — PFS 65 (Cat.No. 241), PFS 180 (Cat.No. 194), PFS 513 (Cat.No. 85), PFS 524 (Cat.No. 2), PFS 1026 (Cat.No. 156)

        Striated — PFS 199* (Cat.No. 305), PFS 774 (Cat.No. 58), PFS 1122 (Cat.No. 228)

        At upper cheek only — PFS 1566* (Cat.No. 218)

    Short or mid-length

        Pointed or blunt-pointed — PFS 10 (Cat.No. 251), PFS 17 (Cat.No. 235), PFS 26 (Cat.No. 299), PFS 30 (Cat.No. 291), PFS 36* (Cat.No. 5), PFS 54* (Cat.No. 277), PFS 79 (Cat.No. 83), PFS 584* (Cat.No. 203), PFS 95 (Cat.No. 25), PFS 120 (Cat.No. 49), PFS 130 (Cat.No. 300), PFS 131 (Cat.No. 170), PFS 132 (Cat.No. 69), PFS 139s (Cat.No. 222), PFS 167 (Cat.No. 255), PFS 190 (Cat.No. 286), PFS 222 (Cat.No. 117), PFS 236 (Cat.No. 213), PFS 247(?) (Cat.No. 245), PFS 249 (Cat.No. 27), PFS 260 (Cat.No. 225), PFS 284* (Cat.No. 111), PFS 297 (Cat.No. 124), PFS 341(?) (Cat.No. 109), PFS 362 (Cat.No. 76), PFS 414 (Cat.No. 280), PFS 496 (Cat.No. 108), PFS 584* (Cat.No. 203), PFS 594 (Cat.No. 103), PFS 614 (Cat.No. 287), PFS 671* (Cat.No. 174), PFS 687 (Cat.No. 119), PFS 719 (Cat.No. 195), PFS 731 (Cat.No. 131), PFS 737 (Cat.No. 281), PFS 740 (Cat.No. 146), PFS 757 (Cat.No. 296), PFS 769* (Cat.No. 278), PFS 781 (Cat.No. 107), PFS 841 (Cat.No. 13), PFS 844 (Cat.No. 59), PFS 849 (Cat.No. 189), PFS 971 (Cat.No. 171), PFS 1030 (Cat.No. 120), PFS 1076 (Cat.No. 193), PFS 1083 (Cat.No. 43), PFS 1123 (Cat.No. 279), PFS 1135 (Cat.No. 66), PFS 1155 (Cat.No. 190), PFS 1227* (Cat.No. 219), PFS 1249 (Cat.No. 294), PFS 1260s (Cat.No. 184), PFS 1309s (Cat.No. 229), PFS 1315s (Cat.No. 253), PFS 1321s (Cat.No. 176), PFS 1325 (Cat.No. 41), PFS 1362 (Cat.No. 30), PFS 1374 (Cat.No. 31), PFS 1406 (Cat.No. 276), PFS 1440 (Cat.No. 42), PFS 1463s (Cat.No. 231), PFS 1483 (Cat.No. 88), PFS 1598 (Cat.No. 63)

        Narrow — PFS 39s (Cat.No. 221), PFS 43* (Cat.No. 207), PFS 63 (Cat.No. 24), PFS 1181 (Cat.No. 210)

        Striated — PFS 959s (Cat.No. 246)

        Rounded — PFS 34 (Cat.No. 73), PFS 80 (Cat.No. 202), PFS 100 (Cat.No. 274), PFS 125 (Cat.No. 250), PFS 149 (Cat.No. 212), PFS 168 (Cat.No. 74), PFS 217 (Cat.No. 135), PFS 225 (Cat.No. 46), PFS 321 (Cat.No. 125), PFS 380 (Cat.No. 95), PFS 673 (Cat.No. 64), PFS 684 (Cat.No. 183), PFS 782 (Cat.No. 105), PFS 818 (Cat.No. 265), PFS 819 (Cat.No. 86), PFS 851 (Cat.No. 60), PFS 882 (Cat.No. 65), PFS 896 (Cat.No. 308), PFS 902 (Cat.No. 243), PFS 931* (Cat.No. 270), PFS 1072 (Cat.No. 61), PFS 1077 (Cat.No. 158), PFS 1090 (Cat.No. 175), PFS 1189 (Cat.No. 8), PFS 1202 (Cat.No. 137), PFS 1236(?) (Cat.No. 159), PFS 1322 (Cat.No. 36), PFS 1375s (Cat.No. 254), PFS 1387 (Cat.No. 72), PFS 1454 (Cat.No. 166), PFS 1465 (Cat.No. 21), PFS 1550 (Cat.No. 14), PFS 1586 (Cat.No. 121), PFS 1624s (Cat.No. 261), PFS 1641 (Cat.No. 18), PFS 1654 (Cat.No. 122)

BEARDS OF HEROES (*cont.*)

    Short or mid-length (*cont.*)

        Rounded (*cont.*)

            Narrow — PFS 632 (Cat.No. 143), PFS 884 (Cat.No. 123), PFS 1020 (Cat.No. 37)

            Segmented — PFS 49 (Cat.No. 23), PFS 65 (Cat.No. 241), PFS 152 (Cat.No. 295), PFS 1217s (Cat.No. 168)

            Striated — PFS 4* (Cat.No. 292), PFS 58 (Cat.No. 242), PFS 146 (Cat.No. 275)

        Squared — PFS 57* (Cat.No. 239), PFS 109 (Cat.No. 197), PFS 123* (Cat.No. 75), PFS 231 (Cat.No. 51), PFS 233 (Cat.No. 52), PFS 234 (Cat.No. 188), PFS 435 (Cat.No. 310), PFS 778 (Cat.No. 11), PFS 795 (Cat.No. 214), PFS 883* (Cat.No. 97), PFS 939 (Cat.No. 267), PFS 970 (Cat.No. 6), PFS 1227* (Cat.No. 219), PFS 1428s (Cat.No. 230), PFS 1630 (Cat.No. 165), PFS 1632* (Cat.No. 244), PFS 1637* (Cat.No. 273), PFS 1684 (Cat.No. 17)

            Narrow — PFS 196 (Cat.No. 224), PFS 1367s (Cat.No. 211), PFS 1489 (Cat.No. 106)

            Segmented — PFS 265 (Cat.No. 240), PFS 266* (Cat.No. 208)

                With mustache shown — PFS 113* (Cat.No. 19)

            Striated — PFS 38 (Cat.No. 16), PFS 64* (Cat.No. 173), PFS 981* (Cat.No. 87), PFS 1101 (Cat.No. 297)

BEARDS OF OTHER HUMANS AND HUMAN-FACED/HUMAN-HEADED CREATURES

    Beardless or close-shaved — PFS 32* (Cat.No. 180), PFS 34 (Cat.No. 73), PFS 38(?) (Cat.No. 16), PFS 49 (Cat.No. 23), PFS 52 (Cat.No. 114), PFS 123* (Cat.No. 75), PFS 168 (Cat.No. 74), PFS 731 (Cat.No. 131), PFS 1023 (Cat.No. 127), PFS 1458(?) (Cat.No. 80), PFS 1658 (Cat.No. 101)

    Long

        Pointed or blunt-pointed — PFS 30 (Cat.No. 291), PFS 58 (Cat.No. 242), PFS 113* (Cat.No. 19), PFS 321 (Cat.No. 125), PFS 526* (Cat.No. 216), PFS 1002 (Cat.No. 196), PFS 1155 (Cat.No. 190)

            Segmented — PFS 4* (Cat.No. 292)

        Rounded — PFS 222 (Cat.No. 117), PFS 514 (Cat.No. 192), PFS 1155 (Cat.No. 190), PFS 1586 (Cat.No. 121)

            Narrow — PFS 222 (Cat.No. 117)

            Segmented — PFS 1632* (Cat.No. 244)

        Squared — PFS 774 (Cat.No. 58), PFS 944 (Cat.No. 129), PFS 1204 (Cat.No. 136), PFS 1641 (Cat.No. 18)

            Curling upward — PFS 1684 (Cat.No. 17)

        Segmented — PFS 4* (Cat.No. 292), PFS 29 (Cat.No. 302), PFS 98* (Cat.No. 217)

            Terminating in beaded segments — PFS 38 (Cat.No. 16)

    Short or mid-length

        Pointed or blunt-pointed — PFS 18 (Cat.No. 15), PFS 26 (Cat.No. 299), PFS 145 (Cat.No. 115), PFS 158 (Cat.No. 94), PFS 217 (Cat.No. 135), PFS 312 (Cat.No. 237), PFS 362 (Cat.No. 76), PFS 370 (Cat.No. 99), PFS 380 (Cat.No. 95), PFS 414 (Cat.No. 280), PFS 514 (Cat.No. 192), PFS 677*(?) (Cat.No. 181), PFS 787 (Cat.No. 79), PFS 902 (Cat.No. 243), PFS 940 (Cat.No. 81), PFS 945 (Cat.No. 96), PFS 1016 (Cat.No. 77), PFS 1026 (Cat.No. 156), PFS 1053 (Cat.No. 45), PFS 1071 (Cat.No. 29), PFS 1454(?) (Cat.No. 166), PFS 1566* (Cat.No. 218)

            Narrow — PFS 916 (Cat.No. 226), PFS 1016 (Cat.No. 77), PFS 1076 (Cat.No. 193), PFS 1454 (Cat.No. 166), PFS 1658 (Cat.No. 101)

        Rounded — PFS 26 (Cat.No. 299), PFS 123* (Cat.No. 75), PFS 326 (Cat.No. 100), PFS 373 (Cat.No. 306), PFS 380 (Cat.No. 95), PFS 538 (Cat.No. 312), PFS 1204 (Cat.No. 136), PFS 1465 (Cat.No. 21), PFS 1586 (Cat.No. 121), PFS 1684 (Cat.No. 17)

            Striated — PFS 164* (Cat.No. 20), PFS 1227* (Cat.No. 219), PFS 1641 (Cat.No. 18)

        Squared — PFS 247 (Cat.No. 245), PFS 399 (Cat.No. 78)

            Narrow — PFS 1613 (Cat.No. 82)

            Segmented — PFS 113* (Cat.No. 19), PFS 516 (Cat.No. 98)

            Striated — PFS 164* (Cat.No. 20)

BIRDS (*see* ANIMALS AND CREATURES AS SECONDARY ELEMENTS OF MAIN DESIGN FIELD, above; TERMINAL FIELD MOTIFS: Animal [non-quadruped], below)

BORDERS (*see also* GROUND LINES, below)

    From seal caps — PFS 2 (Cat.No. 3), PFS 231 (Cat.No. 51), PFS 690(?) (Cat.No. 139)

        Circumstantial evidence of (?) — PFS 594 (Cat.No. 103), PFS 1101 (Cat.No. 297)

    On seal design — PFS 2 (Cat.No. 3), PFS 49 (Cat.No. 23), PFS 43* (Cat.No. 207), PFS 80 (Cat.No. 202), PFS 131 (Cat.No. 170), PFS 146 (Cat.No. 275), PFS 213 (Cat.No. 140), PFS 233 (Cat.No. 52), PFS 263 (Cat.No. 289), PFS 284* (Cat.No. 111), PFS 514 (Cat.No. 192), PFS 594 (Cat.No. 103), PFS 731 (Cat.No. 131), PFS 774 (Cat.No. 58), PFS 778 (Cat.No. 11), PFS 819 (Cat.No. 86), PFS 971 (Cat.No. 171), PFS 1002 (Cat.No. 196), PFS 1072 (Cat.No. 61), PFS 1090 (Cat.No. 175), PFS 1440 (Cat.No. 42), PFS 1550 (Cat.No. 14)

CHAIRS (*see* FURNITURE, below)

COIFFURES OF HEROES

    Mass at back of head or base of neck

        Flattened — PFS 52 (Cat.No. 114), PFS 63 (Cat.No. 24), PFS 64* (Cat.No. 173), PFS 149 (Cat.No. 212), PFS 164* (Cat.No. 20), PFS 199* (Cat.No. 305), PFS 266* (Cat.No. 208), PFS 301 (Cat.No. 54), PFS 435 (Cat.No. 310), PFS 516 (Cat.No. 98), PFS 632 (Cat.No. 143), PFS 749 (Cat.No. 110), PFS 981* (Cat.No. 87), PFS 1458 (Cat.No. 80), PFS 1483 (Cat.No. 88), PFS 1499 (Cat.No. 10), PFS 1566* (Cat.No. 218), PFS 1582 (Cat.No. 232), PFS 1641 (Cat.No. 18)

        Curled upward — PFS 63 (Cat.No. 24), PFS 884 (Cat.No. 123), PFS 1362 (Cat.No. 30)

            Striated — PFS 34 (Cat.No. 73), PFS 1684 (Cat.No. 17)

    Pointed — PFS 916 (Cat.No. 226)

        Curled upward — PFS 853 (Cat.No. 204)

        Narrow — PFS 247 (Cat.No. 245), PFS 1286 (Cat.No. 258), PFS 1309s (Cat.No. 229)

            Curled upward — PFS 58 (Cat.No. 242)

        Thick — PFS 795 (Cat.No. 214)

        Round — PFS 2 (Cat.No. 3), PFS 16* (Cat.No. 22), PFS 18 (Cat.No. 15), PFS 36* (Cat.No. 5), PFS 79 (Cat.No. 83), PFS 86 (Cat.No. 48), PFS 103* (Cat.No. 84), PFS 109 (Cat.No. 197), PFS 130 (Cat.No. 300), PFS 131 (Cat.No. 170), PFS 146 (Cat.No. 275), PFS 222 (Cat.No. 117), PFS 225 (Cat.No. 46), PFS 233 (Cat.No. 52), PFS 234 (Cat.No. 188), PFS 249 (Cat.No. 27), PFS 255 (Cat.No. 233), PFS 312 (Cat.No. 237), PFS 361 (Cat.No. 47), PFS 362 (Cat.No. 76), PFS 514 (Cat.No. 192), PFS 690 (Cat.No. 139), PFS 740 (Cat.No. 146), PFS 882 (Cat.No. 65), PFS 1072 (Cat.No. 61), PFS 1142 (Cat.No. 39), PFS 1146 (Cat.No. 40), PFS 1204 (Cat.No. 136), PFS 1227* (Cat.No. 219), PFS 1325 (Cat.No. 41), PFS 1654 (Cat.No. 122)

        Long, segmented — PFS 180 (Cat.No. 194)

        Rounded — PFS 4* (Cat.No. 292), PFS 7* (Cat.No. 4), PFS 17 (Cat.No. 235), PFS 24 (Cat.No. 298), PFS 26 (Cat.No. 299), PFS 31 (Cat.No. 172), PFS 32* (Cat.No. 180), PFS 39s (Cat.No. 221), PFS 54* (Cat.No. 277), PFS 57* (Cat.No. 239), PFS 67 (Cat.No. 293), PFS 100 (Cat.No. 274), PFS 102 (Cat.No. 1), PFS 113* (Cat.No. 19), PFS 114 (Cat.No. 284), PFS 125 (Cat.No. 250), PFS 131 (Cat.No. 170), PFS 132 (Cat.No. 69), PFS 148 (Cat.No. 311), PFS 153 (Cat.No. 285), PFS 158 (Cat.No. 94), PFS 162 (Cat.No. 249), PFS 167 (Cat.No. 255), PFS 196 (Cat.No. 224), PFS 197 (Cat.No. 116), PFS 201 (Cat.No. 50), PFS 217 (Cat.No. 135), PFS 231 (Cat.No. 51), PFS 243 (Cat.No. 303), PFS 256 (Cat.No. 198), PFS 260 (Cat.No. 225), PFS 263 (Cat.No. 289), PFS 265 (Cat.No. 240), PFS 284* (Cat.No. 111), PFS 298s (Cat.No. 236), PFS 321 (Cat.No. 125), PFS 326 (Cat.No. 100), PFS 344 (Cat.No. 263), PFS 399 (Cat.No. 78), PFS 426 (Cat.No. 55), PFS 494 (Cat.No. 130), PFS 496 (Cat.No. 108), PFS 524 (Cat.No. 2), PFS 536 (Cat.No. 102), PFS 584* (Cat.No. 203), PFS 671* (Cat.No. 174), PFS 684 (Cat.No. 183), PFS 720 (Cat.No. 57), PFS 731 (Cat.No. 131), PFS 737 (Cat.No. 281), PFS 757 (Cat.No. 296), PFS 769* (Cat.No. 278), PFS 774 (Cat.No. 58), PFS 778 (Cat.No. 11), PFS 781 (Cat.No. 107), PFS 818 (Cat.No. 265), PFS 819 (Cat.No. 86), PFS 841 (Cat.No. 13), PFS 844 (Cat.No. 59), PFS 849 (Cat.No. 189), PFS 851 (Cat.No. 60), PFS 859* (Cat.No. 205), PFS 902 (Cat.No. 243), PFS 945 (Cat.No. 96), PFS 959s (Cat.No. 246), PFS 970 (Cat.No. 6), PFS 990 (Cat.No. 256), PFS 1016 (Cat.No. 77), PFS 1018 (Cat.No. 185), PFS 1020 (Cat.No. 37), PFS 1026 (Cat.No. 156), PFS 1030 (Cat.No. 120), PFS 1053 (Cat.No. 45), PFS 1071 (Cat.No. 29), PFS 1076 (Cat.No. 193), PFS 1077 (Cat.No. 158), PFS 1083 (Cat.No. 43), PFS 1090 (Cat.No. 175), PFS 1101 (Cat.No. 297), PFS 1122 (Cat.No. 228), PFS 1123 (Cat.No. 279), PFS 1135 (Cat.No. 66), PFS 1155 (Cat.No. 190), PFS 1181 (Cat.No. 210), PFS 1189

COIFFURES OF HEROES (*cont.*)

   Mass at back of head or base of neck (*cont.*)

      Rounded (*cont.*)

         (Cat.No. 8), PFS 1217s (Cat.No. 168), PFS 1227* (Cat.No. 219), PFS 1249 (Cat.No. 294), PFS 1260s (Cat.No. 184), PSF 1264s (Cat.No. 206), PFS 1300 (Cat.No.191), PFS 1315s (Cat.No. 253), PFS 1320 (Cat.No. 35), PFS 1321s (Cat.No. 176), PFS 1322 (Cat.No. 36), PFS 1367s (Cat.No. 211), PFS 1374 (Cat.No. 31), PFS 1387 (Cat.No. 72), PFS 1406 (Cat.No. 276), PFS 1428s (Cat.No. 230), PFS 1440 (Cat.No. 42), PFS 1444 (Cat.No. 62), PFS 1460 (Cat.No. 9), PFS 1467 (Cat.No. 12), PFS 1485 (Cat.No. 112), PFS 1489 (Cat.No. 106), PFS 1527 (Cat.No. 32), PFS 1550 (Cat.No. 14), PFS 1598 (Cat.No. 63), PFS 1612 (Cat.No. 268), PFS 1624s (Cat.No. 261), PFS 1630 (Cat.No. 165), PFS 1637* (Cat.No. 273), PFS 1658 (Cat.No. 101)

        Curled upward — PFS 29 (Cat.No. 302), PFS 65 (Cat.No. 241), PFS 95 (Cat.No. 25), PFS 120 (Cat.No. 49), PFS 131 (Cat.No. 170), PFS 168 (Cat.No. 74), PFS 614 (Cat.No. 287), PFS 1023 (Cat.No. 127), PFS 1465 (Cat.No. 21), PFS 1475 (Cat.No. 177), PFS 1501 (Cat.No. 238)

        Narrow — PFS 10 (Cat.No. 251), PFS 65 (Cat.No. 241), PFS 98* (Cat.No. 217), PFS 139s (Cat.No. 222), PFS 149 (Cat.No. 212), PFS 594 (Cat.No. 103), PFS 912 (Cat.No. 138), PFS 931* (Cat.No. 270), PFS 939 (Cat.No. 267), PFS 1454 (Cat.No. 166)

        Segmented — PFS 9* (Cat.No. 288), PFS 49 (Cat.No. 23), PFS 123* (Cat.No. 75), PFS 151 (Cat.No. 223), PFS 1391 (Cat.No. 248), PFS 1586 (Cat.No. 121)

        Striated — PFS 38 (Cat.No. 16), PFS 152 (Cat.No. 295), PFS 677* (Cat.No. 181)

        Wavy — PFS 6 (Cat.No. 304), PFS 883* (Cat.No. 97)

      Squared — PFS 896 (Cat.No. 308)

        Long and striated — PFS 33 (Cat.No. 220)

        Narrow — PFS 190 (Cat.No. 286)

        Segmented — PFS 43* (Cat.No. 207), PFS 513 (Cat.No. 85)

   Other hairstyles

      Multiple curls on either side of frontal face — PFS 152 (Cat.No. 295)

      Ponytail — PFS 1375s (Cat.No. 254)

      Rounded mass on either side of frontal face — PFS 538 (Cat.No. 312)

      Short-cropped — PFS 236 (Cat.No. 213), PFS 341(?) (Cat.No. 109), PFS 1202 (Cat.No. 137)

COIFFURES OF OTHER HUMANS AND HUMAN-HEADED CREATURES

   Mass at back of head or base of neck

      Flattened — PFS 26 (Cat.No. 299), PFS 774 (Cat.No. 58), PFS 945 (Cat.No. 96), PFS 1016 (Cat.No. 77), PFS 1641 (Cat.No. 18)

      Pointed — PFS 217 (Cat.No. 135), PFS 787 (Cat.No. 79), PFS 1454 (Cat.No. 166)

        Narrow — PFS 247 (Cat.No. 245)

      Round — PFS 32* (Cat.No. 180), PFS 158 (Cat.No. 94), PFS 312 (Cat.No. 237), PFS 362 (Cat.No. 76), PFS 740 (Cat.No. 146), PFS 1155 (Cat.No. 190), PFS 1458 (Cat.No. 80), PFS 1586 (Cat.No. 121), PFS 1658 (Cat.No. 101)

        Striated — PFS 883* (Cat.No. 97)

      Rounded — PFS 18 (Cat.No. 15), PFS 26 (Cat.No. 299), PFS 49 (Cat.No. 23), PFS 113* (Cat.No. 19), PFS 145 (Cat.No. 115), PFS 164* (Cat.No. 20), PFS 326 (Cat.No. 100), PFS 373 (Cat.No. 306), PFS 380 (Cat.No. 95), PFS 399 (Cat.No. 78), PFS 414 (Cat.No. 280), PFS 447 (Cat.No. 301), PFS 494 (Cat.No. 130), PFS 526* (Cat.No. 216), PFS 538 (Cat.No. 312), PFS 731 (Cat.No. 131), PFS 902 (Cat.No. 243), PFS 1023 (Cat.No. 127), PFS 1053 (Cat.No. 45), PFS 1071 (Cat.No. 29), PFS 1204 (Cat.No. 136), PFS 1586 (Cat.No. 121)

        Curled upward — PFS 516 (Cat.No. 98), PFS 884 (Cat.No. 123), PFS 940 (Cat.No. 81)

        Narrow — PFS 38 (Cat.No. 16), PFS 164* (Cat.No. 20), PFS 321(?) (Cat.No. 125), PFS 916 (Cat.No. 226), PFS 940 (Cat.No. 81)

        Segmented — PFS 29 (Cat.No. 302), PFS 123* (Cat.No. 75)

        Striated — PFS 774 (Cat.No. 58)

      Squared, segmented — PFS 677* (Cat.No. 181)

COIFFURES OF HEROES (*cont.*)
    Other hairstyles
        Pigtail — PFS 38 (Cat.No. 16)
        Ponytail — PFS 4* (Cat.No. 292)
           Wavy — PFS 4* (Cat.No. 292)
        Short-cropped — PFS 18 (Cat.No. 15), PFS 52 (Cat.No. 114)

CRESCENTS (*see* DEVICES AND SYMBOLS, below; TERMINAL FIELD MOTIFS, below; TERMINAL FIELD
    MOTIF CLUSTERS, below)

CROSSED ANIMALS OR CREATURES (*see also* TERMINAL FIELD MOTIF CLUSTERS: Animal/creature groups,
    below)
    Crossed pair — PFS 396 (Cat.No. 178), PFS 912 (Cat.No. 138), PFS 990 (Cat.No. 256)
        Fused with heroic encounter — PFS 737 (Cat.No. 281), PFS 912 (Cat.No. 138), PFS 931* (Cat.No. 270), PFS
            952 (Cat.No. 227)
        With additional animal growing from crossed pair — PFS 213 (Cat.No. 140)
    Faux-crossed pair, fused with heroic encounter — PFS 284* (Cat.No. 111)

CROWNS (*see* HEADDRESSES, below)

CULT ACCOUTREMENTS
    Censer(?) — PFS 38 (Cat.No. 16)
    Drooping lotus(?) — PFS 1641 (Cat.No. 18)

DATE PALMS (*see* TREES, below)

DEVICES AND SYMBOLS (*see also* TERMINAL FIELD MOTIFS, below; TERMINAL FIELD MOTIF CLUSTERS, below)
    Altar with star — PFS 228 (Cat.No. 148)
    Ankh — PFS 284* (Cat.No. 111)
    Arrowhead — PFS 24 (Cat.No. 298)
    Crescent — PFS 1* (Cat.No. 182), PFS 17 (Cat.No. 235), PFS 29 (Cat.No. 302), PFS 38 (Cat.No. 16), PFS 102
        (Cat.No. 1), PFS 112 (Cat.No. 282), PFS 120 (Cat.No. 49), PFS 123* (Cat.No. 75), PFS 153(?) (Cat.No.
        285), PFS 222 (Cat.No. 117), PFS 232 (Cat.No. 26), PFS 294(?) (Cat.No. 53), PFS 326 (Cat.No. 100), PFS
        364 (Cat.No. 149), PFS 494 (Cat.No. 130), PFS 614 (Cat.No. 287), PFS 818 (Cat.No. 265), PFS 896
        (Cat.No. 308), PFS 964 (Cat.No. 260), PFS 1030 (Cat.No. 120), PFS 1076 (Cat.No. 193), PFS 1142 (Cat.No.
        39), PFS 1146 (Cat.No. 40), PFS 1236 (Cat.No. 159), PFS 1440 (Cat.No. 42), PFS 1463s (Cat.No. 231)
        Dotted at center — PFS 720 (Cat.No. 57), PFS 1654 (Cat.No. 122)
        Inverted — PFS 9* (Cat.No. 288), PFS 294(?) (Cat.No. 53), PFS 719(?) (Cat.No. 195), PFS 1101(?) (Cat.No.
            297), PFS 1454(?) (Cat.No. 166)
        Vertical — PFS 1444 (Cat.No. 62)
        V-shaped — PFS 294(?) (Cat.No. 53), PFS 1483 (Cat.No. 88)
    Cross — PFS 1057 (Cat.No. 70)
    Diamond shape (*see also* DEVICES AND SYMBOLS: Rhomb, below) — PFS 385 (Cat.No. 38)
        With projection — PFS 10 (Cat.No. 251)
    Disk
        Winged (*see* DEVICES AND SYMBOLS: Winged symbol, below)
        With radiating nimbus of stars, with figure emergent — PFS 38 (Cat.No. 16)
    Dog, sejant — PFS 1122 (Cat.No. 228)
    Dot(s) (*see also* DEVICES AND SYMBOLS: Rosette, below; Ostrich egg, below; Weapons: Projectile, below)
        Four, in horizontal line — PFS 494 (Cat.No. 130)

DEVICES AND SYMBOLS (cont.)

Dot(s) (cont.)

Seven, in Pleiades formation — PFS 38 (Cat.No. 16)

Single — PFS 10 (Cat.No. 251), PFS 32* (Cat.No. 180), PFS 263 (Cat.No. 289), PFS 1236 (Cat.No. 159)

Small — PFS 145 (Cat.No. 115)

Two small, in diagonal line — PFS 80 (Cat.No. 202)

Drooping lotus(?) — PFS 1641 (Cat.No. 18)

Figure emergent

From nimbus of stars — PFS 38 (Cat.No. 16)

From winged symbol — PFS 7* (Cat.No. 4), PFS 774 (Cat.No. 58), PFS 1053 (Cat.No. 45), PFS 1071 (Cat.No. 29)

Fish — PFS 62(?) (Cat.No. 104), PFS 247 (Cat.No. 245), PFS 263 (Cat.No. 289), PFS 463 (Cat.No. 264)

Floral element/Flower (*see* DEVICES AND SYMBOLS: Trefoil shape(?), below; PLANTS OTHER THAN TREES, below)

Half-oval device — PFS 1375s (Cat.No. 254)

H-shaped device disposed horizontally — PFS 231 (Cat.No. 51)

Infant Horus in papyrus plant — PFS 38 (Cat.No. 16)

Leaf(?) — PFS 38 (Cat.No. 16)

Line, vertical — PFS 152 (Cat.No. 295), PFS 1483 (Cat.No. 88)

Lozenge(s) (*see also* TERMINAL FIELD MOTIFS, below) — PFS 6 (Cat.No. 304), PFS 463 (Cat.No. 264)

One end pointed — PFS 243 (Cat.No. 303)

Nimbus of stars (*see also* DEVICES AND SYMBOLS: Figure emergent from nimbus of stars, above; TERMINAL FIELD MOTIFS: Figure emergent: From nimbus of stars, below) — PFS 38 (Cat.No. 16)

Phallic symbol(?) — PFS 38 (Cat.No. 16)

Rhomb (*see also* DEVICES AND SYMBOLS: Diamond shape, above) — PFS 38 (Cat.No. 16), PFS 944 (Cat.No. 129), PFS 1026 (Cat.No. 156)

Ring shape — PFS 10 (Cat.No. 251)

Bisected by horizontal bar — PFS 1463s (Cat.No. 231)

On pole — PFS 1480 (Cat.No. 257)

With two hooked appendages — PFS 99 (Cat.No. 113)

Rosette — PFS 114 (Cat.No. 284), PFS 145 (Cat.No. 115), PFS 260 (Cat.No. 225), PFS 884 (Cat.No. 123)

Seven dots (*see* DEVICES AND SYMBOLS: Dots: Seven in Pleiades formation, above)

Spade of Marduk — PFS 1501 (Cat.No. 238)

Star (*see also* DEVICES AND SYMBOLS: Altar with star; Nimbus of stars, above; TERMINAL FIELD MOTIFS, below) — PFS 6 (Cat.No. 304), PFS 9* (Cat.No. 288), PFS 26 (Cat.No. 299), PFS 29 (Cat.No. 302), PFS 30 (Cat.No. 291), PFS 95 (Cat.No. 25), PFS 102 (Cat.No. 1), PFS 109 (Cat.No. 197), PFS 112(?) (Cat.No. 282), PFS 123* (Cat.No. 75), PFS 130 (Cat.No. 300), PFS 222 (Cat.No. 117), PFS 280 (Cat.No. 309), PFS 329 (Cat.No. 28), PFS 463 (Cat.No. 264), PFS 538 (Cat.No. 312), PFS 749 (Cat.No. 110), PFS 781 (Cat.No. 107), PFS 853 (Cat.No. 204), PFS 896 (Cat.No. 308), PFS 902 (Cat.No. 243), PFS 1030 (Cat.No. 120), PFS 1081 (Cat.No. 71), PFS 1123 (Cat.No. 279), PFS 1142 (Cat.No. 39), PFS 1236(?) (Cat.No. 159)

Stylus of Nabu — PFS 1501 (Cat.No. 238)

Temple gate — PFS 435 (Cat.No. 310), PFS 709 (Cat.No. 271)

Tree (*see* TERMINAL FIELD MOTIFS: Tree; TREES, below)

Trefoil shape(?) — PFS 112 (Cat.No. 282)

Triangle shape(s) — PFS 247 (Cat.No. 245), PFS 418 (Cat.No. 201)

Large and elongated — PFS 913 (Cat.No. 200)

Uncertain fragmentary element — PFS 123*(?) (Cat.No. 75), PFS 885 (Cat.No. 187), PFS 952 (Cat.No. 227), PFS 1023 (Cat.No. 127), PFS 1081 (Cat.No. 71)

Winged symbol — PFS 62 (Cat.No. 104)

With bird's tail — PFS 62 (Cat.No. 104), PFS 514 (Cat.No. 192), PFS 538(?) (Cat.No. 312), PFS 1189 (Cat.No. 8)

And tendrils — PFS 851 (Cat.No. 60)

With ring atop each wing — PFS 196 (Cat.No. 224)

DEVICES AND SYMBOLS (*cont.*)
    Winged symbol (*cont.*)
        With figure emergent
            With bird's tail — PFS 774 (Cat.No. 58), PFS 1053 (Cat.No. 45)
            And tendrils — PFS 7* (Cat.No. 4), PFS 1071 (Cat.No. 29)
        Y-shaped form — PFS 555 (Cat.No. 93)

EGYPTIANIZING WHITE CROWN (*see* HEADDRESSES OF HEROES: Egyptianizing white crown(?), below)

FLOWERS (*see* DEVICES AND SYMBOLS: Drooping lotus(?); Rosette; Trefoil shape(?), above; PLANTS OTHER THAN TREES, below)

FOOTWEAR
    Boots
        Ankle-length — PFS 690 (Cat.No. 139)
        High — PFS 1202(?) (Cat.No. 137)
    Shoes, strapped Persian type — PFS 301 (Cat.No. 54)

FURNITURE
    Chair, straight-backed — PFS 435 (Cat.No. 310)
        With knob-like finial — PFS 280 (Cat.No. 309)
            And cushion(?) — PFS 148 (Cat.No. 311)

GARMENTS OF HEROES (*see also* FOOTWEAR, above; HEADDRESSES OF HEROES, below)
    Assyrian garment
        Belted — PFS 63 (Cat.No. 24), PFS 79 (Cat.No. 83), PFS 167 (Cat.No. 255), PFS 190 (Cat.No. 286), PFS 197 (Cat.No. 116), PFS 217 (Cat.No. 135), PFS 233 (Cat.No. 52), PFS 236 (Cat.No. 213), PFS 246 (Cat.No. 290), PFS 263 (Cat.No. 289), PFS 362 (Cat.No. 76), PFS 385 (Cat.No. 38), PFS 430 (Cat.No. 56), PFS 494 (Cat.No. 130), PFS 501 (Cat.No. 141), PFS 536 (Cat.No. 102), PFS 807 (Cat.No. 269), PFS 841 (Cat.No. 13), PFS 882 (Cat.No. 65), PFS 885 (Cat.No. 187), PFS 939 (Cat.No. 267), PFS 1030 (Cat.No. 120), PFS 1077 (Cat.No. 158), PFS 1320 (Cat.No. 35)
            With fringe, border, or other detailing — PFS 9* (Cat.No. 288), PFS 16* (Cat.No. 22), PFS 30 (Cat.No. 291), PFS 31 (Cat.No. 172), PFS 32* (Cat.No. 180), PFS 65 (Cat.No. 241), PFS 72 (Cat.No. 147), PFS 86 (Cat.No. 48), PFS 98* (Cat.No. 217), PFS 138 (Cat.No. 186), PFS 199* (Cat.No. 305), PFS 265 (Cat.No. 240), PFS 399 (Cat.No. 78), PFS 513 (Cat.No. 85), PFS 514 (Cat.No. 192), PFS 673 (Cat.No. 64), PFS 740 (Cat.No. 146), PFS 749 (Cat.No. 110), PFS 971 (Cat.No. 171), PFS 1072 (Cat.No. 61), PFS 1101 (Cat.No. 297), PFS 1102 (Cat.No. 132), PFS 1119 (Cat.No. 283), PFS 1122 (Cat.No. 228), PFS 1322 (Cat.No. 36), PFS 1325(?), (Cat.No. 41), PFS 1480 (Cat.No. 257), PFS 1566* (Cat.No. 218), PFS 1582 (Cat.No. 232), PFS 1632* (Cat.No. 244)
            With Persianizing folds — PFS 255 (Cat.No. 233)
            With Persianizing sleeves pushed up — PFS 17 (Cat.No. 235), PFS 1249 (Cat.No. 294)
            With tassel — PFS 222 (Cat.No. 117)
        Not belted (*see also* GARMENTS OF HEROES: Persian court robe, below) — PFS 26 (Cat.No. 299), PFS 29 (Cat.No. 302), PFS 58 (Cat.No. 242), PFS 109 (Cat.No. 197), PFS 112 (Cat.No. 282), PFS 131 (Cat.No. 170), PFS 132 (Cat.No. 69), PFS 145 (Cat.No. 115), PFS 149 (Cat.No. 212), PFS 151 (Cat.No. 223), PFS 162 (Cat.No. 249), PFS 168 (Cat.No. 74), PFS 201 (Cat.No. 50), PFS 228 (Cat.No. 148), PFS 232 (Cat.No. 26), PFS 241 (Cat.No. 252), PFS 260 (Cat.No. 225), PFS 298s (Cat.No. 236), PFS 321 (Cat.No. 125), PFS 329 (Cat.No. 28), PFS 334 (Cat.No. 133), PFS 338 (Cat.No. 262), PFS 396 (Cat.No. 178), PFS 454 (Cat.No. 92), PFS 461 (Cat.No. 90), PFS 526* (Cat.No. 216), PFS 555 (Cat.No. 93), PFS 731 (Cat.No. 131), PFS 781 (Cat.No. 107), PFS 782 (Cat.No. 105), PFS 787 (Cat.No. 79), PFS 795 (Cat.No. 214), PFS 815* (Cat.No. 215), PFS 844 (Cat.No. 59), PFS 853 (Cat.No. 204), PFS 902 (Cat.No. 243), PFS 940 (Cat.No. 81), PFS 944 (Cat.No. 129), PFS 945 (Cat.No. 96),

GARMENTS OF HEROES (cont.)
   Assyrian garment (cont.)
      Not belted (cont.)
         PFS 952 (Cat.No. 227), PFS 964 (Cat.No. 260), PFS 991 (Cat.No. 154), PFS 996 (Cat.No. 155), PFS 1018 (Cat.No. 185), PFS 1023 (Cat.No. 127), PFS 1101 (Cat.No. 297), PFS 1123 (Cat.No. 279), PFS 1135 (Cat.No. 66), PFS 1202 (Cat.No. 137), PFS 1243 (Cat.No. 33), PFS 1249 (Cat.No. 294), PFS 1260s (Cat.No. 184), PFS 1276 (Cat.No. 34), PFS 1311s (Cat.No. 247), PFS 1367s (Cat.No. 211), PFS 1374 (Cat.No. 31), PFS 1387 (Cat.No. 72), PFS 1391 (Cat.No. 248), PFS 1406 (Cat.No. 276), PFS 1437s (Cat.No. 128), PFS 1458 (Cat.No. 80), PFS 1483 (Cat.No. 88), PFS 1485 (Cat.No. 112), PFS 1489 (Cat.No. 106), PFS 1499 (Cat.No. 10), PFS 1501 (Cat.No. 238), PFS 1535 (Cat.No. 164), PFS 1550 (Cat.No. 14), PFS 1586 (Cat.No. 121), PFS 1612 (Cat.No. 268), PFS 1624s (Cat.No. 261), PFS 1630 (Cat.No. 165), PFS 1641 (Cat.No. 18)

         With fringe, border, or other detailing — PFS 6 (Cat.No. 304), PFS 36* (Cat.No. 5), PFS 38 (Cat.No. 16), PFS 64* (Cat.No. 173), PFS 65 (Cat.No. 241), PFS 99 (Cat.No. 113), PFS 114 (Cat.No. 284), PFS 256 (Cat.No. 198), PFS 381 (Cat.No. 179), PFS 480 (Cat.No. 134), PFS 523* (Cat.No. 209), PFS 677* (Cat.No. 181), PFS 778 (Cat.No. 11), PFS 883* (Cat.No. 97), PFS 931* (Cat.No. 270), PFS 981* (Cat.No. 87), PFS 1026 (Cat.No. 156), PFS 1053 (Cat.No. 45), PFS 1083 (Cat.No. 43), PFS 1227* (Cat.No. 219), PFS 1466 (Cat.No. 234), PFS 1475 (Cat.No. 177)

         With Persianizing sleeves pushed up(?) — PFS 247 (Cat.No. 245)
      With Persianizing sleeves pushed up — PFS 1388 (Cat.No. 162)
   Garment of uncertain type
      Belted — PFS 123* (Cat.No. 75), PFS 1091 (Cat.No. 68), PFS 1285 (Cat.No. 44), PFS 1465 (Cat.No. 21)
         Two-tiered, with fringe, border, or other detailing — PFS 818 (Cat.No. 265)
         With fringe, border, or other detailing — PFS 33 (Cat.No. 220), PFS 414 (Cat.No. 280), PFS 503 (Cat.No. 307), PFS 1654 (Cat.No. 122)

      Not belted — PFS 100 (Cat.No. 274), PFS 158 (Cat.No. 94), PFS 180 (Cat.No. 194), PFS 234 (Cat.No. 188), PFS 297 (Cat.No. 124), PFS 312 (Cat.No. 237), PFS 344 (Cat.No. 263), PFS 392 (Cat.No. 91), PFS 426 (Cat.No. 55), PFS 439 (Cat.No. 150), PFS 447 (Cat.No. 301), PFS 516 (Cat.No. 98), PFS 614 (Cat.No. 287), PFS 714 (Cat.No. 152), PFS 720 (Cat.No. 57), PFS 757 (Cat.No. 296), PFS 783 (Cat.No. 153), PFS 896 (Cat.No. 308), PFS 916 (Cat.No. 226), PFS 990 (Cat.No. 256), PFS 1025* (Cat.No. 266), PFS 1071 (Cat.No. 29), PFS 1117 (Cat.No. 67), PFS 1142 (Cat.No. 39), PFS 1153 (Cat.No. 199), PFS 1188 (Cat.No. 144), PFS 1189 (Cat.No. 8), PFS 1236 (Cat.No. 159), PFS 1238 (Cat.No. 160), PFS 1286 (Cat.No. 258), PFS 1447 (Cat.No. 163), PFS 1460 (Cat.No. 9), PFS 1467 (Cat.No. 12)

      With forward leg exposed below knee — PFS 1463s (Cat.No. 231)
      With horizontal lozenge-shaped features — PFS 125 (Cat.No. 250)
   Kilt, belted — PFS 4* (Cat.No. 292), PFS 43* (Cat.No. 207), PFS 152 (Cat.No. 295), PFS 272* (Cat.No. 272), PFS 769* (Cat.No. 278), PFS 1637* (Cat.No. 273)
      With fringed lappet — PFS 57* (Cat.No. 239)
   Nude — PFS 152 (Cat.No. 295), PFS 538 (Cat.No. 312)
   Persian court robe
      Belted (*see also* GARMENTS OF HEROES: Assyrian garment: Belted, with Persianizing sleeves, above)
         Sleeves
            Down
               Spread wide — PFS 1227* (Cat.No. 219)
               Garment folds indicated — PFS 584* (Cat.No. 203)
            Not indicated — PFS 231 (Cat.No. 51)
               Garment folds indicated, lower garment with anomalous hem line — PFS 266* (Cat.No. 208)
            Pushed up — PFS 1684 (Cat.No. 17)
               Folds of lower garment and/or sleeves indicated — PFS 52 (Cat.No. 114), PFS 95 (Cat.No. 25), PFS 113* (Cat.No. 19), PFS 153 (Cat.No. 285), PFS 524 (Cat.No. 2), PFS 632 (Cat.No. 143), PFS 774 (Cat.No. 58), PFS 819 (Cat.No. 86), PFS 851 (Cat.No. 60), PFS 1057 (Cat.No. 70), PFS 1181 (Cat.No. 210)
               Lower garment hitched up over forward leg — PFS 225 (Cat.No. 46), PFS 301 (Cat.No. 54)

GARMENTS OF HEROES (*cont.*)
    Persian court robe (*cont.*)
        Not belted (*see also* GARMENTS OF HEROES: Assyrian garment: Not belted: With Persianizing sleeves pushed up, above; Robe, Not belted, Originally with Persianizing sleeve spread wide, below)
            Sleeves
                Down, garment folds indicated — PFS 39s (Cat.No. 221)
                Not indicated, lower garment hitched up over forward leg(?) — PFS 243 (Cat.No. 303)
                Pushed up — PFS 912 (Cat.No. 138), PFS 1428s (Cat.No. 230)
                    With folds of lower garment and/or sleeves indicated — PFS 7* (Cat.No. 4), PFS 102 (Cat.No. 1), PFS 164* (Cat.No. 20), PFS 196 (Cat.No. 224), PFS 294 (Cat.No. 53), PFS 361 (Cat.No. 47), PFS 859* (Cat.No. 205), PFS 970 (Cat.No. 6), PFS 1020 (Cat.No. 37)
                    With Assyrianizing lower garment — PFS 326 (Cat.No. 100)
                    With lower garment of uncertain type — PFS 24 (Cat.No. 298)
                With lower garment hitched up over forward leg — PFS 1428s (Cat.No. 230)
        Robe
            Belted — PFS 148 (Cat.No. 311), PFS 280 (Cat.No. 309), PFS 849 (Cat.No. 189), PFS 1099 (Cat.No. 169)
                Three-tiered — PFS 594 (Cat.No. 103), PFS 1519 (Cat.No. 167)
                With fringe, border, or other detailing — PFS 2 (Cat.No. 3), PFS 103* (Cat.No. 84), PFS 435 (Cat.No. 310), PFS 709 (Cat.No. 271)
                Two-tiered — PFS 463 (Cat.No. 264)
            Not belted — PFS 62 (Cat.No. 104), PFS 139s (Cat.No. 222), PFS 341 (Cat.No. 109), PFS 364 (Cat.No. 149), PFS 370 (Cat.No. 99), PFS 380 (Cat.No. 95), PFS 418 (Cat.No. 201), PFS 669 (Cat.No. 142), PFS 671* (Cat.No. 174), PFS 687 (Cat.No. 119), PFS 719 (Cat.No. 195), PFS 1016 (Cat.No. 77), PFS 1017 (Cat.No. 126), PFS 1155 (Cat.No. 190), PFS 1264s (Cat.No. 206), PFS 1300 (Cat.No. 191), PFS 1321s (Cat.No. 176), PFS 1444 (Cat.No. 62)
            Originally with Persianizing sleeve spread wide — PFS 373 (Cat.No. 306)
            With frontal Persianizing hemline(?) — PFS 496 (Cat.No. 108)
            With horizontal lozenges— PFS 20 (Cat.No. 145)
                Forming lower garment — PFS 1454 (Cat.No. 166)
        Trousers
            Belted — PFS 737 (Cat.No. 281), PFS 1309s, (Cat.No. 229), PFS 1440 (Cat.No. 42), PFS 1527 (Cat.No. 32)
                With fringe, border, or other detailing — PFS 18 (Cat.No. 15), PFS 34 (Cat.No. 73), PFS 120 (Cat.No. 49), PFS 249 (Cat.No. 27), PFS 1081 (Cat.No. 71), PFS 1598 (Cat.No. 63)
            Not belted — PFS 130(?) (Cat.No. 300), PFS 213(?) (Cat.No. 140), PFS 547 (Cat.No. 151), PFS 1045 (Cat.No. 157), PFS 1146 (Cat.No. 40), PFS 1315s (Cat.No. 253), PFS 1375s (Cat.No. 254)
            Under belted tunic— PFS 1076 (Cat.No. 193)
        Tunic
            Belted — PFS 49 (Cat.No. 23), PFS 54* (Cat.No. 277), PFS 67 (Cat.No. 293), PFS 1165 (Cat.No. 89)
                Over trousers — PFS 1076 (Cat.No. 193)
                With fringe, border, or other detailing — PFS 690 (Cat.No. 139)
                    Upper garment stretched across upper arms — PFS 284* (Cat.No. 111)
            Not belted — PFS 10 (Cat.No. 251), PFS 552(?) (Cat.No. 118), PFS 884(?) (Cat.No. 123), PFS 913 (Cat.No. 200), PFS 959s (Cat.No. 246), PFS 1217s (Cat.No. 168), PFS 1362 (Cat.No. 30)
            With central split or fold — PFS 1090 (Cat.No. 175)
            With side panels and horizontal detailing — PFS 80 (Cat.No. 202)

GARMENTS OF OTHER FIGURES
    Assyrian garment
        Belted — PFS 49 (Cat.No. 23)
            With fringe, border, or other detailing — PFS 538 (Cat.No. 312)
        Not belted — PFS 1641 (Cat.No. 18)

APPENDIX EIGHT: ICONOGRAPHIC FEATURES ON SEALS IN VOLUME I

GARMENTS OF OTHER FIGURES (*cont.*)
    Garment of uncertain type, not belted — PFS 774 (Cat.No. 58), PFS 1053 (Cat.No. 45), PFS 1071 (Cat.No. 29)
    Nude — PFS 38 (Cat.No. 16)
    Persian court robe
        Belted, with sleeves pushed up — PFS 1466 (Cat.No. 234)
        Not belted, with sleeves down — PFS 7* (Cat.No. 4)
    Robe, not belted — PFS 38 (Cat.No. 16), PFS 418 (Cat.No. 201)

GENIES (*see* HUMAN/HUMAN-CREATURE FIGURES OTHER THAN HEROES, below)

GROUND LINES (*see also* BORDERS, above)
    Double — PFS 1260s (Cat.No. 184)
        With exergue — PFS 1321s (Cat.No. 176)
    Single — PFS 146 (Cat.No. 275), PFS 263 (Cat.No. 289), PFS 919s (Cat.No. 259), PFS 971 (Cat.No. 171), PFS 1437s (Cat.No. 128), PFS 1440 (Cat.No. 42), PFS 1624s (Cat.No. 261)
    Under discrete figure — PFS 30 (Cat.No. 291)

HEADDRESSES OF HEROES
    Conical — PFS 225 (Cat.No. 46)
        Turban-like, with projection at front — PFS 883* (Cat.No. 97)
        With projection(s) and knob — PFS 594 (Cat.No. 103)
        With knob — PFS 80 (Cat.No. 202)
    Domed
        Turban-like, with knob — PFS 971 (Cat.No. 171)
        With knob — PFS 298s (Cat.No. 236)
        With projection at front — PFS 1586 (Cat.No. 121)
        With projection at top — PFS 1566* (Cat.No. 218)
        With streamer
            At back — PFS 146 (Cat.No. 275)
            At top — PFS 1315s (Cat.No. 253)
    Domed(?) — PFS 2 (Cat.No. 3), PFS 9* (Cat.No. 288), PFS 18 (Cat.No. 15), PFS 29 (Cat.No. 302), PFS 43* (Cat.No. 207), PFS 49 (Cat.No. 23), PFS 54* (Cat.No. 277), PFS 64* (Cat.No. 173), PFS 65 (Cat.No. 241), PFS 109 (Cat.No. 197), PFS 123* (Cat.No. 75), PFS 131 (Cat.No. 170), PFS 149 (Cat.No. 212), PFS 152 (Cat.No. 295), PFS 162 (Cat.No. 249), PFS 233 (Cat.No. 52), PFS 516 (Cat.No. 98), PFS 769* (Cat.No. 278), PFS 778 (Cat.No. 11), PFS 844 (Cat.No. 59), PFS 959s (Cat.No. 246), PFS 1090 (Cat.No. 175), PFS 1217s (Cat.No. 168), PFS 1227* (Cat.No. 219), PFS 1309s (Cat.No. 229), PFS 1367s (Cat.No. 211), PFS 1458 (Cat.No. 80), PFS 1624s (Cat.No. 261), PFS 1658 (Cat.No. 101)
    Striated — PFS 1465 (Cat.No. 21)
        With projection
            At front — PFS 1072 (Cat.No. 61), PFS 1362 (Cat.No. 30)
            At back — PFS 6 (Cat.No. 304), PFS 690 (Cat.No. 139), PFS 1325 (Cat.No. 41)
        With streamer at top — PFS 1315s (Cat.No. 253)
    Egyptianizing White Crown(?) — PFS 80 (Cat.No. 202)
    Flat — PFS 103* (Cat.No. 84), PFS 114 (Cat.No. 284), PFS 120 (Cat.No. 49), PFS 130 (Cat.No. 300)
        With projection at front — PFS 740 (Cat.No. 146)
        With knob — PFS 4* (Cat.No. 292)
    Persian crown
        Dentate — PFS 34 (Cat.No. 73), PFS 39s (Cat.No. 221), PFS 113* (Cat.No. 19), PFS 139s (Cat.No. 222), PFS 326 (Cat.No. 100), PFS 1428s (Cat.No. 230)
            With studded band — PFS 7* (Cat.No. 4), PFS 79 (Cat.No. 83), PFS 301 (Cat.No. 54)
        Serrated — PFS 1077 (Cat.No. 158)

HEADRESSES OF HEROES (*cont.*)
    Persian fluted tiara — PFS 774 (Cat.No. 58), PFS 1189 (Cat.No. 8)
        With bands — PFS 1155 (Cat.No. 190)
    Polos — PFS 231 (Cat.No. 51), PFS 677* (Cat.No. 181), PFS 1406 (Cat.No. 276), PFS 1483 (Cat.No. 88)
        With band — PFS 196 (Cat.No. 224)

HEADDRESSES OF OTHER HUMANS AND HUMAN-HEADED CREATURES
    Conical
        With knob — PFS 38 (Cat.No. 16)
        With band, knob, and projections — PFS 4* (Cat.No. 292)
    Domed
        Low — PFS 1204 (Cat.No. 136)
        With band — PFS 1155 (Cat.No. 190)
            And projections — PFS 740 (Cat.No. 146)
                With serrated contour — PFS 1155 (Cat.No. 190)
        With band, knob, and projections — PFS 4* (Cat.No. 292)
        With projection(s)
            At back — PFS 1458 (Cat.No. 80)
            At front — PFS 1586 (Cat.No. 121)
            At sides and back — PFS 312 (Cat.No. 237)
        Domed(?) — PFS 32* (Cat.No. 180), PFS 49 (Cat.No. 23), PFS 58 (Cat.No. 242), PFS 362 (Cat.No. 76), PFS 516 (Cat.No. 98)
        Striated — PFS 883* (Cat.No. 97)
    Flat, with projection(s)
        At front (or horn at forehead?) — PFS 740 (Cat.No. 146)
        At front and top — PFS 1454 (Cat.No. 166)
    Persian crown
        Serrated — PFS 113* (Cat.No. 19)
        With point at front, back, and center — PFS 774 (Cat.No. 58)
    Polos — PFS 526* (Cat.No. 216)

HERALDIC COMPOSITIONS OF DISTICTIVE FORM CREATED BY INTERACTION OF ANIMALS/CREATURES OF HEROIC ENCOUNTER WITH THE TERMINAL FIELD (*see also* TERMINAL FIELD MOTIF CLUSTERS: Animals/creatures in self-contained heraldic pairs before plant or tree, below)
    Animals/creatures framing terminal field cluster or single animal, device/symbol, inscription, and/or plant/tree
        Bird (goose) in flight — PFS 31 (Cat.No. 172)
        Crescent — PFS 1076 (Cat.No. 193), PFS 1440 (Cat.No. 42), PFS 1146 (Cat.No. 40)
            And bird — PFS 326 (Cat.No. 100)
        Diamond shape — PFS 385 (Cat.No. 38)
        Floral element — PFS 1204 (Cat.No. 136)
            And rampant creature — PFS 162 (Cat.No. 249)
        Heraldic group of animals before stylized tree — PFS 225 (Cat.No. 46)
        Inscription — PFS 1* (Cat.No. 182), PFS 32* (Cat.No. 180), PFS 64* (Cat.No. 173), PFS 164* (Cat.No. 20), PFS 671* (Cat.No. 174), PFS 677* (Cat.No. 181)
            And palm tree — PFS 113* (Cat.No. 19)
        Plant — PFS 841 (Cat.No. 13)
        Star — PFS 749 (Cat.No. 110), PFS 1142 (Cat.No. 39)
        Tree (conifer) — PFS 131 (Cat.No. 170), PFS 496 (Cat.No. 108)
        Tree (stylized) — PFS 1091 (Cat.No. 68)
        Triangle shape — PFS 913 (Cat.No. 200)

HERALDIC COMPOSITIONS OF DISTICTIVE FORM CREATED BY INTERACTION OF ANIMALS/CREATURES
OF HEROIC ENCOUNTER WITH THE TERMINAL FIELD (*cont.*)
    Animals/creatures framing terminal field cluster or single animal, device/symbol, inscription, and/or plant/tree (*cont.*)
        Winged symbol — PFS 62 (Cat.No. 104)
            And papyrus plant — PFS 514 (Cat.No. 192)
    Animals/creatures not framing a terminal field element — PFS 190 (Cat.No. 286), PFS 778 (Cat.No. 11), PFS 1465 (Cat.No. 21), PFS 1467 (Cat.No. 12), PFS 1519 (Cat.No. 167)

HEROES AS COMPOSITE CREATURES
    Bull creature
        Winged
            With human shoulders and arms — PFS 1* (Cat.No. 182)
                And human-head — PFS 1204 (Cat.No. 136)
            With human head, torso, and arms — PFS 684 (Cat.No. 183)
    Bull or lion creature, winged with human head and torso — PFS 146 (Cat.No. 275)
    Human creature
        With ovoid bird's torso — PFS 1188 (Cat.No. 144)
        With four wings — PFS 6 (Cat.No. 304), PFS 36* (Cat.No. 5), PFS 58 (Cat.No. 242), PFS 64* (Cat.No. 173), PFS 72(?) (Cat.No. 147), PFS 103* (Cat.No. 84), PFS 112 (Cat.No. 282), PFS 180 (Cat.No. 194), PFS 297 (Cat.No. 124), PFS 321 (Cat.No. 125), PFS 463 (Cat.No. 264), PFS 513 (Cat.No. 85), PFS 516(?) (Cat.No. 98), PFS 594 (Cat.No. 103), PFS 782 (Cat.No. 105), PFS 883* (Cat.No. 97), PFS 1026 (Cat.No. 156), PFS 1276(?) (Cat.No. 34), PFS 1387(?) (Cat.No. 72), PFS 1586 (Cat.No. 121), PFS 1658 (Cat.No. 101)
        With ovoid bird's torso — PFS 1202 (Cat.No. 137)
        With single wing — PFS 263 (Cat.No. 289), PFS 896 (Cat.No. 308), PFS 1632* (Cat.No. 244)
        With two wings — PFS 30 (Cat.No. 291), PFS 65 (Cat.No. 241), PFS 98* (Cat.No. 217), PFS 931* (Cat.No. 270), PFS 964 (Cat.No. 260), PFS 1566* (Cat.No. 218)
        With bird's feet — PFS 1321s (Cat.No. 176)

HEROES AS NUDE FRONTALLY-FACED FIGURES — PFS 152 (Cat.No. 295), PFS 538 (Cat.No. 312)

HEROES, MULTIPLE (*see* HEROIC ENCOUNTER IMAGES OF UNUSUAL FORMAT: Double hero encounter, below)

HEROIC ENCOUNTER IMAGES OF UNUSUAL FORMAT (*see also* HEROIC POSTURES OTHER THAN BASIC STANDING PROFILE WITH TORSO FRONTAL, below)
    Control encounter and combat encounter performed simultaneously by one hero
        With one animal/creature — PFS 6 (Cat.No. 304), PFS 896 (Cat.No. 308)
        With two separate animals/creatures — PFS 24 (Cat.No. 298), PFS 29 (Cat.No. 302), PFS 243 (Cat.No. 303), PFS 447 (Cat.No. 301)
    Control encounter with only one animal/creature grasped at two opposing appendages — PFS 284* (Cat.No. 111)
    Double encounter images (two discrete encounters on one seal) — PFS 146 (Cat.No. 275), PFS 152 (Cat.No. 295), PFS 199*(?) (Cat.No. 305), PFS 757 (Cat.No. 296), PFS 1249 (Cat.No. 294)
    Double hero encounter (two heroes deployed in one encounter) — PFS 65 (Cat.No. 241), PFS 931* (Cat.No. 270), PFS 1101 (Cat.No. 297), PFS 1227* (Cat.No. 219)
    Heroic encounter fused with crossed animals motif
        In combat encounter — PFS 737 (Cat.No. 281), PFS 931* (Cat.No. 270), PFS 952 (Cat.No. 227)
        In control encounter — PFS 912 (Cat.No. 138)
            With faux-crossed animal creature group — PFS 284* (Cat.No. 111)

HEROIC ENCOUNTER IMAGES OF UNUSUAL FORMAT (*cont.*)
    Heroic encounter fused with well-defined heraldic motif
        In combat encounter — PFS 162 (Cat.No. 249), PFS 190 (Cat.No. 167)
        In control encounter — PFS 62 (Cat.No. 104), PFS 225 (Cat.No. 46), PFS 496 (Cat.No. 108), PFS 749 (Cat.No. 110), PFS 1204 (Cat.No. 136), PFS 1519 (Cat.No. 167)

HEROIC POSTURES OTHER THAN BASIC STANDING PROFILE WITH TORSO FRONTAL
    Athletic posture — PFS 10 (Cat.No. 251)
    Cupping rather than grasping gesture — PFS 1586 (Cat.No. 121)
    Forward arm (in combat encounter) with elbow up — PFS 57* (Cat.No. 239), PFS 65 (Cat.No. 241), PFS 98* (Cat.No. 217), PFS 272* (Cat.No. 272), PFS 1566* (Cat.No. 218)
    Forward leg bent and/or raised (*see also* HEROIC POSTURES OTHER THAN BASIC STANDING PROFILE WITH TORSO FRONTAL: *Knielauf*-pose, below) — PFS 32* (Cat.No. 180), PFS 58 (Cat.No. 242), PFS 109 (Cat.No. 197), PFS 167 (Cat.No. 255), PFS 190 (Cat.No. 286), PFS 201 (Cat.No. 50), PFS 228 (Cat.No. 148), PFS 233 (Cat.No. 52), PFS 241 (Cat.No. 252), PFS 263 (Cat.No. 289), PFS 265 (Cat.No. 240), PFS 321 (Cat.No. 125), PFS 461 (Cat.No. 90), PFS 795 (Cat.No. 214), PFS 807 (Cat.No. 269), PFS 1026 (Cat.No. 156), PFS 1123 (Cat.No. 279), PFS 1204 (Cat.No. 136), PFS 1227* (Cat.No. 219), PFS 1276 (Cat.No. 34), PFS 1286 (Cat.No. 258), PFS 1475 (Cat.No. 177), PFS 1550 (Cat.No. 14), PFS 1586 (Cat.No. 121)
        With foot on animal or creature — PFS 6 (Cat.No. 304), PFS 30 (Cat.No. 291), PFS 43* (Cat.No. 207), PFS 54* (Cat.No. 277), PFS 57* (Cat.No. 239), PFS 80 (Cat.No. 202), PFS 98* (Cat.No. 217), PFS 272* (Cat.No. 272), PFS 538 (Cat.No. 312), PFS 769* (Cat.No. 278), PFS 815* (Cat.No. 215), PFS 931* (Cat.No. 270), PFS 1227*(?) (Cat.No. 219), PFS 1311s (Cat.No. 247), PFS 1566* (Cat.No. 218), PFS 1632* (Cat.No. 244), PFS 1637* (Cat.No. 273)
    Frontal face — PFS 152 (Cat.No. 295), PFS 418(?) (Cat.No. 201), PFS 538 (Cat.No. 312)
    Knielauf-pose (rear leg as well as forward leg bent) — PFS 67 (Cat.No. 293), PFS 120 (Cat.No. 49), PFS 1527 (Cat.No. 32)
        With foot on animal or creature — PFS 1309s (Cat.No. 229)
    Profile torso — PFS 43* (Cat.No. 207), PFS 199* (Cat.No. 305), PFS 373 (Cat.No. 306), PFS 584* (Cat.No. 203), PFS 859* (Cat.No. 205), PFS 931* (Cat.No. 270), PFS 964 (Cat.No. 260), PFS 1264s (Cat.No. 206)
    Quasi-*knielauf*-pose, hero suspended in design field — PFS 1315s (Cat.No. 253)
    Seated — PFS 148 (Cat.No. 311), PFS 280 (Cat.No. 309), PFS 435 (Cat.No. 310)
    Standing
        On feet of paired creatures — PFS 4* (Cat.No. 292), PFS 1519 (Cat.No. 167)
        On inanimate pedestal element — PFS 62 (Cat.No. 104)
        On pedestal animal(s)/creature(s) — (*see also* PEDESTAL ANIMAL(S)/CREATURE(S), below) — PFS 31 (Cat.No. 172), PFS 36* (Cat.No. 5), PFS 164* (Cat.No. 20), PFS 396 (Cat.No. 178), PFS 523* (Cat.No. 209), PFS 524 (Cat.No. 2), PFS 538(?) (Cat.No. 312), PFS 931* (Cat.No. 270), PFS 1454(?) (Cat.No. 166)
        Striding pose — PFS 1* (Cat.No. 182), PFS 4* (Cat.No. 292), PFS 6 (Cat.No. 304), PFS 9* (Cat.No. 288), PFS 18 (Cat.No. 15), PFS 43* (Cat.No. 207), PFS 54* (Cat.No. 277), PFS 57* (Cat.No. 239), PFS 64* (Cat.No. 173), PFS 72 (Cat.No. 147), PFS 80 (Cat.No. 202), PFS 98* (Cat.No. 217), PFS 109 (Cat.No. 197), PFS 138 (Cat.No. 186), PFS 151 (Cat.No. 223), PFS 164* (Cat.No. 20), PFS 201 (Cat.No. 50), PFS 213 (Cat.No. 140), PFS 217 (Cat.No. 135), PFS 222 (Cat.No. 117), PFS 249 (Cat.No. 27), PFS 256 (Cat.No. 198), PFS 265 (Cat.No. 240), PFS 321 (Cat.No. 125), PFS 381 (Cat.No. 179), PFS 396 (Cat.No. 178), PFS 454 (Cat.No. 92), PFS 461 (Cat.No. 90), PFS 480 (Cat.No. 134), PFS 514 (Cat.No. 192), PFS 538 (Cat.No. 312), PFS 555 (Cat.No. 93), PFS 677* (Cat.No. 181), PFS 684 (Cat.No. 183), PFS 749 (Cat.No. 110), PFS 769* (Cat.No. 278), PFS 778 (Cat.No. 11), PFS 781 (Cat.No. 107), PFS 782 (Cat.No. 105), PFS 795 (Cat.No. 214), PFS 902 (Cat.No. 243), PFS 931* (Cat.No. 270), PFS 945 (Cat.No. 96), PFS 971 (Cat.No. 171), PFS 991 (Cat.No. 154), PFS 1018 (Cat.No. 185), PFS 1026 (Cat.No. 156), PFS 1122 (Cat.No. 228), PFS 1227* (Cat.No. 219), PFS 1321s (Cat.No. 176), PFS 1388 (Cat.No. 162), PFS 1391 (Cat.No. 248), PFS 1437s (Cat.No. 128), PFS 1475 (Cat.No. 177), PFS 1483 (Cat.No. 88), PFS 1489 (Cat.No. 106), PFS 1535 (Cat.No. 164), PFS 1550 (Cat.No. 14), PFS 1566* (Cat.No. 218), PFS 1598 (Cat.No. 63), PFS 1632* (Cat.No. 244), PFS 1637* (Cat.No. 273)

APPENDIX EIGHT: ICONOGRAPHIC FEATURES ON SEALS IN VOLUME I

HUMAN/HUMAN-CREATURE FIGURES OTHER THAN HEROES
    Deity
        Emergent from winged symbol — PFS 7* (Cat.No. 4), PFS 774 (Cat.No. 58), PFS 1053 (Cat.No. 45), PFS 1071 (Cat.No. 29)
        (Female?) emergent from nimbus of stars — PFS 38 (Cat.No. 16)
        Infant Horus — PFS 38 (Cat.No. 16)
    Genie — PFS 418 (Cat.No. 201), PFS 1099 (Cat.No. 169)
    Weapon-bearing figure
        Archer — PFS 49 (Cat.No. 23), PFS 1466 (Cat.No. 234)
        With sheathed sword and flail — PFS 538 (Cat.No. 312)
    Winged nude frontal female — PFS 1485 (Cat.No. 112)
    Worshiper/cult attendant — PFS 1641 (Cat.No. 18)

INSCRIPTIONS (*see also* TERMINAL FIELD MOTIFS, below; TERMINAL FIELD MOTIF CLUSTERS: Device[s]/symbol[s], inscription, and/or plant[s]/tree[s], below)
    Aramaic
        In panel
            Oriented along horizontal axis — PFS 16* (Cat.No. 22), PFS 54* (Cat.No. 277), PFS 981* (Cat.No. 87)
            Oriented along vertical axis, without case lines — PFS 266* (Cat.No. 208)
        Without panel
            Oriented along horizontal axis across top of seal — PFS 123* (Cat.No. 75)
            Oriented along vertical axis — PFS 9* (Cat.No. 288), PFS 164* (Cat.No. 20), PFS 815* (Cat.No. 215)
    Babylonian (*see also* INSCRIPTIONS: Old Persian, Elamite, Babylonian: In panel: Oriented along vertical axis, below)
        Without panel
            Oriented along vertical axis, reversed — PFS 1632* (Cat.No. 244)
    Babylonian(?)
        Without panel
            Oriented along vertical axis, read from bottom to top(?) — PFS 883* (Cat.No. 97)
    Elamite (*see also* INSCRIPTIONS: Old Persian, Elamite, Babylonian: In panel: Oriented along vertical axis, below)
        In panel
            Oriented along horizontal axis — PFS 36* (Cat.No. 5), PFS 43* (Cat.No. 207), PFS 272* (Cat.No. 272), PFS 584* (Cat.No. 203), PFS 769* (Cat.No. 278), PFS 1566* (Cat.No. 218)
                With one sign in design field — PFS 1637* (Cat.No. 273)
            Oriented along vertical axis — PFS 1* (Cat.No. 182)
        Without panel
            Oriented along horizontal axis — PFS 57* (Cat.No. 239)
                With bottom line of inscription integrated into main as well as terminal field — PFS 103* (Cat.No. 84)
                With horizontal case lines — PFS 4* (Cat.No. 292), PFS 98* (Cat.No. 217)
            Oriented along vertical axis — PFS 32* (Cat.No. 180)
    Elamite(?)
        In panel
            Oriented along horizontal axis — PFS 199* (Cat.No. 305)
        Without panel
            Oriented along horizontal axis, with horizontal case line(s) — PFS 931* (Cat.No. 270), PFS 1025* (Cat.No. 266)
    Mock(?) (*see* INSCRIPTIONS: Unknown language, below)
    Old Persian, Elamite, Babylonian
        In panel
            Oriented along vertical axis — PFS 7* (Cat.No. 4), PFS 113* (Cat.No. 19)

INSCRIPTIONS (*cont.*)
    Uncertain language in cuneiform
        In panel
            Oriented along horizontal axis — PFS 523* (Cat.No. 209), PFS 859* (Cat.No. 205), PFS 1227* (Cat.No. 219)
            Oriented along vertical axis — PFS 64* (Cat.No. 173), PFS 526* (Cat.No. 216)
    Unknown language
        In cuneiform-like script
            In panel
                Oriented along vertical axis — PFS 671* (Cat.No. 174)
            Without panel
                Oriented along vertical axis — PFS 677* (Cat.No. 181)
        In Greek script
            Without panel
                Oriented along horizontal axis across top of seal — PFS 284* (Cat.No. 111)

LINE BORDER (*see* BORDERS: On seal design, above)

MUSTACHE — PFS 113* (Cat.No. 19)

OSTRICH EGG — PFS 263 (Cat.No. 289)

PALM TREE (*see* TREES: Date palm; Palm, below)

PEDESTAL ANIMAL(S)/CREATURE(S)
    Couchant
        Addorsed
            Creatures of uncertain type, winged — PFS 396 (Cat.No. 178)
        Heraldic
            Creatures of uncertain type, winged, each supporting one hero — PFS 931* (Cat.No. 270)
    Couchant(?)
        Addorsed
            Bull creatures, winged — PFS 36* (Cat.No. 5)
            Lion creatures, winged, horned — PFS 164* (Cat.No. 20)
        Format and creature not preserved — PFS 1454 (Cat.No. 166)
    Courant
        Addorsed
            Lion creatures (one, winged), horned — PFS 524 (Cat.No. 2)
        Lion — PFS 523* (Cat.No. 209)
    Marchant
        Bull — PFS 538(?) (Cat.No. 312)
        Humped bull — PFS 31 (Cat.No. 172)

PEDESTAL PAIRS WITH FEET ONLY SERVING AS SUPPORTS
    Marchant
        Scorpion creatures — PFS 4* (Cat.No. 292)
    Rampant
        Lion or bull creatures, winged — PFS 1519 (Cat.No. 167)

PEDESTAL DEVICES, INANIMATE
   Winged symbol — PFS 62 (Cat.No. 104)

PERSIAN COURT ROBES (*see* GARMENTS OF HEROES; GARMENTS OF OTHER FIGURES, above)

PERSIAN CROWNS (*see* HEADDRESSES OF HEROES; HEADDRESSES OF OTHER HUMANS AND HUMAN-HEADED CREATURES, above)

PHALLIC SYMBOL(?) — PFS 38 (Cat.No. 16)

PLANTS OTHER THAN TREES (*see also* DEVICES AND SYMBOLS: Drooping lotus; Leaf; Rosette; Trefoil shape, above)
   Plant — PFS 731 (Cat.No. 131), PFS 841 (Cat.No. 13)
   Floral element — PFS 162 (Cat.No. 249), PFS 614 (Cat.No. 287), PFS 632 (Cat.No. 143), PFS 1204 (Cat.No. 136), PFS 1466 (Cat.No. 234)
      Lotus blossoms and buds — PFS 38 (Cat.No. 16)
      Papyrus plant — PFS 38 (Cat.No. 16), PFS 514 (Cat.No. 192)

SHOES (*see* FOOTWEAR, above)

SHRINES (*see* DEVICES AND SYMBOLS: Temple gate, above)

STARS (*see* DEVICES AND SYMBOLS, above; TERMINAL FIELD MOTIFS, below; TERMINAL FIELD MOTIF CLUSTERS, below)

SUPPORTING FIGURES BELOW FIGURE EMERGENT AND/OR WINGED SYMBOL (*see also* ATLAS FIGURES, above; TERMINAL FIELD MOTIFS, below) — PFS 774 (Cat.No. 58), PFS 1053 (Cat.No. 45), PFS 1071 (Cat.No. 29), PFS 1582(?) (Cat.No. 232)

TEMPLE GATE SYMBOLS (*see* DEVICES AND SYMBOLS, above)

TERMINAL FIELD MOTIFS (*see also* TERMINAL FIELD MOTIF CLUSTERS, below)
   Altar with star — PFS 228 (Cat.No. 148)
   Animal (non-quadruped)
      Bird — PFS 30 (Cat.No. 291), PFS 31 (Cat.No. 172), PFS 123*(?) (Cat.No. 75), PFS 326 (Cat.No. 100), PFS 329 (Cat.No. 28), PFS 461 (Cat.No. 90), PFS 939 (Cat.No. 267), PFS 1099 (Cat.No. 169), PFS 1122 (Cat.No. 228), PFS 1374 (Cat.No. 31), PFS 1388 (Cat.No. 162), PFS 1475 (Cat.No. 177), PFS 1527 (Cat.No. 32)
      Bird creature, rampant, winged, human-headed — PFS 247 (Cat.No. 245), PFS 916 (Cat.No. 226)
      Fish, insect, or reptile — PFS 247 (Cat.No. 245), PFS 263 (Cat.No. 289)
   Animal or creature (quadruped)
      Courant — PFS 463 (Cat.No. 264), PFS 1181 (Cat.No. 210)
      Inverted — PFS 17 (Cat.No. 235), PFS 1388 (Cat.No. 162), PFS 1475 (Cat.No. 177)
      Marchant — PFS 246 (Cat.No. 290), PFS 501 (Cat.No. 141), PFS 536 (Cat.No. 102), PFS 1322(?) (Cat.No. 36), PFS 1406(?) (Cat.No. 276)
      Rampant — PFS 9* (Cat.No. 288), PFS 33 (Cat.No. 220), PFS 80 (Cat.No. 202), PFS 153 (Cat.No. 285), PFS 162 (Cat.No. 249), PFS 197 (Cat.No. 116), PFS 236 (Cat.No. 213), PFS 246 (Cat.No. 290), PFS 255 (Cat.No. 233), PFS 265 (Cat.No. 240), PFS 338 (Cat.No. 262), PFS 344 (Cat.No. 263), PFS 687 (Cat.No. 119), PFS 853 (Cat.No. 204), PFS 902 (Cat.No. 243), PFS 916 (Cat.No. 226), PFS 991

TERMINAL FIELD MOTIFS (*cont.*)

    Animal or creature (quadruped) (*cont.*)

        Rampant (*cont.*)

            (Cat.No. 154), PFS 1016 (Cat.No. 77), PFS 1119 (Cat.No. 283), PFS 1123 (Cat.No. 279), PFS 1202(?) (Cat.No. 137), PFS 1243 (Cat.No. 33), PFS 1320 (Cat.No. 35), PFS 1285 (Cat.No. 44), PFS 1444 (Cat.No. 62), PFS 1480 (Cat.No. 257), PFS 1612 (Cat.No. 268)

            Atlas pose/related supporting posture — PFS 774 (Cat.No. 58), PFS 1053 (Cat.No. 45), PFS 1071 (Cat.No. 29), PFS 1582 (Cat.No. 232)

        Suspended vertically in mid-field — PFS 1285 (Cat.No. 44)

        Suspended on its back — PFS 256 (Cat.No. 198)

    Censer(?) — PFS 38 (Cat.No. 16)

    Column — PFS 1099 (Cat.No. 169)

    Crescent — PFS 17 (Cat.No. 235), PFS 102 (Cat.No. 1), PFS 120 (Cat.No. 49), PFS 153(?) (Cat.No. 285), PFS 222 (Cat.No. 117), PFS 232 (Cat.No. 26), PFS 326 (Cat.No. 100), PFS 364 (Cat.No. 149), PFS 494 (Cat.No. 130), PFS 818 (Cat.No. 265), PFS 1030 (Cat.No. 120), PFS 1076 (Cat.No. 193), PFS 1146 (Cat.No. 40), PFS 1440 (Cat.No. 42)

        Dotted at center — PFS 720 (Cat.No. 57), PFS 1654 (Cat.No. 122)

        Inverted — PFS 294(?) (Cat.No. 53)

        V-shaped — PFS 294(?) (Cat.No. 53), PFS 1483 (Cat.No. 88)

        Vertical — PFS 1444 (Cat.No. 62)

    Cross — PFS 1057 (Cat.No. 70)

    Diamond shape — PFS 385 (Cat.No. 38)

    Disk, winged (*see* TERMINAL FIELD MOTIFS: Winged symbol, below)

    Dots

        Four — PFS 494 (Cat.No. 130)

        Seven — PFS 38 (Cat.No. 16)

    Figure emergent

        From nimbus of stars — PFS 38 (Cat.No. 16)

        From winged symbol — PFS 1053 (Cat.No. 45). PFS 1071 (Cat.No. 29)

    Fish (*see* TERMINAL FIELD MOTIFS: Animal [non-quadruped], above)

    Floral element (*see* TERMINAL FIELD MOTIFS: Plant other than tree, below)

    Genie (*see* TERMINAL FIELD MOTIFS: Human/human-creature figure, below)

    H-shape disposed horizontally — PFS 231 (Cat.No. 51)

    Human/human-creature figure (*see also* TERMINAL FIELD MOTIFS: Figure emergent, above)

        Genie — PFS 418 (Cat.No. 201), PFS 1099 (Cat.No. 169)

    Inscription (*see also* INSCRIPTIONS, above) — PFS 1* (Cat.No. 182), PFS 4* (Cat.No. 292), PFS 7* (Cat.No. 4), PFS 16* (Cat.No. 22), PFS 32* (Cat.No. 180), PFS 36* (Cat.No. 5), PFS 43* (Cat.No. 207), PFS 54* (Cat.No. 277), PFS 57* (Cat.No. 239), PFS 64* (Cat.No. 173), PFS 98* (Cat.No. 217), PFS 103* (Cat.No. 84), PFS 113* (Cat.No. 19), PFS 199* (Cat.No. 305), PFS 164* (Cat.No. 20), PFS 272* (Cat.No. 272), PFS 266* (Cat.No. 208), PFS 523* (Cat.No. 209), PFS 526* (Cat.No. 216), PFS 584* (Cat.No. 203), PFS 671* (Cat.No. 174), PFS 677* (Cat.No. 181), PFS 769* (Cat.No. 278), PFS 883* (Cat.No. 97), PFS 815* (Cat.No. 215), PFS 859* (Cat.No. 205), PFS 931* (Cat.No. 270), PFS 981* (Cat.No. 87), PFS 1025* (Cat.No. 266), PFS 1227* (Cat.No. 219), PFS 1566* (Cat.No. 218), PFS 1632* (Cat.No. 244), PFS 1637* (Cat.No. 273)

    Leaf(?) — PFS 38 (Cat.No. 16)

    Line, vertical — PFS 152 (Cat.No. 295)

    Lozenges — PFS 463 (Cat.No. 264)

    Nimbus of stars (*see* TERMINAL FIELD MOTIFS: Figure emergent, above)

    Phallic symbol(?) — PFS 38 (Cat.No. 16)

    Plant other than tree — PFS 38 (Cat.No. 16), PFS 162 (Cat.No. 249), PFS 514 (Cat.No. 192), PFS 614 (Cat.No. 287), PFS 632 (Cat.No. 143), PFS 731 (Cat.No. 131), PFS 841 (Cat.No. 13), PFS 1204 (Cat.No. 136)

TERMINAL FIELD MOTIFS (*cont.*)
    Pole with star (*see* TERMINAL FIELD MOTIFS: Altar with star, above)
    Rosette — PFS 145 (Cat.No. 115), PFS 114 (Cat.No. 284), PFS 260 (Cat.No. 225), PFS 884 (Cat.No. 123)
    Seven dots (*see* TERMINAL FIELD MOTIFS: Dots, above)
    Spade of Marduk — PFS 1501 (Cat.No. 238)
    Star (*see also* TERMINAL FIELD MOTIFS: Altar with star, above) — PFS 9* (Cat.No. 288), PFS 30 (Cat.No. 291), PFS 95 (Cat.No. 25), PFS 130 (Cat.No. 300), PFS 222 (Cat.No. 117), PFS 280 (Cat.No. 309), PFS 463 (Cat.No. 264), PFS 749 (Cat.No. 110), PFS 781 (Cat.No. 107), PFS 853 (Cat.No. 204), PFS 902 (Cat.No. 243), PFS 1030 (Cat.No. 120), PFS 1081 (Cat.No. 71), PFS 1142 (Cat.No. 39)
    Stylus of Nabu — PFS 1501 (Cat.No. 238)
    Supporting figures under figure emergent and/or winged symbol — PFS 774 (Cat.No. 58), PFS 1053 (Cat.No. 45), PFS 1071 (Cat.No. 29)
        Supported element not preserved — PFS 1582 (Cat.No. 232)
    Temple gate — PFS 435 (Cat.No. 310), PFS 709 (Cat.No. 271)
    Tree
        Conifer — PFS 334 (Cat.No. 133), PFS 496 (Cat.No. 108)
            On stand with "arms" — PFS 971 (Cat.No. 171)
        Date palm — PFS 113* (Cat.No. 19), PFS 123* (Cat.No. 75), PFS 125 (Cat.No. 250), PFS 853 (Cat.No. 204), PFS 1276 (Cat.No. 34),
            Pair — PFS 7* (Cat.No. 4)
            With framing floral fronds at base — PFS 1236 (Cat.No. 159)
        Palm — PFS 80 (Cat.No. 202), PFS 148 (Cat.No. 311), PFS 149 (Cat.No. 212), PFS 280 (Cat.No. 309), PFS 503(?) (Cat.No. 307), PFS 1002 (Cat.No. 196)
            With framing fronds at base — PFS 381 (Cat.No. 179), PFS 1362 (Cat.No. 30)
            With multiple shoots at lower trunk — PFS 58 (Cat.No. 242)
        Uncertain type
            Asymmetric long-branched — PFS 234 (Cat.No. 188), PFS 849 (Cat.No. 189)
            Stylized — PFS 225 (Cat.No. 46), PFS 1072 (Cat.No. 61), PFS 1091 (Cat.No. 68), PFS 1123 (Cat.No. 279)
    Triangle shape — PFS 247 (Cat.No. 245)
        Large and elongated — PFS 913 (Cat.No. 200)
    Uncertain fragmentary element — PFS 885 (Cat.No. 187), PFS 1238 (Cat.No. 160)
    Winged symbol — PFS 62 (Cat.No. 104), PFS 196 (Cat.No. 224), PFS 514 (Cat.No. 192), PFS 851 (Cat.No. 60), PFS 1189 (Cat.No. 8)
        With figure emergent — PFS 1053 (Cat.No. 45), PFS 1071 (Cat.No. 29)
    Y-shaped form — PFS 555 (Cat.No. 93)

TERMINAL FIELD MOTIF CLUSTERS
    Animal/creature groups
        Animal of uncertain type
            Above horned animal of undetermined type — PFS 246 (Cat.No. 290)
            Inverted below bird of uncertain type in flight — PFS 1388 (Cat.No. 162)
        Bird (eagle) atop column, beside winged human creature (genie?) — PFS 1099 (Cat.No. 169)
        Crossed pair
            Bulls — PFS 396 (Cat.No. 178)
            Horned-animal creatures, winged, of undetermined type
                With marchant horned animal, of undetermined type, growing from crossed pair
                      With vertically disposed horned animal, of undetermined type— PFS 218 (Cat.No. 140)
            Lions(?) — PFS 912 (Cat.No. 138)
            Lion creature, winged, and lion — PFS 990 (Cat.No. 256)
        Wild goat (inverted) and vulture (pecking) — PFS 1475 (Cat.No. 177)

TERMINAL FIELD MOTIF CLUSTERS (*cont.*)
　Animal/creatures with devices/symbols and/or plants/trees
　　Animal of uncertain type
　　　With lozenges and star — PFS 463 (Cat.No. 264)
　　Bird
　　　With crescent — PFS 326 (Cat.No. 100)
　　　With date palm — PFS 123* (Cat.No. 75)
　　　With star — PFS 30 (Cat.No. 291)
　　Bird creature, winged, human-headed
　　　With fish and triangle — PFS 247 (Cat.No. 245)
　　Bull creature, winged
　　　With date palm and star — PFS 853 (Cat.No. 204)
　　Bull creature, winged, human-faced
　　　With star — PFS 30 (Cat.No. 291)
　　Bull creature, winged, with human arms
　　　Supporting symbol (not preserved)(?) — PFS 1582 (Cat.No. 232)
　　Bull creature, winged, with human head, torso, and arms
　　　Supporting winged symbol with figure emergent — PFS 774 (Cat.No. 58)
　　Bull or lion creatures, winged, human-headed
　　　Supporting winged symbol with figure emergent — PFS 1053 (Cat.No. 45), PFS 1071 (Cat.No. 29)
　　Horned animal
　　　Undetermined type
　　　　With crescent — PFS 17 (Cat.No. 235), PFS 153(?) (Cat.No. 285), PFS 1444 (Cat.No. 62)
　　　Wild goat
　　　　With star — PFS 9* (Cat.No. 288)
　　Horned-animal creature
　　　Wild sheep, winged
　　　　Before stacked floral element — PFS 162 (Cat.No. 249)
　　Lion
　　　With star — PFS 902 (Cat.No. 243)
　Animals/creatures in self-contained heraldic pairs before plant or tree (*see also* HERALDIC COMPOSITIONS OF DISTINCTIVE FORM CREATED BY INTERACTION OF ANIMALS/CREATURES OF HEROIC ENCOUNTER WITH THE TERMINAL FIELD)
　　Horned Animals
　　　Deer
　　　　Before stylized tree — PFS 225 (Cat.No. 46)
　　Horned-animal creatures
　　　Wild goat creatures, winged
　　　　Before stylized tree — PFS 1123 (Cat.No. 279)
　　Lions
　　　Before palm tree — PFS 80 (Cat.No. 202)
　Device(s)/symbol(s)
　　Crescent
　　　And four dots — PFS 494 (Cat.No. 130)
　　　And star — PFS 102 (Cat.No. 1), PFS 222 (Cat.No. 117), PFS 1030 (Cat.No. 120)
　　　Inverted(?) and V-shaped(?) — PFS 294 (Cat.No. 53)
　　Spade of Marduk and stylus of Nabu — PFS 1501 (Cat.No. 238)
　Device(s)/symbol(s), inscription, and/or plant(s)/tree(s)
　　Figure emergent from nimbus of stars, leaf(?), seven dots, censer or phallic symbol, and elaborate floral element — PFS 38 (Cat.No. 16)

TERMINAL FIELD MOTIF CLUSTERS (*cont.*)
    Device(s)/symbol(s), inscription, and/or plant(s)/tree(s) (*cont.*)
        Inscription
            With date palm tree — PFS 113* (Cat.No. 19)
            With framing date palm trees — PFS 7* (Cat.No. 4)
        Star(s)
            With date palm tree — PFS 1236(?) (Cat.No. 159)
            With palm tree — PFS 280 (Cat.No. 309)
        Winged symbol and papyrus plant — PFS 514 (Cat.No. 192)

TREES
    Conifer — PFS 131 (Cat.No. 170), PFS 334 (Cat.No. 133), PFS 496 (Cat.No. 108)
        On stand with "arms" — PFS 971 (Cat.No. 171)
        With framing fronds at base — PFS 1023 (Cat.No. 127)
    Date palm — PFS 7* (Cat.No. 4), PFS 123* (Cat.No. 75), PFS 125 (Cat.No. 250), PFS 853 (Cat.No. 204), PFS 1276 (Cat.No. 34)
        With framing floral fronds or stars — PFS 1236 (Cat.No. 159)
    Palm — PFS 80 (Cat.No. 202), PFS 148 (Cat.No. 311), PFS 149 (Cat.No. 212), PFS 280 (Cat.No. 309), PFS 503(?) (Cat.No. 307), PFS 1002 (Cat.No. 196)
        With framing fronds at base — PFS 381 (Cat.No. 179), PFS 1362 (Cat.No. 30)
        With multiple shoots at lower trunk — PFS 58 (Cat.No. 242)
    Uncertain type
        Asymmetric long-branched — PFS 234 (Cat.No. 188), PFS 849 (Cat.No. 189)
        Stylized — PFS 225 (Cat.No. 46), PFS 1072 (Cat.No. 61), PFS 1091 (Cat.No. 68), PFS 1123 (Cat.No. 279)

WEAPONS
    Arrow(s) — PFS 49 (Cat.No. 23), PFS 266* (Cat.No. 208), PFS 859* (Cat.No. 205), PFS 1101 (Cat.No. 297)
    Bow — PFS 49 (Cat.No. 23), PFS 196 (Cat.No. 224), PFS 709(?) (Cat.No. 271), PFS 859* (Cat.No. 205), PFS 1204 (Cat.No. 136), PFS 1375s(?) (Cat.No. 254), PFS 1466 (Cat.No. 234)
        With duck-head finial — PFS 301 (Cat.No. 54)
    Bow case — PFS 196 (Cat.No. 224)
    Dagger — PFS 17 (Cat.No. 235), PFS 29 (Cat.No. 302), PFS 43*(?) (Cat.No. 207), PFS 54* (Cat.No. 277), PFS 112 (Cat.No. 282), PFS 146 (Cat.No. 275), PFS 246 (Cat.No. 290), PFS 255 (Cat.No. 233), PFS 266* (Cat.No. 208), PFS 523* (Cat.No. 209), PFS 584* (Cat.No. 203), PFS 853 (Cat.No. 204), PFS 859* (Cat.No. 205), PFS 959s (Cat.No. 246), PFS 990 (Cat.No. 256), PFS 1101 (Cat.No. 297), PFS 1122 (Cat.No. 228), PFS 1181 (Cat.No. 210), PFS 1264s (Cat.No. 206), PFS 1428s (Cat.No. 230), PFS 1637* (Cat.No. 273)
    Flail — PFS 538 (Cat.No. 312)
    Hammer-like weapon — PFS 503 (Cat.No. 307)
    Mace — PFS 98* (Cat.No. 217)
    Projectile
        Attached in brace at hero's forearm — PFS 57* (Cat.No. 239)
        Held aloft by hero — PFS 4* (Cat.No. 292)
        Hurled in space by hero — PFS 10 (Cat.No. 251)
    Quiver — PFS 709(?) (Cat.No. 271)
        With tassels — PFS 266* (Cat.No. 208), PFS 859* (Cat.No. 205)
    Saw-like weapon — PFS 247 (Cat.No. 245)
    Sheath — PFS 4* (Cat.No. 292), PFS 38 (Cat.No. 16), PFS 43* (Cat.No. 207), PFS 54* (Cat.No. 277), PFS 102(?) (Cat.No. 1), PFS 138 (Cat.No. 186), PFS 265 (Cat.No. 240), PFS 272* (Cat.No. 272), PFS 321(?) (Cat.No. 125), PFS 547 (Cat.No. 151), PFS 740 (Cat.No. 146), PFS 769* (Cat.No. 278), PFS 807 (Cat.No. 269), PFS 952(?) (Cat.No. 227), PFS 1165(?) (Cat.No. 89), PFS 1181(?) (Cat.No. 210), PFS 1391 (Cat.No. 248), PFS 1637* (Cat.No. 273)

WEAPONS (*cont.*)

    Sheath (*cont.*)

        Strapped to leg(?) — PFS 1122 (Cat.No. 228)

        With hilt of dagger or sword visible — PFS 538 (Cat.No. 312), PFS 1485 (Cat.No. 112)

    Sling — PFS 10 (Cat.No. 251), PFS 57* (Cat.No. 239)

    Spear — PFS 24 (Cat.No. 298), PFS 26 (Cat.No. 299), PFS 130 (Cat.No. 300), PFS 199*(?) (Cat.No. 305), PFS 447(?) (Cat.No. 301)

    Sword — PFS 43*(?) (Cat.No. 207), PFS 80 (Cat.No. 202), PFS 190 (Cat.No. 286), PFS 236 (Cat.No. 213), PFS 818 (Cat.No. 265)

        Curved — PFS 6 (Cat.No. 304), PFS 30(?) (Cat.No. 291), PFS 114 (Cat.No. 284), PFS 125 (Cat.No. 250), PFS 152 (Cat.No. 295), PFS 153 (Cat.No. 285), PFS 162 (Cat.No. 249), PFS 167 (Cat.No. 255), PFS 243(?) (Cat.No. 303), PFS 260 (Cat.No. 225), PFS 263 (Cat.No. 289), PFS 344 (Cat.No. 263), PFS 757 (Cat.No. 296), PFS 1249(?) (Cat.No. 294), PFS 1391(?) (Cat.No. 248), PFS 1466 (Cat.No. 234), PFS 1566* (Cat.No. 218), PFS 1582 (Cat.No. 232), PFS 1632* (Cat.No. 244)

    Throw stick — PFS 9*(?) (Cat.No. 288), PFS 39s (Cat.No. 221), PFS 1367s(?) (Cat.No. 211)

    Weapon of uncertain type — PFS 241 (Cat.No. 252), PFS 526* (Cat.No. 216), PFS 916 (Cat.No. 226), PFS 952 (Cat.No. 227), PFS 1286 (Cat.No. 258), PFS 1309s (Cat.No. 229)

        Not adequately preserved for analysis — PFS 33 (Cat.No. 220), PFS 58 (Cat.No. 242), PFS 65 (Cat.No. 241), PFS 67 (Cat.No. 293), PFS 139s (Cat.No. 222), PFS 146 (Cat.No. 275), PFS 149 (Cat.No. 212), PFS 151 (Cat.No. 223), PFS 196 (Cat.No. 224), PFS 265 (Cat.No. 240), PFS 338 (Cat.No. 262), PFS 435(?) (Cat.No. 310), PFS 737 (Cat.No. 281), PFS 795 (Cat.No. 214), PFS 815* (Cat.No. 215), PFS 939 (Cat.No. 267), PFS 1227* (Cat.No. 219), PFS 1406 (Cat.No. 276), PFS 1480 (Cat.No. 257)

APPENDIX NINE
PERSONAL NAMES

This appendix contains personal names occurring in seal inscriptions and/or mentioned in seal commentaries in the Volume I catalog entries. All personal names found in the PF texts are given in their Elamite forms as transliterated and translated by Hallock (1969), with the exception of Cyrus and Darius, which are rendered in their conventional Greek form. Personal names not found in the PF texts follow standard scholarly convention. See also *General Index*.

Abbatema	PFS 49 (Cat.No. 23)
Abbateya	PFS 98* (Cat.No. 217), PFS 1566* (Cat.No. 218)
Akkiya	PFS 4* (Cat.No. 292)
Ammamarda	PFS 29 (Cat.No. 302), PFS 43* (Cat.No. 207), PFS 190 (Cat.No. 286)
Ammasuzawiš(?)	PFS 1315s (Cat.No. 253)
Apmanya	PFS 1252 (Cat.No. 161)
Appumanya	PFS 1252 (Cat.No. 161)
Arsames	*See* Aršam
Aršam	PFS 16* (Cat.No. 22)
Artadara	PFS 1321s (Cat.No. 176)
Artaphernes	*See* Artadara
Artaxerxes	PFS 913 (Cat.No. 200), PFS 1286 (Cat.No. 258)
Artystone	*See* Irtašduna
Badumašda	PFS 1252 (Cat.No. 161)
Bakabada	PFS 120 (Cat.No. 49), PFS 1320 (Cat.No. 35), PFS 1444 (Cat.No. 62)
Bakabaduš	PFS 34 (Cat.No. 73)
Bakabana	PFS 130 (Cat.No. 300), PFS 298s (Cat.No. 236), PFS 1236 (Cat.No. 159), PFS 1243 (Cat.No. 33), PFS 1252 (Cat.No. 161), PFS 1311s (Cat.No. 247), PFS 1320 (Cat.No. 35), PFS 1322 (Cat.No. 36), PFS 1437s (Cat.No. 128), PFS 1684 (Cat.No. 17)
Bakadada	PFS 1243 (Cat.No. 33)
Bakakeya	PFS 1264s (Cat.No. 206)
Bakanšakka	PFS 1300 (Cat.No. 191)
Bakaradduš	PFS 95 (Cat.No. 25)
Bakena	PFS 32* (Cat.No. 180)
Bakubeša	PFS 43* (Cat.No. 207)
Bakuratsa	PFS 32* (Cat.No. 180)
Baradkama	PFS 113* (Cat.No. 19)
Barnuš	PFS 1612 (Cat.No. 268)
Barušiyatiš	PFS 26 (Cat.No. 299), PFS 1613 (Cat.No. 82)
Battišdana	PFS 32* (Cat.No. 180)
Cyrus	PFS 38 (Cat.No. 16)
Dadaka	PFS 1309s (Cat.No. 229)
Darius	PFS 7* (Cat.No. 4), PFS 9* (Cat.No. 288), PFS 16* (Cat.No. 22), PFS 38 (Cat.No. 16), PFS 113* (Cat.No. 19), PFS 859* (Cat.No. 205), PFS 1286 (Cat.No. 258), PFS 1566* (Cat.No. 218)

Dattaparna	PFS 815* (Cat.No. 215)
Daʾuka	PFS 225 (Cat.No. 46)
Dauma	PFS 1321s (Cat.No. 176)
Daʾupirna	PFS 201 (Cat.No. 50)
Dutukka	PFS 38 (Cat.No. 16)
Hapumanya	PFS 1252 (Cat.No. 161)
Harmasula	PFS 1260s (Cat.No. 184)
Harraštamka	PFS 1362 (Cat.No. 30)
Harrumassula(?)	PFS 1260s (Cat.No. 184)
Hatarbanuš	PFS 6 (Cat.No. 304)
Haturdada	PFS 10 (Cat.No. 251), PFS 32* (Cat.No. 180)
Haturrada	PFS 1458 (Cat.No. 80)
Hiumizza	PFS 63 (Cat.No. 24)
Hiyautarra	PFS 1367s (Cat.No. 211)
Hupanʾahpi	PFS 4* (Cat.No. 292)
Hupan-Kitin	PFS 43* (Cat.No. 207)
Hu…radu	PFS 1637* (Cat.No. 273)
Ir…	PFS 1566* (Cat.No. 218)
Irdabada	PFS 100 (Cat.No. 274)
Iršena	PFS 4* (Cat.No. 292), PFS 120 (Cat.No. 49)
Irtašbada	PFS 32* (Cat.No. 180)
Irtašduna (f.)	PFS 38 (Cat.No. 16)
Irtena	PFS 1249 (Cat.No. 294)
Irtuppiya	PFS 2 (Cat.No. 3)
Irzapparra	PFS 95 (Cat.No. 25)
Išbakatukka	PFS 298s (Cat.No. 236)
Išbaramištima	PFS 49 (Cat.No. 23)
Ištibara	PFS 1612 (Cat.No. 268)
Ištimanka	PFS 4* (Cat.No. 292), PFS 95 (Cat.No. 25)
Kamišdana	PFS 132 (Cat.No. 69)
Kammazikara	PFS 1325 (Cat.No. 41)
Kamnakka	PFS 1374 (Cat.No. 31)
Kandu…	PFS 272* (Cat.No. 272)
Kapiša	PFS 1375s (Cat.No. 254)
Karkašša	PFS 940 (Cat.No. 81)
Karkiš	PFS 1* (Cat.No. 182), PFS 146 (Cat.No. 275), PFS 236 (Cat.No. 213), PFS 1315s (Cat.No. 253), PFS 1428s (Cat.No. 230)
Karukka	PFS 95 (Cat.No. 25)
Kuntukka	PFS 67 (Cat.No. 293)
Ma…ak(?)	PFS 1637* (Cat.No. 273)
Mamannuwiš	PFS 20 (Cat.No. 145)
Manaka	PFS 58 (Cat.No. 242)
Manezza	PFS 1586 (Cat.No. 121)
Manmakka	PFS 1286 (Cat.No. 258)
Mannunda	PFS 72 (Cat.No. 147)

APPENDIX NINE: PERSONAL NAMES

Mannuya	PFS 1286 (Cat.No. 258)
Manukka	PFS 6 (Cat.No. 304), PFS 112 (Cat.No. 282)
Manuš	PFS 1286 (Cat.No. 258)
Manyakka	PFS 32* (Cat.No. 180)
Marduk-nāṣir	PFS 1632* (Cat.No. 244)
Mardukka	PFS 32* (Cat.No. 180)
Matēna	PFS 312 (Cat.No. 237)
Matiša	PFS 162 (Cat.No. 249)
Matukka	PFS 139s (Cat.No. 222), PFS 1428s (Cat.No. 230)
Maudadda	PFS 1315s (Cat.No. 253)
Mawukka	PFS 120 (Cat.No. 49)
Mazamanna	PFS 95 (Cat.No. 25)
Medumannuš	PFS 95 (Cat.No. 25)
Mella	PFS 201 (Cat.No. 50)
Mikrašba	PFS 52 (Cat.No. 114), PFS 62 (Cat.No. 104)
Minduka	PFS 1387 (Cat.No. 72)
Mirara(?)	PFS 1388 (Cat.No. 162)
Mirayauda	PFS 18 (Cat.No. 15), PFS 24 (Cat.No. 298)
Mirinzamna	PFS 1276 (Cat.No. 34)
Mirinzana	PFS 57* (Cat.No. 239)
Misraka	PFS 1391 (Cat.No. 248)
Misranka	PFS 1391 (Cat.No. 248)
Mišmina	PFS 1260s (Cat.No. 184)
Miyara	PFS 1238 (Cat.No. 160)
Mizapirzaka (f.)	PFS 1437s (Cat.No. 128)
Mizirma	PFS 72 (Cat.No. 147)
Murašû	PFS 131 (Cat.No. 170), PFS 247 (Cat.No. 245), PFS 1101 (Cat.No. 297), PFS 1501 (Cat.No. 238)
Naktiš	PFS 1458 (Cat.No. 80)
Nap...	PFS 43* (Cat.No. 207)
Napidan	PFS 1311s (Cat.No. 247)
Napša-Kitin	PFS 43* (Cat.No. 207)
Naptaš	PFS 54* (Cat.No. 277)
Nidintu-Anu	PFS 913 (Cat.No. 200)
ʾN(?)Š...	PFS 981* (Cat.No. 87)
Pandušašša (f.)	PFS 1300 (Cat.No. 191)
Parnaka	PFS 9* (Cat.No. 288), PFS 16* (Cat.No. 22), PFS 1238 (Cat.No. 160), PFS 1309s (Cat.No. 229), PFS 1325 (Cat.No. 41), PFS 1374 (Cat.No. 31), PFS 1388 (Cat.No. 162), PFS 1391 (Cat.No. 248), PFS 1440 (Cat.No. 42), PFS 1460 (Cat.No. 9), PFS 1566* (Cat.No. 218), PFS 1632* (Cat.No. 244)
Parru	PFS 43* (Cat.No. 207), PFS 58 (Cat.No. 242)
Parsauka	PFS 24 (Cat.No. 298)
Paršena	PFS 1460 (Cat.No. 9)
Pharnaces	See Parnaka
Pilpisurmu(?)	PFS 201 (Cat.No. 50)
Pirdukana	PFS 1463s (Cat.No. 231)
Pirišla	PFS 132 (Cat.No. 69)

Rašda	PFS 36* (Cat.No. 5)
Ratešda	PFS 1406 (Cat.No. 276)
Raubasa	PFS 1632* (Cat.No. 244)
Saka	PFS 1* (Cat.No. 182)
Šalamana	PFS 38 (Cat.No. 16)
Šaman	PFS 1612 (Cat.No. 268)
Šanau	PFS 103* (Cat.No. 84)
Šandupirzana	PFS 1325 (Cat.No. 41)
Šappiš	PFS 1447 (Cat.No. 163)
Šarbaladda(?)	PFS 1286 (Cat.No. 258)
Šati-...	PFS 98* (Cat.No. 217)
Šati-Hupan	PFS 4* (Cat.No. 292), PFS 103* (Cat.No. 84)
Šati(?)-Hupan	PFS 272* (Cat.No. 272)
Šatra...	PFS 64* (Cat.No. 173)
Šauša	PFS 1684 (Cat.No. 17)
Šeraš (f.)	PFS 4* (Cat.No. 292)
Šimut-ap	PFS 151 (Cat.No. 223)
Šuddayauda	PFS 1* (Cat.No. 182), PFS 32* (Cat.No. 180), PFS 312 (Cat.No. 237)
Šutur-Nahunte	PFS 43* (Cat.No. 207)
SYNʾ	PFS 266* (Cat.No. 208)
Tiridada	PFS 64* (Cat.No. 173)
Turdumannuš(?)	PFS 1236 (Cat.No. 159)
Turpiš	PFS 1285 (Cat.No. 44)
Umardada	PFS 72 (Cat.No. 147)
Umiša	PFS 1322 (Cat.No. 36)
Ummanana	PFS 10 (Cat.No. 251)
Ummurdak	PFS 190 (Cat.No. 286)
Ušaya	PFS 17 (Cat.No. 235)
Uštana	PFS 36* (Cat.No. 5), PFS 43* (Cat.No. 207), PFS 54* (Cat.No. 277)
URU-kisuna	PFS 1* (Cat.No. 182)
Xerxes	PFS 113* (Cat.No. 19), PFS 931* (Cat.No. 270)
Yap...	PFS 523* (Cat.No. 209)
Yaunaparza	PFS 1440 (Cat.No. 42)
Zakarna	PFS 95 (Cat.No. 25)
Zirra...	PFS 57* (Cat.No. 239)
Zišsabarna	PFS 36* (Cat.No. 5)
Zišanduš	PFS 213 (Cat.No. 140)
Zišsawiš	PFS 1249 (Cat.No. 294), PFS 1315s (Cat.No. 253), PFS 1367s (Cat.No. 211), PFS 1447 (Cat.No. 163), PFS 1566* (Cat.No. 218)

APPENDIX TEN
OCCUPATIONAL DESIGNATIONS

This appendix contains occupational designations occurring in seal inscriptions and/or mentioned in seal commentaries in the Volume I catalog entries. All occupational designations found in the PF texts are given in their Elamite forms as transliterated and translated by Hallock (1969) or in an approximate English translation as provided by Hallock (1969). Occupational designations not found in the PF texts follow standard scholarly convention. See also *General Index*.

accountant	PFS 57* (Cat.No. 239), PFS 99 (Cat.No. 113), PFS 228 (Cat.No. 148), PFS 513 (Cat.No. 85), PFS 1285 (Cat.No. 44), PFS 1582 (Cat.No. 232), PFS 1586 (Cat.No. 121), PFS 1632* (Cat.No. 244)
apportioner of workers	PFS 32* (Cat.No. 180)
barrišdama	PFS 49 (Cat.No. 23), PFS 213 (Cat.No. 140), PFS 1325 (Cat.No. 41), PFS 1460 (Cat.No. 9)
bazikara	PFS 120 (Cat.No. 49)
caravan leader	*See karabattiš*
chief of workers	*See kurdabattiš*
connected with a treasury	PFS 86 (Cat.No. 48)
daʾubattiš	PFS 162 (Cat.No. 249)
delivery man	*See ullira*
director of royal bakery	PFS 72 (Cat.No. 147)
elite guide	*See barrišdama*
grain handler	PFS 1286 (Cat.No. 258), PFS 1309s (Cat.No. 229); *see also tumara*
halla makers, exerters(?)	PFS 139s (Cat.No. 222)
horseman	PFS 32* (Cat.No. 180)
horseman for *kulla* horses	PFS 1285 (Cat.No. 44)
hupika	PFS 1406 (Cat.No. 276)
ištimara(?)	PFS 1264s (Cat.No. 206)
kanzabara	PFS 1* (Cat.No. 182), PFS 32* (Cat.No. 180), PFS 1286 (Cat.No. 258)
karabattiš	PFS 1285 (Cat.No. 44)
karamaraš	PFS 1612 (Cat.No. 268)
kazabara	PFS 1286 (Cat.No. 258)
king	PFS 7* (Cat.No. 4), PFS 43* (Cat.No. 207), PFS 54* (Cat.No. 277), PFS 139s (Cat.No. 222), PFS 146 (Cat.No. 275), PFS 298s (Cat.No. 236), PFS 1260s (Cat.No. 184), PFS 1264s (Cat.No. 206), PFS 1276 (Cat.No. 34), PFS 1285 (Cat.No. 44), PFS 1300 (Cat.No. 191), PFS 1315s (Cat.No. 253), PFS 1362 (Cat.No. 30), PFS 1375s (Cat.No. 254), PFS 1387 (Cat.No. 72), PFS 1406 (Cat.No. 276), PFS 1428s (Cat.No. 230), PFS 1444 (Cat.No. 62), PFS 1463s (Cat.No. 231), PFS 1566* (Cat.No. 218), PFS 1612 (Cat.No. 268), PFS 1632* (Cat.No. 244), PFS 1684 (Cat.No. 17)

m.KUR.lg zakkip	PFS 1632* (Cat.No. 244)
kurdabattiš	PFS 1* (Cat.No. 182), PFS 4* (Cat.No. 292), PFS 32* (Cat.No. 180)
kurtaš abbakkanaš Irdabamana	PFS 36* (Cat.No. 5)
magi	PFS 1315s (Cat.No. 253)
masašiš	PFS 1264s (Cat.No. 206)
matira	PFS 1286 (Cat.No. 258)
messenger	*See pirradaziš*
miller(?)	PFS 1440 (Cat.No. 42)
payers(?) of the land	*See m.KUR.lg zakkip*
pirradaziš	PFS 1260s (Cat.No. 184), PFS 1264s (Cat.No. 206)
police officer(?)	*See da'ubattiš*
queen	*See* wife, royal
raduššara(?)	PFS 1252 (Cat.No. 161)
satrap	PFS 130 (Cat.No. 300)
scribe	PFS 30 (Cat.No. 291), PFS 1264s (Cat.No. 206)
supervisor(?)	*See titikaš*
supplier	PFS 2 (Cat.No. 3), PFS 4* (Cat.No. 292), PFS 6 (Cat.No. 304), PFS 10 (Cat.No. 251), PFS 17 (Cat.No. 235), PFS 18 (Cat.No. 15), PFS 24 (Cat.No. 298), PFS 26 (Cat.No. 299), PFS 33 (Cat.No. 220), PFS 34 (Cat.No. 73), PFS 43* (Cat.No. 207), PFS 52 (Cat.No. 114), PFS 58 (Cat.No. 242), PFS 62 (Cat.No. 104), PFS 95 (Cat.No. 25), PFS 109 (Cat.No. 197), PFS 112 (Cat.No. 282), PFS 132 (Cat.No. 69), PFS 138 (Cat.No. 186), PFS 201 (Cat.No. 50), PFS 940 (Cat.No. 81), PFS 1252 (Cat.No. 161), PFS 1285 (Cat.No. 44), PFS 1300 (Cat.No. 191), PFS 1315s (Cat.No. 253), PFS 1322 (Cat.No. 36), PFS 1387 (Cat.No. 72), PFS 1428s (Cat.No. 230), PFS 1458 (Cat.No. 80), PFS 1586 (Cat.No. 121), PFS 1613 (Cat.No. 82)
tax handler	PFS 1632* (Cat.No. 244)
titikaš	PFS 225 (Cat.No. 46)
treasurer	PFS 1* (Cat.No. 182), PFS 32* (Cat.No. 180), PFS 113* (Cat.No. 19), PFS 1286 (Cat.No. 258); *see also kanzabara*
tumara	PFS 18 (Cat.No. 15), PFS 1286 (Cat.No. 258)
ullira	PFS 1264s (Cat.No. 206), PFS 1286 (Cat.No. 258), PFS 1315s (Cat.No. 253), PFS 1428s (Cat.No. 230)
unsak	PFS 1* (Cat.No. 182)
wife	PFS 1300 (Cat.No. 191)
wife, royal	PFS 38 (Cat.No. 16)

APPENDIX ELEVEN
GEOGRAPHICAL NAMES

This appendix contains geographical names occurring in the seal commentaries in the Volume I catalog entries. All geographical names found in the PF texts are given in their Elamite forms as transliterated and translated by Hallock (1969). Geographical names not found in the PF texts follow standard scholarly convention. See also General Index.

Abu Salabikh	PFS 152 (Cat.No. 295), PFS 1101 (Cat.No. 297)
Antarrantiš	PFS 1322 (Cat.No. 36)
Arachosia	PFS 1406 (Cat.No. 276)
Armenia	PFS 284* (Cat.No. 111)
Aššur	PFS 1099 (Cat.No. 169), PFS 1122 (Cat.No. 228)
Assyria	PFS 1122 (Cat.No. 228), PFS 1527 (Cat.No. 32)
Babylon	PFS 146 (Cat.No. 275)
Babylonia	PFS 1122 (Cat.No. 228)
Baktiš	PFS 34 (Cat.No. 73)
Barrikana	PFS 1315s (Cat.No. 253)
Battirakkan	PFS 120 (Cat.No. 49)
Bessitme	PFS 1276 (Cat.No. 34)
Borsippa	PFS 131 (Cat.No. 170), PFS 152 (Cat.No. 295), PFS 538 (Cat.No. 312)
Dur	PFS 79 (Cat.No. 83)
Elam	PFS 43* (Cat.No. 207), PFS 130 (Cat.No. 300), PFS 1447 (Cat.No. 163), PFS 1460 (Cat.No. 9)
Elam Region	PFS 2 (Cat.No. 3), PFS 4* (Cat.No. 292), PFS 10 (Cat.No. 251), PFS 20 (Cat.No. 145), PFS 29 (Cat.No. 302), PFS 43* (Cat.No. 207), PFS 54* (Cat.No. 277), PFS 57* (Cat.No. 239), PFS 64* (Cat.No. 173), PFS 99 (Cat.No. 113), PFS 100 (Cat.No. 274), PFS 103* (Cat.No. 84), PFS 132 (Cat.No. 69), PFS 151 (Cat.No. 223), PFS 162 (Cat.No. 249), PFS 168 (Cat.No. 74), PFS 190 (Cat.No. 286), PFS 225 (Cat.No. 46), PFS 228 (Cat.No. 148)
Etruria	PFS 263 (Cat.No. 289)
Fara	PFS 243 (Cat.No. 303), PFS 247 (Cat.No. 245), PFS 952 (Cat.No. 227)
Gorgippa	PFS 30 (Cat.No. 291), PFS 38 (Cat.No. 16)
Hadaran	PFS 940 (Cat.No. 81)
Harina	PFS 1444 (Cat.No. 62)
Hibaš	PFS 131 (Cat.No. 170)
Hidali	PFS 64* (Cat.No. 173), PFS 99 (Cat.No. 113), PFS 138 (Cat.No. 186), PFS 201 (Cat.No. 50), PFS 1320 (Cat.No. 35), PFS 1321s (Cat.No. 176), PFS 1322 (Cat.No. 36)
Hiran	PFS 79 (Cat.No. 83)
Hišema	PFS 29 (Cat.No. 302), PFS 190 (Cat.No. 286)
Hutpirri	PFS 100 (Cat.No. 274), PFS 132 (Cat.No. 69)

India	PFS 49 (Cat.No. 23)
Irišdumaka	PFS 79 (Cat.No. 83)
Isana	PFS 1122 (Cat.No. 228)
Kandahar	PFS 213 (Cat.No. 140), PFS 940 (Cat.No. 81)
Kanduma	PFS 131 (Cat.No. 170)
Kansakam	PFS 1286 (Cat.No. 258)
Kansan	PFS 1285 (Cat.No. 44)
Kapišda	PFS 64* (Cat.No. 173)
Kaupirriš	PFS 39s (Cat.No. 221)
Kerman	PFS 1276 (Cat.No. 34)
Kesat	PFS 20 (Cat.No. 145), PFS 64* (Cat.No. 173)
Kinet Höyük	PFS 9* (Cat.No. 288)
Kurarakka	PFS 1387 (Cat.No. 72)
Kurdušum	PFS 10 (Cat.No. 251), PFS 33 (Cat.No. 220)
Kurištiš	PFS 1285 (Cat.No. 44)
Kurpun	PFS 57* (Cat.No. 239), PFS 1586 (Cat.No. 121)
Kurra	PFS 64* (Cat.No. 173)
Kutkuš	PFS 34 (Cat.No. 73)
Liduma	PFS 58 (Cat.No. 242), PFS 99 (Cat.No. 113), PFS 103* (Cat.No. 84), PFS 228 (Cat.No. 148)
Luristan	PFS 190 (Cat.No. 286)
Makarkiš	PFS 79 (Cat.No. 83)
Makkaš	PFS 1612 (Cat.No. 268), PFS 1613 (Cat.No. 82)
Maknan	PFS 1325 (Cat.No. 41)
Manda	PFS 17 (Cat.No. 235)
Marmaš	PFS 64* (Cat.No. 173)
Matezziš	PFS 1286 (Cat.No. 258)
Memphis	PFS 99 (Cat.No. 113)
Mutrizaš	PFS 34 (Cat.No. 73)
Naširmannu	PFS 146 (Cat.No. 275)
Nimrud	PFS 4* (Cat.No. 292), PFS 29 (Cat.No. 302), PFS 38 (Cat.No. 16), PFS 130 (Cat.No. 300), PFS 514 (Cat.No. 192), PFS 1023 (Cat.No. 127), PFS 1586 (Cat.No. 121)
Nineveh	PFS 9* (Cat.No. 288), PFS 10 (Cat.No. 251), PFS 38 (Cat.No. 16), PFS 62 (Cat.No. 104), PFS 196 (Cat.No. 224), PFS 243 (Cat.No. 303), PFS 385 (Cat.No. 38), PFS 496 (Cat.No. 108), PFS 1189 (Cat.No. 8)
Nippur	PFS 1501 (Cat.No. 238)
Parmadan	PFS 26 (Cat.No. 299), PFS 1613 (Cat.No. 82)
Parmizzan	PFS 63 (Cat.No. 24), PFS 1315s (Cat.No. 253)
Parribana	PFS 1315s (Cat.No. 253)
Pasargadae	PFS 152 (Cat.No. 295), PFS 494 (Cat.No. 130), PFS 774 (Cat.No. 58), PFS 1480 (Cat.No. 257)
Persepolis	PFS 1* (Cat.No. 182), PFS 32* (Cat.No. 180), PFS 80 (Cat.No. 202), PFS 99 (Cat.No. 113), PFS 113* (Cat.No. 19), PFS 139s (Cat.No. 222), PFS 190 (Cat.No. 286), PFS 201 (Cat.No. 50), PFS 418 (Cat.No. 201), PFS 435 (Cat.No. 310), PFS 496 (Cat.No. 108), PFS 584* (Cat.No. 203), PFS 709 (Cat.No. 271), PFS 774 (Cat.No. 58), PFS 859* (Cat.No. 205), PFS 1122 (Cat.No. 228), PFS 1181 (Cat.No. 210), PFS 1243 (Cat.No. 33), PFS 1249 (Cat.No. 294), PFS 1252 (Cat.No. 161), PFS 1276 (Cat.No. 34), PFS 1286 (Cat.No. 258), PFS 1300 (Cat.No. 191),

Persepolis (*cont.*)	PFS 1309s (Cat.No. 229), PFS 1311s (Cat.No. 247), PFS 1320 (Cat.No. 35), PFS 1321s (Cat.No. 176), PFS 1322 (Cat.No. 36), PFS 1374 (Cat.No. 31), PFS 1387 (Cat.No. 72), PFS 1428s (Cat.No. 230), PFS 1437s (Cat.No. 128), PFS 1463s (Cat.No. 231), PFS 1480 (Cat.No. 257)
Persepolis Region	PFS 6 (Cat.No. 304), PFS 72 (Cat.No. 147), PFS 112 (Cat.No. 282), PFS 120 (Cat.No. 49)
Pitlan(?)	PFS 168 (Cat.No. 74)
Qasr-i Abu Nasr	PFS 32* (Cat.No. 180), PFS 39s (Cat.No. 221), PFS 919s (Cat.No. 259), PFS 1624s (Cat.No. 261)
Razakanuš	PFS 1252 (Cat.No. 161)
Sagartia	PFS 1276 (Cat.No. 34)
Samos	PFS 4* (Cat.No. 292), PFS 197 (Cat.No. 116), PFS 1122 (Cat.No. 228)
Sardis	PFS 524 (Cat.No. 2), PFS 774 (Cat.No. 58), PFS 1321s (Cat.No. 176), PFS 1325 (Cat.No. 41), PFS 1463s (Cat.No. 231), PFS 1480 (Cat.No. 257)
Šaurakkaš	PFS 34 (Cat.No. 73)
Seleucia on the Tigris	PFS 1501 (Cat.No. 238)
Shiraz Region	PFS 6 (Cat.No. 304), PFS 112 (Cat.No. 282), PFS 1243 (Cat.No. 33)
Šurauša	PFS 146 (Cat.No. 275)
Šurkutur	PFS 43* (Cat.No. 207), PFS 58 (Cat.No. 242)
Šursunkiri	PFS 43* (Cat.No. 207), PFS 64* (Cat.No. 173), PFS 131 (Cat.No. 170)
Susa	PFS 1* (Cat.No. 182), PFS 7* (Cat.No. 4), PFS 43* (Cat.No. 207), PFS 49 (Cat.No. 23), PFS 67 (Cat.No. 293), PFS 120 (Cat.No. 49), PFS 131 (Cat.No. 170), PFS 152 (Cat.No. 295), PFS 180 (Cat.No. 194), PFS 190 (Cat.No. 286), PFS 201 (Cat.No. 50), PFS 213 (Cat.No. 140), PFS 243 (Cat.No. 303), PFS 266* (Cat.No. 208), PFS 321 (Cat.No. 125), PFS 418 (Cat.No. 201), PFS 538 (Cat.No. 312), PFS 594 (Cat.No. 103), PFS 931* (Cat.No. 270), PFS 940 (Cat.No. 81), PFS 1238 (Cat.No. 160), PFS 1276 (Cat.No. 34), PFS 1286 (Cat.No. 258), PFS 1300 (Cat.No. 191), PFS 1309s (Cat.No. 229), PFS 1315s (Cat.No. 253), PFS 1320 (Cat.No. 35), PFS 1325 (Cat.No. 41), PFS 1367s (Cat.No. 211), PFS 1374 (Cat.No. 31), PFS 1437s (Cat.No. 128), PFS 1463s (Cat.No. 231), PFS 1475 (Cat.No. 177), PFS 1480 (Cat.No. 257), PFS 1527 (Cat.No. 32), PFS 1612 (Cat.No. 268)
Syria	PFS 284* (Cat.No. 111)
Tarsus	PFS 196 (Cat.No. 224)
Tašpak	PFS 43* (Cat.No. 207), PFS 58 (Cat.No. 242), PFS 225 (Cat.No. 46)
Tello	PFS 931* (Cat.No. 270)
Tepe Sialk	PFS 10 (Cat.No. 251)
Tiliman	PFS 99 (Cat.No. 113)
Tirazziš (Shiraz)	PFS 36* (Cat.No. 5), PFS 65 (Cat.No. 241), PFS 67 (Cat.No. 293), PFS 86 (Cat.No. 48), PFS 439 (Cat.No. 150)
Tukraš	PFS 1285 (Cat.No. 44)
Turtukkan	PFS 1252 (Cat.No. 161)
Ullu Burun	PFS 10 (Cat.No. 251)
Umpura	PFS 18 (Cat.No. 15)
Umpuranuš	PFS 24 (Cat.No. 298)
Ur	PFS 131 (Cat.No. 170), PFS 243 (Cat.No. 303), PFS 1101 (Cat.No. 297)
Uruk	PFS 243 (Cat.No. 303), PFS 913 (Cat.No. 200)

Western Anatolia	PFS 24 (Cat.No. 298), PFS 99 (Cat.No. 113), PFS 284* (Cat.No. 111), PFS 396 (Cat.No. 178), PFS 1321s (Cat.No. 176)
Zakzaku	PFS 1252 (Cat.No. 161)
Zila-Umpan	PFS 43* (Cat.No. 207)
Zilaba	PFS 33 (Cat.No. 220)
Zinçirli	PFS 952 (Cat.No. 227)
Ziršamattiš	PFS 57* (Cat.No. 239)

APPENDIX TWELVE

CONCORDANCE OF PFS TO CAT.NO. IN VOLUME I

PFS 1*	=	Cat.No. 182	PFS 103*	=	Cat.No. 84
PFS 2	=	Cat.No. 3	PFS 109	=	Cat.No. 197
PFS 4*	=	Cat.No. 292	PFS 112	=	Cat.No. 282
PFS 6	=	Cat.No. 304	PFS 113*	=	Cat.No. 19
PFS 7*	=	Cat.No. 4	PFS 114	=	Cat.No. 284
PFS 9*	=	Cat.No. 288	PFS 120	=	Cat.No. 49
PFS 10	=	Cat.No. 251	PFS 123*	=	Cat.No. 75
PFS 16*	=	Cat.No. 22	PFS 125	=	Cat.No. 250
PFS 17	=	Cat.No. 235	PFS 130	=	Cat.No. 300
PFS 18	=	Cat.No. 15	PFS 131	=	Cat.No. 170
PFS 20	=	Cat.No. 145	PFS 132	=	Cat.No. 69
PFS 24	=	Cat.No. 298	PFS 138	=	Cat.No. 186
PFS 26	=	Cat.No. 299	PFS 139s	=	Cat.No. 222
PFS 29	=	Cat.No. 302	PFS 145	=	Cat.No. 115
PFS 30	=	Cat.No. 291	PFS 146	=	Cat.No. 275
PFS 31	=	Cat.No. 172	PFS 148	=	Cat.No. 311
PFS 32*	=	Cat.No. 180	PFS 149	=	Cat.No. 212
PFS 33	=	Cat.No. 220	PFS 151	=	Cat.No. 223
PFS 34	=	Cat.No. 73	PFS 152	=	Cat.No. 295
PFS 36*	=	Cat.No. 5	PFS 153	=	Cat.No. 285
PFS 38	=	Cat.No. 16	PFS 158	=	Cat.No. 94
PFS 39s	=	Cat.No. 221	PFS 162	=	Cat.No. 249
PFS 43*	=	Cat.No. 207	PFS 164*	=	Cat.No. 20
PFS 49	=	Cat.No. 23	PFS 167	=	Cat.No. 255
PFS 52	=	Cat.No. 114	PFS 168	=	Cat.No. 74
PFS 54*	=	Cat.No. 277	PFS 180	=	Cat.No. 194
PFS 57*	=	Cat.No. 239	PFS 190	=	Cat.No. 286
PFS 58	=	Cat.No. 242	PFS 196	=	Cat.No. 224
PFS 62	=	Cat.No. 104	PFS 197	=	Cat.No. 116
PFS 63	=	Cat.No. 24	PFS 199*	=	Cat.No. 305
PFS 64*	=	Cat.No. 173	PFS 201	=	Cat.No. 50
PFS 65	=	Cat.No. 241	PFS 213	=	Cat.No. 140
PFS 67	=	Cat.No. 293	PFS 217	=	Cat.No. 135
PFS 72	=	Cat.No. 147	PFS 222	=	Cat.No. 117
PFS 79	=	Cat.No. 83	PFS 225	=	Cat.No. 46
PFS 80	=	Cat.No. 202	PFS 228	=	Cat.No. 148
PFS 86	=	Cat.No. 48	PFS 231	=	Cat.No. 51
PFS 95	=	Cat.No. 25	PFS 232	=	Cat.No. 26
PFS 98*	=	Cat.No. 217	PFS 233	=	Cat.No. 52
PFS 99	=	Cat.No. 113	PFS 234	=	Cat.No. 188
PFS 100	=	Cat.No. 274	PFS 236	=	Cat.No. 213
PFS 102	=	Cat.No. 1	PFS 241	=	Cat.No. 252

Concordance of PFS to Cat.No. in Volume I (*cont.*)

PFS 243	=	Cat.No. 303	PFS 494	=	Cat.No. 130
PFS 246	=	Cat.No. 290	PFS 496	=	Cat.No. 108
PFS 247	=	Cat.No. 245	PFS 501	=	Cat.No. 141
PFS 249	=	Cat.No. 27	PFS 503	=	Cat.No. 307
PFS 255	=	Cat.No. 233	PFS 513	=	Cat.No. 85
PFS 256	=	Cat.No. 198	PFS 514	=	Cat.No. 192
PFS 260	=	Cat.No. 225	PFS 516	=	Cat.No. 98
PFS 263	=	Cat.No. 289	PFS 523*	=	Cat.No. 209
PFS 265	=	Cat.No. 240	PFS 524	=	Cat.No. 2
PFS 266*	=	Cat.No. 208	PFS 526*	=	Cat.No. 216
PFS 272*	=	Cat.No. 272	PFS 536	=	Cat.No. 102
PFS 280	=	Cat.No. 309	PFS 538	=	Cat.No. 312
PFS 284*	=	Cat.No. 111	PFS 547	=	Cat.No. 151
PFS 294	=	Cat.No. 53	PFS 552	=	Cat.No. 118
PFS 297	=	Cat.No. 124	PFS 555	=	Cat.No. 93
PFS 298s	=	Cat.No. 236	PFS 584*	=	Cat.No. 203
PFS 301	=	Cat.No. 54	PFS 594	=	Cat.No. 103
PFS 312	=	Cat.No. 237	PFS 614	=	Cat.No. 287
PFS 321	=	Cat.No. 125	PFS 632	=	Cat.No. 143
PFS 326	=	Cat.No. 100	PFS 669	=	Cat.No. 142
PFS 329	=	Cat.No. 28	PFS 671*	=	Cat.No. 174
PFS 334	=	Cat.No. 133	PFS 673	=	Cat.No. 64
PFS 338	=	Cat.No. 262	PFS 677*	=	Cat.No. 181
PFS 341	=	Cat.No. 109	PFS 684	=	Cat.No. 183
PFS 344	=	Cat.No. 263	PFS 687	=	Cat.No. 119
PFS 361	=	Cat.No. 47	PFS 690	=	Cat.No. 139
PFS 362	=	Cat.No. 76	PFS 709	=	Cat.No. 271
PFS 364	=	Cat.No. 149	PFS 714	=	Cat.No. 152
PFS 370	=	Cat.No. 99	PFS 719	=	Cat.No. 195
PFS 373	=	Cat.No. 306	PFS 720	=	Cat.No. 57
PFS 380	=	Cat.No. 95	PFS 731	=	Cat.No. 131
PFS 381	=	Cat.No. 179	PFS 737	=	Cat.No. 281
PFS 385	=	Cat.No. 38	PFS 740	=	Cat.No. 146
PFS 392	=	Cat.No. 91	PFS 749	=	Cat.No. 110
PFS 396	=	Cat.No. 178	PFS 757	=	Cat.No. 296
PFS 399	=	Cat.No. 78	PFS 769*	=	Cat.No. 278
PFS 414	=	Cat.No. 280	PFS 774	=	Cat.No. 58
PFS 418	=	Cat.No. 201	PFS 778	=	Cat.No. 11
PFS 426	=	Cat.No. 55	PFS 781	=	Cat.No. 107
PFS 429	=	Cat.No. 7	PFS 782	=	Cat.No. 105
PFS 430	=	Cat.No. 56	PFS 783	=	Cat.No. 153
PFS 435	=	Cat.No. 310	PFS 787	=	Cat.No. 79
PFS 439	=	Cat.No. 150	PFS 795	=	Cat.No. 214
PFS 447	=	Cat.No. 301	PFS 807	=	Cat.No. 269
PFS 454	=	Cat.No. 92	PFS 815*	=	Cat.No. 215
PFS 461	=	Cat.No. 90	PFS 818	=	Cat.No. 265
PFS 463	=	Cat.No. 264	PFS 819	=	Cat.No. 86
PFS 480	=	Cat.No. 134	PFS 841	=	Cat.No. 13

Concordance of PFS to Cat.No. in Volume I (*cont.*)

PFS		Cat.No.	PFS		Cat.No.
PFS 844	=	Cat.No. 59	PFS 1091	=	Cat.No. 68
PFS 849	=	Cat.No. 189	PFS 1099	=	Cat.No. 169
PFS 851	=	Cat.No. 60	PFS 1101	=	Cat.No. 297
PFS 853	=	Cat.No. 204	PFS 1102	=	Cat.No. 132
PFS 859*	=	Cat.No. 205	PFS 1117	=	Cat.No. 67
PFS 882	=	Cat.No. 65	PFS 1119	=	Cat.No. 283
PFS 883*	=	Cat.No. 97	PFS 1122	=	Cat.No. 228
PFS 884	=	Cat.No. 123	PFS 1123	=	Cat.No. 279
PFS 885	=	Cat.No. 187	PFS 1135	=	Cat.No. 66
PFS 896	=	Cat.No. 308	PFS 1142	=	Cat.No. 39
PFS 902	=	Cat.No. 243	PFS 1146	=	Cat.No. 40
PFS 912	=	Cat.No. 138	PFS 1153	=	Cat.No. 199
PFS 913	=	Cat.No. 200	PFS 1155	=	Cat.No. 190
PFS 916	=	Cat.No. 226	PFS 1165	=	Cat.No. 89
PFS 919s	=	Cat.No. 259	PFS 1181	=	Cat.No. 210
PFS 931*	=	Cat.No. 270	PFS 1188	=	Cat.No. 144
PFS 939	=	Cat.No. 267	PFS 1189	=	Cat.No. 8
PFS 940	=	Cat.No. 81	PFS 1202	=	Cat.No. 137
PFS 944	=	Cat.No. 129	PFS 1204	=	Cat.No. 136
PFS 945	=	Cat.No. 96	PFS 1217s	=	Cat.No. 168
PFS 952	=	Cat.No. 227	PFS 1227*	=	Cat.No. 219
PFS 959s	=	Cat.No. 246	PFS 1236	=	Cat.No. 159
PFS 964	=	Cat.No. 260	PFS 1238	=	Cat.No. 160
PFS 970	=	Cat.No. 6	PFS 1243	=	Cat.No. 33
PFS 971	=	Cat.No. 171	PFS 1249	=	Cat.No. 294
PFS 981*	=	Cat.No. 87	PFS 1252	=	Cat.No. 161
PFS 990	=	Cat.No. 256	PFS 1260s	=	Cat.No. 184
PFS 991	=	Cat.No. 154	PFS 1264s	=	Cat.No. 206
PFS 996	=	Cat.No. 155	PFS 1276	=	Cat.No. 34
PFS 1002	=	Cat.No. 196	PFS 1285	=	Cat.No. 44
PFS 1016	=	Cat.No. 77	PFS 1286	=	Cat.No. 258
PFS 1017	=	Cat.No. 126	PFS 1300	=	Cat.No. 191
PFS 1018	=	Cat.No. 185	PFS 1309s	=	Cat.No. 229
PFS 1020	=	Cat.No. 37	PFS 1311s	=	Cat.No. 247
PFS 1023	=	Cat.No. 127	PFS 1315s	=	Cat.No. 253
PFS 1025*	=	Cat.No. 266	PFS 1320	=	Cat.No. 35
PFS 1026	=	Cat.No. 156	PFS 1321s	=	Cat.No. 176
PFS 1030	=	Cat.No. 120	PFS 1322	=	Cat.No. 36
PFS 1045	=	Cat.No. 157	PFS 1325	=	Cat.No. 41
PFS 1053	=	Cat.No. 45	PFS 1362	=	Cat.No. 30
PFS 1057	=	Cat.No. 70	PFS 1367s	=	Cat.No. 211
PFS 1071	=	Cat.No. 29	PFS 1374	=	Cat.No. 31
PFS 1072	=	Cat.No. 61	PFS 1375s	=	Cat.No. 254
PFS 1076	=	Cat.No. 193	PFS 1387	=	Cat.No. 72
PFS 1077	=	Cat.No. 158	PFS 1388	=	Cat.No. 162
PFS 1081	=	Cat.No. 71	PFS 1391	=	Cat.No. 248
PFS 1083	=	Cat.No. 43	PFS 1406	=	Cat.No. 276
PFS 1090	=	Cat.No. 175	PFS 1428s	=	Cat.No. 230

Concordance of PFS to Cat.No. in Volume I (*cont.*)

PFS 1437s	=	Cat.No. 128	PFS 1519	=	Cat.No. 167
PFS 1440	=	Cat.No. 42	PFS 1527	=	Cat.No. 32
PFS 1444	=	Cat.No. 62	PFS 1535	=	Cat.No. 164
PFS 1447	=	Cat.No. 163	PFS 1550	=	Cat.No. 14
PFS 1454	=	Cat.No. 166	PFS 1566*	=	Cat.No. 218
PFS 1458	=	Cat.No. 80	PFS 1582	=	Cat.No. 232
PFS 1460	=	Cat.No. 9	PFS 1586	=	Cat.No. 121
PFS 1463s	=	Cat.No. 231	PFS 1598	=	Cat.No. 63
PFS 1465	=	Cat.No. 21	PFS 1612	=	Cat.No. 268
PFS 1466	=	Cat.No. 234	PFS 1613	=	Cat.No. 82
PFS 1467	=	Cat.No. 12	PFS 1624s	=	Cat.No. 261
PFS 1475	=	Cat.No. 177	PFS 1630	=	Cat.No. 165
PFS 1480	=	Cat.No. 257	PFS 1632*	=	Cat.No. 244
PFS 1483	=	Cat.No. 88	PFS 1637*	=	Cat.No. 273
PFS 1485	=	Cat.No. 112	PFS 1641	=	Cat.No. 18
PFS 1489	=	Cat.No. 106	PFS 1654	=	Cat.No. 122
PFS 1499	=	Cat.No. 10	PFS 1658	=	Cat.No. 101
PFS 1501	=	Cat.No. 238	PFS 1684	=	Cat.No. 17

INDEX OF ALL SEALS ON FORTIFICATION AND TREASURY TABLETS CITED IN VOLUME I

All of the seals (PFS and PTS), either published or referenced in the *Introduction, Catalog*, and *Appendix One* of Volume I, are indexed in the following order: PFS in Volume I, PFS in Volume II, PFS in Volume III, illegible PFS, and PTS. Page number rendered in boldface gives the first page of the catalog entry of each seal in Volume I.

VOLUME I SEALS (PFS)

PFS 1* (Cat.No. 182) — 2, 16, 43–45, 50, 57, 69, 89, 259, 269, **272**–75, 311, 315, 343, 389, 443–44

PFS 2 (Cat.No. 3) — 20, 45, **66**, 67, 114, 127, 159, 223, 229–30, 251, 294, 430, 444–45

PFS 4* (Cat.No. 292) — 45, 162, 204, 251, 361, 384, **411**–13, 427, 445–46

PFS 6 (Cat.No. 304) — 48, 193, 200, 256, 350, 355, 397, **430**–31, 435, 446–47, 458, 460–61, 466

PFS 7* (Cat.No. 4) — 2, 7, 11, 19, 31–32, 35, 39, 46, 51, 54, 57, 59, **68**–70, 89, 102, 118, 133, 259, 273, 281, 315, 447

PFS 9* (Cat.No. 288) — 2, 6–7, 10, 14, 17–18, 45, 84, 93, 243, 353, **404**–06, 447–48

PFS 10 (Cat.No. 251) — **361**–62, 412, 448–49, 454, 462, 465, 468

PFS 16* (Cat.No. 22) — 7, 10, 14–17, 31, 45, **92**–94, 167, 219, 337, 405–06, 449

PFS 17 (Cat.No. 235) — 13, 246, 265, **340**–41, 449, 454, 459, 466, 468

PFS 18 (Cat.No. 15) — **82**, 421, 450, 466–67

PFS 20 (Cat.No. 145) — 2, 223, **229**–30, 291, 450

PFS 24 (Cat.No. 298) — 82, **421**–23, 450–51, 465, 467

PFS 26 (Cat.No. 299) — 159, 221–22, 228, **423**–24, 451, 467

PFS 29 (Cat.No. 302) — 204, 402–03, 405, 412, **427**–28, 451, 460, 464

PFS 30 (Cat.No. 291) — 107, **409**–10, 443, 451

PFS 31 (Cat.No. 172) — 65, 72, 91, 104, **257**–58, 267, 307, 382, 452, 462

PFS 32* (Cat.No. 180) — 7, 16, **268**–70, 273, 452

PFS 33 (Cat.No. 220) — **321**–22, 452–54, 465

PFS 34 (Cat.No. 73) — 63, **149**–50, 453

PFS 36* (Cat.No. 5) — 65, **71**–72, 91, 267, 307, 382, 453

PFS 38 (Cat.No. 16) — 10–12, 17, 47, **83**–85, 111, 212, 240, 243, 405, 453

PFS 39s (Cat.No. 221) — 321, **323**, 453–54, 459, 464

PFS 43* (Cat.No. 207) — 2, **302**–03, 454

PFS 49 (Cat.No. 23) — **95**–96, 340, 390, 420, 448–49, 452, 454

PFS 52 (Cat.No. 114) — 2, **196**–97, 454–55

PFS 54* (Cat.No. 277) — **391**–92, 454

PFS 57* (Cat.No. 239) — 179, 285, **345**–46, 361, 454–55, 459, 464

PFS 58 (Cat.No. 242) — **349**–50, 455

PFS 62 (Cat.No. 104) — 21, **184**–85, 197, 287, 454–55

PFS 63 (Cat.No. 24) — **96**–97, 291, 385, 455, 461

PFS 64* (Cat.No. 173) — 69, 89, 195, **259**–60, 273, 315, 327, 455, 457, 460

PFS 65 (Cat.No. 241) — 107, **348**–49, 455, 457, 463

PFS 67 (Cat.No. 293) — 105, 123, 333, **414**, 455–56, 463

PFS 72 (Cat.No. 147) — 107, 155, **231**–32, 456, 462–63

PFS 79 (Cat.No. 83) — **160**–61, 456

PFS 80 (Cat.No. 202) — 251, **295**–96, 394, 456, 468

PFS 86 (Cat.No. 48) — 121–22, 234, 410, 455, 457

PFS 95 (Cat.No. 25) — **97**–98, 457, 466–67

PFS 98* (Cat.No. 217) — 107, **316**–17, 319, 346, 348, 410, 457

PFS 99 (Cat.No. 113) — 162, 191, **195**–96, 232–33, 336, 414, 455, 457, 460, 462–64

PFS 100 (Cat.No. 274) — **387**, 457

PFS 102 (Cat.No. 1) — **63**–64, 149, 457

PFS 103* (Cat.No. 84) — **161**–62, 195, 232, 412, 457

PFS 109 (Cat.No. 197) — **290**, 458–59

PFS 112 (Cat.No. 282) — **397**–98, 446, 458

PFS 113*/PTS 4* (Cat.No. 19) — 17, 33, 51, 59, 69, 84, **88**–89, 259, 273, 315, 323, 458

PFS 114 (Cat.No. 284) — **399**–400, 402, 425, 458–59

PFS 120 (Cat.No. 49) — 81, 105, **123**–24, 333, 414, 458

PFS 123* (Cat.No. 75) — **151**–52, 193, 375, 458, 463

PFS 125 (Cat.No. 250) — **360**, 459

PFS 130 (Cat.No. 300) — 215, 400, 420, **424**–25, 458–59, 466–67

PFS 131 (Cat.No. 170) — **254**–55, 305, 389, 416–18, 455, 459, 464

PFS 132 (Cat.No. 69) — **145**, 459

PFS 138 (Cat.No. 186) — **278**–79, 459, 468

PFS 139s (Cat.No. 222) — 282, **324**–25, 334, 459

PFS 145 (Cat.No. 115) — **198**, 206, 459, 465

PFS 146 (Cat.No. 275) — 255, **388**–89, 449, 458–59

PFS 148 (Cat.No. 311) — 57, 437, **439**, 453–54, 459

PFS 149 (Cat.No. 212) — **310**–11, 459

PFS 151 (Cat.No. 223) — **325**–26, 459

PFS 152 (Cat.No. 295) — 203, 208, 255, **416**–18, 441, 459, 466

543

VOLUME I SEALS (PFS) (cont.)

PFS 153 (Cat.No. 285) — **401**, 459, 461
PFS 158 (Cat.No. 94) — **174**, 460
PFS 162 (Cat.No. 249) — 120, 189, 219, 251, **358**–59, 460
PFS 164* (Cat.No. 20) — 65, 72, **90**–91, 267, 307, 382, 460
PFS 167 (Cat.No. 255) — **366**, 460
PFS 168 (Cat.No. 74) — 149, **150**–51, 460, 468
PFS 180 (Cat.No. 194) — 21, 185, **287**–88, 460
PFS 190 (Cat.No. 286) — 400, **402**–03, 451, 460
PFS 196 (Cat.No. 224) — **326**–27, 455, 460
PFS 197 (Cat.No. 116) — **199**, 460
PFS 199* (Cat.No. 305) — 48, **432**–33, 460
PFS 201 (Cat.No. 50) — **124**–25, 252, 460, 467–68
PFS 213 (Cat.No. 140) — 222, **224**–25, 265, 267, 367, 460, 465
PFS 217 (Cat.No. 135) — **218**, 460
PFS 222 (Cat.No. 117) — **200**–01, 446–47, 460
PFS 225 (Cat.No. 46) — **119**–20, 189, 219, 251, 338, 359, 394, 460
PFS 228 (Cat.No. 148) — 162, 195, **232**–33, 457, 460
PFS 231 (Cat.No. 51) — **125**–26, 460
PFS 232 (Cat.No. 26) — **99**, 460
PFS 233 (Cat.No. 52) — **127**, 159, 230, 460
PFS 234 (Cat.No. 188) — **280**, 461
PFS 236 (Cat.No. 213) — 176, **311**–12, 461, 465
PFS 241 (Cat.No. 252) — 267, **363**, 366, 461–62
PFS 243 (Cat.No. 303) — 246, 265–66, 341, **428**–29, 461
PFS 246 (Cat.No. 290) — **408**–09, 461
PFS 247 (Cat.No. 245) — 246, 329, **354**–55, 446–47, 461
PFS 249 (Cat.No. 27) — **100**, 461
PFS 255 (Cat.No. 233) — 120, **338**–39, 461
PFS 256 (Cat.No. 198) — 246, 265–66, **291**, 341, 455, 461
PFS 260 (Cat.No. 225) — 45–46, **328**, 401, 459, 461
PFS 263 (Cat.No. 289) — 405, **407**, 427, 461
PFS 265 (Cat.No. 240) — **347**, 461, 467
PFS 266* (Cat.No. 208) — 13, **304**–05, 308, 461, 466–67
PFS 272* (Cat.No. 272) — **384**–85, 412, 455, 461
PFS 280 (Cat.No. 309) — 57, **436**–37, 439, 461
PFS 284* (Cat.No. 111) — 7, 152, 159, **192**–93, 240, 271, 430, 462
PFS 294 (Cat.No. 53) — 110, **128**, 462
PFS 297 (Cat.No. 124) — **207**, 462
PFS 298s (Cat.No. 236) — **342**, 448, 462
PFS 301 (Cat.No. 54) — 128, **129**–30, 462
PFS 312 (Cat.No. 237) — **312**, 462, 466
PFS 321 (Cat.No. 125) — **208**–09, 375, 462
PFS 326 (Cat.No. 100) — **180**–81, 246, 282, 457, 462
PFS 329 (Cat.No. 28) — **101**, 462
PFS 334 (Cat.No. 133) — **216**, 462
PFS 338 (Cat.No. 262) — **373**, 462
PFS 341 (Cat.No. 109) — **190**, 462
PFS 344 (Cat.No. 263) — **374**, 462
PFS 361 (Cat.No. 47) — **120**–21, 462

PFS 362 (Cat.No. 76) — **153**, 462
PFS 364 (Cat.No. 149) — **233**–34, 452, 462
PFS 370 (Cat.No. 99) — **179**, 452, 462
PFS 373 (Cat.No. 306) — **433**–34, 462
PFS 380 (Cat.No. 95) — **175**, 462
PFS 381 (Cat.No. 179) — **267**–68, 462
PFS 385 (Cat.No. 38) — **111**, 462
PFS 392 (Cat.No. 91) — **171**, 462
PFS 396 (Cat.No. 178) — 65, 72, 91, 222, 224, **266**–67, 307, 363, 367, 382, 461–62
PFS 399 (Cat.No. 78) — **155**, 231–32, 456, 462–63
PFS 414 (Cat.No. 280) — **395**–96, 463
PFS 418 (Cat.No. 201) — **294**–95, 463
PFS 426 (Cat.No. 55) — **130**, 457, 463,
PFS 429 (Cat.No. 7) — **74**, 131, 457, 463
PFS 430 (Cat.No. 56) — 74, **131**, 457, 463,
PFS 435 (Cat.No. 310) — 57, 383, **437**–38, 463
PFS 439 (Cat.No. 150) — 122, **234**, 455, 463
PFS 447 (Cat.No. 301) — **426**, 455, 463
PFS 454 (Cat.No. 92) — **172**, 463
PFS 461 (Cat.No. 90) — **170**, 253, 458, 463
PFS 463 (Cat.No. 264) — 20, 152, **375**, 458, 463
PFS 480 (Cat.No. 134) — 122, **217**, 463
PFS 494 (Cat.No. 130) — 198, **213**, 463
PFS 496 (Cat.No. 108) — 120, **189**, 216, 251, 359, 463
PFS 501 (Cat.No. 141) — **225**, 463
PFS 503 (Cat.No. 307) — 195, **434**–35, 457, 464
PFS 513 (Cat.No. 85) — 16, **163**–64, 464
PFS 514 (Cat.No. 192) — **284**–86, 292, 346, 454, 464
PFS 516 (Cat.No. 98) — 107, **178**–79, 346, 455, 459, 464
PFS 523* (Cat.No. 209) — 65–66, 72, 91, 267, **306**–07, 382, 464
PFS 524 (Cat.No. 2) — **65**–66, 72, 91, 267, 307, 382, 464
PFS 526* (Cat.No. 216) — 69, 89, 259, 273, **314**–15, 464
PFS 536 (Cat.No. 102) — **182**, 464
PFS 538 (Cat.No. 312) — **440**–41, 464
PFS 547 (Cat.No. 151) — **235**, 464
PFS 552 (Cat.No. 118) — **201**, 464
PFS 555 (Cat.No. 93) — **173**, 464
PFS 584* (Cat.No. 203) — **297**–98, 300, 464
PFS 594 (Cat.No. 103) — 177, **183**–84, 464
PFS 614 (Cat.No. 287) — **403**–04, 464
PFS 632 (Cat.No. 143) — **227**, 464
PFS 669 (Cat.No. 142) — **226**, 464
PFS 671* (Cat.No. 174) — 7, 193, 259, **260**–61, 271, 451, 464
PFS 673 (Cat.No. 64) — **140**, 464
PFS 677* (Cat.No. 181) — 7, 193, 261, **271**–72, 464
PFS 684 (Cat.No. 183) — 273, **275**, 464
PFS 687 (Cat.No. 119) — **202**, 464
PFS 690 (Cat.No. 139) — 20, 67, 159, **223**, 229–30, 464
PFS 709 (Cat.No. 271) — **383**, 438, 464

VOLUME I SEALS (PFS) (cont.)

PFS 714 (Cat.No. 152) — **236**, 453, 464
PFS 719 (Cat.No. 195) — **288**, 464
PFS 720 (Cat.No. 57) — **132**, 464
PFS 731 (Cat.No. 131) — 2, **214**, 464
PFS 737 (Cat.No. 281) — 222, 224, 330, 382, **396**–97, 464
PFS 740 (Cat.No. 146) — 20, 67, 159, 223, 229, **230**–31, 464
PFS 749 (Cat.No. 110) — **191**, 195, 414, 464
PFS 757 (Cat.No. 296) — 255, **418**–19, 464
PFS 769* (Cat.No. 278) — **392**–93, 464
PFS 774 (Cat.No. 58) — 2, 69, 102, **133**–34, 282, 337, 465
PFS 778 (Cat.No. 11) — 2, **78**, 465
PFS 781 (Cat.No. 107) — **188**, 465
PFS 782 (Cat.No. 105) — **186**, 465
PFS 783 (Cat.No. 153) — **237**, 465
PFS 787 (Cat.No. 79) — **156**, 465
PFS 795 (Cat.No. 214) — **312**–13, 465
PFS 807 (Cat.No. 269) — **380**, 465
PFS 815* (Cat.No. 215) — **313**–14, 465
PFS 818 (Cat.No. 265) — **376**, 465
PFS 819 (Cat.No. 86) — **165**, 465
PFS 841 (Cat.No. 13) — **80**, 465
PFS 844 (Cat.No. 59) — **135**, 465
PFS 849 (Cat.No. 189) — 280, **281**, 465, 467
PFS 851 (Cat.No. 60) — **136**, 465
PFS 853 (Cat.No. 204) — **298**–99, 448, 452, 465
PFS 859* (Cat.No. 205) — 11, 297–98, **299**–300, 308, 465
PFS 882 (Cat.No. 65) — **141**, 465
PFS 883* (Cat.No. 97) — 16, **177**–78, 183, 465
PFS 884 (Cat.No. 123) — 198, **206**, 219, 465
PFS 885 (Cat.No. 187) — 268, **279**–80, 459, 465
PFS 896 (Cat.No. 308) — 430, **435**–36, 465
PFS 902 (Cat.No. 243) — **351**, 465
PFS 912 (Cat.No. 138) — **221**–22, 224, 330, 367, 382, 396, 423, 465
PFS 913 (Cat.No. 200) — **293**, 465
PFS 916 (Cat.No. 226) — **329**, 354, 450, 465
PFS 919s (Cat.No. 259) — 211, 264, 276, **370**–72, 465
PFS 931* (Cat.No. 270) — 65, 72, 91, 107, 222, 224, 267, 307, 330, **381**–82, 396, 420, 465
PFS 939 (Cat.No. 267) — **378**, 465
PFS 940 (Cat.No. 81) — **158**, 460, 465
PFS 944 (Cat.No. 129) — 84, 148, 194, **212**, 240, 465
PFS 945 (Cat.No. 96) — **176**, 312, 461, 465
PFS 952 (Cat.No. 227) — 222, 224, **330**, 382, 396, 465
PFS 959s (Cat.No. 246) — 18, **355**–56, 465
PFS 964 (Cat.No. 260) — 107, **371**–72, 465
PFS 970 (Cat.No. 6) — **73**, 466
PFS 971 (Cat.No. 171) — 122, 210, **256**–57, 299, 446, 466
PFS 981* (Cat.No. 87) — **166**–67, 466
PFS 990 (Cat.No. 256) — 222, 224, 267, **367**, 466
PFS 991 (Cat.No. 154) — **238**, 466
PFS 996 (Cat.No. 155) — **239**, 466

PFS 1002 (Cat.No. 196) — **289**, 466
PFS 1016 (Cat.No. 77) — **154**, 466
PFS 1017 (Cat.No. 126) — **209**, 466
PFS 1018 (Cat.No. 185) — **277**–78, 466
PFS 1020 (Cat.No. 37) — **110**, 128, 466
PFS 1023 (Cat.No. 127) — **210**, 466
PFS 1025* (Cat.No. 266) — **377**, 466
PFS 1026 (Cat.No. 156) — 84, 212, **240**, 466
PFS 1030 (Cat.No. 120) — **203**, 459, 466
PFS 1045 (Cat.No. 157) — **241**, 466
PFS 1053 (Cat.No. 45) — 69, 102, **118**–19, 450, 466
PFS 1057 (Cat.No. 70) — **146**, 466
PFS 1071 (Cat.No. 29) — 42, 69, **102**, 118, 133–34, 137, 449, 466
PFS 1072 (Cat.No. 61) — 102, **137**, 394, 449, 466
PFS 1076 (Cat.No. 193) — 159, 284, **285**–86, 292, 461, 466
PFS 1077 (Cat.No. 158) — **242**, 466
PFS 1081 (Cat.No. 71) — **147**, 466
PFS 1083 (Cat.No. 43) — 115, **116**, 466
PFS 1090 (Cat.No. 175) — **262**, 457, 466
PFS 1091 (Cat.No. 68) — **144**, 462, 466
PFS 1099 (Cat.No. 169) — **253**–54, 416, 466
PFS 1101 (Cat.No. 297) — 95, 215, 340, 382, **419**–20, 425, 459, 466–67
PFS 1102 (Cat.No. 132) — **215**, 420, 459, 466–67
PFS 1117 (Cat.No. 67) — **143**, 467
PFS 1119 (Cat.No. 283) — **398**–99, 465, 467
PFS 1122 (Cat.No. 228) — 16, **331**–32, 467
PFS 1123 (Cat.No. 279) — 120, 189, 251, **394**–95, 467
PFS 1135 (Cat.No. 66) — **142**, 467
PFS 1142 (Cat.No. 39) — 18, **112**, 246, 457, 467
PFS 1146 (Cat.No. 40) — **113**, 467
PFS 1153 (Cat.No. 199) — **292**, 467
PFS 1155 (Cat.No. 190) — **282**, 467
PFS 1165 (Cat.No. 89) — **169**, 467
PFS 1181 (Cat.No. 210) — 13, 305, **308**–09, 461, 467
PFS 1188 (Cat.No. 144) — 221–22, **228**, 423, 467
PFS 1189 (Cat.No. 8) — **75**, 282, 450, 467
PFS 1202 (Cat.No. 137) — 162, **220**–22, 228, 423, 450, 467
PFS 1204 (Cat.No. 136) — 206, **219**–20, 251, 359, 467
PFS 1217s (Cat.No. 168) — **252**, 416, 460, 467
PFS 1227* (Cat.No. 219) — **320**–21, 323, 467
PFS 1236 (Cat.No. 159) — 84, **243**, 405, 451, 467
PFS 1238 (Cat.No. 160) — **244**, 451, 467
PFS 1243 (Cat.No. 33) — **106**, 451, 467
PFS 1249 (Cat.No. 294) — 246, 255, **415**–16, 451, 467
PFS 1252 (Cat.No. 161) — **245**, 467
PFS 1260s (Cat.No. 184) — 211, 264, **276**–77, 301, 371–72, 467
PFS 1264s (Cat.No. 206) — **301**, 467
PFS 1276 (Cat.No. 34) — **107**, 148, 178, 231, 240, 467
PFS 1285 (Cat.No. 44) — **117**, 467

VOLUME I SEALS (PFS) (cont.)

PFS 1286 (Cat.No. 258) — **369**–70, 467
PFS 1300 (Cat.No. 191) — **283**, 467
PFS 1309s (Cat.No. 229) — 19, 105, 123, 276, **333**–34, 414, 450, 467
PFS 1311s (Cat.No. 247) — **356**–57, 450, 467
PFS 1315s (Cat.No. 253) — **364**–65, 450, 467
PFS 1320 (Cat.No. 35) — **108**, 138, 468
PFS 1321s (Cat.No. 176) — 10, 19, 107, 211, **263**–64, 276, 333, 336, 371–72, 460, 468
PFS 1322 (Cat.No. 36) — **109**, 459, 468
PFS 1325 (Cat.No. 41) — **114**, 468
PFS 1362 (Cat.No. 30) — **103**, 468
PFS 1367s (Cat.No. 211) — **309**–10, 468
PFS 1374 (Cat.No. 31) — **104**, 258, 448, 468
PFS 1375s (Cat.No. 254) — **365**, 468
PFS 1387 (Cat.No. 72) — 107, **148**, 194, 212, 468
PFS 1388 (Cat.No. 162) — **246**–47, 265–66, 291, 341, 468
PFS 1391 (Cat.No. 248) — **357**–58, 468
PFS 1406 (Cat.No. 276) — **390**, 468
PFS 1428s (Cat.No. 230) — 324, **334**–35, 468
PFS 1437s (Cat.No. 128) — **211**, 264, 276, 371–72, 468
PFS 1440 (Cat.No. 42) — **115**–16, 468
PFS 1444 (Cat.No. 62) — **138**, 206, 449, 468
PFS 1447 (Cat.No. 163) — **247**, 449, 468
PFS 1454 (Cat.No. 166) — **250**, 468
PFS 1458 (Cat.No. 80) — 16, **157**–58, 181, 468
PFS 1460 (Cat.No. 9) — **76**, 449, 468
PFS 1463s (Cat.No. 231) — 19, 276, **335**–36, 468
PFS 1465 (Cat.No. 21) — **91**–92, 468
PFS 1466 (Cat.No. 234) — 95, **339**–40, 420, 468

PFS 1467 (Cat.No. 12) — **79**, 468
PFS 1475 (Cat.No. 177) — 246, **265**–66, 291, 341, 429, 468
PFS 1480 (Cat.No. 257) — 16, **368**, 468
PFS 1483 (Cat.No. 88) — **168**, 468
PFS 1485 (Cat.No. 112) — 148, **194**, 212, 456, 468
PFS 1489 (Cat.No. 106) — **187**, 468
PFS 1499 (Cat.No. 10) — **77**, 468
PFS 1501 (Cat.No. 238) — 233, **344**–45, 468
PFS 1519 (Cat.No. 167) — 20, 67, 120, 159, 223, 229–30, **251**, 359, 460, 468
PFS 1527 (Cat.No. 32) — **105**, 123, 333, 414, 468
PFS 1535 (Cat.No. 164) — **248**, 468
PFS 1550 (Cat.No. 14) — **81**, 468
PFS 1566* (Cat.No. 218) — 16–17, 107, 317, **318**–19, 321, 346, 348, 468
PFS 1582 (Cat.No. 232) — 93, **337**, 468
PFS 1586 (Cat.No. 121) — **204**, 412, 427, 468
PFS 1598 (Cat.No. 63) — **139**, 468
PFS 1612 (Cat.No. 268) — **379**, 468
PFS 1613 (Cat.No. 82) — **159**, 223, 229–30, 284, 286, 423, 468
PFS 1624s (Cat.No. 261) — 211, 264, 276, 371, **372**–73, 468
PFS 1630 (Cat.No. 165) — **249**, 468
PFS 1632* (Cat.No. 244) — **352**–53, 468
PFS 1637* (Cat.No. 273) — **385**–86, 468
PFS 1641 (Cat.No. 18) — **87**–88, 468
PFS 1654 (Cat.No. 122) — **205**, 468
PFS 1658 (Cat.No. 101) — 16, 157, **181**, 468
PFS 1684 (Cat.No. 17) — **86**, 468

VOLUME II SEALS (PFS)

PFS 5 — 228, 294, 350, 454, 459, 462, 464, 467–68
PFS 11* — 14, 19
PFS 12a — 45, 134
PFS 12b — 45, 134, 386, 468
PFS 21 — 370, 460, 465–68
PFS 22 — 466
PFS 35* — 300, 455–56
PFS 50* — 462
PFS 51 — 11–12, 195, 303
PFS 60 — 63–64, 149, 453, 457, 463
PFS 61 — 468
PFS 66a* — 69–70, 134, 447
PFS 66b* — 69–70, 134, 447
PFS 66c* — 69–70, 134, 447
PFS 68 — 87, 450
PFS 71*/PTS 33* — 33
PFS 77* — 412
PFS 78 — 180

PFS 84 — 134, 198, 206, 454, 468
PFS 93* — 11, 14, 195, 303
PFS 97 — 229
PFS 101 — 456
PFS 105s — 458–59
PFS 108* — 352, 464
PFS 117 — 468
PFS 122 — 102, 339, 461, 464
PFS 131s — 361
PFS 137 — 450
PFS 141 — 231, 456, 462–63
PFS 143s — 180, 454
PFS 157 — 466
PFS 163 — 122, 382, 462
PFS 166 — 87, 253
PFS 177 — 241, 466
PFS 181* — 463
PFS 184 — 454, 467

VOLUME II SEALS (PFS) (cont.)

PFS 186s — 451
PFS 187s — 148, 451
PFS 189 — 449
PFS 191 — 452
PFS 195 — 451
PFS 198 — 199, 460
PFS 206 — 457
PFS 211 — 455
PFS 220 — 258
PFS 221 — 456
PFS 223 — 450
PFS 224 — 134, 400, 458–59
PFS 239 — 448
PFS 248 — 100, 461
PFS 250 — 468
PFS 261* — 467
PFS 273s — 454
PFS 276 — 456
PFS 281 — 437, 461
PFS 287 — 195
PFS 289*s — 451, 453
PFS 302 — 130, 462
PFS 306 — 458
PFS 307 — 458
PFS 308 — 459
PFS 309 — 461
PFS 310 — 133
PFS 311 — 453
PFS 331 — 460
PFS 349 — 456
PFS 358 — 449
PFS 419 — 463
PFS 451s/PTS 61s — 33
PFS 458 — 457, 462
PFS 465 — 458, 463
PFS 478 — 195, 455, 457
PFS 499s — 463
PFS 546 — 449
PFS 553 — 464
PFS 554 — 173, 464
PFS 556 — 464
PFS 590 — 449
PFS 606 — 402, 451
PFS 611 — 454
PFS 633 — 464
PFS 648s — 450
PFS 650 — 43
PFS 678 — 464
PFS 695 — 457
PFS 706* — 452
PFS 708 — 464
PFS 718 — 464

PFS 784 — 465
PFS 802 — 450
PFS 813* — 454
PFS 843 — 465
PFS 848* — 465
PFS 900s — 465
PFS 901 — 465
PFS 960 — 465
PFS 1000 — 452
PFS 1024 — 229
PFS 1027s — 452
PFS 1044 — 195, 456
PFS 1048s — 457
PFS 1052 — 459
PFS 1054 — 450
PFS 1058 — 466
PFS 1085 — 466
PFS 1121s — 332, 467
PFS 1143 — 467
PFS 1156 — 467
PFS 1159s — 466
PFS 1164 — 169, 467
PFS 1166 — 43, 467
PFS 1193 — 459
PFS 1211 — 456
PFS 1225 — 416
PFS 1250s — 451
PFS 1256 — 448
PFS 1278s — 459
PFS 1308* — 422, 450
PFS 1312s — 43, 450
PFS 1314s — 450
PFS 1316 — 451
PFS 1327 — 452
PFS 1333s — 451
PFS 1342 — 468
PFS 1347s — 452
PFS 1359 — 448
PFS 1371 — 448
PFS 1393s — 11, 39, 105, 457
PFS 1402s — 458
PFS 1414s — 449
PFS 1426s — 459
PFS 1431 — 379
PFS 1434s — 460
PFS 1445s — 449
PFS 1459 — 439, 450
PFS 1486 — 450
PFS 1514 — 451
PFS 1541 — 450
PFS 1548 — 454, 455
PFS 1567* — 14, 33

VOLUME II SEALS (PFS) (cont.)

PFS 1585 — 459
PFS 1591 — 464
PFS 1597 — 468
PFS 1627 — 455

PFS 1662 — 464
PFS 1666 — 286, 461, 466
PFS 1680 — 466
PFS 1689 — 448

VOLUME III SEALS (PFS)

PFS 3 — 45, 222, 382, 410
PFS 8 — 149, 453
PFS 13 — 149, 453
PFS 15 — 134, 451, 464
PFS 19 — 466
PFS 23 — 67, 467, 468
PFS 27* — 134
PFS 37 — 468
PFS 40 — 99, 459, 460, 468
PFS 41 — 6, 460
PFS 42 — 452, 464
PFS 45* — 134, 303, 460
PFS 48 — 280, 461
PFS 53 — 450
PFS 55 — 361, 454, 462, 467
PFS 56 — 462, 468
PFS 59 — 350, 455, 461
PFS 69 — 464
PFS 70s — 458, 459
PFS 73* — 454
PFS 83* — 14, 133
PFS 89 — 464, 466, 468
PFS 90 — 231, 232, 456, 463
PFS 92 — 452, 462
PFS 94 — 462
PFS 106 — 433, 460
PFS 107 — 468
PFS 108* — 352, 464
PFS 111 — 450
PFS 136 — 465
PFS 142 — 148
PFS 150 — 459
PFS 154 — 174, 460, 464
PFS 160* — 416
PFS 171 — 152, 458, 463
PFS 172 — 458, 463
PFS 185 — 464
PFS 188* — 134, 449, 451
PFS 193 — 462, 466
PFS 202 — 408, 461
PFS 205s — 456
PFS 212 — 450
PFS 219 — 458
PFS 227 — 46
PFS 230 — 152, 458

PFS 251 — 448
PFS 258s — 465
PFS 264 — 461, 467
PFS 270s — 449
PFS 282 — 437, 461
PFS 295 — 450, 458
PFS 296* — 207, 462
PFS 303 — 462
PFS 313 — 454
PFS 323 — 459
PFS 328s — 101, 462
PFS 337 — 462
PFS 342 — 134, 462
PFS 357 — 449
PFS 363 — 452
PFS 366 — 452, 462
PFS 372 — 462
PFS 384s — 111, 462
PFS 413 — 459
PFS 415s — 462
PFS 417 — 462
PFS 427 — 457, 463
PFS 428 — 457, 463
PFS 431 — 457, 463
PFS 434 — 463
PFS 460 — 170, 458, 463
PFS 462 — 458, 463
PFS 464 — 375, 458, 463
PFS 477 — 195, 196, 455, 457
PFS 481 — 463
PFS 493 — 463
PFS 495 — 463
PFS 497 — 463
PFS 498 — 463
PFS 502 — 435, 457, 464
PFS 504 — 195, 435, 457, 464
PFS 505 — 195
PFS 527 — 464
PFS 543* — 134
PFS 548 — 464
PFS 557 — 450
PFS 596 — 450
PFS 598 — 450
PFS 628 — 466
PFS 659 — 456

VOLUME III SEALS (PFS) (cont.)

PFS 685 — 453
PFS 689 — 451
PFS 696 — 457
PFS 701s — 459
PFS 702 — 464
PFS 732 — 464, 468
PFS 772 — 451
PFS 776 — 454
PFS 788 — 465
PFS 799 — 459
PFS 831 — 457
PFS 842 — 465
PFS 852s — 449
PFS 856 — 454
PFS 857s — 10, 12
PFS 867s — 460
PFS 881s — 465
PFS 895 — 465
PFS 943 — 446
PFS 972 — 446
PFS 985 — 468
PFS 986 — 452
PFS 1003 — 466
PFS 1015 — 466
PFS 1022 — 466
PFS 1036s — 448
PFS 1051 — 453
PFS 1056 — 146
PFS 1060 — 466
PFS 1063s — 462
PFS 1084*/PTS 42* — 33, 466
PFS 1092 — 462, 466
PFS 1094 — 456
PFS 1097 — 452
PFS 1098 — 449
PFS 1107 — 448
PFS 1116 — 467
PFS 1134s — 467
PFS 1167 — 467
PFS 1173 — 455
PFS 1184 — 112
PFS 1190 — 457, 467
PFS 1191 — 460
PFS 1237s — 451
PFS 1239 — 451
PFS 1242s — 451
PFS 1246 — 451
PFS 1254 — 448
PFS 1255s — 448
PFS 1261s — 454
PFS 1268s — 245
PFS 1280 — 459
PFS 1289s — 452

PFS 1290s — 448
PFS 1292s — 448, 450
PFS 1293 — 457
PFS 1297 — 450
PFS 1298 — 450
PFS 1302s — 450
PFS 1307 — 450
PFS 1310s — 333
PFS 1313s — 450
PFS 1346 — 448
PFS 1373 — 458
PFS 1379 — 452
PFS 1382 — 448
PFS 1386s — 458
PFS 1390s — 358, 448
PFS 1394s — 448
PFS 1396 — 448
PFS 1411s — 452
PFS 1415 — 449
PFS 1418 — 449
PFS 1419 — 449
PFS 1420 — 452
PFS 1438 — 468
PFS 1442 — 449
PFS 1446s — 449
PFS 1464 — 468
PFS 1490 — 468
PFS 1498s — 454
PFS 1505 — 459
PFS 1528 — 468
PFS 1531 — 456
PFS 1532s — 10
PFS 1545s — 452
PFS 1546 — 447
PFS 1547 — 453
PFS 1551 — 468
PFS 1552s — 456
PFS 1556 — 447
PFS 1558 — 453
PFS 1560 — 449
PFS 1562 — 451
PFS 1616s — 6, 11, 39
PFS 1626s — 453
PFS 1631 — 468
PFS 1644 — 462
PFS 1645 — 462
PFS 1648 — 466
PFS 1660s — 455
PFS 1673 — 464
PFS 1685 — 465
PFS 1690 — 448
PFS 1692 — 46
PFS 1693s — 451

ILLEGIBLE SEALS (PFS)

PFS 324 — 159
PFS 333 — 455
PFS 368 — 452
PFS 374 — 452
PFS 376 — 452
PFS 377 — 452
PFS 391 — 462
PFS 452 — 461
PFS 459 — 457, 462
PFS 479 — 195, 233, 457, 460
PFS 486 — 458
PFS 571 — 462
PFS 618s — 455
PFS 697 — 457
PFS 728 — 460
PFS 742 — 464
PFS 758 — 464
PFS 760 — 454
PFS 761 — 456
PFS 762 — 456
PFS 775 — 460
PFS 789 — 465
PFS 796 — 465
PFS 806 — 465
PFS 861 — 447
PFS 886 — 459
PFS 920 — 465
PFS 932 — 107, 465
PFS 1055 — 460
PFS 1059 — 466
PFS 1078 — 464
PFS 1086 — 456
PFS 1100 — 458, 459
PFS 1152s — 467
PFS 1154 — 467
PFS 1251s — 467
PFS 1275 — 467
PFS 1306s — 450
PFS 1323 — 459
PFS 1324 — 459
PFS 1330 — 138
PFS 1332s — 460
PFS 1376 — 468
PFS 1385 — 334, 448
PFS 1389 — 468
PFS 1392 — 468
PFS 1400s — 452
PFS 1433 — 449
PFS 1443s — 449
PFS 1450 — 301, 449
PFS 1455 — 468
PFS 1456s — 117
PFS 1471 — 465
PFS 1474s — 335
PFS 1521 — 451
PFS 1525 — 450
PFS 1554 — 450
PFS 1575 — 460
PFS 1677 — 454

SEALS ON PERSEPOLIS TREASURY TABLETS (PTS)

PTS 1* — 54, 59, 65, 91, 307
PTS 2* — 54, 59
PTS 3* — 54, 59, 65, 91, 307
PTS 4*/PFS 113* (Cat.No. 12) — 33, 51, 54, 59, 88, 89
PTS 5* — 34, 54, 59
PTS 6* — 54, 59, 65, 91, 307
PTS 7* — 54, 59
PTS 8* — 54, 59, 382
PTS 9 — 54, 59
PTS 10 — 54, 59
PTS 11* — 54, 59
PTS 12 — 54, 59
PTS 13 — 54, 59
PTS 14* — 9, 14, 33
PTS 18 — 195
PTS 19 — 34, 102, 133
PTS 28 — 34
PTS 33*/PFS 71* (II) — 33
PTS 37 — 54, 59
PTS 38 — 54, 59
PTS 39* — 54, 59
PTS 42*/PFS 1084* (III) — 33
PTS 54s — 34
PTS 55s — 34
PTS 59s — 54, 59
PTS 60s — 54, 59
PTS 61s/PFS 451s (II) — 33

GENERAL INDEX

This index cites names, terms, and key words occurring in the *Introduction* and *Catalog* of Volume I. In the case of animals and creatures, the index does not duplicate the information contained in *Appendix Seven: Animals and Composite Creatures on Seals in Volume I*. References to specific animals and creatures are included here only if they are supplementary to the *Appendix Seven* apparatus — relating to seal comparanda or to information contained in PF texts. Similarly, the index does not duplicate *Appendix Eight: Iconographical Features on Seals in Volume I*. References to iconographical features are included here only when they are discussed in other contexts of Volume I.

Abbatema — 95
Abbateya — 17, 317–19
Abu Salabikh — 417, 420
account — 123, 162, 195, 232, 346; *see also* text (W text)
    accounting — 27–28, 160, 162–63, 244, 353
accountant — 162–63, 204, 232, 337, 346
Acemhöyük — 14
Achaemenid — *see* Persia
administrator — 7, 34, 55, 57–58, 191, 370
agate — 21, 56, 59, 75, 111, 211, 344
Ahuramazda — 39, 69
Akkadian — 382, 417; *see also* glyptic, iconography, language
Akkiya — 412
Alalakh — 20
Alexander (the Great) — 10, 23–24
ambassador — 10
Ammamarda — 303, 402, 427
Ammasuzawiš — 364
Anahita — 84
Anatolia — 14
    Anatolian — 20, 111
    coastal — 19, 193
    western — 195, 263
animal (as commodity) — 11, 346, 353, 397, 430
ankh-sign — 192
    ankh-shaped sign — 146
anomaly — 7, 14, 67, 162, 168, 225, 231, 258, 299, 310, 333, 335, 339, 355, 420, 431, 434, 399
Anšan — 11, 14
Antarrantiš — 109
antique — 12, 15–18, 39, 44, 54, 57, 60, 185, 354, 368, 417
Antique Style — *see* style
Anu — 293, 355, 429
Apmanya — 245
application — 3, 13, 20, 30–32, 34, 47–49, 52, passim in *Catalog*; *see also* seal (rolling of)
    pattern — 12, 42, 52, 296, 308
apportioner of workers — 269
Appumanya — 245
Arachosia — 390
Aramaic — *see* language
archaism — 21, 417, 441
    archaizing — 15, 17–18, 44, 54, 56, 157, 164, 181, 183, 230, 255, 258, 294, 417, 441
archer — 36, 95–96, 105, 219, 222, 225, 255, 333, 339, 382, 420
    archer scene — 43, 123
    royal archer — 105

archive — 1, 3–17, 19–21, 23–39, 41, 46, 54–56, 65, 67, 89, 91, 93, 192, 255, 273, 303, 307, 319, 321, 344, 346, 405, 412, 420
archival deposition — 26, 29
Armenia — 193
Arsames — *see* Aršam
Aršam — 36–37, 93, 405
art market — 6, 405
Artadara — 263
Artaphernes — *see* Artadara
Artaxerxes — 8, 34–35, 37–38, 293, 369
artifact — 1, 3, 6, 10, 12–15, 17–18, 20–21, 28–30, 33, 41, 49–50, 52, 54, 56, 263
artisan — 10, 39, 55–56, 58, 317
artist — 9, 19–20, 26, 48, 51, 58, 60, 64, 67, 77, 82, 86, 89, 91, 95, 97–100, 103, 105, 112, 118, 120, 123, 125, 129, 138–39, 141, 144–45, 147, 149–50, 153, 159, 162, 168, 170–71, 173, 188, 191, 197–99, 210, 214, 216, 221, 223, 227, 230, 242, 251, 256, 262, 289, 301, 322–23, 329, 335–36, 354, 359, 363, 390, 414, 429, 435
    collection of models — 39
    of the Pendent Robe — 284
Artystone — *see* Irtašduna
Ashmolean Museum — 12, 36
Asia
    Minor — 26, 192
    western — 3, 11, 12, 13, 15, 30, 31, 37, 53, 57, 267, 407, 430
        Asiatic — 3, 4, 8, 13, 28, 41, 53, 55, 59, 60, 123, 222, 333, 414
Aspathines — *see* Ašbazana
Ašbazana — 9, 33
Aššur — 21, 30, 32, 253, 332
Aššurbanipal — 15
Assyria — 16, 84, 87, 105, 251, 331
    Assyrian — 8, 10, 14–18, 43, 58, 60, 71, 77–78, 80–81, 83, 93, 95–96, 99, 101, 104, 106–09, 111, 114, 116, 118, 121–22, 124–25, 127, 131, 135, 137, 140–42, 145, 148, 150, 153, 155–58, 160, 163–64, 166–68, 170, 172–73, 176–77, 180, 182, 186–88, 191, 194–95, 198–200, 203–04, 208, 210–18, 220, 225, 230–32, 238–40, 242, 246, 248–49, 253–57, 259, 265–67, 269, 271, 276–79, 284, 290–91, 298, 306, 309–13, 315–18, 320, 325, 328, 330–32, 337–40, 342, 344, 347–49, 351, 354, 356–57, 359, 361, 363, 366, 368, 371–73, 378–81, 390, 394, 397–99, 402, 405, 407–410, 412, 415–16, 419–20, 423, 430, 432, 440; *see also* language
    Assyrianizing — 15, 84, 93, 319, 348

Assyria (*cont.*)
    Assyrian-type — 338
    Assyro-Babylonian — 14–15, 21, 104, 157, 177, 181, 184, 208, 256, 273, 287, 319, 331, 344, 368, 375, 410, 427, 441
    Middle Assyrian — 12, 30, 32, 405
    Neo-Assyrian — 10, 12, 14–17, 21, 53, 84, 87, 157, 163–64, 183, 185, 199, 208, 210, 213, 254–55, 284, 287, 327, 331–32, 359, 361, 368, 383, 405, 427, 438, 441
    Neo-Assyrian/Neo-Babylonian — 14–15, 21, 53, 255, 287, 331, 429
Athens — 10
    Athenian — 6, 10, 39
Atlit — 56
authority/authorization — 11, 30, 32, 53, 69, 76, 86, 103–04, 106–09, 114–15, 138, 148, 211, 243–47, 263, 276, 283, 301, 309, 324, 333–34, 336, 342, 350, 357–58, 364–65, 379, 388–90, 415; *see also* halmi, *miyatukkam*

Babylon — 21, 37–38, 388
Babylonia — 16, 37, 208, 251, 331
    Babylonian — 3–4, 6–7, 14, 33, 37–38, 43, 55, 68–69, 88–89, 177, 193, 233, 255, 301, 332, 344, 352; *see also* language
    Neo-Babylonian — 14, 16–17, 21, 37, 53, 55–56, 58–59, 84, 87, 105, 146, 183, 185, 208, 233, 255, 287, 301, 331–32, 355, 368, 429
    Old Babylonian — 13–14, 255, 361, 382, 441
Bactria — 32
Badumašda — 245
Bakabada — 108, 123, 138
Bakabaduš — 149
Bakabana — 86, 106, 108–09, 211, 243, 245, 342, 357, 425
Bakadada — 106
Bakakeya — 301
Bakanšakka — 283
Bakaradduš — 98
Bakena — 269
bakery — 231
Baktiš — 149
Bakubeša — 303
Bakuratsa —269
Bal — 59
Baradkama — 89
barley — 346, 402
    loaves — 245
Barnuš — 379
Barrikana — 364
barrišdama — 76, 95, 114, 224–25
Barušiyatiš — 159, 423
Battirakkan — 123
Battišdana — 269
bazikara — 123
beer — 124–25, 145, 211, 322, 324, 334, 379, 388–89
Berlin — 21
Bes — 55–56, 416
"Beschaffungsbeamter" — 369
Bessitme — 107

Biblical Institute of the University of Fribourg — 6
Bibliothèque Nationale — 59
bio-sketches — 21
"blameless one" — 59
Borsippa — 56, 255, 417, 441
Bowman, R. A. — 6, 28, 93
boys — 364
Breasted, Charles — 23, 25, 27
British Museum (BM) — 14, 20–21, 56, 59, 146, 255, 258, 331–32, 344, 361, 398, 416
Broad and Flat Styles — *see* style
bulla — 8, 29, 33–39, 54–55, 58–59, 69, 72
Byron, Robert — 23

C4 text — *see* text
calf (animal) — 258, 416–18
calligraphic — 20, 67, 80, 82, 200, 262
camel (driver/rider) — 10, 332
Cameron, George — 3, 30, 93
Çanakkale Museum — 14
caption — 37, 41, 60, 405
caravan leader — s*ee karabattiš*
carnelian — 56, 254
carver/carving — 13, 18–19, 33, 38, 58, 64, 93, 116, 138, 148, 157, 191, 203, 229, 280, 293–94, 297–98, 305, 323, 362, 396, 399, 431, 433–35, 438; *see also* inscription, seal
    image — 8
    miscarving — 286, 305; *see also* error, flaw/flawed
casemate — 27
cattle — 66, 245, 300
century
    second — 37, 39
    fourth — 35, 38, 296
    fifth — 35–36
    sixth — 7, 9, 15–17, 303
    seventh — 14, 16, 331
    eighth — 191
"Cerealien-Kommissar" — 369
chalcedony — 20, 56, 59, 255, 356
chariot — 43
Chicago — 1, 3, 23–24, 28, 47, 56
    Chicago Expedition — 17
chief of workers — *see kurdabattiš*
chip — 63, 84, 151, 179–80, 183, 187, 195–96, 223, 229, 251, 302–03, 334–35, 341, 375, 384, 405, 412, 417, 420
    chipped — 391
    chipping —183, 420
Chogha Mish — 25, 32
Christian — 60
chronology — 9, 13, 34, 55, 263
*Čiçafarnah — 71
clay sources — 30
clearance — 23–24
coffin — 39, 410
coin — 11, 39, 55, 105, 368; *see also* tetradrachm
collate — 6, 44
    collated — 33, 45–47, 55, 152
    collating — 44, 86
collation — 1, 11, 44–47, 52, 101, 122, 185, 234, 317

commodity (supply)
    exotic — 322
    food — 9–10, 28, 69
"connected pieces style" — *see* style
conoid — 48, 56, 75, 211, 309, 323, 335, 356, 371–72
context, archaeological — 7, 14, 27, 36–38, 56, 263
correspondence — 26, 36–38; *see also* letter, text (T text)
cosmopolitanism — 38
    cosmopolitan — 10, 60
countermark — 368
court — 7–10, 13–15, 17–18, 30, 32–33, 35–36, 57–58
    Persian — 8, 14, 37, 39, 41, 319, 332
    satrapal — 35, 55
Court Style — *see* style
craft — 15
craftsman — 9, 56, 60, 87
cult — 53, 58, 233, 253; *see also* scene
cultic — 10
cultivation — 303, 323, 392
culture — 3–4, 10, 12–13, 38, 53, 58
    cross-cultural — 10
    multi-cultural — 10, 38, 59
    multi-culturalism — 10
cuneiform-like — 193, 261, 271–72
cut down — 12, 18; *see also* recut
Cut Style — *see* style
cylinder — 2, 12, 21, 33, 37, 48, 54, 56, 261, 344; *see also* seal (cylinder)
Cyrus — 10–11, 16, 84
Cyrus of Anšan (grandfather of Cyrus the Great) — 11, 14

Dadaka — 333
damage — 20, 365, 371
    damaged — 18, 28, 88, 142, 159, 204, 236, 239, 245, 291, 307, 319, 337, 353, 379, 420, 435
Daniel, Book of — 59, 68
daʾubattiš — 359
Daʾuka — 120
Daʾupirna — 125
Darius — 1, 5–8, 10–11, 13–14, 18, 23, 26-27, 29, 34, 37–38, 41, 58–59, 65, 68–69, 84, 89, 93, 183, 298, 300, 327, 369, 405, 416
    post-Darius — 29, 327
Daskyleion — 8, 35, 55, 59
Daskyleion-Ergili — 35,
date (the commodity) — 76, 269
date palm — 18–19, 68–70, 88–89, 107, 151–52, 243, 298–99, 360
Dattaparna — 314
Dauma — 263
decontextualized — 6, 36
delivery man — *see ullira*
depot — 229
device
    linear — 19, 126, 146, 195, 336, 422
    geometric — 42, 44
director of royal bakery — 231
disk — 69, 84, 102, 136, 256
    cutting — 251

distortion — 47–48, 67, 70, 72, 82, 85, 91, 93, 96–98, 100, 122–23, 135, 160, 164, 182, 185, 188, 193, 196–98, 200, 207, 220, 229, 232, 255, 258, 260, 270, 272, 274, 280, 285, 296, 303, 305, 311, 317, 321–23, 326, 341–43, 346, 349–50, 355, 362, 387, 389, 392, 398, 400, 403, 406, 410, 413–14, 418, 424–25, 428, 432–33, 439
    distorted — 47
Diverse Styles — *see* style
door sealing — 29
doorjamb — 221, 308
    reliefs — 14, 58, 298, 300
Double Crown of Upper and Lower Egypt — 36
double entendre — 348
drill/drilling — 20, 67, 93, 157, 181, 198, 205, 213, 223, 230, 251, 255, 263, 287, 303
Drilled Style — *see* style
duplicate — 14, 31, 45, 437
Dur — 160
Dutukka — 84
dynamic, aesthetic — 13, 160

Ea — 407
Early Dynastic — 20, 53, 265, 305, 330, 354, 382–83, 400, 402, 417, 420, 429, 438
Ecbatana — 32
Egibi (family archive) — 38
Egypt — 23, 35–37, 55, 193; *see also* language
    Egyptianizing — 35, 38, 84, 193, 295, 327
Egyptianate — 37
Elam — 76, 247, 303, 425
    Elamite — 15, 35, 294, 332, 417; *see also* language
    Neo-Elamite — 14, 177, 183, 208, 221, 305, 412; *see also* glyptic, language
    proto-Elamite — 274
    Region — 66, 120, 145, 150, 162, 195, 229, 232, 260, 303, 325, 346, 359, 361, 387, 392, 402, 412, 427
encounter
    combat — 56, 59–61, 95, 142–43, 156, 172, 193, 211, 217, 222, 225, 230, 242, 245, 249, 255, 288, 298–99, 312, 323, 330, 332–33, 344, 348, 351, 357, 359, 364, 370–71, 380, 383, 385–87, 393, 396, 405, 407, 410, 413–15, 420, 431–32, 434–35
    control — 34, 59, 67, 82, 93, 105, 121, 123, 125, 127, 137–38, 142–43, 156, 167, 191, 208, 211, 215, 222, 230, 240, 249, 254–55, 269, 272, 274, 287, 290, 330, 340, 344, 348, 375, 387, 394, 396, 420, 430
England — 8
engraver, master — 64, 167
equestrian — 36; *see also* horseman
error — 3, 86
    carving — 412; *see also* flaw/flawed, carver/carving (miscarving)
    scribal — 9
Ešnunna — 13
Esther, Book of — 57
ethnicity — 8, 38, 57
    ethnic — 8, 38, 60
Etruria — 407

excavation — 1, 7, 12, 23–25, 28–29, 32–35, 37, 39, 56, 59, 332, 344, 417
    excavated — 3, 12, 14, 17–18, 21, 32–33, 35, 37, 53–54, 56, 65, 134, 170, 193, 213, 263–64, 296, 332, 348, 383, 403, 405, 438
    unexcavated — 21, 23, 54, 56
exergue — 263–64
exerter — 324

F text — *see* text
fanning — 47
Fara — 330, 354, 429
Fars — 15
female — 43, 84, 194
fertility — 204
figs — 98
fill — 27, 34
    construction — 27–28
"filler motif" — 355
fixed point — 13–14, 34, 264
flaw/flawed — 25, 50, 63, 151, 168, 195, 302, 411, 420, 434; *see also* error, carver/carving (miscarving)
floating (artifact) — 14, 56
flour — 11, 69, 82, 86, 98, 103–04, 107–09, 114, 117, 124, 148, 157, 159, 231, 243–46, 263, 278, 283, 290, 309, 322, 334–35, 350, 358, 361, 364–65, 369, 379, 390, 415, 423
Fort. texts — *see* text
fortification — 5, 9, 23, 25–29, 32, 34
    archive — 1, 3, 6–9, 13, 23, 25, 28–29, 32–34, 41, 56, 67, 93, 192, 303, 319, 346, 405
    Style — *see* style
    tablet — 1, 23, 25–29, 33–34
        type — 6, 32, 54, 405
    wall — 27
Freer Gallery of Art and Arthur M. Sackler Gallery Archives — 24

gal makip — 397
Garrison (quarters in Persepolis) — 27
gender — 14
genie — 221, 253, 294
geometric — 20, 42, 44, 67, 75, 114, 127, 223, 251, 282, 294, 401
Gezer — 56
gift — 33
Gilgamesh — 53, 59, 417, 441
Girsu — 36–37
glass — 56
glyptic — 1, 6, 12, 14–15, 18, 20, 27, 32, 37, 39, 42, 54–55, 57–60, 89, 93, 189, 193, 264, 319, 331, 354, 368, 382–83, 410, 430, 438
    Achaemenid — 16, 18, 20, 57, 65, 72, 91, 102, 180, 211, 213, 266, 294, 307, 382, 416
    Aegean — 15
    Akkadian — 441
    Asiatic — 8, 53, 222
    Assyrian — 194
    Assyro-Babylonian — 427, 441

    Early Dynastic — 53
    Early Dynastic II — 265, 402, 429
    Elamite — 67
    Graeco-Persian — 19
    Greek — 34, 55
    Mespotamian — 405, 407
    Neo-Assyrian — 84, 405
    Neo-Assyrian/Neo-Babylonian — 21, 53, 185, 287, 331
    Neo-Elamite — 303
    Old Babylonian — 441
    Ur III/Isin-Larsa — 13
    western Asian — 267
goats (as featured in texts) — 43, 61, 104, 117, 154, 182–84, 187–88, 190, 199–200, 227, 252–55, 258, 265–66, 276, 287–88, 291, 308, 319, 353–56, 358–59, 394–95, 405–06
Gobryas — *see* Kambarma
god — 18, 39, 59, 69, 293, 355, 402
goddess — 331
Godin Tepe — 28
gold — 20
Gorgippa — 84, 410
Graeco-Persian — *see* Persian
Graeco-Persian style — *see* style
grain — 66, 82, 98, 109, 117, 145, 148–49, 159–60, 185, 197, 204, 229, 244–45, 260, 269, 283, 301, 303, 317, 322–23, 334–35, 350, 361, 369–70, 387, 392, 414, 425, 427, 430; *see also tarmu*-grain
    handler — 333, 369; *see also tumara*
Great Depression — 25
Greece — 23
    Greek — 1, 10, 13, 34–35, 39, 125, 263, 407; *see also* language
    Hellenic — 60
    Hellenistic — 18, 38, 39, 293
    Hellenizing — 33, 55
    Ionian — 26, 125
    Ionic — 192–93
Gudea — 37
guide, elite — *see barrišdama*
Gula — 331

H text — *see* text
Hadaran — 158
halla-maker — 324
Hallock, Richard T. — 1, 3–4, 6, 11, 25, 27–28, 30, 33, 44–46, 51–52, 69, 82, 86, 89, 93, 192, 245, 269, 273, 286, 303, 317, 322, 346, 358–59, 361, 389, 410, 412
halmi — 76, 86, 103, 104, 106, 107–109, 114, 115, 138, 148, 211, 243–247, 263, 276, 283, 301, 309, 324, 333, 334, 336, 342, 357, 358, 364, 365, 379, 388, 389, 390, 415; *see also* authority
hamura — 117
hand
    attribution — 14, 15, 37
    of artist — 123, 168, 190, 227, 230, 300, 301, 322, 329, 336, 354, 363, 429
Hapumanya — 245
Harem of Xerxes — 58

Harina — 138
Harmasula — 276
Harraštamka — 103
Harrumassula(?) — 276
Hasanlu — 53
hat, domed — 14–15
Hatarbanuš — 430
Haturdada — 269, 361
Haturrada — 157
headdress, domed — 66, 78, 82, 91, 95, 103, 114, 120, 127, 135, 137, 151, 153, 157, 177–78, 181, 204, 219, 223, 230, 252, 254, 256, 259, 262, 269, 282, 290, 302, 309–10, 318, 320, 333, 342–43, 348, 350, 355, 359, 364, 372, 388, 391, 393, 404, 411, 417, 427, 430
heartland — 9, 19, 55
    Achaemenid — 18, 32, 33, 39, 48, 55
    imperial — 1
    Persian — 9, 35, 38, 39, 41, 55, 193, 344
heirloom — 12, 14, 16–18, 54, 157, 163, 164, 177, 181, 183, 208, 303, 319, 331, 405, 412
Hellenic/Hellenistic/Hellenizing — *see* Greece
Heraion, Samian — *see* Samos
Herakles — 55, 56, 60
hero — 7, 14–18, 20, 21, 36, 42, 43, 50, 52–61, passim in *Catalog*
    heroic combat — 56–61, passim in *Catalog*
    heroic control — 7, 34, 42, 43, 55, 59–61, passim in *Catalog*
    heroic encounter — 8, 14, 30, 34, 42, 43, 49, 50, 53–56, 59–61, passim in *Catalog*
Herodotus — 84
Herzfeld, Ernst E. — 7, 23–29, 34
hexapolis, Doric — 192–93
Hibaš — 255
Hidali — 108, 109, 124, 125, 195, 260, 263, 278
hide (writing medium) — 3; *see also* leather, papyrus, parchment
hieratic — 16, 57, 58, 59
Hiran — 160
Hišema — 402, 427
Hiumizza — 97
Hiyautarra — 309
"Hofintendantur" — 66
"Hofschatzwart" — 269, 369
"Hofspeicherwart" — 66
Hofspeisenmeister" — 69
Horom — 56
horse — 23, 97, 117, 191, 194, 195, 196, 244, 364, 414
    kulla-horses of the king — 117
horseman — 269, 332; *see also* equestrian
    for *kulla*-horses — 117
Horus, birth cycle/infant — 84
Hu...radu — 386
Hupan-Kitin — 302, 303
Hupanʾahpi — 412
hupika — 390
Hutpirri — 145, 387
hybrid — 19, 43, 44, 50, 92, 221
hybridization — 19, 67, 264, 284

ibis — 425
iconography — 6, 8, 14, 16, 18, 36, 37, 39, 43, 55, 56, 69, 75, 84, 93, 121, 157, 193, 255, 264, 275, 305, 317, 327, 331, 335, 412
    Akkadian — 255
    iconographic(al) — 8, 14, 17–18, 35, 37, 39, 41–44, 46, 50–52, 54–55, 69, 95, 253, 263, 273, 275, 315
identification (cultural) — 57
identity — 1, 7, 8, 31, 54–59, 61, 69, 303
ideology — 57
    ideological — 18, 57, 59
    imperial — 8
idiosyncrasy — 13, 15, 17, 47
India — 95
individual, elite — 10, 65, 72, 76, 91, 95, 114, 224–25, 266–67, 307, 311, 382
individuality — 13
Indo-Iranian — 59, 332
information, biographical — 8
ink — 6, 31, 47
inscription — 4, 7–9, 13, 16–17, 20, 26, 30–31, 35–36, 42, 47–52, 57, 59, 68–72, 88–94, 151–52, 160–62, 166–67, 177, 192–93, 259–261, 268–274, 286, 297, 299, 300, 302–307, 313–321, 332, 345–46, 352–53, 377, 381–82, 384–86, 391–93, 404–06, 411–13, 417, 432–33
    carving — 8
    mock — 7, 193, 259, 261, 271
    royal name — 10, 35, 69, 89
    uninscribed — 3, 6, 8, 28, 33–34, 70, 269, 321
"Intendantur" — 66
Ionian/Ionic — *see* Greece
Ir... — 318
Iran National Museum — 3
Iranian riding habit — 14, 57
Irdabada — 387
Irdabama — 11–12
Irišdumaka — 160
Iršena — 123, 412
Irtašbada — 269
Irtašduna — 10–12, 17, 84
Irtena — 415–16
Irtuppiya — 66
Irzapparra — 98
Isana — 332
Isin-Larsa — 13
Israel — 39
Išbakatukka — 342
Išbaramištima — 95
Ištar — 84
Ištibara — 379
Ištimanka — 98, 412
ištimara(?) — 301
Istanbul Archaeological Museum — 14
ivory — 41

J text — *see* text
jamb — 416; *see also* doorjamb
Jerusalem — 38

Jews — 59
　Jewish — 39
Job, Book of — 59
journal — 30, 123, 160, 204, 244, 337, 364, 369; *see also* text (V text)
Judah — 39

Kambarma — 10, 12
Kamišdana — 145
Kammazikara — 114
Kamnakka — 104
Kandahar — 32, 158, 224
Kandu... — 384
Kanduma — 255
Kansakam — 370
Kansan — 117
kanti — 145; *see also* warehouse
Kantor, Helene J. — 25
kanzabara — 269, 273, 369–70; *see also* treasurer
Kapiša — 365
Kapišda — 260
karabattiš — 117
karamaraš — 379
Karkašša — 158
Karkiš — 273, 311, 334, 364, 388–89
Karukka — 98
Kasr — 37
Kassite — 14
Kaupirriš — 323
kazabara — 369
Kedesh of the Upper Galilee — 39
Kelsey Museum of Archaeology — 59, 344
kem — 195
Kerman — 107
Kesat — 229, 260
Khorsabad — 14
Khuzistan — 32
Kinet Höyük — 405
king — 1, 8–12, 23, 33–34, 36, 55, 57–59, 69, 86, 103, 107, 117, 129, 138, 148, 170, 276, 283, 301, 303, 319, 324, 334, 336, 342, 353, 364–65, 379, 388–90, 417, 442
kingship — 57–59
koine — 39, 55–56, 60, 193, 264
Krefter, Friedrich — 23
Kuntukka — 414
Kurarakka — 148
kurdabattiš — 269, 273, 412
Kurdušum — 322, 361
Kurigalzu — 193
Kuristiš — 117
Kurpun — 204, 346
Kurra — 260
kurtaš abbakkanaš Irdabamana — 72
Kutkuš — 149

L1 text — *see* text
label — 29–30, 33–34, 45–46, 54, 59; see also text (U text)
Lahmu — 417, 441
"Landvogt" — 359
language
　Akkadian — 89
　Aramaic — 3, 6–8, 28, 30–32, 36, 51, 90, 92–94, 151–52, 166, 193, 270, 286, 304–05, 313, 391, 404–05
　Assyrian — 111
　Babylonian — 4, 6–7, 33, 37–38, 68–69, 88–89, 177
　bilingual — 6
　Egyptian — 55
　Elamite — 1, 3–4, 6–7, 16–17, 33, 51, 68–69, 71, 88–89, 161–62, 268–69, 272–73, 297, 302–03, 316–18, 345–46, 377, 381–82, 384–86, 392–93, 411–12, 432
　Elamite-Aramaic — 6
　Greek — 1, 6–7, 55, 126, 192–93
　Middle Assyrian — 12
　monolingual — 6–8, 20
　multilingualism — 7–8
　Neo-Elamite — 317, 346
　of uncertain identity — 7, 192, 259–61, 271, 299–300, 306, 314–15, 320
　Old Persian — 4, 7–8, 20, 36, 68–69, 71, 88–89, 382
　Phrygian — 6
　trilingual — 4, 7–8, 51, 69, 89
　uncertain — 7, 259, 299–300, 306, 314–15, 320
　unknown — 7, 192, 260–61, 271
lapis — 417, 420
leather — 36 (writing medium); *see also* hide, papyrus, parchment
"Leiter" — 66,
letter — 11, 17; *see also* correspondence, text (T text)
Liduma — 162, 195, 232, 350
Linear Styles — *see* style
lingua franca — 3
literate — 9, 12
　non-literate — 261
　pre-literate — 12, 53
　protoliterate — 8, 12, 21, 53
Louvre Museum — 14–15, 42, 69, 274, 382
Luristan — 402
Lydia — 35
　Lydian — 56

M text — *see* text
m.KUR.lg zakkip — 353
Ma...ak(?) — 386
Macedonians — 38
Makarkiš — 160
Makkaš — 159, 379
Maknan — 114
"Maltese" cross — 146
Mamannuwiš — 229
Manaka — 350
Manda — 341
Manezza — 204
Manmakka — 370

Mannunda — 231
Mannuya — 369–70
Manukka — 397, 430
Manuš — 369
Manyakka — 269
Marathon — 23
Marcopoli Collection — 21
Marduk — 344
Mardukka — 269
Marduk-nāṣir — 352
Marmaš — 260
Marv Dasht Plain — 9
masašiš — 301
Masjid-i Suleiman — 60
mason's mark — 111, 336, 368
Matēna — 343
Matezziš — 369
matira — 370
Matiša — 359
Matukka — 324, 334–35
Maudadda — 364
Mawukka — 123
Mazamanna — 98
Mazdaism — 39
Mede — 14–15
    Median — 16, 27
Medumannuš — 98
Mella — 124
Memphis — 8, 35, 55, 170, 195
men — 33, 114, 117, 247, 324, 342, 364, 379
Mesopotamia — 36–37, 39, 53, 58–59, 204, 331, 336, 438
    Mesopotamian — 16, 21, 36, 39, 54–56, 146, 170, 233, 258, 278, 293, 344, 354–55, 405, 407, 425
messenger — s*ee pirradaziš*
metalware — 39, 55, 60
metaphor — 57, 59
    metaphorical — 53, 57
Metropolitan Museum of Art — 7, 24, 269
Mikrašba — 185, 197
millennium
    first — 3, 15, 193, 294, 382
    second — 14, 37, 230, 382
    third — 10, 13, 20, 37, 265, 330, 382
miller — 115
milti — 98
Minduka — 148
Mirara — 246
Mirayauda — 82, 421–22
Mirinzamna — 107
Mirinzana — 346
Misraka — 358
Misranka — 358
Mišmina — 276
Mithra — 58
    Mithraic — 58
Mixed Styles — *see* style
Miyara — 244
miyattukam — 342; *see also* authority
Mizapirzaka — 211
Mizirma — 231

Modeled Style — *see* style
modeling — 16, 19, 58, 64, 178, 273, 308, 319, 325, 368, 427
monkey — 253
monumental (architecture, art, sculpture) — 4, 14, 25–26, 32, 56–57, 59, 69, 129, 189, 308
mount/mounting (for seals) — 20, 183, 420
mule — 117
multiple occurrences — 44–47, 269
Munich — 263
Murašû — 37–38, 41, 55, 255, 321, 344, 355, 420
Mutrizaš — 149

Nabopolassar — 37
Nabu — 344
    Temple — 204, 412, 427
Naktiš — 157
Nap… — 302
Napidan — 357
Napša-Kitin — 303
Naptaš — 392
Naqsh-i Rustam — 59
narrative — 1, 42–43, 50, 52, 58, 246, 253, 265, 362, 400, 407, 420, 423
narrativize — 291
Naširmannu — 389
negative space — 67, 78, 127, 160–61, 183, 196, 251, 261, 267, 269, 279, 311, 326, 367, 377, 389
"Nereid Coffin" — 410
neutron activation analysis — 30, 34
Newell Collection — 36, 59
Nidintu-Anu — 293
Nimrud — 84, 204, 210, 284, 412, 425, 427
Nineveh — 16, 75, 84, 111, 185, 189, 327, 361, 405, 429
Nippur — 37–38, 55, 344
Nuzi — 30
office, royal — 10–11
Old Kandahar — 32
'N(?)Š… — 166

orality — 8
Oriental Institute — 28
over-rolling — 70, 84, 130, 137, 169, 185, 435

P texts — *see* text
Palace of Darius — 5, 58, 183, 298, 300, 416
Pandušašša — 283
papyrus (writing medium) — 38; *see also* hide, leather, parchment
paraffin — 24, 28
parasang — 4
parchment (writing medium) — 3; *see also* hide, leather, papyrus
Parmadan — 159, 423
Parmizzan — 97, 364
Parnaka — 7–8, 10, 15, 17–18, 31, 76, 93, 104, 114–15, 244, 246, 319, 333, 353, 358, 405–06

parody — 57
Parribana — 364
Parru — 303, 350
Parša — 1
Parsauka — 422
Paršena — 76
Pasargadae — 9, 14, 32, 56, 134, 213, 221, 368, 417
patron — 10, 38–39, 55, 60, 193
patronage — 14–15, 58, 93
payers(?) of the land — *see* m.KUR.lg zakkip
pedestal — 65, 71–72, 90–91, 185, 210, 250–51, 255, 257–58, 266–67, 306–07, 381–82, 413, 441
penis — 208, 417
permeability — 10, 19
Pers. 6754 — *see* text
Persepolis —
    Persepolitan — 9, 16–17, 32, 75, 92, 157, 164, 181, 420
    region — 9–10, 16, 18, 20, 28, 31, 41, 123, 231, 397, 430
    Treasury — 5, 12, 21, 26–29, 33, 54, 56, 273, 296, 348, 383, 403, 438
    tablet, archive, corpus — 5, 8, 26, 30, 33–34, 46, 54, 59, 65, 69, 89, 91, 273, 307, 369, 382
Persia — 23
    Persian — 1, 3, 8–10, 13, 15, 20, 23, 26, 35–36, 38–39, 41, 43, 54–59, 68–69, 75, 88, 105, 129, 133, 149, 160, 170, 180, 193, 242, 282, 323–24, 334–35, 344, 382, 415
    court — 8, 14, 18, 37, 39, 41, 57, 319, 332
    court robe — 18, 57, 63–65, 68–69, 73, 86, 88–90, 97–98, 110, 119–20, 125, 128–29, 133–34, 136, 146, 165, 180, 189, 197, 221, 227, 246, 297–300, 304–05, 308, 320–21, 323, 326, 334–35, 339, 401, 416, 421, 428, 433
    Empire — 1, 10, 14, 16, 33, 35, 39, 146, 264
        Achaemenid — 1, 4, 7–10, 12, 14–18, 20–21, 26, 32–39, 42, 48, 53–60, 65, 69, 72, 84, 91, 102, 104–05, 111, 180, 185, 208, 211, 213, 255, 258, 266–67, 274, 278, 287, 294, 303, 305, 307, 317, 327, 332, 336, 339, 354, 368, 382, 398, 407, 410, 412, 416–17, 420, 429, 441
        Empire — 1, 3–4, 8–9, 14–15, 32–33, 35, 38, 54–57, 59–60, 294, 344
        imperial — 1, 7–8, 10, 14, 32–33, 37, 39, 53, 56–57, 264, 407
        Persian — 3, 10, 15, 39, 55–56
        pre-Achaemenid — 12, 35, 54, 58, 294, 332, 417
    Seleucid — 37, 60
    Parthian — 60
    Sasanian — 7, 53, 56, 60
    Graeco-Persian — 19, 26, 56, 263–64; *see also* style
    "Man" — 7–8, 57–58
    Old Persian — *see* language
    Persianizing — 189, 338, 340, 354
PFa (texts) — *see* text
PFNN (texts) — *see* text
phallic symbol — 84
Pharnaces — *see* Parnaka
Philippos — 125

Phoenician — 296
    Phoenician-Punic — 126
photography — 25, 46
    photographic — 45–47
Phrygia — 35
    Phrygian — *see* language
Pilpisurmu(?) — 125
Pirdukana — 336
Pirišla — 145
pirradaziš — 276, 301
Pitlan(?) — 150
Plausibly Antique — *see* style
police officer — *see* da'ubattiš
practice, sealing — 12–13, 32
prehistory — 417
    prehistoric — 26, 53, 294
    protohistoric — 294
priest, fish-garbed — 253
prince — 36–37
Princeton — 24, 26
procession — 43, 407
professional — 8, 12–13, 15, 25
    non-professional — 13
prosopographical — 7
protection (imagery) — 400
protocol (sealing) — 11, 31–32, 36, 46, 51, 305, 353
provenance — 36–37, 56
    provenanced — 35, 52
    unprovenanced — 7, 41, 56, 75, 211, 258, 263, 273, 332, 344, 356
"Prüfer" — 255
Ptolemy II — 407
Punic — *see* Phoenician

Q text — *see* text
Qasr-i Abu Nasr — 7, 56, 269, 323, 371–72

raduššara — 245
rank — 8, 319, 353, 369; *see also* status
    high ranking — 84, 106, 273, 389, 412
    ranked — 10
Rašda — 72
Ratešda — 390
Raubasa — 353
Razakanuš — 245
"Rechnungsführer" — 162
"Rechnungsprüfer" — 346
recut — 18, 20, 168, 361, 417, 429; *see also* cut down
    recutting — 15, 20
rations — 72, 76, 86, 103–04, 107–09, 114–15, 117, 120, 138, 148, 159, 211, 243–47, 263, 269, 273, 283, 309, 317, 324, 334–36, 358, 364–65, 369, 379, 388–90, 402, 425
    daily — 124, 278; *see also* text (P text)
    for individual with religious function — 125; *see also* text (K1 text)

rations (*cont.*)
    for persons without qualification — 158; *see also* text
    mothers' — 98; *see also* text (N text)
    regular, for animals — 159, 244; *see also* text (S1 text)
    regular monthly, for named person without qualifications — 397, 412, 415; *see also* text (K3 text)
    regular monthly, with *gal makip* — 397; *see also* text (L1 text)
    royal provisions — 84; *see also* text
    special — 98, 305; *see also* text (M text)
    travel — 51, 95, 322, 364, 370, 421; *see also* text (Q text)
    travel, for animals — 11; *see also* text (S3 text)
religion — 9
religious — 1, 9, 39, 55, 125
repeat (of seal design) — 48, 67, 161, 184, 189, 205, 216, 220, 222–23
    repeated — 67, 134, 406
    repeating — 180
ring
    seal — 18, 34
    signet — 17, 33
ritual — 10, 36
road — 29
    royal — 9
rod (for suspension) — 30
family — 15, 37–38
    heirloom — 163
    royal — 10–11, 303, 319
Royal Ontario Museum — 14

S1 text — *see* text
S3 text — *see* text
Sabi Abyad — 53
"sacred tree" — 284
Sagartia — 107
Saka — 273
Šalamana — 84
Salamis — 23
Šaman — 379
Samaria — 38–39, 55–56
    Samaritans — 38, 55
Samarkand — 399
Sami, Ali — 27–28
Samos — 332
    Samian Heraion — 199, 412
Šanau — 162
Šandupirzana — 114
Šappiš — 247
Šarbaladda — 369
Sardis — 10, 14, 20, 35, 37, 56, 65, 134, 263–64, 336, 368
    Sardian — 26, 114
Šati-Hupan — 162, 384, 412
Šati-... — 316
Šatra... — 260
satrap — 32, 36–37, 425
    satrapal court — 35, 55
Šaurakkaš — 149
Šauša — 86

scarab — 35, 296
scaraboid — 20, 48, 56, 309, 333
scene
    banquet — 43, 383, 438
    cult — 43, 253–54; *see also* cult
    genre — 43
    hunt — 43, 255
    main — 42
    martial — 43
"Schatzwart" — 369
Schmidt, Erich E. — 24–27, 29, 33, 54
scribe — 3, 7, 9, 12–13, 58, 197, 301, 338
    scribal — 9, 15, 410
SD2a — 8
SDa — 69
SDe — 69
SDg — 89
seal
    cap — 20, 66–67, 126, 223
    carver — 38, 59, 261
    carving — 8, 15–16, 18
    counter — 69
    cutter — 8
    cylinder — 7–8, 12, 14, 18, 20–21, 33–34, 36, 42, 48–50, 52, 59, 65, 115, 134, 204, 213, 410, 412, 420, 427, 438
    double-registered — 137
    matrix — 20–21
    new — 6, 14, 18, 54, 159
    office — 32, 45, 58, 63, 69, 71, 98, 163, 197, 269, 273–74, 303, 311, 322–23, 348, 350, 412–13, 422
    official — 10, 31
    personal — 7, 10–12, 36–37, 66–67, 69, 76, 82, 84, 86, 93, 95, 97, 103–04, 107, 109, 114–15, 117, 120, 125, 145, 148–49, 158–60, 162–64, 196, 204, 211, 225, 229, 231–33, 244–45, 247, 260, 264, 269, 273, 276, 279, 283, 300–01, 310, 314, 317, 319, 323–24, 326, 333, 335–37, 341–42, 346, 353, 357–58, 362, 365, 370, 379, 389–90, 397, 405, 414, 423, 428, 430
    pre-owned — 346
    replacement — 405
    ring seal — 34
    rolling of — 12–13, 48–50, 52, passim in *Catalog*; *see also* application
    royal name — 6, 8. 10–11, 13–14, 31–32, 34, 46, 51, 57–59, 65, 69, 89, 259, 273, 315
    stamp — 1, 12, 14, 18–21, 26, 33, 37, 48–50, 52–53, 56, 84, 111, 146, 195, 211, 252, 263–64, 276, 293–94, 301, 309, 323–24, 333–36, 342, 355–57, 364–65, 370–72, 416, 425
        pyramidal — 12, 19, 48, 146, 195, 263–64, 276, 333, 336
        theriomorphic — 21, 56
    tabloid — 12
    western Semitic — 39
seated figure/hero/personage — 36, 42–43, 57, 60–61, 436–37
Seleucia-on-the-Tigris — 59, 344
Sennacherib — 361
separation — 1, 45–46, 52, 315
Šeraš — 412
service access/entrance — 5, 28–29

sesame — 269, 336
sex — 53
sheep — 61, 182, 187, 190, 199–201, 252, 255, 276, 287–88, 353–54, 358–59, 364, 420
Shiraz — 7, 9, 71, 122, 234, 348, 414; *see also* Tirazziš
    Region — 106, 397, 430
silver — 60, 369
Šimut-ap — 325
Sinai — 56
Sippar — 37–38, 55
Širazziš — *see* Tirazziš
Smithsonian Institution — 24, 26
spear — 14, 43, 420–21, 423–24, 426
    spear-bearer — 10
    spearing — 34
    spearman — 255
standard, royal — 170
station — 422
    post station — 322, 342, 421, 423
    way station — 322
statue, guardian — 332
status — 1, 8–9, 11, 16–17, 42, 53, 57–58, 204, 267, 311, 331, 406; *see also* rank
"Steuereinnehmer" — 123, 353
storage — 9, 27–28, 30, 32, 37, 195
storehouse — 117, 364
string — 30, 33, 36
style
    Antique — 16–18, 163, 178
    Broad and Flat — 19, 158, 189, 200, 228, 235, 280, 324, 326–27, 329, 334–35, 354, 360, 364–65, 370, 396, 428, 435, 437–38
    "connected pieces" — 229
    Court — 15, 18–19, 34, 36, 64–65, 67–69, 72–73, 75, 77, 86, 88–89, 91–92, 95, 98, 102, 118, 121, 129, 133–34, 145, 149–50, 165, 167, 180, 197, 210, 227, 239, 242, 281, 289, 297, 299–300, 305, 307–08, 315, 323–24, 327, 335, 377
    Cut — 208, 251, 375
    Diverse — 19–20, 66, 75, 91, 192, 206, 223, 229–30, 251, 263, 265, 294, 302, 333, 375, 398, 401–02, 430
    Drilled — 21, 184–85
    Fortification — 15, 18–19, 49, 63, 67, 71, 76–82, 91–92, 95–100, 103–09, 111–19, 121, 123–25, 127, 129–32, 135–39, 141–45, 147, 149–50, 153–56, 159–61, 167–75, 179, 187–88, 190–91, 196, 198–99, 202–03, 206–07, 209–10, 213–14, 216, 218–21, 225–27, 232–34, 236–39, 242–43, 246–48, 252–54, 256–57, 259–60, 262–64, 266–67, 269, 276–79, 281–85, 289–90, 292, 296, 301, 305, 307, 309–12, 314, 321–22, 325, 328, 330, 335–40, 342, 344, 350–51, 355–56, 358, 361–63, 366–67, 372–74, 378, 383, 387–88, 390, 394–97, 399, 401, 403–05, 408, 414–15, 417–18, 420–21, 423–24, 426, 430, 433–34, 436–39
    Graeco-Persian — 19, 263, 276, 333, 336
    Linear — 19, 110, 128, 176, 205, 215, 224, 241, 245, 250, 288, 291, 293, 295, 361, 368, 383, 394, 438
    Mixed — 19, 65, 80, 90, 101–02, 104, 114, 120, 136–37, 146, 151, 166, 211, 236–37, 244, 256, 281, 292, 298, 304, 306, 337, 343, 349, 357, 379, 419

    Modeled — 16–19, 74, 80–81, 83, 87, 92–93, 104, 114, 140, 148, 157, 163–64, 167, 177–78, 181–82, 186, 194–95, 199, 201, 204, 212, 217, 219, 231, 236–37, 240, 246, 249, 256, 260, 268, 271–72, 275, 292, 303, 310, 312–13, 316, 318–20, 325, 331–32, 337, 345, 347–48, 350, 352, 356, 358, 368–69, 371, 376, 380–81, 384–85, 391–92, 399, 407, 409–12, 416, 420, 427, 432, 434–35, 440–41
    Plausibly Antique — 16–17, 21, 157, 177, 181, 183–84, 208, 287, 303, 331, 368
    Unknown — 19
suckling (a calf) — 258
Šuddayauda — 269, 273, 343
sun
    diurnal — 58
    nocturnal — 58
supervisor — *see titikaš*
supplier — 82, 98, 117, 124–25, 145, 148, 158–59, 185, 197, 245, 278–79, 283, 290, 303, 322, 335, 341, 350, 361, 364, 369, 397, 412, 421–23, 430
Šurauša — 388–89
Šurkutur — 303, 350
Šursunkiri — 255, 260
Susa — 7, 9, 12, 14–15, 32, 35, 38, 54, 56, 58, 69, 72, 95, 104–05, 107–08, 114, 123–24, 158, 183, 208, 211, 224, 244, 258, 265, 274, 283, 287, 294, 303, 305, 309, 333, 336, 352, 364, 368–69, 379, 382, 402, 414, 417, 429, 441
    Susian — 9, 27, 303
Šutur-Nahunte — 303
symbol, winged — 18, 36, 39, 42, 55, 68–69, 75, 102, 118, 133–34, 136, 184–85, 284, 327, 337, 440–41
syncretistic — 59
SYN' — 304–05
Syria — 193
    Syrian —12
Syro-Palestine — 39
    Syro-Palestinian — 193
system, bureaucratic — 1

T text — *see* correspondence, letter, text
tablet, typically shaped — 30–31, 33, 36
Tadjvidi — 34
Takht — 1, 3, 5, 9, 23–25, 28–30, 58
tarmu-grain — 245, 260, 334; *see also* grain
Tarsus — 327
Tašpak — 120, 303, 350
tax — 149, 353
    overtax — 57
    handler — 353
taxation   9
Teispes — 11
Tell el-Heir — 56
Tell Mozan — 10, 13
Tello — 36–37, 382
Tepe Sialk — 361
terminal field — 42, 48, 50–51, passim in *Catalog*
terminus ante quem — 13, 49
terminus post quem — 39
Terqa — 13

GENERAL INDEX

tetradrachm — 6, 39; *see also* coin
text
    account — 30, 107, 117, 123, 148, 163, 245, 276, 346
    C4 text — 353
    F text — 159, 317
    Fort. — 3, 6, 8, 65
        Fort. 1771 — 6, 192
    H text (receipt by official) — 389
    J text (royal provisions) — 11, 69, 84, 300, 333
    K1 text — 125; *see also* rations (for individual with religious function)
    K3 text — 158; *see also* rations (regular monthly, for named person without qualifications)
    L1 text — 397; *see also* rations (regular monthly, with *gal makip*)
    legal — 38, 293, 429
    M text — 98, 305; *see also* rations (special)
    N text — 98; *see also* rations (mothers')
    P text — 124, 278; *see also* rations (daily)
    Pers. 6754 — 3
    PFa — 3, 6
        24 — 244
        29 — 244
        31 — 107
    PFNN — 3, 6, 11, 30, 44, 47, 51
        208 — 307
        1018 — 314
        1046 — 71
        1068 — 71
        2543 — 412
    Q text — 11, 51, 76, 82, 86, 95, 98, 103–04, 106–09, 114–15, 117, 124, 138, 145, 148, 157–59, 211, 224, 243–47, 263, 276, 278, 283, 290, 301, 309, 324, 333–34, 336, 341–42, 350, 357–58, 361, 364–65, 369, 379, 388, 390, 412, 415, 421, 423; *see also* rations (travel)
    S1 text — 159, 244; *see also* rations (regular, for animals)
    S3 text — 11, 159; *see also* rations (travel, for animals)
    T text (letter) — 11, 51, 84, 93, 314, 319; *see also* correspondence, letter
    "Tools" — 29
    U text (label) — 30, 410; *see also* label
    V text (journal) — 30, 123, 204, 337; *see also* journal
    W text (accounts) — 30, 123; *see also* account
Thebes — 14
theophoric name — 293
Throne Hall — 5, 58
thumb — 273, 427
thumbnail — 11
Tiliman — 195
Tirazziš (Shiraz) — 7, 72, 122, 234, 348, 414
Tiridada — 260
titikaš — 120
tongue — 7, 224, 298, 300, 345, 347, 384–86, 391, 393
treasurer — 26, 89, 269, 273, 369; *see also kanzabara*
treasury — 18, 369
    connected with — 122, 348
    Matezziš — 369
    Persepolis — 5, 12, 21, 26–27. 29, 33, 54, 59, 273, 296, 348, 383, 403, 438
    Tirazziš — 122, 234, 348

archive (Persepolis) — 5, 26, 33, 65, 91, 307
    tablet (Persepolis) — 8, 30, 33–34, 46, 69, 89, 273, 369, 382
Troy — 14
Tukraš — 117
tumara — 82, 109, 369–70; *see also* grain (handler)
Turdumannuš(?) — 243
Turpiš — 117
Turtukkan — 245

U text — *see* text
ullira — 301, 335, 364, 369
Ullu Burun — 361
    shipwreck — 361
Umardada — 231
Umiša — 109
Umma-Drehem — 13
Ummanana — 361
Ummurdak — 402
Umpura — 82
Umpuranuš — 421–22
unprovenanced — *see* provenance
unsak — 273
Ur — 39, 55, 255, 420, 429
Ur III — 13
Urartu — 56
    Urartian — 362
urban — 3, 9–10
Urkesh — 10
Uruk — 18, 38, 293, 429
URU-kisuna — 273
Ušaya — 341
Uštana — 72, 303, 392

V text — *see* text
validation — 30
verification — 30–31, 162, 195, 232
"Vize-Intendant" — 273

W text — 30, 123; *see also* account, text
Wadi ed-Daliyeh — 38–39, 55
warehouse — 145, 370; *see also kanti*
warrior — 57, 59
wheel, cutting — 92
wife — 10, 84, 283
    royal — 17
wine — 107, 115, 117, 138, 158, 160, 204, 245, 247, 341, 346, 364, 425
woman — 9, 11, 84, 211, 412
work crew — 9
worker — 23, 72, 76, 120, 149, 247, 260, 269, 273, 303, 352, 364, 397, 412, 425, 430
Works Progress Administration (WPA) — 25
workshop — 14–19, 55, 75, 95, 125, 157, 193, 204, 263, 314, 317, 319, 321, 346–47, 353, 357, 380, 382, 385–86, 392–93, 407, 413

World War II — 1, 25, 36
worldwide web — 3
worship — 43, 59
    scene — 55, 87, 146, 344, 383, 438
    seal — 55
worshiper — 87, 253, 284, 301, 331
wumrudda — 117

Xerxes — 5, 8, 23, 26, 34–35, 37–38, 58, 89, 382

Yahweh — 59
Yale Babylonian Collection — 7
Yap... — 307
Yaunaparza — 115

Zakarna — 98
Zakzaku — 245
zebu — 258
Zilaba — 322
Zila-Umpan — 303
Zinçirli — 330
Zirra... — 346
Ziršamattiš — 346
Zišanduš — 224
Ziššabarna — 71
Zišsawiš — 247, 309, 319, 364, 415
Zoroastrian — 39, 332